THE
QUICKWAY CROSSWORD DICTIONARY

The
Quickway
CROSSWORD
DICTIONARY

Compiled by
COLONEL H. W. HILL
C.M.G., D.S.O.
and
revised by his son

FREDERICK WARNE AND CO. LTD.
LONDON AND NEW YORK

SBN 7232 0163 3

Printed in Great Britain
by Lowe & Brydone (Printers) Ltd., London
150·871

CONTENTS

THE CROSSWORD CURE

To The Times *Crossword Editor*

O nameless coiner of the cryptic clue,
*   O master of delusive definition,*
Embracing in your panoramic view
*   A world of miscellaneous erudition,*
Once more I pay the homage due
*   To your wise conduct of your Inquisition,*
Bringing a daily boon and breathing space
To the tired runners in a mad world's race.

You leave no fruitful avenues unexplored
*   That minister to innocent hilarity,*
But never strike a harsh or jarring chord,
*   Or find a virtue in unveiled vulgarity.*
Rumour and gossip are by you ignored ;
*   You season ridicule with kindly charity,*
Yet on occasion with unerring eyes
Transfix malicious folly as it flies.

You jog my memory with your mental jerks ;
*   To you, in fine, I owe a double debt*
For while the old machinery still works
*   And shows no sign of breaking down as yet—*
Thanks to the stimulus of your quips and quirks—
*   You teach me to remember, and forget.*
For Hell's most grisly gangsters have no power
To crash the gate that guards the Crossword hour.

C. L. GRAVES.

The above poem, which appeared in *The Times* of July 23, 1941, is reproduced by the kind permission of the author's son.

Publisher's Note

In 1967 a revision was undertaken by Rowland and Ingrid Hill. Many modern words and terms were added, while obsolete words were omitted. This crossword dictionary remains, however, substantially that compiled during the years 1920–1951 by Col. H. W. Hill.

PREFACE

This Dictionary has been specially compiled to meet the exacting needs of modern crossword enthusiasts. All the distinctive features of *The Quickway Key* —of which over 100,000 copies have been sold—have been retained ; but notable additions have been made. These include a far greater number of CLUE words, a wide range of synonyms, and a complete vocabulary of the Eight-Letter Words.

The distinctive features are :

1. All CLUE words having the same number of letters are grouped together.
2. Every line begins with a possible CLUE word.
3. All CLUE words are printed in capital letters.
4. Classification letters such as **B.** for Botany, **Z.** for Zoology, **Min.** for Mineral, **Eccl.** for Ecclesiastical ; also the following words in full, **Law, Coin, Tool,** are placed at the extreme right-hand edges of the lines. Words in brackets indicate some correlation, *e.g.* **BYE** (cricket).
5. A very wide range of words has been recorded, and these include many new words of common occurrence such as : **ASDIC, RADAR, CORGI, HAYWIRE, GREMLIN, COMPERE, POLIO, DEVALUE, SNOOPER, CLIPPIE, PHONEY, LANDGIRL, BIZONAL,** etc. ; few of these are to be found in any other dictionary.
6. The present and past participles of nearly all verbs are recorded.

These distinctive features materially reduce the time that has to be spent in the search for interesting clues.

A large number of dictionaries have been consulted ; these include *The Shorter Oxford Dictionary, The Century, Chambers's, Nuttall's, Webster's Collegiate Dictionary* ; also etymological and classical dictionaries, Roget's *Thesaurus*, and Nuttall's *Synonyms and Antonyms*. Clue words have been taken from encyclopædias, *The Statesman's Year Book*, Dr. Brewer's *Reader's Handbook*, and authoritative books on Glass, China, Pewter, Curios, etc.

Words such as **CRITH, HELITE, CHENAR, LIBIDO, ZYGOTE,** etc., have been collected from scientific books and reports dealing with Modern Chemistry, Electricity, Physics, Zoology, Botany, Engineering, Physiology, etc., also from books on Theosophy and New Thought. Store catalogues and the special catalogues referring to wireless apparatus, tools, seeds, drapery, and other trades have been ransacked. A wide range of terms dealing with sports and pastimes has been included, as for example : **SCRUM, CAPPED, STANCE, DORMY, ROQUET, BURNED, GOLD, HYPE, OXER, CRAPS.**

Australian, South African, Canadian, Indian, American, and foreign words, such as **COOEE, TREK, MUSH, BHYLE, PRONTO, DUCE, TCHEKA,** are represented.

The mythological names include many Greek, Roman, Norse, Egyptian, Chaldean, and Hindu Gods.

Nearly all English words have in the course of centuries passed through many variations in their spellings. For example, in Murray's *New English Dictionary* the spelling of the word " POWDER " has between the thirteenth and seventeenth centuries passed through the following variations, *poudre, pudre, puder, powdre, powdir, powdyr, pouder, powdere, poudire, pouldre, pulder, poulder, powlder* ; and to these might be added the Scots variations of *pouther* and *powther*. A number of variations in spelling have been collected, but the range of variations recorded in different dictionaries is so large that those now given should not be regarded as exhaustive.

The selection of suitable definitions or synonyms for the words of three or four letters seldom presents any difficulty ; in fact, these short words often have so many completely different meanings that more than one line is required to

vii

indicate possible clue solutions. For example, **BOX** may refer to a receptacle, a shrub, a driver's seat, a box at the theatre, an affair of fisticuffs, or to some occult nautical rite in which a compass is involved.

The longer words are usually more definite in their meanings; but **BESTED** and **WORSTED** may in some cases be synonymous terms, whilst **CLEAVE** may imply either "adhered to" or "split asunder." Crossword setters, however, have a somewhat similar outlook as that master of the English language, Humpty Dumpty, who declared that : "When *I* use a word, it means just what I choose it to mean—neither more nor less."

No attempt has been made to define well-known words which have precise meanings and have no reasonable synonyms, unless some useful correlation can be suggested. The extreme difficulty of defining the obvious is one of long standing. In Dr. Johnson's famous dictionary, the following entry occurs, "**STRIKER**—one who strikes"; more modern dictionaries amplify the above to "one who, or that which, strikes"; but neither of these definitions can be regarded as helpful or illuminating. In any case, the crossword setter, bound by no inhibitions and having no compunction in splitting up words to suit his nefarious purpose—who insists that **BOOKSHOP** is a voluminous dance—will, in spite of any exact or meritorious definition, persist in evolving his uncanny mystifications.

This particular aspect of crosswords has been delightfully epitomized in the sonnet commemorating the 5,000th Crossword in *The Times*, here reproduced by the kind permission of its author.

TO THE EDITOR OF THE TIMES

Sir,

Much have I travelled in another life,
Taken the golden road to Samarkand,
Rolled down to Rio, wandered down the Strand
(Bananaless), asked after Laban's wife.
I swore, " I will not cease from mental strife
Nor shall my pencil slumber in my hand
Till I have re-discovered Penguinland
And found a cricketer's Malayan knife."

In vain ; the tangled clues still tantalize
And synonyms elude, like runic rhymes.
So would-be solvers with lack-lustre eyes,
Confronted with the anagram for limes,
Look at each other with a wild surmise
Silent, upon a crossword in The Times.

Yours faithfully,

ELTON EDE

The various items enumerated under the heading GENERAL INFORMA-TION will frequently be found of special value in elucidating clues without the necessity of delving into a selection of reference books.

The compiler wishes to express his thanks to those numerous correspondents who so kindly forwarded valuable suggestions. It is his hope that this new volume will be found to fulfil the multifarious requirements of earnest crossword solvers and setters and so enhance the pleasures of the crossword hour.

H. W. HILL.

Avalon

A B a Hebrew month
A D a short advertisement
A E one (Sc.)
A H !
A I South American three-toed sloth   **Z.**
A L " the " in Arabic
A M
A N if, ornate box
A P son of (Welsh)
A S Roman pound
A S an integer; Roman bronze   **Coin**
A T
A X axe   **Tool**
A Y yes; yea; more so

B A the soul (Egypt)
B E exist
B O sacred tree of Buddha   **B.**
B Y

C A' ca' canny (Sc.)
C O company

D O ditto; act; perform
D O 1st note   **Mus.**

E A Chaldean fish god
E A an inlet; drainage canal in Fens
E E eye (Sc.)
E H !
E L " the " in Spanish
' E M them
E M a printing space   **Meas.**
E N a printing space   **Meas.**
E X late; out of

F A 4th note   **Mus.**
F O Chinese Buddha
F U Chinese prefecture
F Y ! fie; denoting disgust

G E Mother-Earth (Gr.)
G O proceed; depart; fare

H A !
H E
H I !
H O !

I D fish (carp) also ide   **Z.**
I F supposing that
I L " the " in Italian
I' M I am
I N
I O triumphal cry
I O beloved by Jupiter
I S
I T personality; sex appeal

J O a sweetheart (Sc.)

K A jackdaw (Sc.)   **Z.**
K A ethereal double (Egypt)
K O knock out
K Y kye; kine; cattle (Sc.)   **Z.**
L A 6th note   **Mus.**
L I Chinese mile   **Meas.**
L O ! behold

M A goddess of Right (Egypt)
M E
M I 3rd note   **Mus.**
M O (half-a-mo); medical Officer   **Med.**
M P a legislator; a politician
M Y

N O

O D magnetic force
O F
O G King of Basan
O H
O K all correct
O N
O P a short work; opus
O R alternatively; heraldic gold
O S bone; mouth   **Med.**
O X   **Z.**

P A Maori fort
P I mixed type (printing)

R A hawk-headed sun-god (Egypt)
R E concerning
R E ra, 2nd note   **Mus.**

S I 7th note   **Mus.**
S O
S T short street; saint

T A thanks
T I tree-lily (Polynesia)   **B.**
T O
T V (television)

U G disgust; a surfeit
U P
U R of the Chaldees
U S
U T 1st note   **Mus.**

V A go on   **Mus.**
V E brother of Odin
V O a creek

W E
W O ! whoa ! stop

Y A !
Y E you; the (obs.)

Z O Image (Jap.)

A

AAH the Moon-God of Egypt
AAM 30-35 gallons, Dutch liquid **Meas.**
ABA Eastern camel-hair fabric
ABB yarn for the warp
ABC a railway guide
ABP abbr. for Archbishop
ABU father (Arabic)
ABY atone ; pay penalty; retribution
ACE aviator; particle; (cards)
ACT deed in writing; do; perform **Law**
ADD join; tag; annex; append; tot
ADO stir ; fuss; commotion; hubbub
ADS. advertisements
ADZ adze **Tool**
AFT abaft ; astern **Naut.**
AGA Turkish officer; agha
AGE era ; period ; epoch ; senility
AGO past; gone
AHA!
AID succour; help; subsidy; assistant
AIK oak (Sc.) **B.**
AIL suffer; pain; peak; pine
AIM object; direct; intend; purpose
AIN own (Sc.)
AIR mien; ventilate; display; tune
AIT river or lake islet; eyot
AKE ache (obs.)
ALA wing or side petal of blossom **B.**
ALB white linen clerical vestment **Eccl.**
ALE mead; beer
ALK resin from turpentine tree
ALL entirely; whole
ALP pasture land
ALS also (Sc.)
ALT high notes in the scale **Mus.**
AMA holy wine or vessel **Eccl.**
AMP electrical unit **Meas.**
ANA miscellaneous facts; Celtic goddess
ANA equal parts **Med.**
AND the ampersand; &
ANE one (Sc.)
ANN annat (Sc.) **Law**
ANT emmet; pismire; termite **Z.**
ANU Celtic goddess; Babylonian sea-god
ANY
APE imitate; copy; mimic; monkey **Z.**
APT appropriate; pertinent; prone
ARC bow; luminous bridge
ARE cf. hectare (Fr.) **Meas.**
ARK chest; coffer; place of refuge **Eccl.**
ARM equip; limb; estuary
ART skill; dexterity; craft
ARY any (Soc.)
ASA gum; Norse God **B.**
ASE Peer Gynt's mother
ASH cinder; forest tree; wood **B.**
ASK interrogate; invite; sue
ASP poisonous snake (Cleopatra) **Z.**

ASS moke; burro; donkey **Z.**
ATE Goddess of Mischief
AUF fool; oaf; simpleton
AUK flightless sea-bird; gare fowl **Z.**
AVA kava; Hawaiian palm-lily drink
AVE prayer; hail **Eccl.**
AWA' away (Sc.)
AWE reverential veneration
AWL the cobbler's tool; bradawl **Tool**
AWN beard in chaff **B.**
AXE to cut down; hatchet **Tool**
AYE yea; for ever

B

BAA to bleat
BAB fishing bob
BAC ferry; brewing tub
BAD depraved; detrimental;evil;baneful
BAG sack; wallet; pouch; steal
BAH ! a derogatory exclamation
BAM bamboozle; hoax
BAN muslin; bar; interdict; outlaw
BAP Scotch scone
BAR ban; prohibit; hinder; stop; ingot
BAT spree; batsman; vampire
BAY mill-dam; bark; laurel **B.**
BBC (broadcasting)
BED couch; berth; layer; plant
BEE emblem of the French Empire **Z.**
BEG crave; implore; entreat; petition
BEL Baal; a Babylonian God
BEN (Big Ben); mountain; within (Sc.)
BEN winged seed of ben-tree **B.**
BET lay; wager; stake; gamble; pledge
BEY or **BEG,** a Turkish title
BIB feeder; sip; tipple; whiting pout **Z**
BID order; charge; direct; offer; invite
BIG huge; swollen; pregnant; barley **B.**
BIN a receptacle for wine, corn, etc.
BIS encore **Mus.**
BIT (horse's bit); piece; fragment **Tool**
BOA snake; fur collar **Z.**
BOB style of hairdressing
BOB sleigh; shilling **Coin**
BOG sog; morass; swamp; marsh
BOK a South African deer **Z.**
BOM boma; boa; snake **Z.**
BOO cry down; decry; hoot; execrate
BOT the larva of the bot-fly **Z.**
BOW arc; bob; bend; a tie; prow **Naut.**
BOX (theatre); (compass); driver's seat
BOX case; chest; encase; shrub **B.**
BOX cuff; buffet; spar; fight
BOY lad; page; stripling; Champagne
BOZ Charles Dickens
BRA woman's garment
BUB yeast; strong drink; boy (U.S.A.)
BUD sprout; blossom; graft **B.**
BUG bed-bug; bugbear **Z.**

BUM hum; bailiff; a loafer
BUN style of coiffure; a confection
BUR burr; rough edge; chestnut shell **B.**
BUS an omnibus
BUT yet; except; nevertheless; unless
BUY purchase; bribe; corrupt
BYE (cricket); (golf); (tournament draw)

C

CAB cabriolet; 3 pints (Heb.) **Meas.**
CAD a vulgarian
CAM (machinery)
CAN to preserve; pannikin
CAP to out-do; (hunt collection)
CAR vehicle
CAT tackle; whip; puss; mouser **Z.**
CAW also kaw
CAY kay; key; shoal; reef; islet
CEE a shape of spring
CID Spanish chief; poem
CIG usually a fag
CIT citizen
CLY to steal
COB pony; male swan; spider **Z.**
COB a head; spike of maize; nut **B.**
COB harbour; clay; basket; dollar **Coin**
COD pod; husk; deceive; codfish **Z.**
C.O.D. cash on delivery
COG toothed wheel; small boat **Naut.**
COG coax; wheedle; cheat; wooden bowl
COL mountain pass; nek
CON study; memorize; steer; a knock
COO (dove)
COP hill; head; tuft
COP policeman ; arrest
COR heart
COS lettuce **B.**
COT cottage; crib; small boat **Naut.**
COW browbeat; intimidate; depress **Z.**
COX coxswain **Naut.**
COY shy; bashful; demure; diffident
COZ cousin
CRI the crackle of pewter
CRU yield; produce; grape-juice (Fr.)
CRY sob; yell; bawl; blazon
CUB enclosure for cattle **Z.**
CUD food for re-chewing
CUE (billiards); (acting)
CUP to bleed; a beverage
CUR mongrel; pariah **Z.**
CUT incision; gash; wound; channel
CUT chop; sever; carve; avoid; shorten
CWT a hundredweight **Meas.**

D

DAB fish; expert **Z.**
DAD a blow; to thrash; to scatter
DAG shred; cut

DAG dagger; pistol
DAH dhar; Burmese curved knife
DAK post; bungalow (Ind.)
DAL lentil **B.**
DAM Indian coin; barrier **Coin**
DAN tub; a title
DAP to fish with a may-fly
DAR dace **Z.**
DAW dawn; jackdaw **Z.**
DAY epoch; era; time
DEB a debutante
DEE die (Sc.)
DEN cave; haunt; snuggery
DEW an aqueous precipitation
DEY Turkish title; bey; dairymaid
DIB dip; make holes
DID diddled; performed
DIE stamp; (dice); perish **Tool**
DIG delve; scoop; excavate
DIK trouble
DIM obscure; vague; tarnish
DIN clamour; racket; row **Phot.**
DIP dop; duck; douse; souse
DIS to fail; Pluto; the underworld
DIT a ditty (Spens.)
DIV evil spirit (Persian)
DOD clip; poll; lop
DOE female of fallow-deer, hare, rabbit **Z.**
DOG follow; trail; track **Z.**
DOM a Portuguese title
DON put on; assume; a Spanish title
DOP to dip; duck **Z.**
DOP Cape brandy
DOR befool; mock; mockery; bedim
DOR dorr; dung-beetle; drone **Z**
DOT dowry; point; stop; speck
DOW fit and able
DRY sere; parch; desiccate
DUB to smooth; rub; confer knighthood
DUD worthless; defective
DUE owing; proper; becoming
DUG udder; nudged; exhumed; excavated
DUN mound; dark colour; gloomy
DUN to cure fish; to demand payment
DUO song in two parts **Mus.**
DUP to open
DUX a leader
DWT a pennyweight **Meas.**
DYE colour; tinge; stain

E

EAN to produce
EAR plough or till; lug; heed
EAT chew; consume; devour; erode
EAU -de-Cologne
EBB recede; wane; subside
ECU five-franc piece **Con.**
EEL **Z.**
EEN eyes (Sc.)

E'EN even
E'ER ever
EFT a newt; forthwith (obs.) **Z.**
EGG incite; impel; stimulate **Z.**
EGO the self-conscious subject
EIK eke; add; addition (Sc.)
EKE increase; likewise; in addition
ELD old age; olden times; decrepitude
ELF sprite; gnome; imp; pixy; fairy
ELK wapiti; the whooper swan **Z.**
ELL 45 inches (cloth) **Meas.**
ELM **B.**
EMU Australian bird, cassowary type **Z.**
END kill; close; conclude; terminate
ENE once (Sc.)
ENS entity
EON eternity; perfection; an age; aeon
EOS Dawn Goddess
ERA age; period; epoch; cycle
ERE before; sooner than
ERF small garden in S. Africa
ERG unit of work **Meas.**
ERN sea eagle **Z.**
ERR offend; sin; wander; trespass
ERS vetch **B.**
ESS the letter " S "
ETC et cetera, and so forth
EVE evening; the day before an event
EWE a female sheep **Z.**
EYE observe; watch; view; bud **B.**

F

FAD whim; craze; crochet; hobby
FAG knot; end; cigarette
FAG drudge; fatigue; a bore
FAM the hand (slang)
FAN a votary; agitate; inflame
FAP drunk; fuddles (Shak.)
FAR distant; remote; buck-wheat **B.**
FAT printing term; vat; obese
FAW gypsy
FAY fairy; elf; fit closely
FAY fey; to clean out
FEB a short month
FED ate; subsisted; supplied
FEE remuneration; pay; reward; toll
FEN marsh lands;(Chinese) **Coin.**
FET get; fetch (obs.)
FEU tenure **Law**
FEW scant; rare; scarce
FEY fay; spiritual exaltation; fated
FEZ cap with tassel
FIB petty falsehood
FID a wedge **Naut.**
FIE !
FIG excrescence; tobacco; a fruit **B.**
FIL (Iraq), (Jordan) **Coin.**
FIN an organ of locomotion **Z.**
FIR a cone-bearing tree **B.**
FIT appropriate; qualified; spasm **Med.**

FIX quandary; dilemma; hitch; tie
FLU influenza **Med.**
FLY vehicle; sly; observant; abscond
FLY printing term; flee; decamp **Z.**
FOB watch pocket; impose; delude
FOE antagonist; opponent; enemy
FOG moss; rank grass; thick mist **B.**
FOH Buddha (Chinese)
FOO Chinese department
FOP a dandy; a nut; beau; coxcomb
FOR on this account
FOU tipsy; full; a bushel (Sc.) **Meas.**
FOX deceive; to stain; reynard **Z.**
FOY farewell feast
FRA brother; (Fra Anselmo)
FRO from; away; back
FRY cook; swarm; smolt **Z.**
FUB fat man; cheat
FUD hare's tail **Z.**
FUG frowsty warmth
FUM Chinese phoenix
FUN merriment; jollification
FUR incrustation; a pelt **Z.**

G

GAB talk; a hook
GAD gauntlet spike; wedge **Tool**
GAD rod; goad; to rove
GAE go (Sc.)
GAG a wheeze; to silence
GAL girl
GAM gossip; talk; school of whales **Z.**
GAM mouth; leg
GAP fissure; rift; cranny; chink
GAR to compel (Sc.); a marine fish **Z.**
GAS to gab; ether; gasoline **Chem.**
GAT pistol; a strait; a gap
GAY gey; lively; merry; blithe; joyous
GED pike or luce **Z.**
GEE turn; go faster
GEL viscous, colloidal
GEM jewel; treasure; a leaf-bud **B.**
GEN detailed information; manna (Heb).
GEO gio; creek; voe; vae; firth; frith
GET win; gain; acquire; breed
GEY gay; fairly; rather (Sc.)
GIB a cat; the Rock **Z.**
GID sheep-disease; sturdy
GIE give (Sc.)
GIF if (Sc.)
GIG whirl; cloth machine; vehicle
GIM neat
GIN machine; snare; schnapps
GIN native woman (Australia)
GIP clean herrings
GNU buffalo (S. Africa) **Z.**
GOA Tibetan antelope **Z.**
GOB mouthful; refuse coal
GOB worked out mine
GOD Deity; idol; image

4

GOG and Magog
GOT seized; procured; achieved
GRU ice
GUE Shetland violin **Mus.**
GUM stick; mucilage; resin **B.**
GUN a revolver or pistol
GUP idle chatter; rumour
GUT narrow channel; intestine **Med.**
GUY rope; oddity; to burlesque **Naut.**
GYM gymnastics
GYP college servant; bedmaker

H

HAD befooled; caught; kept; owned
HAE have (Sc.)
HAG parasite fish; virago; beldam **Z.**
HAH !
HAM Noah's second son
HAM a heavy actor
HAN plural of have (Spens.)
HAP chance; luck; accident; fortuity
HAS owns; possesses; acquires
HAT dignity of Cardinal; bonnet
HAW hawthorn berry **B.**
HAW hedge; boundary
HAY cut grass; hedge; fence
HEL Goddess of Death (Scand.)
HEM a cough; to sew; to edge
HEN a fowl **Z.**
HEP hip; berry of the dog-rose **B.**
HER
HET hot and bothered
HEW chop; hack; fell; cut
HEY !
HIC ! a small hiccup
HID secreted; cached; concealed
HIE a cry; to hasten
HIM
HIN 6 quarts (Heb.) **Meas.**
HIP rafter (Arch.); berry; hep **B.**
HIP-hurray
HIS
HIT success; strike; cosh; beat
HOA ! ahoy
HOB part of grate; hub
HOB a rustic; a fairy
HOD (for bricks); a coal-scuttle
HOE a promontory; to weed **Tool**
HOG scrubbing broom; boar; pig **Z.**
HOG to cut hair; bend
HOO ! hold ! stop !
HOP small dance; plant **B.**
HOT violent; acrid; fervid; ardent
HOW glen; dell; low hill
HOX to hamstring
HOY small ship **Naut.**
HOY ! ahoy ; hoa !
HUB hilt; a boss; a centre
HUB mark on quoits

HUE and cry; tint
HUG embrace; enfold; clasp
HUH !
HUM to croon; drone; impose on
HUN Tartar; savage nomadic Asiatic race
HUP ! a horse hastener
HUT hovel; shed; cabin; cot
HUX method of fishing
HYP depression; hip

I

IBO native of East Nigeria
ICE to cover with sugar
ICH Dien
ICY frigid; cold; chilling; frosty
IDE kind of carp **Z.**
IDO artificial language
ILK like; the same
ILL ailing; evil; badly; sick
IMP extend; strengthen; graft; sprite
INK
INN caravanserai; tavern; hostelry
ION (Electrolysis)
I.O.U. a note of hand
IRE rage; fury; resentment; passion
IRK weary; trouble; distress
ISE I shall (Sc.)
ISH exit; issue (Sc.)
ISM ideological prejudice
ITS belonging to it
IVY a creeper sacred to Bacchus **B.**

J

JAB prod; poke; stab; a thrust
JAD a quarrying cut
JAG a notch; a binge; to stab
JAH Jehovah
JAK bread-fruit tree **B.**
JAM child's garment; squeeze; a conserve
JAP Japanese
JAR discord; jolt; jangle; gallipot
JAT Indo-Aryan
JAW lecture; the mouth; to splash **Med.**
JAY simpleton; nitwit **Z.**
JEE to move; to budge (Sc.)
JET spray; black variety of lignite **Min.**
JEU a game
JEW Hebrew; to overreach
JIB to balk; to shy; a sail **Naut.**
JIG tune; dance; mechanical guide **Tool**
JOB stab; profession; work
JOE a sweetheart (Sc.)
JOG rog; push; nudge; remind; trot
JOT an iota; a tittle; to note
JOW to toll; a stroke of a bell (Sc.)
JOY rapture; ecstasy; bliss; glee
JUD a mass of coal

JUG	incarcerate; an ewer; to stew	
JUR	earth-nut	**B.**
JUT	protrude; project; to collide	

K

KAA	The Rock Python	**Z.**
KAE	jackdaw (Sc.)	**Z.**
KAF	fountain conferring immortality	
KAM	crooked (Shak.)	
KAT	Egyptian weight	**Meas.**
KAW	caw	
KAY	shoal; cay; key; reef	
KEA	parrot that kills sheep (N.Z.)	**Z.**
KEB	ewe; sheep louse	**Z.**
KEF	drugged stupor	
KEG	small cask or barrel	
KEN	know; recognise; knowledge	
KEP	to catch (Sc.)	
KET	carrion; matted wool; a fleece (Sc.)	
KEV	1,000 Electron-Volts	**Meas.**
KEX	fool's parsley; dried stalks	**B.**
KEY	quay; cay; crib; wedge; clamp	**Mus.**
KID	faggot; bundle of sticks	
KID	tub; deceive; hoax; young goat	**Z.**
KIM		
KIN	relationship; affinity; kindred	
KIP	skin of young cattle; play truant	
KIP	doss; dose; snooze; coin	
KIT	tub; bottle; violin; gear	**Mus.**
KOA	acacia (Sandwich Islands)	**B.**
KOB	water antelope	**Z.**
KOP	hill (S. Africa)	
KRI	Hebrew marginal direction	
KRU	Kroo; a Liberian	
KYA	native hut (S. Africa)	
KYE	kine (Sc.)	**Z.**

L

LAC	dye; shellac; transparent resin	**Coin**
LAD	youngster; stripling; boy	
LAG	convict; dawdle; loiter; dally	
LAM	to thrash; weaving device	
LAP	fold; wrap; polish; circuit; drink	
LAR	Roman Household God	
LAR	white-handed gibbon	**Z.**
LAT	inscribed pillar (India)	
LAT	Latvian money	**Coin**
LAV	a word (Gypsy)	
LAW	an allowance; edict; statute; canon	
LAX	slack; loose; remiss	
LAY	lea; ballad; exorcise; put	
LAY	non-clerical; laic; inexpert	
LAZ	las, Black Sea Turks	
LBW	leg before wicket	
LEA	measure of yarn; meadow	**Meas.**
LEA	lay; open land; pasture	
LED	induced; helped; conducted	
LEE	sheltered; lea; meadow	

LEG	a tack in sailing	**Naut.**
LEI	plural of **LEU;** garland	**Coin**
LEK	bird courtship; coin	**Z.**
LEO	5th sign of the Zodiac	
LET	(tennis); permit; allow; lease; hire	
LET	hindrance; prevent; delay	
LEU	Rumanian money	**Coin**
LEW	luke-warm; tepid	
LEX	an enactment	**Law**
LEV	} Bulgarian money	**Coin**
LEY		
LEY	lea; pasture; common pewter	
LIB	ad lib.	
LID	top; cover; coverlet	
LIE	falsehood; rest; recline; repose	
LIN	a waterfall; to cease	
LIP	touch the edge	
LIS	litigation	**Law**
LIS	fleur-de-lis; heraldic lily	**B.**
LIT	lighted; kindled; ignited	
LOB	clumsy; (cricket); worm	**Z.**
LOG	record; tree-trunk	**Naut.**
LOG	¾ pint (Hebrew)	**Meas.**
LOO	card game	
LOP	truncate; amputate; dock	
LOT	to catalogue; fate; portion	
LOW	base; vile; abject; depressed	
LOW	bellow; moo; to flame; to blaze (Sc.)	
LOY	narrow spade	
LSD	money, (Libra; Solidus; Denarius)	
LUD	King Lud	
LUE	to sift	
LUG	ear; tug; haul; drag	
LUM	chimney (Sc.)	
LUX	unit of light	**Meas.**
LUZ	a legendary bone	
LYE	alkaline solution	**Chem.**
LYM	dog on leash	**Z.**

M

MAB	the queen of the fairies	
MAC	son of (Sc.)	
MAD	crazy; demented; raving; insane	
MAG	chatter; steal; magpie	**Z.**
MAG	half-penny	**Coin**
MAM	Madame; ma'am	
MAN	employee; husband; mankind	**Naut.**
MAO	The Peacock	**Z.**
MAP	delineate; chart; draw	
MAR	spoil; deface; impair; disfigure	
MAT	dull surface; weave; interlace; twist	
MAW	craw; crop stomach	
MAX	a kind of gin	
MAY	jet; allow; hawthorn blossom	**B.**
MEL	honey	
MEN	humanity	
MET	Metropolitan; a bushel	**Meas.**
MEV	Million Electron-Volts	**Meas.**
MEW	sea-gull; moult	**Z.**

MEW cage; confine; a cat-call
MHO electrical unit of conductivity **Meas.**
MID central; amid; middle
MIL one-thousandth of an inch **Meas.**
MIM prim; demure; precise
MIR Russian commune
MIX blend; combine; jumble; mingle
MNA mina; 50 shekels **Coin**
MOA extinct bird, emu type (N.Z.) **Z.**
MOB cap; rabble; populace; crowd
MOD assembly; meeting
MOD Gaelic choral contest **Mus.**
MOE mow; grimace; mop
MOG move away
MON Cambodian language
MOO cow noise
MOP swab; a hiring-fair; a grimace
MOT bon mot; witticism
MOW stack; heap; pile of hay; cut down
MOW facial expression; moe
MRS mistress
MUD mire; sludge; slime
MUG fool; face; cup
MUM silence; a special brew of beer
MUN man (dialect)
MUX to spoil; a mess
MYA shell-fish **Z.**

N

NAB seize; nap; grab; a knoll
NAE none (Sc.)
NAG harass; pester; horse **Z.**
NAM distraint (obs.) **Law**
NAP slumber; doze; drouse; forty-winks
NAP a card game; a racing tip
NAY contrariwise
N.C.O. non-commissioned officer
NEB beak; nose; nib; a point
NEE born (Fr.)
NEF silver model ship; cadenas; casket
NEK a pass (S. Africa); a col
NEO new style
NEP catmint; knot in cotton fibre **B.**
NET neat; nett; snare; capture
NEW novel; recent; fresh; modern
NIB beak; point; neb
NIL nihil; zero; nothing
NIM steal; margosa oil
NIP squeeze; pinch; sip; a dram
NIS not so; imp; hobgoblin; mix
NIT insect's egg **Z.**
NIX water elf; nothing
NOB a knave at cribbage; the head
NOD bow; beck; drowse
NOG small pot; tree nail
NOG wooden brick; peg; noggin; ale
NOM de plume
NOR logic
NOT

NOW
NOX Nyx; personification of night
NOY annoy (Spens.)
NUB shove; hang; knob; gist
NUN a religeuse; a sister **Eccl.**
NUR knot in wood
NUT a dandy; screwed bolt end **B.**
NUT boss on anchor **Naut.**
NUX (vomica) **Med., B.**
NYE brood of pheasants **Z.**
NYS none is (Spens.)
NYX Goddess of Night, daughter of Chaos

O

OAF changeling; fool; dolt; idiot
OAK outer door **B.**
OAR to row; an oarsman **Naut.**
OAT a grain; a pan-pipe **B., Mus.**
OBI oby; magic; a fetish (West Indies)
OBI Japanese sash
OCA potato (S. America) **B.**
OCH ! oh ! or ah ! (Sc. & Ir.)
ODD singular; peculiar; quaint; droll
ODE poem or song set to music
ODO Bishop of Bayeux, 1066 A.D.
O'ER poetical over
OES O's; circlets
OFF away; gone
OFT often; frequently; repeatedly
OHM electrical resistance **Meas.**
OHO !
OIL anoint; lubricate; a lubricant
OKE Turkish weight, 2¾ lbs. **Meas.**
OLD antique; archaic; pristine; aged
OLM a blind lizard **Z.**
ONE individual; unity; undivided
OOF money
OOM Uncle (Cape Dutch)
OPE open
OPS Goddess of Wealth; wife of Saturn
OPT to choose; elect; pick
ORB globe; circle
ORC whale; grampus; an ogre **Z.**
ORD edge; beginning
ORE Scandinavian mite **Coin, Min.**
ORT a bit; refuse; a crumb
OUR three-quarters of an hour
OUT without; beyond; get out !
OVA eggs **Z.**
OWE run up an account
OWL to smuggle **Z.**
OWN possess; admit; concede
OZS ounces **Meas.**

P

PAD cushion; stuff; paw **Z.**
PAH !
PAH stockade (New Zealand)

PAL	staunch friend; palooka; mate	
PAM	knave of clubs at loo	
PAN	forest god; small pool	
PAP	conical hill; nipple	
PAR	equality; (golf)	
PAR	parr; young salmon	**Z.**
PAS	pace; precedence	
PAT	dab; tap; rap; caress; aptly	
PAU	bustard (S. Africa)	**Z.**
PAW	pad; handle roughly	**Z.**
PAX	kiss of peace; an osculatory	**Eccl.**
PAY	to cover with pitch; stipend; wages	
PEA	(thimble-rigging)	**B.**
PED	pack-saddle; basket	
PED	small pack-saddle; pedal	**Mus.**
PEG	short drink; spigot; spile	
PEN	pound; enclosure; mountain; indite	
PEN	female swan; quill	**Z.**
PEP	energy; drive (U.S.A.)	
PER	by	
PET	temper; fondle; a favourite	**Z.**
PEW	a seat in church	**Eccl.**
PIA	arrowroot (Polynesian)	**B.**
PIE	magpie; pye	**Z.**
PIE	prayer-book; pi; mixed print	
PIG	earthen vessel; to guzzle	**Z.**
PIN	half a firkin; transfix	**Meas.**
PIN	peg; nail; to fasten	
PIN	cataract; eye disease	**Med.**
PIP	to black-ball; chirp; a depression	
PIP	disease of fowls; melancholy	**B.**
PIT	set; match; mine; abyss	
PIU	more	**Mus.**
PIX	holy box; coin box; pyx	
PLY	fold; layer; bias	**Naut.**
POA	a genus of grass	**B.**
POD	husk; to swell	**B.**
POD	a shoal of whales or seals	**Z.**
POE	or parson-bird (New Zealand)	**Z.**
POH	!	
POM	small Pomeranian dog	**Z.**
POP	burst; explode; pawn	
POT	to shoot ; tankard; mug	
POW	poll; head (Sc.)	
POX	a disease	**Med.**
POY	balancing-pole; a grant	
POZ	positive; certain	
PRO	for; professional	
PRY	peer; snoop; examine	
PUB	public-house	
PUD	paw; pad	**Z.**
PUG	dog; fox or monkey; pugilist	**Z.**
PUN	a form of humour; a paronomasia	
PUP	to whelp; young dog or seal	**Z.**
PUR	purr; curr; (owl or cat noise)	
PUS	matter	**Med.**
PUT	to steer; bud; game at cards; rustic	
PUT	wanton woman; signal of distress	
PUY	volcanic formation	
PYA	Burmese money	**Coin**
PYE	pie; magpie	**Z.**
PYX	pix; holy box; coin box at the Mint	

Q

QUA	as, Latin	
QUI	who, Latin	
QUO	whither, Latin	

R

RAD	radical; afraid (Sc.)	
RAG	a famous club; to torment; garment	
RAI	one-third acre (Siam)	**Meas.**
RAJ	power (India)	
RAM	engine; prow; butt; cram	**Z.**
RAN	raced; scurried; flowed; melted	
RAP	snatch; tap	
RAP	counterfeit Irish halfpenny	**Coin**
RAS	vizier (Abyssinia)	
RAT	to desert; a rodent	**Z.**
RAW	bleak; crude; uncooked	
RAX	reach; strain (Sc.)	
RAY	part of flower; a beam	**B.**
RAY	the skate; sheep scab	**Z.**
RED	to disentangle; revolutionary	
REE	hen-bird of ruff	**Z.**
REE	riddle; tipsy; Portuguese	**Coin**
REF	referee	
REH	saline efflorescence (India)	
REI	Portuguese money of account	**Coin**
REN	the kidney	**Med.**
REP	debauchee; rip	
REP	a fabric; repetition	
RES	a thing; a point	**Law**
RET	to rot flax, hemp or jute	
REV	to speed up ; Reverend	**Eccl**
REX	a king	
RIA	inlet of the sea	
RIB	a petiole; water-cress	**B.**
RID	to free; clear; expel; destroy	
RIE	rye	**B.**
RIG	wanton; manipulate	**Naut., Z.**
RIM	brim; border; edge	
RIO	ounce (Japan); a tael	**Meas.**
RIP	fish-basket; tear; rend; a Lothario	
RIT	strike; tear (Sc.)	
ROB	rook; fleece; strip; fruit syrup	
ROC	fabulous bird; rok	**Z.**
ROD	twig; wand; 5½ yds.	**Meas.**
ROE	of fish; deer	**Z.**
ROG	to jog; to shake	
ROK	roc; fabulous bird	**Z.**
ROM	gipsy; a Romany	
RON	King Arthur's ebony spear	
ROO	a kangaroo	**Z.**
ROT	to decay; putrefy; nonsense	
ROW	line; brawl; a dreadful din; (oars)	
ROY	a king (obs.)	
RUA	storage pit (New Zealand)	

RUB chafe; abrade; dilemma
RUC rok; roc; a fabulous bird **Z.**
RUD rub; polish; flush; ochre
RUE lament; regret; suffer; sorrow
RUE herb of grace **B.**
RUG mat; coverlet; a drink; shaggy dog
RUM grog; queer; quaint; odd; fantastic
RUN hurry; speed; propel; tour; demand
RUT wheel track; groove; desire
RYE rie; (whisky) **B.**
RYE a bird disease

S

SAB sob (Sc.)
SAC bag of liquid **Med.**
SAD sorry; downcast; gloomy; dismal
SAE so (Sc.)
SAG droop; settle; bend; sink
SAI Brazilian monkey **Z.**
SAL Indian timber tree **B.**
SAL salt **Chem.**
SAM together; to collect; to curdle
SAP undermine; juice; a worker **B.**
SAT seated; perched; settled
SAW a saying; an adage; seen **Tool**
SAX a knife; slate-cutter's hammer **Tool**
SAY tell; declare; utter; allege
SEA basin; an ocean; wave surge **Eccl.**
SEC dry flavour
SED (fish-hook); a fillet
SEE watch; descry; heed; a throne **Eccl.**
SEG sedge; a bullock **B., Z.**
SEL self (Sc.)
SEN (Japanese) (Indonesian) **Coin**
SEP sepal; leaf **B.**
SET a twist; squared block; firm fixed
SET group; clique; (filming)
SET Egyptian deity of darkness
SEW stitch; baste
SEX gender
SHA shapo; wild sheep **Z.**
SHE
SHY coy; bashful; diffident; wary
SIB akin to; also syb
SIC as written
SIK to seek (Sc.)
SIL ochre pigment
SIM a Simeonite; low churchman **Eccl.**
SIN transgress; wickedness; iniquity
SIP sup
SIR
SIS girl; sweetheart
SIT brood; incubate; rest; repose
SIX sax (Sc.)
SKI (winter sport)
SKY to loft; heavens; the weather
SLY artful; wily; astute; fly
SNY upward curve
SOB cry; blubber; weep; snivel

SOC privilege; sac **Law**
SOD turf; sward; lawn; grass
SOG a bog; morass; marsh; to saturate
SOL old French halfpenny (Peru) **Coin**
SOL the sun; gold; 5th note **Mus.**
SON off-spring; a disciple
SOP to soak; to steep; a bribe
SOS help !
SOT drunkard
SOU French mite; sol **Coin**
SOW disseminate; plant; broadcast **Z.**
SOX haberdashery
SOY a bean; sauce (Jap.) **B.**
SPA spring; health resort; hydro
SPY espy; behold; detect; observe
STY (in eye); pig-pen **Med.**
SUB subaltern; substitute
SUE prosecute; plead **Law**
SUG a kind of worm **Z.**
SUM add; total; amount; aggregate
SUN Phoebus Apollo; Sol; Helios
SUP sip
SYB sib; akin to
SYN syne; since (Sc.)

T

TAB flap; tally; check
TAD street boy (U.S.A.)
TAG catchword; touch; label; game
TAI Japanese bream **Z.**
TAJ Mahal; headdress (Ind.)
TAN to beat; brown colour
TAP rap; pat; knock; broach
TAP cock; faucet; screw **Tool**
TAR sailor; pitch; bitumen; incite **Naut.**
TAT needlework; pony
TAT native cloth
TAU bug; toad-fish **Z.**
TAU St. Anthony's Cross
TAW a marble; game
TAX accuse; strain; tariff; levy
TEA bohea **B.**
TEC teck; detective
TED spread
TEE (golf); Chinese umbrella
TEG deer; sheep; tag **Z.**
TEN a net drawn up
TER thrice
TEW gear; iron chain; scourge
THE definite article
THO' though
THY
TIB a courtesan
TIC nervous twitch; spasm **Med.**
TIE dead-heat; bind; link; unite
TIG a game; a cup
TIN can; preserve; receptacle; money **Min.**
TIP gratuity; vails; cant; tilt; incline
TIR shooting contest (Fr.)

TIS it is
TIT small bird; pony **Z.**
TOD 28 lbs of wool **Meas.**
TOD bush; fox **B., Z.**
TOE extremity
TOG to dress; a garment
TOK a nesting place of capercaildies **Z.**
TOL take away
TOM male animal **Z.**
TON fashion **Meas.**
TOO more than enough
TOP a toy; vertex; zenith; acme; excel
TOR rocky hill
TOT to add; child **Meas.**
TOW flax; hemp; haul **B.**
TOY to trifle; sport
TRY 3 points at Rugby football
TRY test; essay; attempt; endeavour
TUB a rowing boat **Naut.**
TUG haul; tow; lug **Naut.**
TUI parson-bird (N. Zealand) **Z.**
TUN barrel; large cask **Meas.**
TUP ram; to butt; hammer **Z.**
TUR Caucasian goat **Z.**
TUT !
TUT piece-work; a hassock
TWA two (Sc.)
TWO a pair; brace; couple; deuce
TYE ore washing buddie; tie
TYG tall china cup
TYR a son of Odin

U

UDA purplish brown glaze
UDO Japanese vegetable **B.**
UDO universal language
UGH !
ULE gum (Mexico) **B.**
ULT ultimo
UMA wife of Siva
UNA cat-boat having a centreboard **Naut.**
UNO United Nations Organisation
URE practice; wont; work; exercise
URE wild ox; aurochs **Z.**
URF stunted child (Sc.)
URN jar; vase; receptacle
URY hazy (Sc.)
USE usage; avail; employ; apply; usury
UTA American lizard **Z.**
UTU blood-money; requital (N.Z.)
UVA a bunch **B.**

V

VAC vacation
V.A.D. war worker
VAE voe; gio; creek; firth; frith; fiord
VAG peat (Sc.)
VAN fan; forefront; vehicle; vane

VAS blood vessel **Med.**
VAT also fat; large vessel or tank
VET horse doctor; examine
VEX plague; harass; fret; chafe
VIA by way of
VIE strive; contend; contest
VIM force
VIS power
VIZ namely
VLY vlei; pool (S. Africa)
VOE vae; geo; gio; fiord; estuary; firth
VOL two wings conjoined at base (Her.)
VOW pledge; dedicate; consecrate; oath
VOX voice; song part **Mus.**
VUG rock cavity (Cornish)
VUM vow (Amer.)

W

WAD Manganese ore; mass of paper **Min.**
WAE woe (Sc.)
WAG vibrate; wit; jester; humorist
WAN pale; sickly; languid
WAP whop; a bundle; swat; wrap
WAR strife; enmity; discord; contend
WAS
WAT hare; drunken (Sc.) **Z.**
WAX increase; grow; beeswax
WAY route; passage; track; usage
WEB a textile fabric; cobweb
WED a pledge; to marry
WEE diminutive
WEN (London); tumour; wart **Med.**
WET humid; moist; watery; drench
WEY various weights, salt, corn, &c. **Meas.**
WHO
WHY
WIG vallancy; toupee; periwig; peruke
WIG berate; scold; lecture; upbraid
WIN gain; procure; acquire; achieved
WIS know; also **WIT**
WIT wag; humour; reason; facetiousness
WOE affliction; sorrow; grief; anguish
WOG a coloured gentleman
WON to dwell; an abode (Korea) **Coin**
WON earned; got; swayed; persuaded
WOO to court
WOP whop; whip; Italian
WOT know
WOW event; sound change
WOX waxed (Spens.)
WRY awry; askew; crooked; distorted
WYE a person (Sc.)

Y

YAB jabber (Sc.)
YAH ! exclamation of derision
YAK Thibetan ox **Z.**

YAM sweet potato **B.**
YAP yell; cry; bark
YAW deviate **Naut.**
YEA ay; aye; yes; truly; verily
YEN a gold or silver Japanese **Coin**
YEP yeh; yes (Amer.)
YES yea; aye; ay
YET a gate (Sc.)
YET still; further; besides; however
YEW wood for the bow **B.**
YEX hiccough
YID a Jew
YIP pert forward girl (Sc.)
YOD phonetic sound " y "
YON yonder
YOU

YOW ewe (Sc.) **Z.**
YUG an age of the world (Hind.)

Z

ZAK Kashmir raft
ZAX slate cutter; sax **Tool**
ZEA maize **B.**
ZED or **ZEE** the letter Z
ZEL cymbal **Mus.**
ZHO zobo; hybrid yak and cow **Z.**
ZIP liveliness; a ping; a fastening
ZOO
ZUZ an ancient Jewish coin **Coin**

A

ABBA Chaldean or Coptic divine   **Eccl.**
ABBE French abbot; priest   **Eccl.**
ABED in bed
ABER river mouth (Celtic)
ABET aid; incite; favour; countenance
ABIB 1st month of the Jewish year
ABLE skilful; adroit; expert; competent
ABLY masterly; powerfully; cleverly
ABUT meet; adjoin; rest; terminate
ABYE aby; atone; pay the penalty (obs.)
ACER the maple-tree   **B.**
ACHE pain; pang; agony; anguish
ACID sour; tart; bitter; vitriolic
ACME zenith; apex; pinnacle; pitch
ACNE a skin disease   **Med.**
ACOP atop; on high (obs.)
ACOR acidity   **Med.**
ACOY accoy; to soothe (obs.)
ACRE 4840 square yards; 4 roods **Meas.**
ACTA proceedings in a court   **Law**
ADAM the first man; a gaoler
ADAR 12th month of the Jewish year
ADIT opening or passage; entrance
ADRY athirst
ADZE adz; a mattock   **Tool**
AEON an age; era; cycle; period; eon
AERY eyry; ayry; an eagle's nest   **Z.**
AERY ethereal; visionary
AFAR away; distant; remote; aloof
AFER the South-West wind
AFFY to betroth; trust; confide (obs.)
AGAR ploughman of playing fields, Eton
AGED elderly; ancient; antiquated
AGEE awry; askew; asquint; ajee
AGEN again
AGHA aga; Turkish Officer; ruler
AGIO premium; discount; brokerage
AGNI Hindu fire-god and protector
AGOG astir; eager; excited
AGUA South American toad   **Z.**
AGUE malarial fever; chilliness   **Med.**
AHEM !
AHOY !
AIDE helper; assistant; coadjutor
AINE elder son; cadet
AINT (are not)
AINU aboriginal (Jap.)
AIRA hair-grass   **B.**
AIRE an altar; Irish freeman
AIRT direction; quarter (Sc.)
AIRY blythe; breezy; ethereal; spacious
AJAR slightly opened
AJEE agee; ajar; askew
AJOG jogging along
AKEE West Indian fruit tree   **B.**
AKIN sib; agnate; similar; related
ALAR having wings
ALAS alack; welladay

ALBE albeit; even though
ALCA sea-auk genus   **Z.**
ALEE on the lee-side   **Naut.**
ALEW halloo (obs.)
ALFA esparto grass   **B.**
ALGA sea-weed   **B.**
ALLA in the manner of   **Mus.**
ALLY alley; a marble of real alabaster
ALLY unite; marry; confederate; friend
ALMA or **ALME**; Egyptian dancing girl
ALMS oblations; gifts; bounty
ALOD allod; freehold
ALOE a large genus of bitter herbs   **B.**
ALOW below; ablaze (Sc.)   **Naut.**
ALPS
ALSO in like manner; further
ALTO male voice of highest pitch **Mus.**
ALUM mordant mineral salt   **Chem.**
AMAH ayah; Indian nurse
AMBE ancient surgical instrument **Med.**
AMBO high reading desk   **Eccl.**
AMEN Egyptian deity of the dead
AMIA bow-fin or mud-fish (N. Amer.) **Z.**
AMIC ammoniac   **Chem.**
AMID betwixt; between; amongst
AMIN ammoniate   **Chem.**
AMIR Ameer; Emir
AMMA a truss; Syrian abbess   **Eccl.**
AMMO ammunition
AMOK amuck; frenzy (Malay)
AMOR Roman cupid; Eros
AMOY language (Formosa)
AMYL a tar product   **Chem.**
ANAK a giant of Palestine
ANEW again; freshly; repeatedly
ANIL the indigo plant   **B.**
ANKH life symbol (Egypt)
ANNA 16 annas to the rupee   **Coin**
ANOA wild ox of the Celebes   **Z.**
ANON at once; then again
ANSA decorated vase-handle
ANTA a pilaster
ANTE a stake at poker
APAY to satisfy; to repay (obs.)
APED copied; imitated; mimicked
APER an impersonator
APEX acme; zenith; pinnacle; point
APIS sacred bull (Egypt)
APOD fish without ventral fins   **Z.**
APSE polygonal recess   **Eccl.**
AQUA water; solution   **Chem.**
ARAB Saracen; Moor
ARAF Mohammedan purgatory
ARAK the areca nut   **B.**
ARAR North African timber tree   **B.**
ARBA covered wagon (Tartar)
ARCA chest or coffer   **Eccl.**
ARCH roguish; cunning; shrewd
AREA yard; enclosure; region; district
ARES Mars, the God of War

ARGO the Argonauts' ship   **Naut.**
ARIA air; tune; melody   **Mus.**
ARID dry; parched; sterile; barren
ARIL outer seed cover   **B.**
ARMS armorial emblems
ARMY host; array; throng; force
AROW successively; in a row
'ARRY jovial Cockney
ARTS crafts; guiles
ARTY spuriously aesthetic
ARUM lily genus   **B.**
ASAR eskar; gravel ridges
ASCI bags of spores   **B.**
ASHY ashen; wan; pallid; hueless
ASIA
ATLI a Norse king (Atle)
ATOM jot; tittle; whit; particle
ATOP acop; on top (obs.)
AULA a hall; a court
AULD old (Sc.)
AUNT (Aunt Sally)
AURA a zephyr; emanation   **Coin**
AUTO da fe; autocar
AVAL an endorsement on a bill
AVEL an awn of barley   **B.**
AVER avouch; confirm; authenticate
AVES birds collectively   **Z.**
AVID eager; greedy; voracious
AVON river (Celt.)
AVOW own; aver; admit; confess
AWAY afar; distant; abroad; absent
AWED inspired by reverence; cowed
AWNY bearded   **B.**
AWRY askew; oblique; crooked
AXAL axial (obs.)
AXED discharged; sacked; cut down
AXIL angle between branch and trunk **B.**
AXIN cochineal ointment
AXIS the chital; Indian spotted deer **Z.**
AXLE axis; spindle; shaft
AYAH amah; Indian nurse
AYES supporting votes
AYRY eyry; eyrie; an eagle's nest   **Z.**
AZER native of Central Asia
AZOL developer   **Phot.**

B

BAAL Phoenician god; false god; idol
BAAS the boss; master (Cape Dutch)
BABA Patriarch of Alexandria; a cake
BABE infant; suckling
BABU Hindu clerk
BACK help; support; wager; retreat
BADE (bid); commanded
BAFF biff; smite; buff
BAFT abaft; an oriental fabric
BAHT (Thailand)   **Coin**
BAIL (cricket); hoop-handle; surety **Law**
BAIT worry; badger; a lure; refreshment

BAKE harden; parch
BALD bare; hairless; prosiac; unadorned
BALE bane; harm; misery; bundle
BALK bauk; impede; refuse; timber
BALL party; rout; globe; bullet
BALM salve; unguent; fragrance
BANC bench (obs.)   **Law**
BAND bond; unite; a troupe; a coterie
BANE poison; ruin; sheep-rot
BANI (Romania)   **Coin**
BANG explosion; a fringe of hair
BANG bhang; the assassin's drug
BANK bench of rowers; deposit
BANT adopt a slimming diet
BARB to shave; (fish-hook); horse **Z.**
BARD wandering minstrel; a poet
BARE naked; nude; exposed; bleak
BARK cortex; yelp; yap; a ship **B., Naut.**
BARM yeast; ferment; leaven
BARN granary; store; out-building
BART baronet
BARU fluffy fibre   **B.**
BASE basis; abject; vile; sordid
BASH smite; baff; biff; wallop; buffet
BASK luxuriate; revel
BASS (ale); low; deep; grave   **Mus.**
BASS American linden tree; perch **Z.**
BAST bass; fibre of that tree   **B.**
BAST cat-headed Egyptian goddess
BATE abate; decrease; lessen; curtail
BATH 6 gallons, Jewish liquid **Meas.**
BAUK balk; beam; ridge; hinder
BAWD a hare (Shak.)   **Z.**
BAWL howl; yawl; yell; shout
BAWN fort; cattle-pen
BAYA the Indian weaver bird   **Z.**
BAYS laurels of distinction   **B.**
BEAD bubble; globule; a moulding
BEAK magistrate; prow; bill; mandible
BEAM rafter; ray; shine; emit; smile
BEAM (wireless system); width **Naut.**
BEAN leguminous plant   **B.**
BEAR carry; uphold; suffer; produce **Z.**
BEAT spent; exhausted; batter; throb
BEAT a policeman's perambulation
BEAU fop; dandy; gallant; coxcomb
BECK beckon; a small stream
BEEF grumble (U.S.A.); strength
BEEN the vina; Indian guitar   **Mus.**
BEEP telephonic signal
BEER ale; lager; swipes
BEET the beetroot   **B.**
BEIN comfortable; well-found (Sc.)
BEJA tribe (Africa)
BELL a model of soundness; to bellow
BELT zone; girdle; band; thrash
BEMA judge's seat; pulpit   **Eccl.**
BEND deflect; stoop; incline; a spree
BEND diagonal band on a shield (Her.)
BENE the oil-plant   **B**

BENT curved; crooked; withered grass	**BOIL** seethe; rage; fume
BERE bear; barley (Sc.) **B.**	**BOKO** nasal organ
BERG mountain; iceberg	**BOLD** brave; valiant; daring; doughty
BERM a ledge; slanting bank	**BOLE** a tree-trunk; recess **B**
BEST worst; defeat; overcome	**BOLL** pod; capsule **B.**
BETA rays	**BOLO** Filipino knife
BEVY swarm; flock; throng	**BOLT** abscond; gulp; missile; fasten; sift
BHEL Bengal quince **B.**	**BOMA** boa; anaconda **Z.**
BHIL a Dravidian race (India)	**BOMB** petard; block-buster
BIAS prejudice; prepossession	**BOND** link; band; contract; (bricks)
BICE pale blue or green	**BONE** to steal; os **Med.**
BIDE await; tarry; stay; dwell	**BONT** many coloured (S. Africa)
BIER a conveyance for the dead	**BONY** full of bones; strong; stout
BIFF baff; buff; smite; crash	**BOOB** booby; dunce; blockhead
BIGA two-horsed Roman chariot	**BOOH** ! a derisive interjection
BIGG bere; a kind of barley (Sc.)	**BOOK** tome; volume; manual
BIKE bicycle; wasp's nest; a swarm **Z.**	**BOOM** boost; resound; def. barrier **Naut.**
BILE ill-humour **Med.**	**BOON** benefit; merry; jovial
BILK balk; cheat; deceive; thwart	**BOOR** clophopper; lout; lubber
BILL fondle; account; placard; poster	**BOOT** gain; to eject; luggage recess
BIND tie; fasten; restrain; secure	**BORA** cold Adriatic wind
BINE hop-stems, etc. **B.**	**BORD** coal face (mining)
BING a heap of corn or alum	**BORE** tidal wave; tire; calibre; drill
BINK bench; bank; shelf (Sc.)	**BORN** née; begotten
BINT a girl (Arabic)	**BORT** diamond dust
BIRD (get the bird); a fowl **Z.**	**BOSA** a Persian liquor
BIRK the birch-tree **B.**	**BOSH** tosh; inane chatter; bunkum
BIRL spin; whirl (Sc.)	**BOSK** bosket; thicket; grove
BIRR impetus; violent thrust; a whirr	**BOSS** foreman; stud; protuberance
BIRT the turbot **Z.**	**BOTE** compensation; reparation **Law**
BISE cold northerly wind (Mediterranean)	**BOTH**
BISK bisque; soup; pottery	**BOTS** botts; the larvae of the botfly **Z.**
BITE a nibble; etch; nip; grip; grasp	**BOUD** insect in grain; weevil
BITT (to bitt a cable) **Naut.**	**BOUN** to dress; prepare; set out (Sc.) **Z.**
BLAB divulge; disclose; tell tales	**BOUT** contest; conflict; turn
BLAD fragment; lump; stain; batter (Sc.)	**BOWL** beaker; goblet; (cricket)
BLAE blue (Sc.)	**BOWS** the fore-end of a ship **Naut.**
BLAY ⎫ a river fish; the bleak **Z.**	**BRAD** small nail
BLEY ⎭	**BRAE** steep hill (Sc.)
BLEA inner bark of tree **B.**	**BRAG** boast; vaunt; a game of cards
BLEB transparent blister; bubble **Med.**	**BRAN** refuse of grain **B.**
BLED past tense of bleed	**BRAT** urchin; gamin; child
BLEE complexion; colour	**BRAW** fine; brave; showy (Sc.)
BLET spot on decayed fruit; to rot **B.**	**BRAY** braise; pound; clamour; blare
BLEW sounded; puffed; panted	**BRED** reared; raised; nurtured
BLOB viscous globule	**BREE** eyebrow; liquor
BLOC political or economic control	**BREN** sub-machine gun
BLOT blur; mar; tarnish; erase	**BRER** brother; (brer-rabbit)
BLOW sound; puff; pant	**BRET** a fish of the turbot kind **Z.**
BLUB sob; cry; blubber	**BREW** concoct; devise; plot
BLUE navy; cobalt; ultramarine; glum	**BRIE** a cream cheese
BLUE azure; sapphire ; (Oxford)	**BRIG** two-masted square-rigged ship **Naut.**
BLUR dim; sully; obscure; blot	**BRIM** verge; marge; border; to coast
BOAR hog **Z.**	**BRIN** a fan-stick
BOAT craft; bark; skiff; vessel **Naut.**	**BRIO** vivacity **Mus.**
BOCK light beer	**BRIT** whitebait, etc. **Z.**
BODE portend; presage; augur	**BROB** a wooden wedge
BODY corpse; carcass; substance	**BROC** pewter wine measure
BOER Africander	**BROG** an awl; to pierce **Tool**
BOGY bogey; bugbear; hobgoblin	**BROW** rim; edge; brink; forehead

BUBO the eagle owl **Z.**	**CARD** woolcomb; personality; game
BUCK talk; jump; deer; dollar **Coin., Z.**	**CARE** tend; concern; worry; heed
BUDE a gas burner	**CARK** care; trouble; fret; anxiety
BUFF baff; biff; strike; yellow	**CARL** churl; clown
BUFF pliant leather; the bare skin	**CARP** cavil; censure; goldfish **Z.**
BUHL brass and tortoiseshell inlay	**CARR** reclaimed bog land
BUHR burr-stone; a millstone **Min.**	**CART** van; wagon; transport
BULB (electric); corm; tuber **B.**	**CASE** box; enclose; plight; lawsuit **Law**
BULK mass; volume; magnitude	**CASH** specie; money; small Chinese **Coin**
BULL (papal); (Irish); walrus; moose **Z.**	**CASK** casque; helmet; barrel; tub; cade
BUMP thump; the call of the bittern **Z.**	**CAST** mien; shed; toss; mould; tint
BUND league; embankment; quay	**CATE** dainty food
BUNG barrel-stopper; large cork	**CAUF** live fish box
BUNK depart; sleeping berth **Naut.**	**CAUK** sulphate of baryta **Min.**
BUNT butt; part of a sail **Naut.**	**CAUL** net; membrane **Med.**
BUOY cheer; sustain; float **Naut.**	**CAVE** cavern; grotto; den; beware!
BURG bury; borough; burgh	**CAVY** genus of rodents; guinea-pig **Z.**
BURK burke; murder; smother; hush up	**CAWK** heavy spar **Min.**
BURL a knot in thread or wood	**CEDE** yield; relinquish; apportion; forego
BURN a brook; parch; char; glow	**CEIL** ciel; roof; ceiling
BURR rough edge; the burdock **B.**	**CELL** cavity; dungeon; nucleus; (elec.)
BURT flat-fish, turbot type **Z.**	**CELO** unit of acceleration **Meas.**
BURY burgh; clump of trees; inter	**CELT** Kelt; early Aryan
BUSH thimble; (bearings); a shrub **B.**	**CENT** 10 cents make one dime **Coin**
BUSK to act in the street	**CERE** to wax; to wrap in cerecloth
BUSS to kiss; a fishing boat **Naut.**	**CERT** alleged certainty; a snip
BUST bosom; sculpture; broken	**CESS** sess; to tax; a local rate
BUSY sedulous; officious; industrious	**CEST** cestus; a belt or girdle
BUTT thrust; a mound	**CHAC** Central American rain gods
BUZZ rumour; a whispered report	**CHAD** shad; a fish; sea-bream **Z.**
BYRE a cow-house	**CHAI** gipsy girl
	CHAL gipsy man
C	**CHAM** King of Tartary; Mogul khan
	CHAP jaw; cleft; fellow; guy; chapman
CABA cabas; work-basket; pannier	**CHAR** a lake fish; to scorch; to burn **Z.**
CADE cask of herrings; pet lamb **Z.**	**CHAT** talk; gossip; warbler; wheat-ear **Z.**
CADI kadi; Turkish judge	**CHAW** chew; masticate; champ
CAER camp; fort (Celt.)	**CHAY** shay; chaise; open carriage
CAFE coffee-house; restaurant	**CHEF** expert cook
CAGE crib; cabin; confine; mew	**CHEW** ruminate; munch
CAIC Turkish skiff **Naut.**	**CHIC** charmingly correct
CAID alcayde; Arab judge	**CHID** scolded; rated; rebuked
CAIN kain; rent in kind; a weasel **Z.**	**CHIG** to chew; a quid; chaw
CAKE solidify; harden; a tablet	**CHIN**
CAKY encrusted	**CHIP** fruit basket; cut; to chaff; stake
CALF part of leg; (Golden) **Z.**	**CHIT** pert child; note; memo; voucher
CALK caulk; spike; calkin **Naut.**	**CHOP** the jaw; veer; vary; change
CALL dub; term; summon; visit	**CHOU** ornamental ribbon
CALM still; unflurried; peaceful	**CHOW** Chinese dog **Z.**
CALP shale bed (Irish) **Min.**	**CHOY** Indian madder **B.**
CALX chalk or lime **Min.**	**CHUB** the cheven; a fresh-water carp **Z.**
CAMA South African hartebeest **Z.**	**CHUG** a fussy engine noise
CAME arrived; reached; attained	**CHUM** pal; palooka; buddy; messmate
CAMP encamp; laager	**CHUT** a peevish cry
CANE rattan; bamboo; beat **B.**	**CIEL** ceil; plaster; wainscot
CANG Chinese pillory	**CIMA** cyma; ogee moulding of cornice
CANT incline; thieves' patter; hypocrisy	**CIRC** prehistoric stone circle
CANY made of cane	**CIRE** polished silk fabric (Fr.)
CAPA Spanish cloak	**CIRL** a species of bunting **Z.**
CAPE capa; cope; headland; ness	**CIST** cyst; stone chest; tomb

CITE quote; summon; adduce **Law**
CITY cathedral town
CIVE chive; onion **B.**
CLAD garbed; dressed; clothed
CLAG clog; bemire (Sc.)
CLAM bivalve shell-fish; to clog **Z.**
CLAN family; coterie; clique; set
CLAP beak of hawk; applaud; cheer **Z.**
CLAW tear; scratch; lacerate; talon
CLAY alumina **Min.**
CLEF key **Mus.**
CLEG horse-fly
CLEM to starve
CLEW clue; trace; brail; truss **Naut.**
CLIO Muse of History; molluscs **Z.**
CLIP cut; trim; prune; curtail; embrace
CLOD sod; turf; lump; yokel; rustic
CLOG obstruct; hamper; trammel
CLOT curdle; thicken; coagulate **Med.**
CLOU the essential point
CLOY glut; pall; satiate; surfeit
CLUB cudgel; bludgeon; combine; set
CLUE clew; hint; guide; ball of string
COAK a dowel-pin; metal bush
COAL **Min.**
COAT cover; lay; spread; vesture
COAX cajole; allure; wheedle
COCA the cocaine plant (Peru) **B.**
COCH coach (Spens.)
COCK rooster; cockerel; chanticleer **Z.**
COCK haycock; chief; arrow-notch
COCO coconut palm **B.**
CODA finale **Mus.**
CODE digest of laws or rules; cipher
CO-ED mixed school
COFF to buy (Sc.)
COFT bought (Sc.)
COIF headdress; Judge's black cap **Law**
COIL trouble; bustle; curl; wind
COIN counterfeit; invent; quoin; wedge
COIR coconut fibre; cirdage
COIX a grass; job's tears **B**
COKE slang for cocaine
COLD icy; polar; gelid; passionless
COLE kale; cabbages generally **B**
COLL fondle; embrace
COLT young horse, camel or ass **Z.**
COLT gun; young cricketer
COMA stupor; drowsiness **Med.**
COMA tuft of foilicles; (comet) **B.**
COMB cock's comb; crest; wave; (bees)
COMB combe; coomb; dell; valley
COME reach; attain; ensue; arrive
COMS malt-dust
COND to navigate **Naut.**
CONE (fir-cone) **B.**
CONK the nose
CONN con; cond; steer; navigate **Naut.**
CONS arguments against; cf. pros.
CONY coney; hyrax; rock-rabbit **Z.**

COOF silly coon (Sc.)
COOK cuckoo-noise; chef; falsify
COOL calm; collected; allay; indifferent
COOM soot; axle dirt; coal-dust
COON nigger; sly fellow; raccoon **Z.**
CO-OP co-operative stores
COOP hen-coop; cask; cage; confine
COOT the ankle (Sc.); a water-fowl **Z.**
COPE vie; contend; struggle; cloak **Eccl.**
COPT Egyptian Christian
COPY model; ape; mimic; transcribe
CORB⎰ iron coal basket;
CORF⎱ alms-basket
CORD line; rope; braid; cut wood **Meas.**
CORE centre; heart; kernel
CORK a stopper; bung **B.**
CORM a kind of bulb **B.**
CORN preserve; an excrescence; grain **B.**
COSE to make's one's self cosy (Sc.)
COSH to slug; to smite; cosy
COSS about 1¾ miles (Indian) **Meas.**
COST price; charge; outlay; detriment
COSY tea-pot cover; cozy; snug
COTE sheepfold; pass by; outstrip
COUP exploit; stroke; barter; overturn
COVE bay; bight; harbour; a fellow
COWL a monk's hood; chimney-pot
COXA the hip-joint **Med.**
COXY cocksure; bumptious
COZE to chat; a talk
COZY cosy; snug; comfortable
CRAB bitter apple; peevish person **B.**
CRAB a portable winch; crustacean **Z.**
CRAG ragged rock
CRAM ram; stuff; glut; study
CRAN about 750 herrings **Meas.**
CRAW maw; crop; fowl's stomach
CRAX S. American bird; curassow **Z.**
CREE to soften grain
CREW mob; gang; crowd; crowed **Naut.**
CREX the white bullace **B.**
CRIB manger; cot; coop; copy
CRIS creese; Malay knife; kris
CROP reap; an ox-hide; whip; craw
CROW brag; vaunt; crowbar; croak **Z.**
CROY embankment; fish-trap
CRUP the buttocks; brittle
CRUT a dwarf; shaggy oak-bark **B.**
CRUX the crucial point
CUBE the third power
CUCA coca; cocaine shrub **B.**
CUFF sleeve-end; buffet; slap; a stroke
CUIR leather
CULL pick; pluck; choose
CULM coal-dust; corn or grass stalk **B.**
CULT ritual; worship; system; ism
CURB check; restraint; kerb
CURD coagulated milk
CURE remedy; antidote; panacea; heal
CURE care of souls, priest (Fr.) **Eccl.**

CURL	wind; wave; ringlet; ripple	
CURR	purr; snore like a barn-owl	
CURT	abrupt; terse; brief; laconic	
CUSK	burbot, an eel-like fish	**Z.**
CUSP	a kink in a curve	
CUSS	a curse; cross-grained fellow	
CUTE	shrewd; clever; adroit; chic	
CYAR	the ear-hole	**Med.**
CYMA	moulding of a cornice; ogee	
CYME	young; shoot; inflorescence	**B.**
CYST	water-bag; bladder	**Med.**
CZAR	Ksar; Tsar; Tzar	

D

DACE	small river fish; dare; dart	**Z.**
DADE	hold up by leading-strings	
DADO	decorative skirting	
DAFF	to play the fool (Sc.)	
DAFT	idiotic; absurd; ridiculous	
DAGO	a Southern European	
DAIL	Irish Parliament	
DAIS	raised platform; a canopy	
DAKS	sports trousers	
DALE	vale; valley; dingle	
DALI	Brazilian timber-tree	**B.**
DALL	incised tile; cow-dung fuel	
DALT	a foster-child	
DAME	the wife of a baronet	
DAMN	doom; condemn; ruin	
DAMP	dank; humid; depress; discourage	
DANE	great dane; Dalmatian	**Z.**
DANG	elegant form of damn	
DANK	moist; clammy; humid; damp	
DARE	defy; venture; challenge; presume	
DARG	a day's work; a task (Sc.)	
DARI	Indian millet	**B.**
DARK	ebon; murky; Cimmerian	
DARN	to mend by stitching	
DART	rush; run; hurl; a missile	
DASH	throw; onset; elan; frustrate	
DATA	accepted inferences; premises	
DATE	period; epoch; age; a fruit	**B.**
DAUB	smear; sully; smirch; plaster	
DAUD	dawd; thump; knock; a lump (Sc.)	
DAUK	a flaw in timber	
DAUR	to dare (Sc.)	
DAUW	Burchell's zebra	**Z.**
DAVY	safety-lamp; affidavit	
DAWK	dak; mail carried by relays (India)	
DAWM	a fortieth of a rupee, Indian **Coin**	
DAWN	cock-crow; dayspring; gleam	
DAZE	stun; amaze; astound; confuse	
D-DAY	invasion day	
DEAD	exactly; directly; defunct; late	
DEAF	heedless; inattentive; (no kernel)	
DEAL	pinewood; allot; treat; bargain	
DEAN	president of a guild	**Eccl.**
DEAR	beloved; costly; expensive	
DEBT	liability; arrears; obligation	

DECK	adorn; array; (cards)	**Naut.**
DEED	feat; exploit; document	**Law**
DEEM	opine; judge; imagine; believe	
DEEP	the ocean; profound; recondite	
DEER	a solid-horned ungulate	**Z.**
DEEV	evil spirit (Persia)	
DEFT	dextrous; adroit; handy; skilful	
DEFY	flout; spurn; brave; dare	
DEIL	the devil; scrat; Old Scratch (Sc.)	
DELE	delete; erase; efface; obliterate	
DELF	delftware; pottery; a drain	
DELL	dale; dene; dingle; vale	
DEME	Greek township; tribal division	
DEMY	a size of paper	
DENE	dell; dune; sandhill	
DENT	niche; notch; dint; indentation	
DENY	contradict; gainsay; refute	
DERM	the skin	**Med.**
DERN	durn; secret; dreadful; gatepost	
DERV	diesel oil	
DESK	writing table; a lectern	
DEVA	a benign spirit (Hindu)	
DEVI	the wife of Siva (Hindu mythology)	
DEWY	spangled with dew	
DHAK	East Indian timber-tree	**B.**
DHAR	Burmese curved knife	
DHOW	Arab ship	**Naut.**
DIAL	(telephone) ; face	
DICE	sometimes loaded	
DICK	sworn declaration; detective **Law**	
DIDO	antic; caper; queen of Carthage	
DIEB	North African jackal	**Z.**
DIED	perished; expired; departed	
DIES	(dies non); (screw-taps)	**Tool**
DIET	assembly; viands; sustenance	
DIGS	lodgings	
DIKA	West African mango	**B.**
DIKE	ditch; rine; rhine; mortarless wall	
DILL	medicinal herb	**B.**
DIME	a ten-cent piece (U.S.A.)	**Coin**
DINE	give a dinner to; eat	
DING	ring; urge; enforce; dash	
DINK	braw; neat; trim (Sc.)	
DINT	dent; power; blow; stroke	
DIRE	awful; disastrous; calamitous	
DIRK	dagger; poniard (Sc.); dark (obs.)	
DIRL	to tingle; vibrate (Sc.)	
DIRT	mud; mire; dust; muck; grime; soil	
DISA	S. African orchid	**B.**
DISC	disk; record; flat round plate	
DISH	a culinary conception; frustrate	
DISK	disc; any flat round growth	**B.**
DISS	an Algerian grass	**B.**
DIVA	a prima donna	**Mus.**
DIVE	plunge; descend; a gambling hell	
DOAB	alluvial land (India)	
DOCK	curtail; lessen; deduct; a weed **B.**	
DODD	cut off; clip; poll; a mound	
DODO	extinct bird (Madagascar)	**Z.**
DOER	agent; executive; performer	

DOFF daff; take off; divest
DOGE Venetian magistrate
DOHL pulse; (dried peas) **B.**
DOIT Dutch or Scotch half-farthing **Coin**
DOKE a dint; a dimple
DOLE an allowance; dispense; pain; grief
DOLL to dress up; a toy
DOLT dunce; booby; dullard
DOME a cupola; round roof
DONE ended; finished; transacted
DONG (Vietnam) **Coin**
DONT prelude to a prohibition
DOOB an Indian grass **B.**
DOOD camel or dromedary **Z.**
DOOK a bung; a bathe (Sc.)
DOOL dole; gloom; sorrow (Sc.)
DOOM kismet; condemn; judgment
DOOR portal; entrance; access; egress
DOPE drug; narcotic; doctor; varnish
DORA Defence of the Realm Act
DORN the thorn-back skate **Z.**
DORP burg; town; village
DORR the dor-beetle **Z.**
DORY golden coloured fish; skiff **Z, Naut.**
DOSE draught; drench; physic **Med.**
DOSS a shake-down; a hassock
DOST thou doest
DOTE love tenderly; talk trash
DOTH a poetical 'do'
DOTY decayed; half-rotten
DOUC a highly coloured monkey **Z.**
DOUM the doom-palm **B.**
DOUR stern; grim; relentless; obstinate
DOUT extinguish
DOVE emblem of peace **Z.**
DOWF dull; heavy; spiritless (Sc.)
DOWN fluff; pasture; hill; prone
DOXY loose woman; moll
DOZE nap; slumber; forty-winks
DOZY drowsy; sleepy; dreamy
DRAB khaki colour; a cloth; a trull
DRAD dread; dreaded (Spens.)
DRAG a hunt; a vehicle; haul; pull
DRAM drachm; a tot of spirits **Meas.**
DRAT a mild expletive
DRAW limn; allure; attract; (chimney)
DRAY strong cart for heavy goods
DREE endure; bear; suffer (Sc.)
DREY a squirrel's nest **Z.**
DREW drafted; depicted; extracted
DRIB purloin small pieces; inveigle
DRIP ooze; dribble; trickle; percolate
DROP globule; bead; sink; quit
DROW trow; troll; cave elf (Shetland)
DRUB maul; thrash; beat; pound
DRUG drudge; a narcotic **Med.**
DRUM ridge of hills; tambour **Mus.**
DUAD union of two
DUAL twofold
DUAN a division of a poem; a canto

DUCE leader, dictator (Italian)
DUCK cloth; dive; dip; underplay **Z.**
DUCT tube; canal; pipe; conduit
DUDE a dandy; fop; nut
DUDS clothing; rags
DUEL single combat
DUET composition for two voices **Mus.**
DUFF muff; a pudding; refurbish
DUKE (strawberry leaves)
DUKW amphibious army vehicle
DULE woe (Sc.)
DULL benumb; blunt; abate; stolid
DULY properly; regularly; exactly
DUMA Russian Parliament
DUMB mute; inarticulate; soundless
DUMP unload; rubbish-heap
DUNE dene; sandy waste
DUNG manure; compost; soil
DUNT staggering affection; heavy blow
DUPE gull; delude; outwit; hoodwink
DURA an Indian grass **B.**
DURE endure; harden; severe
DURN dern; a door-post
DUSE deuce; demon; evil spirit
DUSH to throw down (Sc.)
DUSK eventide; twilight; eve
DUST pulverulence; a disturbance
DUTY obligation; excise; tariff
DWAM swoon; qualm; faint (Sc.)
DYAD cf. monad **Chem.**
DYAK a native of Borneo
DYED stained; tinted; tinged
DYER
DYKE dike; ditch; fosse
DYNE the unit of force **Meas.**

E

EACH both; every one
EARL jarl
EARN win; gain; merit; acquire
EASE allay; still; assuage; relief
EAST a cardinal point
EASY facile; affluent; flowing
EBON of ebony; black
ECHE to eke out; augment (Sc.)
ECHO repeat; resound; reverberate
ECRU pale yellowish brown
EDAM spherical Dutch cheese
EDDA Scandinavian saga
EDDY ripple; swirl; vortex
EDEN garden of delight
EDGE brink; fringe; zest; sharpness
EDGY on edge; nervous
EDIT revise; annote; amend
EGAD a refined expletive
EGAL equal (Shak.)
EGER eagre; bore; tidal wave
EGIS aegis; a shield

EIGH exclamation of surprise
EILD dry; not giving milk (Sc.)
EIRE Ireland
EJOO the sago palm **B.**
EKED existed on small pittance
ELAN dash; impetuosity; vivacity
ELIA Charles Lamb
ELMO Elmo's fire; electrical flame
ELMY abounding with elms **B**
ELSE other; otherwise; besides
ELUL 12th month of the Jewish year
EMIR amir; Eastern title
EMIT vent; eject; exhale; discharge
EMYS terrapin genus **Z.**
ENEW drive back; pursue (obs.)
ENOW enough; just now; soon (Sc.)
ENSA forces entertainment organisation
ENTE heraldic engraftment
ENVY ill-will; malice; covet; grudge
EOAN dawning; eastern
EPHA ephah; Hebrew bushel **Meas.**
EPEE foil; rapier (Fr.)
EPIC heroic; lofty; a rhapsody
EPOS epic poem; Homeric narrative
ERGO therefore
ERIC eriach; blood-money (Irish Law)
ERIN the Green Isle
ERNE the sea-eagle **Z.**
EROS God of Love; Cupid
ERSE the Gaelic language
ERSH stubble **B.**
ERST formerly; whilom
ESOX the pike **Z.**
ESPY discover; observe; perceive; notice
ESSE to be in existence (Latin)
ETCH engrave; draw; cropped ground
ETNA small spirit stove
ETON a returnable note
ETUI etwee; a needle-case
EUGE bravo; well done
EUGH obsolete form of yew **B.**
EVEN level; uniform; steady; impartial
EVER aye; always; eternally
EVET eft; newt; ewft **Z.**
EVIL harm; malice; baneful; malign
EVOE a Bacchanalian cry
EWER pitcher; jug with handle
EWFT eft; newt; evet (obs.) **Z.**
EWRY scullery
EXAM examination
EXES expenses
EXIT way out; a stage departure
EXON an officer, Yeoman of the Guard
EXUL an exile (Spens.)
EYAS nyas; young hawk **Z.**
EYED observed; watched; espied
EYER a watcher
EYNE eyes (Sc.)
EYOT ait; river or lake islet
EYRA S. American cat **Z.**

EYRE journey; circuit; court **Law**
EYRY eyrie; ayry; eagle's nest **Z.**

F

FAAM Indian orchid **B.**
FAAP the garfish **Z.**
FABA the broad bean **B.**
FACE defy; dare; surface; confront; dial
FACT incident; actuality; occurrence
FACY impudent
FADE wither; dwindle; insipid
FAIK to abate; to excuse (Sc.)
FAIL wane; flag; decline; neglect
FAIN willingly; gladly; readily
FAIR market; just; equitable; blond
FAIX by my faith
FAKE a cable coil; counterfeit
FALA old madrigal **Mus.**
FALL autumn; the Fall; drop; cascade
FALX a membrane **Med.**
FAMA the goddess of rumour
FAME renown; repute; lustre; celebrity
FANE vane; temple; church **Eccl.**
FANG tooth; claw; talon
FANK sheepfold (Sc.)
FARD face-paint
FARE manage; victuals; passenger
FARL Scotch oatcake
FARM ferm; till; cultivate; lease
FARO a card game
FASH to bother; trouble; annoy (Sc.)
FAST firm; rapid; fleet; dissolute
FATA Morgana; a mirage
FATE kismet; doom; destiny; lot
FAUN woodland deity; Pan
FAUX pas
FAWN cringe; a colour; fallow-deer **Z.**
FAZE disconcert; worry
FEAL faithful; constant; loyal
FEAR awe; alarm; dread; anxiety
FEAT exploit; deed; trick
FECK efficacy; strength (Sc.)
FEED cater; sustain; provender
FEEL sense; touch; experience
FEER or **FERE,** companion
FEET paws; hoofs
FELL hew; cut; tumbled; barren hill
FELL cruel; deadly; spirited; skin
FELO de se; suicide **Law**
FELT fabric; sensed; handled; touched
FEME wife
FEND parry; ward off; make shift
FEOD feud; fief (obs.)
FERM a farm; abode; lodging (Spens.)
FERN vascular cryptogamous plant **B.**
FESS fesse; broad heraldic band
FETE gala; festival; carnival; holiday
FEUD clan warfare; strife; a fief
FIAR freeholder, not a life-renter **Law**

FIAT decree; command; ukase
FICO a snap of the fingers; a fig **B.**
FIEF land held on feudal tenure **Law**
FIFE a variety of flute **Mus.**
FIKE fidget; trivial detail
FIKY fussy (Sc.)
FILE list; dossier; artful dodger **Tool**
FILL sate; glut; replenish
FILM thin skin; scum; thread; pellicle
FIND discover; discovery; decide
FINE forfeit; delicate; tenuous; exact
FINN a Finlander
FIRE discharge; kindle; ignite: blaze
FIRK whip; beat; rouse (Sc.)
FIRM fast; tight; compact; a company
FIRN glacier snow; neve
FISC state treasury; revenue; purse
FISH to angle; search by sweeping **Z.**
FISK to frisk; to move briskly (obs.)
FIST neif; the clenched hand; to punch
FIST calligraphy
FITT fitte; fytte; song; (obs.)
FITZ son of
FIVE the pentad
FIZZ hiss; champagne
FLAG banner; ensign; to signal **Naut.**
FLAG droop; weary; a stone; a plant **B.**
FLAK anti-aircraft gunfire (German)
FLAM whim; fancy; falsehood; impose
FLAN open fruit tart
FLAP flop; wave; vibrate; flutter
FLAT smooth; level; insipid; residence
FLAW blemish; defect; crevice; a gust
FLAX linum; the linen plant **B.**
FLAY skin; excoriate; strip; criticise
FLEA pulex irritans **Z.**
FLED ran; bolted; retreated
FLEE escape; abscond; decamp
FLEW fled; the chap of a hound
FLEX to bend; an electric lead
FLEY flay; frighten; cause to fly
FLIP a joy ride; (egg-flip)
FLIT fly; dart; flicker; migrate
FLIX fur; beaver-down **Z.**
FLOE an icefield
FLOG lash; thrash; scourge; whip
FLOP flap; a failure; a fiasco
FLOT stratified ore **Min.**
FLOW run; emanate; abound; circulate
FLUE smoke pipe; light down; fluff
FLUX flow; mutation; change;(soldering)
FOAL colt or filly **Z.**
FOAM spume; froth; spray; rage
FOGY fogey; an old buffer
FOIE liver (Fr.)
FOIL track of game; baffle; outwit
FOIL thin metal; fencing rapier
FOIN a thrust with spear or sword
FOLD lap; wrap; furl; double; envelop
FOLK kindred; relations; people

FOND loving; doting; attached
FONE foes (Spens.)
FONT fount; source; spring; type **Eccl.**
FOOD viands; victuals; rations
FOOL gull; beguile; hoodwink; ninny
FOOT pay; discharge; settle **Meas.**
FORD wade; a river crossing
FORE a warning cry at golf
FORK branch; divide; divaricate
FORM bench; formula; mould; fashion
FORM bed of hare; mode; ceremony
FORS force; fortitude; fortune (Ruskin)
FORT keep; citadel; fastness
FOSS ditch or moat
FOUD magistrate or bailiff (Orkney)
FOUL noisome; ribald; unfair; sullied
FOUR
FOWL poultry **Z.**
FOXY sly; wily; sour; a colour
FOZY spongy (Sc.)
FRAB to worry
FRAP to bind; to strike
FRAU a German married woman
FRAY rub; brush; quarrel; skirmish
FREE rid; loose; clear; informal
FRET fray; fume; chafe; abrade; grieve
FRIT glass material; a wheat-fly **Z.**
FRIZ frizz; to curl; to crisp
FROE woodcutter's cleaver **Tool**
FROG a batrachian; (of horse) **Z.**
FROG cloak button or tassel
FROM
FROW tool for lathe splitting **Tool**
FROW Dutch lady; a slut
FUAR feuar; landholder (Sc.)
FUEL combustibles
FUFF puff; a burst of anger (Sc.)
FUGH exclamation of abhorrence
FULL replete; copious; ample; thicken
FUME smoke; vapour; exhalation; reek
FUMY vaporous; fumous; fussy
FUND reserve; store; supply; capital
FUNG mythical Chinese pheasant **Z**
FUNK terror; fear; shirk; touchwood
FURL fold; roll; stow; wrap
FURY frenzy; rage; turbulence; shrew
FUSE } melt; liquefy; blend;
FUZE } quickmatch; a timing device
FUSS ado; stir; fume; fidget; fret
FUST shaft of column; musty smell
FUZZ fluff; light particles
FYKE bagnet for fishing
FYRD pre-Conquest Saxon military array

G

GABY a simpleton; nitwit
GADE gaid; gad; goad; graver **Tool**
GAEL Celtic

GAFF low theatre; a hook; a spar **Naut.**
GAGE a pledge; stake; wager; plum **B.**
GAID gade; gad; spike on gauntlet **Tool**
GAIN get; win; acquire; profit
GAIR gore (Sc.)
GAIT walk; bearing; step; pace
GAIT pasturage; charge; sheaf of corn **B.**
GALA festival; festivity; pomp; show
GALE high wind; rent; a bog plant **B.**
GALL vex; torment; provoke; rancour
GALL bile; malignity; glass scum
GALT gault; clay; marl; brick-earth
GAMB leg; shank
GAME lame; plucky; dauntless; pastime
GAMP an umbrella
GAMY high in flavour
GANG crew; band; horde; coterie
GANT to yawn (Sc.)
GAOL jail; prison; objective
GAPE stare; to yawn
GARB dress; costume; heraldic sheaf
GARE greedy (Sc.); beware; look out
GARI Indian carriage
GASH slash; score; slit; wound
GASP pant; puff
GAST to terrify (Shak.)
GATE portal; defile; entrance money
GAUB an Indian tree; guy-rope **B., Naut.**
GAUD a gewgaw; showy ornament; gawd
GAUL old France
GAUM to smear; to daub
GAUN going (Sc.)
GAUP gawp; gape
GAUR a wild Indian ox **Z.**
GAVE presented; granted; yielded
GAWD gaud; a piece of finery
GAWK gowk; simpleton; a cuckoo **Z.**
GAWN small tub; a ladle
GAZE stare; view; regard; contemplate
GEAL to congeal
GEAN wild cherry **B.**
GEAR tackle; harness; dress; mechanism
GEAT hole for metal casting
GECK dupe; mock; simpleton
GEDD the pike **Z.**
GEED went faster
GEEZ archaic Semitic dialect
GEGG a hoax; a trick (Sc.)
GELD gold; tribute; castrate; spay
GELT geld; gilt; money; emasculated
GENA the cheek **Med.**
GENE heredity factor **Med.**
GENS Roman clan
GENT a would-be gentleman
GERM ovule; nucleus; a bacillus **Med.**
GEST an exploit; feat; bearing
GEUM avens and herb-bennet genus **B.**
GHAT Indian mountain; landing-stair
GHEE Indian oil or butter
GIBE jibe; sneer; deride; taunt **Naut.**

GIFT boon; bounty; gratuity; faculty
GILD guild; trade's union; add lustre
GILL a flirt; a ravine; ground ivy **B.**
GILL breathing organ; ¼ pint **Z., Meas.**
GILT gilded; aureate; a young sow **Z.**
GIMP smart; spruce; a trimming
GING gang or company
GINN jinn; djinn; demon; spirit
GIRD bind; reproach; gibe; spasm
GIRL young roe-buck **Z.**
GIRN grin; snarl (Sc.)
GIRR a hoop (Sc.)
GIRT tightly moored; bound **Naut.**
GIST essential point; pith
GITE bed or an abode (Fr.)
GIVE yield; confer; grant; present
GIZZ phiz; face (Sc.)
GLAD (eye); joyous; elated; delectable
GLEE hilarity; merriment; mirth
GLEE squint; part song **Mus.**
GLEG clever; apt; sharp (Sc.)
GLEN vale; dale; dell; dingle; valley
GLEY to squint; to glance (Sc.)
GLIB voluble; fluent; ready; facile
GLIM a light; a glimmer
GLOW fervour; shine; burn; gleam
GLUE cement; an adhesive
GLUM grum; crestfallen; downcast
GLUT surfeit; surplus; cloy; satiate
G-MAN American armed policeman
GNAR knar; yarr; snarl
GNAT mosquito **Z.**
GNAW bite; corrode; erode; champ
GOAD spur; rouse; incite; an ankus
GOAF worked out mine; slag
GOAL jail; end; aim; ambition; object
GOAN Indian; East African Indian
GOAT Capricornus **Z.**
GO-BY evasion
GOBY fish having nests of seaweed **Z.**
GODS lofty theatrical supporters
GOEL an avenger of blood (Heb.)
GOER a mover; a go-between
GOLA a cyma; cyme; a moulding
GOLD or; money wealth; bull at archery
GOLF goff; gowf;
GOME black cart-grease
GOND native Indian tribe
GONE hied; wended; fared; left; parted
GONG prelude to a meal; medal (slang)
GOOD weal; virtuous; upright; proper
GOOF simpleton; silly cuckoo
GOOR coarse sugar from the date-palm
GORE clotted blood; wedge of cloth
GORM sheen; shine of varnish
GORY sanguinary; ensanguined
GOSH an ejaculation
GOTH Teutonic barbarian
GOUM native Algerian soldier (Fr.)
GOUT a drop; taste; relish **Med.**

GOUL } howl;
GOWL } yowl
GOWD gold (Sc.)
GOWF golf; goff
GOWK gouk; simpleton; oaf; cuckoo **Z.**
GOWN robe; garment
GRAB snatch; seize; grip; a card game
GRAB two-masted vessel (Malabar) **Naut.**
GRAF German title; a count
GRAM Indian corn; weight **B., Meas.**
GRAM misery
GRAY grey; ash-coloured
GREE a step; degree; goodwill
GREW thrived; raised; progressed
GREY gray; a neutral tint
GRID lines on a map; (electrical)
GRIG sand-eel; grasshopper; cricket **Z.**
GRIM stern; dire; hideous; grisly
GRIN girn; smirk; a snare
GRIP clutch; handbag; small ditch
GRIT endurance; courage; sand
GROG rum and water
GROS silken fabric
GROT a grotto
GROW wax; develop; expand; raise
GRUB caterpillar; food; (cricket) **Z.**
GRUM glum; surly; morose; guttural
GUAN Brazilian game bird **Z.**
GUDE good (Sc.)
GUFA Tigris ferry boat **Naut.**
GUHR loose earth found in rocks **Min.**
GUIB the harnessed antelope **Z.**
GULA the throat; the gullet **Med.**
GULF chasm; abyss; bight; bay
GULL beguile; hoax; deceive; sea-bird **Z.**
GULP gasp: swallow; choke
GULY coloured red in heraldry
GURU Hindu teacher
GUSH rush; spout; stream; an outburst
GUST squall; burst of passion; relish
GUY'S Guy's Hospital
GYAL gayal; East Indian ox **Z.**
GYBE gibe; sneer **Naut.**
GYLE to ferment; a brew
GYRA embroidered border
GYRE a circular motion
GYRO a gyroscope
GYTE crazy; mad; a child (Sc.)
GYVE fetter; shackle; handcuff; bond

H

HAAF deep-sea fishing ground (Shetland)
HAAR harr; a cold sea mist
HACK notch; gash; kick; chopper **Tool**
HACK literary drudge; sorry jade **Z.**
HADE slope of mineral vein or fault
HADJ or **HAJJ,** a pilgrimage to Mecca
HAET or **HAIT,** a whit (Sc.)
HAFT heft; hilt; handle; to haggle

HA-HA haw-haw; sunken fence; laughter
HAIK hyke; haick; an Arab wrap
HAIL health; greeting; frozen rain
HAIN save; preserve; spare (Sc.)
HAIR jot; iota; quality; character
HAKA native dance (New Zealand)
HAKE a pot-hook; loiter; sea fish **Z.**
HALD hold (Sc.)
HALE haul; drag; healthy; robust
HALF a moiety; a half-back; partial
HALL manor house; a college
HALM haum; haulm; corn-stalk; stubble
HALO a saintly hat-band
HALT to stop; to limp; crippled; waver
HAME bar for trace attachment
HAND manual labour; assistance
HAND proffer; (cards) 4″ **Meas.**
HANG suspend; hover; slope; drift
HANK skein; coil; hoop; ring
HARD firm; compact; arduous
HARE to speed; puss **Z.**
HARK hear; listen; attend
HARL fibres of flax; troll for fish **B.**
HARM hurt; scathe; wrong; injury
HARN coarse linen fabric (Sc.)
HARO an appeal (Channel Islands) **Law**
HARP reiterate; Lyra **Mus.**
HARR haar; a storm; an eagre
HART male red-deer **Z.**
HASH chop; mangle; mince; a jumble
HASP clasp or fastening
HAST " thou havest "
HATE abhor; loathe; enmity; odium
HATH
HAUL tug; pull; drag; draw; heave
HAUM halm; haulm; stubble **B.**
HAVE own; possess; hold; contain
HAWK rapacious bird or person **Z.**
HAWK intentional cough; to peddle
HAWK plasterer's mortar board **Tool**
HAWM to lounge about
HAZE fog; mist; pall; miasma; to bully
HAZY vague; obscure; indistinct; murky
HEAD (bowls); acme; top; steer
HEAL cure; remedy; assuage; compose
HEAP pile; mound; amass; collect
HEAR heed; hark; try judicially **Law**
HEAT rage; passion; ardour; excite
HEBE an Olympian cup-bearer
HECK fish-weir; a rack; river bend
HEED mind; mark; obey; regard; caution
HEEL (cock-spurs); low fellow; twerp
HEFT hilt; handle; heaved
HEIR inheritor; offspring
HELD grasped; adhered; restrained
HELE to conceal; to hide (obs.)
HELL Hades; Gehenna; gambling house
HELM tiller; steering gear; steer **Naut.**
HELM helmet; crown; top; guide; direct
HELP aid; abet; back; second; relieve

22

HEMP rope-fibre; a plant **B.**
HEND to seize; to apprehend (obs.)
HERA (Juno), wife of Zeus
HERB a simple; an annual plant **B.**
HERD drove; rabble; tend; collect
HERE
HERL harl; barb of feather
HERN heron (obs.) **Z.**
HERO a priestess of Aphrodite
HERR German gent
HERS also **HERN**
HEST behest; command (Shak.)
HEWN cut; felled; chiselled
HICK bucolic; country cousin (U.S.A.)
HIDE about 100 acres **Meas.**
HIDE a skin; pelt; secrete; cache
HIED set off
HI-FI high-fidelity sound
HIGH eminent; lofty; arrogant; shrill
HIKE to carry; to ramble
HILA the eyes of beans **B.**
HILL to earth up plants
HILT haft; heft; handle
HIND a rustic; backward; a deer **Z.**
HINK a reaping hook **Tool**
HINT imply; insinuate; innuendo
HIRE rent; charter; lease; salary
HISK to breathe with difficulty
HISS also **HISH** and **HIZZ**
HIST! hush!
HIVE to collect; store up; a skep
HOAR hoary; rime; venerable
HOAX gammon; spoof; dupe; delude
HOBO a tramp; a vagrant (U.S.A.)
HOCK Rhenish wine; a joint, the hough
HOED weeded
HOER manipulator of a hoe
HOGG hog; a two-year old sheep **Z.**
HOIK hike; an upward turn
HOIT to leap; to caper.
HOLD grasp; contain; keep **Naut.**
HOLE cavity; lair; burrow; pierce
HOLM evergreen oak; holly **B.**
HOLM flat land; an islet
HOLT woodland; a copse; a burrow
HOLY sanctified; consecrated; divine
HOME habitat; seat; institution
HOMY homelike
HONE to pine; to moan; a whetstone
HONG Chinese factory
HONK to hoot
HOOD cowl; cover; to blind
HOOF pad the hoof; to walk
HOOK promontory; snare; sickle **Tool**
HOOK to bend; to decamp; to steal
HOOP a whoop; a band; a toy
HOOT honk; boo; decry; execrate
HOPE expect; anticipate; confidence
HOPS beer flavouring **B.**
HORN cornucopia; drinking cup **Mus.**

HORS out of; beyond; hors-de-combat
HOSE stockings; hosiery; to sprinkle
HOSH courtyard of Arab house
HOST multitude; consecrated wafer **Eccl.**
HOUR always passing
HOVA a Malagash
HOVE to heave; to raise; to loiter
HOWE how; hollow; glen; dell (Sc.)
HOWK dig; burrow; extract (Sc.)
HOWL gowl; yowl; wail; yell; squall
HOYA genus of climbing plants **B.**
HUCK a German trout **Z.**
HUED coloured; tinted
HUEL a wheal; a Cornish mine
HUER fish-scout watching for shoals
HUFF swell; bluster; anger; (Draughts)
HUGE vast; colossal; gigantic; immense
HUIA New Zealand starling **B.**
HULK old ship **Naut.**
HULL husk; pod; to pierce **B., Naut.**
HUMP hillock; to carry; depression
HUNG dangled; draped; hovered
HUNK chunk; lump; large slice
HUNT pursue; hound; search; chase
HURL cast; pitch; fling; whirl
HURT pain; offend; mar; an injury
HUSH quiet; calm; still; tranquillize
HUSO the great sturgeon **Z.**
HUSK hull; rind; coating **B.**
HUTU native of Rwanda (Africa)
HWAN (Korea) **Coin**
HYKE haik; loose Arab garment
HYMN panegyric; paean
HYPE a wrestling throw
HYPO sodium thiosulphate **Chem.**

I

IBEX chamois; mountain wild goat **Z.**
IBID in the same place (Latin)
IBIS a wading bird, sacred in Egypt **Z.**
ICED frozen; congealed
ICON also **IKON**, sacred picture; image
IDEA notion; fantasy; conceit
IDEM the same
IDES Roman date
IDLE inert; lazy; futile; inactive
IDLY indolently
IDOL hero; pet; image
IDYL idyll; pastoral poem
ILEX evergreen oak **B.**
ILKA each (Sc.)
IMAM ⎫ Mohammedan priest;
IMAN ⎭ Mohammedan prince
IMPI Zulu regiment
INBY inbye; inwards (Sc.)
INCA ancient king or prince of Peru
INCH creep forward; isle (Sc.) **Meas.**
INIA phrenological bumps **Med.**
INKY black; blotted

INLY inward; secret
INRO Japanese comfit box
INTO
IOTA a jot; tittle; whit; particle
IRID iris of the eye; flag plant **Med., B.**
IRIS Rainbow Goddess, messenger of Zeus
IRON golf club; strength; to smooth **Min.**
IRON gyve; fetter; bond; shackle
ISCA excrescence on oak or hazel **B.**
ISIS Moon Goddess; mother of Horus
ISLE ait; eyot; islet
ITCH constant teasing desire **Med.**
ITEM detail; entry; innuendo
ITIS undiagnosed disease **Med.**
ITMA it's that man again
IWIS ywis; certainly
IXIA South African iridaceous plants **B.**

J

JACA the bread-fruit tree **B.**
JACK knave at cards; national flag **Naut.**
JACK various appliances; (bowls); pike **Z.**
JADE sorry nag; mean woman **Z.**
JADE to fatigue; to tire **Min.**
JAIL gaol; to imprison
JAIN Indian religious sect
JAMB a door-post; to wedge; stick
JANE jean; twilled cloth; Genoese **Coin**
JANN jinn; Moslem demon
JANT jaunt; ramble
JAPE jibe; joke; jest; quip
JARL earl (Norse)
JAUP to bespatter (Sc.)
JAWY with jaws
JAZZ rag-time music **Mus.**
JEAN jane; twilled cloth
JEEP an American car
JEER mock; scoff; taunt; deride
JEFF dicing with quadrats; circus rope
JEHU a coachman
JERK yerk; jolt; pluck; twitch
JESS a leg-strap in falconry
JEST jape; quirk; raillery; banter
JHOW Indian grass **B.**
JIFF a jiffy; a moment
JILL a flirt; Jack's girl friend
JILT deceive; delude; to discard
JIMP neat; slender; elegant (Sc.)
JINK a sharp turn; to dodge
JINN ginn; djinn; Moslem demon
JINX bad joss
JIVE jazz dance (swing)
JOCK a Scotsman
JOEY small kangaroo **Z.**
JOEY small drinking glass; 4d. piece **Coin**
JOHN a variety of pink **B.**
JOIN link together; associate
JOKE jest; banter; witticism
JOLE jowl; jaw; jolt
JOLT jar; jog; jerk; shake

JOSH to rag; ridicule
JOSS Chinese idol; luck
JOUK jook; duck; dodge; bow (Sc.)
JOVE Jupiter; alchemist's tin
JOWL dewlap; the cheek
JUBA negro dance
JUBE rood-loft **Eccl.**
JUDO advanced ju-jitsu
JUDY Mr. Punch's wife
JUGA leaflets in a pinnate leaf **B.**
JU-JU West African black magic
JUKE a head movement
JULY
JUMP leap; skip; bound; purloin
JUNE
JUNK scrap-metal; trask; Chinese ship
JUNO Queen of Heaven
JURY twelve persons; makeshift **Law**
JUST true; exact; impartial; barely
JUTE sack and twine fibre **B.**

K

KADI cadi; Moslem judge
KAGO Japanese palanquin
KAGU crane of New Caledonia **Z.**
KAIF keif; drugged stupor
KAIL a ninepin
KAIN cain; tribute in kind
KAKA New Zealand parrot **Z.**
KAKI the Chinese date **B.**
KALA time; destiny; death (Sanskrit)
KALE kail; colewort; curly cabbage **B.**
KALI prickly saltwort or glasswort **B.**
KALI wife of Siva; goddess of destruction
KAMA Hindu cupid
KAMI Japanese god or title
KANA Japanese handwriting
KANG Chinese water-jar
KANS Indian sugar-cane grass **B.**
KATA Tibetan cloth or scarf
KAVA ava; Polynesian drink; plant **B.**
KECK to retch; dried hemlock **B.**
KEEK to peep (Sc.)
KEEL ruddle; flat-bottomed barge **Naut.**
KEEN lamentation; acute; eager; sharp
KEEP stronghold; provender; retain
KEIF kaif; drugged stupor
KEIR bleaching-vat
KELK a blow; to beat; large stone
KELL caul; cobweb; film; network
KELP kilp; seaweed; wrack
KELT Celt; salmon; woollen cloth **Z.**
KEMB to comb
KEMP coarse rough hairs of wool
KENT pole; pike; bugle with keys **Mus.**
KEPT held; stored; retained; endured
KERB curb; edge of pavement
KERF a saw-cut; a swath
KERN quern; a hand-mill; to granulate

KERN or **KIRN**; Irish foot-soldier
KETA a caviare fish   **Z.**
KHAN Eastern inn; caravanserai; ruler
KHEL a clan (Afghanistan)
KHUD Indian ravine
KIBE chilblain   **Med.**
KIBY affected with chilblains
KICK resist; rebel; spurn; boot; punt
KIEF keif; kef; stupor; drowsiness
KIER keir; bleaching-vat
KILL slay; destroy; despatch; consume
KILN furnace; oven
KILO 2.205 lbs.   **Meas.**
KILP kelp; calcined ashes of seaweed
KILT a philibeg; pleated skirt; tuck up
KIND class; type; genus; benign; gentle
KINE cows   **Z.**
KING monarch; sovereign; ruler; a card
KINK bend; knot; curl; loop; whim
KINO a mixture of gums; catechu
KIPE basket for catching fish
KIRI knobkerrie; Kaffir throwing stick
KIRN kern; last sheaf; harvest image
KIRK a church (Sc.)   **Eccl.**
KISH wicker turf basket; impure graphite
KISS buss; touch gently; (billiards)
KIST chest; coffer
KITE accommodation bill; a toy   **Z.**
KITH kindred; acquaintances; friends
KIVE a mashing vat
KIWI apteryx, N.Z. flightless bird   **Z.**
KNAB to bite; to gnaw
KNAG knot in wood; peg; a wart
KNAP to snap; a swelling; a hillock
KNAR gnar; snarl; growl; a knarl
KNEE a genuflection
KNEW understood; perceived
KNIT draw together; weave; wrinkle
KNOB a bunch; boss; door-handle
KNOP knob; tufted top; button
KNOT knag; small sandpiper; (speed) **Z.**
KNOW comprehend; discern; approve
KNUB knob; a small lump
KNUR knar; gnarl; wooden ball
KNUT a nut; a dandy
KOBA kob; African water antelope   **Z.**
KOEL Indian cuckoo   **Z.**
KOFF Dutch sailing vessel   **Naut.**
KOHL black antimony eye pigment
KOLA African nut tree; a beverage   **B.**
KOTH volcanic mud (S. America)   **Min.**
KOTO Japanese stringed instrument **Mus.**
KRIL plankton; whale food   **Z.**
KRIS creese; Malay dagger
KROO an African race
KUDU a large African antelope   **Z.**
KUNA Panamanian Indian
KURD native of Kurdistan
KYAT (Burma)   **Coin**
KYLE narrow strait or sound

L

LACE tie; fasten; beat; intermix
LACK want; need; deficiency
LACY lace-like texture
LADE load; burden; ladle; bale
LADY a gentle woman
LAIC a layman
LAID deposited; ribbed; prostrate
LAIN rested; reclined; reposed
LAIR den; form; burrow; quagmire
LAIS a courtesan
LAKE mere; pool; crimson colour
LAKH lac; 100,000 rupees   **Coin**
LAKY resembling a lake
LAMA Tibetan priest
LAMB to yean   **Z.**
LAME halt; crippled; feeble; imperfect
LAME gold- or silver-threaded material
LAMP lantern; to shine
LANA the genipap tree of Demerara   **B.**
LAND realm; tract; debark; (fish)
LANE narrow way; passage; by-road
LANG long (Sc.)
LANK lax; loose; languid; drooping; thin
LANX Roman platter
LAPP a Laplander
LARD bacon fat; smear; flatter
LARK frolic; prank; spree; sky-lark   **Z.**
LASH whip; scourge; satirize; a stripe
LASS girl; a sweetheart
LAST final; ultimate; boot-maker's **Tool**
LAST continue; endure; a cargo
LATE overdue; past; recent; deceased
LATH a narrow strip of wood
LAUD extol; praise; eulogy; panegyric
LAVA plutonic rock matter   **Min.**
LAVE to wash; bathe; bath
LAWN fine linen or cambric; sward
LAZE to idle
LAZY inert; torpid; slothful; sluggish
LEAD surpass; guide; precede; plummet
LEAF thin plate; lamina; page of book
LEAK ooze; drip; percolate; rift
LEAL loyal; true; faithful
LEAN rest; rely; depend; incline; lank
LEAP clear; spring; caper; frisk
LEAR to learn; learning (Spens.)
LEAT watercourse to a mill
LEDA beloved of Zeus disguised as swan
LEEK an emblem of Wales   **B.**
LEER ogle; smirk
LEES the dregs   **[Law**
LEET court of record; list of candidates
LEFT sinister; abandoned; bequeathed
LEHR glass annealing oven
LEND advance; loan; furnish; grant
LENE unaspirated

B

LENO a fabric like muslin
LENS optical glass
LENT loaned; inclined; a fast **Eccl.**
LESS smaller; inferior; minor
LEST for fear that
LETO mother of Apollo and Artemis
LETT Baltic tribe
LEUD Frankish vassal
LEVY tribute; exact; muster; impose
LEWD licentious
LIAR an economiser of the truth
LIAS argillaceous limestone **Min.**
LICE insect carriers of typhus **Z.**
LICH or **LYCH** dead body; corpse
LICK to lap; defeat; overcome
LIDO a bathing pool
LIED stated falsely; German ballad
LIEF gladly; willingly; beloved
LIEN right of retention **Law**
LIEU place; stead
LIFE vitality; duration; memoir
LIFT exalt; raise; elevate; steal
LIKE prefer; enjoy; cognate; match
LILT cheerful song or air; ditty **Mus.**
LILY fleur-de-lis **B.**
LIMB edge; border; an imp; branch **B.**
LIME to ensnare; citron or lemon tree **B.**
LIMN to paint; draw; illuminate
LIMP walk lamely; slack; flaccid
LIMY glutinous; viscous
LINE ancestry; business; the Equator
LING sea-fish; common heather **Z., B.**
LINK torch; nexus; tie; connect
LINK (missing); 7.92″ **Meas.**
LINN pool; waterfall
LINO linoleum
LINT surgical linen **Med.**
LINY streaky; wrinkled
LION Hercules killed Nemean lion **Z.**
LIPP a crimson fish **Z.**
LIRA Italian silver coin **Coin**
LIRE the plural of lira **Coin**
LIRK a fold; to hang in creases (Sc.)
LISP
LIST enlist; register; roll; elect; wish
LITH joint; segment
LIVE exist; survive; active; alive; dwell
LOAD lade; cumber; charge; incubus
LOAF lounge; dawdle; (bread)
LOAM rich mould
LOAN lend; advance; imprest
LOBE projecting part; a cotyledon **B.**
LOCH lake; arm of the sea
LOCK close; seal; bolt; hug; ringlet
LOCO locomotive
LODE vein in ore; drain; open ditch
LOFT upper room; to sky
LOGE a box in a theatre
LOIN
LOKE grassy road (East Anglia)

LOKI Norse spirit of evil or mischief
LOLL sprawl; lounge
LOMA lobe; fringe
LOMP the lump fish **Z.**
LONE isolated; solitary; secluded
LONG prolix; lengthy; crave; aspire
LOOF the palm of the hand
LOOK scan; gaze; peer; seem; mien
LOOM machine; approach menacingly
LOON rascal; Great Northern Diver **Z.**
LOOP bight; bend; loophole
LOOS laus; praise (Spens.)
LOOT booty; plunder; sack; ransack
LOPE run with easy strides
LORD dominate; master; ruler; a peer
LORE wisdom; erudition; doctrine
LORN forlorn; lost; forsaken; undone
LORY Australian parrot **Z.**
LOSE mislay; waste; squander; fail
LOSS defeat; reverse; deprivation
LOST missing; astray; vicious; dreamy
LOTE lotus; water-lily **B.**
LOTH averse; unwilling; allergic
LOTO lotto; a game
LOUD stentorian; clamorous; noisy
LOUP loop; to leap
LOUR scowl; frown; glower
LOUT boor; clod; booby; yokel
LOVE adore; affection; courtship
LOWN sheltered; tranquil (Sc.)
LUCE full grown pike **Z.**
LUCK hap; fate; hazard; fortune; chance
LUDO a game
LUES poison; plague; disease
LUFF the weather-gauge **Naut.**
LUGE toboggan
LULL calm; assuage; an interim
LUMP chunk; projection; hunk
LUNA the moon; heraldic argent
LUNE half-moon shape
LUNG respiratory organ **Med.**
LUNT a light; a slow-match
LURE entice; decoy; bait
LURK skulk; lie in wait
LUSH juicy; luscious; succulent; watery
LUSK a sluggard; to laze
LUST desire; cupidity; covet
LUTE tenacious composition; guitar **Mus.**
LUXE luxuriousness (Fr.)
LYAM leam; dog-leash
LYME a coarse grass **B.**
LYNX sharp-eyed animal **Z.**
LYON Heraldic Court (Sc.)
LYRA a constellation
LYRE early form of harp **Mus.**

M

MA'AM marm; madame

MAAR a crater	**MESA** broad, flat, rocky, tableland (Sp.)
MACE staff of authority; spice **B.**	**MESH** ensnare; net-work; brewery grains
MACH supersonic speed	**MESS** muddle; jumble; dish of food; **eat**
MACK or **MAIK** make (Sc.)	**META** Roman racing pylon
MADE formed; fashioned; compelled	**METE** measure; limit; boundary
MAGE a magician	**MEUM** and tuum
MAGI wise men of the East	**MEWL** to squall
MAID lass; lassie; damsel	**MEWS** stables; cages for hawks
MAIL the post; chain-armour	**MIAU** a cat-call
MAIM cripple; mutilate; disable	**MICA** a silicate used as glass **Min.**
MAIN at dice or cockfighting; essential	**MICE** small rodents **Z.**
MAIN the ocean; might; power; pipe	**MICH** lie hid; skulk; sneak; play truant
MAKE do; gain; form; cause; reach	**MICO** vegetable butter or solid oil **B.**
MAKI a Malagasy lemur **Z.**	**MIDA** the larva of the bean-fly **Z.**
MALE masculine	**MIEN** air; bearing; deportment; aspect
MALL hammer; to bruise; public walk	**MIFF** annoyance; resentment
MALM calcareous loam **Min.**	**MIKE** shirk; loiter; microphone
MALT steeped grain	**MILD** suave; bland; placid; soothing
MAMA mamma; mammy	**MILE** 1760 yards **Meas.**
MANE	**MILK** cat-lap
MANX curtailed	**MILL** grind; factory; fight **Coin**
MANY sundry; divers; manifold	**MILO** the strong man of Crotona
MARC oil-cake refuse	**MILT** the spleen; roe; spawn **Z.**
MARE **Z.**	**MIME** mimic; ape; copy; a farce
MARK (letters of) ; brand; stigma **Coin**	**MINA** 50 shekels; Indian bird **Coin, Z.**
MARL mixture of clay, sand and lime	**MIND** mark; heed; dislike; intention
MARM ma'am; madame	**MINE** pit; colliery; sap; weaken
MARS God of War; a planet	**MING** Chinese porcelain; dynasty
MART market; bazaar; emporium	**MINI** compact size
MASH mix; crush; knead; compound	**MINK** furry animal, weasel type **Z.**
MASK veil; cloak; revel; disguise; visor	**MINO** Japanese raincoat
MASS bulk; size; whole; heap **Eccl.**	**MINT** coin; invent; an aromatic plant **B**.
MAST beech-nuts, etc. **Naut.**	**MINX** pert selfish girl; she-puppy **Z.**
MATE comrade; checkmate; tea plant **B.**	**MINY** subterraneous
MATH a mowing	**MIRE** mud; ooze; slime
MATT roughened	**MIRK** murk; gloom; dark
MAUD shepherd's woollen plaid (Sc.)	**MIRY** muddy; marshy; soggy
MAUL mall; hammer; to molest **Tool**	**MISE** cost; expense; a treaty **Law**
MAWK a maggot **Z.**	**MISS** fail; want; need; spinster
MAYA language; Hindu mythology	**MIST** fog; haze; obscurity
MAZE daze; bewilder; a labyrinth	**MISY** mysy; impure iron ore **Min.**
MAZY winding; intricate	**MITE** widow's donation; insect **Coin, Z.**
MEAD spiced ale; meadow; field	**MITT** mitten; a covering for the wrist
MEAL a repast; ground grain	**MITY** full of insects **Z.**
MEAN middle; average; intend; signify	**MIXT** mixed; mingled; blended
MEAT food; flesh	**MOAN** bewail; lament; deplore
MEDE a native of Media	**MOAT**
MEED reward; recompense; guerdon	**MOCK** taunt; flaunt; deride; imitate
MEEK mild; lowly; pacific; unassuming	**MOCO** the rock cavy **Z.**
MEER mere; pool; lake (obs.)	**MODE** style; form; way; vogue
MEET fit; proper; encounter; join	**MODI** methods; (modus)
MELT fuse; thaw; soften; dissolve	**MODS** first B.A. examination, Oxford
MEMO memorandum; note; jotting	**MOFF** Caucasian silk fabric
MEND repair; patch; amend; correct	**MOHR** West African gazelle **Z.**
MENU bill of fare	**MOIL** toil; soil; daub
MERE pool; lake; marsh; boundary	**MOKE** ass; donkey; burro **Z.**
MERE unmixed; simply; alone; only	**MOKO** Maori tattooing
MERI Maori war club	**MOLD** mould
MERK an old Scots silver coin **Coin**	**MOLE** jetty; a blemish; artificial harbour
MERV silk dress material	**MOLE** the gentleman in velveteens **Z.**

MOLL courtesan; gangster's sweetheart
MOLT melt; moult (obs.)
MOLY a countercharm; garlic **B.**
MOME a dullard; buffoon
MONK an ink-stain in printing **Eccl.**
MOOD disposition; humour; temper; vein
MOON wander aimlessly; a satellite
MOOP to nibble; to browse (Sc.)
MOOR fasten; berth; heath; (Othello)
MOOT an assembly; debate; discuss
MOPE to be dull and listless
MOPS a pug-dog **Z.**
MOPY downcast; dejected; sad
MORA game "fingers out"; a tree **B.**
MORE additional; further; again
MORN morning; to-morrow
MORT death tune; a quantity
MOSS a cryptogamic plant **B.**
MOST more than more
MOTE mite; particle; speck; blemish
MOTE moot; assembly; to debate (obs.)
MOTH **Z.**
MOUE a pout; a grimace (Fr.)
MOUL mool; mouldy (Sc.)
MOVE stir; shift; budge; propose
MOWN scythed; cut
MOXA a cauterizer **B., Med.**
MOYA volcanic mud **Min.**
MOZE to raise the nap on cloth
MUCH plenteous; greatly; largely
MUCK refuse; dirt
MUFF a duffer; hand-warmer
MUID hogshead; dry measure for corn
MUIR moor (Sc.)
MULE slipper; machine; a hybrid **Z.**
MULL snuff-box; headland; mistake
MULT multure; fee for grinding corn
MUMM to mask; act; masquerade
MUMP nibble; grin; deceive; beg
MURE immure; a wall
MURK mirk; darkness; obscurity
MUSA banana genus **B.**
MUSE meditate; ponder; contemplate
MUSH pulp; travel by dog-sled
MUSK a scent; a deer **Z.**
MUSS a mess; scramble; disarrange
MUST obliged; necessitated
MUST mould; unfermented grapejuice
MUST elephant frenzy
MUTE dumb; still; a sordine **Mus.**
MUTT a fool
MUXY gloomy; dirty
MYNA the Indian starling **Z.**
MYTH legend; fable; invention

N

NABK a plant in the crown of thorns **B.**
NAGA sacred Hindu snakes **Z.**
NAIB Indian law officer
NAIF naive; artless; ingenuous

NAIK Indian corporal
NAIL to spike; secure; 2¼ inches **Meas.**
NAJA venonous snake; a cobra **Z.**
NAME call; term; nominate; renown
NANA benteak skill
NAND logic
NAOS a shrine (Greek)
NAPE the back of the neck
NAPO (ne plus); finish
NAPU the musk-deer of Java **Z.**
NARD spikenard; an unguent **B.**
NARK police spy; a squealer
NAVE (wheel); hub; main aisle **Ecc.**
NAVY fleet of ships **Naut.**
NAZE cape; mull; headland; ness
NAZI German nationalist
NEAL anneal; to temper
NEAP lowest tide
NEAR nigh; close; stingy; miserly
NEAT trim; tidy; simple; cattle **Z.**
NECK col; an isthmus
NEED want; lack; require; poverty
NEEM margosa oil
NEEP a turnip **B.**
NE'ER never
NEMO nobody
NEON a gas **Chem.**
NEPE flannel footwear
NERO a tyrant
NESH soft; crumbly; tender
NESS naze; cape; promontory
NEST abode; resort
NETT without discount
NEUM neume; a musical phrase **Mus.**
NEVE glacial snow; firn
NEWS tidings; word; report; advice
NEWT an eft **Z.**
NEXT close to; bordering
NIAS nyas; eyas; a young hawk **Z.**
NIBS His Nibs
NICE precise; fine; finical; pleasant
NICK notch; reckoning; winning throw
NIDE a brood of pheasants **Z.**
NIGH near; impending; almost
NIKE Greek goddess of victory
NILL unwilling; incandescent sparks
NINE one over the eight
NIPA Indian palm tree; toddy **B.**
NISI prius; unless previously **Law**
NIXY nixie; malignant water-spirit
NIZY dunce; simpleton
NOCK the notch of an arrow
NODE knot; knob; intersection
NODE plot of play; principal difficulty
NOEL Xmas; Yule
NOES opposition votes
NOIL a knot of combed wool
NOLL ⎫
NOUL ⎬ the head; poll; the crown
NOWL ⎭

NOME tract of land in Egypt or Greece	**ONLY** sole; alone; singly; barely; but
NONE not one	**ONST** once
NOOK cranny; corner; recess; arbour	**ONUS** burden; load; responsibility
NOON mid-day; height; meridional	**ONTO** on to
NOPE American negation	**ONYM** species or zoological group **Z.**
NORM rule; model; standard	**ONYX** agate streaked with chalcedony
NORN one of the three Norse fates	**OOFY** wealthy; opulent; plutocratic
NOSE sagacity; scent; pry; projection	**OOZE** slime; mire; exude; leak; drip
NOSY nosey; inquisitive	**OOZY** viscous; slimy
NOTE heed; mark; record; letter; fame	**OPAH** the king-fish or sunfish **Z.**
NOUN a substantive	**OPAL** iridescent precious stone **Min.**
NOUS talent; gumption; intellect	**OPEN** overt; candid; undo; begin; start
NOUT neat; cattle (Sc.) **Z.**	**O-PIP** observing station
NOVA a new star	**OPUS** a composition; a work **Mus.**
NOWT cattle (Sc.)	**ORAL** by word of mouth
NOWY knotted (Her.)	**ORCA** the whale genus **Z.**
NUDE bare; naked; undraped; stark	**ORFE** a gold fish; ide **Z.**
NULL void; invalid; nugatory	**ORGY** drunken revelry; orge
NUMB torpid; deadened; paralyzed	**ORLE** fillet under an ovolo (Arch.)
NUNG a bale of cloves	**ORRA** odd; worthless (Sc.)
NURL to mill; to indent	**ORYX** Afr. antelope; legendary unicorn **Z.**
NYAS nias; eyas; young hawk **Z.**	**OSSA** and Pelion, mountains in Thessaly
	OTIC a medicine for the ears **Med.**
O	**OTTI** ottar; an essential oil; perfume
	OUCH a jewel socket
OAKS a race for fillies	**OURS** also **OURN**
OAKY hard; tough; strong	**OUSE** bark for tanning
OAST hop-kiln	**OUST** evict; eject; expel; dislodge
OATH vow; pledge; curse; expletive	**OVAL** elliptical
OBEX a barrier; an obstacle	**OVEN** kiln
OBEY heed; mind; comply; submit	**OVER** (cricket); above; besides; very
OBIT R. C. funeral service **Eccl.**	**OVUM** an egg **Z.**
OBOE the hautboy **Mus.**	**OWED** due; outstanding; indebited
OBOL Charon's ferry fee over Styx **Coin**	**OWRE** the wild ox **Z.**
OBUS projectile (Fr.)	**OWSE** tan vat liquor
ODAL udal; absolute tenure in land **Law**	**OXEN** kine; cattle; neat **Z.**
ODDS chances; probabilities	**OXER** a stiff fence
ODIC odylic force	**OYER** the hearing of a law suit **Law**
ODIN Norse father of heaven	**OYES**⎫ the call of the public crier
ODYL magnetic force	**OYEZ**⎭
OFFA King of Mercia	
OGAM ogham; ancient Irish writing	**P**
OGEE a double curve in architecture	
OGLE side glance; leer; smicker	
OGPU Soviet police	**PACA** South American rodent **Z.**
OGRE monster; giant	**PACE** rate; speed; step; walk; peace
OILY greasy; unctuous; oleaginous	**PACK** stow; crowd; bale; load; (cards)
OKAY perfectly correct	**PACO** the alpaca; Peruvian sheep **Z.**
OKRA a vegetable; gumbo **B.**	**PACT** bond; agreement; contract
OLEO oleomargarine; oleograph	**PAFF** piff-paff; jargon
OLIO mess; medley; mixture; stew	**PAGE** buttons; bell-hop; to paginate
OLLA olio; jar; urn; cooking pot	**PAID** requited; defrayed; settled; met
OLPE Grecian jug	**PAIK** a beating (Sc.)
OMAR Khayyam, the tentmaker	**PAIL** bucket
OMEN sign; portent; presage; augury	**PAIN** vex; fret; rack; torment; injure
OMER a Hebrew unit of capacity **Meas.**	**PAIR** two; twain; brace; couple
OMIT miss; skip; exclude; neglect	**PAIS** a jury list **Law**
ONCE also onst	**PALA** South African antelope **Z.**
ONDY wavy (heraldic)	**PALE** wan; sallow; paling; district
ONER singular; a single; an adept	**PALE** a vertical division (Her.)
	PALI Bhuddist sacred language

PALL mantle; cloak; cloy; sate; surfeit	**PESO** (Philippines); dollar **Coin**
PALM to conceal; a token of victory **B.**	**PEST** plague; pestilence; scourge
PALP jointed feeler **Z.**	**PHEW** !
PALT rubbish (Dutch)	**PHIZ** face; visage: physiognomy
PALY ashen; divided vertically (Her.)	**PHON** a decibel; unit of loudness **Meas.**
PAND narrow curtain over a bed (Sc.)	**PHOT** unit of illumination **Meas.**
PANE window glass; a patch	**PIAL** spinal chord membrane **Med.**
PANG throe; paroxysm; to cram	**PIAT** anti-tank mortar
PANT gasp; puff; blow; palpitate	**PICA** type of print; a magpie **Z.**
PAPA Greek parish priest; a bishop **Eccl.**	**PICE** Indian (Nepalese) **Coin**
PARA paragraph; Turkish copper **Coin**	**PICK** cull; select; choice; peck **Tool**
PARA Brazilian rubber **B.**	**PICT** early Scottish race
PARD the leopard; a partner **Z.**	**PIED** spotted
PARE cut; peel; skive; lessen; diminish	**PIER** jetty; mole; pillar
PARK train of artillery; an enclosure	**PIET** the magpie; dipper; water-ousel **Z.**
PARR young salmon **Z.**	**PIKA** small rodent; guinea-pig type **Z.**
PART sever; allot; parcel; divide; quit	**PIKE** peak; a turnpike; a weapon; fish **Z.**
PASS exceed; overstep; ignore; enact	**PILE** nap; heap; mass; stake; (electrical)
PAST gone; done; over; former; bygone	**PILL** to rod; plunder; blackball **Med.**
PATE head; pie; pasty; patty	**PIMP** a pander
PATH way; track; trail; route; access	**PINE** to wilt; pine-apple; fir-tree **B.**
PAUW the South African bustard **Z.**	**PING** the noise of a bullet
PAVE smooth; prepare; facilitate	**PINK** to pierce; to knock; a flower **B.**
PAVE the cobbled roads of France	**PINT** measure of capacity; 4 gills **Meas.**
PAVO peacock; southern constellation **Z.**	**PINY** full of pines **B.**
PAUL ⎱ a check stop	**PIPE** exchequer roll; long tube; calumet
PAWL ⎰	**PIPE** to call; cask; bosun's whistle **Mus.**
PAWK trick; a cunning device (Sc.)	**PIPI** pods for tanning
PAWN pledge; hypothecate; a chessman	**PIPY** tubular
PAYA Honduran Indian	**PIRN** reel; bobbin; thread on a reel
PAYE pay as you earn	**PISE** rammed clay
PEAK to ai; top; acme; apex; zenith	**PISH** !
PEAL clang; echo; resound; thunder	**PITH** quintessence; gist; marrow **B.**
PEAN paean; song of triumph	**PITY** ruth; condolence; compassion
PEAR a fruit **B.**	**PIXY** pixie; a small fairy
PEAT turf used for fuel	**PIZE** term used in execration
PEBA armadillo; the black tatou **Z.**	**PLAN** plot; scheme; design; sketch
PECH also **PEGH**; to pant (Sc.)	**PLAP** plop; plash; splash
PECK strike with beak; 2 gallon **Meas.**	**PLAT** to plait; piece of ground; dish
PEEK to peep (Sc.)	**PLAY** act; romp; game; frolic; farce
PEEL skin; pare; rind; bark; flay	**PLEA** excuse; prayer; claim; argument
PEEL a shovel; a fort; to pillage	**PLED** pleaded; argued; disputed
PEEN the back of a hammer-head	**PLIM** to swell
PEEP a sly look; the cry of a chicken	**PLOD** jog along; toil; moil; drudge
PEER to peep; to appear; a nobleman	**PLOP** to fall into water
PEKE a Pekinese dog **Z.**	**PLOT** plan; concoct; outline; allotment
PELA white wax from a scale-insect	**PLOW** a plough
PELF money; riches; filthy lucre	**PLOY** employment; a frolic (Sc.)
PELL skin; hide; parchment	**PLUG** a stopple; stop; plod
PELT raw hide; throw; rain heavily	**PLUM** £100.000 **B.**
PEND hang; impend; an enclosure	**PLUS** in addition; more
PENT enclosed; confined; shut up	**PNYX** Athenian meeting place
PEON day-labourer; bondsman; police	**POCK** a pustule **Med.**
PEON foot-soldier; messenger (India)	**POCO** little; rather (It.) **Mus.**
PEPO a fruit of the gourd type **B.**	**POEM** ode; lyric; elegy
PERI fairy excluded from paradise	**POET** bard; balladmonger
PERK smarten up; trim; spruce	**POGO** a pastime
PERM a permanent wave	**POKE** bag; bonnet; nudge; prod
PERN the honey-buzzard **Z.**	**POKY** small; cramped; confined; stupid
PERT saucy; forward; impertinent	**POLE** a mast; 5½ yards (Poland) **Meas.**

POLK to dance the polka	
POLL clip; lop; election; head; parrot **Z.**	
POLO	
POLT a blow; a hard knock; a club	
POME an apple; ball of dominion **B.**	
POMP pageantry; ceremony; display	
POND pool; mere; to ponder	
PONE bread made from Indian corn	
PONK a nocturnal spirit (Shak.)	
PONS medical link or bridge **Med.**	
PONY £25; nag; tit; palfrey **Z.**	
POOD Russian weight, 36 lbs. **Meas.**	
POOH !	
POOL mere; tarn; merge; combine	
POON East Indian tree; wood for spars	
POOP nincompoop; stern of ship **Naut.**	
POOR scant; meagre; sterile; needy	
POPE the Bishop of Rome **Eccl.**	
PORE con; study; small orifice **Med.**	
PORK	
PORT bagpipe music; mien; bearing **Mus.**	
PORT wine; haven; entry; larboard **Naut.**	
PORY porous; pervious	
POSE puzzle; nonplus; feign; a posture	
POSH very superior	
POST size of paper; mail; station; record	
POSY motto or verse; nosegay **B.**	
POUF pouffe; large cushion; gauze	
POUR rush; gush; flow; emit; stream	
POUT to register pique; a whiting **Z.**	
PRAD a horse (slang)	
PRAM perambulator; Baltic boat **Naut.**	
PRAY beg; crave; implore; entreat	
PREE to prove; to taste (Sc.)	
PREP preparation; preparatory	
PREX college president (U.S.A.)	
PREY despoil; pillage; devour; quarry	
PRIG pilfer; a coxcomb	
PRIM formal; precise; privet shrub **B.**	
PROA Malay sailing canoe **Naut.**	
PROD goad; poke; nudge; prick	
PROG proctor	
PROM promenade concert **Mus.**	
PROP support; uphold; buttress	
PROS arguments for; cf. cons	
PROW the cutwater **Naut.**	
PROX proximo	
PRYS price (Spens.)	
PSHA ! pshaw	
PTAH Egyptian God, the Creator	
PUCE flea-colour	
PUCK ice hockey ball; an imp	
PUDU a small deer of the Andes **Z.**	
PUFF fuff; pant; blow; flatter; a whiff	
PUGH! interjection of disgust	
PUJA Hindu ritual; obeisance	
PUKE to vomit	
PULE to whine; to cry	
PULK Laplander's sledge	
PULL draw; drag; haul; pluck; pick	

PULP any soft uniform mass	
PULS (Afghan) **Coin**	
PULU Hawaiian tree-fern fibre **B.**	
PUMA Peruvian lion **Z.**	
PUMP raise water; interrogate	
PUMY pumice-stone **Min.**	
PUNA Andean plateau	
PUNK tinder; dud; worthless	
PUNT gamble; kick; flat-boat **Naut.**	
PUNY tiny; weak; petty; Lilliputian	
PUPA also **PUPE**; a chrysalis **Z.**	
PURE chaste; unsullied; unmixed; neat	
PURL knit; flow; ripple; mulled ale	
PURR curr; (a cat or pigeon noise)	
PUSH a gang; urge; jostle; press	
PUSS hare or cat **Z.**	
PUTT an endeavour to hole the ball	
PUXI North Amer. edible caterpillar **Z.**	
PYRE a funeral pile	
PYRO pyrogallic acid **Chem.**	

Q

QUAB quob; tremble (obs.)	
QUAD quadrangle; quadruped; prison **Z.**	
QUAG quagmire; morass; swamp	
QUAT a nonentity; a twerp	
QUAY wharf; landing place	
QUEY a young cow or heifer (Sc.) **Z.**	
QUIB quip; jibe; jest	
QUID £1; a chew of tobacco **Coin**	
QUIN a kind of scallop **Z.**	
QUIP sally; retort; taunt; quirk	
QUIT leave; desert; retire; release	
QUIZ puzzle; chaff; ridicule; an enquiry	
QUOB quab; tremble	
QUOP quap; throb	
QUOD quad; prison	

R

RAAD South African parliament	
RABI the grain crop of Hindustan	
RACA a term of contempt	
RACE run; compete; tribe; nation	
RACE flavour; root; rapid; current	
RACH dog; pointer or setter **Z.**	
RACK torture; stretch; anguish; harass	
RACK a grating; wrack; cloud; to amble	
RACY spirited; piquant; pungent	
RAFF riff-raff; rabble; rubbish	
RAFT a floating framework **Naut.**	
RAGE rave; fume; fury; storm; craze	
RAGG ragstone; siliceous sandstone **Min.**	
RAGI species of millet **B.**	
RAHU the dark planet in Hindu Myth.	
RAID foray; inroad; invasion; irruption	
RAIL fence; scold; genus of birds **B.**	
RAIN pitter-patter; a downpour	
RAJA rajah	

RAKE roué; inclination; gardening **Tool**
RAKI Levant; aniseed brandy
RALE rattling sound in the lungs **Med.**
RAMA heroic incarnation of Vishnu
RAMP a slope; a swindle; climb; spring
RANA amphibian genus, frogs, etc. **Z.**
RANA a Rajput prince or chief
RAND mountain ridge in the Transvaal
RAND edge; border; margin; inner sole
RANG
RANI ranee; the wife of a rajah
RANK row; grade; range; foul; musty
RANT rave; orate; spout; declaim
RAPE land division in Sussex; oil-seed **B.**
RAPE ravish; violate; outrage
RAPT enthralled; absorbed; fascinated
RARE choice; unusual; precious; raw
RASE raze; erase; expunge; level
RASH hasty; headlong; to slice **Med.**
RASP to file; abrade; raspberry **Tool, B.**
RATA a New Zealand ironwood tree **B.**
RATE scold; assess; appraise; speed
RATH Burmese state carriage
RATH rathe; early; soon; Irish fort
RAVE rant; fume; storm; drive
RAZE rase; gut; demolish; overthrow
READ peruse; decipher; study; erudite
REAL true; genuine; a Spanish **Coin**
REAM to enlarge; to froth; 20 quires
REAN rine; rone; rune; a ditch
REAP gain; crop; gather; harvest
REAR raise; breed; erect; end; behind
RECK to care for; regard; heed
REDD to tidy; to arrange; to clear
REDE counsel; advise; advice
REED rush; aquatic grass
REED to thatch; a pipe **Mus.**
REEF rocky ledge; shoal; lode **Naut.**
REEK smoke; vapour; fume; stink
REEL sway; whirl; totter; a bobbin
REEM the unicorn of the Bible **Z.**
REFT bereft; left destitute
REIM riem; raw-hide thong (S. Africa)
REIN govern; restrain; check; curb
REIS Brazilian or Portuguese money **Coin**
RELY depend; lean; confide; trust
REND rip; tear; sunder; sever; rupture
RENT hire; let; lease; schism; tear
REPP ribbed fabric
RESP a sheep disease
REST repose; lean; recline; respite
RETE a plexus; network of vessels **Med.**
REUS a defendant; debtor **Law**
REVE dream; reverie (obs.)
RHEA the South American ostrich **Z.**
RHEA Hellenic nature-goddess
RHEA the ramie plant or fibre **B.**
RHOM parallelogram brick
RHUS cashew-nut genus **B.**
RIAL ryal (Iran); English gold **Coin**

RICE a wedding cereal **B.**
RICH opulent; wealthy; fertile; luscious
RICK stack; wrench; sprain
RIDE domineer; control; a district
RIEL (Cambodia) **Coin**
RIEM reim; leather rope (S. Africa)
RIFE ryfe; prevalent; current; abundant
RIFF a moroccan
RIFT fissure; cleft; gap; split; chink
RIGA deal; balsam; hemp from Riga **B.**
RILE vex; anger; provoke; irritate
RILL rivulet; brook; streamlet
RIMA a wood nymph
RIME hoar-frost; rhyme; poem
RIND peel; bark; external cover **B.**
RINE rind; to touch
RINE rone; rune; rean; water-course
RING encircle; hoop; arena; combine
RINK a sheet of ice
RIOT orgy; broil; uproar; tumult
RIPE mature; ready; mellow; fit
RIPT ripped; torn
RISE soar; mount; tower; rebel
RISK chance; hazard; peril; speculate
RISP to rasp; branch of green stalks **B.**
RITE form; usage; observance
RIVA rift; cleft
RIVE a bank; tear; rend; pierce
RIVO a drinking cry (Shak.)
RIXY quarrelsome; the sea-swallow **Z.**
ROAD route; thoroughfare; highway
ROAM rove; ramble; meander; saunter
ROAN a colour; sheepskin binding
ROAR yell; shout; bellow; howl
ROBE clothe; invest; drape; dress
ROCK a distaff; oscillate; sweetmeat
RODE travelled; a raid; a roadstead
ROER elephant gun
ROIL rile; to stir up; to vex
ROIN royne; whisper; mutter
ROKE reek; smoke; mist
ROKY foggy
ROLE part; function; character
ROLL reel; lurch; enfold; scroll
ROME Catholicism
ROMP sport; frisk; caper; gambol
RONE rine; rune; rean; gutter
RONG rung; tolled (obs.)
RONT runt; stunted; a stump
ROOD The Cross; **Eccl.**
ROOD a quarter of an acre **Meas.**
ROOF cover; canopy; shelter
ROOK cheat; defraud; fleece; castle **Z.**
ROOL to ruffle; to raggle
ROOM chamber; stead; space; scope
ROOM roum; a deep-blue dye
ROON rim; border (Sc.)
ROOP to roar; hoarseness (obs.)
ROOT fix; implant; origin; radix **B.**
ROPE tie; secure; bind; tether

ROPY stringy; viscous; adhesive
ROSE arose; colour; a spray **B.**
ROSS the refuse of plants (Sc.)
ROSY roseate; blooming; blushing
ROTA roster; R.C. court **Eccl.**
ROTE mechanical repetition
ROTI the joint (Fr.)
ROTL a 12 ounce Arab weight **Meas.**
ROUE rake; debauchee; libertine
ROUM room; a deep-blue dye
ROUP a fowl disease; an auction (Sc.)
ROUT vanquish; defeat; disorder
ROUT social function; soirée
ROUX a thickening culinary mixture
ROVE roam; ramble; stray; range
RUBE a rustic (U.S.A.)
RUBY a size of type; a gem **Min.**
RUCK wrinkle; fold; crease
RUDD freshwater fish; the red-eye **Z.**
RUDE boorish; churlish; rough; raw
RUED regretted; repented
RUFF a frill; to trump; a bird **Z.**
RUGA fold; corrugation
RUIN wreck; demolish; subvert
RUKH the jungle (India)
RULE control; sway; precept; custom
RUMP the Parliament of 1648
RUNE incised writing of the Norsemen
RUNG a ladder step; tolled
RUNN low-lying land in India
RUNT ront; dwarf; stump; a pigeon **Z.**
RUSA Indian deer, the sambar **Z.**
RUSA Indian grass; (geranium oil) **B.**
RUSE wile; trick; artifice; stratagem
RUSH dash; fly; career; sally; a reed **B.**
RUSK a biscuit
RUSS a Russian
RUST fust; must; corrosion
RUTA genus of plants; rue **B.**
RUTH mercy; pity; sorrow; misery
RYAL rial; rose-noble old English **Coin**
RYKE to reach (Sc.)
RYND iron millstone support
RYOT Indian cultivator
RYPE the Norwegian ptarmigan **Z.**
RYVE rive; to pierce (Spens.)

S

SACK wine; garment; pillage; pouch
SADR the lote-bush **B.**
SAFE sure; secure; reliable; certain
SAGA heroic Norse legends
SAGE a Solomon; genus salvia **B.**
SAGO edible palm pith **B.**
SAGY seasoned with sage
SAIC Levantine ketch **Naut.**
SAID stated; declared; alleged
SAIL cruise; glide; depart **Naut.**

SAIN to consecrate (Sc.)
SAIR to serve; to satisfy; sore (Sc.)
SAKE cause; regard; reason
SAKI Japanese beer
SAKI South American monkey genus **Z.**
SALE auction; market; vendition
SALP swimming tunicate **Z.**
SALT mariner; wit; pungent; salacious
SALT sodium chloride **Chem.**
SAME ditto.; identical; exactly similar
SAMP porridge made from Indian corn
SAND grit; force of character **Min.**
SANE rational; sound; normal; lucid
SANG chanted; heraldic blood
SANK foundered; subsided; dug
SANS without (Shak.)
SAPO the toad-fish **Z.**
SARD a precious stone; agate **Min.**
SARI Indian garment; scarf
SARK a shirt or chemise
SARN a pavement
SASH window frame; a scarf
SASS impudence; sauce
SATE cloy; glut; gratify; surfeit
SATI suttee; self-immolation(India)
SAUL Indian tree; an oratorio **B., Mus.**
SAUT salt (Sc.)
SAVE except; rescue; husband; retain
SAWN cut with a saw
SAXE a kind of paper; light blue
SCAB a blackleg; a sore **Med.**
SCAD horse-mackerel **Z.**
SCAN view; examine; scrutinize
SCAR mark; blemish; steep rock
SCAT a tax; scare away; be off!
SCAW skaw; a promontory
SCON scun; skim; skip
SCOT a Scotsman; a tax
SCOW flat-bottomed boat **Naut.**
SCRY descry; espy
SCUD rack; wrack; hasten; bustle
SCUG skug; shelter; expiate
SCUM dross; froth; refuse; scoria
SCUN scon; skim
SCUP a swing; the porgy fish **Z.**
SCUR graze; jerk; a stunted horn (Sc.)
SCUT a short tail
SCYE armhole of a garment
SEAH Jewish dry measure, 14 pts. **Meas.**
SEAL fasten; a pinniped **Z.**
SEAM joint; vein; stratum
SEAN seine; a drag-net
SEAR burn; scorch; a pawl; dry; sere
SEAT chair; site; residence; abode
SEAX Celtic sword
SECT faction; schism; party
SEED germ; embryo; progeny **B., Z.**
SEEK try; ask; hunt; search; court
SEEL to close the eye-lids; good fortune
SEEM appear; look; pretend

SEEN observed; regarded; perceived
SEEP to ooze; to trickle; to sipe
SEER augur; prophet; soothsayer
SEER Indian kilogramme **Meas.**
SEGO an American plant **B.**
SEID a descendant of Mohammed
SEIL sile; strain; a sieve (Sc.)
SELF particular; simple; selfishness
SELL vend; barter; hawk; betray
SEME strewn with stars, etc. (heraldic)
SEMI demi; hemi; a prefix
SEND transmit; propel; eject
SENS since (Spens.)
SENT forwarded; despatched; flung
SEPS reptile genus; lizards **Z.**
SEPT a clan in Ireland
SERA a lock of any kind
SERB native of Serbia
SERE sear; withered; parched; dry
SERF thrall; villein; slave; helot
SESS cess; tax
SETA bristle; prickle
SETT squared block; packing piece
SETT badger's home; (mining)
SEWN stitched
SEXT musical interval **Mus.**
SHAD a fish of the herring type **Z.**
SHAG tobacco; green cormorant **Z.**
SHAG coarse hair; roughen; deform
SHAH Persian monarch
SHAM deceive; substitute
SHAN Burmese borderer
SHAW a grove; a thicket
SHAY chaise; a vehicle
SHEA African butter-tree **B.**
SHED emit; diffuse; cot; shack
SHET freed from; get rid of
SHEW show; exhibit; parade
SHIM to wedge up; a packing piece;
SHIN to climb; tramp; trudge
SHIP to export **Naut.**
SHIR shirr; to pucker
SHOD provided with shoes
SHOE
SHOG shake; jog; a shock
SHOO! begone; scare away
SHOP emporium; store; imprison
SHOT a reckoning; a marksman; missile
SHOW flaunt; blazon; expound; pomp
SHUG to shrug; to crawl
SHUN avoid; evade; eschew; elude
SHUT bar; lock; close; slam; secure
SICE the six at dice
SICE syce; groom (India)
SICK to incite; poorly; ailing; disgusted
SIDA genus of mallows **B.**
SIDE verge; border; cause; behalf
SIDY aloof and pretentious
SIFT separate; examine; sort

SIGH mourn; repine; lament
SIGN beckon; endorse; emblem; portent
SIKE syke; Arctic stream
SIKH a Punjab soldier
SILE a sieve; a colander
SILK **Law**
SILL doorstep; window-frame
SILO fodder storage; ensilage
SILT sediment; ooze; percolate
SIMP a simpleton; a mutt
SIND or **SYND** to rinse (Sc.)
SINE syne; since; then (Sc.)
SING relate in verse; chant; squeal
SINK flag; droop; subside; founder
SINN Fein
SIPE to ooze; to seep; to percolate
SIRE your Majesty; progenitor
SIST summon; delay; stay (Sc.) **Law**
SITE location; place; position; spot
SIUM the water-parsnip **B.**
SIVA the Destroyer in Hindu religion
SIZE glue; varnish; bulk; volume
SIZY sticky; viscous
SKAT a card game
SKAW scaw; a promontory
SKEE ski; a winter sport
SKEG stump; branch; wild plum **B.**
SKEP beehive; wicker basket
SKEW or **SKUE** awry; oblique; a squint
SKID heavy timber; drag-shoe; side-slip
SKIM graze; touch; skirt; brush
SKIN peel; pare; flay; hide; pelt
SKIO or **SKEO** a hut in the Orkneys
SKIP skipper; large tub; omit; leap
SKIT a lampoon; burlesque
SKUA the pirate gull **Z.**
SKUG a squirrel **Z.**
SKUG scug; shelter; expiate
SKYE terrier **Z.**
SKYR curds (Iceland)
SLAB chunk; block; thick; mud
SLAE sloe (Sc.); blackthorn **B.**
SLAG scoria; debris; mine waste
SLAM bang; shut with violence; (cards)
SLAP spank; a cleft; a gap in a fence
SLAT strip; lath; slate; sharp blow
SLAV a Slavonic Aryan
SLAW sliced cabbage used as salad
SLAY kill; destroy; despatch; murder
SLED sledge; sleigh
SLEW slue; to twist; turn round; killed
SLEY the reed of a weaver's loom
SLID slipped; skidded; glided; tripped
SLIM slight; slender; lithe; crafty
SLIP trip; fall; scion; twig; cutting **B.**
SLIT rip; rend; tear; slash; sever
SLOB muddy ground
SLOE slae; blackthorn **B.**
SLOG smite; swipe

SLOP a policeman; a mess; a spill
SLOT track of deer; slit; groove
SLOW tardy; dilatory; dull; inactive
SLUB to twist whilst spinning
SLUD sludge; ooze; mud
SLUE slew; to revolve
SLUG sluggard; a pellet   **Z.**
SLUM a purlieu; squalid neighbourhood
SLUR stigma; stain; aspersion; sully **Mus.**
SLUT a slattern; a jade
SMEE widgeon; pintail   **Z.**
SMEW migratory sea duck   **Z.**
SMIT to infect; a stain; infection
SMOG smoky fog
SMUG self-satisfied; to confiscate
SMUR fine misty rain; to drizzle (Sc.)
SMUT soot; a plant disease
SNAG projecting stump; an obstacle
SNAP bite; nip; snip; crack; break
SNAP a snap-shot; a photo; a game
SNAR to snarl (Spens.)
SNEB snib; snub; check; reprimand
SNEE a large knife (Dutch)
SNIG to cut; an eel   **Z.**
SNIP clip; piece; snippet; a certainty
SNOB shoemaker; tuft-hunter
SNOD neat; trim; sleek (Sc.)
SNOW (cocaine)
SNUB snib; check; slight
SNUG cosy; compact; sheltered
SOAK steep; drench; saturate
SOAP to flatter
SOAR rise; mount; tower; aspire
SOCK plough-share; hose
SODA an alkali   **Chem.**
SOFA couch; divan; ottoman
SOFI or **SUFI** religious Persian; dervish
SOFT pliable; plastic; yielding; dulcet
SOHO a sportsman's halloo (Shak.)
SOIL loam; stain; sully; tarnish
SOKE soc; privilege; (East Anglian)**Law**
SOLA hat-plant; sponge-wood; pith **B.**
SOLD retailed; peddled; taken in
SOLE only; unique; solitary
SOLI the plural of solo   **Mus.**
SOLO a card game   **Mus.**
SOMA an intoxicating drink
SOME distinctive (American)
SONG lay; carol; ballad; lullaby   **Mus.**
SOON anon; early; willingly; lief
SOOP to sweep (Sc.)
SOOT sout; grime
SOPH sophomore; a student
SORA Carolina rail   **Z.**
SORB mountain ash; service tree   **B.**
SORE raw; tender; grievous; painful
SORI fern spore-cases   **B.**
SORN to cadge board and lodgings
SORT arrange; classify; kind; race
SORY sulphate of iron   **Chem.**

SO-SO indifferent; moderate
SOSS a mess; a puddle; plump
SOUK bazaar; Eastern market
SOUL spirit; fervour; essence
SOUM sowm; pasturage (Sc.)
SOUP broth; consommé
SOUR tart; acid; rancid; caustic; bitter
SOUT soot; grime (obs.)
SOWL to pull by the ears (Shak.)
SOWN disseminated; scattered; strewn
SOYA Japanese bean   **B.**
SPAE spay; foretell; divine
SPAM spiced ham
SPAN a yoke; to bridge; wholly   **Meas.**
SPAR to box; rafter; pole   **Naut., Min.**
SPAT the spawn of shellfish; a slap **Z.**
SPAY to render unfertile; geld
SPEC speculation
SPED fled; hurried; hastened
SPER to bolt; to shut (obs.)
SPET to spit (obs.)
SPEW spue; vomit
SPIE a keen glance; spy (obs.)
SPIN turn; twist; twirl; prolong
SPIT a shoal; an iron prong
SPIV felonious speculating parasite
SPOT blot; stain; patch; mark; site
SPRY alert; brisk; nimble; lively
SPUD narrow spade; potato   **B.**
SPUE spew; eject; vomit
SPUN whirled; woven; extended
SPUR goad; urge; impel; prick
STAB pierce; spear; gore; thrust
STAG a colt; an ox   **Z.**
STAM to confound; confusion
STAR an asterisk; a heavenly body
STAW to stand still; a surfeit (Sc.)
STAY stop; check; curb; tarry; abide **Law**
STEM dam; hold; resist; stock; stalk **B.**
STEN a tommy-gun
STEP pace; tread; rung; stage
STET let it stand (Latin)
STEW ragout; simmer; fishpond
STIE to ascend (Spens.)
STIR spur; stimulate; tumult; prison
STOA a porch; stoic philosophy
STOB stub; stump; wedge
STOG to stir up mud
STOP block; impede; cease; desist
STOT young ox; steer   **Z.**
STOW pack; arrange; place
STUB stump; to extirpate; a counterfoil
STUD knob; nail; breeding place
STUG a thorn (Sc.)
STUM unfermented wine; must
STUN bewilder; amaze; dumbfound
STYE an inflamed eyelid   **Med.**
STYX river in Hades; (see **Obol**)
SUCH sich; so; like; similar
SUCK imbibe; absorb; engulf

SUDD	flood debris, Nile	**TALK**	parley; prate; palaver
SUDS	soapsuds **Naut.**	**TALL**	towering; elevated
SUED	entreated; prosecuted; high & dry	**TAME**	docile; dull; insipid; domesticate
SUER	a plaintiff **Law**	**TAMP**	pack earth round a mine
SUET	fatty tissue	**TANA**	Indian police station
SUEZ	canal; (Lesseps, the engineer)	**TANE**	ta'en; taken
SUFI	Islamic mystic	**TANG**	point; twang; sea-weed; flavour
SUIT	gratify; beseem; action; case	**TANK**	cistern; reservoir
SULK	glower; be sullen	**TANT**	small scarlet spider **Z.**
SUMA	Nicaraguan Indian	**TAPA**	Polynesian fibre cloth
SUMP	pit; morass	**TAPE**	to bind; ribbon; to measure
SUNG	chanted	**TAPU**	tabu; taboo; bar; veto
SUNK	immersed; engulfed; dug	**TARA**	old Irish Convocation
SUNN	Indian plant; its fibre **B.**	**TARA**	an edible New Zealand fern **B.**
SUPE	a supernumerary; a toady	**TARE**	gross weight; a weed **B.**
SURA	a chapter of the Koran	**TARN**	mountain pool; a marsh
SURA	the sap of the coco-palm **B.**	**TARO**	edible plant of the arum type **B.**
SURD	an irrational number	**TART**	sharp; bitter; pungent; small pie
SURE	certain; secure; reliable; safe·	**TASH**	Indian silk fabric with gold thread
SURF	foaming waters	**TASK**	toil; drudgery; labour
SWAB	swob; mop up	**TASS**	a drinking-cup; a heap
SWAD	pod; podgy person; clump	**TASS**	pouch; thigh-armour
SWAG	plunder; festoon; sag	**TA-TA**	good-bye
SWAM	swum	**TATE**	a London Picture Gallery
SWAN	the Swan of Avon, Shakespeare **Z.**	**TATH**	cattle dung; to manure
SWAP	swop; a blow; a stroke; to barter	**TATU**	tatou; peba; armadillo **Z.**
SWAT	a fly-killer; a smart blow	**TAUT**	tense; strained; stressed
SWAY	rock; roll; reel; influence; power	**TAWS**	tawse; a leather strap (Sc.)
SWIG	gulp down; pulley gear	**TAXI**	motor-cab; (aeroplane)
SWIM	float; overflow; be dizzy	**TAYO**	apronlike garment (S. America)
SWIN	sea river or channel	**TEAK**	hardwood tree; the wood **B.**
SWOB	swab; mop	**TEAL**	small waterfowl; a duck **Z.**
SWOP	swap; exchange; barter;	**TEAM**	side; group; draught animals **Z.**
SWOT	swat; an earnest student	**TEAN**	sorrow; vex; tease (Sc.)
SWUM	swam	**TEAR**	rip; rend; lacerate; (sob)
SYBO	cibol; onion **B.**	**TEAT**	a nipple
SYCE	sice; chauffeur; groom (India)	**TECK**	detective
SYKE	sike; rill; rivulet (Sc.)	**TEDE**	tead; torch; flambeau
SYNE	sine; since (Sc.)	**TEED**	(golf)
		TEEM	swarm; to abound; be prolific
		TEEN	grief; affliction; allot (obs.)
T		**TEER**	to stir; to sieve
		TEFF	Abyssinian cereal grass **B.**
TAAL	Cape Dutch	**TEIL**	the lime tree **B.**
TABU	taboo; ban; veto; prohibit	**TELA**	web; tissue
TACE	be silent **Mus.**	**TELD**	told (Spens.)
TACK	a nail; hard food; hasten **Naut.**	**TELL**	recite; divulge; blab; reckon
TACT	diplomacy; finesse	**TEND**	incline; verge; mind; nurture
TAEL	money of account **Coin**	**TENT**	lint; probe; a pavilion
TAEL	Chinese ounce **Meas.**	**TENT**	sacramental wine **Eccl.**
TA'EN	taken	**TERM**	dub; entitle; phrase; period
TAFT	a plumbing joint	**TERN**	threefold; sea-bird, gull-type **Z.**
TAHA	African weaver-bird **Z.**	**TERN**	a prize in a lottery
TAHR	Himalayan goat **Z.**	**TEST**	refining vessel; essay; assay
TAIC	Indo-Chinese; their language	**TEST**	attest; proof; ordeal; criterion
TAIL	extremity; queue; trail; entail	**TETE**	head; head-dress (Fr.)
TAIN	mirror silver	**TETT**	a plait (obs.)
TAIT	tate; fibre; lock of hair (Sc.)	**TETT**	theme; subject; thesis; treatise
TAKE	grasp; seize; adopt; carry	**THAI**	(Siamese); language
TALC	mica **Min.**	**THAN**	
TALE	story; fable; narration		

THAR goat-antelope of Nepal **Z.**	**TOIL** moil; snare; travail; pains; strive
THAT	**TOIT** a cushion
THAW run; fuse; melt; liquefy	**TOKO** toco; a drubbing
THEA the tea plant **B.**	**TOLA** Indian weight; 180 grains troy
THEE	**TOLD** narrated; related; recounted
THEM	**TOLE** toll; entice; attract
THEN	**TOLL** tribute; (funeral bell); telephone
THEW muscle; sinew; strength	**TOLT** old English writ **Law**
THEY Kipling's pronoun	**TOLU** oleo-resin; balsam **B.**
THIG to beg; to beseech; to sorn	**TOMB** grave; sepulchre; mausoleum
THIN lean; fine; lank; spare; sparse	**TOME** book; volume; work
THIS	**TONE** cadence; inflection; tint
THOR the God of Thunder	**TONG** the tongue of a buckle (Spens.)
THOU treat with familiarity	**TONK** a mighty smite
THRO, THRU through	**TONY** a simpleton; genteel; posh
THUD a dull sound	**TOOK** grabbed; gained; captured
THUG Indian strangler or poisoner	**TOOL** cat's-paw; drive a coach
THUS frankincense; a form of resin **B.**	**TOOM** empty; rubbish-heap
TIAO Chinese money of account	**TOON** Indian cedar **B.**
TIBU Saharan tribe	**TOOT** a wastrel; the devil; honk
TICE entice; a decoy	**TOPE** shark known as the penny-dog **Z.**
TICK credit; bed fabric; mark; insect **Z.**	**TOPE** Buddhist monument
TIDE season; course; current	**TOPE** clump of tree; to booze
TIDY neat; spruce; trim; orderly	**TORE** dead winter grass **B.**
TIED united; constrained; fastened	**TORE** rent; split; a torus; a moulding
TIER row; rank; mountain range	**TORI** mouldings at the base of columns
TIFF also **TIFT**; quarrel; peevishness	**TORN** lacerated; ript
TIFF quaff; a short drink; adorn	**TORT** redress of wrongs **Law**
TIGE the shaft of a column (Arch.)	**TORY** a Conservative
TIKE tyke; dog; cur; Yorkshireman **Z.**	**TOSE** to tease (obs.)
TIKI Maori charm or amulet	**TOSH** bosh; twaddle; boloney
TILE roofing material; a hat	**TOSS** pitch; hurl; cast; throw; lob
TILL cash drawer; cultivate	**TOST** flung; writhed
TILT tent; a covering; a hood	**TOSY** teased; soft (obs.)
TILT to hammer; incline; lean; slant	**TOTE** to carry; totalisator
TIME era; epoch; term; spell; date	**TOUR** trip; round; jaunt; ramble
TINE point of antler; spike; to enclose	**TOUT** paid agent; tipster; to pout
TING ring; tinkle	**TOWN** a city; London
TINK tinkle	**TOWY** like tow; hempen
TINT hue; dye; stain; tinge	**TOZE** to pluck; pull by the ears
TINY pygmy; wee; puny; minute	**TRAM** a beam; tramcar
TIRE tyre; iron hoop; attire; headdress	**TRAP** a gin; igneous rock **Min.**
TIRE weary; harass; vex; fatigue	**TRAP** adorn; drape; ambush; ensnare
TIRL quiver; vibrate; twirl (Sc.)	**TRAY** salver; trez; third
TIRO tyro; novice; beginner	**TREE** the Cross; to tree **B.**
TIRR tear; strip off (Sc.)	**TREK** travel by ox-wagons (S. Africa)
TITI South Amer. squirrel monkey **Z.**	**TRET** a trade allowance
TIVY with speed; tantivy	**TREY** a three at cards or dice
TOAD an amphibious batrachian **Z.**	**TREZ** third; the third tine of antler
TOBY beer-mug; Punch's pet **Z.**	**TRIG** trim; tight; secure; a dandy
TOCO toko; punishment	**TRIG** wedge; skid; boundary line
TO-DO ado; bustle; excitement	**TRIM** neat; tidy; clip; adjust; Corporal
TODY green humming bird **Z.**	**TRIO** composition in three parts **Mus.**
TOED trod; toed the line	**TRIP** tour; err; slip; stumble; dance
TOFF fop; dandy; swell	**TROD** trampled; walked
TOFT grove; messuage **Law**	**TRON** ancient beam balance (Sc.)
TOGA Roman raiment	**TROT** to run; an old woman (Shak.)
TOGE a robe (Shak.)	**TROW** to trust; believe; suppose
TOGS ceremonial garments	**TROY** weights used for gold, etc. **Meas.**
TOHO a dog-call	**TRUE** loyal; staunch; straight; exact

TRUG hod for mortar; gardening basket
TSAR Czar; Ksar; Tzar; Zsar
TSUN Chinese inch **Meas.**
TUAN title of respect (China & Malay)
TUBA bass trumpet; transmitter **Mus.**
TUBE pipe; telescope; Underground
TUCK rapier; fold; net; pull; thrust
TUCK beat of drum; food; to cram
TUFA inexpensive cheroot
TUFA calcareous deposit **Min.**
TUFF volcanic rock-debris **Min.**
TUFT knot; bunch; clump; tuffet
TULE Californian bulrush **B.**
TUMP hillock; to earth up
TUNA the prickly pear **B.**
TUNA the great tunny fish **Z.**
TUNE air; melody; strain; harmony
TURF sod; sward; earth; peat; racing
TURK Ottoman
TURM a troop (obs.)
TURN spin; bend; divert; curdle; hinge
TURR three-stringed Burmese violin **Mus.**
TUSH ! pshaw; tusk (Shak.)
TUSK pointed tooth; sea-fish cod type **Z.**
TUTU New Zealand shrub **B.**
TUUM (meum and teum); thine (Latin)
TUZA tucan; Mexican pouched rat **Z.**
TWAL twelve (Sc.)
TWAS it was
TWAY twain; two (Sc.)
TWIG observe; understand; sprig **B.**
TWIN double; duplex
TWIT taunt; ridicule; upbraid
TYKE tike; Yorkshireman; dog; cur **Z.**
TYMP mouth of blast furnace's hearth
TYNE anxiety; disappear; perish (obs.)
TYPE kind; sort; class; species; emblem
TYPO a compositor
TYRE tire; attire; dress
TYRO tiro; novice; recruit; neophyte
TZAR Tsar; Czar; Ksar; Zsar

U

UDAL odal; freehold estate **Law**
UGLY hideous; unsightly; hateful
ULEX furze genus **B.**
ULNA an arm-bone **Med.**
UMBO boss of a shield; a knob
UMBO the point of a bivalve shell **Z.**
UNAU S. American two-toed sloth **Z.**
UNBE undo; destroy (obs.)
UNCO uncommon (Sc.)
UNDE wavy (Her.)
UNDO open; untie; nullify
UNIO genus of freshwater mussels **Z.**
UNIT a standard quantity **Meas.**
UNTO
UPAS the deadly antiar tree **B.**
UPBY further up (Sc.)

UPON on
URAO American soda **Min.**
URDE pointed; variated (heraldic)
URDU a language much used in India
UREA a crystalline compound **Med.**
URGE push; drive; impel; incite; spur
URIA a genus of sea-birds, guillemots **Z.**
URIC an acid **Med.**
URIM and Thummim
URRY blue clay near a coal seam **Min.**
URSA a constellation
URUS the European wild ox **Z.**
URVA an ichneumon (India) **Z.**
USED habituated; employed; worn
USER consumer; frequenter; expender
UTAS a festivity
UTIS a period
UVAE grapes, raisins, etc. **B.**
UVEA part of the iris of the eye **Med.**

V

VADE fade (Shak.)
VAIL veil; tip; gratuity; submission
VAIN empty; conceited; unavailing
VAIR heraldic fur
VAKE to be vacant (Sc.)
VALE dale; valley; recede; farewell
VAMP boot-uppers; to patch
VAMP cinema character; to strum **Mus.**
VANE weathercock; flag; blade; fane
VANG peak steadying brace **Naut.**
VARA S. Amer. yard of 33 inches **Meas.**
VARE a wand of authority
VARI monkey (Madagascar) **Z.**
VARY alter; change; alternate; differ
VASE urn
VAST huge; spacious; colossal
VEAL dinner for a prodigal son
VEDA sacred Hindu books
VEER vary; turn; shift
VEGA Cuban tobacco-field; a star
VEIL mask; cloak; screen; cover
VEIN lode; seam; ledge; mood; humour
VELD veldt (South Africa)
VELE veil (Spens.)
VELL rennet; to cut turf
VELO speed of one foot per second **Meas.**
VENA a vein **Med.**
VEND sell; hawk; peddle
VENT utter; discharge; orifice; sale
VERB
VERT the greenery of the forest **Law**
VERT convert; pervert; heraldic green
VERY a signal light
VEST endow; endue; clothe; a garment
VETO ban; forbid; taboo; embargo
VETU lozenge **Her.**
VIAL phial; ampulla
VICE vise; a screw-press **Tool**

VICE iniquity; defect; sin; in place of	**WAPP** shroud-tightener **Naut.**
VIDE see (Latin)	**WARD** fend; repel; custody; a minor
VIED contested; competed; strove	**WARE** a caution; aware; sea-weed **B.**
VIEW eye; scan; survey; vista; prospect	**WARK** bulwark; work (obs.)
VILE base; ignoble; paltry; cheap	**WARM** ardent; fervid; keen; zealous
VILL villa; suburban seat	**WARN** caution; admonish; notify
VINA East Indian banjo **Mus.**	**WARP** twist; deviate; pervert; haul
VINE **B.**	**WART** a verruca; an excrescence **Med.**
VINT Russian card game; to make wine	**WARY** canny; cautious; vigilant
VINY producing grapes or vines	**WASE** straw head-pad
VIOL antique violin **Mus.**	**WASH** wake; lave; rinse; cleanse
VIRE crossbow-bolt; heraldic annulet	**WASP**
VISA vise; stamp; permit; authoriz't'n	**WAST** preterite of be
VISE official endorsement	**WATT** unit of work **Meas.**
VIVA Italian applause; (viva-voce)	**WAUL** wawl; caterwaul
VIVE French applause	**WAVE** sway; beckon; brandish; ripple
VIVO lively; with animation **Mus.**	**WAVE** swell; billow; comber; roller
VLEI artificial lake (S. Africa)	**WAVY** curly; sinuous; billowy;
VOCE the voice; (sotto-voce)	**WAWE** a wave (Spens.)
VOID null; invalid; empty; vacant; emit	**WAWL** waul; to howl; caterwaul
VOLA rapid series of notes **Mus.**	**WAXY** pliant; yielding; wrathful
VOLE a grand slam	**WEAK** frail; insipid; watery; fragile
VOLE genus of rodents, water-rats, etc. **Z.**	**WEAL** prosperity; state; wale; stripe
VOLT electrical unit **Meas.**	**WEAN** alienate; detach
VOLT a turn; sudden leap; (fencing)	**WEAR** bear; don; sport; impair
VOTE suffrage; ballot; elect; poll	**WEED** a cigar; to root out; eradicate **B.**
VOYA anchor cable **Meas.**	**WEEK**
VRIL force	**WEEL** fish-trap; whirlpool; well (Sc.)
VROW Dutch woman	**WEEM** underground abode (Sc.)
VULN to wound (heraldic)	**WEEN** to think; consider; guess; judge
	WEEP sob; bewail; lament
	WEFT threads crossing warp; waif
	WEIR wear; a dam across a river

W

WADD manganese ore **Min.**	**WEKA** Maori hen **Z.**
WADE to ford	**WELD** join together; mignonette **B.**
WADI } dry river bed (Arab.)	**WELK** wither; shrivel; wrinkle
WADY	**WELL** fount; source; origin; hale
WAFD Egyptian nationalist party	**WELT** shoe-edging; to flog
WAFF yaff; to bark; weak; paltry (Sc.)	**WEND** wander; a Slavonic race
WAFT float; convey; beckon; ventilate	**WENT** left; departed; decamped
WAGE pay; hire; stipend; salary	**WEPT** cried; lamented; sobbed
WAIF a stray; vagabond; ownerless	**WERE**
WAIL cry; weep; deplore; plaint	**WERT**
WAIN wagon; constellation	**WEST**
WAIR a plank	**WHAP** whop; whip; defeat
WAIT bide; tarry; linger; serve; minister	**WHAT**
WAKA Maori canoe	**WHEN**
WAKE funeral vigil; rouse; trail; wash	**WHET** sharpen; heighten; rouse
WALD weld; mignonette (Sc.) **B.**	**WHEW !**
WALE weal; raised streak; ridge; bruise	**WHEY** skimmed milk
WALK hike; saunter; gait; career; beat	**WHID** to whisk; a lie; a quarrel (Sc.)
WALL	**WHIG** Liberal; sour whey
WALT cranky; tottering	**WHIM** caprice; crotchet; notion
WALY beautiful; alas ! (Sc.)	**WHIN** gorse; furse **B.**
WAME the belly (Sc.)	**WHIP** quirt; flog; driver; coachman
WAND rod; twig; staff; baton	**WHIR** whirl; spin; twirl
WANE ebb; fail; decline; droop	**WHIT** jot; iota; speck; scintilla
WANG cheek-bone; shoe-lace	**WHIZ** whizz; a noise
WANT need; crave; wish; penury	**WHOA !**

WHOM
WHOP whap; whip; defeat
WHOT hot (Spens.)
WHUR a noise
WICK (candle); creek; quick; alive
WIDE spacious; rife; distant; (cricket)
WIFE spouse
WILD rash; disorderly; savage;
WILE ruse; stratagem; dodge; chicanery
WILL wish; desire; bequeath; testament
WILT to droop; to wither
WILY sly; artful; crafty; insidious
WIND coil; twist; turn; breeze; blow
WINE
WING to fly; to wound
WINK to nictitate
WINY having the flavour of wine
WIPE rub; clean; handkerchief
WIRE bind; snare; telegram
WIRY flexible and strong
WISE sagacious; sage; sapient; method
WISH will; want; desire; behest
WISP (of snipe); small broom; a whisk
WISS to wish (Sc.)
WIST knew
WITE to blame; to reproach (Spens.)
WITH withe; a twig
WIVE to marry
WOAD plant yielding a blue dye   **B.**
WOLD wood; a down; a weald
WOLF devour   **Z.**
WOMB
WONT habit; custom; practice; use
WOOD timber; grove; forest   **B.**
WOOF the weft
WOOL fleece; a staple product
WOOM beaver fur
WOON governor of a Burmese province
WORD term; news; advice; pledge
WORE bore; sported; donned; lasted
WORK toil; operate; endeavour
WORM a groveller; to insinuate   **Z.**
WORN rather the worse for wear
WORT malt after mashing; a plant   **B.**
WOVE intertwined; matted; knitted
WOWF crazy (Sc.)
WRAP wind; swathe; enfold; muffle
WREN a war worker   **Z.**
WRIT summons; formal document **Law**
WULL will (Spens.)
WYND a lane; narrow alley

X

XEMA genus of gulls   **Z.**
XMAS Noel; Yule
X-RAY   **Med.**
XYST gymnasium

Y

YAFF waff; to bark (Sc.)
YALD yauld; active; supple (Sc.)
YAMA Hindu Pluto
YANK an American; to heave
YAPP limp leather binding
YARD 36 ins.; enclosed area   **Meas.**
YARD (Scotland); a spar   **Naut.**
YARE dexterous; quick; prompt
YARN spun thread; sailor's story
YARR to snarl; the spurrey plant   **B.**
YAUD a jade (Sc.)
YAUP yelp; hungry; blue titmouse   **Z.**
YAWL yowl; howl; fishing-boat   **Naut.**
YAWN gape
YAWS a form of scurvy   **Med.**
YEAH yes (U.S.A.)
YEAN yeen; to lamb
YEAR
YEEN yean; to produce; to lamb
YEGG hobo; cracksman; safe-breaker
YELD barren, not giving milk
YELK yolk
YELL bawl; scream; screech
YELP yap; cry of pain; bark
YERK jerk; rouse; excite
YEST yeast
YETI abominable snowman   **Z.**
YETT yate; a gate (Sc.)
YILL ale (Sc.)
YITE
YOIT } the yellow bunting   **Z.**
YMIR the Frost Giant (Scand.)
YOGA Hindu philosophy
YOGI Hindu ascetic
YO-HO
YOKE team together; enslave; restrain
YOKO Japanese wood block
YOLK, YOLKY, YELK wool oil
YOND beyond; yonder; mad (Spens.)
YONI Hindu symbol
YOOP an onomatopoetic sob
YORE in olden time
YOUR
YOWL howl; yawl; gowl; bawl
YO-YO a toy; a bandalore
YUAN (China)   **Coin**
YUCK to itch; the itch
YUGA one of the Hindu ages of the world
YULE Xmas; Noel
YUNX the wry-neck bird   **Z.**
Y-WIS i'wis; truly
YURT a Siberian house or tent

Z

ZAIM Turkish military chief
ZANY buffoon; merry-andrew; mimic
ZARF zurf; metal coffee-cup holder

ZATI an Indian parrot   **Z.**
Z-BAR building fixture
ZEAL fervour; intensity; enthusiasm
ZEBU humped domestic ox (India)   **Z.**
ZEIN zeine; a protein found in maize   **B.**
ZEND a Persian dialect
ZEPP zeppelin; airship
ZERO cipher; naught; nothing
ZEST peel-flavouring; gusto; relish
ZETA the Greek Z
ZETA sexton's room over porch   **Eccl.**
ZEUS Olympian deity
ZIMB Abyssinian tse-tse fly   **Z.**
ZINC a metallic element   **Chem.**
ZING pep (U.S.A.)
ZION a hill in Jerusalem
ZOAR a place of refuge

ZOBO zhobo; dsomo; hybrid yak-cow
ZOEA crustaceans in a larval stage   **Z.**
ZOIC pertaining to life
ZOLA Borax hardener   **Chem.**
ZOLL German toll or custom-duty
ZONA zone; belt
ZONE belt; girdle; district
ZOOM aerobatic manoeuvre
ZOON the product of a fertilized ovum
ZOOT fashionable, gaudy
ZSAR Czar; Ksar; Tsar; Tzar
ZULU
ZUNA Angola sheep   **Z.**
ZUNI Mexican Indians
ZUPA Serbian village confederation
ZURF zarf; metal coffee-pot holder
ZYME a ferment; a disease germ   **Med.**

A

AAZIZ Queen of Sheba; also Balkis
ABACA Manila hemp **B**
ABACI counting frames
ABACI crowns of columns
ABACK aft; behind; backwards
ABAFT aft; astern **Naut.**
ABASE lower; reduce; disgrace
ABASH awe; confound; disconcert
ABASK basking in the sun
ABATE wane; diminish; lessen
ABBEY a monastery **Eccl.**
ABBOT the head of an abbey **Eccl.**
ABCEE an abc; an alphabet
ABEAM abreast; on the beam **Naut.**
ABEAR to bear; endure; tolerate
ABELE the hoary poplar **B.**
ABHAL the fruit of the cypress **B.**
ABHOR hate; loathe; abominate; detest
ABIDE lodge; tarry; tolerate; sojourn
ABIES the fir genus **B.**
ABLEN a freshwater fish; the bleak **Z.**
ABLER more competent; more expert
ABLET ablen; the bleak **Z.**
ABODE house; dwelling; home; lived
ABOHM electro-magnetic unit **Meas.**
ABOIL on the boil; boiling
ABOMA boa-constrictor (S. Amer.) **Z.**
A-BOMB nuclear weapon
ABORT to miscarry; sterile
ABOUT almost; around; anent; near
ABOVE aloft; over; before; exceeding
ABRAY rouse; startle; waken (obs.)
ABUSE misuse; defame; traduce; revile
ABUZZ buzzing; humming
ABYSM⎫ chasm; bottomless pit;
ABYSS⎭ gulf; gorge; gap; fissure
ACARI mites and ticks **Z.**
ACERA bubble-shell genus **Z.**
ACERB sour; bitter; acid; harsh
ACHED pained; sorrowed; grieved
ACHOR dandruff **Med.**
ACINI granulations; berries **Med., B.**
ACKEE Jamaican fruit **B.**
ACLIS spiked club; javelin
ACOCK jaunty; defiantly
ACOLD chilly
ACORN terminal of a blind-cord **B.**
ACRED lavishly landed
ACRID sour; pungent; bitter; mordant
ACTED performed; simulated; deputized
ACTIN muscle protein **Bio-Chem.**
ACTON padded jerkin
ACTOR player; trouper; histrion
ACUTE keen; sharp; astute; poignant
ADAGE proverb; dictum; maxim; saw
ADAPT adjust; accommodate
ADAYS now-a-days
ADDAX African antelope **Z.**

ADDED affixed; subjoined; appended
ADDER viper; snake; basilisk; asp **Z.**
ADDLE confuse; putrid; muddled
ADEEM to revoke a legacy **Law**
ADEPS fatty tissue **Med.**
ADEPT adroit; expert; proficient
ADIEU farewell; goodbye
AD-LIB extemporise freely **Mus.**
ADMAN advertising pundit
ADMIT acknowledge; concede; own
ADMIX infuse; blend; mingle
ADOBE sun dried brick
ADOPT accept; assume; espouse; father
ADORE worship; revere; idolize; love
ADORN decorate; deck; enrich; garnish
ADOWN downward
ADOXY a tolerant belief
ADSUM (present at a roll-call)
ADULT a grown-up; mature; ripe
ADUST incinerated; pulverized
ADYTA chancels **Eccl.**
AEGER sick; ill **Med.**
AEGIS Minerva's shield; protection
AERIE eyrie; eagle's nest **Z.**
AESOP a fabulist
AFEAR affear; to terrify (obs.)
AFFIX add; fasten; subjoin; attach
AFIRE aflame; blazing
AFLAT level with the ground
AFOAM foaming
AFOOT astir; happening
AFORE previously; before
AFOUL entangled; in collision with
AFRIC African
AFRIT afreet; evil demon; jinn (Arab)
AFTER later; in imitation of
AGAIN anew; afresh; moreover
AGAIT astir; afoot (Sc.)
AGAMA genus of lizards; saurians **Z.**
AGAMI grallatorial bird of S. Amer. **Z.**
AGAPE staring; a love feast
AGATE a quartz; ruby type **Min.**
AGATY like an agate
AGAVE American aloe **B.**
AGAVE daughter of Cadmus
AGAZE gazing
AGENT doer; factor; deputy; proxy
AGGER a mound; rampart
AGILE nimble; spry; alert; brisk
AGIST pasture rate **Law**
AGLEE⎫ asquint; askew; awry;
AGLEY⎭ off the line (Sc.)
AGLET a pendant; braided tag
AGLOW glowing; gleaming; shining
AGNEL French gold coin (lamb) **Coin**
AGNUS Dei; pascal lamb **Z.**
AGONE ago; past; since; a line
AGONY pangs; anguish; torment; throe
AGOOD in earnest
AGORA Grecian market

AGREE accede; engage; conform; concur
AGRIN grinning
AGROM an Indian tongue disease **Med.**
AGUED fevered; shivering
AHEAD leading; onward; in front
AHEAP trembling with fear
AHIGH on high
AHOLD close to the wind. **Naut.**
AHULL hove to **Naut.**
AIDED abetted; seconded; succoured
AIDER helper; assistant; acolyte
AIERY aerie; eyrie; eagle's nest **Z.**
AIGRE eagre; bore; high tidal wave
AILED afflicted; peaked; pined
AIMED directed; pointed; trained
AIMER purposeful person
AIRED ventilated; spread abroad
AIRER dryer; ventilator
AISLE passage; walk **Eccl.**
AITCH (h); aitch-bone
AJUGA bugle genus of plants **B.**
AKALI Sikh fanatic
AKELA Kipling's lone wolf **Z.**
ALACK alas; lackaday; woe is me
ALAND landed
ALANT heraldic mastiff **Z.**
ALARM fear; scare; dismay; a tocsin
ALARY alar; having wings **Z.**
ALATE winged; of late; lately
ALBIN an opaque white mineral **Min.**
ALBUM book for photos or stamps
ALCES the elk **Z.**
ALDER a tree **B.**
ALERT wary; watchful; vigilant
ALGAE the sea-weeds **B.**
ALGID cold; chilly **Med.**
ALGIN sea-weed extract for iodine
ALGOL a star; computer term
ALGOR unusual coldness **Med.**
ALGUM almug; sandal-wood **B.**
ALIAS otherwise; an assumed name
ALIBI elsewhere
ALIEN strange; exotic; remote; foreign
ALIGN⎫ adjust; rectify; arrange;
ALINE⎭ regulate; conform
ALIKE similar; analogous; equal
ALISH resembling beer
ALIVE vital; quick; alert; brisk
ALLAH Moslem word for the Deity **Eccl.**
ALLAY lull; calm; relieve; repress
ALLEY large marble; taw; passage
ALL-IN (policy) comprehensive
ALL-IN exhausted
ALLIS the allice shad; a fish **Z.**
ALLOD freehold estate
ALLOO halloo
ALLOT distribute; apportion; assign
ALLOW admit; own; concede; grant
ALLOY a base admixture
ALLYL organic radicle **Chem.**

ALMAH⎫ an Egyptian
ALMEH⎭ dancing girl
ALMRY almonry; cupboard
ALMUG algum; sandal-wood **B.**
ALOED⎫ tinctured with aloes;
ALOID ⎬ resembling aloes; **Med.**
ALOIN⎭ bitter aloe extract
ALOES bitter purgative drug **B.**
ALOFT above; overhead; skyward
ALONE only; sole; single; isolated
ALONG by; beside; together
ALOOF apart; away; distant
ALOSE allis; shad-fish **Z.**
ALOUD audibly; loudly; clamorously
ALPEN Alpine
ALPHA the first or beginning
ALPIA bird-seed **B.**
ALTAR shrine; sanctuary **Eccl.**
ALTER vary; change; turn; transform
ALULA bastard wing **Z.**
ALURE cloister; gallery (obs.)
ALUTA leather treated with alum
ALWAY ever; always; regularly
AMAIN forcibly; suddenly; violently
AMASS heap; gather; accumulate; pile
AMATE subdue; daunt; stupefy (obs.)
AMATI violin (Cremona) **Mus.**
AMAZE daze; astound; perplex
AMBER fossilized resin **Min.**
AMBIT precinct; extent; compass
AMBLE dawdle; saunter; stroll
AMBON lectern; pulpit **Eccl.**
AMBRY alms-box; niche; almonry **Eccl.**
AMEER⎫ Afghan king;
AMERE⎭ emir; prince
AMEND emend; better; rectify; correct
AMENT a catkin **B.**
AMICE pilgrim's cloak; linen gown
AMICT amice; cape or hood **Eccl.**
AMIDE⎫ an ammonia compound **Chem.**
AMINE⎭
AMISS wrong; faulty; erroneously
AMITY friendship; fellowship; harmony
AMMON Thibetan sheep **Z.**
AMONG emong; amidst; amongst
AMORT halfdead; dejected; spiritless
AMOUR an affair; a love intrigue
AMOVE stir up; to affect
AMPLE ointment-box; wide; capacious
AMPLY plentifully; bountifully
AMPUL ample; oil-jar; flask
AMSEL⎫ blackbird **Z.**
AMZEL⎭
AMUCK madly; in murderous frenzy
AMUSE entertain; cheer; charm; divert
ANANA the pine-apple **B.**
ANCLE also **ANKLE**
ANCON the elbow; a console **Med.**
ANEAL anele; to anoint **Eccl.**
ANEAR near; nigh

ANELE extreme unction **Eccl.**	**ARBOR** tree genus; bower **B.**
ANENT concerning	**ARBOR** spindle; axis
ANGEL divine messenger; fish **Z., Coin**	**ARDEA** the heron genus **Z.**
ANGER ire; rage; choler; passion	**ARDES** 5½ bushels, Egyptian dry **Meas.**
ANGLE a corner; to entice; to fish	**ARDIL** fibre from groundnuts **B.**
ANGOR acute pain or anxiety	**AREAD**⎤ to divine;
ANGRY irate; wroth; piqued; riled	**AREDE** ⎬ counsel; explain;
ANIGH nigh; near by	**AREED**⎦ interpret; solve
ANILE old womanish; imbecile	**AREAL** (area); superficial
ANIME resin; fiery **Her. B.**	**AREAR** in the rear; to raise; uplift
ANION electro-negative ion	**ARECA** betel-nut palm **B.**
ANISE plant furnishing aniseed **B.**	**AREFY** dry up; shrivel; wither
ANISO unequal	**ARENA** ring; stage; battlefield
ANKER European liquid measure **Meas.**	**ARENG** the sago palm **B.**
ANKLE also **ANCLE** **Med.**	**ARETE** Swiss mountain ridge
ANKUS elephant goad	**ARGAL** crude tartar **Chem.**
ANNAL a Mass **Eccl.**	**ARGIL** potter's earth **Min.**
ANNAT an Ecclesiastical levy **Eccl.**	**ARGOL** argal; crude tartar **Chem.**
ANNET the kittiwake **Z.**	**ARGON** a light gas **Chem.**
ANNEX add; append; join; unite	**ARGOT** slang; jargon (Fr.)
ANNOY badger; worry; affront; molest	**ARGUE** plead; dispute; reason; debate
ANNUL cancel; quash; revoke	**ARGUS** watchful; a pheasant **Z.**
ANODE positive electrical pole	**ARIAN** a sectarian; Unitarian
ANOMY lawlessness; a miracle	**ARIEL** a sprite; a gazelle **Z.**
ANONA custard-apple genus **B.**	**ARIES** the Ram of the Zodiac
ANTIC fantastic; prank; lark; caper	**ARIOT** riotously; uproariously
ANTRE a cave; a cavern	**ARISE** ascend; soar; emerge; rebel
ANURA batrachians **Z.**	**ARLES** earnest money on engagement
ANVIL an ear-bone **Med., Tool**	**ARMED** equipped; protected
ANZAC Australian, N.Z., Army Corps	**ARMET** medieval helmet
AORTA the great artery **Med.**	**ARMIL** insignia of royalty
APACE rapidly; swiftly; at speed	**ARNEE** Indian buffalo
APART aloof; asunder; separately	**ARNOT** pig-nut; earth-nut **B.**
APEAK⎤ anchor aweigh **Naut.**	**AROAR** uproariously; ariot
APEEK⎦ or atrip	**AROID** a plant allied to the arum **B.**
APERT open; public (obs.)	**AROMA** scent; perfume; fragrance; odour
APERY monkey-house **Z.**	**AROSE** got up; began; sprang; revolted
APHID⎤ green-fly;	**ARRAH** Indian lentil **B.**
APHIS⎦ ant-cows **Z.**	**ARRAH** Irish expletive
APIAN relating to bees **Z.**	**ARRAS** tapestry; hangings
APING copying; mimicing; imitating	**ARRAY** range; marshal; deck; hosts
APISH ape-like **Z.**	**ARRET** decree; arrest **Law**
APIUM the celery genus **B.**	**ARRIS** sharp edge; arete
APODA eels, etc. **Z.**	**ARROW** bolt; shaft; dart; reed
APODE limbless creature **Z.**	**ARSIS** vocal inflection; emphasis
APOOP astern **Naut.**	**ARSON** fire-raising; pyromania **Law**
APORT to port **Naut.**	**ARTEL** a Russian guild
APPAL scare; daunt; shock; astound	**ARYAN** Indo-European
APPAY apay; to satisfy (obs.)	**ASCII** dwellers on the equator
APPLE the award of Paris **B.**	**ASCOT** fashionable race meeting
APPLY bestow; use; employ; refer	**ASCUS** spore case **B.**
APPUI⎤ support; reciprocal action	**ASDIC** submarine-detector **Naut.**
APPUY⎦	**ASHEN** wan; pale; hueless; pallid
APRIL	**ASHES** results of cricket on the hearth
APRON short cassock **Eccl.**	**ASHET** a serving dish (Sc.)
APSIS extreme point in an orbit	**ASHUR** Assyrian god
APTLY fittingly; appositely; apropos	**ASIAN** Asiatic
ARABA Turkish ox-cart	**ASIDE** apart; away; aloof; laterally
ARABY Arabia	**ASKED** invited; demanded; requested
ARACK arrack; fermented palm juice	**ASKER** a newt; petitioner; suitor **Z.**

ASKEW awry; aslant; askance; oblique
ASOAK sodden
ASPEN the trembling poplar **B.**
ASPER a small silver Turkish **Coin**
ASPIC savoury meat jelly; sap **Z.**
ASPIC 12 pounder cannon; lavender **B.**
ASSAI enough; very **Mus.**
ASSAY essay; test; try; analysis
ASSER rafter; thin lath
ASSES mokes; donkeys; burros
ASSET a possession
ASSOT besot; infatuate (Spens.)
ASTAY a cable direction **Naut.**
ASTEL a dam; a splinter
ASTER flowering plant **B.**
ASTIR alert; awake; agog; excited
ASTON astun; astonished (obs.)
ASWAY swinging; oscillating
ASWIM afloat
ATAXY confusion; disorder **Med.**
ATCHI Caucasian ibex **Z.**
ATILT on edge; slanting
ATIMY dishonour; disgrace
ATLAS a Titan; a moth **Z.**
ATMAN the Buddhist ego
ATOLL coral island
ATOMY atom; skeleton; a pygmy
ATONE expiate; satisfy; propitiate
ATONY debility; off colour **Med.**
ATRIP anchor clear; aweigh **Naut.**
ATTAR otto; fragrant rose oil
ATTIC Athenian; (salt); garret; loft
ATTLE refuse from mines; rubbish
AUBIN Canterbury gallop
AUDIT examine accounts
AUGER a drill **Tool**
AUGET explosive charge for mines
AUGHT zero; ought; naught; O
AUGUR seer; soothsayer; portend
AULAE Roman halls or courts
AULIC (royal court)
AUMIL amildar; Indian tax collector
AUNTY auntie
AURAL (exhalation); (ear)
AURIC golden
AURIN golden red dye **Chem.**
AURUM gold; chemical element **Chem.**
AVAIL benefit; help; suffice; use
AVAST stop; stay; cease **Naut.**
AVENS the herb bennet **B.**
AVERT avoid; divert; forfend; parry
AVIAN bird-like **Z.**
AVION aeroplane (French)
AVISO a dispatch boat (Span.) **Naut.**
AVOID shun; elude; forsake; eschew
AVOUE French lawyer; advocate **Law**
AWAIT tarry; bide; stay; pause;
AWAKE alert; ready; alive; vigilant
AWARD give; grant; adjudge; prize
AWARE mindful; conscious

AWASH nearly submerged **Naut.**
AWAVE waving; fluttering
AWEEK per week
AWFUL dire; dread; fearful; imposing
AWHIR whirring; spinning
AWING on the wing; flying; cowing
AWNED bearded like barley **B.**
AWNER grain separator
AWOKE bestirred; roused; incited
AWORK at work
AXIAL on the same axis
AXILE
AXIOM truism; assumed truth
AXITE a propellant
AXLED having a spindle
AXOID axoidean
AYELP yelping; howling
AZOIC devoid of life
AZOTE nitrogen **Chem.**
AZOTH the alchemist cure-all; panacea
AZTEC extinct Mexican-Indian
AZURE sky-blue; the sky;
AZURN the vault of heaven
AZURY blue; cerulean
AZYME unleaven bread

B

BABEL tower; din; jargon; clamour
BABOO babu; Indian clerk
BACCA a berry **B.**
BACCY bacco; tobacco **B.**
BACON something to be saved
BADGE sign; mark; emblem; token
BADLY corruptly; wickedly; imperfectly
BAFFY an old golf club
BAGGY loose fitting; bulging
BAHAR 3½ cwts., East Indian **Meas.**
BAIRN a child (Sc.)
BAIZE bayze; a coarse cloth
BAJAN bejan; a freshman (Sc.)
BAKED parched; hardened; dried up
BAKER a small oven
BALAS orange ruby **Min.**
BALED in bundles; (aeronautics)
BALER a bowl; scoop
BALKY apt to stop suddenly
BALMY fragrant; soothing
BALOO the Bear **Z.**
BALSA Peruvian raft; a tree **B.**
BAMBI film faun **Z.**
BANAL commonplace; trivial; trite
BANAT Hungarian division
BANCO bench; bank money **Law**
BANDY ice hockey; crooked; dispute
BANJO job an octaroon would like **Mus.**
BANNS public notice of marriage **Eccl.**
BANNY a minnow **Z.**
BANTU Negroid African tribe

BARBE war-horse armour
BARBE nun's kerchief
BARED naked; unadorned; stripped
BARET a biretta; cardinal's cap   **Eccl.**
BARGE shove; jostle   **Naut.**
BARIA baryta   **Min.**
BARKY of bark
BARMY (yeast); crazy; insane
BARON (of beef); a title
BARRY divided by horizontal bars (Her.)
BARYE unit of pressure dynes   **Meas.**
BASAL basic; fundamental
BASED founded on
BASEL tanned skin; basil
BASIC basal; fundamental   **Chem.**
BASIL chisel edge; leather; a herb   **B.**
BASIN pond; dock; reservoir; bowl
BASIS ground work; first principle
BASON a basin
BASSE bass; fish like a perch   **Z.**
BASSO a bass singer
BASTA stop! enough (It.)   **Mus.**
BASTE cook; sew; stitch; thrash
BASTO ace of clubs
BATAK language
BATCH lot ; quantity; amount; crowd
BATED restrained; repressed; reduced
BATEY gold and silver embroidery
BATHE immerse
BATIK straw-work
BATON staff; wand; sceptre; rod   **Mus.**
BATTA Indian grant
BATTY bat-like; dotty
BAUGE cloth; drugget
BAULK beam; (billiards); thwart
BAVIN faggot of brushwood
BAWDY lewd, immoral
BAYED recessed; howled like a dog
BAYOU channel; outlet
BAZAR bazaar; mart; souk; exchange
BEACH shore; strand; sands; margin
BEADS a rosary   **Eccl.**
BEADY small and bright
BE-ALL sum and substance; ultimate
BEAMY shining; radiant; broad
BEANO jamboree; beanfeast; spree
BEARD defy; oppose; confront
BEAST brute; ruffian; animal   **Z.**
BEAUX gallants (Fr.)
BEBOP dissonant jazz   **Mus.**
BECHE drill extractor   **Tool**
BEDAD ! Irish interjection
BEDEL beadle (obs.)
BEDEW sprinkle; moisten
BEDIM obscure; cloud; darken
BEECH a forest tree   **B.**
BEEFY stolid; powerful
BEELD shelter (Sc.)
BEELE pick-axe   **Tool**
BEERY maudlin; fuddled

BEFIT suit; become
BEFOG confuse, obfuscate
BEFUR cover with fur or scale
BEGAD !
BEGAN started; initiated; originated
BEGAT bred; sired; engendered
BEGEM bejewel
BEGET produce; generate
BEGIN start; initiate; commence
BEGOT procreated; gave rise to
BEGUM Indian native princess
BEGUN originated; opened
BEHEN sea-lavender   **B.**
BEIGE fabric; yellowish grey
BEING existence; actuality
BEISA oryx; unicorn   **Z.**
BEJAN bajan; freshman (Sc.)
BEKAH half shekel; Hebrew   **Coin**
BEKER S. African cup
BELAY fasten; hold   **Naut.**
BELCH eructate; discharge; emit
BELEE on the lee side
BELGA Belgian currency
BELIE falsify; contradict; slander
BELIT rekindled; illuminated
BELLE a beauteous damsel
BELLY stomach; abdomen
BELOW under; beneath; in Hades
BEMAD madden
BENCH seat; form; court; tribunal
BENDY divided into bends (Her.)
BENET to ensnare; an exorcist
BENJY a straw hat
BENNE bene; an oil plant   **B.**
BENTY covered with dry grass
BEPAT pat or tap repeatedly
BERET Basque cap
BEROB rob; plunder; pillage
BEROE luminous medusa   **Z.**
BERRY mound; barrow; fruit   **B.**
BERTH bed; post; situation   **Naut.**
BERYL a gem   **Min.**
BERYX perch-like sea fish   **Z.**
BESET assail; encircle; surround
BESIT besiege
BESOM a broom
BESOT assot; get fuddled
BETEL nut of the areca palm   **B.**
BETON a kind of concrete
BETSO a small Venetian   **Coin**
BETTY flask; jemmy
BEVEL slant; to incline   **Tool**
BEWET to wet; to moisten
BEWIG to don a wig
BEWIT leather strap in falconry
BEZAN Bengal cotton cloth
BEZEL basil; setting; groove
BEZIL bezel
BHANG hashish; Indian hemp   **B.**
BHYLE Indian ox   **Z.**

BIBBS wooden brackets	**Naut.**	
BIBLE The Scriptures		
BIDDY a fowl; a chicken	**Z.**	
BIDET sitz bath; pack-pony	**Z.**	
BIDON about five quarts	**Meas.**	
BIDRI Indian metal-ware		
BIELD shelter; protection		
BIFID two-clefted		
BIGHT cove; bay; coil; loop	**Naut.**	
BIGLY ostentatiously		
BIGOT zealot; fanatic; dogmatist		
BIJOU small; pretty; gem; trinket		
BILBO Spanish rapier		
BILGE bulging part of cask	**Naut.**	
BILIN bile	**Med.**	
BILLY Australian cooking can		
BINGE a carousal		
BINGO brandy; gambling pastime		
BINNY a Nile fish	**Z.**	
BIPED two-footed animal	**Z.**	
BIPOD (c.f. tripod)		
BIRCH to flog; forest tree	**B.**	
BIRLE to carouse (Sc.)		
BIRSE bristle; to bruise		
BIRSY stubbly		
BIRTH genesis; nativity; origin		
BISON American buffalo	**Z.**	
BITCH female dog, wolf, or fox	**Z.**	
BITER nibbler; cheat		
BITTS a cable attachment	**Naut.**	
BITTY incomplete; fragmentary		
BIXIN annatto	**Chem.**	
BLACK ebon; inky; dusky; sombre		
BLADE roisterer; (knife); (oar)	**B.**	
BLAES hardened shale	**Min.**	
BLAIN blister; blotch	**Med.**	
BLAME chide; rebuke; reproach		
BLAND soft; sauve; mild; benign		
BLANK lacuna; vacant; void		
BLARE blazon; proclaim; clangour		
BLASE cloyed; surfeited (Fr.)		
BLASH watery stuff (Sc.)		
BLAST gust; outbreak; shrivel		
BLATE shy; bashful (Sc.)		
BLAZE (horse); flame; proclaim		
BLAZE a mark on trees		
BLEAK drear; desolate; river-fish	**Z.**	
BLEAR dim; rheumy; watery		
BLEAT the cry of a sheep		
BLECK coal-fish	**Z.**	
BLEED exude; secrete; impoverish		
BLEEP radio signal		
BLEND mix; unite; knead; coalesce		
BLENT blended; amalgamated		
BLESS laud; exalt; praise; extol		
BLEST beatified; glorified		
BLIMP small airship; (Colonel)		
BLIND ruse; feint; cover; issueless		
BLINK glance; flicker; ignore		
BLIRT blore; squall; gust	**Naut.**	

BLISS ecstasy; rapture; felicity		
BLITE the plant Good King Henry	**B.**	
BLIVE soon; speedily (Sc.)		
BLOAT blote; dry by smoke; dilate		
BLOCK bar; obstruct; a mass	**Naut.**	
BLOKE a fellow; a man		
BLOND fair; flaxen		
BLOOD cruor; gore; kindred; lineage		
BLOOM bud; blossom; prime; thrive	**B.**	
BLORE blirt; violent gust		
BLOTE bloat; dry by smoke		
BLOWN winded; trumpeted		
BLOWY breezy; gusty; windy		
BLUED tempered; squandered		
BLUER more blue; gloomier		
BLUES Royal Horse Guards	**Mus.**	
BLUEY blanket; bundle (Australia)		
BLUFF sheer; brusque; spoof		
BLUNT blont; dull; abrupt		
BLURB eulogy; panegyric		
BLURT utter hastily		
BLUSH flush; colour; redden		
BOARD embark; victuals; council		
BOAST brag; crow; vaunt		
BOBBY policeman		
BOCAL glass beaker		
BOCHE a Hun		
BODED portended; presaged; augured		
BODGE botch; mess up; fail		
BODHI Buddhist sacred tree	**B.**	
BODLE farthing (Sc.)	**Coin**	
BOGEY (golf); hobgoblin; ghost		
BOGGY soggy; swampy; marshy		
BOGIE four-wheeled truck		
BOGLE bugbear; scarecrow		
BOGUS sham; spurious; false		
BOHEA inferior tea	**B.**	
BOIAR boyar; Russian nobleman		
BOLAS S. American missile		
BOLIN bowline	**Naut.**	
BOLUS large pill	**Med.**	
BONED seized; stole; purloined		
BONES bobbins	**Mus.**	
BONGO African antelope	**Z.**	
BONNE French nurse		
BONNY bonnie; ore pocket		
BONUS award; premium; subsidy		
BONZE Buddhist priest	**Eccl.**	
BOOBY looby; dunce; simpleton		
BOODY to sulk; to mope		
BOOED hooted; noisily objected		
BOOER vociferous interrupter		
BOOPS humpbacked whale	**Z.**	
BOORT (diamond polishing)		
BOOSE booze; drink; swill		
BOOST boom; push; eulogize		
BOOSY boozy; tipsy; fuddled		
BOOTH market stall		
BOOTS last joined; shoe cleaner		
BOOTY loot; spoil; plunder		

BORAK banter; chaff (Australia)		
BORAX tincal; borate of soda	**Chem.**	
BORED drilled; wearied		
BOREE French peasants' dance		
BORER an insect; sea-worm	**Z.**	
BORIC boracic	**Chem.**	
BORNE narrow-minded; carried		
BORON a non-metallic element	**Chem.**	
BOSKY busky; shady; thickly wooded		
BOSOM breast; confidential		
BOSON bo'sun; boatswain	**Naut.**	
BOSSY dictatorial; domineering		
BOTCH to patch; worthless	**Med.**	
BOTHY hut; cottage (Sc.)		
BOTTS larvae; worms	**Z.**	
BOUCH to bush; to debouch		
BOUGH branch; limb; offshoot	**B.**	
BOULE (buhl); inlay work		
BOULE Greek Parliament		
BOUND limit; pale; leap; spring		
BOURG a town; burgh; borough		
BOURN bourne; stream; bound; border		
BOUSE boose; booze; bowze; swill		
BOUSY tipsy; drunken; crapulous		
BOVEY a kind of coal	**Min.**	
BOWED bent; curved; subdued		
BOWEL disembowel	**Med.**	
BOWER arbour; shelter; anchor	**Naut.**	
BOWER the knave at euchre		
BOWET young hawk	**Z.**	
BOWIE a large knife		
BOWLS skittles; a game		
BOWSE to heave; bouse	**Naut.**	
BOXED crated		
BOXEN made of boxwood		
BOXER a pugilist		
BOX-UP mistake, error		
BOYAR boiar; Russian nobleman		
BOYAU ditch; trench (Fr.)		
BOYER Flemish sloop	**Naut.**	
BRACE pair; couple; stiffen	**Tool**	
BRACH bitch-hound	**Z.**	
BRACK a flaw in cloth		
BRACT specialized leaf	**B.**	
BRAID brede; broid; weave; entwine		
BRAIL (falconry); to furl	**Naut.**	
BRAIN cerebellum; intellect		
BRAIT rough diamond	**Min.**	
BRAKE thicket; harrow; wagonette		
BRAKY overgrown with ferns	**B.**	
BRAND brond; stigma; mark; torch		
BRANK buckwheat	**B.**	
BRANK bridle for scolds		
BRANT a goose	**Z.**	
BRASH hasty; brittle; loose rock		
BRASS money; impudence; effrontery		
BRAST burst (Spens.)		
BRAUL striped cloth		
BRAVE to dare; heroic; valiant		
BRAVO well done!; an assassin		

BRAWL wrangle; bicker; quarrel		
BRAWN muscular strength		
BRAXY splenetic sheep disease		
BRAZE to solder		
BREAD food; fare; aliment		
BREAK interval; smash; shatter		
BREAM a fish; to clean	**Z.**	
BREED beget; race; progeny		
BREEM stern; fiery (Spens.);		
BREME clear; raging; celebrated		
BREER to sprout (Sc.)		
BRERE		
BRENT lofty; smooth; a goose	**Z.**	
BREST breast		
BREVE a long note	**Mus.**	
BRIAR a pipe; wild rose	**B.**	
BRIBE suborn; graft; an inducement		
BRICK a stout-hearted fellow		
BRIDE banned but beloved		
BRIEF short; concise; a writ	**Law**	
BRIER briar; wild rose	**B.**	
BRILL prill; type of turbot	**Z.**	
BRINE salt water; the sea; tears		
BRING fetch; convoy; produce		
BRINK brim; brow; verge; marge		
BRINY the sea; salty		
BRISK agile; alert; nimble		
BRITE over-ripe		
BRIZA totter-grass	**B.**	
BRIZE the gadfly	**Z.**	
BROAD wide; spacious; liberal		
BROCH early stone hut		
BROCK badger; a brocket	**Z.**	
BROGH burgh (Sc.)		
BROID braid; to interweave		
BROIL brawl; quarrel; affray		
BROKE ruined; penniless		
BROMA prepared chocolate		
BROME a grass	**B.**	
BROND brand		
BRONX a cocktail		
BROOD incubate; progeny; meditate		
BROOK beck; rill; tolerate; allow		
BROOL a deep murmur		
BROOM a besom; a shrub	**B.**	
BROSE Scotch porridge		
BROTH soup; a decoction		
BROWN tan; ecru; russet; sorrel		
BRUIN a bear	**Z.**	
BRUIT to noise abroad; a rumour		
BRUME fog; mist; vapour		
BRUNT shock; impulse		
BRUSH skirmish; scrap; sweep		
BRUTE savage; senseless; rough		
BUCCO puff-bird genus	**Z.**	
BUCHU African medicinal plant	**B.**	
BUCKO a bully (U.S.A.)		
BUDDY a partner; blooming		
BUDGE lambskin fur; pompous; to stir		
BUFFO comic actor		

BUFFS a famous regiment	**CABLE** wire; 100 fathoms **Meas., Naut.**
BUFFY buff colour	**CABOB** or Kebab Oriental dish of meat
BUGGY a gig; a vehicle	**CABRE** aero-stunt
BUGLE jet bead; horn **Mus.**	**CACAO** the chocolate-tree **B.**
BUGLE genus of flowering plants **B.**	**CACHE** a hide; secret store
BUILD erect; construct; raise	**CADDY** (golf); a tea-caddy
BUILT fabricated; established	**CADET** younger son
BUIST to mark sheep or cattle (Sc.)	**CADGE** peddle; sponge
BULBY bulbous	**CADGY** frolicsome; wanton
BULGE swell; belly	**CADRE** nucleus; framework
BULGY protuberant	**CAGED** captive; mewed
BULKY vast; massive; voluminous	**CAGEY** cautious; irritable; secretive
BULLA Papal seal; a mollusc **Z.**	**CAGOT** Pyrenese pariah race
BULLY hector; intimidate; splendid	**CA-IRA** "on with it"
BULSE a bag of diamonds	**CAIRD** tinker; gipsy
BUMBO rumbo; a drink	**CAIRN** heap of stones; terrier **Z.**
BUMPY uneven	**CAKED** clotted; plastered
BUNCH set; lot; lump; batch	**CALID** hot; fiery; ardent; glowing
BUNIA Indian trader or banker	**CALIF** Caliph; Kalif
BUNKO bunco; a trick; swindle	**CALIN** a Chinese alloy
BUNNY a rabbit **Z.**	**CALIX** calyx; cup **B.**
BUNTY wheat disease	**CALLA** bog-arum **B.**
BURAN blizzard (Central Asia)	**CALLE** caul; callet; net-work cap
BURGH town; borough	**CALMY** calm; quiet; pacific
BURIN engraving tool **Tool**	**CALPA** Kalpa; a day of Brahma **Eccl.**
BURKE murder; hush up	**CALVE** give birth **Z.**
BURLY stout; lusty; portly	**CAMAN** shinty stick (Sc.)
BURNT charred; parched; tanned	**CAMEL** a Bactrian; **Z.**
BURRO donkey; moke **Z.**	**CAMEO** opposite to intaglio
BURRY having burs; prickly **B.**	**CAMPOS** Savanna (Brazil)
BURSA a sac; a pouch **Med.**	**CAMIS** chemise; loose garment
BURSE purse; bourse	**CANAL** channel; duct; waterway
BURST split; exploded; rent asunder	**CANDY** a sweetmeat; to crystallize
BUSBY bearskin headdress	**CANED** thrashed; tanned
BUSES vehicles	**CANNA** arrowroot **B.**
BUSHY overgrown; bosky	**CANNY** shrewd; cautious; knowing
BUSKY bosky; woody; shady	**CANOE** a dug-out **Naut.**
BUTTE hill with flat top; ridge	**CANON** precept; rule **Eccl.**
BUTTS rifle range	**CANTO** a division of a poem
BUTTY mining partner; deputy	**CANTY** cheerful; talkative
BUTYL butter extract **Chem.**	**CAPEL** caple; composite stone **Z., Min.**
BUXOM comely; lively; jolly	**CAPER** dance; gambol; a plant **B.**
BUYER purchaser; shopper	**CAPER** Dutch privateer **Naut.**
BUZZY muzzy; dazed	**CAPLE** capel; capul; a horse **Z.**
BWANA master; boss (Swahili)	**CAPOC** kapok; Indian cotton **B.**
BYARD miner's hauling strap	**CAPON** fish; letter; fowl **Z.**
BY-END subsidiary aim	**CAPOT** to win all tricks at piquet
BY-LAW bye-law	**CAPRA** she-goat **Z.**
BYOUS extraordinary (Sc.)	**CAPUL** caple **Z.**
BY-WAY by-path	**CAPUT** the head **Med.**
	CARAT a weight **Meas.**
	CARED heeded; recked; minded
C	**CARET** the mark ʌ
	CAREX sedge **B.**
CAABA Kaaba; shrine in Mecca **Eccl.**	**CARGO** load; freight **Naut.**
CABAL clique; junto; set	**CARIB** a Caribbean
CABAS rush-basket	**CARLE** rude strong man
CABBY a cab-driver	**CARNY** blarney; flattery
CABER pole; tree-trunk (Sc.)	**CAROB** locust or algaroba tree **B.**
CABIN hut; shed; hovel **Naut.**	**CAROL** lay; ditty; warble; hymn
CABIR nature worship (Lemnos)	

CAROM	cannon in French billiards	
CARRY	convey; urge; accomplish	
CARSE	low-lying land	
CARTE	(fencing); card	
CARUS	unconsciousness	
CARVE	cut; hack; slice; engrave	
CARVY	caraway plant	**B.**
CASAL	belonging to a case (Grammar)	
CASCO	Manila barge	**Naut.**
CASED	boxed; packed; enveloped	
CASSE	broken paper	
CASTE	class; rank; lineage	
CATCH	latch; clutch; ensnare	
CATER	provide food, etc.	
CATES	viands; dainties	
CATTY	feline; spiteful	
CAULD	dam; weir (Sc.)	
CAULK	make water-tight	**Naut.**
CAUSE	reason; object; source	
CAVED	collapsed; fallen	
CAVIE	hen-coop or cage	
CAVIL	carp; censure; criticize	
CAVIN	covered approach	
CAWED	crowed	
CAWKY	of baryta	**Chem.**
CAXON	hairy wig	
CEASE	cesse; end; stop; desist	
CEBUS	S. American monkey	**Z.**
CEDAR	a Lebanon tree	**B.**
CEDED	granted; allotted; yielded	
CELLA	central body of temple	
CELLO	violincello	**Mus.**
CENSE	burn incense	
CENTO	a medley	**Mus.**
CEORL	churl; a freeman	
CERED	covered with wax	
CERES	Harvest Goddess	
CERGE	altar candle	**Eccl.**
CERIC	wax-like	
CERIN	a constituent of wax	**Chem.**
CERTY	certainly (Sc.)	
CETIC	(spermaceti)	**Z.**
CETYL	a radical in spermaceti	
CHACK	the toss of a horse's head	
CHAFE	rub; heat; vex; gall	
CHAFF	husks; deride; raillery	
CHAFT	chaps; the jaw (Sc.)	
CHAIN	fetter; 22 yards	**Meas.**
CHAIR	seat; professorship	
CHAKO	shako; a headdress	
CHALK	to record	
CHAMA	large oyster	**Min.**
CHAMP	(horses); chew; crunch	**Z.**
CHANK	species of conch-shell	**Z.**
CHANT	intone; carol	**Mus.**
CHAOS	anarchy; disorder; confusion	
CHAPE	the catch of a buckle	
CHAPS	the jaws; chops	
CHAPS	cowboy breeches	
CHARD	artichoke	**B.**

CHARE	chore; daily work	
CHARE	narrow street or court	
CHARK	char; charcoal	
CHARM	spell; allure; amulet	
CHARR	char; (trout)	**Z.**
CHART	sea-map	**Naut.**
CHARY	frugal; circumspect; wary	
CHASE	pursue; hunt; follow; race	
CHASE	engrave; frame; type-case	
CHASM	gap; cleft; rift; abyss	
CHEAP	mean; common; paltry	
CHEAT	dupe; fraud; swindle	
CHECK	curb; stay; bridle; tally	
CHEEK	insolence; sauce	
CHEEP	pipe; chirp; churr	
CHEER	gaiety; hearten; encourage	
CHELA	lobster claw	**Z.**
CHELA	a Buddhist disciple	
CHENG	Chinese reed instrument	**Mus.**
CHERT	flint; hornstone	**Min.**
CHESS	a matey game	
CHEST	coffer; coffin; breast	
CHEVY	chivy; chase; scamper	
CHIAN	of Chios	
CHIAO		**Coin**
CHICA	orange-red dye; liquor	
CHICH	a dwarf pea; lentil	**B.**
CHICK	to sprout; child; chicken	**Z.**
CHICK	bamboo screen	
CHIDE	scold; rebuke; reprove	
CHIEF	boss; head; prime; principal	
CHIEL	child; lad (Sc.)	
CHILD	babe; nursling; offspring	
CHILI	pod of cayenne pepper	**B.**
CHILL	cold; frigid; depress	
CHIMB	edge of cask	
CHIME	harmonize; strike; agree	
CHINA	porcelain; Celestial Empire	
CHINE	cleft; ravine; backbone	**Med.**
CHINK	gap; rift; cranny; clink	
CHIPS	a carpenter	
CHIRK	chirp; cheep; cheerful	
CHIRM	bird noises	
CHIRP	chirr; chirl; to trill	
CHIRT	to squeeze	
CHIVE	a type of onion	**B.**
CHIVY	chevy; chase; pursue	
CHOCK	wedge; block; a log	
CHODE	scolded; rated; upbraided	
CHOIR	the chancel	**Eccl.**
CHOKE	gag; stifle; burke; strangle	
CHOKY	prison (slang)	
CHOPS	chaps; the jaws	
CHORD	harmonious sound	**Mus.**
CHORE	chare; household toil	
CHOSE	selected; picked; culled	
CHOUT	blackmail; extortion (Hind.)	
CHUBB	patent lock; a safe	
CHUCK	jerk; throw; cluck	**Tool**
CHUET	a pie of minced meat	

CHUFF clown; boor; surly fellow
CHUMP lump of wood; blockhead
CHUNK thick slice
CHURL ceorl; freeman; clodhopper
CHURN foam; jostle; agitate
CHURR chirp; chirk
CHUTE waterfall; sloping channel
CHYAK tease; chaff (Australia)
CHYLE milky fluid **Med.**
CHYME pulpy food **Med.**
CHYND cleft to the chine (obs.)
CIBOL variety of onion; shallot **B.**
CICER chick-pea **B.**
CIDER cyder; fermented apple-juice
CIGAR a Havana
CILIA filaments; eye-lashes **Med.**
CIMAR cymar; simar; scarf
CIMEX bed-bug **Z.**
CINCH girth; a certainty
CIRCA about (Latin prefix)
CIRCE a glamorous Syren
CIRRI tendrils; clouds
CISCO American char **Z.**
CISSY effeminate youth
CITAL summons; accusation **Law**
CITED quoted; adduced; mentioned
CIVET cat; perfume; fur **Z.**
CIVIC municipal; corporate
CIVIL polite; courteous; suave
CIVVY a civilian
CLACK click; clink; clatter; prate
CLAES clothes (Sc.)
CLAIK the barnacle goose **Z.**
CLAIM right; privilege; usurp
CLAMP clump: fasten **Tool**
CLAMS pincers; vice **Tool**
CLANG clank; clash
CLANK clatter; clangour
CLARE a nun of St. Clare **Eccl.**
CLARO mild in taste (cigars)
CLARY sweet-herb **B.**
CLASH jar; differ; contend; collide
CLASP hasp; catch; grip
CLASS set; grade; category
CLATS slops; (mud wall) (Sc.)
CLAUT rake; scratch (Sc.)
CLAVE clove; cleft; clung
CLEAN immaculate; pure; scour
CLEAR pellucid; serene; free
CLEAT a wedge; slat **Naut.**
CLEEK golf club; hook; peg
CLEFT clift; split; rift; cranny
CLEPE to name; (yclept)
CLERK scribe; scrivener; recorder
CLEVE a cliff; a valley
CLEVY draught-iron of a plough
CLICK klick; tick; a latch
CLIFF crag; headland; precipice
CLIFT cleft; fissure; breach

CLIMB scale; ascend; surmount
CLIME region; place; climate
CLING hold; cleave; embrace
CLINK prison; chink; jingle
CLINT a hard rock **Min.**
CLOAK cover; pretext; mask
CLOAM earthenware
CLOCK chronometer; horologe
CLOFF cleft; a weight allowance
CLOOM cloam; clay
CLOOP pop !
CLOOT cloven hoof (Sc.)
CLOSE estop; end; grapple **Eccl.**
CLOSH skittles
CLOTH woven fabric; the clergy **Eccl.**
CLOUD haze; vapour; obscure
CLOUR to knock; a bump
CLOUT dish-cloth; nail; buffet
CLOVE a spice; a weight **B., Meas.**
CLOWN jester; fool; buffoon; dunce
CLUCK the call of a hen
CLUMP cluster; group; patch
CLUNG clasped; adhered; held
CLUNK a gurgle
CLUNY pillow-lace
CNIDA stinging thread; jelly-fish **Z.**
COACH teach; trainer; vehicle
CO-ACT co-operate; aid; abet
CO-AID helper; assistant
COALY resembling coal
COARB bishop or abbot **Eccl.**
COAST shore; strand; seaside
COATI American racoon **Z.**
COBBY stout; brisk
COBLE fishing boat **Naut.**
COBRA hamadryad **Z.**
COCKY conceited
COCOA a beverage **B.**
COCUS green ebony **B.**
CODED in code; in cipher
CODEX ancient manuscript
CODLE coddle; pamper; caress
COGUE wooden milk bowl (Sc.)
COIGN corner-stone; quoin; wedge
COKED converted into coke
COLIC flatulence **Med.**
COLIN American partridge **Z.**
COLLY coal-smut
COLON punctuation; money **Med.**
COLOR colour; hue tint; pigment
COLZA cabbage; rape oil **B.**
COMBE coomb; wooded valley
COMER an arrival
COMET card game; nebulous body
COMFY comfortable
COMIC droll; farcical; ludicrous
COMMA a butterfly **Z.**
COMPO plaster; stucco
COMPT to count (obs.)

COMUS God of Revelry; a masque	
CONCH shell; trumpet	**Mus.**
CONED tapering	
CONES fine flour	
CONEY cony; bunny	**Z.**
CONGA dance (Afro-Cuban)	**Mus.**
CONGE leave; dismissal (Fr.)	
CONGO black tea	**B.**
CONIA hemolck	**B.**
CONIC conical; tapering	
CONIN conine; hemlock	**B.**
CONNE conn; con; study; steer	
CONTO money of account (Portugal)	
COOED made love	
COOEE cooey; Australian bush-call	
COOKY a cook; cookies; a small cake	
COOLY coolie (Hind.)	
COOMB 4 bushels; wooded valley	**Meas.**
CO-OPT to elect	
COPAL a resin; a varnish	**B.**
COPEC kopeck; a Russian copper	**Coin**
COPED vied; contended; overcame	
COPER dealer	
COPOS lassitude	
COPRA dried coconut kernels	**B.**
COPSE coppice; grove; thicket	
COPSY covered with undergrowth	
CORAL lobster roe	**Min., Z.**
CORED centre removed, bored.	
CORGI small breed of dog (Wales)	**Z.**
CORKY lively; skittish	
CORNO French horn	**Mus.**
CORNU a horn	**Z.**
CORNY horny; (humour) trite (slang)	
CORPS staff; contingent; troops	
CORSE a corpse (obs.)	
COSEY cosy; snug; teapot-cover	
COSTS expenses	**Law**
COTTA a surplice	**Eccl.**
COUCH sofa; divan; squat; grass	**B.**
COUGH tussis; a cold	**Med.**
COULD be able	
COUNT compute; number; reckon	
COUPE closed car	
COURB to stoop; bent (obs.)	
COURT woo; invite; homage; tribunal	
COUTH familiar; agreeable	
COVED arched over	
COVEN a muster of witches	
COVER wrap; cloak; shroud; invest	
COVET desire; hanker after	
COVEY a brood; a bevy	**Z.**
COVIN collusive fraudulence	**Law**
COWAN uninitiated mason	
COWED daunted; overawed; abashed	
COWER fawn; quail; cringe; shrink	
COWRY small shell used as money	
COYLY bashfully; demurely; shyly	
COYPU nutria; S. American rodent	**Z.**
COXAE hip-joints	**Med.**

COZEN cheat; deceive; sponge	
CRACK gap; rift; rent; crevice	
CRAFT skill; dexterity; guile	**Naut.**
CRAIG crag; the neck (Sc.)	
CRAKE the corncrake	**Z.**
CRAME booth; covered stall	
CRAMP a spasm; hinder; impede	
CRANE hoisting machine; wader	**Z.**
CRANK handle; bend; twist; quirk	
CRAPE transparent gauze; to curl	
CRAPS a dice game	
CRAPY resembling crape	
CRARE trading vessel	**Naut.**
CRASH coarse cloth; shatter; smash	
CRASS gross; dense; stupid	
CRATE hamper; packing case	
CRAVE beg; yearn; implore	
CRAWL fish-pen; creep; abase	
CRAZE mania; insane passion; fad	
CRAZY mad; idiotic; rickety	
CREAK grate	
CREAM to mantle	
CRECK the corncrake	**Z.**
CREDO the creed	**Eccl.**
CREED belief; tenet; dogma	
CREEK bay; cove inlet; bight	
CREEL fish-basket	
CREEP crawl; cringe; grovel	
CRENA a furrow; a notch	
CREPE fabric; ribber	
CREPT crawled; fawned; glided	
CRESS watercress, etc.	**B.**
CREST top; apex; summit; device	
CREUX the reverse of relief	
CREWE cruse; earthenware pot	
CRICK cramp; spasm; convulsion	
CRIED wept; sobbed; lamented	
CRIER proclaimer; howler	
CRIES yells; shrieks; shouts	
CRIME felony; enormity; misdeed	
CRIMP corrugate; decoy	
CRINE shrink; shrivel (Sc.)	
CRISP curl; brittle; friable	
CRITH unit weight of a gas	**Meas.**
CROAK grumble; complain; die	
CROAT (Yugoslavian)	
CROCK soot; jar; pitcher; shard	
CROFT a small farm; a pasture	
CROMA crome; a quaver	**Mus.**
CROME cromb; crook; hook	
CRONE old woman; an ewe	**Z.**
CRONY familiar friend	
CROOK crome; bend; crosier	**Eccl.**
CROOL to mutter	
CROOM a pitchfork	**Tool**
CROON low moan	
CROPE a finial; the top	
CRORE 100 lacs of rupees	**Coin**
CROSS crusty; sullen; thwart	
CROUD Welsh violin	**Mus.**

CROUP	rump; throat disease	**Med.**
CROUT	pickled cabbage	
CROWD	mob; throng; herd; swarm	
CROWN	diadem; garland; 5/-	**Coin**
CROZE	cooper's tool; groove	**Tool**
CRUDE	raw; tough; immature	
CRUEL	fell; dire; brutal; inhuman	
CRUET	eucharistic flagon	**Eccl.**
CRUMB	soft part of a loaf	
CRUMP	crooked; wrinkled; a bang	
CRUNT	a blow on the head (Sc.)	
CRUOR	coagulated blood; gore	**Med.**
CRUSE	vial; small bottle	
CRUSH	squeeze; subdue; pulverize	
CRUST	incrustation; coating	
CRWTH	Welsh violin	**Mus.**
CRYPT	vault; tomb; catacomb	
CUBAN	a native of Cuba	
CUBEB	dried pepper-berry	**B.**
CUBED	raised to third power	
CUBIC	volumetric	**Meas.**
CUBIT	length of 18 or 22 inches	**Meas.**
CUDDY	cabin; rent; donkey	**Z.**
CUFIC	an Arabic script	
CUISH	cuisse; thigh-armour	
CULCH	rubbish	
CULET	lower facet of a diamond	
CULEX	a gnat genus	**Z.**
CULLY	silly dupe; to deceive	
CUMIN	cummin; a bitter herb	**B.**
CUPEL	assaying vessel	
CUPID	Eros; the god of love	
CURCH	a kerchief	
CURDY	coagulated	
CURED	healed; remedied; preserved	
CURER	a fish-drier	
CURIA	Senate house; court	
CURIE	unit of radiation	**Meas.**
CURIO	rare bric-à-brac	
CURLY	wavy; sinuous; twisty	
CURRE	golden-eye duck	**Z.**
CURRY	to dress leather; thrash	
CURRY	Indian spiced dish	
CURSE	anathema; execrate; maledict	
CURST	tormented; plagued	
CURVE	turn; bend; inflect	
CUSEC	cubic flow per second	**Meas.**
CUSHY	easy and well-paid	
CUTCH	catechu; couch grass	**B.**
CUTER	more cunning; sharper	
CUT-IN	football; motoring	
CUTIS	true skin	**Med.**
CUTTO	cuttoe; large knife	**Tool**
CUTTY	short; curtailed; clay pipe	
CUVEE	blend of wine (Fr.)	
CYCAD	a palm	**B.**
CYCLE	period; age; era; circle	
CYMRY	Cymric; Welsh	
CYNIC	misanthrope; captious; morose	
CZECH		

D

DADDY	dadda; papa; father	
DAGON	Philistine Fish-God	
DAILY	diurnal; quotidian	
DAIRI	Mikado's palace	
DAIRY	milkshop; creamery	
DAISY	sometimes ox-eyed	**B.**
DAKER	corncrake; crake	**Z.**
DAKIR	daker; dicker; half-a-score	
DALAI	Lama; Tibetan Priest-King	**Eccl.**
DALER	a dalesman	
DALLY	sport; wanton; toy; dawdle	
DAMAN	coney; Syrian hyrax	**Z.**
DAMAR	dammar; resin	**B.**
DAMON	and Pythias	
DAMPS	exhalations	
DAMPY	dejected; moist; humid	
DANCE	hop; caper; prance; pirouette	
DANDY	fop; beau; swell; coxcomb	
DARBY	plasterer's float	**Tool**
DARED	braved; ventured; presumed	
DARIC	gold coin of Darius	**Coin**
DARKY	darkey; negro; lantern	
DAROO	sycamore	**B.**
DASHY	showy; ostentatious; gaudy	
DATED	of an era	
DATUM	something given	
DAUBY	sticky; viscous; glutinous	
DAUNT	cow; appal; scare; intimidate	
DAVIT	usually davits	**Naut.**
DAYAK	Dyak; Malay race	
DAZED	mazed; dazzled; bewildered	
DEADS	ore débris	
DEALT	(cards); trafficked; traded	
DEARN	mournful; lonely; solitary	
DEARY	a dear	
DEATH	demise; decease	
DEAVE	to deafen (Sc.)	
DEBAG	remove trousers forcibly	
DEBAR	ban; deny; prevent; stop	
DEBEL	to conquer; subdue	
DEBIT	due; arrears; liability	
DEBUG	de programme (computer)	
DEBUS	get off a bus	
DEBUT	first appearance	
DECAD	decade; a group of ten	
DECAY	rot; wane; decline	
DECEM	ten; (a prefix)	
DECOR	scheme of decoration	
DECOY	lure; ensnare; inveigle	
DECRY	censure; vilify; disparage	
DEDAL	daedal; intricate	
DEEDY	illustrious; active	
DEFER	delay; adjourn; postpone	
DEIFY	idolize; apotheosize	
DEIGN	condescend; vouchsafe	
DEISM	belief in a god	
DEIST	a free-thinking believer	
DEITY	divinity; providence	

DEKKO to look (Ind.)	**DISME** a tithe; a tenth; a dime
DEKLE deckle; ragged	**DITAL** guitar tuning key **Mus.**
DELAY dally; retard; impede	**DITCH** moat; trench; rine; drain
DELFT glazed earthenware	**DITTO** the same again
DELPH delf; pottery	**DITTY** refrain; sonnet; ode; lilt
DELTA river mouth; alluvial deposit	**DIVAN** council; saloon; sofa; couch
DELVE dig; scoop; excavate	**DIVED** plunged; fathomed; explored
DEMIT release; resign	**DIVER** a sea-bird **Z.**
DEMOB demobilize	**DIVES** the rich man in the Bible
DEMON imp; goblin; devil; troll	**DIVOT** a piece of turf
DEMOS the proletariat	**DIVVY** share; divide
DEMPT deemed; judged (Spens.)	**DIXIE** camp-kettle; Southern U.S.A.
DEMUR pause; object; waver	**DIZEN** to dress gaudily
DENAY deny; denial (obs.)	**DJINN** genie; demon; afrit
DENGU an Indian fever **Med.**	**DO-ALL** factotum
DENIM twilled cotton goods	**DOBBY** a dotard; part of a loom
DENSE compact; close; solid	**DODDY** hornless cow **Z.**
DEPOT depository; storehouse	**DODGE** evade; avoid; shuffle
DEPTH profundity; abyss	**DODGY** artful; tricky
DERAY to disarrange	**DOGAL** (doge of Venice)
DERBY a race; a hat	**DOGGO** concealed
DERMA lobster-skin **Z.**	**DOGGY** fond of dogs
DERRY a prejudice (Australia)	**DOGMA** tenet; doctrine; maxim
DETER prevent; restrain; dissuade	**DOGRA** a Kashmiri
DEUCE the Devil; (cards); (tennis)	**DOILT** crazy; daft (Sc.)
DEVIL imp; to drudge; Lucifer	**DOILY** ornamented napkin
DEWAN Indian fiscal officer	**DOING** performing; swindling
DEWED bedewed	**DOLCE** softly **Mus.**
DHOBI Indian washerman	**DOLED** bestowed sparingly
DHOLE Indian wild dog **Z.**	**DOLLY** camera carriage (Television)
DHOTI loin cloth (Hind.)	**DOLOR** dolour; grief; sorrow
DIANA moon-goddess; Artemis	**DOMAL** relating to a house
DIARY journal; chronicle; record	**DOMED** vaulted
DICED cut into cubes	**DONAH** coster's sweetheart
DICER dice-player	**DONAT** donet; grammer-book; primer
DICHT to wipe (Sc.)	**DONEE** the recipient
DICKY seat; apron; shirt-front	**DONGA** S. African ravine
DICTA pronouncements	**DONNA** donya; a lady don (Sp.)
DIDST	**DONOR** giver; bestower
DIDUS the dodo genus **Z.**	**DONYA** Spanish lady
DIENE unsaturated hydrocarbons **Chem.**	**DOOLE** dole; gloom (obs.)
DIGHT adorned; arrayed	**DOOLY** Indian litter
DIGIT finger; toe; integer	**DOORN** S. African briar **B.**
DIKED banked; ditched	**DOPED** drugged; covered with varnish
DILLY native bag (Australia)	**DOPER** dauber; horse-coper
DILLY diligence; the daffodil **B.**	**DOPEY** slow-witted; dull
DIMLY obscurely; vaguely	**DOREE** dory; golden-yellow fish **Z.**
DINAR (Iran, Jordan, Yugoslavia) **Coin**	**DORIC** (Greek architecture)
DINED postprandially replete	**DORMY** unbeatable at golf
DINER restaurant car	**DORSE** Baltic cod; coal-fish **Z.**
DINGO Australian dog **Z.**	**DORTY** pettish; delicate (Sc.)
DINGY dull; sullied; squalid	**DOSED** physicked; drenched
DINIC dizzy; vertiginous	**DOSEH** religious ceremony (Cairo)
DINKY elegant	**DOSEL** dossal; tapestry **Eccl.**
DIODE thermionic valve; a circuit	**DOSER** dossel; coloured cloths
DIOTA two-handled jar	**DOTAL** referring to a dowry
DIPUS the jerboa **Z.**	**DOTED** loved; drivelled
DIPPY a little insane	**DOTTY** barmy; silly; deranged
DIRGE elegy; requiem; lament	**DOUAR** dowar; Arab camp
DIRTY foul; sordid; mean; paltry	**DOUAY** a Bible edition

DOUBT distrust; indecision; demur
DOUCE dulce; sweet
DOUGH money; the kneadful
DOURA millet **B.**
DOUSE dowse; slacken suddenly; drench
DOVER doze; slumber; a powder **Med.**
DOWDY slovenly; untidy; slatternly
DOWEL a wooden pin
DOWER dowry; dot; bequest
DOWLE fluff; down fibre
DOWNY filamentous; knowing
DOWRY dower; dot; endowment
DOWSE lower; close; put out **Naut.**
DOYEN senior member
DOZED snoozed; drowsed; slumbered
DOZEN apostolic number
DOZER went nap
DRACO a constellation
DRAFF dregs; residue
DRAFT outline; sketch; prepare
DRAIL to trail; to draggle
DRAIN empty; tap; a gutter
DRAKE (bowls); (drum) **Z.**
DRAMA histrionic art ; play
DRANK quaffed; caroused; imbibed
DRANT to drone; to drawl
DRAPE cover; array; deck
DRAWL lag; drag; drone
DRAWN hauled; sketched; eviscerated
DREAD awe; fear; apprehension
DREAM reverie; hallucination
DREAR bleak; dismal; gloomy
DREGS lees; draff; sediment
DRENT drenched (obs.)
DRESS garb; guise; apparel
DREST attired; arrayed
DREUL drool; dribble
DRIED aerified; parched; desiccated
DRIER desiccator; dryer
DRIFT wander; aim; intention **Tool**
DRILL cloth; ape; bore **Z., Tool**
DRILY dryly; sarcastically
D-RING ' D ' shaped ring
DRINK potion; draught; absorb
DRIVE urge; impel; coerce
DROIL ca' canny; drudgery
DROIT right; title
DROLL odd; rummy; whimsical
DROME racecourse; aerodrome
DRONE idler; hum; dawdle; bee **Z.**
DRONE (bagpipes) **Mus.**
DROOK to drench; to duck (Sc.)
DROOL dreul; slaver; drivel
DROOP sag; fade; wilt; languish
DROPS small doses; gouts **Med.**
DROSS scum; dregs; scoria
DROUK drook; to duck (Sc.)
DROVE (cattle); forced; actuated
DROWN swamp; flood; deluge
DRUID bard

DRUNK crapulous; tipsy; quaffed
DRUPE a stone fruit **B.**
DRUSE mining cavity; a Syrian
DRUXY partly decayed timber
DRYAD wood-nymph
DRYAS mountain avens **B.**
DRYER drier
DRYLY drily; insipidly; aridly
DSOMO zhomo; a hydrid **Z.**
DUCAL with strawberry leaves
DUCAT Italian gold or silver **Coin**
DUCHY a dukedom
DUDDY ragged; in tatters
DULCE douce; sweeten; soothe
DULIA angel adoration, R.C. **Eccl.**
DULLY stupidly; inertly; languidly
DULSE edible seaweed **B,**
DUMBA fat-tailed sheep **Z.**
DUMMY declarer's mute partner
DUMPS low spirits; dejection
DUMPY short and thick
DUNCE dolt; dullard; booby
DUNCH punch; jolt; to gore
DUNNE the knot-sandpiper **Z.**
DUNNY deaf; dull of apprehension
DUOMO Italian cathedral **Eccl.**
DUPED deluded; gulled; hoaxed
DUPER trickster; dodger; sharper
DUPLE double; twofold
DUPPY W. Indian ghost
DURED endured (obs.)
DURGA wife of Siva **Eccl.**
DURGY undersized; dwarf
DURIO Malay tree; (durian fruit) **B.**
DUROY corduroy; figured serge
DURRA doura; millet **B.**
DURST dared
DUSKY swarthy; shady; dark; dim
DUSTY powdery
DUTCH a coster's wife; (courage)
DUVET eiderdown
DWALE heretic; heraldic sable
DWALE the deadly nightshade **B.**
DWALM dwaum; swoon; sicken
DWAMY faint; languid; sickly (Sc.)
DWANG a crowbar **Tool**
DWARF imp; pygmy; midget; stunted
DWELL abide; reside; linger
DWELT stayed; tarried; sojourned
DWINE to pine; to fade
DYING moribund; expiring; demise
DYNAM the unit of work. **Meas.**

E

EAGER keen; ardent; avid; zealous
EAGLE (golf); 10 dollar gold **Coin**
EAGLE lectern; standard; erne **Z.**
EAGRE aigre; tidal wave; bore
EARED having lugs

EARLY rathe; forward; betimes
EARST erst; formerly
EARTH world; soil; humus
EASED allayed; soothed; assuaged
EASEL canvas carrier
EASLE hot ashes (Sc.)
EATEN masticated; corroded
EATER consumer; devourer
EAVES over-hanging roof-edges
EBBED waned; receded; declined
EBLIS a djinn; evil spirit
EBONY **B.**
ECLAT splendour; brilliance
ECTAL ectad; outer; external
EDDER top binding of a hedge
EDGED keen; bordered; fringed
EDICT ukase; decree; order
EDIFY uplift; enlighten; instruct
EDILE Roman magistrate
EDUCE elicit; draw; extract
EDUCT deduction
EERIE eirie; uncanny; weird
EGEST throw out; eject; cast
EGGAR egger ; silkworm moth **Z.**
EGGED incited; urged; impelled
EGGER an egg collector
EGRET aigrette; heron **Z.**
EIDAM Dutch cheese
EIDER sea-duck **Z.**
EIGHT
EIGNE eldest son; first born
EIGNE entailed and unalienable **Law**
EIKON ikon; likeness
EIRIE eerie; weird; uncanny
EISEL vinegar **Chem.**
EJECT evict; expel; oust; emit
EKING prolonging
ELAIN clarified oil or fat
ELAND antelope (S. Africa) **Z.**
ELAPS venemous coral snake **Z.**
ELATE exult; rouse; animate
ELBOW jostle; nudge; a bend
ELCHI Turkish envoy
ELDER older; ancestor **B.**
ELECT cull; select; chosen
ELEGY dirge; threnody; lament
ELEMI resin; chewing gum **B.**
ELEOT species of apple **B.**
ELERS designer of china-ware
ELEVE pupil (Fr.)
ELFIN small elf; puckish; pixy
ELGIN (marbles)
ELIDE contract; curtail
ELITE the elect; very select
ELMEN made of elm **B.**
ELOGE funeral oration
ELOGY panegyric; eulogy; encomium
ELOIN banish; remove (obs.)
ELOPE run away; abscond; decamp
ELOPS herring genus **Z.**

ELSIN an awl (Sc.) **Tool**
ELUDE evade; baffle; escape
ELUTE cleanse; purify by washing
ELVAN Cornish rock; elvish **Min.**
ELVAS prune; plum **B.**
ELVER young eel **Z.**
EMBAR prevent; bar; shut; stop
EMBAY to shelter; to landlock
EMBED imbed; set firmly
EMBER glowing fuel
EMBOG engulf
EMBOW to arch; to vault
EMBOX encase; pack
EMBUS to put in a bus
EMEER Ameer; Emir
EMEND amend; rectify; correct
EMERY carborundum **Min.**
EMMER bucket; pail (S. Africa)
EMMET an ant; a pismire **Z.**
EMMEW enmew; immew; confine
EMPTY void; vacant; vacuous; inane
EMURE immure (obs.)
ENACT ordain; decree; authorize
ENATE growing out
ENDED finished; concluded; ceased
ENDER a finale; a cropper
END-ON abutting
ENDOR home of a witch
ENDOW endue; indue; endew
ENDUE to invest; provide
ENEID epic poem
ENEMY foe; rival; antagonist
ENGLE Angle; early English
ENJOY relish; appreciate
ENNUI weariness; boredom (Fr.)
ENODE jointless; knotless
ENORM enormous (obs.)
ENROL list; enlist; chronicle
ENSKY to sky
ENSUE pursue; result; follow
ENTAL internal
ENTER invade; record; insert
ENTRY adit; inlet; portal; note
ENURE inure; accustom
ENVOI } diplomatic agent; legate;
ENVOY } postscript
ENZYM a ferment; yeast **Chem.**
EOLIC Eolian; Aeolian
EOLUS God of the Winds
EOSIN red dye or ink **Chem.**
EPACT moon's age at new year
EPHAH Hebrew bushel **Meas.**
EPHOD vestment; surplice **Eccl.**
EPHOR Greek magistrate
EPOCH era; cycle; remarkable period
EPODE part of an ode
EPOPT an Eleusinian initiate
EPSOM salts **Med.**
EPURE large working plan (Fr.)

EQUAL peer; competent; equable
EQUES Roman Knight
EQUIP rig; arm; accoutre; array
EQUUS the horse genus   **Z.**
ERASE blot; delete; cancel; efface
ERATO Muse of lyric poetry
ERECT build; upright; vertical
ERGOT parasitical fungus   **B.**
ERICA the heath genus   **B.**
ERICK a blood-fine (Irish)   **Law**
ERODE eat away; corrode; consume
EROSE a leaf shape   **B.**
ERRED strayed; sinned; wandered
ERROR mistake; fault; fallacy
ERUCA the salad plant; a larva **B., Z.**
ERUPT eject; eruct; burst forth
ERVUM the lentil   **B.**
ESCOT scot; an ancient tax
ESCAR⎫
ESKAR⎬ glacial gravel ridge
ESKER⎭
ESSAY assay; attempt; trial; paper
ESTER ethereal salt   **Chem.**
ESTOC short cavalry sword (Fr.)
ESTOP stop; bar; impede   **Law**
ETERN eternal; endless
ETHAL (spermaceti)   **Chem.**
ETHER upper air; volatile gas   **Chem.**
ETHIC ethical; moral
ETHOS individuality
ETHYL alcohol radical   **Chem.**
ETTLE intend; guess (Sc.)
ETUDE a composition (Fr.)   **Mus.**
ETWEE etui; pocket-case
EUPAD (antiseptic)   **Chem.**
EURUS the east wind
EUSOL (antiseptic)   **Chem.**
EVADE elude; avoid; foil; dodge
EVENS fifty-fifty
EVENT incident; outcome; occurrence
EVERT turn inside out
EVERY all; each
EVICT eject; dislodge; dispossess
EVITE evade; avoid; shun
EVOKE arouse; excite; summon
EWEST near (Sc.)
EWHOW alas ! (Sc.)
EXACT precise; extort; mulct
EXALT raise; extol; magnify
EXCEL outvie; surpass; exceed
EXEAT a short leave
EXEME exempt (Sc.)
EXERT strive; try; endeavour
EXIES ecstasy; hysterics (Sc.)
EXILE refugee; banish; proscribe
EXIST be; live; endure; last
EX-LEX outlaw   **Law**
EXODE dramatic climax
EXPEL eject; dislodge; oust
EXTOL exalt; laud; glorify

EXTRA supernumerary; additional
EXUDE ooze; percolate; sweat
EXULT crow; gloat; triumph
EYING watching; observing
EYRIE aerie; eagle's nest

F

FABLE myth; legend; allegory
FACED defied; confronted; covered
FACER a blow
FACET small polished surface
FACIA fascia; shop name-board
FADDY crotchety; particular
FADER   **Radio**
FADGE suit; prosper; burden
FAERY fairy
FAGIN (beech mast); a Jew   **B.**
FAGOT faggot; bundle of sticks
FAGUS the beech tree   **B.**
FAHAM Indian orchid   **B.**
FAINT swoon; dim; indistinct
FAIRY faery; peri; elf; pixie
FAITH tenet; dogma; belief
FAKED spurious; counterfeit
FAKER forger; cheat; swindler
FAKIR monkish mendicant; magician
FALSE sham; erroneous; untrue
FAMED illustrious; renowned
FANAL lighthouse; beacon
FANAM Madras money of account **Coin.**
FANCY pugilism; whim; idea; caprice
FANGO radio-active mud   **Med.**
FANON napkin; scarf   **Eccl.**
FARAD unit of electrical capacity
FARED fed; travelled; prospered
FARCE comedy; travesty; parody
FARCY glanders; equine malady
FARLE oatcake (Sc.)
FARSE a Bible extract   **Eccl.**
FARSI, Parsi (Persian) language
FASTI Roman calendar of festivals
FATAL lethal; baneful; ruinous
FATED doomed; destined
FATES Clotho, Lachesis & Atropos
FATLY obesely; grossly
FATTY adipose; pudgy; plump
FAULT blemish; (tennis); (geology)
FAUNA animal life   **Z.**
FAUST a drama by Goethe
FAVUS scalp disease   **Med.**
FEAST banquet; carousal; delight
FEAZE unravel
FECIT he (or she) made it (art)
FED-UP disgruntled; browned off
FEEZE to twist; worry
FEIGN pretend; simulate; assume
FEINT stratagem; artifice; trick
FELID one of the cat tribe   **Z.**
FELIS the cat tribe   **Z.**

c

FELIX the cartoon cat
FELLY felloe; part of rim of wheel
FELON criminal; miscreant; outlaw
FEMUR thigh bone   Med.
FENCE receiver of stolen goods
FENDY shifty
FENKS finks; blubber refuse
FENNY marshy; swamp; boggy
FEOFF a fief; grant of land   Law
FERAE wild animals   Z.
FERAL wild; deadly; funereal
FERLY fearful; a wonder
FERNY   B.
FERRY river transport
FESSE heraldic band
FETAL also FŒTAL; embryonic   Med.
FETCH trick; ghost; bring; carry
FETED honoured; lionized
FETID noxious; mephitic; noisome
FETOR offensive odour
FETUS an embryo; the young   Med.
FETWA a judgment (Arab)   Law
FEUAR a lease-holder (Sc.)
FEVER ferment; passion; ardour   Med.
FEWER rather less
FIARS the prices of grain (Sc.)
FIBRE staple; filament; strand
FICHU small lace or muslin shawl
FICUS the fig   B.
FIDGE to fidget; to be eager (Sc.)
FIELD glebe; (cricket); (racing)
FIEND imp; demon; monster; wretch
FIERI facias; a writ   Law
FIERY ardent; fierce; igneous
FIFED fluted   Mus.
FIFER fife-player
FIFTH
FIFTY L
FIGHT fray; brawl; combat; contest
FILAR threadlike; filamentous
FILCH steal; pilfer; purloin
FILED smooth; polished
FILER one who files; artful
FILLY girl; foal   Z.
FILMY diaphanous
FILTH dirt; muck; impurity
FINAL last; ultimate; terminal
FINCH a passerine   Z.
FINED mulcted; amersed
FINER refiner; keener; smaller
FINIS the end; conclusion
FINOS merino wool
FIORD   ⎤ rock-bound inlet;
FIRTH   ⎬ river mouth;
FJORD   ⎦ frith; arm of the sea
FIRED discharged; kindled; sacked
FIRER an incendiary; igniter
FIRRY full of pines   B.
FIRST chief; premier; primeval
FISHY questionable; unreliable
FISTY left-handed person (Sc.)

FITCH pole-cat; fur-brush   Z.
FITCH vetch; chick-pea   B.
FITLY aptly; properly; seemly
FITTE fytte; ballad
FIVER £5
FIVES horse disease; a ball-game
FIXED secured; placed; settled
FLACK ⎤ to flap; to flick (Sc.);
FLAFF ⎦ to flutter; to pant
FLAIL a threshing implement   Tool
FLAIR intensive perception
FLAKE hurdle; hanging platform
FLAKE scale; lamina; to peel off
FLAKY fissile
FLAME ardour; blaze; flare
FLAMY lambent
FLANG miner's pick   Tool
FLANK side; border; touch
FLARE a signal light; glare
FLARY flaming; flickering
FLASH glint; sparkle; showy
FLASK ampulla; vial; phial
FLAWN custard; pancake
FLAWY defective; gusty
FLAXY light in colour
FLEAD pork fat for lard
FLEAK a small lock
FLEAM surgical knife   Med.
FLECK dapple; speckle; variegate
FLECK the flounder   Z.
FLEER to mock; to flout
FLEET a creek; swift; flotilla   Naut.
FLESH mankind; to accustom
FLEWS bloodhound's chaps
FLICK flip; fleece; wound
FLIER flyer; aeronaut
FLIES back-stage appliances
FLIMP watch-snatching (slang)
FLING hurl; dance; escapade
FLINT variety of quartz   Min.
FLIPE to fold back (Sc.)
FLIRT philander; coquet; flip
FLISK a comb; frisk; caper
FLITE flyte; scold; brawl (Sc.)
FLOAT waft; drift; raft; buoy
FLOCK wool; swarm; herd   Z.
FLONG stereotyping paper
FLOOD spate; downpour; deluge
FLOOK fluke
FLOOR to stump; nonplus
FLORA flowers collectively   B.
FLORY fleury (heraldic); boat   Naut.
FLOSS silky substance; slag
FLOTA Spanish fleet   Naut.
FLOUR meal
FLOUT scoff; mock; taunt; jeer
FLOWN swollen with insolence
FLUEY fluffy; downy
FLUFF nap; down; lint
FLUID liquid; unsettled; gaseous

FLUKE parasite worm; (whale)	**Z.**	
FLUKE (anchor); fortunate shot		
FLUKY accidently good		
FLUME a water-chute		
FLUMP plump down		
FLUNG tossed; hurled; pitched		
FLUOR calcium spar	**Min.**	
FLUSH blush; level; (poker)		
FLUTE kind of boat	**Mus.**	
FLUTY flutelike		
FLYER flier; aviator		
FLYTE flite; scold; brawl (obs.)		
FOAMY frothy; spumy		
FOCAL converging		
FOCUS point of convergence		
FOEHN a hot wind in the Alps		
FOGEY old-fashioned person		
FOGGY obscure; hazy; indistinct		
FOGLE silk handkerchief (slang)		
FOISM Chinese Buddhism	**Eccl.**	
FOIST impose; thrust; palm		
FOLIO a sheet of paper		
FOLLY inanity; absurdity; fatuity		
FOMES absorbent substance		
FONDU colour blending in calico		
FOOTS refuse; sediment		
FORAY raid; inroad; sally; invasion		
FORBY adjacent		
FORCE power; energy; army; coerce		
FORDO undo; ruin; destroy		
FOREL thin parchment		
FORET a drill	**Tool**	
FORGE smithy; falsify; fabricate		
FORGO renounce; go without		
FORKY branching		
FORME bed of type		
FORTE strong point; loudly	**Mus.**	
FORTH forward; onward; ahead		
FORTY		
FORUM tribunal; court; market-place		
FOSSA Malagasy civet cat	**Z.**	
FOSSE ditch; moat; canal		
FOUAT⎱ an onion (Sc.);		
FOUET⎰ the house-leek	**B.**	
FOUND to cast; establish; start		
FOUNT spring; well; source; type		
FOUTH fowth; abundance (Sc.)		
FOVEA pit; a pock-mark	**Med.**	
FOXED stained; repaired; deluded		
FOYER lobby; fire-grate		
FRACK freck; eager; bold; hale		
FRAIL weak: infirm; rush-basket		
FRAME fashion; concoct; mood		
FRAME a game at snooker		
FRANC 100 centimes	**Coin**	
FRANK candid; open; gannet	**Z.**	
FRATE friar	**Eccl.**	
FRATI friars; brethren	**Eccl.**	
FRAUD guilt; imposture; deception		
FREAK monstrosity; quirk; vagary		

FRECK frack; eager; hale (Sc.)		
FREED emancipated; exempted		
FREER deliverer; more lavish		
FREET friet; superstition (Sc.)		
FREMD strange; a stranger (Sc.)		
FRESH novel; recent; unsalted		
FRETT ore refuse		
FREYA wife of Odin		
FRIAR frier; frate	**Eccl.**	
FRIED simmered		
FRILL ruffle; border; mannerism		
FRISK romp; search; flisk		
FRITH firth; forest; peace		
FRITZ a German		
FRIZZ to curl; to crisp		
FROCK smock; costume		
FROND fern leaf	**B.**	
FRONS part of skull	**Med.**	
FRONT van; face; assurance		
FRORE flory; frozen (Spens.)		
FROST rime; iciness; a failure		
FROTH spume; foam; effervesce		
FROWN glower; scowl		
FROWY rank; musty		
FROZE became ice		
FRUIT produce; crop; issue	**B.**	
FRUMP a joke; dowdy woman		
FRUSH brittle; broken; thrush		
FRYER a frying pan		
FUBBY⎱ fat and squat;		
FUBSY⎰ chubby		
FUCUS dye; disguise; seaweed	**B.**	
FUDGE fake; nonsense; sweetmeat		
FUERO statute; charter (Sp.)	**Law**	
FUFFY fluffy; soft; downy		
FUGAL like a fugue	**Mus.**	
FUGIE a runaway; a coward (Sc.)		
FUGLE to act as ringleader		
FUGUE polyphonic composition	**Mus.**	
FULLY amply; entirely; completely		
FUMET deer-dung		
FUMID smoky; vaporous		
FUNDI a West African grain	**B.**	
FUNGI mushrooms; toadstools, etc.	**B.**	
FUNIS umbilical cord	**Med.**	
FUNKY nervous; timid; cowardly		
FUNNY droll; comical; boat	**Naut.**	
FUROR wave of enthusiasm		
FURRY incrusted		
FURZE gorse; whin	**B.**	
FURZY whinny		
FUSED melted; merged; blended		
FUSEE vesuvian; firelock fuzee		
FUSIL fusible; a musket		
FUSSY fidgety; bustling		
FUSTY musty; rank; mouldy		
FUZED provided with a fuze		
FUZEE fusee; (clockwork)		
FUZZY woolly; shaggy; blurred		
FYTTE fitte; song; ballad		

G

GABEL excise duty; salt tax (Fr. obs.)
GABLE
GADGE instrument of torture
GADUS the cod genus   **Z.**
GAFFE a social solecism
GAGED pledged; pawned; engaged
GAGER gauger
GAILY gayly; blithely; lively
GALAH Australian cockatoo   **Z.**
GALEA helmet-shaped   **B.**
GALLY like gall; scare; daze
GALOP a round dance
GAMBA a viol   **Mus.**
GAMBE leg (often animal)   **Z.**
GAMED gambled; hazarded; wagered
GAMIC sexual
GAMIN urchin (Fr.)
GAMMA surgical instrument   **Med.**
GAMUT range; scope   **Mus.**
GANCH Turkish form of execution
GANIL limestone   **Min.**
GANJA Indian drink made of hemp
GANZA a wild goose   **Z.**
GAPED wide open; yawned
GAPPY crannied
GARRY Indian carriage
GARTH fish-weir; yard; garden
GARUM fish sauce
GASSY gaseous; aerated
GATED confined
GAUCY gawsy; buxom; jolly (Sc.)
GAUDY garish; tawdry; flashy
GAUGE estimate; measure   **Tool**
GAULT clay   **Min.**
GAUMY dauby; smeary
GAUNT lean; lanky; emaciated
GAUSS unit of magnetic intensity **Meas.**
GAUZE transparent fabric
GAUZY filmy
GAVEL mason's hammer; mallet
GAVEL sheaf of corn
GAVOT gavotte; a dance
GAWKY awkward; ungainly; clumsy
GAYAL wild ox   **Z.**
GAYER merrier; brighter
GAZED looked intently
GAZEL gazelle   **Z.**
GAZER starer; rubber-neck
GAZON turf (Fr.)
GEACH a thief; to steal (slang)
GECKO lizard   **Z.**
GEESE   **Z.**
GEEST alluvial deposit   **Min.**
GEIST mental drive
GELID cold; freezing
GEMEL a twin
GEMMA leaf-bud   **B.**
GEMMY glittering

GEMOT moot; assembly (obs.)
GENET civet-cat fur
GENIE jinee; Arabian sprite
GENII men of ingenuity
GENIO ingenious person (It.)
GENOA a cake
GENRE painting of every day life
GENRO Japanese elder statesmen
GENTY graceful (Sc.)
GENUS group of a species   **Z.**
GEODE crystaline cavity
GEOID the figure of the earth
GERAH twentieth of a shekel   **Coin**
GERBE sheaf; firework (Fr.)
GESSO stucco; plaster
GET-UP style of dress
GHAUT Indian mountain; pass
GHAZI Arab fanatic
GHOST spook; spectre; phantom
GHOUL a gruesome fiend
GHYLL goyal; ravine; gully
GIANT Cyclops; colossus; huge
GIBBE a worn-out animal (Shak.)
GIBED jibed; taunted; jeered   **Naut.**
GIBEL Prussian carp   **Z.**
GIBER scoffer; joker; derider
GIBUS an opera hat
GIDDY dizzy; fickle; mutable
GIGOT jigot; leg of mutton (Fr.)
GIGUE lively tune   **Mus.**
GILLY gillie; keeper (Sc.)
GILPY a tom-boy (Sc.)
GIPSY gypsy; zingaro
GIRTH girdle; thong; cinch
GIUST joust (Spens.)
GIVEN presented; conceded
GIVER bestower; donor; granter
GIVES gyves; fetters; bonds
GLACE smooth; iced
GLADE woodland avenue
GLAIK trick (Sc.)
GLAIR white of egg; varnish
GLAND a secretory organ   **Med.**
GLARE glower; frown; glitter
GLARY dazzling; lustrous
GLASS mirror; telescope; tumbler
GLAUM to grasp eagerly (Sc.)
GLAUR glower (Sc.)
GLAUX sea milkwort   **B.**
GLAVE glaive; kind of halbert
GLAZE lustre; burnish; (windows)
GLAZY shiny; filmy
GLEAD glede; buzzard; kite   **Z.**
GLEAM ray; beam; glimmer; shine
GLEAN cull; collect; harvest
GLEBE sod; church land   **Eccl.**
GLEBY turfy; cloddy
GLEDE glead; buzzard; kite   **Z.**
GLEED glowing ember

GLEEK three-handed card game
GLEET (Sc)ooze, inflammation **Med.**
GLENE eye-ball; socket **Med.**
GLIDE slide; slip; skim; flow
GLIFF glift; an alarm (Sc.)
GLINT gleam; a flash
GLISK a glimpse (Sc.)
GLIST glimmer; mica **Min.**
GLOAM to darken
GLOAT exult; crow; revel
GLOBE orb; sphere; ball; earth
GLOBY spherical
GLOME globular head of flowers **B.**
GLOOM sadness; depression; darkness
GLORY exult; honour; renown
GLOSS comment; polish; veil
GLOUT to be sulky
GLOVE gauntlet; mitten
GLOZE wheedle; flattery; adulation
GLUED stuck together; adhered
GLUER a user of mucilage
GLUEY adhesive; viscous; glutinous
GLUME husks **B.**
GLYPH vertical fluting
GNARL snarl; growl; grumble
GNARR a knot in wood; a snag
GNASH to grind the teeth
GNOME dwarf; a maxim
GOBBO okra; a fruit **B.**
GODLY holy; pious; devout
GOETY black magic
GOFER gauffre; wafer
GOING wending; faring; elapsing
GOLDY goldfinch **Z.**
GOLLY negroid exclamation
GONAD germ-gland **Med.**
GONER irretrievably lost
GOODS chattels; effects
GOODY a sweet
GOOSE tailor's iron **Tool, Z.**
GORAL Indian antelope **Z.**
GORED (bull-fighting); (tailoring)
GORGE gulch; defile; gulp; cram
GORSE whin **B.**
GORSY abounding in gorse
GOUDA a Dutch cheese
GOUGE scoop; circular chisel **Tool**
GOURA a pigeon genus **Z.**
GOURD drinking cup; (cucumber) **B.**
GOUTY swollen; boggy **Med.**
GOWAN a daisy **B.**
GOYAL ghyll; kloof; combe
GRAAL Holy Grail; sacred cup **Eccl.**
GRACE adorn; embellish; favour
GRADE step; rank; slope; degree
GRAFF graft; ditch; moat
GRAFT intrigue; swindle; engraft
GRAIL Holy Grail; sacred cup **Eccl.**
GRAIN corn; seed; grist **B., Meas.**
GRAIP dung-fork **Tool**

GRAMA pasture land (U.S.A.)
GRAME gram; misery
GRAND lordly; 1,000 dollars **Coin**
GRANT cede; confer; gift; largess
GRAPE fruit of the vine **B.**
GRAPH a diagram
GRAPY like a grape
GRASP clasp; clutch; hold; scope
GRASS herbage; pasture; to turf **B.**
GRATE abrade; rasp; jar; fireplace
GRAVE solemn; engrave; tomb
GRAVY meat juice
GRAZE skim; browse; touch lightly
GREAT eminent; bulky; huge
GREBE web-footed bird **Z.**
GRECE grize; steps; staircase
GREED voracity; avidity; gluttony
GREEK Attic; Doric; Hellenic
GREEN raw; fresh; inexperienced
GREEN verdant; (village); (golf)
GREES grece; steps; stairway
GREET cry; weep; lament (Sc.); hail
GREIT greet; weep; cry
GREYS cavalry regiment
GRIAS species of pear **B.**
GRICE young wild boar **Z.**
GRIDE gryde; grate; pierce
GRIEF woe; anguish; mishap
GRILL broil; grid-iron; question
GRIME dirt; soil; sully; befoul
GRIMY filthy; smutty; unclean
GRIND abrade; pulverize; sharpen
GRIPE grasp; squeeze; ditch
GRIST corn; provision
GRITS coarse oatmeal (Sc.)
GRIZE grece; grees; staircase
GROAN moan; complain; grumble
GROAT Joey; fourpenny piece **Coin**
GROCK a kindly clown
GROIN sea-wall; side of body **Med.**
GROOM syce; equerry; bridegroom
GROPE search by feeling
GROSS coarse; 12 dozen **Meas.**
GROUP clump; cluster; arrange
GROUT coarse meal; mortar
GROVE wood; thicket; spinney
GROWL snarl; grumble; complain
GROWN raised; waxed; extended
GRUEL thin porridge
GRUFF surly; rude; churlish
GRUME a blood-clot **Med.**
GRUNT snort like a pig
GRYDE gride; grate
GUACO plant; snake-bite antidote **B.**
GUANA American lizard **Z.**
GUANO sea-fowl's manure
GUARD shield; watch; bulwark
GUAVA pear-shaped fruit **B.**
GUESS surmise; conjecture; divine
GUEST visitor; lodger

GUIDE pilot; signpost; control
GUILD trade's union; fraternity
GUILE craft; duplicity; cunning
GUILT sin   **Law**
GUIRD Cuban instrument   **Mus.**
GUISE garb; aspect; manner
GULAR (throat)
GULCH gully; gorge; ravine
GULES heraldic red-
GULFY full of whirlpools
GULLY water-worn channel; (cricket)
GUMBO a stew; okra soup
GUMMY viscous, sticky
GUNNY Bengal sacking
GURGE whirlpool (obs.)
GURRY fish-offal
GUSTO zest; relish; enjoyment
GUSTY squally; stormy; puffy
GUTTA Doric ornament
GUTTY old type golf ball
GUYED mocked; ridiculed; derided
GUYOT submarine mountain
GYALL gayal; jungle bull   **Z.**
GYBED (a sailing manoeuvre)   **Naut.**
GYGIS tern genus   **Z.**
GYPSY gipsy; zingaro
GYRAL revolving; whirling
GYRON heraldic device
GYRUS convolution of the brain   **Med.**
GYVES bonds; fetters; shackles

H

HABIT dress; usage; wont; custom
HABLE habile; able (Spens.)
HADES the abode of the dead
HADJI pilgrim (Arab); hajji
HAFIZ knowledge of the Koran
HAICK Arab wrap
HAIKH an Armenian
HAILY apt to hail; icy
HAIRY vairy; furry
HAJJI hadji; pilgrim (Arab)
HAKIM wise man; physician (Arab)
HALED hauled; dragged along
HALFA esparto grass   **B.**
HALLO ! hello ! hillo !
HALMA a game
HALVE bisect; divide
HANAP pewter goblet
HANCE haunch (Arch.)
HANCH to snap
HANDY near; dexterous; adroit
HANKY handkerchief
HANSE a league (German)
HAPLY perchance; peradventure
HAPPY joyous; lucky; opportune
HARAS stud; breeding establishment
HARDS hurds; refuse of flax
HARDY bold; intrepid; robust

HARED sprinted; sped; ran
HAREM seraglio; zenana
HARLE harl; flax-fibre
HARPY fabulous monster; vulture   **Z.**
HARPY golden eagle; extortioner   **Z.**
HARRY harass; ravage; raid
HARSH raucous; strident; caustic
HASTE alacrity; speed; hustle
HASTY swift; reckless; headlong
HATCH to plot; doorway; to shade
HATED loathed; abominated
HATER abhorrer; detester
HATHI wild Indian elephant   **Z.**
HATTO bishop eaten by rats
HAULM halm; stubble   **B.**
HAUNT frequent; importune; resort
HAURL harl; rough-cast
HAUSA Northern Nigerian
HAVAS news-agency
HAVEN port; refuge; asylum
HAVER to drivel; blather
HAVOC waste; carnage; devastation
HAWSE part of ship's bows   **Naut.**
HAZED bullied; punished
HAZEL a colour; nut-tree   **B.**
HAZRI Indian breakfast
HEADS or tails; latrines   **Naut.**
HEADY rash; hasty; wilful
HEADY intoxicating
HEALD warp guide in a loom
HEAPY in piles
HEARD listened to; tried   **Law**
HEART core; centre; spirit
HEATH shrubs; common land   **B.**
HEAVE to raise, push, haul   **Naut.**
HEAVY weighty, serious
HEDGE lay off; enclose; fence
HEFTY heavy; strong; powerful
HEIGH !
HELIO a heliograph
HELIX a spiral; a snail   **Z.**
HELLO ! hallo ! hillo ! hollo !
HELOT Spartan slave; serf
HELVE axe-handle; haft
HEMAL haemal; (blood)   **Med.**
HE-MAN
HEMPY like hemp
HENCE henceforth; away; therefore
HENNA a dye; a shrub   **B.**
HENRY electrical induction unit   **Meas.**
HEPAR a sulphur compound   **Chem.**
HERBY herbaceous; herbous
HEROD a tyrant
HERON a wading bird   **Z.**
HERSE a portcullis
HERTZ unit of electrical frequency   **Mea**
HERUT political party (Israel)
HET-UP annoyed, angry
HEVEA rubber-tree   **B.**
HEWED axed; hacked; fashioned

HEWER cutter; sculptor; miner
HIDER one who conceals
HIGHT hecht; to command; to call
HIKED tramped
HIKER rambler; pedestrian
HILCH to hobble; a limp (Sc.)
HILLY undulating
HILUM the eye of a bean   **B.**
HINDI Indian dialect
HINDU
HINGE depend; turn; hang
HINNY whinny; a mule   **Z.**
HIPPO the river-horse   **Z.**
HIRED chartered; leased; rented
HIRER an employer of labour
HITCH fasten; catch; obstacle; knot
HITHE hythe; haven; port
HIVED stored; gathered
HIVER an apiarist
HIVES the croup; nettle-rash   **Med.**
HOARD amass; garner; save; secrete
HOARY venerable; ancient; silvery
HOAST a cough; to cough
HOBBY recreation; horse; falcon   **Z.**
HOBIT mortar; short gun
HOCUS to cheat; to drug
HODGE a rustic
HOGAN strong liquor
HOIST hoise; heave; elevate
HOLEY holed; riddled
HOLLA!
HOLLO!
HOLLY an evergreen   **B.**
HOMER homing pigeon   **Z., Meas.**
HONED whetted; sharpened
HONEY sweetness
HOOCH fire-water
HOOEY HOO-HA balderdash
HOOKA hookah; Turkish pipe
HOOKY full of barbs
HOOLY carefully; softly (Sc.)
HOOSH a stew; a mixture
HOOVE a cattle disease
HOPED desired; anticipated
HOPPO Chinese overseer
HOPPY flavoured with hops
HOSED drenched; watered
HORAL horary; hourly
HORDE clan; throng; gang; crew
HORNY callous
HORSE steed; palfrey; nag; cob   **Z.**
HORSE cavalry; flogging frame
HORSY horsey; equine
HORUS son of Osiris (Egypt)
HOTEL inn; tavern; hostel
HOTLY eagerly; ardently; fervidly
HOUGH hamstring; the ham
HOUND pursue; chase   **Z.**
HOURI a nymph of paradise; peri
HOUSE mansion; domicile; lineage

HOVEL shelter; hut; cabin; shed
HOVER hang; vacillate; wave
HOWDY a midwife (Sc.); howdie
HOWEL cooper's tool   **Tool**
HOWFF houff; a haunt; resort (Sc.)
HOWSO howsoever; although
HUBBY husband
HUFFY petulant; irritable
HULCH hunch; bump; bunch
HULKY unwieldy; clumsy
HULLO! hallo!
HULLY husky
HUMAN mortal; cosmical; rational
HUMET abbreviated fesse (Her.)
HUMIC wet; dank; mouldy
HUMID damp; moist
HUMPH!
HUMPY Australian native hut
HUMUS rich soil
HUNCH presentiment; hump; lump
HUNKS miser; niggard
HUNYA fighting rams   **Z.**
HURDS hards; flax refuse
HURLY confusion; flurry
HURRY hasten; expedite; speed
HURST a grove; a wood
HUSKY Canadian sled-dog   **Z.**
HUSKY hoarse; raucous; guttural
HUSSY housewife; brazen girl
HUTCH coop; chest; bin
HUTIA West Indian hog-rat   **Z.**
HUZZA also hurra
HYADS hyades; cluster of stars
HYDRA many headed water-snake   **Z.**
HYDRO a spa; a hotel
HYENA hyen; a carnivore   **Z.**
HYLEG ruling planet in horoscope
HYLIC materialistic
HYMEN God of Marriage
HYOID tongue-bone   **Med.**
HYPHA a fungus filament   **B.**
HYRAX rock-rabbit; cony   **Z.**
HYSON green tea (China)   **B.**
HYTHE hithe; haven; port

I

ICENI Ancient British tribe
ICHOR a god's blood; a fluid   **Med.**
ICIER colder
ICILY frigidly; frostily
ICING a sugar-coating
ICKER an ear of corn (Sc.)   **B.**
ICTIC abrupt; sudden
ICTUS a stroke; accentuation
IDEAL Utopian; fanciful; visionary
IDIOM peculiarity of phraseology
IDIOT Gothamite; Bedlamite; moron
IDIST Ido linguist
IDLED slacked

IDLER drone; lounger; trifler
IDOLA phantasies; apparitions
IDRIS mythical Welsh giant; (water)
IDYLL pastoral poem
IGLOO Esquimo snow-hut
ILEAC colicky; iliac   **Med.**
ILEUM (intestine)   **Med.**
ILIAD epic poem; (siege of Troy)
ILIUM part of hip-bone   **Med.**
IMAGE ikon; idol; copy; likeness
IMAGO perfect state of insect   **Z.**
IMAUM imam; Islamic priest
IMBAR embar; exclude
IMBED embed
IMBER the great northern diver   **Z.**
IMBOW to arch
IMBUE dye; steep; stain; permeate
IMMEW emmew; to confine
IMMIT inject
IMMIX to mingle
IMPEL urge; drive; incite; actuate
IMPEN to pen; to write
IMPLY mean; hint; signify; involve
IMPUT input; charge
INAJA Brazilian palm   **B.**
INANE fatuous; empty; void; vapid
INAPT unfit; inapposite; clumsy
INARM to encircle
INCOG incognito; disguised
INCUR contract; gain; acquire
INCUS ear-bone like an anvil   **Med.**
INCUT inset
INDEX pointer; forefinger; exponent
INDRA Hindu God of Rain
INDRI babakoto; large lemur   **Z.**
INDUE endue; invest; endow
INEPT inane; futile; pointless
INERM without prickles   **B.**
INERT slack; dull; torpid; inactive
INEYE to graft
INFER deduce; gather; surmise
INFIX implant; ingraft; instil
INGLE fireside
INGOT a mass of metal
INION the nape of the neck   **Med.**
INKED
INKER recording device
INKLE broad linen tape
INKOS Zulu chief
INLAW c.f. outlaw
INLAY (buhl); tesselate
INLET bay; bight; creek; entrance
INNER interior; (next to a bull)
INPUT c.f. output; charge
INSET an insertion; implant
INTER bury; inhume; entomb
INULA herb, a   **B.**
INURE enure; harden; toughen; train
INURN bury; entomb
INUUS Barbary ape   **Z.**

INVAR an alloy of nickel and steel
INWIT intuition; conscience
IODAL } containing iodine   **Chem.**
IODIC }
IONIC (Ionia)
IRADE Turkish written decree   **Law**
IRAQI, IRAKI dwellers in Iraq
IRATE wroth; ireful; angry; incensed
IRENE Roman goddess of peace
IRIAN relating to the iris   **Med.**
IRISH Hibernian
IRITE an iridium compound   **Min.**
IRKED bored; wearied; jaded
IRONS gyves; golf clubs   **Naut.**
IRONY satire; sarcasm; mockery
ISIAC referring to Isis
ISLAM (Mohammedanism)   **Eccl.**
ISLET isle; eyot; atoll
ISSUE egress; vent; outcome; result
ISTLE } aloe fibre   **B.**
IXTLE }
ITCHY scratchy; desirous; uneasy
IULUS julus; catkin; wireworm   **B., Z.**
IVIED ivyed; covered with ivy
IVORY dentine   **Z.**
IVRIT modernised Hebrew (language)
IXION wheel-bound king; (Hell)
IZARD Pyrenean ibex or chamois   **Z.**

J

JABOT lace frill
JACKS wooden wedges
JADED weary; tied; fagged; exhausted
JADOO artificial silk
JAFFA orange
JAGER the great skua; pirate gull   **Z.**
JAGGY uneven; serrated; notched
JALAP a cathartic root   **B., Med.**
JAMBE a piece of leg armour
JAMBU rose-apple tree   **B.**
JAMES a flunkey
JAMMY smothered in jam
JANTU Indian water-raising device
JANTY jaunty; airy; showy
JANUS god of doorways
JAPAN varnish; lacquer; enamel
JARDE tumour on a horse's leg
JASEY worsted wig
JASPE veined jaspar   **Min.**
JAUNT trip; outing; excursion
JAWED talked; lectured
JEANS overalls
JEDGE gauge; dean's warrant (Sc.)
JEHAD Islamic Holy War
JELLY gelatin; aspic
JEMMY gemmy; spruce; lever   **Tool**
JENNY spinning machine; billiard shot
JERID Turkish javelin
JERKY spasmodic; convulsive; irregular

JERRY a German
JESSE candlestick; stained window **Eccl.**
JETTY jut; projection; a pier **Naut.**
JEWEL gem; trinket
JEWRY Judaea
JHEEL Indian marsh
JHOOM jungle cultivation
JIBED gibed; sneered; taunted **Naut.**
JIFFY a moment; an instant
JIMMY jemmy; a lever **Tool**
JIMPY, JINTY slender; elegeant (Sc.)
JINGO ultra-militarist
JINKS high jinks; merry-making
JIPPO jupon; vest
JOCKO a chimpanzee **Z.**
JODEL yodel; Tyrolese singing **Mus.**
JOINT splice; seam; united; concerted
JOIST floor beam
JOKED bantered; rallied
JOKER jester; wag; humorist; a card
JOLLY a marine; mirthful; a boat **Naut.**
JONAH
JORAM }
JORUM } drinking bowl or its contents
JOTUN Norse giant
JOUGS iron neck-ring; pillory
JOULE electrical unit of work **Meas.**
JOUST giust; tilt; encounter; a tourney
JUDAS traitor; spy-hole; tree **B.**
JUDGE decide; arbiter; critic **Law**
JUGAL malar; (cheek-bone) **Med.**
JUICE sap; fluid extract; petrol
JUICY succulent; moist; lush
JULAP } sweet medicine;
JULEP } mixed liquor **Med.**
JULIS a wrasse; a small fish **Z.**
JULUS iulus; catkin; wire-worm **B., Z.**
JUMBO elephant; locomotive **Z.**
JUMPY nervous; nervy
JUNCO North American snow-bird **Z.**
JUNTA Spanish Grand Council; cabal
JUNTO coterie; clique; faction
JUPON jippo; surcoat; petticoat
JURAL legal; lawful
JURAT an alderman; (affidavit) **Law**
JUROR a juryman
JUSSI Manilla textile fabric
JUTES invaders from Jutland
JUTTY a jetty

K

KAABA caaba; sacred stone at Mecca
KAAMA hartebeest; S. Afr. antelope **Z.**
KABOB, KEBAB oriental food
KADIR (cup for pig-sticking)
KAFIR Kaffir
KALAN sea otter of North Pacific **Z.**
KALIF Calif; Caliph
KALPA calpa; a day of Brahma **Eccl.**

KAMES glacial deposits **Min.**
KAMIS Eastern tunic
KANDY candy; S. Indian weight **Meas.**
KANEH caneh; 6 cubits Hebrew **Meas.**
KAPOK fibre of silk-cotton tree **B.**
KARMA theory of inevitable consequence
KAROB 24th part of a grain **Meas.**
KAROO South African plateau
KARST limestone caves (Yugoslavia)
KASHA dress material
KASSU catechu made from betel-nut **B.**
KAURI New Zealand fir tree **B.**
KAYAK, Kaiak Eskimo seal-skin canoe
KAYLE ninepin; skittle
KECKS fool's parsley **B.**
KEDGE small anchor **Naut.**
KEDGE kidge; brisk; lively
KEDGY cadgy; happy; merry; wanton
KEEPS permanent possession
KEESH carburet of iron **Min.**
KEEVE vat; fermenting tub
KEFIR fermented milk
KELPY malignant water-sprite (Sc.)
KELTY a penalty drink (Sc.)
KEMPS the plantain
KERNE Irish foot-soldier; boor
KETCH two-masted vessel **Naut.**
KETEN colourless gas **Chem.**
KEVEL belaying pin **Naut.**
KEVEL young gazelle **Z.**
KEYED wedged
KHAKI
KHEDA elephant enclosure
KHMER people and language (Cambodia)
KIANG Tibetan wild horse **Z.**
KIBED chapped with cold
KIDDY youngster
KIDEL kiddle; fish-trap
KIDGE kedge; brisk; pot-bellied
KILEY kyley; boomerang
KINGS two Biblical books
KINKY crotchety; entangled
KINSH stone-mason's lever **Tool**
KIOSK covered stall
KITTY pool; kitten **Z.**
KLANG complex musical tone **Mus.**
KLICK click
KLOOF S. African ravine
KNACK skill; dexterity; faculty
KNARL gnarl; a knot in wood
KNAVE rascal; rogue; caitiff
KNEAD mix; blend; incorporate
KNEED baggy
KNEEL (KNELT) bend (bent) knee: submit
KNELL toll; ring; sound
KNEPH an Egyptian diety
KNIFE to stab; to lance **Tool**
KNOCK rap; beat; buffet
KNOLL knell; hillock; mound

KNOSP ornamental flower-bud
KNOTE (rope-making)
KNOUD the grey gurnard   **Z.**
KNOUT Russian whip
KNOWN understood; recognized
KNUBS waste silk
KNURL knob; milled edge   **Tool**
KNURR knot in wood
KOALA Australian bear   **Z.**
KOBIL cobble; small boat   **Naut.**
KODAK a camera
KOKOB venomous serpent   **Z.**
KOKRA wood used for flutes   **B.**
KONDO bronze-gilt finish
KOPEC kopek; Russian farthing   **Coin**
KOPJE S. African hill
KORAN Moslem Bible   **Eccl.**
KOTOW kow-tow; make obeisance
KRAAL native village
KRAIT venemous snake   **Z.**
KRANG kreng; whale flesh
KRONE Austrian coin   **Coin**
KRUPP a gun
KUDOS credit; prestige; fame
KUFIC early Arab alphabet
KUKRI Gurkha knife
KULAK Russian peasant proprietor
KUNDA lawyer-vine   **B.**
KUTCH cutch; catechu   **B.**
KVASS Russian beer
KWELA tin whistle (African)
KYACK American pack saddle
KYLEY kiley; boomerang
KYLIN Chinese or Japanese dragon
KYLIX Greek drinking vessel
KYLOE Hebridean cattle   **Z.**
KYOTO Japanese pottery
KYPOO extract of catechu
KYRIE (Mass)   **Eccl., Mus.**

L

LABEL an adhesive stamp; (Her.)
LABEL dripstone; codicil
LABIS cochlear; eucharistic spoon **Eccl.**
LACED stiffened; twined
LACET lace-work
LADAS a classic runner
LADED burdened; loaded
LADEN freighted
LADIN Swiss Latin
LADLE scoop; bale; dole
LAGAN ligan; (flotsam)   **Law**
LAGER beer
LAINE woollen fabric
LAIRD Scottish landowner
LAITY laymen
LAKIN ladykin; small damsel
LAMED crippled
LAMIA sorceress; witch

LAMMY sailor's quilted jumper
LANCE lancet; spear; pierce
LANCH launch
LANDE sterile tract (Fr.)
LANKY lean; tall; gaunt
LAPEL part of a coat
LAPIS stone; (calico-printing)   **Min.**
LAPSE slip; slide; indiscretion
LARCH genus of trees   **B.**
LARDY full of lard
LARES Roman household gods
LARGE massive; bulky; copious
LARGO slowly   **Mus.**
LARKY sportive; frolicsome
LARRY lorry; truck
LARUM alarm
LARUS aquatic bird   **Z.**
LARVA caterpillar; grub; maggot   **Z.**
LASER resin; searing ray   **Med.**
LASSO rope with running noose
LATCH catch; fasten
LATER tardier; more recent
LATEX sap   **B.**
LATHE county division; machine   **Tool**
LATHI bamboo cudgel
LATHY thin; long and slender
LATIN Roman
LAUGH deride; guffaw
LAURA a hermitage
LAUTU royal Inca badge
LAVED washed; bathed
LAVER brazen washing basin
LAVER edible sea-weed   **B.**
LAXLY loosely; slackly; remissly
LAY-BY parking bay
LAYER seam; stratum; bed; hen   **Z.**
LAZAR leper
LAZED tranquillized
LEACH to wash by percolation
LEADY leaden
LEAFY leavy; full of leaves
LEAKY not water tight; tattling
LEANT inclined; reposed; trusted
LEAPT jumped; sprang
LEARN acquire; hear; memorize
LEARY old mine-shaft
LEASE let; hire; tenure
LEASH three; bind; thong
LEAST smallest; minutest
LEAVE forsake; quit; depart
LEAVY leafy
LEDGE shelf; ridge; layer
LEDGY full of ridges
LEECH blood-sucker; doctor   **Z.**
LEECH edge of a sail   **Naut.**
LEERY sly
LEGAL lawful; licit; proper
LEGER a race; light; small
LEGGY lanky
LEMAN lover; gallant; paramour

LEMON a citrus	**B.**
LEMUR ghost; noctural monkey	**Z.**
LENCA Honduran Indian	
LENTO slowly	**Mus.**
LEPER lazar	**Med.**
LEPID jocose; pleasant	
LEPIS a scale	**Z.**
LEPRA leprosy	**Med.**
LEPTA (Greece)	**Coin**
LETCH to separate by percolation	
LETHE the river of oblivion	
LET-UP an alleviation	
LEVEE embankment; reception	
LEVEL raze; plane; even; flush	
LEVER a jemmy; prise	**Tool**
LEWIS a grip for masonry	
LIANA tropical climbing plant	**B.**
LIANG Chinese ounce	**Meas.**
LIART liard; lyart; dapple-gray	
LIBEL slander; defame; traduce	**Law**
LIBER bast; inner bark; a book	
LIBRA the Balance (Zodiac)	
LICIT lawful; permissible	
LIEGE vassal; subject; faithful	
LIFER prisoner sentenced for life	
LIGAN lagan; (flotsam)	**Law**
LIGHT kindle; illume; buoyant	
LIKED enjoyed; relished	
LIKEN to compare	
LIKIN Chinese transport duty	
LILAC a colour; a shrub	**B.**
LIMBO hell; paradise of fools	
LIMED cemented; ensnared; treated	
LIMEN threshold (Psychology)	
LIMIT restraint; bound; border	
LIMMA a semitone	**Mus.**
LINCH ledge; projection; cliff	
LINED care-worn; with lines	
LINEN flax cloth; underwear	
LINER a shim; a vessel	**Naut.**
LINGO speech; language	
LINGY active; limber; heathery	
LININ (cell nucleus)	
LINKS (cuff); golf course	
LIPPY half-a-gallon (Sc.)	**Meas.**
LISLE thread	
LISSE warp threads in tapestry	
LISTS the combat-ground	
LITAS Lithuanian currency	
LITHE⎱ lythe; active; supple; pliant;	
LITHY⎰ pliable; easily bent; limber	
LITHO a lithograph	
LITRE nearly 1¾ pints	**Meas.**
LIVED dwelt; abode; survived	
LIVEN enliven; animate; vivify	
LIVER internal organ	**Med.**
LIVID black and blue	
LIVRE old French franc	**Coin**
LLAMA Peruvian camel	**Z.**
LLANO S. American plain	

LOACH loche; a river-fish	**Z.**
LOAMY soil	
LOATH reluctant; unwilling	
LOBAR, LOBED lobate	**B. Med.**
LOBBY passage; to seek votes	
LOCAL an inn; topical; regional	
LOCHE a loach; a river-fish	**Z.**
LOCUM locum tenens; a deputy	
LOCUS locality	
LODGE reside; sojourn; deposit	
LOESS alluvial deposits	
LOFTY stately; imposing; towering	
LOGAN poised rock; a berry	**B.**
LOGGE miller's thumb; small fish	**Z.**
LOGIA oracles; dicta	
LOGIC reasoning; dialectics	
LOGIE sham jewels	
LOGOS the Divine Word	
LOKUM Turkish delight (sweetmeat)	
LOLLY lollipop; a lump; money	
LOLOS aboriginal race (China)	
LOOFA luffa; flesh-brush	**B.**
LOONY mad; lunatic	
LOOPY kinky; dotty	
LOOSE liberate; slack; vague; lax	
LOPED ran with easy strides	
LORAN Radio-navigation system	**Naut.**
LORDS cricket ground	
LORIS Cingalese monkey	**Z.**
LORRY larry; truck; vehicle	
LOSER also ran; (billiards)	
LOTTO a game	
LOTUS lotos; water lily	**B.**
LOUGH loch; an arm of the sea	
LOUIS obsolete French gold coin	
LOUSE parasitic insect	**Z.**
LOUSY mean; contemptible	
LOVAT a tweed	
LOVED adored; liked; esteemed	
LOVER a Romeo; admirer; swain	
LOWER depress; degrade; frown	
LOWLY meek; humble; modest	
LOXIA cross-bill birds	**Z.**
LOYAL leal; true; devoted	
LUBRA black woman (Australia)	
LUCID clear; limpid; sane; pure	
LUCKY fortunate; auspicious	
LUCRE gain; profit; wealth	
LUGER automatic pistol	
LUMEN unit of luminous flux	**Meas.**
LUMPY coagulated	
LUNAR	
LUNCH luncheon; tiffin	
LUNGE, LONGE thrust; (equitation)	
LUNIK artificial moon satellite	
LUPIN a flower	**B.**
LUPPA cloth of gold or silver	
LUPUS skin disease	**Med.**
LURCH stagger; sway; roll; toss	
LURED enticed; decoyed; inveigled	

LURID glowing; sensational
LUSHY tipsy
LUSTY robust; vigorous; sturdy
LUSUS a freak; an exception
LUTED sealed with luting
LUTER lute-player   **Mus.**
LYART liart; liard; dapple-gray
LYCEE French school
LYING mendacious; recumbent
LYMPH a fluid; vaccine   **Med.**
LYNCH mob law; kill
LYRIC a short poem; tuneful
LYRID meteor from Lyra
LYRIE Manx shearwater gull   **Z.**
LYSIS recovery   **Med.**
LYSOL a disinfectant   **Chem.**
LYSSA hydrophobia; rabies
LYTHE the pollack   **Z.**
LYTHE lithe; flexible; agile

M

MACAW parrot; palm   **Z., B.**
MACER a court usher (Sc.)   **Law**
MACHE materials for papier maché
MACLE double crystal   **Min.**
MACON a French wine
MADAM madame
MADGE leaden hammer; magpie   **Z.**
MADIA the tar-weed; oil-plant   **B.**
MADID moist; wet; damp
MADLY deliriously; insanely
MAFIA Sicilian secret society
MAGAR Indian crocodile   **Z.**
MAGIC witchery; sorcery; charm
MAGMA plutonic rock   **Min.**
MAGOG
MAGOT Barbary ape   **Z.**
MAHDI Moslem prophet (dervish) **Eccl.**
MAHWA butter-tree   **B.**
MAIZE Indian corn   **B.**
MAJOR a rank; greater
MAKER creator; manufacturer
MAKWA Chinese jacket
MALAR cheek-bone   **Med.**
MALAY
MALIC (apples)   **B.**
MALIK village headman (Ind.)
MALTY malt-flavoured
MAMBA S. African snake   **Z.**
MAMBO dance   **Mus.**
MAMMA mother
MAMMY negro nurse
MANED having a mane
MANEH mina; 50 shekels   **Coin**
MANES ghosts; departed souls
MANET stage direction " remain "
MANGA covering for a cross
MANGE parasitic disease   **Med.**
MANGO a fruit   **B.**

MANGY scabious
MANIA frenzy; delirium; craziness
MANIS the scaly ant-eater   **Z.**
MANLY hardy; intrepid; bold
MANNA food; a form of sap   **B.**
MANOR freehold estate
MANSE the minister's house (Sc.)
MANTA ox-ray; a sea-fish   **Z.**
MANUS the hand   **Med.**
MAORI native race (N. Zealand)
MAPLE sugar-tree   **B.**
MAQUI Chilian evergreen shrub   **B.**
MARAH bitterness (Hebrew)
MARAY moray; muray; eel-like fish   **Z.**
MARCH border; advance; walk
MARDY spoilt; naughty
MARGE brink; brim; verge; edge
MARID powerful jinn
MARLY clay-like
MARRY unite; wed; espouse; join
MARSH bog; swamp; fen; morass
MASAI African tribe
MASER micro-wave amplifier   **El.**
MASHY mashie; a golf club
MASON stone-worker
MASSA master
MASSE a billiard stroke
MASSY massive; bulky
MASTY full of beech-mast   **B.**
MATCH suit; tally; agree; lucifer
MATED (chess); married; matched
MATER mother
MATEY friendly
MATIN morning
MATTE crude black copper   **Min.**
MAUND an Eastern weight   **Meas.**
MAUVE a mallow colour
MAVIS the thrush   **Z.**
MAWKY crotchety; maudlin
MAXIM gun; adage; saw; precept
MAYAN native of Honduras
MAY-BE perhaps
MAYOR
MAZDA Supreme Deity (Zend-Avesta)
MAZED bewildered; dazed; astounded
MAZER goblet; bowl
MEALY farinaceous
MEANS mode; agency; method; wealth
MEANT signified; purposed
MEASE a group of 500   **Meas.**
MEATY fleshy
MEBOS salted apricots (S. Africa)
MECCA desired objective
MEDAL
MEDIA agencies
MEDIC clover, lucerne, etc.   **B.**
MEDOC a red French wine
MEINY a retinue (Shak.)
MELEE fray; brawl; scuffle; mixture
MELES badger genus   **Z.**

MELIC lyric; a grass **B.**
MELON a gourd **B.**
MERCY pity; lenity; clemency; grace
MERGE coalesce; immerse; submerge
MERIT desert; worth; credit; earn
MERLE the blackbird **Z.**
MERRY the English wild cherry **B.**
MERRY gay; blithe; jocund; lively
MESAL mesial; median; central
MESHY netted; reticulated
MESNE intermediate **Law**
MESON cosmic ray constituent
MESSY mussy; muddled; disordered
METAL bullion; courage; ore
METAL broken stone for roads
METED measured; apportioned
METER a measuring instrument
METIC alien; foreign resident
METIF octaroon
METIS American half-breed
METOL (photography) **Chem.**
METRA a measuring instrument
METRE (verse); 39.37 inches **Meas.**
METRO Underground railway (Fr.)
MEUTE mew; cage for hawks
MEWED (cats); moulted; confined
MEZZO middle **Mus.**
MIAOW miaul; caterwaul
MIASM miasma; effluvia **Med.**
MICHE hide; skulk; pilfer
MICKY Irish lad; young bull **Z.**
MIDAS had a golden touch
MIDDY a midshipman **Naut.**
MIDGE dwarf; gnat **Z.**
MID-ON (cricket)
MIDST among; middle
MIGHT force; power; main
MILCH giving milk
MILER a mile runner
MILKY lacteal; lactic
MIMED mimicked; acted
MIMIC ape; copy; mime; mock
MINCE chop fine; palliate
MINED dug; undermined
MINER sapper
MINIE old type rifle
MINIM dwarf; single drop; note **Mus.**
MINOR petty; lesser; small **Mus.**
MINOS King of Crete
MINUS less; lacking; wanting
MIRED bogged; unit of colour temperature **Meas.**
MIRTH glee; gaiety; hilarity
MIRZA a Persian title
MIS-DO err; sin; trespass
MISER skinflint; hoarder; niggard
MISLE mizzle; rain in small drops
MISLY drizzly
MISSY sentimental; namby-pamby
MISTY dim; obscure; cloudy
MITRA Persian sun-god

MITRE angle of 45 degrees; cap **Eccl.**
MITTS mittens
MIXED blended; mingled; confused
MIXEN midden
MIXER a good companion
MIX-UP mêlée; scuffle; brawl
MIZZY bog; swamp; quagmire
MOBBY fermented fruit juice
MOBLE wrap the head in a hood
MOBUS motor-bus
MOCHA agate; coffee **Min.**
MOCHE packet of spun silk
MODAL moody; (logic)
MODEL example; pattern; copy
MODER matrix of astrolobe
MODUS style; a method **Law**
MOGUL a Mongolian
MOHUR Indian gold coin **Coin**
MOIRE watered silk
MOIST dank; clammy; humid
MOLAR grinding; a tooth
MOLLY the wagtail bird **Z.**
MOLTO very; much **Mus.**
MOMUS God of Ridicule
MONAD **Chem.**
MONAL a pheasant **Z.**
MONDE society (Fr.)
MONEL an alloy
MONEY cash; coin; currency; wealth
MONGO (Mongolia) **Coin**
MONOX the crowberry **B.**
MONTE a game like faro
MONTH
MOOCH slouch; loiter
MOODY sullen; morose; glum; captious
MOOED lowed
MOOLA mollah; Moselm judge **Law**
MOONY dreamy
MOORY sterile; boggy
MOOSE the elk **Z.**
MOPED pined; motor cycle
MOPPY tipsy; fuddled
MOPSY mopsey; untidy woman
MOPUS a mope; drone; money
MORAL ethical; virtuous; meaning
MORAT mulberry juice
MORAY maray; fish of eel-type **Z.**
MOREL cherry; nightshade **B.**
MORIL morel; mushroom **B.**
MORMO bugbear
MORNE blunt head of a lance
MORON childish imbecile
MORSE signalling; the walrus **Z.**
MORUS mulberry **B.**
MOSES a law-giver
MOSEY hurry off (U.S.A.)
MOSSY cryptogamous **B.**
MOTED dusty
MOTEL motorists' hotel
MOTET sacred melody **Mus.**

MOTHY moth-eaten
MOTIF theme; feature **Mus.**
MOTOR automobile
MOTTO pithy maxim; slogan
MOUCH mooch; skulk; slouch
MOULD blight; create; shape; form
MOULT to cast feathers
MOUND knoll; tumulus; hillock
MOUNT climb; scale; ascend; tower
MOURN bewail; lament; deplore
MOUSE **Z.**
MOUSY mouselike; quiet
MOUTH opening; orifice; declaim
MOVED shifted; budged; roused
MOVER proposer
MOWED scythed; cut
MOWER a mowing machine
MOYEN means; influence
MPRET Albanian ruler
MUCIC an acid **Chem.**
MUCID musty; mouldy; slimy
MUCKY dirty; filthy; muddy
MUCOR mould; fungus **B.**
MUCRO stiff sharp point **B.**
MUCUS slime **Med.**
MUDAR madar; medicinal herb **B.**
MUDDY turbid; impure; obscure
MUDIR Eastern Governor
MUFTI Moslem priest or lawyer
MUFTI civilian clothing
MUGGY damp and warm
MUGIL the mullet fish **Z.**
MULCH mulsh; litter· manure
MULCT fine; penalize **Law**
MULEY mooly; hornless
MULGA Australian acacia **B.**
MULLA mullah; fanatic
MULSE mulled wine
MULSH mulch; litter; manure
MUMMY bituminous drug; (Egypt)
MUMPS epidemic parotitis **Med.**
MUNCH chew; crunch; masticate
MUNGO shoddy; inferior cloth
MURAL fixed to a wall
MURAY cf. moray; murry **Z.**
MURED immured; pent
MUREX Tyrian dye; molluscs **Z.**
MURKY lurid; dark; lowering
MURRA fluor-spar **Min.**
MURRE razorbill or guillemot **Z.**
MURRY also **MORAY**; eel-like fish **Z.**
MUSCA fly genus **Z.**
MUSCI the mosses **B.**
MUSED pondered; contemplated
MUSER ruminator
MUSET a gap in a fence (Fr.)
MUSHY pulpy
MUSIC melody; harmony **Mus.**
MUSKY fragrant like musk
MUSSY messy; disordered

MUSTY mucid; fusty; mouldy
MUTCH a woman's cap (Sc.)
MUTED muffled; pianissimo **Mus.**
MUZZY dazed; confused
MYALL Australian hard-wood tree **B.**
MYOID like muscle **Med.**
MYOPE myops; short-sighted person
MYOPY myopia; short-sight **Med.**
MYRRH scented resin **B.**
MYSIS the opossum shrimp **Z.**
MYXON fish of mullet family **Z.**

N

NABEE aconite poison **Med.**
NABIT crushed candy
NABOB nawab; wealthy individual
NACRE mother-of-pearl
NADIR opposite to zenith
NAEVE a birthmark **Med.**
NAGGY querulous ; quarrelsome
NAGOR Senegal antelope **Z.**
NAIAD water-nymph
NAIVE artless; ingenuous; candid
NAKED stark; open; bare; denuded
NAKER a kettle-drum **Mus.**
NAKIR examiner of the dead (Koran)
NAMED yclept; specified; dubbed
NAMER nominator
NANDU rhea; American ostrich **Z.**
NANNY nurse; goat **Z.**
NAPOO (ne plus); finished
NAPPY drowsy; a dish
NARES nostrils **Med.**
NARIS nostril **Med.**
NARRE near (Spens.)
NASAL an errhine **Med.**
NASTY foul; loathsome; ribald
NATAL nascent; initial
NATCH notch; the rump
NATTE interlaced ornamentation
NATTY neat; spruce; trig
NAVAL nautical; maritime; marine
NAVEL the centre **Med.**
NAVEW wild turnip **B.**
NAVVY excavator; canal digger
NAWAB nabob; Eastern ruler
NAZIR Indian bailiff
NAZIS German national socialists
NEATH beneath
NEBBY saucy (Sc.)
NEBEL the Jew's harp **Mus.**
NEDDY donkey; moke; burro **Z.**
NEEDS perforce; necessarily
NEEDY poor; indigent; penniless
NEELE neeld; needle; sharp point
NEESE neeze; sneeze
NEGRE nigger-colour (Fr.)
NEGRO a nigger; a darkie
NEGUS Abyssinian King

NEGUS a drink; hot punch	**NONCE** the present	
NEIGH to whinny	**NONES** (Roman calendar)	
NEIST next	**NONET** piece for 9 singers	**Mus.**
NEMPT named; yclept (Spens.)	**NOOPS** the cloud-berry	**B.**
NEPER power ratio unit **Meas.**	**NOOSE** loop; lasso; lariat	
NERVE brace; pluck; hardihood **Med.**	**NOPAL** Mexican cactus	**B.**
NERVY vigorous; nervous; fearful	**NORIA** Persian water-wheel	
NESKI Arabic script	**NORMA** a rule; a model	
NETTY meshy; reticulated	**NORNS** Scandinavian Fates	
NEUME a musical phrase **Mus.**	**NORSE**	
NEVEL to punch (Sc.)	**NORTH** septentrion (Shak.)	
NEVER not at any time	**NOSED** snooped	
NEWEL finial of a staircase	**NOSEY** inquisitive	
NEWLY recently; freshly	**NOTCH** natch; dent; nick; incision	
NEWSY chatty; gossipy	**NOTED** famous; recorded; remarked	
NEXUS connecting link; bond **Law**	**NOTUM** back of a bug	**Z.**
NICER more pleasant; more exact	**NOTUS** southerly wind	
NICHE nook; corner; recess	**NOVEL** recent; new; book of fiction	
NICOL (polarizing light)	**NOWAY** in no manner; nohow	
NIDGE to dress stones	**NOWED** tied in a knot (Her.); coiled	
NIDOR the smell of cooking	**NOWEL** foundry loam	
NIDUS nest; a breeding place **Med.**	**NOYAU** almond cordial	
NIECE daughter of brother or sister	**NUCHA** nape of the neck	**Med.**
NIFFY smelly	**NUDGE** jog; jostle; elbow	
NIFTY classy; stylish	**NULLO** a game	
NIGHT darkness; obscurity	**NURSE** tend; foster; nurture	
NIHIL nil; zero; nothing	**NUTTY**	
NIKAU New Zealand palm **B.**	**NYALA** African antelope	**Z.**
NINNY simpleton; nitwit; palooka	**NYLON** artificial silk	
NINON dress material	**NYMPH** maiden	
NINTH	**NYULA** parasite insect	**Z.**
NIOBE a weeper		
NIPPY a waitress; alert; parsimonous	**O**	
NIRLS herpes; shingles **Med.**		
NISAN Jewish April	**OAKEN**	
NISUS an effort; an endeavour	**OAKUM** picked; tarred rope **Naut.**	
NITID gleaming; shining	**OARED** rowed	
NITON gaseous element **Chem.**	**OASIS** fertile spot in desert	
NITRE saltpetre **Chem.**	**OATEN**	
NITTY full of nits	**OAVES** dolts; changelings	
NIVAL nivose; niveous; snowy	**OBANG** an old Japanese gold **Coin**	
NIXIE water-elf	**OBEAH** obi; West African magic	
NIZAM Indian prince	**OBESE** abnormally fat; corpulent	
NOBBY smart; ornate	**OBOLE** weight of 10 or 12 grs. **Meas.**	
NOBEL invented dynamite; prize	**OCCUR** happen; befall; chance	
NOBLE patrician; obsolete gold **Coin**	**OCEAN** main; the deep	
NOBLY grandly; splendidly	**OCHRE** ocher; yellow pigment	
NODAL knotty **Mus.**	**OCHRY** yellowish-brown	
NODDY fool; sea-mew **Z.**	**OCREA** armoured shin-guard **Z., B.**	
NODUS knotty point	**OCTAD** series of eight	
NOHOW in no way	**OCTET** group of eight **Mus.**	
NOILS wool-combings	**OCTYL** organic radical **Chem.**	
NOINT anoint (Shak.)	**OCUBA** vegetable wax **B.**	
NOISE din; clamour; uproar	**ODDLY** queerly; quaintly	
NOISY blatant; vociferous; riotous	**ODEON** ⎫ ancient Grecian	
NOKES a boob	**ODEUM** ⎭ music hall	
NOMAD a wanderer; vagrant	**ODIUM** obloquy; hatred; enmity	
NOMEN name (Latin)	**ODOUR** scent; fragrance; perfume	
NOMIC customary	**ODYLE** mesmerism	
NOMOS Greek province	**OFBIT** devil's bit; a scabious **B.**	
	OFFAL carrion; garbage; refuse	

OFFER bid; tender; proposal
OFTEN oft; frequently; repeatedly
OGHAM Irish alphabet
OGIVE pointed arch
OGLED leered
OGLER
OILED lubricated
OILER oilcan; oilman
OKAPI type of giraffe   **Z.**
OLDEN ancient; aged; antique
OLDER more elderly
OLEIC an acid   **Chem.**
OLEON olein; fatty oil   **Chem.**
OLEUM fuming sulphuric acid   **Chem.**
OLIVE emblem of peace   **B.**
OLLAM Irish doctor   **Med.**
OLOGY theory in general
OMAHA a Sioux Indian of Nebraska
OMATI a Mexican Indian
OMBRE a card game
OMEGA last letter of Greek alphabet
ONCER he did not do it again
ONION a shallot   **B.**
ON-OFF control and keying electron
ONSET assault; attack; storm
ONYMY group nomenclature
OOMPH magnetic personality
OOPAK black tea
OOZED seeped; percolated
OPERA works   **Mus.**
OPINE suppose; surmise; ween
OPIUM a narcotic   **B.**
OPTED chosen; elected
OPTIC optical; the eye   **Med.**
ORACH a kind of spinach   **B.**
ORALE Papal veil   **Eccl.**
ORANG an ape   **Z.**
ORANT worshipper
ORATE spout; declaim; harangue
ORBED globular; spherical
ORBIT ambit; heavenly path; circuit
ORBIT the eye-socket   **Med.**
ORCIN purple dye   **B.**
ORDER bid; decree; enact; ukase
OREAD mountain nymph
ORGAL argal; crude tartar   **Chem.**
ORGAN medium; means   **Mus.**
ORIBI South African antelope   **Z.**
ORIEL mullioned window
ORION a constellation
ORIYA (Orissa, India) language
ORLON artificial textile fabric
ORLOP a ship's deck   **Naut.**
ORMER ear-shell   **Z.**
ORNIS avifauna; a bird   **Z.**
ORPIN yellow pigment
ORRIS gold or silver lace   **B.**
ORTYX American quail   **Z.**
ORVAL the herb clary   **B.**
ORYZA grass genus; rice   **B.**

OSCAN early Italic tribe
OSCAR film award
OSHAC gum-plant   **B.**
OSIER a willow   **B.**
OSMIC (osmium)   **Chem.**
OSRAM osmium and wolfram
OTARY genus of seals   **Z.**
OTHER different
OTTAR attar; aromatic oil
OTTER fishing device   **Z.**
OUBIT a hairy caterpillar   **Z.**
OUGHT aught; nought; a cipher
OUIJA planchette
OUNCE snow-leopard   **Meas., Z.**
OUNDY wavy; scalloped
OUPHE oaf; dolt; idiot (Shak.)
OUSEL ouzel; blackbird   **Z.**
OUTBY out of doors (Sc.)
OUTDO exceed; surpass; eclipse
OUTED ejected; thrown out; sacked
OUTER exterior; external; outside
OUTGO expenditure
OUTRE odd; bizarre; strange
OUZEL ousel; blackbird   **Z.**
OVARY seed-vessel   **Med.**
OVATE oval; egg-shaped
OVERT open to view; apparent
OVINE sheep-like   **Z.**
OVOID oval; oviform
OVOLO a moulding
OVULE small seed   **B.**
OWCHE ouch; jewel socket
OWING due; outstanding
OWLER smuggler of wool
OWLET young owl
OWNED admitted; confessed; allowed
OWNER the captain   **Naut.**
OWSEN oxen   **Z.**
OWSER tan vat liquor
OX-BOT bot-fly   **Z.**
OXBOW part of yoke
OX-EYE daisy; marguerite   **B.**
OX-FLY bot-fly   **Z.**
OXIDE   **Chem.**
OXLIP species of primrose   **B.**
OXTER armpit; to hug (Sc.)
OZENA an ulcer   **Med.**
OZONE   **Chem.**

P

PAAUW African bustard   **Z.**
PACED stepped; walked; hurried
PACER speed-maker
PADAR coarse flour or meal
PADDY Irishman; temper; rice   **B.**
PADMA lotus   **B.**
PADRA black tea (China)   **B.**
PADRE army chaplain   **Eccl.**
PAEAN song of triumph

PAEON a poetical foot		
PAGAN paynim; heathen; idolator		
PAGED found by the bell-hop		
PAGLE paigle; cowslip	**B.**	
PAGUS county division (obs.)		
PAINS meticulous care		
PAINT limn; depict; portray		
PAIRK a park; a field (Sc.)		
PALAS Punjab bean	**B.**	
PALAY ivory-tree	**B.**	
PALEA inner husk; chaff	**B.**	
PALED blanched; encompassed		
PALES Goddess of cattle		
PALKI palanquin		
PALMY flourishing; thriving		
PALPI jointed feelers	**Z.**	
PALSY paralysis; benumb	**Med.**	
PANAX ginseng; medicinal plant	**B.**	
PANCH thick mat; fender	**Naut.**	
PANDA bear-cat	**Z.**	
PANDY a slap on the open hand		
PANED variegated; glazed		
PANEL list; board; schedule	**Law**	
PANIC fear; fright; terror; alarm		
PANSY overdressed weakling	**B.**	
PANTS pantaloons		
PAPAL popish; pontifical	**Eccl.**	
PAPAW a fruit tree	**B.**	
PAPER journal; sheet; essay		
PAPPY succulent; juicy; easy		
PARCH dry; scorch; shrivel		
PARDI ⎫ perdy; pardieu;		
PARDY ⎭ in truth (Spens.)		
PARED cut; shaved		
PARER trimmer		
PAREU Polynesian wrap		
PARKA Alaskan fur coat with hood		
PARKY cold; chilly		
PAROL oral; by word of mouth		
PARRY avert; evade; prevent		
PARSE analyse grammatically		
PARSI Parsee; Indo-Persian		
PARTI eligible suitor		
PARTS abilities; talents		
PARTY set; clique; cabal; faction		
PASCH Passover (Hebrew); Easter		
PASHA pacha; Turkish governor		
PASHM under-fur of Cashmere goat		
PASSE faded; out of date (Fr.)		
PASSE 17 to 36 at Roulette		
PASTE to stick; an adhesive		
PASTY glutinous; patty; a pie		
PATCH cobble; botch; mend		
PATED with a head		
PATEN patin; eucharistic plate	**Eccl.**	
PATER father		
PATIO courtyard		
PATLY aptly; fitly; apropos		
PATTE sash-band (Fr.)		
PATTY a small pie		

PAUSE halt; delay; tarry; hesitate		
PAVAN paven; pavin; a dance (Sp.)		
PAVED tesselated		
PAVER pavier; pavement layer		
PAVID timid		
PAVON lance pennon		
PAWED fingered; scraped		
PAWKY sly; crafty; shrewd		
PAYED coated with pitch		
PAYEE the receiver		
PAYER rewarder; liquidator		
PAYSE paise; peise; poise		
PEACE harmony; concord; repose		
PEACH to divulge	**B.**	
PEAKY sickly		
PEARL a gem; a size of type		
PEASE peas collectively	**B.**	
PEATY like peat		
PEAVY lumberman's hook	**Tool**	
PECAN hickory; a nut	**B.**	
PECUL Chinese weight, 133 lbs.	**Meas.**	
PEDAL to cycle	**Mus.**	
PEDUM shepherd's crook		
PEERY peg-top		
PEGGY a warbler	**Z.**	
PEINE (squeeze to death)		
PEKAN the fisher-marten	**Z.**	
PEKOE black tea (China)	**B.**	
PELLS records; rolls of parchment		
PELMA sole of foot	**Med.**	
PELTA light shield or buckler		
PENAL punitive; disciplinary		
PENCE pennies; (Peter)	**Coin**	
PENNA a feather	**Z.**	
PENNY a denarius	**Coin**	
PEONY piony; a plant	**Z.**	
PERCH pole; 5½ yards	**Meas., B.**	
PERDU lost (Fr.)		
PERIL risk; hazard; danger; jeopardy		
PERKY smart; lively; brisk		
PERRY cf. cider		
PERSE dark blue; a cloth		
PESKY irksome; trying; vexatious		
PETAL a flower-leaf	**B.**	
PETAR petard; firework (Shak.)		
PETER blue flag; (Cards); (out)		
PETIT mignon; petty; trivial		
PETRE saltpeter	**Chem.**	
PETTY trivial; mean		
PEWIT pewet; peewit; lapwing	**Z.**	
PHARE pharos; lighthouse; beacon		
PHARO faro; a game of chance		
PHASE appearance; aspect; guise		
PHEON the broad arrow		
PHIAL vial; ampulla; small flask		
PHLOX a plant	**B.**	
PHOCA the seal genus	**Z.**	
PHONE to telephone		
PHOTO photograph; snap-shot		
PHREN the mind	**Med.**	

PHYLA classifications		
PHYMA tubercle	Med.	
PIANO softly	Mus.	
PICEA spruce genus	B.	
PICOT little lace loop		
PICRA powdered aloes	Med.	
PICUL pecul; Chinese weight	Meas.	
PICUS woodpecker	Z.	
PI-DOG Indian pariah dog	Z.	
PIECE unite; bit; part; scrap		
PIEND peen; hammer-point		
PIENO all performing	Mus.	
PIETA holy picture	Eccl.	
PIETY holiness; sanctity		
PIGMY pygmy; dwarf; midget		
PIKED pointed; sharp; spiked		
PIKER a tramp		
PILAR hairy; hirsute		
PILAU } pillau; pilaff; pilav		
PILAW } a savoury stew (rice)		
PILCH fur or flannel gown		
PILED amassed; heaped; erected		
PILER gatherer		
PILOT guide; steer; direct	Naut.	
PILUM heavy javelin		
PILUS a botanical hair	B.	
PINCH squeeze; take	Meas.	
PINED languished; drooped		
PINIC an acid	Chem.	
PINKY small boat; dinghy	Naut.	
PINNA a wing	Z.	
PINNY pinafore		
PINTO variety of kidney bean	B.	
PIN-UP cut-out romantic wall picture		
PIONY peony; a flowering plant	B.	
PIOUS devout; godly; religious		
PIPAL pipul; sacred fig-tree	B.	
PIPED hollow		
PIPER (bagpipes)	Mus.	
PIPIT tit-lark	Z.	
PIQUE vexation		
PISTE track; footprint; ski-way		
PITCH toss; hurl; locate; tar		
PITHY terse; concise; laconic		
PITOT tube recording air speed		
PIVOT hinge; axle; axis; centre		
PIXIE pixy; a fairy; elf		
PLACE site; scene; post; assign		
PLAID a tartan; a maud		
PLAIN prairie; obvious; simple		
PLAIT weave; twine; braid		
PLANE level; flat; a tree	Tool, B.	
PLANK sawn timber; lay down		
PLANT inculcate; sow; machinery	B.	
PLASH plesh; pool; weave; splash		
PLASM mould or matrix		
PLATE silver-ware; to overlay		
PLATO Greek philosopher		
PLATT ore dump		
PLAZA public square; market-place		

PLEAD argue; reason; entreat		
PLEAT fold		
PLEBS the people; populace		
PLESH plash; splash		
PLICA a hair disease	Med.	
PLIED folded; carried on		
PLUCK animal offal; pick; cull		
PLUCK valour; daring; mettle		
PLUFF to puff		
PLUMB vertical; to fathom; level		
PLUME feather; crest; to pride		
PLUMP stout; chubby; corpulent		
PLUMY feathered		
PLUSH a material		
PLYER transport worker		
POACH (eggs); (game)		
POCKY pitted		
PODGE a fat man; a puddle		
PODGY short and fat; pudgy		
POESY poetry; a posy		
POGGE armed bull-head fish	Z.	
POILU French soldier		
POIND distrain	Law	
POINT aim; tip; apex; sharpen		
POISE paise; payse; peise; weigh		
POKAL a drinking-cup		
POKED thrust; jabbed; prodded		
POKER (cards); the pochard duck	Z.	
POLAR opposite		
POLEY polled; without horns		
POLIO infantile paralysis	Med.	
POLKA a Bohemian dance		
POLLY parrot	Z.	
POLYP many-limbed animal	Z.	
PONGO African ape	Z.	
POOJA Hindu ritual; obeisance		
POORT col or pass (S. Africa)		
POPPY (opium)	B.	
PORCH portico; entrance; stoa		
PORED examined diligently		
PORER student		
PORGY porgie; a sea-fish	Z.	
PORKY fat		
PORTA transverse fissure; liver	Med.	
PORTE Turkish Government		
POSED perplexed; masqueraded		
POSER an attitudiniser		
POSIT to affirm; postulate		
POSSE power; force of constables		
POTCH thrust (Spens.)		
POTIN Roman coin-metal		
POTTO West African sloth; racoon	Z.	
POTTY petty; small; dotty		
POUCH bag; wallet; sack; steal		
POULP a cephalopod	Z.	
POULT a young bird	Z.	
POUND pen; to crush	Coin, Meas.	
POWAN Loch Lomond fish	Z.	
POWER force; faculty; control		
POYOU armadillo	Z.	

PRAAM a barge — **Naut.**
PRADO Art Gallery, Madrid
PRAHU Malay boat — **Naut.**
PRANG a crash landing; destroy
PRANK prink; bedizen; caper; frolic
PRASE green quartz — **Min.**
PRATE babble; chatter; jabber
PRAWN a crustacean — **Z.**
PREDY ready for action — **Naut.**
PREEN to clean the feathers
PRESS crush; urge; crowd; hurry
PREST at hand; ready money; to loan
PREXY college president (U.S.A.)
PRICE cost; charge; rate; reward
PRICK perforate; puncture; mark
PRIDE arrogance; hauteur; conceit
PRIED peeped; spied; snooped
PRIER pryer; a nosey Parker
PRILL brill; a fish — **Z.**
PRIMA first; leading
PRIME chief; principal; zenith
PRIMO leading part — **Mus.**
PRIMY blooming
PRINK prank; to dress up
PRINT stamp; brand; impress
PRIOR previous; earlier — **Eccl.**
PRISE to lever
PRISM
PRIVY private
PRIZE esteem; reward; booty
PROBE scrutinize; examine; prove
PROEM preface
PRONE face downwards; apt to
PRONG the tine of a fork
PROOF test; ordeal; impenetrable
PROPS theatrical properties
PRORE the prow of a ship — **Naut.**
PROSE talk without rhyme or reason
PROSY prolix; tedious; vapid
PROUD vain; imperious; stately
PROVE evince; verify; examine
PROWL prey; stalk; rove; slink
PROXY substitute; deputy; agent
PRUDE lady of affected modesty
PRUNE dried plum — **B.**
PRYAN felspathic clay — **Min.**
PRYER prier; snooper
PSALM sacred song
PSHAW!
PSOAS tenderloin — **Med.**
PSORA the itch — **Med.**
PTERE an alate organ; a wing — **Z.**
PUBIS pelvic bones — **Med.**
PUDGY podgy; fat; fleshy
PUFFY tumid; swollen; bombastic
PUGIL a pinch of
PUKKA veritable; genuine
PULED whined
PULER a whimperer
PULEX the flea — **Z.**

PULKA Lapland sledge
PULPY soft; succulent
PULSE a lentil; to throb — **Med., B.**
PUMPS evening shoes
PUNCH pummel; pierce; horse — **Z.**
PUNIC Carthaginian; faithless
PUNKA punkah; Indian fan
PUNTO fencing; Cuban dance
PUNTY glass-blower's iron — **Tool**
PUPAL in the chrysalis state — **Z.**
PUPIL scholar; tyro; alumnus
PUPPY a whelp — **Z.**
PUREE thick soup; strained pulp
PURER cleaner; more chaste
PURGE cleanse; absolve; shrive
PURIM Jewish feast
PURRE the dunlin bird — **Z.**
PURSE to wrinkle; money-bag
PURSY fat and asthmatic
PUSSY willow catkin — **B., Z.**
PUTID putrid; worthless
PUTOO nut-meal
PUTTY cement with linseed oil
PUT-UP preconcerted
PUTZI Chinese game
PYGAL relating to backsides
PYGMY pigmy; midget; Lilliputian
PYLON gateway; turning mark; tower
PYOID pus-like — **Med**
PYRAL (funeral pyre)
PYRUS apple or pear genus — **B.**
PYXIS pyx; sacred box — **Eccl.**

Q

Q-BOAT disguised, armed ship — **Naut.**
QUACK charlatan; humbug; empiric
QUADS a quadruplet
QUAFF gulp; swallow; drink deep
QUAID quelled (Spens.)
QUAIL blench; cower; flinch — **Z.**
QUAIR quire; a book
QUAKE tremble; quiver; rock
QUAKY unstable; shaky
QUALM scruple; pang; throe
QUANT punt or jumping pole
QUARL a segment of fireclay
QUARL jelly-fish — **Z.**
QUART (cards); 2 pints — **Meas.**
QUASH nullify; annul; override
QUASI as it were; virtually
QUASS kvass; Russian beer
QUEAN a saucy girl (obs.)
QUEEN (cards); (chess)
QUEER odd; rummy; curious; strange
QUEET an ankle; a gaiter (Sc.)
QUELL suppress; crush; quench
QUERK to throttle; to grunt
QUERL to twirl; a coil
QUERN primitive stone handmill
QUERY question; dispute; ask

QUEST	search; pursuit; inquiry		
QUEUE	a hopeful tail		
QUICK	fleet; agile; brisk; alive		
QUIET	still; clam; lull; pacify		
QUIFF	a curly lock		
QUI-HI	Anglo-Indian		
QUILL	a feather; a pen	Z.	
QUILP	a hideous dwarf		
QUILT	twilt; counterpane		
QUINA	quinine	Med.	
QUINS	a quintuplet		
QUINT	sequence of five		
QUIPO⎫	mnemonic Inca language;		
QUIPU⎭	coloured and knotted cords		
QUIRE	choir; 24 sheets	Meas.	
QUIRK	twist; subterfuge; evasion		
QUIRT	riding whip		
QUITE	fully; exactly; entirely		
QUITS	acquittance; clear of debt		
QUOAD	as far as		
QUOIF	coif; headdress		
QUOIN	wedge		
QUOIT	discus		
QUOOK	quaked (Spens.)		
QUOTA	share; portion; allotment		
QUOTE	cite; mention; adduce		
QUOTH	spake; said; remarked		
QURAN	Koran		
QURSH	(Arabia)	Coin	

R

RABBI	Jewish teacher		
RABID	furious; violent		
RABOT	marble-polisher		
RACED	ran; hurried; competed		
RACER			
RADAR	radio-location		
RADGE	rodge; gray duck; gadwall	Z.	
RADII	plural of radius		
RADIO	a radio-telegram		
RADIX	(logarithms); a root	B.	
RAFFE	three-cornered sail	Naut.	
RAFTY	damp; musty		
RAGED	raved; fumed; stormed		
RAINY	showery		
RAISE	erect; uplift; exalt; breed		
RAJAH	Indian prince		
RAKED	enfiladed; searched; combed		
RAKER	ransacker; scraper		
RALLY	banter; recover; (tennis)		
RALPH	a mischievous raven	Z.	
RAMAL	branching		
RAMED	framed on the stocks	Naut.	
RAMIE	ramee; rope fibre	B.	
RAMMY	strongly scented		
RAMUS	branch; twig; spray	B.	
RANCE	a rocket trough		
RANCH	farm; cattle farm		
RANDY	a virago; a romp; a beggar		

RANEE	rani; Indian queen		
RANGE	array; align; tier; scope		
RANGY	long-limbed and slender		
RANTY	boisterous; vociferous		
RAPHE	seam; rib; partition		
RAPED	violated; outraged		
RAPID	fast; fleet; swift; hasty		
RAPIN	devouring animal	Her.	
RARER	scarcer; more uncommon		
RASED⎫	erased; effaced;		
RAZED⎭	demolished; blotted out		
RASPY	rough; scratchy; abrasive		
RASSE	small civet	Z.	
RATAL	rate value		
RATAN	rattan; a cane	B.	
RATCH	pawl; ratchet; rack		
RATED	valued; scolded; chid		
RATEL	honey-badger	Z.	
RATER	assessor; (yachting)		
RATHE	early; quickly; rapidly		
RATIO	proportion; rate; quota		
RATTY	irascible; irate; angry		
RAVED	raged; ranted; drivelled		
RAVEL	entangle; untwist		
RAVEN	the emblem of Denmark	Z.	
RAVER	a maniac		
RAVIN	raven; prey; plunder; rapine		
RAWLY	unskillfully; immaturely		
RAYAH	non-Mohammedan Turk		
RAYED	shone; arrayed		
RAYON	artificial silk		
RAZEE	to cut down; prune	Naut.	
RAZOR			
REACH	expanse; stretch; scope		
REACT	recoil; resist; repeat		
READY	prompt; alert; willing		
REALM	kingdom; domain		
RE-ARM	re-equip		
REAST	to dry by smoke		
REATA	riata; lariat; lasso		
REAVE	to bereave; ravage		
REBEC	Moorish fiddle	Mus.	
REBEL	revolt; rise; insurgent		
REBID	(auction)		
REBUS	a pictorial puzzle		
REBUT	confute; disprove; rebuff		
RECAP	redescribe briefly		
RECCE	reconnaisance		
RECIF	reef or bar (S. Africa)		
RECTO	right-hand page		
RECUR	reappear; revert; resort		
REDAN	earthwork; redoubt		
REDLY	blushingly		
REDUX	re-appearance; return		
RE-DYE			
REEDY	a thin tone	B.	
REEFY	full of rocks		
REEKY	smoky; vaporous		
REESK	rank grass; waste land (Sc.)		
REEST	reist; arrest; stop (Sc.)		

REEVE steward; sheriff; (rope)
REEVE the female ruff   **Z.**
REFEL refute; disprove (Shak.)
REFER submit; relate; advert
REFIT repair; re-equip
REFIX
REGAL royal; kingly; princely
REGET regain; recover
REGIE government monopoly
REGMA botanical capsule   **B.**
REICH German realm
REIFY to materialize
REIGN rule; govern; control
REIST reest; to baulk; arrest
REIVE reave; to ravage
RELAX abate; slacken; loosen
RELAY (race); (electrical)
RELET to re-lease
RELIC memento; souvenir; keepsake
RELIT rekindled
REMAN get a fresh crew
REMEX a flight feather   **Z.**
REMIT replace; diminish; release
RENAL (kidneys)   **Med.**
RENES the kidneys   **Med.**
RENEW renovate; refurbish; restore
RENTE annuity from French funds
REPAY refund; recompense; avenge
REPEL repulse; parry; withstand
REPET repeat; the same again   **Med.**
REPLY echo; answer; respond
REPOT transplant
RESAW saw again; revisualized
RESET set again; (stolen goods)
RESIN rosin   **B.**
RESOW to sow again
RESTY indolent; restive
RETCH reach; strain
RETEX to annul
RETRY try again
REVEL feast; carouse; luxuriate
REVET (revetment)
REVIE outdo; retort
REVUE variety entertainment   **Mus.**
REWET part of a wheel-lock
REWIN regain
RHEIC (rhubarb)   **B.**
RHEIN chrysophanic acid   **Chem.**
RHEUM rhubarb   **B.**
RHINE rine; a ditch
RHINO money   **Z.**
RHOMB a rhombohedron
RHONE eaves gutter
RHUMB vertical circle; (compass)
RHYME rime; poetry; metre
RHYNE Russian hemp   **B.**
RIANT laughing; smiling (Fr.)
RIATA reata; lariat; lasso
RIBES currant genus   **B.**
RIDER horseman; added clause

RIDGE ledge; crest; weal
RIDGY furrowed
RIFLE ransack; strip; to groove
RIGEL a star in Orion
RIGHT due; equity; privilege
RIGID staunch; unbending; strict
RIGOL a diadem; crown; coronet
RIGOR rigour; rigidity   **Med.**
RILED angered; annoyed
RILLE lunar valley
RIMED frosted
RIMER an enlarging tool   **Tool**
RINGE heather whisk
RINSE lave; clean; wash
RIOJA Spanish wine
RIPEN mature; develop; perfect
RIPER further advanced
RIPON a spur
RISEL support for a vine
RISEN ascended; mounted; revolted
RISER rebel; stair-board
RISHI poet; Vedic seer
RISKY hazardous; speculative
RISSA kittiwake genus   **Z.**
RITHE small stream
RITZY luxurious
RIVAL vie; emulate; match; equal
RIVEL to wrinkle; shrivel
RIVEN rived; rent; split
RIVER stream; torrent; tributary
RIVET clinch; fasten
RIYAL (Sudan)   **Coin**
RIZOM head of corn or oats   **B.**
ROACH part of sail; a fish   **Naut. Z.**
ROAST parch; chaff outrageously
ROBED garbed; attired; arrayed
ROBIN sometimes round   **Z.**
ROBLE Californian white oak   **B.**
ROBOT an automaton
ROCKY stony; shaky; unsteady
ROCTA ancient violin   **Mus.**
RODEO cattle round-up
RODGE radge; gray duck; gadwall   **Z.**
ROGER a ram; a rogue   **Z.**
ROGUE knave; scamp; rascal; caitiff
ROHAN red-wood mahogany tree   **B.**
ROIST to bluster; to swagger
ROKER thornback ray; skate   **Z.**
ROMAL kerchief; raw hide whip
ROMAN type of type
ROMEO a lover
ROMIC a phonetic notation
ROMPU heraldic fracture
ROMPY rampageous
RONDE round-hand type (Fr.)
RONDO music in several strains   **Mus.**
RONIN Japanese outcast
ROODY coarse; luxuriant
ROOFY having roofs
ROOKY inhabited by rooks

ROOMY spacious
ROOPY roupy; hoarse
ROOSE to extol (Sc.)
ROOST a fowl support; to perch
ROOTY radical; bread (India)
ROPED tied; lashed; bound
ROQUE a form of croquet (Fr.)
RORAL dewy; roscid
RORIC moist with dew
RORTY exuberant; rampageous
ROSET a red colour; rosin
ROSIN resin **B.**
ROTAL according to roster
ROTOR a machine; airfoil
ROUGE (Eton wall game); polish
ROUGH rugged; crude; coarse
ROUND convex; rotund; period; tour
ROUPY roupy; hoarse
ROUSE carouse; disturb; awaken
ROUST rouse; stir up; incite
ROUSY noisy; riotous
ROUTE way; course; itinerary
ROUTH plentiful; abundant (Sc.)
ROVED roamed; wandered; rambled
ROVER nomad; pirate; (croquet)
ROWAN mountain ash **B.**
ROWDY ruffian; rough; boisterous
ROWED sculled; upbraided
ROWEL part of a spur
ROWEN second hay crop
ROWER oarsman
ROYAL regal; superb; august
ROYLE to rile; to salt fish
ROYNE to bite; to gnaw; whisper
RUBIA madder genus **B.**
RUBLE rouble ; Russian silver **Coin**
RUBUS bramble genus **B.**
RUCHE plaited trimming
RUDAS a hag; virago (Sc.)
RUDDY rubicund; red
RUDER coarser; cruder
RUDGE a partridge **Z.**
RUFFE ruff; fresh-water perch **Z.**
RUGBY (football); (school)
RUING regretting; lamenting
RULED lined; governed; decided
RULER monarch; regent; dictator
RUMAL romal; shawl (Hind.)
RUMBA Cuban dance
RUMBO rum punch
RUMEN paunch of ruminant
RUMEX sorrel genus **B.**
RUMMY odd; queer; card game
RUNCH crunch; the wild charlock **B.**
RUNER bard
RUNIC Ancient Scandinavian script
RUN-IN the finish in racing
RUNNY liquid
RUPEE 16 annas **Coin**
RUPIA skin disease **Med.**

RURAL Arcadian; sylvan; pastoral
RUSHY full of rushes
RUSMA rhusma; a depilatory **Med.**
RUSTY corroded; out of practice
RUTAL⎫
RUTIC⎬ derived from rue **B.**
RUTTY uneven; furrowed; grooved
RUVID rough
RYPER ptarmigans **Z.**

S

SABAL a fan palm genus **B.**
SABLE antelope; marten; fur **Z.**
SABLE black (Her.); dusky; sombre
SABOT wooden shoe
SABRA native of Israel
SABRE also **SABER**; cavalry sword
SACRA an artery **Med.**
SACRE saker; falcon; cannon **Z.**
SADDA abbreviated Zendavesta
SADHU Hindu ascetic
SADLY gloomily; dismally; mournfully
SAFER surer; more secure
SAGAN Jewish priest
SAGER wiser; cleverer
SAGRA beetle genus **Z.**
SAGUM Roman cloak
SAHIB a white man; gentleman (India)
SAIGA puff-nosed antelope **Z.**
SAILY like a sail **Naut.**
SAINT to canonize **Eccl.**
SAITH (says)
SAIVA votary of Siva **Eccl.**
SAJOU American monkey **Z.**
SAKER sacre; hawk; old gun **Z.**
SAKIA Persian water-wheel
SALAD **B.**
SALAL evergreen shrub **B.**
SALDA a bug genus **Z.**
SALEP salop; dried orchis root **B.**
SALIC (Salic Law)
SALIN saline; a salt **Chem.**
SALIX willow genus **B.**
SALLE salon; hall (Fr.)
SALLY bell-rope tuffing; outburst; wit
SALLY a stone-fly; a wren **Z.**
SALMI hashed game
SALMO salmon genus **Z.**
SALON saloon; hall
SALOP salep; dried orchis root **B.**
SALPA genus of sea-squirts **Z.**
SALSE volcanic mud
SALTS saline draughts **Med.**
SALTY witty; briny; saline
SALVE save; rescue; heal; a remedy
SALVO an exception; a volley
SAMBA dance (S. America) **Mus.**
SAMBO a negro

SAMIA silkworm genus   **Z.**
SAMMY American Tommy
SANDY yellowish red
SANER less idiotic; more normal
SANSA tambourine   **Mus.**
SAPID savoury; affected; palatable
SAPOR flavour; taste
SAPPY juicy; succulent; weak
SARDA mackerel, tunny genus   **Z.**
SAROH Indian guitar   **Mus.**
SAROS an astronomical cycle
SARSE a fine sieve
SARUM Salisbury; (rotten borough)
SASIA pigmy woodpeckers (Ind.)   **Z.**
SASIN antelope; Indian blackbuck   **Z.**
SASSE Dutch weir with flood-gates
SATAN clootie; Devil; Lucifer
SATED replete; surfeited; cloyed
SATIN glossy fabric
SATIS enough (Latin)
SATYR goat-like sylvan deity
SAUCE impudence; a condiment; relish
SAUCY pert; bold; malapert; flippant
SAUCH, SAUGH the willow (Sc.)   **B.**
SAUDI gold sovereign (Arabia)   **Coin**
SAULT a rapid (Canadian)
SAUNA Finnish steam-bath
SAURY skipper-fish   **Z.**
SAUTE fried in fat
SAVED rescued; freed; redeemed; kept
SAVER a hoarder; an economist
SAVIN evergreen conifer   **B.**
SAVOR savour; taste; odour; relish
SAVOY curly cabbage   **B.**
SAVVY common-sense; nous; gumption
SAWED cut with a saw; sawn
SAWNY or **SAWNEY**; a Scotsman
SAXIN saccharin   **Chem.**
SAXON
SAYER a speaker; an assayer
SAYON medieval peasant's jacket
SAY-SO a dictum
SCAFF food of any kind (Sc.); scoff
SCAIL skail; scatter; disperse (Sc.)
SCALA a surgical instrument   **Med.**
SCALD the dodder-plant; a burn   **B.**
SCALD skald; Scandinavian bard
SCALE climb; balance; flake; lamina
SCALL leprosy; a scab; mean   **Med.**
SCALP token of victory; trophy
SCALY incrusted; shabby; mean
SCAMP rogue; knave; stint
SCANT to stint; scarcely sufficient
SCAPE shaft of column; a fault
SCAPE stem; escape; miss
SCARD shard; sherd; fragment
SCARE alarm; appal; dismay; daunt
SCARF neckerchief; a carpenter's joint
SCARF cormorant; scart; skart   **Z.**
SCARP heraldic scarf; rampart slope

SCART to scratch; scrape; a niggard
SCARY timid; frightened; windy
SCATE skate; a fish   **Z.**
SCATH scathe; damage; injury; harm
SCATT scat; tax (Shetland Is.)
SCAUD scald; scold (Sc.)
SCAUP a sea-duck   **Z.**
SCAUR river bank; rocky cliffs; scar
SCELP skelp; iron for gun-barrels
SCENA stage of an ancient theatre
SCEND ascend; to heave upwards
SCENE show; pageant; sight; view
SCENT perfume; odour; redolence; trail
SCHUT cattle-pound (South Africa)
SCION offshoot; branch; descendant
SCISE to cut (obs.)
SCOAT scote; to scotch; to wedge
SCOBS shavings; sawdust; dross
SCOBY or **SCOBBY**; the chaffinch   **Z.**
SCOFF (food); sneer; mock; deride
SCOLD rate; upbraid; censure; chide
SCOMM a buffoon (obs.)
SCONE coronation stone; a confection
SCOON skim along the water
SCOOP dig; hollow; excavate; a ladle
SCOOT decamp; bolt; run
SCOPA stiff hairs of moths   **Z.**
SCOPE room; space; liberty; object
SCOPS screech-owl   **Z.**
SCORE record; mark; furrow; scratch
SCORN spurn; scout; disdain; deride
SCOTE a scotch; a wedge; a prop
SCOTS Scottish
SCOUP to run; to scamper (Sc.)
SCOUR scrub; scrape; purge
SCOUT contemn; spurn; reconnoitre
SCOUT the guillemot; razor-bill   **Z.**
SCOVE to tamp; to poise
SCOVY smeared; blotched
SCOWL frown; lower; glower
SCRAB crab-apple; to scratch; scrape **B.**
SCRAG to throttle; odd lean bit
SCRAM ! clear off! get out!
SCRAN skran; scraps of food
SCRAP bit; atom; particle; tussle
SCRAT a devil; a goblin; monster
SCRAW a turf; a sod (Ir.)
SCRAY sea-swallow   **Z.**
SCREE steep stony slope
SCREW twist; distort; force; old horse
SCRIM lining cloth
SCRIP wallet; purse; satchel
SCRIP (receipt for) share certificates
SCROD to shed; young codfish   **Z.**
SCROG stunted bush; thicket
SCRUB underwood; clean; scour   **B.**
SCRUM (football)
SCUDO Italian silver dollar   **Coin**
SCUFF scurf; a scale; to shuffle
SCUFT the nape of the neck

SCULK skulk; lurk; slink	**SEWEN** sewin; salmon type **Z.**
SCULL an oar; a cockboat; to row **Naut.**	**SEWER** taster; butler; drain
SCULL skua-gull; a shoal of fish **Z.**	**SEXTE** sixth hour service **Eccl.**
SCULP to carve; to engrave; to flay	**SEXTO** a size of book
SCURF dandruff; scum; bull-trout **Z.**	**S'FOOT** an imprecation
SCUSE excuse me	**SHACK** a shed; to tramp; a vagabond
SCUTE a shield; scale of fish **Z.**	**SHADE** hue; tint; veil; cover; screen
SEAMY dark; sordid; nasty	**SHADY** shadowy; obscure; doubtful
SEA-OX the walrus **Z.**	**SHAFT** arrow; missile; handle; pit
SEAVE a wick made of a rush	**SHAHI** Persian copper coin **Coin**
SEAVY overgrown with rushes **B.**	**SHAKE** jar; jolt; agitate; quiver; dance
SEBAT 5th month of the Jewish year	**SHAKO** chako; military cap
SECCO a fresco; unaccompanied **Mus.**	**SHAKY** tottering; unstable loose
SEDAN carrying chair; a disaster	**SHALE** shaly clay; husk **Min.**
SEDGE flock of herons **Z., B.**	**SHALL**
SEDGY overgrown with sedge or rushes	**SHALM** ⎫
SEEDY shabby; run to seed; unwell	**SHAWM** ⎭ type of oboe **Mus.**
SEGNO repetition **Mus.**	**SHALT**
SEINE large fishing net	**SHALY** laminated and friable
SEISM an earthquake	**SHAMA** Indian song-bird; warbler **Z.**
SEITY personality; selfhood	**SHAME** abash; mortify; infamy
SEIZE grasp; clutch; grapple; impound	**SHAND** shame; base coin; worthless
SEKOS Greek sanctuary	**SHANK** (golf); the tibia **Med.**
SELAH a pause in the Psalms	**SHAPE** mould; fashion; form; image
SELVA tropical rainforest (Brazil)	**SHAPO** wild sheep of Tibet **Z.**
SEMIS Roman bronze coin, half an as	**SHAPS** chaps; cowboy breeches
SENAL a landmark (South America)	**SHARD** sherd; fragment; wing case **Z.**
SENCH to cause to founder	**SHARE** quota; part; portion; divide
SENEX S. American hawk; a swift **Z.**	**SHARK** a cheat; artful greedy fellow **Z.**
SENNA dried cassia leaves **Med.**	**SHARN** cow-dung (Sc.)
SENOR Spanish title of address	**SHARP** fine; thin; keen; caustic **Mus.**
SENSE perceive; wisdom; reason	**SHAVE** pare; clip; shear; skim; graze
SENZA without **Mus.**	**SHAWL** a wrap
SEPAL calyx segment **B.**	**SHEAF** a bundle; a collection
SEPIA genus of cuttlefish; pigment **Z.**	**SHEAL** to shell; to husk
SEPIC done in sepia	**SHEAL** shiel; shepherd's hut
SEPOY native Indian soldier	**SHEAR** clip; cut; fleece; strip
SERAC glacial ice	**SHEEN** gloss; lustre; shine; polish
SERAI caravanserai; a Persian inn	**SHEEP** a woolly ruminant **Z.**
SERGE twilled fabric	**SHEER** absolute; precipitous; turn aside
SERIC Chinese; silken	**SHEET** a bed-cloth; wide expanse; rope
SERIF short cross-line in typography	**SHEIK** Arab chief
SERIN song-bird; canary **Z.**	**SHELF** ledge; shoal; sandbank
SERON bale of exotic produce	**SHELL** case; husk; projectile; bombard
SEROW Asiatic goat **Z.**	**SHEND** to disgrace (Spens.)
SERRA a saw; sierra; mountain ridge	**SHEOL** pit; Hades (Heb.)
SERRY to crowd together	**SHERD** shard; fragment; scard
SERUM whey; (inoculations) **Med.**	**SHETH** part of plough
SERVE do; act; suit; aid; obey; attend	**SHEVA** (Hebrew vowel point)
SESHA Serpent-King (Hindu Myth.)	**SHEWN** displayed; revealed; taught
SESIA clear-wing moths **Z.**	**SHIAH** Mohammedan sect
SESSA hurry! (Shak.)	**SHIED** (coconuts); (horses)
SETON a dressing **Med.**	**SHIEL** shieling; shelter for sheep (Sc.)
SETAE bristles; cat's whiskers **B., Z.**	**SHIER** shyer; more bashful
SET-TO an affray	**SHI-ER** snow-runner
SET-UP scheme; plot	**SHIFT** chemise; vary; alter; trick; wile
SEVEN	**SHIKO** prostrate veneration (Burma)
SEVER cut; part; sunder; detach	**SHILY** shyly; coyly; timidly
SEWED stitched, threaded	**SHINE** radiate; glitter; flash; gloss
SEWEL a scarecrow	**SHINY** the East; gleaming

SHIRE county; draught-horse	**Z.**	
SHIRK evade; avoid; neglect; malinger	
SHIRL to slide	
SHIRR to pucker; to wrinkle	
SHIRT a blouse; distinctive garment	
SHIST schist; crystalline rock	**Min.**
SHIVE a slice; a wooden bung	
SHOAD fragments of ore	**Min.**
SHOAL swarm; throng; bank; bar	
SHOAT young hog	**Z.**
SHOCK stouk; sheaf; onset; to disgust	
SHOER a farrier	
SHOLA a wood; a thicket (Ind.)	
SHOLE ground plank	
SHONE radiated; sparkled; flashed	
SHOOK cask staves; trembled; quaked	
SHOOL beg; grimace; shovel (Sc.)	
SHOON shoes	
SHOOT emit; dart; fire; sprout	**B.**
SHORE prop; brace; strand; beach	
SHORL tourmaline	**Min.**
SHORN shaven: fleeced; clipped	
SHORT terse; abrupt; laconic; pithy	
SCHOTT, CHOTT seasonal salt lake	
SHOUT cry; cheer; call; bellow	
SHOVE jostle; push; press; elbow	
SHOWN presented; paraded; revealed	
SHOWY gay; garish; loud; gaudy	
SHRAB shrub; a drink (Arab)	
SHRED scrap; tatter; atom; piece	
SHREW vixen; virago; scold	**Z.**
SHROF Indian money-lender	
SHROW shrew; dormice type	**Z.**
SHRUB a cordial; dwarf tree	**B.**
SHRUG to draw up; contract	
SHUCK a husk, shell or pod	**B.**
SHUNT divert; electrical device	
SHYLY shily; coyly; bashfully	
SIBBE sib; akin	
SIBYL prophetess; witch; sorceress	
SICCA newly coined; a rupee	**Coin**
SIDED flattened; biassed	
SIDER partisan; protagonist	
SIDLE to go crabwise	
SIEGE besiege; invest; a throne	
SIELD ceiled; plastered (Spens.)	
SIEUR title of respect (Fr.)	
SIEVE to sift; to strain; a temse	
SIGHT see; view; observe; scene	
SIGIL signature; occult mark	
SIGMA a Greek letter; reactor circuit	
SILEX silica	**Min.**
SILKY silken	
SILLY inane; inept; unwise; stupid	
SILVA sylva; forest trees	**B.**
SIMAR cymar; cimar; scarf; loose dress	
SIMIA genus of apes	**Z.**
SINCE after; subsequently; because	
SINEW a tendon	**Med.**
SINGE sear; burn; scorch	
SINIC Seric; Chinese	

SINTO shinto; ancestor-worship (Jap.)	
SINUS a cavity; a bay	**Med.**
SIOUX Dakota Indian	
SIPED oozed; exuded; percolated	
SIRED fathered; generated	
SIREN syren; seducer; hooter	
SIRIH betel-leaf (Malay)	**B.**
SIRUP sorop; syrup	
SISAL fibrous plant, (ropemaking)	**B.**
SISON stone parsley	**B.**
SISSY sweetheart; a weakling	
SITED placed, situate	
SITTA the nut-hatch	**Z.**
SIVAN Jewish month	
SIXTH	
SIXTY	
SIZAR a rationed student	
SIZED graded; glued	
SIZEL scissel; metal clipping	
SIZER sizing machine	
SKALD scald; Scandinavian bard	
SKAIL scail; disperse; scatter; empty	
SKAIN skein; coil of yarn	
SKATE scate; the ray; a roller-skate	**Z.**
SKEAN skene; a dagger; a dirk (Sc.)	
SKEEL a milking-pail; a tub (Sc.)	
SKEET the pollack; a long scoop	**Z.**
SKEIN tangle; wild geese flying	**Z.**
SKELP a blow; a large portion (Sc.)	
SKENE skean; dagger; dirk (Sc.)	
SKIED skyed; lofted; elevated	
SKIER skyer; a lofted shot at cricket	
SKIES the firmament	
SKIFF a light boat; to skim	**Naut.**
SKILL knack; address; art; facility	
SKIMP stint; scamp; scanty	
SHINK African lizard; a shin-bone	**Z.**
SKIRL a shrill cry or sound	
SKIRR scurry; hasten; scour	
SKIRT hem; border; skim; edge	
SKITE skyte; to glide or slip (Sc.)	
SKITE the yellow bunting	**Z.**
SKIVE pare; split	
SKOAL Hail! a toast! (Scand.)	
SKRAN scran; scraps; rubbish; refuse	
SKULK lurk; slink; cower; sneak	
SKULL the sconce; the noddle	
SKYEY skiey; ethereal	
SKYTE skite; glide; slip (Sc.)	
SLACK lax; loose; lazy; sluggish	
SLACK shallow dell; small coal	
SLADE valley; spade; Art School	
SLAIE weaver's reed	
SLAIN killed; despatched; murdered	
SLAKE quench; extinguish; allay	
SLANG argot; to scold; to abuse	
SLANT tilt; list; lean; slope	
SLASH cut; gash; slit; swipe	
SLATE reprimand; slang	**Min.**
SLATT slat; a lath	

SLATY like slate
SLAVE serf; thrall; drudge; menial
SLEEK smooth; soft; glossy; silken
SLEEP doze; slumber; nap; siesta
SLEET snow mingled with rain
SLEPT drowsed; slumbered; rested
SLICE fire-shovel; cut; sever; piece
SLICK plausible; easily done; ore **Min.**
SLICY apt to slice
SLIDE glide; skid; grace notes **Mus.**
SLIER slyer; more crafty
S'LIFE an imprecation
SLILY slyly; artfully; astutely
SLIME mire; sludge; ooze; mud
SLIMY viscid; viscous; clammy
SLING a drink; hurl; hang; cast
SLINK untimely beast; skulk; lurk
SLIPE slype; mining skip
SLIPS men's bathing costumes
SLIPS (theatre); (shipbuilding)
SLISH slice; slash; cut
SLIVE to slide; to skulk
SLOAM clay between coal-beds **Min.**
SLOAT slot; bar; bolt
SLOID, SLOYD handicrafts
SLOOM to slumber; to sleep
SLOOP a warship **Naut.**
SLOPE slant; shelve; grade; a ramp
SLOPS ready-made clothes
SLOSH slush; sludge; sentimentality
SLOTH torpor; inaction; laziness **Z.**
SLOYD sloid; Swedish manual training
SLUED turned round; tipsy
SLUGS half-roasted ore
SLUMP collapse; sudden fall; marsh
SLUNG flung; thrown; suspended; cast
SLUNK lurked; cowered; skulked
SLUSH slosh; sludge; mire; bathos
SLYLY slily; astutely; craftily
SLYNE face of a jointed rock
SLYPE narrow passage
SMACK slap; flavour; spice; dash **Naut.**
SMALL tiny; petty; trivial; minute
SMALT blue glass; blue pigment
SMART rankle; pungent; trim; witty
SMASH crash; crack; disrupt; ruin
SMEAR daub; plaster; sully; begrime
SMELL scent; aroma; odour; perfume
SMELT stank; melt ore; small fish **Z.**
SMIFT a fuse
SMILE smirk; grin; simper
SMIRK an affected smile
SMITE hit; buffet; knock; chasten
SMITH a metal worker; blacksmith
SMITT ore used for marking sheep
SMOCK a chemise; pastoral garment
SMOKE fume; reek; exhale; vapour
SMOKY steamy; vaporous
SMOLT young river salmon **Z.**
SMOOT journeyman printer; smout

SMORE smother (Sc.)
SMOTE struck; blasted; slew
SMOUT smowt; speckled trout **Z.**
SMUCK a crowd of jellyfishes **Z.**
SNACK hasty light repast; a share
SNAIL spiral cam **Z.**
SNAKE serpent; reptile **Z.**
SNAKY sly; cunning; serpentine
SNAPE to bevel
SNARE gin; net; toil; wile; trap
SNARL gnarl; gird at; entangle
SNARY insidious; complicated
SNASH insolence; abusive language (Sc.)
SNATH curved handle of a scythe
SNEAD snath; snathe; sned
SNEAK lurk; slink; skulk; blab
SNEAP check; rebuke; nip
SNECK snick; cut; a latch
SNEER gibe; mock; jeer; scoff
SNELL keen; sharp; severe (Sc.)
SNICK a notch; nick; (cricket)
SNIDE spurious; dishonest; counterfeit
SNIFF to smell; inhale; scent; snuff
SNIFT snort; sniff
SNIPE to shoot from ambush **Z.**
SNIRT a smothered laugh; snigger
SNOEK S. African fish; barracouta **Z.**
SNOOD hair ribbon; a fillet
SNOOK lurk; snoop; derisive action
SNOOL to cringe; a sniveller (Sc.)
SNOOP to pry
SNORE
SNORT
SNOUK snook; lurk; snoop
SNOUT nose; nozzle; proboscis
SNOWY pure; unblemished; niveous
SNUFF sniff; (tobacco)
SOAPY unctuous; emollient; flattering
SOAVE sweetly **Mus.**
SOBER staid; sedate; steady; grave
SOBOL the Russian sable **Z.**
SOCKS a drubbing
SOCLE plinth
SODDY covered with sod; turfy
SOFTA Moslem student
SOGER a shirker
SOGGY boggy; marshy; wet; saturated
SOKEN socage district
SOKOL Czech organisation
SOLAH solar; sola; sponge-wood **B.**
SOLAR sunshine parlour; solarium
SOLDO Italian copper coin **Coin**
SOLED (boots)
SOLEN razor-fish genus **Z.**
SOL-FA (singing) **Mus.**
SOLID hard; dense; stout; stable
SOLON wise legislator; wiseacre **Z.**
SOLUM piece of ground; soil
SOLUS alone
SOLVE elucidate; unravel; interpret

SOMAJ a Hindu society
SONDE upper atmospheric probe
SONIC relating to sound
SONNY term of endearment
SONSY soncy; buxom; jolly; cordial
SONTY sanctity (Shak.)
SOOJA soya bean **B.**
SOOTE sweetly (Spens.)
SOOTH truth; reality; true; indeed
SOOTY begrimed
SOPHA a sofa; seat of a king
SOPHI Persian king
SOPOR deep sleep; moral lethargy
SOPPY moist; wet; silly
SOPRA above **Mus.**
SORBO porous rubber
SORDA damped with a mute **Mus.**
SOREL a buck of the third year **Z.**
SORER more grieved; tenderer
SOREX a genus including shrew-mice **Z.**
SORRA not; never (Irish)
SORRY sad; dejected; regretful; abject
SORUS cluster of capsules on ferns **B.**
SOUGH low moan; whine; drain
SOUND probe; fathom; hale; valid
SOUPY like soup
SOUSE pickle; sauce; douse; swoop
SOUTH the Southern regions
SOWAR Indian cavalryman
SOWED strewn; spread; cast
SOWER propagator; disseminator
SOWLE to pull by the ears (Shak.)
SOWTH to whistle softly (Sc.)
SPACE extent; capacity; duration
SPADE (cards); gelding; dig **Tool**
SPADO spade; eunuch; a sword
SPAER a diviner (Sc.)
SPAHI Algerian cavalryman
SPAKE discoursed; declared; told
SPALE spail; a splinter (Sc.)
SPALL break; split; clip
SPALT a flux; brittle
SPANE spean; to wean (Sc.)
SPANG a spangle; to leap; to hurl
SPANK a blow; a slap
SPARE save; hoard; store; frugal
SPARK to flash; bright lad
SPASM tic; throe; twitch; paroxysm
SPATE spait; a sudden flood
SPAVE to geld; to spay
SPAWL to spit; to slaver
SPAWN offspring; ova; sperm **Z.**
SPEAK express; declare; talk
SPEAR a lance; to pierce
SPEAR male descent (cf. **DISTAFF**)
SPECS spectacles
SPECK stain; blemish; blubber; lard
SPEED haste; urge; celerity; rate
SPEER speir; to ask (Sc.)
SPELD chip; splinter

SPELK rod; switch
SPELL charm; cantrip; period
SPELT spelled; German wheat **B.**
SPEND lavish; disburse; exhaust
SPENT consumed, worn, wasted
SPERM spawn; semen **Z.**
SPEWY wet; boggy
SPHEX the wasp genus **Z.**
SPICA spur; spike; bandage **Med.**
SPICE to season; flavour; relish
SPICK spike; nail; tidy; fresh
SPICY aromatic; piquant; racy
SPIED observed; beheld
SPIES secret agents
SPIKE large nail; lavender **B.**
SPIKY spiny; sharp; pointed
SPILE spigot; peg
SPILL upset; shed; effuse; lighter
SPILT diffused; scattered; dropped
SPINE spina; spike; back-bone **Med.**
SPINK chaffinch; primrose **Z., B.**
SPINY thorny; spiky; difficult
SPIRE steeple; a curl; sedge **B.**
SPIRT spurt; spout; gush; jet
SPIRY spiral
SPITE gall; pique; hatred; malice
SPIZA a finch genus **Z.**
SPITZ Pomeranian dog **Z.**
SPLAT part of a chair-back
SPLAY wide; to slant; to slope
SPLIT divulge; rent; cleave
SPODE china-ware
SPOIL mar; booty; snake's skin **Z.**
SPOKE orated; spouted; said
SPOLE spool; a small wheel
SPOOF hoax; humbug; bamboozle
SPOOK phantom; ghost; spectre
SPOOL spole; small wheel
SPOOM to scud down wind **Naut.**
SPOON ladle; to court
SPOOR track or trail of an animal
SPORE reproductive cell **B.**
SPORT play; gambol; romp; frolic
SPOSH slush
SPOTS a leopard **Z.**
SPOUT pawn; gush; issue; nozzle
SPRAG a check-stop; young salmon **Z.**
SPRAT small sea-fish **Z.**
SPRAY foam; sprig; diffuse
SPREE a carousal
SPRIG shoot; twig; a brad
SPRIT a sprout; boom; spar **Naut.**
SPROD a second year salmon **Z.**
SPRUE a disease **Med.**
SPUME froth; spray
SPUMY foaming
SPUNK tinder; pluck
SPURN scorn; scout; slight; disdain
SPURT spout; sprint; rush; speed
SQUAB clumsy; curt; unfledged; coy

SQUAD	band; gang; crew; bevy	
SQUAT	crouch; cower; dumpy; stocky	
SQUAW	Indian woman	
SQUIB	firework; skit; lampoon	
SQUID	cuttle-fish; a calamary	**Z.**
SRUTI	Hindu tradition	
STACK	to pile; chimney; (cards)	
STADE	stadium; arena	**Meas.**
STAFF	rod; pole; stick; personnel	
STAGE	produce; present; platform	
STAGY	theatrical; histrionic	
STAID	steady; grave; sedate	
STAIN	sully; taint; tarnish; soil	
STAIR	a step; a stairway	
STAKE	picket; wager; risk; hazard	
STALE	musty; vapid; effete; trite	
STALK	hunt; strut; stride	**B.**
STALL	(flying); stop; halt; booth	
STAMP	impress; brand; mark; type	
STAND	provide; stay; stall; rostrum	
STANG	wooden pole; to throb	
STANK	stunk; smelt	
STARE	gape; gaze; the starling	**Z.**
STARK	rigid; still; sheer; bare	
STARR	Jewish deed or bond	
START	evoke; rouse; shrink; wince	
STATE	aver; avow; plight; phase	
STAVE	avert; fend; burst	**Mus.**
STEAD	bedstead; use; help	
STEAK		
STEAL	filch; purloin; pilfer; creep	
STEAM	vapour; fume; reek	
STEAN	steen; crockery	
STEED	warhorse; palfrey; mount	**Z.**
STEEK	stitch; pierce; shut (Sc.)	
STEEL	brace; nerve; vigour; blade	
STEEP	imbue; dip; soak; excessive	
STEER	guide; pilot; bullock	**Z.**
STEIN	glass beer mug	
STELA \}	inscribed column; tablet;	
STELE /	sap system	**B.**
STEND	leap; walk with long strides	
STENT	to stint; restrain; limit	
STERE	cubic metre	**Meas.**
STERN	dour; grim; rigorous	**Naut.**
STEVE	to stow	
STICA	Saxon farthing	**Coin**
STICH	stave; a verse	**Mus.**
STICH	a row of trees	
STICK	stab; fix; attach; adhere	
STIED	penned like pigs	
STIFF	stark; rigid; prim; starchy	
STILB	unit of luminance	**Meas.**
STILE	the gnomon of a sundial	
STILL	not sparkling; calm; distil	
STILP	to go on crutches (Sc.)	
STILT	a pole; a snipe	**Z.**
STIME	styme; a glimmer; ray (Sc.)	
STIMY	stymie; (golf)	
STING	prick; wound; hurt; afflict	

STINK	stench, odour, smell	
STINT	allotted task; limit; scrimp	
STINT	sandpiper; dunlin	**Z.**
STIPA	the feather grasses	**B.**
STIPE	stalk; stem	**B.**
STIRK	young ox or cow	**Z.**
STIRP	line of descent	
STIVE	to stew	
STIVY	stuffy; close	
STOAK	to stop; to choke	**Naut.**
STOAT	ermine; weasel	**Z.**
STOCK	cravat; store; garner; fund	
STOEP	stoop; verandah (S. Africa)	
STOIC	a disciple of Zeno	
STOKE	replenish; refuel	
STOLA	Roman lady's dress	
STOLE	peculated; plagarised	**Eccl.**
STOLE	a stolon; a sucker	**B.**
STOMA	breathing pore	**B.**
STOMP	stamp; prance	
STONE	boulder; pelt; 14 lbs.	**Meas.**
STONY	hard; flinty; obdurate; broke	
STOOD	allowed; brooked; bore	
STOOK	stouk; 12 sheaves	**B.**
STOOL	a seat without a back; ramify	
STOOM	stum; renew fermentation	
STOOP	flagon; condescend; yield	
STOOR	stour; dust; commotion	
STOPE	mining ledge; to excavate	
STORE	hoard; garner; stock; supply	
STORK	infant conveyor	**Z.**
STORM	fume; rage; scold; turmoil	
STORY	narrative; recital; account	
STOSH	fish-offal; pomace	
STOUK	stook; sheaves of corn	**B.**
STOUP	stoop; flagon; tankard	
STOUR	stoor; tumult; paroxysm	
STOUT	resolute; robust; a drink	
STOVE	oven; kiln; to heat	
STOWN	stolen (Sc.)	
STRAD	a Stradivarius violin	**Mus.**
STRAE	straw (Sc.)	**B.**
STRAP	a strop; chastise; beat	
STRAW	strae (Sc.); valueless trifle	
STRAY	err; rove; wander; deviate	
STREW	scatter; spread; broadcast	
STRIA	stripe; streak; small channel	
STRIG	stalk; footstalk	**B.**
STRIP	peel; divest; dismantle; shred	
STRIX	screech-owl	**Z.**
STROB	measure of angular velocity	
STROP	strap; sharpen; a rope	**Meas.**
STROW	strew; scatter	
STRUB	to rob	
STRUM	thrum	**Mus.**
STRUT	support; brace; walk; swagger	
STUCK	set; fixed; adhered; stabbed	
STUDY	con; scan; reflect; learning; den	
STUFA	jet of steam	
STUFF	cram; pack; cloth; fabric	

STULL cross-timber in a mine
STULM shaft used to drain a mine
STULP a stump
STUMP log; block; stub; nonplus
STUNG pricked; afflicted; had
STUNK stank; smelt
STUNT to dwarf; check; exploit
STUPA Buddist monument; a dagoba
STUPE hot bandage; fomentation **Med.**
STURT strife; wrath; vexation
STYCA Saxon half-farthing **Coin**
STYLE pen; dub; entitle; vogue
STYLO a pen; a stylograph
STYME stime; stimie (golf)
SUAGE to assuage (Milt.)
SUAVE bland; pleasant; polite
SUBAH province; viceroyship (Ind.)
SUDAK the pike-perch **Z.**
SUDRA the lowest Hindu caste
SUEDE unglazed leather
SUENT neat and tidy
SUETY (suet)
SUFIC (Islamic mysticism)
SUGAR flattery
SUING legal prosecution **Law**
SUINT lanoline
SUIST self-seeker
SUITE retinue; series; train
SULKS grumpiness
SULKY light vehicle; sullen; morose
SULLY soil; taint; stain; defame
SUMAC sumach; plant used in dyeing **B.**
SUMPH dunce; blockhead (Sc.)
SUNNA Moslem traditions **Law, Eccl.**
SUNNI orthodox Muslim **Eccl.**
SUNNY bright; brilliant; unclouded
SUN-UP sunrise; dawn; cock-crow
SUPER a supernumerary; special
SURAH Indian silk
SURAL (calf of the leg) **Med.**
SURAT coarse Indian cotton
SURER more certain; safer
SURFY covered with surf
SURGE roll; swell; heave; a billow
SURGY swirling; towering; surfy
SURLY churlish; morose; crusty; gruff
SURRA Eastern horse disease
SURYA Hindu sun-god
SUTOR a cobbler
SUTRA (Brahminical ritual) **Eccl.**
SWACK active; nimble; to gulp (Sc.)
SWAGE assuage; soften; mitigate **Tool**
SWAIN a peasant; a country lover
SWALE shady spot; a vale; melt; sweal
SWAMP flood; inundate; fen; slough
SWANG swamp; greensward
SWANK brag; swagger
SWAPE handle; oar; sconce
SWARD turf; bacon rind
SWARE testified; deposed; cursed

SWARF to faint; to swoon; grit
SWARM throng; teem; cluster; bevy
SWART swarthy; tawny; dusky
SWASH dash; splash; soft
SWATH swathe; the sweep of a scythe
SWATS new ale (Sc.)
SWAZI (Swaziland)
SWEAL scorch; melt; gutter; swale
SWEAR affirm; vow; vouch; blaspheme
SWEAT exude; ooze; perspire; toil
SWEDE a turnip **B.**
SWEEP (chimney); brush; lottery
SWEEP a bend; scope; curve; oar **Naut.**
SWEER sweir; lazy; reluctant (Sc.)
SWEET luscious; honeyed; dulcet
SWELL expand; dilate; amplify; bulge
SWELT to swelter (Spens.)
SWEPT brushed; scoured; scrubbed
SWIFT fleet; quick; sudden; prompt **Z.**
SWILL boose; quaff; wash; rinse
SWINE pigs **Z.**
SWING sway; vibrate; dangle; hang
SWINK labour; to toil; to drudge
SWIPE smite; slog; steal
SWIRE a col; a hollow between 2 hills
SWIRL whirl; gyrate; eddy
SWISH to birch; thrash
SWISS Helvetian
SWITH quickly; away! begone !
SWOON to faint
SWOOP rush; stoop; descent
SWORD hanger; rapier; cutlass; blade
SWORE sworn; sware; testified
SWORN under oath; affirmed
SWOTE sweetly (Spens.)
SWUNG rocked; vacillated; dangled
SYCEE silver in small ingots (China)
SYKER surely (Spens.)
SYLPH an airy fairy; (Pope)
SYLVA silva; forest trees
SYNOD ecclesiastical Council **Eccl.**
SYREN siren; enticer; hooter
SYRUP sirup; sirop; sweetened liquid
SYTHE scythe (obs.)

T

TABAC snuff-colour
TABBY brindled; watered silk; a cat **Z.**
TABES emaciation; atrophy **Med.**
TABID consumptive; phthisical **Med.**
TABLE index; list; schedule; board
TABOO ban; bar: prohibit; interdict
TABOR camp; laager; small drum **Mus.**
TACCA tropical plant genus **B.**
TACET be silent ! **Mus.**
TACHE a catch; stain; freckle; loop
TACIT silent; implicit; inferred
TACKY viscous; gummy; sticky
TAFFY a Welshman; toffy; blarney

TAFIA Malay rum
TAGAL Filippino
TAHLI Hindu gold ornament
TAIGA coniferous region (Siberia)
TAILS evening dress
TAINT stain; tarnish; sully; defile
TAIPO taepo; vicious animal (N.Z.) **Z.**
TAKEN seized; captured; won; assumed
TAKER grasper; acceptor
TALES equals in kind; (Jurors) **Law**
TALLY agree; correspond; match
TALMA loose cloak
TALON claw; concave moulding
TALPA the mole genus; a wen **Z., Med.**
TALUK Indian subdistrict
TALUS a slope; ankle-bone **Med.**
TAMBU tamboo; taboo; ostracism
TAMED docile; domesticated; curbed
TAMER subjugator; subduer
TAMIL a Dravidian language (Ceylon)
TAMIN glazed worsted stuff
TAMIS tammy; straining cloth
TAMMY tamis; a tam-o'-shanter
TAMUS black bryony **B.**
TANGO Argentine dance
TANGY piquant; sharp in taste
TANIA African farinaceous tuber **B.**
TANKA Canton boat population
TANNA tana; Indian police station
TANSY Easter cake; bitter herb **B.**
TANTO so; so much **Mus.**
TANTY Hindu loom
TAPED measured; sized up
TAPEN made of tape
TAPER wax-candle; slender and conical
TAPET tapestry; tapis
TAPIR kind of rhinoceros **Z.**
TAPIS tapet; tapestry; lie hid
TAPPA tapa; fibre for mats **B.**
TARDO slowly **Mus.**
TARDY late; sluggish; dilatory
TARED tare allowance recorded
TARFA tamarisk; (exudes manna) **B.**
TARGE target; shield or buckler
TARIN the siskin **Z.**
TAROC card game in which there
TAROT were 78 cards in the pack
TARRY stay; linger; sojourn; loiter
TARSE the tarsus; foot; ankle **Med.**
TARSI feet of insects **Z.**
TARVE a curve; a bend
TASSE thigh armour
TASSO Italian poet, 16th Century
TASTE savour; smack; experience
TASTY piquant; savoury; appetising
TATAR native of Tartary
TATOU tatu; peba; armadillo **Z.**
TAT-TA goodbye; a stroll
TATTA Indian screen; of cuscus grass
TATTY tattered; worn out

TAUNT gibe; deride; revile; twit
TAWED treated with alum
TAWER a leather-dresser
TAWIE tame (Sc.)
TAWNY fulvous; fulvid; tanned
TAWSE taws; leather strap (Sc.)
TAXEL N. American badger **Z.**
TAXED burdened; accused
TAXER inspector of taxes
TAXIN yew extract **B.**
TAXIS classification; manipulation
TAXUS yew genus **B.**
TAZZA bowl
TEACH coach; edify; instruct
TEASE vex; annoy; plague; harass
TECHY tetchy; touchy; testy; petulant
TEDDY a bear **Z.**
TEENS thirteen to nineteen
TEENY wee; tiny; minute
TEETH
TE-HEE titter; snigger
TEIAN Ionian, (Anacreon)
TEINT colour; tinge; tint; hue
TELAR web-like; woven; spun
TELEX teleprinter exchange
TELIC final; conclusive
TEMPE amusement park in Thessaly
TEMPO (cards); relative rapidity **Mus.**
TEMPT allure; lure; decoy; entice
TEMSE sieve; to sift
TENCH a fish **Z.**
TENET rigid doctrine; dogma; belief
TENNE an orange-brown colour
TENON mortise projection
TENOR purport; trend; course **Mus.**
TENSE taut; tight; intent; strained
TENTH a tithe
TENTY attentive; alert
TEPAL a perianth leaf **B.**
TEPEE Sioux tent
TEPID, TEPOR lukewarm; moderate
TERCE about 42 gallons **Meas.**
TEREK a sand-piper
TERES a muscle **Med.**
TERMA terminal lamina of brain **Med.**
TERNE inferior tin-plate
TERRA earth
TERRY a fabric
TERSE abrupt
TESLA magnetic-flux density **Meas.**
TESTA husk; integument **B.**
TESTY techy; fretful; irritable
TEUCH teugh; tough (Sc.)
TEWEL chimney flue
THANE, THEGN Anglo-Saxon title
THANK express gratitude
THARM twisted gut
THAWY inclined to thaw
THECA seed or spore case **B.**
THEFT larceny; robbery; pilfering

THEIC tea-pot devotee
THEIN tea **B.**
THEIR
THEMA ⎫ subject for discussion;
THEME ⎭ short melody **Mus.**
THERE
THERM thermal unit of gas **Meas.**
THESE
THETA a Greek letter
THEWY muscular; strong
THICK dense; solid; turbid; friendly
THIEF pickpocket; an Autolycus
THIGH
THILK the same
THILL shaft of a cart; fire-clay
THINE thy
THING object; article; entity
THING Scandinavian Parliament
THINK deem; muse; cogitate
THIRD
THIRL a restriction; to pierce
THOFT a rowing bench
THOLE pin for an oar; to suffer **Naut.**
THONG lash of whip; strap
THORN prickle; spine **B.**
THORP homestead; hamlet; dorp
THOSE
THOTH Egyptian god of wisdom
THOUS African jackal genus **Z.**
THOWL thole; pin for an oar **Naut.**
THRAP to fasten
THRAW to wrench; to twist (Sc.)
THREE brace and a half; a leash
THREW flung; hurled; projected
THRID to thread
THROB beat; palpitate; quiver
THROE pang; agony; anguish
THROW cast; toss; fell; pitch
THRUM yarn; fringe; to strum **Mus.**
THULE Ultima Thule
THUMB finger clumsily
THUMP bang; whack; pommel
THURL thirl; passage in a mine
THUYA arbor vitae **B.**
THYME a genus of plants **B.**
THYMY fragrant
TIARA ornamental head-dress
TIBBY cat
TIBET heavy goat-hair fabric
TIBIA the large shinbone **Med.**
TICAL Siamese rupee **Coin**
TICED enticed; decoyed
TIDAL
TIDED surmounted
TIDDY the wren **Z.**
TIFFY an artificer
TIGER diminutive groom **Z.**
TIGHT taut; tense; close; compact
TIKUL Indian tree **B.**
TILDE diacritical mark: ~

TILED tessellated
TILER tyler; Masonic doorkeeper
TILIA lime-tree **B**
TILKA Hindu caste mark
TILTH cultivation
TIMED
TIMES the newspaper
TIMID shy; fearful; diffident
TIMON Athenian misanthrope
TINEA moth genus; ringworm **Z., Med.**
TINED pronged
TINGE hue; tint; stain; **dye**
TINGI Brazilian soap-tree **B.**
TINNY like tin; sharp in sound
TINTY crudely tinted
TIPSY tight; drunk; fuddled
TIRAZ Moorish silk fabric
TIRED weary; harassed; attired
T'IRON a webbed bar
TISIC consumptive (Shak.)
TISRI Hebrew month
TITAN giant; Cyclops; Goliath
TITHE a tenth; a tax **Eccl.**
TITLE claim; right; due; name
TITUP tittup; skip; canter
TIVER ochre sheep dye
TIZZY a sixpence **Coin.**
TOADY a sycophant
TOAST scorch; health proposal
TOBAS S. American native race
TOBIT Apocryphal book
TO-DAY
TODDE 28 lb. weight (obs.) **Meas.**
TODDY a cordial
TOFFY toffee; taffy
TOGED arrayed in a toga
TOGUE mackinaw; lake-trout **Z.**
TOILE twill; quilting
TOILS a snare
TOISE old French linear **Meas.**
TOKAY Hungarian wine
TOKEN sign; symbol; mark; badge
TOMAN Persian gold coin **Coin**
TOMIN a weight of 12 grains **Meas.**
TOMMY Atkins; soldier; lever **Tool**
TONAL accented; harmonious
TONED moderated; shaded; tinted
TONGA Eastern cart
TONIC bracing; key-note **Med., Mus.**
TOOTH prong; fang; tusk **B.**
TOPAU rhinoceros-bird **Z.**
TOPAZ a gem **Min.**
TOPEE sun helmet
TOPER toss-pot; sot; tippler
TOPET crested titmouse **Z.**
TOPIA Roman mural decoration
TOPIC theme; subject; a remedy **Med.**
TOQUE tuque; bonnet
TORAH the Mosaic law **Law**
TORAN Buddhist porch **Eccl.**

TORCH flambeau; link; fire-brand	**TRIOR** an examiner **Law**
TORIC type of lens	**TRIPE** offal; rubbish
TORSE heraldic wreath	**TRIST** sorrowful; sad
TORSK a cod **Z.**	**TRITE** hackneyed; obvious; worn
TORSO body; trunk **Med.**	**TROCO** a ball game
TORUS an architectural moulding	**TROIC** Trojan
TOSSY contemptous	**TROKE** exchange; small wares (Sc.)
TOTAL all; sum; whole; gross	**TROLL** to fish; sing; cave-elf
TOTEM superstitious symbol	**TRONA** Egyptian soda **Min.**
TOTED carried; borne; transported	**TRONC** tipping system
TOUCH handle; concern; effect	**TRONE** steelyard; a drain **Meas.**
TOUGH tenacious; coriaceous	**TROOP** throng; crowd; cluster
TOUSE tousle; haul; tease	**TROPE** a metaphor; figure of speech
TOUSY disarranged	**TROTH** to plight; confidence; faith
TOWED hauled; dragged; tugged	**TROUT** fish of Salmo genus **Z.**
TOWEL an altar cloth **Eccl.**	**TROVE** treasure trove
TOWER soar; mount; turret	**TRUCE** lull; respite; armistice
TOWNY a townsman	**TRUCK** a wheel; barter; a vehicle
TOXIC toxicological	**TRUCK** wagon; mast-head **Naut.**
TOXIN poison; virus **Med.**	**TRUER** more worthy of belief
TOYED dallied; sported	**TRULL** vagrant; a drab
TOYER trifler	**TRULY** verily; exactly; veritably
TRACE vestige; trail; follow	**TRUMP** (the last trump); to ruff
TRACK spoor; pathway; race-course	**TRUMP** a trumpet; Jew's harp **Mus.**
TRACT region; pamphlet; homily	**TRUNK** torso; butt; stem; saratoga
TRADE barter; traffic; craft	**TRUSS** bind; fasten **Med.**
TRAIK to wander (Sc.)	**TRUST** credit; reliance; merger
TRAIL haul; tow; track; follow	**TRUTH** probity; fact; candour
TRAIN drill; school; retinue	**TRYMA** a stone fruit; a drupe **B.**
TRAIT characteristic	**TRY-ON** a bluff
TRAMP hike; trudge; vagrant; hobo	**TRYST** rendezvous; (Lutheran carol)
TRANK skin for glove cutting	**TSUBA** Japanese sword hilt
TRANT to hawk; to peddle	**TUBAL** tubar; tubular; hollow
TRAPA the water-chestnut **B.**	**TUBBY** fat; obese; dull
TRAPE traipse; tramp	**TUBED** piped
TRAPS luggage	**TUBER** bulbous growth **B.**
TRASH poor whites (U.S.A.)	**TUCAN** Mexican pouched rat **Z.**
TRASS volcanic earth **Min.**	**TUCUM** S. American palm **B.**
TRAVE beam; wooden frame	**TUDEH** political party (Iran)
TRAWL a drag-net	**TUDOR** a royal house
TREAD trample; step; press	**TUFTY** feathery
TREAT doctor; manage; deal	**TUILE** tuille; armour plates
TREED cornered	**TUISM** a curious theory
TREEN wooden	**TULIP** **B.**
TREND tend; incline; lean	**TULLE** a delicate fabric
TRESS ringlet; lock of hair	**TUMBA** instrument S. Domingo **Mus.**
TREST a beam; a stool (Sc.)	**TUMID** swollen; bombastic
TREWS Scottish trousers	**TUMPY** lumpy; uneven
TRIAD a trinity **Mus.**	**TUNED** attuned; harmonized; adapted
TRIAL test; ordeal; case **Law**	**TUNER** (wireless) **Mus.**
TRIAS sandstone **Min.**	**TUNIC** surcoat; a membrane **Med.**
TRIBE clan; race; class; order	**TUNNY** large fish, mackerel type **Z.**
TRICE an instant; to haul **Naut.**	**TUQUE** toque; Canadian knitted cap
TRICK dupe; cheat; artifice	**TURBO** whelk and winkle genus **Z.**
TRIED essayed; attempted **Law**	**TURCO** Algerian soldier
TRIER experimentalist	**TURFY** swardy; grassy; cespitose
TRIES (Rugby football, 3 points)	**TURPS** turpentine
TRILL warble; quaver; shake **Mus.**	**TUSKY** with long teeth
TRINE triple; threefold; a triad	**TUTOR** coach; instruct; guardian
TRINE favourable planet aspect	**TUTSI** native of Burundi (Africa)

TUTTI all in; (Mozart opera)	**Mus.**
TUTTY impure oxide of zinc	**Chem.**
TUZZY tuft; tuffet; cluster	
TWAIN a couple; brace; pair	
TWAIT species of shad	**Z.**
TWANG tang; flavour	
TWANK twang; a nasal note	**Mus.**
TWEAK pinch; twist; twitch	
TWEED twilled cloth	
TWEEN between; twixt	
TWEER twier; blast-furnace	
TWERE it were	
TWERP nasty nitwit	
TWICE twofold; doubly; encore	
TWILL, TWEEL woven fabric	
TWILT a quilt (Sc.)	
TWINE entwine; wind; cord; string	
TWINK twinkle; twitter; chirp	
TWIRE to gleam; twist; twirl	
TWIRK a twitch (Sc.)	
TWIRL whirl; rotate; revolve	
TWIST writhe; hunger; (tobacco)	
TWITE mountain linnet	**Z.**
TWIXT betwixt; between	
TWYER tweer; blast-furnace	
TYCHE Greek goddess of fortune	
TYING fastening; shackling	
TYLER tiler; Masonic doorkeeper	
TYPAL typical; representative	
TYPED	
TYPHA bulrush	**B.**
TYPIC emblematic; symbolic	
TYRED wheeled, pneumatic	
TYTHE tithe; a tenth	**Eccl.**

U

U-BOAT a submarine	**Naut**
UDDER mammary gland	**Z.**
UGRIC Finns, Magyars, etc.	
UHLAN Prussian cavalryman	
UKASE Russian decree	
ULCER	**Med.**
ULEMA Turkish hierarchy	
ULMIC (elm exudations)	**B.**
ULMIN humus; a brown pigment	
ULMUS elm genus	**B.**
ULNAD toward the ulna	**Med.**
ULNAR (forearm bone)	**Med.**
ULTRA extreme	
UMBEL inflorescent flower	**B.**
UMBER brown pigment	**Z.**
UMBRA a shadow	
UMBRE umber; the grayling	**Z.**
UMIAK Eskimo boat	**Naut.**
UNAPT inept; irrevelant	
UNARM disarm	
UNBAR open; permit	
UNBAY to open up	
UNBED arouse	

UNBID uninvited; spontaneous	
UNBIT not bitten	
UNBOW to unbend	
UNBOX uncase; unpack	
UNCAP unhat; uncover	
UNCLE pawnbroker	
UNCLE oom; Sam; Tom; Remus	
UNCUS hook or claw	**Z.**
UNCUT untrimmed	
UNDAM release	
UNDER below; lower; subject to	
UNDID untied; nullified	
UNDUE excessive; inordinate	
UNFED	
UNFIT unqualified; improper	
UNFIX detach; undo; loosen	
UNGUM unstick	
UNHAT uncover; uncap	
UNIAT Russian Christian	**Eccl.**
UNIFY unite; combine	
UNION coalition; guild; league	
UNITE join; concert; bind	
UNITY concord; harmony; accord	
UNKED unkid; strange; ugly	
UNLAP unfold	
UNLAY untwist; unravel	
UNLED without guidance	
UNLET vacant; tenantless	
UNMAN dishearten; unnerve	
UNMEW release from confinement	
UNNUN unfrock	
UNODE a geometric conception	
UNOIL free from oil	
UNPAY make undone	
UNPEG	
UNPEN release	
UNPIN	
UNRIG dismantle	
UNRIP rip open	
UNSAY retract; disavow	
UNSET unmounted; runny; sticky	
UNSEX geld	
UNSON disinherit	
UNTAX remove a tax	
UNTIE undo; unbind; unknot	
UNTIL till	
UNTIN uncan	
UNWEB unweave; unravel	
UNWED unmarried	
UNZIP Undo patent fastening	
UP-END tilt	
UPLAY to hoard	
UPPER superior; higher	
UPRUN run up; ascend	
UPSEE after the manner of	
UPSET capsize; overturn; disconcert	
UPUPA hoopoe genus	**Z.**
URATE (uric acid)	**Chem.**
URBAN	**B.**
UREDO fungus genus	

D

URENA Indian mallow   **B.**
URGED pleaded; drove; impelled
URGER inciter; prompter; agitator
URIAL Asiatic wild sheep   **Z.**
URILE cormorant   **Z.**
URITE tail of insect   **Z.**
URMAN Siberian forest land
URNAL urn-shaped
URNED (cremated)
URSON Canadian porcupine   **Z.**
URSUS the bear genus   **Z.**
URUBU American turkey-buzzard   **Z.**
URVED curved upward
USAGE habit; wont; custom
USHAS Hindu aurora
USHER herald; introduce; precede
USING applying; employing
USUAL normal; ordinary; habitual
USURP arrogate; assume; seize
USURY usure; exorbitant; interest
UTTER declare; enunciate; total
UVULA (soft palate)   **Med.**
UZBEG, UZBEK Turkish Tatar

V

VAGUE dim; indistinct; indefinite
VAGUS a cranial nerve   **Med.**
VAILS tip; gratuity; backsheesh
VAIRE ⎫
VAIRY ⎬ charged with heraldic fur
VAKIL Indian attorney   **Law**
VALED lowered; receded
VALES vails; pourboire; douceur
VALET gentleman's gentleman
VALID cogent; substantial; strong
VALSE waltz
VALUE worth; price; cost; utility
VALVE mechanical device
VAMPS short hose
VANED having vanes or blades
VANIR three Norse deities
VAPID insipid; feeble; jejune
VAPOR vapour; miasma; steam
VAREC seaweed; kelp   **B.**
VARIX uneven dilation   **Med.**
VARUS knock-kneed   **Med.**
VASAL (blood-vessel)   **Med.**
VASTY spacious; immense; boundless
VATIC prophetic; oracular
VAULT leap; cell; tomb; crypt
VAUNT boast; exult; swagger
VEALY calflike; immature
VEDAS Hindu sacred writings   **Eccl.**
VEDIC according to the Vedas
VEERY American thrush   **Z.**
VEHME German secret society
VEINY full of veins
VELAR guttural; (Arch.)
VELDT grass lands (S. Africa)

VELIA water-bugs   **Z.**
VELUM soft palate   **Med.**
VENAL mercenary; corrupt; sordid
VENEY ⎫ a thrust or hit
VENEW ⎬ in fencing
VENGE avenge (Shak.)
VENOM virus; poison; rancour; gall
VENUE location; district   **Law**
VENUS Aphrodite
VEREY signal light
VERGE edge; staff; mace   **Eccl.**
VERSE poetry; stanza; stich; stave
VERSO left-hand page
VERST Russian mile   **Meas.**
VERTU virtu; rarity in art
VERVE energy; vigour; inspiration
VESPA wasp genus   **Z.**
VESTA goddess of the hearth
VESTA match; lucifer; taper
VETCH ers; the tare   **B.**
VEXED troubled; bothered; piqued
VEXER provoker; annoyer
VEXIL a banner; a petal   **B.**
VIAND food
VIBEX a blood spot   **Med.**
VICAR parish parson   **Eccl.**
VIDEO Recorded Television film
VIEWY visionary; speculative
VIFDA vivda; dried meat
VIGIA charted rock (Sp.)
VIGIL watch; wake; eve
VILER more degraded
VILLA country residence
VILLI small fibres   **Med., B.**
VIMEN slender shoot   **B.**
VINCA periwinkle   **B.**
VINED with tendrils
VINIC alcoholic
VINYL plastic fibre
VIOLA plant genus   **Mus., B.**
VIPER adder; asp   **Z.**
VIREO American song-birds   **Z.**
VIRGO (Zodiac); a constellation
VIRID green
VIRTU vertu; rarity in art
VIRUS poison; venom; toxin   **Med.**
VISIE a searching glance (Sc.)
VISIT frequent; call; drop in
VISON American mink   **Z.**
VISOR ⎫ movable part of
VIZOR ⎬ a helmet; a mask
VISTA view; scene; prospect
VITAL essential; animate; living
VITEX verbena   **B.**
VITIS the vine   **B.**
VITTA a headband; garland
VIURE heraldic ribbon (Fr.)
VIVAT (applause)
VIVDA vifda; dried meat
VIVES a disease of horses

VIVID	intense; brilliant; graphic	
VIZEN	scold; shrew; termagant	**Z.**
VIZIR	vizier; vezir; minister (Turkish)	
VLACH	a Wallachian	
VOCAL	articulate	
VODKA	Russian drink	
VOGAD	telephony	
VOGIE	vain; merry (Sc.)	
VOGUE	fashion; mode; practice	
VOICE	express; declare; utter	
VOILE	gauzy material	
VOLAR	(palm of the hand)	**Med.**
VOLEE	rapid phrase	**Mus.**
VOLET	part of triptych	
VOLTA	an old dance; repeat	**Mus.**
VOLTE	old dances; turns	
VOLTI	turn over	**Mus.**
VOLVE	ponder; turn over (obs.)	
VOMER	ploughshare; nose-bone	**Med.**
VOMIT	spew; eject; disgorge	
VOTED	polled; balloted	
VOTER	elector	
VOUCH	guarantee; affirm; aver	
VOWED	swore; pledged; dedicated	
VOWEL		
VOWER	devotee	
VUGGY	full of cavities	
VYING	striving; competing	

W

WACKE	basalt; trap-rock	**Min.**
WADDY	Australian war club	
WADED	forded	
WADER	long-legged bird	**Z.**
WAFER	crisp cake	
WAGED	pledged; conducted	
WAGEL	black gull	**Z.**
WAGER	bet; hazard; stake; gamble	
WAGES	stipend; remuneration	
WAGON	wain; lorry; truck	
WAHOO	cascara sagrada	**Med., B.**
WAIST	bodice; corsage	
WAITS	Yule minstrels	
WAIVE	remit; forego; relinquish	
WAKED	kept vigil; stimulated	
WAKEN	awaken; excite; animate	
WALAN	amboyna tree	**B.**
WALED	striped	
WALER	Australian horse	**Z.**
WALTY	unstable	**Naut.**
WALTZ	valse	
WANDY	wandlike; flexible	
WANED	ebbed; decreased; declined	
WANLY	sickly; languidly	
WANTY	a loading strap	
WARES	merchandise; commodities	
WARTY	excrescent	
WASHY	watery; thin; feeble	
WASTE	dissipate; squander; fritter	

WATCH	guard; tend; mark	**Naut.**
WATER	irrigate; moisten; sprinkle	
WAVED	fluctuated; brandished	
WAVER	sway; totter; vacillate	
WAVEY	the snow-goose	
WAXED	cered; grew; increased	
WAXEN	ceruminous	
WEALD	wold; woodland	
WEARY	jaded; spent; fatigue; tire	
WEAVE	plait; mat; entwine; interlace	
WEBBY	filmy; reticulated	
WEBER	magnetic flux	**Meas.**
WEDGE	coign; a scotch	
WEEDS	widow's mourning apparel	
WEEDY	weak and lanky	**B.**
WEELY	wicker fish trap	
WEEPY	lacrimose; oozy	
WEIGH	balance; ponder; (anchor)	**Naut.**
WEIRD	eerie; uncanny; supernatural	
WEISM	excessive use of 'we'	
WELCH	Welsh; Cymric	
WELSH	Cymric; abscond	
WENCH	maid; damsel	
WENNY	(sebaceous cyst)	**Med.**
WERSH	tasteless; unsalted (Sc.)	
WHACK	thwack; defeat; smite	
WHALE	the orc; a cetacean	**Z.**
WHALL	wall-eye	
WHAME	the burrel-fly	**Z.**
WHANG	bang; whack; leather thong	
WHARE	Maori hut	
WHARF	quay; dock; pier	
WHAUP	curlew	**Z.**
WHEAL	wale; weal	
WHEAT	a cereal	**B.**
WHEEL	turn; revolve; whirl	
WHEEN	a small quantity (Sc.)	
WHEFT	a knotted flag	
WHELK	a gasteropod	**Z.**
WHELM	overwhelm	
WHELP	puppy; cub; pup; to litter	
WHERE		
WHICH		
WHIFF	puff; outrigger boat	**Naut.**
WHIFT	a breath; a snatch; glimpse	
WHILE	pass the time	
WHILK	the scoter; sea duck	**Z.**
WHINE	whimper; snivel; cry	
WHIPT	scourged; thrashed	
WHIRL	twirl; spin; gyrate; eddy	
WHISK	a brush; stir; hasten; rush	
WHIST	keep silence; (cards)	
WHITE	pale; wan; pallid; chalky	
WHIZZ	whiz	
WHOLE	entire; intact; total	
WHOOP	a shout of joy	
WHOOT	hoot	
WHORL	convolution; spiral	
WHORT	whurt; whortleberry	**B.**
WHOSE		

WHOSO		
WICKY	mountain ash	B.
WIDDY	widow; withy; withe	B.
WIDEN	extend; enlarge	
WIDER	broader; more remote	
WIDOW	to bereave	
WIDTH	span; amplitude; beam	
WIELD	control; exert; ply; brandish	
WIERY	wet; moist; miry (obs.)	
WIGAN	stiff canvas	
WIGHT	a creature; strong; nimble	
WILED	beguiled; hoaxed; cheated	
WILLY	wool cleaning machine	
WINCE	flinch; blench; shrink	
WINCH	hoisting machine	
WINDY	timid; nervous; bombastic	
WINED	drank wine	
WINGY	rapid	
WINZE	ventilating shaft; a curse	
WIPED	rubbed; mopped; cleansed	
WIPER	mechanical device	
WIRED	telegraphed; snared	
WISER	sager; more expedient	
WISPY	flocculent; nebulous	
WITAN	Witanagemote (Anglo-Saxon)	
WITCH	hag; crone; sibyl	
WITHE	willow twig	B.
WITHY	species of willow	B.
WITTY	droll; facetious; humorous	
WIVES	spouses	
WIZEN	shrivelled; dried up	
WODEN	Odin; Wotan	
WOMAN		
WOMBY	capacious (Shak.)	
WOMEN		
WONGA	Australian pigeon	Z.
WOODY	sylvan; ligneous	
WOOED	courted	
WOOER	a lover; a swain	
WOOFY	dense; close in texture	
WOOLD	to twist; dyer's weed	B.
WOONT	the mole	Z.
WOOTZ	Bengal steel	
WORDY	verbose; prolix; garrulous	
WORLD	universe; globe; earth	
WORMY	vermigerous	Z.
WORRY	fret; chafe; fidget; badger	
WORSE		
WORST	best; defeat; conquer	
WORTH	value; cost; merit; desert	
WOTAN	Odin; Woden	
WOULD		
WOUND	harm; hurt; lacerate	
WOVEN	plaited; interlaced	
WRACK	ruin; seaweed	B.
WRAPT	wrapped; hidden; enveloped	
WRANG	wrung; twisted and squeezed	
WRATH	ire; rage; fury; passion	
WRAUL	wrawl; to caterwaul	
WREAK	avenge; inflict; indulge	

WRECK	ruin; blight; shatter	
WREST	twist; wrench; strain	
WRICK	to sprain	
WRIER	more contorted	
WRING	extort; wrest; writhe	
WRIST		
WRITE	indite; scrawl; scribble	
WRONG	injure; falsify; error; tort	
WROTE	inscribed; penned; engrossed	
WROTH	wrathful; angry; furious	
WRUNG	tormented; racked	
WRYLY	distorted; askew	

X

XEBEC	Algerian pirate ship	Naut.
XENON	a gas	Chem.
XERES	sherry	
X-MARK	face-mark (carpentry)	
X-RAYS		Med.
XYLEM	woody tissue	
XYLIC	benzoic acid	Chem.
XYLOL	aromatic fluid	
XYLYL	xylene	Chem.

Y

YACCA	Jamaican tree	B.
YACHT		Naut.
YACOU	guan; a game bird	Z.
YAGER	Jaeger; light infantry	
YAHOO	hooligan	
YAMEN	mandarin's house	
YAMUN	Chinese office	
YAPOK	S. American water-opossum	Z.
YAPON	evergreen shrub; cassine	B.
YAQUI	Mexican Indians	
YASHT	Zend-Avesta prayer book	Eccl.
YAWED	out of course	Naut.
YAWEY	(tropical disease)	Med.
YEARN	crave; hanker; desire	
YEAST	leaven; balm; ferment	
YELEK	a long vest (Turk.)	
YERBA	Paraguay tea	B.
YESTY	yeasty	
YEWEN	made of yew	B.
YEXED	hiccupped	
YIELD	submit; render; supply	
Y-MOTH		Z.
YODEL	yodle; Tyrolese singing	
YOGIN	Hindu philosopher	
YOICK	to encourage	
YOJAN	about 5 miles (E. Ind.)	Meas.
YOKED	coupled; linked; paired	
YOKEL	rustic; churl; clodhopper	
YOLKY	egg-yolk consistency	
YORKY	slate with curved cleave	
YOUNG	boyish; juvenile; recent	
YOURS		
YOUTH	lad; stripling; heyday	
YUCCA	lily genus	B.

YUCKY itchy
YULAN Chinese magnolia   **B.**

Z

ZABRA Spanish coasting vessel   **Naut.**
ZAMBO cross-bred Indian
ZAMIA a palm genus   **B.**
ZANJE irrigation canal (S. America)
ZANTE satin-wood   **B.**
ZAYAT Burmese inn
ZEBEC xebec; Algerian ship   **Naut.**
ZEBRA an ungulate   **Z.**
ZEBUS Abyssinian tsetse-fly   **Z.**
ZEINE the gluten of maize   **B.**
ZEMNI the blind mole-rat   **Z.**
ZENER semi-conductor current
ZERDA African fox   **Z.**
ZHOBO ⎫
ZHOMO ⎬ hybrid, yak and cow
ZIBET Asiatic civet   **Z.**
ZIMBA Am. Indian and Eskimo game
ZIMBI cowry used as money   **Z.**
ZINCO zincograph
ZINKE old type of cornet   **Mus.**
ZINKY zincy; partly zinc

ZIZEL marmot; ground-squirrel   **Z.**
ZLOTY Polish money   **Coin**
ZOAEA ⎫
ZOOEA ⎬ larval crustacean   **Z.**
ZOCCO ⎫
ZOCLE ⎬ square base
ZOEAL early crustacean life   **Z.**
ZOFRA Moorish carpet
ZOGAN Japanese inlay work
ZOHAR sacred Jewish book   **Eccl.**
ZOISM theory of life origin
ZOIST a believer in zoism
ZONAL zonic
ZONAR like a girdle
ZONDA the dry wind of the Andes
ZOOID an organism   **Z.**
ZOOKS gadzooks
ZOPPO occasional syncopation   **Mus.**
ZORIL African skunk   **Z.**
ZORRA American skunk   **Z.**
ZORRO S. American fox-wolf   **Z.**
ZUPAN Serbian rural council
ZYGAL like an " H "
ZYGON connecting bar
ZYMIC relating to fermentation

A

ABACOT cap of state
ABACUS a counting device
ABALYN synthetic resin; lacquer
ABASED humbled; debased; sunk
ABATED mitigated; subsided
ABATER reducer; assuager
ABATIS abattis; obstacles
ABBACY Eccl.
ABBATE a title Eccl.
ABBESS Eccl.
ABDALS Moslem fanatics (Pers.)
ABDEST Mohammedan rite
ABDIEL the faithful seraph
ABDUCE separate; retract
ABDUCT remove; kidnap
ABIDED abode; sojourned; tarried
ABIDER dweller; settler
ABIENT avoidance reflex Psych.
ABJECT servile; base; ignoble
ABJURE renounce; recant; repudiate
ABKARI ⎫
ABKARY ⎬ Persian excise duty on wine
ABLAUT (vowel change)
ABLAZE flaming; excited
ABLEST most competent; cleverest
ABLINS perhaps
ABLOOM thriving
ABLUSH blushing; flushing
ABOARD afloat; inside Naut.
ABORAL remote from the mouth
ABOUND flow; team; swarm
ABRADE scrape; grate
ABRAYD to awaken (Spens.)
ABROAD apart; far; widely
ABROOK endure
ABRUPT steep; hasty; brusque; curt
ABSENT away; left; distracted
ABSORB engulf; consume; swallow
ABSURD irrational; asinine
ABUSED reviled; violated; traduced
ABUSER reviler; slanderer
ACACIA B.
ACACIO acajou; cashew nut B.
ACADIA Nova Scotia
ACAJOU gum; acacio B.
ACARUS insect genus Z.
ACETAL plastic; cosmetic base Chem.
ACATES food
ACCEDE assent; agree; comply
ACCEND kindle (obs.)
ACCENT tone; stress; cadence
ACCEPT take; receive; admit
ACCESS entry; approach; fit
ACCITE to cite
ACCLOY to cloy; satiate; surfeit
ACCOIL to collect (Spens.)
ACCORD concede; deign; tally

ACCOST confront; hail; greet
ACCREW ⎫ to result in; inure;
ACCRUE ⎬ proceed; accumulate
ACCUSE charge; cite; censure
ACEDIA torpor; fish Med., Z.
ACERIC (maple) B.
ACETIC an acid Chem.
ACHENE seeded fruit B.
ACHING continued pain; sorrowing
ACIDIC acid Chem.
ACINUS berry B.
ACK-ACK anti-aircraft
ACLIDE spiked club
ACOPIC invigorating Med.
ACORUS sweet flag B.
ACQUIT absolve; release; exonerate
ACRISY poor judgment
ACRITA sponges B., Z.
ACROSS athwart; transversely
ACTING performing; pretending
ACTION deed; feat; gesture Law
ACTIVE agile; alert; nimble; busy
ACTUAL real; true; genuine; positive
ACUATE pointed
ACUITY sharpness
ACULEI prickles B., Z.
ACUMEN keenness of perception
ADAGIO leisurely Mus.
ADAMIC (Adam)
ADDEEM judge
ADDICT accustom; habituate; devote
ADDING totting; summing
ADDLED deranged; rotten
ADDUCE allege; assign; advance; cite
ADHERE cohere; cling; cleave
ADIEUS or **ADIEUX** farewells
ADIPIC fatty; adiposé
ADJECT to add to
ADJOIN abut; annex; touch; unite
ADJURE exhort; urge; beg; pray
ADJUST arrange; trim; rectify; fit
ADMASS common consumers; the masses;
ADMIRE esteem; prize; revere; respect
ADNATE growing B.
ADNOUN an adjective
ADONAI lord (Hebrew)
ADONIC species of short verse
ADONIS bird's eye; pheasant's eye B.
ADONIS youth loved by venus
ADOORS at the door
ADORED worshipped; idolized; beloved
ADORER admirer; lover; venerator
ADREAD fearful; apprehensive
ADRIFT afloat; distracted; loose
ADROIT expert; skilful; masterly
ADSORB to condense a gas
ADVENE accede
ADVENT arrival; approach Eccl.
ADVERT to notice; to regard
ADVICE counsel; warning; tidings; rede

ADVIEW to view (Spens.)
ADVISE urge; recommend; inform
ADVISO news; intelligence
ADYTUM chancel   **Eccl.**
AEDILE Roman magistrate
AENEID epic poem
AEOLIC Greek dialect
AEOLUS god of the winds
AERATE
AERIAL etherial; empyreal; airy
AERIFY aerate
AEROBE an organic growth   **Med.**
AEROSE coppery; brassy
AERUGO verdigris; patina; rust
AETHER ether   **Chem.**
AFEARD affrighted
AFFAIR incident; concern; skirmish
AFFEAR to terrify
AFFECT assume; feign; influence
AFFEER settle a price   **Law**
AFFIRM vouch; ratify; endorse; allege
AFFLUX to flow
AFFORD produce; impart; confer; spare
AFFRAY onset; brawl; strife; fracas
AFFRET effray; broil; startle; frighten
AFFUSE sprinkle; pour upon
AFGHAN
AFIELD in the open
AFLAME blazing; afire
AFLOAT at sea; unfixed
AFOCAL without focal length   **Phot.**
AFRAID timid; fearful; anxious
AFREET evil spirit (Arab.)
AFRESH anew; again
AFRONT in front (obs.)
AFRIDI (Afghan.)
AGALMA impression of a seal
AGAMAE cryptogamic plants   **B.**
AGAMIC asexual
AGARIC fungus; mushroom   **B.**
AGAZED thunder-struck; amazed
AGEING maturing; mellowing
AGENCY intervention; mediation
AGENDA items of business
AGHAST appalled; astounded
AGNAIL a whitlow   **Med.**
AGNAME nickname
AGNATE (relationship) akin; allied
AGNISE acknowledge; confess
AGNOSY ignorance
AGOING current
AGONIC zero declination
AGOUTA Haytian rat   **Z.**
AGOUTI } guinea-pig;   **Z.**
AGOUTY } S. American rodent
AGRAIL narrow-gauge railway
AGREED reconciled; concerted; tallied
AGUISE to dress (Spens,)
AGUISH shivering; chilly   **Med.**
AIDANT helpful

AIDFUL helpful; co-operative
AIDING assisting; succouring
AIGLET aglet; pendant; young eagle **Z.**
AIGRET aigrette; plume
AILING sick; unwell; indisposed
AIMING pointing; endeavouring
AIR-ACE super-airman
AIR-BED
AIR-DRY dry to parity with atmosphere
AIR-GAS
AIR-GUN
AIRILY buoyantly; gaily
AIRING stroll; ventilation
AIR-LOG linear travel recorder
AIRMAN aeronaut
AIR-SAC air-cell
AIRWAY
AISLED   **Eccl.**
AKIMBO arched; bent
ALALIA loss of speech   **Med.**
ALARUM alarm clock; alarm
ALATED alate; winged   **B.**
ALBATA an alloy
ALBEDO light reflective power
ALBEIT although
ALBERT a watch chain
ALBINO
ALBION England (Morte D'Arthur)
ALBITE (felspar)   **Min.**
ALBUGO eye-trouble   **Med.**
ALCADE } judge; magistrate
ALCAID } (Spain)
ALCAIC poetic metre
ALCEDO } kingfisher
ALCYON }
ALCLAD an aluminium alloy
ALCOVE a bower; arbour; recess
ALDERN made of alder
ALDINE 16th century books by Aldus
ALECTO a Fury
ALEGAR sour ale
ALEGER lively; cheerful
ALERCE cedar wood   **B.**
ALETTE pilaster (Arch.)
ALE-VAT
ALEVIN salmon fry   **Z.**
ALEXIA inability to read   **Med.**
ALEXIN defensive proteid   **Med.**
ALGATE always; nevertheless
ALGOID (seaweeds)   **B**
ALGOUS (algoid)   **B.**
ALIGHT descend; ignited; flaming
ALINED, ALIGNED brought into line, allied
ALIPED bat-like beast   **Z.**
ALKALI   **Chem.**
ALLEGE also alegge; assert; maintain
ALLICE Severn shad; fish   **Z.**
ALLIED united; related; cognate; akin
ALLIES affinities; associates

ALL-OUT top speed
ALLUDE refer; imply; hint; insinuate
ALLURE tempt; decoy; seduce; cajole
ALMAIN German; dance (obs.)
ALMNER almoner; dispenser
ALMOIN alms; alms-chest (tenure)
ALMOND **B.**
ALMOST well-nigh; nearly
ALMUCE amice or furred hood
ALNAGE measuring by the ell **Meas.**
ALPACA llama; Peruvian sheep
ALPHOS⎫ leprosy; psoriasis **Med.**
ALPHUS⎭
ALPINE very high
ALPINI Italian mountain troops
ALPIST bird-seed **B.**
ALSIKE Swedish clover **B.**
ALTERN alternate
ALUDEL distilling apparatus **Chem.**
ALUMNA a woman graduate
ALUMNI collegiates; pupils; scholars
ALVINE intestinal **Med.**
ALWAYS age; evermore; eternally
AMADOU dried fungus; tinder
AMATOL explosive **Chem.**
AMAZED astounded; nonplussed
AMAZON female warrior; virago; shrew
AMBAGE circumlocution; subterfuge
AMBERY amber-like
AMBLED at an easy pace; strolled
AMBLER saunterer
AMBURY⎫ a disease in turnips **B.**
ANBURY⎭
AMBUSH troops in waiting
AMENDE⎫ reparation (Fr.) recompense;
AMENDS⎭ compensation; apology
AMENED ratified
AMENTA catkins **B.**
AMERCE to fine arbitrarily
AMIDIN starch solution **Chem.**
AMIDOL **Chem.**
AMINOL an explosive **Chem.**
AMNION⎫ membrane **Med.**
AMNOIS⎭
AMOEBA protozoa **Z.**
AMOMUM cardamom; aromatic shrub
AMORAL non-moral
AMORCE toy detonator; percussion cap
AMORET sweetheart; love knot
AMOUNT sum; total; aggregate; attain
AMPERE (electrical) **Meas.**
AMPLER more copious; fuller; richer
AMREET water of immortality
AMRITA nectar; ambrosia
AMULET charm; talisman; safeguard
AMURCA olive-oil extract
AMUSED diverted; beguiled; enlivened
AMYLIC, AMYLUM starch **Chem.**
ANABAS tree climbing fish **Z.**
ANADEM garland; chaplet

ANANAS West Indian penguin **Z.**
ANARAK windcheater garment (Eskimo)
ANATTO⎫ orange-red dye used
ANOTTO⎭ for cheeses
ANCHOR often dropped; (sheet) **Naut.**
ANCOME a boil; a whitlow **Med.**
ANCONA a fowl **Z.**
ANDEAN (Andes)
ANDRON men's meeting room (Gr.)
ANELED anointed (extreme unction)
ANGARY angaria; war-rights
ANGINA quinsy **Med.**
ANGLED fished; schemed
ANGLER the fishing frog **Z.**
ANGLES early East Anglican settlers
ANGORA⎫ cloth; mohair, **Z.**
ANGORA⎭ goat; rabbit; cat **Z.**
ANHIMA horned screamer bird **Z.**
ANICUT dam for irrigation (Ind.)
ANIGHT at night
ANIMAL creature; beast; carnal **Z.**
ANIMUS malice; bias; animosity
ANKLED having ankles
ANKLET ornament or fetter
ANLACE dagger
ANNALS historical records
ANNATE⎫ first fruits **Eccl.**
ANNATS⎭
ANNEAL to temper
ANNEXE an addition
ANNONA year's produce
ANNUAL yearly
ANODIC anodal; positively polar
ANOINT anele; consecrate
ANOLIS lizard genus (Amer.) **Z.**
ANONYM pseudonym
ANOURA frog genus **Z.**
ANOXIA deficiency of oxygen **Med.**
ANSATE handled
ANSWER respond; reply; fulfil; refute
ANT-COW an aphis **Z.**
ANTHAX wood coal **Min.**
ANTHEM song of praise **Mus.**
ANTHER part of stamen **B.**
ANTIAR upas tree **B.**
ANTLER a horn **Z.**
ANTLIA proboscis of insects **Z.**
ANTRUM cavity; cave; den **Med.**
ANUBIS jackal-headed Egyptian deity
ANYHOW in any case
ANYWAY anyhow
AONIAN (Muses)
AORIST a past tense (Greek)
AORTAL⎫ arterial **Med.**
AORTIC⎭
APACHE Parisian assassin ; dance
APATHY torpor; lethargy; dulness
APEDOM apishness
APEPSY poor digestion **Med.**
APERCU a precis; a summary

APHONY loss of voice; dumbness **Med.**
APHTHA thrush disease **Med.**
APIARY (bees)
APICAL topmost
APICES culminations; highest points
APIECE to each
APINCH pinching
APLOMB self-possession; poise
APLOME garnet **Min.**
APNOEA breath cessation **Med.**
APODEL without feet or fins **Z.**
APOGEE furthest point; apex **Astr.**
APORIA rhetorical doubt
APOZEM a decoction **B.**
APPEAL entreat; implore; invoke **Law**
APPEAR seem; emerge; dawn; look
APPEND add; fasten; subjoin
APPOSE to seal; superimpose
APTERA wingless insects **Z.**
APTOTE (indeclinable)
APULSE pulsing
ARABIC
ARABIN gum arabic **B.**
ARABIS rock-cress **B.**
ARABLE tillable; cultivable
ARAISE to raise from the dead
ARANGO cornelian **Min.**
ARBOUR bower; recess; retreat; spindle
ARBUTE strawberry tree **B.**
ARCADE arched gallery
ARCADY pastoral district; (Sir Philip
ARCANA mysteries [Sidney]
ARCANE secret
ARCHED vaulted; concave
ARCHER a bowman; Zodiac sign
ARCHIL violet dye **B.**
ARCHLY roguishly; merrily; shrewdly
ARCHON Greek magistrate
ARCING electrical leakage
ARCTIC northern; boreal; cold
ARDENT fiery; fervent; intense
ARDOUR warmth; heat; passion; zeal
AREOLA⎫ cell nucleus; small area; **Med.**
AREOLE⎭ interstitial space **B.**
ARETTE entrust (Spens.)
ARGALA adjutant bird (Hind.) **Z.**
ARGALI wild sheep of Asia **Z.**
ARGAND (burner); (diagram)
ARGEMA optical ulcer **Med.**
ARGENT silver **Her.**
ARGIVE (Argos); Greek
ARGOSY richly laden vessel
ARGUED reasoned; implied; mooted
ARGUER disputed; debated; pleaded
ARGUFY wrangle
ARGUTE subtle; ingenious
ARIDAS East Indian taffeta
ARIGHT rightly
ARIOSE⎫ melodious
ARIOSO⎭ song-like recitation **Mus.**
ARISEN appeared; cropped up

ARISTA beard of corn **B.**
ARKITE Noachian
ARMADA fleet; flotilla **Naut.**
ARMIES
ARMING preparing for war
ARMLET band; creek; (armour)
ARMORY armoury; heraldry
ARMOUR defensive arms
ARMPIT the axilla **Med.**
ARNAUT Albanian mountaineer
ARNICA a plant genus **B.**
AROINT⎫ begone!
AROYNT⎭
AROUND about; encompassing
AROURA 100 square feet (Egyptian)
AROUSE excite; stir; provoke
ARPENT 100 square perches **Meas.**
ARRACH plant; the orache **B.**
ARRACK fermented toddy
ARRANT errant; unmitigated
ARREAR backward
ARRECT erect; intent; alert
ARREST stem; curb; detain; capture
ARRIDE to please; to laugh at
ARRIVE reach; attain; land; come
ARROBA Spanish 25 lbs. weight **Meas.**
ARROWY like an arrow
ARROYO ravine; gully (Sp.)
ARSHIN 30 inches (Russ.) **Meas.**
ARSINE poison gas **Chem.**
ARTERY **Med.**
ARTFUL sly; wily; subtle; astute
ARTIST painter; master; adept
ARUNDO reed genus **B.**
ASCEND climb; scale; mount
ASCENT rise; elevation; eminence
ASCIAN equator dweller
ASEITY self-origination
ASGARD abode of Norse gods
ASHAKE ashiver; aquake
ASHAME to feel shame (obs.)
ASHERY ash-heap
ASH-FLY
ASHIER more ashen; paler
ASHLAR⎫ hewn stones (Arch.)
ASHLER⎭
ASHORE stranded; aground
ASH-PAN dust-pan
ASH-PIT
ASITIA off one's oats **Med.**
ASKANT askance; obliquely
ASKARI African soldier
ASKING requesting; begging; inviting
ASLAKE to slake; to mitigate
ASLANT sloping; askew; awry
ASLEEP dormant; slumbering
ASLOPE obliquely; aslant; atilt
ASNORT snorting
ASPECT outlook; mien; bearing; view
ASPICK lavender; asp **Z., B.**

97

ASPIRE crave; soar; yearn; aim
ASPORT remove feloniously
ASPOUT spouting
ASQUAT squatting
ASSAIL attack; defame; asperse
ASSART to grub up trees, etc.
ASSENT concur; agree; accord
ASSERT declare; maintain; allege; aver
ASSESS compute; tax; rate; value
ASSETS possessions; effects
ASSIGN allot; appoint; adduce
ASSIST aid; help; succour; abet
ASSIZE to assess **Law**
ASSOIL to pardon; to soil
ASSORT group; arrange; classify
ASSUME feign; sham; arrogate
ASSURE aver; guarantee; warrant
ASTARE staring
ASTART suddenly
ASTERN aft; abaft **Naut.**
ASTERT astart; suddenly (Spens.)
ASTHMA **Med.**
ASTRAL starry; stellar; sidereal
ASTRAY erring; wandering; missing
ASTRUT puffed up (obs.)
ASTUTE artful; subtle; wily
ASWARM swarming
ASWING asway
ASWOON in a swoon
ASYLUM a sanctuary; refuge
ATABAL Moorish drum **Mus.**
ATAMAN Cossack chief
ATAVIC inherent; hereditary
ATAXIA paralysis **Med.**
ATAXIC irregular **Med.**
ATHENE goddess of wisdom and war
AT-HOME a reception
ATHROB throbbing
ATKINS British private soldier
ATOMIC minute
ATONAL lacking tone **Mus.**
ATONED reconciled; propitiated
ATONER an expiator
ATONIC unaccented; debilitated **Med.**
ATRIUM Roman hall
ATTACH annex; adhere; cement
ATTACK storm; charge; assail; impugn
ATTAIN acquire; achieve; reach; grasp
ATTASK to task
ATTEND serve; guard; hearken; heed
ATTENT intention; attentive (Spens.)
ATTEST ratify; confirm; endorse
ATTIRE garb; rig; accoutre; outfit
ATTORN transfer homage **Law**
ATTRAP array; adorn
ATTUNE harmonize; accord; adapt
ATWAIN in sunder
ATWEEN between
ATWIXT betwixt
ATYPIC unclassified; unusual **Med.**

AUBADE dawn; concert; morning song
AUBURN carroty; Titian
AUDILE (mental image of sound)
AUDION wireless amplifier
AUGEAN foul; arduous and toilsome
AUGITE volcanic rock **Min.**
AUGURY omen; portent; sign; presage
AUGUST majestic; venerable; imposing
AUMBRY ambry; cupboard **Eccl.**
AUMUCE amice; furred hood
AUNTIE aunty
AURATE a gold compound **Chem.**
AUREAT gilded; golden; auric
AUREUS Roman gold coin **Coin**
AURIGA a constellation; the Charioteer
AURIST ear specialist **Med.**
AURORA goddess of dawn
AUROUS golden; aureate
AUSPEX seer; diviner; prophet
AUSSIE an Australian
AUSTER South wind
AUSTIN Augustine
AUTHOR write; creator; cause; agent
AUTUMN the fall
AVALON a western fairy isle
AVATAR incarnation of Brahma **Eccl.**
AVAUNT begone; to boast
AVENER ⎫ master of the Horse
AVENOR ⎭ in feudal times
AVENGE vindicate; retaliate; visit
AVENUE entry; access; approach
AVERSE loath; allergic; reluctant
AVIARY a large bird-cage **Z.**
AVIATE to fly
AVIDLY voraciously; greedily; eagerly
AVISED hue; complexion
AVITAL hereditary; ancestral
AVOCAT advocate (Fr.) **Law**
AVOCET ⎫ wading birds **Z.**
AVOSET ⎭
AVOUCH maintain; guarantee
AVOURE confession; justification(Spens.)
AVOWAL frank admission; confession
AVOWED openly declared; owned
AVOWEE (advowson) **Law**
AVOWRY (replevin) **Law**
AVULSE to grab
AWAKEN rouse; stir up; kindle
AWASTE wasting
AWATCH watching; alert
AWEARY tired; faded; spent
AWEIGH atrip; apeak **Naut.**
AWHEEL cycling
AWHILE sometime; briefly; soon
AWNING tilt; canopy; baldequin
AWRACK wrecked
AXENIC free from parasites **Med.**
AXICLE sheave; pulley wheel
AXILLA armpit **Med.**

AXUNGE hog's lard; wheel-grease	
AYE-AYE squirrel-like lemur	**Z.**
AZALEA plant, rhododendron type	**B.**
AZARIN brilliant crimson dye	**Chem.**
AZAZEL Satan's standard-bearer	
AZONAL recent formation (soil)	
AZONIC not local	
AZOTIC lifeless	
AZRAEL destroying angel	
AZURED colour of azure	
AZURIN blue dye	**Chem.**
AZYGOS occurring singly	

B

BAAING bleating	
BAALIM false gods (Baal)	
BABBIT Babbit metal	
BABBLE chatter; prattle; drivel	
BABIES infants; twins; triplets	
BABISH infantile; foolish	
BABLAH acacia-rind	**B.**
BABOON	**Z.**
BACKED retired; aided; betted	
BACKER supporter; partisan	
BACKET coal-box	
BADGER pester; annoy; bait; tool	**Z.**
BAFFLE balk; thwart; acoustics	
BAFTAS cotton; muslin	
BAGFUL	
BAGGED stolen; shot	
BAGGIT salmon after spawning	**Z.**
BAGMAN commercial traveller	
BAGNIO bath-house; gaol	
BAGWIG an 18th century wig	
BAILED released on security	**Law**
BAILEE (trustee)	**Law**
BAILER one who stands bail	
BAILEY a prison; castle wall	
BAILIE alderman (Sc.)	**Law**
BAILOR bailee	
BAITED badgered; lured; enticed	
BAJREE Indian grass	**B.**
BAKERY bake-house	
BAKING cooking	
BALAAM unimportant newsprint	
BALASS a ruby	**Min.**
BALATA rubberlike gum	**B.**
BALBOA (Panama)	**Coin**
BALDER less hirsute	
BALDLY inelegantly; plainly	
BALDUR son of Odin (mistletoe)	
BALEEN whalebone	**Z.**
BALING bundling	
BALIZE a sea-mark	
BALKAN	
BALKED refused; frustrated	

BALKER fish-spotter	
BALKIS Queen of Sheba; also Aaziz	
BALLAD epic song	
BALLED clogged	
BALLET	
BALLOT vote; ticket; to elect	
BALSAM aromatic balm	**B.**
BALTIC shipping exchange	
BAMBOO	**B.**
BANANA	**B.**
BANATE ⎫ Hungarian territorial	
BANNAT ⎭ divisions (military)	
BANCOR monetary unit	
BANDED united; bound	
BANDIT outlaw; brigand; footpad	
BANDLE 2 feet (Irish)	**Meas.**
BANDOG watch-dog	**Z.**
BANGED with hair cut square	
BANGLE bracelet; armlet; ring	
BANGUE bhang; a narcotic	
BANG-UP slap-up; stylish	
BANIAN Hindu caste; fig-tree	**B.**
BANISH exile; expell; eject	
BANKED (road construction)	
BANKER fishing-boat	**Naut.**
BANKER mason's bench; card game	
BANKET auriferous rock (Transvaal)	
BANNED barred; tabooed; vetoed	
BANNER petal; flag; standard	**B.**
BANTAM carved work; small	**Z.**
BANTER twit; rally; deride; bandy	
BANYAN Indian fig; banian	**B.**
BANZAI! Japanese hurrah	
BAOBAB African tree	**B.**
BARBED bearded; hooked; pointed	
BARBEL carp	**Z.**
BARBER hairdresser	
BARBET bird; dog	**Z.**
BARCOO grass (Australia)	
BARDIC poetic; epic	
BAREGE fabric	
BARELY only just	
BAREST bleakest; baldest; plainest	
BARGED charged into; shoved	
BARGEE bargeman	
BARING uncovering; unsheathing	
BARISH rather bare	
BARIUM metallic element	**Chem.**
BARKED grazed (shins); helped	
BARKEN to become like bark	
BARKER shop-tout	
BARKIS the carrier " is willing "	
BARLEY a cereal	**B.**
BARMAN pot-man; bar-tender	
BARNED stored	
BARNEY humbug; prize fight	
BARONY	
BARQUE three-masted ship	**Naut.**
BARRAS resin	**B.**
BARRED banned; excluded; ostracized	

BARREL 36 gallon cask   **Meas.**
BARREN bare; sterile; unfertile
BARRET beret; cap   **Eccl.**
BARROW mound; tumulus; truck
BARSAC white wine (Fr.)
BARTER trade; exchange; traffic
BARTON domain lands; farm-house
BARYTA barium oxide   **Chem.**
BASALT igneous rock   **Min.**
BASELY spuriously; corruptly
BASHAW pasha (Turkish)
BASHED coshed; biffed
BASIAL osculatory
BASIFY make into a salifiable salt
BASING founding; establishing
BASKED warmed by the sun
BASKET pannier; creal; punnet; trug
BASNET helmet; basinet
BASQUE Biscayan
BASSET outcrop; (cards); hound   **Z.**
BASTED (cooking); (sewing)
BASTON heraldic baton
BASUTO African
BASYLE radicle   **Chem.**
BATATA sweet potato   **B.**
BATEAU light boat   **Naut.**
BATHED laved; suffused
BATHER
BATHOS anti-climax; bombast
BATING except; abating; deducting
BATLET linen-beater
BATMAN an officer's servant
BATOON baston; bar; staff; truncheon
BATTED (cricket)
BATTEL Oxford kitchen account
BATTEN grow fat; a lath
BATTER culinary mixture; smite
BATTLE war; strive; contest; fight
BATTON batten; a slat
BATTUE a beat; slaughter
BAUBEE, BAWBEE halfpenny (Sc.)
BAUBLE⎫ showy finery; gee-gaw;
BAUBLE⎬ jester's wand
BAWSON⎫ a badger   **Z.**
BAWSIN⎭
BAWLED clamoured; shouted; yelled
BAWLER a howler
BAWLEY Thames fishing-boat   **Naut.**
BAWTIE a hare; a dog   **Z.**
BAXTER (prints)
BAYARD a famous steed   **Z.**
BAYARD a very perfect knight
BAYEUX famous for its tapestry
BAYING in full cry
BAYRAM Mohammedan festival
BAY-RUM hair lotion
BAZAAR mart; emporium; exchange
BEACHY pebbly
BEACON signal-fire; lighthouse
BEADED strung together
BEADLE parish officer; servitor

BEAGLE a hound; jammer (radio)   **Z.**
BEAKED sharp-pointed
BEAKER a cup; glass vessel
BEAMED (antlers); smiled
BEARER a carrier; (funerals)
BEATEN defeated; hackneyed
BEATER striker; (game)
BEAUNE a French wine
BEAUTY grace; comeliness; fairness
BEAVER a hat; fur   **Z.**
BECALL miscall; vituperate
BECALM still; pacify; soothe
BECAME grew into; graced
BECKED nodded; signed
BECKET a loop   **Naut.**
BECKON call; wave; signal; invite
BECOME suit; befit; grace; adorn
BECURL to curl
BEDASH bespatter
BEDAUB smear; befoul; stain
BED-BUG cimex   **Z.**
BEDDED planted out
BEDDER millstone; a plant   **B**
BEDECK array; gild; adorn
BED-KEY bedstead tightener   **Tool**
BEDLAM mad-house; uproar
BEDRAL a beadle
BEDRID bedridden
BEDROP sprinkle; to speckle
BEDUCK to plunge under water
BEDUIN a Bedouin Arab
BEDUST cover with dust
BEENAH marriage (Ceylon)
BEEPER remote controlled aircraft
BEETLE maul; heavy mallet   **Z.**
BEEVES oxen; kine   **Z.**
BEFALL betide; happen; chance
BEFANA Epiphany present; a fairy
BEFOAM bespatter with foam
BEFOOL dupe; hoodwink; hoax
BEFORE prior to; formerly; above
BEFOUL defoul; defile; sully
BEGAUM princess (E. Indies)
BEGGAR ruin; surpass; pauper
BEGGED entreated; cadged
BEGIFT to make a presentation
BEGILD gild
BEGILT gilt
BEGIRD enclose; encircle; environ
BEGNAW to corrode
BEGONE! go away; avaunt!
BEHALF benefit; interest; advantage
BEHAVE act; comport; demean
BEHEAD decapitate; execute
BEHELD saw; surveyed; contemplated
BEHEST command; mandate; order
BEHIND abaft; following
BEHOLD regard; discern; look
BEHOOF profit; advantage; benefit
BEHOTE promised; vowed (Spens.)

BEHOVE befit; suit; beseem
BEHOWL to howl at (Shak.)
BEHUNG draped
BEJANT bejan; freshman (Sc.)
BEJUCO a cane **B.**
BEKISS kiss intensively; osculate
BELACE adorn with lace; beat
BELAMY good friend (Spens.)
BELATE delay; retard; hinder
BELAUD overpraise; bepuff
BELDAM a hag; beldame
BELFRY bat habitat; bell-tower
BELGIC Belgian
BELIAL a low and profligate devil
BELIED falsified; counterfeited
BELIEF faith; creed; dogma; tenet
BELIER a confidence-man
BELIKE likely; perhaps; maybe
BELIVE speedily; ere long (Sc.)
BELLED bellowed
BELLIS the daisy **B.**
BELLOW lead colic **Med.**
BELLOW roar; bawl; clamour
BELOCK to fasten; to lock
BELONE garfish **Z.**
BELONG to appertain
BELTED girt; zoned; girdled
BELUGA sturgeon; dolphin **Z.**
BEMASK to conceal
BEMAUL wound; disfigure; bruise
BEMBEX genus of sand-wasps **Z.**
BEMIRE bedaub; soil; besmirch
BEMOAN lament; bewail; mourn
BEMOCK deride; jeer; flout
BEMOIL bemire; bedraggle
BEMUSE daze; bewilder
BENDER spree; a stretcher
BENGAL fabric; (Lancer)
BENIGN kindly; amiable; friendly
BENNET herb **B.**
BEN-NUT oil-nut of horse-radish tree **B.**
BENSHI banshee; Irish fairy
BENUMB stupefy; deaden; blunt
BENZOL benzene **Chem.**
BEPELT pelt vigorously
BEPITY to sympathize
BEPUFF belaud; overpraise
BERATE rate; scold; chide; reprove
BERBER Moroccans of Atlas mountains
BERBER a Barbary dialect
BEREAN extinct Scottish sect
BEREFT stripped; deprived; destitute
BERLIN a vehicle; wool
BERTHA Hun gun
BESANT⎫ Byzantine gold; **Coin**
BEZANT⎭ gold heraldic circlet
BESEEM behove; befit; suit; become
BESEEN comely
BESIDE near; close to; alongside
BESIGH to sigh

BESING celebrate in song
BESMUT begrime; blacken
BESOIL defile; besmirch
BESORT to fit; to become
BESPAT spat upon
BESPED helped on
BESPIT to spit upon
BESPOT to mark with spots
BESTED overwhelmed; worsted
BESTIR hasten; rouse; strive; labour
BESTOW confer; grant; give; award
BESTUD to stud
BETAIL curtail
BETAKE remove or repair to
BETEEM produce; shed
BETHEL a chapel
BETIDE befall; happen; chance
BETIME betide; befall
BETONY a plant **B.**
BETOOK went away; left
BETORN torn to pieces
BETOSS agitate violently
BETRAP ensnare
BETRAY divulge; reveal; entrap
BETRIM arrange; to deck
BETTED wagered
BETTER superior; amend; rectify
BETTOR punter; wagerer
BEVIES flocks; crowds
BEVILE heraldic device
BEWAIL moan; lament; grieve; deplore
BEWARE achtung! heed; mind
BEWEEP bewail
BEWEPT disfigured by weeping
BEWRAP envelope; enclose
BEWRAY betray; accuse
BEWTER bittern **Z.**
BEYLIK a Bey's province
BEYOND over; past; farther
BEZANT besant; Dutch ship **Naut.**
BEZOAR a stony concretion
BHARAL wild sheep (Tibet) **Z.**
BHISTI Indian water-carrier
BIACID **Chem.**
BIASED prejudiced
BIAZAL having two optical axes
BIBBER wine-bibber; toper
BIBLUS papyrus; paper-reed **B.**
BICEPS a muscle **Med.**
BICKER bowl; quarrel; nipple
BICORN having 2 horns
BIDALE a benefit
BIDDED (auction)
BIDDER tenderer
BIDENT two-pronged
BIDING pausing; awaiting
BIFFED coshed; bashed
BIFFIN apple-pie; dried apple
BIFLEX double curve
BIFOIL twayblade plant **B.**

BIFOLD two-fold; double
BIFORM having two shapes
BI-FUEL propelled with two fuels
BIGAMY
BIG-END crank end of connecting rod
BIGGEN } child's cap
BIGGIN } small wooden bowl
BIGGER larger; greater; bulkier
BIG-WIG
BIKING cycling
BIKINI minimum two-piece garment
BILGED broad-bottomed
BILGED fractured in the bilge
BILKED defrauded
BILKER an absconder
BILLED advertised
BILLET a log; note; lodgings
BILLIE tin can; billy
BILLON an alloy
BILLOT gold or silver bar
BILLOW roll; heave; surge; swell
BIMANA bimane; two-handed
BINARY double
BINATE double; in pairs
BINDER a bandage
BINOUS binate; double
BIOTIC biological
BIOTIN B vitamin
BIPACK two-film colour photography
BIPONT (printing); bipontine
BIRDED snared
BIRDER bird catcher
BIRDIE one under bogey at golf
BIREME cf. trireme   Naut.
BIRKEN made of birch-wood
BIRKIE lively lad (Sc.)
BIRLER a carouser
BIRSLE to scorch; to toast (Sc.)
BISECT to halve
BISHOP a drink; dress   Eccl.
BISHOP horse-faking
BISLEY (rifle shooting)
BISMAR Orkney steel-yard
BISQUE (croquet handicap)
BISSON blind; blinding (Shak.)
BISTRE, BISTER brown pigment
BISTRO small eating house (Fr.)
BITING mordant; champing
BITTED (horse's bit)   Naut.
BITTEN tricked; corroded
BITTER acrimonious; sour; tart
BITTLE flat club; beetle
BITTOR the bittern   Z.
BIZARD carnation   B.
BLADED having a blade
BLAGUE blarney; swagger
BLAMED reproached; censured
BLANCH bleach; whiten; fade
BLARED trumpeted; pealed
BLASHY watery
BLAZED proclaimed; (trees)

BLAZER bright coloured sports jacket
BLAZON, BLASON to display; blare
BLEACH blanch; whiten
BLEAKY bleak; cheerless
BLEARY blear-eyed
BLEBBY bubbly; blistered
BLENCH blink; shrink; flinch
BLENDE an ore of zinc   Min.
BLENNY fish   Z.
BLEWIT mushroom   B.
BLEYME inflammation
BLIGHT mildew; wither; shrivel
BLINDS camouflage
BLINKS chickweed   B.
BLINKY blink-eyed
BLITHE merry; gay; vivacious; joyous
BLONDE silk lace; fair lady
BLOODY sanguinary
BLOOMY blooming
BLOSME bloom (Spens.)
BLOTCH a blemish; pustule
BLOTTO fuddled
BLOUSE loose outer garment
BLOWED blasted; confounded
BLOWER a whale; telephone, voice pipe
                                            Z.
BLOWSE see blouse
BLOWTH bloom; blossoms
BLOWZE coarse woman
BLOWZY fat; tawdry; unkempt
BLUELY, BLUISH of a blue colour
BLUEST most blue; gloomiest
BLUFFY rather bluff
BLUING tempering steel
BLUISM (blue stocking)
BLUNGE (clay mixing)
BOATER straw hat
BOBBED (hair); (winter sports)
BOBBIN spool; reel
BOBBLE pobble; ripple
BOBWIG wig of short hair
BOCAGE boscage; leafy underwood   B.
BODEGA wine-shop (Sp.)
BODGER pedlar; botcher
BODICE
BODIED embodied
BODIES organizations
BODILY corporeally
BODING an omen; portending
BODKIN dagger; needle for tape
BODKIN 3 crowded up
BOFFIN back-room scientist
BOGGLE to waver; to dissemble
BOGLET a small bog
BOG-OAK   B.
BOG-ORE   Min.
BOILED seethed
BOILER
BOIOBI green snake   Z.
BOLARY clay-like
102 **BOLDEN** to make bold; embolden

BOLDER more daring; saucier	**BOTONE** heraldic budding
BOLDLY confidently; valiantly	**BO-TREE** sacred tree; pipal **B.**
BOLERO Spanish dance	**BOTTLE** bundle of hay
BOLIDE meteor	**BOTTOM** basis; foot; foundation
BOLLED⎫ podded	**BOUCAN** dried meat
BOLLEN⎭ swollen	**BOUCHE** metal plug
BOLTED barred; swallowed	**BOUCLE** tube of woven cloth
BOLTER bran-machine	**BOUFFE** farcical (Fr.)
BOMBAX cotton-tree **B.**	**BOUGHT** purchased; bribed **[Med.**
BOMBED blitzed	**BOUGIE** instrument; form of music
BOMBIC, BOMBYX silkworm **Z.**	**BOULET** sloping pastern
BON-BON sugar-plum; Xmas cracker	**BOUNCE** dog-fish; rebound **Z.**
BONDED (warehoused)	**BOUNDS** (out of bounds)
BONDER binding stone or brick	**BOUNTY** gift; reward; liberality
BONGOS Conga twin drums **Mus.**	**BOURNE** destination
BONING levelling; removing bones	**BOURSE** exchange; money market
BONITO (tunny) (Sp.) **Z.**	**BOVATE** peasant holding (20 acres)
BON-MOT witticism	**BOVINE** dull; stupid
BONNET cap; (sail) **Naut.**	**BOVRIL** an extract of beef
BONNIE blithe; fair; joyous; pretty	**BOW-BOY** Cupid; Eros
BONTEN woollen stuff	**BOW-CAP** on extreme bow of airship
BON-TON chic; good style	**BOW-DYE** scarlet
BONXIE skua-gull **Z.**	**BOWELS** entrails **Med.**
BONZER lucky strike (Aust.)	**BOWERY** shady; (New York)
BOODLE money; marigold **B.**	**BOWESS** a young hawk **Z.**
BOOHOO weep aloud	**BOWFIN** mudfish (N. Amer.) **Z.**
BOOING noisily disapproving; hooting	**BOWING** fiddling; submitting
BOOKED entered; recorded	**BOWLED** (cricket); (bowls)
BOOKIE bookmaker	**BOW-LEG** a crooked leg
BOOMED advertised; resounded	**BOWLER** a hat; (cricket)
BOOMER Kangaroo **Z.**	**BOWMAN** archer; toxophilite
BOOPIC ox-eyed	**BOW-NET** lobster-pot
BOOSED, BOOZED drank, swilled	**BOW-OAR** No. 1 of a racing crew
BOOTED sacked	**BOW-PEN** a drawing instrument
BOOTEE short boot	**BOW-SAW** **Tool**
BOOTES constellation	**BOWSIE** cleat **Naut.**
BO-PEEP	**BOW-TIE**
BORAGE a plant **B.**	**BOW-WOW** **Z.**
BORATE **Chem.**	**BOWYER** bowman (obs.)
BORCER rock-drill **Tool**	**BOX-BED**
BORDAR cottage	**BOX-DAY** day for lodging papers **Law**
BORDEL bawdy-house	**BOXING** pugilism; the fancy
BORDER margin; boundary; edge	**BOYISH** youthful; puerile; young
BOREAL (North wind)	**BOYUNA** serpent **Z.**
BOREAS the North wind	**BRACED** supported; propped
BOREEN Irish lane or track	**BRACER** pick-me-up
BORING tedious; drilling	**BRAGLY** braggingly; boastfully (Spens.)
BORLEY bawley; Thames barge **Naut.**	**BRAHMA** lock
BORROW copy; assume; feign	**BRAINY** intellectual; clever
BORZOI Russian hound **Z.**	**BRAIRD** germination **B.**
BOSCHE a Hun; German soldier	**BRAISE** to stew
BOSKET a grove; small wood **B.**	**BRAIZE** red pandora fish **Z.**
BOSSED controlled; dominated	**BRAKED** put on the brake
BOSTAL hill road	**BRANCH** limb; bough; off-shoot
BOSTON a dance	**BRANDY** cognac
BOTANY Australian wool **B.**	**BRANKS** scold's bridle
BOTCHY ill-done; clumsy	**BRANKY** showy (Sc.)
BOT-FLY gad-fly **Z.**	**BRANNY** like bran
BOTHER pother; pester; worry	**BRASEN**⎫ made of brass;
BOTHIE a house; a hut (Sc.)	**BRAZEN**⎭ impudent
	BRASHY fragmentary

BRASIL Brazil wood; **B.**	**BRUCIA** a poison **Med.**
BRAZIL sappan tree	**BRUISE** batter; crush; contuse; wale
BRASSE perch **Z.**	**BRUMAL** (wintry)
BRASSY brassie; a golf club	**BRUMBY** unbroken horse **Z.**
BRAVED dared; defied; challenged	**BRUNCH** early lunch
BRAVER nobler; more daring	**BRUSHY** rough; shaggy
BRAWLY bravely; excellently	**BRUTAL** inhuman; ruthless; savage
BRAWNY hefty; lusty; sturdy; robust	**BRUTUS** a kind of wig
BRAYED ground in a mortar	**BRYONY** briony; a plant **B.**
BRAYER (printing) roller **Tool**	**BUBBLE** gurgle; cheat
BRAYLE hawk leash	**BUBBLY** champagne; effervescent
BRAZED soldered	**BUCCAL** (cheek) **Med.**
BREACH rupture; crack; rift; quarrel	**BUCCAN** dried meat
BREAST a torus: bosom; oppose; stem	**BUCKED** bleached; exhilarated
BREATH aroma; pause; exhalation	**BUCKET** pail; ride furiously
BREECH the hinder part	**BUCKIE** large whelk **Z.**
BREEKS trousers	**BUCKLE** brooch; clasp; wrinkle
BREESE breeze	**BUCKRA** white man
BREEZE gad-fly; cinders **Z.**	**BUDDED** grafted
BREEZY gusty; windy; hearty	**BUDDHA**
BREGMA part of skull **Med.**	**BUDDLE** (ore-washing)
BREHON Irish judge **Law**	**BUDGER** a stirrer; a mover
BRETON	**BUDGET** package; batch; (finance)
BREVET a patent; nominal rank	**BUDLET** a little bud **B.**
BREWED plotted; concocted	**BUFFED** buffeted; polished
BREWER a brewster; maltster	**BUFFEL** an American duck **Z.**
BRIBED seduced; hired	**BUFFER** (old); bumper; fender
BRIBER a corrupter	**BUFFET** cuff; smite; sideboard
BRICKY of brick	**BUGLED** **Mus.**
BRIDAL nuptial; conjugal	**BUGLER** **Mus.**
BRIDGE card game; span; surmount	**BUGLET** a small glass bead
BRIDLE curb; control; restrain; check	**BUGONG** a moth **Z.**
BRIERY set with brambles	**BUKSHA** (Yemen) **Coin**
BRIGHT vivid; shining; gay; merry	**BUKSHI** tip; percentage (India)
BRIGUE intrigue; cabal; strife	**BULBAR** bulbous; bulbiform;
BRILLS eye-lashes (horse)	**BULBED** bulby; bulbaceous **B.**
BRIONY bryony; a plant **B.**	**BULBIL** bud developing into a plant **B.**
BRISKY brisk; effervescing	**BULBUL** nightingale; Turkish sweet **Z.**
BRITON	**BULBUS** a corm; a bulb **B.**
BROACH hint; suggest; tap **Tool**	**BULGAR** Bulgarian
BROADS waterways	**BULGED** protruded
BROCHE brocade; embroider	**BULGER** a golf club
BROGAN leather shoe	**BULGUR** cracked wheat (Levant)
BROGUE shoe; Irish accent	**BULIMY** morbid appetite; voracity **Med.**
BROKEN fractured; snapped; smashed	**BULKED** in bulk
BROKER dealer	**BULKER** street thief
BROLLY umbrella	**BULLED** (Stock Exchange)
BROMAL oily fluid **Chem.**	**BULLER** torrential turmoil
BROMIC **Chem.**	**BULLET** projectile; slug
BRONCO unbroken horse (Amer.) **Z.**	**BUMKIN** short broom **Naut.**
BRONZE an alloy of copper and tin	**BUMMED** hummed
BRONZY bronze-like	**BUMMEL** meander; cycle seat
BROOCH (a painting); ornamental clasp	**BUMMER** camp follower; loafer
BROODY pensive; hen	**BUMMLE** to blunder; an idler
BROOKY abounding with streams	**BUMPED** thumped
BROOMY full of broom	**BUMPER** buffer; full; generous
BROUGH town; burgh; borough	**BUNCHY** clustered; tufty
BROWNY of a brown colour	**BUNDLE** parcel; package; packet; roll
BROWSE nibble; crop; feed	**BUNGED** closed up
BRUANG Malayan bear	**BUNGLE** miss; fail; botch

BUNION a swelling   **Med.**
BUNKED decamped
BUNKER (golf); (coal); bin; crib
BUNKUM blather; nonsense
BUNSEN lamp   **Chem.**
BUNTED butted
BUNTER mottled sandstone   **Min.**
BUNYIP Australian monster
BUOYED sustained; upheld
BURBLE confusion; trouble
BURBOT eel-pout   **Z.**
BURDEN chorus; incubus; load; onus
BUREAU office; department
BURGEE pennant; flag; coal   **Min.**
BURGLE to steal by night
BURGOO savoury mess
BURHEL Asiatic goat   **Z.**
BURIAL
BURIED interred; inhumed
BURKED hushed up; smothered
BURLAP coarse canvas
BURLED with knots removed
BURLER cloth-dresser
BURMAN native of Burma
BURNED (bowls); scorched; charred
BURNER flame controller
BURNET plant; moth   **B., Z.**
BURRED roughened
BURRELL pear; russet cloth   **B.**
BURROW tunnel; mine; excavate
BURSAL, BURSAE, cavity   **Med.**
BURSAR treasurer; cashier; (college)
BURSCH German student
BURTON a tackle   **Naut.**
BURYAT Central Asian Turkmens
BUS-BAR metallic rod link   **El.**
BUSHED lost in the bush
BUSHEL 8 gallons   **Meas.**
BUSIED actively employed
BUSIES detectives (slang)
BUSILY diligently; assiduously
BUSKED wearing a busk; corseted
BUSKER tragedian; street actor
BUSKIN kind of boot; cothurnus
BUSMEN transport workers
BUSSED kissed; osculated
BUSTED gone bust (slang); bankrupt
BUSTER frolic; a roisterer
BUSTLE stuffed pad; stir; tumult
BUST-UP violent quarrel
BUTANE a paraffin   **Chem.**
BUTLER
BUTTED rammed; bunted
BUTTER to flatter
BUTTON to fasten
BUXINE (alkaloid)   **Chem.**
BUYING bribing; corrupting
BUZZED spread abroad; bruited
BUZZER tatler; tell-tale

BY-BLOW illegitimate child
BYE-BYE (golf); adieu
BYE-LAW
BY-FORM a variant
BYGONE past; of yore
BY-LANE side road
BYLINA Russian poem, song
BY-NAME nickname
BY-PASS a shunt; (motoring)
BY-PAST past; gone by
BY-PATH
BY-PLAY significant acting in dumb show
BY-PLOT subsidiary plot
BY-ROAD secondary road
BY-ROOM small ante-chamber
BYSSUS fine linen cloth
BYSSUS a tuft of filaments   **Z.**
BY-TIME leisure time
BY-VIEW self-interest
BY-WALK by-path
BY-WIPE a sarcastic allusion
BY-WORD taunt; saw; adage; maxim
BY-WORK by-time work
BYZANT bezant; Turkish gold   **Coin**

C

CABALA Jewish traditional doctrine
CABANA a brand of cigars
CABBLE smash into small pieces
CABECA Indian silk
CABIRI ancient Semitic divinities
CABLED telegraphed
CABLET tow-rope
CABMAN cabby
CABRIE ⎫
CABRIT ⎬ prong-horn antelope   **Z.**
CABURN spun-yarn
CACHED hidden; concealed
CACHET a seal; distinctive stamp
CACHOU a sweetmeat
CACKLE titter; snigger; chatter
CACOON bean   **B.**
CACTAL (cactus)
CACTUS prickly plant   **B.**
CADANE Turkish carpet
CADDIE caddy (golf); messenger
CADDIS tape; a worm   **Z.**
CADENT falling; dropping
CADGED sponged; begged; importuned
CADGER huckster; beggar; mendicant
CADMIA sulphide of cadmium
CAECUM a blind sac   **Med.**
CAESAR an autocrat
CAFARD Algerian desert melancolia
CAFFRE Caffrarian
CAFTAN kaftan; Persian vest
CAGING confining; mewing; penning
CAGMAG meat unfit for food
CAHIER book; report; an issue

CAHOOT partnership
CAIMAN alligator (S. Amer.) **Z.**
CAIQUE a Turkish skiff **Naut.**
CAKING coagulating; clotting
CAJOLE coax; wheedle; beguile
CALADE (manege ground)
CALASH vehicle; hood
CALCAR glass furnace
CALCED wearing shoes; shod
CALCIC containing calcium **Chem.**
CALICO cotton cloth
CALIGO dimness of sight **Med.**
CALIPH Calif; Khalif
CALKED caulked
CALKER ⎫
CALKIN ⎭ part of horseshoe
CALLED left cards; dubbed
CALLER fresh; visitor
CALLET a scold
CALLID skilled; expert; shrewd
CALLOW unfledged; inexperienced
CALL-UP military induction
CALLUS a callosity **Med.**
CALMED quiescent; lulled; allayed
CALMLY sedately; serenely; placidly
CALORY caloric; thermal unit **Meas.**
CALPAC Eastern cap
CALTHA king-cup **B.**
CALVED
CALVER caller; fresh; cool
CALVES **Z.**
CAMAIL chain-mail
CAMASS lily (edible bulbs) **B.**
CAMATA acorns **B.**
CAMBER convexity; to arch; dock
CAMERA judge's room **Law**
CAMESE, CAMISE, CAMISO Arab shirt
CAMION motor truck, waggon
CAMLET fabric
CAMPED
CAMPER
CAMPOS Savannah (Brazil)
CAMPUS college grounds
CANAPÉ cocktail delicacy
CANARD a hoax; rumour
CANARY wine; bird; dance **Z.**
CANCAN a dance
CANCEL quash; annul; blot
CANCER the Crab (Zodiac) **Med.**
CANDID frank; honest; sincere
CANDIE 500 lbs. (Ind). **Meas.**
CANDLE light; taper
CANGUE Chinese criminal yoke
CANINE doggy
CANING thrashing
CANKER corrode; infect **Med.**
CANNED preserved; drunk
CANNEL bituminous coal **Min.**
CANNON (artillery); (billiards)
CANNOT unable

CANOPY awning; tilt; firmament
CANTAB Cambridge
CANTAR about 1 cwt. (Syrian) **Meas.**
CANTED atilt
CANTER
CANTHI corners of the eye **Med.**
CANTLE (saddle); fragment
CANTON Swiss province
CANTOR a precentor **Eccl.**
CANTUS chant **Mus.**
CANUCK Canadian
CANVAS sails in general **Naut.**
CANYON deep ravine; gulch
CAPFUL
CAPIAS writ **Law**
CAPITE royal tenant, feudal **Law**
CAPIVI balsam; copaiva **Med.**
CAPLIN small smelt **Z.**
CAPOTE long cloak (Fr.)
CAPPED (international); (hunting)
CAPRIC acid **Chem.**
CAPRID goaty
CAPRIN an acid found in butter
CAPTOR capturer
CARACK cargo-boat **Naut.**
CARACT mark; sign; character
CARAFE glass water-jug
CARANX mackerel **Z.**
CARAPA crab-wood tree (S. Amer.) **B.**
CARBOL (carbolic) **Chem.**
CARBON charcoal **Chem.**
CARBOY glass jar
CARDED combed (wool)
CARDOL cashew-nut oil **Med.**
CAREEN to heel over
CAREER rush; progress; race; life
CARESS fondle; wheedle; embrace; hug
CARFAX (cross-roads)
CARFOX carfax; four-forked
CARICA paw-paw tree **B.**
CARIES decay **Med.**
CARINA keel-like structure **B., Z.**
CARING tending; feeling
CARKED worried; perplexed
CARLOT churl; peasant
CARMAN
CARMEN carriers; an opera
CARNAL fleshy; sensual
CARNET motor passport
CARNEY horse-disease
CARPAL of the wrist **Med.**
CARPED cavilled; grumbled
CARPEL seed vessel **B.**
CARPER censurer; critic
CARPET floor fabric
CARPUS the wrist **Med.**
CARRAT carat **Meas.**
CARREL cross-bow arrow; quarry
CARROT **B.**
CARTED removed

CARTEL (exchange); challenge
CARTER wagoner
CARTON (bulls-eye); pasteboard box
CARVED hewn; chiselled; engraved
CARVEN cut; sliced; shaped
CARVEL jelly fish; caravel   **Naut., Z.**
CARVER sculptor; a knife
CASEIC (cheese)   **Chem.**
CASEIN milk protein
CASERN barracks
CASEUM caseine   **Chem.**
CASHED converted into specie
CASHEW tropical American tree   **B.**
CASHOO catechu; an astringent   **B.**
CASING boxing; packing; wrapping
CASINO saloon; gaming-house
CASKET jewel case; reliquary
CASQUE a helmet; morion
CASSIA plant; cinnamon   **B.**
CASTER cruet; small wheel
CASTLE citadel; fortress; stronghold
CASTOR beaver genus   **Z.**
CASTOR a hat; plant   **B.**
CASUAL accidental; fortuitous
CASULA a chasuble   **Eccl.**
CATCHY deceptive; infectious
CATENA a chain; a series
CATGUT cord; violin string   **Z.**
CATHAY China; (Marco Polo)
CATION (electrical)
CATKIN pendulous inflorescence   **B.**
CAT-LAP tame tipple
CATLOG catalogue
CATNAP forty winks; doze
CATNIP mint; catmint   **B.**
CATSUP a relish; ketchup
CATTED anchor housed
CATTLE kine; oxen   **Z.**
CAUCUS political organization
CAUDAL tail-bearing
CAUDEX palm-stem   **B.**
CAUDLE hot spiced wine
CAUGHT trapped; entangled
CAUKED ⎫
CAWKED ⎬ water-tight   **Naut.**
CAUKER ⎰ (caulking oakum);
CAWKER ⎱ a dram; a tall story   **Naut.**
CAULIS stem   **B.**
CAUSAL producing; resulting
CAUSED occasioned; created; effected
CAUSER instigator; prime mover
CAUSEY pavée; causeway (obs.)
CAUTEL craft; wariness (obs.)
CAUTER searing-iron
CAVASS kavass; Turkish policeman
CAVEAT a warning   **Law**
CAVERN cave; grotto; den
CAVIAR fish-roe of the sturgeon   **Z.**
CAVIES guinea-pig   **Z.**
CAVING giving way
CAVITY void; pocket; vacuum

CAVORT prance; buck
CAWASS attendant (Arab)
CAXTON a book in black letter
CAYMAN alligator; caiman   **Z.**
CAYUSE Wild West bronco; nag   **Z.**
CEASED stopped; desisted; terminated
CECILS rissoles
CECITY blindness   **Med.**
CEDARN ⎫ made of cedar-wood;   **B.**
CEDARY ⎰ of cedar colour
CEDING yielding; resigning
CEDRAT citron   **B.**
CEDULA S. American mortgage   **Law**
CELERY   **B.**
CELIAC coeliac; abdominal   **Med.**
CELLAR vault
CELLED honeycombed; alveolate
CELTIC Keltic
CEMENT cohere; unite; attach
CENSED redolent with incense
CENSER tray for burning incense   **Eccl.**
CENSOR critic; inspector; carper
CENSUS official enumeration
CENTAL 100 lbs.   **Meas.**
CENTRE also center; middle; midst
CEPOLA snake-fish   **Z.**
CERAGO pollen   **B.**
CERATE an ointment   **Med.**
CEREAL grain; corn   **B.**
CEREUS a cactus genus   **B.**
CERINE an ore of cerium   **Min.**
CERING covering with wax
CERIPH serif; (printing)
CERISE cherry-colour
CERITE cerium silicate   **Chem.**
CERIUM metallic element   **Chem.**
CEROON seroon; a bale
CERRIS the bitter oak   **B.**
CERTES ⎫ in sooth;
CERTIE ⎰ certainly (Sc.)
CERUSE white-lead   **Chem.**
CERVUS the stag genus   **Z.**
CESSED taxed
CESSIO an assignment   **Law**
CESTUI a beneficiary   **Law**
CESTUS a girdle; boxing glove
CESURA ⎫ metrical pause;
CESURE ⎰ an interruption
CETATE   **Chem.**
CETINE spermaceti   **Z.**
CHABUK Eastern ship   **Naut.**
CHACMA baboon   **Z.**
CHAFED fretted by rubbing; galled
CHAFER a beetle; cockchafer   **Z.**
CHAFFY light; worthless; jovial
CHAGAN a Khan
CHAISE vehicle; shay
CHALET Swiss cottage
CHALKA Zulu king
CHALKY

CHANCE happen; betide; fortune	**CHITAL** spotted deer	**Z.**
CHANCY hazardous; risky; fortuitous	**CHITIN** horny material	**Z.**
CHANGE alter; vary; shift; veer	**CHITON** a mollusc; Greek tunic	**Z.**
CHANTY sailor's song **Naut.**	**CHITTY** childish; infantile	
CHAPEL a printer's association **Eccl.**	**CHIVVY** hasten, nag, pester	
CHAPPY cleft; chinky	**CHOICE** select; dainty; option; election	
CHARET a chariot (Spens.)	**CHOKED** stifled; throttled; suppressed	
CHARGE command; bid; trust; ward	**CHOKER** a tie; a neckerchief	
CHARON ferryman of the Styx	**CHOKEY** prison	
CHARRY like charcoal	**CHOLER** anger; ire; spleen; rage	
CHASED followed; tracked; engraved	**CHOLIC** (bile); bilious **Med.**	
CHASER hunter; pursuer **Tool**	**CHOOSE** pick; elect; adopt; prefer	
CHASMY gaping; yawning	**CHOOSY** pernickety; fastidious	
CHASSE a liqueur; dance step	**CHOPIN** quart (Sc.) **Meas.**	
CHASTE pure; incorrupt; virtuous	**CHOPPY** irregular	
CHATON the head of a ring (Fr.)	**CHORAL** chanted	
CHATTA umbrella (Ind.)	**CHOREA** St. Vitus' dance **Med.**	
CHATTY talkative; gossipy	**CHOREE** trochee	
CHAWED } gnawed; crunched	**CHORIA** external membranes **B.**	
CHEWED }	**CHORIC** (chorus)	
CHECKY checkered	**CHORUS** **Mus.**	
CHEEKY insolent; impudent	**CHOSEN** elected; selected; picked	
CHEERY buoyant; merry; blithe	**CHOUAN** Breton guerilla	
CHEESE	**CHOUGH** a crow **Z.**	
CHEESY chic	**CHOUSE** to cheat; a trick	
CHEKOA porcelain-clay **Min.**	**CHOWRY** fly-whisk (Ind.)	
CHENAR Kashmir tree **B.**	**CHRISM** Holy oil **Eccl.**	
CHEQUE a draft	**CHROME** metal **Chem.**	
CHERRY ruddy; a fruit tree **B.**	**CHUBBY** plump; buxom	
CHERTY flinty **Min.**	**CHUFFY** puffy; surly	
CHERUB angel; child	**CHUKKA** period of play at polo	
CHERUP to chirp; to urge	**CHUMMY** sociable; matey	
CHESIL gravel; shingle **Min.**	**CHUNAM** lime; stucco (Ind.) **Min.**	
CHESTY low pitched	**CHURCH** temple; kirk **Eccl.**	
CHETAH leopard **Z.**	**CHURLY** churlish; surly; sullen	
CHEVAL a frame	**CHUTNY** chutnee; chutney	
CHEVEN chevin; chub **Z.**	**CHYLDE** churlish; surly; sullen	
CHEVET an apse (Arch.)	**CHYMIC** chemical **Chem.**	
CHEWET chough; chatterer **Z.**	**CHYPRE** a perfume	
CHIASM (optic nerve) **Med.**	**CICADA** } a chirping insect **Z.**	
CHIAUS chouse; a cheat (obs.)	**CICALA** }	
CHICHA liquor from maize (S. Amer.)	**CICELY** a genus of plants; myrrh **B.**	
CHICLE chewing gum **B.**	**CICERO** a fount of type	
CHICLY fashionably modishly	**CICUTA** hemlock; cow-bane **B.**	
CHICOT jester to Henri III.	**CIGALE** cigala; cicada **Z.**	
CHILDE chylde; nobleman's son	**CIERGE** wax candle **Eccl.**	
CHILLI cayenne pepper **B.**	**CILERY** carving; carved foliage (Arch.)	
CHILLY bleak; frigid	**CILICE** hair-cloth	
CHIMED struck; accorded	**CIMBEX** the saw-fly **Z.**	
CHIMER bishop's robe **Eccl.**	**CIMBIA** a fillet (Arch.)	
CHINCH grain insect; bed-bug; cimex **Z.**	**CIMIER** crest of helmet (Fr.)	
CHINED cleft to the back-bone	**CIMISE** bed-bug; cimex **Z.**	
CHINEE a Chinaman	**CIMNEL** simnel; Saffron cake	
CHINKY gaping; chappy	**CINDER** ember; ash	
CHINSE to caulk **Naut.**	**CINEMA** kinema; movies; talkies	
CHINTZ floral cotton cloth	**CINGLE** surcingle; girth; cinch	
CHIPPY off colour	**CINQUE** (cards or dice); (ports)	
CHIRPY chatty; cheerful; cheery	**CINTRE** centering (Arch.)	
CHISEL to cheat **Tool**	**CIPHER** zero; dot; nought; device	
CHISIL chesil; gravel **Min.**	**CIPPUS** funereal column	

CIRCAR district (Hind.)		
CIRCLE ring; compass; circuit; set		
CIRCUS		
CIRRUS tendril; cloud	**B.**	
CISLEU a Jewish month		
CISSUS wild vine	**B.**	
CISTED in a cyst; entombed		
CISTIC cystic	**Med.**	
CISTIL pewter box		
CISTUS rock-rose	**B.**	
CITESS citizeness		
CITHER zither (guitar)	**Mus.**	
CITIED with many cities		
CITING quoting; summoning		
CITOLE a dulcimer; psaltery	**Mus.**	
CITRIC (lemons)	**Chem.**	
CITRIL song bird; a finch	**Z.**	
CITRIN vitamin P		
CITRON a fruit	**B.**	
CITRUL the pumpkin	**B.**	
CITRUS plant genus	**B.**	
CIVICS science of citizenship		
CIVISM good citizenship		
CIVIES mufti		
CLAGGY sticky; cloggy; cledgy		
CLAMMY dank; viscous; sticky		
CLAQUE hired applause		
CLARET a wine; a colour		
CLARTY miry; muddy		
CLASSY superior; high-toned		
CLATCH botch; daub		
CLAUSE paragraph; proviso; condition		
CLAVER gossip (Sc.)		
CLAVES Cuban percussion	**Mus.**	
CLAVIS a translation; a key		
CLAWED torn; scratched; lacerated		
CLAYES hurdles; wattles		
CLAYEY like clay; cledgy		
CLEAVE cling; cohere; split; rend		
CLECHE a cross voided (Her.)		
CLEDGE fuller's earth	**Min.**	
CLEDGY clayey; tenacious		
CLENCH clinch; secure; fasten; grapple		
CLERGY the cloth	**Eccl.**	
CLERIC clerical; a clerk		
CLEUCH clough (Sc.); ravine		
CLEVER able; adroit; gifted; dexterous		
CLEVIS draught-iron of plough		
CLEWED coiled; trussed	**Naut.**	
CLICHE artist's proof; trite phrase		
CLIENT customer; dependant		
CLIFFY ⎫ craggy; broken		
CLIFTY ⎭		
CLIMAX acme; zenith; height; top		
CLINCH clench; clutch; catch; grasp		
CLINGY adhesive; sticky		
CLINIC (bedside); hospital	**Med.**	
CLIONE "whales' food"; small fish	**Z.**	
CLIQUE coterie; junto; cabal; set		
CLOACA a sewer		

CLOCHE bell-glass; (hat)		
CLODDY clodly; earthy; gross; boorish		
CLOGGY adhesive; clingy		
CLOKED cloaked; concealed		
CLONIC convulsive		
CLONUS a spasm	**Med.**	
CLOSED united; grappled; shut		
CLOSER closure; tighter		
CLOSET small room		
CLOTHE attire; drape; invest; robe		
CLOTTY curdy		
CLOUDY dim; overcast; gloomy; murky		
CLOUGH ravine; cleft; chine		
CLOUGH trade allowance		
CLOVEN cleft; split asunder		
CLOVER trifolium	**B.**	
CLOYED satiated; cumbered; surfeited		
CLUMPS a numskull; nitwit; dullard		
CLUMPY massive; shapeless		
CLUMSY awkward; heavy-handed		
CLUNCH marl; clay	**Min.**	
CLUPEA sprat genus	**Z.**	
CLUTCH (of eggs); grasp; clench; grip		
COACHY a coachman		
COAITA S. American monkey coati	**Z.**	
COALED stoked		
CO-ALLY fellow-helper; partner		
COARSE crude; impure; rough; rude		
COATED spread; covered		
COATEE coat with short tails		
COAXED persuaded; allured; seduced		
COAXER cajoler; flatterer; wheedler		
COBALT metal; blue	**Chem.**	
COBBLE a stone; to repair	**Min.**	
COBCAL sandal		
COBNUT hazel-nut	**B.**	
COBRES S. American indigo	**B.**	
COBRIC cobra-type	**Z.**	
COBURG a twilled fabric		
COBWEB flimsy fly-trap		
COCCUS seed-vessel; microbe	**Med., B.**	
COCCYX terminal bone of spine	**Med.**	
COCHIN a fowl	**Z.**	
COCKAL the game of knuckle-bones		
COCKED erect; inebriated		
COCKER to pamper; a spaniel	**Z.**	
COCKER famous for his arithmetic		
COCKET customs seal; a certificate		
COCKLE a weed	**B.**	
COCKLE shell-fish; to pucker	**Z.**	
COCKSY bumptious; conceited		
COCOON	**Z.**	
CODBER pillow-slip		
CODDED in a pod; hoaxed		
CODDER a gatherer of peas		
CODDLE indulge; pamper; humour		
CODGER an eccentric old man		
CODIFY digest; regulate		
CODING putting into cipher		
CODIST summarist; arranger		

CODLIN an apple **B.**
COELOM the body cavity **Med.**
COERCE force; impel; constrain
COEVAL contemporaneous
COFFEE **B.**
COFFER panel (Arch.); chest
COFFIN a printing frame
COFFLE a slave gang
COGENT potent; urgent; forcible
COGGED toothed; cheated
COGGIE small bowl
COGGLE small boat **Naut.**
COGNAC brandy
COHEIR joint heir
COHERE cleave; unite; join; stick
COHORN obsolete trench-mortar
COHORT tenth part of a legion
COHUNE palm **B.**
COIGNE enforced billeting (Ir.)
COILED spiral; wound
COINED invented; minted
COINER counterfeiter; inventor
CO-JOIN join together; unite
COKING taking cocaine
COLDER chillier
COLDLY frigidly
COLLAR
COLLED embraced; hugged
COLLET collar; setting of a jewel
COLLIE colley; sheep-dog **Z.**
COLLOP a slice of meat
COLLUM lowest part of stem **B.**
COLMAR pear **B.**
COLMEY the coal-fish **Z.**
COLONY a settlement
COLOUR tint; hue; dye; shade
COLTER ploughshare
COLUMN pillar; file; row; line
COLURE (astronomical term)
COMARB abbot; coarb **Eccl.**
COMART an agreement
COMATE comose; hairy; hirsute
COMBAT contest; war; resist; oppose
COMBED
COMBER foaming billow
COMEDO a blackhead **Med.**
COMEDY a play
COMELY seemly; graceful; shapely
COMFIT sweetmeat; confit
COMFRY comfrey; wild plant **B.**
COMING approach; future; expected
COMITY courtesy; civility
COMMIS waiter's assistant; deputy
COMMIT entrust; enact; consign
COMMIX to mix; mingle
COMMON public; ordinary; usual
COMOSE hairy; downy; comate
COMPEL coerce; oblige; make
COMPLY agree; submit; yield; conform
COMPOT a preserve

CONCHA ear-cavity; conch **Med.**
CONCHY conscientious objector
CONCUR agree; harmonize; help
CONDED navigated; steered;
CONNED memorized; studied
CONDER pilot; fish-scout
CONDOR vulture **Z.**
CONFAB pow-wow; conference
CONFER bestow; grant; consult
CONFIT comfit; sweetmeat
CONFIX fasten; attach; append
CONGEE conjee; dismissal; farewell
CONGER eel **Z.**
CONGOU black tea **B.**
CONICS geometry of the cone
CONIES rabbits; pikas; **Z.**
CONEYS hyrax genus
CONIIN conin; hemlock extract **Med.**
CONIMA gum resin **B.**
CONINE an alkaloid **Med.**
CONIUM hemlock **B.**
CONJEE congee; rice-water
CONKED petered out
CONKER chestnut **B.**
CON-MAN trickster; swindler
CONNER an inspector; look-out **[Med.**
CONOID pineal gland; a paraboloid
CONSUL a government official
CONTRA against; opposite
CONVEX protuberant
CONVEY carry; transport; transfer
CONVOY escort; guard; protect
CONYZA fleabane **B.**
COOEED (Australian bush call)
COOING and billing
COOKED done to a turn
COOKER cooking-range
COOKIE super-heavy bomb; a bun
COOLED calmed; allayed; moderated
COOLER a drink; colder
COOLIE labourer (China)
COOLLY calmly; placidly; impudently
COOMBE combe; deep valley
COONTY arrowroot (Florida) **B.**
COOPED cabined and confined
COOPER a mixed drink; cask-maker
COOTIE feathered legs (Sc.)
COPANG Japanese gold coin **Coin**
COPECK 1/100th part of rouble **Coin**
COPIED transcribed; aped
COPIER copyer; scribe; plagiarist
COPIES reduplications; imitations
COPING top course of a wall; striving
COPPED caught; run in
COPPER a P.C.; a penny **Coin**
COPPIN ball of thread
COPTIC (Egyptian Christianity)
COPULA a link
COQUET to flirt
CORBAN, KURBAN gift; ceremony

CORBEL stone bracket (Arch.)
CORBIE a raven; carrion crow **Z.**
CORCLE embryo seed **B.**
CORCUR purple dye
CORDED ribbed; furrowed
CORDON a ribbon of honour; a guard
COREAN or **KOREAN**
CORING boring; drilling
CORIUM true skin **Med.**
CORKED (wine)
CORKER a poser; a finisher
CORKIR red or purple lichen dye
CORMUS stem **B.**
CORNEA eye-membrane **Med.**
CORNED preserved; granulated; salted
CORNEL dog-wood **B.**
CORNER bend; angle; nook; cranny
CORNET an officer; trumpet **Mus.**
CORNUA horns **Z.**
CORODY an allowance; a pension
CORONA a halo; a crown; a cigar
COROZO vegetable ivory **B.**
CORPSE carcass; corse; remains
CORPUS a body; association **Med.**
CORRAL cattle-pen; to round up
CORRIE a hollow; a valley (Sc.)
CORSAC, CORSAK Central Asian fox **Z.**
CORSET a bodice; stays
CORTES Spanish Parliament
CORTEX treebark; covering **B.**
CORVEE forced levy (pre-1789 Fr.)
CORVEE recruitment for road service
CORVET curvet; leap; frolic
CORVUS a crow **Z.**
CORVUS grappling iron
CORYMB a panicle; a raceme **B.**
CORYZA snuffy cold **Med.**
COSHED bashed; slugged
COSHER to pamper; to chat
COSIER a botcher; cozier; cobbler
COSILY snugly
COSINE (geometry)
COSMIC cosmical; orderly
COSMOS universe; order
COSSAS Indian Muslims
COSSET a pet lamb; to pet **Z.**
COSTAL (rib) **Med.**
CO-STAR actors cast together
COSTER costermonger; apple-seller
COSTLY dear; sumptuous; rich
COTISE a bendlet (Her.)
COTTAR a cottager; cotter
COTTER wedge; pin
COTTON to harmonize; attract **B.**
COTYLA a sucker **Z.**
COTYLE bone-cavity; cup **Med.**
COUCAL cuckoo **Z.**
COUGAR puma **Z.**
COULEE ravine; couloir
COUPED bartered for; cut off

COUPEE an antic; a salute
COUPER a dealer
COUPLE pair; brace; connect
COUPON a voucher
COURAP disease (E. Ind.) **Med.**
COURSE circuit; orbit; progress; series
COUSIN a Kinsman
COUTER £1 (slang)
COUTIL strong cotton fabric
COVENT a convent **Eccl.**
COVERT concealed; secret; thicket
COVESS female cove or chap
COVING (fireplace); (jutting out)
COWAGE a leguminous plant **B.**
COWARD craven; dastard; recreant
COW-BOY
COWDIE cowrie-pine **B.**
COWING intimidating; browbeating
COWISH like a cow
COWLED hooded
COW-MAN cow-herd
COW-POX
COWRIE sea-shell; cowry **Z.**
COYISH coy; rather reserved
COYOTE prairie wolf **Z.**
COYPOU coypu; rodent (S. Amer). **Z.**
COZIER tramp; cosier
CRABBY perplexing; peevish
CRABER water-vole **Z.**
CRABRO hornet genus **Z.**
CRADLE crib; a frame; to compose
CRAFTY artful; deceitful; cunning
CRAGGE the neck
CRAGGY rugged; rough; jagged
CRAMBO a game; a rhyme
CRAMPY affected with cramp
CRANCH crunch; chew
CRANED with neck out-stretched
CRANIA skulls (cranium) **Med.**
CRANKY eccentric; crotchet
CRANNY chink; fissure; cleft; rift
CRANTS funeral garlands
CRAPED curled
CRASIS temperament **Med.**
CRATCH hay-rack; manger
CRATED boxed; encased
CRATER bomb-hole
CRAVAT necktie
CRAVED entreated; desired
CRAVEN coward; recreant; dastard
CRAVER beggar; an addict
CRAYER small trading ship **Naut.**
CRAYON chalk pencil
CRAZED decrepit; loony; deranged
CREACH } foray (Sc.);
CREAGH } booty; raid
CREAKY crepitative
CREAMY
CREANT forming; creative
CREASE Malay dagger; creese

CREASE (cricket); a fold
CREASY crumpled
CREATE cause; fashion; invent
CRECHE a day-nursery ·
CREDIT trust; loan; merit; belief
CREEKY winding
CREEPY, CREEPS eerie; horrific
CREESE Malay dagger; crease
CREESH grease (Sc.)
CREMOR creamy juice
CRENEL loophole or notch
CRENIC acid   **Chem.**
CREOLE West Indian half-breed
CREPON crepe fabric
CRESOL tar product   **Chem.**
CRESSY like water-cress   **B.**
CRESTA the ice-run at St. Moritz
CRETIC a metric foot
CRETIN deformed; idiot; moron
CREVET goldsmith; crucible
CREWEL embroidery
CRIKEY !
CRIMED charged with
CRIMPY frizzy, waved
CRINAL hairy; comate; hirsute
CRINGE fawn; stoop; cower
CRISES decisive moments
CRISIS emergency; turning point
CRISPY curled; brittle
CRISTA a crest
CRITIC arbiter; reviewer; judge
CROAKY harsh; guttural
CROATS Croatia (Yugoslavia)
CROCUS the saffron   **B.**
CRONET horse-hoof hair
CROOKS tubular devices   **Mus.**
CROPPY crop-eared
CROSSE lacrosse stick
CROTCH a crutch; a fork
CROTON oil plant   **B.**
CROUCH cringe; stoop; cower
CROUPY affected with croup   **Med.**
CROUSE lively; pert (Sc.)
CROWDY gruel (Sc.)
CROWED exulted; boasted
CRUCKS tree trunk framework   **Arch.**
CRUDER rougher; coarser; harsher
CRUISE ocean travel
CRUIVE fish trap
CRUMBY in crumbs; crummy
CRUMMY cow with crumpled horn   **Z.**
CRUNCH cranch; munch; bite
CRURAL leggy   **Med.**
CRUSET crucible; crevet
CRUSIE lamp with rush wick (Sc.)
CRUSTA engraved gem; a shell
CRUSTY surly; peevish; morose; crabby
CRUTCH to support
CRYING notorious; outcry; clamour
CUBAGE solid content

CUBICA shallon cloth
CUBING raising to third power
CUBISM modern artistic geometry
CUBIST geometrical daubist
CUBOID (cubical)
CUBSHA Indian drug
CUCKOO   **Z.**
CUDDIE a donkey; a silly ass   **Z.**
CUDDLE hug; embrace; fondle
CUDGEL bludgeon; club; batter
CUE-BID (Contract bridge)
CUE-OWL scops-owl; a migrant owl   **Z.**
CUERPO querpo; undress; partial array
CUISSE thigh-armour
CUITER fondle; pamper
CULDEE order of monks   **Eccl.**
CULLED picked; gathered
CULLER a selector
CULLET scrap-glass
CULLIS broth; jelly; gutter; groove
CULMEN summit; highest point
CULTCH oyster-spawn   **Z.**
CULTUR Kultur, German culture
CULTUS a cult
CULVER pigeon; wood-pigeon   **Z.**
CUMBER hamper; impede; clog
CUMMER kimmer; godmother; gossip
CUMMIN, CUMIN spice seed; anti-colic
CUNEAL wedge-shaped
CUPFUL   **Meas.**
CUP-MAN boon companion
CUPOLA dome; furnace
CUPPED bled; hollowed
CUPPER cup-bearer
CUPRIC (copper)   **Chem.**
CUP-TIE football
CUPULA acorn-cup   **B.**
CUPULE filbert-husk; cupula   **B.**
CURACY   **Eccl.**
CURARA ⎫
CURARE ⎬ arrow poison used by
CURARI ⎭ South American Indians
CURATE an incumbent   **Eccl.**
CURBED restrained; held back
CURCAS a nut   **B.**
CURDLE coagulate; congeal
CURFEW time to rake out the fires
CURIET cuirass (Spens.)
CURING preserving; healing; remedying
CURLED rippled; waved; twisted
CURLER (ice); (hair)
CURLEW the whaup   **Z.**
CURRED purred; cooed
CURRIE quarry (obs.)
CURSED anathematized; tormented
CURSER vituperator
CURSOR a slide-rule adjunct
CURSUS a course; curriculum
CURTAL docked; curt
CURTER more brusque; terser

CURTLY concisely; shortly; briefly	**DAGGLE** bedraggle; defile; sully
CURTSY curtesy; an obeisance	**DAGOBA** Buddhist shrine **Eccl.**
CURULE Roman chair	**DAGOES** Spaniards and Italians
CURVED arched; bent; bowed	**DAHLIA** a flower genus **B.**
CURVET corvet: leap: frolic	**DAIKER** to adorn; to deck
CUSCUS fibre; North African dish **B.**	**DAIMIO** Japanese noble
CUSCUS flying squirrel **Z.**	**DAINTY** choice; exquisite; tasty; chic
CUSHAT ring-dove **Z.**	**DAKOIT** pirate; robber; dacoit
CUSPID a canine tooth **Med.**	**DALILA** Delilah; a betrayer
CUSSED cursed (slang)	**DALLOP** a tuft of grass; a lump
CUSTOM habit; usage; wont; tax	**DAMAGE** mar; hurt; impair; injury
CUSTOS a keeper	**DAMASK** linen fabric
CUTCHA temporary (Ind.)	**DAMMAR** resin; damar **B.**
CUTEST most cunning; slyest	**DAMMED** embanked; confined
CUTLER a dealer in knives	**DAMNED** condemned; doomed
CUTLET	**DAMPED** moderated; deadened
CUT-OFF	**DAMPEN** moisten; discourage; depress
CUT-OUT (motoring)	**DAMPER** (food); a regulator
CUTTER a tailor **Naut.**	**DAMPLY** unenthusiastically
CUTTLE squid **Z.**	**DAMSEL** lass; maiden; girl
CUTTOE large knife (U.S.)	**DAMSON** small plum **B.**
CYANIC **Chem.**	**DANCED** capered; frisked; hopped
CYCLED	**DANCER** a ballerina; Pavlova; Salome
CYCLIC periodic; epic	**DANDER** saunter; anger
CYCLUS a bicycle or tricycle	**DANDIE** terrier **Z.**
CYGNET young swan **Z.**	**DANDLE** pet; fondle; caress
CYGNUS swan genus **Z.**	**DANGER** risk; peril; hazard; jeopardy
CYMBAL **Mus.**	**DANGLE** to fondle; swing; suspend
CYMENE (camphor) **Med.**	**DANIEL** a wise judge
CYMOID having a waving profile	**DANISH**
CYMOSE ⎫ (inflorescence definite **B.**	**DANITE** (Mormon sect)
CYMOUS ⎭ or centrifugal)	**DANTON** to daunt; to subdue (Sc.)
CYMRIC Welsh	**DAPHNE** evergreens **B.**
CYNARA artichoke genus **B.**	**DAPPED** fished with a may-fly
CYNICS Athenian philosophical sect	**DAPPER** neat; nimble; sprightly
CYPHEL flowering shrub **B.**	**DAPPLE** to variegate with spots
CYPHER cipher; naught; a nonentity	**DARGER** day-worker
CY-PRES near **Law**	**DARING** lark snaring; audacious
CYPRIS shrimp species **Z.**	**DARKEN** darkle; cloud
CYPRUS black fabric	**DARKEN** obscure; perplex
CYSTIC, CYSTIS bladder **Med.**	**DARKER** blacker; duskier
CYTASE an enzyme **Med.**	**DARKEY, DARKIE** negro
CYTOID cell-like	**DARKLE** to grow dark
	DARKLY opaquely; mysteriously
	DARNED repaired; mended
D	**DARNEL** rye grass; tares **B.**
	DARNER a darning machine
DABBED pecked; patted	**DARTED** sprang out; shot; flew
DABBER an inking ball	**DARTER** Brazilian pelican **Z.**
DABBLE mix; meddle; sprinkle	**DARTLE** spring out
DABOIA venomous snake **Z.**	**DARTRE** skin-disease; herpes **Med.**
DACKER to saunter; to lounge (Sc.)	**DASHED** cast; sped; rushed; shattered
DACOIT pirate; robber (Burma)	**DASHER** plunger
DACRON polyester fibre	**DASSIE** badger; hyrax **Z.**
DACTYL finger or toe	**DATARY** papal officer
DADDLE walk totteringly	**DATING** reckoning; beginning
DAEDAL intricate; mazy; complex	**DATIVE** a case
DAEMON friendly spirit	**DATURA** thorn-apple **B.**
DAFTLY idiotically; crazily	**DAUBED** smeared; plastered
DAGGED cut into slips	**DAUBER** inferior painter
DAGGER dirk; stiletto; poniard	

DAUBRY the work of a dauber
DAUCUS the carrot **B.**
DAUNER dander; perambulate
DAVINA volcanic substance **Min.**
DAVITS **Naut.**
DAWDLE lag; dally; idle; trifle
DAWISH like a jack-daw
DAWNED began to appear
DAY-BED a sofa
DAY-BOY non-resident schoolboy
DAY-FLY an ephemeral insect **Z.**
DAZING mazing; stunning
DAZZLE daze; confuse; bewilder
DEACON **Eccl.**
DEADEN benumb; blunt; obtund
DEADLY fatal; mortal; baneful; lethal
DEAFEN confuse; stun
DEAFLY unhearingly
DEALER vendor; monger; trader
DEARER costlier; fonder
DEARIE term of endearment
DEARLY expensively
DEARTH scarcity; lack; shortage
DEASIL opp. to widdershins
DEBARK disembark; land
DEBASE degrade; lower; humble
DEBATE dispute; contest; argue
DEBLAI cf. remblai; excavated soil
DEBOSH debauch (obs.)
DEBOUT to expel
DEBRIS bits and pieces
DEBTED indebted; owed
DEBTEE the lender **Law**
DEBTOR the borrower
DEBUNK expose; unmask; reveal
DECADE ten of
DECAMP abscond; bolt; fly
DECANI deans **Eccl.**
DECANT to pour gently
DECARE 1000 sq. metres **Meas.**
DECEIT guile; fraud; chicanery
DECENT proper; seemly; suitable
DECERN to judge; to decree
DECIDE settle; determine; resolve
DECILE (astronomical aspect)
DECIMA a tenth **Mus.**
DECIME a tenth of a franc **Coin**
DECKED adorned; arrayed **Naut.**
DECKER adorner **Naut.**
DECKLE paper gauge
DECOCT to boil; to devise; digest
DECODE decipher
DECREE ordain; ukase; fiat; edict
DECREW to decrease (Spens.)
DECURY squad of ten (Roman)
DEDANS gallery (tennis)
DEDUCE infer; gather; conclude
DEDUCT bate; subtract; withdraw
DEEDED conveyed by deed **Law**
DEEMED believed; determined; judged

DEEPEN darken
DEEPER further down
DEEPLY profoundly
DEFACE disfigure; injure; sully
DEFAME asperse; vilify; traduce
DEFEAT rout; frustrate; overwhelm
DEFECT flaw; blemish; fault
DEFEND ward; protect; guard
DEFIED challenged; braved
DEFIER scorner; ignorer; spurner
DEFILE violate; taint; vitiate; a gorge
DEFINE specify; explain; limit
DEFLEX bend down
DEFLUX a discharge **Med.**
DEFORM distort; deface; spoil
DEFRAY pay; meet; liquidate; bear
DEFTLY deftly; dextrously; adroitly
DEGAGE unconstrained (Fr.)
DEGREE grade; rank; class; order
DEGUST to taste
DEHORN remove horns from cattle
DEHORS irrelevant (Fr.) **Law**
DEHORT dissuade
DE-ICER anti-wing-ice device
DEIFIC divine; godlike
DEJECT cast down; depress; dishearten
DELATE to sneak; to inform
DELETE erase; obliterate; efface
DELIAC, DELIAN (of Delas) a vase
DELICE, DELUCE fleur-de-lis
DELICT an offence; crime **Law**
DELUDE dupe; beguile; trick; cozen
DELUGE flood; cataclysm; inundate
DELVED dug; excavated; searched
DELVER a digger
DEMAIN demesne; an estate
DEMAND query; claim; require; exact
DEMEAN behave; lower; degrade
DEMENT madden; derange
DEMISE a death; to bequeath
DEMODE old fashioned
DEMOTH prepare stored arms (war)
DEMURE modest; grave; discreet
DENARY ten
DENGUE a fever **Med**
DENIAL dementi; refutation; refusal
DENIED refused; contradicted; refuted
DENIER disowner; silk; nylon
Meas. Coin
DENNET light two-wheeled carriage
DENOTE signify; imply; indicate
DENSER more compact; thicker; closer
DENTAL
DENTED, DINTED notched, concussed
DENTEL, DENTIL dog toothed **Arch**
DENTEX sea perch **Z**
DENTIN, DENTINE tooth ivory
DENUDE strip, bare, divest
DEODAR sacred tree
DEPART start; vanish; retire; die

DEPEND rely; hang; hinge; rest
DEPICT sketch; limn; portray; draw
DEPLOY open; expand; extend; unfold
DEPONE to testify under oath **Law**
DEPORT banish; expel; deportment
DEPOSE oust; divest of office; depone
DEPUTE delegate; authorize; charge
DEPUTY envoy; proxy; agent
DERAIL upset; leave rail track
DERAIN vindicate; prove; justify
DERATE reduce
DERBIO a green sea-fish **Z.**
DERHAM dirhem; Attic coin **Coin**
DERIDE ridicule; mock; lampoon; scorn
DERIVE obtain; draw; trace; receive
DERMAL dermic; relating to skin **Med.**
DERMIS skin **Med.**
DERNED darned; damned
DERNLY secretly
DERRIS plant insecticide
DESCRY to espy; detect; discern
DESERT quit; abandon; forsake; merit
DESERT a Sahara; fruit, etc.
DESIGN plan; devise; concoct; scheme
DESINE denote; (Spens.)
DESIRE covet; crave; want; passion
DESIST stay; stop; forbear; pause
DESMAN musk-rat **Z.**
DESMID river-weed **B.**
DESPOT dictator; tyrant; autocrat
DETACH sever; divide; part; disengage
DETAIL delineate; recount; relate; item
DETAIN retain; keep; hold; confine
DETECT discover; reveal; unmask
DETENT a check-stop
DETEST hate; abhor; loathe
DETORT to pervert **Law**
DETOUR deviation; circumambulation
DETUNE (wireless)
DEUCED devilish; confounded
DEUNME Jew turned Moslem
DEVALL cease; a stop (Sc.)
DEVEST strip; denude
DEVICE gadget; ruse; artifice; emblem
DEVISE scheme; plan; bequeath **Law**
DEVOID lacking; vacant; empty
DEVOIR politeness; duty
DEVOTE dedicate; give; resign
DEVOUR gorge; gobble; consume
DEVOUT pious; saintly; sincere
DEWANI a dewan's office
DEWING bedewing
DEWITT to lynch
DEWLAP pendulous neck-flesh
DEXTER on the right-hand side
DEZINK (zinc extraction)
DHARMA law of Buddha **Eccl.**
DHOBIE Indian washerman
DHOOLY Indian litter
DHURRA millet **B.**

DIADEM crown; coronet; tiara
DIALED (telephone)
DIAMYL (amyl) **Chem.**
DIAPER a napkin
DIATOM a sea-weed **B.**
DIBBED (gardening)
DIBBER pointed tool **Tool**
DIBBLE dibber; to make holes
DICAST dikast; Athenian judge
DICING gaming
DICKER ten; to barter
DICKEY bird; ass; unwell **Z.**
DICKEY false shirt-front; back-seat
DICTUM maxim
DICTUM precept; award **Law**
DIDDER to shiver
DIDDLE cheat; totter; dodder
DIESEL heavy oil engine
DIESIS printing mark
DIETED, DIETAL, DIETER food regime
DIFFER deviate; vary; wrangle
DIGAMY second marriage
DIGEST peptonize; summary **Law**
DIGGED delved; dug
DIGGER Australian
DIGLOT bi-lingual
DIGRAM a digraph
DIKAST dicast; Athenian judge
DIK-DIK S. African antelope **Z.**
DIKING ditching
DIKKAH tribune in a mosque
DIKKOP bustard (S. African) **Z.**
DILATE amplify; expand; enlarge
DILOGY double-entendre
DILUTE water; thin; attenuate
DIMITY figured cloth
DIMMED obscured; clouded; dulled
DIMMER more indistinct; fainter
DIMOUT partial black-out
DIMPLE a cheery depression
DIMPLY
DIMWIT fool
DIN-DIN Indian cymbals **Mus.**
DINDLE ⎱ to tingle (Sc.);
DINNLE ⎰ a thrill
DINFUL clamorous; noisy
DINGED hurled; enforced; urged
DINGES what's its name (S. Africa)
DINGHY dingey; boat **Naut.**
DINGLE dell; dale; vale; glen
DINGUS gadget; contraption
DINING
DINKUM honest; genuine (Australia)
DINNED persistently repeated
DINNER
DIODON globe fish genus **Z.**
DIPLEX simultaneous transmission
DIPLOE skull tissue **Med.**
DIPNOI fish with lungs and gills **Z.**
DIPODY two footed

DIPOLE type of wireless aerial
DIPPED immersed; doused; soused
DIPPER water ousel; ladle   **Z.**
DIP-ROD oil gauge   **Meas.**
DIPSAS serpent   **Z.**
DIPYRE a silicate of alumina   **Min.**
DIRDUM uproar; a scolding (Sc.)
DIRECT straight; bid; order; address
DIREST most calamitous; cruellest
DIRHAM ⎱ ancient oriental weight **Meas.**
DIRHEM ⎰ derham; silver coin   **Coin**
DIRKED stabbed
DIRZEE Indian needlewoman
DISARM
DISBAR to expel   **Law**
DISBUD remove buds
DISCAL (disc)
DISCUS quoit; (Greek Games)
DISCUS flower centre   **B.**
DISEUR (diseuse) raconteur (Fr.)
DISHED frustrated
DISMAL dull; doleful; lugubrious
DISMAN unman
DISMAY appal; scare; daunt; alarm
DISOWN deny; disclaim; reject; ignore
DISPEL banish; scatter; dismiss
DISTAL terminal; furthest from axis **B.**
DISTIL vaporize; drip; emanate
DISUSE desuetude; neglect
DITHER didder; tremble; quake
DITION dominion; rule; power
DITONE an interval   **Mus.**
DITTAY an indictment (Sc.)   **Law**
DITTOS a mono-coloured suit
DIURNA insects; ephemerae   **Z.**
DIVALI Feast of Lanterns (Hind.)
DIVERS diverse; different; sundry
DIVERT distract; amuse; relax; deflect
DIVEST devest; strip; denude; bare
DIVIDE sever; sunder; cleave; share
DIVINE predict; augur; angelic; sacred
DIVING plunging; penetrating; swooping
DIVOTO solemnly   **Mus.**
DIZAIN poem in ten stanzas
DJIBBA Eastern garment
DOABLE practical
DOBBIE a dotard; a brownie
DOBBIN old horse   **Z.**
DOCENT teaching
DOCILE pliant; amenable; compliant
DOCITY docility
DOCKED cut short   **Naut.**
DOCKER dock-labourer; stevedore
DOCKET doquet; a summary   **Law**
DOCTOR a fish; medico; to falsify
DODDED hornless   **[B.**
DODDER parasitic plant; didder; shake
DODDLE a pollard   **B., Z.**
DODGED evaded; quibbled; avoided
DODGER trickster; shifter

DODKIN a doit;   **Coin**
DODMAN a snail   **Z.**
DOFFED removed; took off
DOFFER carding mechanism
DOGANA custom house
DOGATE dignity of doge
DOG-BEE a drone   **Z.**
DOG-BOX (Railing dogs)
DOG-FLY   **Z.**
DOG-FOX renard   **Z.**
DOGGAR ironstone   **Min.**
DOGGED sullen; obstinate; determined
DOGGER fishing boat   **Naut.**
DOG-MAD rabid; crazy; insane
DOILED doilt; crazy (Sc.)
DOINGS multifarious activities
DOITED crazy; stupid
DOLENT full of woe (obs.)
DOLING distributing
DOLIUM molluscs   **Z.**
DOLLAR 100 cents   **Coin**
DOLLED prinked up
DOLLOP viscous mass
DOLMAN hussar's jacket
DOLMEN stone table; cromlech
DOLOSE fraudulent; deceitful
DOLOUR anguish; sorrow; pain
DOMAIN demesne; dominion; sway **Law**
DOM-BOC Saxon book
DOMETT shroud fabric
DOMIFY (horoscope)
DOMINO priest's cape; cloak
DOMITE variety of trachyte   **Min.**
DONARY a gift   **Eccl.**
DONATE present; give
DONJON the keep
DONKEY burro; moke; ass   **Z.**
DONSIE perverse (Sc.)
DONZEL budding knight; a page
DOOCOT dovecote (Sc.)
DOODLE a simpleton; a trifler
DOOLIE Indian litter
DOOMED destined; condemned
DOPING doctoring; varnishing
DOPPER Dutch baptist
DORADO constellation; a dolphin   **Z.**
DORBIE the dunlin   **Z.**
DORCAS charitable society
DORIAN Dōric
DORING lark-catching
DORISM Doricism
DORMER window (Arch.)
DORMIE dormy; unbeatable at golf
DORNIC figured linen
DORSAL (back)   **Med**
DORSEL fabric; pannier
DORTER dormitory   **Eccl**
DOSAGE, DOSING taking medicine
DOSSAL, DOSSEL altar cloth   **Eccl**
DOSSIL pledget; slug   **Med**

DOTAGE senility	**DROPSY** Med.
DOTANT a dotard	**DROSKY** Russian vehicle
DOTARD imbecile; driveller	**DROSSY** impure; foul; worthless
DOTERY drivel	**DROUGE** harpoon drag
DOTING madly fond	**DROUMY** troubled; muddy
DOTISH daft; imbecile; demented	**DROUTH** dryness; thirst
DOTTED stippled	**DROVER** cattle-driver
DOTTLE pipe-ash	**DROWSE** nap; slumber; doze
DOUANE custom-house (Fr.)	**DROWSY** lethargic; comatose; soporific
DOUBLE dual; twofold; duplicate	**DRUDGE** menial; scullion; toil; slave
DOUCHE shower-bath	**DRUIDS** a sacred order
DOUGHY soft like dough	**DRUMLY** turbid; muddy
DOUKAR dabchick Z.	**DRUPEL** a stone-fruit; a drupe B.
DOURLY grimly; sternly; obstinately	**DRUSED** crystalline
DOUSED ⎫ extinguished;	**DRUSES** Moslem sect
DOUTED ⎬ struck;	**DRY-BOB** (Eton)
DOWSED ⎭ drenched	**DRY-FLY** (fishing)
DOUTER extinguisher	**DRYING** parching; desiccating
DOWERY dowry; dot	**DRYISH** somewhat sarcastic
DOWLAS coarse cloth	**DRYITE** fossil wood Min.
DOWNED floored	**DRY-ROT**
DOWSER water-diviner	**DRY-RUB** nettoyage à sec
DOYLEY lace mat; a doily	**DUALIN** an explosive Chem.
DOZING somnolent; drowsy	**DUBASH** an interpreter
DRABBY sluttish	**DUBBED** styled; greased
DRACHM drachma; a dram Coin	**DUBBER** Indian bottle; dupper
DRAFFY dreggy; waste; worthless	**DUBBIN** a grease; dubbing
DRAFTS draughts; a game	**DUCKED** bobbed; immersed
DRAGEE sweetmeat	**DUCKER** a plunger; bird Z.
DRAGON monstrous saurian Z.	**DUDDER** to shake; to deafen
DRAPED dressed; robed; clothed	**DUDEEN** Irish clay pipe
DRAPER haberdasher	**DUELLO** duelling (It.)
DRAPET coverlet	**DUENNA** chaperone
DRAPPY a wee drop (Sc.)	**DUETTO** a duet Mus.
DRAWEE (Bill of Exchange)	**DUFFED** stole cattle (Australia)
DRAWER pot-man; an attraction	**DUFFEL** ⎫ coarse cloth with thick nap
DRAZEL a slut	**DUFFLE** ⎭
DREAMT imagined; fancied	**DUFFER** a pedlar; muff
DREAMY fanciful; visionary	**DUGONG** sea-cow; halicore; manatee Z.
DREARY dismal; lonely; dull; gloomy	**DUG-OUT** canoe; shelter
DREDGE a drag-net; to sprinkle	**DUG-OUT** retired officer
DREGGY (dregs); muddy	**DUIKER** duyker; antelope Z.
DREICH tiresome (Sc.)	**DUKERY** seat of a duke
DRENCH (tenure); soak; imbrue Law	**DUKKER** to tell fortunes
DRESSY dapper; dandified	**DULCET** melodious; honeyed
DRIEST very dry	**DULLED** blunted; assuaged; softened
DRIFTY (snow-drifts)	**DULLER** more listless
DRIVEL twaddle; prate; balderdash	**DUMBLY** silently; mutely
DRIVEN urged; compelled; overworked	**DUM-DUM** soft-nosed bullet
DRIVER a golf club	**DUMOSE** ⎫ abounding with
DROGER a coaster; drogher Naut.	**DUMOUS** ⎭ bushes and briars
DROGUE sea anchor; sleeve target Naut.	**DUMPED** unloaded; deposited; heaped
DROLLY droll; laughable	**DUMPLE** to cook a dumpling
DROMIC (race-course)	**DUN-COW** species of ray Z.
DROMON medieval war-ship Naut.	**DUNDER** dregs; lees
DROMOS Greek race-course	**DUNKER** tunker; baptist
DRONED buzzed; drawled; idled	**DUNLIN** sandpiper Z.
DRONGO king crow Z.	**DUNLOP** a cheese; a tyre
DROPAX a depilatory	**DUNNED** importuned
DROP-IN computer error; visit	**DUNNER** debt-collector

DUPERY duping; chicanery
DUPING gulling; deceiving
DUPION double cocoon **Z.**
DUPLET electrons bonding atoms
DUPLEX two-fold; double
DUPPER Indian bottle; dubber
DURAIN type of coal **Min.**
DURANT glazed fabric
DURATE harsh to the ear **Mus.**
DURBAR audience-chamber
DURDEN a thicket; a copse
DURDUM dirdum; an uproar
DURESS restraint; imprisonment
DURGAN dwarf
DURHAM breed of cattle **Z.**
DURIAN Malay fruit **B.**
DURING throughout; pending
DURION see durian **B.**
DURITY hardness; firmness
DURRIE Indian cotton fabric
DUSKEN to grow dark
DUSKLY duskily; gloomily
DUSTER a cloth
DUST-UP quarrel
DUTIED taxed
DUTIES obligations; excises
DUYKER duiker; African antelope **Z.**
DYADIC (two) **Chem.**
DYEING colouring; staining
DYNAMO
DYNAST a ruler; dynasty
DYNODE (electronic)
DYVOUR a bankrupt (Sc.) **Law.**
DZEREN ⎫
DZERON ⎬ Mongolian antelope **Z.**

E

EADISH aftermath; second crop
EAGLET a young eagle **Z.**
EAR-BOB an earring
EAR-CAP ear-muff
EARFUL a diatribe
EARING ploughing; rope **Naut.**
EARLAP tip of ear **Med.**
EARNED merited; won; deserved
EARNER wage taker; breadwinner
EARTHY material; gross; unrefined
EAR-WAX
EAR-WIG informer **Z.**
EASIER more tranquil; more pliant
EASILY tranquilly; calmly
EASING relieving; calming; soothing
EASSEL easterly (Sc.)
EASTER **Eccl.**
EATAGE cattle food
EATING eroding; devouring
EBBING waning; declining; subsiding
ECARTE card game
ECBOLE a digression

ECHOED repeated; resounded
ECHOES reverberations
ECLAIR a confection
ECLEGM oil and syrup **Med.**
ECTYPE a cast (Arch.); a copy
ECURIE stable (Fr.)
ECZEMA a skin disease **Med.**
EDDIED swirled; rippled
EDDISH eadish; aftermath
EDDOES W. Indian potatoes **B.**
EDENIC (Eden)
EDGING border; frill; rim
EDIBLE eatable; esculent
EDITED revised; emended
EDITOR corrector; reviser; annotator
EDUCED extracted; elicited; derived
EEL-OIL
EEL-POT an eel-trap
EERILY weirdly; uncannily
EFFACE erase; expunge; delete
EFFECT achieve; cause; create
EFFEIR effere; affair (Sc.)
EFFETE spent; worn; barren; abortive
EFFIGY image; statue; figure; likeness
EFFLUX flow; effusion; discharge
EFFORM to shape
EFFORT essay; trial; striving; strain
EFFRAY affray (Sc.)
EFFUSE emanate; issue; pour; spill
EGENCE exigence
EGERAN garnet **Min.**
EGERIA spiritual adviser
EGG-CUP
EGGERY nesting-place
EGGING inciting
EGGLER an egg-dealer
EGG-NOG a drink
EGOISM conceit; vanity; self-praise
EGOIST egotist; not an altruist
EGOITY identity; personality
EGRESS exit; outlet; emergence
EGROIT a sour cherry **B.**
EIDENT diligent (Sc.)
EIDOLA apparitions
EIFFEL tower, 985 ft. high
EIGHTH an interval **Mus.**
EIGHTS (boat-racing)
EIGHTY four-score
EIRACK young hen (Sc.) **Z.**
EITHER one of two
EKEING eking; adding; stretching
ELAEIS African oil palm **B.**
ELAINE the lily-maid of Astolat
ELANCE throw out; launch
ELANET insectivorous kite **Z.**
ELAPSE intervene; pass; slip
ELATED exalted; proud; excited
ELATER click-deetle genus **Z.**
ELATOR a rouser
ELCHEE eltchi; Turkish ambassador

ELDEST oldest
ELDING fuel (dial.)
ELEGIT writ   **Law**
ELEMIN oil from resin
ELENCH a disproof; a refutation
ELEVEN a cricket team
ELFISH puckish; impish; mischievous
ELICIT deduce; evoke; extract
ELIDED cut off a syllable
ELISOR (jury selection)   **Law**
ELIXIR a cordial; quintessence
ELK-NUT oil-nut   **B.**
ELLECK red gurnet   **Z.**
ELLOPS snake or fish (obs.)   **Z.**
ELODES sweating sickness   **Med.**
ELOHIM the Creator (Hebrew)
ELOIGN to carry away
ELOPED bolted; absconded; disappeared
ELTCHI elchee; Turkish ambassador
ELUDED evaded; dodged; foiled
ELVANS felspar veins   **Min.**
ELVISH elfish; elf-like; tricksy
ELWAND an ellwand   **Meas.**
ELYSEE French president's residence
EMBACE⎱ to degrade (obs.)
EMBASE⎰ depreciate; debase
EMBALE to pack; to bundle
EMBALL encircle; ensphere
EMBALM perfume; to preserve
EMBANK
EMBARK imbark; start; enter; launch
EMBERS live cinders
EMBLEM badge; token; device; symbol
EMBODY imbody; incorporate; include
EMBOIL imboil; boil with anger (Spens.)
EMBOSS conceal; cover
EMBRUE imbrue; soak; drench; steep
EMBRYO germ; nucleus; rudiment
EMERGE emanate; appear; issue
EMESIS vomiting   **Med.**
EMETIC   **Med.**
EMETIN an emetic   **Med.**
EMEUTE riot; disorder; insurrection
EMIGRE French royalist abroad
EMMESH immesh; enmesh; entrap
EMPALE impale; to enclose
EMPARK to enclose; to fence
EMPASM a deodorant powder
EMPAWN pawn; impawn; pledge
EMPERY empire; power
EMPIRE rule; sway; dominion
EMPLOY use; engross; occupy
EMPUSA⎱ spectre or goblin
EMPUSE⎰ sent by Hecate
EMUCID mouldy
ENABLE allow; permit; empower
ENAMEL
ENCAGE to coop; emmew; incage
ENCAMP camp; pitch; settle
ENCASE incase; enclose

ENCASH pay in cash
ENCAVE to cache
ENCOPE an incision   **Med.**
ENCORE a repeat
ENCYST put in a bag
END-ALL finish; conclusion
ENDEAR captivate; charm; win
ENDING finale; closing; finis
ENDIVE species of chicory   **B.**
ENDOSS endorse; sanction; ratify
ENDUED indued; endowed; supplied
ENDURE abide; brook; tolerate
ENECIA fever   **Med.**
ENERGY vigour; power; intensity
ENFACE superscribe
ENFEST infest
ENFOLD infold; wrap up
ENFORM to fashion; to mould
ENFREE to release
ENGAGE contend; agree; promise
ENGAOL to put in prison; enjail
ENGILD to gild; brighten
ENGINE machine; device; method
ENGIRD surround; encircle
ENGLUT to swallow; to fill
ENGOBE ceramic technique
ENGORE to gore; to wound
ENGRAM essence of memory   **Med.**
ENGULF ingulf; overwhelm
ENHALO surround with a halo
ENIGMA puzzle; riddle; mystery; rebus
ENISLE isolate
ENJAIL imprison; incarcerate
ENJOIN bid; direct; command
ENKOMO small Cuban drum   **Mus.**
ENLACE enfold; entwine
ENLARD to baste
ENLINK to connect; concatenate
ENLIST engage; enroll; secure
ENLOCK lock up
ENMESH emmesh; entrap
ENMITY animus; hatred; aversion
ENMURE to immure; imprison
ENNEAD group of nine
ENNUYE bored (Fr.)
ENODAL without knobs
ENOSIS political union (Gr.)
ENOUGH ample; adequate; sufficient
ENRACE to enroot; implant
ENRAGE incense; infuriate; madden
ENRAIL entrain
ENRANK place in order
ENRAPT in an ecstasy
ENRICH fertilize; endow; adorn
ENRING encircle; surround
ENROBE invest; attire; array
ENROLL enlist
ENROOT enrace; implant
ENSATE sword-shaped   **B.**
ENSEAL seal up; impress

ENSEAM to sew up
ENSEAR to cauterize
ENSIGN an officer; a flag
ENSILE store in a pit
ENSPAN to yoke up (S. Africa)
ENSUED followed; resulted; accrued
ENSURE insure; assure; secure; fix
ENTAIL leave; bequeath; involve **Law**
ENTAME to tame; domesticate
ENTENT intention; design
ENTERA intestines **Med.**
ENTICE seduce; allure; decoy; cajole
ENTIRE (stout); complete; perfect
ENTITY being; essence; existence
ENTOIL to ensnare
ENTOMB bury; inter; inhume
ENTRAP inveigle; ensnare; entangle
ENTREE freedom of access; a dish
ENTUNE chant; sing
ENURED inured; hardened **Law**
ENVIED grudged; coveted
ENVIER rival
ENWALL inwall; enclose
ENWIND entwine; enlace
ENWOMB to bury; make pregnant
ENWRAP envelop; engross; perplex
ENZONE to girdle; surround
ENZYME (fermentation); leavened bread
EOCENE a geological period
EOLIAN Aeolian; Eolic
EOLITH prehistoric flint implement
EOSTRE Saxon goddess; (Easter)
EOTHEN from the East
EOZOIC ⎱ rock containing
EOZOON ⎰ fossilized foraminifera **Min.**
EPARCH Greek governor
EPAULE part of bastion
EPEIRA genus of spiders **Z.**
EPHEBE young Athenian
EPHORI Spartan magistrates
EPIGEE perigee; astronomical point
EPIZOA parasites **Z.**
EPODIC lyric
EPONYM derived name
EPOPEE epic poem
EPULIS gum disease **Med.**
EQUANT imaginary circle
EQUATE to equalize; to average
EQUINE horsey
EQUITY impartial justice
ERASED expunged; cancelled; deleted
ERASER a scraper
ERBIUM rare metal **Chem.**
EREBUS darkness; son of Chaos
ERENOW before this time
ERIACH a fine; blood-money (Irish) **Law**
ERINGO eryngo; sea-holly **B.**
ERINYS one of the Furies
ERMINE the stoat's winter coat **Z.**
ERODED corroded; eaten; consumed

EROTIC amatory
ERRAND mission; charge; message
ERRANT roving; rambling; wandering
ERRATA errors; mistakes
ERRING straying; mistaking
ERSATZ German reserve; a substitute
ERYNGO sea-holly genus **B.**
ESCAPE shun; evade; elude; flee
ESCARP steep slope
ESCARS gravel ridges
ESCHAR burnt wounds; scab **Med.**
ESCHEW to shun; avoid; miss
ESCORT protect; guard; convoy
ESCROL heraldic scroll
ESCROW deed; escrol **Law**
ESCUDO Portugese coin **Coin**
ESKIMO an Innuit
ESLOIN eloign; to carry away
ESNECY privilege of choice **Law**
ESPADA bull-fighting sword
ESPIAL spying; discovery; notice
ESPIED discovered unexpectedly
ESPIER a spy; a watcher
ESPRIT wit; sprightliness
ESSENE ascetic Hebrew
ESSERA skin eruption **Med.**
ESSOIN excuse for absence **Law**
ESTAIN French pewter
ESTATE condition; rank; property
ESTEEM deem; consider; value
ESTRAY to stray; a stray
ETCHED engraved; corroded by acid
ETCHER an engraver
ETERNE eternal (obs.)
ETHICS moral science
ETHIOP an Ethiopian
ETHNIC racial; ethnological
ETNEAN (Etna)
ETYMON derivation; meaning
ETYPIC unique
EUCAIN drug similar to cocaine **Med**
EUCHRE card game
EUCLID a geometer
EULOGY panegyric; encomium
EUNOMY good government
EUNUCH
EUONYM a suitable name
EUPION vegetable oil **B**
EUPODA (beetles) **Z**
EUREKA Found! (Archimedes)
EURITE a granite **Min**
EUSTON a railway terminus
EUTAXY regularity
EVADED eluded; dodged; avoided
EVANID faint; evanescent
EVENER leveller
EVENLY smoothly; fairly; uniformly
EVILLY wickedly; maliciously
EVINCE display; show; exhibit
EVIPAN soporific injection **Med**

EVOKED roused; inflamed; elicited
EVOLVE unfold; unroll; develop
EXAMEN a disquisition; an enquiry
EXARCH a title; viceroy **Eccl.**
EXCEED cap; outdo; surpass; transcend
EXCEPT bar; ban; exclude; omit
EXCERN to sweat
EXCESS surplus; glut; balance
EXCIDE to cut off
EXCISE duty; impost; tax; (Walpole)
EXCITE wake; rouse; incite; kindle
EXCUSE acquit; pardon; exempt
EXCUSS to decipher; shake off
EXCUSS to seize and detain **Law**
EXEDRA a hall; a recess
EXEMPT free; released; immune
EXEQUY funeral rites
EXEUNT all quit the stage
EXHALE emit; reek; emanate; breathe
EXHORT urge; encourage; counsel
EXHUME unearth; disinter; resurrect
EXILED banished; outlawed
EXILIC (Jewish exile)
EXITUS yearly rent; issue **Law**
EXODIC (Exodus); migratory
EXODUS departure
EXOGEN a class of plant **B.**
EXOMIS Greek sleeveless tunic
EXOTIC not native; extraneous; foreign
EXPAND spread; dilate; swell; extend
EXPECT hope; await; forecast
EXPEND disburse; consume; exert
EXPERT apt; adroit; skilful; able
EXPIRE end; die; stop; finish
EXPIRY conclusion; extinction
EXPORT ship; produce; send; carry
EXPOSE an exposure; reveal; unmask
EXPUGN take by assault; conquer
EXSECT to cut away; cut out
EXSERT to protrude
EXTANT existent; current
EXTASY ecstasy; rapture; trance
EXTEND stretch; reach; expand
EXTENT amount; scope; range; field
EXTERN day-boy
EXTERN not inherent; external
EXTINE (pollen grain) **B.**
EXTORT exact; extract; wrench; elicit
EXUDED sweated; oozed; percolated
EYALET Turkish province; a vilayet
EYE-CUP (used for eye lotion) **Med.**
EYEFUL a glance
EYEING watching
EYELET loop-hole
EYELID
EYEPIT eye socket
EYRANT bird of prey on nest **Z.**

F

FABIAN policy of patiently waiting
FABLED fabricated; fictional
FABLER an Aesop
FABRIC structure; texture; web
FACADE front view; face
FACIAL frontal **[Med.**
FACIES external appearance; the face
FACILE easy; dexterous; pliant
FACING confronting; opposing
FACTOR broker; middleman
FACTOR agent or manager of estate
FACTUM a deed **Law**
FACULA sun-spot
FADDLE to trifle; to play
FADGED suited; prospered
FADING (wireless); withering
FAERIE fairy; fairyland; (Spens.)
FAFFLE to stammer
FAG-END butt (cigarette)
FAGGED tired
FAGGOT fagot; bundle of sticks
FAILED miscarried; declined
FAILLE nun's veiling
FAINTY feeble; languid
FAIRER more equitable
FAIRLY moderately; passably
FAITOR rogue; impostor; evil-doer
FAKEER Indian beggar
FAKING forging; doctoring **Naut.**
FALCON hawk; cannon **Z.**
FALLAL finery; streamer
FALLEN sunk; lapsed; ebbed
FALLOW untilled; idle; dormant
FALSER more fallacious
FALTER totter; waver; vacillate
FALUNS miocene deposits
FAMBLE the hand (slang)
FAMILY household; race; lineage
FAMINE dearth; scarcity; starvation
FAMISH starve; exhaust; hunger
FAMOUS renowned; eminent
FANGED toothed; taloned
FANGLE a contraption; novelty
FANGOT a quantity of wares
FANNED inflamed
FANNEL, FANION flag; banner; splint
FANNER winnower
FANTAN Chinese gambling game
FANTOM phantom
FAQUIR religious mendicant
FARCIN glanders; farcy
FARDEL a bundle; burden; load
FARINA pollen; flour **B.**
FARING experiencing; feeding
FARMED leased
FARMER tiller; cultivator
FARROW litter of pigs

FASCES Roman badge	**FENNEL** (plant) **B.**
FASCIA a band; name-board	**FEODAL** feudal
FASHED vexed; worried (Sc.)	**FERIAE** Roman holidays
FASTED abstained from food	**FERIAL** (holidays)
FASTEN bind; secure; tie; latch	**FERINE** wild; savage; untamed; fierce
FASTER quicker; speedier	**FERITY** wildness
FASTLY firmly	**FERRET** silk ribbon; pole cat **Z.**
FAT-HEN goose-foot **B.**	**FERRIC** (iron) **Chem.**
FATHER adopt; beget; sire	**FERULA** fennel **B.**
FATHOM 6 feet; comprehend **Naut.**	**FERULE** a rod; cane
FATTED fattened	**FERVID** fervent; eager; ardent
FATTEN grow plump	**FESCUE** a pointer; a grass **B.**
FATTER more obese	**FESTAL** joyous; gay
FAUCAL throaty; guttural	**FESTER** rankle; rot; putrefy
FAUCES (mouth) **Med.**	**FETIAL** fecial; Roman priest
FAUCET a tap; fosset	**FETISH** fetich; charm; amulet; talisman
FAULTY defective; blameworthy	**FETTER** manacle; shackle; bond; gyve
FAUNAL relating to animals **Z.**	**FETTLE** good condition; fitness
FAUNUS Pan	**FEUDAL**
FAUTOR a supporter	**FEWEST** greatest paucity
FAVOSE honeycombed; cellular	**FIACRE** French cab
FAVOUR gift; patronize; bias	**FIANCE** betrothed
FAWNED flattered; knelt	**FIASCO** a failure; a flask
FAWNER sycophant; clinger; parasite	**FIBBED** prevaricated
FAYING fitting closely **Naut.**	**FIBBER** a liar
FEALTY fidelity; loyalty; homage	**FIBRED** having fibres
FEARED apprehended; dreaded	**FIBRIL** small fibre; slender thread
FEATLY neatly; dexterously; adroitly	**FIBRIN** gluten; clot formative **Med. B.**
FEAZED untwisted; unravelled	**FIBULA** leg-bone; buckle **Med.**
FECIAL Roman priest; fetial	**FICKLE** volatile; mercurial; unstable
FECKLY effectually	**FICTOR** a modeller
FECULA (plants); starch **B.**	**FIDDLE** a railing **Mus.**
FECUND prolific; fertile; fruitful	**FIDGET** fret; chafe; worry
FEDARY a confederate	**FIERCE** savage; cruel; violent
FEDORA trilby hat (U.S.A.)	**FIFING** **Mus.**
FEEBLE faint; frail; weak	**FIGARO** a schemer; French newspaper
FEEBLY languidly	**FIGGED** all dressed up
FEEDER a bib; a channel	**FIGURE** reckon; digit; diagram
FEEING hiring; recompensing	**FIJIAN** (Fiji Islands)
FEELER organ of animals, plants	**FIKERY** fuss (Sc.)
FEELER tentative suggestion	**FILAGO** cudweed **B.**
FELINE catty; spiteful **Z.**	**FILFOT** fylfot; a swastika
FELLAH an Egyptian peasant	**FILIAL**
FELLED cut down	**FILING** particle; (documents)
FELLER wood-cutter	**FILLED** replete
FELLIC (bile) **Med.**	**FILLER** (Hungary) **Coin**
FELLOE felly; rim of wheel	**FILLET** hair-ribbon; a band
FELLOW peer; mate; equal	**FILL-IN** shadow technique **Photo.**
FELONY crime; misdemeanour **Law**	**FILLIP** to flip; an incitement
FELTED covered with felt	**FILMED**
FELTER to mat together	**FILOSE** thread-like
FELTRE cuirass	**FILTER** strain; percolate
FEMALE feminine	**FILTHY** foul; dirty; corrupt
FENCED equivocated	**FIMBLE** hemp **B.**
FENCER hedger; prevaricator	**FINALE** climax; conclusion; finis
FENDED warded off; parried	**FINDER** discoverer
FENDER **Naut.**	**FINDON** dried haddock
FENIAN an Irish conspirator	**FINEER** (fraudulent credit)
FEN-MAN fen-lander	**FINELY** excellently; delicately
FENNEC African fox **Z.**	**FINERY** splendour; trappings; fallals

FINEST keenest; sharpest; purest		**FLAYER** skinner	
FINGER digit; pilfer; touch		**FLECHE** a redan; spire	
FINIAL a pinnacle (Arch.)		**FLEDGE** grow feathers	
FINING refining		**FLEDGY** feathery; downy	
FINISH end; terminate; accomplish		**FLEECE** to strip; plunder	
FINITE limited; restricted		**FLEECH** flatter; coax (Sc.)	
FINLET small fin		**FLEECY** woolly; flocculent	
FINNAN findon haddock	**Z.**	**FLENCH** } to cut up the blubber	
FINNED		**FLENSE** } of a whale	
FINNER fin-backed whale; torqual	**Z.**	**FLESHY** carnal; corporeal	
FINNIC Finnish		**FLETCH** to feather an arrow	
FINNOC white trout	**Z.**	**FLEURY** (fleur-de-lis)	
FIORIN bent-grass	**B.**	**FLEWED** deep-mouthed	
FIRING igniting; kindling; expelling		**FLEXED** bent	
FIRKIN 9 imperial gallons	**Meas.**	**FLEXOR** muscle	**Med.**
FIRLOT a quarter boll	**Meas.**	**FLICKS** movies	
FIRMAN passport; decree		**FLIGHT** retreat; exodus; rout	
FIRMED confirmed; established		**FLIMSY** frail; trivial; weak	
FIRMLY steadily; compactly		**FLINCH** wince; blench; quail	
FISCAL treasurer	**Law**	**FLINTY** obdurate; hard; miserly	
FISHED strengthened	**Naut.**	**FLISKY** frisky (Sc.)	
FISHER weasel; black fox	**Z.**	**FLITCH** a side of bacon	
FISHES	**Z.**	**FLITTY** flighty; unstable	
FISSLE rustle; whistle (Sc.)		**FLOATS** (paddle-wheels)	
FISTED struck with the fist		**FLOATY** buoyant; light	
FISTIC (boxing); pugilistic		**FLOCCI** woolly filaments	
FITCHE } pointed (Her.)		**FLOCKS** waste wool	
FITCHY }		**FLOCKY** downy	
FITFUL irregular; unreliable		**FLOPPY** flaccid; drooping	
FITTED apt; seemly; adjusted		**FLORAL** flowery	
FITTER an artificer; more seemly		**FLORAN** tin ore	**Min.**
FIXING deciding; settling		**FLORET** floweret	**B.**
FIXITY permanence; fastness		**FLORID** ornate; meretricious	
FIXIVE gummy; adhesive; glutinous		**FLORIN** once coined at Florence	**Coin**
FIXURE stability; firmness (Shak.)		**FLOSSY** silky	
FIZGIG fisgig; a flirt; damp squib		**FLOURY** like flour	
FIZZED hissed		**FLOUSE** } to turn the edge of	
FIZZER a fast one		**FLOUSH** } a tool; to splash (Sc.)	
FIZZLE a fiasco; splutter		**FLOWER** blow; bloom; blossom	**B.**
FLABBY tabid; flaccid; lax		**FLUATE** fluoride	**Chem.**
FLACON scent-bottle; small flask (Fr.)		**FLUCAN** clay	**Min.**
FLAGGY drooping; languishing		**FLUENT** flowing; voluble; fluid	
FLAGON a flask		**FLUFFY** downy; fluey	
FLAKED peeled off		**FLUKED** was fortunate	
FLAMED glazed; excited		**FLUNKY** a lackey; snob	
FLAMEN Roman official of rites		**FLURRY** agitation; bustle; perturb	
FLANCH a flange		**FLUSHY** reddish	
FLANGE projecting rim		**FLUTED** channelled	**Mus.**
FLANKS sore back (horse)		**FLUTER** flutist; flautist	**Mus.**
FLARED burnt unsteadily		**FLUXED** melted; purged	
FLASHE a sluice		**FLYING** aviation; fleeing; soaring	
FLASHY gaudy; impulsive; vapid		**FLYMAN** cabman	
FLATLY positively; plainly		**FLY-NET** mosquito curtain	
FLATTY a policeman (slang)		**FLY-NUT** winged nut	
FLATUS puff of wind		**FOALED**	
FLAUNT vaunt; parade; display		**FOAMED** spumed; frothed	
FLAVIN yellow dye		**FOBBED** imposed on; tricked	
FLAWED defective		**FOCILE** a bone (arm or leg)	**Med.**
FLAXEN pale yellow		**FOCOSO** spiritedly	**Mus.**
FLAYED skinned		**FO'C'SLE** forecastle: bows	**Naut.**

FODDER a weight; food   **Meas.**
FOEMAN foe; antagonist; enemy
FOETOR a stench; offensive odour
FOETUS an embryo   **Med.**
FOG-BOW white rainbow
FOGGED blurred; overcast
FOGRAM antiquated; a fogey
FOIBLE faible; weak point; defect
FOILED baffled; thwarted; balked
FOILER a frustrator
FOISON plenty; autumn
FOKKER type of aeroplane
FOLDED doubled; wrapped; furled
FOLDER paper jacket
FOLIAR (leaves); laminar
FOLIER goldsmith's foil
FOLIOT goblin
FOLIUM thin geological stratum
FOLKSY imitation rustic
FOLLIA (composition)   **Mus.**
FOLLOW succeed; chase; pursue; heed
FOMENT fan; excite; stimulate
FONDER tenderer; sillier
FONDLE pet; caress; dandle
FONDLY affectionately; foolishly
FONDUS calico-printing
FONTAL primary; baptismal
FOOLED duped; hoodwinked; hoaxed
FOOLEN (embankment)
FOOTED walked; paid; kicked
FOOTER football (slang)
FOOTLE twaddle; bunkum
FOOZLE bungle; mishit
FORAGE fodder; search; pillage
FORBID ban; inhibit; taboo; veto
FORBYE besides; hard by
FORCED unnatural; compulsory
FORCER compeller
FORDED crossed by wading
FORE-BY besides (Sc.)
FOREDO to destroy; undo; overpower
FOREGO yield; resign; relinquish
FOREST woodland; grove; boscage
FORFEX scissors   **Tool**
FORGAT forgot
FORGED fabricated; spurious
FORGER falsifier; hammerman
FORGET overlook; slight
FORGOT neglected
FORINT (Hungary)   **Coin**
FORKED bifurcated
FORLAY to ambush; lie in wait for
FORMAL precise; exact; stiff; set
FORMAT (book-production)
FORMED arranged; moulded; shaped
FORMER prior; previous; bygone
FORMIC (acid)   **Chem.**
FORNIX (shell); (brain)   **Med.**
FORPET } a fourth part
FORPIT } a quarter (Sc.)

FORREL forel; parchment
FORRIT forward (Sc.)
FORROW not with calf (Sc.)   **Z.**
FORSAY forbid; renounce
FORTED guarded
FOSSIL petrified   **Min.**
FOSTER cherish; nourish; encourage
FOTHER leak-stopping   **Naut.**
FOTMAL 70 lbs. of lead   **Meas.**
FOUGHT strove; contended; warred
FOULED polluted; sullied
FOULLY scurvily; unfairly; basely
FOURBE a cheat; trickster
FOURTH
FOWLER bird-shooter
FOX-BAT flying fox   **Z.**
FOXING deceiving; duping; deluding
FOXISH cunning; sly; shrewd
FOYBLE part of sword-blade
FRACAS an uproar; brawl; riot
FRACID overripe; rotten
FRAGOR a crash
FRAISE defence of pointed stakes
FRAMED constructed; devised
FRAMER contriver; frame-maker
FRANCO free of expense   **Naut.**
FRANZY crotchety (dial.)
FRAPPE chilled with ice (Fr.)
FRATCH a quarrel; a brawl (dial.)
FRATER refectory; brother; friar   **Eccl.**
FRAYED worn; chafed; fretted
FRAZIL anchor-ice; spicular ice
FREELY unimpeded; willingly; readily
FREEZE chill; numb; congeal
FRENCH Gallic
FRENUM a ligament   **Med.**
FRENZY delirium; madness; fury
FRESCO drink; paint
FRESCO coolness; wall painting
FRETTE a strengthening band
FRETTY ornate
FRIARY monastery   **Eccl.**
FRIDAY (Robinson Crusoe)
FRIDGE ice-box
FRIEND ally; chum; intimate
FRIEZE rough stuff (Arch.)
FRIGGA wife of Odin
FRIGHT alarm; dismay; panic; dread
FRIGID icy; cold; formal
FRILLY fluted; overdressed   **Photo.**
FRINGE border; edge
FRINGY adorned with fringes
FRISKY gay; lively; sportive
FRIVOL to trifle
FRIZEL (flint-lock)
FROGGY abounding in frogs
FROISE pancake; fraise
FROLIC romp; gambol; play; lark
FRONDE political party (Fr.) 17th c.
FROSTY chilling; wintry

FROTHY empty; unsubstantial; foamy
FROUZY rank; musty; rancid
FROWER a cleaver   **Tool**
FROWST stuffy and hot
FROWSY frowzy; unkempt; disorderly
FROZEN froren; frosty; iced
FRUGAL thrifty; saving; parsimonious
FRUITY fruitful; luscious
FRUMPY dowdy
FRUTEX a shrub   **B.**
FRYING cooking with fat
FUCATE painted; sham
FUCOID a fossil sea-weed   **Min.**
FUDDLE muddle; inebriate
FUDGED cheated; faked; bungled
FUFFED puffed
FUGATO like a fugue   **Mus.**
FUGILE ear trouble   **Med.**
FULANI tribe (South Sahara)
FULFIL meet; effect; satisfy
FULGID fulgent; flashing; steaming
FULGOR splendour
FULHAM⎫
FULLAM⎬ a die loaded at one
FULLAN⎭   corner to throw high
FULICA coot genus   **Z.**
FULLED scoured and thickened
FULLER hammer   **Tool**
FULMAR sea-fowl; the petrel   **Z.**
FULVID tawny; yellow
FUMADO smoked pilchard (Sp.)
FUMAGE chimney tax; hearth money
FUMBLE grope; bungle; stammer
FUMILY sulkily; smokily
FUMING ammonia process   **Photo.**
FUMMEL funnel; mule   **Z.**
FUMOUS (fumes); vaporous
FUNDED endowed
FUNDUS back part
FUNEST doleful; lamentable
FUNGAL, FUNGIN (fungi) mushrooms
    B.
FUNGIA genus of corals   **Z.**
FUNGUS plant   **B.**
FUNKED played the coward
FUNKIA a lily genus   **B.**
FUNNEL fummel; smoke-stack
FURFUR dandruff   **Med.**
FURIES avenging deities
FURLED closely rolled
FURORE outburst of enthusiasm
FURROW rut; groove; seam; corrugate
FURZEN furzy; whinny   **B.**
FUSAIN friable coal   **Min.**
FUSING liquefaction
FUSION melting; amalgamation
FUSSED worried; fretted; fidgeted
FUSTED mouldy; rancid; malodorous
FUSTET shrub; the sumac   **B.**
FUSTIC tropical American tree   **B.**

FUSURE smelting; fusion
FUTILE bootless; vain; useless
FUTTAH⎫ rat-proof raised
FUTTER⎭   store-house (N.Z.)
FUTURE hereafter; prospective
FUZZED ground to powder
FUZZLE intoxicate; fuddle

G

GABBED talked; prattled
GABBLE jabber; prate; chatter
GABBRO (felspar)   **Min.**
GABION basket for earthworks
GABLED
GABLET small gable
GADDED wandered about
GADDER a gadabout; a rover
GADFLY horse-fly   **Z.**
GADGET a cunning device; contraption
GADINE gadean; cod-type   **Z.**
GADOID codfish type   **Z.**
GAELIC Scottish-Highland dialect
GAFFED (fishing)
GAFFER rustic; foreman
GAFFLE spur (cock-fight)
GAGGED silenced; joked
GAGGER an interpolator   **Tool**
GAGGLE a flock of geese   **Z.**
GAGMAN joke-writer; comic
GAIETY gayety; merriment; vivacity
GAINED acquired; reached; won
GAINER winner, beneficiary
GAINLY comely; conveniently
GAINST against
GAITED having a distinctive walk
GAITER gamash
GALAGE galosh; golosh
GALAGO lemur (Madagascar)   **Z.**
GALAXY Milky Way; brilliant assembly
GALBAN a gum used in medicine   **B.**
GALEAS galley   **Naut.**
GALEGA goat's rue   **B.**
GALENA lead sulphide   **Chem.**
GALIOT brigantine   **Naut.**
GALIUM bed-straw genus   **B.**
GALLED chagrined; fretted; vexed
GALLEY ship; boat; cook-house   **Naut.**
GALLIC French; an acid   **Chem.**
GALLIO insouciance personified
GALLON 4 quarts   **Meas.**
GALLOP a dance; speed
GALLOW to terrify
GALLUP poll; voting system
GALOON galloon; silk fabric
GALOOT lout
GALORE golore; in abundance
GALOSH galage; overshoe
GAMASH gaiters
125 **GAMBET** a bird; red-shank   **Z.**

GAMBIT (chess)	
GAMBLE stake; hazard; risk; wager	
GAMBOL frolic; romp; caper	
GAMELY pluckily	
GAMETE egg cell	**Z.**
GAMING gambling	
GAMMER old woman	
GAMMON (bacon); hoax; cozen	
GANDER a glance (U.S.A.)	**Z.**
GANESA Hindu elephant god	
GANGER foreman; overman	
GANGUE veinstone	**Min.**
GANNET solan goose	**Z.**
GANOID sturgeon type of fish	**Z.**
GANTRY travelling crane	
GAOLED imprisoned; incarcerated	
GAOLER jailer; prison warder	
GAPING yawning; staring; gazing	
GARAGE motor shed	
GARBED clothed	
GARBLE separate; pervert; misquote	
GARCON waiter (Fr.)	
GARDEN a pleasance	
GARDON roach; ide (Fr.)	**Z.**
GARGET throat inflammation	
GARGIL goose disease	
GARGLE a mouth-wash	
GARGOL swine disease	
GARIAL gavial; crocodile	**Z.**
GARISH gaudy; ornate; florid	
GARLIC genus of plants	**B.**
GARNER to store; collect; hoard	
GARNET carbuncle	**Min.**
GAROUS garum, a fish sauce	
GARRAN horse; galloway (Sc.)	**Z.**
GARRET loft; attic	
GARRON (see garran)	
GARROT a tourniquet	**Med.**
GARROT ocean duck	**Z.**
GARRYA flowering evergreen	**B.**
GARTER	
GARUDA Hindu demi-god	
GARVIE the sprat	**Z.**
GAS-BAG a blimp; chatter-box	
GASCON of Gascony	
GASHED severely wounded	
GASHLY ghastly; frightful	
GASIFY convert into gas	
GAS-JET a burner	
GASKET ⎱ cord for lashing	**Naut.**
GASKIN ⎰ sails to yards	
GAS-MAN	
GASPED panted; blew; puffed	
GASPER cigarette; fag (slang)	
GASSED poisoned by gas	
GAS-TAR coal-tar	
GATEAU cake; brioche (Fr.)	
GATHER assemble; muster; fold	
GATING a university restriction	**Electron**
GATTEN dogwood	**B.**
GAUCHE boorish; clumsy (Fr.)	

GAUCHE bad-mannered (Fr.)	
GAUCHO cow-boy; shepherd (S. Amer.)	
GAUGED measured; estimated	
GAUGER excise officer	
GAUPUS ⎱ a silly person	
GAWPUS ⎰	
GAVIAL garial; crocodile (Asia)	**Z.**
GAYEST liveliest; merriest; blithest	
GAY-YOU fishing boat (Annam.)	
GAZEBO summer house; balcony	
GAZING viewing; gaping; regarding	
GAZOON Hogg's body	
GEARED harnessed	
GEBBIE the stomach (Sc.)	
GEEZER a seedy gent	
GEIGER radio-activity counter	
GEISHA mousmee; Jap dancing girl	
GELDED castrated; enfeebled	
GELERT Llewellyn's faithful hound	**Z.**
GEMARA (Talmud) (Heb.)	**Eccl.**
GEMINI Castor and Pollux; (Zodiac)	
GEMMAE leaf-buds	**B.**
GEMMAN gentleman	
GEMMED jewelled; budded	
GEMMHO inverse meg-ohm	**Meas.**
GEMOTE meeting; gemot	
GENDER to beget; sex	
GENERA plural of genus	
GENEVA gin; hollands	
GENIAL hearty; kindly; cordial	
GENIUS adept; gift; talent; djinn	
GENNET jennet; small Spanish horse	**Z.**
GENTLE larva of fly	**Z.**
GENTLY tenderly; gradually	
GENTOO a Hindu; a penguin	**Z.**
GENTRY "the nobs"; "the upper ten"	
GENUAL (knee)	
GEODIC (crystalline cavity)	**Min.**
GEOGEN environmental factor	
GEOMYS rodents (U.S.A.)	**Z.**
GEORGE a jewel	**Coin**
GERANT gerent; manager	
GERBIL a rodent	**Z.**
GERMAN related to; germana	
GERMEN ⎱ an ovary	**B.**
GERMIN ⎰ a germ	
GERUND verbal noun	
GERVAO West Indian shrub	**B.**
GERVAS plant (W. Indies)	**B.**
GESTIC legendary	
GETTER a sire	
GEW-GAW bauble; trinket; gaud	
GEYSER hot spring	
GHARRY gharri; Indian cart	
GHAZAL ⎱ a form of	
GHAZEL ⎰ Persian verse; gazelle	**Z.**
GHEBER ⎱ Zoroastrian	
GHEBRE ⎰ also Guebre	
GHETTO Jewish quarter	
GHURKA Gurkha; native of Nepal	

GIAOUR unbeliever (Turk)	
GIBBER jabber; gabble; babble	
GIBBET the gallows; to hang	
GIBBON an ape	**Z.**
GIB-CAT worn-out cat	**Z.**
GIBING scoffing; jibing	**Naut.**
GIBLET internal part of a fowl	
GIFTED intellectual; able; talented	
GIGGIT to move rapidly (U.S.A.)	
GIGGLE snigger; titter; cackle	
GIGLET } a giddy girl	
GIGLOT } a wanton	
GIGMAN would-be gent	
GIGOLO dancing partner; kept man	
GILDED gilt	
GILDER a guilder	
GILLIE attendant; game-keeper (Sc.)	
GILPEY boisterous boy or girl (Sc.)	
GILPIN the coal-fish	**Z.**
GIMBAL (compass)	**Naut.**
GIMLET a boring tool	**Tool**
GIMMAL (machinery)	**Z.**
GIMMER 2 year-old ewe	
GINETE Spanish trooper	
GINGAL Indian musket; swivel gun	
GINGER sandy; reddish	**B.**
GINGKO } Chinese yew	**B.**
GINKGO } maiden-hair tree	
GINGLE jingle; Irish car	
GINNED snared; (cotton)	
GINNET a nag; a jennet	**Z.**
GIRDED reproached; braced; surrounded	
GIRDER a cross-beam	
GIRDLE belt; zone; enclosure	
GIRKIN gherkin	**B.**
GIRNEL granary; meal-chest	
GITANA Spanish gipsy woman	
GITANO Spanish gipsy man	
GIUSTO in time; regular	**Mus.**
GIVING yielding; allowing	
GIZZEN to wither; leaky	
GLACIS gentle slope; parapet	
GLADLY with pleasure; joyously	
GLAGOL Slavonic alphabet	
GLAIRY viscous	
GLAIVE broadsword or falchion	
GLANCE glimpse; look; ricochet	
GLARED stared; glowered; frowned	
GLASSY, GLAZED vitrified	
GLAZER polisher; calico-smoother	
GLEAMY casting rays of light	
GLEDGE cunning look; to squint	
GLEETY limpid; ichorous	
GLIBLY volubly; oily tongued	
GLIDED skimmed; skated	
GLIDER engineless aeroplane	
GLOBAL globular; world-wide	
GLOBIN (haemoglobin)	**Med.**
GLOOMY dim; dismal; obscure	
GLORIA a hymn	**Eccl.**

GLOSSY smooth; sheeny; bright	
GLOVED	
GLOVER glove-maker	
GLOWED flushed; shone; gleamed	
GLOWER scowl; frown; glare	
GLOZED palliated; wheedled	
GLOZER flatterer; sycophant	
GLUCIC (glucose)	**Chem.**
GLUING cementing; uniting	
GLUISH (glue); sticky; viscous	
GLUMAL husky	**B.**
GLUMLY sulkily; sullenly	
GLUMPS the sulks	
GLUTEN (wheat); glutin	**B.**
GLYCIN gelatin-sugar	**Chem.**
GLYCOL a liquid	**Chem.**
GNARLY } knotted; crabbed	
GNARRY } gnarled	
GNAWED fretted; tormented	
GNAWER a rodent; masticator	
GNEISS laminated granite	**Min.**
GNETUM plant (E. Indies)	**B.**
GNOMIC didactic	
GNOMON style of sundial	
GNOSIS esoteric knowledge	
GOADED impelled; spurred; stung	
GOALIE goalkeeper (football)	
GOANNA iguana (Australia)	**Z.**
GOATEE a beard	
GO-BANG a game	
GOBBET lump; swallow; mouthful	
GOBBIN coal refuse	
GOBBLE to swallow; bolt; (turkey)	
GOBLET tumbler; glass cup; rummer	
GOBLIN sprite; gnome; spectre	
GO-CART two-wheeled cart	
GO-DOWN warehouse	
GODSON	
GODWIT bird of passage	**Z.**
GOETIC (black magic)	
GOFFER to plait; to crimp	
GOGGLE to roll the eyes	
GOGLET porous vase	
GOIDEL Celtic; gael	
GOITER } a tumour	**Med.**
GOITRE } bronchocele	
GOLDEN gilt; excellent; auric	
GOLFER	
GOLIAS medieval nom de plume	
GOLLAR to scold; speak loudly	
GOLORE abundance; galore	
GOLOSH overshoe	
GOMMER soup ingredient	
GOMUTI } sago palm	**B.**
GOMUTO } black fibre	
GONGED prelude to a fine	
GOODLY fair; comely; seemly	
GOOGLY a strange delivery	
GOORAL Asiatic goat	**Z.**
GOOROO Hindoo teacher	**Eccl.**

GOPHER American rodent   **Z.**
GOPHER timber used for the Ark   **B.**
GOPURA Hindu temple tower
GORAMY gourami; fish (E. Arch.)   **Z.**
GORGED glutted; stuffed; (Her.)
GORGET throat armour; lady's ruff
GORGET instrument   **Med.**
GORGIO gipsy term for a non-gipsy
GORGON ugly monster
GORHEN hen grouse   **Z.**
GORIER more blood-stained
GORING a pricking; puncture
GOSHEN land of plenty
GOSPEL glad tidings
GOSSAN } ferruginous rock   **Min.**
GOZZAN }
GOSSIP chatter; boon companion
GOTHIC rude; barbarous
GOTTEN got; acquired
GOUGED scooped out
GOUDIE } goldfinch (Sc.)   **Z.**
GOWDIE } a jewel; gold lace
GOURDE (Haiti)   **Coin·**
GOURDY swelling (horse)
GOUSTY dreary (Sc.)
GOVERN rule; sway; control; restrain
GOWNED robed; arrayed
GOWPEN a handful (Sc.)
GRACED virtuous; chaste
GRACES the Greek Charities
GRADED classified; arranged
GRADIN raised step or seat
GRADUS dictionary of prosody
GRAFIN German count
GRAINS malt husks; prongs; harpoons
GRAINY granulated
GRAITH accoutrements; equipment (Sc.)
GRAKLE starling   **Z.**
GRAMME weight (Fr.)   **Meas.**
GRANGE farmers' union; farm-house
GRANNY knot   **Naut.**
GRANTH Sikh Scriptures   **Eccl.**
GRASSY green
GRATER kitchen implement
GRATIN (brown crust)
GRATIS without payment
GRAVED cleaned; chiselled; cut   **Naut.**
GRAVEL disease   **Med.**
GRAVEL embarrass; puzzle
GRAVEN engraved; carved
GRAVER (engraver); more sedate   **Tool**
GRAVES white wine (Fr.)
GRAVES melted tallow
GRAVID pregnant
GRAZED scratched; brushed
GRAZER browser
GREASE lubricate; bribe
GREASY unctuous; sebaceous; slippery
GREATS final exam. in classics, Ox. B.A.
GREAVE leg armour; greave

GREECE } flight of steps
GREESE } staircase
GRIECE } a degree
GREEDY eager; voracious; grasping
GREENS vegetables   **B.**
GREENY greenish
GREEVE greave; steward; a reeve
GREGAL gregarious
GRIDED grated; pierced
GRIEVE greve; sadden; lament
GRILLE iron grating
GRILSE young salmon   **Z.**
GRIMED begrimed; foul
GRIMLY fiercely; dourly
GRINGO Yankee in S. America
GRIPED furrowed; trenched
GRIPER extortioner; oppressor
GRIPPE influenza (Fr.)
GRISLY grim; ferocious; fierce; dire
GRISON weasel (S. Amer.)   **Z.**
GRITER teasel spade   **Tool**
GRITTY sandy
GRIVET Abyssinian monkey   **Z.**
GRIZEL meek patient wife
GROATS hulled oats
GROCER
GROGGY tipsy; staggering
GROMEL gromil; gromwell; a plant   **B.**
GROMET a rope ring   **Naut.**
GROOVE furrow; rut; cutting
GROPED searched; picked; sought
GROSER gooseberry   **B.**
GROSZY (Poland)   **Coin**
GROTTO cavern; cave
GROUND earth; clod; domain; cause
GROUSE complaint   **Z.**
GROUTS coarse meal
GROUTY thick; muddy; sulky
GROVEL crawl; cringe; fawn
GROWER husbandman
GROWTH increase; progress
GROYNE sea wall
GRUBBY grimy; dirty
GRUDGE envy; covet; enmity; dislike
GRU-GRU edible insect   **Z**
GRUMLY morosely; surlily
GRUMPH grunt (Sc.)
GRUMPY surly; sullen; churlish
GRUNDY (Mrs.)
GRYFON griffin (obs.)
GUACHO gaucho; shepherd (S. Amer.)
GUANIN (GUANO)
GUDDLE to tickle trout (Sc.)
GUEBRE Gueber; Parsee fire-worshipper
GUELPH German medieval faction
GUENON African monkey   **Z**
GUFFAW boisterous laugh
GUGGLE to gurgle
GUIDED regulated; instructed; steered
GUIDER a director; leader; pilot

GUIDON flag; signal (Fr.)
GUILED beguiled; treacherous
GUILLS corn marigold **B.**
GUILTY criminal; culpable; sinful
GUINEA fowl; worm; pig **Coin, Z.**
GUISER mummer
GUITAR type of lute **Mus.**
GULDEN florin **Coin**
GULLED duped; tricked; hoaxed
GULLER a cheat; impostor
GULLET throat **Med.**
GULLEY large knife (Sc.)
GULPED swallowed; bolted
GUMLAC resinous matter
GUMMED stuck; cemented
GUN-MAN armed bandit
GUN-MEN desperadoes
GUNNEL a blenny; butterfish **Z.**
GUNNEL ship's side; gunwale **Naut.**
GUNNER artillery-man
GUN-SHY
GUNTER instrument; sail **Naut.**
GUN-WAD
GUNYAH Australian native hut
GURGLE purl; ripple; murmur
GURJUN Indian balsam **B.**
GURHKA a native of Nepal
GURNET fish; gurnard **Z.**
GURRAH Indian earthen jar
GUSHED rushed; spurted; spouted
GUSHER oil-well
GUSSET an insertion
GUTTAE Doric ornamentation
GUTTED plundered; eviscerated
GUTTEE bedewed (Her.)
GUTTER conduit; sweal; rhine
GUTTLE to guzzle
GUZZLE swill; swallow greedily
GYBING jibing **Naut.**
GYMNIC gymnastic (obs.)
GYPSEY gipsy
GYPSUM lime sulphate **Chem.**
GYRATE spiral; revolve; spin
GYROSE like a crook **B.**

H

HABBLE perplex; stutter (Sc.)
HACHEL a sloven (Sc.)
HACKED mangled; hired; kicked
HACKEE chipmunk; American squirrel **Z.**
HACKET kittiwake **Z.**
HACKLE cock's neck feathers
HACKLE fly (angling); comb
HACKLY rough
HADDIE haddock (Sc.)
HADDIN a holding; residence (Sc.)
HADING (mining); geological fault
HADITH Moslem oral tradition **Eccl.**
HAEMAL, MAEMIC relating to the blood **Med.**

HAFFET the temples (Sc.)
HAFFLE to lie; prevaricate
HAFTED handled
HAGBUT arquebuse; hackbut
HAGDEN shearwater gull **Z.**
HAGGED ugly; lean; haggish
HAGGIS Scotch dish
HAGGLE to mangle; higgle; bargain
HAGLET shearwater gull **Z.**
HAIDUK Hungarian yeoman
HAIGHA a king's messenger
HAILED greeted; came from
HAIQUE Arab wrap
HAIRDO hairstyle; coiffure
HAIRED hairy; hirsute; comate
HAIRST harvest (Sc.)
HAKEEM physician (Arabic)
HALFER fallow deer **Z.**
HALING hauling
HALION skipper fish **Z.**
HALLAN a partition (Sc.)
HALLEL Passover hymn **Eccl.**
HALLOA hallo!
HALLOO a hunting cry
HALLOW to reverence
HALLUX hind toe of bird **Z.**
HALOED sainted
HALOID (salt) **Chem.**
HALSED embraced by the neck
HALSER hawser **Naut.**
HALTED limped; hesitated; stopped
HALTER rope; cord
HALVED bisected; fifty-fifty
HALVES moieties
HAMATE set with hooks
HAMBLE mutilate the foot
HAMITE fossil; native (E. Africa) **Min.**
HAMLET cluster of cottages
HAMMAL Turkish porter
HAMMAM Turkish bath
HAMMER forge; a gavel **Tool**
HAMOSE ⎫ hooked **B.**
HAMOUS ⎭
HAMPER basket; impede; embarrass
HANDED served; conducted; led on
HANDLE touch; feel; manipulate
HANGAR aircraft shed
HANGED dangled; depended
HANGER broadsword; wood on hill-side
HANGER the sword of Damocles
HANJAR Persian dagger
HANKED skeined; jibbed **Naut.**
HANKER desire; crave; yearn; want
HANSEL earnest penny; handsel
HANSOM a cab
HANTLE considerable number (Sc.)
HAPPEN occur; betide; chance; befall
HARASS annoy; tire; vex; worry
HARDEN nerve; steal; brace; inure

HARDER stiffer; firmer
HARDLY barely; scarcely; narrowly
HARD-UP impecunious; indigent
HARELD sea-duck   **Z.**
HARIER a harrier   **Z.**
HARING speeding
HARISH like a hare
HARKED listened; hurried
HARKEN hearken; listen; attend
HARLED covered with rough-cast
HARLOT strumpet; moll; trollop
HARMAN policeman; a copper
HARMED damaged; injured
HARMEL Syrian rue   **B.**
HARPED iterated; dwelt   **Mus.**
HARPER lyrist; harpist   **Mus.**
HARRIS a tweed
HARROW lacerate; tear
HARTAL Indian boycott
HASHED chopped, mixed
HASLET hog's heart
HASTED hastened; hurried
HASTEN hurry; speed; despatch; urge
HAT-BOX
HATHOR goddess of love (Egypt)
HATING detesting; loathing; abhoring
HAT-PEG
HAT-PIN
HATRED odium; enmity; rancour
HATTED
HATTER independent miner (Australia)
HAULED dragged; tugged; towed
HAULER haulier; carter
HAUNCH part of an arch
HAUSSA West African race
HAUTIN sea-fish in fresh water   **Z.**
HAUYNE a silicate   **Min.**
HAVANA (cigar)
HAVERS twaddle; empty talk
HAVING holding; possessing
HAWHAW sunk fence; guffaw
HAWKED peddled; streaked
HAWKER pedlar; retailer; falconer
HAWKEY ⎫ dark cow with white   **Z.**
HAWKIE ⎭ streaked face (Sc.)
HAWSER halser; cable   **Naut.**
HAY-BOX cooking appliance
HAYMOW hay in barn
HAYSEL hay-makers' festival
HAZARD risk; chance; peril; jeopardy
HAZILY obscurely; foggily; mistily
HAZING bullying; brutal horse-play
HEADED (cask); (football)
HEADER (brick); (diving)
HEAD-ON
HEALED cured; remedied
HEALER doctor; restorer
HEALTH soundness; hygiene; haleness
HEAPED massed; accumulated; piled
HEARER one of an audience

HEARSE funeral car
HEARTH fireplace; fireside; home
HEARTY robust; sincere; cordial
HEATED agitated; excited; hectic
HEATER
HEATHY heathery   **B.**
HEAUME heavy helmet
HEAVED hoisted; dilated; panted
HEAVEN Elysium; Paradise; bliss
HEAVER a lever
HEAVES disease (horse); broken wind
HEBREW a Jew
HECATE goddess of witchcraft
HECKLE to comb; to question
HECTIC feverish; heated; hot
HECTOR to bully; bluster; vaunt
HEDDLE (weaving)
HEDERA ivy   **B.**
HEDGED skulked; (betting)
HEDGER a trimmer of fences
HEEDED attended; noticed
HEE-HAW to bray
HEELED armed; equipped; leant
HEELER hanger-on (U.S.A.)
HEGIRA ⎫ Mohammed's flight from
HEJIRA ⎭ Mecca to Medina, A.D. 622
HEIFER young cow   **Z.**
HEIGHT altitude; acme; zenith
HELIAC heliacal; (sun)
HELION virago; shrew; hell-cat
HELITE an amalgam   **Chem.**
HELIUM a gaseous element   **Chem.**
HELLAS ancient Greece
HELLER German copper coin   **Coin**
HELMED with a helmet; directed
HELMET part of retort
HELPED prevented; aided; succoured
HELPER assistant; abettor; ally
HELVED having a handle; hafted
HELVIN mineral   **Min.**
HEMINA about 10 ounces   **Meas.**
HEMMED bordered; enclosed
HEMMER a stitcher; a sewer
HEMPEN made of hemp   **B.**
HENBIT dead nettle   **B.**
HEPTAD series of seven
HERALD harbinger; crier; proclaim
HERBAL book describing plants
HERDED tended; massed
HERDIC a cab (U.S.A.)
HEREAT at this point
HEREBY by this
HEREIN
HEREOF
HEREON
HERESY schism; heterodoxy; recusancy
HERETO in addition
HERIOT a fine   **Law**
HERMAE sculptured busts
HERMES Mercury (Greek)

HERMIT anchorite; recluse
HERNIA rupture   **Med.**
HEROES demi-gods
HEROIC bold; intrepid; valiant
HEROIN a drug   **Med.**
HERPES skin disease; shingles   **Med.**
HERREN German gentlemen
HERSED in harrow form (Her.)
HESPER evening star
HESVAN Heshvan; Jewish month
HETMAN Cossack chief
HEWING hacking; shaping
HEXADE series of six
HEXANE paraffin
HEXODE a thermionic valve
HEYDAY frolic; period of vigour
HIATUS a chasm; gap; lacuna
HICCUP hiccough
HIDAGE a tax   **Law**
HIDDEN latent; covert; recondite
HIDING a beating; screening; masking
HIEING going along; hiking
HIEMAL wintry; hyemal
HIGGLE to bargain; haggle
HIGHER superior; nobler
HIGHLY eminently; loftily   [**Eccl.**
HI-JACK kidnap; rob
HIJRAH Hegira; flight from Mecca
HIKING walking; foot-slogging
HILARY Law Court session; (Oxford)
HILLED earthed up
HILSAH fish (Ganges)   **Z.**
HILTED hafted; helved
HINDEE North Indian tongue
HINDER delay
HINGED depended on
HINTED implied
HINTER suggester
HIPPED melancholic; roof   **Arch.**
HIPPIC horsy; equine
HIPPUS clonic spasm of iris   **Med.**
HIRCIN mutton suet
HIRCUS the goat   **Z.**
HIRING bribing; engaging
HIRMOI ⎱ hymns   **Eccl.**
HIRMOS ⎰ ode (Greek church)
HIRSEL ⎱ flock of sheep (Sc.)
HIRSLE ⎰ a throng; to slide
HISPID bristly
HISSED hizzed
HISSER disapprover
HITCHY catchy
HITHER to this place
HITTER smiter; slogger; striker
HIVING storing; clustering
HOARSE guttural; husky; raucous
HOAXED tricked; gulled; gammoned
HOAXEE the victim
HOAXER practical joker
HOAZIN (S. Amer.) pheasant   **Z.**

HOBBLE halt; limp; shackle; clog
HOBJOB an odd job
HOBNOB familiarity
HOCKEY an outdoor game
HOCKLE to mow; hamstring
HODDEN grey cloth
HODMAN mason's labourer
HOEING weeding
HOGGED clipped; bent
HOGGER (whole)
HOGGET young sheep; colt or boar   **Z.**
HOGGIN sand and gravel mixture
HOGPEN hogsty
HOGSTY pig pen
HOIDEN hoyden; a romp; rude; rustic
HOLDER a tenant
HOLD-UP robbery under arms
HOLIER more sacred
HOLILY piously
HOLISM evolution
HOLLER, HOLLOA shout (distress)
HOLLOW empty; vacant; void; cavity
HOLMIA oxide of holmium   **Chem.**
HOLMIC (holmium)   **Chem.**
HOMAGE fealty; devotion; loyalty
HOMELY plain; simple; domestic
HOMILY sermon; address; discourse
HOMING (pigeons); aerial navigation
HOMINY boiled maize
HONEST fair; just; trusty; sincere
HONING whetting
HONKED (cry of wild geese)
HONOUR exalt; dignify; fame; renown
HOODED cowled; cloaked
HOODIE carrion-crow (Sc.)   **Z.**
HOODOO voodoo; witchcraft; (W.Indies)
HOOFED ungulate
HOOKAH Turkish pipe
HOOKED (golf); hamate
HOOKER fishing boat   **Naut.**
HOOK-UP radio connections
HOOPED encircled; whooped
HOOPER (tubs); a cooper
HOOP-LA game at fairs
HOOPOE ⎱ crested birds,   **Z.**
HOOPOO ⎰ horn-bill type
HOOTCH hooch; firewater (U.S.A.)
HOOTED honked
HOOTER a siren
HOOVEN (cattle-disease)
HOOVER dust removing appliance
HOOVES
HOPDOG pale tussock moth   **Z.**
HOP-FLY plant louse   **Z.**
HOPING desiring; trusting
HOPPED danced; bounced
HOPPER wooden trough; hop-picker
HOPPER young locust   **Z.**
HOPPET hand-basket

HORARY hourly
HORNED with horns; butted
HORNER dealer in horns; sand-eel **Z.**
HORNET **Z.**
HORNIE the devil; old Nick
HORRID horrific; terrible; dreadful
HORROR terror; panic; alarm; dismay
HORSED mounted
HOSIER dealer in stockings
HOSTEL an inn; lodging house
HOT-BED earth-bed (Hort.)
HOT-DOG sausage sandwich
HOT-POT peppery stew
HOT-ROD supercharged car
HOTTER more ardent
HOUDAH howdah; seat on an elephant
HOUDAN breed of fowls **Z.**
HOUNDS (mast head) **Naut.**
HOURLY horary
HOUSED resided; sheltered; stored
HOUSEL the Eucharist **Eccl.**
HOUSTY a sore throat (dial.)
HOWDAH houdah; seat on an elephant
HOWDIE midwife (Sc.)
HOWKER hooker; vessel (Dutch) **Naut.**
HOWLED yowled; cried; lamented
HOWLER (monkey); grievous error **Z.**
HOWLET (owlet) **Z.**
HOYDEN hoiden; tomboy; romp
HUBBLE an uproar; hubbub
HUBBLY rowdy
HUBBUB disorder; noise; uproar; din
HUCKLE the hip; a haunch
HUDDLE crowd; confuse; jumble
HUDDUP get up !
HUFFED blustered; (draughts)
HUFFER a bully; blusterer
HUGELY enormously; immensely
HULLED pierced; husked
HULLER hulling machine
HUMANE kind; benign; merciful
HUMBLE degrade; abash; meek; lowly
HUMBLY unobtrusively
HUMBUG quackery; charlatan
HUMECT⎫ to moisten
HUMEFY⎰ to dampen
HUMERI bones of the upper arm **Med.**
HUMETE abbreviated fesse (Her.)
HUMHUM coarse cloth (Ind.)
HUMIAN (David Hume)
HUMINE black ground powder; humus
HUMITE limestone **Min.**
HUMMED buzzed; droned
HUMMEL hornless; awnless
HUMMER a sledge-runner
HUMMIE small bulge
HUMOUR indulge; pamper **Med.**
HUMOUS mouldy
HUMPED shouldered
HUMPER meat-porter; carrier

HUNGER hanker; desire; crave
HUNGRY ravenous; famishing
HUNKER to squat down; old fogey
HUNNIC Hunnish
HUNTED searched; sought; hounded
HUNTER chaser; stalker **Z.**
HURDLE wattle fence
HURLED flung; heaved; slung; cast
HURLER a thrower
HURLEY shinty; (hockey)
HURRAH
HURRAY
HURTER a buffer plank
HURTLE to whirl; to crash
HUSHED quietened; calmed; stilled
HUSKED hulled
HUSKER a remover of husks
HUSSAR light cavalryman
HUSSIF (housewife); a holdall
HUSTLE bustle; jostle; elbow; rush
HUTTED in huts
HUZOOR Indian title of respect
HYADES 5 stars in Taurus
HYAENA hyena **Z.**
HYBRID cross-bred; mongrel
HYDRIA Grecian water-vase
HYDRIC (hydrogen) **Chem.**
HYDRID hydrogen compound **Chem.**
HYDRUS constellation; water-snake **Z.**
HYEMAL hiemal; wintry
HYETAL (rainfall)
HYGEIA Goddess of Health
HYKSOS Egyptian dynasty
HYLISM materialism
HYMNAL collection of hymns
HYMNED celebrated in song
HYMNIC
HYPHAE fungoid filaments **B.**
HYPHEN
HYPNUM a moss genus **B.**
HYSSOP aromatic herb **B.**

I

IAMBIC rhythmic
IAMBUS Greek satiric metre
IATRIC medicinal **Med.**
IBERIS candytuft **B.**
IBEXES wild goats (Alps.) **Z.**
IBIDEM in the same place
ICARUS an early aeronaut
ICE-AGE
ICE-AXE
ICE-CAP
ICE-MAN
ICE-SAW
ICICLE
ICIEST frostiest
ICONIC illustrative
IDEATE to fancy
IDIASM a peculiarity

IDIOCY lunacy; dementia; craziness

IDLING nothing doing

IDOLUM ⎫
IDOLON ⎬ mental picture

I'FAITH indeed; truly; verily

IGNITE kindle; inflame; fire

IGNORE disregard; overlook; skip

IGOROTE Filipino

IGUANA lizard; a saurian   **Z.**

ILEXES holm-oaks   **B.**

ILL-GOT ill-gotten

ILLISH somewhat unwell

ILLUDE to deceive; delude

ILLUME illumine; brighten

ILL-USE mistreat

IMAGED imagined; fancied

IMBALM embalm

IMBAND form into band

IMBANK embank

IMBARK embark; board

IMBIBE absorb; assimilate; drink

IMBODY embody; incorporate

IMBOIL emboil; burn with anger

IMBREX pantile; curved roof-tile

IMBRUE to moisten; to drench

IMBUED dyed; inspired; steeped

IMMANE huge; savage (Shak.)

IMMASK to cover

IMMESH entangle; enmesh

IMMUNE secure against attack

IMMURE enclose; incarcerate; confine

IMPACT shock; stroke; collision

IMPAIR mar; injure; harm; vitiate

IMPALA South African antelope   **Z.**

IMPALE transfix

IMPALM to grasp

IMPARK enclose

IMPARL to hold mutual discourse

IMPARL parley

IMPART bestow; confer; divulge

IMPAVE to pave

IMPAWN to pledge

IMPEDE obstruct; hinder; thwart

IMPEND threaten; hover; approach

IMPING ekeing; extending; grafting

IMPISH puckish; mischievous

IMPLEX complicated

IMPONE to stake; to wager

IMPORT imply; purport; gist; drift

IMPOSE lay; inflict; charge; dictate

IMPOST a tax; a duty; a cess

IMPUGN attack; contradict; question

IMPURE unclean; sullied; tarnished

IMPUTE charge; ascribe; imply

INARCH to graft

INBOND (brick-laying)

INBORN innate; inherent; congenital

INBRED natural; inborn

INCAGE encage; confine

INCARN to incarnate

INCASE encase; enclose; enshrine

INCASK to put in a cask

INCAST a bonus; thrown in

INCAVO incised part of an intaglio

INCEPT to begin; to commence

INCEST prohibited co-habitation

INCHED advanced by inches

INCISE engrave; scribe

INCITE stir; goad; foment; rouse

INCLIP to grasp; enclose; surround

INCOME revenue; annual receipts

INCONY delicate; fine; pretty (Shak.

INCULT uncultivated

INCUSE to stamp

INCUSS incuse; forge

INDABA native council

INDART to rush in (Shak.)

INDEED really; truly; verily; actually

INDENT to notch; order

INDIAN

INDICT to charge in writing   **Law**

INDIGN unworthy

INDIGO a blue dye   **B.**

INDITE endite; write; pen; dictate

INDIUM metallic element   **Chem.**

INDOOR within the house

INDUCE urge; actuate; incite

INDUCT introduce; install; initiate

INDUED endued; invested with

INDUNA Zulu chief

INEUNT a cusp

INFALL an inroad

INFAME defame

INFAMY shame; obloquy; disgrace

INFANT babe; suckling; minor

INFECT corrupt; vitiate; taint

INFEFF, INFEFT (land transfer)   **Law**

INFELT heart-felt

INFEST enfest; overrun; throng; beset

INFIRM frail; weak; decrepit

INFLOW

INFLUX importation in abundance

INFOLD enfold; embrace

INFORM tell; notify; apprize

INFULA Roman priestly badge

INFUSE instil; inculcate; steep

INGATE aperture in a mould

INGEST absorb; swallow

IN-GOAL rugby football

INGULF engulf; overwhelm

INHALE breathe in

INHAUL (a rope)   **Naut.**

INHERE to be innate

INHIVE to hive

INHOOP to confine

INHUME to inter; to bury; entomb

INJECT interpolate; insert

INJURE harm; hurt; mar; impair

INJURY ill; detriment; wrong

INK-BAG (cuttle-fish)   **Z.**

INKING marking with ink
INKNIT to knit in
INKNOT to knot
INK-POT
INK-SAC (cuttle-fish) **Z.**
INLACE to lace
INLAID fitted flush to surface
INLAND remote from the sea
INLIER geological formation
INLOCK enlock
INMATE resident; guest; denizen
INMOST innermost; deepest
INNATE inherent; congenital; inborn
INNING harvest grain
INNUIT an Eskimo
INRAIL enclose with rails
INROAD raid; foray; incursion
INROLL enroll (obs.)
INRUSH invasion; irruption
INSANE mad; crazy; deranged
INSEAM mark with a seam
INSECT mean; contemptible
INSECT a fly **Z.**
INSERT inject; introduce; infix
INSHIP embark; to ship
INSIDE inner; internal; interior
INSIST maintain; demand; urge
INSOLE inner sole
INSPAN to yoke
INSTAL install; induct; invest
INSTAR adorn with stars
INSTEP part of the foot
INSTIL infuse; ingraft; implant
INSTOP make fast; to stop
INSULT abuse; affront; ridicule
INSURE ensure; assure; guarantee
INTACT inviolate; integral; scatheless
INTAKE inlet of a pipe
INTEND mean; purpose; contemplate
INTENT set; bent; eager; attentive
INTERN confine; segregate
INTINE inner coat of pollen grain **B.**
INTOED with toes turned in
INTOMB entomb; bury; inter
INTONE to chant
INTORT to twist; to wreathe; to wind
INTRAP entrap (obs.)
INTUSE a bruise (Spens.) **Med.**
INULIN vegetable base (elecampane)
INURED hardened; accustomed **Law**
INVADE raid; infringe; assault; violate
INVENT devise; contrive; create; make
INVERT reverse; upset; overturn
INVEST indue; bedeck; array; beset
INVITE ask; bid; call; request; solicit
INVOKE adjure; conjure; implicate
INWALL enclose; enwall
INWARD inside; inner; internal
INWICK curling cannon
INWITH within (Sc.)

INWORK work within
INWORN inwrought
INWRAP to perplex; enwrap
INYALA nyala; bushbuck **Z.**
IODATE (iodic acid) **Chem.**
IODIDE **Chem.**
IODINE **Chem.**
IODISM morbid state
IODIZE treat with iodine
IOLITE a translucent silicate **Min.**
IONIAN (Ionia) (Arch.)
IONISM Ionic architecture
IONIUM (radium) **Chem.**
IONIZE convert into ions
IRANIC from Iran
IREFUL angry; wroth; incensed
IRENIC pacific
IRIDAL prismatic; iridian
IRIDIN active principle of iris
IRISED like a rainbow
IRITIC (iritis); inflamed **Med.**
IRITIS (eye disease) **Med.**
IRKING irksome; tedious; wearying
IRONED in irons; (laundry)
IRONER a laundry operative
IRONIC satirical; sarcastic
IRRUPT to interrupt; invade
ISABEL brownish yellow
ISAGON equi-angular figure
ISATIC woad-like **B.**
ISATIN an indigo product **Chem.**
ISATIS woad **B.**
ISLAND isle; to insulate
ISOBAR line of equal barometric press.
ISODIA Jewish sacred feast
ISOGON an isagon
ISOHEL sunshine contour
ISOMER (similar substance) **Chem.**
ISONYM paronym
ISOPOD (crustaceans) **Z.**
ISRAEL Jacob
ISSUED distributed; emitted; emerged
ISSUER publisher; utterer
ITALIC Italian
ITCHED wanted to; craved; hankered
ITSELF
IVIGAR sea-urchin **Z.**
IZZARD the letter Z

J

JABBED poked; prodded
JABBER much talk; prattle; gabble
JABBLE rough sea; splash (Sc.)
JABIRU Brazilian stork **Z.**
JACANA wading bird **Z.**
JACENT lying at length
JACKAL **Z.**
JACKED lifted with a jack
JACKET cover; jerkin; coat
JADERY tricks of a jade

JADISH vicious; unchaste
JAEGER gull; hunstman (Ger.) **Z.**
JAGGED notched; ragged; serrated
JAGGER brass wheel
JAGHIR a reward (Hind.)
JAGUAR American leopard **Z.**
JAILED gaoled; incarcerated
JAILER⎫ gaoler; warder
JAILOR⎭
JAMBEE a cane; walking-stick
JAMBOK sjambok; hide whip
JAMBUL Indian evergreen **B.**
JAMMED crushed; squeezed
JAMPAN sedan chair (Ind.)
JANGLE wrangle; clash; bicker
JANKER log-transporter (Sc.)
JARGON nonsense; gibberish; palaver
JAROOL Indian blood-wood **B.**
JARRAH tree (W. Australia) **B.**
JARRED wrangled; grated
JARVEY cab driver
JASHER lost Hebrew book
JASMIN climbing shrub **B.**
JASPER quartz **Min.**
JATAKA nativity (Buddha) **Eccl.**
JAUNCE to jolt; a jaunt (Shak.)
JAUNTY airy; sprightly; finical
JAW-BOX a sink (Sc.)
JAWING scolding
JAZZED
JEAMES a flunkey
JEERED mocked; derided; taunted
JEERER scoffer; sneerer
JEJUNE void of interest; meagre
JENNET gennet; small Spanish horse **Z.**
JERBOA a jumping rodent **Z.**
JEREED jerid; blunt javelin
JERKED twitched; flipped; jolted
JERKER underhand thrower
JERKIN a coat; jacket
JERKIN a hawk; gyrfalcon **Z.**
JERSEY cow; knitted garment **Z.**
JERVIN alkaloid (hellebore) **Chem.**
JESSED (Heraldic ornamentation)
JESTED joked; made merry; quizzed
JESTER joker; buffoon; wag; fool
JESUIT an intriguer
JETSAM goods thrown overboard **Law**
JETSOM jetson; jetsam
JETTEE projection (Arch.)
JETTON metal counter
JEWESS
JEWISH Hebrew
JEZAIL Afghan rifle
JIBBAH jubbah; Eastern garment
JIBBED refused to go; baulked
JIBBER restive horse
JIBING sneering; quizzing; taunting
JIBOYA boa-constrictor **Z.**
JIFFEY an instant

JIGGED danced
JIGGER an insect; a device **Z.**
JIGGLE wriggle; joggle; jolt
JIGJOG jolting
JIG-SAW fret-saw; a puzzle
JILLET a flirt; a wanton
JILTED discarded
JIMSON thorn-apple **B.**
JINGAL Eastern cannon
JINGLE Irish covered car; tinkle; rhyme
JINKER dodged; eluded; turned sharply
JINKER timber-cart (Australia)
JINNEE djinn; jinn; genie
JITTER instability **Electron**
JOBBER a dealer; stock-broker
JOB-LOT odds and ends
JOCKEY to cheat; rider of races
JOCOSE facetious; humorous; waggish
JOCUND sportive; merry; cheerful
JOGGED travelled slowly; shook
JOGGER jostler
JOGGLE a notch; to jar; to shake
JOHNNY gay spark
JOINED united; coupled; connected
JOINER a carpenter
JOKING jesting; bantering; rallying
JOLTED jogged; shook; jounced
JOLTER hustler
JORDAN a river; chamber pot
JOSEPH riding habit; unsized paper
JOSKIN yokel; clown
JOSSER a fellow; a chap; a palooka
JOSTLE hustle; elbow; joggle; justle
JOTTED noted; recorded
JOTTER memorandum book
JOUNCE to jolt; shake
JOVIAL genial; convivial; blithe
JOVIAN (Jupiter)
JOWDER, JOWTER fish hawker
JOWLER hunting dog **Z.**
JOYFUL happy; pleased; glad; blithe
JOYOUS gay; airy; merry; jocund
JUBATE maned; having a fringe
JUBBAH Eastern garment
JUDAIC Jewish; Hebrew; Israelitish
JUDDER jar and shudder **Aeronaut**
JUDEAN native of Judea
JUDGED considered; sentenced
JUDGER a judge; umpire; arbitrator
JUDICA Passion Sunday **Eccl.**
JUGATE coupled; yoked **B.**
JUGFUL **Meas.**
JUGGED (hare); imprisoned
JUGGLE conjure; shuffle; swindle
JUG-JUG nightingale's notes
JUJUBE shrub; lozenge **B.**
JULIAN (calendar)
JUMART hybrid animal (Fr.) **Z.**
JUMBAL crisp sweet cake
JUMBLE confuse; mix; muddle

JUMBUK a sheep (Australia) **Z.**
JUMENT a mare **Z.**
JUMPED bounded; grabbed; sprang
JUMPER chisel **Tool**
JUMPER religious sect; over-blouse **Z.**
JUNCUS plants (rush) **B.**
JUNGLE the rukh
JUNGLY jungli; unsophisticated
JUNIOR younger; a son
JUNIUS anonymous writer
JUNKER a Prussian
JUNKET a sweetmeat; to feast; regale
JUPATI palm yielding raphia fibre **B.**
JURANT swearing
JURIST a lawyer **Law**
JUSTER more equitable
JUSTLE jostle; nudge; elbow
JUSTLY fairly; impartially; rightly
JUTTED projected; protruded
JUZAIL Afghan heavy rifle
JYMOLD gimmal; gimbal

K

KABAKA ruler of Buganda
KABALA Moslem Holy of Holies **Eccl.**
KABOOK iron-stone (Ceylon) **Min.**
KABYLE Algerian Berber
KACHIN Burmese borderer
KAFFIR a Kafir
KAFILA caravan; train of camels
KAFTAN robe (Turk)
KAISER German emperor
KAKAPO New Zealand parrot **Z.**
KALIUM potassium **Chem.**
KALMIA American laurel **B.**
KALONG Malay fox-bat **Z.**
KALPIS Grecian water-vase
KAMEES kamis; Eastern garment
KAMELA ⎫ orange dye **B.**
KAMILA ⎭ (E. Indies)
KAMERA camera; private room
KAMSIN a hot wind of the Sahara
KANAKA South Sea Islander
KANTEN a sea-weed **B.**
KANUCK a Canadian
KAOLIN China clay
KARMIC relating to Karma
KAROSS skin blanket (S. Africa)
KARROO tableland (S. Africa)
KATION (electrical)
KAVASS Turkish constable
KEBBIE a cudgel (Sc.)
KEBLAH, KIBLAH towards Mecca
KECKLE cackle; (rope protection)
KECKSY dried stalks **B.**
KEDDAH kheda; elephant trap
KEDGED warped **Naut.**
KEDGER a kedge; small anchor
KEEKER mine inspector (Sc.)
KEELED carinated; navigated

KEELER tub; bargee
KEELIE kestrel; street Arab (Sc.) **Z.**
KEENED wailed; lamented
KEENER professional mourner
KEENLY sharply; acutely; astutely
KEEPER guard-ring; warden
KEEVED tubbed
KELKEL dried sole
KELPIE water spirit
KELSON keelson; inner keel **Naut.**
KELTIC Celtic
KELTIE kittiwake gull **Z.**
KELVIN thermo-dynamic temperature **Meas.**
KENCHI ivory carving tool
KENNED recognized; knew
KENNEL channel; gutter; a haunt
KENTLE (100 lb.); quintal **Meas.**
KERION hair disease **Med.**
KERITE insulating material
KERMES crimson dye; cochineal **Z.**
KERMIS kermess; Dutch fair
KERNEL nucleus; heart **B.**
KERRIA Japanese rose **B.**
KERRIE knob-kerrie
KERSEY woollen cloth
KESLOP (rennet)
KETONE acetone **Chem.**
KETTLE
KEUPER sandstone **Min.**
KEYAGE quayage
KEYING signals by modulation **Electron**
KEY-MEN the indispensables
KEY-PIN key-pivot
KHALIF Calif; Caliph
KHILIM reversible rug (Turkey)
KIBBLE iron bucket; well-bucket
KICKED hacked; objected; punted
KICKER
KICKUP small dance
KIDDED hoaxed; duped; spoofed
KIDDER a corn cornerer; a carpet
KIDDER forestaller; huckster
KIDDLE weir
KIDDOW guillemot **Z.**
KID-FOX young fox **Z.**
KIDNAP abduct; capture; steal
KIDNEY kind; humour **Med.**
KIEKIE a New Zealand shrub **B.**
KIKUYU tribe (Kenya)
KILERG 1,000 ergs **Meas.**
KILLAS slate **Min.**
KILLED fascinated; neutralized
KILLER dolphin **Z.**
KILLOW a black earth **Min.**
KILLUT Indian robe of honour
KILTED
KILTIE kilted soldier
KIMMER woman neighbour
KIMONO Japanese robe

KINATE salt   Chem.
KINCOB Indian thread work
KINDER more benevolent
KINDLE provoke; animate; ignite
KINDLY congenial; benevolent
KINEMA cinema; the movies; talkies
KINGLY regal; imperial; august
KINKED snarled; twisted
KINKLE a kink
KIPPER a salmon after spawning   Z.
KIRBEH Arab water-skin
KIRKIN (church attendance)   Eccl.
KIRPAN Sikh 3 foot knife
KIRSCH wild cherry liqueur
KIRTLE a gown; a mantle
KIRTLE weight of flax   Meas.
KISMET fate; destiny
KISSED bussed; (billiards)
KISSER
KIT-BAG
KITTEN   Z.
KITTLE ticklish; intractable (Sc.)
KITTLY ticklish; sensitive
KLAXON a motor horn
KLEPHT Greek bandit
KNACKY cunning
KNAGGY knotty; rough in temper
KNARRY knotty; rugged
KNAWEL a plant   B.
KNICKS knickers
KNIFED stabbed
KNIGHT a chess-man; a paladin
KNITCH faggot (dial.)
KNOBBY knotty; stubborn
KNOTTY intricate; difficult
KNOWER an erudite man
KOBALT cobalt   Chem.
KOBANG old Japanese gold coin   Coin
KOBOLD goblin; gnome
KOODOO antelope (S. Africa)   Z.
KOPECK Russian farthing   Coin
KOREAN Corean
KORKIR corkir; purple dye   B.
KORUNA crown (Czech)   Coin
KOSHER pure; (meat, Heb.)
KOSMOS Cosmos; opposite to chaos
KOTWAL Indian police officer
KOUSSO plant (Abys.)   B.
KOWHAI Maori trees   B.
KOW-TOW salutation (China)
KRAKEN sea monster (Danish)
KRANTZ rocky summit (S. Africa)
KRASIS Eucharistic wine with water
KREESE creese; Malay dagger
K-THIBH (Hebrew Scriptures)
KUKANG lemur or loris (Malay)   Z.
KULTUR education; German culture
KUMBAR Indian coarse wood   B.
KUMBUK E. Indian tree   B.
KUMISS koumiss; drink (Tartar)

KUMMEL a liqueur
KUNKUR Indian limestone
KURKEE coarse blanket
KURUSH (Turkey)   Coin
KUSKUS cuskus; Indian fibre   B.
KUTTAR short Indian dagger
KYBOSH insurmountable obstruction
KYLOES Highland cattle   Z.

L

LAAGER Boer wagon encampment
LABEFY impair; weaken
LABIAL (lips)
LABILE unstable; liable to err
LABIUM a lip   B., Med.
LABOUR toil; drudge; industry
LABRET lip ornament
LABRUM upper lip   Med.
LACCIC (a resinous dye)   Chem.
LAC-DYE (dye); shellac
LACHES negligence   Law
LACING twining; beating; intermixing
LACKED short of; needed; wanted
LACKER one in want
LACKEY flunkey; footman; attendant
LACMUS litmus; lichen-dye   Chem.
LACTIC (milk)
LACUNA a void; gap; blank; hiatus
LADDER (stockings); (Jacob's)
LADDIE youngster; lad; boy
LA-DI-DA affected manner
LADIES gentlewomen
LADING freight; cargo; burden
LADINO Spanish dialect
LADLED spooned; dispensed
LAGENA amphora; vase
LAG-END the bitter end
LAGGED loitered; apprehended
LAGGEN barrel projection (Sc.)
LAGGER laggard; loafer; idler
LAGOON lake; bayou
LAGUNE lagoon; pool
LAICAL (laity)
LAIDLY loathly; clumsy (dial.)
LAID-UP ill; out of action
LAITHE pollack fish   Z.
LAKIST (Lake school of poetry)
LALLAN Lowland (Sc.)
LAMBED yeaned
LAMBIE small lamb   Z.
LAMELY haltingly
LAMENT deplore; wail; a jeremiad
LAMINA thin plate
LAMING crippling; disabling
LAMISH somewhat lame
LAMMAS 1st August
LAMMED thrashed; drubbed
LAMMER amber (Sc.)
LAMMIE quilted jumper; lammy

LAMPAS swelling in horse's palate
LAMPIC (alcohol) **Chem.**
LANARY wool store
LANATE woolly
LANCED cut open; pierced
LANCER a cavalry-man
LANCET a cutting instrument **Med.**
LANCET window (Arch.)
LANDAU a carriage
LANDED disembarked; owning estates
LANDER a miner
LANGET coarse Dutch lace
LANGUE tongue (linguistics)
LANGUR Indian monkey **Z.**
LANKLY laxly; languidly
LANNER hawk; falcon **Z.**
LAPDOG small pet dog **Z.**
LAPFUL
LAPPED (gem cutting); (racing)
LAPPEL lapel; folded flap
LAPPER folder
LAPPET loose flap; a lobe
LAPSED slipped; became void; sank
LARDED smeared with lard
LARDER store-house
LARDON slice of bacon
LARGER bigger; wider; greater, bulkier
LARIAT lasso; rope with noose
LARRUP to beat; to flog
LARVAE caterpillars; grubs; maggots **Z.**
LARVAL (larva) **Z.**
LARYNX (throat); (wind pipe) **Med.**
LASCAR East Indian sailor
LASHED secured; scourged
LASHER rope; pool below a weir
LASHES thongs; eye-lashes
LASKET loop line in a sail **Naut.**
LASQUE flat diamond **Min.**
LASSIE damsel; maid; lass
LASTED endured; remained; continued
LASTER boot-maker; cobbler
LASTLY ultimately; finally; endwise
LATEEN triangular sail **Naut.**
LATELY recently; latterly
LATENT dormant; concealed; potential
LATEST most up-to-date
LATHEN made of laths
LATHER soapy froth; foam
LATISH somewhat late
LATRIA highest kind of worship **Eccl.**
LATTEN sheet brass
LATTER modern; recent; previous
LAUDED praised; extolled; magnified
LAUDER eulogist; encomiast; panegyrist
LAUNCE a balance; an eel **Z.**
LAUNCH hurl; inaugurate; start
LAUREL the bay-tree **B.**
LAURIN an extract from laurel
LAVABO ritualistic washing **Eccl.**
LAVAGE washing **Med.**

LAVING bathing
LAVISH squander; dissipate; prodigal
LAVOLT medieval dance; lavolta
LAW-DAY day of open court **Law**
LAWFUL legal; legitimate; rightful
LAWING litigation; tavern-bill **Law**
LAWYER solicitor; counsel; advocate
LAXIST amoral philanderer
LAXITY slackness; latitude; neglect
LAY-DAY a lading day
LAYING placing; betting; imputing
LAYMAN not a cleric
LAY-OFF dismissal (industrial)
LAY-OUT set-out; plan
LAZIER more indolent and inert
LAZILY slothfully; drowsily; supinely
LAZING idling
LAZULI blue spar **Min.**
LEADED set in lead
LEADEN heavy; dull
LEADER head; chief; guide; director
LEAD-IN wire connecting an aerial
LEAFED having leaves
LEAGUE combine; union; cabal
LEAKED oozed; percolated
LEALTY loyalty; fidelity
LEAMER dog on leam **Z.**
LEANED relied; leant; inclined
LEANER thinner; skimpier
LEANLY lankly; slenderly; scantily
LEAN-TO a shed
LEAPED sprang; skipped; gambolled
LEAPER jumper; vaulter; chaser **Z.**
LEASED let out
LEASER gleaner
LEAVED interleaved **B.**
LEAVEN yeast; balm; ferment; imbue
LEAVER a forsaker; quitter; deserter
LECTOR reader **Eccl.**
LEDGER scaffold (Arch.); account book
LEERED ogled; gloated
LEEWAY arrears of work **Naut.**
LEGACY bequest; gift; devise **Law**
LEGATE ambassador; envoy; delegate
LEGATO smoothly **Mus.**
LEG-BYE (cricket)
LEGEND myth; fable; fiction; caption
LEGGED dashed off
LEGION host; multitude; horde; army
LEGIST skilled in law; jurist **Law**
LEGUME seed vessel; pod **B.**
LEIGER a resident ambassador (Shak.)
LEIPOA Australian game-bird **Z.**
LENDER loaner
LENGTH extent; duration; reach
LENIFY assuage; mollify
LENITY clemency; leniency
LENTEN (Lent); sparing
LENTIL a bean; pulse **B**
LENTOR slowness; tenacity; viscosity

LENVOY postscript
LEONID a meteor from Leo
LEPCHA native of Sikkim
LEPTON hundredth of a drachma **Coin**
LESION injury; wound **Med.**
LESSEE (lease); tenant **Law**
LESSEN reduce; mitigate; decrease
LESSER lower; minor; inferior
LESSON task; precept; warning
LESSOR lease holder **Law**
LETHAL fatal; deadly; mortal
LET-OFF a reprieve
LETTER note; epistle; missive
LETTIC Lettish; (Latvia)
LEUCOL coal-tar product
LEVANT to decamp; eastern
LEVIED mustered; taxed
LEVITE Jewish tribe; priest
LEVITY frivolity; flippancy; giddiness
LEWDLY lustfully
LEYDEN electrical jar
LIABLE accountable; likely; obnoxious
LIAISE to form a liaison
LIBANT sipping
LIBATE to make a libation
LIBIDO life force
LIBYAN (N. Africa)
LICHEN flowerless plant **B.**
LICHEN skin disease **Med.**
LICKED lapped; lammed; defeated
LICTOR Roman officer
LIDDED having lids
LIEDER German ballads
LIERNE cross-rib (Arch.)
LIFTED elevated; stole; upraised
LIFTER a thief; raiser
LIGATE to tie up **Med.**
LIGGER bed-spread; night-line
LIGHTS (ancient); (Northern); offal
LIGNIN wood-fibre
LIGNUM hardwood **B.**
LIGULA, LIGULE grass; petal **B.**
LIGURE precious stone **Min.**
LIKELY probable; credible; pleasing
LIKING love; fondness; regard
LILIED adorned with lilies
LILITH Adam's first wife
LILTED sung rhythmically
LIMBEC a still; a distilling vessel
LIMBED with limbs
LIMBER flexible; pliant; supple
LIMBUS limbo; paradise of fools
LIMING snaring; treating with lime
LIMMER mongrel; idler; jade **Z.**
LIMNED painted; illuminated
LIMNER artist; delineator
LIMOUS muddy; slimy; sticky
LIMPED halted
LIMPER a lame man
LIMPET univalve mollusc **Z.**

LIMPID clear; pellucid; pure
LINAGE (penny-a-line)
LINDEN lime tree **B.**
LINEAL in a direct line
LINEAR slender; rectilinear
LINE-UP show of unity
LINGAM sacred symbol (Hindu) **Eccl.**
LINGEL waxed thread (Sc.)
LINGER lag; loiter; dawdle; tarry
LINGET ⎞ an ingot
LINGOT ⎠
LINHAY farm shed
LINING aligning; inner cover
LINKED connected; united; coupled
LINNET bird; lintie **Z.**
LINSEY mixed wool and linen cloth
LINTEL the top of a door
LINTER cotton fibre
LINTIE linnet; a song-bird (Sc.) **Z.**
LIONEL, LIONET young lion
LIPASE enzyme **Chem.**
LIPLET little lip
LIPOID fatty; sebaceous **Med.**
LIPOMA a fatty tumour **Med.**
LIPPED labiate; (golf)
LIPPEN to rely; to trust (Sc.)
LIPPER a rippling; surface roughness
LIPPIE quarter of a peck (Sc.) **Meas.**
LIQUID fluid; fluent; melting; dulcet
LIQUOR spirits; drink
LISBON a Portuguese wine
LISPED (Pope)
LISPER
LISSOM lithe; agile; pliant; supple
LISTED enlisted; canted over; chose
LISTEL fillet (Arch.)
LISTEN hark; attend; eavesdrop
LISTER arranger; recorder
LITANY solemn supplication **Eccl.**
LITCHI fruit (China) **B.**
LITHER lazy; worthless; smooth
LITHIA oxide of lithium **Med.**
LITHIC (stone) **Med.**
LITMUS dye from lichen **Chem.**
LITTER scatter; disorder; bedding **Z.**
LITTLE tiny; pygmy; brief; trivial
LITUUS augur's staff
LIVELY joyful; active; vigorous; quick
LIVERY uniform; costume
LIVERY writ of possession **Law**
LIVING livelihood; animate **Eccl.**
LIZARD saurian reptile **Z.**
LLANOS plains of South America
LLOYD'S (underwriters)
LOADED laden; filled; cumbered
LOADER one of the gun's crew
LOAFED lounged
LOAFER idler; vagrant; flaneur; drone
LOANED lent; advanced
LOATHE hate; detest; abhor

LOAVES of bread
LOBATE (lobes)
LOBBED pitched
LOBOLA wife-purchase (S. Africa)
LOBOSE lobate **B.**
LOBULE small lobe
LOCALE a locality (Fr.)
LOCATE fix; place; settle; find
LOCHAN a pond; a loch (Sc.)
LOCKED grappled; embraced; clasped
LOCKER a cupboard; a drawer
LOCKET an ornament; a fastening
LOCK-UP
LOCULI cells **B.**
LOCUST acacia tree **Z., B.**
LODGED deposited; dwelt; harboured
LODGER temporary resident
LODORE a cataract
LOFTED skied
LOFTER (golf)
LOGGAN rocking stone; logan
LOGGAT ⎱ medieval ninepin ;
LOGGET ⎰ heavy wooden pole
LOGGED recorded **Naut.**
LOGGER lumberman
LOGGIA gallery or arcade (Italian)
LOG-HUT log-cabin
LOG-LOG logarithm of a logarithm
LOGMAN woodman; logger
LOHOCK syrup **Med.**
LOIMIC (plague) **Med.**
LOITER linger; dawdle; delay; tarry
LOLIGO cuttle-fish; squid **Z.**
LOLIUM genus of grass **B.**
LOLLED hung out; reclined
LOLLER lounger; flaneur
LOLLOP to lounge
LOMENT a type of legume **B.**
LONELY solitary; remote; forlorn
LONGAN Chinese fruit tree **B.**
LONGED craved; desired
LONGER more extensive; taller
LOOFAH also loofa; skeleton; gourd **B.**
LOOKED examined; observed; glanced
LOOKER onlooker; spectator
LOOK-IN hasty visit ; glance
LOOMED rose to view
LOOPED encircled
LOOPER a caterpillar **Z.**
LOOSED set free
LOOSEN slacken; release; untie; relax
LOOTED ransacked
LOOTER plunderer; pillager; despoiler
LOP-EAR a lop-eared rabbit **Z.**
LOPING running easily
LOPPED trimmed; truncated
LOPPER to curdle; trimmer; a cutting
LOQUAT Chinese fruit **B.**
LORATE thong-shaped
LORCHA junk-rigged Chinese ship **Naut.**

LORDED domineered
LORDLY noble; magnificent; arrogant
LORICA a cuirass
LORING learning (Spens.)
LORIOT golden oriole **Z.**
LOSING mislaying; squandering; failing
LOSSES casualties; damages; privations
LOTION a wash
LOUDER noisier; more stentorian
LOUDLY uproariously; clamorously
LOUNGE loll; loaf; recline; idle
LOURED frowned; scowled
LOUSED infested with lice
LOUVER louvre; ventilator
LOUVRE open turret (Fr.)
LOVAGE genus of herb; angelica type **B.**
LOVELY beauteous; delectable
LOVING adoring; liking; esteeming
LOWERY gloomy; overcast; murky
LOWEST most debased; deepest
LOWING bellowing; mooing
LUBBER heavy, clumsy fellow
LUBRIC slippery; lewd
LUCAMA fruit (Chile) **B.**
LUCENT bright; shining; clear
LUCINA Diana or Juno
LUCKIE elderly woman (Sc.)
LUCUMO Etruscan title
LUETIC pestilential **Med.**
LUFFED **Naut.**
LUFFER (see Louvre); open turret
LUGGED tugged; hauled; dragged
LUGGER small sailing ship **Naut.**
LUGGIE vase with ears
LULLED soothed; assuaged; calmed
LUMBAL, LUMBAR vertebrae **Med.**
LUMBER junk; rubbish; trash; refuse
LUMPED heaped up
LUMPER stevedore
LUNACY mania; dementia; craziness
LUNARY lunar; moonwort fern **B.**
LUNATE like a crescent-moon
LUNGED thrust
LUNKAH Indian cheroot
LUNULA ⎱ crescent-like; lunate
LUNULE ⎰
LUPINE wolf-like; wolfish
LUPINE lupin; a fodder plant **B.**
LURING enticing; inveigling; decoying
LURKED hid; laid in wait
LURKER skulker
LUSIAD Portuguese epic poem
LUSTED eagerly desired
LUSTIC lusty; vigorous
LUSTRA periods of five years
LUSTRE Roman purification ceremony
LUSTRE gloss; splendour; glory
LUTEIN egg yellow
LUTINE (Lloyd's bell)
LUTING a composition; clay

LUTIST lute player   **Mus.**
LUTOSE miry
LUXATE dislocate
LUXURY epicurism; voluptuousness
LUZULA a rush genus   **B.**
LYCEUM lecture hall
LYDIAN effeminate
LYDITE black slate; touchstone   **Min.**
LYMPHY (lymph)   **Med.**
LYRATE lyre-shaped
LYRISM playing the lyre   **Mus.**
LYRIST lyrical writer

M

MABOLA Philippine tree   **B.**
MACACO a tropical tree   **B.**
MACHAN platform for tiger-shooting
MACIES emaciation; wasting   **Med.**
MACKLE macule; a blur in printing
MACLED spotted
MACRON a mark (-) long vowel
MACULA sun-spot; a spot on skin **Med.**
MACULE mackle; a blotch; stain
MADCAP hair-brained; frolicsome
MADDEN enrage; infuriate; provoke
MADDER a plant; a red dye   **B.**
MADMAN maniac; bedlamite; moron
MADRAS bright kerchief; cotton fabric
MAENAD a frenzied woman
MAFFIA mafia; Sicilian secret society
MAGGOT worm; grub; larva; a whim **Z.**
MAGIAN (Wise Men of the East)
MAGILP megilp; painters' varnish
MAGISM Persian philosophy
MAGNET lodestone; attraction; lure
MAGNUM 2 quart bottle
MAGNOX magnesium alloy   **Chem.**
MAGPIE (target shooting)   **Z.**
MAGUEY Mexican aloe   **B.**
MAGYAR Hungarian
MAHOUN mahound; evil spirit (Arabic)
MAHOUT elephant driver
MAHSIR mahseer; an Indian fish   **Z.**
MAIDAN Indian parade ground; a plain
MAIDEN lass; damsel; virgin; guillotine
MAILED posted; clad in armour
MAIMED crippled; disabled; mutilated
MAINLY chiefly; principally; largely
MAINOR stolen goods; theft   **Law**
MAJLIS parliament (Iran)
MAKE-UP fiction; facial embellishment
MAKING forcing; compelling; reaching
MALADY ailment; disorder; complaint
MALAGA a Spanish wine
MALATE a salt of malic acid   **Chem.**
MALAWI native of E. Africa
MALEIC obtained from malic acid
MALGRE maugre; in spite of
MALICE spite; rancour; malevolence
MALIGN defame; slander; traduce

MALISM pessimistic belief
MALKIN scarecrow; mawkin
MALLEE Australian tree   **B.**
MALLET maul; beetle; hammer
MALLOW plant   **B.**
MALTED (brewing)
MALTHA petroleum
MAMMAL   **Z.**
MAMMEE West Indian fruit   **B.**
MAMMER stammer; hesitate; hover
MAMMET puppet; scarecrow
MAMMON god of riches; wealth
MANAGE contrive; control; regulate
MANANA to-morrow (Spanish)
MANCHE sleeve (Her.); the channel (Fr.)
MANCHU ruling Chinese race
MANDOM humanity
MANEGE riding school; equitation
MANFUL virile; courageous; bold
MANGAL charcoal brazier (Turk.)
MANGER a trough
MANGLE mutilate; to calender
MANIAC madman; lunatic; moron
MANILA Manilla cheroot
MANIOC tapioca; cassava   **B.**
MANITO Great Spirit (American Ind.)
MANNED provided a crew
MANNER behaviour; style; deportment
MANQUE 1 to 18 in roulette
MANTEL a beam; mantel-shelf
MANTIC inspired; prophetic; vatic
MANTIS a praying insect   **Z.**
MANTLE cloak; hood; covering; suffuse
MANTON Spanish shawl
MANTRA a Vedic hymn
MANTUA lady's cloak or gown
MANUAL handbook; organ key-board
MANURE compost; fertilizer; dressing
MAOISM, MAOIST follower of Mao
Tse-Tung
MAPPED charted; drew; delineated
MAQUIS French Resistance Force   **B.**
MAQUIS French Resistance Force
MARAUD raid; plunder; pillage
MARBLE small ball   **Min.**
MARBLY like marble
MARCEL a hair wave; style of coiffure
MARCID wasting
MARGAY American tiger-cat   **Z.**
MARGED bordered; edged
MARGIN verge; brim; brink; reserve
MARGOT fish (perch)   **Z.**
MARIAN (Mary)
MARIET violet campanula   **B.**
MARINE nautical; naval; maritime
MARISH a marsh; swamp
MARIST (Virgin Mary)
MARKED unmistakable; notable
MARKER recorder
MARKET mart; emporium; sale; vend
141 MARMOT desert rodent   **Z.**

MAROON claret-colour; firework	**MAZDAH** supreme deity (Zend Avesta)
MAROON runaway negro slave	**MAZILY** confusedly; distractedly
MARQUE (letters of); boundary	**MAZING** bewildering; perplexing
MARRAM sand dune; bent grass **B.**	**MAZOUT** petroleum extract
MARRED disfigured; impaired	**MEADOW** mead; lea; sward; field
MARRER spoiler; bungler; botcher	**MEAGER**⎫ thin; skinny; lean; gaunt
MARRON chestnut (Fr.) **B.**	**MEAGRE**⎭ lank; mean; emaciated
MARROT guillemot **Z.**	**MEAKER** a minnow **Z.**
MARROW medulla; essence; pith	**MEALER** (out-boarder)
MARSHY boggy; fenny; paludal	**MEALIE** maize **B.**
MARTEN (weasel) **Z.**	**MEANLY** ignobly; basely; sordidly
MARTIN swallow **Z.**	**MEASLY** stingy; miserly; meagre
MARTYR victim; sacrifice; persecute	**MEATHE** mead; a liquor
MARVEL wonder; prodigy; miracle	**MEATUS** passage in the body **Med.**
MARVER glass blower's table	**MEDDLE** muddle; intrude; interfere
MASCLE heraldic lozenge	**MEDIAL** average; mean; mediocre
MASCOT charm; talisman; halidom	**MEDIAN** traversal; a Mede
MASHAQ Persian goat-skin water-bag	**MEDICK** lucerne or clover **B.**
MASHED bruised; pulped; kneaded	**MEDICO** doctor or student **Med.**
MASHER fop; dandy; lady-killer	**MEDISM** Grecian treachery
MASHIE a golf-club	**MEDIUM** moderate; means; agency
MASJID masjed; a mosque	**MEDIUS** the middle finger **Med.**
MASKED disguised; cloaked; screened	**MEDLAR** fruit **B.**
MASKER masquerader; mummer	**MEDLEY** farrago; jumble; olio **Mus.**
MASLIN rye-bread	**MEDUSA** jelly-fish; a gorgon **Z.**
MASORA Hebrew traditions	**MEEKEN** to humble; to abase
MASQUE mask; a play; revel	**MEEKLY** lowly; submissively
MASSED collected; heaped; lumped	**MEETLY** fitly; suitably; correctly
MASSES the proletariat	**MEGASS** bagasse; cane refuse
MASSIF central mountain-mass	**MEGERG** million ergs **Méas.**
MASTED having masts **Naut.**	**MEGGER** insulation recorder
MASTEL maple tree **B.**	**MEGILP** magilp; linseed-oil and varnish
MASTER maestro; tutor; teacher	**MEGOHM** a million ohms **Meas.**
MASTIC resin **B.**	**MEGRIM** neuralgic pain; migraine **Med.**
MATHES may-weed **B.**	**MELLAY** mêlée; affray; broil; brawl
MATICO Peruvian astringent plant **B.**	**MELLEY** scuffle; contest; conflict
MATIES herring; a wrasse **Z.**	**MELLIT** a horse-scab
MATING matching; check-mating	**MELLOW** mature; ripe; genial; soften
MATINS morning service **Eccl.**	**MELODY** air; tune; descant; theme
MATRIX original die; mould; cavity	**MELTED** molten; dissolved; relaxed
MATRON head nurse; dame	**MELTER** liquefier
MATTED entangled; interlaced	**MELTON** woollen cloth
MATTER signify; import; stuff; affair	**MEMBER** part; limb; component
MATURE ripen; mellow; full grown	**MEMNON** desert crier
MAUGRE in spite of	**MEMOIR** life; biography; journal
MAULED hammered; mangled; bruised	**MEMORY** remembrance; recollection
MAUMAU (Kenya)	**MENACE** threat; alarm; intimidate
MAUNDY Thursday before G. Friday	**MENAGE** housekeeping; household
MAUSER rifle	**MENDED** restored; rectified; improved
MAWMET maumet; mammet; puppet	**MENDER** repairer; restorer
MAXIMA highest or top limits	**MENHIR** obelisk; long grave stone
MAXIXE dance (Brazil) **Mus.**	**MENIAL** slave; flunkey; lackey; servile
MAY-BUG cockchafer **Z.**	**MENINX** a brain-membrane **Med.**
MAY-DAY distress signal	**MENNAD** the minnow **Z.**
MAY-DEW	**MENSAL** monthly
MAY-FLY a species of Ephemera **Z.**	**MENTAL** intellectual; psychical
MAYHAP perhaps	**MENTOR** guide; monitor; counsellor
MAYHEM criminal mutilation **Law**	**MENURA** lyre-bird **Z.**
MAYING gathering may	**MERCER** a dealer in silks
MAZARD skull; cherry **B.**	**MERELY** simply; solely; only; purely

MERGED sunk; absorbed; immersed
MERGER an amalgamation
MERINO sheep; wool   **Z.**
MERKIN false hair; a mop
MERLIN falcon; small hawk   **Z.**
MERMAN cf. mermaid
MEROPS bird; bee-eater   **Z.**
MERULA thrush; blackbird   **Z.**
MESAIL vizor of helmet
MESCAL Mexican drink
MESETA tableland (S. Amer.)
MESHED reticulated; engaged
MESIAL } middle;
MESIAN } median
MESJID masjid; a mosque   **Eccl.**
MESLIN maslin; mixed grain   **B.**
MESPOT Mesopotamia
MESSED mussed; confused
MESSIN a mongrel (Sc.)   **Z.**
MESTEE half-caste; octaroon
METAGE measurement   **Meas.**
METEOR aerolite; shooting star
METHER vessel for mead
METHOD order; system; process
METHYL spirit   **Chem.**
METIER role (Fr.); profession
METING measuring
METOPE forehead; (frieze) (Arch.)
METRIC decimal
METTLE courage; ardour; pluck
MEWING caterwauling; confining
MEWLED yowled; squalled
MEWLER a crying child
MIASMA bad air; exhalation
MICHED concealed; played truant
MICHER skulker; beggar; pilferer
MICKLE muckle; great; much
MICMAC an American Indian
MICRON millionth part of metre **Meas.**
MID-AGE middle time of life
MID-AIR
MIDDAY noon; meridian
MIDDEN dunghill
MIDDLE centre; intermediate; medial
MIDGET sand-fly; dwarf   **Z.**
MID-LEG (cricket)
MID-OFF (cricket)
MID-RIB leaf-vein   **B.**
MID-SEA
MIDWAY half-way
MIFFED ruffled; annoyed
MIGHTY puissant; potent; dynamic
MIGNON dainty; pretty
MIHRAB (direction of Mecca)
MIKADO Emperor of Japan
MILADY my lady
MILDEN to mollify
MILDER calmer; softer; gentler
MILDEW mould; blight; rust; must
MILDLY leniently; placidly; suavely

MILIEU environment
MILIUM millet grass   **B.**
MILKED
MILKEN milk-like
MILKER cow-man
MILLED ground; struggled; levigated
MILLER
MILLET grain
MILORD my lord
MILSEY milk strainer
MILTER male fish   **Z.**
MIMBAR } pulpit in a mosque
MINBAR }
MIMING mimicking; aping; acting
MIMOSA plant genus   **B.**
MINCED affected; abbreviated
MINCER mincing machine
MINDED heeded; noted; objected
MINDER care-taker
MINGLE blend; mix; join; jumble
MINIFY diminish; depreciate
MINIMA the lowest
MINING burrowing; sapping
MINION a favourite; sycophant
MINISH diminish; reduce; minify
MINIUM vermilion
MINNIE trench mortar
MINNOW meaker; mennad   **Z.**
MINOAN Cretan
MINTED coined; stamped: invented
MINTER inventor; creator
MINTON china ware
MINUET a dance   **Mus.**
MINUTE small; tiny; minikin; record
MIOSIS rhetorical understatement
MIRAGE optical illusion
MIRING muddying
MIRROR exemplar; reflector
MISCUE (billiards)
MISDID erred; blundered
MISERE (solo whist, no tricks)
MISERY distress; woe; grief; anguish
MISFIT square peg in round hole
MISGET obtain unjustly
MISHAP accident; ill chance
MISHMI vegetable drug
MISHNA the text of the Talmud
MISKEN to ignore; be unaware (Sc.)
MISKIN a little bagpipe   **Mus.**
MISLAY misplace; lose
MISLED (mislead); deluded; deceived
MISSAL Mass-book   **Eccl.**
MISSAY say wrongly; slander
MISSED failed; wanted; needed
MISSEE view erroneously
MISSEL thrush; storm cock   **Z.**
MIS-SET to arrange unfitly
MISSIS missus; mistress
MISTER
MISTLE missel-thrush   **Z.**

MISUSE abuse; profane; misapply
MITHAN Indian ox; gayal **Z**
MITHRA sun-god (Pers.)
MITRAL like a mitre; somewhat conical
MITRED (carpentry)
MITTEN a boxing glove
MIURUS dactylic hexameter
MIXING mingling; jumbling
MIZZEN a sail **Naut.**
MIZZLE fine rain; to drizzle; decamp
MIZZLY misty
MOANED lamented; bewailed; deplored
MOATED surrounded with a ditch
MOBBED thronged; set about
MOBCAP a frilly cap
MOBILE volatile; mercurial; motile
MOB-LAW lynch-law **Law**
MOCKED derided; jeered; aped
MOCKER scorner; scoffer; taunter
MOCK-UP a non-working model
MODENA crimson
MODERN present; current; up-to-date
MODEST chaste; unassuming; diffident
MODIFY alter; change; vary; moderate
MODISH stylish; fashionable; chic
MODIST a follower of fashion
MODIUS 2 gallons (Roman) **Meas.**
MODOCS Oregon Indian tribe
MODULE model; proportion (Arch.)
MOFFLE bungle
MOHAIR hair of the Angora goat
MOHAWK ruffian; N. Amer. Indian
MOHOLE penetration of earth's crust
MOIDER to toil; confuse; spend (Sc.)
MOIETY a half; a share
MOILED drudged; toiled; soiled
MOIRAE the Fates
MOLECH ⎫ Phoenician god; Semitic
MOLOCH ⎭ deity; Australian lizard
MOLEST vex; harry; worry; pester
MOLINE mill-stone rynd
MOLLAH ⎫ judge;
MOOLAH ⎬ Moslem teacher;
MULLAH ⎭ fanatic
MOLTEN melted; liquefied; fused
MOMENT instant; trice; import
MONDAY Solomon Grundy's birthday
MONERA simple protozoans **Z.**
MONGER dealer; to deal in
MONGOL native of Mongolia
MONIED rich; opulent
MONIES coins; means; specie
MONISM a doctrine
MONIST believer in monism
MONKEY a primate; bandar; rhesus **Z.**
MONKEY £500; pile-driver; meddle
MONODY a dirge **Mus.**
MONOID (versification)
MONOSY abnormal condition **B.**
MONTEM Eton custom of money-raising

MONTON ore (Sp.) **Min.**
MONTRE organ stop; ceramic **Mus.**
MOO-COW
MOOING lowing
MOONED wandered aimlessly
MOONER listless lounger
MOONET little moon
MOORUK Bennett's cassowary **Z.**
MOORVA fibre; bowstring-hemp
MOOTED debated; discussed
MOOTER disputer
MOPING languishing
MOPISH gloomy; spiritless; despondent
MOPOKE Australian owl **Z.**
MOPPED swabbed
MOPPET ⎫ puppet
MOPSEY ⎭
MORALE courageous endurance
MORASS bog; fen; swamp; quagmire
MORBID diseased; vitiated; sickly
MOREEN watered woollen fabric
MORGAY shark; dog-fish **Z.**
MORGEN about 2 acres **Meas.**
MORGUE mortuary (Fr.)
MORIAN a Moor
MORION open helmet
MORKIN dead beast
MORLOP jasper **Min.**
MORMON a polygamist of Utah
MORNED blunted (Her.)
MORONE a deep crimson colour
MOROSE sullen; surly; churlish
MORRIS dance
MORROW the next day
MORSED signalled by Morse
MORSEL titbit; piece; fragment
MORTAL human; deadly; fatal
MORTAR trench weapon; cement
MORULA button-scurvy **Med.**
MOSAIC (Moses); inlaid ornamentation
MOSLEM Muslim; Mohammedan **Eccl.**
MOSQUE temple; mesjid **Eccl.**
MOSTIC maulstick (painting)
MOSTLY chiefly; mainly
MOTHER (liquors); dam; generatrix
MOTILE mobile; capable of movement
MOTION proposal; action; impulse
MOTIVE spur; incentive; reason
MOTLEY mixed; clown's costume
MOT-MOT American bird **Z.**
MOTORY giving motion
MOTTLE to stain
MOUJIK muzhik; Russian peasant
MOULDY fusty; musty; rusty
MOULIN glacial crevasse
MOUNTY the rise of a hawk
MOUSED bound with spun-yarn **Naut.**
MOUSER capable cat **Z.**
MOUSSE culinary confection
MOUTAN tree-peony **B.**

MOUTHY ranting; bombastic
MOUTON sheep; ancient French coin
MOVIES moving pictures
MOVING stirring; budging; touching
MOWGLI
MOWING grass cutting
MOZING raising nap (cloth)
MUCATE ⎫
MUCITE ⎬ mucic acid   **Chem.**
MUCHLY rather much
MUCKED muddled; dirtied
MUCKER a failure; a fall
MUCKLE much (Sc.)
MUCOUS mucoid; slimy; viscous **Med.**
MUDDLE confuse; chaos; derange
MUD-PIE child's inedible confection
MUFFED fumbled and failed
MUFFIN a winter's delicacy
MUFFLE (furnace); deaden; shroud
MUGGED crammed up
MUGGER Indian crocodile   **Z.**
MUGGET lily of the valley   **B.**
MULIER wife   **Law**
MULISH obstinate
MULLAH (see Mollah); teacher
MULLED heated; dispirited
MULLEN mullein plant   **B.**
MULLER a miller (Sc.)
MULLER heating vessel; pestle
MULLET genus of fish   **Z.**
MULLET a star (Her.); a rowel
MULLEY mooly; a cow; hornless   **Z.**
MULTUM adulterant used in brewing
MUMBLE mutter; chew
MUMMER masquerader; actor; histrion
MUMPED nibbled; grinned; chewed
MUMPER a beggar
MUNDIC iron pyrites   **Min.**
MUNDIL a turban
MUNSHI Eastern teacher
MURAGE money for town repairs (Fr.)
MURDER kill; assassinate; slaughter
MURINE (mice)   **Z.**
MURING immuring; walling up
MURMUR whisper; complain; repine
MURPHY potato   **B.**
MURREN a murrain (obs.)
MURREY dark red
MUSANG East Indian coffee-rat   **Z.**
MUSCAL (mosses)   **B.**
MUSCAT a grape; a wine   **B.**
MUSCLE thew; sinew   **Med.**
MUSEUM
MUSHED sledded (Alaska)
MUSHER snow traveller (Canada)
MUSING ruminating; reflecting
MUSIVE mosaic
MUSKEG swamp; marsh (Canada)
MUSKET hawk; smooth-bore gun   **Z.**
MUSK-OX N. American ox   **Z.**

MUSLIM Moslem; Mohammedan
MUSLIN soft cotton fabric
MUSMON moufflon; European sheep **Z.**
MUSNUD Persian throne of state
MUSSAL Indian torch
MUSSED messed; disarranged
MUSSEL a shell-fish   **Z.**
MUSTAC small tufted monkey   **Z.**
MUSTEE mestee; an octaroon
MUSTER parade; assemble; rally
MUTAGE (checking fermentation)
MUTATE to change
MUTELY dumbly; silently
MUTING the dung of birds; silencing
MUTINY riot; sedition; revolt
MUTISM dumbness; speechlessness
MUTTER murmur; grumble; maunder
MUTTON proverbially dead
MUTUAL reciprocal; correlative
MUTULE projection (Arch.)
MUTUUM loan contract   **Law**
MUZHIK moujik; Russian peasant
MUZZLE curb; restrain
MUZZLE snout: mouth
MARIA bivalves   **Z.**
MYELON spinal cord   **Med.**
MYGALE genus of spiders   **Z.**
MYOPIA near-sightedness   **Med.**
MYOPIC short-sighted; purblind
MYOSIN ⎫
MYOSIS ⎬ disease of the eye   **Med.**
MYOTIC ⎭
MYRIAD countless; innumerable
MYRTLE genus of shrub   **B.**
MYRTUS wax-myrtle; bay-berry   **B.**
MYSELF
MYSTIC occult; recondite; enigmatic
MYTHIC legendary; fictitious; fanciful
MYTHUS a myth; a fable
MYXINE hag-fish   **Z.**
MYXOMA a tumour   **Med.**

N

NABBED grabbed
NABKET snuff; small cake (Sc.)
NAEVUS birth-mark   **Med.**
NAGANA tse-tse fly disease   **Med.**
NAGARI Sanskrit script
NAGGED scolded; upbraided; pestered
NAGGER a fault-finder
NAHOOR sheep (Nepal)   **Z.**
NAIANT (swimming) (Her.)   **Z.**
NAILED caught; secured; exposed
NAILER nail-maker
NAKONG water-koodoo (S. Africa)   **Z.**
NAMELY viz., specifically
NAMING christening; nominating
NANDOO S. American ostrich   **Z.**

NANISM dwarfishness		
NANKIN nankeen; cotton cloth		
NANNAR Chaldean moon-god		
NANOID dwarf; pigmy		
NAPERY household linen		
NAPKIN serviette		
NAPPAL soaprock	**Min.**	
NAPPED dozed; slumbered		
NARDOO Australian plant	**B.**	
NARDUS mat-grass	**B.**	
NARGIL coconut tree; hubble-bubble	**B.**	
NARIAL⎫ nasal		
NARINE⎭	**Med.**	
NARROW strait; close; contracted		
NARWAL sea-unicorn	**Z.**	
NASARD organ stop	**Mus.**	
NASION part of nose	**Med.**	
NASUTE captious; critical		
NATANT swimming; naiant (Her.)		
NATION people; race; country		
NATIVE aboriginal; intrinsic; congenital		
NATRIX genus of snakes	**Z.**	
NATRON carbonate of soda	**Chem.**	
NATTER to nag (dial.)		
NATTES surface decoration		
NATURE universe; species; quality		
NAUGHT O; zero; nought; nothing		
NAUSEA sea-sickness; disgust; qualm		
NAUTCH dancing girl; a dance		
NAUTIC nautical; naval; maritime		
NEAPED aground at low tide		
NEARBY adjacent; nigh; at hand		
NEARED approached; drew nigh		
NEARER more adjacent		
NEARLY closely; all but; almost		
NEATLY smartly; featly; dexterously		
NEBBUK (crown of thorns)	**B.**	
NEB-NEB acacia pods	**B.**	
NEBRIS fawn-skin worn by Bacchus		
NEBULA heavy cloud; mist		
NEBULE nebula; mist; fog		
NEBULY wavy		
NECKED embraced; hugged; beheaded		
NECTAR ambrosia; honey		
NEED-BE a necessity		
NEEDED wanted; lacked; necessitated		
NEEDER requirer		
NEEDLE critical	**Tool**	
NEEDLY thorny		
NEESED, NEEZED sneezed		
NEGATE deny; mollify		
NEMEAN (lion killed by Hercules)		
NEPALI language (Nepal)		
NEPHEW		
NEREID sea-nymph		
NEREUS sea-god		
NERINE Guernsey lily	**B.**	
NERITE mollusc	**Z.**	
NERIUM oleander	**B.**	
NEROLI oil from orange flowers		

NERVAL nervous; sinewy		
NERVED fortified; plucky; courageous		
NESHEN to soften		
NESHKI Arabic script		
NESSUS a Centaur		
NESTED		
NESTLE snuggle; rest; cherish		
NESTOR genus of parrots (N. Z.)	**Z.**	
NETHER lower; under		
NETTED reticulated; gained; trapped		
NETTLE to irritate; fret	**B.**	
NEURAL (nerves)	**Med.**	
NEURIC nervous		
NEURON nerve cell	**Med.**	
NEUTER neutral; non-partisan		
NEWING yeast; barm		
NEWISH somewhat novel		
NEW-SAD recently bereaved (Shak.)		
NEWTON gravity force	**Meas.**	
NIACIN nicotinic acid; B Vitamin		
NIBBED complete with nib		
NIBBLE bite; gnaw		
NICELY exactly; accurately; adroitly		
NICENE creed (Asia)		
NICEST daintiest; choicest		
NICETY precision; delicacy		
NICHED in a niche or recess		
NICHER neigh; snigger		
NICKED notched		
NICKEL 5 cent piece	**Coin, Chem.**	
NICKER a cheat; woodpecker	**Z.**	
NIDDER shiver; molest		
NIDGED nudged (stone-cutting)		
NIDGET a fool		
NID-NOD nod repeatedly		
NIDOSE olfactory		
NIELLO engraving; ornamentation		
NIFFLE pilfer		
NIGGER negro; denizen of wood-pile		
NIGGLE trifle; to be finicky		
NIGHLY nearly; adjacent		
NIGRIC black		
NILGAI Indian antelope	**Z.**	
NIMBLE agile; lively; swift		
NIMBLY alertly; briskly; quickly		
NIMBUS a halo; rain cloud		
NIMROD a mighty hunter		
NINETY		
NINGAL Nannar's wife		
NIPPED pinched; compressed; gripped		
NIPPER tooth (horse)		
NIPPLE teat; dug; pap; mamilla		
NIPPON Japan		
NIPTER feet washing ceremony		
NIRLES herpes; shingles	**Med.**	
NITRIC (nitre)	**Chem.**	
NITTER bot-fly	**Z.**	
NITWIT numskull		
NIVOSE 4th French month (Revol.)		
NO-BALL (cricket)		

NOBBLE dope; doctor; get at
NOBLER more illustrious
NOBODY a nonentity
NOCAKE parched corn
NOCENT hurtful; mischievous
NOCTUA large moth genus **Z.**
NODDED bowed; acknowledged
NODDER a drowsy person
NODDLE the head
NODOSE knotted
NODULE small knot
NOETIC intellectual
NOGGIN small cup; ¼ pint **Meas.**
NO-GOOD useless
NOISED reported; rumoured
NOMIAL a single term in algebra
NONAGE immature; minority
NONARY group of nine
NON-COM an N.C.O.
NON-CON not content
NON-EGO (metaphysics)
NONIUS a graduating instrument
NOODLE simpleton; baked dish
NOOSED snared; caught; lassooed
NORDIC Germanic
NORMAL regular; perpendicular
NORMAN
NORROY king at arms
NOSEAN a silicate **Min.**
NO-SIDE end of a game of Rugby
NOSING projection (Arch.); snooping
NOSTOC genus of seaweed **B.**
NOTARY a court official **Law**
NOTICE see; remark; heed; intimation
NOTIFY warn; advise; apprise
NOTING recording; registering
NOTION idea; belief; theory; concept
NOTOUR notorious (Sc.)
NOUGAT a confection
NOUGHT O; naught; zero; a cypher
NOUNAL (noun)
NOUSLE to nurse; nuzzle
NOVENA nine days' devotion **Eccl.**
NOVENE by nines
NOVICE tyro; neophyte; probationer
NOWAYS in no way
NOWISE nohow
NOWYED (heraldic branches)
NOYADE execution by drowning (Fr.)
NOZZLE snout; projecting mouthpiece
NUANCE a subtle distinction
NUBBIN stunted maize **B.**
NUBBLE punch; small lump
NUBBLY bumpy; knotty
NUBIAN
NUBILE marriageable
NUCHAL (nape of neck) **Med.**
NUCLEI cell-centres; cores; kernels
NUCULE a little nut
NUDELY barely; nakedly

NUDGED jogged; poked; pushed
NUDISM, NUDIST naked sun worshipper
NUDITY nakedness
NUGGAR mugger; alligator **Z.**
NUGGET a lump of gold **Min.**
NULLAH watercourse; ravine (Ind.)
NUMBED torpid; paralyzed; dazed
NUMBER count; compute; figure
NUMBLY in a frozen manner
NUMNAH saddle cloth
NUNCIO Papal representative
NUNCLE mine uncle (Shak.)
NUNOME mesh fabric
NUPHAR water lily **B.**
NURLED milled like a coin
NURSED fostered; encouraged
NURSER tender; cherisher
NUTANT nodding
NUT-MEG an aromatic kernel **B.**
NUT-OIL
NUTRIA the fur of the coypu **Z.**
NUTTER a nut-gatherer
NUZZER a presentation (India)
NUZZLE nousle; fondle
NYANZA African lake
NYLGAU nilgai; an Indian antelope **Z.**
NYMPHA pupa; chrysalis **Z.**

O

OAFISH idiotic; dull; doltish
OARAGE rowing
OARING sculling
OARIUM an ovary; ovarium **B.**
OARLAP a distinctive rabbit **Z.**
OBDUCE draw over
OBELUS mark (†); obelisk
OBERON king of the fairies
OBEYED complied; yielded
OBEYER heeder; minder
OBIISM West Indian witchcraft
OBITER incidentally
OBJECT protest; demur; goal; intent
OBJURE to swear
OBLATE secular body **Eccl.**
OBLIGE compel; bind; favour; serve
OBLONG longer than broad
OBOIST oboe-player **Mus.**
OBOLUS Charon's fee, about 1½d. **Coin**
OBSESS besiege; beset; haunt
OBTAIN get; win; acquire; attain
OBTEST to beseech; supplicate
OBTUND deaden; blunt
OBTUSE dull; stolid; stupid
OBVERT turn toward; to face
OCCAMY silvery alloy
OCCULT mystic; hidden; obscure
OCCUPY fill; possess; inhabit
OCELLI peacock's " eyes "
OCELOT American leopard **Z.**

O'CLOCK an indefinite time
OCTANE petrol purification figure **Chem.**
OCTANS constellation (South Pole)
OCTANT measuring instrument [**Mus.**
OCTAVE ottava; consisting of eight
OCTAVO (eight leaves to the sheet)
OCTILE octant; eighth of a circle
OCTODE a thermionic valve
OCULAR visible
ODDITY singularity; strangeness
ODIOUS hateful; detested; obnoxious
ODYLIC mesmeric
OECIST founder of Greek colony
OEDEMA localized dropsy **Med.**
OFF-DAY unlucky occasion, free day
OFFEND affront; insult; trespass
OFFICE post; function; bureau **Eccl.**
OFFING the sea beyond the harbour
OFFISH haughty; snobbish
OFFSET counter-balance
OFFSET (printing)
OGAMIC ancient Irish script
OGHAMS ancient Irish alphabet
OGIVAL arched
OGLING an amorous advance
OGRESS a monstrous lady
OGRISH ogreish
OIDIUM fungus; vine-mildew **B.**
OIL-BAG oil gland
OIL-CAN
OILERY oilman's stock
OIL-GAS inflammable gas
OILING lubricating
OIL-MAN oil-dealer
OIL-NUT butternut **B.**
OIL-RIG boring apparatus for oil
OLDEST most senile; eldest
OLDISH somewhat ancient
OLEATE (oleic acid) **Chem.**
OLEINE liquid fat
OLEOSE oily; oleic
OLERON ancient code of sea laws **Naut.**
OLIVER small tilt-hammer; (Roland)
OLIVET mock pearl
OLIVIL gum from the olive tree
OLLAMH ancient Irish doctor **Med.**
OMASAL (cow's stomach)
OMASUM ruminant's third stomach
OMBROS madder
OMELET omelette
OMENED predicted; augured; presaged
OMNIFY to render universal
OMNIUM (Stock Exchange)
ONAGER wild ass; ghorkhar **Z.**
ONCOME deluge; approach
ONCOST extraneous mining charges
ONDINE undine; water-spirit
ONDING fall of rain or snow
ONE-MAN soloist
ONE-WAY (traffic)

ONEYER (of uncertain origin)
ONFALL storm; attack; assault
ONFLOW gush; stream
ONIONY **B.**
ONRUSH onset; charge
ON-SIDE (football)
ONWARD forward; advancing
ONYMAL (technical group name) **Z.**
OOCYTE ovicell **Z.**
OODLES quantities; heaps
OOGENY embryonic development
OOIDAL egg-shaped
OOLITE a limestone **Min.**
OOLOGY the study of birds' eggs
OOLONG oulong; tea
OOMIAK Eskimo boat **Naut.**
OORIAL wild sheep (India) **Z.**
OOZING exuding; seeping; percolating
OPAQUE impermeable to light
OPENED undid; disclosed; revealed
OPENER beginner; cutter
OPENLY publicly; above-board
OPHITE porphyry **Min.**
OPHITE gnostic serpent-worshipper
OPIANE narcotine **Chem.**
OPIATE a sedative medicine **Med.**
OPINED supposed; thought; fancied
OPPOSE prevent; hinder; combat
OPPUGN oppose; obstruct; resist
OPTANT volunteer
OPTICS science of light and vision
OPTIME almost a wrangler
OPTING choosing; co-opting
OPTION choice; wish; selection
ORACHE genus of plants, spinach **B.**
ORACLE wiseacre; ambiguous response
ORALLY by word of mouth
ORANGE Citrus Aurantium **B.**
ORATED harangued; prated; spouted
ORATOR declaimer; spell-binder
ORBATE bereaved; fatherless
ORBITA eye-sockets **Med.**
ORCHID orchis **B.**
ORCHIL archil; purple dye; a lichen **B.**
ORCINE lichen dye
ORDAIN prescribe; enjoin; appoint
ORDEAL test; trial; assay; scrutiny
ORDURE excrement
OREIDE imitation gold
OREXIS desire; appetite **Med.**
ORGASM sexual climax **Med.**
OR-GATE pulse circuit **Electron**
ORGEAT liquor (barley)
ORGIES revels; carousals
ORIENT eastern; the east
ORIGAN marjoram **B.**
ORIGIN fount; spring; source; root
ORIOLE a bird species **Z.**
ORISON prayer; supplication **Eccl.**
ORMULU, ORMOLU gilt brass

ORMUZD (Magian system)
ORNARY ordinary; mean; low
ORNATE florid; embellished
OROIDE alloy; oreide **Min.**
ORPHAN
ORPHIC (Orpheus)
ORPINE a yellow plant **B.**
ORRERY model of solar system
ORRICE dried iris root **B.**
ORTIVE rising; eastern
OSCULE small mouth
OSELLA Doge's medal
OSIERY osier-bed **B.**
OSIRIS greatest Egyptian god
OSMIUM metallic element **Min.**
OSMOSE (diffusion of fluids)
OSPREY sea-hawk; an egret plume **Z.**
OSSEIN bone-cartilage
OSSIFY to become bone
OSTENT portent; show; appearance
OSTIUM an opening; mouth of river
OSTLER stableman; groom
OSTMEN Danish settlers in Ireland
OSTREA oyster **Z.**
OTALGY ear-ache **Med.**
OTARIA genus of seals **Z.**
OTIOSE at ease; lazy; idle
OTITIS ear-trouble **Med.**
OTTAVA an octave
OUSTED deposed; ejected; thrown out
OUSTER ejection; dispossession
OUTAGE electrical failure
OUTASK ask for the last time
OUTBAR to shut out
OUTBID offer more
OUTBYE out of doors (Sc.)
OUTCRY hue; clamour; tumult; bruit
OUTDID excelled; surpassed; exceeded
OUTFIT equipment
OUTFLY
OUTING expedition; trip; holiday
OUTJET project
OUTLAW brigand; bandit; proscribe
OUTLAY expense; disbursement
OUTLET exit; vent; loophole
OUTLIE excel in lying
OUTMAN outnumber
OUTPUT production
OUTRUN outstrip; beat; surpass
OUTSET start; beginning; opening
OUTSIT
OUTSUM outnumber
OUTTOP over-reach
OUTVIE surpass; out-rival; eclipse
OUTWIT dupe; overreach; circumvent
OVALLY elliptically
OVERBY adjacent
OVERDO carry too far
OVERGO exceed
OVIBOS musk-ox; buffalo-cow **Z.**

OVISAC (ovary) **Z.**
OVULAR embryonic **B.**
OWLERY haunt of owls **Z.**
OWLING smuggling, especially wool
OWLISH not very wise
OWNING possessing; conceding
OXALIC an acid **Chem.**
OXALIS wood sorrel **B.**
OXBIRD the dunlin **Z.**
OX-EYED
OXFORD (blue); (shoe)
OXGALL
OXGANG ⎫ a bovate; about 15 acres of
OXGATE ⎬ land, amount that could
OXLAND ⎭ be cultivated with one ox
OXHEAD block-head; dolt (Shak.)
OX-HEEL the setter-wort **B.**
OX-HIDE leather
OXLIKE
OXTAIL
OXYGEN **Chem.**
OXYGON a triangle with 2 acute angles
OXYMEL honey and vinegar
OYSTER ostrea **Z.**
OZALID copy of engineering drawing
OZONIC

P

PACIFY calm; appease; reconcile
PACING setting the pace
PACKED crowded; compressed
PACKER stower
PACKET parcel; bale; a vessel **Naut.**
PADANG a field (Malay)
PADDED travelled slowly; (cell)
PADDER foot-pad; highwayman
PADDLE also pattle
PADNAG ambling horse **Z.**
PADUAN (Padua); the pavan
PAGING marking pages
PAGODA pagode; temple **Coin**
PAID-UP shares or capital **Law**
PAIGLE cowslip **B.**
PAINED hurt; distressed; grieved
PAINIM (see Paynim); pagan
PAINTY
PAIRED coupled; yoked; mated; (voting)
PAKEHA white man (Maori)
PALACE (Crystal)
PALAMA toe-webbing **Z.**
PALATE roof of mouth; taste; relish
PALELY wanly; ashy; pallidly
PALING a fence; blanching
PALISH wan
PALKEE palanquin (Ind.)
PALLAH African antelope **Z.**
PALLAS Athene goddess of wisdom
PALLED cloaked **Eccl.**
PALLET palette; small bed

PALLID pale; sallow; cadaverous
PALLOR pallidness
PALMAR (hand)
PALMED concealed; handled
PALMER pilgrim
PALOLO edible worm   **Z.**
PALPAL ⎫ (antennae-like feelers)   **Z.**
PALPED ⎭
PALPUS feeler of an insect   **Z.**
PALTER dodge; shuffle; prevaricate
PALTRY mean; petty; despicable
PAMPAS treeless plains, (S. Amer.)   **B.**
PAMPER indulge; coddle; humour
PANADA bread pulp
PANAMA hat
PANARY store-house for bread; pantry
PANDER a procurer
PANDIT pundit; a learned man
PANDUR robber; Austrian soldier
PANFUL
PANGED emotionally upset
PANISC Pan as a satyr
PANMUG crockery; butter-pan
PANNED yielded (mining)
PANNEL rustic saddle
PANNER a nagger; faultfinder
PANNUS birthmark; a dressing   **Med.**
PANSER belly-armour (obs.)
PANTED gasped; blew; palpitated
PANTER a snare; panther   **Z.**
PANTON a special kind of horseshoe
PANTRY
PANZER armoured corps (Ger.)
PAPACY (Pope); popery   **Eccl.**
PAPAIN digestive enzyme   **Med.**
PAPERY resembling paper
PAPISH papist
PAPISM Popery
PAPIST Roman Catholic
PAPPUS hairy tuft   **B.**
PAPUAN from New Guinea
PAPULA pimple   **Med.**
PAPYRI scrolls of papyrus (Egypt)
PARADE show; display; flaunt
PARAMO wind-swept desert in Andes
PARANG heavy Malay knife
PARAPH a flourish to a signature
PARCAE the Fates
PARCEL packet; bundle; piece; share
PARDON remit; condone; forgive
PARDON mercy
PAREIL an equal
PARENT author; producer; cause
PARFAY ! by or in faith !
PARGET rough plaster; gypsum
PARIAH outcast; mongrel   **Z.**
PARIAN (marble); (porcelain)
PARING rind; shaving; reducing
PARISH a county subdivision
PARITY equality; parage

PARKED (motors); enclosed; assembled
PARKER park-keeper; (nosey)
PARKIN perkin; Lancashire cake
PARLAY expand, exploit
PARLEY confer; discuss; talk
PARODY travesty; burlesque; caricature
PAROLE word of honour
PARRAL ⎫ collar to prevent spars from
PARREL ⎭ slipping from the mast **Naut.**
PARROT to repeat by rote   **Z.**
PARSEC interstellar distance unit **Meas.**
PARSED analysed grammatically
PARSEE Persian living in India
PARSON rector   **Eccl.**
PARTAN crab (Sc.)   **Z.**
PARTED left; broke; separated
PARTER distributor; sharer
PARTIM in part
PARTLY not altogether
PARURE set of jewels
PARVIS court; portico   **Eccl.**
PASSED ignored; spent; elapsed
PASSEE faded (Fr.)
PASSER a passer-by
PASSIM here and there
PASTED basted; gummed
PASTEL crayon; chalk drawing
PASTIL medicated lozenge
PASTOR shepherd; starling   **Eccl., Z.**
PASTRY confiserie
PATCHY unequal
PATENT spreading; open; copyright **Law**
PATERA shallow circular dish
PATHAN Afghan
PATHIC (diseases)   **Med.**
PATHOS deep emotion
PATINA green encrustation
PATINE paten; eucharistic plate **Eccl.**
PATOIS dialect (Fr.)
PATROL mobile armed guard
PATRON friend; helper; protector
PATTED tapped
PATTEN a clog
PATTER high speed talk
PATTLE a paddle
PAUNCH the belly
PAUPER indigent person
PAUSAL ceasing; pausing
PAUSED hesitated; halted; tarried
PAUSER a deliberator; a demurrer
PAVAGE paving cost
PAVANE Spanish dance; pavan
PAVIER ⎫ paver; pavement layer
PAVIOR ⎭
PAVING surfacing
PAVISE great shield
PAWING flattering: scrapping; handling
PAWNED pledged; risked; hazarded
PAWNEE N. American Indian tribe
PAWNEE pawnbroker

PAWNER a borrower on security	
PAWPAW papaw; a tropical fruit	**B.**
PAWWAW powwow; a palaver	
PAXWAX tendon; faxwax	**Z.**
PAY-DAY	
PAYING gainful; punishing; tarring	
PAYNIM painim; infidel; heathen	
PAY-OFF	**Naut.**
PEACHY like a peach	
PEACOD pea-pod	**B.**
PEAHEN a peafowl	**Z.**
PEAKED looked ill; pointed	**Naut.**
PEALED resounded; reverberated	
PEA-NUT the ground-nut	**B.**
PEA-ORE oxide of iron	**Min.**
PEA-POD	**B.**
PEARLY transparent; translucent	
PEBBLE a stone; an agate	**Min.**
PEBBLY shingly	
PECKED stumbled	
PECKER woodpecker; courage	**Z.**
PECTEN bivalve genus; scallop	**Z.**
PECTEN eye membrane of a bird	**Z.**
PECTIC congealing; gelatinizing	
PECTIN (apple jelly)	
PEDALE altar foot-cloth	**Eccl.**
PEDANT schoolmaster; precisian	
PEDATE divided like a foot	**B.**
PEDDLE to sell retail; to trifle	
PEDLAR } hawker; vendor; bagman	
PEDLER }	
PEECED imperfect (Spens.)	
PEELED stripped; skinned; pillaged	
PEELER policeman (Sir Robert Peel)	
PEENGE whimper (Sc.)	
PEEPED chirped; glimpsed; snooped	
PEEPER (chicken); the eye	**Z.**
PEEPUL sacred tree; Indian bo-tree	**B.**
PEERER a peeping Tom	
PEERIE peg-top (Sc.)	
PEEVED annoyed; fretful	
PEEWIT green plover; lapwing	**Z.**
PEGGED fixed; toiled	
PEG-LEG wooden leg	
PEG-TOP a spinning top	
PELAGE animal fur	**Z.**
PELIKE double-handled Greek vase	
PELION and Ossa, mountains	
PELLET small ball or shot	
PELMET curtain housing	
PELOTA a Basque ball game	
PELTER rainstorm; shower of missiles	
PELTRY skins with fur on them	
PELVIC (pelvis)	**Med.**
PELVIS a bony cavity	**Med.**
PENCIL light rays; small brush	
PENDED held up; balanced	
PENFUL	
PENMAN scribe; author; clerk	
PENNAL freshman (Ger.)	

PENNED wrote; indited; enclosed	
PENNER writer; scribe	
PENNON pennant; flag; streamer	
PENSEE thought (Fr.)	
PENSUM an imposition	
PENTAD set of five	
PENT-UP confined; mewed	
PENULT last but one	
PENURY need; want; indigence	
PEOPLE mob; rabble; populace; nation	
PEPITA nugget of gold (Sp.)	
PEPLIS water-purslane	**B.**
PEPLUM } robe worn by	
PEPLUS } Greek women	
PEPPER pelt with shot	**B.**
PEPSIN (gastric juice)	**Med.**
PEPTIC digestive	
PERDIE ! pardieu !	
PERDUE perdu; hidden; concealed	
PERIOD age; era; term; epoch; stage	
PERISH die; wither; expire; pass	
PERKED smartened up	
PERKIN perry; see parkin	
PERMIT let; grant; sanction; tolerate	
PERNIS honey-buzzard	**Z.**
PERONE fibula	
PERRON external stairway	
PERSIC Persian	
PERSON individual; party; someone	
PERSUE a track (Spens.)	
PERTLY impudently; saucily	
PERUKE a periwig; a vallancy	
PERUSE read; scrutinize; observe	
PESADE an equine evolution	
PESETA Spanish money	**Coin**
PESHWA Mahratta chief	
PESTER vex; worry; harass; nettle	
PESTLE a pulveriser	
PETARD explosive machine; bomb	
PETARY a peat-bog	
PETITE small (Fr.)	
PETREL sea-bird	**Z.**
PETROL gasoline	
PETTED fondled; caressed; indulged	
PETTLE indulge (Sc.)	
PEWTER an alloy of tin and lead	
PEYOTE cactus; source of mescalin	
PEZIZA cup-shaped fungi	**B.**
PHAROS lighthouse	
PHASEL French bean	**B.**
PHASIS a phase	
PHASMA leaf insects, etc.	**Z.**
PHEESE to beat; to worry (Sc.)	
PHENIC carbolic	**Chem.**
PHENIX fabulous bird; phoenix	**Z.**
PHENOL carbolic acid	
PHENYL an organic radicle	**Chem.**
PHINOC sea trout	**Z.**
PHLEGM calmness; indifference	
PHLEME lancet	**Med.**

PHLEUM cat's tail grass, etc. **B.**
PHLOEM bast tissue **B.**
PHOBIA morbid fear or aversion **Med.**
PHOBOS a satellite of Mars
PHOCAL (seal) **Z.**
PHOEBE the moon-goddess
PHOLAS stone boring molluscs **Z.**
PHONED telephoned
PHONEY specious; sham; bogus
PHONIC phonetic
PHOTON unit of light energy **Meas.**
PHRASE idiom; diction; style
PHYLON }
PHYLUM } biological group
PHYSIC dose; drug; medicine **B.**
PHYTON bud
PIAFFE a horse gait (Sp.)
PIAZZA square; market place (It.)
PICARD high shoe (Fr.)
PICKED chose; culled; pilfered
PICKER selector; collector
PICKET sharp stake; guard
PICKLE preserve
PICK-UP (motoring); (wireless)
PICNIC alfresco meal
PICRIC trinitro-phenol; lyddite **Chem.**
PIDGIN Chinese English
PIECED mended; joined; augmented
PIECER patcher
PIEDOG a pariah; pye-dog **Z.**
PIELED peeled; bare; bald (Shak.)
PIEMAN (Simple Simon)
PIERCE drill; bore; perforate
PIFFLE nonsense; worthless talk
PIGEON sometimes a gull **Z.**
PIGGIN small bowl
PIGNON pine seed **B.**
PIGNUT ground nut **B.**
PIG-STY
PILAFF spiced chicken and rice
PILARY hairy; comate
PILEUM head of bird **Z.**
PILE-UP crash (motoring)
PILEUS mushroom cap **B.**
PILFER purloin; filch; peculate
PILING amassing; stacking; heaping
PILLAR post; column; support
PILLED black-balled
PILLOW a block; bearing **Naut.**
PILOSE }
PILOUS } hairy; comate
PILULA }
PILULE } a small pill **Med.**
PIMPLE a pustule **Med.**
PIMPLY
PINANG betel nut **B.**
PINARD red Algerian wine
PINCOP weft in power loom
PINDAR Greek poet
PINDER pinner; impounder

PINEAL like a pine cone
PINERY hothouse **B.**
PINGED whistled by
PINGLE dawdle
PINING languishing; desiring
PINION feather; wheel; to shackle
PINITE (iolite) **Min.**
PINKED pierced; pricked; stabbed
PINNED transfixed
PINNER pinmaker; pinder
PINNET pinnacle (Sc.)
PINOLE meal of sorts (U.S.A.)
PINTLE iron bolt **Naut.**
PINXIT he painted it
PIONED full of peonies (Shak.)
PIONER a pioneer (Shak.)
PIPAGE pipe-distribution
PIPING boiling; shrill; feeble
PIPKIN boiler; small pot
PIPPED pilled; just defeated
PIPPIN apple **B.**
PIQUED offended; irritated
PIQUET card game; picket
PIRACY buccaneering; (copyright)
PIRATE freebooter; corsair; picaroon
PIRNIE night cap (Sc.)
PISANG plantain; banana **B.**
PISCES the fishes (Zodiac sign)
PISTIL part of flower **B.**
PISTOL a fire-arm
PISTON
PITAKA Buddhist scriptures **Eccl.**
PITCHY black; dark; tarry
PITHOS round Greek vase
PITIED commiserated
PITIER a compassionate party
PITMAN a miner
PITSAW large saw **Tool**
PITTED pock-marked; matched
PLACED invested; ascribed; put
PLACER auriferous gravel
PLACET Latin affirmation, "so be it"
PLACID serene; calm; even; tranquil
PLAGAL (Gregorian music) **Mus.**
PLAGUE pest; contagion; pester
PLAGUY vexatious; harassing
PLAICE plaise; fish **Z.**
PLAINT lamentation; dirge; wail **Law**
PLAISE plaice **Z.**
PLANCH to cover with planks
PLANED smoothed; (aeroplane)
PLANER planing machine **Tool**
PLANET a celestial body
PLANISH to hammer smooth
PLAQUE an ornament
PLASHY sloppy
PLASMA quartz; congealed blood **Med**
PLATAN plane tree **B**
PLATED overlaid; armoured
PLATEN the roller of a typewriter

PLATER race-horse **Z.**	**POLLER** voter; tree-trimmer
PLATEY flat	**POLLEX** thumb **Med.**
PLAYED sported; trifled; acted	**POLLUX** twin brother of Castor
PLAYER professional cricketer **-Mus.**	**POLONY** sausage
PLEACH interweave	**POLYAD** polygamous element **Chem.**
PLEASE like; prefer; delight; oblige	**POLYPE** polyp; aquatic animal **Z.**
PLEDGE security; plight; pawn; toast	**POMACE** crushed fruit
PLEIAD a star	**POMADE** perfumed hair unguent
PLENTY abundance; profusion	**POMELO** the grape fruit; shaddock **B.**
PLENUM space; a full assembly	**POMMEL** part of saddle; belabour
PLEUGH plough (Sc.)	**POMONA** goddess of fruit
PLEURA (lungs) **Med.**	**POM-POM** quick-firing gun
PLEVIN assurance **Law**	**POMPON** ornament; a tuft
PLEXOR hammer used with pleximeter	**PONCHO** cloak (S. America)
PLEXUS nerve centre **Med.**	**PONDER** weigh; meditate; ruminate
PLIANT flexible; limber; lithe; facile	**PONENT** western
PLIERS plyers **Tool**	**PONGEE** soft woven silk
PLIGHT promise; dilemma; predicament	**PONGYI** Buddhist priest (Burma)
PLINTH pedestal (Arch.)	**PONTAC** claret
PLONGE superior slope of parapet	**PONTEE** pontil (glassmaking) **Tool**
PLOUGH plow; furrow; to pluck	**PONTIC** (Black Sea)
PLOVER bird **Z.**	**PONTIL** glass-maker's iron rod **Tool**
PLOWED ploughed	**PONTON** lighter; pontoon
PLUCKY courageous; brave; bold	**POODLE** **Z.**
PLUFFY puffy (Sc.)	**POOGYE** nose-flute (Ind.) **Mus.**
PLUG-IN (wireless) electricity	**POOLED** shared; amalgamated
PLUMED took pride in	**POOLER** (tanning)
PLUMPY plump; fat; burly	**POONAC** pulp refuse
PLUNGE dip; dive; sink; souse	**POOPED** overtaken by a wave
PLURAL	**POORER** more impecunious; inferior
PLUSHY like plush	**POORLY** indisposed
PLUTUS the god of wealth	**POPERY** Roman Catholicism
PLYERS pliers **Tool**	**POPGUN** an air gun of sorts
PLYING folding; touting; urging	**POPISH**
PNEUMA breath; spirit	**POPLAR** genus of trees; abele **B.**
POACHY set and soft	**POPLIN** silk stuff (Fr.)
POCKED pitted	**POPPED** pawned; proposed; exploded
POCKET pouch; cavity; a poke	**POPPER** a pistol; maize-popper
PODDED	**POPPET** puppet; head of a lathe
PODIAL stalk-like **B.**	**POPPLE** to bob about
PODITE lobster's limb **Z.**	**PORGIE** bream fish **Z.**
PODIUM pedestal; balcony; stylobate	**PORING** sweating; brooding; studying
POETIC lyrical; metrical	**PORISM** corollary
POETRY poesy; verse	**PORITE** a species of coral **Min.**
POGROM plunder and massacre (Rus.)	**PORKER** young pig **Z.**
POISED suspended in equilibrium	**PORKET** porker **Z.**
POISER a balancer	**POROUS** porose; interstitial limestone
POISON taint; venom; pest; bane	**PORRET** small onion; leek **B.**
POKING thrusting	**PORTAL** gate; entry; entrance
POLACK a Pole	**PORTED** conveyed **Naut.**
POLDER drained land in Holland	**PORTER** door-keeper; carrier
POLICE constabulary	**PORTLY** burly; stout; imposing
POLICY statesmanship; strategy; plan	**POSADA** a Spanish inn
POLING scaffolding	**POSEUR** poser; an affected person
POLISH furbish; burnish; lustre	**POSING** feigning; puzzling; posturing
POLITE courtly; urbane; civil	**POSNET** small bowl
POLITY the constitution	**POSSET** a bed-time drink
POLLAN a salmon-type of Irish fish **Z.**	**POSSUM** opossum **Z.**
POLLED cropped; lopped; voted	**POSTAL** (order); (Union) **[Law**
POLLEN (flowers); fine bran **B.**	**POSTEA** record of subsequent events

F

POSTED set; stationed; hastened
POSTER bill; placard; advertisement
POSTIL marginal note; a homily
POT-ALE distillery refuse
POTALE grain refuse
POTASH alkali; potass **Chem.**
POTATO murphy; a tuber **B.**
POTBOY a junior tapster
POTEEN Irish whisky
POTENT efficacious; powerful; cogent
POTHER bother; bristle; fuss; ado
POTION dose; draught; philter
POT-LID a cover
POTMAN barman; general factotum
POTTED preserved; abbreviated
POTTER clay-worker
POTTLE (four pints); a tankard **Meas.**
POTTLE a small basket for fruit
POUDRE powdered (Fr.)
POUFFE a cushion (Fr.)
POULPE octopus; poulp **Z.**
POUNCE suddenly snatch; seize
POUNCE claw of a bird of prey **Z.**
POUNCE fine blotting powder
POURED uttered; flowed; gushed
POURER the lady of the tea-pot
POUTED registered displeasure
POUTER ⎫ pigeon having an
POWTER ⎭ inflated breast **Z.**
POWDER crush; pulverize; sprinkle
POW-WOW incantation; conference
PRAISE laud; extol; eulogize; encomium
PRANCE to bound; to spring
PRATED orated; gabbled; talked
PRATER a chatter-box
PRAXIS use; practice; an example
PRAYED supplicated; craved; besought
PRAYER petition; entreaty; orison
PREACH teach; exhort; declare
PRECES prayers **Eccl.**
PRECIS summary; abstract
PRECUT uniformity of size, shape
PREDAL rapacious; voracious; ravenous
PREFAB a prefabricated house
PREFER pick; select; choose; promote
PREFIX appoint beforehand
PREPAY pay in advance
PRESEE foresee; anticipate; foretell
PRESES chairman (Sc.)
PRESTO quickly; (conjuror) **Mus.**
PRETER a prefix; beyond
PRETOR praetor; Roman judge
PRETTY neat; comely; pleasing; canning
PRETTY the fairway of a golf course
PRE-WAR
PREYED ravened; ravaged; despoiled
PREYER a plunderer; freebooter
PRICED appraised; valued
PRICEY expensive
PRIDED plumed; arrogated

PRIEST pastor; divine; minister **Eccl.**
PRIMAL primary; main; first; original
PRIMER detonator
PRIMER prayer-book; type of type
PRIMET privet (dialect) **B.**
PRIMLY precisely; formally; demurely
PRIMUS bishop (Sc.); first **Eccl.**
PRINCE sovereign; lord; ruler
PRIORY monastery **Eccl.**
PRISED prized; levered
PRISMY prismatic
PRISON jail; gaol; quod; restrain
PRIVET genus of shrub; primet **B.**
PRIZED valued; esteemed
PRIZER an appraiser
PROCES law-suit (Fr.) **Law**
PROFIT gain; benefit; advantage
PROJET a proposal; draft
PROKER a poker (dial.)
PROLEG a caterpillar's leg **Z.**
PROLIX long-winded; verbose
PROMPT urge; incite; quick; apt
PRONTO precipitately
PROPED pseudo-leg **Z.**
PROPEL hurl; cast; throw; impel
PROPER correct; accurate; seemly
PROSED conversed in lengthy periods
PROSER tedious speaker
PROSIT! here's luck!
PROTEA S. African flowering shrubs **B.**
PROTON electrical nucleus
PROVED tested; verified; established
PROVEN proved; justified
PROVER demonstrator; assayer
PRUNED trimmed; clipped; lopped
PRUNUS genus of trees and shrubs **B.**
PRUTAH (Israel) **Coin**
PRYING peeping; curious; inquisitive
PSEUDO false; spurious
PSORIC (psora); itchy **Med.**
PSYCHE maiden beloved by Cupid
PTERIS fern genus **B.**
PTERNA heel-pad in birds **Z.**
PTERON Greek portico
PTISAN barley water; tisane
PTOSIS (fallen eyelid) **Med.**
PUBLIC open; common; general
PUCKER wrinkle; crease; furrow
PUDDER tumult; pother
PUDDLE muddy pool; (iron)
PUDDLY dirty; foul
PUEBLO S. American town or village
PUFFED fuffed; blown
PUFFER globe-fish **Z.**
PUFFIN bird; an auk **Z.**
PUG-DOG a lap-dog **Z.**
PUGREE Indian hat scarf
PUISNE inferior in rank
PUKKHA pucka; real (Ind.)
PULING whimpering; whining

PULLED drawn; hauled; extracted
PULLER hauler; an attraction
PULLET young hen   **Z.**
PULLEY grooved wheel
PULL-IN, PULL-UP roadside halt
PULL-ON boxing gloves
PULPED, PULPER mashed; machine shredded
PULPIT rostrum; ambo   **Eccl.**
PULQUE a Mexican beverage
PULSED throbbed; vibrated
PULVIL scented powder
PULWAR Ganges boat
PUMELO pomelo; shaddock; grape fruit
PUMICE spongy lava   **Min.**
PUMPED exhausted; interrogated
PUMPER cross-examiner
PUNCHI Kaskmiri people
PUNCHY fat; stocky
PUNCTO point (fencing); punctilio
PUNDIT savant; wiseacre
PUNICA pomegranate   **B.**
PUNIER weaker; feebler
PUNISH correct; chasten; scourge
PUNKAH fan (Ind.)
PUNNER a ram; maul   **Tool**
PUNNET basket for fruit
PUNTED betted; kicked
PUNTER gambler
PUPATE become a pupa   **Z.**
PUPOID like a chrysalis   **Z.**
PUPPED whelped; littered
PUPPET doll; marionette; pawn
PURANA sacred Sanscrit books
PURDAH curtain; seclusion
PURELY simply; clearly; really
PUREST without blemish
PURFLE embroider
PURFLY wrinkled
PURGED cleared; purified; shriven
PURGER an aperient
PURIFY cleanse; clean
PURINE uric acid compound   **Chem.**
PURISM precision; nicety; exactness
PURIST stickler for style
PURITY chastity; fineness; simplicity
PURLED curled; swirled; knitted
PURLER a fall; a cropper
PURLIN a roof timber
PURPLE a cardinalate   **Eccl.**
PURRED curred, (cats or pigeons)
PURSED contracted; wrinkled
PURSER paymaster   **Naut.**
PURSUE follow; track; chase; practise
PURVEY sell; cater; retail; procure
PUSHED urged; impelled; jostled
PUSHER type of plane; thruster
PUSHTU Afghan tongue
PUTEAL well-curb

PUTELI Ganges boat
PUTLOG short board; putlock
PUTRID corrupt; rotten; decaying
PUTSCH German revolt
PUTTED endeavoured to hole out
PUTTEE cloth legging; puttie (Ind.)
PUTTER a golf club
PUTTOO goat's wool cloth
PUZZLE bewilder; enigma; problem
PYCNID (fungus' spores)   **B.**
PYCNON a semi-tone   **Mus.**
PYEDOG piedog; a pariah   **Z.**
PYEMIA blood-poisoning   **Med.**
PYEMIC septicaemic   **Med.**
PYGARG antelope (Herodotus)   **Z.**
PYGARG osprey or sea-eagle   **Z.**
PYOSIS formation of pus   **Med.**
PYRENE fruit stone   **B.**
PYRENE tar product   **Chem.**
PYRITE pyrites   **Min.**
PYROLA winter green   **B.**
PYROPE garnet   **Min.**
PYTHIA Delphic oracle priestess
PYTHON serpent slain by Apollo   **Z.**

Q

QUADRA square frame or border
QUAERE enquire; seek (Latin)
QUAGGA zebra (S. Africa)   **Z.**
QUAGGY boggy; marshy
QUAHOG clam (N. America)   **Z.**
QUAICH } drinking cup;
QUAIGH } tassie (Sc.)
QUAINT droll; fantastic; curious; odd
QUAKED shook; quivered; rocked
QUAKER a Friend
QUARRY pit; prey; victim; an arrow
QUARTE guard (fencing)
QUARTO a size of book
QUARTZ silica   **Min.**
QUATCH squat; flat (Shak.)
QUAVER quiver; tremble; vibrate **Mus.**
QUAYED having a wharf
QUBBAH domed tomb (Arabic)
QUEASY squeamish; fastidious
QUEEST ring-dove   **Z.**
QUEINT quaint (Spens.)
QUELCH squelch
QUELEA weaver-bird   **Z.**
QUENCH repress; extinguish; quash
QUERRY an equerry; groom
QUESAL } resplendent trogon;
QUEZAL } brilliant green bird;   **Z.**
QUIJAL } badge of Guatemala
QUEUED lined up
QUHILK whilk; which (Sc.)
QUIDAM somebody (Latin)
QUIHYE Anglo-Indian (Bengal)
QUILLS clerk

QUINCE fruit **B.**
QUINIC (quinine) **Med.**
QUINOA Mexican oats **B.**
QUINOL reducing agent **Photo.**
QUINSY tonsillitis **Med.**
QUINTA villa in Madeira
QUINZE card game
QUIRED in quires; sang in harmony
QUIRKY evasive; artful; illusive
QUITCH couch grass **B.**
QUIVER case for arrows; vibrate
QUORUM a valid executive **Law**
QUOTED referred; repeated; mentioned
QUOTER a citer
QUOTHA forsooth
QUOTUM share; proportion

R

RABATE beat down; an abatement
RABATO turned-down collar; rebato
RABBAN super-rabbi
RABBET a groove in a plank
RABBIN Jewish lawyer or rabbi
RABBIT **Z.**
RABBLE the mob; iron puddling bar
RABIES madness **Med.**
RACEME a cluster **B.**
RACHIS backbone; spine **B., Z.**
RACIAL lineal; ancestral
RACILY piquantly; spicily; pungently
RACING contesting; competing
RACISM superiority theory,
RACKED strained; wrestled; ambled
RACKER a torturer
RACKET snow-shoe; clamour; (tennis)
RACKLE rattle; crackle
RACOON raccoon; kind of bear **Z.**
RADDLE twist; red ochre
RADIAL like a ray
RADIAN an angle of 57.3 degrees
RADISH plant **B.**
RADIUM metal **Min.**
RADIUS bone of forearm **Med., B.**
RADOUB refitting of a ship
RADULA mollusc's tongue **Z.**
RAFALE burst of fire; squall
RAFFED swept; huddled together
RAFFEE, RAFFIE schooner sail **Naut.**
RAFFIA palm fibre **B.**
RAFFLE sweepstake; draw; lottery
RAFTER roof-timber; lumberman
RAGBAG odd scraps of fabric
RAGDAY students' carnival
RAGGED jagged; uneven; torn
RAGGEE Indian millet **B.**
RAGGLE notch irregularly
RAGING wroth; rabid; furious
RAGLAN loose overcoat
RAGMAN rag-picker

RAGOUT stew; a spicy mixture
RAG-TAG riff-raff
RAGULY jagged (Her.)
RAIBLE rabble (Sc.)
RAIDED forayed; irrupted
RAIDER invader; plunderer
RAILED mocked; nagged; upbraided
RAILER scoffer; sneerer
RAILEX postal express service
RAINED pelted
RAISED exalted; extolled; lifted
RAISER producer
RAISIN a dried grape **B.**
RAJPUT Royal Hindu
RAKERY debauchery
RAKING inclining; enfilading
RAKISH dissolute; licentious
RALLUS water-rails, etc. **Z.**
RAMBLE excursion; stroll; roam
RAM-CAT tom-cat **Z.**
RAMEAL branching **B.**
RAMENT bristle-shaped leaflet **B.**
RAMIFY branch; divide; sub-divide
RAMISM system of logic
RAMJET open duct combustion
Aeronaut
RAMMED butted; crammed
RAMMEL refuse wood
RAMMER
RAMOON mulberry (W. Indies) **B.**
RAMOUS, RAMOSE branched
RAMPED bounded; sprang
RAMPER race-course rough
RAMROD
RAMSON hedgerow garlic **B.**
RAMULE small branch **B.**
RANCHO ranch; stock farm; ranche
RANCID sour; musty; fetid
RANDAN a row boat **Naut.**
RANDLE plate rack
RANDOM casual; haphazard; fortuitous
RANGED extended; disposed
RANGER park-keeper; rover
RANGIA a bivalve genus **Z.**
RANINE frog-like **Z.**
RANKER fouler; officer from the ranks
RANKLE fester; burn; smoulder
RANKLY rampantly; excessively
RANSOM a fine for redemption
RANTAN clatter of pots and pans
RANTED orated; declaimed
RANTER spouter; boisterous preacher
RANULA frog-tongue **Med.**
RAPHIA raffia; palm fibre **B.**
RAPHIS crystal in plant cell **B.**
RAPIDO with rapidity **Mus.**
RAPIER a thrusting sword
RAPINE pillage; spoliation; plunder
RAPING ravishing; violating
RAPPED tapped; struck
RAPPEE snuff

RAPPEL call to arms		
RAPPEN (Swiss)	**Coin**	
RAPPER knocker; arouser		
RAPTOR a ravisher; a hawk	**Z.**	
RAREFY attenuate		
RARELY seldom; infrequently		
RAREST sparsest; thinnest; scarcest		
RARITY scarcity; fewness; tenuity		
RASANT flanking; raking		
RASCAL rogue; scamp; knave; caitiff		
RASHER thin slice; hastier		
RASHLY audaciously; recklessly		
RASING razing; levelling		
RASION rasure; an erasure		
RASPED filed; abraded; grated		
RASPER scraper; stiff fence		
RASTER cathode ray projector (Television)		
RASURE an erasure		
RATANY Peruvian shrub	**B.**	
RATEEN ratteen; woollen fabric		
RATHER sooner; preferably; slightly		
RATIFY confirm; endorse; approve		
RATING tonnage; class	**Naut.**	
RATION share; quota; portion		
RATITE raft-breasted	**Z.**	
RATLIN (shrouds)	**Naut.**	
RATOON sugarcane sprout	**B.**	
RAT-PIT		
RATTAN drum-beat; basketry	**B.**	
RAT-TAT postman's knock		
RATTED deserted		
RATTEN stealing non-unionists' tools		
RATTER rat-catcher		
RATTLE chatter; vibrate; a herb	**B.**	
RAUCID raucous; hoarse		
RAUCLE rough; fearless (Sc.)		
RAVAGE spoil; lay waste; ransack		
RAVINE gulch; gulley; gorge; defile		
RAVING delirious; raging; frenzied		
RAVISH rape; violate; delight		
RAWISH somewhat raw		
RAYING radiating; shining		
RAY-OIL ray-fish oil	**Z.**	
RAZING overthrowing; rasing		
RAZURE rasure; an erasure		
RAZZIA a foray (Algerian)		
READER proof corrector; reading book		
REALLY truly; verily; actually		
REALTY real estate	**Law**	
REAMED frothed; enlarged		
REAMER rotatory cutter	**Tool**	
REAPED acquired; cropped; obtained		
REAPER harvester; a machine		
REARED erected; educated		
REARER an up-bringer		
REASON argue; intelligence; motive		
REASTY rancid		
REAVED bereaved; robbed		
REAVER reiver; freebooter		
REAVOW avow again		

REBATE blunt; abatement; a rabbet		
REBATE freestone	**Min.**	
REBATO a ruff; rabato		
REBECK Moorish violin	**Mus.**	
REBIND refasten		
REBITE (engraving)		
REBOIL seethe again		
REBORN re-incarnated		
REBUFF snub; repel; repulse		
REBUKE upbraid; reprove; chide		
REBURY inter again		
RECALL revoke; rescind; retract		
RECANT adjure; renounce; deny		
RECAST compute again		
RECEDE ebb; retire; withdraw		
RECENT modern; late; new; novel		
RECEPT extraneous idea		
RECESS niche; alcove; nook		
RECIPE prescription; formula		
RECITE tell; relate; repeat; recount		
RECKED regarded; heeded		
RECKON deem; calculate; estimate		
RECOAL refuel		
RECOCT re-cooked; to vamp up		
RECOIL kick; rebound; shrink		
RECOIN remint		
RECORD enter; note; achievement		
RECORD a gramophone disc		
RECOUP indemnify; make good		
RECTOR parson; vicar	**Eccl.**	
RECUIL } recoil (Spens.)		
RECULE }		
RECUMB to repose		
RECURE recover		
RECUSE reject	**Law**	
REDACT to reduce; to edit		
REDBUD Judas tree	**B.**	
REDCAP goldfinch	**Z.**	
REDDED tidied; arranged (Sc.)		
REDDEN blush		
REDDER		
REDDLE raddle; red chalk		
RED-DOG low-grade flour		
REDEEM ransom; free; retrieve		
RED-EYE rudd; carp	**Z.**	
RED-GUM eucalyptus	**B.**	
RED-HOT extreme		
RED-LAC Japanese wax-tree	**B.**	
RED-OAK N. American oak	**B.**	
REDOUT fort		
REDOWA Bohemian dance	**Mus.**	
REDRAW redraft; copy		
RED-TOP kind of grass	**B.**	
REDUCE degrade; curtail; abridge		
REDUCT a diminution in size		
REDUIT redoubt; redout		
RED-WUD stark mad (Sc.)		
RE-DYED		
REEBOK rhebok; S. African antelope	**Z.**	
RE-ECHO repeat; reverberate		

REECHY smoke-stained
REEDED covered with reeds
REEDEN (reeds)
RE-EDIT compile new edition
REEFED   **Naut.**
REEFER jacket; drug   **Naut.**
REEFER refrigerated ship
REEKED exhaled; fumed; smelt
REELED staggered; span; swayed
REELER the grasshopper warbler   **Z.**
REFAIT a drawn game (Fr.)
REFILL replenish; film cassette **Photo.**
RE-FIND retrieve
REFINE clarify; purify; cleanse
REFLET iridescent glaze
REFLEX reactive; introspective
REFLOW re-issue
REFLUX ebb; return; redound
REFOLD replicate
REFOOT
REFORM amend; remodel; better
REFUEL
REFUGE security; sanctuary; asylum
REFUND repay; return; restore
REFUSE veto; decline; deny; trash
REFUTE disprove; confute
REGAIN retrieve; recover; recapture
REGALE feast; entertain; gratify
REGALO a gift; a sumptuous repast
REGARD note; watch; repute
REGENT ruling; a ruler
REGILD
REGIME diet; system; administration
REGINA a queen
REGION province; tract; vicinity
REGIUS
REGIUM } appointed by the Crown
REGIVE restore
REGLET flat moulding
REGLET spacing block (printing)
REGLOW to recalesce; rekindle
REGNAL during the reign of
REGNUM badge of royalty
REGRET rue; deplore; remorse
REGULA book of rules
REHANG
REHASH
REHEAD head again
RE-HEAL to heal again
REHEAR   **Law**
REHEAT
REIGLE a channel or guide
REINED curbed
REITER German trooper
REIVER reaver; robber; freebooter
REJECT jilt; spurn; discard; repudiate
REJOIN reunite
REJOLT a new shock
RELAID (carpets); (wireless)
RELAIS a rampart walk

RELAND land again
RELATE tell; recite; narrate; report
RELENT relax; yield; soften
RELICT a widow (obs.)
RELIED depended on; confided
RELIEF aid; redress; alleviation
RELIER a trusting person
RELISH appreciate; zest; gusto; taste
RELIVE revive
RELOAD recharge; refill
RELOVE
RELUCT to resist (obs.)
RELUME to rekindle
REMADE (golf balls); refashioned
REMAIN persist; tarry; stop; survive
REMAKE revamp
REMAND send back to custody
REMARK also re-mark; say; comment
REMAST   **Naut.**
REMBLE remove (dial.)
REMEDY cure; panacea; specific
REMIND call to remembrance
REMISE release; give back   **Law**
REMISS slack; dilatory; negligent
REMORA a sucking fish   **Z.**
REMORD strike with remorse (obs.)
REMOTE far; distant; secluded; slight
REMOVE dislodge; transport; eject
REMPLI Heraldic colouring
RENAME rechristen
RENARD Reynard, a fox   **Z.**
RENATE renewed; born again
RENDER return; assign; supply; restore
RENEGE to revoke (cards)
RENNET apple; (junket)   **B.**
RENOWN fame; eminence; repute
RENTAL rent-roll; schedule
RENTED endowed; leased
RENTER lease-holder
RENTES French Government securities
RENULE small kidney   **Med.**
RENVOY return; dismissal (obs.)
RE-OPEN restart
REPACE retrace one's steps
REPACK
REPAID requited; rewarded; liquidated
REPAIR patch; mend; restore; wend
REPAND bent back
RE-PART share; divide
REPASS
REPAST a meal; victuals; food
RE-PAVE
REPEAL annul; rescind; nullify
REPEAT iterate; renew; echo
REPENT creeping; rue; regret; deplore
REPINE fret; complain; murmur
RE-PLAN re-design; re-arrange
REPLUM a botanical structure   **B.**
REPONE re-appoint   **Law**
REPORT rumour; relate; promulgate

REPOSE lie; recline; rest; respite
REPOUR re-issue
REPPED ribbed
REPUGN oppose (Shak.)
REPUTE reputation; renown; regard
REQUIT requited; repaid (Spens.)
RE-RAIL
RE-READ
RESAIL put to sea again
RESALE a second sale
RESCUE save; redeem; release
RESEAT repair a seat
RESEAU a net work
RESECT cut off; (surveying)
RESEDA mignonette genus   **B.**
RESELL revend
RESEND
RESENT dislike; repel; resist; hate
RESHIP
RESIDE live; dwell; lodge; sojourn
RESIGN also re-sign; forgo; yield
RESILE recede; start back
RESINY resinous; rosiny
RESIST oppose; thwart; withstand
RESOLD
RESORB swallow up
RESORT recourse; assemble; haunt
RESOWN
RESTED reposed; quieted; desisted
RESTEM force back; recheck
RESTIO plant genus   **B.**
RESULT ensue; outcome; sequel; end
RESUME renew; summarize; synopsis
RETAIL hawk; peddle; recount
RETAIN hold; keep; reserve; detain
RETAKE recapture
RETARD clog; hinder; impede; check
RETENT retained; held back
RE-TEST try again
RETINA a network of optic nerves **Med.**
RETIRE recede; withdraw; shrink
RETOLD already narrated
RETOOK regained; recaptured
RETORT rejoinder; repartee
RETOSE reticulated   **B.**
RETOSS throw again
RETOUR return (Sc.)
RETRAD backward
RETRAL posterior; retrorse
RETREE paper refuse; wastage
RETRIM embellish; smarten up
RETUND to dull; to blunt
RETURN also re-turn; restore; recur
RETUSE blunt
RETYRE
RE-URGE
REUTER news agency
REVAMP renovate; remake
REVEAL disclose; divulge; unveil
REVERB reverberate (Shak.)

REVERE adore; venerate; honour
REVERS revere; lapel
REVERT return; reverse; relapse
REVERY reverie; dream; trance
REVEST revert; clothe again (obs.)
REVIEW survey; inspect; critique
REVILE asperse; traduce; defame
REVISE reconsider; improve; correct
REVIVE rouse; invigorate; quicken
REVOKE annul; cancel; quash
REVOLT rebel; nauseate; mutiny
REVVED rotated at speed
REWARD guerdon; repay; premium
REWOOD afforest
REWORD change the phraseology
REXISM   Anti-Communist
REXIST   Belgian party
RHAGON form of sponge
RHAPIS genus of Chinese palms   **B.**
RHESUS bandar; Indian monkey   **Z.**
RHEUMY watery; rheumatic   **Med.**
RHEXIA genus of flowering plants   **B.**
RHINAE shark genus   **Z.**
RHINAL nasal   **Med.**
RHIZIC radical; root-like   **B.**
RHUSMA a depilatory   **Chem.**
RHYMED harmonized
RHYMER versifier
RHYMIC almost poetic
RHYSSA ichneumon flies   **Z.**
RHYTHM cadence; metre; symmetry
RHYTON Greek vase
RIALTO a bridge in Venice
RIANCY gaiety; laughter
RIBALD coarse; rude; gross; lewd
RIBAND a ribbon
RIBBED ridged; furrowed
RIBBON riband; strip
RIBIBE rebec; old woman (obs.)   **Mus.**
RIBLET rudimentary rib
RICCIA a plant genus   **B.**
RICHEN enrich; enhance
RICHER wealthier
RICHES abundance; affluence
RICHLY opulently; sumptuously
RICKED piled; sprained
RICKLE small pile or rick (Sc.)
RICTAL gaping
RICTUS open mouth
RIDDEL altar-curtain   **Eccl.**
RIDDEN
RIDDER a remover
RIDDLE sieve; enigma; rebus
RIDEAU curtain (Fr.)
RIDGED ribbed; furrowed
RIDGEL   riglan; riggot;
RIDGIL   defective male   **Z.**
RIDING county sub-division
RIEVER reaver; robber; pirate
RIFELY abundantly

RIFFLE engraving tool **Tool**	**RIZZER** a red currant (Sc.) **B.**
RIFLED pillaged; grooved	**RIZZLE** to creep; frizzle (dial.)
RIFLER robber; freebooter; plunderer	**ROAMED** ranged; rambled
RIFTED cleft; split	**ROAMER** nomad; vagrant; stroller
RIGGED (the market) **Naut.**	**ROARED** bawled; guffawed
RIGGER an air-mechanic **Naut.**	**ROARER** broken-winded horse **Z.**
RIGGLE sand-eel **Z.**	**ROBALO** a fish (U.S.A.) **Z.**
RIGLET (see reglet); flat piece of wood	**ROBBED** stole; despoiled; purloined
RIGOUR rigidity; austerity; harshness	**ROBBER** brigand; bandit; burglar
RIG-OUT complete outfit	**ROBBIN** spun-yarn
RILING annoying; irritating	**ROBERD** chaffinch **Z.**
RILLED trilled; flowed	**ROBING** attiring; dressing
RILLET rivulet; stream	**ROB-ROY** a canoe **Naut.**
RIMIST writer of doggerel	**ROBUST** sturdy; vigorous; hale; hearty
RIMLET thin rim	**ROCCUS** striped bass fish **Z.**
RIMMED bordered	**ROCHEA** a plant genus **B.**
RIMMER pastry cutter	**ROCHET** fish; the roach **Z.**
RIMMON Syrian god	**ROCHET** bishop's surplice **Eccl.**
RIMOSE ⎱ gnarled	**ROCKED** reeled; tottered
RIMOUS ⎰	**ROCKEL** a woman's cloak
RIMPLE wrinkle; rumple	**ROCKER** mining cradle
RIMSAW **Tool**	**ROCKET** Stephenson's locomotive 1829
RIMULA fossil limpits **Min.**	**ROCKET** cabbage plant **B.**
RINDED peeled	**ROCKIE** rock-linnet **Z.**
RINDLE gutter; runnel; rine	**ROCOCO** florid style
RINGED encircled	**RODDIN** rowan-tree (Sc.) **B.**
RINGER expert shearer (Australia)	**RODENT** gnawing
RINKED roller-skated	**RODING** evening flight
RINSED laved; cleansed; cleared	**ROGGAN** logan; rocking stone
RINSER a washer	**ROGGLE** shake (dial.)
RIOTED brawled; luxuriated	**ROILED** riled; vexed
RIOTER disturber of the peace	**ROINEK** Boer name for British soldier
RIPECK ⎫	**ROLAND** legendary hero
REPECK ⎬ punt pole for mooring	**ROLLED** trundled; rotated; turned
RYPECK ⎭	**ROLL-IN** hockey
RIPELY maturely	**ROLLER** wave; crow; a sect **Z.**
RIPEST mellowest	**ROMAGE** tumult (Shak.)
RIPPED torn; rent	**ROMAIC** modern Greek
RIPPER fog-horn; cutter **Tool**	**ROMANT** exaggerate; romance
RIPPLE flax-comb; small wave	**ROMANY** gipsy; gipsy language
RIPPLY rippling	**ROMERO** pilot-fish **Z.**
RIPPON a spur from Ripon	**ROMIST** papist
RIPRAP broken stone used for walls	**ROMPED** frolicked; gambolled; sported
RIPSAW a ripper **Tool**	**ROMPER** garment
RISALA troop of native cavalry	**RONDEL** short poem
RISBAN defended ground	**RONDLE** bastion turret
RISING insurrection; towering	**RONION** ⎱ mangy animal; **Z.**
RISKED chanced	**RONYON** ⎰ leprous lounger
RISKER gambler; venturer	**ROOFED** covered
RISLEY an acrobat	**ROOFER** tiler
RISQUE indelicate; audacious (Fr.)	**ROOKED** cheated
RITELY with due rites	**ROOKER** swindler
RITTER a knight (Ger.)	**ROOKIE** a recruit
RITUAL rite; ceremony; usage	**ROOKLE** rootle
RIVAGE the coast; shore; bank	**ROOMED** lodged
RIVERY riparian	**ROOMER** lodger
RIVINA the pokeweed genus **B.**	**ROOPIT** hoarse; roopy; roupy
RIVING splitting; rending	**ROOTED** rootled; deep-set
RIVOSE tabby; furrowed	**ROOTER** grubber
RIZZER dry in the sun (Sc.)	**ROOTLE** rookle; poke about like a pig

ROPERY rope walk	**RUDEST** most savage; crudest
ROPING lassoing	**RUEFUL** mournful; sad; melancholy
ROQUET (croquet)	**RUELLE** a coterie
ROSARY a chaplet; string of beads	**RUFFED** trumped
ROSCID dewy; roric	**RUFFER** comb for flax
ROSEAL rose-like	**RUFFIN** fresh-water perch **Z.**
ROSERY a rose garden	**RUFFLE** a pleated border; disorder
ROSIED adorned with roses	**RUFOUS** ruddy; florid
ROSILY	**RUGATE** wrinkled; furrowed
ROSING sprinkling	**RUGGED** ragged; harsh; austere
ROSINY resiny **B.**	**RUGGER** Rugby football
ROSSER policeman (slang)	**RUGINE** surgeon's rasp **Tool**
ROSTEL embryo root; radicle **B.**	**RUGOSA** corals **Min.**
ROSTER duty list; roll of names	**RUGOSE**⎫ wrinkled; rugate
ROSULA small rose **B.**	**RUGOUS**⎭
ROTARY rotatory	**RUINED** wrecked; destroyed; beggared
ROTATE spin; whirl; twirl; revolve	**RUINER** demolisher
ROTCHE little auk **Z.**	**RULING** governing; ascendant
ROT-GUT bad liquor	**RULLEY** a dray
ROTHER roaring; lowing (Shak.)	**RUMBLE** carriage-seat; reverberate
ROTTED disintegrated; decayed	**RUM-BUD** grog-blossom
ROTTEN corrupt; rank; moribund	**RUMKIN** tailless fowl **Z.**
ROTTER a pestilent person	**RUMMER** drinking glass
ROTULA knee-cap **Med.**	**RUMOUR** report; bruit; hearsay
ROTUND round; spherical	**RUMPLE** rimple; crumple; pucker
ROTURE plebian rank (Fr.)	**RUMPUS** uproar; disturbance
ROUBLE 100 kopecks (Russian) **Coin**	**RUM-TUM** Thames sculling boat
ROUCOU a dye (anotto)	**RUNDLE** a ladder-rung; a spoke
ROUGED powdered	**RUNKLE** wrinkle
ROUGET swine-fever	**RUNLET, RUNNEL** rivulet **Naut.**
ROUMAN Romanian	**RUN-MAN** naval deserter **Naut.**
ROUNCE a pulley; card game	**RUNNER** racer; messenger
ROUNCY a nag; a hack **Z.**	**RUNNET** rennet
ROUSED ruffled; agitated; provoked	**RUN-OUT** cricket
ROUSER a stimulator; inciter	**RUNRIG** land tenure (Sc.)
ROUTED fled in disorder; defeated	**RUNWAY** track; airfield take-off
ROUTER sash-plane **Tool**	**RUPIAH** (Indonesia) **Coin**
ROUTLE grub up; rootle	**RUPPIA** a grass genus **B.**
ROVERY roving; nomadism	**RUSCUS** butcher's broom **B.**
ROVING rambling; ranging	**RUSHED** dashed; flew; ran; plunged
ROWING sculling	**RUSHEN** of rushes
ROYENA ebony **B.**	**RUSHER** impetuous person; thruster
RUBACE rock crystal **Min.**	**RUSSEL** woollen fabric; fox **Z.**
RUBATO change of rhythm **Mus.**	**RUSSET** homespun; apple **B.**
RUBBED wiped; scoured; chafed; galled	**RUSSIA** leather
RUBBER coagulated latex	**RUSTED** oxidized
RUBBLE undressed stone	**RUSTIC** rural; bucolic; pastoral
RUBBLY broken	**RUSTLE** quiver; whisper
RUBIAN madder colour	**RUSTRE** Heraldic lozenge
RUBIED red as a ruby	**RUSURE** earth-slide
RUBIFY to redden	**RUTELA** beetle genus **Z.**
RUBIGO mildew; rust **B.**	**RUTILE** an oxide of titanium **Min.**
RUBINE crimson dye; rubin	**RUTTED** grooved; furrowed
RUBRIC a heading in red **Eccl.**	**RUTTER** a chart; trooper
RUCKLE wrinkle; pucker	**RUTTLE** gurgle; rattle (Dial.)
RUDDER **Naut.**	**RYPECK** ripeck; repeck; punt-pole
RUDDLE red chalk or ochre	
RUDDOC robin red-breast **Z.**	**S**
RUDDOC kind of apple; gold coin **B.**	**SABALO** the tarpon
RUDELY boorishly; insolently	**SABEAN** zabian

SABIAN star worshipper
SABINE plant; the savin **B.**
SABLED darkened **[Mus.**
SACBUT sackbut; stringed instrument
SACCOS Oriental vestment **Eccl.**
SACHEL satchel
SACHEM Red Indian chief
SACHET scent bag
SACKED plundered; dismissed
SACKER sack-filling machine
SACRAL (pelvic arch) **Med.**
SACRED holy; divine; consecrated
SACRUM a pelvis bone **Med.**
SADDEN to grieve; depress
SADDLE burden; clog; encumber
SADDLE earth formation
SADINA sort of sardine **Z.**
SADISM lustful cruelty
SADIST torturer; tormentor
SAETER Norwegian mountain hut
SAFARI caravan
SAFARI expedition
SAFELY securely; surely; reliably
SAFEST surest
SAFETY security; protection; safeguard
SAGELY wisely; sagaciously
SAGENE fishing net; a net work
SAGENE seven feet, Russian **Meas.**
SAGEST wisest
SAGGAR sagger; fire-clay pot
SAGGED drooped; bent
SAGGER clay retort for stoneware
SAGINA pink genus **B.**
SAGOIN S. American monkey **Z.**
SAGUIN capuchin monkey **Z.**
SAHARA a desert
SAILED cruised **Naut.**
SAILER **Naut.**
SAILOR A.B.; tar; seaman **Naut.**
SAIRLY sorely (Sc.)
SAITHE cod, ling, etc. **Z.**
SAJENE sagene; seven feet (Russian)
SAKIEH Persian water-wheel **[Meas.**
SALAAM salutation (India)
SALAME spiced sausage (It.)
SALARY pay; wages; stipend
SALIAN (Mars); salic
SALIFY (chemistry) **Chem.**
SALINA salt-marsh (Sp.)
SALINE salty; briny
SALITE to season with salt
SALIVA spittle **Med.**
SALLAL a fruit **B.**
SALLET light helmet
SALLIE ⎫
SALUIE ⎬ hired mourner (Sc.)
SALLOW yellow; a willow **B.**
SALMIS ragout; salmi; a hash
SALMON **Z.**
SALOON meeting room

SALOOP a decoction of sassafras **B.**
SALTED preserved
SALTER salt-seller
SALTIE a dab **Z.**
SALTLY salty; saline
SALTUS a mental jump
SALUKI hunting dog (Iran)
SALUTE hail; greet; accost
SALVED soothed; rescued
SALVER a tray
SALVIA sage **B.**
SALVOR a salvage expert
SAMARA winged fruit **B.**
SAMARE old-fashioned jacket
SAMBOO ⎫
SAMBUR ⎬ sambar; Indian elk **Z.**
SAMELY monotonous; unvaried
SAMIAN (Samos)
SAMIEL the simoon; hot wind
SAMIOT native of Samos
SAMITE silk
SAMLET a parr; salmon **Z.**
SAMOAN native of Samoa
SAMPAN sanpan; Chinese boat **Naut.**
SAMPLE try; taste; specimen
SAMSHU rice spirit (China)
SAMYDA West Indian birch **B.**
SANCHO negro guitar **Mus.**
SANDAL a Barbary vessel **Naut.**
SANDED
SANDIX ⎫ red lead;
SANDYX ⎬ vermilion
SANELY rationally
SANEST most intelligent; soundest
SANGAR stone breastwork
SANGHA Buddhist church
SANIES serum **Med.**
SANIFY to restore to health
SANITY wisdom; normality; lucidity
SANNOP ⎫ a brave;
SANNUP ⎬ American Indian
SANTIR ⎫
SANTUR ⎬ Eastern dulcimer **Mus.**
SANTON Dervish priest
SAPFUL juicy
SAPIUM gum-tree **B.**
SAPPED undermined
SAPPER Royal Engineer
SAPPHO Greek poetess
SAP-ROT dry rot
SAPYGA digger-wasps **Z.**
SARCEL pinion of a hawk's wing
SARCEN ⎫ Stonehenge sandstone; **Min.**
SARSEN ⎬ tin-worker
SARDEL herring type of fish **Z.**
SARGUS fish of mullet type **Z.**
SARLAK sarlac; the yak **Z.**
SARONG Eastern petticoat
SARSEN large sandstone boulder
SARSIA jelly-fish **Z.**

SARTOR a tailor	**SCARUS** parrot fish **Z.**
SASHES window-framings; scarves	**SCATCH** a horse-bit
SASINE seizin (Sc.) **Law**	**SCATHE** injury; damage
SASTRA sacred book (Hindu.) **Eccl.**	**SCATHY** dangerous; mischievous (Sc.)
SATANG (Thailand) **Coin**	**SCATTY** showery
SATARA lustred woollen cloth	**SCAURY** gull (Shetlands) **Z.**
SATEEN fabric	**SCAZON** imperfect rhythm
SATINE a hard wood **B.**	**SCELIO** parasite insects **Z.**
SATING satisfying; cloying	**SCENIC** dramatic; theatrical
SATINY glossy	**SCHANS** Zulu fort
SATIRE irony; sarcasm; lampoon	**SCHEIK** sheik (Arabic)
SATIVE sown	**SCHELM** a rascal (Boer)
SATRAP Persian provincial governor	**SCHEMA** scheme; synopsis
SATURN planet; god of agriculture	**SCHEME** plan; plot; intrigue; devise
SAUCED cheeked	**SCHEMY** cunningly devised
SAUCER a piece of china-ware	**SCHENE** $7\frac{1}{2}$ miles (Egyptian) **Meas.**
SAUGER American pike **Z.**	**SCHISM** a split; discord; dissent
SAUMER white wine	**SCHIST** slatey rock **Min.**
SAUREL the horse-mackerel **Z.**	**SCHOOL** train; educate; academy
SAURIA reptile genus **Z.**	**SCHORL** tourmaline **Min.**
SAURUS lizard-fish genus **Z.**	**SCHOUT** Dutch colonial official
SAVAGE barbaric; ferocious; brutal	**SCIARA** gnats and midges **Z.**
SAVANT a scientist; professor	**SCIATH** Irish wicker shield
SAVATE French boxing	**SCIENT** knowing
SAVINE medicinal shrub; red cedar **B.**	**SCILLA** hyacinth **B.**
SAVING husbanding; excepting	**SCLATE** slate (obs.)
SAVORY aromatic pot-herb **B.**	**SCLAVE** a Slav; Slavonian
SAVOUR taste; flavour; odour	**SCLERA** hard coating **Med.**
SAVVEY nous; common-sense	**SCOBBY** chaffinch **Z.**
SAWDER flattery	**SCOGIE** a drudge (Sc.)
SAW-FLY **Z.**	**SCOLEX** a worm **Z.**
SAWING	**SCOLIA** burrowing insects **Z.**
SAW-NEB sawbill **Z.**	**SCONCE** skull; bulwark
SAWNEY Sandy	**SCONCE** to fine; candle-stick
SAW-PIT	**SCOPUS** genus of wading-birds **Z.**
SAW-SET **Tool**	**SCORCH** singe; char; parch; scar
SAWYER plank-cutter	**SCORED** registered; scratched
SAXONY flannel	**SCORER** recorder
SAYING saw; dictum; adage; proverb	**SCORIA** dross **Min.**
SAYNAY a lamprey **Z.**	**SCORSE** exchange (Sc.)
SBIRRO Italian policeman	**SCORZA** variety of epidote **Min.**
S'BLOOD an imprecation	**SCOTCH** to cut; wedge
SCABBY rough; itchy; leprous	**SCOTER** a sea-duck **Z.**
SCAEAN western (gate of Troy)	**SCOTIA** Scotland; a concave moulding
SCAITH harm; damage (Sc.)	**SCOUSE** meat and vegetable broth
SCALAR magnitude without direction	**SCOUTH** scope (Sc.)
SCALED measured; ascended; mounted	**SCOVAN** tin lode (Cornish)
SCALER climber	**SCOVED** smeared (dial.)
SCALES a balance **Mus.**	**SCOVEL** oven-mop
SCALMA a horse disease	**SCRAMB** } scrape together (dial.) ;
SCAMEL bar-tailed godwit **Z.**	**SCRAMP** } snatch
SCAMPI prawns	**SCRAPE** grate; abrade; rasp; difficulty
SCANTY meagre; niggardly; chary	**SCRAWL** hasty writing
SCAPHA (helix of ear) **Med.**	**SCRAWM** to scratch (dial.)
SCAPUS shaft of column	**SCREAK** a screech; scream
SCARAB beetle; gem **Z.**	**SCREAM** cry; yell; squall; shriek
SCARCE rare; infrequent; uncommon	**SCREED** tiresome harangue; a shred
SCARED affrightened; panic struck	**SCREEN** shroud; cloak; hide; sieve
SCARPH to scarf (carpentry)	**SCREES** stony debris
SCARRY scarred; disfigured	**SCREWY** nefarious; underhand; exacting

SCRIBE writer; notary; scrivener	
SCRIKE shriek (Spens.)	
SCRIME to fence	
SCRIMP to stint	
SCRINE a shrine (Spens.)	
SCRIPT handwriting; typescript	
SCRIVE scribe; engrave	
SCROBE groove in mandible	**Z.**
SCROLL roll; list; register; flourish	
SCROOP to grate; to crack	
SCRUFF of neck	
SCRUNT miser (Sc.)	
SCRUTO theatrical trap	
SCRUZE squeeze (Spens.)	
SCUFFY shabby; seedy	
SCULPT to sculpture; carve	
SCULSH rubbish; lollypops	
SCUMMY covered with scum	
SCURFF bull-trout	**Z.**
SCURFY leprous	**Med.**
SCURRY skurry; a race; scamper	
SCURVY vile; shabby	
SCUTCH to beat; to comb	
SCUTUM Roman shield	
SCYLLA six-headed monster; (Charyb.)	
SCYTHE a reaping implement	**Tool**
S'DEATH an imprecation	
SDEIGN disdain (Spens.)	
SEA-APE sea-otter	**Z.**
SEA-BAR tern	**Z.**
SEA-BAT flying fish	**Z.**
SEA-BOY sailor lad	**Naut.**
SEA-BUN sea-urchin	**Z.**
SEA-CAP a sponge	
SEA-CAT cat-fish	**Z.**
SEA-COB a gull	**Z.**
SEA-COW manatee; walrus	**Z.**
SEA-DOG common seal	**Z.**
SEA-EAR a mollusc; ormer shell	**Z.**
SEA-EEL conger	**Z.**
SEA-EGG sea-urchin	**Z.**
SEA-FAN a polyp	**Z.**
SEA-FIR another polyp	**Z.**
SEA-FOX thrasher shark	**Z.**
SEA-GOD Neptune	
SEA-HEN guillemot	**Z.**
SEA-HOG porpoise	**Z.**
SEALED ratified; confirmed; shut	
SEALER seal hunter	
SEAMAN A.B.; tar; sailor	
SEA-MAT polyzoa	**Z.**
SEA-MAW sea-mew	**Z.**
SEAMED united by sewing; lined	
SEAMER seamster	
SEA-MEW a gull	**Z.**
SEA-MUD ooze	
SEANCE spiritualistic session	
SEA-ORB globe fish	**Z.**
SEA-OWL lump-fish	**Z.**
SEA-PAD star-fish	**Z.**

SEA-PEA beach-pea	**B.**
SEA-PEN quill zoophyte	**Z.**
SEA-PIE a seafowl	**Z.**
SEA-PIG the dugong	**Z.**
SEA-RAT herring-king; a fish	**Z.**
SEARCE to sift; a sieve (Sc.)	
SEARCH scrutiny; seek; inquire; quest	
SEARED cauterized; burnt; scorched	
SEA-ROD a polyp	**Z.**
SEASON time; period; flavour	
SEATED sited; established	
SEA-WAY steerage way	
SEBATE a fatty compound	**Chem.**
SECALE plant	**B.**
SECANT (geometrical); cutting	
SECEDE withdraw; segregate	
SECERN secrete; discriminate	
SECESH secessionist (U.S.A.)	
SECKEL variety of pear	**B.**
SECOHM electrical unit	**Meas.**
SECOND support; assist; inferior	**Meas.**
SECRET covert; occult; privy; cryptic	
SECTOR an area; a cutting	
SECUND unilateral	
SECURE get; obtain; safe; firm	
SEDATE staid; placid; serene; calm	
SEDENT inactive; quiet; torpid	
SEDGED flagged	**B.**
SEDILE seat in chancel	**Eccl.**
SEDUCE decoy; tempt; entice; inveigle	
SEEDED (Tournaments); sown	
SEEDER seed-drill	**Tool**
SEEING observing; viewing; watching	
SEEKER inquirer; searcher	
SEELDE seldom (Spens.)	
SEEMED befitted; appeared	
SEEMER pretentious person; pretender	
SEEMLY proper; becoming; decorous	
SEEPED oozed; percolated	
SEE-SAW	
SEETHE to boil; to soak	
SEGGAN sedge (Sc.)	**B**
SEGGAR fire-clay pot; sagger	
SEGHOL Hebrew vowel point	
SEICHE change of water level (Fr.)	
SEINER net-fisherman	
SEISED possessed of	
SEISON a parasite genus	**Z**
SEIZED lashed; grasped; stuck fast	
SEIZER grasper; snatcher	
SEIZIN } possession	**Law**
SEISIN }	
SEIZOR bailiff	**Law**
SEJANT sitting up (Heraldic)	
SEJOIN separate (obs.)	
SELDOM rarely; hardly ever	
SELECT cull; pick; choose; prefer	
SELENE Greek Moon-goddess	
SELION a ridge of land	
SELJUK Turkish warrior: dynasty	

SELLER vendor; hawker; retailer
SELVES individualities
SEMBLE to dissemble (obs.)
SEMELE genus of bivalves **Z.**
SEMESE half-eaten
SEMITA (sea-urchins) **Z.**
SEMITE descendant of Shem
SEMMIT undershirt (Sc.)
SEMOLA semolina
SEMPLE simple (Sc.)
SEMPRE in the same style **Mus.**
SENARY six of
SENATE assembly; council
SENDAL thin linen
SENDER transmitter; despatcher
SEND-UP compliment; ridiculous
SENEGA snake-root; an antidote **B.**
SENHOR Portuguese signor
SENILE aged; doting; tottering; infirm
SENIOR elder; older; higher; superior
SENNET trumpet call (Shak.)
SENNIT braided cord; plaited straw
SENORA lady (Spanish)
SENSED perceived; felt
SENTRY sentinel; watchman; guardian
SEPAWN maize-meal
SEPHEN sting-ray **Z.**
SEPIUM cuttle-bone **Z.**
SEPSIN a ptomaine **Med.**
SEPSIS (blood poison); putrefaction **Med.**
SEPTAL partitional (Irish)
SEPTAN weekly
SEPTET party of seven **Mus.**
SEPTIC rotten; putrid **Med.**
SEPTON (putrefaction)
SEPTUM a partition **B.**
SEQUEL consequence; upshot; result
SEQUIN a spangle; Venetian **Coin**
SERAIL seraglio; harem; serai; palace
SERANG Lascar boatswain
SERAPE zarafe; Mexican scarf
SERAPH six-winged angel
SERDAB secret chamber (Egypt)
SEREIN rain from a cloudless sky
SERENA damp evening air
SERENE calm; placid; tranquil; clear
SERIAL a periodical
SERIAN Chinese; Seric
SERICA beetle genus **Z.**
SERIES sequence; succession; order
SERIPH serif in printing
SERMON address; homily; discourse
SEROON package of drugs **Meas.**
SEROUS watery; thin **Med.**
SERPET basket (obs.)
SERULA red-breasted merganser **Z.**
SERVAL small African leopard **Z.**
SERVED ministered; acted; obeyed
SERVER salver; waiter
SESAME plant having oily seeds **B.**

SESBAN a marsh plant **B.**
SESELI saxifrage **B.**
SESTET sextet **Mus.**
SET-OFF (printing term)
SETOSE } bristly
SETOUS }
SET-OUT display
SETTEE sofa; Mediterranean ship **Naut.**
SETTER sporting dog **Z.**
SETTLE wooden seat; colonize; pay
SETULE small bristle **B.**
SEVERE harsh; cruel; rigorous; plain
SEVRES porcelain (Fr.)
SEWAGE drainage
SEWING needlework
SEXFID six-cleft **B.**
SEXTAN recurring every sixth day
SEXTET group of six **Mus.**
SEXTIC of the 6th degree
SEXTON gravedigger **Eccl.**
SEXUAL
SHABBY threadbare; paltry; beggarly
SHADED screened; obscured
SHADOW umbrage
SHADUF Nile water-raising device
SHAGGY rugged; rough; uneven
SHAHPU Tibetan wild sheep **Z.**
SHAIRL Cashmere cloth
SHAIRN cow-dung (Sc.) **Z.**
SHAKAL jackal **Z.**
SHAKEN jarred; agitated; moved
SHAKER (religious sect)
SHALLI Indian cotton stuff
SHALOT (garlic); shallot **B.**
SHAMAH shama; Indian song-bird **Z.**
SHAMAN animist; wizard (Siberia)
SHAMED abashed; disgraced
SHAMMY shamoy; chamois-leather **Z.**
SHANNY blenny fish **Z.**
SHANTY hut; hovel; shack; sea chant
SHAPED moulded; formed; regulated
SHAPER metal-planing machine **Tool**
SHARED partook; divided
SHARER participator
SHARPY oysterman's boat **Naut.**
SHAVED swindled
SHAVER a sharp dealer; a barber
SHAVIE a trick; a prank (Sc.)
SHAYAK coarse cloth (Tripoli)
SHEAFY (sheaves)
SHEARS sheers **Tool**
SHEATH scabbard
SHEAVE pulley-wheel
SHEENY bright; showy; a Jew
SHEERS shears; a hoisting appliance
SHEIKH Arab chief; scheik
SHEKEL Jewish half-crown **Meas., Coin**
SHELFY shelvy; shallow
SHELLY abounding with shells
SHELTA beggars' cant

SHELTY Shetland pony **Z.**
SHELVE put aside; to incline
SHELVY sloping shallow
SHE-OAK Australian shrub **B.**
SHEPPY sheep-cote
SHERIF shereef; Arab title
SHERRY a wine from Xeres
SHEUCH⎱ ditch; drain;
SHEUGH⎰ trench; furrow (Sc.)
SHEWEL scarecrow
SHICER welsher (Australia)
SHIELD shelter; cover; screen; guard
SHIFTY tricky; fertile in resources
SHIING skiing; a winter sport
SHIISM Moslem schism
SHIITE believer in Shiism
SHIKAR big game hunting (Ind.)
SHIMMY chemise; a dance
SHINDY trouble; quarrel; spree
SHINER £1 ; a boot-black
SHINNY⎱ bandy-ball;
SHINTY⎰ West Highland hockey
SHINTO Japanese ancestor worship
SHIPOV small sturgeon **Z.**
SHIPPO Japanese enamel
SHIPPY ship-shape
SHIRAZ a Persian drink
SHIRES the Shires (counties)
SHIRTY indignant; wroth; angry
SHIVER tremble; quiver; slate **Min.**
SHOALY shallow; shelfy
SHODDY coarse cloth
SHODER goldbeater's packet
SHOFAR ram's horn trumpet (Heb.)
SHOGUN Japanese C. in C.
SHOOED drove away
SHOPPY commercial
SHORED propped; buttressed; braced
SHORER a support
SHORTS bran; knicks
SHOUGH shaggy dog **Z.**
SHOULD
SHOVED obtruded; pushed; jostled
SHOVEL (clergyman's hat) **Tool**
SHOVER pusher
SHOWER distribute liberally; rain
SHRANK contracted; recoiled
SHREWD astute; cunning; wise; canny
SHRIEK cry; scream; yell; screech
SHRIFT confession; absolution **Eccl.**
SHRIKE butcher-bird **Z.**
SHRILL high; sharp; piping
SHRIMP a pink dwarf **Z.**
SHRINE tomb; reliquary
SHRINK shrivel; wrinkle
SHRITE missel; thrush **Z.**
SHRIVE to absolve **Eccl.**
SHROFF Indian banker
SHROUD winding sheet **Naut.**
SHROVE Tuesday

SHRUFF dross
SHRUNK contracted
SHUCKS! nonsense !
SHYING throwing; starting
SICCAN such (Sc.)
SICCAR⎱ sure (Sc.);
SICKER⎰ certain
SICKEN to disgust; to languish
SICKLE reaping hook **Tool**
SICKLY faint; unhealthy; morbid
SICSAC crocodile bird **Z.**
SICYOS gourds **B.**
SIDDHA⎱ Buddhist who has
SIDDHI⎰ attained perfection
SIDDOW soft; pulpy (dial.)
SIDING parallel set of rails
SIDLED moved furtively
SIENNA yellow paint
SIERRA mountain range
SIESTA nap; forty winks; doze
SIFAKA a lemur **Z.**
SIFFLE to whistle
SIFTED winnowed; bolted
SIFTER scrutinizer; separatist
SIGHED lamented; mourned
SIGHER repiner
SIGNAL eminent; a sign
SIGNED signified; endorsed
SIGNER one who subscribes
SIGNET a seal
SIGNOR Mr. in Italian
SILAGE ensilage; stored fodder
SILENE bladder-campion **B.**
SILENT mute; dumb; taciturn
SILICA flint; quartz; etc. **Min.**
SILKEN delicate; tender
SILLER silver; money (Sc.)
SILLON a mound in a moat
SILPHA carrion beetles **Z.**
SILTED oozed; choked with debris
SILURE cat-fish **Z.**
SILVAN woody; rustic
SILVER money; bright **Chem.**
SIMBIL African stork **Z.**
SIMIAL⎱ ape-like; **Z.**
SIMIAN⎰ monkey-like
SIMILE parable; comparison
SIMKIN champagne (Ind.)
SIMMER a gentle boil; stew
SIMNEL sweet fruit cake
SIMONY buying preferment **Eccl.**
SIMOOM simoon
SIMOON hot suffocating desert wind
SIMORG⎱ fabulous Persian bird **Z.**
SUMURG⎰
SIMOUS snub-nosed; concave
SIMPAI Sumatra monkey **Z**
SIMPER silly affected smile
SIMPLE naive; artless; frank; ingenuou
SIMPLY merely; only ; barely; solely

SIMSON groundsel **B.**
SINAIC (Mount Sinai)
SINDON a wrapper; winding sheet
SINEWY strong; vigorous; muscular
SINFUL wrong; iniquitous; depraved
SINGED scorched; slightly burnt
SINGER warbler **Mus.**
SINGLE choose; select; alone; celibate
SINGLY uniquely; individually
SINIAN Chinese rock formation **Min.**
SINISM Chinese custom
SINKER a plummet
SINNED erred; transgressed
SINNER transgressor
SINNET sennet; braided cordage **Naut.**
SINTER a siliceous deposit **Min.**
SINTOC cinnamon bark **B.**
SIOUAN Sioux; American Indian tribe
SIPAHI sepoy
SIPHON syphon
SIPING percolating; oozing; leaking
SIPPED tasted
SIPPER drinker of small draughts
SIPPET small sop
SIPPLE to sup in sips
SIRCAR sirkar; Hindu clerk
SIRDAR Egyptian commander
SIRENE a pitchpipe **Mus.**
SIRING begetting
SIRIUS the Dog Star
SIRRAH sir; sirree
SIRUPY like syrup; syrupy
SISKIN bird; a finch **Z.**
SISSOO Indian timber-tree **B.**
SISTED summoned (Sc.) **Law**
SISTER nun; nurse
SITTER painter's patient model
SIWASH N. American Indian
SIZING size; weak glue; grading
SIZZLE fry
SKATED
SKATER
SKATHE scathe; injury; harm; damage
SKEARY scary; scared
SKEELY skilful (Sc.)
SKELLY to squint (Sc.)
SKERRY rocky island
SKETCH limn; portray; outline; draught
SKEWER to impale
SKILLY thin gruel
SKILTS trews (Sc.)
SKIMPY scanty; meagre
SKINNY emaciated; lean; lank
SKITTY water-rail **Z.**
SKIVED sliced; split
SKIVER split sheep-skin
SKIVIE askew (Sc.)
SKLENT to slant; to split (Sc.)
SKRYER a diviner
SKURRY or **SCURRY** (Sc.)

SKYISH ethereal
SLABBY viscous; thick; sloppy
SLACKS women's trousers
SLAGGY (slag); scoriaceous
SLAKED quenched
SLANGY colloquial
SLAP-UP posh
SLASHY muddy (Sc.)
SLATCH fair weather **Naut.**
SLATED abused; upbraided; chid
SLATER a wood louse **Z.**
SLAVED drudged
SLAVER dribble; slave ship **Naut.**
SLAVEY serving wench
SLAVIC Slavonic
SLAYER murderer; killer
SLEAVE unwrought silk; floss ·
SLEAZY, SLEEZY flimsy; worn out
SLEDGE heavy hammer; sled **Tool**
SLEEKY of smooth appearance
SLEEPY soporous; drowsy; somnolent
SLEETY wet and cold
SLEEVE drogue
SLEIGH sled; sledge
SLEUTH detective; bloodhound **Z.**
SLEWED swung askew
SLICED (golf); chopped; pared
SLICER cutter
SLIDER a moveable part
SLIEST slyest; most artful; most crafty
SLIGHT scorn; ignore; disdain
SLIMSY flimsy; frail
SLINKY lean; furtive
SLIP-ON easily put on (clothing)
SLIPPY nimble; unstable
SLIP-UP error; mistake
SLITHY lithe and slimy
SLIVER to cut; a splinter
SLOGAN Scottish war-cry
SLOKEN quench; slocken
SLOPED decamped; at an angle
SLOPPY maudlin; slipshod
SLOSHY ⎫ muddy; boggy;
SLUSHY ⎭ watery; miry
SLOUCH a clown; depress; hang down
SLOUGH deep mud; morass; swamp
SLOUGH a cast skin
SLOVAK Slav
SLOVEN slattern; slut
SLOWER not so fast
SLOWLY gradually; tardily; sluggishly
SLUDGE mire; wet refuse
SLUDGY muddy
SLUGGA subterranean cavity
SLUICE floodgate; wash
SLUICY streaming
SLUING turning round
SLUMPY marshy
SLURRY to smear; to dirty
SLUSHY swampy; muddy; miry

SLUTCH sediment; muck; mire	**SNUDGE** sneak; miser
SLYEST sliest; most artful	**SNUFFY** irritable; peevish
SMALLS exams.; underwear	**SNUGLY** cosily; comfortably
SMARMY oily; ingratiating	**SOAKED** sodden; drenched; steeped
SMARTY over-bright youth	**SOAKER** confirmed toper
SMATCH taste; tincture (Shak.)	**SOAPED** lathered
SMEARY bedaubed; adhesive; glutinous	**SOARED** aspired; towered; ascended
SMEATH aquatic bird; smew **Z.**	**SOBBED** wept; cried
SMEECH⎱ smell of burning (dial.)	**SOBEIT** if it be so **[Law**
SMITCH⎰	**SOCAGE** tenure of land by service
SMEGMA an unguent **Med.**	**SOCCER** (football)
SMELLY odoriferous	**SOCIAL** genial; civic; civil; festive
SMIDDY a smithy (Sc.)	**SOCKED** biffed; whanged; coshed
SMIGHT smite (Spens.)	**SOCKET** a cavity
SMILAX sarsaparilla plant **B.**	**SOCMAN** tenant by socage **Law**
SMILED grinned; simpered	**SODAIC** containing soda
SMILER	**SODDED** turfed
SMILET a little smile	**SODDEN** soaked; wet; drenched
SMIRCH depreciate; foul	**SODIUM** metallic element **Chem.**
SMIRKY smart	**SO-EVER** indefinite suffix
SMITER slogger	**SOFFET** small sofa
SMITHY also **SMIDDY**	**SOFFIT** ceiling (Arch.)
SMOKED ridiculed; fumed; reeked	**SOFISM** form of Moslem belief
SMOKER a tobacco addict	**SOFTEN** enervate; relent; alleviate
SMOOTH level; flatten; suave; bland	**SOFTER** tenderer; milder
SMOUCH smack; to kiss	**SOFTLY** pliably; quietly; dulcetly
SMOUSE pedlar (S. Africa)	**SOGGED** saturated; sopped
SMUDGE stain; blot	**SOILED** tarnished; smirched
SMUDGY stained; smeary	**SOIREE** evening party (Fr.)
SMUGLY primly; neatly; complacently	**SOLACE** consolation; cheer; relief
SMURRY misty (Sc.)	**SOLAND** the gannet **Z.**
SMUTCH to blacken	**SOLANO** hot Mediterranean wind
SMUTTY sooty	**SOLDER** fusible metallic cement
SNABBY chaffinch (Sc.) **Z.**	**SOLELY** singly; alone; solitarily
SNACOT pipe-fish **Z.**	**SOLEMN** august; grave; staid; serious
SNAGGY full of snags	**SOLEUS** a leg muscle **Med.**
SNAKED coiled; crept **Naut.**	**SOLION** audio signal detector **Electron**
SNAPED bevelled	**SOLITO** in the usual manner **Mus.**
SNAPPY abrupt; tart	**SOLIVE** joist; cross-timber
SNARED netted; caught	**SOLLAR**⎱ upper gallery;
SNARER trapper	**SOLLER**⎰ garret
SNATCH grab; seize; grasp; fragment	**SO-LONG** good-bye
SNATHE scythe-handle	**SOLUTE** loose; cheerful
SNEEZE	**SOLVED** removed; resolved
SNIFFY disdainful	**SOLVER** elucidator; interpreter
SNIFTY having a luscious smell	**SOMALI** native (Somalia)
SNIPER concealed marksman	**SOMALO** (Somalia) **Coin**
SNIPPY fragmentary; stingy	**SOMBRE** dismal; gloomy; lugubrious
SNITCH nose	**SOMITE** body segment **Z.**
SNIVEL snuffle; blubber; whine	**SOMNUS** sleep personified
SNOBBY snobbish	**SONANT** sounding; resonant
SNOOTY conceited snob	**SONATA** instrumental piece **Mus.**
SNOOZE a nap; doze; siesta; drowse	**SONCIE**⎱ buxom; lucky;
SNORED	**SONSIE**⎰ good-natured (Sc.)
SNORER	**SONNET** a short poem
SNORTY	**SONTAG** knitted cap
SNOTTY midshipman **Naut.**	**SOODRA** Hindu caste
SNOUTY protuberant	**SOOJEE**⎱ specially fine flour;
SNOWED	**SOUJEE**⎰ sujee (Ind.)
SNUBBY somewhat snub; rather blunt	**SOONER** earlier; more readily

SOORMA an antimony cosmetic		**SPARKE** battle-axe (Spens.)	
SOOSOO river dolphin	**Z.**	**SPARKS** wireless operator	**Naut.**
SOOTHE calm; pacific; lull; palliate		**SPARRE** bolt; bar (Spens.)	
SOPHIC teaching wisdom; wise		**SPARRY** (spar); (crystalline)	**Min.**
SOPITE to quash		**SPARSE** scanty; meagre; thin	
SOPPED very wet; sogged		**SPARTH** halberd; mace	
SOPPER wet feeder		**SPARVE** hedge-sparrow	**Z.**
SORAGE phase of hawk's life	**Z.**	**SPATHE** flower sheath	**B.**
SORBET an ice; sherbet		**SPAVIN** a swollen joint	
SORBIC (sorbin)	**B.**	**SPECIE** bullion; coin; cash	
SORBIN mountain ash	**B.**	**SPECKY** speckled	
SORDES dregs; filth		**SPEECH** harangue; oration; palaver	
SORDET a mute for an instrument	**Mus.**	**SPEEDY** prompt; fast; rapid; hasty	
SORDID base; vile; ignoble; foul		**SPEISS** metallic dross	**Min.**
SORDOR dregs; filth; sordes		**SPELIN** form of Esperanto	
SORELY grievously; deeply; sadly		**SPENCE** buttery; pantry	
SOREST most grievous		**SPETCH** strip of hide	
SORNER gate-crasher; uninvited guest		**SPEWED** spat; vomited	
SOROSE clustered	**B.**	**SPHENE** titanite	**Min.**
SORREL colour; buck	**B., Z.**	**SPHERE** globe; orb; ball; domain	
SORROW woe; distress; affliction		**SPHERY** spherical; round	
SORTED grouped; suited		**SPHINX** the Guinea baboon	**Z.**
SORTER classifier; arranger		**SPICAL** spiky	**B.**
SORTIE sally; raid		**SPICED** seasoned	
SOSSLE dabble		**SPICER** spice-merchant	
SOTHIC (dog-star)		**SPIDER** a weaver of webs	**Z.**
SOTNIA Cossack troop		**SPIFFY** spruce; smart (slang)	
SOTTED besotted		**SPIGHT** spite (Spens.)	
SOUARI butter-nut tree (Brit. Guiana)	**B.**	**SPIGOT** spile; peg for a cask	
SOUGHT quested; hunted; tried		**SPIKED** pointed; put out of action	
SOULED full of feeling		**SPILTH** anything spilt	
SOUPER (a convert)		**SPILUS** birth-mark; a naevus	**Med.**
SOUPLE flail arm		**SPINAL** (back-bone)	**Med.**
SOURCE fount; cause; spring; origin		**SPINED** thorny	
SOURER more acid		**SPINEL** (corundum)	**Min.**
SOURLY tartly; bitterly		**SPINET** form of harpsicord	**Mus.**
SOUSED ⎫		**SPINNY** a small copse	
SOWSED ⎬ pickled; rushed; struck		**SPIRAL** cork-screw; winding	
SOUTAR ⎱		**SPIRED** having a spire; sprouted	
SOUTER ⎬ a cobbler; shoemaker		**SPIRIC** like an anchor-ring	
SOWTER ⎰		**SPIRIT** zeal; soul; essence; spook	
SOVIET Russian government		**SPITAL** hospital (obs.)	
SOVRAN sovereign; monarch (obs.)		**SPITED** thwarted; vexed	
SOWANS ⎱ flummery from		**SPLASH** spatter; splurge; a sensation	
SOWENS ⎰ oat husks		**SPLEEN** anger; melancholy	**Med.**
SOW-BUG a millipede	**Z.**	**SPLENT** a splint	
SOWING disseminating; propagating		**SPLICE** to marry; a junction	
SOZZLE sossle; muddle		**SPLINE** flexible ruler	
SOZZLY sloppy		**SPLINT** splent	**Med.**
SPACED extended		**SPLORE** a jollification (Sc.)	
SPACER distance piece		**SPOFFY** officious	
SPADED dug		**SPOKEN** told; articulated	
SPADIX a spike	**B.**	**SPONGE** spunge; cadge	**Z.**
SPAHEE Algerian cavalryman		**SPONGY** absorbent	
SPALAX mole-rats	**Z.**	**SPOOKY** eerie; ghostly	
SPANDY wholly; completely		**SPOONY** weak-minded; amorous	
SPARED saved; refrained; withheld		**SPOSHY** slushy	
SPARER economiser		**SPOT-ON** accurately placed	
SPARES spare parts; duplicates		**SPOTTY** speckled	
SPARGE to sprinkle		**SPOUSE** husband or wife	

SPRACK	sprightly; alert	
SPRAID	chapped with cold	
SPRAIN	strain; ridge; wrench	
SPRANG	jumped; leapt; bounded; tea	
SPRAWL	lounge; spread; straggle	
SPREAD	open; broadcast; scatter	
SPRENT	sprinkled	
SPRING	well; fount; rise; emanate	
SPRINT	also sprent; a spurt	
SPRITE	elf; fay; pixy; fairy; hobgoblin	
SPRONG	sprung (Spens.)	
SPROUT	bud; germinate; shoot; spire	
SPRUCE	fir-tree; neat; trim; finical	**B.**
SPRUIT	water-course (S. Africa)	
SPRUNG	tipsy; bent	
SPRUNT	leap; sprout	
SPRYER	more vigorous	
SPUDDY	chubby; podgy	
SPULYE	to spoil (Sc.)	
SPUNGE	sponge	
SPUNKY	mettlesome; spirited	
SPURGE	a plant	**B.**
SPURNE	to spur (Spens.)	
SPURRY	pink weed	**B.**
SPYING	detecting; discerning	
SPYISM	spy-craft; espionage	
SQUAIL	a disc or counter	
SQUALL	blast; gust; yell; squeal	
SQUAMA	a bract;	**B.**
SQUAME	a scale	**Z.**
SQUARE	fair; just; bribe; adjust	
SQUASH	a gourd; a game; crush	**B.**
SQUAWK		
SQUEAK		
SQUEAL	to inform	
SQUILL	(hyacinth)	**B., Z.**
SQUINT	a strabismus; glance	**Med.**
SQUIRE	escort; gallant	
SQUIRM	writhe; twist; wriggle	
SQUIRT	syringe; spout; eject	
STABLE	durable; fixed; constant	
STABLY	firmly; steadfastly; securely	
STACTE	myrrh	**B.**
STADDA	comb-cutting saw	**Tool**
STADIA	a range-finder	
STAGED	performed; produced	
STAGER	old hand	
STAGEY	melodramatic	
STAITH	coaling stage; staithe	
STAKED	(a claim); wagered	
STALAG	prisoners-of-war camp (Ger.)	
STALER	less fresh; older	
STALKY		
STAMEN	stamina	**B.**
STAMIN	harsh woollen stuff	
STANCE	(golf); attitude; station	
STANCH	staunch; firm; stop the flow	
STANZA	(poetry); (Arch.)	
STAPES	ear-bones	**Med.**
STAPLE	mart; raw material; chief	

STARCH	to stiffen; rigid	
STARED	gazed; glared; gaped	
STAREE	one who is stared at·	
STARER	beholder	
STARRY	stellate	
STARVE	famish; lack; deprive	
STASIS	stagnation	**Med.**
STATED	settled; regular; asserted	
STATER	ancient Greek gold coin	**Coin**
STATHE	landing stage	
STATIC	motionless; in equilibrium	
STATOR	cf. Rotor; circuit holder	
STATUA	an image (obs.)	
STATUE	image; figurine	
STATUS	rank; standing; position	
STAVED	burst; delayed	
STAVES	(staff); rods; sticks	
STAYED	waited; propped; stopped	
STAYER		
STAY-IN	(strike)	
STAYNE	deface; stain (Spens.)	
STAYRE	a stair (Spens.)	
STEADY	equable; regular; uniform	
STEAMY	vaporous	
STEARE	a steer; an ox (Spens.)	**Z.**
STEBOY!	go seek; (dog talk)	
STEEDY	steady (Spens.)	
STEELY	hard; firm; obdurate	
STEEPY	precipitous	
STEEVE	to stow; pack closely	
STEMMA	pedigree; family tree	
STENCH	fetor; odour; effluvium	
STEPPE	Russian plain	
STEREO	stereotype	
STERIC	(atomic arrangement)	**Chem.**
STEROL	solid alcohol	**Chem.**
STERVE	starve (Spens.)	
STEVEN	a clamour (Spens.)	
STEWED	simmered; seethed	
STIBIC	(antimony)	**Chem.**
STICKY	gummy; adhesive; viscid	
STIDDY	a forge; smiddy; smithy	
STIFLE	suffocate; choke; smother	
STIGMA	brand; mark; tarnish	
STIGME	a dot; disgrace	
STILAR	(sundial stile)	
STILLY	calm; tranquil; silent	
STILTY	stilted; high-hat	
STIMIE	stimy; (golf)	
STINGO	strong ale	
STINGY	near; close; mean; parsimonious	
STINTY	stinted; limited	
STIPEL	stipule	**B.**
STIPES	stalk; stipe; stem	**B.**
STIRPS	progenitor; ancestor	
STITCH	sew; a twinge	
STITHY	anvil; forge	
STIVER	Dutch halfpenny	**Coin**
STOCKY	sturdy; thick-set; robust	
STODGE	to cram	

STODGY heavy; indigestible
STOKED fuelled
STOKER furnace operator
STOLEN filched; purloined; taken
STOLID obtuse; phlegmatic
STOLON a runner   **B.**
STONED lapidated
STONER wall builder
STOOGE a butt; foil; dummy
STOORY dusty
STORAX resinous balsam   **B.**
STORED garnered; treasured
STORER hoarder; stocker
STORES an emporium
STOREY (building); a floor
STORGE natural affection (Greek)
STORMY wild; rough; tempestuous
STOUND moment; mishap (Spens.)
STOVED dried; baked
STOVER fodder for cattle
STOWED packed; placed
STOWER stevedore; packer
STRAFE punish (Ger.)
STRAIK ⎱ a stroke (Sc.);
STRAKE ⎰ tire of wheel
STRAIN exert; race; filter   **Mus.**
STRAIT narrow; distress; dilemma
STRAKE (wheel); planging   **Naut.**
STRAND shore; beach; thread; fibre
STRASS flint glass
STRATA layers; beds
STRATH valley (Sc.)
STRAWY straw-like
STREAK stripe; line; band; bar
STREAM flow; pour; brook; burn
STREET roadway; avenue; terrace
STRENE race; strain (obs.)
STRESS accent; force; urgency; tension
STREWN strewed; scattered
STRIAE stripes; streaks
STRICH see strick (obs.)
STRICK screech-owl; flax   **Z.**
STRIDE stalk; step; gait
STRIFE discord; conflict; quarrel
STRIGA bristle; stripe   **B.**
STRIKE buffet; clash; lock-out
STRING cord; twine; series
STRIPE band; line; stroke
STRIPY streaky
STRIVE vie; compete; attempt
STROAM to stroll; to roam (dial.)
STRODE straddled; bestrode
STROKE blow; knock; caress
STROLL ramble; rove; stray
STROMA tissue   **Med.**
STROMB a gasteropod   **Z.**
STROND strand; beach (Shak.)
STRONG puissant; bold; lusty
STROOK struck (obs.)
STROUP spout; nozzle (Sc.)

STROUT strunt; to strut (obs.)
STROVE vied; toiled; tried; attempted
STRUCK smote; hit; collided; revolted
STRUMA goitre; scrofula   **Med.**
STRUNG threaded; filed
STUBBY stocky; blunt; truncated
STUCCO plaster
STUDIO atelier; broadcasting chamber
STUFFY close; fusty; musty; angry
STUGGY thick-set; stumpy (dial.)
STUMER worthless cheque
STUMPS (cricket)
STUMPY stubby; short and thick
STUPID witless; dull; idiotic; asinine
STUPOR torpor; coma; lethargy
STURDY robust; stalwart; vigorous
STYING penning
STYLAR pillar-like; pointed
STYLED designated
STYLET dagger; poniard   **Med.**
STYLUS pen; style
STYMIE (golf); stimy
STYRAX gum plants; storax   **B.**
STYTHE after-damp
SUABLE liable to be sued   **Law**
SUBDUE quell; overpower; tame
SUBFEU (subinfeudation)   **Law**
SUBITO quickly   **Mus.**
SUBLET underlet
SUBMIT yield; capitulate; acquiesce
SUBORN to bribe; commit perjury
SUBTIL subtle; crafty
SUBTLE subtile; sly; crafty; clever
SUBTLY slyly; artfully; astutely
SUBURB outskirt; neighbourhood
SUBWAY underground passage
SUCCIN amber
SUCCUS juice   **B.**
SUCKED absorbed; imbibed
SUCKEN mill district (Sc.)
SUCKER a fish; nitwit   **B., Z.**
SUCKET sweetmeat
SUCKLE to wet-nurse
SUDARY a sweat-cloth
SUDDEN abrupt; quick; rapid; fleet
SUDDER chief; supreme (Ind.)
SUEING prosecuting; entreating
SUFFER brook; endure; allow; undergo
SUFFIX an affix
SUFISM Moslem doctrine
SUGARY sweet; honeyed; dulcet
SUIDAE pigs, hogs; etc.   **Z.**
SUITED contented; dressed
SUITOR wooer; admirer; litigant
SUIVEZ follow the soloist   **Mus.**
SUKAMA native of Tanganyika
SULCUS furrow; groove
SULKED
SULLEN morose; sulky
SULTAN a fowl; a Turkish ruler   **Z.**

SULTRY stuffy; oppressive; stifling
SUMACH plant used in tanning **B.**
SUMMED counted; added
SUMMER stretcher (Arch.)
SUMMIT top; acme; zenith; vertex
SUMMON bid; cite; invoke; prosecute
SUMPIT poisoned dart (Borneo)
SUNBOW rainbow
SUNDAE ice cream
SUNDAY
SUNDER cleave; sever; disrupt; part
SUN-DEW a bog plant **B.**
SUN-DOG a parhelion; mock sun
SUNDRY several; various; manifold
SUN-GOD Phoebus; Apollo; Re or Ra
SUN-HAT solar topee
SUNKEN submerged; engulfed
SUNKET an idler; food (Sc.)
SUNLIT
SUNNED
SUNSET sundown
SUN-TAN
SUPAWN Indian porridge
SUPERB magnificent; splendid
SUPINE indolent; torpid; inert
SUPPED
SUPPER
SUPPLE lithe; pliant; flexible
SUPPLY provide; furnish; grant
SURBED (stone-laying)
SURCLE little shoot; sucker **B.**
SURELY certainly; positively
SUREST safest; most certain
SURETY bond; guarantee; pledge
SURGED billowed
SURREY a fowl; a chay (U.S.A.) **Z.**
SURTAX an impost
SURVEY see; review; look; observe
SUSLIK marmot; ground squirrel **Z.**
SUTILE (stitching)
SUTLER camp follower; caterer
SUTTEE self-immolation
SUTTLE neat; (tare and tret)
SUTURE seam **Med., B.**
SVELTE lissom; slender
SWADDY militia-man (slang)
SWAGED mitigated; forged; burnt
SWAGGY bending
SWALED wasted; consumed
SWAMPY marshy; spongy
SWANKY swipes; boastful
SWANNY swan-like
SWARAJ home-rule (India)
SWARDY grassy
SWARMY oleaginous; unctuous
SWARTH tawny; apparition
SWARVE to swerve
SWASHY over-ripe
SWATCH a sample of cloth
SWATHE to bind; a bandage

SWATHY like a scythe-cut
SWAYED vacillated; tottered; wielded
SWEATY laborious
SWEENY emaciation; atrophy **Med.**
SWEEPY strutting; wavy
SWERVE deviate; turn aside
SWINGE to belabour; chastise
SWIPED lashed out; slogged
SWIPER a smiter
SWIPES small beer
SWIPEY fuddled
SWIRLY curly
SWITCH twig; whip; bypass; shunt
SWIVEL to turn; revolve
SWOUND to swoon (obs.)
SYCITE fig-stone **Min.**
SYCOMA tumour **Med.**
SYLVAN rustic; rural; woodland
SYMBAL cymbal **Mus.**
SYMBOL token; sign; badge; emblem
SYNDAW a plant **B.**
SYNDIC magistrate; Andorran council
SYNEMA column of filaments **B.**
SYNEPY interjunction
SYNTAX grammatical sequence
SYPHER to join flush
SYPHON siphon
SYRIAC ⎫ relating to Syria;
SYRIAN ⎭ the language
SYRINX Pan's pipes **Mus.**
SYRTIC like a quicksand
SYRTIS quicksand
SYRUPY sirupy; sugary
SYSTEM rule; method; order; plan
SYZYGY astronomical conjunction

T

TABARD ⎫ herald's coat;
TABERD ⎭ a tunic
TABBED having tabs; tagged
TABEFY to emaciate
TABLED catalogued; boarded
TABLER boarder
TABLES (back-gammon)
TABLET flat monument **Med.**
TABOUR tabor; drum **Mus.**
TABRET small tabour or drum **Mus.**
TACKED attached; stitched
TACKER
TACKET hob-nail (Sc.)
TACKLE gear; implements; grapple
TACTIC tactical; mode of operation
TACTUS sense of touch
TAENIA tape-worm; a fillet **Z.**
TAG-END fag-end
TAGGED tabbed; touched; fastened
TAGGER an appendage
TAGLIA a hoisting device

TAG-RAG and bobtail
TAGUAN Malayan flying squirrel **Z.**
TAHONA ore crusher (Sp.)
TAIGLE entangle; delay; tarry
TAILED docked; followed
TAILOR
TAILYE entail (Sc.) **Law**
TAISCH 'second sight'; apparition (Sc.)
TAJACU Mexican hog; peccary **Z.**
TAKE-IN a hoax
TAKE-UP tailoring
TAKING alluring; attractive; winning
TALBOT sporting dog **Z.**
TALCKY containing talc **Min.**
TALENT genius; aptitude **Coin, Meas.**
TALIAN Bohemian dance **Mus.**
TALION retaliation **Law**
TALKED discoursed; prated; spoke
TALKER chatterbox; gossip
TALLAT⎫
TALLET ⎬ a hay-loft (dial.)
TALLOT⎭
TALLER sturdier; bolder; higher
TALLOW hard fat
TALMUD Hebrew Bible **Eccl.**
TALWEG deep valley (Ger.)
TAMALE Mexican porridge
TAMANU gamboge tree (E. Ind.) **B.**
TAMARA mixed spice
TAMBAC alloy; also aloes-wood **Min., B.**
TAMBOO taboo; tambu
TAMBOR globe-fish **Z.**
TAMELY meekly; submissively
TAMEST flattest; dullest
TAMINE⎫ worsted stuff;
TAMINY⎬ tamise; tammy
TAMING domesticating
TAMKIN tampion
TAMMUZ Syrian sun-god
TAMPAN South Afr. venomous tick **Z.**
TAMPED packed with earth
TAMPER meddle; interfere
TAMPIN turning pins
TAMPOE an E. Indian fruit **B.**
TAMPON surgical plug **Med.**
TAN-BED bark bed
TANDEM one behind the other
TANGED banged; twanged; flavoured
TANGLE Orcadian water-spirit
TANGLE mat; twist; involve; jumble
TANGLY complicated; intricate
TANGUM Thibetan piebald horse
TANIST land owner (Irish)
TANITE a cement
TANJIB⎫ figured muslin (Ind.)
TANZIB⎬
TANKED stored; fuddled
TANKER oil steamer **Naut.**
TANKIA boat population, Canton
TANNED browned off; leathered

TANNER sixpence; leather worker **Coin**
TANNIC an acid
TANNIN an astringent **Chem.**
TANNOY amplified; loud speaker
TAN-PIT
TANREC⎫ insect eater **Z.**
TENREC⎬ (Madagascar)
TANTRA Sanscrit holy book
TAN-VAT
TAOISM Chinese religion **Eccl.**
TAOIST Chinese religionist **Eccl.**
TAO-TAI Chinese official
TAPETI Brazilian hare **Z.**
TAPING binding; measuring
TAPPED screw-threaded; rapped
TAPPER rapper
TAPPET (motor valves); small lever
TAPPIT crested
TARGET aim; butt; mark; objective
TARGUM Bible in Chaldee
TARIFF tax; impost; schedule
TARING recording tare allowance
TARMAC road material
TARNAL eternal or infernal
TARPAN wild horse (Asia) **Z.**
TARPON⎫ the Jew-fish **Z.**
TARPUM⎬
TARRED payed
TARSAL (tarsus); (the ankle)
TARSEL hawk; tiercel **Z.**
TARSIA marquetry
TARSUS instep; ankle **Med.**
TARTAN chequered fabric; ship **Naut.**
TARTAR argol **Chem.**
TARTLY sharply; pungently; acidly
TASCAL informer's reward
TASKED employed; burdened
TASKER taskmaster; overseer
TASLET tasset; thigh armour
TASSEL a pendant
TASSET thigh armour
TASSIE drinking cup (Sc.)
TASTED experienced; savoured
TASTER
TATLER a gossip; sandpiper **Z.**
TATTED (lace making)
TATTER a rag
TATTIE Indian trellis; tatta
TATTLE prattle; gossip; babble
TATTOO pageant; beat of drum
TAUGHT imparted; tutored; coached
TAURUS a sign of the Zodiac; the Bull
TAUTEN stretch; strain
TAUTER tighter
TAUTOG N. American black-fish **Z.**
TAVERN inn; hostel; caravanserai
TAVERT fuddled; muddled (Sc.)
TAWDRY gaudy, garish
TAWERY white leather factory
TAWING leather dressing

173

TAWPIE taupie (Sc.)	
TAWTOG tautog	**Z.**
TAXEME linguistic selection	
TAXIED (aeroplane on ground)	
TAXING accusing; straining; costing	
TCHEKA Soviet secret police	
TCHICK a click	
TEA-BAG tea sachet: tisane	
TEA-CUP	
TEAGLE a tackle; a hoist	
TEAGUE an Irishman	
TEAMED associated conjointly	
TEA-POT	
TEA-POY small table	
TEARER render; ripper	
TEASED combed; tantalized	
TEASEL plant with burs used	
TEAZEL for raising nap	**B.**
TEAZLE on cloth	
TEASER a puzzle; aggravator	
TEA-SET	
TEATHE (manure)	
TEA-URN a samovar	
TEBETH Jewish month	
TEDDED spread (new-mown hay)	
TEDDER a tether; hay-maker	
TE DEUM thanksgiving	**Eccl.**
TEDIUM boredom; ennui; monotony	
TEEING (golf)	
TEEMED full of life; in myriads	
TEEMER a producer	
TEENED troubled; excited	
TEE-TEE S. Amer. squirrel monkey	**Z.**
TEETER see-saw (U.S.A.)	
TEETHE to grow teeth	
TEGMEN inner seed coat	**B.**
TEGULA sub-title (printing)	
TEINDS tithes (Sc.)	
TELARY web-like	
TELEDU stinkard; Malayan badger	**Z.**
TELEGA Russian springless cart	
TELESM amulet; charm	
TELLER bank cashier; tale-bearer	
TELLUS Goddess of Earth (Roman)	
TELSON tail segment	**Z.**
TELUGU dialect (S. India)	
TEMPER anger; passion; spleen; tantrum	
TEMPER mitigate; alleviate; anneal	
TEMPLE (Inns of court)	
TEMPLE fane; part of head	
TENACE (bridge)	
TENANT lease-holder	**Law**
TENDED cared for; contributed	
TENDER mild; lenient; offer	**Naut.**
TENDON a ligament	**Med.**
TENNER £10	
TENNIS	
TENORA Catalan instrument	**Mus.**
TENREC hedgehog genus (Madagascar)	**Z.**
TENSED keyed up; taut; stretched	

TENSER under greater strain	
TENSON tournament of song	
TENZON	
TENSOR muscle	**Med.**
TENTED probed	
TENTER machine attendant	
TENURE possession; holding	
TENUTO sustained	**Mus.**
TEPEFY to warm	
TERAPH Hebrew household god	
TERBIC containing terbium	**Chem.**
TERCEL male falcon	**Z.**
TERCET triplet	**Mus.**
TEREDO boring worm; ship-worm	**Z.**
TERETE cylindrical	
TERGAL dorsal	
TERGUM the back	
TERMED terminated; designated	
TERMER holder of an estate for a	
TERMOR term of years	
TERMES white ant genus	**Z.**
TERMLY term by term	
TERREL a spherical magnet	
TERRET territ; harness pad ring	
TERROR awe; dismay; dread; panic	
TESTED proved; assayed	
TESTER canopy; Henry VIII shilling	
TETCHY testy; peevish	
TETHER tie; fasten; stake	
TETRAD group of four	
TETRAO capercaille	**Z.**
TETTER a rash	**Med.**
TETTIX cicada; tree-cricket	**Z.**
TEUTON	
TEWHIT peewit; lapwing	**Z.**
TEXTUS authoritative version	
THAIRM catgut (Sc.)	
THALER German dollar	**Coin**
THALIA comic Muse	
THANKS an expression of gratitude	
THATCH roof with straw	
THAWED melted	
THEAVE ewe of the 1st year	**Z.**
THEBAN	
THECAL sac-like	**B.**
THECLA hair-streak butterflies	**Z.**
THEINE tea alkaloid	**Chem.**
THEIRS	
THEISM	
THEIST a believer in God	
THEMIS goddess of law	
THENAL (palm or sole)	**Med.**
THENAR palm or sole	**Med.**
THENCE for that reason	
THEORY speculation; hypothesis	
THESIS a theme; a dissertation; essay	
THETIC dogmatic (thesis)	
THETIS sea-nymph; the sea	
THEWED trained; muscular	
THIBET heavy woollen fabric	

THIBLE a dibble
THIEVE filch; pilfer; purloin; rob
THINLY scantily; sparsely
THIRDS widows' rights   **Law**
THIRST crave; yearn; hanker; desire
THIRTY
THOLUS dome; cupola (Greek)
THORAH the Pentateuch
THORAL nuptial
THORAX (chest)   **Med.**
THORNY spiny; prickly; sharp
THORPE a homestead
THOUGH notwithstanding
THOWEL thole-pin   **Naut.**
THRALL a slave; slavery
THRASH drub; castigate
THRAVE two stooks (Iceland)
THRAWN twisted (Sc.)
THREAD cord; filament; drift; gist
THREAP⎱ contradict; urge
THREEP⎰ insist on (Sc.)
THREAT menace; intimidation
THRENE a lament (Gk.)
THRESH thrash; drub; maul; trounce
THRICE three times; very
THRIFT frugality; economy
THRIFT the sea-pink   **B.**
THRILL excite; rouse; electrify
THRIPS corn-bugs   **Z.**
THRIST thirst-(Spens.)
THRIVE wax; prosper; flourish
THROAT the fauces   **Med.**
THRONE sovereign power and dignity
THRONG crowd; flock; congregate
THROVE thrived
THROWN cast; propelled; flung
THRUSH (horse disease)   **Z.**
THRUST lunge; tilt; stab
THUSLY as follows
THWACK belabour; whack; thump
THWART balk; frustrate; obstruct
THYITE pale green clay   **Min.**
THYMOL oil of thyme   **Med.**
THYMUS a gland   **Med.**
THYRSE panicle   **B.**
TIBIAL (bone); (flute)   **Med.**
TICING enticing; decoying; luring
TICKED speckled; clicked; beat
TICKEN bed ticking; cloth
TICKER a watch
TICKET voucher; coupon; pass
TICKEY 3d. piece (S. Africa)
TICKLE gratify; divert; amuse
TICKLY ticklish; risky; difficult
TIC-TAC bookie's signalling system
TID-BIT tit-bit
TIDDER to fondle
TIDDLE to potter; to trifle
TIDIED cleared up; shipshape
TIDIER neater

TIDILY methodically
TIEING binding; confining
TIE-PIN ornament for a cravat
TIERCE 42 gallon cask   **Mus., Meas.**
TIE-ROD connecting rod
TIE-WIG court-wig
TIFFIN Indian lunch
TIGHTS theatrical wear
TIKKER electrical make and break device
TILERY tilework; tile factory
TILING roofing
TILLED cultivated; ploughed
TILLER helm; drawer; till
TILMUS floccillation   **Med.**
TILTED covered with awning; aslant
TILTER tent-pegger
TIMBAL tymbal; kettledrum   **Mus.**
TIMBER wood
TIMBRE resonance; tone; quality
TIMELY opportune; punctual; apropos
TIMING clocking
TIMIST timekeeper   **Mus.**
TIN-CAN food container
TINDAL Lascar bo'sun's mate
TINDER touchwood
TINEID (small moths)   **Z.**
TINGAL, TINKAL crude borax   **Min.**
TINGED tinkled; imbued; flavoured
TINGIS an insect genus   **Z.**
TINGLE thrill; small nail
TINGUY Brazilian soap-tree   **B.**
TINIER much smaller
TINKED tinged; tinkled
TINKER bungler; a fish   **Z.**
TINKLE
TINMAN a manufacturer
TINNED preserved
TINNER tin miner
TIN-POT
TINSEL finery; glittering; gaudy
TINTED tinged; imbued
TINTER colourist
TIP-CAT a children's game
TIP-OFF secret information
TIPPED overturned; (racing)
TIPPET garment; small cape
TIPPLE drink
TIP-TOE great expectation
TIP-TOP first class
TIPULA insect genus; daddy-longlegs **Z.**
TIRADE diatribe; invective; harangue
TIRING dressing; wearying
TIRLED vibrated; twisted
TIRRET handcuff; manacle; fetter
TIRRIT terror (Shak.)
TIRWIT lapwing   **Z.**
TISANE barley-water
TISSUE web; fabric; series   **Med.**
TIT-BIT tid-bit
TITELY quickly

TITHED taxed
TITHER tithe collector
TITLED yclept; inscribed; named
TITLER stickle-back   **Z.**
TI-TREE the manuka   **B.**
TITTER giggle; snigger; laugh
TITTLE an iota; small particle
TITTUP canter
TMESIS rhetorical intersection
TOBINE twilled silk
TOCHER dowry (Sc.)
TOCSIN an alarm
TODDLE saunter
TOE-CAP
TOEING
TOFFEE
TOFORE before; heretofore
TOGGED arrayed
TOGGLE wooden pin   **Naut.**
TOILED moiled; strove
TOILER labourer; worker; striver
TOILET dress; costume; attire
TOISON a fleece
TOLEDO sword-blade
TOLLED annulled; (bells)   **Law**
TOLLER toll-gatherer
TOLLER bell-ringer
TOL-LOL goodish
TOLSEY toll-booth; mart
TOLTEC early Mexican
TOLTER to flounder (dial.)
TOLUIC (benzene)   **Chem.**
TOLUOL methylbenzene   **Chem.**
TOMAND Arabian grain   **Meas.**
TOMATO   **B.**
TOMAUN Persian gold coin   **Coin**
TOMBAC, TOMBAK a copper alloy
TOMBED buried
TOMBIC like a tomb
TOMBOC Javanese weapon
TOMBOY a romping girl; hoyden
TOM-CAT   **Z.**
TOMCOD a fish   **Z.**
TOMIAL } cutting edge
TOMIUM }   of a bird's bill   **Z.**
TOMPON inking pad
TOMPOT blenny fish   **Z.**
TOM-TIT blue tit   **Z.**
TOMTOM Hindu drum; tumtum
TONAME nickname; byname
TONGAN native of Tonga
TONGUE language; speech; scold
TONING intoning   **Eccl.**
TONING tinting
TONISH stylish; having " ton "
TONITE an explosive   **Chem.**
TONSIL   **Med.**
TOOART Australian eucalyptus   **B.**
TOOLED ornamented; drove
TOOTED hooted

TOOTER a piper
TOOTHY
TOOTLE play on the flute   **Mus.**
TOO-TOO quite so; super
TOPAZA humming birds   **Z.**
TOP-DOG
TOPFUL brimming
TOP-HAT topper
TOPHET place of torment (Hebrew)
TOPHUS (gout)   **Med.**
TOPMAN top sawyer   **Naut.**
TOPPED surpassed; filled up; (golf)
TOPPER high hat
TOPPLE fall; tumble; collapse; totter
TORERO bull-fighter on foot
TOROID a symmetrical geometrical fig.
TOROSE }
TOROUS } swelling; protuberant
TORPID inert; numb; lethargic
TORPOR apathy; dulness; dormancy
TORQUE twisting force
TORQUE collar; necklace
TORRID sultry; scorching; fiery
TORSEL twisted scroll
TORULA yeast plant   **B.**
TOSSED thrown; pitched
TOSSER pitcher
TOSS-UP an even chance
T'OTHER the other
TOTING carrying; humping
TOTTED added up
TOTTER topple; reel; rock; stagger
TOTTIE a small tot
TOUCAN S. American bird   **Z.**
TOUCHY testy; irascible; petulant
TOUPEE } a tuft; a curl; lock of
TOUPET }   false hair
TOURED journeyed
TOUSED hauled; torn; rumpled
TOUSER a teaser; a worrit
TOUSLE to rumple; ruffle; derange
TOUTED canvassed
TOUTER a tout
TOUTIE petulant (Sc.)
TOWAGE haulage
TOWARD apt; docile; tractable
TOWERY lofty
TOWHEE American marsh robin   **Z.**
TOWING dragging; drawing
TOWSER a dog   **Z**
TOY-DOG   **Z**
TOYFUL trifling
TOYING dallying; trifling
TOYISH playful; wanton
TOY-MAN a dealer in playthings
TRABAL beamy
TRABEA Roman consular robe
TRACED trailed; drawn; limned
TRACER investigator; (bullet)
TRADED bartered; vended; sold

TRADER merchant; trafficker		**TROUGH** groove; trench; furrow	
TRAGIC shocking; calamitous		**TROUPE** a company	
TRAGUS (ear portal)	**Med.**	**TROVER** (finding)	**Law**
TRANCE coma; rapture; ecstasy		**TROWED** trusted; believed	
TRANKA juggler's box		**TROWEL**	**Tool**
TRAPAN to ensnare; stratagem		**TRUANT** vagrant; vagabond; shirker	
TRAPES a slut; a tramp		**TRUDGE** tramp; plod; march	
TRAPPY treacherous		**TRUEST** exactest; most veracious	
TRASHY rubbishy; worthless		**TRUISM** axiom; platitude	
TRAUMA a wound; shock **Psych. Med.**		**TRUITE** crackled (porcelain)	
TRAVEL tour; trip; journey; move		**TRUSTY** reliable; staunch; faithful	
TRAVIS stable partition		**TRYGON** sting-ray	**Z.**
TREATY pact; covenant; alliance		**TRYING** irksome; difficult; arduous	
TREBLE triple; threefold	**Mus.**	**TRY-OUT** preliminary trial	
TREBLY triply		**TSAMBA** black barley (Thibet)	**B**
TREFLE trefoil		**TSETSE** deadly fly (S. Africa)	**Z.**
TREMEX an insect genus	**Z.**	**TSONGA** language (Mozambique)	
TREMOR shock; vibration		**TSWANA** language (Africa)	
TRENCH cut; furrow; ditch		**T-TOTUM** teetotum	
TREPAN (skull-cütting)	**Med.**	**TUAREG** tribe (Sahara)	
TREPAN a cheat; ensnare; trapan		**TUBAGE** inserting a tube	
TREPID quaking; trembling		**TUBBED** bathed	
TRESSY curly		**TUBFUL** the contents of a barrel	
TRIACT having three rays		**TUB-GIG** Welsh car	
TRIAGE sorting		**TUBING** piping	
TRIBAL clannish		**TUBULE** small tube	
TRICAR motor-cycle		**TUCHUN** Chinese military governor	
TRICKY intricate; difficult		**TUCKED** stuffed; folded; pleated	
TRICOT knitted fabric		**TUCKER** bib; frilling	
TRIFID three-cleft	**B.**	**TUCKET** trumpet-call	**Mus.**
TRIFLE a sweet; gewgaw; dally		**TUCK-IN** large meal; picnic	
TRIGLA gurnards	**Z.**	**TUFFET** Miss Muffet's seat; grass	
TRIGLY dandified		**TUFTED** tufty	
TRIGON ancient harp; triangle	**Mus.**	**TUFTER** a stag-hound	**Z.**
TRILBY a hat		**TUGGED** lugged	
TRIMLY neatly; compactly		**TUGGER** a heaver	
TRINAL three-fold		**TUILLE** thigh armour	
TRINGA sand-piper genus	**Z.**	**TULWAR** Eastern sabre	
TRIODE thermionic valve (wireless)		**TUMBLE** trip; stumble; somersault	
TRIPLE treble		**TUMBLY** uneven; unstable	
TRIPLY threefold		**TUMEFY** to swell; distend; inflate	
TRIPOD three-legged stool		**TUMOUR** morbid swelling	**Med.**
TRIPOS Cambridge examination		**TUMPED** hilled (gardening)	
TRISTE sad; sorrowful; gloomy	**Mus.**	**TUM-TUM** W. Indian food; tomtom	
TRITON one of Neptune's trumpeters		**TUMULI** ancient mounds	
TRITON genus of molluscs	**Z.**	**TUMULT** uproar; hubbub; turmoil	
TRIUNE (Trinity)		**TUNDRA** Russian swamp	
TRIVET trevet; small hob		**TUNDUN** a toy; a bull-roarer	
TROCAR surgical instrument	**Med.**	**TUNE-IN** set radio to a station	
TROCHE a lozenge; tabloid		**TUNGUS** Turanian tribe	
TROGGS clothes (Sc.)		**TUNING** (wireless); syntonizing	
TROGON Central American bird	**Z.**	**TUNKER** dunker; baptist	
TROIKA Russian 3-horsed sleigh		**TUNNED** casked	
TROJAN a champion; a plucky fellow		**TUNNEL** funnel; passage; burrow	
TROLLY small truck		**TUPAIA** tree-shrew (Malay)	**Z.**
TROPHI (insect's mouth)	**Z.**	**TUPELO** gum-tree	**B.**
TROPHY prize; laurels		**TUPPED** butted; rammed	
TROPIC (Cancer and Capricorn)		**TURACO** Afr. plantain-eating bird	**Z.**
TROPPO excessively	**Mus.**	**TURBAN** oriental head-dress	
TROTYL explosive	**Chem.**	**TURBID** muddy; cloudy; confused	

TURBOT, TURBIT a flat fish   **Z.**
TURDUS the thrush   **Z.**
TUREEN a receptacle for soup
TURFED sodded; kicked out
TURFEN (turf); covered with sward
TURGID bloated; tumid; bombastic
TURGOR fullness   **Med.**
TURION runner; underground shoot   **B.**
TURKEY (straight talk)   **Z.**
TURKIS turquoise   **Min.**
TURMUT turnip (dial.)   **B.**
TURNED hinged; applied (lathe)
TURNER lathe-worker; pigeon   **Z.**
TURNIP old-fashioned watch   **B.**
TURN-UP an altercation
TURNUS swallow-tail butterfly   **Z.**
TURREL tool used by coopers   **Tool**
TURRET minaret; cupola; pinnacle
TURTLE marine tortoise   **Z.**
TURVES plural of turf; sods
TUSCAN a classic order of architecture
TUSKAR peat cutter
TUSKED tusky; toothy
TUSKER elephant   **Z.**
TUSSAC a tussock
TUSSER tussore silk
TUSSIS a cough   **Med.**
TUSSLE scuffle; wrestle; contend
TUTRIX female guardian
TUTSAN a plant   **B.**
TU-WHIT ⎫
TU-WHOO ⎬ owlishness
TUXEDO dinner jacket (U.S.A.)
TUYERE a pipe; twyer
TWAITE species of shad   **Z.**
TWAITE arable land
TWEENY maid; small cigar
TWELVE a dozen
TWENTY a score
TWICER compositor and pressman
TWIGGY abounding in shoots
TWILLY cotton-cleaning machine
TWINED twisted; meandered
TWINER climbing plant   **B.**
TWINGE pang; twitch; spasm
TWITCH twinge; jerk
TWO-PLY
T'WOULD it would
TWO-WAY (a switch)
TYBURN (executions); (Marble Arch)
TYCOON Japanese prince
TYLOTE sponge-spicule
TYMBAL kettledrum; timbal   **Mus.**
TYMPAN printing frame
TYPHON evil genius (Egypt)
TYPHUS gaol fever   **Med.**
TYPIFY exemplify; symbolize
TYPING
TYPIST
TYRANT autocrat; despot

TYRIAN purple
TYRITE a mineral   **Min.**
TYSTIE the black guillemot   **Z.**
TZETZE Abyssinian guitar

U

UAKARI S. American monkeys   **Z.**
UBERTY fruitfulness
UBIETY local relation
UBIQUE Royal Artillery motto
UDMURT native of Central Asia
UGLIER
UGLIFY to make hideous
UGLILY in an ungainly manner
UGRIAN Ugro-Finnic
UGSOME hideous; gruesome
UIGITE a silicate of aluminium   **Min.**
ULITIS gum inflammation   **Med.**
ULLAGE lack of fulness in a cask
ULLING ullage
ULMOUS (elm exudation)   **B.**
ULNARE cuneiform bone   **Med.**
ULOSIS cicatrisation   **Med.**
ULSTER overcoat
ULTIMO last; in last month
ULTION revenge
UMBERY of umber colour
UMBLES entrails of deer
UMBRAL shady; darksome
UMBRIL umbrel; helmet vizor
UMLAUT vowel inflection
UMPIRE arbiter; referee; judge
UNABLE powerless; impotent
UNAWED undismayed; undaunted
UNBANK (stoking)
UNBEAR to unharness; ungear
UNBEND to relax; undo   **Naut.**
UNBENT relaxed; untied
UNBIAS to free from prejudice
UNBIND release; unfetter
UNBITT (release cable)   **Naut.**
UNBOLT unfasten; unbar
UNBONE remove the bones
UNBOOT
UNBORN non-existent; uncreated
UNBRED rude; underbred
UNBURY disinter; exhume
UNCAGE to free
UNCALM to disturb; agitate
UNCAMP dislodge
UNCAPE unhood
UNCART unload
UNCASE unpack; display; unsheath
UNCATE hooked
UNCIAL a script used in ancient MSS.
UNCLAD naked; berserk
UNCLEW unwind
UNCLOG unhamper
UNCOCK (shooting); (hay-making)

UNCOIF remove cap
UNCOIL unwind
UNCOIN withdraw from currency
UNCOLT unhorse (Shak.)
UNCORD unbind
UNCORK open
UNCOWL unveil
UNCURL untwist
UNDATE wavy; undose
UNDEAF to free from deafness
UNDEAN deprive of that office **Eccl.**
UNDECK divest of ornaments
UNDERN 9 a.m.; the third hour
UNDIES nether-wear
UNDINE water-nymph
UNDOCK to leave dock **Naut.**
UNDOER subversionary agent
UNDONE untied; awaiting performance
UNDOSE undulated; undate; wavy
UNDRAW draw aside
UNDUKE deprive of duke's rank
UNDULL sharpen; whet
UNDULY excessively; improperly
UNEASE mental unrest; anxiety
UNEASY restive; disturbed
UNEATH uneasily (Spens.)
UNEDGE blunt
UNEVEN rugged; rough; odd
UNEYED unnoticed; unobserved
UNFACE expose
UNFAIR dishonest; foul; partial
UNFAST insecure
UNFEED without fee
UNFELT unimpressed; callous
UNFILE remove from a file
UNFINE shabby
UNFIRM weak; unstable
UNFIST to release; unhand
UNFOLD open; expand; reveal
UNFOOL restore from folly; unhoax
UNFORM to destroy
UNFREE not free; tied; restricted
UNFURL display; unroll
UNGAIN ungainly; clumsy (obs.)
UNGEAR to unharness; unbear
UNGILD remove the gilding
UNGILL release from a gill-net
UNGILT not gilt
UNGIRD unbind
UNGIRT unconfined
UNGLUE ungum; unstick
UNGOWN disrobe
UNGUAL having claws, nails, etc.
UNGUIS claw; hoof **Z., B.**
UNGULA instrument **Med.**
UNGULA section of a cylinder
UNGYVE unfetter
UNHAIR deprive of hair
UNHAND let go; release
UNHANG take off the line

UNHASP unfasten
UNHEAD behead; decapitate
UNHEAL ⎱ to uncover (Spens.)
UNHELE ⎰
UNHELM (helmet)
UNHEWN rough
UNHIVE deprive of habitation
UNHOLD release
UNHOLY impious; profane; ungodly
UNHOOK disconnect
UNHOOP
UNHUNG unhanged
UNHURT scatheless
UNHUSK to shell
UNIATE Greek Catholic sect. **Eccl.**
UNIBLE ⎱ unifiable
UNIFIC ⎰
UNIOLA American grass genus **B.**
UNIPED single-footed
UNIPOD single support camera mounting
UNIQUE peculiar; sole; unexampled
UNISON harmony; concord; accord
UNITAL unique; singular
UNITED combined; coalesced
UNITER joiner; merger
UNJUST biassed; partial
UNKARD ⎱ uncouth; ugly;
UNKETH ⎰ strange (dial.)
UNKENT unknown
UNKEPT discarded; rejected
UNKIND cruel; harsh; unfriendly
UNKING dethrone
UNKNIT unravel
UNKNOT untie; unfasten
UNLACE loose; loosen
UNLADE disburden; unload
UNLAID not allayed; untwisted
UNLASH let loose; unbind; untie
UNLEAD remove lead (printing)
UNLEAL unloyal
UNLENT not loaned
UNLESS if not; except
UNLICH unlike (Spens.)
UNLIKE dissimilar; heterogeneous
UNLIME extract the lime
UNLINE remove the lining
UNLINK unfasten
UNLIVE kill; dull; not electrified
UNLOAD relieve; lighten
UNLOCK unfasten
UNLORD deprive of that dignity
UNLOVE cease to love
UNLUTE unglue
UNMADE not manufactured
UNMAKE destroy; dismantle
UNMASK expose; denounce; reveal
UNMEET unworthy; unbecoming
UNMIRY not muddy
UNMIXT pure; unalloyed; sheer
UNMOOR to weigh anchor **Naut.**

UNNAIL extract the nails
UNNEST eject; evict
UNNETH uneath; not easily (Spens.)
UNOWED not due
UNPACK disburden
UNPAID still owing; outstanding
UNPICK unravel; unknit
UNPRAY revoke a prayer
UNPROP remove a support
UNPURE impure; adulterated
UNQUIT not discharged
UNREAD not perused; ignorant
UNREAL fantastic; visionary; illusory
UNREIN slacken the rein
UNRENT untorn; unripped
UNREST disquiet; unease; fidgetiness
UNRING
UNRIPE immature; crude; green
UNROBE undress
UNROLL open out; uncoil; evolve
UNROOF untile
UNROOT extirpate; eradicate
UNROPE untie; unlash
UNRUDE civil; complaisant
UNRULY riotous; turbulent
UNSAFE risky; hazardous; insecure
UNSAID unspoken
UNSEAL
UNSEAM rip; cleave; unpick
UNSEAT unhorse
UNSEEL to open the eyes
UNSEEN invisible
UNSELF eliminate personality
UNSENT not despatched
UNSEWN unstitched
UNSHED retained; kept
UNSHIP remove; unload **Naut.**
UNSHOD barefoot
UNSHOE
UNSHOT not discharged
UNSHUT open
UNSOFT not softly (Spens.)
UNSOLD not purchased
UNSOUL materialize; deaden
UNSOWN not propagated
UNSPAR remove spars
UNSPED undone
UNSPIN unravel
UNSTEP remove (a mast) **Naut.**
UNSTOP release
UNSUNG
UNSURE uncertain
UNTACK disjoin
UNTAME wild; undomesticated
UNTELL never to narrate
UNTENT uncover
UNTIDY slovenly; disorderly
UNTIED undone; unloosed
UNTILE unroof
UNTOLD uncounted; numberless

UNTOMB exhume
UNTORN unrent
UNTRIM disarray
UNTROD
UNTRUE false; fallacious; spurious
UNTUCK unfold
UNTUNE to disorder
UNTURF
UNTURN untwist; unscrew
UNUSED new; unaccustomed
UNVEIL uncover; reveal; unmask
UNVOTE out-vote
UNWARM chillsome
UNWARP **Naut.**
UNWARY rash; incautious; indiscreet
UNWELL ailing; sick; indisposed
UNWEPT not lamented
UNWILY lacking in craft
UNWIND uncoil; disentangle
UNWIRE
UNWISE indiscreet; imprudent
UNWISH wish not to be (Shak.)
UNWOOF unweave
UNWORK undo
UNWORN unimpaired
UNWRAP unfold; uncloak
UNYOKE separate; disjoin
UPBEAR sustain; elevate
UPBEAT unaccentuated rhythm **Mus**
UPBIND confine
UPCAST uptoss
UPCOIL to coil
UPCURL
UP-DATE bring into line; modernise
UPFILL to fill
UPFLOW upgush
UPGAZE look upwards
UPGROW develop; evolve
UPGUSH upflow
UPHAND lift
UPHEAP pile up; amass
UPHILL toilsome; arduous; strenuous
UPHOLD advocate; maintain; champio
UPHROE awning support **Nau**
UPKEEP maintenance
UPLAND highland
UPLEAN to incline towards
UPLIFT upheaval; exaltation
UP-LINE line to London (railway)
UPLOCK lock up
UPLOOK raise the eyes
UPMOST topmost
UP-PILE accumulate; upheap
UPPING swan marking
UPPISH bumptious
UP-PROP to shore; support
UPREAR to raise
UPRISE ascend; revolt
UPRIST up-risen; uprose
UPROAR riot; hubbub; turmoil

UPROLL furl	**VADIUM** surety (Sc.) **Law**
UPROOT eradicate; extirpate	**VAGARY** whim; crotchet; fancy
UPROSE stood up; rebelled	**VAGOUS** wandering; erratic
UPRUSH	**VAGUER** more indefinite; dimmer
UPSEEK seek	**VAIDIC** Vedic; (philosophical)
UPSEES after the manner of	**VAILED** submitted; tipped
UPSEND throw up	**VAILER** a yielder
UPSHOT outcome; issue; result	**VAINER** more conceited; falser
UPSIDE topside	**VAINLY** ineffectually; proudly
UPSOAR zoom	**VAISYA** (Hindu caste)
UPSTAY sustain; support	**VAKASS** Armenian clerical vestment
UPSWAY swing up	**VAKEEL** Indian attorney **Law**
UPTAKE mental agility	**VALGUS** knock-kneed man; club-foot
UPTEAR rend	**VALING** receding; lowering
UPTILT incline; tip	**VALISE** portmanteau; holdall
UPTOSS pitch	**VALKYR** a Valkyrie; Walkyr
UPTOWN	**VALLAR** (rampart)
UPTURN overturn; overthrow	**VALLEY** dale; vale; dell; glen; dingle
UPWARD ascending; uphill	**VALLUM** Roman rampart
UPWAYS upward	**VALOUR** heroism; courage; prowess
UPWELL upspring; gush	**VALUED** esteemed; prized; treasured
UPWIND to wind up	**VALUER** appraiser
URAEUM tail-end of bird **Z.**	**VALVED**
URAEUS serpent emblem (Egypt)	**VAMOSE** vamoose; to clear out
URANIA Muse of astronomy	**VAMPED** improvised; patched; repaired
URANIC (uranium); celestial	**VAMPER** a pianist; siren **Mus.**
URANIN yellow dye **Chem.**	**VANDAL** barbarian; destroyer
URANUS a planet; father of Saturn	**VANISH** fade; disappear; depart
URBANE courteous; polite; affable	**VANITY** conceit; egotism; futility
URCHIN hedgehog; brat; gamin **Z.**	**VAN-MAN**
UREASE enzyme **Chem.**	**VANNER** light cart horse **Z**
URETIC a medicine **Med.**	**VAPORS** vapours; nervous dejection **Med.**
URGENT pressing; imperative	**VAPOUR** steam; reek; fume; to boast
URGING impelling; inciting	**VARIED** diverse; motley; altered
URNFUL	**VARIER** an inconsistent person
URNING consigning to an urn	**VARLET** scoundrel; rascal; knave
UROPOD abdominal limb **Z.**	**VARMIN** vermin; varmint **Z.**
URSINE bear-like	**VARSAL** universal
URTICA nettle genus **B.**	**VARUNA** The Creator (Hindu Myth.)
URVANT turned up (Heraldry)	**VASSAL** retainer; dependant; bondman
USABLE employable; applicable	**VASTER** on a grander scale
USAGER a religionist **Eccl.**	**VASTLY** spaciously; widely; immensely
USANCE usury	**VASTUS** a thigh muscle **Med.**
USEFUL helpful; beneficial	**VAT-DYE** oxidation of textiles
USTION combustion	**VATTED** mellow
USURER money-lender; a Shylock	**VAUDOO** voodoo; witchcraft (Afr.)
USWARD towards us	**VAULTY** arched
UTGARD abode of Loki (Scand.)	**VAWARD** vanward; in the van
UTMOST extreme; farthest	**VEADER** Jewish intercalary month
UTOPIA a political romance	**VECTOR** (direction and magnitude)
UVEOUS grape-like **Med.**	**VEDDAH** native Cingalese
UVULAR (uvula) **Med.**	**VEERED** changed course; shifted **Naut.**
	VEHMIC (vehmgericht)
V	**VEILED** concealed; shrouded; glozed
	VEINED streaked; variegated; venose
VACANT void; empty; inane	**VELARY** a sail or awning
VACATE quit; leave; annul; rescind	**VELATE** enveloped; veiled **B.**
VACHER cow-keeper	**VELETA** waltz **Mus.**
VACUNA Roman goddess of horticulture	**VELITE** lightly armed Roman soldier
VACUUM void; vacuity; emptiness	**VELLED** removed turf

VELLET velvet (Spens.)
VELLON Spanish money of account
VELLUM parchment from calf-skin
VELOCE very quick **Mus.**
VELOUR velvet
VELURE velvet; smoothing pad
VELVET soft silky stuff
VENDED sold; peddled; hawked
VENDEE the buyer; purchaser
VENDER ⎤
VENDOR ⎦ the seller
VENDUE an auction; roup
VENEER coating; layer; cover
VENERY sport; hunting
VENEUR head-keeper
VENGER an avenger (Spens.)
VENIAL excusable; pardonable
VENITE 95th Psalm
VENNEL an alley-way (Sc.)
VENOSE ⎤
VENOUS ⎦ veined
VENTED poured forth; uttered; emitted
VENTER the abdomen **Med.**
VENTIL (cornet valve) **Mus.**
VERBAL oral; by word of mouth
VERDOY charged with heraldic flowers
VERDUN antique rapier (Fr.)
VERGED sloped; inclined; bordered on
VERGEE about half acre **Meas.**
VERGER pew-opener **Eccl.**
VERIFY confirm; authenticate; identify
VERILY truly; really; certainly
VERITY actuality; fact; reality
VERMES worms **Z.**
VERMIL vermilion
VERMIN noxious animal; rabble **Z.**
VERNAL springlike
VERREL ferrule; see Virole
VERREY vaire; furry (Her.)
VERSAL universal (Shak.)
VERSED skilled; familiar; accomplished
VERSER versifier; poetaster
VERSET prelude **Mus.**
VERSUS against; opposing
VERTEX top; apex; acme; zenith
VERVET South African monkey **Z.**
VESICA a bladder; a sac **Med.**
VESPER evening star, Venus
VESSEL receptacle; utensil **Naut.**
VESTAL chaste
VESTED fixed; legalized; established
VESTRY sacristy **Eccl.**
VETCHY (vetch) **B.**
VETOED prohibited; banned; forbidden
VETTED carefully examined
VETUST ancient
VEXING annoying; tormenting; trying
VIABLE capable of existence
VIANDS food; provisions
VIATIC (journey)

VIATOR wayfarer
VIBRIO spiral bacillus **Z.**
VICARY a vicarage **Eccl.**
VICTIM a dupe; martyr; saçrifice
VICTOR conqueror; winner; champion
VICUNA the wild llama **Z.**
VIDAME French noble
VIDUAL widowed
VIELLE antique viol (Fr.) **Mus**
VIEWED beheld; surveyed; scanned
VIEWER examiner; inspector
VIEWLY striking
VIGOUR force; energy; manliness
VIHARA Buddhist temple
VIKING Norse sea-rover
VILELY basely; ignobly; malignantly
VILEST lowest; abject
VILIFY defame; traduce; disparage
VILLUS hair; wool **Med**
VILNED wounded beast **Her.**
VINAGE wine doctoring
VINERY grape house
VINNEY a blue Dorset cheese
VINOSE ⎤
VINOUS ⎦ (wine)
VINTED turned into wine
VINTRY wine shop; bodega; bistro
VIOLAN violet blue **Min**
VIOLET a colour **F**
VIOLIN fiddle; a kit **Mus**
VIRAGO a termagant; vixen; shrew
VIRENT verdant; green; fresh
VIRGIN maiden; damsel; spinster
VIRILE manly; robust; masculine
VIROLE ferrule; hoop (Her.)
VIROSE ⎤
VIROUS ⎦ poisonous
VIRTUE integrity; probity; goodness
VISAED endorsed (passport)
VISAGE face; aspect; countenance
VISCID sticky; glutinous; tenacious
VISCUM mistletoe **F**
VISCUS an entrail **Me**
VISHNU The Preserver (Hindu God)
VISIER ⎤
VIZIER ⎦ wizier; Turkish minister
VISION sight; spectre; ghost; dream
VISIVE visual
VISUAL visible; perceptible
VITALS essential organs
VITRIC glassy
VIVACE lively **Mu**
VIVARY small zoo; vivarium
VIVERS victuals (Sc.)
VIVIFY animate; enliven; quicken
VIZARD mask; visor
VOCULE a feeble cry
VOICED said; declared; uttered
VOICER spokesman
VOIDED evacuated; quitted; left

VOIDER shallow basket
VOLANT flying; nimble; active   **Her.**
VOLATA rapid phrase   **Mus.**
VOLERY flight of birds
VOLLEY salvo; shower; storm
VOLUME book; tome; bulk; mass
VOLUTE spiral scroll
VOLVOX fresh-water algae   **B.**
VOMICA an abscess in the lungs   **Med.**
VOMITO yellow fever   **Med.**
VOODOO ⎱ witchcraft, vaudoo
VOUDOU ⎰ (Hayti and West Indies)
VORAGO whirlpool; vortex; gulf
VORANT devouring (Her.)
VORTEX whirlpool; whirlwind
VOTARY a fan; devotee; zealot
VOTING electing; polling
VOTIVE vowed; devoted
VOULGE ancient form of pike (Fr.)
VOWING pledging; promising
VOYAGE trip; cruise; passage
VULCAN god of fire
VULGAR coarse; ordinary; vernacular

W

WABBLE wobble
WABBLY insecure; unstable
WADDED stuffed with tow
WADDIE Australian war club
WADDLE walk like a duck
WADING fording
WADMAL thick woollen cloth
WADSET a mortgage   **Law**
WAEFUL woeful; sorrowful
WAFERY wafer-like
WAFFLE a cake; a gauffre
WAFTED floated; waved; beckoned
WAFTER a fan
WAGGED shook; vibrated; swayed
WAGGEL great gull   **Z.**
WAGGLE vibrate; oscillate
WAGGON wagon; dray
WAGING betting; venturing; conducting
WAG-WIT a would-be wit
WAHABI Puritan Moslem   **Eccl.**
WAHINE Maori woman
WAILED bemoaned; lamented
WAILER howler; weeper
WAITED attended; tarried; lingered
WAITER attendant; servitor; garçon
WAIVED relinquished; forwent
WAIVER yielder; renouncer
WAKING arousing; stimulating
WALING chastising
WALKED perambulated; strolled
WALKER hiker; pedestrian
WALKYR Valkyr; a Valkyrie
WALLAH a fellow (Ind.)
WALLED enclosed

WALLER a wall-builder
WALLET purse; scrip; pouch
WALLOP to boil; to beat; beer·
WALLOW welter; grovel; flounder
WALNUT   **B.**
WALRUS the morse; sea-horse   **Z.**
WAMBLE to be queasy
WAMMUS knitted jacket (U.S.A.)
WAMPEE a Chinese fruit   **B.**
WAMPUM beads used as cash (N.A.In.)
WANDER stroll; stray; roam
WANDLE supple; nimble (dial.)
WANDOO Australian white gum   **B.**
WANGLE get by craft
WANING declining; ebbing; paling
WANION bad luck (Sc.)
WANKLE weak; unstable
WANNED made pale
WANTED needed; lacked; desired
WANTER a requirer; craver
WANTON sportive; frolicsome; frisky
WAPITI stag; American elk   **Z.**
WAPPER gudgeon   **Z.**
WAPPET yelping cur   **Z.**
WARBLE cattle tumour; quaver; sing
WAR-CRY slogan
WARDED guarded; fended; parried
WARDEN ⎱ keeper; guardian; protector;
WARDER ⎰ curator; custodian; turnkey
WARELY warily (Spens.)
WARIER more cautious
WARILY cautiously; carefully; cannily
WARMAN warrior; man-at-arms
WARMER hotter; keener
WARMLY earnestly; ardently; zealously
WARMTH heat; enthusiasm; fervency
WARNED cautioned; notified; apprised
WARNER an admonisher
WARPED distorted; perverted; biassed
WARPER a weaver; a twister
WARRAY to ravage by war (Spens.)
WARREN rabbit burrows; enclosure
WAR-TAX
WARTED verrucose   **B.**
WASHED laved; abstersed; purged
WASHER metal ring
WASH-UP
WASTED frittered; squandered
WASTEL a fine sort of bread
WASTER a cudgel; spendthrift
WATERY aqueous; dilute; thin; insipid
WATTLE fowl's gills   **Z.**
WATTLE an acacia; a hurdle   **B.**
WAUGHT ⎱ a deep draught;
WAUGHT ⎰ to quaff (Sc.)
WAULED ⎱
WAWLED ⎰ caterwauled
WAVERY unsteady; tremulous
WAVING undulating; swaying
WAVURE procrastination

WAX-END cobbler's thread
WAXIER more irate
WAXING growing; increasing; rising
WAX-RED
WAYLAY to ambush
WAYOUT advanced; unusual
WEAKEN impair; enfeeble; enervate
WEAKER more dilute; thinner; feebler
WEAKLY delicately; infirmly; frailly
WEALTH riches; opulence; abundance
WEANED alienated; withdrawn
WEAPON sometimes blunt
WEARER bearer; waster
WEASEL explosive carnivore   **Z.**
WEAVER bird; see webster   **Z.**
WEAZEN wizened; sharp; shrivelled
WEBBED arachnoid; woven
WEB-EYE a disease of the cornea   **Med.**
WEDDED married; espoused; spliced
WEDGED scotched; compressed; ceramics
WEEDED hoed; eradicated; purged
WEEDER
WEEKLY hebdomadary; a periodical
WEENED imagined; thought
WEEPER Niobe; a monkey   **Z.**
WEEVER sting-fish   **Z.**
WEEVIL a beetle   **Z.**
WEIGHT onus; incubus; load; burden
WELDED united
WELDER Irish sub-tenant
WELKIN sky
WELLED poured forth; spouted; gushed
WELTED edged; bordered
WELTER wallow; flounder; heavy
WENDED journeyed; wandered
WENDIC a Sorabian
WESAND⎫ weazand; wind-pipe
WEZAND⎭
WESTER to turn westward
WET-BOB Eton aquatic sportsman
WETHER a castrated ram   **Z.**
WETTER damper; more showery
WHALER whale-boat   **Naut.**
WHALLY having greenish-white eyes
WHATEN⎫ what kind of (Sc.)
WHATNA⎭
WHATSO of whatever kind
WHEELY circular
WHEEZE puff; blow; ancient joke
WHEEZY asthmatic
WHELKY rounded; protuberant
WHENAS when; whereas (Shak.)
WHENCE wherefrom
WHERRY a liquor; sailing boat   **Naut.**
WHEUGH ! exclamation of surprise
WHEWER the wigeon   **Z.**
WHEYEY whey-like
WHILED beguiled
WHILES⎫ meanwhile
WHILST⎭

WHILLY to cajole; to wheedle
WHILOM formerly
WHILST while
WHIMSY fad; caprice; fancy; crotchet
WHINED whimpered
WHINER sniveller
WHINGE to whine (Sc.)
WHINNY (horse); (gorse)
WHIPPY flexible; springy
WHIRRY to hurry off (Sc.)
WHISHT ! hush !
WHISKY a light gig
WHITEN blanch; bleach; turn pale
WHITER purer; brighter
WHITES (flannels)
WHOLLY entirely; fully; utterly
WHOMSO every one whom
WHYDAH⎫ African weaver bird   **Z.**
WHIDAH⎭
WICKED evil; sinful; ungodly; nefarious
WICKEN mountain ash   **B.**
WICKER pliant twig; osier   **B.**
WICKET small gate; (cricket)
WICOPY American basswood   **B.**
WIDELY spaciously; extensively; rifely
WIDEST broadest; remotest
WIELDY manageable
WIFELY wively
WIGEON widgeon   **Z.**
WIGGED berated; reproved; chid
WIGGLE wriggle; waggle
WIGWAG flag-wag; twist
WIGWAM Indian hut
WILDER bewilder
WILDLY fiercely; recklessly; savagely
WILFUL wanton; perverse; obdurate
WILIER craftier; slyer
WILILY artfully; cunningly; insiduously
WILING beguiling; deceiving
WILLED resolved; bequeathed   **Lav**
WILLER one who wills
WILLET North American snipe   **Z**
WILLOW a cricket bat   **B**
WILTED drooped; withered
WIMBLE to drill; gimlet   **Too**
WIMBLE nimble; active
WIMPLE a headdress; to ripple
WINCED flinched; quailed
WINCER a shrinker
WINCEY winsey; a fabric
WINDED blew; blown; caught scent
WINDER to fan; to winnow; a key
WINDLE a spindle; reel
WINDOW lattice; casement
WIND-UP alarm; trepidation
WINGED alate; rapid; wounded
WINGER (football)
WINKED twinkled; flickered; acquiesce
WINKER horse's blinker
WINKLE periwinkle   **B.,**

WINNER victor; conqueror; champion
WINNOW sift; examine; fan
WINSEY wincey; twilled cotton
WINTER hyemal
WINTLE stagger; writhe (Sc.)
WINTRY icy; frosty; cheerless
WIPING deterging; rubbing
WIRIER capable of greater strain
WIRILY vigorously; tenaciously
WIRING (electrical); telegraphing
WISARD ⎫ conjuror; sorcerer;
WIZARD ⎬ necromancer; marabout
WISDOM sagacity; knowledge
WISELY sagely; sensibly; sapiently
WISEST most learned and judicious
WISHED listed; wanted; longed for
WISHER desirer; yearner
WISKET a basket
WISTLY earnestly; attentively
WITHAL together with; likewise
WITHED bound with a withe
WITHER fade; pine; languish
WITHIN not exceeding; indoors
WITTED alert; wise
WITWAL popinjay; wood-pecker　**Ż.**
WIVELY wifely
WIVERN wyvern; winged dragon
WIZIER vizier; visier; minister
WOBBLE wabble; oscillate; vibrate
WOBBLY unstable; unsteady
WOEFUL waeful; tragic; grievous
WOLFER voracious feeder
WOLVES predacious animals　**Z.**
WOMBAT burrowing marsupial　**Z.**
WONDER marvel; miracle; prodigy; awe
WONING a dwelling
WONTED accustomed; usual
WOODED afforested
WOODEN clumsy; impassive
WOODIE the gallows (Sc.)
WOOFER base loudspeaker (acoustics)
WOOING courting; courtship
WOOLLY lanate
WORDED expressed; phrased
WORKED moiled; strove; slaved
WORKER hand; toiler; operative
WORMED crept; insinuated; crawled
WORMUL a wornil　**Z.**
WORNIL cow-maggot　**Z.**
WORREL lizard (Egypt)　**Z.**
WORRIT an annoyance
WORSEN to defeat
WORSEN to deteriorate
WORSER far worse
WORTHY exemplary; noble; meritorious
WOUNDY excessive; injurious
WOU-WOU silver gibbon wow-wow (Java)
WOWSER kill-joy; fanatical Puritan
WRAITH apparition; ghost; spectre
WRASSE prickly fish　**Z.**

WRATHY apt to wrath; choleric
WREATH festoon; garland; chaplet
WRENCH strain; sprain; twist　**Tool**
WRETCH villain; vagabond; miscreant
WRIEST most distorted
WRIGHT an artificer; mechanic
WRITER scribe; author; scribbler
WRITHE squirm; wriggle; contort
WUTHER to low (dial.)
WUZZLE to jumble (U.S.A.)
WYVERN wivern; heraldic dragon

X

XANADU Khan's pleasure house
XANGTI Zeus (Chinese)
XENIAL genial; friendly
XENIUM gift; picture of still life
XENOPS tree-creeper birds (S. Amer.)　**Z.**
XERXES Persian King; Ahasuerus
X-FLASH　　　**Electron, Photo.**
X-GUIDE transmission line
XOANON primitive Greek statue
X-RAYED (Rontgen rays)　**Med.**
XYLENE a benzene derivative　**Chem.**
XYLITE asbestos　**Min.**
XYLOID like wood
XYLOSE wood sugar　**Chem.**
XYSTER a bone scraper　**Med.**
XYSTOS ⎫ covered portico used by
XYSTUS ⎬ athletes (Greek)

Y

YABBER speech (Australian)
YAFFLE the green woodpecker　**Z.**
YAGGER pedlar; hawker (Sc.)
YAHVEH Jahveh; Jehovah　**Eccl.**
YAKSKA Hindu gnome
YAMMER whine; blather; grumble
YANKED heaved
YANKEE Northern American
YANKEE a specially large jib　**Naut.**
YANKER a big lie (Sc.)
YAOURT Turkish fermented milk
YAPOCK S. Amer. water-opossum　**Z.**
YAPPED yelped
YAPPER a yapping dog　**Z.**
YARDED confined
YARNED related; narrated
YARPHA peaty soil (Shetland)
YARRAH Australian red gum tree　**B.**
YARROW the milfoil　**B.**
YAUPED yelped (U.S.A.)　**B.**
YAUPON holly (used as tea)
YAWING deviating from course　**Naut.**
YAWLED howled; cried
YAWNED gaped; oscitated
YCLEPT by name of
YEANED, YEENED brought forth

YEARLY annual
YEASTY turbid; frothy; foamy
YELLED bawled; howled; screamed
YELLOW cowardly
YELPED yauped; yapped; barked
YELPER yapper
YEMENI native of Yemen
YENITE a silicate of iron   **Min.**
YEOMAN a beefeater; a farmer   **Naut.**
YERKED jerked
YER-NUT pig-nut   **B.**
YES-MAN sycophant
YESTER previous; last
YEXING hiccuping
YOGISM a Hindu philosophy
YOICKS! a hunting cry
YOJANA about 5 miles (Indian)   **Meas.**
YOKING coupling; linking
YOLKED having a yolk
YONDER over there
YONKER a stripling
YORICK jester to court of Denmark
YORKER (cricket)
YORUBA tribe (South Sahara)
YOUTHY young; callow
YOU-UNS you, you ones
YOWLED howled; yelled
YOWLEY yellow bunting   **Z.**
Y-TRACK reversing lines for trains
YTTRIA oxide of yttrium   **Chem.**
YTTRIC containing yttrium   **Chem.**
YUCKER American woodpecker   **Z.**

Z

ZABIAN Sabian; non-Christian gnostic
ZABISM Sabianism
ZABRUS beetle genus   **Z.**
ZACCAB Yucatan wall plaster
ZACCHO the base of a pedestal
ZAFFER } cobalt ore   **Min.**
ZAFFRE }
ZAMITE fossil-plant   **B.**
ZANDER sander; pike-perch   **Z.**
ZANIES clowns; buffoons
ZANTHA knitted fabric
ZAPOTE plums (Mexico)   **B.**
ZARAPE serape; Mexican scarf
ZAREBA zeraba; zariba; fortified camp
ZARNEC orpiment   **Min.**
ZEALOT fanatic; bigot; partisan
ZEBECK Algerian pirate-ship   **Naut.**

ZECHIN sequin; Venetian gold **Coin**
ZEEKOE hippopotamus (S. Africa)   **Z.**
ZEETAK red-coral (S. Africa)
ZEMZEM sacred fountain at Mecca
ZENANA women's quarter (Ind.)
ZENDIK Eastern heretic; magician
ZENITH acme; apex; climax; summit
ZEPHYR the west wind; soft breeze
ZEREBA zareba; thornbush stockade
ZEUGMA grammatical conjunction
ZIAMET Turkish military district
ZICSAC sicsac; crocodile bird   **Z.**
ZIG-ZAG tortuous
ZILLAH Indian district
ZIMONE (gluten)
ZINCKY like zinc
ZINGEL perch; Danube fish   **Z.**
ZINNIA a flower   **B.**
ZIPPED whizzed
ZIPPER zip-fastener
ZIRCON a silicate   **Min.**
ZITHER the cithern   **Mus.**
ZIVOLA yellow-hammer   **Z.**
ZODIAC a heavenly girdle; the ecliptic
ZOETIC vital
ZOMBIE moron; drugged person
ZONARY } resembling a girdle
ZONOID }
ZONATE belted
ZONING area allocation; planning
ZONNAR girdle worn in the Levant
ZONULE zonula; small zone
ZONURE lizard covered with spikes   **Z.**
ZOONAL embryonic   **Z.**
ZOONIC zoological   **Z.**
ZOO-ZOO wood-pigeon   **Z.**
ZOSTER shingles   **Med.**
ZOUAVE Algerian soldier
ZOUNDS 'God's wounds'
ZUFOLO zuffolo; flageolet   **Mus.**
ZUMATE } a salt of zymic acid   **Chem.**
ZYMATE }
ZUNIAN Pueblo-Indian
ZYGITE an oarsman in a trireme
ZYGOMA the cheek-bone   **Med.**
ZYGOSE (fertilization)   **B.**
ZYGOTE a spore; a germ-cell   **B., Z.**
ZYMASE a ferment; an enzyme
ZYMITE priest using leavened bread **Eccl.**
ZYMOID like a ferment; yeasty   **Chem.**
ZYMOME insoluble gluten
ZYTHUM ancient type of beer

A

AARONIC (Jewish priest-hood)   **Eccl.**
ABACIST an accountant
ABACTOR cattle thief; rustler
ABADDON Apollyon; bottomless pit
ABALONE mother-of-pearl
ABANDON joie-de-vivre; forsake; quit
ABASHED shamed; embarrassed
ABASING degrading; humbling
ABATING mitigating; stopping
ABATTIS military obstacles
ABATURE beast tracks
ABAXIAL oblique rays   **Photo.**
ABB-WOOL warp-yarn
ABDOMEN the belly   **Med.**
ABDUCED abducted; separated
ABETTED incited; aided; assisted
ABETTER an abettor; instigator   **Law**
ABEYANT in abeyance
ABIDING residence; lasting; durable
ABIETIC (conifers)   **B.**
ABIETIN (resin)
ABIGAIL serving-girl; Hebe; waitress
ABIGEAT cattle theft   **Law**
ABILITY legal power; wealth; talent •
ABIOSIS absence of life
ABJUDGE deprive by law   **Law**
ABJURED recanted; repudiated
ABJURER forswearer
ABLEPSY blindness   **Med.**
ABLINGS aiblins; perhaps
ABLUENT detergent
ABOLISH destroy; extirpate; annul
ABRADED scraped; worn away
ABRAXAS Gnostic god; amulet
ABREAST side by side
ABRIDGE curtail; epitomize; summarize
ABROACH tapped; afoot; astir
ABSCESS boil; ulcer   **Med.**
ABSCIND cut off
ABSCISS a geometric line
ABSCOND decamp; bolt; quit; levant
ABSENCE lack; want; deficiency
ABSIDAL apse-like
ABSINTH liqueur; wormwood
ABSOLVE release; exonerate; shrive
ABSTAIN refrain; desist; avoid
ABUSING perverting; violating
ABUSION deception; disparagement
ABUSIVE ribald; reviling; calumnious
ABUTTAL the boundary of lands
ABUTTED contiguous; bordered on
ABUTTER neighbour   **Law**
ABYSMAL fathomless; profound
ABYSSAL bottomless
ACADEMY also academe; institution
ACADIAN Nova Scotian
ACALEPH jelly-fish   **Z.**
ACANTHA prickly plant   **B.**
ACARDIA heart-less

ACARINA mites; ticks   **Z.**
ACCABLE overwhelm; crush (obs.)
ACCEDED assented; succeeded
ACCEDER one who concurs
ACCIDIE sloth; torpor (obs.)
ACCLAIM applaud; applause; proclaim
ACCOAST (low flying)
ACCOLLE collared (Her.)
ACCOMPT account
ACCOUNT deem; reckon; recital; bill
ACCOURT to court (Spens.)
ACCRETE grow together
ACCRUED resulted; accumulated
ACCURSE curse; condemn; execrate
ACCURST accursed; damned; diabolical
ACCUSAL an accusation; indictment
ACCUSED defendant; arraigned   **Law**
ACCUSER plaintiff   **Law**
ACERATE (aceric acid)   **Chem.**
ACERBIC sour; caustic; astringent
ACEROSE acerous; prickly   **B.**
ACETARY acid pulp
ACETATE (vinegar)   **Chem.**
ACETIFY acidify   **Chem.**
ACETONE liquid ketone   **Chem.**
ACETOUS also acetose; sour
ACHAEAN of Archaia (Greek)
ACHAENE seeded fruit   **B.**
ACHATES a true friend
ACHERON river of woe
ACHIEVE perform; perfect; attain
ACHOLIA lack of bile   **Med.**
ACHTUNG beware !; look out !
ACICULA spiked crystals
ACIDIZE to add acid
ACIDITY sourness; tartness
ACIDOID potentially acid (soil)
ACIFORM needle-shaped
ACINOUS acinose; granular
ACK-EMMA a.m. (signalling)
ACLINIC no magnetic dip
ACOLOGY the healing art   **Med.**
ACOLYTE also acolyth; assistant   **Eccl.**
ACONITE plant genus; monkshood   **B.**
ACOUCHY guinea pig; agouti   **Z.**
ACQUEST acquisition   **Law**
ACQUIRE get; gain; procure; win
ACREAGE area in acres
ACRISIA therapeutic uncertainty   **Med.**
ACROBAT a tumbler; funambulist
ACROGEN (club-moss); (tree-fern)   **B.**
ACRONIC non-cosmical (astronomy)
ACROTER pinnacle (arch.)
ACROTIC (superficial)   **Med.**
ACTABLE performable
ACTINIA (sea-anemones)   **Z.**
ACTINIC chemical ray action (solar)
ACTRESS a lady of parts
ACTUARY statistical expert; registrar

ACTUATE impel; urge; instigate; incite
ACULEUS sting; prickle   **Z., B.**
ACUSHLA darling (Irish)
ACUTELY keenly; intensely; poignantly
ADACTYL fingerless
ADAGIAL proverbial
ADAMANT the diamond   **Min.**
ADAMITE a nudist
ADAPTED conformed; attuned; adjusted
ADAPTER adaptor: a fitment
ADDENDA appendix; augmented matter
ADDIBLE addable
ADDLING going rotten; confusing
ADDRESS skill; accost; speech; (golf)
ADDUCED cited; brt. forwd.; alleged
ADDUCER a deducer
ADDULCE to sweeten
ADELPHI
ADENOID growth in nasal pharynx **Med.**
ADENOSE⎫
ADENOUS⎭ glandular   **Med.**
ADHERED stuck; clung; held; cleaved
ADHERER partisan; ally; parasite
ADHIBIT attach; administer
ADIPOMA morbid obesity   **Med.**
ADIPOSE fatty; adipous; sebaceous
ADIPSIA never thirsty   **Med.**
ADJOINT united; connected
ADJOURN suspend; postpone; defer
ADJUDGE condemn; decree; ordain
ADJUNCT a concomitant
ADJURED charged on oath
ADJURER adjuror
ADJUTOR a helper; colleague; ally
ADMIRAL also ammiral   **Naut.**
ADMIRED wondered; appreciated
ADMIRER a lover; adorer
ADMIXED adulterated; infused
ADOLODE distillation tester
ADONAIS Shelley's elegy on Keats
ADONIZE adonise; beautify
ADOPTED appropriated; fathered
ADORING worshipping; idolizing
ADORNED embellished; decked
ADORSED back to back (Her.)
ADRENAL (kidneys)   **Med.**
ADULATE flatter; cajole; belaud
ADULLAM (a cave of refuge)
ADUSTED sunburnt; parched
ADVANCE to extoll; loan; promote
ADVENED acceded
ADVENER an assentor
ADVERSE contrary; hostile; inimical
ADVISED notified; informed; apprised
ADVISOR adviser; counsellor
ADVOWEE a patron of a benefice **Eccl.**
ADYNAMY weakness   **Med.**
AEOLIAN aerial   **Mus.**
AEOLIST wind-bag
AEONIAN eternal

AERATED gassy
AERATOR soda-water machine
AEROBAT an aerial stunter
AEROBIA bacteria   **Med.**
AEROBIC microbial   **Med.**
AEROBUS passenger plane
AEROSOL sprayed mist   **Chem.**
AETATIS at the age of
AFFABLE benign; gracious; sociable
AFFABLY cordially; courteously
AFFICHE notice; placard
AFFINAL akin; related
AFFINED united; allied; related
AFFIXED attached; appended; annexed
AFFLICT distress; torment; chasten
AFFORCE reinforce
AFFRONT insult; outrage; abuse
AFFUSED sprinkled
AFFYING betrothing
AFGHANI native (Afghanistan)   **Coin**
AFLAUNT flaunting
AFRICAN
AGAINST opposite; counter; despite
AGALAXY lack of milk   **Med.**
AGAMIST matrimonial objector
AGAMOUS cryptogamic
AGATINE like agate   **Min.**
AGATIZE turn into agate
AGELESS timeless
AGELONG ancient; antiquated
AGENDUM a business item
AGEUSIA loss of taste   **Med.**
AGGRACE to favour
AGGRATE to gratify
AGGRESS encroach; assault; intrude
AGGROUP group together
AGILELY quickly; actively
AGILITY nimbleness; readiness
AGISTER⎫
AGISTOR⎭ grazing controller
AGITATE ruffle; perturb; confuse
AGITATO spasmodic   **Mus.**
AGNAMED known as
AGNATIC akin
AGNOMEN added surname
AGONISM a competition
AGONIST a contestant
AGONIZE agonise; torture; suffer
AGRAFFE clasp for armour; a hook
AGROUND stranded
AGYNOUS non-reproductive   **B.**
AHRIMAN evil spirit (Persian)
AIBLINS ablings; perhaps
AIDANCE help; succour; bounty
AIDLESS unsupported; unbacked; solo
AIGULET aglet; pendant
AILANTO tree of Heaven   **B.**
AILERON wing lateral-control
AILETTE armoured epaulet
AILMENT malady; complaint; disorder

AIMLESS pointless; random; haphazard
AIR-BALL
AIR-BASE strategic air supply point
AIR-BATH
AIR-BONE hollow bone
AIR-BUMP (air travel)
AIRCAST sow seed from the air
AIR-CELL
AIR-FLUE hot air distributor
AIRFOIL aileron
AIRGLOW atmospheric luminosity
AIRHEAD airport (forward supply)
AIR-HOLE ventilator
AIRLESS stuffy
AIRLIFT aerial transportation
AIR-LINE
AIR-LOCK
AIR-MAIL
AIRMARK par avion
AIRPARK fleet of aeroplanes
AIR-PORT
AIR-PUMP
AIR-RAID
AIR-SACS quill vesicles **Z.**
AIR-SHED a hangar
AIR-SHIP dirigible
AIR-TRAP
AIR-WAYS air-lines
AJUTAGE vent pipe
ALADDIN
ALAMEDA shaded promenade
A-LA-MODE stylish
A-LA-MORT till death
ALANTIN starch **B.**
ALARMED shocked; appalled; daunted
ALASKAN (Alaska)
ALASTOR Nemesis
ALBERIA shield without arms (Her.)
ALBITIC (felspar) **Chem.**
ALBORAK Mahomet's mount to heaven
ALBOREA
ALBUMEN white of egg
ALBUMIN (endosperm) **Med.**
ALCAICS Alcaic verse
ALCALDE judge
ALCANNA henna **B.**
ALCAYDE Spanish governor; judge
ALCAZAR Moorish palace
ALCHEMY alchymy; medieval chemistry
ALCOHOL **Chem.**
ALCYONE star in Pleiades
ALECOST costmary; ale flavouring **B.**
ALE-GILL medicated liquor
ALE-HOOP ground ivy **B.**
ALEMBIC distilling retort
ALENGTH full length
ALERTER brisker; more wakeful
ALERTLY vigilantly; actively; warily
ALETUDE fatness; bulkiness

ALEURON albuminoid **B.**
ALE-WIFE kind of skad **Z.**
ALFALFA lucerne grass **B.**
ALGAROT antimony emetic **Med.**
ALGATES by all means; always
ALGEBAR the constellation, Orion
ALGEBRA
ALGIFIC producing cold
ALHENNA henna; alkenna; orange dye
ALICANT Spanish wine,
ALIENEE transferree
ALIENER a parter
ALIFORM wing-like
ALIGNED adjusted; regulated; aimed
ALIMENT nutriment; sustenance; food
ALIMONY maintenance **Law**
ALIQUOT integral factor
ALKANET henna dye **B.**
ALKORAN alcoran; the Koran **Eccl.**
ALLAYED quieted; alleviated; pacified
ALLEGED averred; asserted; declared
ALLEGRO gaily **Mus.**
ALLERGY distaste; repugnance
ALL-GOOD a plant **B.**
ALL-HAIL a greeting
ALL-HEAL a panacea; valerian, etc. **B.**
ALLONAL soporific drug **Med.**
ALLONGE added leaf; lunge
ALLOWED abated; authorized
ALLOYED debased; tempered
ALLSEED flax **B.**
ALL-TIME unprecedented occurrence
ALLUDED suggested; insinuated; hinted
ALLURED enticed; inveigled; decoyed
ALLUVIA waterborne deposit
ALL-WAVE (wireless)
ALL-WISE of infinite wisdom
ALLYING betrothing; leaguing
ALMADIE bark canoe
ALMANAC calendar
ALMOIGN charitable endowment
ALMONER giver of alms
ALMONRY almsgiving place; cupboard
ALMS-BOX
ALMS-FEE Peter's pence
ALMSMAN receiver of alms
ALNAGER wool inspector
ALODIUM freehold **Law**
ALOETIC purgative **Med.**
ALONGST along with
ALOPECY baldness **Med.**
ALP-HORN Swiss cow-horn **Mus.**
ALREADY before; previously
ALSIRAT bridge to paradise
ALTERED modified; transmuted
ALTHAEA hollyhock genus **B.**
ALTHING Iceland Parliament
ALT-HORN saxhorn **Mus.**
ALUMINA aluminium clay **Min.**

189

ALUMINE oxide of aluminium
ALUMING impregnating with alum
ALUMISH resembling alum
ALUMNUS college student
ALUNITE alum-stone   **Min.**
ALVEARY hive; ear cavity   **Med.**
ALVEATE to hollow out
ALVEOLE tooth socket   **Med.**
ALYSSUM a rock plant   **B.**
AMALGAM mercury alloy   **Chem.**
AMANDIN (almonds)   **B.**
AMARANT amaranth; a fadeless flower
AMASSED heaped; collected
AMATEUR not a professional
AMATIVE loving; lovesome
AMATORY ardent; erotic; passionate
AMAZING astounding; bewildering
AMBAGES circumlocution; subterfuge
AMBARIE covered howdah
AMBIENT encompassing; enfolding
AMBITUS outer edge
AMBLING at an easy gait; sauntering
AMBOYNA a decorative wood   **B.**
AMBREIN (ambergris)
AMBROID moulded amber
AMBS-ACE, AMES-ACE double-ace
(dice)
AMBULET small ambulance
AMELLUS purple star-wort   **B.**
AMENAGE domesticate; manage
AMENDED emended; ameliorated
AMENING ratifying; sanctioning
AMENITY pleasantness; agreeableness
AMENTAL bearing catkins   **B.**
AMENTIA imbecility   **Med.**
AMENTUM a catkin   **B.**
AMERCED fined
AMHARIC language (Ethiopia)
AMIABLE lovable; benign; winsome
AMIABLY kindly; charmingly
AMIDINE wheat extract
AMILDAR Indian official
AMMETER (electrical)   **Meas.**
AMMONAL an explosive   **Chem.**
AMMONIA   **Chem.**
AMNESIA loss of memory   **Med.**
AMNESTY pardon; absolution; oblivion
AMONGST amid; between
AMORIST philanderer
AMOROSA, AMOROSI sweethearts
gallants
AMOROSO tenderly   **Mus.**
AMOROUS amative; passionate
AMORPHA indigo   **B.**
AMOTION deprivation   **Law**
AMPASSY ampersand, the &
AMPHORA two-handled wine jar
AMPLEST most lavish; most copious
AMPLIFY expand; enlarge; augment
AMPOULE⎱ glass container for
AMPULLA⎰ hypodermic dose   **Med.**

AMUSING entertaining; droll; ludicrous
AMUSIVE amusing
AMUTTER muttering
AMYLENE (amyl)   **Chem.**
AMYLINE starch cellulose
AMYLOID, AMYLOSE starchy
    B., Chem.
ANACARD cashew-nut   **B.**
ANAEMIA general debility   **Med.**
ANAEMIC bloodless   **Med.**
ANAGOGE⎱ mystical
ANAGOGY⎰ interpretation
ANAGRAM letter puzzle
ANALECT anthology
ANALOGY similarity; likeness
ANALYSE examine critically
ANALYST a resolver
ANAPEST poetic metre
ANARCHY chaos; disorder; violence
ANATASE titanium oxide   **Chem.**
ANATOMY a skeleton; dissection **Med.**
ANATRON glass scum
ANCHOVY a small fish   **Z.**
ANCIENT antique; pristine ensign
ANCONES ornamental brackets
ANCRESS⎱ female anchorite
ANKRESS⎰
ANDANTE rather slow   **Mus.**
ANDARAC a red pigment
ANDIRON endiron; fire-dog
ANDROID automaton; robot
ANDVARI a dwarf (Norse myth.)
ANELACE anlace; a broad dagger
ANELING anointing with oil   **Eccl.**
ANEMONE anemony; windflower **B., Z.**
ANEROID a kind of barometer
ANETHOL oil of anise   **B.**
ANGARIA war rights
ANGELIC seraphic; cherubic; heavenly
ANGELOT ancient lute; cheese   **Coin**
ANGELUS a prayer
ANGERED exasperated; enraged; roused
ANGERLY angrily; wrathfully
ANGEVIN of Anjou
ANGLICE in English
ANGLIFY to anglicize
ANGLING hopeful occupation
ANGLIST expert in English
ANGRILY wrathfully; irately
ANGUINE snake-like
ANGUISH agony; distress; rack; pang
ANGULAR sharp cornered
ANIGHTS at night
ANILINE indigo derivative   **Chem.**
ANILITY dotage; senility; imbecility
ANIMATE actuate; vivify; excite
ANIMISM⎱ religious theory that the
ANIMIST⎰ soul is the vital principle
ANISEED the seed of the anise   **B.**
ANNATES first fruits   **Eccl., Law.**
ANNATTO annotto; a reddish dye   **B.**
ANNELID worm   **Z.**

190

ANNEXED affixed; subjoined; attached
ANNOYED harassed; pestered; molested
ANNOYER an irritator; teaser
ANNUENT nodding
ANNUITY a yearly payment
ANNULAR ring-like
ANNULET small fillet round a column
ANODISE dyeing aluminium
ANODONT a fresh-water mussel   **Z.**
ANODYNE pain-killer; opiate; sedative
ANOMALY irregularity; eccentricity
ANOREXY lack of appetite   **Med.**
ANORMAL abnormal
ANOSMIA loss of smell power   **Med.**
ANOTHER
ANSATED with a handle
ANT-ACID a corrective   **Med.**
ANT-BEAR American ant-eater   **Z.**
ANTE-ACT an act preceding
ANTEFIX ornamental tiling
ANT-EGGS the pupae of ants   **Z.**
ANTENNA a feeler; (wireless)   **Z.**
ANT-HILL a formicary   **Z.**
ANTHOID flower-like   **B.**
ANTHONY saint; piglet   **Eccl.**
ANTHRAX wool-sorter's disease   **Med.**
ANTICLY oddly; fantastically; quaintly
ANTICOR animal disease
ANTICUM a front porch
ANTI-GAS
ANTIGEN cause of antibodies   **Med.**
ANTILOG anti-logarithm
ANTIQUE archaic; old; ancient
ANTI-RED anti-communist
ANT-LIKE industrious
ANT-LION a neuropterous insect   **Z.**
ANTONYM the opposite of a synonym
ANVILED forged; wrought by a smith
ANXIETY concern; disquiet; uneasiness
ANXIOUS troubled; apprehensive
ANYBODY
ANYWAYS anyhow
ANYWHEN any old time
ANYWISE somehow
APAGOGE ⎱ progressive argument
APAGOGY ⎰ reductio ad absurdum
APANAGE natural attribute; perquisite
APATITE lime phosphate   **Min.**
APAUMEE open hand (Her.)
APE-HOOD apishness
APELIKE imitative; simian
APELLES finished painter
APEPSIA poor digestion   **Med.**
APERTOR eye-opener; muscle   **Med.**
APHASIA temporary dumbness   **Med.**
APHELIA plural of aphelion
APHEMIA loss of speech   **Med.**
APHESIS ⎱ vowel elision
APHETIC ⎰

APHIDES plant-lice; ant-cows   **Z.**
APHONIA loss of voice   **Med.**
APHONIC speechless
APHORIA sterility   **Med.**
APHRITE carbonate of lime   **Min.**
APHTHAE ulceration of the mouth   **Med.**
APICIAN epicurean; gastronomic
APIECES in pieces (obs.)
APISHLY monkey-like
APITPAT palpitating
APOCOPE elision; verbal curtailment
APOGEAN culminating; climactic
APOLOGY excuse; explanation; plea
APOPLEX apoplexy (obs.)   **Med.**
APOSTIL marginal note; postscript
APOSTLE a divine messenge
APOTOME ⎱ mathematical difference
APOTOMY ⎰ a major semitone   **Mus.**
APPAREL equipment; attire; vesture
APPEACH impeach; censure (obs.)
APPEASE pacify; assuage; placate
APPERIL peril (Shak.)
APPLAUD praise; commend; extol
APPLIED referred; exercised; used
APPOINT nominate; prescribe; enjoin
APPOSED placed side by side
APPOSER an examiner; questioner
APPRISE inform; acquaint; warn
APPRIZE appreciate; appraise
APPROOF sanction; praise; trial
APPROVE ratify; assent; encourage
APPULSE rapprochement
APRICOT abricock   **B.**
APRICOT (brandy)
APRONED wearing an apron
APROPOS pertinent; opportune; timely
APSIDAL absidal; apse
APSIDES perigree and apogee
APTERAL wingless   **Z.**
APTERYX kiwi-bird (New Zealand)   **Z.**
APTHOUS (thrush); ulcerous   **Med.**
APTNESS suitability; felicity
APTOTIC indeclinable
APYREXY absence of fever   **Med.**
APYROUS unchanged by heat
AQUARIA (aquariums)   **Z.**
AQUATIC
AQUEOUS watery; humid; damp
AQUILON the north wind
ARABIAN
ARABINE gum arabic   **B.**
ARABISM Arab idiom
ARABIST Arabic expert
ARACHIS pea-nut genus   **B.**
ARAMAIC Syriac; Aramite
ARAMEAN Chaldaic
ARBITER umpire; judge; referee
ARBLAST crossbow
ARBORED arboured
ARBORET shrub   **B.**

ARBUTUS an evergreen **B.**
ARCADED
ARCADIA pastoral country
ARCADIA (Sir Philip Sidney)
ARCANUM a mystery; a secret
ARCHAIC Noachian; antiquated
ARCHERY a pastime
ARCHEUS vital principle in alchemy
ARCH-FOE Satan
ARCHING curved; vaulting
ARCHLET small arch
ARCHWAY
ARC-LAMP
ARCUATE bow-shaped
ARDENCY passion; warmth; fire
ARDUOUS laborious; toilsome
AREFIED withered; arid; parched
ARENOSE sandy; arenaceous
AREOLAR areolic; cell nucleus **B.**
ARGHOOL Arab reed pipe **Mus.**
ARGOTIC slangy
ARGUING discussing; debating
ARGYRIA silver poisoning **Med.**
ARICINA ⎫
ARICINE ⎭ alkaloid drug **Med.**
ARIDITY dryness; aridness; sterility
ARIETTA ariette; air **Mus.**
ARIGHTS correctly
ARILLED having a husk **B.**
ARILLUS seed coating **B.**
ARIPPLE aglinting
ARISING emerging; originating
ARMHOLE
ARMIGER an esquire; armour-bearer
ARMILLA antique bracelet
ARMLESS
ARMOIRE cupboard; aumbry
ARMORIC Breton dialect
ARMOURY arsenal; magazine
ARNOTTO annatto; orange dye **B.**
AROUSAL awakening; uprising
AROUSED excited; provoked
ARRAIGN accuse; summon **Law**
ARRANGE group; classify; dispose
ARRAYED marshalled; equipped
ARREARS payments overdue
ARRIDED pleased; gratified; scorned
ARRIERE rear; back; remote (Fr.)
ARRIVAL advent; coming; newcomer
ARRYISH festive; jovial
ARSENAL armoury; depository
ARSENIC a metallic element **Chem.**
ARTICLE essay; paper; indenture
ARTISAN artizan; workman; operative
ARTISTE a fine performer
ARTLESS simple; ingenuous; naive
ARTSMAN a craftsman
ARUSPEX soothsayer; seer; diviner
ASARONE form of camphor
ASBOLIN oil from soot

ASCARIS parasite worms **Z.**
ASCETIC austere; rigid; abstemious
ASCIANS equator dwellers
ASCIDIA molluscs **Z.**
ASCITES dropsy **Med.**
ASCITIC dropsical **Med.**
ASCRIBE attribute; assign; impute
ASEPSIS sterilization **Med.**
ASEPTIC sterilized
ASEXUAL agamic; sexless
ASHAMED abashed; confused
ASH-CAKE
ASH-FIRE
ASH-HEAP
ASH-HOLE
ASHIVER atremble
ASH-TRAY
ASH-WORT a weed **B.**
ASIARCH Asiatic Proconsul
ASIATIC
ASINEGO a dolt; asinico
ASININE ass-like; idiotic; obstinate
ASKANCE obliquely; aslant; awry
ASPERGE sprinkle
ASPERSE slander; vilify; traduce
ASPHALT bitumen **Min.**
ASPHYXY suffocation **Med.**
ASPIRED soared; aimed high; yearned
ASPIRER aspirant; competitor
ASPIRIN a drug **Med.**
ASPRAWL sprawling
ASPREAD scattered
ASPROUT sprouting
ASQUINT obliquely; askew
ASSAGAI assegai; spear
ASSAPAN flying squirrel (N.Amer.) **Z.**
ASSAULT onset; attack; storm; assail
ASSAYED tested; tried; endeavoured
ASSAYER metallurgist; analyst
ASSEGAI assegay; Zulu spear
ASSEVER asseverate; allege; aver
ASS-HEAD blockhead
ASSIEGE to besiege
ASSIZER inspector of weights
ASSIZES Courts of jurisdiction **Law**
ASSIZOR juror **Law**
ASSUAGE allay; pacify; mollify; quell
ASSUMED usurped; feigned; implied
ASSUMER an arrogant person
ASSURED pledged; guaranteed
ASSURER ⎱ underwriter **Law**
ASSUROR ⎰ insurer
ASSWAGE assuage (obs.)
ASTATIC unstable; lacking polarity
ASTEISM refined irony
ASTERIA (sapphire) **Min.**
ASTERID star-fish **Z.**
ASTHORE darling; acushla (Irish)
ASTONED astonished; confounded
ASTOUND amaze; daze; stupefy

ASTRAEA Goddess of Justice	**AUREOLA** aureole
ASTRAND stranded	**AUREOLE** golden halo
ASTRICT restrict; bind	**AURICLE** external ear **Med.**
ASTRIDE astraddle	**AURIFIC** gold bearing
ASTRITE star-stone **Min.**	**AURITED** having ears
ASTYLAR without columns	**AUROCHS** urus; wild ox; Eur. bison **Z.**
ASUDDEN suddenly	**AURORAL** (dawn); eoan
ASUNDER apart; divided; divergent	**AUSONIA** Italy
ATAGHAN Turkish dagger	**AUSPICE** augury; omen; portent
ATARAXY impassiveness; coolness	**AUSTERE** severely simple; ascetic
ATAVISM reversion to type	**AUSTRAL** southern
ATELENE amorphous; imperfect	**AUTARCH** autocrat; tyrant
ATELIER studio; sculptor's workshop	**AUTOBUS**
ATHALIA saw-fly **Z.**	**AUTOCAR**
ATHANOR alchemist's furnace	**AUTONYM** true name
ATHEISE atheize	**AUTOPSY** post-mortem exam. **Med.**
ATHEISM disbelief	**AUTO-VAC** (motoring)
ATHEIST a nullifidian	**AUXESIS** hyperbole
ATHIRST eager; dry; thirsty	**AUXETIC** amplifying
ATHLETE athleta; a contestant	**AVAILED** answered the purpose; helped
ATHRILL thrilling	**AVARICE** greed; rapacity; cupidity
ATHRONG crowded	**AVENAGE** barley-corn rent **Law**
ATHWART across; askew; aslant	**AVENGED** retaliated; revenged
ATOBOMB atomic bomb	**AVENGER** vindicator
ATOMISM atomic theory	**AVERAGE** mean; moderate; ordinary
ATOMIST atomic theorist	**AVERNUS** infernal regions
ATOMIZE vaporize	**AVERRED** affirmed; alleged; stated
ATONING expiating; reconciling	**AVERTED** warded off; prevented
ATROPAL not inverted; upturned **B.**	**AVERTER** preventer; diverter
ATROPHY wasting away **Med.**	**AVIATED** flew; planed
ATROPIA bella-donna **Med.**	**AVIATOR**
ATROPIN deadly nightshade **B.**	**AVIDITY** greed; voracity; eagerness
ATTABOY a panegyric (U.S.A.)	**AVIETTE** a glider
ATTACHE (embassy)	**AVIFORM** bird-shaped
ATTAGAS a pheasant **Z.**	**AVOCADO** alligator-pear **B.**
ATTAINT corrupt; convicted	**AVODIRE** African hard-wood **B.**
ATTEMPT try; aim; endeavour; effort	**AVOIDED** eschewed; annulled; eluded
ATTICAL classical	**AVOIDER** dodger; shunner
ATTINGE touch	**AVOWANT** defendant in replevin **Law**
ATTIRED garbed; dressed; arrayed	**AVOWING** owning; admitting; averring
ATTRACT draw; allure; charm; decoy	**AWAITED** eagerly expected; tarried
ATTRIST to sadden	**AWAKING** rousing; bestirring
ATTRITE worn by friction; penitent	**AWARDED** bestowed; granted; allotted
ATTUNED in harmony	**AWARDER** a judge; donor; giver **Law**
AUBERGE an inn (Fr.)	**AWAVING** fluttering
AUCTION roup; vendue	**AWELESS** without fear
AUDIBLE able to be heard	**AWESOME** full of awe; fearsome
AUDIBLY spoken clearly	**AWFULLY** dreadfully; portentously
AUDIENT listening; attentive	**AWKWARD** clumsy; ungainly; inapt
AUDITED examined; checked	**AWL-BIRD** woodpecker **Z.**
AUDITOR examiner; accountant	**AWL-WORT** an aquatic plant **B.**
AUGITIC (augite); (pyroxene) **Min.**	**AWNLESS** beardless **B.**
AUGMENT amplify; increase; enhance	**AXIALLY** from pole to pole
AUGURAL soothsaying; ominous	**AXIFORM** like a spindle or aborr
AUGURED portended; foretold	**AXILLAR** a feather **Z., B.**
AURALLY (ear)	**AXLE-BOX**
AURATED aureate; golden	**AXLE-PIN** linch-pin
AUREATE gilded	**AXOLOTL** larval salamander **Z.**
AUREITY the property of gold	**AZAROLE** medlar **B.**
AURELIA a chrysalis **Z.**	**AZILIAN** pre-Neolithic

AZIMUTH zenith
AZOTITE nitrous acid   **Chem.**
AZOTIZE to nitrogenise
AZOTOUS nitrous
AZTECAN Aztec
AZUREAN sky-blue
AZURINE azure
AZURITE copper carbonate   **Min.**
AZYGOUS not in pairs
AZYMITE Armenian churchman   **Eccl.**
AZYMOUS unleavened; unfermented

B

BAALISM idolatry
BAALITE worshipper of Baal
BABBLED chattered; jabbered
BABBLER tropical thrush   **Z.**
BABIISM Persian religion
BABYISH infantile
BABYISM infancy
BABYLON
BACCARA baccarat
BACCARE, BACKACHE stand back!
BACCATE berry-shaped; pulpy   **B.**
BACCHIC roistering; carousing
BACCHUS the god of Wine
BACILLI bacteria; microbes   **Med.**
BACKEND
BACKING aiding; abetting; retiring
BACK-LOG log at back of the fire
BACK-OUT reversal of missile drill
BACKSET an eddy
BACTRIS peach-palm   **B.**
BADDISH rather bad
BADIAGA small sponge
BADIANE bandian; aniseed   **B.**
BADNESS depravity; evil; wickedness
BAFFLED foiled; checked; bewildered
BAFFLER thwarter; confounder
BAGASSE refuse sugar stalks
BAGGAGE luggage; belongings; traps
BAGGING bag-cloth; pouching
BAGPIPE has 3 drones and a chanter
BAHADUR Indian title
BAILAGE ancient export duty
BAILIFF land steward; overseer   **Law**
BAILING confining; releasing
BAILLIE a bailiff (Sc.)
BAITING victuals; badgering; harassing
BALANCE poise; weigh; surplus
BALANUS crustacean; acorn-shell   **Z.**
BALCONY
BALDEST barest; plainest
BALDING loss of hair
BALDISH somewhat bald
BALDRIC baudric; shoulder-belt
BALEFUL evil; noxious; pernicious
BALISTA large Roman catapult
BALKING baulking; swerving; shying

BALLADE a form of poetry
BALLAST filling; discretion; stability
BALL-BOY (tennis)
BALLING becoming clogged
BALLIUM bulwark
BALLOON anything inflated and empty
BALMIER sweeter; milder
BALMILY soothingly; fragrantly
BALMING assuaging; embalming
BALNEUM a bath   **Chem.**
BALSAMY fragrant; aromatic
BAMBINO a child (It.)
BAMMING hoaxing; cheating
BANABAN micronesian language
BANBURY a cake
BANDAGE ligament; ligature
BANDANA silk handkerchief
BANDBOX
BANDEAU brow-band
BANDIAN badiane; aniseed   **B.**
BANDIED discussed; tossed; agitated
BANDING uniting together
BANDLET bandelet; a flat moulding
BANDORE ancient kind of lute   **Mus.**
BANDROL banderole; small flag
BAND-SAW   **Tool**
BANEFUL baleful; deadly; venomous
BANGING overwhelming; clattering
BANGLED with bangles
BANKING (aeroplane); relying
BANKSIA dwarf yellow climbing rose **B.**
BANNING cursing; proscribing; barring
BANNOCK oaten-cake
BANQUET feast; regalement
BANSHEE ghost (Irish)
BANTERY raillery
BANTING reducing the diet
BAPTISM immersion at christening **Eccl.**
BAPTIST
BAPTIZE christen
BARACAN camel-hair cloth
BARBARY a Saracen country
BARBATE bearded; awned   **B.**
BAR-BELL dumb-bell
BARBING shaving; trimming; piercing
BARBOLA modern gesso
BARBULE small beard   **B.**
BARDISH bardic; (poetry)
BARDISM the lore of bards
BARDLET bardling; poetaster
BARGAIN chaffer; haggle; compact
BARGING shoving; elbowing; jostling
BARILLA raw sea-weed alkali
BAR-IRON mallable iron in bars
BARK-BED tanner's hot-bed
BARKBUG   **Z.**
BARKERY tan-house
BARKING peeling; (shins)
BARK-PIT tan-vat
BARMAID Hebe; tavern server

BARMIER flightier more crazy	**BAUSOND** badger-like **Z.**
BARMKIN,BARNEKIN outer castle ward	**BAUXITE** (aluminium) **Min.**
BARNABY the apostle, Barnabas	**BAWCOCK** fine fellow
BARNAGH large whelk **Z.**	**BAWDILY** lewdly; obscenely
BARNING storing; garnering	**BAWDKIN** baldachin; canopy **Eccl.**
BARN-OWL screech owl **Z.**	**BAWLING** shouting; clamouring
BARONET bart	**BAYONET** a weapon of offence
BAROQUE rococo; whimsical; odd	**BAY-SALT** evaporated sea-water
BARRACE lists (tournament)	**BAY-TREE** the laurel **B.**
BARRACK (booing)	**BAYWOOD** mahogany **B.**
BARRAGE embankment; dam	**BAY-YARN** woollen yarn
BARRAGE (artillery fire)	**BAZOOKA** anti-tank gun
BARRENS elevated plateaux	**BEACHED** on the beach
BARRICO small keg (Sp.)	**BEADING** narrow moulding
BARRIER hindrance; embargo; obstacle	**BEADMAN** an almsman
BARRING excluding; banning	**BEAKING** (cock-fighting)
BARRULY Heraldic division	**BEAMILY** broad on the beam
BAR-SHOE special horseshoe	**BEAMING** radiant; gleaming; bright
BAR-SHOT double connected shot	**BEAN-FLY** a garden pest **Z.**
BARTRAM the plant pellitory **B.**	**BEARDED** awned; defied; opposed
BARWOOD red dye-wood **B.**	**BEARDIE** the whitethroat bird **Z.**
BARYTES barium sulphate **Chem.**	**BEARING** (magnetic); (rein)
BARYTIC (baryta)	**BEARISH** uncouth; boorish; rude
BASBLEU blue stocking	**BEAR-PIT**
BASCULE balanced drawbridge	**BEASTLY** brutal; sensual; bestial
BASENET bascinet; basnet; a helmet	**BEATIFY** (saint-hood); canonize
BASENJI Congo barkless dog **Z.**	**BEATING** chastisement; battering
BASHFUL strikingly modest; shy	**BEAUISH** foppish
BASHING coshing; slugging	**BEBEERU** greenheart tree **B.**
BASHLYK Russian hood	**BECAUSE** owing to
BASILAR serving as a basis	**BECHARM** captivate; fascinate
BASILIC basilican style	**BECKING** nodding; bowing
BASINED in a basin	**BECLOUD** obscure; darken; bedim
BASINET basnet; round helmet	**BEDDING** planting out
BASKING luxuriating; revelling	**BEDEAUX** piece-work system
BASLARD a small dagger	**BEDELRY** beadlery
BASSOCK fibre mat	**BEDEMAN** beadman
BASSOON bass oboe **Mus.**	**BEDEVIL** bewitch
BASTARD spurious; base-born; natural	**BEDEWED** covered with dew; affused
BASTILE castle on wheels	**BEDEWER** a sprinkler
BASTING coarse stitching	**BEDFAST** bed-ridden
BASTION an out-work	**BED-GOWN** night gown
BATABLE debatable; controversial	**BEDIGHT** adorned
BATATAS sweet potatoes **B.**	**BEDIZEN** gaudily attired
BAT-BOAT sea-plane	**BED-MATE** bed-fellow
BATEFUL contentious; disputable	**BEDOUIN** nomadic Arab
BATHBUN a comestible	**BED-POST**
BATHING	**BED-REST**
BATHMAN	**BED-ROCK**
BATH-MAT	**BEDROOM** sleeping apartment
BATISTE cambric	**BEDROPT** besprinkled; bedewed
BATSMAN a cricketer	**BEDSIDE** clinic
BATTELS provisions (Oxford)	**BED-SORE** **Med.**
BATTERY (artillery); (electrical)	**BED-TICK** cotton cloth
BATTING quilting; (cricket)	**BEDTIME**
BATTISH bat-like	**BEDWARD** to bed
BATTLED battlemented; fought	**BEDWARF** to belittle; to dwarf
BATTLER resident at Oxford	**BEDWORK** easy toil
BAUDRIC shoulder sash	**BEE-BIRD** fly-catcher **Z.**
BAULKED shied; balked; jibbed	**BEECHEN** of beech

BEEF-TEA
BEE-GLUE beeswax
BEE-HIVE
BEE-LINE straight line
BEE-MOTH wax-moth   Z.
BEESWAX
BEET-BUG agricultural pest   Z.
BEET-FLY a dipterous insect   Z.
BEETLED jutted out; smote
BEE-TREE American linden   B.
BEFFANA befana; Epiphany fairy
BEGGARY mendicancy; indigence
BEGGING soliciting; craving; imploring
BEGHARD beguine; religious order Eccl.
BEGLOOM sadden
BEGONIA elephant's ear plant   B.
BEGORED gory; ensanguined
BEGRIME (grime); sully; foul
BEGROAN lament; complain
BEGUARD a beghard; lay mendicant
BEGUILE pass pleasantly; amuse
BEGUILE deceive; delude; trick
BEGUILE soothe (obs.)
BEGUINE beghard; (religious order)
BEHAVED acted with propriety
BEHONEY sweeten
BEHOOVE to be necessary
BEHOVED was necessary; befitted
BEINKED smudged
BEJEWEL set with gems
BEKNAVE to call a knave
BEKNOWN known
BELACED adorned with lace
BELATED over-due; retarded
BELAYED fastened; held   Naut.
BELCHED eructated
BELCHER coloured kerchief
BELDAME old hag
BELEPER infect with leprosy
BELGARD kind regard (obs.)
BELGIAN
BELIBEL libel; traduce; slander
BELIEVE credit; opine; accept
BELL-HOP page boy
BELLIED dilated
BELLING full and ripe; bellowing
BELL-MAN town crier
BELLONA goddess of War
BELLOWS (organ); wind producer
BELOVED dear; darling
BELTANE May Day fire festival
BELTING beating; a belt
BELYING calumniating; counterfeiting
BEMAZED astounded; stupefied; dazed
BEMIRED soiled; besmirched
BEMOUTH to mouth; declaim
BEMUSED dazed; bewildered; confused
BENCHED seated
BENCHER (inns of court)   Law
BENDING curving; flexing; inclining

BENDLET small Heraldic bend
BENEATH inferior; subordinate; under
BENEFIT boon; profit; gain; enrich
BENELUX Belgium, Netherlands and
BENGALI of Bengal   [Luxemburg
BENIGHT obscure; cloud
BENISON benediction
BENOTED amply annotated
BENTEAK Nana-wood   B.
BENTHOS ocean-bed organisms   Z.
BENZENE benzine   Chem.
BENZOIN resinous incense   B.
BENZOLE tar product   Chem.
BENZOYL benzoic acid   Chem.
BEPAINT paint; daub; smear
BEPATCH patch; cobble; mend
BEPEARL adorn with pearls
BEPINCH marked with pinches
BEPLUME feather
BEPROSE discuss tediously
BEQUEST legacy; inheritance
BEQUOTE quote frequently
BERATED scolded; nagged; chided
BEREAVE deprive; divest; despoil
BERGYLT red sea-fish   Z.
BERHYME to lampoon in verse
BERLINE berlin; a vehicle
BERRIED
BERSERK Norse warrior; in a fury
BERTHED moored; situated   Naut.
BERTHON collapsible boat   Naut.
BERTRAM bastard pellitory   B.
BESAINT beatify; canonize   Eccl.
BESAYLE great-grandfather   Law
BESEECH implore; entreat; crave
BESHAME put to shame
BESHINE light up; illuminate
BESHMET grape pulp
BESHONE sparkled; glittered
BESHREW curse; execrate
BESIDES except; save; moreover
BESIEGE beset; invest; beleaguer
BESLAVE enthral; enslave
BESLIME to soil; besmirch; defile
BESMEAR to daub; dirty; begrime
BESMOKE blacken with smoke
BESNUFF foul with snuff
BESOGNO besonio; a beggar; Besonian
BESPATE spit upon
BESPEAK stipulate; betoken; order
BESPEED help along
BESPICE to season; to drug
BESPIRT to asperse; sprinkle
BESPOKE ordered
BESPOUT orate; declaim; harangue
BESPURT besputter
BESTAIN mark with spots
BESTEAD avail; help; relieve
BESTIAL brutal; live-stock (Sc.)
BESTICK to stick; prick

BESTILL to quiet	**BILLOWY** roughish
BESTING worsting; winning	**BILOBED** doubled-lobed
BEST-MAN groomsman	**BILTONG** dried meat (S.Africa)
BESTORM assail	**BIMANAL** two-handed
BESTREW scatter; spread	**BINDERY** bookbinding
BESTRID stepped across	**BINDING** obligatory; a fillet
BESTUCK transfixed	**BINDWEB** (nervous system) **Med.**
BETAINE beet alkaloid **Chem.**	**BINNING** (wine)
BETAKEN departed; applied	**BINOCLE** double-telescope
BETHANK thank effusively	**BIOGENY** life origin science
BETHINK recall to mind	**BIOLOGY** science of life
BETHRAL enslave; captivate	**BIONICS** living electronic systems **Med.**
BETHUMB crease	**BIOTAXY**⎫ grouping of **Z.**
BETHUMP belabour; pommel	**BIOTICS**⎬ organisms
BETIDED happened; befell	**BIOTINE** (alumina) **Min.**
BETIMES early; soon	**BIOTITE** magnesia mica **Min.**
BETITLE give a name to	**BIOTOPE** uniform habitat
BETOKEN indicate; foreshow	**BIOTYPE** uniform genetic make-up
BETREAD step on	**BIPEDAL** having two feet
BETROTH affiance; plight	**BIPLANE** (aeroplane)
BETTING wagering; staking	**BIPOLAR** with two poles
BETTONG kangaroo rat **Z.**	**BIRCHED** flogged
BETUTOR instruct	**BIRCHEN** of birch
BETWEEN amid	**BIRDEYE** bird's-eye
BETWIXT amidst	**BIRDING** snaring
BEWARED took care; heeded; minded	**BIRDMAN** fowler
BEWITCH fascinate; enchant; charm	**BIRETTA** clerical cap **Eccl.**
BEZIQUE card game	**BIRLING** whirling; spinning
BHISTEE water-carrier (India)	**BIRLINN** Gaelic barge
BIASING prejudicing; influencing	**BISCUIT**
BIAXIAL with two axes	**BISMITE** bismuth-ochre **Min.**
BIBASIC **Chem.**	**BISMUTH** a metal **Chem.**
BIBBING tippling	**BISSEXT** (leap year)
BIBELOT small work of art	**BISTORT** snake-weed **B.**
BIBLIST a faithful one	**BITLESS** no bit
BICHORD doubly strung **Mus.**	**BITTERN** also bittour **Z.**
BICKERN pointed anvil **Tool**	**BITTERN** brine
BICOLOR	**BITTERS** spirituous liquor
BICYCLE bike	**BITTING** (horse)
BIDDERY metal alloy	**BITTOCK** small bit
BIDDING enjoining; directing	**BITTOUR** the bittern **Z.**
BIFFINS dried apples	**BITUMED** bituminous
BIFIDLY cleft	**BITUMEN** asphalt; pitch **Min.**
BIFILAR double-threaded	**BIVALVE** a mollusc **Z.**
BIFOCAL (spectacles)	**BIVIOUS** two ways
BIFROST Rainbow Bridge (Norse)	**BIVOUAC** tentless camp
BIGENER cross-breed	**BIZARRE** fantastic; whimsical; strange
BIGGEST largest; greatest	**BIZONAL** under dual control
BIGGISH somewhat massive	**BLABBED** babbled; told; revealed
BIG-HORN wild sheep **Z.**	**BLABBER** sneak; tell-tale; prattler
BIGNESS of a size; bulkiness	**BLACKED** inked; obscured
BIGOTED dogmatic; intolerant	**BLACKEN** darken; defame; decry
BIGOTRY zealotry; fanaticism	**BLACKER** darker; more sullen
BILBOES bars and shackles	**BLACKEY** a negro
BILGING pumping **Naut.**	**BLACKLY** sombrely
BILIARY, BILIOUS (bile) **Med.**	**BLADDER** **Med.**
BILKING defrauding; eluding	**BLADING** fitting a blade to
BILLING love-making	**BLAMING** censuring; reproaching
BILLION a large number	**BLANDLY** mildly; benignly; affably
BILL-MAN hedger; pruning hook	**BLANKET** the mullein **B.**

BLANKLY vacantly
BLARING strident
BLARNEY whimsical flattery
BLASTED withered; blighted; ruined
BLASTER froth-blower; golf
BLATANT obtrusively vulgar
BLATHER⎫ also blether,
BLATTER⎰ to babble
BLAWORT hare-bell **B.**
BLAZING flaming; proclaiming
BLEAKER more exposed; barer
BLEAKLY cheerlessly; drearily
BLEATED
BLEMISH defect
BLENDED mingled; blent; mixed
BLENDER a mixer
BLESBOK S.African antelope **Z.**
BLESSED extolled; glorified; adored
BLETHER blather
BLETTED decayed
BLEWART the germander speedwell **B.**
BLEWITS mushrooms **B.**
BLIGHTY England (soldiers' slang)
BLINDED shuttered; deceived
BLINDER more obtuse; a blinker
BLINDLY ignorantly; heedlessly
BLINKED twinkled; flickered; connived
BLISTER protective hull **Naut.**
BLOATED swollen; distended
BLOATER smoked herring **Z.**
BLOBBER blubber **Z.**
BLOCKED obstructed; stopped; jammed
BLOMARY a forge
BLONDIN tight-rope walker
BLOODED (fox-hunting)
BLOOMED flowered; blossomed; throve
BLOOMER an error
BLOSSOM bloom; bud; flower **B.**
BLOTCHY patchy; smeary
BLOTING drying by smoke
BLOTTED stained; sullied
BLOTTER a blotting pad
BLOWFLY blue-bottle **Z.**
BLOW-GUN blow-pipe
BLOWING puffing; disclosing
BLOW-OUT a spread; banquet
BLOWZED frowsy
BLUBBER wail; (whale)
BLUCHER a booting
BLUE-CAP tit-mouse; a Scot (Shak.) **Z.**
BLUE-CAT Siberian cat **Z.**
BLUE-EYE honey-eater bird **Z.**
BLUE-GUM eucalyptus **B.**
BLUEING a metal finish; expending
BLUE-JAY North American jay **Z.**
BLUFFED concealed; spoofed
BLUFFER a deceiver
BLUFFLY bluntly; frankly; openly
BLUNDER gross mistake; howler
BLUNGER clay-mixer

BLUNTED took the edge off; dulled
BLUNTER more outspoken
BLUNTLY stolidly; obtusely
BLURRED dimmed; obscured
BLURTED uttered abruptly
BLUSHED flushed; coloured
BLUSHET a damsel
BLUSTER turbulence; swagger; storm
BOARDED lodged; embarked **Naut.**
BOARDER paying guest
BOARISH swinish; brutal
BOASTED vaunted; bragged; blustered
BOASTER a broad chisel **Tool**
BOAT-CAR canal trolley
BOAT-FLY water-boatman **Z.**
BOATFUL ship-load
BOATING an aquatic pastime
BOATMAN a rower; an oarsman
BOBADIL a swaggering captain
BOBBERY rampageous
BOBBING cheating; curtseying
BOBBING (winter sports); angling
BOBBISH hearty; energetic; uppish
BOB-SLED bob-sleigh
BOB-STAY bowsprit stay **Naut.**
BOBTAIL rabble; caudal abbreviation
BOCKING red herring **Z.**
BOCLAND feudal freehold **Law**
BODEFUL ominous
BOG-BEAN marsh plant **B.**
BOGGARD⎫ bugbear; scarecrow
BOGGART⎰ hobgoblin; spectre
BOGGLED hesitated; vacillated
BOGGLER a waverer; demurrer; doubter
BOG-LAND fen; marsh; swamp
BOG-MOSS sphagnum **B.**
BOG-RUSH a sedge **B.**
BOGYISM dreadfulness
BOILING enraged; seething
BOLDEST bravest; most valiant
BOLETIC fungoid extract **B.**
BOLETUS fungus genus **B.**
BOLIVAR Venezuelan currency unit
BOLLARD mooring post **Naut.**
BOLLING a pollard; a lopped tree **B.**
BOLOGNA Polony sausage
BOLONEY phoney palaver
BOLSTER to support; prop; pillow
BOLTING sifting; swallowing
BOMBARD to attack with artillery
BOMBAST fustian; rodomontade
BOMBING blitzing
BONANZA stroke of luck
BONASUS bison or wild ox **Z.**
BONDAGE captivity; thraldom; helotry
BONDING (customs); (bricklaying)
BONDMAN villein; peon
BONE-ACE card game
BONE-ASH
BONE-BED strata with fossils

BONETTA tunny fish **Z.**
BONFIRE a beacon
BONNILY handsomely
BOOKFUL theoretical
BOOKING reserving; buying
BOOKISH studious
BOOKLET brochure; pamphlet
BOOKMAN scholar
BOOMING in demand; resounding
BOOMKIN short boom **Naut.**
BOONDER Rhesus monkey **Z.**
BOORISH mannerless; clumsy; lubberly
BOOSING tippling; bousing
BOOSTED advertised; eulogized
BOOSTER electrical device
BOOTIED laden with booty
BOOTING foot-wear; sacking
BOOT-LEG rum-runner
BOOZING boosing; toping
BORACIC a boron derivative **Chem.**
BORDAGE feudal tenure
BORDMAN feudal tenant
BORDURE Heraldic border
BOREDOM ennui; tedium; dulness
BORNITE erubiscite; copper ore **Min.**
BOROUGH electoral division
BORSTAL a reformatory
BOSCAGE undergrowth
BOSHBOK bush-buck **Z.**
BOSOMED embraced
BOSQUET an arbour
BOSSAGE (projecting stones)
BOSSING controlling
BOSSISM political dictatorship
BOSWELL a biographer
BOTANIC botanical; floral
BOTARGO special sausage
BOTCHED bungled; patched
BOTCHER incompetent worker
BOTTINE small boot
BOTTLED inebriated
BOTTLER
BOTTONY Heraldic cross
BOUCHET a pear **B.**
BOUDOIR a lady's private room
BOUILLI boiled meat
BOULDER bowlder; a large rock
BOULIMY morbid appetite **Med.**
BOULTER fishing line
BOULTIN convex moulding
BOUNCED rebounded; bluffed
BOUNCER chucker-out; bad cheque
BOUNDED sprang; limited; bordered
BOUNDEN obligatory
BOUNDER inconsiderate ass
BOUQUET nosegay **B.**
BOURBON Kentucky corn whisky
BOURDON bass stop **Mus.**
BOURDON mule; pilgrim's staff **Z.**
BOURLAW local jurisprudence

BOW-BACK crooked; hog-back
BOW-BENT bent as a bow
BOW-HAND left hand (archery)
BOWLDER a boulder
BOWLESS no bow
BOWLINE a rope **Naut.**
BOWLING (bowls); (cricket); trundling
BOW-SHOT about 80 yards
BOX-CALF tanned calfskin
BOX-COAT heavy coat
BOXHAUL a luffing turn **Naut.**
BOX-IRON
BOX-KITE
BOX-TREE **B.**
BOX-WOOD
BOYCOTT ostracize
BOYHOOD puerility
BRABBLE squabble; a quarrel; broil
BRACCIA plural of braccio
BRACCIO Italian cubit **Meas.**
BRACING fortifying; invigorating **Naut.**
BRACKEN brake-fern **B.**
BRACKET brace; corbel; a support
BRACTED (irregular leaf) **B.**
BRADAWL **Tool**
BRAGGED boasted; blustered
BRAHMAN } Hindu priest **Eccl.**
BRAHMIN }
BRAIDED plaited; embroidered
BRAILED trussed **Naut.**
BRAILLE raised letters
BRAINED brainy; bashed
BRAISED stewed
BRAKING retarding
BRAMBLE brier-bush **B.**
BRAMBLY thorny; prickly
BRANCHY spreading; ramifying
BRANDED marked; disgraced
BRANDLE waver; shake
BRANGLE wrangle; a brawl
BRANLIN striped worm **Z.**
BRAN-NEW brand-new
BRANTLE a dance
BRASIER } brass-worker;
BRAZIER } charcoal pan
BRASERO }
BRA-SLIP women's combination garment
BRASSET casque or helmet
BRASSIE a golf club
BRASSIE small fish **Z.**
BRATTLE clatter
BRAVADO arrogant bluster
BRAVELY gallantly; daringly
BRAVERY valour; heroism
BRAVEST most courageous
BRAVING defying; daring
BRAVOES hired assassins
BRAVURA florid **Mus.**
BRAWLED wrangled; quarrelled
BRAWLER rowdy ruffian

BRAWNER boar-meat **Z.**
BRAYING clamour; pounding
BRAZIER brasier
BRAZING soldering
BREACHY unruly
BREADTH broadness; beaminess
BREAKER small water cask
BREAKER wave; (ice)
BREAK-IN interruption; burglary
BREAK-UP disrupt; disillusion
BREAMED cleaned of barnacles **Naut.**
BREATHE respire; exhale; express
BRECCIA conglomèrate **Min.**
BREEDER begetter; sire
BREVIER a size of type
BREVITY terseness; conciseness
BREWAGE a brew
BREWERY brewhouse
BREWING plotting; hatching
BRIABOT angler-fish **Z.**
BRIBERY palm-oil; graft
BRIBING suborning
BRIBRIS Costa Rican Indian
BRICKED blocked completely
BRICKLE brittle
BRICOLE rebound; bounce
BRIDGED spanned; traversed
BRIDLED curbed; checked
BRIDLER controller
BRIDOON snaffle bit
BRIEFED instructed **Law**
BRIEFER shorter; more concise
BRIEFLY curtly; pithily; in short
BRIERED set with briars
BRIGADE
BRIGAND bandit; outlaw; freebooter
BRIMFUL almost over-flowing
BRIMMED edged
BRIMMER a hat; a full glass
BRINDLE streaky-brown
BRINING salting
BRINISH salty; brackish
BRINJAL egg-plant (Indian) **B.**
BRIOCHE light cake (Fr.)
BRISKER sharper; quicker; sprier
BRISKET breast
BRISKLY vivaciously
BRISTLE a stiff hair
BRISTLY rough and prickly
BRISTOL (glass); (china)
BRISURE rampart deviation
BRITISH
BRITTLE easily broken; fragile
BRITZKA, BRITSKA Polish carriage
BROADEN enlarge; extend; amplify
BROADER wider; more liberal
BROADLY tolerantly; spaciously
BROCADE woven silk
BROCAGE brokerage; brokery
BROCARD maxim or canon
BROCKED black and white

BROCKET young red deer **Z.**
BRODKIN a buskin; brodekin
BROIDER embroider
BROILED grilled
BROILER grid-iron; brawler
BROKAGE brokerage
BROKERY brokerage
BROKING bargaining; negotiating
BROMATE a salt of bromic acid **Chem.**
BROMIDE a sedative **Chem.**
BROMINE a liquid element **Chem.**
BROMISM condition after overdose **Med.**
BROMIZE (photography)
BROMOIL oil pigment prints **Photo.**
BRONCHO unbroken horse **Z.**
BRONZED tanned
BROODED cherished; meditated
BROOKED allowed; enjoyed; endured
BROOMED swept
BROTHEL bawdy-house
BROTHER kinsman; comrade; friar
BROUGHT conducted; led; fetched
BROWNED bronzed; tanned
BROWNER more sunburnt
BROWNIE elf; young guide
BROWSED pastured; grazed
BRUCHUS pea-beetle **Z.**
BRUCINE nux vomica **B.**
BRUCITE hydrate of magnesia **Chem.**
BRUISED injured; contused; pounded
BRUISER a boxer
BRUITED rumoured; noised abroad
BRULZIE broil; quarrel
BRUMMER large fly (S. Africa) **Z.**
BRUMOUS foggy; wintry
BRUNION nectarine **B.**
BRUSHED swept; grazed
BRUSQUE abrupt; gruff; blunt
BRUSTLE rustle; bully
BRUTIFY brutalize
BRUTISH bestial; savage
BRUTISM animalism
BRYOZOA incrustations **Z.**
BUBALIS antelope genus **Z.**
BUBALUS buffalo **Z.**
BUBBLED gurgled; burbled
BUBBLER a cheat
BUBONIC plague **Med.**
BUCEROS rhinoceros horn-bill **Z.**
BUCKEEN Irish squireen
BUCKEYE horse-chestnut **B.**
BUCKING boasting; soaking
BUCKISH foppish; gay; dashing
BUCKLED bent; fastened
BUCKLER round shield
BUCKRAM stiffened cloth
BUCKSAW frame-saw **Tool**
BUCOLIC Arcadian; pastoral; rural
BUDDING germinating; blossoming
BUDGERO Bengal boat **Naut.**

200

BUDGING shifting; stirring
BUDLESS barren; sterile **B.**
BUFFALO **Z.**
BUFFING polishing
BUFFOON a merry-andrew; jester
BUGBEAR bugaboo; hobgoblin; bogey
BUGLOSS borage **B.**
BUGWORT a plant **B.**
BUILDED built; erected; raised
BUILDER constructor
BUILD-UP favourable publicity
BUILT-UP urban area
BUIRDLY stalwart; burly (Sc.)
BUKSHEE paymaster (Indian)
BULBING bulging
BULBOUS bulb-shaped **B.**
BULBULE small bulb
BULCHIN bull-calf **Z.**
BULGING protuberant; distended
BULIMTA insatiable appetite **Med.**
BULKIER more massive
BULKING looming large; blending
BULLACE wild-plum **B.**
BULLARY (papal bulls)
BULLATE blistered
BULL-BAT night-hawk **Z.**
BULL-BEE stag-beetle **Z.**
BULL-DOG college police **Z.**
BULL-FLY gadfly **Z.**
BULLIED blustered; hazed; (hockey)
BULLIES browbeaters; hectors
BULLING boosting
BULLION uncoined metal
BULLISH obstinate; mulish
BULLOCK steer **Z.**
BULL-PUP **Z.**
BULRUSH the reed-mace **B.**
BULWARK ship's side
BUMBAZE bamboozle
BUMBOAT provision boat **Naut.**
BUMMALO Bombay duck (dried fish)
BUMMING humming
BUMMOCK ale
BUMPING thumping; jarring; knocking
BUMPKIN short boom; rustic; swain
BUNCHED clustered; concentrated
BUNDLED wrapped
BUNGLED failed; mismanaged
BUNGLER muff; botcher
BUNKAGE coaling charge **Naut.**
BUNKING decamping; bolting
BUNTING bird; fabric **Z.**
BUOYAGE placing buoys **Naut.**
BUOYANT light; floating
BUOYING sustaining
BUPHAGA beef-eater bird **Z.**
BURDASH fringed sash
BURDOCK dock with prickly head **B.**
BURETTE graduated glass tube; phial
BURGAGE tenure in socage

BURGEON to bud; germinate
BURGESS borough freeman
BURGHAL of a borough
BURGHER inhabitant
BURGLAR house-breaker; cracksman
BURGLED stole at night
BURKING smothering; concealing
BURLACE a variety of grape **B**
BURLIER more robust; sturdier
BURLING removing knots
BURMESE (Burma)
BURNING vehement; ardent; fervent
BURNISH polish; furbish; brighten
BURNOUS Arab attire
BUR-REED a plant **B.**
BURRHEL wild sheep of Tibet **Z.**
BURRING raising a ridge
BURROCK small weir
BURSARY treasury
BURTHEN burden
BUR-WEED a plant **B.**
BURYING burial; concealing; sepulture
BUSH-CAT the serval **Z.**
BUSHIDO Japanese code of chivalry
BUSHING detachable lining
BUSHMAN
BUSH-TIT long tailed titmouse **Z.**
BUSKING cruising; preparing
BUSSING kissing heartily
BUS-STOP here by request
BUSTARD a bird **Z.**
BUSTLED hastened; fussed
BUSTLER booster; hustler
BUSY-BEE socially active person
BUSYING meddling; interfering
BUTCHER murder; slay; slaughter
BUTLERY pantry
BUTMENT an abutment
BUTT-END fag-end
BUTTERY store-room
BUTTING ramming; abutting
BUTTOCK stern
BUTTONS a page; tansy **B.**
BUTTONY adorned with buttons
BUTYRIC rancid **Chem.**
BUXEOUS (box-tree) **B.**
BUXOMLY gaily; pliably; blithely
BUYABLE on sale
BUZZARD rapacious bird **Z.**
BUZZING
BUZZ-SAW circular saw **Tool**
BY-AND-BY presently
BYE-ROAD secondary road
BY-GOING passing by
BYNEMPT by name
BYOUSLY outlandishly
BY-PLACE a quiet spot
BYRONIC cynical
BYSSINE of flax
BYSSOID fringed

BY-THING a minor detail
BYWONER squatter (S. Africa)

C

CABARET tavern; inn; wine-shop
CABARET variety entertainment
CABBAGE to purloin **B.**
CABBALA rabbinic mysticism
CABBLED fragmented
CABEIRI deities of Semitic origin
CABESSE Indian silk
CAB-FARE
CABINED confined; cribbed
CABINET chamber; ministry
CABINET a show case
CABIRIC (nature worship)
CABLING telegraphing
CABOOSE ship's galley **Naut.**
CAB-RANK
CA'CANNY work in slow time
CACHEXY morbid state **Med.**
CACIQUE cazique; Mexican chieftain
CACKLED clacked
CACKLER a noisy fowl **Z.**
CACODYL oily compound **Chem.**
CACOEPY false pronunciation
CACOLET mule-chair
CADAVER corpse; dead body **Med.**
CADDICE caddis-worm **Z.**
CADDISH on the boundary line
CADENAS condiment casket
CADENCE modulated flow; tone
CADENCY regularity of movement
CADENUS Dean Swift
CADENZA a flourish **Mus.**
CADGING hawking; sponging; sorning
CADMEAN (Cadmus)
CADMIUM a metal **Chem.**
CADRANS (jewel cutting) **Tool**
CAESIUM a metal **Chem.**
CAESURA poetic pause
CAFENET Turkish inn
CAFFEIC (coffee)
CAFFEIN vegetable alkaloid **Med.**
CAINITE (Cain); a Gnostic
CAISSON tumbril; (engineering)
CAITIFF knave; miscreant; churl
CAJEPUT cajuput; oil yielding tree **B.**
CAJOLED coaxed; inveigled
CAJOLER a wheedler; beguiler
CAJUPUT pungent oil **B.**
CALABER squirrel-fur
CALAMAR cuttle-fish **Z.**
CALAMUS dragon's blood palm **B.**
CALAMUS antique pen
CALANDO diminuendo **Mus.**
CALCIFY petrifaction
CALCINE pulverize by heat
CALCITE calc-spar **Min.**
CALCIUM a metallic element **Chem.**

CALCULI gall-stones **Med.**
CALDRON cauldron; boiler; kettle
CALECHE a vehicle; calash (Fr.)
CALENDS first of month
CALIBAN a tempestuous monster
CALIBER } diameter of bore; gauge
CALIBRE } capacity; faculty; talent
CALICHE sodium nitrate **Chem.**
CALICLE small cup **B.**
CALIPEE turtle fat
CALIPER measuring instrument **Tool**
CALIVER a musket
CALKING stopping seams **Naut.**
CALLANT a lad (Sc.)
CALL-BOY prompter's attendant
CALLING vocation; profession; trade
CALLOUS insensitive; hard; obdurate
CALLUNA heather **B.**
CALMANT a sedative **Med.**
CALMING tranquillizing
CALMUCK Kalmuck; Mongolian
CALOMEL mercuric chloride **Med.**
CALORIC heating
CALORIE unit of heat **Meas.**
CALOTTE skull-cap
CALOYER Greek monk **Eccl.**
CALPACK felt cap (Turk)
CALTRAP } spiked obstacle for use
CALTROP } against cavalry
CALUMBA climbing plant **B.**
CALUMET Indian peace-pipe
CALUMNY slander; aspersion; obloquy
CALVARY the place of skulls **Eccl.**
CALVING bringing forth
CALYCLE coral-polype **Z.**
CALYPSO sea nymph; (Odysseus) **B.**
CAMAIEU cameo; a monochrome
CAMBISM art of exchange
CAMBIST banker; financier
CAMBIUM cellular tissue
CAMBLET camel-hair cloth
CAMBOGE gamboge **B.**
CAMBREL meat-hook
CAMBRIC white linen
CAMBUCA pastoral staff **Eccl.**
CAMELOT King Arthur's Court
CAMELRY camel corps
CAMORRA secret society (It.)
CAMPANA an anemone **B.**
CAMPHOR aromatic laurel **B.**
CAMPING encamping; struggling
CAMPION plant **B.**
CAMWOOD a red wood **B.**
CANAKIN small can
CANASTA two-pack card game
CAN-BUOY conical buoy
CANDELA luminous intensity **Meas.**
CANDENT incandescent; glowing
CANDIED sugary
CANDIFY preserve in sugar

CANDOCK yellow water-lily **B.**	**CARAWAY** seed; plant; spice **B.**
CANDOUR frankness; openness	**CARBIDE** carburet **Chem.**
CANELLA West Indian tree **B.**	**CARBINE** short rifle
CANHOOK cask-hook	**CARCAKE** pancake
CANKERY cankered	**CARCASE** body; bomb; framework
CANNERY factory	**CARCASS** a fire-work; shell arch
CANNIER more pawky (Sc.)	**CARDECU** French quarter-crown **Coin**
CANNING preserving; tinning	**CARDIAC** (heart); cordial **Med.**
CANNULA surgical tube **Med.**	**CARDING** combing flax
CANONIC canonical **Eccl.**	**CARDOON** artichoke **B.**
CANONRY canon's benefice **Eccl.**	**CARDUUS** thistle genus **B.**
CANOPIC (Canopic case)	**CAREFUL** meticulous; heedful; wary
CANOPUS star in Argo	**CARGOES** argosies
CANTATA narrative poem **Mus.**	**CARIAMA** bird of prey **Z.**
CANTEEN cooking tin	**CARIBOU** Arctic reindeer (N. Amer.) **Z.**
CANTHUS corner of the eye **Med.**	**CARIOLE** light cart
CANTING hypocritical; sanctimonious	**CARIOUS** decayed
CANTION a song (Spens.)	**CARKING** anxious
CANTLET fragment; cantle; a cutting	**CARLINE** a witch; thistle genus **B.**
CANTOON cotton material	**CARLISM** (Don Carlos)
CANTRED hundred; county division	**CARLIST** Spanish Royalist
CANTRIP a witch's spell	**CARLOCK** isinglass
CANVASS discuss; lobby	**CARMINE** a pigment
CANZONE song or melody **Mus.**	**CARNAGE** slaughter; butchery
CAPABLE efficient; able	**CARNIFY** turn to flesh
CAPABLY competently; skilfully	**CARNOSE, CARNOUS** fleshy, meat-
CAP-A-PIE from head to foot	like
CAP-CASE travelling case	**CAROCHE** coach (Fr.)
CAPELIN small smelt **Z.**	**CAROLUS** sovereign of Charles I **Coin**
CAPERED frolicked; frisked; bounded	**CAROSSE** sheepskin or fur rug (S.A.)
CAPERER a dancer	**CAROTID** arterial **Med.**
CAPITAL money; main; excellent	**CAROTIN** carrot pigment,vitamin **Med.**
CAPITAN Turkish naval officer	**CAROUSE** revel; feast; tipple
CAPITOL Roman temple	**CAR PARK** parking area
CAPOTED won all tricks at piquet	**CARPING** captious; cavilling; objecting
CAPOUCH monk's cowl **Eccl.**	**CARPORT** open garage
CAPPING topping; (hunt subscription)	**CARRACK** armed trading ship
CAPRATE a salt **Chem.**	**CARRIED** borne; upheld; transported
CAPRICE whim; vagary; humour	**CARRIER** transporter; conveyor
CAPRINE like a goat	**CARRION** putrid meat
CAPROIC goatish	**CARROTY** rufous
CAPRONE flavouring oil	**CARTAGE** conveyance
CAPSIZE upset; overturn	**CARTING** transporting
CAPSTAN windlass **Naut.**	**CARTOON** topical sketch
CAPSULA seed-vessel; a cap **B.**	**CARVING** slicing; cutting; engraving
CAPSULE soluble envelope **Med.**	**CARVIST** hawk on hand **Z.**
CAPTAIN leader; chief; master **Naut.**	**CARYOTA** fish-tail palms **B.**
CAPTION certificate; title; arrest	**CASCADE** waterfall; collar
CAPTIVE prisoner	**CASCARA** a laxative **Med.**
CAPTURE take; apprehend; catch	**CASEATE** (cheese) **Chem.**
CAPUCHE a Capuchin's hood **Eccl.**	**CASE-LAW** (a precedent) **Law**
CAPULET father of Romeo's Juliet	**CASEMAN** compositor
CAPULIN Mexican cherry **B.**	**CASEOUS** like cheese
CARACAL Persian lynx **Z.**	**CASHIER** discharge with ignominy
CARACOL spiral shell; an evolution	**CASHING** (cheques)
CARACUL Bukhara Sheep **Z.**	**CASSADA** tapioca **B.**
CARAMEL a sweetmeat; caromel	**CASSAVA** tapioca **B.**
CARANNA aromatic resin (Amazon) **B.**	**CASSINO** casino, card game
CARAVAN house on wheels	**CASSIUS** (purple)
CARAVEL four-masted ship **Naut.**	**CASSOCK** a vestment **Eccl.**
	CASSONE bridal chest (It.)

CASTING rejecting; pitching
CASTLED (chess)
CASTLET small castle
CAST-OFF laid aside
CASTRAL (camp)
CASUIST a quibbler; sophist
CATALAN Catalonian
CATALLO hybrid, buffalo and cow **Z.**
CATALOG university calendar (U.S.A.)
CATALPA Shawnee-wood **B.**
CATAPAN Byzantine governor
CATARRH (inflammation) **Med.**
CATASTA slave-block
CATAWBA Ohio grape **B.**
CAT-BIRD American thrush **Z.**
CAT-BOAT boat with mast in bow
CAT-CALL derisive yell
CATCHER (base-ball)
CATCHES songs; (fish)
CATCHUP ketchup sauce
CATECHU an astringent **Med.**
CATERAN freebooter (Sc.)
CATERED provided with food, etc.
CATERER purveyor
CAT-EYED (night vision)
CAT-FALL anchor rope **Naut.**
CAT-FISH wolf-fish; nurse-hound **Z.**
CATHEAD anchor rest
CATHECT to direct feelings **Psych.**
CATHODE negative electrode
CAT-HOLE hawser hole **Naut.**
CATHOOD c.f. spinsterhood
CATLIKE feline; pussy
CATLING small cat; cat-gut **Z.**
CAT-MINT a species of Nepeta **B.**
CAT-SALT rough salt
CAT'S-EYE a quartz **Min.**
CAT'S-PAW a dupe; a ripple
CATTALO hybrid; buffalo and cow **Z.**
CATTISH spiteful
CATWALK narrow plank bridge **Naut.**
CATWHIN needle-gorse **B.**
CAUDATE with a tail
CAULINE stalky **B.**
CAULKED rendered watertight
CAULKER a dram; a whopper
CAUSING resulting in; occasioning
CAUSTIC corrosive; mordant
CAUTERY a searer **Med.**
CAUTION care; heed; warning
CAVALRY horse-soldiers
CAVEMAN a troglodyte
CAVETTO hollow moulding
CAVIARE sturgeon's roe **Z.**
CAYENNE red pepper **B.**
CAZIQUE cacique; West Ind. chief
CEASING desisting; ending; stopping
CEBIDAE class of monkeys **Z.**
CEDARED lots of cedars
CEDILLA " c " like " s "

CEDRATE the citron **B.**
CEDRELA a tropical cedar **B.**
CEDRINE (cedar)
CEILING (aeroplane height)
CELADON green porcelain
CELLIST violoncellist **Mus.**
CELLULE small cell
CELSIUS (centigrade thermometer)
CEMBALO Italian stringed instrument
CENACLE supper-room
CENSING burning incense
CENSION assessment
CENSUAL (census)
CENSURE blame; rebuke; chide
CENTAGE percentage
CENTAUR mythological horse-man
CENTAVO Portuguese half-penny **Coin**
CENTIME hundredth part of a franc
CENTNER foreign cwt. **Meas.**
CENTRAL mediate; middlemost
CENTRED concentrated
CENTRIC central
CENTURY centenary; hundred
CERAMIC (pottery)
CERASIN plum-gum **B.**
CERATED waxed
CEREALS breakfast food
CEREOUS, CERESIN wax
CEROTIC beeswax extract
CERTAIN assured; infallible; undeniable
CERTIFY avouch; attest; witness
CERULIN indigo
CERUMEN ear-wax **Med.**
CERUSED white-leaded
CERVINE (stags)
CESIOUS bluish-grey
CESSING taxing
CESSION relinquishment; surrender
CESS-PIT midden
CESTOID tape-worm **Med.**
CETACEA whales, etc. **Z.**
CHABLIS white wine
CHABOUK Eastern whip
CHACONE slow dance **Mus.**
CHAFERY welding furnace
CHAFFED bantered; scoffed; derided
CHAFFER haggle; bargain
CHAFING fretting; fuming; rubbing
CHAGRIN vexation; irritation
CHAINED fettered; measured
CHAIRED carried in triumph
CHALAZA the base of an ovule **B.**
CHALDEE Chaldean
CHALDER 96 bushels **Meas.**
CHALICE communion cup; goblet **Eccl.**
CHALKED scored; recorded
CHALLIS fine silk
CHALONE an internal secretion **Med.**
CHAMADE invitation to a parley
CHAMBER room; closet; hall; cavity

CHAMFER	groove; polish	
CHAMLET	camlet; camel-hair	
CHAMOIS	leather	**Z.**
CHAMPAC	Indian tree; champak	**B.**
CHAMPED	crunched; chewed; bit	
CHANCED	happened; befell; risked	
CHANCEL		**Eccl.**
CHANGED	altered; varied; shifted	
CHANGER	exchanger; shifter	
CHANNEL	canal; duct; strait; gutter	
CHANSON	song (Fr.)	**Mus.**
CHANTED	(horse-coping); intoned	
CHANTER	a precentor	**Eccl.**
CHANTER	(bagpipes)	**Mus.**
CHANTRY	chapel for mass	**Eccl.**
CHAOTIC	confused; disordered	
CHAPEAU	a hat (Fr.)	
CHAPLET	garland; wreath; coronal	
CHAPMAN	pedlar; hawker	
CHAPNET }	pewter salt-cellar	
CHAPNUT }		
CHAPPED	seamed; cleft; cracked	
CHAPPIE	ghost (Sc.)	
CHAPTER	a decretal epistle	**Eccl.**
CHARACT	a character (Shak.)	
CHARADE	dramatic enigma	
CHARGED	loaded; accused	
CHARGER	platter; warhorse	**Z.**
CHARILY	stingily; warily; reluctantly	
CHARING	drudgery	
CHARIOT	state carriage	
CHARISM	miraculous power	
CHARITY	benevolence; alms	
CHARLEY	night-watchman	
CHARLIE	pointed beard	
CHARMED	enchanted; fascinated	
CHARMER	a syren	
CHARNEL	mortuary	
CHARPIE	lint	**Med.**
CHARPOY	Indian bedstead	
CHARQUI	dried beef (Peru)	
CHARRED	scorched; seared; burnt	
CHARTED	tabulated; recorded	**Naut.**
CHARTER	right; privilege; hire	
CHASING	engraving; pursuing; hunting	
CHASSIS	frame-work	
CHASTEN	correct; punish; humble	
CHATEAU	country seat	
CHATTAH	Indian umbrella	
CHATTED	gossiped; prattled	
CHATTEL	movable property	**Law**
CHATTER	talk; prate; tattle	
CHAUVIN	French patriot	
CHAWING	chewing; munching	
CHEAPEN	belittle; depreciate	
CHEAPER	not so dear	
CHEAPLY	inexpensively	
CHEATED	bobbed; duped; gulled	
CHEATER	trickster; swindler	
CHECHIA	Arab skull-cap	

CHECKED	restrained; hindered; verified	
CHECKER	chess board; to variegate	
CHEDDAR	a cheese	
CHEEKED	sauced; was impertinent	
CHEEPED	chirped	
CHEEPER	young game bird	**Z.**
CHEERED	applauded; enlivened	
CHEERER	vociferous supporter	
CHEERIO	convivial salutation	
CHEETAH	hunting leopard	**Z.**
CHELATE	(claw)	**Z.**
CHELONE	tortoise; shell flower	**B., Z.**
CHELSEA	china	
CHEMISE	shift; smock; slip	
CHEMISM	chemical action	**Chem.**
CHEMIST	chymist; pharmacist; druggist	
CHEMOSH	a Moabite god	
CHENILE	fluffy cord	
CHEQUER	checker; diversify	
CHERISH	to foster; harbour; treasure	
CHERMES	kermes; a crimson dye	
CHEROOT	Burmese or Manila cigar	
CHERVIL	culinary herb	**B.**
CHESNUT	a hoary jest	**B.**
CHESSEL	a cheese mould or vat	
CHESTED	boxed	
CHESTON	a species of plum	**B.**
CHETNIK	Yugoslav guerrilla	
CHEVIED	chased; pursued; hunted	
CHEVIOT	sheep bred on the Cheviots	**Z.**
CHEVRON	zig-zag badge	
CHEWING	chawing; munching	
CHIANTI	Italian red wine	
CHIASMA	nerve intersection	**Med.**
CHIBOUK	Turkish pipe	
CHICANE	trick; artifice; (cards)	
CHICKED	sprouted; vegetated	
CHICKEN	a child	**Z.**
CHICORY	(often mixed with coffee)	**B.**
CHIDDEN	reproved; censured; rebuked	
CHIDING	rating; scolding; blaming	
CHIEFLY	principally; mainly; mostly	
CHIEFRY	rent; chief's lands	
CHIFFON	gauzy material	
CHIFFRE	denoting harmony (Fr.)	**Mus.**
CHIGGER	chigoe; West Indian flea	**Z.**
CHIGNON	a coiffure	
CHIKARA	an Indian antelope	**Z.**
CHIKARA	Indian guitar	**Mus.**
CHILDED	having a child (Shak.)	
CHILDLY	childishly	
CHILEAN	Chilian; native of Chile	
CHILIAD	a thousand years	
CHILLED	discouraged; depressed	
CHILLER	an iceberg or wet blanket	
CHILLUM	hookah	
CHILOMA	camel's lip	**Z.**
CHIMERA	mythical monster; illusion	**Z.**
CHIMERE	bishop's robe	**Eccl.**
CHIMNEY	funnel; smoke-stack	

CHINCHA S. American rodent	**Z.**	
CHINDIT Burmese guerilla		
CHINESE Sinesian		
CHINGLE shingle; gravel	**Min.**	
CHINING cutting the backbone		
CHINKED jingled; clinked		
CHINOOK N. American Indian tribe		
CHINSED caulked		
CHINTHE Burmese leogriff		
CHINWAG chatty conversation		
CHIPAXE light axe	**Tool**	
CHIP-HAT hat made of palm leaves		
CHIPPED chaffed; chopped		
CHIPPER lively; twitter		
CHIRPED— bird song; grasshopper		
— clicking		
CHIRRED— also **CHURRED**		
CHIRPER grasshopper	**Z.**	
CHIRRUP bird noise		
CHISLEU a Jewish month		
CHISLEY gravelly		
CHITTER shiver with cold		
CHITWAH panda; red bear-cat	**Z.**	
CHLORAL a narcotic	**Med.**	
CHLORIC chlorine derivative	**Chem.**	
CHLORID chloride	**Chem.**	
CHOBDAR servant to a rajah		
CHOCTAW (skating); a tribe		
CHOIRED in chorus	**Mus.**	
CHOKING stifling; strangling		
CHOLEIC (bile)	**Med.**	
CHOLERA deadly infectious disease	**Med.**	
CHOLINE B vitamin; organic base	**Med.**	
CHOLTRY caravanserai; Eastern inn		
CHOOSER a picker; a selector		
CHOPINE clog or patten		
CHOPPED cut; minced; changed		
CHOPPER cleaver	**Tool**	
CHORALE choral composition	**Mus.**	
CHORDED strung	**Mus.**	
CHOREUS a trochee		
CHORION a membrane	**B.**	
CHORIST chorister	**Eccl.**	
CHOROID eye-membrane	**Med.**	
CHORTLE chuckle noisily; exult		
CHOWDER dish of clams		
CHOWTER grumble; croak		
CHRISOM baptismal cloth	**Eccl.**	
CHROMIC	**Chem.**	
CHRONIC long continuing; inveterate		
CHUCKED pitched; tossed; thrown		
CHUCKIE a chicken	**Z.**	
CHUCKLE exult; crow		
CHUDDAH chudder; cloak or cloth (Ind.)		
CHUKKUR chukka; period of play (polo)		
CHUMMED roomed together		
CHUPATI unleavened bread (Ind.)		
CHURCHY pious; ritualistic	**Eccl.**	
CHURNED agitated; jostled; upset		
CHURRED see chirmed		
CHURRUS Indian resin	**B.** 206	

CHUTNEE chutney	**B.**	
CHYAZIC (hydro-cyanic)	**Chem.**	
CHYMIFY to digest	**Chem.**	
CHYMIST chemist; pharmacist		
CIBORIA canopies	**Eccl.**	
CICHLID Tanganyika fish	**Z.**	
CICONIA storks	**Z.**	
CIDARIS sea-urchins	**Z.**	
CILIARY (eyelashes)	**Med.**	
CILIATE with hairs		
CIMBRIC a language		
CIMELIA stored treasures		
CIMETER scimitar		
CINDERY full of cinders; ashy		
CINEREA nerve tissue	**Med.**	
CIPOLIN green marble	**Min.**	
CIRCEAN fatefully fascinating		
CIRCLED went round		
CIRCLER circlet; small ring		
CIRCLET an orb; a ring		
CIRCUIT tour; revolution; journey		
CIRRATE curly		
CIRROSE ⎱ with tendrils;	**B.**	
CIRROUS ⎰ with curls		
CISSOID geometric curve		
CISTERN wine-cooler		
CITABLE quotable		
CITADEL keep; stronghold; fortress		
CITATOR a summoner	**Law**	
CITHARA Greek lyre	**Mus.**	
CITHERN guitar	**Mus.**	
CITIZEN burgher; burgess; resident		
CITRATE lemon salts	**Chem.**	
CITRENE oil of lemons		
CITRINE a yellow		
CITTERN cithern; zither	**Mus.**	
CIVILLY courteously; politely		
CIVVIES mufti		
CLABBER thicken		
CLACHAN small village (Sc.)		
CLACKED clucked; clicked; jabbered		
CLACKER clack-valve		
CLADODE leaflike branch	**B.**	
CLAIMED demanded; insisted; usurped		
CLAIMER claimant; appellant		
CLAMANT crying; insistent		
CLAMBER climb; scramble		
CLAMMED clogged; smeared		
CLAMOUR din; uproar; hubbub		
CLAMPED clumped; held down		
CLAMPER iron patch		
CLANGED clashed; pranged		
CLANKED clinked; clanged		
CLAP-NET bird fowler's net		
CLAPPED applauded; shut		
CLAPPER tongue of a bell		
CLAQUER claqueur; hired applauder		
CLARAIN fine coal		
CLARIFY make clear; strain; purify		
CLARION a shrill trumpet	**Mus.**	

CLARITY clearness; distinctness
CLARKIA a flowering annual **B.**
CLASHED clattered; opposed
CLASPED grasped; gripped
CLASPER tendril; embracer **B.**
CLASSED ranked; grouped; ranged
CLASSIC first rate; standard; masterly
CLASSIS assembly or convention **Eccl.**
CLASTIC fragmental; brittle
CLATTER clash; rattle; crash
CLAUGHT to snatch; catch (Sc.)
CLAVATE club-shaped
CLAVIER keyboard **Mus.**
CLAWING scratching; fawning
CLAYING puddling; purifying
CLAYISH clay-like
CLAY-PIT marl-pit
CLEANED purified; washed; scoured
CLEANER dirt remover
CLEANLY spotlessly; adroitly
CLEANSE clear; purge; elutriate
CLEAN-UP a purge; cartoon technique
CLEARED acquitted; absolved
CLEARER more obvious; less opaque
CLEARLY distinctly; patently
CLEAVED split; parted; adhered
CLEAVER butcher's chopper
CLEDDYO Celtic sword
CLEMENT merciful; lenient; mild
CLEMENT (Pope)
CLEMMED starved; hungered
CLEPING naming (obs.)
CLERISY the clergy **Eccl.**
CLERKLY learnedly; scholarly
CLEWING coiling; securing **Naut.**
CLICKED found favour; ticked
CLICKER cobbler; compositor
CLICKET knocker; door-latch
CLIMATE clime; weather
CLIMBED scaled; swarmed; ascended
CLIMBER a creeper; mountaineer **B.**
CLINKED clanked; jingled
CLINKER slag; (ship design)
CLINOID like a bed
CLIPPED shorn; pared; snipped; docked
CLIPPER schooner; cutter; trimmer
CLIPPIE bus-conductress **[Naut.**
CLITTER clatter
CLIVERS goose-grass **B.**
CLIVITY slope; incline
CLOAKED disguised; concealed; hidden
CLOBBER clothing; cobbler's paste
CLOCKED timed; clucked
CLOCKER time-keeper; a hen **Z.**
CLODDED clotted; mired
CLOGGED congested; coalesced
CLOGGER clog-maker
CLOISON partition (Fr.)
CLOOTIE cloven hoof; the Devil
CLOSELY intimately; accurately

CLOSEST nearest; densest
CLOSE-UP (movies)
CLOSING conclusion; sealing; clogging
CLOSURE also cloture; enclosure
CLOT-BUR the burdock **B.**
CLOTHED attired; arrayed; draped
CLOTHES apparel
CLOTTED curdled
CLOTTER to coagulate
CLOTURE closure; conclusion
CLOUDED obscured; blended; dimmed
CLOUTED patched; buffeted
CLOVATE inverse taper
CLOWNED played the fool
CLUBBED coshed; bludgeoned
CLUBBER clubbist; club member
CLUB-LAW might is right
CLUB-MAN
CLUCKED clocked; cackled
CLUMBER a spaniel **Z.**
CLUMPED in clusters; mustered
CLUMPER to form clumps
CLUNIAC Benedictine monk **Eccl.**
CLUSTER bunch; clump; assembly
CLUTTER confused mass
CLYPEAL like a shield; scutate
CLYPEUS insect's forehead **Z.**
CLYSMIC cleansing
CLYSTER an injection **Med.**
COACHED tutored; trained
COACHEE a coachman
COACTED compelled; concentrated
COAGENT an associate; colleague
COAKING dowelling
COAL-BED
COAL-BOX
COAL-GAS
COALING **Naut.**
COALISE form a coalition
COALITE a form of fuel
COALMAN
COAL-PIT mine
COAL-TAR
COAL-TIT a passerine bird **Z.**
COAMING raised border **Naut.**
CO-ANNEX join jointly
COARSEN roughen
COARSER cruder; rougher; ruder
COASTAL littoral
COASTED free-wheeled **Naut.**
COASTER decanter stand
COASTER small ship **Naut.**
COATING layer; covering
CO-AXIAL
COAXING cajoling; wheedling
COBBING pulling the ears
COBBLED mended; tinkered; patched
COBBLER boot-maker; botcher
COBIRON andiron; firedog
COBLOAF crusty loaf

COB-SWAN male swan **Z.**
COB-WALL mud-wall
COBWORK log-house construction **Arch.**
COCAINE drug **Med.**
COCALON large cocoon **Z.**
COCHLEA ear-cavity **Med.**
COCINIC cocoa extract **Chem.**
COCKADE hat badge
COCKEYE imperfect vision; a squint
COCKING strutting; (trigger)
COCKLED puckered; wrinkled
COCKLER cockle merchant
COCKNEY true Londoner
COCKPIT
COCK-SHY a target; Aunt Sally
COCO-NUT cocoa-nut **B.**
COCOTTE light o' love (Fr.)
COCTILE baked
COCTION digestion; cooking
CODDING hoaxing
CODDLED pampered; simmered
CODEINE an alkaloid from opium **B.**
CODFISH **Z.**
CODICES manuscript books
CODICIL supplement to a will **Law**
CODILLA coarse hemp **B.**
CODILLE card-term at ombre
CODLING young cod **Z.**
GODLING codlin apple **B.**
COELEBS bachelor
COELIAC abdominal **Med.**
COENURE young tape-worm **Z.**
COEQUAL a peer; a compeer
COERCED concussed; compelled
COEXIST be coeval
COGENCE convincing power; force
COGENCY urgency; potency
COGGERY trickery
COGGING cheating
COGNATE related; allied; akin; sib
COGNIZE to be aware of; recognize
COG-WOOD a Jamaican tree **B.**
COHABIT live together
COHERED adhered; cleaved; coalesced
COHERER (wireless)
COHIBIT restrain; hinder; prevent
COIFFED (hair-dressing)
COIGNED billeted (Irish)
COILING entangling; winding up
COINAGE money; specie
COINING minting; counterfeiting
COJUROR witness to credibility **Law**
COLA-NUT the kola-nut **B.**
COLDEST iciest; frostiest
COLDISH chillsome
COLD-PIG cold douche
COLIBRI species of humming-bird **Z.**
COLICKY with pains
COLITIS colic; colonic infection **Med.**
COLLAGE real objects on art forms **B.**

COLLARD cole-wort
COLLATE collect and compare
COLLAUD unite in praising
COLLECT a prayer; assemble; amass
COLLEEN Irish girl
COLLEGE academy; seminary; guild
COLLIDE crash; encounter; clash
COLLIED begrimed; coal-black (Shak.)
COLLIER miner; vessel **Naut.**
COLLING embracing; necking
COLLOID gelatinous
COLLUDE act in collusion; connive
COLOBUS a monkey genus **Z.**
COLONEL highest regimental rank
COLOSSI gigantic statues
COLOURS (army); (awards)
COLOURY coloured
COLTISH frisky
COLUBER a snake genus **Z.**
COLUMBA holy vessel; (Iona) **Eccl.**
COLUMEL a small column
COMBINE unite; blend; coalesce
COMBING breaking into foam
COMBUST Astrological term
COMETIC (comets)
COMFORT console; solace; ease; cheer
COMFREY a plant **B.**
COMICAL droll; diverting; farcical
COMITIA assemblies
COMMAND govern; rule; enjoin; decree
COMMARK a frontier
COMMEND laud; praise; eulogize
COMMENT remark; note; criticize
COMMERE a gossip
COMMODE chest of drawers
COMMONS food; fare; provisions
COMMOVE agitate
COMMUNE converse; discourse
COMMUTE exchange; replace; barter
COMPACT united; a treaty; close
COMPANY party; group; society
COMPARE liken; assimilate
COMPART to divide
COMPASS to encircle; scope; limit **Naut.**
COMPEAR appear in court (Sc.) **Law**
COMPEER equal; comrade; associate
COMPEND compendium; epitome
COMPERE the leader of a troupe
COMPETE strive; emulate; rival
COMPILE combine; arrange; amass
COMPLEX intricate; complicated
COMPLEX mental inhibition
COMPLIN evening service **Eccl.**
COMPLOT conspiracy
COMPORT behave; agree; tally
COMPOSE create; calm; pacify
COMPOST a mixture
COMPOTE dish; fruit (Fr.)
COMPTER counter (obs.)
COMPUTE reckon; count; rate

COMRADE pal; mate; associate
COMTISM Positivism
COMTIST disciple of Comte
CONACRE sublet (Irish)
CONATUS volition; effort; impulse
CONCAVE hollow; scooped
CONCEAL cloak; disguise; screen
CONCEDE yield; allow; grant
CONCEIT vanity; egotism; notion
CONCENT harmony; concord of sounds
CONCEPT general notion; fancy
CONCERN trouble; regard; firm
CONCERT devise; concoct   **Mus.**
CONCISE terse; pithy; laconic
CONCOCT plot; hatch; brew
CONCORD harmony; amity; union
CONCREW to concrete (obs.)
CONCUPY a concubine (Shak.)
CONCUSS coerce; overawe; agitate
CONDEMN doom; convict; blame
CONDIGN deserved; merited
CONDING navigating   **Naut.**
CONDITE to pickle; to preserve
CONDOLE console; sympathize
CONDONE pardon; overlook; forgive
CONDUCE lead to; tend; promote
CONDUCT guide; escort; deportment
CONDUIT passage; pipe; channel
CONDYLE knuckle   **Med.**
CONEINE coniine; hemlock   **B.**
CONFECT a sweetmeat; to prepare
CONFESS admit; own; disclose; avow
CONFEST confessed
CONFIDE rely; trust; depend
CONFINE limit; boundary; restrain
CONFIRM ratify; endorse; establish
CONFLUX confluence; a crowd
CONFORM comply; tally; adapt
CONFUSE confound; derange; perplex
CONFUTE disprove; refute
CONGEAL coagulate; benumb
CONGEED took leave
CONGEST to swell; accumulate
CONGREE to agree (obs.)
CONGRUE congree; agree; harmonize
CONGRUE to accord (obs.)
CONICAL conic; tapering
CONIFER pine; fir; etc.   **B.**
CONIINE conine; hemlock   **B.**
CONJECT conjecture; guess (obs.)
CONJOIN unite; link; fasten
CONJURE invoke; juggle
CONJURY conjuring; legerdemain
CONNATE congenital; innate; inherent
CONNECT couple; conjoin; hyphenate
CONNING steering; studying   **Naut.**
CONNIVE permit; wink at; abet
CONNOTE imply a sequence
CONQUER overpower; vanquish
CONSENT concur; agree; assent

CONSIGN despatch; send; transmit
CONSIST subsist; make up of
CONSOLE comfort; pier table
CONSOLS funds
CONSORT compeer; fraternize
CONSTAT certificate of a record
CONSULT deliberate; confer
CONSUME devour; waste; expend
CONSUTE like stitching
CONTACT touch; juncture; taction
CONTAIN include; embody; comprise
CONTEMN despise; disregard; scorn
CONTEND strive; cope; vie; argue
CONTENT volume; satisfy; mollify
CONTEST struggle; contend; dispute
CONTEXT texture; firm; extract
CONTORT writhe; distort; twist
CONTOUR outline; height line; profile
CONTROL direct; sway; mastery
CONTUND contuse; bruise
CONTUSE bruise; crush
CONVENE assemble; muster; summon
CONVENT a nunnery   **Eccl**
CONVERT change; alter; transform
CONVICT sentence; felon; lag
CONVIVE boon companion; a guest
CONVOKE convene; gather; summon
COOKERY cuisine
COOKING concocting; manipulating
COOLEST most impudent
COOLING moderating
COOLISH somewhat cool
COONCAN card game
COONTIE arrowroot   **B.**
COOPERY barrel production
COOPING confining; penning
CO-OPTED elected
COPEPOD minute water organism   **Z.**
COPAIBA copaiva; balsam   **B.**
CO-PILOT
COPIOUS abundant; plenteous; ample
OOPLAND angular piece of land
COPPERY like copper
COPPICE spinney
COPPING catching; arresting
COPULAR linking
COPYCAT apeing others' ideas
COPYING aping; transcribing
COPYISM copyist's work
COPYIST plagiarist; imitator
COQUITO honey-palm   **B.**
CORACLE Ancient British boat
CORANTO dance; news-letter
CORBEAU raven-black
CORBEIL sculptured basket
CORCASS Irish salt marsh
CORCULE an embryo   **B.**
CORDAGE rope
CORDATE heart-shaped   **B.**
CORDIAL cocktail; hearty; ardent

CORDING cordage; binding
CORDITE a propellant
CORINTH a currant   **B.**
CO-RIVAL competitor
CORKAGE an imposition at hotels
CORKING stopping
CORK-LEG artificial limb
CORNAGE (land tenure)
CORN-COB spike of maize   **B.**
CORNEAL (eye-membrane)   **Med.**
CORN-FLY destructive insect   **Z.**
CORNICE ledge; a top moulding
CORNINE quinine type   **B.**
CORNING preserving; granulating
CORNISH (Cornwall)
CORNIST cornet blower   **Mus.**
CORN-LAW   **Law**
CORN-RIG strip of growing corn
CORNUAL horny
CORNUTE horny
CORN-VAN winnowing machine
COROLLA floral whorl   **B.**
CORONAL circlet; wreath
CORONER an inquirer   **Law**
CORONET a moth; tiara   **Z.**
CORONIS elision; contraction
CORRECT O.K.; exact; precise; true
CORRODE gnaw; rust; canker
CORRODY allowance; pension
CORRUPT putrid; depraved; bribe
CORSAGE part of a dress
CORSAIR pirate; pirate ship   **Naut.**
CORSITE diorite   **Min.**
CORSLET sleeveless armour
CORSNED an ordeal
CORTEGE procession
CORTILE courtyard
CORUBIN aluminium oxide   **Chem.**
CORVINE like a crow
CORYDON a rustic lover
CORYLUS hazel   **B.**
CORYPHA fan-palm   **B.**
COSAQUE cracker; bon-bon (Fr.)
COSHERY billeting (Irish)
COSHING bashing; slugging
COSIEST snuggest; coziest
COSMISM a philosophy
COSMIST a secularist
COSSACK Russian cavalryman
COSTARD apple   **B.**
COSTATE ribbed
COSTEAN (prospecting)
COSTING accounting
COSTIVE obstructive; constipated
COSTREL pilgrim's bottle
COSTUME dress; uniform; livery
COTERIE social circle
COT-FOLK cottars (Sc.)
COTHURN buskin
COTIDAL contemporaneous tides

COTINGA chattering birds   **Z.**
COTLAND cottage land
COTTAGE cot; lodge; hut
COTTICE heraldic barrulet
COTTIER Irish tenant
COTTOID fish genus; miller's thumb **Z.**
COTTONY downy; nappy
COT-TOWN town of cottages
COUCHED expressed; reclined
COUCHEE soirée; evening reception (Fr.)
COUCHER a cataract removed   **Med.**
COUGHED
COUGHER one having a tussis
COULDST (could)
COULEUR colour
COULOIR dredge; mountain cleft
COULOMB electrical unit of quantity
COULTER fore-end of plough
COUNCIL ministry; assembly; diet
COUNSEL advice; barrister   **Law**
COUNTED reckoned; relied; numbered
COUNTER contrary; adverse; opposed
COUNTRY region; nation; state
COUPLED paired; bracketed; joined
COUPLER connector
COUPLET two lines; a pair
COURAGE pluck; valour; heroism
COURANT a disseminator
COURIER messenger; runner; dragoman
COURLAN S. American crane   **Z.**
COURSED hunted; pursued; chased
COURSER war-horse; plover   **Z.**
COURSES some sails   **Naut.**
COURTED wooed; invited; solicited
COURTER a wooer; swain
COURTLY elegant; urbane; debonair
COUTEAU long knife
COUTHIE kindly; friendly (Sc.)
COUVADE a curious custom
COVELET small bay
COVERED enveloped; veiled; spread
COVERTS certain feathers   **Z.**
COVER-UP boxing
COVETED longed for; desired
COW-BANE water-hemlock   **B.**
COW-BIRD American cuckoo   **Z.**
COW-CALF female calf   **Z.**
COWERED cringed; shrank; crouched
COWHAGE a bean (Hind.)
COW-HEEL ox-foot stewed to a jelly
COWHERD a cow tender
COWHIDE leather
COW-ITCH cowhage   **B.**
COWLICK a lock of hair
COWLIKE ruminant; placid
COWLING hood; (aeroplane)
COWSLIP paigle   **B.**
COW-TREE moraceous tree   **B.**
COW-WEED   **B.**
COXCOMB conceited fellow; dandy

COYNESS shyness; bashfulness
COZENED deceived; gulled
COZENER white collar bandit
CRABBED morose; surly; disparaged
CRABITE fossil crab
CRAB-OIL carap-oil **B.**
CRACKED crazy; snapped; split; broke
CRACKER cosaque; biscuit; firework
CRACKLE glazed fissures in china
CRACK-UP breakdown; crash **Psych.**
CRACOWE pointed shoe
CRADLED nurtured
CRAGGED rugged; jagged
CRAKING cawing
CRAMBUS grass moth **Z.**
CRAMESY crimson
CRAMMED stuffed; studied
CRAMMER intensive teacher
CRAMPED confined; cabined
CRAMPON mountaineering spike
CRANAGE crane dues
CRANIAL (skull)
CRANING stretching the neck
CRANIUM a skull **Med.**
CRANKED bent; turned; wound
CRANKLE crinkle; wrinkle; a turn
CRANNOG lake dwelling
CRAPING curling
CRAPNEL grapnel; hook
CRASHED smashed; shattered; fell
CRASHER uninvited guest
CRATING boxing; encasing
CRAUNCH crunch; gnaw
CRAVING longing; yearning; desiring
CRAWLED crept; (swimming)
CRAWLER a reptile; a baby's overall
CRAZIER madder; insaner
CRAZILY daftly; distractedly
CRAZING weakening; breaking **Arch.**
CREAKED grated
CREAMED mantled; foamed
CREANCE hawk-leash line
CREASED folded; wrinkled; rugate
CREATED originated; produced
CREATIN muscular constituent **Med.**
CREATOR maker; originator; inventor
CREDENT credulous; trusting
CREEING softening grain
CREEPER crawler; ski-aid; cricket
CREEPIE a cutty-stool (Sc.)
CREMATE reduce to ashes; incinerate
CREMONA a violin **Mus.**
CRENATE notched **B.**
CRENAUX loop-holes
CREOSOL (phenol) **Chem.**
CREPANE wound due to brushing
CRESSET beacon; torch
CRESTED surmounted
CRETIFY impregnate with lime
CRETISM a falsehood

CRETOSE chalky
CREVICE fissure; rift; breach
CREWELS embroidery
CRIBBED confined; plagiarized
CRIBBLE coarse sieve; a temse
CRICKED sprained
CRICKET a low stool; an insect **Z.**
CRICOID ring-shaped
CRIMINE⎱ an interjection
CRIMINI⎰ of surprise
CRIMING charging; accusing
CRIMPED plaited; shanghied
CRIMPER corrugating machine
CRIMPLE shrink; curl
CRIMSON cramesy
CRINGED cowered; fawned
CRINGER a yes-man; sycophant
CRINGLE eyelet in sail **Naut.**
CRINITE hairy; a fossil
CRINKLE crankle; wrinkle; crimp
CRINOID fossilized sea-lily **Min.**
CRINOSE crinite; pilose; hairy
CRIPPLE disable; impair; hobble
CRISPED frizzled; made brittle
CRISPER curler; more friable
CRISPIN the cobbler's Saint
CRISPLY briskly
CRIZZEL⎱ roughness on glass
CRIZZLE⎰ making it cloudy
CROAKED died; grumbled; decried
CROAKER a fish; a pessimist **Z.**
CROCHET fancy-work
CROCKED blackened; broken down
CROCKET pinnacle adornment (Arch.)
CROESUS a wealthy man
CROFTER small farmer
CROODLE lie snug; cower
CROOKED tortuous; awry; bent
CROONED moaned; lamented
CROONER sentimental singer
CROP-EAR
CROPFUL satiated
CROPPED mowed; reaped; cut
CROPPER printing machine; heavy fall
CROQUET up to date pall-mall
CROSIER crozier; bishop's crook **Eccl.**
CROSLET crossed cross (Her.)
CROSSED thwarted; interbred
CROSSLY peevishly; testily; petulantly
CROTALO Turkish cymbal **Mus.**
CROTTLE lichen-dye
CROUTON chopped fried bread
CROWBAR lever; jemmy **Tool**
CROWDED huddled; thronged
CROWDER Welsh fiddler **Mus.**
CROWDIE porridge (Sc.)
CROWGER striped wrasse, fish **Z.**
CROWING exulting; rejoicing; boasting
CROWNED honoured; completed
CROWNER coroner

CROWNET coronet (Shak,)
CROW-TOE the butter-cup **B.**
CROZIER crosier; pastoral staff **Eccl.**
CRUCIAL cross-like; critical; decisive
CRUCIAN gold-fish; crusian **Z.**
CRUCIFY mortify
CRUCITE red iron ore **Min.**
CRUDELY unpolished; roughly
CRUDEST rawest; coarsest
CRUDITY rawness; immaturity
CRUELER more brutal; harsher
CRUELTY savagery; barbarity
CRUISED sailed
CRUISER rover **Naut.**
CRUISIE primitive lamp
CRULLER a cake
CRUMBED fragmented
CRUMBLE pulverize; disintegrate
CRUMBLY friable
CRUMPED blasted; blown up
CRUMPET an indigestible comestible
CRUMPLE wrinkle; crunkle; ruffle
CRUNKLE crumple; crimp; crinkle
CRUORIN haemoglobin **Med.**
CRUPPER saddle-strap
CRUSADE fanatical enterprize
CRUSADO Portuguese coin **Coin**
CRUSHED overwhelmed; compressed
CRUSHER pulverizer
CRUSIAN crucian; carp; goldfish **Z.**
CRUSTED encrusted; incrusted
CRY-BABY a weakling
CRYOGEN a freezing mixture
CRYPTIC hidden; occult; secret
CRYPTON krypton; a gas **Chem.**
CRYSTAL (Palace); (fortune-telling) **Min.**
CTENOID comb-shaped
CUBBING whelping; hunting
CUBBISH ill-mannered
CUBEBIN cubeb extract **Med.**
CUBICAL cubic
CUBICLE little bed-room
CUBITAL about 20 inches
CUBITED measured in cubits
CUBITUS a cubit **Meas.**
CUCKOLD husband of loose wife
CUCULUS cuckoo **Z.**
CUDBEAR a lichen; a purple dye **B.**
CUDDLED hugged; fondled; caressed
CUDWEED a plant **B.**
CUE-BALL (billiards)
CUFFING scuffling; buffeting
CUINAGE tin stamping
CUIRASS breast-plate
CUISINE cookery
CUITTLE cajole; curry (Sc.)
CUL-DE-SAC dead-end
CULETTE hip-armour
CULICID mosquito **Z.**
CULLIED duped; gulled; hoaxed

CULLING selecting; gathering; picking
CULLION bulbous root **B.**
CULPRIT delinquent; offender
CULTIST a pedant; dilettante
CULTURE refinement; education
CULVERT small bridge
CUMBENT recumbent; lying down
CUMQUAT kumquat; Chinese fruit **B,**
CUMSHAW gift; tip; present (Ind.)
CUMULUS a heap; a large cloud
CUNEATE wedge-shaped
CUNNING crafty; sly; wily; astute
CUP-GALL an oak-gall **B.**
CUP-MOSS a lichen **B.**
CUPPING blood-letting
CUPRITE oxide of copper **Min.**
CUP-ROSE poppy **B.**
CUPROUS copper compound **Chem.**
CURABLE remedial
CURACAO orange liqueur
CURATOR custodian; keeper; warden
CURBING repressing; restraining
CURCUMA (arrowroot, etc.) **B.**
CURDING coagulating
CURDLED congealed; thrilled
CURE-ALL panacea
CURETTE surgical scraper **Med**
CURIOSO virtuoso; a collector
CURIOUS rum; prying; unusual; queer
CURLING a pastime; coiling; bending
CURRACH curragh; coracle
CURRANT ribes; a dried raisin **B**
CURRENT accepted; present; tide; flov
CURRIED groomed; (leather)
CURRIER leather-dresser
CURRING purring; cooing
CURRISH snarling; spiteful; quarrelsom
CURSING swearing; execrating
CURSIVE flowing; running
CURSORY hasty; superficial; transient
CURTAIL abridge; contract; shorten
CURTAIN theatrical drapery
CURTANA sword of mercy, (Coron.)
CURTATE reduced; abbreviated
CURT-AXE short broad-sword
CURTEST bluntest; briefest; shortest
CURVATE bent; curved
CURVING turning; inflecting
CURVITY regular bend
CUSHION pad; hassock; pouffe
CUSSING swearing (slang)
CUSTARD sometimes cowardly
CUSTODE a watchman; custodian
CUSTODY care; imprisonment; duress
CUSTOMS duties on merchandise
CUSTREL buckler-bearer; a costrel
CUT-AWAY (tailoring)
CUT-BACK decrease production (indu-
trial)
CUT-DOWN reduce; cheapen
CUTICLE outer-skin **Me**

CUTLASS short broad sword   **Naut.**
CUTLERY edged tools
CUTTING satirical; sardonic; sarcastic
CUT-WORM caterpillar pest   **Z.**
CUVETTE crucible; trench; cunette
CYANATE cyanide   **Chem.**
CYANINE cyanite   **Chem.**
CYCLING
CYCLIST
CYCLOID geometric curve
CYCLONE tornado; hurricane; typhoon
CYCLOPS one-eyed Sicilian giant
CYCLORN a cycle-horn
CYMBALO the dulcimer   **Mus.**
CYNICAL disparaging; ironical
CYPERUS a sedge   **B.**
CYPRESS funereal tree   **B.**
CYPRIAN licentious; (Cyprus)
CYPRINE (cypress); funereal   **B.**
CYPRIOT courtesan; (Cyprus)
CYSTINE calculus growth   **Med.**
CYSTOID⎫ cystlike   **Med.**
CYSTOSE⎭ cystlike   **Med.**
CYSTOMA tumour   **Med.**
CYTISUS the broom genus   **B.**
CYTITIS dermatitis   **Med.**
CZARDAS Hungarian dance
CZARINA Tsarina
CZARISM despotism
CZECHIC Slavic

D

DABBING tapping; patting
DABBLED sprinkled; meddled; trifled
DABBLER dilettante; trifler
DABSTER an expert; adept
DACOITY dakoity; brigandage
DADAISM art movement
DADDLED tottered
DADDOCK the heart of a rotten tree
DAFTEST silliest; maddest; craziest
DAGGING cutting into strips
DAGGLED befouled; smirched
DAG-LOCK hanging lock of wool
DAGONET King Arthur's fool
DAGWOOD dog-wood; sandwich   **B.**
DAHLINE dahlia starch   **B.**
DAIRIES dairy farms
DAISIED
DAKOITY dacoity
DALLIED trifled; dawdled; sported
DALLIER a trifler; flaneur
DALRIAD an Ulster Scot
DAMAGED marred; injured; hurt
DAMBROD a draught-board (Sc.)
DAMMING embanking
DAMNIFY to injure
DAMNING conclusive; condemning
DAMOSEL damozel; damsel
DAMPING (wireless); discouraging

DAMPISH moist; dank; humid
DANAKIL nomad fisher tribe
DANCING capering; pirouetting
DANDIFY smarten; beautify
DANDLED fondled
DANELAW Danelagh; Danish England
DANGLED suspended; swung; hung
DANGLER hanger-on
DANKISH damp and dark
DANSKER a Dane (Shak.)
DANTEAN sombre (Dante)
DANTIST a Dante scholar
DAPHNAL (laurels)   **B.**
DAPHNIA water-fleas   **Z.**
DAPHNIN bay-extract   **B.**
DAPIFER meat-bearer; royal steward
DAPPING may-fly fishing
DAPPLED variegated
DARBIES handcuffs
DARCALL long-tailed duck   **Z.**
DARCOCK water-rail   **Z.**
DARIOLE rich cake
DARKEST most secret; blackest
DARKISH gloomy
DARLING beloved; dear; pet; idol
DARNING mending
DARREIN (benefice)   **Eccl.**
DARTARS sheep ulcers
DARTING casting; sprinting
DASHING rushing; impetuous; spirited
DASH-POT snubber (electronic)
DASTARD poltroon; coward; craven
DASYPUS armadillo genus   **Z.**
DASYURE Australian cat   **Z.**
DATABLE assignable to a period
DATARIA (papal chancery)   **Eccl.**
DATISCA hemp   **B.**
DATIVAL (dative)
DAUBERY poor painting
DAUBING daubery; smearing
DAUNTED discouraged; cowed
DAUPHIN King's eldest son (Fr.)
DAWDLED lagged; dallied; tarried
DAWDLER time-waster; laggard
DAWNING day-break; day-spring
DAY-BOOK
DAY-COAL (upper stratum)   **Min.**
DAY-GIRL non-resident schoolgirl
DAY-LILY the hemerocallis   **B.**
DAY-MAID dairy-maid; daily girl
DAY-PEEP dawn
DAY'S-MAN umpire
DAY-STAR the morning star
DAYSURE a wolf genus   **Z.**
DAY-TIME
DAY-WORK
DAZZLED dazed; bewildered; confused
DEAD-END cul-de-sac
DEAD-EYE three-eyed naval block   **Naut.**
DEADISH rather moribund; decaying

DEADMEN empty bottles
DEADPAN expressionless (facial)
DEAD-PAY (pay drawn; death concealed)
DEAD-SET determined effort
DEAD-TOP arboreal disease **B.**
DEAF-AID hearing device
DEAF-NUT (no kernel) **B.**
DEALING negotiating; (cards)
DEANERY **Eccl.**
DEAREST most expensive; costliest
DEARNLY secretly; grievously
DEASIUL, DEASOIL opposite Widdershins
DEISEAL sun-wise
DEATHLY mortal; deadly; destructive
DEBACLE a rout; collapse; stampede
DEBASED adulterated; degraded
DEBASER contaminator
DEBATED deliberated; disputed
DEBATER arguer; controversialist
DEBAUCH carouse; corrupt; deprave
DEBITED charged with
DEBITOR debtor (Shak.)
DEBOUCH come into the open
DECADAL in tens
DECAGON ten-sided figure
DECANAL (deanery) **Eccl.**
DECAPOD having ten limbs; (lobster)**Z.**
DECAYED rotted; degenerated; wasted
DECAYER source of decay
DECEASE perish; die; expire; demise
DECEIVE beguile; mislead; overreach
DECENCY propriety; decorum
DECHARM disenchant
DECIARE tenth of an are (Fr.) **Meas.**
DECIBEL unit of noise **Meas.**
DECIDED resolute; firm; unwavering
DECIDER final heat
DECIMAL a tenth
DECKING ornament; embellishment
DECKLED with edges uncut
DECLAIM orate; harangue; rant; spout
DECLARE avouch; assert; proclaim
DECLINE refuse; decay; wane; languish
DECODED deciphered
DECORUM seemliness; decency
DECOYED allured; snared; inveigled
DECREED ordered; resolved; enacted
DECREET announce court judgment
DECRIAL clamorous censure
DECRIED disparaged; traduced
DECRIER vilifier
DECROWD (slum clearance)
DECROWN discrown; dethrone
DECUMAN main gate; tenth; principal
DECUPLE tenfold
DECURVE straighten
DEDIMUS judicial commission **Law**
DEDUCED inferred; concluded; reasoned
DEEDFUL manful; doughty
DEEDILY valiantly

DEEDING conveying by deed **Law**
DEEMING opining; considering
DEEPEST most profound; lowest
DEEP-FRY cooking
DEEP-SEA
DEFACED disfigured; mutilated
DEFACER spoiler
DEFAMED libelled; vilified
DEFAMER detractor; slanderer
DEFAULT to fail; failure; lapse
DEFENCE plea; excuse; protection
DEFIANT provocative; contumacious
DEFICIT shortage
DEFILED polluted; vitiated
DEFILER contaminator; seducer
DEFINED accurately described; limited
DEFINER a precisian
DEFLATE release the air
DEFLECT divert; turn aside
DEFORCE resist **Law**
DEFRAUD trick; cheat; deceive
DEFUNCT deceased
DEFYING challenging; flouting
DEGAUSS antimagnetic device
DEGLAZE to clear thick gravy
DEGRADE lower; humble; debase
DEHISCE to gape
DEICIDE a god-destroyer
DE-ICING removing ice
DEICTIC clearly proving
DEIFIED exalted; idolized
DEIFORM godlike
DEIGNED condescended; vouchsafed
DEISTIC freethinking
DEITIES gods
DELAINE woollen fabric
DELATED gave information; squealed
DELATOR accuser; informer; relator
DELAYED procrastinated; deferred
DELAYER a cunctator; dawdler
DELEBLE delible; erasable
DELENDA things to be erased
DELETED expunged; effaced
DELIGHT charm; ravish; joy; ecstasy
DELILAH a charming hairdresser
DELIMIT fix limits
DELIVER cede; consign; rescue; save
DELOUSE to remove lice
DELPHIC oracular
DELPHIN classical edition
DELTAIC delta-like
DELTOID a muscle **Me**
DELUDED misled; beguiled; gulled
DELUDER deceiver; trickster; hoaxer
DELUGED flooded; inundated; swampe
DELVING digging; excavating
DEMENTI official denial (Fr.)
DEMERIT a fault; defect
DEMERSE immerse; drown
DEMESNE lord's farming land (feudal

DEMIGOD	**DESPAIR** hopelessness; despondency
DEMIREP a lady of doubtful virtue	**DESPISE** disdain; contemn; scorn; scout
DEMISED bequeathed; willed	**DESPITE** in spite of; malice
DEMODED old fashioned	**DESPOIL** rob; bereave; strip; rifle
DEMONIC fiendish; satanic; diabolical	**DESPOND** despair; dejectedness
DEMONRY devilry	**DESSERT** a fruit course
DEMOTIC popular; common	**DESTINE** to ordain; appoint
DENIZEN alien inhabitant; resident	**DESTINY** fate; fortune; doom; Kismet
DENOTED indicated; signified	**DESTROY** devour; demolish; raze
DENSELY closely; thickly	**DETERGE** cleanse; wipe
DENSEST thickest; closest	**DETERMA** a useful wood from Guiana
DENSITY compactness; stolidness	**DETINUE** writ of distraint **Law**
DENTARY (teeth)	**DETRACT** defame; disparage; traduce
DENTATE toothed	**DETRAIN**
DENTELS toothed ornaments	**DETRUDE** force down
DENTINE ivory tissue	**DEUTZIA** a white flower **B.**
DENTING dinting; notching	**DEVALUE** depreciate
DENTIST **Med.**	**DEVELOP** grow; unfold; expand
DENTIZE (dental work)	**DEVIATE** swerve; turn; tack; digress
DENTOID tooth-like	**DEVILET** small demon; imp
DENTURE false teeth	**DEVILRY** cruel mischief; diabolism
DENUDED stripped; bared; divested	**DEVIOUS** wandering; erratic; tortuous
DENYING controverting; refuting	**DEVISED** contrived; willed; concocted
DEODAND a forfeit (obs.) **Law**	**DEVISEE** legatee
DEODATE heavenly gift	**DEVISER** inventor; schemer; planner
DEPLANE cf. detrain	**DEVISOR** testator
DEPLETE to empty; exhaust; drain	**DEVOLVE** deliver; depute; impose
DEPLORE lament; grieve; bewail	**DEVOTED** loving; ardent; attached
DEPLUME to pluck	**DEVOTEE** an addict; a fan; zealot
DEPONED testified **Law**	**DEVOTER** worshipper
DEPOSAL dismissal; sacking	**DEWANNY** office of dewan (India)
DEPOSED bore witness; ousted	**DEW-CLAW** rudimentary claw **Z.**
DEPOSIT store; lodge; intrust	**DEW-DROP**
DEPRAVE corrupt; debase; vitiate	**DEW-FALL** aqueous precipitation
DEPRESS damp; dishearten; sadden	**DEWLAPT** with a dewlap
DEPRIVE reprive; strip; rob; divest	**DEWLESS**
DEPUTED delegated; authorized	**DEW-POND**
DERAIGN darrain; justify (obs.)	**DEW-WORM** the earth-worm **Z.**
DERANGE disturb; upset; ruffle	**DEXTRAL** (not left)
DERATED freed from liability	**DEXTRAN** synthetic blood plasma
DERBEND Turkish guard house	**DEXTRIN** starch gum
DERIDED jeered; scorned; lampooned	**DHAGOBA** Buddhist mound **Eccl.**
DERIDER a mocker; scoffer	**DHOOLIE** covered litter
DERIVED deduced; traced; obtained	**DHURRIE** Indian curtain
DERMOID like skin	**DIABASE** basalt **Min.**
DERNFUL solitary; mournful	**DIABOLO** a game
DERNIER final; last (Fr.)	**DIACOPE** tmesis
DERRICK form of crane **Naut.**	**DIADROM** a beat; a vibration
DERRING daring	**DIAGRAM** graph; sketch; drawing
DERVISH Moslem monk	**DIALECT** idiom; parlance
DESCANT comment freely; dilate	**DIALIST** dial-maker
DESCANT part song; a commentary	**DIALIZE** separate **Chem.**
DESCEND dismount; alight; drop; sink	**DIALLED** rang up
DESCENT slope; decline; origin; raid	**DIAMOND** **Min.**
DESERVE earn; win; merit; justify	**DIANDER** (two stamens) **B.**
DESIRED wanted; solicited; coveted	**DIAPASM** toilet powder
DESIRER craver; yearner; fancier	**DIARAIN** diarial; daily
DESKILL simplify industrial work	**DIARCHY** dual monarchy
DESMINE stilbite; zeolitic mineral **Min.**	**DIARIES** daily records
DESMOID tufty	**DIARISE** to record

DIARIST a chronicler
DIATOMS sea-weed **B.**
DIBASIC giving two salts **Chem.**
DIBATAG N. African gazelle **Z.**
DIBBING dipping
DIBBLED made holes in the ground
DIBBLER planted
DICE-BOX
DICEING throwing dice
DICERAS clams **Z.**
DICHORD lyre **Mus.**
DICKENS Boz
DICTATE enjoin; command; bid
DICTION style; speech; phraseology
DIDACHE apostolic teaching
DIDDLED out-witted; cajoled; cozened
DIDDLER a cheat; swindler; cajoler
DIDIDAE the dodo, etc. **Z.**
DIE-AWAY languishing
DIE-CAST (condenser construction)
DIEDRAL dihedral
DIE-HARD last ditcher
DIETARY course of diet
DIETING banting; slimming
DIETIST dietitian
DIE-WORK die-cutting
DIFFORM irregular
DIFFUSE spread; copious; prolix
DIGAMMA obsolete Greek letter
DIGGING delving; grubbing; thrusting
DIGHTLY finely apparelled (obs.)
DIGITAL integral
DIGLYPH grooved face
DIGNIFY ennoble; exalt; grace
DIGNITY majesty; decorum; rank
DIGRAPH (two letters)
DIGRESS deviate; wander; swerve
DIGYNIA curious plant; (two pistils) **B.**
DILATED enlarged; expatiated
DILATER an expander; amplifier
DILATOR a muscle **Med.**
DILEMMA quandary; plight; strait
DILLING darling; weakling
DILL-OIL a carminative **Med.**
DILUENT a diluter; reducer
DILUTED watered; attenuated
DILUTEE unskilled worker (industrial)
DILUTER thinner
DIMETER (poetry)
DIM-EYED
DIMMING blurring; clouding; dulling
DIMMISH somewhat obscure
DIMNESS vagueness; dinginess
DIMPLED
DINETTE a light meal
DINGING ringing; urging
DINGOES wild dogs of Australia **Z.**
DINMONT shorn wether **Z.**
DINNING advocating clamorously
DINTING denting; striking

DIOCESE a bishopric **Eccl-**
DIOECIA genus of plants **B.**
DIONAEA Venus's fly-trap **B.**
DIOPSIS fly-genus **Z.**
DIOPTER optical measurement **Meas.**
DIOPTER speculum; theodolite
DIOPTRE unit of lens power **Photo.**
DIORAMA panorama
DIORISM definition
DIORITE igneous rock **Min.**
DIOXIDE **Chem.**
DIPHONE a shorthand sign
DIPLOID twin chromosomes **Med.**
DIPLOMA a certificate
DIPOLAR with two poles
DIPPING dibbing; plunging; immersing
DIPTERA two-winged insect **Z**
DIP-TRAP bend in a pipe
DIPTYCH pictorial altar-piece **Eccl**
DIREFUL calamitous; baleful; awful
DIRKING stabbing
DIRT-BED (quarrying)
DIRTIED soiled; sullied; begrimed
DIRTIER grubbier
DIRTILY filthily
DIRT-PIE mud-pie
DISABLE unfit; incapacitate; maim
DISALLY separate; sunder
DISAVOW repudiate; disown; deny
DISBAND disperse; disembody
DISBARK disembark
DISBEND unbend (obs.)
DISCAGE release; unmew
DISCANT descant; discourse
DISCARD cast; reject; abandon
DISCASE strip; unpack
DISCEPT debate; dispute
DISCERN espy; perceive; discriminate
DISCERP tear off; separate
DISCOID flat like a disc
DISCORD strife; brawl; animosity
DISCOUS broad; flat
DISCUSS debate; argue; consume
DISDAIN spurn; contemn; ignore
DISEASE malady; complaint **Me**
DISEDGE to blunt
DISEUSE woman reciter (Fr.)
DISFAME disrepute; evil reputation
DISFORM alter; deform; disfigure
DISGOWN unfrock
DISGUST nausea; aversion; loathing
DISHELM remove helmet
DISHFUL
DISHING thwarting; frustrating
DISH-MAT
DISHOME evict
DISHORN remove horns
DISJOIN part; detach; sunder; sever
DISJUNE dejeuner; lunch (Sc.)
DISLEAF deprive of leaves

DISLEAL disloyal; dishonourable
DISLIKE hate; detest; antipathy
DISLIMB dismember
DISLIMN obliterate; efface (obs.)
DISLINK unlink; disjoin
DISLOAD unburden; unload
DISMALS mournings
DISMASK unmask; uncover; reveal
DISMAST Naut.
DISMISS cashier; discharge; sack
DISNEST eject
DISOBEY transgress; disregard; infringe
DISPAIR separate; uncouple
DISPARK set at large
DISPART separate
DISPEND expend; disburse (obs.)
DISPLAY parade; flaunt; show; evince
DISPONE hand over Law
DISPORT sport; gambol; frolic; wanton
DISPOSE sell; transfer; arrange
DISPOST displace
DISPUTE argue; wrangle; bicker
DISRANK degrade
DISRATE reduce to lower rating
DISROBE unrobe; strip; divest; bare
DISROOT uproot; eradicate
DISRUPT break up; disintegrate
DISSEAT unseat
DISSECT anatomize; analyse; cut
DISSENT disagree; differ
DISSERT discourse; dissertation (obs.)
DISTAFF staff for holding unspun flax
DISTAFF the opposite to spear-side
DISTAIN sully; stain
DISTANT remote; far; aloof; reserved
DISTEND dilate; swell; expand; bloat
DISTENT distended (Spens.)
DISTICH rhyming couplet
DISTOMA genus of worms Z.
DISTORT pervert; misrepresent
DISTUNE put out of tune
DISTURB molest; confuse; vex; annoy
DISTYLE portico
DISUSED obsolete; neglected; abandoned
DISWARN dissuade
DISWONT deprive of wonted usage
DISYOKE unyoke
DITCHED fallen into the sea (R.A.F.)
DITCHER ditch clearer
DITHERY nervous; agitated; tremulous
DITTANY candle-plant B.
DITTIED sung
DITTIES sonnets; shanties
DIURNAL daily; quotidian; journal
DIVERGE fork; radiate; part
DIVERSE unlike; different; varied
DIVIDED severed; sundered; separated
DIVIDER distributor; apportioner
DIVINER predictor; seer; magician
DIVISOR (arithmetic)

DIVORCE dissever; part; alienate
DIVULGE tell; reveal; disclose; impart
DIVVY-UP divide
DIZENED bedecked
DIZZARD block-head
DIZZIED dazed; bewildered; confused
DIZZIER giddier
DIZZILY confusedly
DJEREED } blunt Turkish javelin
DJERRID }
DJIBBAH } Eastern garment
DJUBBAH }
DOBHASH interpreter (Hind.)
DOCETAE an ungodly sect
DOCETIC heretical
DOCIBLE docile; tractable; amenable
DOCIOUS docile
DOCKAGE dock dues
DOCKING curtailing; clipping Naut.
DOCKIZE to construct docks
DOCQUET docket; summary; list
DODDART hockey (obs.)
DODDING lopping; polling
DODGERY trickery; prevarication
DODGING evading; quibbling
DOESKIN
DOFFING divesting; putting off
DOG-BANE plant with a bitter root
DOG-BELT part of dog harness
DOG-BOLT arrow; dog-meal
DOG-CART two-wheeled vehicle
DOG-DAYS (occur in July and August)
DOGEATE office of doge
DOG-FISH tope; small shark Z.
DOGGING following closely; tailing
DOGGISH rather posh
DOGGREL doggerel; trashy verse
DOGHEAD gunlock hammer
DOG-HOLE not a luxurious abode
DOGHOOD cf. manhood
DOGLIKE having canine attributes
DOG-NAIL large nail
DOG-ROSE wild rose B.
DOG'S-EAR a fold in a page in a book
DOGSHIP personality of a dog
DOG-SICK sick as a dog
DOGSKIN
DOG'S-RUE a plant; Scrophularia B.
DOG-STAR Sirius
DOG-TICK a parasite Z.
DOGTROT jog
DOG-VANE wind-vane Naut.
DOGWOOD a plant B.
DOLABRA Roman hatchet
DOLEFUL woe-begone; dismal; rueful
DOLLIED hammered; laundered
DOLLIER an ore-crusher
DOLLMAN Turkish robe
DOLPHIN fish; a spar Z.
DOLTISH stupid; stolid; witless

DOMABLE tamable; tractable	**DRABBLE** befoul; draggle
DOMICAL dome-shaped	**DRABLER** additional sail **Naut.**
DOMINIE schoolmaster (Sc.)	**DRACHMA** Greek silver coin **Meas.**
DOMINUS Master; Lord	**DRACINA** dragon's blood palm **B.**
DONATOR donor; presenter; giver	**DRACINE** dracina; a dye **B.**
DONNERD donnert; stunned (Sc.)	**DRACULA** Bram Stoker's batman
DONNING putting on; assuming	**DRAFTED** out-lined; detached
DONNISH like a don	**DRAFT-OX** draught-ox **Z.**
DONNISM self-importance	**DRAG-BAR** draw-bar
DONSHIP	**DRAGGED** tugged; hauled; lingered
DOOMING condemning; judging	**DRAGGLE** bemire; drabble
DOORING door-case	**DRAG-MAN** a fisherman
DOORMAT	**DRAG-NET** his net
DOORWAY portico	**DRAGOON** compel; coerce; cavalryman
DOPPLER change of frequency **Electron.**	**DRAINED** filtered; exhausted; emptied
DORHAWK nightjar **Z.**	**DRAINER** a colander
DORKING a fowl **Z.**	**DRAPERY** haberdashery
DORLACH bundle; valise (Sc.)	**DRAPIER** a Swift 'nom de plume'
DORMANT quiescent; latent	**DRAPING** covering; dressing
DORMICE sleepy rodents **Z.**	**DRAPPIE** a wee drop (Sc.)
DORNICK ⎫ figured linen	**DRASTIC** severe; forcible; efficacious
DORNOCK ⎭	**DRATTED** confounded
DORTOUR dorter; dormitory **Eccl.**	**DRAUGHT** dose; breeze; outline
DOSSIER file of papers; a brief (Fr.)	**DRAWBAR** connecting rod
DOTTARD decayed tree	**DRAWBOY** a weaving assistant
DOTTIER barmier; more foolish	**DRAWING** pulling; sketch; plan
DOTTING spotting; stippling	**DRAWLED** dawdled; droned
DOTTREL plover **Z.**	**DRAWLER** monotonous speaker
DOUBLED turned; ran; repeated	**DRAW-NET** bird net
DOUBLER duplicator	**DRAYAGE** charge for a dray
DOUBLET jerkin; one of a pair	**DRAYMAN** dray-driver
DOUBTED distrusted; suspected	**DREADED** apprehended; feared
DOUBTER an unbelieving Thomas	**DREADER** an alarmist
DOUCELY sweetly	**DREAMED** dreamt; imagined
DOUCETS ⎫ stones of deer **Z.**	**DREAMER** visionary; idealist; enthuse
DOWCETS ⎭	**DREDGED** sprinkled
DOUCEUR tip; vail; gratuity	**DREDGER**
DOUCHED sprayed	**DREEING** enduring; bearing (Sc.)
DOUCINE ornamental moulding	**DRESDEN** Meissen porcelain
DOUGHTY valiant; intrepid; dauntless	**DRESSED** cooked; decked; arrayed in
DOUPION double cocoon **Z.**	**DRESSER** kitchen sideboard
DOUREST grimmest; staunchest	**DREULED** slavered; dribbled
DOUSING ⎫ dipping; extinguishing;	**DRIBBED** inveigled; filched
DOWSING ⎭ water-divining	**DRIBBLE** (football); trickle; drip; ooze
DOUTING extinguishing; quenching	**DRIBLET** driplet; a small quantity
DOVECOT dove-cote **Z.**	**DRIFTED** floated; enlarged
DOVEKIE little auk **Z.**	**DRIFTER** wanderer **Naut.**
DOVELET young dove **Z.**	**DRILLED** trained; perforated; pierced
DOVERED slumbered	**DRINKER** reveller; carouser; toper
DOWABLE endowable	**DRIPDRY** non-iron fabric
DOWAGER widow with a jointure	**DRIPPED** dropped; oozed; trickled
DOWDILY untidily; slovenly	**DRIP-TIP** a leaf-point **B.**
DOWERED gifted	**DRIVE-IN** service for motorists
DOWN-BED feather bed	**DRIVING** dragooning; urging; forcing
DOWNING felling; overcoming	**DRIZZLE** fine rain
DOWSING water-divining	**DRIZZLY**
DOYENNE senior lady	**DROGHER** coasting vessel **Naut.**
DOZENTH 12th	**DROGMAN** dragoman; interpreter
DRABBER more dingy	**DROGUET** ribbed fabric
DRABBET smocking	**DROICHY** dwarfish (Gael.)

DROILED toiled tediously
DROLLED jested; clowned
DROLLER farceur; funnier; odder
DROMOND fast sailing ship **Naut.**
DRONING prosing; humming
DRONISH lazy
DROOLED slavered; dribbled
DROOPED withered; declined
DROPLET a drip; bead of moisture
DROP-NET a fishing-net
DROP-OUT resign; computer error
DROPPED dripped; fell; quitted
DROPPER end fly of a cast
DROSERA sun-dew **B.**
DROSHKY Russian vehicle
DROUGHT aridity; dryness
DROUTHY thirsty; very dry
DROWNED overflowed; submerged
DROWNER
DROWSED dozed; slumbered; dovered
DRUBBED thrashed; thumped; mauled
DRUBBER a beater
DRUDGED plodded; toiled; slaved
DRUDGER toiler; menial; scullion
DRUGGED stupefied; physicked **Med.**
DRUGGER drogher; small ship **Naut.**
DRUGGET carpet covering
DRUIDIC (Druids)
DRUMBLE to drone
DRUMLIN small drum **Mus.**
DRUMMED expelled **Mus.**
DRUMMER commercial traveller **Mus.**
DRUNKEN inebriated; crapulous; tipsy
DRUSIAN a Syrian
DRYADES wood nymphs; trees **B.**
DRY-BEAT (blows without blood)
DRY-BONE silicate of zinc **Min.**
DRY-CELL (electrical)
DRY-DOCK
DRY-EYED tearless
DRY-FOOT
DRYNESS aridity; drought; thirst
DRY-PILE voltaic battery
DRY-RENT (no distress) **Law**
DRY-SALT preserve; cure
DRYSHOD
DUALINE dualin; form of dynamite
DUALISM a doctrine; Manichaeism
DUALIST (twofoldness in the universe)
DUALITY doubleness
DUALIZE split in twain
DUARCHY diarchy; dual control
DUBBING dubbin; grease; entitling
DUBIATE to doubt; to hesitate
DUBIETY doubtfulness; uncertainty
DUBIOUS undecided; vacillating
DUCALLY in ducal style
DUCHESS
DUCK-ANT Jamaican termite
DUCKING a soaking; diving **Z.**

DUCTILE tractile; malleable
DUDDERY rags; old clo' shop
DUDGEON dagger; sullenness
DUE-BILL accepted debt
DUELIST fighter
DUELLED
DUELLER combatant in single fight
DUENESS fitness; propriety; seemliness
DUFFING sham; furbishing up
DUKEDOM
DULCIFY sweeten
DULCINE manna-sugar; mannite
DULCITE saccharine **Chem.**
DULCOSE dulcine
DULLARD stupid fellow; blockhead
DULLEST bluntest; most obtuse
DULLING allaying; benumbing
DULLISH rather dull; somewhat inert
DULNESS dullness; stupidity; apathy
DUMPING heaping (exporting)
DUMPISH in the dumps
DUN-BIRD pochard duck **Z.**
DUNCERY dulness; stupidity
DUNCIAD Pope's epic poem
DUNCISH not clever
DUNEDIN Edinburgh
DUNFISH cured cod-fish
DUNGEON dark prison; cell
DUNKERS Tunkers; triple baptists
DUNNAGE packing; baggage; timber
DUNNING debt collecting; fish curing
DUNNISH dirty brown
DUNNOCK hedge-sparrow **Z.**
DUODENA ancient jury **Law**
DUPABLE credulous; gullible
DUPPING opening as a door
DURABLE lasting; abiding; stable
DURABLY permanently; long lasting
DURAMEN heart-wood **B.**
DURANCE captivity; duress; restraint
DURANTE for life
DUREFUL long lasting
DURESSE severity; constraint (Fr.)
DURMAST an oak **B.**
DURSLEY bloodless blows **Law**
DUSKIER more sable or swarthy
DUSKILY dimly; darkly
DUSKISH shadowy
DUSTBIN
DUSTIER more flocculent
DUSTING a beating
DUSTMAN
DUSTPAN
DUTEOUS obsequious; deferential
DUTIFUL obedient; respectful
DUUMVIR Roman magistrates
DVORNIK Russian concierge
DWARFED stunted; eclipsed
DWELLED sojourned; abode; inhabited
DWELLER resident; inmate; indigene

DWINDLE diminish; decrease; shrink
DYARCHY duarchy; dual control
DYE-WOOD (various woods) **B.**
DYE-WORK dyeing establishment
DYINGLY deathly
DYNAMIC forceful
DYNASTY house; family; succession
DYSLOGY disapproval; disapprobation
DYSNOMY bad laws
DYSOPSY poor sight **Med.**
DYTICUS water-beetles **Z.**
DYVOURY bankruptcy **Law**

E

EAGERLY avidly; ardently; fervently
EANLING young lamb **Z.**
EAR-ACHE a pain in the ear **Med.**
EAR-DROP a pendant; earring
EAR-DRUM tympanum **Med.**
EAR-HOLE aural portal
EARLDOM the seignory of an earl
EARLESS reluctant to hear
EARLIER sooner
EARLOCK love-lock
EARMARK identity mark for sheep
EARNEST pledge; steady; persevering
EARNING winning; meriting; acquiring
EAR-PICK
EARRING pendant; eardrop
EARSHOT hearing distance
EARTHED burrowed; (wireless)
EARTHEN of clay
EARTHLY carnal; mundane; terrestrial
EASEFUL restful; tranquil; contented
EASIEST least difficult; simplest
EAST-END
EASTERN oriental; auroral
EASTING east of any meridian **Naut.**
EATABLE edible; succulent; esculent
EBB-TIDE retrogression
EBONIST ebony worker
EBONITE vulcanite
EBONIZE ebonise
EBRIETY intoxication; intemperance
EBRIOSE fuddled; crapulous; tipsy
EBRIOUS fond of the bottle; temulent
ECBASIS } rhetorical treatment
ECBATIC }
ECDEMIC foreign; not endemic
ECDYSIS moulting; sloughing
ECHAPPE (horse-breeding)
ECHELLE scale; ladder
ECHELON a ladder formation; cycling
ECHIDNA Australian ant-eater **Z.**
ECHIMYD S. American dormouse **Z.**
ECHINUS sea-urchin **Z.**
ECHOING resounding; repeating
ECHOISM onomatopœia
ECHOIST a yes-man

ECLIPSE shroud; veil; surpass
ECLOGUE pastoral poem
ECOLOGY biological geography
ECONOMY care; thrift; providence
ECOUTES listening posts (Fr.)
ECSTASY rapture; fervour; delight
ECTASIS mispronunciation
ECTHYMA a rash **Med.**
ECTOPIA dislocation **Med.**
ECTOPIC displaced
ECTOZOA parasites **Z.**
ECTYPAL actual copy
EDACITY greed; voracity; rapacity
EDDERED bound by an edder
EDDYING swirling; whirling; vortical
EDELITE a silicate **Min.**
EDENTAL toothless
EDICTAL laid down; ordered
EDIFICE a stylish building
EDIFIED benefited spiritually
EDIFIER an uplifter
EDITING revising; annotating
EDITION issue; number; impression
EDUCATE teach; tutor; school; train
EDUCING extracting; eliciting
EDUCTOR cork-screw
EELBUCK basket-net
EEL-FARE a young eel **Z.**
EEL-POUT blenny **Z.**
EEL-PUNT
EFFABLE explicable; utterable
EFFACED erased; defaced
EFFECTS personal estate
EFFENDI Turkish title
EFFORCE ravish; rape
EFFULGE gleam; glisten; coruscate
EFFUSED emanated; diffused
EGALITY parity; equality
EGESTED cast out; ejected
EGG-BIRD tern **Z.**
EGG-CELL a zygote **Z.**
EGG-COSY oval muff
EGG-FLIP a bracer; drink
EGGHEAD intellectual
EGILOPS goat's eye; an abscess **Med.**
EGOTISM self-sufficiency; vanity
EGOTIST egoist
EGOTIZE (excess of 'I')
EGRETTE spray of gems; aigrette
EIDOLON apparition; phantom
EIRENIC irenic; peaceful
EJECTED threw out; dispossessed
EJECTOR chucker-out
ELAIDIC } oil products **Chem.**
ELAIDIN }
ELANCED threw; darted
ELAPSED intervened; slid away; passed
ELASTIC resilient; springy
ELASTIN elastic
ELATERY elastic force; elasticity

ELATINE water-wort **B.**
ELATING crowing; exalting
ELATION gratification; exhilaration
ELBOWED thrust aside; nudged
ELDERLY somewhat senile
ELEATIC philosophic
ELECTED chosen; picked; preferred
ELECTOR voter; German title
ELECTRO plated metal
ELEGANT refined; graceful; tasteful
ELEGIAC a lament; dirge
ELEGIST plaintive writer
ELEGIZE
ELEMENT part; component; ingredient
ELEVATE elate; raise; hoist; promote
ELEVENS an interim
ELF-BOLT elf-arrow
ELF-LAND fairy-land
ELF-LOCK fairy mono-mark
ELF-SHOT flint arrow-head
ELF-WORT elecampane **B.**
ELIDING rebutting; shortening
ELIMATE to file; to polish
ELISION metric suppression
ELK-WOOD umbrella-tree **B.**
ELLAGIC (gall-nuts) **B.**
ELLIPSE oval
ELL-WAND (a yard and a quarter)
ELOGIST orator at a funeral
ELOGIUM panegyric
ELOHIST Pentateuch author
ELOINED removed; separated; banished
ELOPING sloping; bolting; decamping
ELUDING dodging; evading; baffling
ELUSION evasion; avoidance
ELUSIVE illusory; deceptive; fugitive
ELUSORY hard to solve; intangible
ELUTION ablution
ELYSIAN delightful; heavenly
ELYSIUM Greek paradise
ELYTRAL shield-like **Z.**
ELYTRON ⎫ wing-sheath of beetles **Z.**
ELYTRUM ⎭
ELZEVIR edition of classics
EMANANT proceeding from
EMANATE originate; issue; flow
EMBALED packed; bundled
EMBARGO a prohibition; veto
EMBASSY ambassadorial residence
EMBATHE to bathe
EMBAYED land-locked
EMBLAZE embellish; imblaze
EMBLEMA inlaid ornament
EMBLICA Indian tree **B.**
EMBLOOM bloom
EMBOGUE debouch; discharge
EMBOLUS wedge; a clot **Med.**
EMBOSOM to hug; embrace; enfold
EMBOWER imbower; to shelter
EMBOXED enclosed

EMBRACE clasp; welcome; include
EMBRAID to braid (obs.)
EMBRAIL brail; lash
EMBRAVE embellish; inspirit
EMBREAD embraid
EMBROIL implicate; start trouble
EMBROWN to brown
EMBRUED ensanguined heraldically
EMBRUTE to deteriorate; brutalize
EMBRYON an embryo **B., Z.**
EMENDED amended; corrected
EMERALD smaragdus; brilliant green
EMERGED resulted; emanated; arose
EMERITI honourably discharged
EMICANT sparkling; sparking
EMINENT exalted; prominent
EMIRATE the office of Emir
EMITTED circulated; exhaled; gushed
EMITTER transistor electrode **Electron.**
EMMEWED ⎫ confined; cooped up
ENMEWED ⎭ also inmewed
EMOTION passion; agitation; feeling
EMOTIVE emotional; passionate
EMPALED impaled; transfixed; fenced
EMPANEL enrol
EMPATHY sympathetic reaction
EMPERIL endanger
EMPEROR a size of drawing paper
EMPIGHT placed; fixed
EMPIRIC based on practical experience
EMPIRIC a quack; charlatan
EMPLANE cf. embark
EMPLEAD prosecute **Law**
EMPLUME to feather
EMPOWER authorize; warrant; allow
EMPRESS
EMPRISE a dangerous enterprise
EMPTIED drained; depleted; discharged
EMPTIER more inane and vacuous
EMPTION purchase
EMULATE to vie; compete; rival
EMULOUS striving to equal
EMULSIC emulsive **Med.**
EMULSIN almond ferment **Chem.**
EMU-WREN an Australian bird **Z.**
ENABLED authorized; allowed
ENACTED decreed; ordained
ENACTOR law-maker **Law**
ENAMOUR charm; fascinate; enslave
ENARMED Heraldic term
ENCAGED incaged; cooped
ENCASED incased; enclosed
ENCAUMA a burn mark **Med.**
ENCAVED cached in a cave
ENCENIA commemorations; festivals
ENCHAFE to rub warm
ENCHAIN bind; fetter; shackle
ENCHANT enamour; bewitch; captivate
ENCHASE set with jewels; engrave
ENCHEER hearten; exhilarate

ENCHYMA injection; infusion **Med.**
ENCLASP embrace; hug; enfold
ENCLAVE an inlier
ENCLOSE envelop; fence; wrap
ENCLOUD mystify
ENCORED repeated by request
ENCRATY abstinence; self-control
ENCRUST coat; plaster
ENDEMIC local; indigenous
ENDERON true skin **Med.**
ENDEWED endowed (obs.)
END-GAME chess
ENDIRON andiron; firedog
ENDLESS eternal; interminable
ENDLONG not sideways
ENDMOST uttermost
ENDOGEN botanical growth **B.**
ENDORSE indorse; assign; ratify
ENDOSIS respite from fever **Med.**
ENDOWED supplied; bequeathed
ENDOWER benefactor; donor
END-SHIP a village (obs.)
ENDUING induing; investing
ENDURED tolerated; brooked; bore
ENDURER stayer; patient sufferer
ENDWAYS on end; upright
ENDWISE endways
ENERGIC active; energetic
ENFACED opposite to endorsed
ENFELON make fierce (obs.)
ENFEOFF assignment **Law**
ENFILED Heraldic sword thrust
ENFLESH turn into flesh
ENFORCE compel; oblige; coerce
ENFRAME
ENGAGED plighted; stipulated
ENGAGER employment agent
ENGINED powered; racked
ENGLISH
ENGLOBE inglobe; ensphere
ENGLOOM to depress
ENGORGE stuff with food; engulf
ENGRACE bring into favour
ENGRAFT insert; graft
ENGRAIL spot with dots (Her.)
ENGRAIN dye; permeate
ENGRASP clutch; seize
ENGRAVE cut; chisel; carve
ENGROSS monopolize; absorb; copy
ENGUARD defend
ENHANCE to intensify; heighten
ENISLED isolated
ENJOYED relished; liked; fancied
ENJOYER appreciator; gourmet
ENLACED entwined; inlaced
ENLARGE amplify; extend; expand
ENLIVEN wake; arouse; quicken
ENMURED immured; imprisoned
ENNICHE to enshrine
ENNOBLE exalt; raise; aggrandize

ENNUIED bored stiff
ENODING unknotting
ENOMOTY Spartan band
ENOUNCE proclaim; announce
ENPLANE to board an aeroplane
ENPRINT small enlargement **Photo.**
ENQUIRE inquire; investigate; ask
ENQUIRY inquiry; question; search
ENRACED enrooted
ENRAGED exasperated; incensed
ENRHEUM to have a cold **Med.**
ENRIDGE to furrow
ENRIPEN to mellow; mature
ENROBED attired; invested
ENROUGH to roughen
ENSILED stored in a pit
ENSKIED raised to heaven
ENSLAVE enthral; captivate; subjugate
ENSNARE entrap; allure; inveigle
ENSNARL entangle; ravel
ENSOBER to calm down
ENSTAMP impress; imprint
ENSTEEP immerse; duck; souse
ENSTYLE to call; to name
ENSUING resulting; issuing; accruing
ENSURED insured; made certain
ENSWEEP pass over rapidly
ENSWEPT scoured
ENTAMED subdued; domesticated
ENTASIA spasm **Med.**
ENTASIS architectural swell
ENTENTE understanding
ENTERED began; recorded; penetrated
ENTERER entrant; competitor
ENTERIC typhoid fever **Med.**
ENTHEAL divinely inspired
ENTHRAL inthral; enslave
ENTHUSE to gush
ENTICED allured; attracted
ENTICER seducer; cajoler; wheedler
ENTITLE intitle; qualify; allow
ENTOMIC (insects) **Z.**
ENTONIC of high tension
ENTOTIC (interior of ear) **Med.**
ENTOZOA internal parasites **Z.**
ENTRAIL interweave; plait
ENTRAIN to board a train
ENTRANT intrant; competitor
ENTREAT beg; implore; importune
ENTROPY dissipation of energy
ENTRUST intrust; confide
ENTUNED chanted; sang
ENTWINE weave; interlace; twist
ENTWIST intwist; wring; contort
ENURING inuring; hardening
ENVAULT entomb
ENVELOP enwrap; enfold; encase
ENVENOM to poison
ENVIOUS jealous; invidious; grudging
ENVIRON envelop; encompass; engird

ENVYING grudging; coveting
ENWHEEL encircle; surround
ENWOUND entwined; woven
ENWOVEN interwoven
ENZONED girdled; belted
EPACRID heathlike shrubs **B.**
EPAGOGE figure of speech
EPARCHY prefecture
EPAULET shoulder-piece
EPERGNE ornamental stand
EPHEBUS young Greek citizen
EPHELIS freckles **Med.**
EPICARP the rind **B.**
EPICEDE funeral ode
EPICENE common to both sexes
EPICISM sagas; heroic poems, etc.
EPICIST epic writer
EPICURE gourmet; voluptuary
EPIDEMY epidemic disease **Med.**
EPIDOTE a silicate **Min.**
EPIGEAL low growing
EPIGENE mineral change
EPIGONE a descendant
EPIGONE spore-bag **B.**
EPIGRAM barbed wisdom
EPISODE interesting incident
EPISTLE lengthy letter
EPITAPH monumental inscription
EPITHEM lotion; poultice **Med.**
EPITHET an appellative; adjective
EPITOME brief summary; abstract
EPIZOON epizoan; parasite **Z.**
EPOCHAL remarkable; outstanding
EPOXIDE plastic resin
EPULARY festive
EQUABLE fair; serene; uniform; calm
EQUABLY uniformly; justly
EQUALLY evenly
EQUATED made equal; balanced
EQUATOR a great circle
EQUERRY mounted officer
EQUINAL horsy
EQUINIA glanders **Med.**
EQUINOX (fifty-fifty)
EQUITES noble Romans
ERASING expunging; deleting
ERASION erasure; deletion; obliteration
ERASURE effacement; cancellation
ERECTED raised; constructed; uplifted
ERECTER a builder; prefabricator
ERECTLY uprightly; upstanding
ERECTOR erecting lens
ERELONG before long
EREMITE hermit; a solitary
EREPSIN an enzyme
ERGOTED afflicted with fungus **B.**
ERINEUM leafy excrescence **B.**
ERINITE arseniate of copper **Min.**
ERINOID a plastic material (milk)
ERINYES the Furies

ERISTIC controversial
ERL-KING (Norse mythology)
ERMELIN ermine; the stoat **Z.**
ERMINED adorned with fur
ERMINES white spots (Her.)
ERODENT consuming; erosive
ERODING corroding; eating away
EROSION corrosion
EROSIVE gnawing; virulent; acid
EROTEME interrogation mark
ERRABLE fallible; aberrant
ERRATIC rambling; vagrant; capricious
ERRATUM an error; misprint; mistake
ERRHINE medical snuff **Med.**
ERUDITE scholarly; learned
ERUGATE smoothed
ERUPTED exploded; ejected
ESCAPED eluded; avoided; leaked
ESCAPER danger dodger
ESCHARA net-like coral **Z.**
ESCHEAT forfeiture; confiscate **Law**
ESCRIME fencing; swordsmanship (Fr.)
ESCROLL heraldic scroll
ESCUAGE feudal tenure
ESCULIN alkaloid (horse chestnut) **Chem.**
ESERINE alkaloid (Calabar bean) **Chem.**
ESKIMOS God's frozen people
ESOPIAN fabulous (Aesop)
ESOTERY mysticism; necromancy
ESPADON Spanish sword
ESPARTO grass (Spain & Algeria) **B.**
ESPINEL kind of ruby **Min.**
ESPOUSE to marry; betroth
ESPYING observing; discovering
ESQUIRE originally a shield-bearer
ESSAYED assayed; tested; tried
ESSAYER essay writer
ESSENCE extract; quiddity
ESSENES Jewish fraternity
ESSOIGN essoin; excuse for absence
ESTIVAL (summer)
ESTOILE Heraldic star
ESTRADE a dais (Fr.)
ESTREAT true extract **Law**
ESTUARY river mouth; firth; frith
ESURINE aperitif; a cocktail
ETAERIO berried fruit (strawberry) **B.**
ETAGERE set of shelves (Fr.) .
ETATISM central control (government)
ETCHING engraving; an impression
ETERNAL endless; perennial; immortal
ETESIAN Levant wind
ETHERIA river-oyster **Z.**
ETHICAL moral
ETHIOPS dark-coloured
ETHMOID sieve-like; like a temse
ETOILIN yellow chlorophyll **Chem.**
ETONIAN
EUAEMIA healthy blood **Med.**
EUCAINE a cocaine-type of drug **Med.**

EUCHRED outwitted (U.S.A.)
EUCHYMY sound fluids   **Med.**
EUCLASE beryl   **Min.**
EUCRASY soundness; health   **Med.**
EUGENIA a large genus of spices   **B.**
EUGENIC (birth influence)
EUGENIN clove camphor   **B.**
EULALIA an ornamental grass   **B.**
EULOGIA praises; panegyrics
EULOGIC commendatory; laudatory
EUPEPSY hearty digestion   **Med.**
EUPHONY melodious sound
EUPHROE ridge-pole (Dut.)
EUPNAEA free respiration   **Med.**
EURIPUS strait having violent tides
EURITIC like granite   **Min.**
EURYALE water-lilies   **B.**
EUSTYLE columnar building style
EUTERPE Muse of music
EUTONIA firmness of tone   **Med.**
EVACUEE a displaced person
EVADING eluding; dodging; foiling
EVANGEL the gospel; good news
EVANISH vanish; disappear
EVASION subterfuge; prevarication
EVASIVE elusive; elusory; slippery
EVENING eventide; night-fall; twilight
EVERTED turned inside out
EVICTED dispossessed; ejected   **Law**
EVICTOR chucker-out   **Law**
EVIDENT obvious; patent; manifest
EVIL-EYE a bewitching look
EVINCED manifested; proved
EVIRATE castrate; geld
EVITATE to avoid (Shak.)
EVOCATE to summon spirits
EVOKING rousing; exciting; eliciting
EVOLUTE geometric curve
EVOLVED unfolded; emitted; educed
EWE-LAMB poor man's only possession
EXACTED demanded; levied
EXACTER extortioner
EXACTLY just so; precisely; literally
EXACTOR a tax collector
EXALGIN an anodyne   **Med.**
EXALTED lofty; ennobled; elevated
EXALTER magnifier; extoller
EXAMINE inquire; scrutinize
EXAMPLE model; pattern; sample
EXANGIA blood-vessel   **Med.**
EXARCHY a vice-royalty
EXCERPT an extract; cutting; citation
EXCHEAT escheat; confiscate   **Law**
EXCISED cut out; removed
EXCITED provoked; irritated; inflamed
EXCITER rouser; stimulant; agitator
EXCLAIM vociferate; ejaculate
EXCLAVE opposite to enclave
EXCLUDE prohibit; debar; preclude
EXCURSE to digress; to wander

EXCUSED released; pardoned; condoned
EXECUTE accomplish; behead   **Law**
EXEDRAE halls; recesses
EXEGETE theological exponent
EXERGUE date space on coin
EXERTED strove; applied; used
EXHALED emitted; evaporated; breathed
EXHAUST drain; empty; expend; tire
EXHIBIT display; manifest; evince
EXHUMED disinterred; unearthed
EXHUMER a resurrectionist
EXIGENT urgent; critical; importunate
EXILIAN exiled Jew
EXILING banishing; proscribing
EXILITY tenuity; slenderness
EXISTED was; lasted; endured; subsisted
EXITIAL destructive to life
EXODIST an emigrant
EXOGAMY mixed marriage
EXOMION Greek sleeveless vest
EXOTISM (not indigenous)
EXPANSE stretch; extent; space
EX-PARTE prejudiced; biassed
EXPENSE cost; outlay; charge; price
EXPIATE atone
EXPIRED exhaled; ended; stopped
EXPLAIN elucidate; interpret; expound
EXPLODE burst; detonate; discharge
EXPLOIT feat; deed; achievement
EXPLORE search; prospect; examine
EXPOSAL exposure; revelation
EXPOSED unmasked; debunked
EXPOSER revealer; nark
EXPOUND explain; unfold; interpret
EXPRESS explicit; exude; speedy
EXPUNGE erase; abrogate; cancel
EXPURGE purify; expurgate
EXSCIND cut out; exsect
EXTATIC ecstatic; rapturous
EXTINCT defunct; obsolete; quenched
EXTRACT decoction; essence; juice
EXTRACT extort; derive; select
EXTREME utmost; ultimate; excessive
EXTRUDE expel; eject; force out
EXUDING sweating; oozing; dripping
EXULTED crowed; triumphed; boasted
EXUVIAE cast-off skins, etc.   **Z.**
EXUVIAL (cast skins)   **Z.**
EYE-BALL the pupil of the eye
EYE-BATH eye basin
EYE-BEAM a glance
EYE-BOLT (for hooks)   **Naut**
EYE-BROW a hairy arch
EYE-DROP a tear
EYE-FLAP blinker
EYE-HOLE peep-hole
EYE-LASH cilliary hair
EYELESS blind; unobservant
EYELIAD wanton glance
EYESHOT range of vision; by eye

EYESORE a hideosity
EYESPOT (peacock's feather)
EYEWASH humbug; window dressing
EYE-WINK a wink (Shak.)

F

FABLIAU 12th cent. topical verse (Fr.)
FABLING romancing
FABRILE (handicraft)
FABULAR legendary
FACETED having facets
FACTION cabal; clique; dissension
FACTORY works; mill; workshop
FACTUAL real; actual; authentic
FACTURE manufacture; workmanship
FACULAR, FACULAE sunspots;
  spotted
FACULTY knack; skill; dexterity
FADAISE trivial remark (Fr.)
FADDING shellac lacquering
FADDISH rather crotchety
FADDIST pernickety person
FADDLED trifled; played
FADEDLY insipidly
FADE-OUT (films); an evanescence
FADGING suiting; prospering
FAGGERY drudgery
FAGGING enforced service
FAGOTTO bassoon   Mus.
FAHLERZ copper crystal ore   Min.
FAIENCE fayence; glazed pottery
FAILING a foible; declining; miscarry
FAILURE fiasco; ruin; collapse
FAINING wishing; desiring
FAINTED swooned; languished
FAINTER weaker; paler; dimmer
FAINTLY dimly; indistinctly
FAIREST clearest; purest
FAIRIES enchantresses; pixies
FAIRILY like a fairy; elf-like
FAIRING a present; streamlining
FAIRISH reasonably fair
FAIR-WAY (golf); navigable channel
FAITOUR imposter; scoundrel
FALANGE Spanish fascist party
FALBALA furbelow; puckered flounce
FALCADE (equitation); curvetting
FALCATE hooked; like a crescent
FALCULA claw   Z.
FALDAGE a farming privilege
FALDFEE grazing fee
FALERNE sweet white wine
FALLACY a sophism; chimera; untruth
FALLALS showy trifles
FALLING erring; tumbling; dropping
FALLOUT radioactive contamination
FALSELY fallaciously; untruly
FALSEST most disloyal
FALSIES artificial bust

FALSIFY counterfeit; belie; fake
FALSISH somewhat erroneous
FALSISM obvious falsity
FALSITY fallacy; fabrication
FAMULUS magician's assistant
FANATIC bigot; zealot; visionary
FANCIED favoured; imagined; thought
FANCIER expert; breeder
FANFARE flourish of trumpets
FANGLED newly contrived
FAN-MAIL letters of adulation
FANNING extending; winnowing
FAN-PALM the talipot palm   B.
FANTAIL pigeon; a gas burner
FANTASM spook; phantasm
FANTAST visionary; enthusiast
FANTASY caprice; mental conception
FARADAY unit of electrolysis
FARADIC inductive
FARAWAY distant; remote
FARCEUR satirical jester
FARCING edible stuffing; force-meat
FARCIFY to burlesque
FARDAGE dunnage; packing (Fr.) Naut.
FARMERY homestead
FARMING leasing of taxes
FARMOST uttermost; furthest
FARNESS remoteness
FARRAGO a medley; hodge-podge
FARRIER shoeing-smith; a vet
FARTHEL farl; oatcake
FARTHER besides; further; beyond
FASCETS glass-making tools   Tool
FASCIAE fillets; name boards
FASCIAL (fasces)
FASCINE bound brushwood
FASCISM anti-socialism
FASCIST political party (Italy)
FASHERY annoyance; vexation
FASHING worrying; bothering
FASHION mode; vogue; style; mould
FAST-DAY   Eccl.
FASTEST swiftest; fleetest; closest
FASTING abstaining from food
FASTISH rather dissipated
FATALLY mortally; ; calamitously
FATEFUL ominous; portentous
FAT-HEAD block-head; moron; dunce
FATIDIC prophetic; oracular
FATIGUE tire; jade; lassitude
FATLING   Z.
FATLUTE luting
FATNESS obesity; corpulence; fertility
FATTEST most obese
FATTING fattening
FATTISH rather plump; adipose
FATUITY self-complacency; folly
FATUOUS illusory; imbecile; witless
FAULTED displaced; (tennis)
FAULTER defaulter

FAUNIST naturalist
FAVOURS party badges
FAWNING sycophantic; cringing
FAYENCE faience; pottery
FEARFUL dismayed; dire
FEARING dreading; revering; timid
FEASTED caroused; gratified
FEASTER a Lucullus
FEATHER adorn; quill; (oar)   **Z.**
FEATURE characteristic; aspect; trait
FEAZING unravelling
FEBRILE feverish
FECULUM starchy extract
FEDERAL confederated
FEEDING pasture; eating; subsisting
FEE-FARM tenure without fealty
FEELING sensibility; perception
FEERING first furrow (Sc.)
FEE-TAIL entailed estate
FEEZING twisting; unscrewing
FEIGNED simulated; shammed
FEINTED feigned
FELIDAE, FELINAE the cat genus **Z.**
FELLING hewing; cutting down
FELONRY the convict class
FELSITE igneous rock   **Min.**
FELSPAR metamorphic rock   **Min.**
FELTING felt cloth
FELUCCA Mediterranean vessel   **Naut.**
FELWORT mullein   **B.**
FEMINAL womanly
FEMORAL (thigh)   **Med.**
FENCING hedging; evading
FENDING warding off; averting
FEN-DUCK shoveller-duck   **Z.**
FEN-FIRE will o' the wisp
FENGITE alabaster   **Min.**
FENNISH marshy; boggy; swampy
FEODARY feudal tenure
FEOFFEE receiver of a fief
FEOFFOR feoffer; fief-granter
FERDWIT a quittance; penalty
FERINGI European in India
FERMATA a pause   **Mus.**
FERMENT inflame; commotion; yeast
FERNERY   **B.**
FERN-OWL night-jar   **Z.**
FERRARA a sword-blade (It.)
FERRATE an iron salt   **Chem.**
FERRIED transported
FERRIES ferry-boats
FERRITE ferro-magnetic (ceramics)   **Chem.**
FERROUS (iron)   **Chem.**
FERRUGO plant-rust; fungus   **B.**
FERRULE protecting cap
FERTILE inventive; prolific; fruitful
FERULED caned; punished
FERVENT zealous; ardent; glowing
FERVOUR eagerness; intensity; ardour
FESTIVE joyous; convivial; gay

FESTOON wreath; garland
FESTUCA grass genus   **B.**
FETCHED brought; conveyed; reached
FETCHER collector; heaver
FETLOCK a tuft of hair   **Z.**
FEUDARY feodary   **Law.**
FEUDING quarrelling (ice hockey)
FEUDIST writer on feudal law   **Law**
FEU-DUTY annual payment (Sc.)
FEVERED agitated; febrile
FEWNESS paucity; scarcity; sparsity
FIANCEE betrothed lady
FIBBERY mendacity
FIBBING prevaricating
FIBROID like fibre
FIBROIN cobweb material
FIBROMA fibrous tumour   **Med.**
FIBROSE filamental
FIBROUS stringy
FIBSTER petty liar
FIBULAR (leg bone)   **Med.**
FICARIA celandine   **B.**
FICTILE plastic; mouldable
FICTION romance; fantasy; invention
FICTIVE imaginative; feigned
FIDALGO Portuguese hidalgo
FIDDLED trifled; meddled   **Mus.**
FIDDLER a crab; violinist
FIDDLEY hatchway railing   **Naut.**
FIDGETY restless; uneasy; impatient
FIELDED (cricket); (base-ball)
FIELDER not one of the batting side
FIERCER more violent
FIERILY vehemently; ardently
FIFTEEN a Rugby side
FIFTHLY
FIG-CAKE
FIGGERY dressy ornament
FIGGING dressing up
FIG-GNAT   **Z.**
FIGHTER combatant; warrior
FIG-LEAF early dress material   **B.**
FIGMENT a fabrication
FIG-TREE   **B.**
FIGURAL pictorial; figurate
FIGURED computed; depicted
FIGWORT a plant   **B.**
FILACER } Law officer dealing with
FILAZER } writs and pleas   **Law**
FILARIA parasitic worms   **Z.**
FILBERT hazel-nut   **B.**
FILCHED purloined; stole
FILCHER pick-pocket; pilferer
FILEMOT dead-leaf colour
FILIATE affiliate; adopt
FILIBEG the kilt
FILICAL (ferns)   **B.**
FILICES the ferns   **B.**
FILINGS file fragments
FILLING satisfying; replenishing

FILM-FAN a devotee; star-worshipper
FILMING recording in celluloid
FIMBRIA fringe
FIMETIC foul in thought
FINABLE liable to a fine; amerceable
FINALLY ultimately; lastly; eventually
FINANCE money affairs; revenue
FINBACK rorqual whale **Z.**
FINCHED striped; spotted
FINDING verdict; discovering
FINECUT chopped into small pieces
FINESSE subtlety; craft; artifice
FIN-FISH fin-back whale **Z.**
FIN-FOOT tropical bird **Z.**
FINICAL fastidious; dainty; faddy
FINICKY niggling; meticulous
FINIKIN finicking; finicky
FINLESS having no flipper
FINLIKE
FINNACK } white sea-trout **Z.**
FINNOCK
FINNISH the language of the Finns
FIN-TOED web-footed
FIORITE volcanic residue **Min.**
FIRE-ARM weapon
FIRE-BAR furnace bar
FIRE-BOX
FIRE-BUG an incendiary
FIREDOG an andiron
FIREFLY a luminous beetle **Z.**
FIREMAN
FIRE-NEW brand-new
FIRE-PAN brazier; priming pan
FIRE-POT incendiary bomb
FIRMARY tenant's rights **Law**
FIRMING confirming; establishing
FIRSTLY
FISH-DAY fast day
FISHERY
FISH-FAG fish-wife
FISH-FLY a bait **Z.**
FISH-GIG fishing appliance
FISH-GOD Dagon
FISHIFY to turn into a fish (Shak.)
FISHILY in a fishy manner
FISHING angling; piscatorial pursuit
FISH-MAW swimming bladder
FISH-OIL
FISHWAY fish-ladder
FISKERY friskiness
FISSILE cleavable; laminate
FISSION fissure; rent; rift; fracture
FISSIVE fissile
FISSURE cleft; crevice; interstice
FISTING pommelling
FIST-LAW might is right
FISTUCA pile-driver
FISTULA ulcer; reed **Med.**
FITCHED pointed (Her.)
FITCHEE fitched

FITCHET polecat; foumart **Z.**
FITMENT a fitting
FITNESS aptness; decency; seemliness
FITTAGE brokerage
FITTING a fixture; appropriate
FITWEED anti-hysteric plant **B.**
FIXABLE securable
FIXEDLY firmly; steadfastly
FIXTURE appointment; engagement
FIZZING spluttering; hissing
FIZZLED failed; flopped
FLACCID flabby; tabid; loose; limp
FLACKER flutter like a bird
FLACKET flask; flasket
FLACKIE straw packing
FLAFFER to flutter (Sc.)
FLAG-DAY
FLAGGED signalled; drooped
FLAG-MAN signaller
FLAKING crumbling
FLAMING blazing; burning; glowing
FLAMMED hoaxed
FLAMMER splitting knife **Tool**
FLANEUR an idling gossip
FLANGED having a raised edge
FLANKED bordered by; side by side
FLANKER
FLANNEL woollen fabric; mullein genus
FLAPPED waved; vibrated; wagged
FLAPPER bird; girl **Z.**
FLARING funnel-shaped; glaring
FLASHED glistened; sparkled; gleamed
FLASHER would-be wit
FLASKET basket; flask
FLATLET a small flat
FLATTED flattened; depressed
FLATTEN level; lay low
FLATTER coax; cajole; compliment
FLAUNTY showy; gaudy
FLAVIAN (Flavius Vespasian)
FLAVINE a yellow dye **B.**
FLAVOUR zest; savour; taste; relish
FLAWING cracking; marring
FLAYING skinning; excoriating
FLEABAG sleeping bag
FLEAPIT shabby room; theatre
FLECKED spotted
FLECKER to dapple
FLEDGED ready for flight
FLEECED clipped; shorn
FLEECER white collar bandit
FLEEING absconding; retreating
FLEERED mocked; scoffed
FLEERER a derider; flouter
FLEETED flitted; flew; sped
FLEETER swifter; faster
FLEETLY swiftly; nimbly; rapidly
FLEMING a native of Flanders
FLEMISH language of Flemings
FLENSED cut blubber
FLESHED satiated; glutted

FLESHER butcher; red-backed shrike **Z.**
FLESHLY carnal; sensual; fat; obese
FLEURET floral decoration; fencing-foil
FLEXILE pliable; pliant; supple
FLEXING bending; turning
FLEXION inclination; a bow
FLEXURE bending; curvature
FLICKED flipped
FLICKER twinkle; scintillate
FLIGHTY volatile; mercurial; fickle
FLINDER splinter; fragment
FLINGER hurler
FLIP-DOG liquor heater **Z.**
FLIPPED filliped; flicked
FLIPPER fore-limb of a cetacean **Z.**
FLIRTED coquetted; flicked
FLITTED flew; hovered
FLITTER flutter; a tatter
FLOATED drifted; wafted
FLOATER not a sinker
FLOCCUS tuft of hair; down
FLOCKED crowded; swarmed; thronged
FLOCKLY like sheep
FLOGGED scourged; lashed
FLOODED swamped; inundated; deluged
FLOOKAN slimy clay
FLOORED overthrown; baffled
FLOORER knockdown blow
FLOPPED failed; fizzled
FLOREAL 8th month (Fr. Revolution)
FLORIST a nurseryman
FLOROON flower border
FLORUIT a life-time
FLOTAGE buoyancy
FLOTSAM recovered wreckage
FLOUNCE a jerky movement
FLOURED powdered
FLOUTED jeered; insulted
FLOUTER mocker; derider
FLOWAGE flow; current; discharge
FLOWERY florid; ornate; figurative
FLOWING fluent; copious; smooth
FLUENCY also fluence; exuberance
FLUEWAY smoke and gas duct
FLUFFED bungled; foozled
FLUIDAL flowing; liquid
FLUIDIC fluid
FLUIDLY liquidly
FLUKILY by a fluke
FLUKING scoring by chance
FLUMMOX perplex; defeat
FLUMPED slumped
FLUNKEY footman; snob; toady
FLUORIC (fluorine) **Chem.**
FLUSHED blushed; roused; disturbed
FLUSHER lesser butcher-bird **Z.**
FLUSTER agitation; disconcert; bustle
FLUSTRA sea-mat; polyzoa **Z.**
FLUTINA accordion **Mus.**
FLUTING grooving

FLUTIST flautist
FLUTTER speculation; palpitate
FLUVIAL (rivers)
FLUXIDE fusible
FLUXING melting
FLUXION fusion; variation; change
FLYAWAY flighty
FLYBACK electronics
FLY-BILL hand-bill
FLY-BLOW fly-larva **Z.**
FLY-BOAT canal boat
FLY-BOMB pilotless aerial torpedo
FLY-BOOK (fishing)
FLY-FLAP fly-whisk
FLY-HALF (football)
FLY-LEAF blank page
FLY-LINE fishing line
FLY-OVER road or rail crossing
FLY-PAST flight by aircraft
FLY-RAIL table leaf support
FLY-TRAP an insectivorous plant **B.**
FOALING colt-birth
FOAMING raging; bubbling; creaming
FOBBING cheating; tricking
FOCUSED concentrated
FOE-LIKE hostile; inimical; adverse
FOG-BANK
FOG-BELL
FOGGAGE coarse grass **B.**
FOGGIER murkier; more opaque
FOGGILY mistily
FOGGING obscuring
FOGHORN
FOGLAMP penetrating headlight
FOGLESS clear
FOG-RING bank of fog
FOGYISH antiquated
FOGYISM dull notions
FOILING tracery; deer track
FOILIST fencer
FOINING thrusting; tilting
FOISTED falsified; thrust
FOISTER palmer; imposer; cheat
FOLDAGE sheep folding rights
FOLDING a fold; sheep penning
FOLIAGE leafage; boscage
FOLIATE a curve; laminate
FOLIOED in folios or pages
FOLIOLE leaflet **B.**
FOLIOSE leafy
FOLIOUS thin; unsubstantial
FOLLIES imbecilities; inanities
FOMITES porous substances **Chem.**
FONDANT soft sweet
FONDEST most affectionate
FONDING doting
FONDLED caressed; dandled
FONDLER sugar daddy
FONTEIN S. African spring
FONTLET small font **Eccl.**

FOODFUL nourishing; nutritious
FOOLERY clowning; buffoonery
FOOLING hoodwinking; beguiling
FOOLISH doltish; stupid; irrational
FOOT-BAR aeroplane rudder control
FOOTBOY page; bell-hop
FOOTHOT hot-foot; immediately
FOOTING basis; entrance fee
FOOTLED pottered
FOOTMAN flunkey; lacquey
FOOTPAD highwayman
FOOT-ROT disease of sheep
FOOT-TON a measure of work **Meas.**
FOOTWAY footpath
FOOZLED footled; mishit
FOOZLER bungler
FOPLING young dandy
FOPPERY affectation; coxcombry
FOPPISH finical; dressy
FORAGED plundered; pillaged
FORAGER ravager; a cap
FORAMEN a pore **Med.**
FORAYED invaded; raided
FORAYER marauder
FORBADE vetoed; banned; inhibited
FORBEAR ancestor; refrain; abstain
FORBORE desisted; withheld; shunned
FORCEPS pliers **Tool**
FORCING plant culture; coercing
FORCITE dynamite
FORCQUE fork; mine sump
FORDING crossing
FORDONE tired out
FOREARM **Med.**
FORE-BOW front of saddle
FORE-CAR (motor-cycle)
FOREDAY forenoon
FOREDID overpowered; undid
FORE-END the front end
FOREIGN alien; exotic; strange
FORELAY ambush
FORELEG
FOREMAN boss; overseer; ganger **Law**
FORERAN preceded; ushered
FORERUN herald
FORESAW foretold; forecast
FORESAY predict; presage; augur
FORESEE anticipate; forecast
FORETOP **Naut.**
FOREVER everlasting; always
FORFANG an ancient felony **Law**
FORFEIT alienate; penalty; fine
FORFEND to avert; ward off
FORGAVE pardoned; absolved
FORGERY counterfeiting
FORGING shaping; hammering
FORGIVE remit; excuse
FORGONE past; predetermined
FORKFUL
FORKING branching; dividing

FORLORN desolate; lost; hapless
FORMATE (formic acid) **Chem.**
FORMFUL imaginative; creative
FORMING shaping; moulding
FORMULA set of symbols
FORNENT directly opposite (Sc.)
FORPINE waste away (obs.)
FORSAKE abandon; quit; desert
FORSOOK renounced; relinquished
FORTIFY strengthen; brace
FORTLET small redoubt
FORTUNE luck; Kismet; felicity
FORWARD bold; brazen; quicken
FORWENT foregone
FORWORN tired out (obs.)
FOSSICK prospect; rummage
FOSSWAY Roman road
FOUDRIE jurisdiction (Sc.)
FOUGADE fougasse; mine
FOULARD silk
FOULDER to flame; gleam (obs.)
FOULING (gun-barrels); soiling
FOUMART the polecat; fitchew **Z.**
FOUNDED started; established
FOUNDER collapse; originator
FOUNDRY (metal-casting)
FOURGON baggage wagon
FOVEATE pitted **B.**
FOVEOLA dent; depression **Med.**
FOVILLA (pollen) **B.**
FOWLING falconry
FOWLRUN poultry yard
FOX-CASE fox-skin
FOX-EVIL baldness **Med.**
FOXHOLE defensive trench
FOXHUNT
FOXLIKE cunning
FOXSHIP craftiness
FOXTAIL a grass **B.**
FOX-TRAP a snare
FOX-TROT a dance
FRABBIT peevish
FRACHES glass annealing trays
FRACTED broken (Her.)
FRAGILE delicate; infirm; brittle
FRAILLY weakly; feebly
FRAILTY foible; weakness; infirmity
FRAISED defended by pointed stakes
FRAME-UP a plot
FRAMING forming; devising
FRAMPEL quarrelsome; peevish
FRANCIC Frankish
FRANION boon companion; paramour
FRANKED exempt; post paid
FRANKLY candidly; openly; unreserved
FRANTIC frenzied; raving; distracted
FRAPPED bound **Naut.**
FRATCHY quarrelsome
FRATERY refectory in monastery **Eccl.**
FRAUGHT laden; pregnant; surcharged

FRAYING peel of deer's horn
FRAZZLE tatters; shreds
FREAKED streaked; checkered
FRECKLE macula
FRECKLY
FREEDOM liberty; informality; scope
FREEING loosing; liberating
FREEMAN privileged citizen
FREESIA bulbous plant **B.**
FREEWAY by pass; motorway
FREEZER refrigerator
FREIGHT cargo; burden; burthen
FRENATE bristly **Z.**
FRESHEN refresh; invigorate; revive
FRESHER freshman; less faded
FRESHES a flood; a spate
FRESHET flooding of a river
FRESHLY recently; briskly; newly
FRETFUL petulant; testy; fractious
FRET-SAW **Tool**
FRETTED frayed; abraded; harassed
FRETTEN pock-pitted
FRETTER a worried woman
FRIABLE crumbly; powdery
FRIARLY unsophisticated
FRIBBLE frivolous; to trifle; totter
FRIEZED shaggy with nap; ornamented
FRIGATE a war-ship **Naut.**
FRIJOLE Mexican bean **B.**
FRILLED adorned like a ham
FRINGED bordered; edged
FRIPPER old clo' merchant
FRISEUR hair-dresser
FRISIAN Frieslander; cattle **Z.**
FRISKED gambolled; searched
FRISKER a gad-about; a searcher
FRISKET a printing frame
FRISLET small ruffle
FRISURE a crisping of the hair
FRITTED fused; baked
FRITTER pancake; fragment; dissipate
FRIZZED curled
FRIZZLE to fry; to crisp; to splutter
FRIZZLY curly
FROCKED
FROGBIT aquatic plant **B.**
FROGERY a frog pool **Z.**
FROGGED braided
FROG-MAN special type of diver **Naut.**
FRONDED leafy **B.**
FRONTAL a pediment; head on
FRONTED faced; encountered
FRONTON a pelota ground (Sp.)
FROSTED roughened
FROTHED foamed
FROUNCE wrinkle; frown
FROWARD perverse; wayward
FROWNED scowled; glowered
FROWSTY foul and stuffy
FRUCTED bearing fruit

FRUGGIN oven stirring pole
FRUITED bore fruit
FRUITER fruit grower
FRUMPED jeered
FRUMPER scoffer; mocker
FRUSTUM a conic section
FRUTIFY fructify; teem; produce
FUBBERY deception
FUCATED painted deceptively
FUCHSIA a flowering shrub **B.**
FUCHSIN red fuchsia dye
FUDDLED bemused; fuzzled
FUDDLER drunkard; toper
FUDGING faking
FUEHRER German dictator
FUELLED
FUELLER stoker
FUFFING puffing
FUGUIST fugue composer **Mus.**
FULCRUM support for lever
FULGENT dazzling; radiant; brilliant
FULGORA lantern fly **Z.**
FULGOUR splendour
FULLAGE fuller's pay
FULLERY cloth works
FULLEST amplest; most exhaustive
FULL-HOT vehement; blazing
FULLING (cloth process)
FULL-PAY
FULMINE fulminate
FULNESS repletion; plenty; plentitude
FULSOME obsequious; nauseous
FULVOUS tawny; fulvid
FUMARIA genus of plants **B.**
FUMARIC a vegetable extract **B.**
FUMBLED bungled; groped
FUMBLER foozler
FUMETTE smell of high game
FUMITER the fumitory plant **B.**
FUNARIA genus of mosses **B.**
FUNDING forming a reserve
FUNERAL sepulture; obsequies
FUNFAIR amusement park
FUNGATE (fungic acid) **Chem.**
FUNGITE fossil coral **Min.**
FUNGOID fungus **B.**
FUNICLE ligature; a fibre **B.**
FUNKING panicking; fearing
FUNNILY comically; humorously
FUNNING joking; diverting
FURACIN drug for surface infections **Med**
FURBISH burnish; rub; polish
FURCATE forked
FURCULA the merrythought **Z.**
FURFAIR dandruff **Med.**
FURIOSO all out **Mus.**
FURIOUS frantic; raging; frenzied
FURLANA forlana; Venetian dance
FURLING wrapping; rolling
FURLONG 220 yards **Meas.**

FURMETY frumenty; porridge
FURNACE firebox
FURNISH equip; supply; produce
FURRIER a dealer in furs
FURRING (lathing); encrusting
FURROWY in furrows
FURTHER farther; promote; encourage
FURTIVE stealthy; sly; clandestine
FUSCINE an oil extract   **Chem.**
FUSCITE crystallized pyrargillite **Min.**
FUSCOUS swarthy
FUSIBLE able to be melted
FUSSIER more fidgety
FUSSILY restlessly
FUSSING making trouble
FUSS-POT anxious busy-body
FUSTIAN coarse cloth; bombastic
FUSTIER mouldier; mustier
FUTCHEL supporting bar
FUTHORC Runic alphabet
FUTTOCK ship's timber
FUZZIER curlier; more crinkled
FUZZLED fuddled; inebriated
FYRDUNG Saxon martial array

G

GABBARD gabbart; a barge   **Naut.**
GABBING gossiping
GABBLED gaggled; chattered
GABBLER a babbler
GABELER salt tax collector
GADELLE currant (Fr.)   **B.**
GADDING roving; wandering
GADDISH restless
GADLING gauntlet spike
GADROON ornamented edge
GADSMAN ploughman
GADWALL migratory duck   **Z.**
GAEKWAR Gaikwar; (Baroda)
GAFFING (fishing); gambling
GAGGING interpolation; silencing
GAGGLED gabbled
GAINFUL lucrative; beneficial
GAINING profiting; winning; acquiring
GAINSAY dispute; contradict
GAIRISH garish; gaudy
GAITERS gambadoes
GALANTY (shadow pantomime)
GALATEA Pygmalion's statue
GALATEA cotton fabric
GALEATE crested   **Z.**
GALEENY guinea-fowl   **Z.**
GALENIC (lead)
GALETTE a gateau
GALILEE West porch   **Eccl.**
GALILEO eminent astronomer
GALIPOT pine-resin   **B.**
GALLANT courtly; valiant; a beau
GALLA-OX Abyssinian ox   **Z.**

GALLATE (gallic acid)   **Chem.**
GALLEON treasure ship   **Naut.**
GALLERY corridor; passage; balcony
GALL-FLY a pest   **Z.**
GALLICE in French
GALLING irritating; exasperating
GALLIOT galiot; brigantine   **Naut.**
GALLIUM a metallic element   **Chem.**
GALLIZE (wine-making)
GALL-NUT a pestiferous growth **B.**
GALLOON woven fabric; lace
GALLOWS (Tyburn)
GALOCHE galosh; rubber over-shoe
GALOPIN kitchen-boy (Sc.)
GALUMPH bound exultingly
GAMBADO mud-gaiter; caper
GAMBIAN native of Gambia (W. Africa)
GAMBIER catechu; a dye   **B.**
GAMBIST a viol player   **Mus.**
GAMBLED staked; ventured; hazarded
GAMBLER speculator; wagerer
GAMBOGE also camboge
GAMBREL butcher's crook; roof **Arch.**
GAME-BAG
GAME-EGG a bad egg   **Z.**
GAMEFUL sportive
GAME-LEG lameness   **Med.**
GAMETAL gametic; reproductive
GAMMOCK sky-larking; gammon
GAMPISH bulging; slatternly
GANCHED (Turkish execution)
GANGING going (Sc.); joining **Electron.**
GANGLIA nerve-centre   **Med.**
GANGREL vagrant; vagabond
GANG-SAW multiple saw   **Tool**
GANGWAY a passage   **Naut.**
GANOIDS fish of sturgeon type **Z.**
GANTLET gauntler
GAPPING opening; cleaving
GARAGED
GARBAGE refuse; offal
GARBLED (suppressio veri)
GARBLER (suggestio falsi)
GARBOIL uproar; turmoil (Shak.)
GARDANT full faced (Her.)
GARFISH sea-fish; belone   **Z.**
GARGLED warbled
GARLAND wreath; chaplet; festoon
GARMENT vesture; raiment; apparel
GARNISH adorn; pewter ware
GAROTTE garrotte; throttle
GARPIKE the garfish   **Z.**
GARVOCK a sprat; garvie (Sc.) **Z.**
GAS-BUOY   **Naut.**
GAS-COAL anthracite
GAS-COKE
GASEITY gaseousness
GASEOUS
GAS-FIRE
GASHFUL mutilated; hideous

GASHING slicing; slitting
GASKINS leggings
GAS-LAMP
GAS-LIME (gas filtration)
GAS-MAIN
GAS-MASK
GAS-OVEN
GASPING spasmodic breathing
GAS-PIPE
GAS-RING
GASSING loquacity
GASSOUL mineral soap (Morocco)
GAS-TANK
GASTRIC gastral; (stomach) **Med.**
GATEMAN gate-keeper
GATEWAY entrance
GATLING a gun
GAUDERY finery; gew-gaws
GAUDIED embellished
GAUDILY ostentatiously
GAUFFER to crimp
GAUFFRE a batter cake
GAUGING mensuration; estimating
GAULISH (Gaul)
GAULTER gault or clay digger
GAUMING daubing; smearing
GAUNTLY lankily; leanly
GAUNTRY gantry; travelling crane, &c.
GAVELET land forfeiture **Law**
GAVILAN species of hawk **Z.**
GAVOTTE a country dance **Mus.**
GAYNESS merriment; hilarity
GAYSOME blithe; vivacious; jolly
GAZEFUL regardant; contemplative
GAZELLE **Z.**
GAZETTE journal; newspaper; record
GEAR-BOX motor-engine
GEARING train of wheels
GEGGERY trickery (Sc.)
GEHENNA place of abomination
GELABLE congealable
GELATIN gelatine
GELDING **Z.**
GELIDLY frigidly
GELLOCK crowbar; gavelock **Tool**
GEMMATE budding
GEMMERY, GEMMARY jewellery
GEMMING budding
GEMMULE small bud **B.**
GEMSBOK S. African antelope **Z.**
GENAPPE worsted yarn
GENERAL vague; inexact; usual
GENERIC collective; characteristic
GENESIS starting point
GENETIC originating
GENETTE genet; civet **Z.**
GENEVAN Calvinist **Eccl.**
GENIPAP orange-like fruit
GENISTA broom plant; (Plantagenet) **B.**
GENITAL generic

GENITOR creator
GENOESE
GENTEEL elegant; polite; mincing
GENTIAN plant genus **B.**
GENTILE not a Jew
GENTLER milder; more kindly
GENUINE sincere; authentic; veritable
GEODESY (earth measurements)
GEOGONY (earth formations)
GEOIDAL earth-shaped
GEOLOGY
GEONOMY physical geography
GEORAMA globular map
GEORDIE mine-lamp; guinea **Coin**
GEORGIC rural poetry
GERMANE relevant; apposite; pertinent
GERMULE a small germ **Med.**
GESTAPO German secret police
GESTURE sign; signal; action
GETABLE obtainable; procurable
GET-AWAY escape
GETTING acquisition; gaining; reaching
GHASTLY fearsome; spectral; awful
GHERKIN small cucumber **B.**
GHILGAI Australian dewpond
GHILLIE game-keeper (Sc.)
GHOSTLY weird; spiritual; spectral
GIANTLY gigantic; Cyclopean
GIANTRY giants collectively
GIBBOSE humped
GIBBOUS convex **Astron.**
GIBLETS kidneys and liver
GIDDILY vertiginously
GIFTING endowing; bestowing
GIGGLED
GIGGLER
GIG-MILL nap-raising device
GILBERT magnetic potential
GILDING
GILLIAN sweetheart
GILL-LID gill covering **Z.**
GIMBALS compass suspender
GIMBLET gimlet **Tool**
GIMMICK publicity trick
GIN-FIZZ a beverage
GINGALL swivel gun
GINGERY hot-flavoured
GINGHAM umbrella; gamp; (material)
GINGILI sesame-oil **B.**
GINGING mine-shaft lining
GINNING cotton making
GINSENG a Chinese pick-me-up **B.**
GIN-SHOP gin-palace
GINTRAP
GIPPING gutting
GIPSIES Zingari
GIRAFFE the camelopard **Z.**
GIRASOL fire-opal **Min.**
GIRDING a covering; reproaching
GIRDLED zoned; belted

GIRDLER girdle maker
GIRLISH very young; lady-like
GIRNING grumbling (Sc.)
GIRROCK garfish **Z.**
GIRTHED girdled; bound
GISARME battle-axe; bill; halberd
GITTERN cithern; guitar **Mus.**
GIZZARD entrails of a bird
GLACIAL icy
GLACIER
GLADDEN delight; gratify; rejoice
GLADDER brighter; more cheerful
GLAD-EYE an invitation
GLADIUS sword-fish **Z.**
GLADWYN purple iris **B.**
GLAIDIN glutin; (wheat)
GLAIKIT giddy; foolish (Sc.)
GLAIRED varnished
GLAMOUR fascination; witchery
GLANCED glimpsed; ricocheted
GLARING refulgent; bare-faced
GLASSES specs
GLAUCUS genus of molluscs **Z.**
GLAZIER pane-setter
GLAZING (windows); (pottery)
GLEAMED shone; flashed; glinted
GLEANED gathered; culled; harvested
GLEANER Ruth
GLEBOUS gleby; turfy
GLEDGED squinted
GLEEFUL gay; lively; hilarious
GLEEMAN minstrel
GLENOID cupped **Med.**
GLEYING squinting
GLIADIN gliadine; glutin **Chem.**
GLIDING flowing; skimming; sliding
GLIMMER gleam; inkling
GLIMPSE glance; view; look
GLINTED gleamed; sparkled
GLISTEN shine; coruscate; scintillate
GLISTER glitter; lustre; sparkle
GLITTER glisten; brilliance; radiance
GLOAMED grew dark
GLOATED exulted; revelled
GLOBARD a glow-worm **Z.**
GLOBATE spheroidal
GLOBING encircling
GLOBOID spherical
GLOBOSE round
GLOBOUS globular
GLOBULE corpuscle
GLOOMED obscured; dimmed; moped
GLORIED exalted; took pride in
GLORIFY honour; magnify; extol; bless
GLOSSED explained; palliated
GLOSSER polisher; commentator
GLOSSIC phonetic alphabet
GLOTTIC glottal **Med.**
GLOTTIS (larynx) **Med.**
GLOWING vehement, ardent; fervid

GLOZING specious representation
GLUCIDE saccharin **Chem.**
GLUCINA an oxide **Chem.**
GLUCOSE sugar
GLUE-POT
GLUMMER more dismal and dejected
GLUMOUS husky **B.**
GLUTTED gorged; surfeited; crammed
GLUTTON the wolverine **Z.**
GLYPHIC word picture; plastic model
GLYPTIC engraved; figured
GMELINA (verbena) **B.**
GNARING snarling; growling
GNARLED knotty; gnarred
GNARRED gnarled; knotty
GNASHED ground
GNATHIC (jaws); gnathal **Med.**
GNAT-NET mosquito-net
GNAWING champing; eroding
GNOSTIC speculative believer
GOADING inciting; annoying
GO-AHEAD enterprising
GOATISH lustful
GOBBING coal refuse
GOBBLED gulped; bolted
GOBBLER turkey-cock **Z.**
GOBBLER gormandizer
GOBELIN French tapestry
GODDARD pewter cup
GODDESS
GODETIA a garden annual **B.**
GODHEAD
GODHOOD
GODLESS atheistic; irreligious; profane
GODLIER more righteous
GODLIKE deific
GODLILY devoutly
GODLING an inferior deity
GODROON gadroon; beading
GODSEND wind-fall; a crowning mercy
GODSHIP deification
GODWARD heavenward
GOGGLED lobster-eyed
GOGGLES eye-protectors
GOITRED afflicted with bronchocele
GOLD-CUP butter-cup **B.**
GOLDING an apple; hops **B.**
GOLDNEY a bream **Z.**
GOLFING
GOLIARD wandering jester
GOLIATH large beetle **Z.**
GOMBEEN money-lending; usury (Irish)
GOMELIN cotton starch
GOMERIL a lout; stupid fellow (Sc.)
GONAGRA gout **Med.**
GONDOLA car of an airship **Naut.**
GONGING prelude to a fine
GONIDIA lichen-spores **B.**
GOOD-BYE adieu
GOOD-DAY

GOOD-DEN ⎫ good evening
GOOD-E'EN ⎭
GOOD-EGG! cordial approval
GOODISH not so bad
GOODMAN a husband
GOOD-NOW exclamation of wonder
GOONDIE Australian native hut
GOOSERY cf. swannery　Z.
GOPURAM Hindu gate tower　Arch.
GORCOCK red grouse　Z.
GOR-CROW carrion crow　Z.
GORDIAN intricate; (knot)
GORDIUS hair-worm　Z.
GORGING cramming; stuffing
GORILLA largest anthropoid ape　Z.
GORMAND gourmand; glutton
GORSEDD Welsh bardic assembly
GOSHAWK short-winged hawk　Z.
GOSLING a young goose　Z.
GOSNICK small sea-fish; skipper　Z.
GOSSIPY chatty; loquacious
GOSSOON a boy (Irish)
GOUACHE (water-colour painting)
GOUGING scooping
GOULARD lead acetate　Chem.
GOULASH a ragout; (cards)
GOURAMI tropical fish　Z.
GOURMET a dainty feeder; epicure
GOURNET gurnet　Z.
GOUTILY
GOWN-MAN a divine, etc.
GRAB-BAG lucky-dip bag
GRABBED clutched; snatched
GRABBER gripper; pincher
GRABBLE sprawl; grope; paw
GRACILE slender
GRACING adorning; decking
GRACKLE Indian thrush　Z.
GRADATE to blend colour
GRADELY orderly; really good
GRADINE sculptor's chisel　Tool
GRADING a decoration; classifying
GRADUAL step by step
GRAFFER notary; scrivener　Law
GRAFTED incorporated
GRAFTER swindler
GRAINED (painted wood)
GRAINER grain-painter
GRALLAE wading birds　Z.
GRALLIC stilted
GRAMARY magic; wizardry
GRAMMAR a treatise
GRAMPUS dolphin; killer whale　Z.
GRANARY grain-store
GRANDAD grand-pa
GRANDAM a grannie
GRANDEE Spanish nobleman
GRANDER finer; superior; sublime
GRANDLY splendidly; superbly
GRANDMA grandam

GRANGER farm bailiff
GRANITE igneous crystalline rock　Min.
GRANNOM grandam
GRANTED ceded; allotted; vouchsafed
GRANTEE the receiver　Law
GRANTER the bestower
GRANTOR conveyor　Law
GRANULE small particle
GRAPERY vinery　B.
GRAPHIC pictorial; striking; vivid
GRAPNEL grappling-iron
GRAPPLE grasp; clutch; grip
GRASPED clasped; gripped; understood
GRASPER clasper; grabber
GRASSED brought down
GRASSER extra printing hand
GRASSUM a premium　Law
GRATIFY please; humour; gladden
GRATING harsh; offensive; jarring
GRAVELY seriously; staidly; soberly
GRAVEST most serious; very cogent
GRAVIED served with gravy
GRAVING engraving; scraping
GRAVITA gravely　Mus.
GRAVITY enormity; importance
GRAVURE photogravure
GRAZIER a pastor; shepherd
GRAZING glancing; touching; browsing
GREASED lubricated; oiled
GREASER lubricator; a dago
GREATEN enhance; enlarge; augment
GREATER bulkier; bigger; larger
GREATLY vastly; notably; immensely
GREAVES leg-armour
GREAVES tallow refuse; cracklings
GRECIAN
GRECISM Greek idiom
GRECIZE to Hellenize
GRECQUE coffee-machine
GREENED hoaxed; duped; gulled
GREENER more verdant
GREENLY verdantly
GREENTH verdure
GREETED accosted; welcomed
GREMIAL Bishop's pinafore　Eccl.
GREMLIN aerial imp
GRENADE hand-bomb
GREY-HEN stone bottle
GREY-HEN female grouse　Z.
GREY-FLY gray-fly　Z.
GREY-LAG wild goose　Z.
GREY-OWL tawny owl　Z.
GREYISH grayish
GREYLAG gray-lag; grey goose　Z.
GRIDDED marked in squares
GRIDDLE sieve; a grid
GRIDING grating; jarring
GRIEVED lamented; mourned
GRIFFIN greenhorn; a duenna
GRIFFIN Heraldic monster

GRIFFON griffin; a dog **Z.**	**GRYSBOK** S. African antelope **Z.**
GRILLED broiled; cross-examined	**GUAJIRA** peasant dance (Cuba)
GRIMACE a moué	**GUANACO** huanco; camel **Z.**
GRIMILY grimly; dourly; steadfastly	**GUANINE** (guano)
GRIMING fouling; soiling	**GUARANA** Brazil cocoa **B.**
GRIMMER dourer; fiercer; more grisly	**GUARANI** (Paraguay) **Coin**
GRINDER a molar	**GUARDED** wary; watchful; defended
GRINNED	**GUDGEON** an axle; a fish **Z.**
GRIPING grasping; trenching	**GUELDER** rose; snowball tree **B.**
GRIPPED seized; held; clutched	**GUENONS** a monkey genus **Z.**
GRIPPER a bailiff	**GUERDON** a reward; recompense
GRIPPLE usurious; tenacious	**GUEREZA** the Abyssinian monkey **Z.**
GRIQUAS Dutch half-castes	**QUERITE** watch-tower
GRISKIN lean bacon	**GUESSED** divined; solved; supposed
GRISLED grizzled; grey	**GUESSER** a conjecturer
GRISTLE a cartilage	**GUESTAN** to be a guest (Sc.)
GRISTLY cartilaginous	**GUIACUM** lignum vitae **B.**
GRITTED grated; ground	**GUICHET** small window as for tickets
GRIZZLE whimper; gray	**GUIDING** leading; directing; piloting
GRIZZLY grey; a bear **Z.**	**GUILDER** Dutch gold coin **Coin**
GROANED moaned; bewailed	**GUILDRY** a guild
GROBIAN clumsy lout	**GUINEAN** (W. African)
GROCERY	**GUIPURE** a heavy lace
GROGRAN fabric of silk and mohair	**GUISARD** a Christmas mummer
GROINED arched	**GULLERY** imposture
GROLIER (bookbinding)	**GULLIED** water-worn
GROMMET ring of rope	**GULLIES** ravines; knives
GROOMED	**GULLING** greening; duping
GROOVED furrowed; scooped	**GUM-BOIL** **Med.**
GROPING seeking blindly; stumbling	**GUM-BOOT** rubber shoe
GROSSER coarser; rougher	**GUMDROP** a confection
GROSSLY flagrantly; outrageously	**GUMMING** fruit-tree disease; cementing
GROTIAN (legal philosophy)	**GUMMOUS** gummy; mucilaginous
GROUNDS reasons; dregs; lees	**GUM-RASH** red gum; strophulus **Med.**
GROUPED graded; classified	**GUM-TREE** (quandary) **B.**
GROUPER an arranger	**GUNBOAT** **Naut.**
GROUSED complained; murmured	**GUN-DECK** **Naut.**
GROUSER grumbler	**GUN-FIRE** time signal
GROUTED filled with cement	**GUNLOCK** firing mechanism
GROWING raising; waxing	**GUNNAGE** (number of guns) **Naut.**
GROWLED snarled	**GUNNERY** the craft of the artillery
GROWLER a four-wheeled cab	**GUNNING** shooting
GROWN-UP an adult	**GUN-PORT** port-hole **Naut.**
GRUB-AXE a hoe **Tool**	**GUN-ROOM** a mess-room **Naut.**
GRUBBED dug up	**GUNSHOT** range
GRUBBER an investigator	**GUN-SITE**
GRUBBLE grope; grabble	**GUNWALE** topmost plank **Naut.**
GRUDGED envied; coveted	**GURGLED** purled; rippled
GRUDGER	**GURNARD** gurnet fish **Z.**
GRUFFER surlier; rougher	**GUSHING** spouting; flowing; effusive
GRUFFLY churlishly; roughly; bluntly	**GUSTILY** in gusts; fitfully; breezily
GRUMBLE grouse; complain; repine	**GUTTATE** spotted
GRUMMET a grommet; a rope ring	**GUTTING** gipping; eviscerating
GRUMOSE clustered	**GUTTLED** gulped; swallowed
GRUMOUS clotted	**GUTWORT** a tord-boyau **B.**
GRUNDEL loach or rock-goby **Z.**	**GUZZLED** swilled; gorged; caroused
GRUNTED	**GUZZLER** gourmand
GRUNTER a pig; a gurnet **Z.**	**GWINIAD** fresh water salmon **Z.**
GRUYERE a Swiss cheese	**GWYNIAD** small white fish **Z.**
GRYPHON griffin; heraldic monster	**GYMNAST** athlete

GYRATED twirled; span; spun; rotated
GYRONNY Heraldic triangulation
GYTRASH a ghost

H

HABITAT home; abode; domicile
HABITED dressed; attired
HABITUE a frequenter
HACHURE engraved line
HACKBUT an arquebus
HACKERY Bengal ox-cart
HACKING cutting; notching; kicking
HACKLED combed
HACKLER flax-comber
HACKLET sea-bird; shear-water gull **Z.**
HACKLOG chopping block
HACKNEY horse; cab; trite **Z.**
HACK-SAW a saw for metal **Tool**
HADDING a holding on lease (Sc.)
HADDOCK a haddie (Sc.) **Z.**
HAEMONY witch's bane plant **B.**
HAFFETS the temples (Sc.)
HAFFLED prevaricated
HAFFLIN half-grown (Sc.)
HAFNIUM metallic element **Chem.**
HAFTING fitting a handle
HAGANAH Jewish militia
HAGDOWN shearwater gull **Z.**
HAGFISH parasite fish **Z.**
HAGGADA Jewish commentary
HAGGARD stackyard; lean; hollow-eyed
HAGGING nagging; harassing
HAGGISH ugly; repulsive
HAGGLED mangled; bargained
HAGGLER higgler; bargainer
HAGSEED witch's offspring
HAGSHIP haggishness
HAGWEED broom **B.**
HAILING raining; greeting
HAIR-CUT
HAIRNET coiffure cover
HAIR-OIL
HAIRPIN
HAITIAN native of Haiti
HALACHA⎫ Jewish oral laws
HALAKAH⎭ and traditions
HALBERD pike-like weapon
HALCYON kingfisher; calm **Z.**
HALF-ONE a golf handicap
HALF-PAY
HALFWAY intermediate position
HALF-WIT nit-wit; moron
HALIBUT the largest flounder **Z.**
HALIDOM mascot; sanctuary
HALITUS a vapour **Med.**
HALLAGE market-hall dues
HALLIER bird net
HALLION hallyon; hallian; rascal
HALOGAN salt producer group **Chem.**
HALTING faltering; hesitating

HALVING tieing; bisecting
HALYARD halliard; running rope **Naut.**
HAMBLED mutilated the foot
HAMBURG domestic fowl **Z.**
HAMITIC (Ham)
HAMMOCK canvas hanging bed **Naut.**
HAMSTER a rodent **Z.**
HAMULAR, HAMULUS small hook; hooked
HANAPER hamper; treasury
HANDBAG a reticule
HANDFUL gowpen (Sc.)
HANDIER more dexterous
HANDILY conveniently; adjacently
HANDING presenting; delivering
HANDJAR Persian dagger
HANDLED dealt with; manipulated
HANDLER dealer
HANDOUT prepared statement; sample
HANDSAW **Tool**
HANDSEL earnest money; a present
HANDSET telephone
HANGDOG sullen; morose
HANGING dangling; depending
HANGMAN topsman; public executioner
HANG-NET vertical net
HANKIES kerchiefs
HANKING making into skeins
HANKLED entangled; involved
HANSARD Parliamentary records
HANSTER a freeman of a guild
HANUKKA Jewish feast day **Eccl.**
HANUMAN Hindu monkey-god
HAPLESS luckless
HAPLOID single chromosomes
HAP'ORTH (half-penny)
HAPPIER more expert; luckier
HAPPILY joyously; blissfully; gaily
HAPPING happening
HARBOUR shelter; haven; asylum
HARDEST densest; firmest; harshest
HARDIER pluckier; braver; tougher
HARDILY stoutly; intrepidly; resolutely
HARDISH somewhat hard
HARDOCK harlock; burdock **B.**
HARD-PAN bed-rock
HARD-RUN greatly pressed
HARDSET beset by difficulty; hungry
HARDTOP fixed-roof on a car
HARDWON barely victorious
HAREING speeding
HARELIP fissured lip **Med.**
HARICOT French bean **B.**
HARKING listening; hurrying
HARMALA wild rue **B.**
HARMFUL noxious; baneful; baleful
HARMINE wild rue extract **Chem.**
HARMING molesting; scathing
HARMONY unison; concord; amity
HARNESS gear; tackle; equipment

HARPING nagging; reiterating **Mus.**
HARPIST a harper **Mus.**
HARPOON barbed spear
HARRIED harassed; raided; ravaged
HARRIER hound; hawk **Z.**
HARSHEN stiffen; embitter
HARSHER rougher; severer; sterner
HARSHLY raucously; stridently
HARTALL orpiment **Min.**
HARTLEY unit of information; bits
HARVEST crop; yield; produce
HAS-BEEN diminished fame
HASHING muddling; mangling
HASHIRA narrow print (Jap')
HASHISH bhang; the assassin's drug
HASSOCK cushion; tuft; pouffe
HASTATE spear-shaped
HASTIER quicker; rasher; brisker
HASTILY rapidly; hurriedly; abruptly
HASTING ripening early; expediting
HASTLER turn-spit
HATABLE odious; obnoxious
HATBAND
HATCASE bonnet-box
HATCHED shaded; incubated
HATCHEL to heckle; to tease
HATCHER plotter; conspirator
HATCHES coverings **Naut.**
HATCHET an axe **Tool**
HATEFUL detestable; execrable; odious
HATLESS bare-headed
HAT-RACK
HAT-RAIL
HAUBERK coat of mail
HAUGHTY arrogant; proud
HAULAGE a charge for conveyance
HAULIER carter
HAULING tugging; drawing; dragging
HAUNCHY with full hips
HAUNTED frequented; followed
HAUNTER frequent visitor
HAURLED dragged; rough-cast
HAUTBOY strawberry; oboe **Mus., B.**
HAUTEUR disdain; arrogance; loftiness
HAUTPAS a dais
HAVENOT under-privileged
HAW-BUCK a clown
HAWKBIT a plant **B.**
HAWKING falconry; peddlery
HAWK-OWL snowy owl **Z.**
HAYBAND hay-rope
HAYCOCK
HAYFORK **Tool**
HAYLOFT
HAYRICK
HAYSEED **B.**
HAY-TIER hay bundler
HAYWARD a warden
HAYWIRE in confusion
HAZELLY light brown

HAZIEST foggiest; vaguest
HEADILY impetuously; precipitately
HEADING adit; headline; intercepting
HEADMAN chief; boss
HEAD-SEA
HEADWAY progress
HEAL-ALL valerian; a panacea **B.**
HEALING mollifying; remedying
HEALTHY hygienic; bracing; hale
HEAPING collecting; amassing
HEARING audition; trying **Law**
HEARKEN listen; attend; heed
HEARSAY rumour; report; gossip
HEARSED put in a hearse
HEARTED emboldened; cheered
HEARTEN encourage; rally; inspire
HEATHEN pagan; paynim; infidel
HEATHER ling; erica **B.**
HEATING warming; exciting
HEAVERS stevedores
HEAVE-TO storm tactics **Naut.**
HEAVIER weightier; denser
HEAVILY ponderously; onerously
HEAVING a rising; hoisting; throwing
HEBENON hen-bane; poison **B.**
HEBRAIC Hebrew
HECKLED combed; questioned
HECKLER political enquirer
HECTARE 100 ares (Fr.) **Meas.**
HECTOID flushed; feverish; hectic
HEDEOMA penny-royal **B.**
HEDERAL of ivy
HEDGING guarding against loss
HEDONIC pleasure-seeking
HEEDFUL mindful; wary; cautious
HEEDING paying attention; regarding
HEELING (cockfighting); (football)
HEFTIER stronger; more vigorous
HEFTILY vigorously; powerfully
HEGUMEN Greek abbot **Eccl.**
HEIGH-HO
HEINOUS infamous; flagrant; atrocious
HEIRDOM succession
HEIRESS
HELCOID ulcerous **Med.**
HELIBUS, HELICAB helicopter bus/taxi
HELICAL spiral
HELICES circumvolutions; spirals
HELICON mount beloved by the Muses
HELIXIN an ivy extract **Chem.**
HELL-CAT malignant hag
HELLENE Greek
HELL-HAG
HELLISH diabolical; infernal; fiendish
HELMAGE guidance
HELOSIS eye-trouble **Med.**
HELOTRY serfdom; bondage; (Sparta)
HELPFUL assistant; useful; beneficial
HELPING share; aiding; abetting
HELVING hafting; fitting a handle

HEMIONE half-ass; dziggetal   **Z.**
HEMLOCK conine; poison   **B.**
HEMMING edging; besetting; sewing
HENBANE   **B.**
HENCOOP a fowl abode
HENNAED dyed with henna
HENNERY poultry farm
HENOTIC conciliatory
HENPECK nag; dominate
HENTING final furrow
HENWIFE chicken-girl
HEPATIC liverish   **Med.**
HEPTADE seven
HEPTODE type of electric valve
HERBAGE pasture
HERBARY herb garden
HERBIST herbalist; collector of simples
HERBLET small herb
HERBOUS herbaceous; herbose
HERDING tending; crowding
HERDMAN herdsman; ranchero
HEREOUT out of this
HERETIC unorthodox; schismatic
HERISSE bristled
HERITOR inheritor
HERLING young sea-trout   **Z.**
HERNIAL (rupture)   **Med.**
HEROINE intrepid damsel
HEROISM valour; bravery; fortitude
HEROIZE lionize
HERONRY   **Z.**
HERRING   **Z.**
HERSELF
HERSHIP cattle-theft (Sc.)
HESSIAN jute fabric
HETAIRA Greek dancing girl
HEXAGON a six-sided figure
HEXAPLA a Bible edition
HEXAPOD with six feet
HEYDUCK Haiduk; Hungarian
HEY-PASS conjuror's command
HICATEE Central American tortoise **Z.**
HICKORY American nut-bearing tree **B.**
HICKWAY small woodpecker   **Z.**
HIDALGO Spanish Don; asteroid **Astron.**
HIDEOUS unshapely; monstrous; grisly
HIDE-OUT a cache
HIEMATE hibernate; to winter
HIGGLED negotiated; peddled; chaffered
HIGGLER haggler; bargainer; hawker
HIGHDAY holiday
HIGHEST tallest; loftiest
HIGH-FED pampered
HIGH-HAT high-brow
HIGHLOW sort of shoe
HIGH-TOP a mast-head (Shak.)
HIGHWAY public road
HILDING paltry; base; a deceiver
HILLIER steeper
HILLING earthing

HILLMAN a mountaineer
HILLOCK small hill
HILLTOP
HIMSELF
HINDBOW saddle cantle
HINNIED whinnied
HINTING implying; suggesting
HIP-BATH portable sitting bath
HIP-BELT sword-belt
HIP-GOUT sciatica   **Med.**
HIP-KNOT gable ornament
HIP-LOCK wrestling trick
HIPPING grieving; glooming
HIP-ROOF a type of roof
HIPSHOT dislocated hip
HIPSTER clothes held by a belt
HIRABLE for hire; leasable
HIRCINE goatish   **Z.**
HIRSUTE hairy; rude
HISKING breathing heavily
HISSING audible disapproval
HISTORY chronicle; annals; account
HISTRIO histrion; an actor
HITCHED caught; fastened; attached
HITTING smiting; striking; succeeding
HITTITE
HIVE-BEE honey-bee   **Z.**
HOARDED garnered; amassed; secreted
HOARDER miser; husbandman
HOATZIN S. American bird   **Z.**
HOAXING duping; gammoning
HOBBISH clownish
HOBBISM a moral philosophy
HOBBIST follower of Hobbes
HOBBLED hoppled; tethered
HOBBLER horse-soldier
HOBLIKE boorish; clownish
HOBNAIL boot-nail
HOBOISM vagrancy (U.S.A.)
HOCK-DAY old English festival
HOCKLED houghed; hamstrung
HOE-CAKE Indian meal cake
HOGBACK ridge; eskar
HOGCOTE pig-sty
HOGGERS miner's leg-wear
HOGGING bending
HOGGISH swinish; sordid; greedy
HOG-HERD swine-herd
HOG-MANE clipped mane
HOG-PLUM tropical tree   **B.**
HOGSKIN pigskin
HOGWASH swill
HOGWEED cow parsnip   **B.**
HOISTED raised; heaved
HOISTER an elevator; lift
HOITING capering
HOLDALL a pack; luggage
HOLDING tenure; retaining; grasping
HOLIDAY festival; vacation
HOLIEST most sacred

HOLLAND coarse linen
HOLMIUM metallic element **Chem.**
HOLM-OAK evergreen oak **B.**
HOLSTER leather pistol case
HOLY-DAY **Eccl.**
HOMAGER a vassal
HOMBERG gentleman's hat
HOMELOT home-plot
HOMELYN spotted ray **Z.**
HOMERIC
HOMINID man (ancient and modern)
HOMONYM equivocation
HONESTY best political creed
HONEYED flattering; sweet
HONITON lace
HONKING (motoring); (geese)
HOODING covering; blinding
HOODLUM hooligan; rowdy; mobster
HOODOCK miserly (Sc.)
HOOFING walking
HOOKING ensnaring; bending
HOOKPIN floor nail
HOOP-ASH nettle-tree **B.**
HOOPING binding; encircling
HOOTING decrying; booing
HOP-BACK brewer's vessel
HOPBIND, HOPBINE hop-vine **B.**
HOPEFUL eager; expectant; confident
HOP-FLEA a parasite **Z.**
HOPKILN an oast
HOPLITE Greek heavy-armed soldier
HOP-OAST hop-kiln
HOPPERS a hopping game
HOPPING skipping; leaping
HOPPLED hobbled; tethered
HOPPLES hobbles; rope shackles
HOP-POLE
HOP-TREE American shrub **B.**
HOP-VINE hopbind **B.**
HOP-YARD hop-garden
HORDEIN, HORDEUM barley starch/
genus **B.**
HORDING crowding; herding; amassing
HORIZON
HORMONE gland secretion **Med.**
HORNBAR cross-bar
HORN-BUG stag beetle **Z.**
HORNING debtor's summons **Law**
HORNISH ungual
HORNITO volcanic smoke-hole
HORN-NUT a water-plant **B.**
HORN-OWL tufted owl **Z.**
HORRENT bristling
HORRIFY appal; terrify; alarm; shock
HOSANNA beatific invocation **Eccl.**
HOSEMAN fireman
HOSIERY stock of stockings
HOSPICE guest-house **Eccl.**
HOSTAGE personal pledge
HOSTESS

HOSTILE inimical; adverse; opposed
HOSTLER ostler
HOTFLUE drying room
HOT-FOOT in haste
HOT-HEAD impetuous; rash
HOTNESS fieriness; ardency; fervency
HOT-SPOT internal combustion
HOTSPUR impetuous
HOTTEST most vehement
HOT-TROD Border pursuit
HOT-WALL (fruit culture)
HOUGHED hockled; hamstrung
HOUNDED pursued; harassed; dogged
HOUSAGE storage fee
HOUSING saddle-cloth; sheltering
HOVERED vacillated; lingered
HOVERER waverer; flutterer
HOWBEIT nevertheless
HOWDY-DO ado; fuss; commotion
HOWEVER notwithstanding
HOWLING dreary; lamenting; wailing
HUANACO guanaco; llama **Z.**
HUDDLED heaped; piled; mixed
HUDDLER bungler; confused cogitator
HUELESS colourless
HUFFILY petulantly; angrily; irritably
HUFFING puffing; swelling; (draughts)
HUFFISH hectoring; furious
HUGGING clasping; embracing; necking
HULKING big and clumsy
HULLING husking; shelling
HUMANLY ethically; rationally
HUMBLED abashed; humiliated
HUMBLER an abaser; mortifier
HUMBUZZ a bull-roarer
HUMDRUM commonplace; prosaic
HUMERAL Jewish veil
HUMERUS shoulder **Med.**
HUMETTE heraldic fesse
HUMIDLY damply; dankly
HUMMING bumming; droning
HUMMOCK hommock; hillock
HUMORAL vapourish
HUMULIN, HUMULUS hop extract/
genus **B.**
HUNCHED bunched; crooked
HUNDRED cantred; county division
HUNGRED hungry; famished
HUNKERS the hams; haunches
HUNTING chasing; searching
HURDLED enclosed with a wattle fence
HURDLER
HURKARU Hindu errand boy
HURLING casting; flinging; pitching
HURRIED scurried; accelerated; ran
HURRIED cursory; superficial
HURRIER hastener; quickener; urger
HURTFUL noxious; baleful; detrimental
HURTLED whizzed; crashed
HURTOIR a bumper
HUSBAND spouse

HUSHABY lullaby
HUSHING repressing; calming
HUSHION sort of sock (Sc.)
HUSKIES Eskimo dogs; toughs **Z.**
HUSKING removing husks
HUSSIES worthless women
HUSSITE (John Huss)
HUSTING an assembly; a council
HUSTLED bustled; elbowed
HUSTLER energiser; jostler
HUSWIFE hussif; housewife
HUTCHED cooped; boxed; confined
HUTMENT a hut
HUTTING temporary building
HYALINE glassy
HYALITE clear opal **Min.**
HYALOID vitreous
HYDRANT fire-plug
HYDRATE hydride; hydrous **Chem.**
HYDRIAD water-nymph
HYDROID hydra-like
HYGEIAN hygienic
HYGIENE sanitary science
HYLOIST materialist
HYMNARY hymn-book
HYMNING lauding
HYMNIST hymn-writer
HYMNODY hymn-singing
HYODONT pig-toothed
HYPNOID resembling sleep
HYPOGEA cellars; basement
HYPPISH hippish; depressing
HYSTRIX the porcupine **Z.**

I

IAMBICS classic verse
IAMBISE satirize
IBERIAN Spanish
ICARIAN rash; headlong; adventurous
ICEBELT
ICEBERG
ICEBIRD little auk **Z.**
ICEBOAT
ICE-FALL a glacier
ICE-FERN frosty incrustations
ICE-FLOE
ICE-FOOT belt of ice
ICE-HILL tobogganing slope
ICEPACK
ICEPAIL
ICE-RINK
ICE-SPAR ryacolite **Min.**
ICHABOD calamity (Heb.)
ICHNITE fossil foot-print
ICHTHYS Christian emblem
ICINESS frigidity
ICTERIC jaundiced
ICTERUS jaundice **Med.**
ICTINUS designer of the Parthenon

IDALIAN sacred to Venus
IDEALLY intellectually; mentally
IDENTIC identical
IDIOTCY imbecility; insanity
IDIOTIC fatuous; witless; inane
IDLESSE idleness
IDOLISM idolatry
IDOLIST idolater
IDOLIZE idolise; deify; adore; venerate
IDYLIST writer of idylls
IDYLLIC pastoral; poetic
IGNEOUS volcanic in origin
IGNITED lit; kindled; inflamed
IGNITER primer; detonator
IGNITOR electrode of ignition
IGNOBLE dishonourable; low; base
IGNOBLY infamously; unworthily
IGNORED disregarded; neglected
IGRAINE King Arthur's mother
ILLAPSE glide; slip; a seizure
ILL-BRED
ILLEGAL unlawful; illegitimate; illicit
ILLEISM too much " he "
ILL-FAME of bad repute
ILLICIT forbidden; banned; prohibited
ILLNESS malady; disease; ailment
ILLOCAL not local
ILL-TIME mis-time
ILL-TURN unkindly act
ILLUDED deceived; deluded
ILLUMED elucidated; brightened
ILL-USED badly treated
ILL-WILL enmity; odium; spite; malice
IMAGERY fanciful concept
IMAGINE dream; think; suppose
IMAGING imagining
IMAMATE the Caliphate
IMBATHE bathe
IMBIBED swallowed; absorbed
IMBIBER a toper; drunkard
IMBLAZE emblaze; illuminate
IMBOSOM embosom; caress
IMBOUND impound
IMBOWED embowed; arched
IMBOWER embower; shelter
IMBREED inbreed
IMBREKE houseleek **B.**
IMBROWN embrown; tan
IMBRUED drenched; soaked; stained
IMBRUTE to brutalize
IMBUING pervading; drenching
IMBURSE to finance
IMITANT counterfeit
IMITATE ape; copy; mimic; parody
IMMENSE titanic; colossal; boundless
IMMERGE ⎫ plunge into; souse;
IMMERSE ⎭ to engross; duck
IMMIXED mixed; blended
IMMORAL depraved; vicious
IMMURED shut up; imprisoned

IMPAINT to colour
IMPALED fenced in; spiked; transfixed
IMPALSY strike with palsy
IMPANEL empanel; enrol
IMPASSE deadlock
IMPASTE knead
IMPASTO thick colour
IMPAVID fearless; undaunted
IMPEACH call to account
IMPEARL decorate with pearls
IMPEDED hindered; obstructed
IMPERIL endanger; hazard; jeopardize
IMPETUS momentum
IMPEYAN Indian pheasant   **Z.**
IMPFING crystallisation technique
IMPIETY iniquity; profanity
IMPINGE to touch upon; infringe
IMPIOUS irreverent; ungodly
IMPLANT to graft; infuse; instil
IMPLATE to sheathe
IMPLEAD impeach; plead
IMPLIED understood; insinuated
IMPLORE entreat; crave; adjure
IMPONED wagered; inflicted
IMPOSED forced; misled
IMPOSER impostor; charlatan
IMPOUND confine; confiscate
IMPREGN impregnate
IMPRESS stamp; mark; imprint
IMPREST advanced cash
IMPRINT impress; fix on the mind
IMPROVE amend; ameliorate; raise
IMPULSE stimulus; urge to action
IMPUTED attributed; implied
IMPUTER ascriber
IN-AND-IN inbreed
INANELY vapidly; stupidly
INANITY fatuity; emptiness
INAPTLY untimely; unsuitably
INBEING inherence
INBOARD within the ship
INBOUND inward bound
INBREAK inburst
INBREED
INBURST irruption
INCAGED encaged; confined
INCENSE to inflame; madden; enrage
INCHASE enchase; engrave
INCHEST embox; encase
INCHING moving gradually
INCHPIN deer's sweetbread
INCISED cut; engraved
INCISOR cutting tooth
INCITED roused; fomented; egged
INCITER agitator; agent provocateur
INCIVIL uncivil; impolite (obs.)
INCLASP embrace; enclasp
INCLAVE heraldic dovetail
INCLINE slope; tend; predispose
INCLOSE enclose; envelop; wrap

INCLUDE embody; comprise; contain
INCOMER new arrival
INCRUST encrust
INCUBUS incumbrance; dead weight
INCURVE bend
INCUSED hammered; stamped
INDEXED
INDEXER
INDICES mathematical exponents
INDICIA indications
INDITED scribbled; wrote; dictated
INDITER a writer; composer; penman
INDOORS
INDORSE endorse; countersign; ratify
INDRAFT inflow; indraught
INDRAWN retracted
INDUCED impelled; prompted
INDUCER persuader; instigator
INDUING enduing; investing; endowing
INDULGE pamper; humour; gratify
INDWELL inhabit; occupy
INEARTH inter; bury; inhume
INEPTLY not aptly; pointlessly
INERTIA inertness; indolence
INERTLY sluggishly; torpidly
INEXACT unexact; incorrect; faulty
INEYING inoculating; grafting
INFAMED defamed; libelled; aspersed
INFANCY under 21
INFANTA Spanish princess
INFANTE Spanish prince
INFAUST unlucky; unfortunate
INFERNO hell
INFIDEL disbeliever; paynim; heathen
INFIELD cultivated ground
INFIELD cf. outfield (cricket)
INFIXED fastened; clamped
INFLAME excite; fan; kindle; incense
INFLATE elate; expand; distend; bloat
INFLECT deflect; curve; bend
INFLICT impose; lay; punish
INFULAE priestly badges   **Eccl.**
INFUSED inspired; instilled; inculcated
INFUSER a coffee machine
INGENER a designer (Shak.)
INGENUE naive girl
INGESTA food   **Med.**
INGLOBE englobe; encircle; ensphere
INGOING entrance; entry
INGRAFT engraft; instil; introduce
INGRAIN engrain; permeate
INGRATE ungrateful person (obs.)
INGRESS entrance; portal
INGROSS engross (obs.)
INHABIT dwell; occupy
INHALED breathed
INHALER a respirator
INHAUST to drink in (obs.)
INHERED adhered; stuck
INHERIT acquire by bequest

INHERSE to bury (Shak.)
INHIBIT ban; prohibit; restrain
INHUMAN merciless; fell; ruthless
INHUMED interred; buried
INITIAL incipient; primary letter
INJELLY gelatinise
INJOINT to join (obs.)
INJURED offended; marred; maltreated
INJURER abuser; impairer
INKHORN portable inkpot
INKLING hint; suggestion; innuendo
INKNEED knock-kneed
INKWELL ink-cup
INLACED enlaced; entwined
INLAWED cf. outlawed
INLAYER inlay worker
INMEATS the entrails
INNERVE invigorate; insinew
INNINGS reclaimed land; (cricket)
INNUENT significant
IN-PHASE (electrical)
INQUEST judicial inquiry **Law**
INQUIRE enquire; ask; interrogate
INQUIRY enquiry; examination
INSANER madder; crazier
INSANIE insanity **Med.**
INSCULP engrave; carve (obs.)
INSHELL to hide as in a shell (obs.)
INSHORE close to the beach
INSIDER in the know
INSIGHT vision; perception
INSINEW innerve; invigorate
INSIPID tasteless; vapid; flat; tedious
INSNARE ensnare; entrap; inveigle
INSOOTH in truth
INSPECT supervise; investigate
INSPIRE animate; inflame; imbue
INSTALL instal; instate; induct; invest
INSTANT current; urgent; prompt
INSTATE install; inaugurate; introduce
INSTEAD in place of; in lieu
INSTEEP immerse; souse; duck
INSTILL instil; implant; inculcate
INSTYLE entitle; to name
INSULAR isolated; narrow-minded
INSULIN (diabetes treatment) **Med.**
INSURED ensured; guaranteed
INSURER underwriter
INSWEPT narrowed
INTEGER whole; a whole number
INTENSE acute; vehement; extreme
INTERIM a pause; in the meantime
INTERNE inmate; boarder
INTHRAL enthral; enslave; captivate
INTITLE entitle; intitule (obs.)
INTONED chanted
INTRANT entrant; entering; penetrating
INTREAT entreat; crave; importune
INTROIT opening anthem **Eccl.**
INTRUDE obtrude; trespass; butt in

INTRUST entrust; commit; confide
INTWINE entwine; reticulate; weave
INTWIST entwist; ravel; interlace
INULASE an enzyme **Med.**
INURING enuring; habituating
INUTILE useless (Fr.)
INVADED violated; entered; occupied
INVADER aggressor; raider; attacker
INVALID null and void; infirm; weak
INVEIGH revile; reproach; upbraid
INVERSE reciprocal; inverted
INVEXED arched (Her.)
INVIOUS impassable; untrodden
INVITED bid; bequested; asked
INVITER allurer; solicitor; enticer
INVOICE bill; schedule; inventory
INVOKED adjured; implored; besought
INVOKER summoner; conjuror
INVOLVE implicate; entangle; embrace
INWARDS internally
INWEAVE complicate; intwine
INWHEEL encircle; surround
INWOVEN intertwined
IODIZED treated with iodine
IONIZED electrified
IPOMAEA convolvulus **B.**
IRACUND irascible; choleric; petulant
IRANIAN Persian
IRENICS pacific theology
IRICISM Irish bull
IRIDEAE iris plants **B.**
IRIDISE make iridescent
IRIDIUM metallic element **Chem.**
IRISHRY Irish people
IRKSOME wearisome; tiresome; tedious
IRONIES sarcastic censures
IRONING flattening
IRONIST ironical talker
ISAGOGE a treatise
ISATINE isatin; indigo; woad **Chem.**
ISCHAIL (hip-bone) **Med.**
ISERINE titanic steel
ISHMAEL an outcast
ISIDIUM excrescence on lichen **B.**
ISLAMIC Mohammedan; Moslem
ISLEMAN islander
ISMATIC faddish; fond of isms
ISODOMA form of masonry
ISODONT uniform teeth
ISOETES quill-worts **B.**
ISOGENY similar origin
ISOLATE insulate; segregate; dissociate
ISONOMY equal rights
ISONYMY paronymy; equal **Law**
ISOPODA crustaceans **Z.**
ISOPYRE impure opal **Min.**
ISOTONE stable nucleus (atom)
ISOTOPE allied element **Chem.**
ISOTYPE picture writing
ISRAELI Jew (Israel)

ISSUANT issuing (Her.)
ISSUING emanating; proceeding
ISTHMUS
ITACISM Greek egotism
ITALIAN
ITALICS sloping letters
ITCHING desirous
ITEMIZE particularize
ITERACY repetition
ITERANT repeating
ITERATE recapitulate
IVORIED provided with teeth
IVY-BUSH Bacchus's bush   **B.**
IXOLITE fossil resin   **Min.**

J

JABBING prodding; stabbing
JACAMAR tropical king-fisher   **Z.**
JACCHUS marmoset   **Z.**
JACINTH hyacinth; a gem   **B.**
JACKASS male moke   **Z.**
JACKDAW a daw   **Z.**
JACKING lifting; abandoning
JACKPOT (poker)
JACKSAW goosander   **Z.**
JACK-TAR a sailor   **Naut.**
JACOBIN revolutionary
JACOBUS James I sovereign   **Coin**
JACONET muslin
JADEDLY wearily
JADEITE a silicate   **Min.**
JAGGERY palm sap sugar
JAGGING notching; carousing
JAGHIRE land revenues (Hind.)
JAHVIST scriptural writer
JAILING gaoling; imprisoning
JAINISM an Indian religion
JALAPIN a purge   **Med.**
JALOUSE to suspect (Sc.)
JAMADAR jemidar; Indian lieutenant
JAMBONE (cards on table at euchre)
JAMDANI flowery muslin
JAMDARI figured muslin
JAMEWAR goat hair cloth
JAMMING squeezing; pressing
JAMRACH animal mart
JAMSHID King of the genii
JANEITE (Jane Austen)
JANGADA timber raft
JANGLED jingled; discordant
JANGLER wrangler
JANITOR doorkeeper
JANIZAR Janissary; Turkish soldier
JANNOCK bannock; a cake
JANNOCK straightforward
JANTILY jauntily; airily; finically
JANTING jaunting; rambling
JANUARY
JAP-SILK

JARGOON a gem; zircon   **Min.**
JARKMAN begging letter writer
JARRING discordant; grating; clashing
JASHAWK young hawk   **Z.**
JASMINE fragrant flower   **B.**
JASPERY like jasper   **Min.**
JASPOID jaspery
JAUNDER gossip (Sc.)
JAUNTED rambled; strolled
JAUPING spattering (Sc.)
JAVELIN a throwing spear
JAWBONE Samson's lethal weapon **Med.**
JAW-FALL depression
JAW-FOOT maxilliped   **Z.**
JAW-HOLE a sink
JAW-ROPE   **Naut.**
JAZZING dancing   **Mus.**
JEALOUS envious; covetous; resentful
JEDCOCK jack snipe   **Z.**
JEDDART rough justice (Sc.)
JEERING derision; taunting; scoffing
JEHOVAH
JEJUNUM digestive organ   **Med.**
JELLIED
JELLIFY to become gelatinous
JELLYBY (a philanthropist)
JEMIDAR jamadar; Indian officer
JEMIMAS elastic-sided boots
JENKINS society reporter; toady
JEOFAIL an oversight   **Law**
JEOPARD to hazard; to endanger
JERICHO
JERKING twitching; jolting
JESSAMY jasmine; a dandy   **B.**
JESSANT heraldic uprising
JESTFUL humorous; witty; sportive
JESTING joking; quipping
JETTIED projected; jutted
JETTING spouting; emitting
JEWELRY gems; trinkets
JEW'S-EAR edible fungus   **B.**
JEZEBEL a courtesan
JEZHAIL jezail; Afghan rifle
JIBBING balking; shying
JIB-BOOM   **Naut.**
JIB-DOOR flush door
JIGAJOG jig-jog; also jickajog
JIGGING sieving; dancing
JIGGISH frivolous; frolicsome
JIGGLED joggled; wriggled
JILTING discarding; rejecting
JIMCROW a crow-bar   **Tool**
JIM-JAMS nervous apprehension
JINGLED jangled; tingled
JINGLET sleigh-bell clapper
JINKING dodging; twisting
JITTERS fear; distortion   **Electron.**
JITTERY nervy; agitated; dithery
JOBBERY intrigue
JOBBING doing small jobs

JOBLESS unemployed
JOCULAR jocose; facetious; droll
JOGGING stimulating; nudging
JOGGLED jostled; shook
JOGGLES stone jointing
JOG-TROT
JOHNIAN (St. John's Col. Cam.)
JOINDER united action **Law**
JOINERY carpentry
JOINING uniting; linking; connecting
JOINTED articulated
JOINTER smoothing plane **Tool**
JOINTLY in concert; unitedly
JOISTED (floor-laying)
JOLLIER merrier; more genial
JOLLIFY celebrate; carouse
JOLLILY heartily; mirthfully
JOLLITY joviality; hilarity; frolic
JOLTING jerking; shaking
JONGLER a wandering minstrel
JONQUIL narcissus **B.**
JOOKERY jokery; trickery
JOSTLED hustled; elbowed
JOTTING a memorandum
JOUNCED shook; jolted
JOURNAL diary; newspaper; log
JOURNAL spindle bearing; gazette
JOURNEY jaunt; excursion; travel
JOUSTED tilted
JOYANCE gaiety; festivity
JOYLESS dismal; downcast
JOY-RIDE
JUBILEE fiftieth anniversary
JUDAISE practice Judaism
JUDAISM Jewish rites
JUDAIST
JUDAIZE to enforce Judaism
JUDCOCK jack snipe **Z.**
JUDGING trying; deeming; estimating
JUFFERS square timber
JUGATED coupled; yoked
JUGGING imprisoning; stewing
JUGGINS a simpleton
JUGGLED conjured; swindled
JUGGLER conjuror; wizard; marabout
JUGLANS walnut-genus **B.**
JUGULAR (vein) **Med.**
JUICIER more succulent
JUJITSU ⎫
JUJUTSA ⎬ Japanese wrestling
JUKE-BOX electric gramophone (U.S.A)
JUMBLED disordered; confused
JUMBLER a muddler
JUMPING bounding; (claims)
JUNCATE junket; picnic; spree
JUNCOUS rush-like
JUNIPER coniferous tree; gin-berry **B.**
JUNKMAN junk-dealer
JUPETTE short petticoat
JUPITER a planet

JURALLY lawfully; legally **Law**
JURY-BOX
JURY-MAN juror **Law**
JUSSIVE imperative
JUSTICE equity; fairness; impartiality
JUSTIFY vindicate; exonerate; excuse
JUTTING projecting; beetling
JUVENAL a youth
JUWANZA camel-thorn **B.**

K

KABBALA cabbala; shrine
KABBALA Jewish oral tradition
KACHINA doll (Amer. Indian)
KADDISH Jewish funeral prayer
KAINITE chemical fertilizer **Chem.**
KAKODYL cacodyl; noisome liquid
KALENDS 1st day of Roman month
KALMUCK Calmuck; Mongolian
KAMERAD (surrender)
KAMICHI Brazilian tropical bird **Z.**
KAMPONG (Malay) court-yard
KANAGAI lacquer work (Japan)
KANTIAN (Kant); Kantist
KANTISM a philosophy
KAPITIA lacquer (Ceylon)
KARAGAN Russian fox **Z.**
KARAITE strict Jewish sect **Eccl.**
KARATAS W. Indian pineapple **B.**
KATHODE negative electrode
KATYDID N. Amer. grasshopper **Z.**
KEBBOCK kebbuck; a cheese (Sc.)
KECKLED cackled
KEDGING warping **Naut.**
KEDLACK wild mustard **B.**
KEEKING peeping; prying
KEELAGE harbour duty
KEELING a codling **Z.**
KEELMAN bargee
KEELSON keel-plate **Naut**
KEENEST sharpest; shrewdest
KEENING wailing; mourning
KEEPING lasting; retaining; observing
KEEVING (fermentation)
KEITLOA S. African rhinoceros **Z**
KELKING beating; thrashing
KENNICK tinker jargon
KENNING range of vision; knowing
KENOSIS ⎫
KENOTIC ⎬ divine abnegation
KENTISH ⎭
KERATIN (horn and hair) **Med**
KERMESS Dutch fair
KERNING granulating
KERNISH clownish
KESTREL a falcon **Z**
KETCHUP a sauce
KEYBOLT
KEYCOLD cold as a key

KEYED-UP tense with suspense
KEYHOLE
KEYNOTE Mus.
KEY-RING
KEY-SEAT a groove
KHALIFA khalif; calif
KHAMSIN hot wind of the Sahara
KHANATE khan's jurisdiction
KHEDDAH enclosure; (eleph. hunting)
KHEDIVA⎫ wife of the
KHEDIVE⎭ Egyptian Viceroy
KHOTBAH⎫ Mahommedan
KHUTBAH⎭ prayer and service **Eccl.**
KIBBUTZ communal farm (Israel)
KIBITKA Russian vehicle
KICKING spurning; punting
KICK-OFF
KIDDIES youngsters
KIDDING bluffing
KIDLING a young kid **Z.**
KIDSKIN goat leather
KIKUMON imperial crest of Japan
KILLDEE N. Amer. ring plover **Z.**
KILLICK a small anchor **Naut.**
KILLING slaying; butchering; tiring
KILL-JOY a sour-puss
KILLOCK killick; small anchor **Naut.**
KILN-DRY desiccate
KILTING trussing up (Sc.)
KINDEST most benevolent
KINDLED ignited; fired; incited
KINDLER an igniter
KINDRED relations; related; kin
KINETIC force in motion
KINGCUP marsh marigold **B.**
KINGDOM monarchy; realm; dominion
KINGLET golden-crested wren **Z.**
KING-PIN head of organisation
KINKING twisting; looping
KINLESS without kindred
KINSHIP relationship
KINSMAN a connection
KIP-SHOP house of ill-fame
KIPSKIN kip-leather
KIRGHIZ Central Asian
KIRIMON kikumon; a chrysanthemum
KIRKTON a village (Sc.)
KIRTLED with petticoat
KIRUNDI language of Burundi (Africa)
KISSING bussing
KITCHEN cook-house; galley
KLICKED clicked
KLIPDAS S. African rock-badger **Z.**
KNABBED gnawed; bitten
KNACKER cat's meat purveyor
KNAPPED snapped; nibbled
KNAPPER flint worker
KNAPPLE snap; nibble
KNARRED knotted
KNAVERY roguery; trickery; fraud

KNAVISH rascally; fraudulent
KNEADED massaged; mixed
KNEADER dough-mixer
KNEECAP knee-pan **Med.**
KNEELER
KNELLED knolled; tolled
KNESSET Israeli Parliament
KNIFING stabbing
KNITTED contracted
KNITTER
KNITTLE a draw-thread
KNOBBED knobby
KNOBBLE small boss
KNOBBLY knobby; knotty
KNOCKED buffeted; rapped; hit
KNOCKER a rapper
KNOCK-ON (Rugby)
KNOCK-UP practice game (tennis)
KNOLLED knelled; tolled
KNOLLER bell-toller
KNOPPER gall-nut **B.**
KNOTTED tied; kinked; entangled
KNOW-ALL a wiseacre
KNOW-HOW technical expertise and skill
KNOWING pawky; shrewd; astute
KNUCKLE submit **Med.**
KOFTGAR metal inlayer (Hind.)
KOLA-NUT cola-nut **B.**
KOLKHOZ Soviet collective farm
KORANIC (Koran)
KO-TOWED made obeisance
KOUMISS fermented mare's milk
KREATIN creatin; muscle constituent
KREMLIN citadel (Moscow)
KRIMMER grey lambskin fur
KRISHNA an incarnation of Vishnu
KRUPSIS a theological doctrine
KRYPTOL electrical resistant
KRYPTON gaseous element **Chem.**
KUH-HORN Alpine horn **Mus.**
KUMQUAT Chinese citron **B.**
KURBASH Arab hippo-hide whip
KURDISH (Kurd)
KURSAAL the pump-room of a spa
KUWAITI native of **KUWAIT**
KYANISE rot-proofing of timber
KYANITE aluminium silicate **Min.**

L

LABARUM symbolical banner
LABIATE lip-like
LABROSE thick-lipped
LACCINE (shellac)
LACEMAN lace-dealer
LACERTA lizard genus **Z.**
LACINA fringes
LACK-ALL destitute
LACKING needing; wanting
LAC-LAKE lac dye

245

LACONIC concise; pithy; curt; terse
LACQUER varnish
LACQUEY lackey; footman; flunkey
LACTATE (lactine) **Chem.**
LACTEAL lactean; milky
LACTOSE, LACTINE sugar of milk
LACTUCA lettuce genus **B.**
LACUNAE gaps; blanks; chasms
LACUNAL discontinuously
LACUNAR (panelled ceiling)
LADANUM resinous extract **Med.**
LADINOS mixed race (El Salvador)
LADLING spooning
LADY-BUG lady-fly **Z.**
LADY-COW the ladybird **Z.**
LADY-DAY March 25th
LADYISH genteel; affected
LADYISM gentility
LAETARE 4th Sunday in Lent
LAGGARD lagging; sluggard
LAGGING hysteresis; dawdling
LAGOMYS (tailless hares) **Z.**
LAGOPUS grouse genus **Z.**
LAGOTIC rabbit-eared
LAICISE, LAICIZE commit to laymen
LAIRAGE cattle depot; lair
LAKELET pool; mere; pond
LAKSHMI wife of Vishnu **Eccl.**
LALIQUE artistic glassware
LALLANS Lowland Scots (dial)
LALLING repetition of a sound linguistics
LAMAISM Tibetan Buddhism **Eccl.**
LAMAIST spirit-worshipper **Eccl.**
LAMB-ALE shearing feast
LAMBENT softly radiant
LAMBERT unit of brightness **Meas.**
LAMBING yeaning
LAMBKIN **Z.**
LAMBOYS armoured kilts
LAMELLA thin plate or scale **Z.**
LAMETER ⎫ lamiter; a cripple
LAMIGER ⎭
LAMETTA metal foil
LAMINAR laminal; in plates
LAMMING thrashing
LAMPATE a salt **Chem.**
LAMPERN lamprey **Z.**
LAMP-FLY fire-fly **Z.**
LAMPION fairy lamp
LAMP-LIT
LAMPOON a satirical article
LAMPREY eel-like fish **Z.**
LANATED woolly
LANCERS (cavalry); a dance
LANCING piercing; cutting
LANDING disembarking; floor; (fish)
LANDMAN landsman
LANDTAG governing body
LAND-TAX
LANGAHA snake (Madagascar) **Z.**

LANGATE bandage **Med.**
LANGITE copper sulphate **Min.**
LANGLEY unit of radiation **Meas.**
LANGREL chain-shot
LANGUED heraldic tongue
LANGUET tongue-shaped
LANGUID feeble; listless; enervated
LANGUOR langure; lassitude
LANIARY slaughter house
LANIARY canine tooth
LANIATE tear in pieces
LANKIER taller and thinner
LANOLIN an ointment **Med.**
LANTANA verbena **B.**
LANTERN lanthorn
LANYARD laniard; short rope
LAOCOON (sculptured group)
LAOTIAN native of Laos
LAO-THAI language of Laos
LAPILLI volcanic stones
LAPPING polishing; wrapping; drinking
LAPPISH Laplandish; Lapp
LAPSING slipping; failing
LAPUTAN visionary
LAPWING peewit **Z.**
LAPWORK overlapping work
LARCENY theft; pilfering **Law**
LARCHES conifers **B.**
LARDING smearing with lard
LARD-OIL a lubricant
LARDOON strip of bacon
LARGELY greatly; abundantly
LARGESS bounty; alms; gift
LARGEST most capacious; biggest
LARGISH somewhat extensive
LARIKIN larrikin; hooligan (Aust.)
LARKING sporting; on the spree
LARMIER drip-stone; corona
LARVATE larval; masked **Z.**
LASHING scourging; upbraiding
LASHKAR N. Indian tribal force
LASKETS gaskets **Naut.**
LASSOED noosed
LASSOES lariats
LASTAGE ballast; fishing dues
LASTING abiding; enduring; durable
LATAKIA Syrian tobacco **B.**
LATCHED fastened; grasped
LATCHES laskets **Naut.**
LATCHET shoe-fastening
LATCHET sapphirine gurnet **Z**
LATEBRA an egg cavity **Z**
LATENCE suspended activity
LATENCY force in suspense
LATERAL side by side
LATERAN Roman cathedral **Eccl**
LATHING lath work
LATRINE camp privy; toilet
LATROBE a form of stove
LATTICE a network

LATVIAN Lettish
LAUDING extolling; praising
LAUGHED derided
LAUGHER L'homme qui rit
LAUNDER wash; ore trough
LAUNDRY the wash
LAURELS bays of victory **B.**
LAURITE a sulphide **Min.**
LAUWINE avalanche
LAVOLTA an old dance
LAVROCK lark **Z.**
LAW-BOOK case book **Law**
LAW-CALF (bound in calf)
LAWLESS wild; rebellious; disorderly
LAW-LORD **Law**
LAW-LORE
LAW-SUIT **Law**
LAXATOR a muscle **Med.**
LAXNESS slackness; negligence
LAY-DAYS (cargo lading)
LAYERED stratified
LAYETTE infant's outfit
LAYLAND pasture land
LAYLOCK lilac **B.**
LAY-LORD civil lord **Naut.**
LAZARET hospital
LAZARLY leprous
LAZARUS a poor man
LAZIEST most sluggish; idlest
LAZY-BED potato-bed
-DRIVER learner driver
EACHED strained through wood-ash
EADING chief; principal; main
LEAD-OFF beginning
LEAFAGE foliage; boscage
LEAF-BED gemma **B.**
LEAF-FAT fat in layers
LEAFING leaf-growth
LEAFLET handbill; small pamphlet
LEAGUED united; coalesced
LEAGUER camp; ally
LEAKAGE divulgence; percolation
LEAKING oozing; escaping
LEANDER channel swimmer
LEANEST thinnest; lankiest
LEANING penchant; bias; relying
LEAPING jumping; springing
LEARNED erudite; scholarly
LEARNER pupil; tyro; student
LEASHED bound; under control
LEASING falsehood; letting
LEASOWE a pasture
LEATHER to thrash; to tan
LEAVING desisting; bequeathing
LECTERN lettern; reading desk **Eccl.**
LECTION a reading
LECTURE reproof; rebuke; discourse
LEECHED healed **Med.**
LEECHEE Chinese fruit **B.**
LEEFANG jib sheet **Naut.**

LEEMOST most leeward
LEERILY wideawake; sly; fly
LEERING ogling
LEE-SIDE, LEEGAGE sheltered side **Naut.**
LEE-TIDE tide with the wind
LEEWARD down wind
LEFT-ARM cricket
LEGALLY legitimately; licitly
LEGATEE inheritor **Law**
LEG-BAIL (absconding)
LEGGERS barge-pushers
LEGGING a gaiter
LEGGISM black-leggism
LEGHORN straw hat; fowl **Z.**
LEGIBLE readable
LEGIBLY clearly written
LEG-IRON a fetter
LEGITIM Bairn's Part **Law**
LEGLESS apodal
LEG-PULL a draw
LEGTRAP (cricket)
LEGUMEN vegetable casein **B.**
LEISTER fishing spear (Ice.)
LEISURE restful ease
LEMMATA logical premises
LEMMING Arctic rodent **Z.**
LEMNIAN (Lemnos)
LEMPIRA Honduras **Coin**
LEMURES ghosts of evil doers
LENDING loaning; advancing
LENGTHY extended; protracted
LENIENT mild; clement; merciful
LENTIGO a rash; freckle **Med.**
LENTISK mastic tree **B.**
LENTOID lens-shaped
LENTOUS viscous; tenacious
LEONERO puma hunting dogs **Z.**
LEONIDS meteor shower
LEONINE like a lion
LEOPARD also libbard **Z.**
LEPROSE scurfy **Med.**
LEPROSY, LEPROUS **Med.**
LESBIAN female homosexual
LESOTHO Basuto (S. Africa)
LETCHED percolated; filtered
LET-DOWN an avoidable failure
LETHEAN oblivious
LETHEON an anaesthetic **Med.**
LETTERN lectern; reading desk
LETTING preventing; hindering
LETTISH Latvian; Lettic
LETTUCE **B.**
LEUCINE (decomposition) **Med.**
LEUCITE volcanic rock **Min.**
LEUCOMA wall-eye **Med.**
LEUCOUS albino
LEVATOR a muscle **Med.**
LEVELER leveller
LEVELLY evenly; horizontally
LEVERED raised; lifted

LEVERET young hare   **Z.**
LEVITIC (Levi)
LEVYING collecting; exacting
LEXICAL alphabetically arranged
LEXICON dictionary
LIAISON co-ordination; intrigue
LIASSIC geological formation
LIBERAL bounteous; generous
LIBERTY freedom; emancipation
LIBRARY a voluminous apartment
LIBRATE to balance; poise; oscillate
LICENCE permission; excess; warrant
LICENSE to permit; allow; authorize
LICH-OWL screech-owl   **Z.**
LICH-WAY lych-way
LICITLY lawfully; legally; legitimately
LICKING a flogging; a thrashing
LIE-ABED a sluggard
LIFT-BOY,LIFTMAN elevator operator
LIFTING elating; stealing; raising
LIGATED bandaged   **Med.**
LIGHTED lit; ignited; illumined
LIGHTEN enlighten; alleviate; ease
LIGHTER barge; brighter; igniter
LIGHTLY buoyantly; airily; joyfully
LIGNIFY become woody
LIGNINE woody fibre   **B.**
LIGNITE brown coal   **Min.**
LIGNOSE cellulose
LIGROIN paraffin
LIGULAR strap-shaped   **B.**
LIKABLE attractive; lovable; amiable
LIKENED resembled; compared
LILY-PAD water-lily leaf   **B.**
LIMBATE bordered; edged
LIMBING dismembering
LIME-LIT illuminated
LIME-PIT limestone quarry
LIMINAL almost conscious
LIMITED restricted; circumscribed
LIMITER restrainer
LIMNING water-colour painting
LIMNITE iron ore   **Min.**
LIMOSIS acute hunger   **Med.**
LIMPING halting; walking lamely
LIMPKIN tropical crane   **Z.**
LINCTUS soothing syrup   **Med.**
LINEAGE ancestry; extraction; race
LINEATE lined
LINEMAN (electricity)
LINE-OUT rugby football
LINGISM Swedish drill
LINGUAL (tongue)
LINKAGE (mechanics)
LINKBOY torch bearer
LINKING connecting; joining
LINKMAN linkboy
LINNEAN (Linnaeus, botanist)
LINSANG Indian civet   **Z.**
LINSEED flax-seed   **B.**

LIONCEL small lion (Her.)
LION-CUB   **Z.**
LIONESS   **Z.**
LIONISM tuft hunting
LIONIZE heroize
LIP-BORN hearsay; not genuine
LIP-GOOD good promiser
LIPPING uttering; (golf)
LIQUATE liquefy
LIQUEFY dissolve; melt; fuze
LIQUEUR a cordial
LISPING expressing childishly
LISSOME svelte; lissom; agile
LISTFUL attentive; heedful
LISTING tabulation; choosing
LITERAL au pied de la lettre
LITHATE (lithium)   **Chem.**
LITHELY actively; pliantly
LITHIUM metallic element   **Chem.**
LITHOID stone-like
LITOTES (figure of speech)
LITTERY covered with litter
LITUATE forked
LITURGE leader in public worship **Eccl.**
LITURGY ritual   **Eccl.**
LIVABLE habitable
LIVENED cheered up; enlivened
LIVE-OAK American oak   **B.**
LIVERED (lily-livered)
LLANERO S. American plain dweller
LOADING cargo; lading; charging
LOAFING loitering; idling
LOAMING earthing
LOANING lending; advancing
LOATHED hated; detested
LOATHER an abhorrer
LOATHLY reluctant; unwilling; hateful
LOBBIED sought votes
LOBBIES vestibules
LOBBING pitching
LOBCOCK a lubber; a lubbard
LOBELET small lobe
LOBELIA a flower genus   **B.**
LOBIPED having lobate feet   **Z.**
LOBSTER a decapod   **Z.**
LOBULAR lobed
LOBULUS small lobe
LOBWORM lug-worm   **Z.**
LOCALLY in the vicinity
LOCATED placed; fixed; found
LOCATOR finder
LOCKAGE canal dues
LOCKIAN (Locke's philosophy)
LOCKING grappling; securing
LOCKIST philosopher
LOCK-JAW   **Med**
LOCK-MAN Under-sheriff (I. of M.)
LOCK-OUT (industrial); computer   **Electron**
LOCKRAM coarse linen
LOCULAR cell-like

LOCULUS small cell
LOCUSTA carob-tree **B.**
LODGING quarters; abode; harbour
LOFTIER of greater eminence
LOFTILY arrogantly
LOFTING raising; lifting
LOGBOOK official record **Naut.**
LOG-CHIP log-line board **Naut.**
LOGGATS (ninepins)
LOGGING recording **Naut.**
LOG-HEAD a blockhead
LOG-HEAP log-pile; wood-pile
LOGICAL reasonable; deductive
LOGLINE **Naut.**
LOG-REEL **Naut.**
LOG-ROLL pull strings
LOG-SHIP log-chip **Naut.**
LOGWOOD (red dye) **B.**
LOLLARD religious sect
LOLLING lounging; (tongue)
LOMARIA ferns **B.**
LOMBARD a banker; a money lender
LONG-AGO remote in time
LONGBOW
LONGEST most protracted
LONG-HOP (cricket)
LONGING eager desire; yearning
LONGISH somewhat long
LONG-LEG (cricket)
LONG-RUN final issue
LOOBILY like a looby
LOOKING search; watching; scanning
LOOKOUT sentinel; gazeboo; view
LOOK-SEE glance; hasty visit
LOOMING a mirage; threatening
LOONING cry of the loon
LOOPERS (moth caterpillars) **Z.**
LOOPING circling
LOOSELY vaguely; diffusely; slackly
LOOSING relaxing; releasing
LOOTING pillaging; rifling
LOPPING amputating; curtailing
LORDING lordling
LORELEI a syren; rock
LORETTE a Delilah
LORGNON an eye-glass
LORIMER loriner
LORINER bridle-maker
LOSABLE easily mislaid
LOTTERY
LOTTING cataloguing
LOUDEST showiest; noisiest
LOUKOUM, LOKUM Turkish delight
LOUNDER to beat; a blow (Sc.)
LOUNGED reclined; lolled
LOUNGER flaneur; loafer; idler
LOURING threatening; menacing
LOUSILY
LOUTISH clumsy
LOVABLE amiable; charming; winsome

LOVE-ALL no score tennis
LOVE-DAY settling day (Shak.)
LOVEMAN a plant **B.**
LOVERED having a lover
LOVERLY passionate; devoted
LOW-BELL (night-fowling)
LOW-BORN
LOW-BRED
LOWBROW unintellectual
LOWDOWN rascally
LOWERED threatened; frowned
LOW-GEAR (motoring)
LOWLAND
LOW-LIFE humble life
LOWLILY humbly; meekly
LOWNESS dejection; depression
LOW-TIDE
LOYALLY faithfully; devotedly
LOYALTY fealty; fidelity
LOZENGE a rhomb; cachou **Tool, Med.**
LOZENGY lozenged (Her.)
LUBBARD a lubber
LUCANUS stag beetle **Z.**
LUCARNE luthern; dormer window
LUCENCE⎱ brightness; sheen;
LUCENCY⎰ radiance; effulgence
LUCERNE plant for fodder **B.**
LUCIDLY clearly; limpidly; radiantly
LUCIFER Satan; a match
LUCIGEN powerful oil lamp
LUCKIER more fortunate
LUCKILY happily; fortunately
LUFFING turning toward wind **Naut.**
LUGGAGE baggage; impedimenta
LUGGING tugging; dragging; hauling
LUGMARK earmark
LUGSAIL **Naut.**
LUGWORM lob-worm **Z.**
LUK-CHIN hybrid Chinese
LULLABY soporific song
LULLING soothing; waning; subsiding
LUMBAGO muscular rheumatism **Med.**
LUMINAL narcotic drug **Med.**
LUMPIER bumpier; more awkward
LUMPING bulky
LUMPISH dull; heavy
LUMP-SUM cashdown payment
LUNATIC maniac; crazy; insane
LUNCHED
LUNETTE bastion; watch glass
LUNULAR crescent shaped
LUNULET lunular spot
LUPULIN hop extract
LUPULUS hop plant **B.**
LURCHED pitched; lurked; shifted
LURCHER a lurker; dog **Z.**
LURKING skulking; awaiting
LUSHING swilling; toping
LUSTFUL lascivious
LUSTIER stronger; sturdier

I

LUSTILY vigorously
LUSTING desirous
LUSTRAL (purification)
LUSTRUM period of 5 years
LUTEOUS fulvous; tawny
LUTETIA old name for Paris
LUTHERN lucarne; dormer-window
LUTRINE (otter) **Z.**
LUXATED dislocated
LYCHNIC (vespers, Greek church)
LYCHNIS campion plants **B.**
LYCOPOD a moss **B.**
LYDDITE a high explosive
LYING-IN
LYINGLY falsely; mendaciously
LYMPHAD sailing vessel (Sc.) **Naut.**
LYNCEAN lynx-eyed **Z.**
LYNCHED summarily dealt with
LYNCHET unploughed strip
LYRATED lyre-shaped
LYRICAL musically poetic

M

MACABRE gruesome; grisly
MACACUS baboon **Z.**
MACADAM road material
MACAQUE monkey **Z.**
MACE-ALE spiced ale
MACHAIR low-lying ground (Gael.)
MACHETE West Indian knife
MACHINE
MACKITE asbestos plaster
MACRAME fringe; corded edging
MACULAE dark sun-spots
MAD-BRED passionately conceived
MADDEST craziest
MADDING raging; distracted
MADEIRA a wine; a cake
MADLING a lunatic
MADNESS mania; delirium; frenzy
MADONNA
MADOQUA Abyssinian antelope **Z.**
MADRIER mine-plank
MADRONA⎱ ever-green tree of
MADRONO⎰ California **B.**
MADWORT mugwort; cure for rabies **B.**
MAESTRO eminent composer
MAFFICK rejoice riotously
MAFFLED muddle-headed
MAGENTA red aniline dye
MAGGOTY whimsical
MAGICAL talismanic; supernatural
MAGINOT French defensive line
MAGNATE one of the great
MAGNETO a generator
MAGNIFY praise; enlarge; augment
MAHALEB cherry (Arab.) **B.**
MAHATMA adept in esoteric Buddhism
MAHDISM (Mahdi) **[Eccl.**

MAHDIST Moslem dervish
MAHJONG Chinese game
MAHOUND Moslem evil spirit
MAHSEER Indian river fish **Z.**
MAIL-BAG
MAIL-CAR
MAILING posting
MAIL-VAN
MAIMING mutilating; crippling
MAINOUR stolen property **Law**
MAINTOP **Naut.**
MAISTER maestro; master
MAIZENA maize-meal **B.**
MAJESTY grandeur; magnificence
MAJORAT primogeniture (Fr.)
MALACCA cane **B.**
MALAISE unease; disquiet
MALARIA fever **Med.**
MALAYAN (Malay)
MALEFIC maleficent; baneful; noxious
MALICHO villainy
MALISON a curse; malediction
MALLARD wild duck **Z.**
MALLEUS ear bone **Med.**
MALLING beating; mauling
MALMSEY canary wine
MALTASE an enzyme **Z.**
MALTESE native or language of Malta
MALTING brewing
MALTMAN maltster
MALTOSE starch sugar **Chem.**
MAMELON rounded mound
MAMMARY (breasts)
MAMMATE (mammals) **Z.**
MAMMOCK shapeless mass; to mangle
MAMMOSE like a bosom
MAMMOTH elephantine; colossal **Z.**
MAMMULA small protuberance
MANACLE handcuff; shackle; fetter
MANAGED contrived; administered
MANAGER controller; director
MANAKIN small bird; manikin **Z.**
MANATEE sea-cow; dugong **Z.**
MANCHET small French loaf
MANCHOO Chinese ruler
MANDATE command; charge; edict
MANDIOC cassava shrub **B.**
MANDOLA mandora; guitar **Mus.**
MANDREL lathe-head
MANDRIL mandrel; spindle
MANGABY monkey (Madagascar) **Z.**
MANGLED calendered
MANGLER indifferent carver
MANGOLD mangel-wursel **B.**
MANHOLE
MANHOOD
MAN-HOUR **Meas.**
MAN-HUNT
MANIHOT⎱ mandioc; tapioca;
MANIHOT⎰ cassava **B.**

MANIKIN manakin; dwarf; a bird	**Z.**	
MANILIO arm-ring; copper coin	**Coin**	
MANILLA cheroot		
MANILLE a card value		
MANIPLE handful; scarf	**Eccl.**	
MANITOU Great Spirit		
MANKIND		
MANLESS		
MANLIKE		
MAN-MADE hand-made		
MANNING providing a crew		
MANNISH masculine		
MANNITE manna-sugar	**B.**	
MAN-ROPE handrail	**Naut.**	
MANSARD (roof)	**Arch.**	
MANSION residence; house; seat		
MANTLED cloaked; disguised		
MANTLET cloak; testudo		
MAN-TRAP		
MANTUAN Virgil		
MANUMIT free from slavery		
MANURED fertilized		
MANURER cultivator		
MANX-CAT	**Z.**	
MAORMOR royal steward (Sc.)		
MAPPERY map-work		
MAPPING surveying; delineating		
MAPPIST cartographer		
MARABOU adjutant stork	**Z.**	
MARACAN parrot	**Z.**	
MARACAS Cuban instrument	**Mus.**	
MARATHI Mahratta language		
MARBLED		
MARBLER (decorator)		
MARCATO precisely	**Mus.**	
MARCHED bordered; advanced		
MARCHEN folk-stories		
MARCHER border-defender		
MARCHES boundaries		
MARCONI		
MAREMMA marsh; malaria	**Med.**	
MARGODE bluish stone	**Min.**	
MARGOSA Indian tree	**B.**	
MARIKIN marmoset	**Z.**	
MARINER sailor; sea-farer	**Naut.**	
MARIPUT civet	**Z.**	
MARITAL (husband)		
MARKHOR wild goat	**Z.**	
MARKING branding; labelling		
MARLINE rope		
MARLING binding	**Naut.**	
MARLITE variety of marl	**Min.**	
MARLPIT clay-pit		
MARMITE cooking vessel		
MARMOSE opossum	**Z.**	
MARPLOT spoil-sport		
MARQUEE large tent		
MARQUIS		
MARRIED spliced; wedded		
MARRING spoiling; interrupting		

MARROWY full of marrow		
MARSALA a light wine		
MARSHAL arrange; harbinger		
MARTEXT careless preacher		
MARTIAL warlike; military		
MARTINI rifle; cocktail		
MARTLET house martin	**Z.**	
MARXIAN a socialist		
MARXISM communism		
MARXIST communist		
MARYBUD marigold	**B.**	
MASCLED net-like		
MASCULE } lozenge-shaped,		
MASCULY } (Her.)		
MASHING mixing		
MASHLIN } mashlum; mashlim		
MASHLIM } mixed grain		
MASH-TUB		
MASKING revelling; disguising		
MASONIC (freemasonry)		
MASONRY stonework		
MASSAGE friction	**Med.**	
MASSEUR		
MASSING accumulating; heaping		
MASSIVE bulky; weighty; ponderous		
MASSORA Biblical references		
MASTABA Egyptian tomb		
MASTERY skill; supremacy		
MASTFUL full of beech-nuts		
MASTICH gum; mastic	**B.**	
MASTIFF	**Z.**	
MASTING system of masts	**Naut.**	
MASTOID nipple-shaped	**Med.**	
MATADOR bull-fighter		
MATADOR a domino game		
MATCHED tallied; harmonized		
MATCHES contests; lucifers		
MATCHET machete; cutlass		
MATELOT a sailor (Fr.)		
MATERIA matter	**Med.**	
MATINAL a.m.		
MATINEE afternoon performance		
MATRASS chemical retort		
MAT-REED reed-mace	**B.**	
MATRICE matrix; die		
MATROSS assistant gunner		
MATTERY purulent	**Med.**	
MATTING mat-work		
MATTINS daily service	**Eccl.**	
MATTOCK pick-adze	**Tool**	
MATURED mellow; ripened; payable		
MATZOTH unleaven bread		
MAUDLIN drunk and whining		
MAULING malling; hammering		
MAUNDER mutter; to drivel		
MAURIST a Benedictine	**Eccl.**	
MAUTHER mother (dialect)		
MAWKISH squeamish		
MAW-SEED poppy-seed	**B.**	
MAW-WORM tape-worm	**Z.**	

MAXILLA upper jaw-bone **Med.**
MAXIMAL aphoristic
MAXIMED proverbial
MAXIMUM highest value
MAXWELL unit of magnetic flux **Electr.**
MAY-BIRD wood-thrush **Z.**
MAY-DUKE cherry **B.**
MAYFAIR fashionable locality
MAY-GAME May-day sport
MAY-LADY May-queen
MAY-LILY **B.**
MAY-MORN freshness
MAYORAL (mayor)
MAY-POLE
MAY-TIME season of May
MAY-WEED camomile **B.**
MAZAGAN bean **B.**
MAZARIN deep blue
MAZDEAN godlike
MAZEFUL intricate; daedalian
MAZURKA dance **Mus.**
MAZZARD skull; cherry **B.**
MEADOWY pasturable
MEAL-ARK meal-chest
MEALMAN grain merchant
MEANDER wander; twist and turn
MEANEST
MEANING purport; import; signifying
MEASLED spotted **Med.**
MEASLES **Med.**
MEASURE mete; gauge; value; degree
MEAT-FLY blow-fly **Z.**
MEAT-TEA high-tea
MEAT-TUB pickling tub
MECCANO constructional devices
MECHLIN lace
MECONIC (opium) **Med.**
MEDALET small medal **Eccl.**
MEDDLED interfered; muddled
MEDDLER busybody
MEDIACY interposition
MEDIANT a tone **Mus.**
MEDIATE intermediate
MEDICAL curative; sanatory **Med.**
MEDINAL soporific drug **Med.**
MEDULLA marrow; pith **Med.**
MEDUSAE Gorgons; hydrozoans **Z.**
MEDUSAN (petrifying)
MEERKAT mongoose (S. Africa) **Z.**
MEETING encounter; concourse; duel
MEGAERA one of the Furies
MEGA-ERG a million ergs **Meas.**
MEGAFOG multiple foghorn
MEIOSIS hyperbole
MEISSEN (Dresden china)
MELANGE medley; farrago; jumble
MELANIC black
MELANIN black skin pigment **Med.**
MELASMA black spots **Med.**
MELILOT sweet-scented clover **B.**

MELLITE honey-stone **Min.**
MELLOWY mellow; soft; unctuous
MELODIC melodious; harmonious
MELROSE honey of roses
MELTING fusing; softening; melting
MEMBRAL (limbs) **Med.**
MEMENTO keepsake; souvenir
MENACED alarmed; frightened
MENACER threatener; intimidator
MENDING repairing; amending
MEN-FOLK
MENGITE **Min.**
MENIVER miniver; ermine & lambskin
MENTHOL peppermint camphor **Chem.**
MENTION remark; state; cite; declare
MERCERY haberdashery
MERCIES usually small
MERCURY planet; quicksilver **Chem.**
MERCURY Hermes; messenger **B.**
MERGING absorbing; involving
MERITED deserved; earned; incurred
MERLING the whiting **Z.**
MERMAID famous Inn at Rye
MERRIER more cheerful
MERRILY joyously; blithely; happily
MERSION immersion
MESALLY centrally
MESEEMS it seems to me
MESHING ensnaring; netting
MESODIC (intermediate system)
MESSAGE despatch; missive; errand
MESSIAH also Messias
MESSING muddling; communal feeding
MESS-TIN a soldier's canteen
MESTINO⎫ half-caste Spanish-Indian
MESTIZO⎬
METAZOA multicellular animalculae **Z.**
METHANE marsh-gas **Chem.**
METOCHE an architectural interval
METONIC lunar cycle of 19 years
METOPIC superficial
METOPON opium-based drug **Med.**
METRICS versification; mensuration
METRIFY versify; poetise
METRIST a ballad-monger
METTLED courageous; (road)
MEWLING squalling
MEXICAN
MEZQUIT mesquit; a Mexican tree **B.**
MIASMAL air-borne infection **Med.**
MIAUING mewing
MIAULED caterwauled
MICHING pilfering
MICROBE germ; bacillus **Med.**
MICROHM electrical resistance **Meas.**
MIDDEST middlemost
MIDGARD cf. Asgard (Scand.)
MID-HOUR
MID-IRON golf-club
MIDLAND some way from the coast

MID-LENT
MID-LIFE
MIDMOST middlemost; central
MID-NOON midday
MIDRASH Jewish commentary
MIDRIFF diaphragm; garment   **Med.**
MIDSHIP   **Naut.**
MID-WIFE
MIEMITE lime-stone   **Min.**
MIGRANT nomad; wandering; roving
MIGRATE emigrate
MILDEST calmest; blandest
MILDEWY mouldy; musty; rusty
MILEAGE
MILFOIL the yarrow   **B.**
MILIARY a fever   **Med.**
MILIOLA (fossil millet)   **Min.**
MILITIA citizen army
MILK-BAR snack bar
MILKILY
MILKING
MILKMAN
MILK-RUN routine round
MILKSOP effeminate fellow
MILL-COG water-wheel tooth
MILL-DAM
MILLIER a thousand kilos   **Meas.**
MILLING struggling; grinding
MILLION
MILLREA ⎫ Portuguese and Brazilian
MILREIS ⎬   **Coin**
MILTING spawning
MILVINE (kite family)   **Z.**
MIMESIS mimicry
MIMETIC imitative
MIMICAL mocking
MIMICRY impersonation; miming
MIMULUS musk plant   **B.**
MINARET slender tower
MINCING affected; chopping; cutting
MINDFUL heedful; wary; attentive
MINDING marking; disliking; objecting
MINERAL
MINERVA Pallas Athene
MINEVER ⎫ meniver; ermine & lambskin
MINIVER ⎬
MINGLED joined; associated; jumbled
MINGLER a mixer; blender; compound
MINIATE to paint red
MINICAB hired car
MINIBUS four-wheeled vehicle
MINIKIN small pin; pet; favourite
MINIMAL smallest
MINIMUM least quantity
MINIMUS smallest; youngest
MINIOUS vermilion
MINORCA a fowl   **Z.**
MINSTER cathedral   **Eccl.**
MINTAGE coinage; mint dues
MINTING coining; inventing

MINTMAN coiner
MINUEND (subtraction)
MINUTED briefly recorded
MIOCENE geological period
MIOLNIR Thor's hammer
MIRACLE prodigy; supernatural event
MIRADOR balcony or gallery (Sp.)
MIRBANE (bitter almonds)
MIRIFIC marvellous; wondrous
MISBORN born to misfortune
MISCALL revile; abuse
MISCAST (wrong addition)
MISCITE quote erroneously
MISCOPY copy amiss
MISCUED (billiards)
MISDATE
MISDEAL
MISDEED fault; crime; trespass
MISDEEM judge wrongly
MISDOER delinquent; malefactor
MISDONE ill-done
MISDRAW draft badly
MISERLY parsimonious; niggardly
MISFALL mishap; misadventure
MISFIRE fail to go off
MISFORM
MISGAVE filled with doubt
MISGIVE mistrust; doubt
MISHEAR
MISHMEE a bitter tonic   **Med.**
MISHNAH ⎫ Jewish Oral Law
MISHNIC ⎬
MISJOIN
MISKICK football
MISLAID temporarily lost
MISLEAD dupe; delude; hoodwink
MISLIKE dislike; aversion
MISLIVE live a bad life
MISLUCK ill fortune; misfortune
MISMARK
MISNAME misterm; miscall
MISPLAY foozle
MISRATE rate erroneously
MISREAD
MISRULE anarchy; chaos; riot
MISSAID incorrectly stated
MISSEEM appear falsely
MISSEND ⎫ wrongly addressed
MISSENT ⎬
MISS-HIT cricket
MISSILE bullet; projectile
MISSING lost; lacking; absent
MISSION trust; errand; embassy
MISSISH girlish; affected
MISSIVE missile; letter; message
MISSTEP a false step
MISSUIT not harmonize
MISTAKE err; error; fault; oversight
MISTELL misstate; misrepresent
MISTERM mischance; miscall

MISTERY a craft or trade
MISTFUL clouded; foggy
MISTICO coasting vessel   **Naut.**
MISTILY hazily; obscurely
MISTIME
MISTRAL a northerly wind
MISTUNE
MISTURN
MISUSED abused; squandered
MISWEEN judge wrongly
MISWEND wander; stray
MISYOKE yoke improperly
MITHRAS a Persian divinity
MITOSIS complex cell division
MITRING (carpentering)
MIXABLE
MIXEDLY confoundedly
MIXTION gold-leaf fixative
MIXTURE medley; hotch-potch
MIZMAZE a labyrinth; a maze; amazed
MIZZLED decamped
MJOLNIR, MIOLNIR Thor's hammer
MOABITE a tribe
MOANFUL mournful; grievous
MOANING deploring; repining
MOBBING crowding around
MOBBISH tumultuous; disorderly
MOBILES free-hanging ornaments
MOB-RULE a form of democracy
MOBSMAN well-dressed swindler
MOBSTER gangster; hoodlam; ruffian
MOCKERY scorn; derision; ridicule
MOCKING taunting; jeering
MOCK-ORE a zinc ore   **Min.**
MOCK-SUN a parhelion
MODALLY conditionally
MODESTY chastity; propriety
MODICUM small quantity
MODISTE dress-maker
MODULAR proportional
MODULUS factor of a function
MODWALL bee-eater   **Z.**
MOELLON masonry-filling
MOFETTE (earth-fissures)
MOHICAN Algonquin Indian
MOHSITE titanite of iron   **Min.**
MOIDERT bewildered (Sc.)
MOIDORE Portuguese gold coin   **Coin**
MOILING toiling; drudging
MOINEAU bastion (Fr.)
MOISTEN damp; add water
MOLASSE sand stone   **Min.**
MOLE-RAT a rodent   **Z.**
MOLLIFY pacify; alleviate; soothe
MOLLINE emollient base
MOLLUSC ⎱ snails; gasterpods;   **Z.**
MOLLUSK ⎰ cuttle-fish; cephalopods **Z.**
MOLOSSI (3 long syllables)
MOMENTA masses having velocity
MONACID   **Chem.**

MONADIC   **Chem.**
MONARCH despot; king; ruler
MONERAL
MONERAN ⎱ protozoans   **Z.**
MONERON ⎰
MONEYED rich; wealthy; opulent
MONEYER coiner
MONGREL mixed breed
MONIKER nick-name
MONITOR mentor; advisor; lizard   **Z.**
MONKERY monk-life
MONKEYS Primates   **Z.**
MONKISH monastic
MONOCLE eye-glass
MONODIC monotonous and mournful
MONODON narwhal   **Z.**
MONOGYN type of plant   **B.**
MONSOON Indian rainy season
MONSTER ogre; marvel; prodigy
MONTAGE film editing
MONTANT fencing term
MONTERO horseman-cap (Sp.)
MONTHLY
MONTOIR mounting-stone (Fr.)
MONTURE saddle-horse (Fr.)
MOOCHED loitered; mouched
MOODILY morosely; capriciously
MOOKTAR Indian lawyer   **Law**
MOONEYE lake fish   **Z.**
MOONING day-dreaming
MOONISH fickle; variable
MOONLIT
MOON-MAD moonstruck
MOON-SET the setting of the moon
MOORAGE anchorage
MOOR-HEN water-hen   **Z.**
MOOR-ILL cattle disease (Sc.)
MOORING   **Naut.**
MOORISH Moresque; arabesque
MOOTING suggesting; debating
MOOTMEN law students   **Law**
MOPPING dabbing; wiping
MORAINE glacial debris
MORALER moraliser (Shak.)
MORALLY ethically; virtuously
MORASSY marshy; swampy; boggy
MORBLEU a French oath
MORBOSE diseased; unsound   **Med.**
MORCEAU morsel (Fr.)
MORDANT biting; caustic
MORDENT a trill   **Mus.**
MORELLA ⎱ dark-red cherry   **B.**
MORELLO ⎰
MORESCO arabesque; morisco
MORGANA (Fata)
MORGLAY claymore
MORICHE American palm   **B.**
MORINGA Malay tree   **B.**
MORISCO Moorish; moresco
MORLING dead sheep or its wool

MORMOPS repulsive looking bats **Z.**
MORNING dayspring; daybreak
MOROCCO goatskin leather
MORPHEW scurf **Med.**
MORPHIA opium extract **Med.**
MORPHIC morphological
MORRHUA (cod) **Z.**
MORRICE Morris; Moorish
MORRION open helmet
MORSURE the act of biting
MORTISE, MORTICE a joint in car-
pentry
MORTIER cap of state (Fr.)
MORTIFY putrefy; fester; corrupt
MORTIFY bodily self-denial; humiliate
MOSAISM (Moses)
MOSCHUS musk deer **Z.**
MOSELLE light wine
MOSS-HAG a slough in a bog
MOTACIL wag-tail **Z.**
MOTH-EAT
MOTHERY concreted; maternal
MOTORED
MOTTLED variegated; spotted
MOTTOED
MOTTOES pithy maxims
MOUCHER skulker
MOUFLON wild sheep **Z.**
MOUILLE liquid tone
MOULDED kneaded; shaped
MOULDER metal-caster; crumble
MOULDIE a torpedo **Naut.**
MOULTED shed
MOULVIE ⎫ Mahommedan priest,
MOULWEE ⎭ a learned man **Eccl.**
MOUNDED banked; fortified
MOUNTED on horseback; ascended
MOUNTER climber
MOURNED grieved; keened; wailed
MOURNER bewailer
MOUSING cat-work; lashing
MOUSMEE geisha
MOUTHED orated; chewed
MOUTHER stump-orator; ranter
MOVABLE portable; mobile
MOVABLY
MOW-BURN (hay)
MOZARAB (Christian Spaniard)
MOZETTA cardinal's cape **Eccl.**
MUCKING muffing; muddling
MUD-BATH
MUD-BOAT dredger **Naut.**
MUD-CART
MUD-CONE mud volcano
MUDDIED fouled; dirtied; soiled
MUDDIER more turbid
MUDDILY
MUDDING smearing with mud
MUDDLED misused; confused; fuddled
MUD-FISH the bow-fin **Z.**
MUD-FLAT

MUD-HOLE
MUD-LARK a gamin
MUD-SCOW (dredging)
MUD-SILL
MUD-WALL
MUD-WORT aquatic plant **B.**
MUEDDIN ⎫ Moslem priest **Eccl.**
MUEZZIN ⎭
MUFFING botching; fluffing
MUFFLED deadened; dulled
MUFFLER scarf
MUFFLON wild sheep **Z.**
MUGGARD sullen; displeased
MUGGENT wild fresh-water duck **Z.**
MUGGING swotting
MUGGINS simpleton; a juggins
MUGGISH damp and warm
MUGWORT wormwood plant **B.**
MUGWUMP independent politician
MULATTO half-breed
MULCHED ⎫ applied top dressing
MULSHED ⎭
MULCTED fined; penalized; amerced
MULETTE Portuguese sailing vessel
MULLEIN yellow plant **B.**
MULLING warming and spicing
MULLION munnion; uprt. window bar
MULLOCK rubbish; dirt
MULTOCA Turkish law **Law**
MULTURE grain grinding
MUMBLED muttered
MUMBLER indistinct articulator
MUMMERY masquerading; buffoonery
MUMMIED mummified
MUMMIFY embalm
MUMMING mummery; burlesquing
MUMMOCK ragged coat
MUMPING mockery; begging tricks
MUMPISH dull; sullen
MUNCHED crunched; chewed
MUNCHER a masticator
MUNDANE worldly; secular; temporal
MUNDIFY cleanse; purify
MUNJEET Siberian madder **B.**
MUNNION a mullion
MUNTING a door upright
MUNTJAK barking deer **Z.**
MURAENA eel genus **Z.**
MUREXAN purple dye
MUREXES ⎫ shell fish **Z.**
MURICES ⎭ Tyrian dye
MURGEON a wry face; grimace (Sc.)
MURIATE hydro-chloric **Chem.**
MURKIER more overcast
MURKILY duskily; luridly; darkly
MURRAIN cattle-disease
MURRINE fluor-spar **Min.**
MURRION morion; helmet
MURTHER murder
MUSCITE fossil moss **Min.**

MUSCLED muscular
MUSCOID moss-like   **B.**
MUSEFUL pensive; meditative
MUSETTE small bagpipe   **Mus.**
MUSHING dog-sleighing
MUSICAL tuneful; harmonious
MUSIMON moufflon   **Z.**
MUSK-BAG perfume sachet
MUSK-CAT civet cat   **Z.**
MUSKILY like musk
MUSK-RAT the musquash   **Z.**
MUSROLE nose-band of a bridle
MUSTANG wild horse   **Z.**
MUSTARD sinapis   **B.**
MUSTELA weasel   **Z.**
MUSTILY sourly; acridly; frowsily
MUSTING growing mouldy and rank
MUTABLE changeful; fickle; unstable
MUTABLY variably; inconstantly
MUTAGEN mutation producer   **Med.**
MUTANDA things to be altered
MUTTONY resembling mutton
MUZZILY confusedly; dizzily
MUZZLED forcibly restrained
MYALGIA cramp   **Med.**
MYALGIC tense; stiff   **Med.**
MYARIAN (mussels)   **Z.**
MYCELIA mushroom spawn   **B.**
MYCETES ⎱ howling monkeys   **Z.**
MYCETIS ⎰
MYCOSIS fungoid growth   **Med.**
MYCOTIC fungoid   **B.**
MYELOID marrow-like
MYIASIS a disease due to insects   **Med.**
MYLODON extinct sloth   **Z.**
MYNHEER Dutchman
MYOGRAM (muscular movement)
MYOLOGY (muscles)   **Med.**
MYOTOMY dissection   **Med.**
MYRRHIC (myrrh)   **B.**
MYRRHIN extract of myrrh   **B.**
MYRRHOL myrrh-oil   **B.**
MYSTERY mistery; a craft; enigma
MYSTICS a sect
MYSTIFY nonplus; perplex; bewilder
MYTHIST a recorder of legends
MYTILUS mollusc genus; mussels   **Z.**
MYXOPOD a protozoan   **Z.**

N

NABBING grabbing; seizing
NACARAT bright orange-red colour
NACELLE body of aeroplane
NACODAH Arab sea-captain
NACRITE pearl-like   **Min.**
NACROUS pearly
NAEVOID (birthmark)   **Med.**
NAEVOUS freckled
NAGGING incessant scolding

NAIADES water nymphs
NAILERY nail factory
NAILING spiking; fastening
NAIL-ROD nail material
NAIVELY artlessly; candidly
NAIVETE ingenuousness
NAIVETY unaffected simplicity
NAKEDLY starkly
NAMABLE nameable; nomenclatory
NANDINE civet cat (W. Africa)   **Z**
NANKEEN buff-coloured cloth (Nankin
NAPHTHA rock-oil   **Min**
NAPLESS threadbare
NAPPING dozing; snoozing; unalert
NARDINE spikenard   **B**
NARGILE Eastern pipe; hubble-bubble
NARRATE chronicle; describe; report
NARTHEX porch with lean-to roof **Eccl**
NARWHAL sea-unicorn   **Z**
NASALIS proboscis monkey   **Z**
NASALLY through the nose
NASARDE organ stop   **Mus**
NASCENT natal; originating; incipient
NASMYTH inventor of steam hammer
NASTIER more disagreeable
NASTILY offensively; nauseously
NATTERY peevish; captious
NATTIER French blue; smarter
NATTILY neatly; sprucely
NATURAL an idiot; normal; inherent
NATURED temperamentally disposed
NAUGHTY froward; perverse
NAUPLII crustaceans   **Z**
NAUTILI cuttle-fish   **Z**
NAVARCH an admiral (Greek)
NAVETTE rape plant   **B**
NAVY-CUT rope-bound tobacco sliced
NAVVIES labourers; canal diggers
NAYWORD by-word; watch-word
NAZI-ISM German nationalism
NEAD-END show end
NEALOGY embryology   **Med**
NEAREST closest; stingiest
NEARING approaching, drawing nigh
NEATEST sprucest; tidiest; trimmest
NEBULAE gaseous matter
NEBULAR cloudy; vague; hazy
NECKING embracing; an annulet (Arch
NECKLET small necklace
NECKTIE cravat
NECTARY honey-gland   **B**
NEEDFUL essential; vital; requisite
NEEDIER rather worse off
NEEDILY necessitously
NEEDING wanting; lacking
NEEDLED pierced; embroidered
NEEZING, NEESING sneezing
NEGATED denied; mollified
NEGATUR it is denied   **La**

NEGLECT disregard; omission
NEGLIGE loose attire; negligee
NEGRESS coloured lady
NEGRITO pygmy (Polynesia)
NEGROID negro-type
NEGUNDO box-elder **B.**
NEIGHED whinnied
NEITHER
NELUMBO water lily; lotus **B.**
NEMESIC retributive
NEMESIS goddess of vengeance
NEMORAL arboreal
NEOCENE geological formation
NEOLITE silicate of aluminium **Min.**
NEOLOGY (new terms); rationalism
NEOZOIC geological system
NEPOTIC favouring the family
NEPTUNE sea-god; planet
NEREITE fossil centipede **Min.**
NERVATE veined **B.**
NERVINE nerve tonic **Med.**
NERVING summoning resolution
NERVOUS sensitive; timid; fearful
NERVOSE having nerves
NERVULE } vein in leaf **B.**
NERVURE } or insect's wing **Z.**
NEST-EGG cash savings
NESTING nidification
NESTLED cherished; lay close
NESTLER a snuggler; cuddler
NET-BALL a girl's game
NET-CORD (tennis)
NET-FISH **Z.**
NETSUKE Japanese fastening
NETTING snaring
NETTLED stung; fretted; irritated
NETTLER a provoker
NETWORK reticulation; mesh
NEURINE nerve-matter **Med.**
NEUROMA tumour **Med.**
NEUROSE veined
NEUTRAL unbiassed; indifferent
NEUTRON uncharged particle (nuclear physics)
NEVADOS Andean winds (Ecuador)
NEW-BORN
NEWCOME recently arrived
NEW-LAID fresh eggs
NEW-MADE novel; fresh; neoteric
NEWNESS novelty
NEWSBOY
NEWSMAN
NIAGARA cataract; deluge; torrent
NIBBLED bit; pilfered; carped
NIBBLER dainty feeder
NIBLICK a golf club
NICKING stealing; notching
NICTATE wink
NIDGING stone dressing
NIGELLA love-in-a-mist **B.** 257
NIGGARD a miser; covetous; sparing

NIGGERY negroid
NIGGLED trifled
NIGGLER fuss-pot
NIGHTED benighted
NIGHTIE night attire; robe de nuit
NIGHTLY every evening
NIGRINE an ore of titanium **Min.**
NIGRITE insulating material
NILLING unwilling
NILOTIC (Nile)
NIMBLER more agile; quicker; swifter
NIMIETY excessiveness
NINE-PIN skittle
NINTHLY
NIOBEAN (Niobe); lachrymose; tearful
NIOBIUM metallic element **Chem.**
NIPPERS small pincers **Tool**
NIPPIER quicker; more agile
NIPPIES waitresses
NIPPING biting; pinching
NIRVANA tranquillity; earthly paradise
NITENCY effort; brightness
NITHING poltroon
NITRATE nitrite **Chem.**
NITRIFY convert to nitre **Chem.**
NITROUS nitrose **Chem.**
NIVEOUS snowy
NJORTHR a Vanir (Norse)
NOACHIC of Noah's time
NOBBLED injured; stole
NOBBLER confederate; doper
NOBLESS noblesse; nobility
NOBLEST most illustrious
NO-CLAIM (insurance)
NOCTUID nocturnal moth **Z.**
NOCTULE bat **Z.**
NOCTURN a service of psalms **Eccl.**
NOCUOUS harmful; noxious; baleful
NODATED knotted
NODDING (auction); unwary; nutation
NODICAL (ecliptic point, Astron.)
NODULAR (intersections)
NODULED knotted
NODULUS small knop
NOEMICS intellectual science
NOETIAN a dogmatic theologian
NOGGING brick and wood-work
NOISILY rowdily; loudly; uproariously
NOISING bruiting; rumouring
NOISOME noysome; disgusting
NOMADIC wandering; migratory
NOMANCY divination
NOMARCH Greek provincial governor
NOMBLES entrails of deer
NOMBRIL escutcheon centre
NOMINAL titular; ostensible
NOMINEE prospective candidate
NON-ACID
NON-AGED under 21
NONAGON nine-sided figure

NONPLUS perplex; astound; bewilder
NON-SKID steady grip tyres
NONSTOP perpetual motion
NONSUCH fodder plant **B.**
NON-SUIT **Law**
NON-TERM vacation **Law**
NON-USER
NOOLOGY psychology
NOONDAY 12 o'clock midday
NOONING siesta
NOOSING lassoing; snaring
NORFOLK loose jacket
NORIMON Japanese palanquin
NOR-LAND north country
NORTHER north wind
NORWICH school of painting
NOSE-BAG
NOSEGAY bouquet
NOSE-LED befooled
NOSTRIL
NOSTRUM panacea; quack; medicine
NOTABLE signal; famous; memorable
NOTABLY conspicuously; notoriously
NOTAEUM bird's back **Z.**
NOTANDA memoranda
NOTCHED scored; nicked
NOTCHEL to repudiate
NOTEDLY markedly; particularly
NOTELET small note
NOTHING nihil; zero; naught
NOTICED observed; heeded; marked
NOTITIA a catalogue
NOUMENA opp. to phenomena
NOURISH cherish; foster; encourage
NOURSLE to bring up; to nurse
NOVALIA reclaimed land
NOVELLA supplemental decrees
NOVELTY newness
NOWHERE
NOXIOUS hurtful; nocuous; baneful
NOYADES organised drownings (Fr.)
NOYSOME noisome; nauseating
NUCLEAL nuclear; (nucleus)
NUCLEAR central, like a kernel
NUCLEUS kernel; centre; head of comet
NUCLEIN cell matter
NUDGING elbowing; jostling
NULLIFY annul; rescind; revoke; repeal
NULLITY invalidity; noughtiness
NUMBERS a Biblical book **Eccl.**
NUMBING deadening; paralyzing
NUMBLES entrails of deer
NUMERAL digit; figure
NUMERIC numerical
NUMMARY (coins); numismatics
NUNATAK projecting rock (Esquimo)
NUN-BUOY conical buoy
NUNDINE market day (Roman)
NUNHOOD
NUNNERY convent **Eccl.**

NUNNISH sisterly; conventual
NUPTIAL conjugal; bridal; hymeneal
NURAGHE Sardinian fort
NURLING milling an edge
NURSERY (canons); training centre
NURSING fostering; developing
NURTURE up-bringing; sustenance
NUT-BUSH hazel **B.**
NUT-GALL **B.**
NUT-HOOK crooked stick
NUT-LOAF, NUT-MEAT vegetarian
NUT-MEAL nut-flour
NUT-PINE **B.**
NUTTING gathering nuts
NUT-TREE hazel **B.**
NUT-WOOD panel wood **B.**
NUZZLED nestled; cuddled
NYCTALA genus of owls **Z.**
NYLGHAU antelope (Ind.) **Z.**
NYMPHAL young and beautiful
NYMPHLY, NYMPHIC girlish

O

OAFLIKE doltish; stupid; idiotic
OAK-BARK
OAK-FERN **B.**
OAK-GALL **B.**
OAK-LEAF **B.**
OAKLING young oak **B.**
OARFISH ribbon-fish **Z.**
OARLOCK rowlock
OARSMAN sculler
OAT-CAKE
OAT-MALT
OAT-MEAL
OBCONIC funnel-shaped
OBDUCED drawn over; covered
OBDURED hardened; inured
OBELION part of skull **Med.**
OBELISK printer's dagger (†)
OBELIZE mark as spurious
OBESITY corpulence; fatness
OBEYING submitting; complying
OBITUAL funereal
OBLIGED gratified; forced; bound
OBLIGEE under bond
OBLIGER favourer
OBLIGOR bond giver **Law**
OBLIQUE askew; crooked; aslant
OBLOQUY calumny; censure; odium
OBOLARY poverty-stricken
OBOVATE, OBOVOID egg-shaped
OBSCENE repulsive; lewd
OBSCURE recondite; indistinct
OBSEQUY funeral rite
OBSERVE mark; notice; espy; remark
OBTRUDE intrude; thrust; interfere
OBVERSE head of coin
OBVIATE get round; preclude

OBVIOUS evident; patent; palpable	
OCARINA instrument (Sicily)	**Mus.**
OCCIPUT back of head	**Med.**
OCCLUDE absorb; include	
OCEANIC	
OCEANID ocean nymph	
OCEANUS ocean god	
OCELLAR ocellate; with 'eyes'	**Z.**
OCELLUS single eye; a spot	
OCELOID of the leopard type	**Z.**
OCHROID pale yellow	
OCTAGON	
OCTAPLA eight-fold	
OCTAVUS eighth (Latin)	
OCTETTE group of eight	
OCTOBER	
OCTOFID eight segments	**B.**
OCTOPOD eight-footed	**Z.**
OCTOPUS cuttle-fish; squid	**Z.**
OCTUPLE eightfold	
OCTYLIC (organic radicle)	**Chem.**
OCULATE eyed	
OCULIST	**Med.**
OCYPETE one of the Harpies	
ODALISK woman slave (Turk.)	
ODDMENT remnant	
ODDNESS oddity; eccentricity	
ODFORCE mesmeric force	
ODORANT odorous; fragrant	
ODORINE a bone distillate	
ODOROUS fragrant; redolent	
ODYSSEY perilous journey	
OEDEMIA surf-ducks	**Z.**
OEDIPUS a solver; King of Thebes	
OENOMEL wine and honey	
OERSTED magnetic field intensity	
	Meas.
OESTRUM frenzy; orgasm	
OESTRUS gadfly	**Z.**
OFF-BEAT unusual, advanced	**Mus.**
OFFCOME apology; pretext (Sc.)	
OFFENCE crime; injury; assault;	
OFFERED proffered; tendered; essayed	
OFFERER a bookie; volunteer	
OFFHAND casual; impolite	
OFFICER	
OFF-LINE aside from (computer)	
OFFSCUM offscouring	
OFFSIDE the right-hand side; football	
OFFWARD leaning off	
OGHAMIC (Irish script)	
OGREISH like an ogre	
OGYGIAN pre-historic; primeval	
OIL-BATH bicycle accessory	
OIL-BIRD the guacharo	**Z.**
OIL-CAKE cattle food	
OIL-GOLD (gold leaf)	
OIL-MEAL	
OIL-MILL	
OIL-PALM	**B.**
OIL-SHOP	

OIL-SILK	
OIL-SKIN waterproof garment	
OIL-SUMP drainage cavity in motor	
OIL-WELL petroleum well	
OJIBWAY Algonquian Indian	
OLDNESS senility	
OLDSTER middle-aged	
OLD-TIME old fashioned; quondam	
OLEFINE hydro-carbons	**Chem.**
OLIFANT elephant	**Z.**
OLIGIST haematite	**Min.**
OLITORY (kitchen-garden)	
OLIVARY olive shaped; oval	
OLIVINE chrysolite	**Min.**
OLYMPIC	
OLYMPUS abode of the gods	
OMENING auguring; presaging	
OMENTAL ⎫ peritoneum	**Med.**
OMENTUM ⎭	
OMICRON Greek letter " o "	
OMINOUS portentous; inauspicious	
OMITTED left out; neglected; dropped	
OMNIBUS bus; compendium	
OMNIFIC all-creating	
ONCOSTS overhead costs (Sc.)	
ONE-EYED limited in vision	
ONEFOLD single	
ONENESS unity; concord	
ONERARY operose; oppressive	
ONEROUS burdensome; weighty	
ONESELF me	
ONE-STEP a dance	
ONE-TIME former; previous	
ONGOING proceeding; event	
ONICOLO cameo-onyx	**Min.**
ONOCLEA fern genus	**B.**
ONOLOGY prattle	
ONSHORE towards the land	
ONSTEAD farmstead (Sc.)	
ONWARDS forward; advancing	
ONYCHIA a whitlow	**Med.**
ONYMISE categorise	
ONYMOUS not anonymous	
OOGRAPH egg drawing device	
OOLITIC granular	
OOLOGIC (birds' eggs)	**Z.**
OOMETRY egg measurement	
OOTHECA egg-carrying structure	**Z.**
OPACITY opaqueness; obscurity	
OPACOUS opaque; untransparent	
OPALINE opalescent	
OPALIZE opalise	
OPEN-AIR out-door	
OPEN-END radio; contract	
OPENING aperture; breach; orifice	
OPEN-JAW air ticket (two way)	
OPERANT a worker; artisan; employee	
OPERATE function; manipulate	**Med.**
OPEROSE tedious; onerary	
OPEROUS laborious; toilsome	
OPETIDE spring-tide	

259

OPHIDIA snakes **Z.**
OPHIURA starfish **Z.**
OPIATED drugged
OPINANT of opinion
OPINING opinion; a notion; supposing
OPINION conception; idea; conjecture
OPORICE preserved fruit
OPOSSUM a marsupial **Z.**
OPPIDAN town boy (Eton)
OPPOSED combatted; competed
OPPOSER rival; resister
OPPOSIT to negative
OPPRESS persecute; crush; maltreat
OPSONIC ⎱ germ-resisting corpuscles
OPSONIN ⎰ **Med.**
OPTICAL
OPTIMUM best value
OPULENT wealthy; affluent
OPUNTIA cactus family **B.**
OPUSCLE opusculum; a small work
ORAISON orison; a prayer **Eccl.**
ORARIAN coastal
ORARION, ORARIUM stole **Eccl.**
ORATING spouting; declaiming
ORATION speech; harangue; address
ORATORY eloquence; chapel **Eccl.**
ORATRIX lady speaker
ORBITAL revolutionary; elliptic
ORBLESS without knobs
ORBLIKE globular
ORCHARD garden of fruit-trees
ORDERED regulated; commanded
ORDERER controller; manager
ORDERLY methodical; (military)
ORDINAL a number
ORDINEE young deacon **Eccl.**
OREADES mountain nymphs
ORGANIC vital; radical; fundamental
ORGANON ⎱ organised enquiry
ORGANUM ⎰
ORGANRY organ music **Mus.**
ORGIAST a Bacchanalian
ORIENCY brightness of colour
ORIFICE aperture; vent; pore
ORLEANS cloth; plum **B.**
OROGENY (mountain formation)
OROLOGY mountain lore
OROTUND full voiced
ORPHEAN enchanting
ORPHEUS a maker of melodies
ORPHISM cult of Bacchus
ORPHREY embroidered border
ORTHITE allanite **Min.**
ORTHROS morning service (Greek)
ORTOLAN garden bunting **Z.**
ORVIETO a white wine
OSBORNE convalescent home
OSCINES singing birds **Z.**
OSCULAR (kissing)
OSIERED with withes

OSMANLI a Turk; Ottoman dynasty
OSMIOUS containing osmium **Chem.**
OSMOSIS diffusion **Chem.**
OSMOTIC diffusible
OSMUNDA royal fern **B.**
OSSELET morbid growth
OSSEOUS bony
OSSICLE small bone
OSSIFIC bony **Med.**
OSSUARY charnel-house
OSTEOID like bone
OSTIARY church janitor **Eccl.**
OSTIOLE spore-door **B.**
OSTITIS inflammation **Med.**
OSTRICH also estrich **Z.**
OTALGIA ear-ache **Med.**
OTARINE referring to seals **Z.**
OTOCYST auditory vesicle **Med.**
OTOLITH ear-stone **Med.**
OTOLOGY ear science **Med.**
OTTOMAN Turk; sofa; divan
OURSELF our kingly self
OUSTING ejecting; evicting; dislodging
OUT-BACK one from the back country
OUTBRAG out-boast
OUTBURN burn away
OUTCAST pariah; exile
OUTCOME issue; sequel; upshot
OUTCROP geological fault
OUTDARE outventure
OUTDONE surpassed; eclipsed
OUTDOOR open air
OUTEDGE farthest extremity
OUTFACE to brave
OUTFALL the place of discharge
OUTFLEW
OUTFLOW outlet
OUTFOOT out-pace; outsail
OUTGATE exit
OUTGAZE
OUTGIVE surpass in liberality
OUTGOER
OUTGONE over-reached; went beyond
OUTGROW
OUTGUSH outpour; outwell
OUTHAUL a rope **Naut.**
OUTHIRE to let out
OUTJEST
OUTLAND foreign
OUTLASH sudden outburst
OUTLAST survive; outlive; outwear
OUTLEAP a sally
OUTLIER outcrop
OUTLINE draft; sketch; profile
OUTLIVE survive
OUTLOOK prospect; future; view
OUTMATE overmatch; checkmate
OUTMOST furthest outward
OUTMOVE out-manoeuvre
OUTNAME surpass in reputation

OUTNESS externality; objectiveness
OUTPACE outrun
OUTPART remote part
OUTPEER excel
OUTPLAY out-manoeuvre
OUTPORT branch port
OUTPOST detached fort
OUTPOUR stream; spout
OUTPRAY surpass in prayer
OUTRAGE wanton mischief; abuse
OUTRANK precede
OUTRAZE exterminate
OUTRIDE
OUTROAD a foray (Sc.)
OUTROAR an uproar
OUTRODE
OUTROOT up-root; eradicate
OUTRUSH a raid; a foray
OUTSAIL
OUTSELL
OUTSHOT a projection
OUTSIDE external; exterior; superficial
OUTSIZE
OUTSOAR
OUTSOLD outvend
OUTSOLE outer sole
OUTSPAN to unyoke
OUTSTAY
OUTSTEP overstep
OUTTALK
OUTTURN output; production
OUTVIED surpassed; exceeded
OUTVOTE
OUTWALK outpace
OUTWALL outer wall
OUTWARD ostensible; apparent
OUTWEAR last longer; outlast
OUTWELL outgush
OUTWENT outstripped
OUTWIND extricate
OUTWING out-flank
OUTWITH beyond the scope of (Sc.)
OUTWORE lasted longer than
OUTWORK redoubt; ravelin
OUTWORN worn out; exhausted
OUVRAGE work (Fr.)
OVARIAN (ovary)
OVATION enthusiastic applause
OVEN-TIT willow-warbler   **Z.**
OVERACT act too much
OVERALL protective garment
OVERARM bowling (cricket)
OVER-ATE surfeited
OVERAWE intimidate; daunt; cow
OVERBID
OVERBUY buy too much
OVERDID
OVERDUE in arrears; outstanding
OVERDYE dye too deeply
OVEREAT

OVEREYE to overlook
OVERFAR
OVERFLY soar beyond
OVERJOY
OVERLAP
OVERLAY overwhelm
OVERLIE to smother
OVERMAN foreman
OVERPAY
OVERPLY over-exert
OVERRAN outran; invaded
OVERRUN swarm; infest; printing
OVERSAW superintended
OVERSEA foreign
OVERSEE superintend
OVERSET upset
OVERSEW
OVERTAX
OVERTLY openly; publicly; patently
OVERTOP surpass
OVIDIAN (Ovid)
OVIDUCT ovary passage   **Med.**
OVIFORM oval
OVOIDAL ovoid; egg-shaped
OVOLOGY egg-lore
OVULARY (seed)   **B.**
OVULITE fossil egg   **Min.**
OWENITE (Robert Owen)
OWL-EYED
OWL-LIKE fairly wise
OXALATE   **Chem.**
OXALITE oxalate of iron   **Min.**
OXIDANT combustive agent   **Chem.**
OXIDASE enzyme   **Chem.**
OXIDATE   **Chem.**
OXIDIZE to rust   **Chem.**
OXONIAN of Oxford
OX-STALL
OXY-ACID   **Chem.**
OXYOPIA acute vision   **Med.**
OXYSALT   **Chem.**
OXYTONE accented syllable
OZONIZE charge with ozone
OZONOUS ozonic

P

PABULAR yielding food
PABULUM aliment; fodder; nutriment
PACABLE appeasable
PACATED calmed; quieted; pacified
PACHISI pachesi; Indian backgammon
PACHYMA fungus genus   **B.**
PACIFIC peaceful; tranquil; irenic
PACKAGE bale; bundle; parcel
PACK-ICE
PACKING crowding; stowing
PACKMAN peddler; hawker; tallyman
PACKWAX tendon in animals' necks **Z.**
PACKWAY bridle path

PACTION a pact; covenant; bond
PADDING stuffing
PADDLED dabbled; propelled
PADDLER canoeist
PADDOCK frog or toad **Z.**
PADDOCK puddock; field
PADELLA small lamp
PADISHA Persian title
PADLOCK
PADRONE Italian employer
PAD-TREE harness frame
PAENULA chasuble **Eccl.**
PAEONIN red colouring matter
PAGEANT spectacle; display; pompous
PAGINAL (pages)
PAHLEVI pehlevi, early Persian dialect
PAILFUL the contents of a bucket
PAILLON metal backing
PAINFUL grievous; vexatious; sore
PAINING afflicting; tormenting; aching
PAINTED limned; bedizened; daubed
PAINTER artist in colour; depictor
PAINTER R.A.; mooring rope **Naut.**
PAIRING mating; (voting)
PAJAMAS pyjamas; slumber wear
PAKFONG⎫ German silver
PAKTONG⎭
PALABRA palaver (Sp.)
PALADIN knight errant
PALAMAE toe-webbings **Z.**
PALATAL (palate) **Med.**
PALAVER conference; pow-wow
PALE-ALE
PALEOUS like chaff
PALETOT loose overcoat
PALETTE artist's board
PALFREY saddle-horse **Z.**
PALINAL retrogressive **Med.**
PALLIAL (mantle of mollusc) **Z.**
PALLING covering; surfeiting
PALLIUM archbishop's pall **Eccl.**
PALLONE Italian ball-game
PALMARY worthy; capital
PALMATE web-footed **Z.**
PALMERY palm-house **B.**
PALMING concealing; handling
PALMIST fortune teller
PALM-OIL bribery
PALMYRA East Indian palm **B.**
PALOOKA guy; nitwit; simpleton
PALPATE to handle
PALSHIP comradeship
PALSIED paralyzed
PALUDAL marshy; malarial; fenny
PAMPERO westerly wind (S. America)
PANACEA universal remedy
PANACHE plume; self-esteem
PANAGIA all holy; an ornament **Eccl.**
PANCAKE (aviation); facial make-up (cosmetic)
PANDEAN of Pan

PANDECT digest of Roman Law
PANDION osprey genus **Z.**
PANDORA (her fateful box); sea-bream
PANDORE a lute **Mus.**
PANDOUR⎫ Hungarian soldier;
PANDOOR⎭ a robber
PANDURA Neapolitan guitar **Mus.**
PANGANI East African ivory
PANGING paining; causing anguish
PANICKY jumpy; nervous; fearful
PANICLE a small web **B.**
PANICUM millet **B.**
PANIKIN tin mug
PANNADE curvetting
PANNAGE swine food
PANNIER (dress); basket; corbel
PANNING washing; yielding
PANNOSE like felt
PANOCHA coarse sugar (Mexico)
PANOPLY complete armour
PAN-PIPE mouth-organ **Mus.**
PANSIED with pansies
PANTHER leopard **Z.**
PANTHOS Divinity made manifest
PANTIES undies
PANTILE pentile; curved tile
PANTING palpitating; desirous
PANTLER butler
PANURGE a Rabelaisian rascal
PANURGY skill in all work
PAPALLY popishly
PAPERED sand-papered
PAPERER paper-hanger
PAPHIAN (worship of Venus)
PAPILIO butterfly **Z.**
PAPILLA nerve extremity **Med.**
PAPMEAT soft food
PAPOOSE Indian infant
PAPPING feeding with pap
PAPPOSE pappous; downy
PAPRIKA red pepper (Turkish) **B.**
PAPULAR pimply **Med.**
PAPYRUS sedge; scroll **B.**
PARABLE allegorical similitude
PARACME decline; decadence
PARADED displayed; vaunted
PARADOS rampart
PARADOX surprising statement
PARAGON model of perfection
PARAMOS semi-tundra (Andes, S. Amer.)
PARAPET rampart
PARASOL sunshade
PARBAKE bake partially
PARBOIL seething action
PARCHED scorched; dried; shrivelled
PARDIEU in truth
PAREIRA drug (Brazilian plant) **Med.**
PARELLA⎫ litmus lichen **B.**
PARELLE⎭ perelle
PARERGY subsidiary work

262

PARESIS paralysis **Med.**
PARETIC partially paralyzed **Med.**
PARGING pargeting; external plaster work
PARITOR beadle; apparitor
PARKING lodging; collecting
PARLOUR the Mayor's sanctum
PARLOUS perilous; difficult; precarious
PARODIC (parody); farcical
PAROTIC auricular **Med.**
PAROTID }
PAROTIS } (salivary gland) **Med.**
PARQUET flooring; pit of theatre
PARRIED avoided; warded off; fended
PARSING grammatical exercise
PARSLEY a culinary herb **B.**
PARSNIP parsnep; a vegetable **B.**
PARTAKE to share; participate
PARTIAL biased; restricted; fond
PARTIES sides; jamborees
PARTING division; separating; breaking
PARTITE partially parted **B.**
PARTLET a ruff; a collar; a hen **Z.**
PARTNER colleague; associate; buddy
PARVENU upstart
PARVISE porch; church garden **Eccl.**
PASCHAL (Easter)
PASCUAL grazing; pasturing
PASQUIL }
PASQUIN } lampoon; satire
PASSADE } sword thrust;
PASSADO } equestrian exercise
PASSAGE alley; clause; contest
PASSANT walking (Her.)
PASSING brief; transient; exceeding
PASSION ardour; fervour; wrath
PASSIVE patient; resigned; inert
PASS-KEY a master-key
PASSMAN (honours)
PASTERN (fetlock)
PASTIES patties; pies
PASTIME recreation; sport; diversion
PASTING cementing; gumming
PASTURE herbage; meadowland
PATAMAR coasting vessel (Indian)
PATBALL tennis of sorts
PATCHED repaired clumsily
PATCHER repairer; botcher
PATELLA limpet **Z.**
PATELLA knee-cap; saucer **Med.**
PATERAE shallow dishes
PATHWAY footway; track; trail
PATIENT long-suffering **Med.**
PATNESS celerity in the uptake
PATONCE heraldic curved cross
PATRIAL racial; national
PATRICO gipsy priest; patercove
PATRIOT staunch non-cosmopolitan
PATRIST a theologian
PATROON American proprietor
PATTERN model; exempler; paragon

PATTIES pasties; pies
PATTING tapping
PATTRAS wooden wall-plug
PAUCITY fewness; exiguity; lack
PAULINE (St. Paul)
PAUNCHY obese; stout
PAUSING halting; wavering; tarrying
PAVIAGE road tax (Fr.)
PAVIOUR pavement layer
PAWNING pledging; hypothecating
PAXIUBA South American palm **B.**
PAYABLE due; profitable
PAY-BILL
PAY-BOOK
PAY-DIRT alluvial deposit
PAY-LIST pay-roll
PAY-LOAD plane's cargo
PAYMENT recompense; reward
PAYNISE to preserve wood
PAY-ROLL pay-list
PAYSAGE landscape
PEACHED divulged
PEACHER an informant
PEA-COAT pea-jacket
PEA-COCK pavonine **Z.**
PEA-CRAB small crustacean **Z.**
PEA-FOWL a species of Pavo genus **Z.**
PEAKING raising a yard obliquely **Naut.**
PEAKISH off colour; sickly
PEALING ringing; resounding
PEANISM song of praise or triumph
PEARLED
PEARLIN lace made of silk thread
PEASANT a rustic; swain; hind
PEASCOD pea-pod **B.**
PEA-SOUP London fog
PEAT-BED
PEAT-BOG
PEAT-HAG peat-hole
PEAVIES lumbermen's levers
PEBBLED shingled
PEBRINE silk-worm disease
PECCANT sinning; guilty; criminal
PECCARY S. American pig **Z.**
PECCAVI confession of error
PECKING picking up; striking
PECKISH hungry
PECTATE pectose; gelatinous
PECTINE jelly
PEDDLED retailed; trifled
PEDDLER hawker; huckster
PEDESIS molecular vibration
PEDICEL }
PEDICLE } small stalk **B.**
PEDLARY hawking
PEDRAIL tracked vehicle
PEELING excoriating; skinning
PEELITE follower of Sir R. Peel
PEEPING snooping; peering
PEERAGE Debrett

263

PEERESS consort of a peer	**PEP-TALK** encouragement
PEERING prying; gazing; appearing	**PEPTICS** digestion **Med.**
PEEVERS hop-scotch (Sc.)	**PEPTONE** digestive product **Med.**
PEEVISH querulous; snappish	**PERBEND** bonding stone
PEEWEEP peewit; pewit **Z.**	**PERCALE** woven cambric
PEGASUS winged horse of the Muses	**PERCASE** perhaps
PEGASUS (fish); constellation **Z.**	**PER-CENT**
PEGGING fastening; (croquet)	**PERCEPT** that which is perceived
PEHLEVI pahleri; early Persian dialect	**PERCHED** roosted; settled
PEISHWA Mahratta prime minister	**PERCHER** candle; rooster **Z.**
PELAGIC (deep sea)	**PERCINE** like a perch; percoid **Z.**
PELAMID bonito; mackerel type **Z.**	**PERCOCT** well cooked
PELASGI Greek tribe	**PERCOID** perch-like **Z.**
PELICAN genus of birds **Z.**	**PERCUSS** strike; tap
PELISSE fur-coat	**PERDURE** endure; persist
PELLAGE duty on skins	**PEREGAL** fully equal
PELOPID a son of Pelops	**PEREION** thorax of crustacea **Z.**
PELORIA⎫ abnormalism **Med.**	**PERELLE**⎫ parella; lichen **B.**
PELORIC⎭	**PARELLE**⎭
PELTAST soldier with buckler	**PERFECT** to complete; faultless
PELTATE shield-like	**PERFIDY** betrayal; treachery
PELTING pouring; throwing	**PERFORM** fulfil; act; execute; effect
PENALLY by way of punishment	**PERFUME** scent; aroma; fragrance
PENALTY handicap; retribution	**PERFUSE** sprinkle; bedew; permeate
PENANCE punishment; humiliation	**PERGOLA** pergula; arbour
PENATES Roman household gods	**PERHAPS** aiblins; peradventure
PEN-CASE pen-holder	**PERIAPT** amulet; charm; talisman
PENDANT an ornament; pennant	**PERIDOT** green jewel; olivine **Min.**
PENDENT hanging; dangling	**PERIGEE** orbital distance
PENDING awaiting decision	**PERIKON** wireless detector
PENEIAN (river Peneus in Vale Tempe)	**PERIQUE** Louisiana tobacco
PEN-FISH sparoid fish **Z.**	**PERIWIG** peruke
PENFOLD pinfold; enclosure for cattle	**PERJURE** forswear
PENGUIN pinguin **Z.**	**PERJURY** false testimony **Law**
PENICIL paint-brush	**PERKIER** more irrepressible
PENICIL lint compress; a pledget **Med.**	**PERKILY** saucily; jauntily; airily
PEN-NAME pseudonym; nom de plume	**PERKING** peering; smartening up
PENNANT a long streamer **Naut.**	**PERLITE** vitreous rock **Min.**
PENNATE winged; pinnate **Z.**	**PERMAGY** small Turkish boat
PENNIED having a cash asset	**PERMIAN** geological formation
PENNIES pence **Coin**	**PERMUTE** commute; change
PENNILL stanza (Eisteddfod)	**PEROPOD** rudimentary leg **Z.**
PENNING inditing; cooping	**PERPEND** ratiocinate; cogitate
PENSILE pendulous; suspended	**PERPEND** bonding stone
PENSION (boarding house); annuity	**PERPLEX** puzzle; nonplus; embarrass
PENSIVE meditative; thoughtful	**PERRIER** catapult; a table water
PENTACT five-rayed	**PERSEID** a meteor from Perseus
PENTANE (paraffin) **Chem.**	**PERSEUS** slew Medusa; a constellation
PENTICE pent-house; a sloping roof	**PERSIAN** Iranian
PENTODE pentone; wireless adjunct	**PERSIST** persevere; continue; last
PENTOSE a form of sugar **Chem.**	**PERSONA** (grata); actor's mask
PENTZIA S. African shrub **B.**	**PERSPEX** a glazing material
PEONAGE⎫ agricultural	**PERTAIN** to relate to; concern
PEONISM⎭ servitude	**PERTURB** disturb; agitate; disquiet
PEONIES paeonies **B.**	**PERTUSE** riddled; bored
PEOPLED inhabited	**PERUSAL** careful reading
PEPERIN volcanic tufa **Min.**	**PERUSED** read; studied; examined
PEPPERY irascible; choleric	**PERUSER** a scrutineer of pages
PEPSINE an enzyme **Med.**	**PERVADE** perfuse; impregnate; imbue
PEP-PILL stimulant	**PERVERT** deviate; lead astray

PESHITO Syriac Testament **Eccl.**
PESKILY annoyingly
PESTLED pounded in a mortar
PETASUS Mercury's winged cap
PETERED pottered; exhausted; (cards)
PETEREL petrel; Mother Carey's chick **Z.**
PETIOLE leaf-stalk; pedicle **B.**
PETRARY catapult for stones
PETREAN stony
PETRIFY stupefy; dumbfound; stun
PETRINE according to St. Peter **Eccl.**
PETROUS rocklike
PETTILY meanly; trivially
PETTING fondling; canoodling
PETTISH peevish; fretful; querulous
PETUNIA a flower **B.**
PEW-RENT **Eccl.**
PEWTERY (pewter)
PFENNIG German copper coin **Coin**
PHACOID lenticular **Med.**
PHAETON sky-hog; four-wheel carriage
PHAETON boatswain-bird **Z.**
PHALANX compact body
PHALLIC Bacchanalian
PHALLUS symbol of procreation
PHANTOM spectral; illusive; ghost
PHARAOH Egyptian title
PHARYNX upper part of gullet **Med.**
PHASING adjustment of television picture
PHENATE (phenol) **Chem.**
PHENOIC carbolic **Chem.**
PHIDIAS Greek sculptor
PHILTRE philter; love potion
PHINEAS mascot of Univ. Coll. Hosp.
PHLOEUM phloem; bark-fibre **B.**
PHOCINE (seals) **Z.**
PHOEBUS Apollo; the sun
PHOENIX date palm; fabulous bird **Z.**
PHONATE to utter inarticulately
PHONEME relevant sounds (linguistics)
PHONICS harmony; phonetics
PHONING telephoning
PHORESY assisted flight
PHOTICS science of light
PHOTISM colour sensation
PHRASED expressed; styled
PHRASER phrase-monger
PHRATRY tribal subdivision
PHRENIC diaphragmatic **Med.**
PHRENSY frenzy; madness; delirium
PHYSICS a science
PHYTOID plant-like **B.**
PIACERE at pleasure **Mus.**
PIAFFER a horse gait
PIANINA small piano **Mus.**
PIANISM musical technique **Mus.**
PIANIST an expert on the ivories **Mus.**
PIANOLA self-playing piano **Mus.**
PIARIST philanthropist, A.D. 1617
PIASTRE (Egypt) **Coin**

PIBROCH a tune; bagpipe (Sc.) **Mus.**
PICADOR mounted bull-fighter
PICAMAR tar extract
PICCAGE pitch-money **Law**
PICCOLO small flute **Mus.**
PICEOUS pitch-black
PICKAXE **Tool**
PICKING petty larceny; choosing
PICKLED preserved
PICOTEE carnation **B.**
PICOTTE little lace loop
PICQUET piquet; card game
PICRATE an explosive; lyddite **Chem.**
PICRINE foxglove extract **B.**
PICRITE olivine; peridot **Min.**
PICTISH Celtic
PICTURE portrait; drawing; imagine
PIDDOCK mollusc **Z.**
PIEBALD pyebald
PIECING patching; uniting
PIERAGE pier-tolls
PIERCED transfixed; impaled
PIERCER borer; gimlet; drill
PIERIAN (Muses); (Mount Pierus)
PIERROT an entertainer
PIETISM sanctimoniousness
PIETIST religious sect
PIEWIFE lap-wing **Z.**
PIFFERO oboe; organ-stop **Mus.**
PIFFLED chattered; drivelled
PIG-DEER **Z.**
PIGEYED
PIGGERY pig-sty
PIGGING living higgledy-piggledy
PIGGISH hoggish; swinish; messy
PIGHTLE small enclosure
PIG-IRON
PIG-LEAD cast lead
PIGMEAN pygmean; Lilliputian
PIGMENT paint; colour; tincture
PIGMIES pygmies
PIGNONS fir-cone seeds **B.**
PIGSKIN (leather); (saddle)
PIGTAIL (Chinaman)
PIG-WASH hog-wash
PIKELET ⎱ a crumpet;
PIKELIN ⎰ a tea-cake
PIKEMAN turnpike gatekeeper
PIKRITE igneous rock **Min.**
PILCHER a scabbard
PILEATE cap-shaped
PILFERY petty theft; larceny **Law**
PILGRIM palmer; devotee; wayfarer
PILKINS pill-corn; oats **B.**
PILLAGE rifle; sack; ravage; loot
PILLBOX concrete emplacement
PILLING blackballing
PILLION padded saddle
PILLORY expose to ridicule
PILLOWY yielding; soft

265

PILOTED steered; conducted; guided
PILOTIS building on columns   **Arch.**
PILTOCK coalfish   **Z.**
PILULAR (pills)
PIMELIC a fat product   **Chem.**
PIMENTA ⎱ allspice;   **B.**
PIMENTO ⎰ Jamaica pepper
PIMPLED blotched
PIN-CASE
PINCERS pliers   **Tool**
PINCHED gripped; purloined
PINCHER sea fish   **Z.**
PINCHES nips
PINDARI Indian freebooter
PINE-OIL oil from resin
PINETUM plantation of pine-trees   **B.**
PIN-FIRE (cartridge)
PIN-FISH a scaly fish; sailor's choice **Z.**
PINFOLD cattle pound
PINGING like a bullet
PINGUID fat; greasy; unctuous
PINHEAD top of a pin; minute
PIN-HOLD pin-housing
PINHOLE
PINK-EYE a horse disease
PINKING scalloping; knocking
PINKISH somewhat pink
PINNACE a man-of-war's boat   **Naut.**
PINNATE pennate; feathered   **B.**
PINNING making fast
PINNOCK tom-tit   **Z.**
PINNULA ⎱ branchlet;   **B.**
PINNULE ⎰ small feather   **Z.**
PINTADO guinea-fowl; chintz   **Z.**
PINTAIL a duck   **Z.**
PINT-POT   **Meas.**
PIN-WORK (flexing flax)
PIONEER forerunner; initiator
PIONING pioneering (Spens.)
PIOUSLY devoutly; religiously
PIP-EMMA p.m., (signalling)
PIPERIC peppery
PIPETTE graduated tube
PIPLESS seedless   **B.**
PIPPING pilling; defeating
PIQUANT stimulating; caustic; tart
PIQUING irritating; nettling
PIRAGUA a dug-out canoe   **Naut.**
PIRATED plundered; marauded
PIRATIC infringing; piratical
PIROGUE flat-bottomed boat (Sp.)
PISCARY fishing rights
PISCINA basin; fish-pond   **Eccl.**
PISCINE fishy
PISMIRE an ant; emmet   **Z.**
PISTOLE Spanish golden coin   **Coin**
PITAPAT in a flutter
PITCHED flung; tossed; planted; cast
PITCHER eared jug; (base-ball)
PITCOAL   **Min.**

PITEOUS woeful; sorry; compassionate
PITFALL a trap; snare; danger
PIT-HEAD
PITHILY tersely; concisely; briefly
PITHING extracting the marrow
PITIFUL humane; lenient; wretched
PIT-MIRK dark as pitch (Sc.)
PITTING corrosion; striving
PITTITE play-goer
PITUITA ⎱ phlegm   **Med.**
PITUITE ⎰
PITYING commiserating; condoling
PIVOTAL axial
PIVOTED hinged; centred on
PIXY-LED bewildered
PLACARD bill; poster; notice
PLACATE pacify; conciliate; appease
PLACEBO R.C. mass   **Eccl.**
PLACING identifying; assigning
PLACKET slit; pocket
PLACOID scaly
PLACULA small plate; plaque
PLAFOND ceiling; a soffit
PLAGIUM kidnapping   **Law**
PLAGUED distracted
PLAGUER a vexatious person
PLAIDED wearing a tartan
PLAINER clearer; more obvious
PLAINLY simply; clearly; candidly
PLAITED folded; woven
PLAITER an interlacer
PLANARY flat; level
PLANING smoothing; aeroplaning
PLANISH to hammer smooth
PLANKED laid down; floored
PLANNED sketched; schemed
PLANNER a projector; designer
PLANTAR (sole of foot)
PLANTED instilled; inculcated; sown
PLANTER settler; grower
PLANULA embryo protoplasm   **Z.**
PLANXTY Welsh lament
PLASHED splashed; dabbled
PLASMIC proto-plasmic
PLASMON flour-like food
PLASTER sinapism; daub; stucco
PLASTIC elastic; pliable; yielding
PLASTID living cell   **Z.**
PLATANE plane-tree   **B.**
PLATEAU tableland; highland
PLATINA platinum   **Chem.**
PLATING sheathing
PLATOON a squad
PLATTED plaited; weaved
PLATTER wooden plate
PLAUDIT applause; approbation
PLAY-BOX
PLAY-BOY
PLAY-DAY holiday
PLAYFUL sportive; frolicsome

PLAYING acting; competing; romping
PLEADED entreated; argued **Law**
PLEADER barrister; advocate **Law**
PLEASED delighted; contented; obliged
PLEASER charmer; gratifier
PLEATED platted; interlaced
PLECTRE plectrum; plectron **Mus.**
PLEDGED pawned; engaged
PLEDGEE pawnbroker
PLEDGER pawnbroker's customer
PLEDGET lint compress **Med.**
PLEIADS the Pleiades; 7 stars in Taurus
PLENARY in full; complete; entire
PLENISH provide; equip
PLENIST spacious materialist
PLEROMA abundance; fullness
PLEURAL (lungs) **Med.**
PLEURON shell extension **Z.**
PLEXURE weaving; texture
PLIABLE limber; tractable; supple
PLIABLY flexibly; lithely
PLIANCY flexibility
PLICATE folded; plaited
PLIFORM in the form of a fold
PLIMMED swollen
PLIMSOL rubber shoe; sand-shoe
PLISKIE plight (Sc.)
PLODDED toiled; drudged
PLODDER steady worker
PLOPPED plumped
PLOTFUL full of schemes
PLOTTED planned; schemed; concocted
PLOTTER intriguer; conspirator
PLOTTIE mulled wine (Sc.)
PLOUTER to paddle or dabble
PLOW-BOY plough-boy
PLOWING ploughing
PLUCKED failed to pass; culled
PLUCKER feather remover
PLUGGED plodded; shot; sealed
PLUGGER stopper
PLUMAGE plumery; feathers
PLUMBED measured; made vertical
PLUMBER lead-worker
PLUMBUM, PLUMBIC lead **Chem.**
PLUMCOT plum-apricot **B.**
PLUMERY display of plumes
PLUMING self-congratulation
PLUMIST feather-dresser
PLUMMET lead bob
PLUMOSE plumous; feathery
PLUMPED fell suddenly
PLUMPER chubbier; fatter; stouter
PLUMPLY roundly; fully
PLUMULE plumula; bud **B.**
PLUNDER loot; spoil; pillage; booty
PLUNGED dived; gambled heavily
PLUNGER part of a pump
PLUNKET blue colour
PLUVIAL rainy; humid

PLUVIUS Jupiter pluvius
PLY-WOOD
POACEAE the grasses **B.**
POACHED trespassed; stabbed; (eggs)
POACHER a toiler; setter of snares
POCHARD a duck **Z.**
POCK-PIT pock-mark **Med.**
PODAGRA gout **Med.**
PODDING producing pods
PODESTA Italian magistrate
PODITIC (crab's leg) **Z.**
PODRIDA Spanish stew
POE-BIRD tui; parson bird; (N.Z.) **Z.**
POETESS lyrical lady
POETICS criticism of poetry
POETIZE poetise; versify
POINDED pounded; distrained **Law**
POINTED acute; sharp; keen; signific't
POINTEL pencil; spike; style
POINTER fescue; indicator **Z.**
POISING balancing; loading
POITREL horse-armour
POLACCA Mediterranean sailing vessel
POLDERS reclaimed land
POLE-AXE poll-axe **Tool**
POLE-CAT civet **Z.**
POLEMIC controversial; contentious
POLENTA Italian porridge
POLICED regulated
POLITER more courteous or civil
POLITIC statesmanlike; discreet
POLLACK sea-fish; pollock; chub **Z.**
POLARIS guided missile
POLLARD stag after casting his antlers
POLLARD lopped; bran; the chub **Z.**
POLL-AXE pole-axe **Tool**
POLLENT strong; mighty; puissant
POLLING voting; lopping
POLL-MAN pass-man (Cam.)
POLL-TAX capitation tax
POLLUTE defile; profane; corrupt
POLOIST polo player
POLYACT rayed
POLYGON angular figure
POLYGYN plant genus **B.**
POLYMER complex compound **Chem.**
POLYOPY multiple vision
POLYPUS sea-anemone; coral **Z.**
POLYZOA barnacles **Z.**
POMATUM an unguent
POMELOE citron of shaddock kind **B.**
POMEROY the king-apple **B.**
POMFRET a fish **Z.**
POMMAGE crushed apples
POMMARD a Burgundy wine
POMPANO edible fish (N. Amer.) **Z.**
POMPION pumpkin **B.**
POMPIRE an apple **B.**
POMPOSO with due pomp **Mus.**
POMPOUS self-important; grandiose

PONCEAU poppy; poppy-coloured **B.**
PONDAGE water in a pond
PONDING collecting into a pond
PONIARD dagger
PONTAGE bridge toll
PONTIFF high priest; pope **Eccl.**
PONTINE Roman marsh
PONTOON bridge of boats; card game
POOH-BAH a pluralist
POOLING merging; combining
POOPING (following sea)
POOR-BOX alms for the poor
POOREST most necessitous; neediest
POOR-LAW
POPCORN parched maize **B.**
POPEDOM **Eccl.**
POP-EYED
POPPIED drowsy; slumbrous; narcotic
POPPING exploding; pawning; darting
POPPLED rippled; bubbled
POP-SHOP pawn-shop
POPULAR familiar; prevailing; current
POP-WEED bladder-wort **B.**
PORCATE ridged
PORCINE piggy; swinish; suiform **Z.**
PORIFER a sponge
PORK-PIE type of hat
POROSIS bone formation **Med.**
POROTIC (porosis); callous **Med.**
PORRECT extended
PORRIGO dandruff **Med.**
PORTAGE porterage
PORT-BAR harbour bar
PORTEND foretell; augur; bode
PORTENT an evil omen; presage
PORTICO porch; stoa; colonnade
PORTIFY aggrandise
PORTING carrying; conveying **Naut.**
PORTION bit; part; share; division
PORTRAY paint; describe
PORZANA water-rail; crake **Z.**
POSAUNE German trombone **Mus.**
POSITED postulated
POSSESS own; hold; keep; control
POSTAGE
POST-BAG
POST-BOY
POST-BOX letter-box
POST-DAY
POSTEEN Kashmir sheepskin coat
POSTERN back-door; small gate
POSTFIX affix; suffix; append
POSTING mailing; recording
POSTMAN letter carrier
POSTURE pose; attitude; position
POST-WAR
POTABLE drinkable; liquid
POTAGER porringer
POTANCE part of a watch
POTARGO a pickle

POTASSA potash **Chem.**
POTATOR an imbiber; toper
POTENCE Heraldic gibbet
POTENCY ability; power; influence
POT-HEAD dunderhead
POTHEEN Irish whisky
POT-HERB
POT-HOLE
POT-HOOK
POTICHE porcelain vase
POT-LUCK
POTOROO rat kangaroo **Z.**
POT-SHOP small inn
POT-SHOT random round
POTTAGE a mess; a stew
POTTERY earthenware
POTTING preserving; shooting
POUCHED bagged; marsupial **Z.**
POULARD plump pullet **Z.**
POULTER poulterer (Shak.)
POULTRY fattened fowls **Z.**
POUNCED with claws; sprang; swooped
POUNDAL unit of force **Meas.**
POUNDED confined; bruised
POUNDER pestle
POURING streaming; gushing
POUTING registering displeasure
POVERTY want; penury; indigence
POWDERY pulverous; floury; dusty
POWERED engined
PRACTIC deceitful; skilful (Shak.)
PRAETOR Roman magistrate
PRAIRIE treeless grassy lands
PRAISED lauded; glorified
PRAISER laudator; extoller; eulogizer
PRAKARA temple passage (India)
PRAKRIT Sanskrit and allied languages
PRALINE sweetmeat; nuts in sugar
PRANCED strutted; bounded
PRANGED bombed heavily; struck
PRANKED all dressed up; prinked
PRANKER practical joker; a dude
PRATIES potatoes (Ir.) **B.**
PRATING babbling; boasting
PRATTLE idle chatter
PRAYING imploring; craving; begging
PREACHY tediously didactic
PREBEND canon's stipend **Eccl.**
PRECEDE herald; usher; introduce
PRECEPT behest; maxim; rule; canon
PRECIPE writ **Law**
PRECISE exact; accurate; finical
PREDATE ante-date
PREDIAL (farm estate)
PREDICT presage; portend; foretell
PREDONE worn out; exhausted
PREDOOM prejudge
PREEMPT bespeak at a high price
PREENED tidied up
PREFACE preamble; proem; prologue

PREFECT French magistrate; monitor
PREFINE limit; delimit
PREFORM form beforehand
PRELACY episcopacy   **Eccl.**
PRELATE church dignitary   **Eccl.**
PRELECT discourse; lecture; address
PRELUDE preface; exordium   **Mus.**
PREMIAL at a premium
PREMIER first; principal; P.M.
PREMISE antecedent proposition
PREMISS logical premise
PREMIUM bounty; fee; reward; bonus
PRENDER right of seizure   **Law**
PREORAL in front of the jaw
PREPAID
PREPARE make ready; manufacture
PRESAGE foretell; predict; prophesy
PRESEEN foreseen
PRESELL promote products in advance
PRESENT here; now; existing; current
PRESENT exhibit; proffer; gift
PRESIDE officiate; direct; control
PRESSED urged; crushed; encroached
PRESSER squeezer
PRESTER mythical mediaeval priest
PRESUME assume; reckon; venture
PRETEND feign; simulate; claim
PRETEXT excuse; plea; cloak
PRETONE (accented syllable)
PRETZEL crisp biscuit
PREVAIL dominate; win; succeed
PREVENE precede
PREVENT hinder; hamper; thwart
PREVIEW foresee
PREVISE forewarn; foresee
PREWARN give notice of
PREYFUL predatory
PREYING plundering; wasting; robbing
PRIAPUS God of procreation
PRICING costing; valuing; rating
PRICKED spurred; punctured; bored
PRICKER prickle; light horseman
PRICKET early candlestick
PRICKET a young buck   **Z.**
PRICKET stone-crop   **B.**
PRICKLE to prick; a thorn   **B.**
PRICKLY spinate; spicate
PRIDIAN of yesterday
PRIDING valuing; esteeming highly
PRIDWIN King Arthur's shield
PRIGGED filched; purloined; nabbed
PRIGGER thief; pincher
PRIMACY Archbishopric   **Eccl.**
PRIMAGE a lading charge
PRIMARY main; first; pristine; initial
PRIMATE Archbishop   **Eccl.**
PRIMELY originally; excellently
PRIMERO card game
PRIMINE outer husk   **B.**
PRIMING (powder); (paint)

PRIMMED formed precisely
PRIMSIE demure; prim (Sc.)
PRIMULA primrose genus   **B.**
PRINKED pranked; all dressed up
PRINKER (dressed showily)
PRINTED published; pressed; issued
PRINTER typographer
PRISAGE a levy on wines
PRISING forcing open; levering
PRISTIS saw-fish   **Z.**
PRITHEE I pray thee
PRIVACY seclusion; solitude; retreat
PRIVATE soldier; personal; unofficial
PRIVILY privately; confidentially
PRIVITY secrecy; cognizance
PRIZAGE prisage; crown levy
PRIZING appreciating; valuing
PROBANG whalebone swab   **Med.**
PROBATE proof of a will   **Law**
PROBING scrutinizing; testing; sifting
PROBITY proved integrity; sincerity
PROBLEM enigma; query; conundrum
PROCEED advance; continue; act
PROCESS operation; course; progress
PROCTOR university official   **Law**
PROCURE get; obtain; induce
PROCYON lesser Dog-star
PRODDED goaded; shoved; poked
PRODDER inciter; stimulator
PRODIGY marvel; wonder; portent
PRODUCE engender; show; bear
PRODUCT proceeds; yield; result
PROFACE May it profit you !
PROFANE desecrate; secular
PROFESS own; aver; proclaim
PROFFER offer; tender; volunteer
PROFILE outline; side view
PROFUSE lavish; prodigal; copious
PROGENY off-spring; issue; young
PROGGED begged; prodded; (proctored)
PROGRAM programme; syllabus
PROJECT propel; contrive; jut
PROLATE extended
PROLEGS legs of caterpillars   **Z.**
PROLONG protract; lengthen; sustain
PROMISE pledge; engage; stipulate
PROMOTE further; aid; elevate
PRONAOS temple porch
PRONATE face or palms downwards
PRONELY lying down
PRONGED fork-like; bifurcated
PRONOTA beetles' backs   **Z.**
PRONOUN
PROOFED tried; tested
PROOTIC an ear-bone   **Med.**
PROPALE to disclose
PROPANE paraffin gas
PROPEND to favour; lean forward
PROPHET seer; augur; preacher
PROPINE pledge; guarantee

PROPOSE suggest; intend; purpose
PROPPED shored; strutted; supported
PROPUGN vindicate; defend
PRORATE assess pro rata
PRORSAD prorsal; anterior **Med.**
PROSAIC unexciting; dull; humdrum
PROSECT dissect beforehand **Med.**
PROSIFY turn into prose
PROSILY unimaginatively
PROSING talking tediously
PROSODY (harmonious writing)
PROSOMA forepart of body **Med.**
PROSPER thrive; flourish; succeed
PROTEAN in many guises
PROTECT shield; defend; ward
PROTEGE trusted nominee
PROTEID⎫ complex substances in food,
PROTEIN⎭ necessary for diet **Chem.**
PROTEND hold out; extend
PROTEST expostulate; exclaim; object
PROTEUS sea-god of Carpathian Sea
PROTYLE hypothetical nucleus
PROUDER more arrogant and haughty
PROUDLY majestically; imperiously
PROVAND provision; provend (Shak.)
PROVANT of inferior quality
PROVERB saw; adage; aphorism
PROVIDE supply; produce; purvey
PROVINE (vine culture)
PROVING establishing; testing
PROVISO a condition
PROVOKE infuriate; enrage; rouse
PROVOST magistrate **Eccl.**
PROWESS valour; skill; dexterity
PROWEST most valiant, (obs.)
PROWLED slunk; roved; roamed
PROWLER stealthy stalker
PROXIME nearest
PROXIMO next month
PRUDENT wise; cautious; frugal
PRUDERY mock modesty
PRUDISH very formal; puritanical
PRUNING lopping; clipping; trimming
PRURIGO an itch **Med.**
PRUSSIC acid; a cyanide **Chem.**
PRYTANY Athenian Council division
PRYTHEE I pray thee!
PSALTER psalm book; rosary
PSCHENT royal crown of ancient Egypt
PSOATIC (tenderloin) **Med.**
PSYCHAL spiritualistic
PSYCHIC not based on materialism
PTARMIC sneezing mixture **Med.**
PTERION (craniology) **Med.**
PTEROMA Greek peridrome; side-wall
PTEROPE flying fox; fruit-bat **Z.**
PTOMAIN ptomaine; toxic matter **Med.**
PTYALIN (saliva) **Med.**
PUBERAL of age
PUBERTY the generative age

PUBLISH announce; disclose; blazon
PUCELLE Joan of Arc
PUCERON plant louse **Z**
PUCKERY wrinkled
PUCKISH impish; mischievous
PUDDING fruity farinaceous food
PUDDLED stirred up the mud
PUDDLER iron-worker
PUDENCY modesty; bashfulness
PUEBLAN Mexican aborigine
PUERILE childish
PUFF-BOX
PUFFERY⎫ extravagant;
PUFFING⎭ advertisement
PUFFIER more swollen
PUFFILY bombastically
PUGAREE puggree; puggery; Ind. scar
PUGGING (sound prevention); ceramic
PUGGREE Indian scarf for topee
PUGMILL clay mill
PUG-NOSE retroussé
PULLIES pulley-wheels
PULLING extracting; wresting; towing
PULLMAN (railway carriage)
PULL-OUT extensible
PULPIFY mash
PULPING reducing to pulp
PULPOUS pulpy
PULSATE throb; palpitate; quiver
PULSING beating; vibrating; throbbin
PULSION propulsion
PUMMACE crushed apples
PUMPAGE the amount pumped
PUMPING extracting information
PUMPKIN pumpion; quashey; a gourd **B**
PUMP-ROD
PUNCHED perforated; struck
PUNCHER a bruiser; a drover
PUNCH-UP fist-fight (boxing)
PUNCTUM a dot
PUNGENT acrid; caustic; tart
PUNJABI an Indo-Aryan language
PUNNAGE punning
PUNNING quipping
PUNSTER a pun maker
PUNT-GUN
PUNTING gaming; (football)
PUPATED formed a chrysalis **Z**
PURANIC (Brahmin scriptures) **Eccl**
PURBECK Dorset stone **Mir**
PURFLED decorated (arch.)
PURFLEW wrought border
PURGING cleaning up; pruning
PURITAN
PURLIEU slum; environs
PURLINE timber-work
PURLING rippling
PURLOIN steal; pilfer; filch
PURPLED dyed purple
PURPLES livid spots **Me**

PURPORT signification; import
PURPOSE aim; intent; object
PURPURA Tyrian purple   **Z.**
PURPURE Heraldic purple
PURRING curring; (feline felicitude)
PURROCK paddock
PURSING wrinkling
PURSUED continued; hunted; practised
PURSUER plaintiff (Sc.)   **Law**
PURSUIT chase; search; calling
PURVIEW extent; scope; range
PUSHFUL enterprising; self-assertive
PUSHING vigorous; jostling; thrusting
PUSHPIN a game
PUSTULE pimple   **Med.**
PUTAMEN fruit-stone; husk   **B.**
PUTAMEN lenticular nucleus   **Med.**
PUTREFY rot; decay; decompose
PUTTIED fixed with putty
PUTTIER glazier
PUTTIES leg-wear; puttees
PUTTING (golf); (the weight)
PUTTOCK kite; buzzard   **Z.**
PUZZLED perplexed; mystified
PUZZLER poser; riddler
PYAEMIA blood-poisoning   **Med.**
PYAEMIC suffering from pyaemia **Med.**
PYCNITE topaz   **Min.**
PYEBALD piebald
PYGMEAN pigmean; dwarfish
PYJAMAS also pajamas; slumber-wear
PYLORUS an outlet   **Med.**
PYRAMID
PYRETIC fever-reducer   **Med.**
PYREXIA fever   **Med.**
PYREXIC feverish   **Med.**
PYRITES an iron ore
PYRITIC (pyrites)
PYROGEN fever inducer   **Med.**
PYROSIS indigestion   **Med.**
PYROTIC caustic; burning   **Med.**
PYRRHIC war dance; costly
PYTHIAD a period
PYTHIAN oracular
PYXIDIA capsules   **B.**

Q

QUABIRD night heron   **Z.**
QUACKED boasted; practised quackery
QUACKLE croak; quack
QUADRAT filling piece in printing
QUADREL square tile
QUADRIC quadratic
QUAFFED tippled; swilled; caroused
QUAFFER deep drinker; soaker; toper
QUAHAUG American clam   **Z.**
QUAILED flinched; cowered; blenched
QUAKERS a sect
QUAKERY quakerism

QUAKING shaking; quivering
QUALIFY entitle; regulate; dilute
QUALITY trait; attribute; grade
QUAMASH camass lily   **B.**
QUANACO S. American llama   **Z.**
QUANNET flat file   **Tool**
QUANTIC algebraic function
QUANTUM a sufficiency
QUARREL wrangle; brawl; bicker
QUARREL cross-bow bolt; diam. pane
QUARTAN every fourth day
QUARTER district; region; clemency
QUARTET quartette   **Mus.**
QUARTIC of the fourth degree
QUARTZY (quartz)
QUASARS quasi-stellar radio sources
QUASHED rendered void; nullified
QUASHEY pumpkin; a gourd   **B.**
QUASSIA bitter tonic   **B.**
QUASSIN bitter extract   **B.**
QUATERN a quarter; 4 pound loaf
QUAVERY tremulous; quivery; tottery
QUAYAGE quay dues
QUEACHY bog-like; unsteady; yielding
QUEENED played the queen
QUEENLY
QUEERED put at a disadvantage
QUEERER odder; rummier; stranger
QUEERLY quaintly; whimsically
QUELLED crushed; allayed; quenched
QUELLER subduer; represser
QUERCUS oak   **B.**
QUERELA complaint   **Law**
QUERENT inquirer; plaintiff
QUERIED doubted; challenged
QUERIST questioner; interrogator
QUERLED twirled
QUERNAL oaken
QUESTED sought; requested
QUESTER a seeker; searcher; candidate
QUESTOR Roman treasury official
QUETZAL resplendent trogon **Coin, Z.**
QUIBBED quipped; sneered
QUIBBLE prevaricate; cavil; trifle
QUICKEN revive; rouse; expedite
QUICKER faster; more swiftly
QUICKIE a fatuous film
QUICKLY rapidly; speedily; pronto
QUIDDIT a quibble
QUIDDLE to potter
QUIESCE be still; calm; be silent
QUIETED calmed; assuaged; mollified
QUIETEN lull; allay; pacify; soothe
QUIETER more placid or secluded
QUIETLY peacefully; serenely
QUIETUS discharge; death
QUILLED pleated; crimped
QUILLET a quibble; a furrow
QUILLON part of a sword-guard
QUILTED

QUILTER coverlet maker
QUINARY in fives
QUINATE five-leafed **B.**
QUININE (cinchona) **Med., B.**
QUINNAT king salmon **Z.**
QUINONE (benzene) **Chem.**
QUINTAD pentad
QUINTAL a hundredweight **Meas.**
QUINTAL 100 lbs. or 100 kg. **Meas.**
QUINTAN recurring ague **Med.**
QUINTAR (Albania) **Coin**
QUINTET **Mus.**
QUINTIC fifth degree
QUINTUS the fifth (Latin)
QUIPPED quibbed; taunted
QUIRING singing in unison
QUITTAL repayment; requital
QUITTED abandoned; forsook; left
QUITTER shirker; horse ulcer; deserter
QUI-VIVE alert
QUIXOTE a chivalrous Don
QUIZZED bantered; chaffed
QUIZZER a joker
QUODLIN codlin; an apple **B.**
QUONDAM former
QUOTING citing; pricing
QUOTITY quantity

R

RABATED beaten down; abated
RABBANA raffia matting (Madagascar)
RABBITY petty; rabbit-like
RABBLER puddler; iron-worker
RABBONI Jewish title
RABIDLY frantically; maniacally
RABIFIC causing hydrophobia **Med.**
RABINET ancient gun
RABIOUS raging mad
RACCOON N. American racoon **Z.**
RACE-CUP a trophy
RACEMED clustered **B.**
RACEMIC acid from grapes **Chem.**
RACEWAY sluice
RACKETY bobbery; clamorous
RACKING decanting; straining
RACQUET racket
RADDLED interwoven; painted
RADDOCK ruddock; robin **Z.**
RADIALE radiocarpal bone **Med.**
RADIANT beaming; effulgent; shining
RADIATE sparkle; glitter; emit
RADICAL innate; extreme; inborn
RADICEL small root **B.**
RADICLE root; corm; rootlet **B.**
RADIOED transmitted by wireless
RADULAR rasping; rough
RAFFING sweeping; snatching
RAFFISH rakish; dissipated
RAFFLED notched; (lottery)

RAFFLER lottery organizer
RAFT-DOG iron clamp
RAFTING raft-work
RAG-BOLT iron holdfast
RAG-BUSH heathen shrine **B.**
RAG-DUST rag refuse
RAGEFUL angered; wroth; ireful
RAG-FAIR old clo' sale
RAGGERY rags collectively
RAGGING plaguing; rampaging
RAG-SHOP ragpicker's emporium
RAGTIME syncopation **Mus.**
RAGULED jagged (Her.)
RAG-WEED rag-wort **B.**
RAG-WOOL shoddy
RAGWORK mason's work using stones
RAGWORT rag-weed **B.**
RAIDING foraying; pillaging
RAIL-CAR rail-bus; tram
RAILING fencing; nagging; rating
RAILSAW portable saw **Tool**
RAILWAY railroad
RAIMENT garb; vesture; apparel
RAINBOW
RAINING pouring; showering
RAINMAP weather chart
RAISING erecting; levying; growing
RAKE-OFF rebate
RAKSHAS ghouls (Hindu mythology)
RALLIED recovered; reformed
RALLIES bouts; jamborees
RALLINE (water-rails, etc.) **Z.**
RAMADAN Mohammedan fast **Eccl.**
RAMAZAN Ramadan **Eccl.**
RAMBADE boarding platform **Naut.**
RAMBLED sauntered; maundered
RAMBLER Dr. Johnson's magazine
RAMBLER a climbing rose **B.**
RAMEKIN a cheese savoury
RAMENTA scales on ferns **B.**
RAMEOUS branching; ramulous
RAM-HEAD iron lever; a cuckold
RAMLINE guide line in ship-building
RAMMING thrusting; forcing
RAMMISH rank; strong-scented
RAMPAGE frolic
RAMPANT exuberant
RAMPART rampire; fortified mound
RAMPICK⎫ dead-tree;
RAMPIKE⎰ tree-stump
RAMPING creeping; climbing; bound'
RAMPION campanula **B.**
RAMPLER a rover (Sc.)
RAMSKIN cheese cake; ramekin
RAMSONS garlic, broad-leaved
RAMSTAM reckless; headlong (Sc.)
RAMULUS small branch
RANCHED (stock farming)
RANCHER stock-breeder
RANCOUR deep-seated enmity

RANGERS riflemen
RANGIER scythe (heraldic)
RANGING ranking; roving; extending
RANIDAE the frogs **Z.**
RANKEST coarsest; most rancid
RANKING grading; ranging
RANKLED festered; smouldered
RANSACK rummage; pillage; plunder
RANTING orating; declaiming; raving
RANTING fustian; rodomontade
RANTOCK goosander **Z.**
RAPE-OIL cole-seed oil **B.**
RAPFULL full of wind **Naut.**
RAPHAEL an archangel; a painter
RAPIDLY speedily; swiftly; despatch
RAPLOCH homespun (Sc.)
RAPPING knocking; hitting; beating
RAPPORT harmony; consonance
RAPTURE ecstasy; beatitude; bliss
RAREBIT dainty morsel
RASHEST most precipitate
RASORES gallinaceous birds **Z.**
RASPING grating; abrading
RASTRUM a music-pen **Mus.**
RATABLE taxable; assessable
RATABLY by rate
RATAFIA almond-flavoured biscuit
RATATAT drumming **Mus.**
RATCHED stretched; racked
RATCHEL ratchil; loose stones
RATCHET pawl; toothed bar
RAT-HOLE
RATITAE (ostriches, emus, kiwis.) **Z.**
RATLINE } step of rigging ladder **Naut.**
RATLING }
RAT-RACE career competition
RAT-TAIL tapering
RATTEEN twilled wool
RATTERY apostacy
RATTING quitting; abandoning
RATTLED clattered; shaken
RATTLER snake **Z.**
RATTOON young sugar-cane **B.**
RAT-TRAP bicycle pedal
RAUCITY hoarseness
RAUCOUS harsh; roopy
RAVAGED laid waste; devastated
RAVAGER despoiler; plunderer
RAVELIN part of a fort
RAVENED preyed; plundered
RAVENER ravager; devourer
RAVINED gullied
RAVIOLI meat-filled pasta cases (It.)
RAWBONE gaunt, lean person
RAWCOLD damp and cold (Shak.)
RAWHEAD bugaboo
RAWHIDE untanned skin
RAWNESS immaturity; callowness
RAWPORT porthole for an oar **Naut.**
RAYLESS dark

REACHED attained; arrived; stretched
REACHER stretcher
REACTED took violent action
REACTOR atomic power generator
READIED prepared
READIER prompter; more glib
READILY willingly; cheerfully
READING recital; version; studying
READMIT
READOPT
READORN
REAGENT active agent **Chem.**
REAGREE reconcile
REALGAR red arsenic **Min.**
REALISM naturalism
REALIST a facer of facts
REALITY actuality; truth; verity
REALIZE realise; convert into cash
REALLOT re-assign
REALTOR estate agent U.S.A.
REAMING enlarging
REANNEX reunite
REAPING harvesting; gathering
REAPPLY
REARGUE
REARING breeding; lifting; raising
REARISE reascend
REARMED re-equipped
RE-AROSE got up again
REAUMUR (thermometer)
REAVING bereaving; ravaging
REAWAKE rouse again
REBATED blunted; diminished
REBIRTH
REBLOOM
REBOANT resounding; reverberating
REBORED
REBOUND bounce; recoil
REBRACE
REBUILD re-edify
REBUILT re-erected
REBUKED chidden; upbraided
REBUKER reproacher
REBURSE repay
RECARRY carry anew
RECEDED retreated; withdrew
RECEIPT a recipe; formula; quittance
RECEIVE welcome; acquire; get
RECENCY newness
RECHEAT recall hounds
RECITAL concert; narration
RECITED narrated; rehearsed
RECITER relater
RECKING caring; heeding
RECLAIM rescue; salve; regain
RECLAME notoriety
RECLASP refasten
RECLINE lean; lie; rest; repose
RECLOSE
RECLUSE sequestered; a hermit

RECOAST coast back
RECOUNT tell; relate; enumerate
RECOUPE heraldic division
RECOURE recover (Spens.)
RE-COVER cover anew
RECOVER rally; revive; retrieve
RECROSS
RECRUIT enlist; recuperate; novice
RECTIFY amend; correct; redress
RECTION grammatic influence
RECTORY rector's benefice   **Eccl.**
RECTRIX steering feather   **Z.**
RECURVE reflex
RED-BIRD bull-finch   **Z.**
RED-BOOK a register
RED-CENT copper cent   **Coin**
RED-CLAY raddle; reddle   **Min.**
RED-COAT a soldier
RED-COCK incendiary fire
RED-CRAG Pliocene rock   **Min.**
RED-DEER the common stag   **Z.**
REDDEST ultra-radical
REDDING arranging (Sc.)
REDDISH rubicund; Titian
RED-DRUM red-bass   **Z.**
RED-EYED
RED-FISH Pacific salmon   **Z.**
RED-HAND (Ulster)
RED-HEAD a duck   **Z.**
RED-LEAD minium
RED-LEGS purple sandpiper   **Z.**
REDNESS ruddiness
REDORSE reverse of dorsal
REDOUBT fort
REDOUND conduce; lead; tend
REDPOLL linnet   **Z.**
REDRAFT second copy
REDRAWN drawn again
REDRESS remedy; reparation
REDRIVE drive back
RED-ROOT buckthorn   **B.**
RED-SEAR to break when too hot
RED-SEED small crustaceans   **Z.**
REDSKIN N. American Indian
RED-TAIL North American buzzard **Z.**
RED-TAPE routine
REDUCED curtailed; abridged
REDUCER contractor
RED-WEED the poppy   **B.**
REDWING fieldfare   **Z.**
REDWOOD sequoia   **B.**
RE-EDIFY rebuild
REEDING moulding (arch.)
REEFING shortening sail   **Naut.**
REEKING fuming; smoking
RE-ELECT
REELING staggering; vacillating
REEMING caulking   **Naut.**
RE-ENACT
RE-ENDOW

RE-ENJOY
RE-ENTER
RE-ENTRY regress; return
RE-EQUIP rearm
RE-ERECT rebuild
REEVING (passing a rope)   **Naut.**
REFEOFF reinvest in a fief
REFEREE umpire; arbitrator; judge
REFINED highly cultivated
REFINER purifier; clarifier
REFLAME flare up again
REFLECT mirror; muse; meditate
REFLOAT
REFORGE fashion anew
RE-FOUND
REFRACT to bend at an angle
REFRAIN chorus; forgo; abstain
REFRAME
REFRESH invigorate; revive; brace
REFUGED took sanctuary
REFUGEE a displaced person
REFUSAL declination; denial
REFUSED declined; denied; vetoed
REFUSER repudiator
REFUTED disproved; confuted
REFUTER rebutter
REGALED entertained sumptuously
REGALIA insignia of sovereignty
REGALLY royally
REGATTA gondola race   **Naut.**
REGENCY also regence
REGIBLE governable
REGIMEN regulation; diet
REGNANT ruling
REGORGE vomit
REGRADE re-assess
REGRAFT
REGRANT grant again
REGRATE retail
REGREDE regrade (obs.)
REGREET welcome again
REGRESS return; re-entry
REGULAR steady; systematic; normal
REGULUS star in Leo
REHOUSE
REIGNED ruled; administered
REINING curbing; restraining
REINTER to bury again
REISSUE
REIT-BOK S. African buck   **Z.**
REJOICE revel; exult; gladden
REJOINT make a new joint
REJOURN adjourn; defer
REJUDGE
RELABEL
RELAPSE delapse; backsliding; revert
RELATED akin; connected; recited
RELATER relator; delator
RELATOR informant   **Law**
RELAXED loosened; slackened; abated

RELAYED (wireless)
RELEASE set free; emancipate; liberate
RE-LEASE lease again
RELIANT confident; self-assured
RELIEVE release; allay; assuage
RELIEVO rilievo; in relief
RELIGHT rekindle; reignite
RELIQUE a relic (Fr.)
RELIVED lived again
RELUMED rekindled
RELYING depending; trusting
REMAINS (literary productions)
REMANET delayed lawsuit **Law**
REMARRY
REMEANT coming back (obs.)
REMEGIA a moth genus **Z.**
REMERCY to thank (Spens.)
REMERGE merge again
REMIGES flight feathers **Z.**
REMIPED oar-shaped feet **Z.**
REMISED released; surrendered **Law**
REMNANT residue; odd lot; fragment
REMODEL refashion; remake; redesign
REMORSE anguish; compunction
REMOTER further off
REMOULD shape anew
REMOUNT a fresh horse **Z.**
REMOVAL euphemism for murder
REMOVED dislodged; abstracted
REMOVER shifter
REMPHAN Israelitish idol
REMPLOY for disabled workers
RENAMED rechristened
RENDING ripping; tearing; severing
RENEGED denied; revoked
RENEWAL refreshment
RENEWED repeated; rejuvenated
RENEWER renovator
RENT-DAY
RENTIER estate or fund holder
RENTING letting; leasing
RENUENT nodding
REORDER bid again
REPAINT (a golf ball)
REPAPER (a palindrome)
REPINED fretted; murmured; envied
REPINER plaintive person
REPIQUE (piquet)
REPLACE reinstate; refund
REPLAIT refold
REPLANT
REPLETE crammed; fraught
REPLEVY to bail **Law**
REPLICA a copy; duplicate
REPLIED answered; folded back
REPLIER respondent
REPLUME to preen
REPOINT sharpen; accentuate
REPONED replaced; relied
REPOSAL rest; sleep; ease

REPOSED settled; reclined
REPOSER slumberer
REPOSIT deposit
REPRESS crush; check; restrain
REPRIEF reproof (obs.)
REPRINT a subsequent edition
REPRISE a deduction **Law**
REPRIVE deprive (obs.)
REPROOF reprief; censure
REPROVE chide; upbraid
REPRUNE
REPTANT creeping; reptilian
REPTILE snake; serpent **Z.**
REPULSE rebuff; deter; reject
REPUTED alleged; deemed; reckoned
REQUERE request (Spens.)
REQUEST demand; entreat; solicit
REQUIEM a mass **Eccl.**
REQUIRE want; lack; desire; need
REQUITE repay; reward; avenge
REREDOS altar screen **Eccl.**
RESCIND revoke; quash; cancel
RE-SCORE **Mus.**
RESCUED freed; liberated
RESCUER deliverer; saviour
RESEIZE (legal confiscation) **Law**
RESERVE withhold; restraint
RESHAPE remould; remodel
RESIANT resident **Law**
RESIDED abode; inhered
RESIDER sojourner; dweller
RESIDUE remainder; dregs
RESILED started back; receded
RESOLVE determine; resolution
RESOUND reverberate; extol
RE-SOUND sound again; echo
RESPEAK repeat; reply
RESPECT revere; honour; esteem
RE-SPELL
RE-SPELT
RESPIRE breathe; inhale
RESPITE reprieve; pause; rest
RESPLIT
RE-SPOKE reiterated
RESPOND answer; accord; tally
RESSAUT a projection (arch.)
RESTAMP
RESTANT persistent; remaining
RESTATE re-assert; recite
RESTAUR claim for indemnity **Law**
REST-DAY the Sabbath
RESTFUL tranquil; quiescent; irenic
RESTIFF restive (obs.)
RESTILY stubbornly; recalcitrantly
RESTING reposing; relaxing; leaning
RESTIVE refractory; obstinate
RESTOCK replenish
RESTORE reinstate; repair; heal
RE-STORE return to store
RESUMED renewed; continued

RESURGE rise again   **Eccl.**
RETABLE altar shelf for candles
RETAKEN recaptured
RETAKER recaptor
RETIARY net-like; (gladiator)
RETICLE small net; reticule
RETINAL (retina)   **Med.**
RETINOL resin oil
RETINUE suite; escort; bodyguard
RETIPED having veined feet   **Z.**
RETIRAL withdrawal ; departure
RETIRED left; retreated; secluded
RETOUCH re-engrave; revise
RETOURN to turn back (obs.)
RETRACE return by the same road
RETRACT adjure; recant; revoke
RETRAIT portrait; retired (Spens.)
RETRATE retreat (Spens.)
RETREAD repair of a tyre
RETREAT recede; asylum; refuge
RETRIAL   **Law**
RETRIED   **Law**
RETRUDE to thrust back
RETRUSE abstruse; hidden; occult
RETTERY flax mill
RETTING preparing flax
RETYPED
RETYRED (motoring)
REUNIFY rejoin
REUNION social gathering
REUNITE reconcile; recombine
REURGED entreated again
REUTTER repeat; reiterate
REVALUE re-assess
REVELRY carousal; debauch; orgy
REVENGE requite; retaliate; vindicate
REVENUE income; return; reward
REVERED honoured; worshipped
REVERER venerator
REVERIE dreaminess; trance; vision
REVERSE misfortune; opposite
REVERSI a counter-game
REVERSO left-hand page of a book
REVESTU heraldic squaring
REVILED aspersed; vilified; abused
REVILER traducer; upbraider
REVINCE refute; disprove (obs.)
REVISAL revision; reviewal
REVISED amended; altered
REVISER also revisor ; editor
REVISIT return to the same place
REVIVAL a religious awakening
REVIVED quickened; resuscitated
REVIVER invigorator; rouser
REVIVOR renewed action   **Law**
REVOKED reneged; repealed; quashed
REVOLVE rotate; spin; whirl; circle
REVOMIT regorge
REVVING spinning at speed
REWAKEN re-arouse

REWEIGH
REWRITE transcribe
REWROTE copied
REYNARD the fox   **Z.**
RHABDOM part of the eye   **Med.**
RHABDOS a straight spicule   **B.**
RHAETIC Rhaetian
RHAGOSE spongy
RHAMNUS buckthorn, etc.   **B.**
RHATANY Peruvian shrub   **B.**
RHEMISH (Rheims)
RHENISH (Rhine)
RHENIUM metallic element   **Chem.**
RHESIAN (Indian sacred monkey)   **Z.**
RHIZINE ⎱ rhizina; root-like   **B.**
RHIZOID ⎰
RHIZOMA ⎱ sucker-root   **B.**
RHIZOME ⎰
RHIZOTA small aquatic animals   **Z.**
RHIZOTE rooted   **B.**
RHODIAN Rhodesian; (Rhodes)
RHODIUM hard white metal   **Chem.**
RHODORA rhododendron   **B.**
RHOMBIS ⎱ oblique angled
RHOMBUS ⎰ parallelogram
RHOPODE a marine invertebrate   **Z.**
RHUBARB   **B.**
RHYMING versifying
RHYMIST ballad-monger
RHYNCHO snouted
RHYPHUS genus of gnats   **Z.**
RHYTINA dugong; manatee, etc.   **Z.**
RIB-BAND (shipbuilding)   **Naut.**
RIBBING
RIBBONS driving reins
RIBLESS
RIBLIKE
RIBSTON pippin; an apple   **B.**
RICASSO part of rapier-blade
RICE-HEN American fowl   **Z.**
RICHEST most affluent
RICINUS castor-oil plant   **B.**
RICKERS tree stems for spars
RICKETS softness of the bones   **Med.**
RICKETY shaky; unstable; feeble
RICKING wrenching; spraining
RICKSHA jinricksha; carriage
RIDABLE rideable
RIDDING freeing; banishing; clearing
RIDDLED full of holes
RIDDLER propounder of riddles
RIDERED stakes laid across bars
RIDOTTO musical entertainment (It.)
RIETBOK rietboc; reedbuck   **Z.**
RIFFLER curved file   **Tool**
RIFLING spiral grooving; ransacking
RIFTING riving; cleaving; splitting
RIGGING manipulating; tackle   **Naut.**
RIGGISH wanton
RIGGITE jester; trickster (obs.)

RIGHTED redressed; rectified; adjusted
RIGHTEN set right; settle
RIGHTER redresser of wrongs
RIGHTLY properly; correctly
RIGIDLY inflexibly; staunchly
RIGSDAG Danish Parliament
RIG-VEDA Vedic doctrine **Eccl.**
RIKSDAG Swedish Parliament
RILIEVO relievo; in relief
RILLING flowing; purling; rippling
RIMFIRE a cartridge
RIMLESS
RIMMING making a border or edge
RIMPLED wrinkled; rumpled
RINDING peeling; excoriating
RING-DOG used for hauling timber
RINGENT irregular and gaping
RINGHAL spitting cobra **Z.**
RINGING resounding
RINGLET circlet
RINGMAN third finger; Zulu chief
RING-NET butterfly-net
RING-SAW scroll-saw **Tool**
RINKING roller-skating
RINSING cleansing
RIOLITE silver selenide **Min.**
RIOTING disorder; lawlessness
RIOTISE riot; extravagance (Spens.)
RIOTOUS turbulent; tumultuous
RIPCORD parachute release cord
RIPIENO supplementary **Mus.**
RIPOSTE lightning repartee
RIPPING splendid; tearing
RIPPLED purled; rilled
RIPPLER comb for flax **Tool**
RIPPLET tiny ripple
RIPSACK Californian whale **Z.**
RIPTIDE fast flowing current
RISBERM glacis below jetties
RISIBLE laughable; droll; absurd
RISIBLY amusingly; farcically
RISKIER more hazardous
RISKING venturing; chancing; hazarding
RISOTTO rice and onions
RISSOLE an entrée
RISTORI woman's jacket
RITTOCK tern **Z.**
RIVALRY emulation; competition
RIVERET small river; stream; rivulet
RIVETED fastened
RIVETER clincher
RIVIERA fashionable resort
RIVIERE a necklace of jewels
RIVULET stream; brook; riveret
RIZOMED heraldic grains
ROADBED road foundation
ROADCAR
ROAD-HOG a motor pest
ROADING team racing
ROADMAN road repairer

ROAD-MAP
ROADWAY highway; turnpike; autobahn
ROAMING roving; wandering
ROARING bellowing; shouting; bawling
ROASTED parched; bantered
ROASTER gridiron
ROBBERY piracy; spoliation; pillage
ROBBING stealing; depriving; theft
ROBINET chaffinch **Z.**
ROBINIA acacia **B.**
ROCK-CAM cam on rocking shaft
ROCK-DOE chamois **Z.**
ROCK-EEL **Z.**
ROCKERY rock garden
ROCKIER more unstable
ROCKILY reeling; tottery
ROCKING lulling; staggering
ROCK-OIL petroleum; naphtha **Min.**
ROCK-TAR petroleum **Min.**
RODLIKE cylindrical
ROD-LINE fishing line
RODOMEL roses and honey
ROD-RING (fishing-rod)
RODSTER an angler
ROE-BUCK male roe-deer **Z.**
ROE-DEER **Z.**
ROGUERY knavery; fraudulence
ROGUISH arch; wanton; puckish
ROILING riling; angering
ROINISH roinous; mangy
ROISTER to bluster; swagger; bully
ROKEAGE parched Indian corn
ROKELAY short cloak; roguelaure
ROLLICK frolic
ROLLING trundling; wallowing; lurching
ROLLOCK rowlock; also rullock **Naut.**
ROLLWAY an incline; a shoot
ROMAIKA modern Greek dance
ROMALEA a locust genus **Z.**
ROMANCE historical fiction
ROMANIC derived from Latin
ROMAUNT a romance; exaggeration
ROMEINE (antimony and lime) **Min.**
ROMMANY gipsy language
ROMPERS children's overalls
ROMPING frolicking; capering
ROMPISH frisky; sportive; frolicsome
RONCHIL ronquil, a N. Pacific fish **Z.**
RONDEAU verse with a refrain **Mus.**
RONDENA Andalusian serenade **Mus.**
RONGEUR surgical forceps **Med.**
RONQUIL ronchil, sea-fish **Z.**
RONTGEN (X-rays)
ROOFING
ROOFLET small roof
ROOINEK an Englishman (S. Africa)
ROOKERY (rooks); (seals); (penguins) **Z.**
ROOKING defrauding; fleecing
ROOK-PIE
ROOMAGE stowage

ROOMFUL	
ROOMIER more extensive	
ROOMILY spaciously	
ROOMING lodging	
ROOSTED perched; slept	
ROOSTER chanticleer	**Z.**
ROOTAGE manner of rooting	
ROOTCAP tip at end of root	**B.**
ROOTERY pile of stumps	
ROOTING eradicating; implanting	
ROOTLED rummaged; dug	
ROOTLET radicle; a root fibre	**B.**
ROPALIC club-shaped	
ROPEWAY aerial transport	
RORQUAL a whale	**Z.**
ROSALIA progressive melody	**Mus.**
ROSATED crowned with roses	
ROSEATE rosy; blushing	
ROSEBAY willow-herb	**B.**
ROSE-BIT (for countersinking)	**Tool**
ROSE-BOX a plant	**B.**
ROSE-BUD	**B.**
ROSE-BUG rose-chafer	**Z.**
ROSE-CUT (diamond-cutting)	
ROSE-HAW ⎱ the fruit of	
ROSE-HIP ⎰ the wild rose	**B.**
ROSELET ermine's summer fur	
ROSELLA a parakeet	**Z.**
ROSELLE rose-mallow	**B.**
ROSEOLA a rash	**Med.**
ROSE-RED	
ROSETTA inscribed stone (Ptolemy V)	
ROSETTE a favour	
ROSIEST	
ROSINED resined; gingered up	
ROSLAND moorland	
ROSOLIO raisin brandy	
ROSSING removing bark	
ROSTRAL beak-like	
ROSTRUM platform; pulpit; a beak	
ROSULAR (leaves in clusters)	
ROTALIA foraminifers	**Z.**
ROTATED revolved; spun; twirled	
ROTATOR a rotor	
ROTCHET red gurnard	**Z.**
ROTCHIE little auk; sea-dove	**Z.**
ROTELLA round shield	
ROTIFER an animalcule	**Z.**
ROTODIP car-painting technique	
ROTONDE ruff; cope (Fr.)	
ROTTING decaying; fooling	
ROTTOLO Levantine weight	**Meas.**
ROTULAR (patella)	**Med.**
ROTUNDA circular building	
ROUCHED puckered	
ROUELLE wheel-like amulet	
ROUERIE debauchery	
ROUGHED rasped; (horse-shoes)	
ROUGHEN scarify; coarsen	
ROUGHER ruder; harsher; coarser	

ROUGHIE dried heath (Sc.)	
ROUGHLY boisterously; crudely	
ROUGH-UP violent fight	
ROUGING painting with rouge	
ROULADE melodious passage	**Mus.**
ROULEAU packet of coins	
ROUNDED curved; turned	
ROUNDEL a Norman shield; a ballad	
ROUNDER more like a circle	
ROUNDLY boldly; openly; plainly	
ROUND-UP a rodeo	
ROUPING selling by auction (Sc.)	
ROUSANT starting up (Her.)	
ROUSING stimulating; brisk; lively	
ROUSTER vagrant; vagabond	
ROUTHIE plentiful; abundant (Sc.)	
ROUTIER armed brigand (Fr.)	
ROUTINE regularity; system	
ROUTING rooting; defeating	
ROUTISH clamorous; disorderly	
ROWABLE a truly oarful state	
ROWBOAT	**Naut.**
ROWDIER more uproarious or rampant	
ROWDILY turbulently; noisily	
ROWLOCK rollock; rullock	**Naut.**
ROWPORT oar-hole	
ROYALET petty king; princelet	
ROYALLY regally; imperially	
ROYALTY author's perquisite	
ROYNISH roinish; mangy	
ROYSTON hooded crow	**Z.**
ROYTISH rowdy; wild (obs.)	
ROZELLE hibiscus	**B.**
RUB-A-DUB beat of drum	
RUBASSE Ancona ruby	**Min.**
RUBBING chafing; tracing; scouring	
RUBBISH trash; litter; lumber	
RUB-DOWN	
RUBELLA rubeola; measles	**Med.**
RUBIATE madder	
RUBICAN roan	
RUBICEL variety of ruby	**Min.**
RUBICON boundary; fateful river	
RUBIFIC making red	
RUBIOUS ruby-red	
RUBYING reddening	
RUCHING a plaited frilling	
RUCKING creasing; ruffling	
RUCKLED wrinkled; rucked	
RUCTION uproar; turmoil; disturbance	
RUDDIED reddened	
RUDDIER rosier; more rubicund	
RUDDILY glowingly	
RUDDLED interwoven; ochred	
RUDDOCK robin; apple	**B., Z.**
RUDERAL waste growth	**B.**
RUDESBY uncivil fellow (Shak.)	
RUELLIA a plant genus	**B**
RUE-WORT herb of grace	**B**
RUFFIAN desperado; apache; rascal	

RUFFING trumping; ruffling
RUFFLED disordered; agitated
RUFFLER a bully
RUGGING heavy napped cloth
RUINATE demolish; destroy (Shak.)
RUINING wrecking; demolishing
RUINOUS pernicious; calamitous
RULABLE allowable; governable
RULLION veldt-shoe; virago
RUMBLED reverberated
RUMBLER
RUMINAL ruminant Z.
RUMMAGE search; ransack
RUMMIER stranger; droller; quainter
RUMMILY oddly; whimsically
RUMNESS queerness; oddity
RUMPLED rimpled; crushed
RUM-SHOP a tavern
RUNAWAY fugitive; deserter; renegade
RUNDALE land tenure
RUNDLED rounded like a rung
RUNDLET small barrel; runlet
RUN-DOWN exhausted; weak; anaemic
RUNNING in succession; careering
RUPTION eruption
RUPTIVE ruptile; liable to snap
RUPTURE fracture; breach; rift
RURALLY rustically
RUSALKA water-nymph (Russ.)
RUSHING dashing; careering; flying
RUSH-MAT
RUSH-NUT edible tuber B.
RUSSETY reddish-brown
RUSSIAN
RUSSIFY
RUSSULA red fungus B.
RUSTFUL rusty
RUSTIER less practised
RUSTILY fustily; mustily
RUSTING oxidizing
RUSTLED stirred
RUSTLER cattle-thief
RUSTRED lozenge-shaped (Her.)
RUTHFUL compassionate
RUTTING grooving; furrowing; pairing
RUTTISH lustful
RYE-MOTH a harvest pest Z.
RYE-WOLF (German folk lore) Z.
RYE-WORM larva of rye-moth Z.

S

ABAISM ⎫ star worship, ancient religion
ABEISM ⎬ of Persia and Chaldea
ABAOTH armies (Hebrew)
ABBATH day of rest
ABELLA sea-worms Z.
ABRING cutting with a sabre
ABURRA grittiness of the tongue
ACCADE sudden check Mus.

SACCATA molluscs Z.
SACCATE sack-like
SACCULE small pouch
SACELLA altars; sanctuaries
SACKAGE pillage
SACKBUT sacbut; dulcimer Mus.
SACKFUL bagful
SACKING looting; plundering
SACODES beetle genus Z.
SACRARY a holy place (obs.)
SACRING consecration Eccl.
SACRIST sacristan; a sexton Eccl.
SADDEST most dismal and depressing
SADDLED loaded; hampered
SADDLER
SAD-EYED mournful
SADIRON box-iron; flat-iron
SADNESS sorrowfulness; melancholy
SADTREE night jasmine B.
SAFFIAN (tanned skins)
SAFFRON plant; a colour B.
SAGAMAN a bard; narrator of sagas
SAGATHY woollen stuff
SAGESSE wisdom (Fr.)
SAGGARD box for baking porcelain
SAGGING bending; inclining
SAGITTA a Northern constellation
SAGOUIN capuchin monkey Z.
SAGUARO giant cactus B.
SAHLITE augite Min.
SAIL-ARM (windmill)
SAILING cruising Naut.
SAIMIRI squirrel monkey Z.
SAINTED canonized
SAINTLY holy; devout; religious
SAIRING enough (Sc.)
SAIVISM worship of Siva Eccl.
SALABLE saleable; vendible
SALADIN a Soldan; a Sultan
SALAMBA fishing device (Manila)
SALAMIS insect genus Z.
SALIANT salient; leaping; projecting
SALICIN willow extract Chem.
SALIENT Ypres; prominent
SALIERE salt-cellar (Fr.)
SALIGOT water caltrops B.
SALIQUE salic (male succession)
SALIVAL salivary
SALLIED dashed out
SALLOWY yellowish; jaundiced
SALMIAC sal-ammoniac Chem.
SALPIAN ascidian Z.
SALPINX Eustachian tube Med.
SALSAFY ⎫ oyster plant; B.
SALSIFY ⎬ purple goat's beard
SALSOLA glass-wort B.
SALTANT dancing; leaping
SALTATE to dance; leap: jump; skip
SALT-BOX
SALT-CAT pigeon medicine

SALTERN salt factory
SALTIER saltire
SALTING sea-marsh; pickling; curing
SALTIRE St. Andrew's cross
SALTISH brackish; briny
SALT-PAN evaporating pan
SALT-PIT
SALUTED honoured; kissed; greeted
SALUTER
SALVAGE rescue; compensation
SALVING healing; restoration
SAMBHUR sambhur; Indian stag   **Z.**
SAMBUCA ancient harp   **Mus.**
SAMBUKE sambuca   **Mus.**
SAMIOTE native of Samos
SAMISEN Japanese guitar   **Mus.**
SAMNITE Sabine tribe
SAMOLUS primrose genus   **B.**
SAMOVAR Russian tea-urn
SAMOYED sledge dog; Mongolian   **Z.**
SAMPLED tried; tasted
SAMPLER needlework; pattern
SAMSHOO rice spirit (China)
SAMURAI Japanese military class
SANCTUM a refuge; a shrine   **Eccl.**
SANCTUS a hymn   **Eccl.**
SANDBAG a convenient weapon
SAND-BAR estuarine barrier
SANDBED a mould
SANDBOX also a W. Indian tree   **B.**
SAND-BOY proverbially a happy lad
SANDBUG digger-wasp   **Z.**
SANDBUR a weed   **B.**
SAND-DAB plaice   **Z.**
SAND-EEL small fish   **Z.**
SANDERS red sandal-wood   **B.**
SAND-FLY a biting midge   **Z.**
SANDING burying oysters
SANDISH gritty; friable
SANDJET sand-blast
SAND-LOB lug-worm   **Z.**
SANDMAN children's sleep-giver
SAND-PIT
SAND-RAT the camass rat   **Z.**
SANHITA Vedic hymns
SANICLE healing plant   **B.**
SANKHYA Hindu philosophy
SAPAJOU S. Amer. spider-monkey   **Z.**
SAPERDA boring beetles   **Z.**
SAP-HEAD (fortification)
SAPHENA prominent vein   **Med.**
SAPIENT wise; sage; clever; astute
SAPLESS dry; not juicy
SAPLING young tree   **B.**
SAPLING young grey-hound   **Z.**
SAPONIN soapwort extract
SAPPHIC (Sappho)
SAPPING undermining
SAPPLES soap-suds (Sc.)
SAPSAGO a green Swiss cheese

SAP-TUBE
SAPWOOD the alburnum   **B.**
SARACEN Arab
SARAFAN Russian gala-dress
SARAWAK glossy yellow cane
SARCASM irony; satire; ridicule
SARCELE partly cut through
SARCINA fungoid plant   **B.**
SARCINE (muscular tissue)   **Med.**
SARCODE proto-plasm
SARCOID flesh-like
SARCOMA tumour   **Med.**
SARCOUS fleshy
SARDANA folk dance (Catalan)
SARDINE the young of the pilchard   **Z.**
SARDIUS sard; a quartz   **Min.**
SARGINA mullet genus   **Z.**
SARIGUE opossum (Brazil)   **Z.**
SARKING roof sheathing
SARMENT a runner; filiform stem   **B.**
SARPLAR sarpler; packing cloth
SARSNET fine woven silk
SARTAGE forest clearing
SASHERY sashes
SASHING window framing
SASSABY tsessebe; hartebeest   **Z**
SASSING cheeking; saucing
SATANIC infernal; diabolical; devilish
SATCHEL small sack or container
SATIATE glutted; to cloy; to gorge
SATIETY a surfeit
SATINET thin satin
SATIRIC sarcastic; ironical; mordant
SATISFY gratify; requite; settle
SATRAPY Persian province
SATSUMA Japanese pottery
SATTARA ribbed woollen material
SATTEEN ratteen; thick woollen fabri
SATYRAL Satyr-like
SATYRIC lustful
SATYRUS orang-utan genus   **Z**
SAUCIER ruder; more impudent
SAUCILY pertly; flippantly; pungently
SAUCING sassing; seasoning
SAUNTER dawdle; stroll; dally
SAURIAN lizard; reptile   **Z**
SAUROID reptilian
SAUSAGE an observation balloon
SAUTOIR diagonal ribbon (Her.)
SAVABLE salvable
SAVAGED attacked brutally
SAVANNA treeless plain
SAVE-ALL an economizer
SAVIGNY red Burgundy wine
SAVINGS a nest-egg
SAVIOUR
SAVOURY of grateful savour
SAW-BACK a caterpillar   **:**
SAWBILL goosander; merganser   **:**
SAWBUCK sawhorse   **To**

SAWDUST		
SAWFILE triangular file	**Tool**	
SAWFISH	**Z.**	
SAWHORN an insect	**Z.**	
SAWMILL		
SAWWHET Acadian owl	**Z.**	
SAWWORT a plant	**B.**	
SAXHORN brass wind-instrument	**Mus.**	
SAXONIC Saxon		
SAYETTE serge; woollen yarn		
SCABBED mean; worthless		
SCABBLE scapple; (stone-dressing)		
SCABIES the itch	**Med.**	
SCABRID scabrous; rough; rugged		
SCADDLE skaddle; hurtful; impish		
SCAGLIA Italian calcareous rock	**Min.**	
SCALADE } assault by escalade		
SCALADO		
SCALARY stepped like a ladder		
SCALDED immersed in boiling water		
SCALDER Norse minstrel or bard		
SCALDIC (Norse ballads)		
SCALENE irregular triangle		
SCALING (fish or boilers)		
SCALLED scurfy; scabby		
SCALLOP scollop; shell-fish	**Z.**	
SCALLOP pilgrim badge; (border)		
SCALOPS American shrew-moles	**Z.**	
SCALPED laid bare		
SCALPEL dissecting knife	**Med.**	
SCALPER hair-raising savage		
SCAMBLE shamble; scramble; mangle		
SCAMMEL bar-tailed godwit	**Z.**	
SCAMMUM geometrical figure		
SCAMPED skimped		
SCAMPER scurry; run; hasten		
SCANDAL disgrace; infamy; discredit		
SCANDIX Venus' comb	**B.**	
SCANNED scrutinized; perused		
SCANNER television or radar beam		
SCANTED limited; stinted		
SCANTLE cut into small pieces		
SCANTLY scantily; niggardly		
SCAPNET minnow-net		
SCAPPLE stone-dressing		
SCAPULA shoulder blade	**Med.**	
SCARCER rarer; less plentiful		
SCARFED (timber joint)		
SCARIFY to scratch; to harrow		
SCARING affrighting; daunting		
SCARLET		
SCARPED made precipitous		
SCARRED disfigured		
SCARVES kerchiefs; cravats		
SCATHED injured; damaged; hurt		
SCATTER disperse; strew; dispel		
SCAUPER engraver's tool	**Tool**	
SCENERY prospect; view; landscape		
SCENTED perfumed; smelt; suspected		
SCEPSIS philosophic doubt		

SCEPTIC skeptic; a doubter		
SCEPTRE royal mace		
SCEPTRY rather royal		
SCHAPPE spun silk		
SCHELLY white fish	**Z.**	
SCHEMED plotted; planned; contrived		
SCHEMER intriguer; plotter		
SCHEPEN magistrate (Dutch)		
SCHERZO playfully	**Mus.**	
SCHESIS habitude; wont		
SCHETIC constitutional; habitual		
SCHINUS mastic-tree	**B.**	
S-CHISEL well-boring cutter	**Tool**	
SCHISMA tonal difference	**Mus.**	
SCHLICH ore slime		
SCHNAPS schnapps; Akvavit }		
SCHOLAR student; pupil; disciple		
SCHOLIA marginal notes		
SCHORLY tourmaline	**Min.**	
SCIATIC affecting the hip	**Med.**	
SCIBILE knowable		
SCIENCE knowledge; reduced to system		
SCINCUS lizard; skink; a saurian	**Z.**	
SCIOLTO with abandon	**Mus.**	
SCIRPUS bulrush genus	**B.**	
SCISSEL } metal clippings		
SCISSIL		
SCISSOR to cut		
SCIURUS squirrel genus	**Z.**	
SCLERAL hard; ossified	**Med.**	
SCLERIA sedges	**B.**	
SCOBINA ends of grass	**B.**	
SCOFFED mocked; jeered; derided		
SCOFFER a taunter; ridiculer		
SCOLDED chided; nagged; rebuked		
SCOLDER railer; upbraider		
SCOLITE fossil worm	**Min.**	
SCOLLOP scallop	**Z.**	
SCOMBER mackerel genus	**Z.**	
SCOONED skimmed; glided		
SCOONER a schooner	**Naut.**	
SCOOPED hollowed out; dredged		
SCOOPER a water-fowl; the avocet	**Z.**	
SCOOTED bolted; squirted		
SCOOTER ice-boat; toy		
SCOPATE brush-like		
SCOPTIC bantering; jesting		
SCORIAC ashy		
SCORIAE volcanic ashes	**Min.**	
SCORIFY reduce to ashes		
SCORING recording; scratching		
SCORNED disdained; spurned		
SCORNER contemner; flouter		
SCORPER a gouge	**Tool**	
SCORPIO (Zodiac); scorpion	**Z.**	
SCOTICE in Scottish	**[Eccl.**	
SCOTISM doctrine of Duns Scotus		
SCOTIST a theologian	**Eccl.**	
SCOTOMY scotoma; dizziness	**Med.**	
SCOURED scurried; purged; rinsed		

K

SCOURER scrubber; polisher; scraper
SCOURGE lash; chastise; plague
SCOUTED scorned; ridiculed
SCOUTER stone-flaker
SCOWLED registered displeasure
SCRAGGY lean and bony
SCRANCH scrunch; grind
SCRANKY scraggy; lank (Sc.)
SCRANNY lean; spare
SCRAPED erased; rubbed; rasped
SCRAPER miser; indifferent fiddler
SCRAPPY fragmentary
SCRATCH lacerate; zero handicap
SCRAWLY scribbled; ill-formed
SCRAWNY raw-boned
SCREECH scraich; scraigh
SCREEVE to write begging letters
SCREWED twisted; tipsy
SCREWER screw-driver; extortioner
SCRIBAL clerical
SCRIBED wrote; recorded; marked
SCRIBER engraving tool   **Tool**
SCRIEVE glide swiftly (Sc.)
SCRIMER fencer (Shak.)
SCRINGE cringe; flinch; grate
SCRITCH screech; a thrush   **Z.**
SCROGGY having thick undergrowth
SCROOGE scrudge; squeeze
SCROUGE squeeze; to crowd
SCRUBBY stunted; squabby
SCRUFFY scurfy; scaly
SCRUNCH crunch; crush
SCRUPLE 20 grains, troy weight **Meas.**
SCRYING crystal gazing
SCUDDED ran before the wind   **Naut.**
SCUDDLE scuttle; skuttle
SCUDLER a scullion
SCUFFLE struggle; a hoe   **Tool**
SCULLED rowed   **Naut.**
SCULLER an oarsman
SCULPIN sea-fish; dragonet; bull-head
SCUMBER fox-dung   **Z.**
SCUMBLE overlay painting
SCUMMER a skimmer of scum
SCUNNER loathing; prejudice (Sc.)
SCUPPER vent; annihilate
SCUPPET scoppet; shovel
SCURRIL scurrilous; foul-mouthed
SCURRIT lesser tern   **Z.**
SCURVEY vitamin deficiency disease
   Med.
SCUTAGE feudal tax
SCUTATE like a shield
SCUTTER scurry
SCUTTLE (coal); hatchway; sink **Naut.**
SCYMNUS lady-birds; sharks   **Z.**
SCYPHUS a large drinking-cup (Greek)
SCYTALE secret message (Greek)
SCYTALE coral snake   **Z.**
SCYTHED mowed; cut
SCYTHIC scythian

SEA-BANK protective bank
SEA-BASS marine fish   **Z.**
SEA-BEAN small univalve shell   **B., Z.**
SEA-BEAR seal; polar bear   **Z.**
SEA-BEAT lashed by the waves
SEA-BEET   **B.**
SEA-BELT fucus plant   **B.**
SEA-BIRD   **Z.**
SEA-BOAT (sea-worthy)
SEA-BORN produced by the sea
SEA-CALF common seal   **Z.**
SEA-CARD compass card   **Naut.**
SEA-CLAM a bivalve   **Z.**
SEA-COAL cash   **Min.**
SEA-COCK gurnard; a valve   **Z.**
SEA-COOK   **Naut.**
SEA-COOT   **Z.**
SEA-CORN spawn   **Z.**
SEA-CRAB   **Z.**
SEA-CROW cormorant   **Z.**
SEA-DACE bass   **Z.**
SEA-DOVE little auk   **Z.**
SEA-DUCK eider-duck   **Z.**
SEA-FIRE phosphorescence
SEA-FISH   **Z.**
SEA-FOAM meerschaum   **Min.**
SEA-FOLK
SEA-FOWL   **Z.**
SEA-GAGE depth gauge
SEA-GATE
SEA-GIRT insular
SEA-GOWN
SEA-GULL   **Z.**
SEA-HAAR sea-mist
SEA-HALL hall below the sea
SEA-HARE mollusc   **Z.**
SEA-HAWK a skua   **Z.**
SEAHOLM sea-holly   **B.**
SEAKALE a cruciferous plant   **B.**
SEA-KING a viking
SEA-LACE (sea-weed)   **B.**
SEA-LARK the dunlin   **Z.**
SEA-LEGS
SEALERY seal-fishing station
SEALIKE
SEA-LILY sea-urchin   **Z.**
SEA-LINE horizon; sky-line
SEALING confirming
SEA-LION large seal   **Z.**
SEAL-OFF closure
SEA-LUCE hake   **Z.**
SEA-MAID mermaid
SEA-MALL sea-gull   **Z.**
SEA-MARK land or sea-mark
SEA-MILE geographical mile; 6080 feet
SEAMING sewing together; scarring
SEA-MINK whiting   **Z.**
SEA-MONK monk-seal   **Z.**
SEA-MOSS seaweed   **B.**
SEAM-SET tinman's punch   **Tool**

SEA-OOZE soft mud	**SEEABLE** visible	
SEA-PASS passport	**SEE-CAWK** the American skunk	**Z.**
SEA-PEAR sea-squirt	**Z.**	**SEED-BAG**
SEA-PECK the dunlin	**Z.**	**SEED-BED**
SEA-PERT the opah fish	**Z.**	**SEED-BUD** germ of the fruit	**B.**
SEA-PIKE pike	**Z.**	**SEED-COD** seed-basket; husk
SEA-PINK the thrift	**B.**	**SEEDFUL** promising; hopeful
SEA-PORK an ascidian	**Z.**	**SEEDILY** shabbily
SEA-PORT	**SEEDING** (tournaments); sowing
SEA-REED mat grass	**B.**	**SEED-LAC** dried resin
SEARING cauterizing	**SEED-LOP** seed container	**B.**
SEA-RISK marine hazard	**SEED-OIL** linseed oil
SEA-ROLL sea-cucumber	**Z.**	**SEEKING** inquiring; questing
SEA-ROOM manoeuvre space	**SEELING** closing the eye-lids
SEA-ROSE sea-anemone	**Z.**	**SEEMING** specious; guise; apparent
SEA-RUFF sea-bream	**Z.**	**SEEPAGE** leakage; oozings
SEA-SALT	**Min.**	**SEETHED** boiled; soaked
SEA-SICK mal-de-mer	**SEETHER** boiling pot
SEASIDE	**SEGGROM** ragwort	**B.**
SEA-SLUG a nudibranch	**Z.**	**SEGMENT** a portion; section
SEA-TANG sea-tangle-weed	**SEINING** netting fish
SEATING installing; settling	**SEISING** taking possession	**Law**
SEA-TOAD	**Z.**	**SEISMAL** seismic; (earthquake)
SEA-TOST	**SEISURA** Australian fly-catchers	**Z.**
SEA-TURN a gale from the sea	**SEIURUS** wagtail genus	**Z.**
SEAVIEW	**SEIZING** (ropes); grappling; binding
SEA-WALL	**SEIZURE** grasp; possession	**Law**
SEA-WANE wampum	**SEJEANT** sitting (heraldic)
SEA-WARD	**SELACHE** shark genus	**Z.**
SEA-WARE seaweed; sea-wrack	**B.**	**SELENIC** (selenium)	**Chem.**
SEAWEED tangle; algae	**B.**	**SELF-FED** automatic
SEA-WHIP a zoophyte	**Z.**	**SELFISH** egotistical; mean; ungenerous
SEA-WIFE wrasse	**Z.**	**SELFISM** selfishness
SEA-WING a sail	**SELFIST** egoist
SEA-WOLD imaginary tract	**SELINUM** milk-parsley	**B.**
SEA-WOLF wolf fish ; pirate	**Z.**	**SELLING** vending; hawking; betraying
SEA-WORM marine annelid	**Z.**	**SELTZER** mineral water
SEBACIC fatty acid	**Chem.**	**SELVAGE** selvedge; border
SEBILLA wooden bowl	**SEMATIC** significant
SEBUNDY a sepoy	**SEMEION** metrical mark
SECANCY intersection	**SEMI-APE** a lemur	**Z.**
SECEDED withdrew; separated	**SEMI-GOD** demi-god
SECEDER separationist	**SEMILOR** imitation gold
SECHIUM genus of gourds	**B.**	**SEMINAL** rudimentary; original
SECLUDE segregate; shut up	**SEMINAR** teacher in a seminary
SECONDO bass of duet	**Mus.**	**SEMIPED** (prosody); a half-foot
SECRECY privacy; stealth; reticence	**SEMITIC** Jewish; Hebrew
SECRETE hide; conceal; cache; yield	**SENATOR** a counsellor
SECTANT geometric figure	**SENATUS** governing body
SECTARY sectarian	**SENCION** ⎫ groundsel; ragwort	**B.**
SECTILE sliceable	**SENECIO** ⎭
SECTION portion; division; segment	**SENDING** despatching; forwarding
SECTIST dissenter	**SEND-OFF** farewell party
SECTIVE divisible	**SENEGAL** African fire-bird	**Z.**
SECULAR of the world; lay; temporal	**SENIORY** council of elders
SECURED obtained; ensured; fastened	**SENSATE** sensible
SECURER protector; guardian; safer	**SENSILE** sensitive
SEDILIA altar seats	**Eccl.**	**SENSING** understanding; feeling
SEDUCED enticed; led astray	**SENSION** perception
SEDUCER a libertine	**SENSISM** sensualism

SENSIST sensationalist
SENSORY nerve system **Med.**
SENSUAL voluptuous
SEPIARY } referring to cuttle-fish **Z.**
SEPIOID
SEPIOST cuttle-bone **Z.**
SEPPUKU hara-kiri (Jap.)
SEPTATE partitioned
SEPTIME fencing posture
SEQUELA a consequence **Med.**
SEQUENT following; succeeding
SEQUOIA Californian red-wood **B.**
SERAPIS Apis; Goddess of fertility
SERBIAN Servian
SERENED tranquillized
SERENER calmer; more placid
SERENOA dwarf-palms (Florida) **B.**
SERFAGE serfdom; slavery
SERFDOM villenage; thraldom
SERIATE in series; serial
SERICIN silk
SERICON alchemic red
SERIEMA cariama; (heron) **Z.**
SERINGA flowering shrub **B.**
SERINUS canary genus **Z.**
SERIOLA amber fish **Z.**
SERIOUS grave; sedate; staid
SERPENT snake; reptile **Z.**
SERPIGO ring-worm **Med.**
SERPULA sea-worms **Z.**
SERRATE serrous; notched
SERRIED at close interval
SERVAGE servitude; enthralment
SERVANT retainer; henchman; menial
SERVIAN Serbian; Serb
SERVICE duty; performance; utility
SERVILE fawning; sycophantic
SERVING ministering; (tennis) **[Eccl.**
SERVITE mendicant monk, 13th Cent.
SESAMUM sesame genus **B.**
SESOTHO Basuto language (S. Africa)
SESSILE (no stalk) **B.**
SESSION meeting; assize; sitting
SESTINA sestine; verse (Fr.)
SESTOLE sextuplet
SETARIA spiky grasses **B.**
SET-BACK check; reverse; recess **Arch.**
SET-DOWN a rebuff
SETLESS no score; tennis **[Mus.**
SETTIMA } the interval of a seventh
SETTIMO
SETTING appointing; congealing
SETTLED fixed; paid; sank; serene
SETTLER coloniser; arbitrator
SETWALL valerian **B.**
SETWORK (boat-building); (plaster)
SEVENTH
SEVENTY
SEVERAL sundry; diverse; various
SEVERED cut; rent; divided

SEVERER stricter; simple.
SEVRUGA caviare-fish **Z.**
SEXFOIL six-leafed plant **B.**
SEXLESS
SEXTAIN (six lines)
SEXTANS Roman bronze coin **Coin**
SEXTANT optical instrument **Naut.**
SEXTILE planet aspect
SHACKED tramped; hibernated
SHACKLE manacle; gyve; bond; fetter
SHADFLY May-fly **Z.**
SHADIER more dubious
SHADILY umbrageously
SHADINE American sardine **Z.**
SHADING screening; tinting
SHADOOF water raising device (Nile)
SHADOWY obscure; dim; gloomy
SHAFTED handled; hafted
SHAGGED shaggy; rough; rugged
SHAHEEN peregrine falcon **Z.**
SHAITAN Satan (Arabic)
SHAKE-UP upheaval reorganisation
SHAKILY insecure; precariously
SHAKING quaking; jarring; jolting
SHALLON an edible fruit **B.**
SHALLOP rowing boat; skiff **Naut.**
SHALLOT small type of onion **B.**
SHALLOW superficial; rudd-fish **Z.**
SHAMBLE shuffle along
SHAMING humiliating; abasing
SHAMMED simulated; feigned
SHAMMER impostor; malingerer
SHAMPOO
SHANDRY rickety conveyance (Irish)
SHANGIE shackle (Sc.)
SHANGTI Chinese for God **Eccl.**
SHANKED (golf)
SHAPELY finely formed
SHAPING moulding; fashioning
SHARDED beetle-winged **Z.**
SHARING apportioning; dividing
SHARKED cheated; duped; gulled
SHARKER shark-hunter
SHARPED tricked; defrauded; duped
SHARPEN strop; point; whet
SHARPER a trickster; cheat; rogue
SHARPIE oysterman's boat **Naut.**
SHARPLY keenly; acutely; tartly
SHASTER Hindu Bible **Eccl.**
SHASTRA sacred Hindu book **Eccl.**
SHATTER splinter; disrupt; smash
SHAVIAN (Bernard Shaw)
SHAVING slicing; paring; grazing
SHEAFED bundled in sheaves
SHEARED reaped; cut through
SHEARER clipper; reaper; cutter
SHEATHE encase; cover
SHEATHY like a scabbard
SHEAVED collected in sheaves
SHEBANG store; saloon

SHEBEEN Irish whisky shop	**SHOPPED** imprisoned; framed
SHEDDER emitter; diffuser	**SHOPPER** peripatetic buyer
SHEERED moved away	**SHORAGE** landing charge
SHEETED covered with sheets	**SHORING** props; buttressing
SHELLAC resin lac **B.**	**SHORTED** (electrical fault)
SHELLED bombarded; husked	**SHORTEN** abbreviate; abridge; curtail
SHELLER huller; shucker	**SHORTER** briefer; terser; curter
SHELTER screen; asylum; refuge	**SHOTGUN**
SHELTIE Shetland pony **Z.**	**SHOT-PUT** putting the weight (sport)
SHELVED put aside; pigeonholed	**SHOTTED** loaded
SHELVES ledges	**SHOTTEN** dislocated; curdled
SHEPPEY sheep-cote	**SHOUTED** yelled; bawled; roared
SHERBET a cooling drink	**SHOUTER** crier; vociferator
SHEREEF an Amir; Emir	**SHOVING** propelling; pushing; jostling
SHERIAT Islamic law **Law**	**SHOW-BOX**
SHERIFF county officer **Law**	**SHOW-END** (roll of cloth)
SHEWING showing; demonstrating	**SHOWERY** pluvial
SHIFTED changed; altered; quitted	**SHOWILY** ostentatiously; flashily
SHIFTER remover; contriver	**SHOWING** representation; displaying
SHIITES Persian sectarians	**SHOWMAN** exhibitor
SHIKARI hunter (India)	**SHOW-OFF** play for admiration; swank
SHILPIT washy; feeble (Sc.)	**SHREDDY** ragged; fragmentary
SHIMMED wedged	**SHRILLY** piercingly; sharply
SHIMMER gleam; glisten; glimmer	**SHRINAL** sacred; hallowed
SHINGLE tile; style of hair-cutting	**SHRINED** enshrined
SHINGLY pebbly	**SHRIVEL** to dry up; parch
SHINING resplendent; coruscating	**SHRIVEN** given absolution **Eccl.**
SHINNED climbed	**SHRIVER** a confessor; absolver **Eccl.**
SHIP-BOY **Naut.**	**SHROUDS** winding sheets **Naut.**
SHIPFUL boat-load	**SHROUDY** giving shelter
SHIP-MAN a sailor **Naut.**	**SHRUBBY** full of shrubs **B.**
SHIPPED embarked; (oars)	**SHUCKER** husker; huller; sheller
SHIPPEN sheep-pen; stable	**SHUDDER** shake; quiver; shiver
SHIPPER exporter	**SHUFFLE** mix; cavil; quibble; (cards)
SHIPTON a prophetess	**SHUNNED** avoided; eluded
SHIP-WAY (dry dock)	**SHUNNER** eschewer; evader
SHIRKED evaded; avoided; scamped	**SHUNTED** turned aside
SHIRKER malingerer; dodger	**SHUNTER** a railway-man
SHIRLEY bull-finch **Z.**	**SHUT-EYE** sleep; a nap
SHIRLEY poppy **B.**	**SHUTTER** window **Photo.**
SHIRRED puckered	**SHUTTLE** sliding thread-holder
SHIRTED wearing a shirt	**SHYLOCK** rapacious usurer
SHITTAH⎫ acacia; **B.**	**SHYNESS** bashfulness; coyness
SHITTIM⎭ (Tabernacle wood)	**SHYSTER** rascally lawyer
SHIVERY brittle; chilly	**SIALOID** (saliva) **Med.**
SHIZOKU Japanese gentry	**SIAMANG** Malay gibbon **Z.**
SHOALED became shallow	**SIAMESE** (inseparables)
SHOALER coasting-vessel **Naut.**	**SIBLING** child; stepchild
SHOCKED offended; surprised	**SICCATE** desiccate; dry; parch
SHOCKER sensational novel	**SICCITY** aridity; dryness
SHOE-BOY a shiner	**SICKBAY** hospital ward **Naut.**
SHOEING farrier's work	**SICKBED** clinic
SHOE-PEG a nail	**SICKEST** very poorly
SHOE-TIE shoe-lace	**SICKISH** unwell; out of sorts
SHOGGED jolted; jogged	**SICKLED** with sickle
SHOOING scaring away	**SICK-PAY** wages during illness
SHOOKED packed	**SIC-LIKE** such like
SHOOTER marksman; sniper	**SIDEARM** sword or bayonet
SHOPBOY assistant, errand boy	**SIDEBOX** (theatre)
SHOPMAN	285 **SIDECAR** cocktail (motor-cycle)

SIDECUT branch canal			**SINGULT** a sob; a sigh	
SIDE-ROD coupling rod			**SINICAL** (sine)	
SIDLING edging away			**SINKING** foundering; declining	
SIENESE of Sienna			**SINLESS** innocent; blameless	
SIENITE syenite; hornblende	**Min.**		**SINNING** transgressing	
SIFFLED whistled			**SINOPIA⎱** red pigment;	
SIFFLET small whistle			**SINOPIS⎰** sinople; sinoper	
SIFTING scrutinizing; sorting; sieving			**SINSICK** repentant	
SIGHFUL grievous			**SINSYNE** since (Sc.)	
SIGHING lamenting; repining			**SINUATE** insinuate; curved	
SIGHTED seen; viewed; glimpsed			**SINUOUS** sinuose; winding	
SIGHTER a trial shot			**SINWORN**	
SIGHTLY handsome			**SIPPING** supping	
SIGMATE (sigma)			**SIREDON** larval salamander	**Z.**
SIGMOID curve of beauty			**SIRENIA** sea-cows	**Z.**
SIGNATE designate			**SIRGANG** green jackdaw	**Z.**
SIGNIFY indicate; betoken; portend			**SIRLOIN** surloin	
SIGNING subscribing; gesturing			**SIROCCO** hot desert wind	
SIGNIOR signor (It.)			**SISTINE,SIXTINE** (Pope Sixtus)	**Eccl.**
SIGNORA an Italian lady			**SISTING** summoning (Sc.)	**Law**
SIGNORY seigniory; overlordship			**SISTRUM** holy rattle (Egypt)	**Mus.**
SIKHISM monotheistic sect			**SITFAST** ulcer	**Med.**
SILENCE quiescence; dumbness			**SITHENS** since; after that	
SILENUS foster-father of Bacchus			**SITTINE** (nut-hatches)	**Z.**
SILESIA cotton fabric			**SITTING** session; incubating	
SILICIC (silica)	**Chem.**		**SITUATE** permanently fixed	
SILICLE broad pod	**B.**		**SIVAITE** follower of Siva	**Eccl.**
SILICON an element	**Chem.**		**SIXFOLD**	
SILIQUA⎱ seed vessel;	**B.**		**SIXTEEN**	
SILIQUE⎰ carat	**Meas.**		**SIXTHLY**	
SILKIER more lustrous			**SIZABLE** of a size; bulky	
SILKMAN silk-mercer			**SIZZLED** frizzled	
SILLAGO a fish genus	**Z.**		**SJAMBOK** S. Afr. raw hide whip	
SILLERY a white wine			**SKATING** gliding	
SILLIER more witless			**SKEETER** mosquito	**Z.**
SILLILY inanely; foolishly; ineptly			**SKELDER** swindle	
SILTING depositing mud			**SKELLUM** a rascal; scamp; scoundrel	
SILURUS cat-fish	**Z.**		**SKELTER** skedaddle	
SILVERN of silver			**SKEPFUL** basketful	
SILVERY bright; clear; sweet			**SKEPTIC** sceptic; doubting	
SIMARRE a cymar; a costume			**SKETCHY** vague; incomplete	
SIMILAR alike; analogous; twin			**SKEWGEE** crooked; skewed	
SIMILIA similes; metaphors			**SKIDDED** scotched; slipped	
SIMILOR semilor; imitation gold			**SKIDLID** crash helmet	
SIMIOUS ape-like; simian	**Z.**		**SKID-PAN** motorists' training ground	
SIMITAR scimitar			**SKIFFLE** folk-song and jazz	**Mus.**
SIMPKIN champagne			**SKI-JUMP**	
SIMPLER herbalist; plainer; easier			**SKILFUL** dexterous; adept; expert	
SIMPSON groundsel	**B.**		**SKI-LIFT** cable or funicular lift	
SIMULAR counterfeit; feigned			**SKILLED** expert; artful; adroit	
SIMURGH fabulous bird (Pers.)			**SKILLET** iron cooking pot	
SINAPIS sinapin; mustard	**B.**		**SKIMMED** glided; grazed	
SINBORN			**SKIMMER** scoop; bird	**Z.**
SINBRED			**SKIMPED** stinted	
SINCERE true; genuine; honest			**SKINFUL**	
SINEWED powerful; vigorous			**SKINKER** tapster; barman	
SINGING the vocal art			**SKINNED** peeled; fleeced	
SINGLED selected; separated			**SKINNER** a furrier	
SINGLES tennis; reeled silk			**SKIPPED** omitted; jumped	
SINGLET undervest			**SKIPPER** a fish; a captain	**Z.**

SKIPPET seal-box; boat	**Naut.**
SKIRLED shrieked shrilly	
SKIRRET water-parsnip	**B.**
SKIRTED bordered	
SKIRTER a dodger	
SKI-SUIT winter costume	
SKITTER glide; skim	
SKITTLE bowl out; knock down	
SKIVING leather splitting	
SKULKED lurked	
SKULKER a shirker; malingerer	
SKULPIN sea-fish	**Z.**
SKYBLUE azure	
SKYBORN heaven-born	
SKYHIGH	
SKYLARK the laverock	**Z.**
SKYLINE horizon; sea-line	
SKYSAIL	**Naut.**
SKYWARD	
SLABBED cut into thick slices	
SLABBER slobber; dribble; slaver	
SLACKED eased off	
SLACKEN relax; mitigate; abate	
SLACKER skulker; sluggard; idler	
SLACKLY negligently; laxly	
SLAINTE ! Good health ! (Irish)	
SLAKING quenching; allaying	
SLAMKIN a slut; loose gown	
SLAMMED banged	
SLANDER malign; traduce; obloquy	
SLANGED abused; vituperated	
SLANKET strip of land; slang	
SLANTED sloped; tilted	
SLANTLY slantwise; atilt; obliquely	
SLAPPED smacked; spanked	
SLAPPER slap-up affair	
SLASHED gashed; cut	
SLASHER cutting tool	**Tool**
SLATHER lots of	
SLATING roofing; reprimand; abusing	
SLATTER to be wasteful; slovenly	
SLAVDOM Slavs collectively	
SLAVERY serfdom; thraldom; bondage	
SLAVING drudging; moiling	
SLAVISH servile; obsequious	
SLAYING destroying; despatching	
SLEAVED not spun; raw	
SLEAVED separated; divided	
SLEDDED on a sled	
SLEDGED sledded; mushed	
SLEEKED glided; smoothed	
SLEEKEN to smooth	
SLEEKER slicker	**Tool**
SLEEKIT smooth-tongued (Sc.)	
SLEEKLY fair spoken; glossily; silky	
SLEEPER (various meanings)	
SLEETED hailed and snowed	
SLEIDED unwoven; sleaved	
SLEIGHT dexterity; skill; adroitness	
SLENDER frail; slim; slight	

SLEYING swinging askew	
SLICING severing; (golf)	
SLICKER smarter; more deft	
SLIDDER to slither; slip; slide	
SLIDING a lapse; varying	
SLIGHTY superficial	
SLIMILY viscously; muddily	
SLIMMER more slender; lankier	
SLINGER	
SLIPPED conveyed secretly	
SLIPPER steel cradle; mule	
SLIPWAY (shipbuilding)	
SLITHER slide about	
SLITTED slashed; split	
SLITTER a cutter	**Tool**
SLOBBER slabber; dribble; slaver	
SLOCKEN slake; quench	
SLOE-GIN	
SLOGGED hit hard	
SLOGGER mighty smiter	
SLOPING inclined; declinous; oblique	
SLOPPED spilt	
SLOTTED grooved	
SLOTTER to foul; filth	
SLOUCHY slackly	
SLOUGHY swampy; miry; queachy	
SLOVENE language and people (Yugo-slavia)	
SLOWEST dullest; tardiest	
SLOWING delaying; retarding	
SLUBBER to scamp; slabber	
SLUDGER sewage dumping vessel	**Naut.**
SLUGGED bashed; coshed	
SLUICED drenched; flushed	
SLUMBER sleep; repose; doze	
SLUMMER slum visitor	
SLUMPED fell heavily	
SLUNKEN shrivelled	
SLURRED sullied; disparaged	**Mus.**
SLUTCHY residual; mucky	
SLYNESS sliness; craft; cunning	
SMACKED slapped; spanked	
SMACKER a resounding kiss	
SMARAGD the emerald	**Min.**
SMARTED endured sharp pain	
SMARTEN brighten; quicken	
SMARTER brisker; sprucer	
SMARTLY promptly; readily; alertly	
SMASHED disrupted; broken	
SMASHER snide coin passer	
SMASH-UP a crash	
SMATTER slight superficial knowledge	
SMEARED daubed; contaminated	
SMEDDUM energy; powder	
SMELLED had an odour; smelt	
SMELLER the proboscis	
SMELTED melted; fused	
SMELTER ore-worker	
SMERLIN loach fish	**Z.**
SMICKER to smirk; ogle; leer	
SMICKET a smock	

SMICKLY amorously
SMIDGEN a bittock; a trifle
SMILING smirking
SMIRKED simpered
SMITING striking; buffeting; hitting
SMITTEN afflicted; chastened
SMITTLE to infect
SMOKIER reekier
SMOKILY fumily
SMOKING bloating; quizzing
SMOLDER smoulder
SMOOTHE palliate; flatter; flatten
SMOTHER stifle; suppress (cricket)
SMOUSER pedlar (S. Africa)
SMUDGED blurred; blotted
SMUDGER plumber
SMUGGLE convey secretly; snuggle
SMYTRIE a crowd of children (Sc.)
SNABBLE snaffle; plunder; eat
SNAFFLE a bit; appropriate; filch
SNAGGED snaggy
SNAGGER a cutter **Tool**
SNAKING rope-winding **Naut.**
SNAKISH reptilian; serpentine
SNAPING bevelling
SNAPPED caught; broke; photographed
SNAPPER a turtle **Z.**
SNARING entrapping; catching
SNARLED entangled; complicated
SNARLER growler; grumbler
SNATCHY irregular
SNEAKED told tales; peached
SNEAKER soft soled shoe
SNEAKER short drink
SNECKED latched; fastened (Sc.)
SNECK-UP go hang !
SNEDDEN sand-eel **Z.**
SNEERED jeered; gibed; mocked
SNEERER derider; taunter
SNEEZED
SNICKED nicked; snipped
SNICKER snigger; giggle
SNIFFED snuffed; inhaled
SNIFFLE snuffle
SNIFTED snorted; sniffed
SNIFTER dram; radio-detector
SNIGGER snicker; giggle
SNIGGLE ensnare
SNIPING shooting from ambush
SNIPPED cut off; clipped
SNIPPER a tailor
SNIPPET a cutting
SNIRTLE snigger
SNOODED wearing a fillet
SNOOKER (pool)
SNOOPED pried
SNOOPER a nosy Parker
SNOOZED dozed
SNOOZER a daydreamer
SNORING

SNORKEL breathing pipe (U-boat)
Naut.
SNORTED snifted
SNORTER a fast one (cricket)
SNOTTER bowsprit housing **Naut.**
SNOUTED with snout
SNOW-BOX (stage snowstorm)
SNOW-FED (streams)
SNOW-FLY a stone-fly **Z.**
SNOW-ICE frozen slush
SNOWILY
SNOWISH like snow
SNOW-MAN
SNOW-OWL the great white owl **Z.**
SNUBBED deliberately slighted
SNUBBER shock absorber
SNUFFED sniffed
SNUFFER a snuff taker
SNUFFLE nasal catarrh **Med.**
SNUGGLE smuggle; cuddle; fondle
SNUGIFY to make cosy
SNUZZLE nuzzle
SOAKAGE absorption
SOAKING drenching; steeping; imbruing
SO-AND-SO a vague definition
SOAP-BOX orator's platform
SOAP-PAN soap boiler
SOAPING flattering; lathering
SOARANT heraldic flying
SOARING mental uplift; aspiring
SOBBING lamentation; ululation
SOBERED
SOBERLY staidly
SOBOLES botanical suckers **B.**
SOCAGER socage tenant
SOCCAGE land tenure **Law**
SOCIETY company; sodality; elite
SOCKEYE Pacific salmon **Z.**
SOCKING beating; throwing
SODDING turfing
SOFA-BED day-bed; divan; ottoman
SOFTEST gentlest; easiest
SOFTISH yielding; compliant
SOGGING saturating
SOIGNEE admirably turned out (Fr.)
SOILING staining; tarnishing
SOILURE pollution
SOJOURN visit; tarry; remain; abide
SOKEMAN tenant by socage **Law**
SOLACED consoled; comforted
SOLANUM night-shade genus **B.**
SOLDIER warrior; man-at-arms
SOLICIT importune; canvass; crave
SOLIDLY compactly; firmly; densely
SOLIDUM complete sum
SOLIDUS (" s " for shilling) **Coin**
SOLIPED not cloven-hoofed **Z.**
SOLOIST **Mus.**
SOLOMON wisdom personified
SOLONIC wise like Solon
288 SOLPUGA a spider genus **Z.**

SOLUBLE capable of solution
SOLVEND a substance to be dissolved
SOLVENT able to pay all debts
SOLVING elucidating; unravelling
SOMATIC corporeal; bodily
SOMEHOW
SOMEONE
SOMNIAL dreamy
SONANCE sonancy; a call (Shak.)
SONCHUS sow-thistle genus **B.**
SONDELI Indian musk-rat **Z.**
SONGFUL full of glee
SONGMAN ballad-monger
SONLESS **[Eccl.**
SONNITE Sunnite; orthodox Moslem
SONSHIP
SOOTHED assuaged; pacified; cajoled
SOOTHER diplomatist; mollifier
SOOTHLY truly
SOOTING (sparking plugs)
SOOTISH like soot
SOPHISM a fallacy; specious argument
SOPHIST captious reasoner
SOPHORA pagoda tree **B.**
SOPIENT a soporific
SOPPING soaking; steeping
SOPRANI several sopranos **Mus.**
SOPRANO female treble **Mus.**
SORBENT an absorbent
SORBIAN⎫ Slavonic race in Saxony
SORBISH⎬
SORBINE⎱ sorbate; sweetberry
SORBITE⎰ extract **B.**
SORCERY witchcraft; enchantment
SORDINE a mute **Mus.**
SORDONO (oboe) **Mus.**
SOREHON Irish tenure
SORGHUM sugar-cane **B.**
SORITES syllogistic argument
SORNING obtruding; sponging on
SORONYL soporific drug **Med.**
SORORAL sisterly
SOROSIS mulberry type of fruit **B.**
SOROSIS woman's club
SORRILY meanly; pitiably
SORTING disposing; classifying
SOSPIRO a breathing rest **Mus.**
SOSTRUM life saving reward (Greek)
SOTTING tippling; toping; boozing
SOTTISH besotted; foolish
SOUBISE onion sauce
SOUCHET boiled fish
SOUFFLE frothy egg-dish
SOULFUL spiritually emotional
SOUNDLY thoroughly; validly
SOUNDED vibrated; tested **Naut.**
SOUNDER (Morse)
SOUNDER boar; herd of swine **Z.**
SOUPCON a suspicion; a taste (Fr.)
SOUREST most acid; rankest

SOURING acidulating
SOURISH tart; acetous; acrid
SOUROCK sorrel **B.**
SOURSOP American custard apple **B.**
SOUSING pickling; drenching
SOUTANE cassock **Eccl.**
SOUTHER south wind
SOUTHLY southerly
SOU'WEST S.W.
SOWBACK gravel ridge
SOZZLED sossled; tipsy; fuddled
SPACIAL extensive; commodious
SPACING arranging intervals
SPADDLE spittle; small spade **Tool**
SPADING digging
SPADONE double-handed sword
SPAEMAN diviner (Sc.)
SPAIRGE sparge; sprinkle
SPALING a bracing; cross-band
SPALLED chipped; splintered
SPANCEL cow-hobble
SPANDAU German light machine gun
SPANGLE glittering disc
SPANGLY sparkling
SPANIEL fawning; mean **Z.**
SPANISH Iberian
SPANKED slapped; speeded
SPANKER a sail **Naut.**
SPANNED measured; embraced
SPANNER monkey-wrench
SPAN-NEW brand-new
SPARELY sparingly; charily
SPARGED sprinkled; sprayed
SPARGER sprinkler; diffuser
SPARING frugal; parsimonious
SPARKED played the gallant
SPARKLE coruscate; twinkle
SPARRED disputed; wrangled; boxed
SPARRER boxing partner
SPARROW a small finch **Z.**
SPARTAN austere; hardy; undaunted
SPASTIC spasmodic
SPATHED ensheathed
SPATHIC laminated; foliated
SPATIAL spacial; wide; spacious
SPATTER asperse; besprinkle; splash
SPATTLE⎫ spaddle; spittle;
SPATULA⎰ a blade; a small spade **Med.**
SPATULE (tail feather) **Z.**
SPAWLED slavered
SPAWNED deposited eggs
SPAWNER female fish **Z.**
SPAYING gelding
SPEAKER (House of Commons)
SPEARED lanced; pierced; impaled
SPEARER spearman
SPECIAL distinctive; particular
SPECIES group; genus; class; kind
SPECIFY definite; indicate; detail
SPECKED spotted; speckled

SPECKLE small speck or stain	**SPIZINE** (buntings; finches) **Z.**
SPECTRA (spectrum); images	**SPLASHY** wet and muddy
SPECTRE apparition; spook; hobgoblin	**SPLAYED** sloped; slanted
SPECULA mirrors; reflectors	**SPLEENY** ill-humoured; fretful
SPEEDED ran; hastened; executed	**SPLEGET** a swab **Med.**
SPEEDER pace-maker	**SPLENIC** spleeny; fretful; melancholy
SPEED-UP accelerate	**SPLICED** interwoven; married
SPELDER a splinter; chip	**SPLINTS** surgical appliances **Med.**
SPELEAN troglodytic	**SPLODGE** daub; patch
SPELLED charmed; entranced; spelt	**SPLODGY** stained; blotched
SPELLER spelling book	**SPLOTCH** smear; stain
SPELTER soldering alloy	**SPLURGE** rowdiness
SPENCER butler; jacket	**SPLURGY** boisterous
SPENCER gaff-sail **Naut.**	**SPODIUM** ivory-black
SPENDER prodigal; wastrel; waster	**SPOFFLE** to bustle; to fuss
SPERKET spirket; harness hook	**SPOILED** pillaged; ruined; marred
SPEWING vomiting	**SPOILER** plunderer; bungler
SPHENIC wedge-like	**SPOLIUM** church property **Eccl.**
SPHERAL ball-like; globular	**SPONDEE** poetic foot (2 long syllables)
SPHERED englobed	**SPONDYL** a vertebra; a joint **Med.**
SPHERIC spherical	**SPONGED** deleted; purged; sorned
SPHYRNA hammer-headed sharks	**SPONGER** a parasite; sorner
SPICATE⎫ spicous; prickly;	**SPONSAL** (marriage)
SPICOSE⎭ spinous; thorny; spinate	**SPONSON** protecting bracket **Naut.**
SPICERY (spices)	**SPONSOR** guarantor; a surety
SPICILY pungently; piquantly	**SPOOFED** hoodwinked; hoaxed
SPICING seasoning; varying	**SPOOLED** wound on spools
SPICULE⎫ small pine; **B.**	**SPOOMED** scudded before the wind
SPICULA⎭ spike or ear	**SPOONED** hit into the air; courted
SPIDERY	**SPOONEY** love-sick
SPIEGEL steel alloy	**SPOORER** tracker
SPIGNEL baldmoney, a plant **B.**	**SPOROID** sporous; sporelike **B.**
SPIKING impaling; transfixing	**SPORRAN** kilt-pouch
SPILING building-piles	**SPORTED** wore; trifled; romped
SPILLED spilt; wasted; slopped	**SPORTER** jester; player
SPILLER reefing rope **Naut.**	**SPORULE** small spore **B.**
SPILOMA birthmark; a naevus **Med.**	**SPOTTED** spied; detected; pied
SPINACH spinage **B.**	**SPOTTER** sharp-sighted look-out
SPINATE spiky; spicate **B.**	**SPOUSAL** nuptial; matrimonial
SPINDLE axis; arbor	**SPOUTED** orated; spirted; pawned
SPINDLY fusiform; slender	**SPOUTER** declaimer; whale **Z.**
SPINNER a bait; textile operator	**SPRAICH** shriek; cry (Sc.)
SPINNEY spinny; copse	**SPRAYED** sprinkled; spumed; affused
SPINODE cusp in a curve	**SPRAYEY** branching
SPINOSE spinous; thorny **B.**	**SPREAGH** plunder (Sc.)
SPINULA spicule **B.**	**SPRIGGY** full of sprigs
SPINULE small spine **B.**	**SPRIGHT** sprite; a spirit; a ghost
SPIRAEA a plant genus **B.**	**SPRINGE** spring trap; a gin
SPIRANT fricative consonant; a sibilant	**SPRINTS** bicycle wheels
SPIRING tapering; sprouting	**SPRINGY** vernal; elastic
SPIRITY mettlesome; alcoholic	**SPRUCED** smartened up; prinked
SPIRKET sperket; harness hook	**SPRUNNY** spruce; a sweetheart
SPIRTED spurted; spouted; gushed	**SPRYEST** spriest; gayest; pertest
SPIRTLE to spirt; to spurt	**SPUMING** spumous; frothy; foamy
SPIRULA cephalopods; cuttle-fish **Z.**	**SPUN-HAY** twisted hay
SPITBOX a cuspidor	**SPUN-OUT** long drawn
SPITING grudging; thwarting	**SPUR-DOG** a shark **Z.**
SPITTED (cooking); transfixed	**SPURIAE** bastard quills **Z.**
SPITTER young deer	**SPURNED** rejected; scouted; contemned
SPITTLE small spade; saliva **Z.**	**SPURNER** a disdainer

SPURRED goaded; impelled; galloped
SPURRER inciter; instigator
SPURREY a plant   **B.**
SPURTED spirted; gushed; sprinted
SPURTLE spurt; spirtle
SPURWAY bridle-path
SPUTNIK earth satellite (Russian)
SPUTTER splutter
SPY-BOAT   **Naut.**
SPY-HOLE peep-hole; Judas' hole
SQUABBY squaddy; squat; tubby
SQUACCO crested heron   **Z.**
SQUALID sordid; unclean; filthy
SQUALLY gusty; blustering
SQUALOR dirtiness; foulness
SQUALUS shark   **Z.**
SQUARED adjusted; tallied; bribed
SQUASHY pulpy; soft
SQUATTY squabby; clumsy
SQUEASY scrupulous; squeamish
SQUEEZE compress; crush; pinch; nip
SQUEEZY congested; squashy
SQUELCH crush; suppress; quash
SQUIFFY tipsy; inebriated; sozzled
SQUINCH small stone arch; tight squeeze
SQUINNY to look asquint; meagre
SQUIRED escorted
SQUITCH quitch-grass   **B.**
SRADDHA Hindu devotional offerings
STABBED wounded; pierced   [**Eccl.**
STABBER awl; marlinspike   **Tool**
STABLED
STABLER stable-keeper
STABLES a trumpet call   **Mus.**
STACHYS hedge-nettle genus   **B.**
STACKED piled; (cards)
STACKER haymaker
STADDLE crutch; support
STADIUM arena; running track
STAFFED manned by
STAGERY scenic exhibition
STAGGER astound; lurch; reel; sway
STAGING a structure; producing
STAIDLY steadily; sedately; soberly
STAINED foxed; tarnished; sullied
STAINER a dyer
STAITHE coaling stage
STAKING hazarding; wagering
STALDER cask rack
STALELY mustily; effetely; insipidly
STALEST most trite
STALKED with peduncle   **B.**
STALKER stealthy sportsman
STALLED fatted; lost speed
STAMINA endurance; vitality; vigour
STAMMEL rough red cloth
STAMMER stutter
STAMNOS Greek urn
STAMPED impressed; crushed; branded
STAMPER ore crusher

STAND-BY a reserve
STANDER provider; candidate
STAND-IN deputy; substitute
STAND-TO military readiness
STAND-UP well fought
STANIEL ⎱ stanyel; kestrel;
STANNEL ⎰ windhover   **Z.**
STANNIC (of tin)
STANNUM tin, metallic element   **Chem.**
STAPLED connected together
STAPLER a dealer; clipping machine
STARCHY stiff; formal; precise
STARDOM film eminence
STARING glaring; gaping; prominent
STARKEN stiffen; make obstinate
STARKLY completely; absolutely
STARLET junior actress
STAR-LIT
STARRED shone; bespangled
STARTED winced; roused; began
STARTER also ran
STARTLE alarm; frighten; surprise
STARVED famished; emaciated
STASIMA choral odes (Greek)
STATANT standing (Her.)
STATELY lofty; magnificent; imposing
STATICE sea-lavender   **B.**
STATICS conditions for equilibrium
STATING narrating; affirming
STATION Australian stock-farm; place
STATISM policy; art of government
STATIST statistical expert
STATIVE fixed; standing still
STAT-OHM   **Meas. Elect.**
STATUED with statues
STATURE natural height
STATUTE an enactment; decree   **Law**
STAUNCH stanch; trusty; steadfast
STAVING delaying; broaching
STAYING enduring; detaining; abiding
STAY-PUT semi-permanent
STEALER purloiner; peculator
STEALTH furtiveness; secrecy
STEAMED vaporized
STEAMER cooking vessel   **Naut.**
STEARIC   **Chem.**
STEARIN fat; wax; stearic acid
STEELED hardened; nerved
STEEPED soaked; drenched; imbrued
STEEPEN to make steep
STEEPER soaking vat
STEEPLE a spire   **Eccl.**
STEEPLY almost sheer; abruptly
STEERED conned; controlled; directed
STEERER pilot; guide; director
STEEVED packed closely
STELENE pillar-like; columnar
STELLAR astral; starry
STEMLET small stalk
STEMMED compressed

STEMPLE, STEMPEL cross-beam
STEMSON jointing timber   **Naut.**
STENCHY odoriferous
STENCIL pattern plate
STENGAH whisky and soda (Malay)
STENTOR a loud speaker
STEP-INS elastic-held shoes
STEPNEY spare wheel; (born at sea)
STEPPED paced; walked; fixed
STEPPER horse with high action
STEPSON
STERILE barren; germ-free; acarpous
STERLET sturgeon   **Z.**
STERNAL (breast-bone)   **Med.**
STERNER harsher; more austere
STERNLY severely; strictly; dourly
STERNUM breast-bone   **Med.**
STEROID sterol compound   **Chem.**
STETSON a hat (U.S.A.)
STEVING stowing   **Naut.**
STEWARD seneschal; bailiff   **Naut.**
STEWING simmering; worrying
STEW-CAN
STEW-PAN, STEW-POT
STHENIA strength   **Med.**
STHENIC vigorous; active
STIBIAL (antimony)
STIBIUM antimony.   **Chem.**
STICHIC rhymic
STICHOS a line of verse
STICKER last ditcher; adherent
STICKLE a rapid in a stream
STIFFEN harden
STIFFER more rigid; harder; primmer
STIFFLY rigidly; firmly; starchy
STIFLED suffocated; smothered
STILLED hushed; calmed; distilled
STILLER pacifier; composer
STILTED pompous; bombastic
STILTON a cheese
STIMIED obstructed; (golf)
STIMULI incentives; spurs
STINGER
STINKER
STINTED restricted; rationed
STINTER pincher; restrainer
STIPEND salary; emolument
STIPPLE to make dots
STIPTIC astringent   **Med.**
STIPULA⎱ leaf appendage   **B.**
STIPULE⎰
STIRPES fore-fathers; races
STIRRED roused; incited; bustled
STIRRER thriller; agitator; disturber
STIRRUP
STIVING stewing
STOAKED choked; stopped   **Naut.**
STOCKED stored; saved; hoarded
STOICAL passionless; unfeeling
STOKING adding fuel

STOMACH to brook; to resent   **Med.**
STOMATA breathing pore   **Med.**
STONIED astonished; mazed
STONILY obdurately; unrelentingly
STONING pelting; (fruit)
STOOGED loitered; filled in time
STOOKED set up in sheaves
STOOKER harvest worker
STOOMED fermented
STOOPED condescended; swooped
STOOPER bender
STOOTER Dutch silver coin   **Coin**
STOPGAP locum tenens
STOPING series of ledges
STOPPED restrained; repressed; closed
STOPPER⎱ plug; cork; tampion
STOPPLE⎰
STORAGE safe custody
STORIED
STORIES floors; tales
STORING garnering; hoarding
STORMED assaulted; raved; raged
STORMER blusterer
STOTTER rebound; a bounce (Sc.)
STOUTEN hearten; encheer
STOUTER more corpulent; braver
STOUTLY sturdily; stalwartly; robust
STOVING a heat treatment
STOWAGE packing; loading
STOWING arranging; packing
STRAIKS wheel-plates; strakes
STRANGE unfamiliar; abnormal; exotic
STRAPPY strong; fit; many straps
STRATUM rock formation
STRATUS cloud formation
STRAWED strewed
STRAYED erred; roved; deviated
STRAYER wandered; vagrant
STRAYNE strain; stress (Spens.)
STREAKY striped
STREAMY well watered
STRETCH reach; strain; expand
STRETTO quick and sharp   **Mus.**
STREWED strewn; scattered
STRIATE streaky; scratched
STRIDOR harsh noise; a jar
STRIGES the owl genus   **Z.**
STRIGIL skin-scraper
STRIKER bashful worker; firing pin
STRINGY filamentous
STRIPED streaked
STRIPES a tiger   **Z.**
STRIVEN strove; struggled; tussled
STRIVER emulator; trier; competitor
STROBIC rate of turning; spinning
STROCAL glass-maker's shovel
STROKED rubbed gently; (rowing)
STROKEN struck (Spens.)
STROKER rubber; soother
STROPHE a stanza (Greek)

STUBBED blunted; obtuse; extirpated
STUBBLE corn stumps **B.**
STUBBLY like stubble; unshaven
STUCKLE clump of sheaves
STUCK-UP arrogant; pompous
STUDDED (shirts); (nails)
STUDDLE a trestle
STUDENT pupil; scholar; philomath
STUDIED conned; pondered; worked
STUDIER student; scrutinizer
STUFFED padded; crowded; rammed
STUFFER packer; crammer
STUMBLE trip; slip; blunder; lurch
STUMBLY apt to stumble
STUMMED fortified; doctored
STUMMEL tobacco pipe (German)
STUMPED at a loss; (cricket)
STUMPER wicket-keeper
STUNNED dumbfounded; amazed
STUNNER an astonisher; stupefier
STUNTED dwarfed; pygmean; runty
STUPEFY bemuse; dope; benumb
STUPENT struck with stupor
STUPOSE tufted; scaly; matted
STURNUS starling genus **Z.**
STUTTER stammer; hesitant utterance
STYGIAN infernal; black; murky
STYLATE styloid; like a style or pen
STYLING naming; designating
STYLISH modish; chic; elegant
STYLIST fine writer
STYLITE pillar-dweller
STYLIZE to make conventional
STYLOID pen-like
STYMIED stimied; obstructed; (golf)
STYPTIC stiptic; astringent **Med.**
SUASION persuasion
SUASIVE urbane; agreeable
SUASORY convincing
SUAVELY pleasantly; blandly
SUAVITY affability; sweetness
SUBACID rather acid
SUBADAR⎤ Mogul governor;
SUBEDAR⎦ native captain
SUBBASS low organ note **Mus.**
SUBBING acting as substitute
SUBDEAN under-dean **Eccl.**
SUBDUAL conquest; subjugation
SUBDUCE withdraw
SUBDUCT subtract
SUBDUED piano; routed; worsted
SUBDUER queller; vanquisher
SUBEDIT (edit)
SUBERIC of cork
SUBFUSC subfusk; dusky
SUBGENS sub-clan
SUB-HEAD sub-title
SUBJECT thesis; topic; subservient
SUBJOIN append; affix; postfix
SUBLATE carry off; take away

SUBLIME exalted; lofty; superb
SUBNUDE almost leafless **B.**
SUBOVAL almost ovate
SUBPENA subpoena; writ **Law**
SUBRENT sublet
SUBSALT **Chem.**
SUBSIDE sink; ebb; wane; abate
SUBSIDY a grant; dole; monetary aid
SUBSIGN undersign
SUBSIST live; exist; endure
SUBSOIL the under-soil
SUBSUME include as comprehended
SUBTACK an under-lease (Sc.)
SUBTEND embrace; enfold
SUBTILE subtle; cunningly devised
SUBTLER wilier; craftier
SUBTYPE subdivision
SUBURBS outlying districts
SUBVENE aid; support
SUBVERT overthrow; ruin; corrupt
SUCCADE candied fruit
SUCCEED follow; prosper; win
SUCCESS prosperity; victory; triumph
SUCCORY chicory **B.**
SUCCOSE sappy
SUCCOUR aid; help; support; foster
SUCCUBA a harlot
SUCCULA capstan; winch
SUCCUMB yield; submit; die; capitulate
SUCCUSS to shake suddenly
SUCKING absorbing; imbibing
SUCKLED nursed
SUCKLER an infant; a suckling
SUCROSE cane sugar
SUCTION
SUDANIC group of languages (Sudan)
SUDORAL sweaty; perspiring
SUFFETE Punic official
SUFFICE to content; be enough; avail
SUFFUSE diffuse; blush; overspread
SUGARED candied; sweetened
SUGGEST hint; insinuate; propose
SUICIDE felo-de-se
SUIFORM pig-like; swinish
SUITING pleasing; according; (cloth)
SULCATE grooved; furrowed
SULKIER more sullen
SULKILY morosely; sullenly; surlily
SULKING glowering
SULLAGE dross; scum
SULLENS morose; temper; the sulks
SULLIED tainted; tarnished; defamed
SULPHUR brimstone **Chem.**
SULTANA raisin; marsh bird **B, Z.**
SUMLESS beyond count
SUMMARY epitome; abstract; digest
SUMMERY summerlike
SUMMING summary; adding; counting
SUMMIST writer of a compendium
SUMMONS writ; citation **Law**

SUMPTER pack-horse .... **Z.**
SUNBATH
SUNBEAM
SUNBEAT struck by the sun's rays
SUNBIRD humming bird .... **Z.**
SUNBURN tan
SUNCLAD radiant
SUNDARI hardwood tree (Borneo) **B.**
SUNDAWN dawn-light
SUNDIAL stylish timepiece
SUNDOWN sun-set
SUNDROP primrose (Amer.)
SUNFISH shark .... **Z.**
SUN-KIST kissed by the sun
SUN-LAMP ultra-violet ray
SUNLESS cloudy; overcast
SUNLIKE solar
SUNMYTH a solar myth
SUNNING sun-bathing
SUNNITE Sonnite; orthodox Muslim
SUNRISE dawn; cock-crow
SUNROSE sun-flower .... **B.**
SUNSPOT
SUNWARD towards the sun
SUNWISE clock-wise
SUPPING sipping
SUPPLED made pliant
SUPPORT prop; uphold; assist
SUPPOSE surmise; fancy; deem
SUPREME dominant; paramount
SURBASE cornice; base moulding
SURCOAT coat worn over chain mail
SURDITY lack of resonance
SURFACE exterior; superficies
SURFEIT excess; plethora; cloy; gorge
SURFMAN skilled boatman
SURGENT swelling; heaving
SURGEON chirurgeon .... **Med.**
SURGERY .... **Med.**
SURGING swirling; billowing
SURLIER more churlish and crusty
SURLILY gruffly; sullenly; morosely
SURLOIN sirloin beef
SURMISE conjecture; suppose; imagine
SURNAME sirname; cognomen
SURPASS excel; exceed; outdo
SURPLUS residuum; balance; excess
SURSIZE feudal penalty .... **Law**
SURTOUT overcoat
SURVIVE outlive; endure; outlast
SUSPECT doubtful; mistrust; distrust
SUSPEND hang; postpone; relieve
SUSPIRE sigh; yearn; breathe
SUSTAIN uphold; bear; endure
SUTLERY ⎫ sutler's occupation
SUTLING ⎭ commissariat
SUTURAL sewn; seamy; stitched
SUTURED sewn together
SWABBED washed; mopped
SWABBER scrubber; mopper-up

SWABIAN (South German)
SWADDLE swathe; wrap; bind
SWAGGED sagged; leant
SWAGGER strut; ruffle; boast
SWAGING assuaging; mitigating
SWAGMAN burglar
SWAHILI Zanzibari language
SWALING wasting; consuming; burning
SWALLET underground stream
SWALLOW voracity; engulf; absorb **Z.**
SWAMPED overwhelmed; inundated
SWANKED boasted; bragged
SWANKIE swipes; thin beer
SWANPAN Chinese abacus
SWAPPED bartered; exchanged
SWARAJI home rule (India)
SWARDED grassy; turfy
SWARFED fainted; swooned; dwamed
SWARMED thronged; teemed; clustere
SWARTHY tawny; swart; dark
SWASHED blustered; swanked
SWASHER swash-buckler
SWATTED hit with a fly-swat
SWATTER fly-killer
SWAYING governing; oscillating
SWEALED guttered like a candle
SWEARER blasphemer
SWEATED drudged; oozed; reeked
SWEATER a pull-over; jersey
SWEDISH (Sweden)
SWEEPER an artist of the brush
SWEETEN to palliate; dulcify
SWEETER more fragrant
SWEETIE sweetmeat; confectionery
SWEETLY dulcetly; fragrantly
SWELLED inflated; heaved; bulged
SWELLEL American squirrel .... **Z.**
SWELLET rush of water in a mine
SWELTER perspire; sweat
SWELTRY sultry; oppressive
SWERVED deviated; turned aside
SWERVER jinker
SWIFTER faster; nimbler; quicker
SWIFTLY rapidly; promptly; suddenly
SWIGGED drank deep; quaffed
SWILLED rinsed; washed; boozed
SWILLER copious absorber
SWIMMER water-spider .... **Z.**
SWINDLE fraud; dupe; cheat
SWINERY piggery
SWINGED beaten up; punished
SWINGEL ⎫ loose end of flail
SWINGLE ⎭ swipple
SWINGER
SWINISH hoggish; suiform
SWINKED drudged; moiled; toiled
SWIPING slogging; lashing out
SWIRLED whirled; eddied
SWISHED flogged
SWISHER a wielder of the birch

SWITHER hesitate; doubt; fright
SWITZER Swiss bodyguard; a Swiss
SWIZZLE a mixed drink
SWOLLEN distended; enlarged; bloated
SWOONED fainted; swarfed; dwamed
SWOOPED caught on the wing
SWOPPED swapped; bartered
SWOTTED studied hard
SYCOSIS barber's itch   **Med.**
SYENITE Egyptian granite   **Min.**
SYLPHID small sylph; fairy
SYLVINE potassium chloride   **Chem.**
SYLVITE potassium chloride   **Chem.**
SYMBION symbiotic organism   **Z.**
SYMPTOM token; indication; sign
SYNACMY floral maturity   **B.**
SYNAPSE nerve junction   **Med.**
SYNAPTE Greek litany   **Eccl.**
SYNAXIS an assembly for worship
SYNCOPE contraction; collapse
SYNERGY co-operation
SYNESIS harmonious construction
SYNOCHA fever   **Med.**
SYNOCIL a growth on sponges
SYNODAL bishop's benefit   **Eccl.**
SYNODIC (synod); conventional
SYNONYM a word of similar significance
SYNOTUS long-eared bat   **Z.**
SYNOVIA lubrication   **Med.**
SYNTONY wireless tuning
SYRINGA mock-orange   **B.**
SYRINGE a squirt; to spray
SYSTOLE contraction of the heart **Med.**
SYSTYLE a stylish portico

T

TABANAC French white wine
TABANUS horse-fly or gad-fly   **Z.**
TABARET satin striped silk
TABELLA lozenge   **Med.**
TABETIC consumptive   **Med.**
TABIDLY tabific; tabetic
TABINET curtain material
TABLEAU vivid picture (Fr.)
TABLIER apron; chess-board
TABLING setting down in order
TABLOID multum in parvo   **Med.**
TABOOED banned; barred; accursed
TABORER drummer   **Mus.**
TABORET small drum   **Mus.**
TABULAR listed; tabulated
TACITLY noiselessly implied
TACKILY stickily; adhesively
TACKING stitching; fastening   **Naut.**
TACKLED seized; grappled with
TACTFUL diplomatic and sensitive
TACTICS cunning moves
TACTILE tangible; perceptible
TACTION sense of touch; contact

TACTUAL tactile; palpable
TADORNA duck genus   **Z.**
TADPOLE embryonic frog; polliwog   **Z.**
TADZHIK Central Asian people
TAFFETA wavy fabric
TAFFETY taffeta; lustrous silk
TAGALOG language (Philippines)
TAGETES asters   **B.**
TAGGERS thin sheet iron
TAGGING following; tailing; tacking
TAGSORE sheep disease
TAGTAIL worm; parasite
TAILAGE entail   **Law**
TAILEND fag-end
TAILING following; a winter sport
TAILZIE deed of entail   **Law**
TAINTED infected; stained; sullied
TAIPING Chinese rebel
TAKE-OFF a burlesque; a start
TAKINGS cash receipts
TAKSPAN pine-roof shingles   **Arch.**
TALARIA Mercury's winged sandals
TALCITE nacrite   **Min.**
TALCOSE talcous; of talc
TALEFUL newsy
TALIPED club-footed
TALIPES club-foot   **Med.**
TALIPOT } talipat; fan-palm   **B.**
TALIPUT }
TALKIES talking films
TALKING prating; discoursing
TALLAGE ancient tax
TALLBOY chest of drawers
TALLEST loftiest; highest
TALLIED agreed; corresponded; fitted
TALLIER tally-keeper
TALLISH rather tall
TALLITH praying mantle (Heb.)
TALLOWY fatty
TALLY-HO
TALONED with claws
TAMABLE docile; tractable
TAMANOA ant-eater   **Z.**
TAMARIN S. American monkey   **Z.**
TAMASHA entertainment (India)
TAMBOUR drum; embroidery   **Mus.**
TAMILIC } Tamil; a dialect of Ceylon
TAMULIC }
TAMMANY political organisation, U.S.
TAMPING (blasting)
TAMPION also tompion; a stopper
TANADAR Hindu police officer
TANAGER American finch   **Z.**
TANAGRA finches   **Z.**
TANAGRA terra cotta ware
TANGENT
TANGHIN poison tree (Madagascar)   **B.**
TANGING twanging; flavouring
TANGLED jumbled; matted; twisted
TANGRAM Chinese jigsaw

295

TANKAGE storage
TANKARD drinking vessel
TANKCAR tanker; oil-tank
TANKING waterproofing a basement
TANLING sun-bather
TANNAGE tanning materials
TANNATE a salt of tannic acid **Chem.**
TANNERY
TANNING leathering
TANRIDE riding school
TANSPUD bark-peeling tool **Tool**
TANTARA fanfare **Mus.**
TANTITY tantamount
TANTIVY at speed
TANTONY smallest pig in litter **Z.**
TANTRUM temper; petulance
TANYARD
TAPBOLT screw bolt
TAPERED conical; pointed
TAPETUM (retina) **Med.**
TAPIOCA cassava **B.**
TAPLASH stale swipes
TAPPING broaching; screwcutting
TAPROOM bar
TAPROOT **B.**
TAPSTER, TAPSMAN bartender
TARBUSH tarboosh; fez
TARDIER slower; later; slacker
TARDILY slowly; reluctantly
TARNISH sully; soil; stain
TARRACE volcanic earth
TARRIED loitered; lingered; sojourned
TARRIER dawdler; estate register **Law**
TARRING covering with bitumen
TARROCK arctic tern **Z.**
TARSIER lemur; the malmag **Z.**
TARTARY Tartarus; nethermost hell
TARTISH somewhat sharp
TARTLET small tart
TASKING taskwork; drudgery; toiling
TASTIER choicer; more succulent
TASTILY artistically
TASTING relishing; enjoying; gustation
TATARIC Mongolian, Turkish, etc.
TATOUAY armadillo; peba; tatou **Z.**
TATTERY in rags
TATTING lace work
TATTLED gossiped; chatted; prated
TATTLER tale-bearer
TAUNTED derided; flouted; scorned
TAUNTER mocker; upbraider; reviler
TAURIAN (bulls)
TAURIDS meteoric shower
TAURINE ox extract **Med.**
TAUTEST tightest; tensest
TAXABLE rateable
TAXCART small farm cart
TAXFREE scot free
TAXICAB
TAXI-ING runway movements **Aeron.**

TAXI-MAN
TEA-CAKE
TEA-COSY
TEA-GOWN
TEA-LEAD (tea-chest linings)
TEA-LEAF **B.**
TEA-ROSE **B.**
TEA-SHOP
TEA-TIME
TEA-TRAY
TEA-TREE **B.**
TEACHER master; tutor; pedagogue
TEAMING grouping; selecting
TEARBAG lachrymal gland **Med.**
TEARFUL maudlin; weeping; Niobean
TEAR-GAS riot repellant; eye irritant **Chem**
TEARING rending; raving; raging
TEARPIT a lachrymal depression
TEASING tantalizing; plaguing
TEATHED manured by live stock
TECHILY fretfully; peevishly
TECHNIC technique; technical
TECTRIX a wing or tail feather **Z.**
TEDDING spreading
TEDIOUS wearisome; hum-drum
TEEMFUL prolific; swarming
TEEMING fruitful; abundant
TEENAGE thirteen to nineteen
TEENING troubling; provoking
TEGULAR (tiles)
TELAMON statue supporting masonry
TELECAR mobile telegraph office
TELEOST osseous
TELERGY telepathy
TELESIA sapphire **Min.**
TELLING effective; informing
TELPHER system of electric traction
TEL-QUEL exchange rate
TELSTAR television satellite
TEMENOS temple precinct (Greek)
TEMPEAN delightful; (Vale of Tempe)
TEMPERA oilless paint; distemper
TEMPEST hurricane; typhoon; gale
TEMPLAR student of law **Law**
TEMPLED in a temple
TEMPLET template; jig **Tool**
TEMPTED allured; tried; solicited
TEMPTER a decoy; an enticer
TENABLE maintainable; rational
TENANCY tenure
TENDING tendentious; trending
TENDRIL twining shoot **B.**
TENERAL immature **Z.**
TENFOLD decuple
TENIOID like tapeworms **Z.**
TENONED mortised
TENONER tenon cutter **Tool**
TEN-PINS cf. Nine-pins
TENSELY tautly; tightly
TENSEST stiffest; most emotional

TENSILE ductile
TENSION strain; stress; exigency
TENSITY tenseness; urgency
TENSIVE intensive
TENTBED canopied bed
TENT-FLY part of a tent
TENTFUL tent fully occupied
TENTGUY tent-rope not its occupant
TENTHLY
TENTING probing; searching **Med.**
TENTORY the awning of a tent
TENTPEG, TENTPIN
TENTURE wall hangings
TENUATE thin; attenuate
TENUITY rarity; thinness
TENUOUS diffused; slender
TERBIUM a metallic element **Chem.**
TERCINE seed-coat **B.**
TEREBIC (turpentine) **B.**
TEREBRA Roman ram; ovipositor **Z.**
TEREKIA sand-piper genus **Z.**
TERGANT recursant (Her.)
TERGITE back of an anthropod **Z.**
TERM-FEE **Law**
TERMING naming; denominating
TERMINI boundaries; extremities
TERMITE white ant **Z.**
TERNARY in threes
TERNATE three-leafed **B.**
TERNERY tern breeding ground
TERNION (twelve pages)
TERPENE terebene **Chem.**
TERRACE raised beach
TERRAIN geological features
TERRENE terrestrial; earthy
TERRIER fine fighter **Z.**
TERRIER tarrier; register **Law**
TERRIFY alarm; appal; dismay
TERRINE earthenware cooking dish
TERSELY concisely; briefly; laconically
TERSION wiping
TERTIAL wing feather **Z.**
TERTIAN on alternate days
TESSERA mosaic block
TESTACY testate **Law**
TESTATE leaving a will **Law**
TEST-BAN nuclear weapons agreement
TESTERN testril; a sixpence **Coin**
TESTIER more irritable or irascible
TESTIFY affirm; avow; depose; depone
TESTILY peevishly; petulantly
TESTING proving; trying
TESTOON 1s. (Henry VIII) **Coin**
TESTRIL a tester; a sixpence **Coin**
TESTUDO tortoise; early tank **Z.**
TETANIC **Med.**
TETANUS lock-jaw **Med.**
TETRACT having four rays
TETRODE a thermionic valve
TEXTILE woven fabric

TEXT-MAN a quoter
TEXTUAL authoritative
TEXTURE a web; structure; fabric
THALIAN comic
THALLUS a stem formation **B.**
THALWEG valley path
THAMMUZ Osiris; Adonis
THANAGE thanedom
THANKED gratefully acknowledged
THAPSIA plant genus **B.**
THAWING melting; dissolving
THEATRE (operations) **Med.**
THEBAIA thebain; opium **Med.**
THEBAIC Thèban
THECATE sheathed; encased **B.**
THECIUM spore-case **B.**
THEORBO lute with 11 strings **Mus.**
THEOREM logical proposition
THERAPY the curative art **Med.**
THEREAT on that account
THEREBY in consequence
THEREIN
THEREOF
THEREON
THERETO
THERIAC alleged antidote **Med.**
THERMAL thermic; warm
THERMIT incendiary mixture
THERMOS flask
THEROID animal-like **Z.**
THESEUS slew Minotaur in Labyrinth
THESPIS founder of Greek drama
THEURGY miracle making
THIAMIN B vitamin **Chem.**
THICKEN condense; coagulate; curdle
THICKER closer; duller; muddier
THICKET underwood
THICKLY solidly; densely; closely
THICKUN £1; a sovereign **Coin**
THIEVED stole; peculated; purloined
THIGGED cadged; begged
THIGGER threatening beggar; sorner
THILLER wheel-horse; shaft-horse **Z.**
THIMBLE iron rope ring **Naut.**
THINKER cogitator; (Rodin)
THINNED attenuated; reduced
THINNER slimmer; slighter
THIRDLY
THIRSTY dry; parched; craving
THISTLE emblem of Scotland; weed **B.**
THISTLY overgrown with thistles
THITHER
THOLING enduring; yielding
THOMISM } doctrines of Thomas
THOMIST } Aquinas **Eccl.**
THORITE thorium silicate **Min.**
THORIUM a metallic element **Chem.**
THOUGHT solicitude; concern; care
THOUING treating with familiarity
THRATCH gasp for breath (Sc.)

THREADY filamentous
THREAVE 24 sheaves
THRIFTY frugal; economical; thriving
THRIVED waxed; luxuriated
THRIVEN flourished; grown
THRIVER prosperer
THROATY guttural
THRONAL like a throne
THRONED exalted
THROUGH clear; unobstructed
THROWER caster; hurler; heaver
THROW-IN football
THRUMMY shaggy cloth; fringed
THUGGEE thug; assassin
THULITE Norwegian rock — **Min.**
THULIUM a metallic element — **Chem.**
THUMBED beckoned for a lift
THUMMIM a perfect mystery
THUMPED struck heavily; drubbed
THUMPER whacker
THUNDER denounce; rumble
THURIFY to cense frankincense
THWAITE reclaimed land
THYROID shield-like gland — **Med.**
THYRSUS ivy staff (Bacchus)
THYSELF
TIARAED wearing a tiara
TIBETAN
TIBICEN flute-player — **Mus.**
TICKING bedding material; marking
TICKLED titillated; amused
TICKLER enlivener
TIDDLER small fry — **Z.**
TIDERIP rough water
TIDEWAY a channel
TIDIEST neatest; sprucest
TIDINGS news; intelligence; message
TIE-BEAM rafter retainer
TIERCEL male hawk — **Z.**
TIERCET triple rhyme
TIFFANY gauze; thin silk
TIGHTEN increase the strain
TIGHTER more compact; closer
TIGHTLY tautly; tensely
TIGLINE croton oil — **B.**
TIGRESS — **Z.**
TIGRINE marked like a tiger
TIGRISH fierce
TILBURY dog-cart
TILE-ORE copper ore — **Min.**
TILE-RED brownish-red
TILLAGE cultivation
TILLING husbandry
TILSEED seed of sesamum indicum — **B.**
TILTING slanting; forging
TIMBALE a fowl dish
TIMBREL tambourine — **Mus.**
TIMEFUL seasonable; timely
TIMEGUN
TIME-LAG an interim; delay

TIME-OFF leisure; break
TIMIDLY fearfully; diffidently
TIMOTHY cat's tail grass — **B.**
TIMPANI tympani — **Mus.**
TIMPANO kettle-drum — **Mus.**
TINAMOU S. American quail — **Z.**
TINCHEL
TINCHIL } deer battue
TINDERY inflammable
TIN-FISH torpedo — **Naut.**
TINFOIL
TINGING ringing; tinking
TINGLED thrilled; smarted
TINIEST smallest; puniest; microscopic
TINKING tinkling; ringing
TINKLED rang; clinked
TINKLER small bell
TIN-MINE
TINNING
TINNOCK blue tit — **Z.**
TIN-TACK
TINTAGE colouring; shading
TINTIES coloured films
TINTING tingeing
TINTYPE ferro-type
TINWARE
TIPCART
TIPPING (flute playing); hinting — **Mus.**
TIPPLED drank deep
TIPPLER steady absorber
TIPSIFY inebriate
TIPSILY drunkenly
TIPSTER racing tout
TIPTOED walked warily
TIRASSE pedal coupling — **Mus.**
TIRLING quivering; vibrating; twisting
TISSUED woven; variegated
TITANIA fairy queen
TITANIC gigantic; colossal
TITHING township
TITLARK meadow pipit — **Z.**
TITLING title pages
TITLING hedge sparrow — **Z.**
TITMICE tits — **Z.**
TITOISM political practice
TITRATE (volumetric analysis) — **Chem.**
TITTUPY frisky
TITULAR nominal
TIVERED marked with ochre
TOADIED cringed; truckled; fawned
TOADIES sycophants
TOASTED dried; warmed
TOASTER
TOBACCO
TOBASCO red pepper
TOBOGAN toboggan
TOBYMAN highwayman
TOCCATA a touchy composition — **Mus.**
TODDLED strolled; meandered
TODDLER a tiny tot

TOE-HOLD climbing
TOENAIL
TOFTMAN a cottager
TOGGERY raiment
TOILFUL wearisome
TOILING moiling; labouring; snaring
TOKENED spotted; marked
TOLLAGE dues
TOLLBAR toll-gate
TOLLING knelling; annulling **Law**
TOLLMAN toll-gatherer
TOLUENE methyl benzene **Chem.**
TOMALLY lobster liver **Z.**
TOMATIN tomato; anti-biotic **Chem.**
TOMBOLA a form of lottery
TOMFOOL buffoon
TOMPION inking pad; clockmaker
TONGUED
TO-NIGHT
TONNAGE
TONSILE clippable
TONSURE shaving; (shorn)
TONTINE co-operative loan
TOOL-BOX
TOOLING (bookbinding); driving
TOOTHED dentate
TOOTING prying; hornblowing
TOOTLED played the flute **Mus.**
TOPARCH a Greek governor
TOPBOOT
TOPCOAT
TOPFULL brimming (Shak.)
TOPHOLE first-rate
TOPIARY ornamental clipping
TOPICAL local; particular; allusive
TOPKNOT plume or crest of feathers **Z.**
TOPLESS without a lid
TOPMAST **Naut.**
TOPMOST highest
TOPONYM topographical name
TOPPING of a high order
TOPPLED tumbled down
TOPSAIL **Naut.**
TOPSIDE the upper part
TOPSMAN bailiff; public hangman
TOPSOIL
TORBITE peat fuel
TORCHER torch-bearer; linkman
TORCHON geometric lace
TORGOCH a species of char **Z.**
TORMENT rag; rack; plague; harry
TORMINA griping pains **Med.**
TORNADO cyclone; hurricane; typhoon
TORPEDO ray fish; the tin-fish **Z.**
TORPENT torpid; inert
TORPIFY benumb
TORQUED wreathed (Her.)
TORREFY parch; roast; scorch
TORRENT stream; flood; current
TORSADE twisted scroll

TORSION twisting force
TORSIVE spiral
TORSTEN an iron ore **Min.**
TORTEAU red circlet (Her.)
TORTILE coiled; wreathed
TORTIVE twisted; tortile; tortuous
TORTRIX a moth genus **Z.**
TORTURE torment; agony; pang
TORULUS antenna socket **Z.**
TORVOUS grim; stern in aspect
TORYISM Conservatism
TOSSILY pertly
TOSSING (deciding); agitating; shaking
TOSS-POT toper
TOTALLY wholly; entirely; completely
TOTEMIC (totems); emblematic
TOTTERY shaky; unsteady
TOTTING adding up
TOUCHED sympathetic; impinged
TOUCHER a close call
TOUGHEN indurate; harden
TOUGHLY stubbornly; tenaciously
TOURACO African bird **Z.**
TOURING journeying
TOURISM co-ordinated travel
TOURIST tripper; excursionist
TOURNEY tournament
TOUSING teasing; worrying
TOUSLED unkempt; in disarray
TOUTING seeking custom
TOWARDS
TOWBOAT tug **Naut.**
TOWERED with towers
TOWIRON whaling toggle-iron
TOWLINE
TOWNISH urban
TOWPATH
TOWROPE
TOXEMIA blood poisoning **Med.**
TOXEMIC septicaemic **Med.**
TOXICAL poisonous
TOXODON extinct rhinoceros **Z.**
TOYSHOP
TOYSOME playful
TOYWORT shepherd's purse **B.**
TRACERY ornamental stonework
TRACHEA wind-pipe **Med.**
TRACHLE to draggle (Sc.)
TRACING a copy; traversing
TRACKED trailed; traversed
TRACKER a sleuth
TRACTOR mechanical plough
TRADE-IN part-exchange
TRADING commerce; barter
TRADUCE misrepresent; libel; slander
TRAFFIC intercourse; transport; deal
TRAGEDY drama; calamity
TRAIKET worn out (Sc.)
TRAILED followed; dragged; dogged
TRAILER tracker; towed vehicle

TRAINED proficient; skilled
TRAINEE man under instruction
TRAINER a coach
TRAIPSE to tramp
TRAITOR quisling; betrayer
TRAJECT ferry; tranect; project
TRAMCAR
TRAMMEL bird-net; compass; hamper
TRAMPED toured; walked; trudged
TRAMPER vagrant; stroller; hiker
TRAMPLE crush; spurn; squelch
TRAMPOT socket for a spindle
TRAMWAY
TRANCED in a dream; enraptured
TRANECT ferry; traject
TRANGLE small band (Her.)
TRANKUM a gew-gaw
TRANNEL wooden nail
TRANSIT conveyance; passage
TRANSOM cross-beam   **Naut.**
TRANTER pedlar
TRAPEZE swinging cross-bar
TRAPPED adorned; caught
TRAPPER setter of snares
TRASHED lopped; crushed; hindered
TRAVAIL toil; labour; affliction
TRAWLED fished
TRAWLER   **Naut.**
TRAYLED interwoven (Spens.)
TREACLE
TREACLY viscous and sweet
TREADER trampler
TREADLE pedal
TREASON treachery; disloyalty
TREATED entertained; doctored
TREATER negotiator
TREBLED tripled; threefold
TREDDLE a treadle (obs.)
TREEING cornering
TREFOIL (clover); (Arch.)
TREHALA Turkish manna   **B.**
TREKKED migrated
TREKKER (ox-wagons, S. Africa)
TRELLIS lattice work
TREMBLE quiver; shake; oscillate
TREMBLY tottery; unsteady
TREMOLO vibrato   **Mus.**
TRENAIL wooden nail
TRENDED tended; inclined; gravitated
TRENDLE a roller
TRENTAL 30 masses   **Eccl.**
TREPANG sea-slug   **Z.**
TRESSED curled
TRESSEL trestle; a movable framework
TRESTLE a support
TREVISS cross-beam
TRIABLE (jurisdiction)   **Law**
TRIADIC trivalent   **Chem.**
TRIATIC jumper stay   **Naut.**
TRIAXON with three axes

TRIBBLE paper drying frame
TRIBLET a goldsmith's mandril   **Tool**
TRIBUNE Roman magistrate; platform
TRIBUTE tax; impost; toll; offering
TRICEPS extensor muscle   **Med.**
TRICHAS American warblers   **Z.**
TRICING hauling; clewing   **Naut.**
TRICKED defrauded; hoaxed
TRICKER trickster
TRICKLE drip; ooze; percolate
TRICKLY trickling
TRICKSY artful; deft
TRICORN three-cornered
TRIDARN having three tiers
TRIDENT Neptune's sceptre
TRIDUAN every third day
TRIDUUM period of three days
TRIFLED dallied; toyed; played
TRIFLER philanderer; idler; fribbler
TRIFOLY trefoil   **B.**
TRIFORM triple form
TRIGAMY cf. bigamy
TRIGGED skidded; obstructed
TRIGGER a detent
TRIGLOT in three languages
TRIGRAM a triphthong; a trigraph
TRILABE surgical fork   **Med.**
TRILITH stone doorway
TRILLED warbled; quavered
TRILOGY a series of three dramas
TRIMERA type of beetle   **Z.**
TRIMMED clipped; balanced; rebuked
TRIMMER fishing float; time-server
TRINARY ternary; threefold
TRINDLE trundle; trickle
TRINGLE curtain rod
TRINITY   **Eccl.**
TRINKET small ornament
TRINKLE trickle or tinkle
TRIOLET poetic stanza
TRIONAL hypnotic drug   **Med.**
TRIONES 7 stars in Ursa Major
TRIPERY tripe-booth
TRIPLED trebled
TRIPLET three of a kind   **Mus.**
TRIPOLI polishing powder; diatomite
TRIPOLY Michaelmas daisy   **B.**
TRIPPED erred; slipped; stumbled
TRIPPER excursionist; dancer
TRIPSIS shampooing; pulverizing
TRIREME a galley   **Naut.**
TRISECT cut into three
TRISEME (tribrach)
TRISMUS lock-jaw; tetanus   **Med.**
TRISULA Siva's trident
TRITELY jejunely; hackneyed
TRITOMA red-hot poker   **B.**
TRITONE dissonant interval   **Mus.**
TRIUMPH exultation; success; ovation
TRIVIAL trifling; slight; paltry

TRIVIUM grammar; logic and rhetoric		**TUB-FISH** sapphirine gurnard	**Z.**
TROATED called like a buck		**TUBICEN** trumpeter	**Mus.**
TROCHEE long and short foot metre		**TUBULAR** hollow; fistular; capillary	
TROCHUS gastropod genus	**Z.**	**TUCK-BOX**	
TRODDEN trampled		**TUCKING** cramming; folding; gathering	
TROGGIN peddlery		**TUCK-OUT** tuck-in; blow-out	
TROLLED sang; fished; rambled		**TUEFALL** a pent-house	
TROLLER trolley; trolly		**TUESDAY**	
TROLLEY truck; metal pulley		**TUESITE** slate pencil material	**Min.**
TROLLOL sing; troll; trill		**TUFTING** adorning with tufts	
TROLLOP a slattern; a slut		**TUGBOAT**	**Naut.**
TROMMEL mining sieve		**TUGGING** lugging; pulling; hauling	
TROMPIL blast regulating device		**TUGHRIK** (Mongolia)	**Coin**
TRONAGE wool-tax		**TUITION** instruction; education	
TROOPED thronged; (the colours)		**TULCHAN** spoof calf	
TROOPER mounted man; ship	**Naut.**	**TULLIAN** (Tullius Cicero)	
TROPHIC (nutrition)		**TUMBLED** rumpled; fallen; twigged	
TROPICS (Cancer and Capricorn)		**TUMBLER** pigeon; glass; acrobat	**Z.**
TROPINE constituent of atropine	**Med.**	**TUMBREL** tumbril; two-wheeled cart	
TROPISM enforced turning movement		**TUMIDLY** pompously; turgidly; puffily	
TROPIST figurative speaker		**TUMPING** humping; carrying	
TROTTED		**TUMULAR** heaped	
TROTTER pig's foot		**TUMULUS** burial mound	
TROUBLE disturb; worry; trial; dolour		**TUNABLE** melodious; musical	
TROUNCE to larrup; castigate		**TUNABLY** harmoniously	
TROUPER strolling player		**TUNDISH** wine funnel	
TROUSSE set of instruments	**Med.**	**TUNEFUL** musical; dulcet	
TROWING trusting; believing		**TUNG-OIL** wood-oil	**B.**
TRUANCY vagrancy		**TUNICIN** animal cellulose	**Z.**
TRUCKED bartered; trafficked		**TUNICLE** small tunic	
TRUCKER exchange agent		**TUNMOOT** village council	
TRUCKLE roller; yield; submit		**TUNNAGE** (and poundage) wine tax	
TRUDGED walked wearily; tramped		**TUNNERY** tunny-netting area	
TRUDGEN a swimming stroke		**TUPPING** hammering; butting	
TRUFFLE an edible fungus	**B.**	**TURACIN** carmine	
TRUMEAU part of a wall		**TURAKOO** gaudy bird; plantain-eater	**Z.**
TRUMPED deceived; ruffed		**TURBARY** turf digging rights	
TRUMPET proclaim; blazon	**Mus.**	**TURBINE** rotary engine	
TRUNCAL main; principal		**TURCISM** Turkish mode of life	
TRUNDLE wheel; truck; to roll		**TURDINE** thrush-like	
TRUNDLE spool of golden thread		**TURFING** laying turf; swarding	
TRUSSED bound; tied up		**TURFITE** racing fan	
TRUSTED credited; confided		**TURGENT** swelling; distended; tumid	
TRUSTEE guardian; fiduciary		**TURGITE** a form of haemitite	**Min.**
TRUSTER an optimist; creditor		**TURKISH, TURKMEN** (Turkestan)	
TRYABLE triable	**Law**	**TURKOIS** turquoise	**Min.**
TRYPETA boring flies	**Z.**	**TURMOIL** tumult; ado; hubbub	
TRYPSIN pepsin	**Med.**	**TURNCAP** chimney cowl	
TRYPTIC peptic; digestive	**Med.**	**TURNERY** lathe work	
TRY-SAIL	**Naut.**	**TURNING** flexure; spinning; fermenting	
TRYSTED rendezvoused; appointed		**TURNKEY** prison warder	
TRYSTER tryst convener		**TURN-OUT** an equipage	
TSABIAN star-worshipper; sabian		**TURN-UPS** trouser legs	
TSANTSA head-shrinking technique		**TURPETH** purgative plant	**B.**
TSARINA Empress of Russia		**TURTLER** turtle-hunter	
TSARIST Russian Royalist		**TUSSIVE** afflicted with a cough	
T-SQUARE		**TUSSLED** struggled; fought; battled	
TUATERA tuatara; N. Z. lizard	**Z.**	**TUSSOCK** tuffet; tuft	
TUBBING mine shaft lining; bathing		**TUSSORE** coarse silk	
TUBBISH rotund	**Z.**	**TUTAMEN** a protection; a defence	

TUTANIA Britannia metal
TUTELAR protective
TUTENAG a Chinese alloy; zinc
TUTORED taught; educated; instructed
TUTULUS Etruscan head-dress
TUTWORK (mining); dead-work
TWADDLE verbiage; balderdash; prattle
TWANGED played the banjo   **Mus.**
TWANGLE to twang
TWANKAY green tea
TWANKED twanged; twangled
TWATTLE gabble
TWEAKED twitched; pinched
TWEEDLE (fiddle); wheedle
TWEELED twiller (Sc.)
TWEENIE a maid; tiny
TWEETER loudspeaker   **Acoustics**
TWELFTH
TWIBILL mattock; axe   **Tool**
TWIDDLE twist; tweedle
TWIGGED understood; observed
TWIGGEN of wicker
TWINGED twitched; pained
TWINING twisting; meandering; coiling
TWINKLE wink; glimmer; scintillate
TWINNED two at a time
TWINSET woollen combination garment
TWINTER beast, two winters old
TWIN-TOP (motoring)
TWIRLED span; rotated; whirled
TWIRLER spinner; twister
TWISTED spun; contorted; tangled
TWISTER a puzzle; perverter; tornado
TWISTLE twist; a wrench (Sc.)
TWISTOR computer memory device
TWITTED reproached; rallied; taunted
TWITTEN by-lane
TWITTER an upbraider; chirp; palpitate
TWIZZLE turn and twist
TWO-FOLD twi-fold; double
TWO-LINE size of printing type
TWONESS doubleness
TWOSOME twofold
TWOSTEP a dance
TWO-TIME double-cross   **Mus.**
TYLARUS padded hoof   **Z.**
TYLOPOD camel-footed
TYLOSIS eye-trouble   **Med.**
TYLOTIC (eye-inflammation)   **Med.**
TYMPANA ear-drums   **Med.**
TYMPANO timpano; a drum   **Mus.**
TYMPANY turgidity; flatulence   **Med.**
TYNWALD parliament (Isle of Man)
TYPE-BAR a line of type
TYPHOID a fever   **Med.**
TYPHOON cyclone; hurricane
TYPHOUS enteric   **Med.**
TYPICAL emblematic; characteristic
TYPONYM type-name

TYRANNY despotism; iron rule
TZARINA Tsarina (Russia)
TZIGANE gipsy (Hungary)

U

UBEROUS fruitful
UDALLER odaller; free-holder
UKULELE Hawaian guitar   **Mus.**
ULLALOO Irish lament
ULNARIA arm-bones   **Med.**
ULONCUS swollen gums   **Med.**
ULULANT wailing; sobbing
ULULATE howl; hoot
ULYSSES Odysseus; a wanderer
UMBERED tinged with umber
UMBONAL protuberant
UMBONES bosses on shields
UMBONIC humpy
UMBRAGE shade; resentment
UMBRERE helmet visor
UMBRIAN (Raphael)
UMBRINE a fish   **Z.**
UMBROSE shady; umbrageous
UMPIRED arbitrated; judged
UMPTEEN more than ten
UNACTED never staged
UNAGING immortal
UNAIDED single-handed
UNAIRED possibly damp; stuffy
UNALIST holding one benefice   **Eccl.**
UNAPTLY not à propos
UNARMED defenceless
UNASKED gratuitously
UNAWARE ignorant; uninformed
UNBAKED
UNBATED unblunted; non-stop
UNBAYED opened up
UNBEGUN not started
UNBLIND restore vision
UNBLOCK to clear; (cards)
UNBLOWN not sounded; in the bud
UNBORNE not carried
UNBOSOM freely disclose
UNBOUND loose
UNBOWED unsubdued
UNBRACE relax; free from tension
UNBRAID disentangle
UNBRUTE domesticate; tame
UNBUILT not yet constructed
UNBURNT unconsumed
UNCAGED released; freed
UNCANNY eerie; weird; mysterious
UNCARED untended; unheeded
UNCASED taken out; displayed
UNCEDED not transferred or granted
UNCHAIN free; let loose; unfetter
UNCHARM unspell; exorcise
UNCHARY heedless; not frugal
UNCINAL hook-shaped
UNCINUS small hook   **Med**

UNCIVIL incivil; impolite
UNCLASP unfasten; disconnect
UNCLEAN foul; dirty; leprous
UNCLEAR confused; unintelligible
UNCLING unclasp; disengage
UNCLOAK disrobe; unveil; unmask
UNCLOSE open; babbling
UNCLOUD free from obscurity
UNCOUTH boorish; rustic; rough
UNCOVER lay open; disclose
UNCROSS (the legs)
UNCROWN dethrone
UNCTION an anointing   **Eccl.**
UNCULAR avuncular
UNDATED waved
UNDEIFY remove a god
UNDERDO cook insufficiently
UNDERGO experience; bear; suffer
UNDIGHT to undress
UNDOING opening; unravelling; ruining
UNDRAPE strip; uncover
UNDRAWN not delineated
UNDRESS not full parade uniform
UNDRIED wet; green
UNEARED untilled (Shak.)
UNEARTH disclose; reveal; discover
UNEATEN not consumed
UNEQUAL varying; not uniform
UNEXACT inexact; inaccurate
UNFADED unwithered
UNFAITH infidelity
UNFENCE remove a hedge
UNFILED unrasped; (papers)
UNFITLY unsuitably; improperly
UNFIXED unsettled
UNFLESH reduce to a skeleton
UNFLUSH lose colour
UNFOUND still lost; not met with
UNFROCK deprive of office   **Eccl.**
UNFUMED not fumigated
UNFUSED not melted
UNFUZED (shells); (mines)
UNGIVEN not conceded
UNGLAZE remove the glass
UNGLOVE bare the hand
UNGLUED unstuck
UNGODLY sinful; impious; profane
UNGRATE ungrateful person
UNGUARD leave defenceless
UNGUENT an ointment   **Med.**
UNGULAR (hoofs; nails; etc.)   **Z.**
UNGYVED unfettered
UNHABLE incapable (Spens.)
UNHANDY awkward; clumsy
UNHAPPY sad; grievous; sorrowful
UNHARDY irresolute; delicate
UNHASTY slow; deliberate
UNHEARD inaudible; obscure
UNHEART to discourage (Shak.)
UNHEEDY careless; rash

UNHINGE to unsettle; derange
UNHIRED not engaged
UNHITCH loosen; unfasten
UNHIVED driven from shelter
UNHOARD dissipate; spend
UNHOPED unexpected
UNHORSE force to dismount
UNHOUSE evict
UNIAXAL uniaxial
UNICITY oneness; sameness
UNICORN a fabulous animal; oryx   **Z.**
UNIDEAL realistic; prosaic
UNIFIED united; merged
UNIFIER amalgamator; merger
UNIFOIL bearing only one leaf   **B.**
UNIFORM consistent; steady
UNITAGE measurement
UNITARY monistic; integral
UNITATE remainder after division
UNITING combining; concerting
UNITION conjunction
UNITIVE harmonising
UNITIZE to treat as one unit
UNJOINT disconnect
UNKEMPT uncombed; rough
UNKNOWN nameless; anonymous
UNLACED not done up; untied
UNLADEN unloaded; unloaded
UNLATCH to open
UNLEARN to forget
UNLEASH remove all constraint
UNLEAVE strip of leaves
UNLEVEL uneven; rough
UNLIMED freed from lime
UNLINED (paper); unruled
UNLIVED bereft of life (Shak.)
UNLOOSE unleash; unfasten
UNLOVED disliked
UNLUCKY ill-starred; hapless
UNLUSTY weak; infirm; sickly
UNLUTED unglued; uncemented
UNMANLY effeminate; cowardly
UNMARRY divorce
UNMEANT not intended
UNMETED not measured
UNMEWED set free; released
UNMIXED pure; unadulterated
UNMOIST dehydrated; dry; arid
UNMORAL immoral; licentious
UNMOULD change the form of
UNMOVED impassive; serene; quiet
UNNAMED anonymous
UNNERVE frighten; intimidate
UNNOBLE ignoble (Spens.)
UNNOTED undistinguished
UNOFTEN infrequently
UNOILED free from lubrication
UNORDER countermand
UNOWNED unacknowledged
UNPAINT efface

UNPANEL to unsaddle
UNPAVED uncobbled
UNPENAL without penalty
UNPERCH dislodge; unroost
UNPLACE displace
UNPLAIT unbraid; unravel
UNPLUMB not vertical
UNPLUME pluck
UNQUEEN dethrone
UNQUIET unease; restless
UNQUOTE end quotation
UNRAKED untilled
UNRAVEL disentangle; solve
UNREADY irresolute; slow
UNREEVE withdraw a rope   **Naut.**
UNRIVET undo; loosen; detach
UNROBED undressed
UNROUGH moderately smooth
UNROYAL unkingly
UNRULED uncontrolled; unlined
UNSATED rapacious; not satisfied
UNSCALY having no scales   **Z.**
UNSCREW untwist; unfasten
UNSENSE to stun
UNSEXED lacking femininity
UNSHELL unhusk; release
UNSHORN unshaven; unclipped
UNSHOWN not exhibited
UNSIGHT cricket
UNSIZED not stiffened
UNSLING release from slings
UNSLUNG not projected
UNSMOTE unsmitten
UNSNARL disentangle; unravel
UNSOLID fluid; unsubstantial
UNSOUND erroneous; defective
UNSPELL uncharm; exorcise
UNSPENT unexhausted; still moving
UNSPIED unobserved; undetected
UNSPIKE
UNSPILT not shed; not slopped
UNSPLIT undivided
UNSPOIL restore
UNSTACK
UNSTAID unsteady; unstable
UNSTATE deprive of dignity
UNSTEEL soften; disarm
UNSTICK ungum; tear free
UNSTRAP loosen
UNSTUCK loosened
UNSTUNG
UNSUNNY dull; shady
UNSWEAR recall an oath
UNSWEET inharmonious; acid
UNSWEPT unbrushed
UNSWORN not on oath
UNTAKEN left; relinquished
UNTAMED savage; barbaric
UNTAXED not charged
UNTHINK dismiss from the mind

UNTILED
UNTIRED unwearied
UNTOOTH extract
UNTRIED inexperienced; new
UNTRULY falsely; erroneously
UNTRUSS take apart; dissect
UNTRUTH lie; imposture; error
UNTUNED (wireless)   **Mus.**
UNTWINE untwist; unravel
UNTWIST disentangle
UNTYING unknotting
UNURGED unsolicited
UNUSUAL bizarre; queer; odd; rum
UNVEXED unharassed; untroubled
UNVOWED not bound by oath
UNWAGED unsalaried
UNWAYED trackless
UNWEARY unspent; unflagging
UNWEAVE unplait
UNWHIPT unbirched
UNWIRED
UNWITCH uncharm; unspell
UNWITTY lacking humour; prosaic
UNWOOED uncourted; unsolicited
UNWOUND untwined; uncoiled
UNWOVEN
UNWRUNG not galled
UNYOKED unrestrained (Shak.)
UNZONED unbelted
UPBLAZE to flare up
UPBORNE carried aloft
UPBOUND tied; restricted
UPBRAID rebuke; chide; taunt
UPBREAK shoot up
UPBURST outburst
UPCHEER encourage
UPCLIMB ascend
UPENDED stood on end
UPFIELD cricket
UPGAZED looked upwards
UPGRADE on the rise
UPHEAVE lift up; raise
UPHOARD secrete; amass; garner
UPLYING elevated
UPPLUCK gather up; uproot
UPRAISE to nurture; uplift
UPRIGHT vertical; honest; just
UPRISEN ascended
UPROUSE awaken
UPSHIFT change gear
UPSHOOT a sprout   **B.**
UPSPEAR shoot up straight
UPSTAGE (theatrical)
UPSTAND to stand up; to rise
UPSTARE upgaze
UPSTART parvenu; meadow saffron   **B.**
UPSURGE upswell
UPSWARM
UPSWEEP woman's coiffure
UPSWELL upsurge

UPTHROW an upheaval
UPTRACE to trace
UP-TRAIN train to London
UPTRILL sing high
UPWARDS upward; upwardly
UPWHIRL
URALITE fireproof material **Min.**
URANIAN astronomical
URANITE a green uranium ore **Min.**
URANIUM metallic element **Chem.**
URANOUS containing uranium **Chem.**
URGENCY importunity; stress
URINANT bent fish (Her.)
UROCYON American grey fox **Z.**
URODELE having a tail **Med.**
UROHYAL a tail-bone **Med.**
UROSOME caudal segment **Med.**
URSINAL ursine; bearish **Z.**
URTICAL (nettles) **B.**
USELESS vain; bootless; abortive
USHERED introduced; foreran;heralded
USITATE usually; customary
USUALLY normally; generally
USURPED arrogated; seized; assumed
USURPER a dictator
UTENSIL implement; vessel
UTILISE utilize; employ; apply
UTILITY usefulness
UTOPIAN imaginary; chimerical; ideal
UTOPISM unpractical hopefulness
UTOPIST optimist; visionary
UTRICLE small cell or bladder **Med.**
UTTERED issued; pronounced; said
UTTERER promulgator; (counterfeit)
UTTERLY absolutely; completely
UXORIAL dotingly fond of a wife

V

VACANCY void; emptiness; listlessness
VACATED left; abandoned
VACATOR a quitter
VACATUR annulment **Law**
VACCINE lymph **Med.**
VACHERY cow-house; dairy
VACUATE make a vacuum
VACUIST vacant believer
VACUITY emptiness; a void
VACUOLE minute cavity
VACUOUS void; unfilled
VAGITUS cry of a new-born child
VAGRANT vagabond; nomad; tramp
VAGUELY dimly; indefinitely
VAGUEST most uncertain
VAILING veiling; tipping
VAINEST most conceited
VALANCE draped border
VALENCE } combining power **Chem.**
VALENCY
VALERIC derived from valerian **B.**

VALIANT intrepid; gallant; doughty
VALIDLY with legal force
VALINCH cask tap
VALLARY (rampart)
VALLATE cup-shaped
VALONIA acorn-cup (Levant) **B.**
VALUING esteeming; appraising
VALVATE valvular
VALVLET } valvula; small valve
VALVULE
VAMOOSE to retire
VAMOSED decamped
VAMPING patching; bewitching **Mus.**
VAMPIRE blood-sucker; a bat **Z.**
VAMPLET spear buckler
VANADIC of vanadium **Chem.**
VANDYKE lace collar
VANESSA butterfly genus (Swift) **Z.**
VAN-FOSS a moat
VANILLA orchid; a flavour **B.**
VANNING mining operation
VANSIRE mongoose (Madagascar) **Z.**
VANTAGE (tennis); advantage
VANWARD vanguard
VAPIDLY inertly; insipidly; languidly
VAPOURS nervous malady **Med.**
VAPOURY hypochondriac
VAQUERO S. American cow-puncher
VARANUS monitor lizard **Z.**
VARIANT different; diverse
VARIATE to vary; alter
VARICES knotted veins **Med.**
VARIETY diversity; assortment
VARIOLA smallpox **Med.**
VARIOLE pitted
VARIOUS sundry; several; numerous
VARMINT vermin **Z.**
VARNISH to gloss over; palliate
VARSITY university
VARVELS vervels; rings on a hawk
VARYING differing; deviating; altering
VASTEST bulkiest; greatest
VATICAN papal power
VATTING mixing wines; customs
VAUDOIS Waldensian
VAULTED arched; sprang
VAULTER bounder
VAUNTED boosted; bragged
VAUNTER braggart; boaster
VAVASOR titled land-owner
VECTION porterage; convection
VEDANGA Veda commentary
VEDANTA Veda philosophy
VEDETTE vidette; mounted scout
VEERING shifting; changing; varying
VEGETAL vegetable; plant **B.**
VEHICLE (painting); car; conveyance
VEILING veil material
VEINAGE vein system **B., Med.**
VEINING ramification

VEINLET small vein	**VESPINE** wasp-like
VEINOUS (veins)	**VESTIGE** foot-print; trace; mark
VEINULE veinlet	**VESTING** fabric for vests; investing
VELAMEN a membrane **Med.**	**VESTLET** a sea-anemone **Z.**
VELARIA Roman amphitheatre awning	**VESTRAL** (vestry)
VELLING cutting turf	**VESTURE** clothing; garment; dress
VELLUMY like vellum	**VETERAN** experienced; seasoned
VELOURS plush fabric	**VETIVER** a fragrant grass **B.**
VELVETY smooth	**VETOING** prohibiting; barring; banning
VENALLY mercenary	**VETTING** examining
VENATIC sporting	**VETTURA** Italian cab
VENDACE a lake fish **Z.**	**VEXILLA** processional banners
VENDING selling; bartering	**VIADUCT** raised road
VENERER gamekeeper	**VIALFUL** a bottleful
VENISON deer meat	**VIARIAN** wayfarer
VENOMED poisoned	**VIBICES** feverish spots **Med.**
VENTAGE escape hole	**VIBRANT** resonant; undulous
VENTAIL helmet visor	**VIBRATE** oscillate; quiver; sway
VENTING releasing; uttering; emitting	**VIBRATO** tremolo **Mus.**
VENTOSE windy; breezy	**VIBRION** mobile bacterium **Med.**
VENTOSE Republican month (Fr.)	**VICEROY**
VENT-PEG a spile; spigot	**VICINAL** adjoining; near; neighbouring
VENTRAD ventrally **Z.**	**VICIOUS** depraved; sinful; defective
VENTRAL abdominal **Med.**	**VICTORY** success; mastery; triumph
VENTRIC ventral	**VICTRIX** a lady winner
VENTURE hazard; chance; dare	**VICTUAL** provide provisions
VERANDA verandah; open portico	**VICUGNA** vicuna; wild llama **Z.**
VERBENA vervain **B.**	**VIDENDA** things to be seen
VERBIFY verbalise	**VIDETTE** vedette; mounted scout
VERBOSE wordy; prolix; loquacious	**VIDIMUS** an inspection; summary
VERDANT unsophisticated; green	**VIDUAGE** ⎱ viduity; widowhood
VERDICT decision; finding; judgment	**VIDUATE** ⎰
VERDURE green growth	**VIDUOUS** widowed
VERGENT bordering; tending	**VIEWING** surveying; scanning; eyeing
VERGING inclining; adjacent to	**VIGONIA** llama wool fabric
VERIEST absolute; truest	**VILAYET** Turkish province
VERITAS French shipping bureau	**VILLAGE** hamlet; thorpe
VERMEIL a glaze; ormolu	**VILLAIN** miscreant; rascal; rogue
VERMIAN wormlike **Z.**	**VILLEIN** serf; villager
VERMILY vermilion	**VILLOSE** shaggy
VERMUTH vermouth; absinth	**VILLOUS** hairy
VERNANT spring-like; vernal	**VIMINAL** of twigs
VERNATE to flourish	**VINALIA** Roman wine festival
VERNIER measuring device	**VINASSE** wine dregs
VERONAL an opiate **Med.**	**VINEGAR** acetic acid; sour wine
VERRUCA a wart **B., Med.**	**VINGT-UN** card game
VERSANT conversant; familiar	**VINTAGE** gathering of grapes
VERSIFY relate in verse	**VINTNER** wine-seller
VERSING relating in rhyme	**VIOLATE** outrage; break; profane
VERSION an account; interpretation	**VIOLENT** fierce; vehement; furious
VERSUAL paragraphic	**VIOLINE** poisonous extract **B**
VERSUTE crafty; wily	**VIOLIST** viola player **Mus**
VERTIGO dizziness; giddiness **Med.**	**VIOLONE** double-bass **Mus**
VERULED ringed (Her.)	**VIRELAY** roundelay (Fr.)
VERULES concentric rings (Her.)	**VIRGATE** wand-like; slender & straigh
VERVAIN verbena **B.**	**VIRGATE** a quarter of a hide **Meas**
VERVELS varvels; rings on a hawk	**VIRGULE** small rod; a comma
VESANIA insanity **Med.**	**VIROSIS** viral infection **Med.**
VESICAL ⎱ bladder-like **Med.**	**VIRTUAL** potential; implicit
VESICLE ⎰ cavity or cell	**VISAGED** envisaged

VIS-A-VIS face to face
VISCERA internal organs   **Med.**
VISCOUS sticky; glutinous; tenacious
VISIBLE patent; evident; apparent
VISIBLY obviously; manifestly
VISITED stayed; chastised; afflicted
VISITOR visiter; a caller
VISNOMY physiognomy (Spens.)
VISORED masked
VIS-VIVA striking energy
VITALLY essentially
VITAMIN a food element
VITIATE to spoil; impair; debase
VITRAIN a type of coal   **Min.**
VITREUM eye-fluid   **Med.**
VITRICS glass-making
VITRIFY to glaze
VITRINA glass snails   **Z.**
VITRINE glass show case
VITRIOL sulphuric acid   **Chem.**
VITULAR (calf); (veal)
VIVENCY existence
VIVERRA civet genus   **Z.**
VIVIDLY animatedly; brilliantly
VIVIFIC enlivening
VIXENLY snappish
VOCABLE a word; a name
VOCALIC containing vowels
VOCALLY by voice
VOCODER synthetic speech device
VOCULAR vocal
VOETSAK begone ! (S. Africa)
VOGLITE uranium ore   **Min.**
VOICING expressing
VOIDING ejecting; emptying
VOIVODE, VAIVODE Polish governor
VOLABLE nimble-witted; volatile
VOLANTE Spanish vehicle
VOLAPUK universal language
VOLCANO eruptive mountain
VOLSUNG Odin's grandson
VOLTAGE (electrical)   **Meas.**
VOLTAIC galvanic
VOLUBLE having the gift of the gab
VOLUBLY glibly; fluently
VOLUMED bulky
VOLUSPA song of the sybil (Scand.)
VOLUTED with spiral scroll
VOTABLE enfranchised
VOUCHED warranted; attested
VOUCHEE warrantee   **Law**
VOUCHER a witness; a pass
VOWELLY full of vowels
VOYAGED cruised; traversed
VOYAGER ocean traveller
VULGATE authentic Latin Bible   **Eccl.**
VULPINE foxy; cunning
VULTURE carrion-eating bird   **Z.**
VULTURN Australian turkey   **Z.**

W

WABBLER a wobbler
WABSTER webster; weaver
WADABLE fordable
WADDING stuffing
WADDLED walked like a duck
WADDLER wobbly walker
WAD-HOOK an extractor   **Tool**
WADMOLL woollen cloth
WADSETT a mortgage   **Law**
WAENESS sadness (Sc.)
WAESOME woesome; woeful; pitiful
WAFERED sealed; secured
WAFTAGE transportation
WAFTING floating; airing; beckoning
WAFTURE waftage; wavure
WAGERED hazarded; risked; staked
WAGERER a better
WAGGERY sportive merriment
WAGGING vibrating; stirring
WAGGISH droll; facetious; jocular
WAGGLED wiggled; swayed
WAGONED carted; transported
WAGONER cart-driver
WAGSOME whimsical; witty
WAGTAIL bird; joinery   **Z.**
WAGWANT totter-grass   **B.**
WAHABEE primitive Moslem   **Eccl.**
WAILFUL mournful; sorrowful; grievous
WAILING bemoaning; lamenting
WAINAGE transport
WAISTED narrowed
WAISTER whaling greenhorn
WAITING attendance; biding; tarrying
WAIVING relinquishing; remitting
WAIVODE Polish governor
WAKEFUL alert; wary; vigilant
WAKEMAN watchman
WAKENED stimulated; excited
WAKENER a rouser; knocker-up
WALKING pedestrianism; hiking
WALK-OUT industrial strike; protest
WALLABA timber tree (Guiana)   **B.**
WALLABY young kangaroo   **Z.**
WALLACH Wallack; a Wallachian
WALL-EYE glaucoma   **Med.**
WALLING wall material
WALLOON Belgian dialect
WALL-RUE a fern   **B.**
WALTZED
WALTZER
WAMBLED rumbled
WAME-TOW belly-band
WAMPISH to flourish; to brandish (Sc.)
WAN-EYED languid; sad
WANGHEE a cane; a stick
WANGLED acquired by craft
WANHOPE despair

WANHORN a plant **B.**	**WAX-BEAN** butter-bean **B.**
WANNESS pallor; paleness	**WAXBILL** (weaver-bird) **Z.**
WANNISH sickly	**WAX-DOLL** poupée (Fr.)
WANTAGE deficiency; lack	**WAX-MOTH** (a bee scourge) **Z.**
WANTING absent; desiring; needing	**WAX-PALM** **B.**
WANTWIT a numskull; nitwit	**WAX-TREE** American gamboge tree **B.**
WAPACUT American snowy owl **Z.**	**WAXWING** a crested bird **Z.**
WARATAH Australian plant **B.**	**WAXWORK**
WARBLED quavered; trilled; carolled	**WAYBILL** a list (transport)
WARBLER a songster **Z.**	**WAYFARE** to walk
WARBLES saddle-sores; tumours	**WAYGONE** exhausted; wayworn
WARDAGE watch-tax	**WAYLAND** a legendary smith
WARDIAN botanist's case	**WAYLESS** pathless; trackless
WARDING repelling; fending; guarding	**WAY-MARK** sign-post
WARD-WIT warder's quittance	**WAY-POST** guide-post
WAREFUL wary; cautious; vigilant	**WAYSIDE**
WARFARE strife; hostilities	**WAYWARD** froward; wilful; unruly
WARHOOP war-cry; slogan	**WAYWISE** directional capacity
WARIEST most circumspect	**WAYWODE** waivode; Polish governor
WARISON a reward; a gift	**WAYWORN** exhausted; spent
WARLIKE belligerent; martial	**WEAKEST** puniest
WARLOCK wizard; a spell	**WEALDEN** (weald of Kent)
WARLORD Junker militarist	**WEALTHY** opulent; affluent; rich
WARMEST keenest; most ardent	**WEANING** alienating; detaching
WARMING heating	**WEARIED** fatigued; jaded; careworn
WARNING caution; notification; omen	**WEARIER** more jaded and tired
WARPATH hostile expedition	**WEARILY** tediously
WARPING twisting; distorting	**WEARING** exhausting
WARRANT authority; right; justify	**WEARISH** withered; washy
WARRING contending; striving	**WEASAND**⎫ wind-pipe; throat **Med.**
WARRIOR veteran fighter	**WEAZAND**⎭
WAR-RISK (insurance)	**WEATHER** climate; endure; overcome'
WAR-SCOT war-tax; a levy	**WEAVING** cloth-making
WARSHIP **Naut.**	**WEBBING** hempen fabric
WARSONG	**WEB-EYED** filmy-eyed **Med.**
WART-HOG an African ungulate **Z.**	**WEB-FOOT** **Z.**
WARWOLF military engine	**WEBSTER** wabster; a weaver
WARWORN battle-weary	**WEB-TOED**
WASH-DAY laundry day	**WEDDING** nuptials; espousal; marriage
WASHING ablution; rinsing	**WEDGING** a timber joint; compressing
WASH-OUT a failure	**WEDLOCK** matrimony
WASHPOT (Moab)	**WEEDERY** cf. fernery
WASHTUB	**WEEDING** eliminating; purging
WASP-FLY **Z.**	**WEE-FREE** Independent Liberal
WASPISH resentful; irritable	**WEEKDAY**
WASSAIL an occasion; punch	**WEEK-END**
WASTAGE dissipation	**WEENING** thinking; imagining
WASTING emaciation	**WEEPING** sobbing; crying; bewailing
WASTREL waif; a dud	**WEEVILY** full of weevils **Z.**
WATCHED guarded; tended; noted	**WEFTAGE** texture
WATCHER watchman	**WEIGHED** pondered; pressed; (anchor)
WATCHET light blue	**WEIGHER** weighing machine
WATERED wavy; moistened; sprinkled	**WEIGH-IN** pre-contest weight check
WATERER irrigator	**WEIGHTY** ponderous; onerous; grave
WATTLED (hurdles); (cocks-comb)	**WEIRDER** more fantastic
WAULING howling; caterwauling	**WEIRDLY** eerily; uncannily
WAVELET a ripple	**WELAWAY** alas!
WAVERED faltered; swayed	**WELCHER** welsher; absconding bookie
WAVERER hesitator	**WELCOME** salutation; greeting
WAVESON flotsam	**WELDING** welded joint

WELFARE comfort; prosperity; weal	**WHEWING** whistling with surprise
WELLING springing; gushing	**WHEYISH** like whey
WELL-MET all hail!; welcome!	**WHEY-TUB** cream-tub
WELL-OFF well-to-do; prosperous	**WHIFFED** puffed
WELL-SET firmly set	**WHIFFER** a puffer
WELL-WON honestly gained	**WHIFFET** whipper-snapper
WELSHED decamped; absconded	**WHIFFLE** a flute; prevaricate **Mus.**
WELSHER absconding bookie	**WHILERE** recently
WELTING shoe-edging	**WHILING** loitering; passing the time
WENDING wandering; strolling	**WHIMPER** whine; cry; moan
WENDISH the Wend dialect	**WHIMPLE** wimple; head-dress
WENLOCK limestone **Min.**	**WHIMSEY** whimsy; a caprice; crotchet
WENNISH cyst-like	**WHINGER** dirk; hangar (Sc.)
WERGILD ⎫ fine for murder;	**WHINING** complaining; snivelling
WERGOLD ⎭ blood money	**WHIPCAT** a tailor
WERWOLF werewolf; wolf-man	**WHIPPED** lashed; beaten; thrashed
WEST-END fashionable; stylish	**WHIPPER** a flagellant
WESTERN occidental	**WHIPPET** greyhound; small tank **Z.**
WESTING westerly	**WHIP-RAY** a sea-fish **Z.**
WET-DOCK	**WHIPSAW** **Tool**
WETNESS dampness; humidity	**WHIP-TOP** whipping top
WET-SHOD with wet feet	**WHIRLED** span; spun; revved
WETTEST supersaturated	**WHIRRED** whurred; rotated
WET-TIME wages for rainy days	**WHIRLER** a whirligig
WETTING moistening; drenching	**WHIRRET** wherrit; vex; a blow
WETTISH rather rainy	**WHISHED** whizzed
WHACKED beaten; defeated; smitten	**WHISKER**
WHACKER of large size; formidable	**WHISKET** a basket
WHAISLE wheeze (Sc.)	**WHISKEY** whisky; a light dog-cart
WHALERY whale-fishing industry	**WHISPER** murmur; disclose
WHALING thrashing	**WHISTLE** boson's pipe **Naut.**
WHANGEE bamboo cane **B.**	**WHISTLY** silently
WHAPPED struck; fluttered	**WHITELY** palely; pallidly
WHARFED brought to shore **Naut.**	**WHITEST** purest; lightest
WHARVES quays; docks	**WHITHER** to which place
WHATNOT a piece of furniture	**WHITING** white-wash; a fish **Z.**
WHATTEN what kind of (Sc.)	**WHITISH** near white
WHEATEN **B.**	**WHITLOW** an abscess **Med.**
WHEEDLE to coax; to cajole	**WHITSUL** curds and whey
WHEELED with wheels	**WHITSUN** Whitsuntide
WHEELER shaft-horse; cyclist **Z.**	**WHITTAW** a saddler
WHEELER wheel-wright	**WHITTLE** shawl; to cut; pare
WHEEZED breathed asthmatically	**WHIZZED** tore through the air
WHEEZLE whaizle; whaisle; obtain	**WHIZZER** a fast one
WHELKED ridged	**WHOEVER**
WHELPED littered	**WHOMBLE** whemmle; whummle
WHEMMLE an upset (Sc.)	**WHOMMLE** confusion; overwhelm
WHEREAS	**WHOOBUB** hubbub
WHEREAT	**WHOOPEE** a joyous cry; a revel
WHEREBY	**WHOOPED** hooted; yelled; shouted
WHEREIN	**WHOOPER** the hooper swan **Z.**
WHEREOF	**WHOPPED** beat; defeated
WHEREON	**WHOPPER** whacker
WHERESO	**WHORLED** spiral; convoluted
WHERETO	**WICKING** cannoning when curling
WHERRET to worrit; a blow	**WICKIUP** shelter (Amer. Indian)
WHETHER	**WIDENED** extended; broadened
WHETILE woodpecker **Z.**	**WIDENER** an enlarger; a reamer
WHETTED stimulated; urged	**WIDGEON** migratory duck **Z.**
WHETTER a sharpener	**WIDOWED** bereaved; viduous

WIDOWER	**WITLOOF** chicory **B.**
WIELDED handled; plied; governed	**WITNESS** attest; testimony; see
WIELDER a controller; user	**WITTIER** droller; more facetious
WIGGERY false hair	**WITTILY** jocularly; humorously
WIGGING a scolding; reprimand	**WITTING** wotting; knowing
WIGGLED waggled	**WITWALL** golden oriole **Z.**
WIGGLER a wriggler	**WIZENED** shrivelled; wimpled
WIGHTLY courageously; nimbly	**WOBBLED** deviated
WIGLESS	**WOBBLER** wabbler; vacillator
WILD-ASS the onager **Z.**	**WOESOME** woeful; waesome
WILDCAT speculative; strike (indust.) **Z.**	**WOLF-CUB** young Boy Scout **Z.**
WILDEST most turbulent and rash	**WOLF-DOG** sheep-dog **Z.**
WILDING growing wild; crab-apple **B.**	**WOLFISH** wolvish; rapacious; ravenous
WILDISH rather wild	**WOLFKIN** young wolf
WILD-OAT youthful crop **B.**	**WOLF-NET** large fishing net
WILIEST craftiest; pawkiest	**WOLFRAM** tungsten **Chem.**
WILLING inclined; devising	**WOLSUNG** grandson of Odin
WILLOCK young guillemot **Z.**	**WOMANED** chaperoned
WILLOWY slender; pliant	**WOMANLY** feminine
WILSOME wilful; stubborn; wayward	**WOMMERA**⎫ spear throwing
WILTING drooping; fading	**WOOMERA**⎬ stick (Australian)
WIMBERY whortleberry **B.**	**WONGSHY** yellow dye (Chinese)
WIMBLED drilled; bored	**WOOD-ANT** the red ant **Z.**
WIMBREL whimbrel; small curlew **Z.**	**WOODCUT** a print from a wooden block
WIMPLED puckered; wrinkled	**WOOD-GOD** sylvan deity
WINCHED hoisted; hauled up	**WOODMAN** a forester
WINDAGE clearance	**WOODNUT** hazel-nut **B.**
WINDBAG a would-be orator	**WOOD-OIL** balsam **B.**
WIND-EGG an addled egg **Z.**	**WOOD-OWL** brown owl **Z.**
WIND-GUN air-gun	**WOOD-TAR** a distillate **Chem.**
WINDIER breezier; more alarmed	**WOOD-TIN** tin-stone **Min.**
WINDILY breezily; panic-struck	**WOOLDED** roped; lashed
WINDING tortuous; changing; scenting	**WOOLDER** lashing stick
WINDROW hay or peat in rows	**WOOLFAT** lanolin **Z.**
WINDSOR Royal House	**WOOLLEN**
WINEBAG wine-skin; a tippler	**WOOLMAN** wool dealer
WINEFAT a vat	**WOOLSAW** evil spirit (C. American)
WINESAP American winter apple **B.**	**WOOLSEY** a dress material
WING-ICE (ice on aircraft)	**WOORALI**⎫ wourali; curari;
WINGING flying; wounding	**WOORARA**⎬ arrow poison
WINGLET bastard wing **Z.**	**WORDILY** verbose; prolix; garrulous
WINKERS flashing lights (motoring)	**WORDING** phrasing; expressing
WINKING nictitating; conniving at	**WORDISH** wordy; loquacious
WINNING charming; acquiring; getting	**WORKBAG**
WINNOCK windock; a window (Sc.)	**WORKBOX**
WINSOME engaging; taking; seductive	**WORKDAY**
WINTERY wintry; hyemal	**WORKING** fermenting; drudging
WIREMAN linesman	**WORKMAN** a toiler; operative
WIREWAY telpherage; aerial transport	**WORK-OUT** gymnastic exercise
WIRIEST leanest; toughest	**WORKSHY** allergic to labour
WISE-GUY a Solomon; a Solon	**WORLDLY** earthly; secular; mundane
WISHFUL desirous; eager and anxious	**WORMIAN** (skull bones) **Med.**
WISTFUL pensive; meditative; yearning	**WORMING** (rope); squirming
WISTITI marmoset **Z.**	**WORN-OUT** exhausted
WITCHED bewitched; charmed	**WORRIED** harassed; bothered; troubled
WITCHEN mountain ash; rowan **B.**	**WORRIER** a worrit; a hector
WITHERS (horse's neck)	**WORSHIP** adoration; idolize; venerate
WITHIES willow twigs **B.**	**WORSTED** wool yarn
WITHOUT outside; except; lacking	**WOULD-BE** aspiring
WITLESS indiscreet; thoughtless	**WOULDST**

WOUNDED injured; hurt; damaged
WOUNDER a pain-giver
WRANGLE brangle; bicker; brawl
WRAPPED covered; swathed; wound
WRAPPER envelope; scarf
WRAULED ⎫ caterwauled;
WRAWLED ⎭ howled
WREAKED inflicted
WREAKER an avenger
WREATHE entwine; to garland
WREATHY twisted; interlaced
WRECKED shattered; ruined; destroyed
WRECKER saboteur; blighter
WREN-TIT Californian bird   **Z.**
WRESTED wrenched; forced; pulled
WRESTER a twister
WRESTLE grapple; strive; contend
WRICKED ricked; sprained
WRIGGLE worm; squirm; writhe
WRIGGLY tortuous; sinuous
WRINGER a mangle
WRINKLE crinkle; pucker
WRINKLY creased; rumpled
WRITE-UP flattering-notice
WRITHED squirmed; wriggled
WRITHEN contorted; coiled
WRITHLE to wrinkle; to shrivel
WRITING caligraphy; penmanship
WRITTEN inscribed; indited
WRONGED maltreated; oppressed
WRONGER a wrong-un; evil-doer
WRONGLY falsely; unjustly
WROUGHT worked; effected
WRYBILL a New Zealand plover   **Z.**
WRYNECK (wood-pecker)   **Z.**
WRYNESS crookedness
WUZZENT wizened (Sc.)
WYANDOT Iroquoian Indian; fowl   **Z.**
WYCH-ELM witch-elm   **B.**

X

XANTHIC an acid; yellow   **Chem.**
XANTHIN yellow extract   **B.**
XENURUS genus of armadillos   **Z.**
XERASIA ⎫ hair disease; dryness of
XEROSIS ⎭   the scalp   **Med.**
XERODES dry tumour   **Med.**
XEROTES ⎫ dryness of the body   **Med.**
XEROTIC ⎭
XIPHIAS sword-fish genus   **Z.**
XIPHIAS a Southern constellation
XIPHOID ensiform
X-RAYING (Rontgen rays)   **Med.**
XYLOPIA bitter plants   **B.**
XYLOLIN wood pulp fabric

Y

YACHTED cruised
YACHTER yachtsman
YAHWISM worship of Jehovah   **Eccl.**
YAHWIST Jehovist   **Eccl.**
YAMADOU nutmeg oil   **B.**
YANKING jerking; heaving; hauling
YAPPING yelping; yauping
YAPSTER a yelper
YARDAGE yard dues
YARD-ARM   **Naut.**
YARDING enclosing
YARD-MAN (farm); (railway)
YARNING narrating
YARRING snarling
YARRISH rough dry taste
YASHMAK Moslem woman's double veil
YATAGAN Turkish knife
YAUPING yelping
YAWLING howling; screaming
YAWNING gaping
YEANING ⎫ bringing forth young;
YEENING ⎭ lambing
YEARNED desirous; grieved
YEGGMAN criminal tramp (U.S.A.)
YELDRIN yellow bunting   **Z.**
YELLING howling
YELLOCH to yell; a yell (Sc.)
YELLOWS an animal disease
YELLOWY yellowish; sallowy
YELPING yauping; yapping
YERKING chucking; jerking
YESTERN (yesterday)
YEW-TREE (bow-wood)   **B.**
YEZIDIS devil worshippers
YIDDISH Jewish dialect
YIELDED rendered; resigned; conceded
YIELDER capitulator; abdicator
YODELER Tyrol singer
YOGHURT fermented milk
YOICKED shouted Yoicks
YOLDING ⎫ yorling; yellow-hammer **Z.**
YOLDRIN ⎭
YORKIST (War of Roses)
YOUGHAL needle-point lace
YOUNGER not so old
YOUNGLY inexperienced; juvenile
YOUNKER a stripling; youngster
YOUTHLY youthful; immature
YOWLING howling; bawling
YPERITE poison gas   **Chem.**
YTTRIUM a metallic element   **Chem.**
YULE-LOG

Z

ZABAISM star worship
ZABTIEH Zaptieh; Turkish policeman
ZADKIEL (almanac)
ZALACCA dragon's blood palm   **B.**
ZAMOUSE W. African ox   **Z.**
ZANELLA umbrella fabric
ZANJERO irrigation officer
ZANONIA cucumber   **B.**
ZANYING fooling
ZANYISM buffoonery
ZAPATEO shoe dance (S. Amer.)
ZAPHARA sky blue dye used in pottery
ZAREEBA zareba; stockade
ZARNICH realgar; orpiment   **Min.**
ZEALANT a zealot; enthusiast; bigot
ZEALFUL zealous; enthusiastic; eager
ZEALOUS fervent; ardent; fervid
ZEBRASS a cross-breed; zebra & ass   **Z.**
ZEBRINE zebra type   **Z.**
ZEBRULA (zebra and horse)   **Z.**
ZEDOARY aromatic root   **B.**
ZEMSTVO Russian local assembly
ZEOLITE aluminium silicate   **Min.**
ZESTFUL piquant; eager; keen
ZESTING flavouring; relishing
ZETETIC a seeker; a Pyrrhonist
ZEUXITE a silicate of aluminium   **Min.**
ZIMOCCA bath-sponge
ZINCATE zinc oxide   **Chem.**
ZINCIFY coat with zinc
ZINCITE red zinc ore   **Min.**
ZINCODE } positive pole
ZINCOID } electrode; anode
ZINCOUS (zinc)
ZINCALI Spanish gipsies
ZINGARI (cricket); gipsies (It.)
ZINGARO zingane; zingano (It.)
ZIONISM Jewish Nationalism
ZIONIST
ZIPCORD parachute release cord
ZIPHIUS sword-fish genus   **Z.**

ZIPPING pinging; whizzing; fastening
ZITHERN cithara   **Mus.**
ZITHERN or zither   **Mus.**
ZIZANIA aquatic grasses; (rice)   **B.**
ZOARIUM polyzoan   **Z.**
ZOCCOLO square base (arch.)
ZOILEAN supercritical
ZOILISM carping criticism
ZOILIST a caviller
ZOISITE a silicate; an epidote   **Min.**
ZOLAISM excessive naturalism
ZONALLY girdling
ZONULAR belted
ZONULET small girdle
ZONURUS saurian genus   **Z.**
ZOOECIA polyp cells   **Z.**
ZOOGAMY reproduction
ZOOGENY }
ZOOGONY } zoological origins   **Z.**
ZOOIDAL animal-like   **Z.**
ZOOLITE }
ZOOLITH } a fossil animal   **Min. Z.**
ZOOLOGY   **Z.**
ZOOMING flying low
ZOONITE articulated segment
ZOONOMY natural laws
ZOOTAXY systematic zoology
ZOOTOMY animal anatomy
ZOPISSA pitch used medicinally   **Med.**
ZORGITE a metallic ore   **Min.**
ZORILLA }
ZORILLE } American skunk   **Z.**
ZORRINO }
ZOTHECA alcove (Greek)
ZUFFOLO Italian flute   **Mus.**
ZURLITE a Vesuvian mineral   **Min**
ZYGAENA a shark genus   **Z**
ZYGOSIS conjugation   **Z**
ZYMOGEN a fermentor   **Chem**
ZYMOSIS inflammation   **Med**
ZYMOTIC bacteriological   **Med**
ZYMURGY fermentation   **Chem**

A

AARD-VARK ant-bear (S. Africa)   **Z.**
AARD-WOLF African wolf   **Z.**
AARONITE Hebrew priest   **Eccl.**
ABACTION cattle-theft; rustling
ABACULUS counting-frame; tablet
ABASHING humiliating; shaming
ABATABLE reducible; alleviable
ABAT-JOUR sky-light; reflector
ABATTOIR slaughter-house
ABAT-VOIX canopy over pulpit   **Eccl.**
ABBATESS abbess; Lady Superior   **Eccl.**
ABBATIAL under abbey control   **Eccl.**
ABDALAVI Egyptian musk melon   **B.**
ABDERIAN given to laughter
ABDERITE a Thracian; Democrites
ABDICANT renouncing; an abdicator
ABDICATE resign; cede; renounce
ABDITORY secret repository   **Eccl.**
ABDUCENT retracting; separating
ABDUCING abducting; kipnapping   **Law**
ABDUCTED removed; took by fraud
ABDUCTOR kidnapper; a muscle   **Med.**
ABELIANS ⎱ a sect practising
ABELITES ⎰ marriage chastity (Abel)
ABELMOSK Syrian mallow   **B.**
ABERDEEN a terrier   **Z.**
ABERRANT abnormal; rambling
ABERRATE deviate; diverge; wander
ABERRING straying; digressing
ABETMENT aiding and abetting   **Law**
ABETTING conniving; encouraging
ABEYANCE suspension; dormancy
ABEYANCE cessation; contemplation
ABHORRED hated; loathed; detested
ABHORRER Tory nickname, A.D. 1680
ABIDANCE abode; dwelling; habitation
ABIETENE abietine; balsam   **B.**
ABIOGENY spontaneous generation
ABJECTLY servilely; despicably
ABJURING apostacy; forswearing
ABLATION removal; attrition
ABLATIVE the sixth case in Latin
ABLEGATE despatch; depute; delegate
ABLEGATE a Papal envoy   **Eccl.**
ABLENESS ability; skill, vigour
ABLEPSIA ablepsy; blindness   **Med.**
ABLOCATE hire; lease; let
ABLUTION purification; baptism   **Eccl.**
ABLUVION water-deposited detritus
ABNEGATE deny; adjure; renounce
ABNODATE untie; remove the knots
ABNORMAL odd; irregular; monstrous
ABOCOCKE peaked cap of 15th century
ABOMASUS abomasum; cow's stomach
ABORTING miscarrying; frustrating
ABORTION a hideosity; vain effort
ABORTIVE premature; ineffectual
ABRADANT disintegrator; scraper

ABRADING grinding; abrasing; fraying
ABRASION surface wound; attrition
ABRASIVE scratchy; gritty; rough
ABRASTOL a preservative   **Chem.**
ABRIDGED epitomized; curtailed
ABROGATE cancel; repeal; quash
ABRUPTED rent; torn asunder
ABSCISSA an axial line in geometry
ABSENTED played truant
ABSENTEE deliberate duty dodger
ABSENTLY dreamily; inattentively
ABSINTHE wormwood; French liqueur **B**
ABSOLUTE pure; despotic; supreme
ABSOLVED acquitted; excused
ABSOLVER a pardoner; forgiver
ABSONANT irrational; discordant
ABSONOUS incongruous; out of tune
ABSORBED imbibed; preoccupied
ABSTERGE purge; wipe away
ABSTRACT detach; purloin; abstruse
ABSTRACT gist; summary; epitomize
ABSTRUSE recondite; occult; obscure
ABSURDLY irrationally; foolishly
ABUNDANT profuse; plentiful; copious
ABUSABLE violable; misapplicable
ABUTILON plant genus; the jute   **B.**
ABUTMENT an arch support; adjacency
ABUTTALS estate boundaries   **Law**
ABUTTING bordering; alongside
ACADEMIC scholastic; literary
ACALEPHA hydrozoa (jelly-fish)   **Z.**
ACANTHUS a 'capital' plant   **B.**
ACARDIAC heartless
ACARIDAE mites; ticks, etc.   **Z.**
ACARPOUS sterile; barren   **B.**
ACAUDATE tailless; acaudal   **Z.**
ACAULOUS acauline; stalkless   **B.**
ACCEDING complying; consenting
ACCENSOR R.C. candle-trimmer   **Eccl.**
ACCENTED stressed; emphasized
ACCENTOR the hedge-sparrow   **Z.**
ACCENTOR leading singer   **Mus.**
ACCEPTED admitted; acknowledged
ACCEPTER ⎱ the recipient of a
ACCEPTOR ⎰ Bill of Exchange
ACCIDENT mischance; fortuity; hap
ACCLINAL sloping; atilt
ACCOLADE (knighthood); an embrace
ACCOLENT neighbour; borderer
ACCOLLED collared (heraldic term)
ACCORDED harmonized; granted
ACCOSTED hailed; greeted; addressed
ACCOUNTS recorded transactions
ACCOUPLE to link together
ACCOUTRE dress in military array
ACCREDIT authorize; empower; entrust
ACCRETED grew; increased
ACCROACH usurp; encroach
ACCRUING accumulating; resulting
ACCURACY precision; exactness; truth

L

ACCURATE correct; unerring
ACCURSED execrable; doomed
ACCUSANT informer; accuser   **Law**
ACCUSING charging; impeaching
ACCUSTOM habituate; familiarize
ACELDEMA the field of blood (Hebrew)
ACENTRIC out of centre
ACEPHALA oyster genus   **Z.**
ACERBATE exasperate; embitter
ACERBENT caustic; astringent
ACERBITY bitterness; sour taste
ACERVATE clustered
ACESCENT turning sour
ACETATED (acetic acid)   **Chem.**
ACHENIUM single-seeded fruit   **B**
ACHERSET 8 bushel measure   **Meas.**
ACHEWEED gout-weed   **B.**
ACHIEVED won; attained; perfected
ACHIEVER a performer; an executant
ACHILOUS lipless   **B.**
ACHIRITE dioptase   **Min.**
ACHROITE tourmaline   **Min.**
ACICULAE spikes and prickles   **B., Z.**
ACICULAR needle-shaped
ACIDIFIC producing acid   **Chem.**
ACIDNESS bitterness; tartness
ACIDOSIS acidity   **Med.**
ACIERAGE steel electro-plating
ACIERATE turn into steel
ACNESTIS part of spine   **Z.**
ACOEMETI religious community
ACONITIC (wolf's-bane, monk's-hood) **B.**
ACORN-CUP   **B.**
ACOUSTIC relating to sound
ACQUAINT notify; apprize; teach
ACQUIRED scrounged; won; procured
ACRIDIAN locust   **Z.**
ACRIDITY pungency; harshness
ACRIMONY sharpness of temper
ACRITUDE corrosive quality
ACROATIC esoteric; (oral instruction)
ACROLITH statue with wooden body
ACROSTIC word puzzle in verse
ACROTISM lack of pulsation   **Med.**
ACTINISM effect of light rays
ACTINIUM radio-active element **Chem.**
ACTIVATE to move to activity
ACTIVELY energetically; sedulously
ACTIVISM practical idealism
ACTIVIST production promoter (indust.)
ACTIVITY agility; alertness
ACTUALLY really; as a fact
ACTUATED influenced; set in motion
ACUITION accentuation
ACULEATE spiky; pointed   **B.**
ACUTANCE clarity of enlargement **Photo.**
ADAMITIC Adamic; nudistic
ADAPTING adjusting; suiting
ADAPTIVE adaptable; conformable
ADDEEMED adjudged; considered

ADDENDUM adjunct; appendix
ADDER-FLY dragon-fly   **Z.**
ADDICTED wont; prone; inclined
ADDITION accession; summation
ADDITIVE additional; further   **Chem.**
ADDORSED back to back (Her.)
ADDUCENT retracting (muscles)   **Med.**
ADDUCING citing; alleging
ADDUCTOR a muscle   **Med.**
ADENITIS } inflammation of
ADENOIDS } the nasal glands   **Med.**
ADEPTION attainment; perfection
ADEQUACY sufficiency; fitness
ADEQUATE suitable; condign
ADFECTED compounded
ADHERENT partisan; adhesive
ADHERING cohering; cleaving
ADHESION coalescence; attachment
ADHESIVE tenacious; gummy
ADIANTUM maiden-hair fern   **B.**
ADJACENT contiguous; close by
ADJECTED added to; joined
ADJOINED connected; neighbouring
ADJUDGED awarded; deemed
ADJURING charging on oath   **Law**
ADJUSTER arranger; fitter
ADJUTAGE tubular connection
ADJUTANT assistant; regimental officer
ADJUTANT Indian scavenging stork **Z.**
ADJUTRIX lady help
ADJUVANT helping; intensifier   **Med.**
ADMIRING respecting; marvelling
ADMITTED included; conceded
ADMIXING mingling with
ADMONISH warn; reprove; exhort
ADOPTING choosing; embracing
ADOPTION formal acceptance
ADOPTIVE selective
ADORABLE reverential; venerable
ADORABLY worshipfully; devotedly
ADORNING embellishing; decking
ADROITLY dextrously; adeptly
ADSCRIPT conscript; postscript
ADSORBED condensed
ADULARIA moonstone   **Min.**
ADULATED lauded; flattered
ADULATOR sycophant; yes-man
ADULTERY ex-marital cohabitation
ADUSTION cauterization   **Med.**
ADVANCED in the van; lent; marched
ADVANCER promoter
ADVENING acceding
ADVERTED drew attention to
ADVISING counselling; notifying
ADVISORY hortative
ADVOCACY defence; support
ADVOCATE barrister; recommend **Law**
ADVOWSON patronage of benefice **Eccl.**
ADYNAMIA loss of vitality   **Med.**
ADYNAMIC slack; lifeless; listless

AEGROTAT medical certificate **Med.**
AERARIAN voteless Roman freeman
AERATING charging with gas
AERATION gasification
AERIALLY ethereally
AERIFIED inflated
AERIFORM unsubstantial
AEROBOMB a bomb
AEROCYST sea-weed air cell **B.**
AERODART dart dropped by airman
AERODYNE aircraft **Aeron.**
AEROFOIL lifting surface
AEROGRAM wireless message; letter
AEROLITE⎫ meteoric stone;
AEROLITH⎭ meteorite **Min.**
AEROLOGY meteorology
AERONAUT airman; balloonist
AEROSTAT barrage balloon
AESCULIN horse-chestnut extract **B.**
AESTHETE professed beauty lover
AESTIVAL estival; (summer)
AFFECTED moved; unnatural; insincere
AFFEERED fixed; confirmed
AFFERENT conducting inwards **Med.**
AFFIANCE confidence; betroth
AFFINAGE metal refining
AFFINING refining; purifying
AFFINITY relationship; attraction
AFFIRMED confirmed; ratified
AFFIRMER testifier; a Quaker **Eccl.**
AFFIXING attaching; connecting
AFFLATUS inspiration; ecstasy
AFFLUENT a tributary; wealthy
AFFORCED ravished
AFFORDED yielded; bore the cost
AFFOREST convert into forest
AFFRIGHT sudden terror; frighten
AFFRONTE confronting (heraldic)
AFFUSING spraying; bedewing
AFFUSION baptismal sprinkling **Eccl.**
AFTER-ALL in conclusion
AFTER-WIT wisdom after the event
AGAL-WOOD aloes-wood **B.**
AGAR-AGAR seaweed **B.**
AGASTRIC stomachless **Z.**
AGATIZED turned into agate
AGEDNESS antiquity; senility
AGENESIS imperfect development
AGENTIAL acting through an agent
AGEUSTIA loss of taste **Med.**
AGGRIEVE give sorrow; injure
AGIOTAGE (stock-jobbing)
AGISTAGE tax on pasturage **Law**
AGITABLE excitable; tremulous
AGITATED roused; instigated
AGITATOR agent provocateur
AGLIMMER shimmering
AGNATION male descent **Law**
AGNOSTIC humanist; positivist
AGONISED tormented

AGRAPHIA inability to write **Med.**
AGRARIAN relating to land
AGREEING matching; tallying
AGRESTIC rustic; unpolished
AGRIMONY liver-wort **B.**
AGRONOMY scientific farming
AGRYPNIA insomnia **Med.**
AGUE-CAKE a tumour **Med.**
AGUE-TREE sassafras tree **B.**
AIGRETTE egret's plume **Z.**
AIGUILLE spire; peak; rock-drill
AILLETTE ailette; epaulet
AIR-BORNE no earthly connection
AIR-BRAKE brake operated by air
AIR-BRICK ventilating brick
AIRBRUSH fixative spray
AIR-BUILT chimerical; baseless
AIRCRAFT flying machines
AIR-DRAIN an airspace (arch.)
AIR-DRAWN imaginary; visionary
AIREDALE terrier **Z.**
AIRFIELD landing ground
AIR-FLEET
AIRFRAME fusilage **Aeron.**
AIRGRAPH air mail letter; microfilm
AIRINESS lightness; gaiety
AIR-LINER
AIR-PILOT a flyer; a navigator
AIRPLANE aeroplane
AIRPOISE aneroid barometer
AIR-POWER
AIRSCREW propeller
AIRSHAFT ventilation shaft
AIRSPACE cubic content
AIR-STOVE heating apparatus
AIR-STRIP landing strip
AIRTIGHT impermeable to air
AIRTRUNK ventilating shaft
ALACRITY briskness; agility; readiness
ALARM-GUN signal of distress
ALARMING calling to arms; ominous
ALARMIST Jeremiah; panic-monger
ALBACORE⎫ tunny-fish; **Z.**
ALBICORE⎭ species of thynnus
ALBANIAN (Albania)
ALBINESS female albino
ALBINISM deficiency of pigment
ALBORADA folk music (Sp.) **Mus.**
ALBUMESS Lamb's album-keeper
ALBURNUM sap-wood **B.**
ALCAHEST⎫ universal solvent
ALKAHEST⎭ of the alchemists
ALCATRAS ocean birds; pelican **Z.**
ALCHEMIC relating to alchemy
ALDEHYDE a volatile liquid **Chem.**
ALDERMAN a civic dignitary
ALEATORY depending on dice
ALEBENCH alehouse bench
ALEBERRY hot ale with sops
ALEHOUSE (no spirit licence)

ALEMBDAR Sultan's standard-bearer
ALE-STAKE an alehouse sign
ALEURONE a protein in seeds   **B.**
ALFRESCO in the open air
ALGERINE Algerian; pirate
ALGIDITY chilliness
ALGOLOGY the study of seaweeds   **B.**
ALGONKIN Canadian Indian
ALGORISM the decimal system
ALGRAPHY aluminium printing
ALHAMBRA Moorish palace;
ALICANTE Spanish red wine
ALIENAGE estrangement
ALIENATE transfer; misapply
ALIENISM study of insanity   **Med.**
ALIENIST mental specialist   **Med.**
ALIGHTED stepped off; descended
ALIGNING adjusting; dressing
ALIQUANT a remainder
ALITRUNK winged segment   **Z.**
ALIZARIN madder; synthetic dye
ALKALIES caustic bases
ALKALIFY⎱ neutralize an acid;
ALKALIZE⎰ alkalise   **Chem.**
ALKALINE salty   **Chem.**
ALKALOID active part of a drug   **Med.**
ALKERMES a crimson cordial
ALLANITE cerium silicate   **Chem.**
ALLAYING stilling; mitigating
ALL-CLEAR a bugle call
ALLEGING asserting as a fact
ALLEGORY parable; metaphor
ALLELUIA alleluyah; halleluiah
ALLERGIC antipathetic
ALLERION heraldic beakless eagle
ALLEY-WAY narrow passage
ALL-FIRED infernal; hell-fired
ALL-FOURS (cards); mode of progress
ALLIANCE union by treaty; coalition
ALLIGATE to bind together
ALLOCATE allot; assign; share
ALLODIAL freehold; not feudal
ALLODIUM freehold estate   **Law.**
ALLOGAMY cross-fertilization   **B.**
ALLOPATH user of healing drugs   **Med.**
ALLOTTED meted; assigned; dispensed
ALLOTTEE a sharer
ALL-OUTER extremist; zealot
ALLOWING conceding; admitting
ALLOYAGE the alloying of metals
ALLOYING blending; debasing
ALLSPICE Jamaica pepper   **B.**
ALLUDING hinting; insinuating
ALLURING enticing; tempting
ALLUSION hint; reference
ALLUSIVE relative; innuent
ALLUSORY symbolical; figurative
ALLUVIAL sedimentary
ALLUVION alluvial land
ALLUVIUM water-borne silt

ALMAGEST astronomical problems
ALMIGHTY all-powerful; omnipotent
ALMSDEED act of charity
ALMSGATE (where alms were given)
ALOMANCY divination by salt
ALOPECIA baldness; fox-evil   **Med.**
ALPHABET order or list of letters
ALPHA-RAY a radio-active ray
ALPHENIC white barley-sugar
ALPINIST mountaineer
ALQUIFOU Cornish lead ore   **Min.**
ALSATIAN sheep-dog; debauchee   **Z.**
ALTARAGE altar offerings   **Eccl.**
ALTERANT production of change
ALTER-EGO second self
ALTERING varying; changing
ALTERITY being otherwise
ALTERNAT precedence by rotation
ALTHEINE asparagine   **B.**
ALTHOUGH notwithstanding
ALTINCAR unrefined borax   **Chem.**
ALTITUDE height; eminence
ALTO-CLEF C on 3rd line of staff   **Mus.**
ALTRUISM self-sacrifice
ALTRUIST philanthropist
ALUMINIC containing aluminium   **Min.**
ALUMINUM aluminium   **Chem.**
ALUNOGEN aluminium sulphite   **Chem.**
ALVEATED hollowed out; saucer-shape
ALVEOLAR like a honey-comb
ALVEOLUS alveole; tooth socket   **Med.**
AMADAVAT a weaver-bird   **Z.**
AMANDINE sweet almond ointment
AMANDOLA green marble   **Min.**
AMANITIN poison in fungi   **Chem.**
AMARACUS marjoram   **B.**
AMARANTH love-lies-bleeding   **B.**
AMASSING piling up; accumulating
AMAZEDLY confusedly; dazedly
AMBERITE smokeless explosive   **Chem.**
AMBITION desire; aspiration
AMBIVERT   **Psych.**
AMBLYGON obtuse-angled
AMBREADA spurious amber
AMBREATE salt of ambreic acid   **Chem.**
AMBROSIA food of the gods; bee-bread
AMBROSIN Milanese coin   **Coin**
AMBULANT peripatetic; hiking
AMBULATE saunter; walk; stroll; hike
AMBUSHED caught unaware; lurked
AMENABLE liable; pliant; subject
AMENABLY docilely; responsively
AMENANCE conduct; behaviour
AMENDING rectifying; correcting
AMERCING fining; mulcting
AMERICAN Yankee
AMETHYST anti-inebriation jewel   **Min.**
AMIANTUS fibrous asbestos   **Min.**
AMICABLE friendly; neighbourly
AMICABLY benignly; peacefully

AMIDMOST in the very centre
AMISSING lost; wanting
AMMODYTE sand-eel   **Z.**
AMMONIAC   **Chem.**
AMMONITE explosive
AMMONITE spiral fossil   **Z.**
AMMONIUM base of ammonia   **Chem.**
AMNIOTIC a membrane   **Med.**
AMOEBEAN alternately answering
AMOEBEUM poetic dialogue
AMOEBOID ⎫ of simple structure   **Z.**
AMOEBOUS ⎭ like a protozoon   **Z.**
AMORETTO cupid; a lover
AMORTIZE transfer property   **Law**
AMOUNTED reached; rose; resulted
AMPELITE anti-pest earth   **Min.**
AMPHIBIA amphibians
AMPHIGEN a lichen-like plant   **B.**
AMPHIONT a zygote; an egg-shell   **Z.**
AMPHORAL like a two-handled vase
AMPHORIC hollow sounding   **Med.**
AMPULLAR like a two-handled flask
AMPUTATE lop; prune; sever
AMULETIC like an amulet; charming
AMURCOUS foul with dregs
AMUSABLE capable of enjoyment
AMUSETTE light field gun
AMYLASES pancreatic enzyme   **Med.**
ANABASIS a military advance
ANABLEPS a genus of fish   **Z.**
ANACONDA python (S. America)   **Z.**
ANAGLYPH a cameo; sterioscopic
ANAGOGIC mystical; allegorical
ANAGRAPH catalogue; inventory
ANALEMMA pedestal of sun-dial
ANALEPSY recurring epilepsy   **Med.**
ANALOGIC analogous; alike; akin
ANALOGON ⎫ similarity; synonym;
ANALOGUE ⎭ a corresponding part
ANALYSED examined
ANALYSER scrutator; analyst
ANALYSIS opposite of synthesis
ANALYTIC inductive
ANAPAEST a reversed dactyl
ANAPHORA rhetorical repetition   **Eccl.**
ANARCHIC lawless and turbulent
ANASARCA dropsy   **Med.**
ANATHEMA excommunication   **Eccl.**
ANATOMIC internal   **Med.**
ANCESTOR forefather; forebear
ANCESTRY lineage; descent
ANCHORED fixed securely
ANCHORET anchorite; hermit   **Eccl.**
ANCONEAL relating to the elbow   **Med.**
ANDERSON a steel shelter
ANDESINE felspar; andes   **Min.**
ANDESITE igneous rock, Andes   **Min.**
ANDORRAN (Andorra)
ANDIRONS fire-dogs
ANECDOTE a chatty relation

ANEURISM ⎫ dilated artery;   **Med.**
ANEURYSM ⎭ abnormal enlargement
ANGEL-BED open bed without posts
ANGELICA plant; Californian wine   **B.**
ANGERING inflaming; infuriating
ANGLICAN English; High Church   **Eccl.**
ANGLOMAN anglo-maniac
ANGRIEST exceedingly irate
ANGSTROM light wave-length unit
ANGULATE angular
ANIENTED annulled
ANIMALLY beastly
ANIMATED enlivened
ANIMATOR a rouser
ANIMETTA cloth for chalice   **Eccl.**
ANIRIDIA hereditary eye-defect   **Med.**
ANISETTE liqueur from aniseed
ANNALISE record historical events
ANNALIST writer of annals
ANNAMITE native of Annam, Vietnam
ANNEALED tempered
ANNELIDA worms   **Z.**
ANNEXING attaching; taking over
ANNOTATE add notes to; commentate
ANNOUNCE pronounce; proclaim
ANNOYING irritating; vexatious
ANNUALLY yearly; every year
ANNULARY ring bearing (fourth finger)
ANNULATE divided into rings
ANNULLED rendered void; abolished
ANNULLER a voider
ANNULOSE annular; ringed   **Z.**
ANODISED treated electrically
ANOINTED consecrated; Messiah   **Eccl.**
ANOREXIA loss of appetite   **Med.**
ANORTHIC oblique angled (crystal)
ANSERINE gooselike; stupid; silly
ANSWERED solved; responded; refuted
ANTACRID a medicine   **Med.**
ANTALGIC anodyne; pain-killer   **Med.**
ANT-EATER ant-bear, etc.   **Z.**
ANTECEDE precede
ANTEDATE anticipate
ANTEFIXA ornamental tiling
ANTELOPE antilope   **Z.**
ANTENATI born before a given date
ANTENNAE feelers; wireless wires   **Z.**
ANTENNAL relating to the above
ANTENODE (maximum displacement) **El.**
ANTEPORT outer gate or harbour
ANTERIOR prior; before
ANTEROOM antechamber
ANTHELIA luminous rings around sun
ANTHELIX antihelix; part of the ear
ANTHEMIS plant genus; camomile   **B.**
ANTHERAL (pollen bearing anthers)   **B.**
ANTHESIS full bloom   **B.**
ANTHOZOA sea-anemones; corals   **Z.**
ANTIACID antacid medicine   **Med.**
ANTIADES the tonsils   **Med.**

ANTI-ARMY pacifist
ANTIBODY a counteractive   **Med.**
ANTICIZE to play antics
ANTICOUS centripetal   **B.**
ANTIDOTE counter-measure
ANTI-ICER anti-freeze
ANTILOGY contradiction; antinomy
ANTILOPE antelope   **Z.**
ANTIMASK grotesque interlude
ANTIMONY stibium; a white metal
ANTI-NAZI anti-Hitlerite   **[Chem.**
ANTINODE radio
ANTINOMY legal contradiction   **Law**
ANTINOUS ideal of youthful beauty
ANTIPHON anthem; alternate chanting
ANTIPODE⎫ directly opposite;
ANTIPOLE⎭ the opposite
ANTIPOPE opposition pope; (Avignon)
ANTISERA antibiotics   **Med.**
ANTISTES chief priest or prelate   **Eccl.**
ANTI-TANK (guns, mines, etc.)
ANTITYPE typical example
ANTLERED furnished with antlers
ANTRORSE up-turning   **B.**
ANYTHING an unspecified object
ANYWHERE an undefined locality
AORISTIC indefinite as to time
AORTITIS inflammation of artery **Med.**
APAGOGIC reducing to an absurdity
APELLOUS without a skin   **Med.**
APERIENT a laxative; an opening
APERITIF a cocktail
APERTURE gap; hole; lens   **Photo.**
APHANITE horn-blende, quartz, etc.
APHELION an astronomical distance
APHIDIAN (green-fly)   **Z.**
APHONOUS voiceless; dumb   **Med.**
APHORISM a maxim; a saw
APHORIST a writer of adages
APHORIZE aphorise; define briefly
APHTHOUS ulcerous   **Med.**
APIARIAN concerning bees   **Z.**
APIARIST a bee expert
APICALLY top-most; at the apex
APLASTIC not easily moulded
APLUSTRE ornament on stern   **Naut.**
APODOSIS consequent clause
APOGAEIC (apogees and aphelions)
APOGRAPH a copy; transcript
APOLLYON the destroying angel
APOLOGIA vindication; formal defence
APOLOGIA excuses
APOLOGUE moral fable; allegory
APOPHYGE base of column (arch.)
APOPLEXY loss of mental control **Med.**
APOSITIA aversion to food   **Med.**
APOSTACY⎫ abandonment of principle;
APOSTASY⎭ recantation   **Eccl.**
APOSTATE a renegade
APOSTEME apostume; an abscess **Med.**

APOTHEGM sententious maxim
APPALLED terrified; dismayed
APPANAGE territorial dependency
APPARENT obvious; evident; palpable
APPEALED implored; entreated
APPEALER a suppliant; invoker
APPEARED emerged; dawned; arrived
APPEASED soothed; allayed; mollified
APPEASER pacifier; tranquillizer
APPELLEE defendant in an appeal
APPELLOR prosecutor   **Law**
APPENDED subjoined; attached
APPENDIX supplement; addendum **Med.**
APPETENT desirous; solicitous
APPETITE craving; longing; hunger
APPETIZE to create a desire
APPLAUSE praise; laudation
APPLE-PIE neat; orderly; bed
APPLE-PIP apple-seed   **B.**
APPLIQUE applied work
APPLYING employing; requesting
APPOSITE fit; suitable; pertinent
APPRAISE set a value to; rate; survey
APPRISED informed; notified; told
APPRIZED appreciated; valued
APPROACH advance; resemble; avenue
APPROVAL approbation; sanction
APPROVED commended; ratified
APPROVER ratifier; king's evidence
APPULSED driven; struck; attacked
APRON-MAN a mechanic
APTEROUS wingless   **Z.**
APTITUDE readiness; knack; faculty
APYRETIC feverless   **Med.**
APYREXIA intermittent fever   **Med.**
AQUACADE musical water show
AQUALUNG diver's oxygen pack
AQUARIUM tanks of aquatic animals
AQUARIUS water-carrier (zodiac)
AQUASTAT boiler temperature regulator
AQUATINT a print; (engrav. on copper)
AQUEDUCT artificial water channel
AQUIFORM liquid
AQUILINE like an eagle; hooked
AQUOSITY sloppiness
ARACHNID spider; mite or scorpion **Z.**
ARAINGEE gallery of a mine
ARAMAISM an Aramaic idiom
ARANEOUS araneose; cobwebby   **Z.**
ARAPUNGA the bell-bird; campanero**Z.**
ARBALIST arbalest; cross-bow
ARBITRAL arbitrational
ARBOREAL tree-like   **B.**
ARBORETA shrubberies
ARBORIST tree expert; herbalist
ARBOROUS woody; arboreal
ARBOURED with shady bowers
ARBUSCLE dwarf tree   **B.**
ARBUSTUM copse; shrubbery
ARBUTEAN (strawberry tree)   **B.**

ARCADIAN pastoral; rustic
ARCATURE a small arcade
ARCHAEAN geologically remote
ARCHAISM an archaic expression
ARCHAIZE archaise; use archaisms
ARCHDUKE a princely title
ARCHICAL chief; primary
ARCHIVAL documentary
ARCHIVES record office; records
ARCHLIKE arcuate; iridian
ARCHLUTE double-stringed lute **Mus.**
ARCH-MOCK the height of mockery
ARCHNESS roguishness
ARCH-POET Poet Laureate
ARCHWISE bowed
ARCTURUS Bear-guard; star in Boötes
ARDENTLY fiercely; zealously
AREFYING withering; desiccating
ARENARIA sand-wort; chick-weed **B.**
AREOLATE divided into small areas
ARGEMONE silver-weed **B.**
ARGENTAN German silver
ARGENTIC argental; silvery
ARGENTUM silver; Ag. **Chem.**
ARGONAUT (golden fleece); cuttle-fish
ARGOSIES richly laden vessels
ARGUABLE debatable
ARGUFIED wrangled
ARGUMENT discussion; an abstract
ARGUTELY keenly; shrewdly; piercing
ARIANISE convert to Arianism **Eccl.**
ARIANISM doctrine of Arius **Eccl.**
ARIDNESS dryness; sterility
ARILLARY (exterior coating of a seed) **B.**
ARISTATE awned; bearded **B.**
ARMAMENT munitions; arms; guns
ARMATURE armour; rotor of dynamo
ARM-CHAIR an elbow-chair
ARMENIAN a native; a sect **Eccl.**
ARMIGERO esquire; armour-bearer
ARMILLET small bracelet; armlet
ARMINIAN (opposed to Calvinism) **Eccl.**
ARMORIAL relating to coats-of-arms
ARMORIST expert in heraldry
ARMOURED plated
ARMOURER artificer; manufacturer
ARMOZEEN⎫ taffeta or silk,
ARMOZINE⎭ used for clerical gowns
AROMATIC fragrant; pungent
AROUSING stirring
ARPEGGIO harplike chord **Mus.**
ARQUEBUS heavy musket
ARRANGED settled; grouped
ARRANGER planner: orchestrator
ARRANTLY infamously; notoriously
ARRASENE Arras embroidery
ARRAUGHT taken by force
ARRAYING disposing; adorning
ARRECTED erect; upright
ARRESTED halted; seized; captured

ARRESTER an apprehender **Law**
ARRETTED accused
ARRIDING gratifying; pleasing
ARRIVING reaching; attaining; landing
ARROGANT haughty; overbearing
ARROGATE usurp; assume
ARRONDEE segmented heraldic cross
ARROSION corrosion; gnawing
ARSENATE⎫ arsenical salts **Chem.**
ARSENITE⎭
ARSONIST⎫ felon who deliberately
ARSONITE⎭ sets fire to property
ARTERIAL (arteries); (roads) **Med.**
ARTESIAN (deep wells)
ARTFULLY craftily
ARTICLED bound by agreement **Law**
ARTIFACT product of primitive art
ARTIFICE stratagem; trick; device
ARTISTIC tasteful; aesthetic
ARTISTRY vocation; workmanship
ARUSPICE haruspex; soothsayer
ARUSPICY divination by augury
ARVICOLA vole genus **Z.**
ASBESTIC made of asbestos **Min.**
ASBESTOS incombustible material
ASCENDED rose; mounted
ASCIDIUM bottle-like appendage **B.**
ASCORBIC acid; vitamin 'C' **Chem.**
ASCRIBED attributed; assigned
ASH-LEACH tub for washing wood-ash
ASH-PLANT ash sapling; walking stick
ASH-STAND ash-tray
ASHY-GRAY ashy in colour
ASPARTIC obtained from asparagus **B.**
ASPERATE to roughen
ASPERGES ceremonial sprinkling **Eccl.**
ASPERITY harshness; sourness; acerbity
ASPERSED sprinkled; slandered; abused
ASPHODEL a lily; a daffodil **B.**
ASPHYXIA suffocation **Med.**
ASPIRANT suitor; candidate
ASPIRATE to emphasize the 'h' sound
ASPIRING longing; hoping; soaring
ASPOROUS without spores **B.**
ASPORTED stolen away
ASSAILED assaulted; attacked; vilified
ASSAILER aggressor; invader; traducer
ASSAMESE native of Assam (language)
ASSARTED grubbed up trees and bushes
ASSASSIN a thug primed with hashish
ASSAYING testing; analysing
ASSEMBLE convene; muster; congregate
ASSEMBLY meeting; company
ASSENTED concurred; agreed; acquiesced
ASSENTER assentor; approver
ASSERTED maintained; averred
ASSESSED taxed; rated; appraised
ASSESSOR tax-master; valuer **Law**
ASSIDENT alongside; accompanying
ASSIETTE oblong dish; plate (Fr.)

ASSIGNAT paper currency, Fr. Rev.
ASSIGNED allotted; specified
ASSIGNEE a recipient
ASSIGNOR transferrer of an interest
ASSINEGO small donkey; fool; dolt **Z.**
ASSISTED aided; abetted; sustained
ASSIZING assessing; regulating
ASSONANT harmonious; rhythmical
ASSONATE correspond in sound **Mus.**
ASSORTED mixed; varied; classified
ASSUAGED allayed; abated; appeased
ASSUAGER mitigator; alleviator
ASSUMING arrogant; presumptuous
ASSURANT holder of insurance policy
ASSURING affirming; pledging
ASSYRIAN a descendant of Shem
ASTACIAN shell-fish, lobster type **Z.**
ASTERIAS star-fish genus **Z.**
ASTERISK the mark (*)
ASTERISM small cluster of stars
ASTERNAL not joined to breast-bone
ASTEROID minor planet; star-shaped
ASTHENIA lack of vitality; debility
ASTHENIC feeble; weak **Med.**
ASTOMATA an order of infusoria **Z.**
ASTOMOUS astomatous; mouthless
ASTONIED astounded; stunned; dazed
ASTONISH amaze; startle; surprise
ASTRAGAL a rounded moulding
ASTRINGE constrict; constrain
ASTUNNED astonied; mazed; dazed
ASTUTELY cunningly; craftily
ASYSTOLE heart failure **Med.**
ATABRINE quinine type **Med.**
ATARAXIA stoical indifference
ATHEIZED converted to disbelief
ATHELING Anglo-Saxon noble (King)
ATHENIAN a Greek capitalist
ATHERINE fish genus; mullets; smelts **Z.**
ATHEROMA wen or tumour **Med.**
ATHLETIC strong; vigorous; sinewy
ATLANTES male supporting figures
ATLANTIC the herring pond
ATLANTIS legendary island
ATMOLOGY science of vaporization
ATOMICAL atomic; minute
ATOMIZED vaporized
ATOMIZER a spray
ATONABLE expiable; amendable
ATREMBLE dithering
ATROCITY a Hunnish act
ATROPHIC emaciated; withered
ATROPINE bella-donna **Med.**
ATROPISM illness due to atropine **Med.**
ATROPOUS upturned; erect **B.**
ATTACHED fond; bound; arrested **Law**
ATTACKED assaulted; set about
ATTACKER assailant; invader; violator
ATTAINED achieved; secured; won
ATTENDED served; escorted; hearkened

ATTENDER attendant; close listener
ATTESTED invoked; endorsed
ATTESTOR attester; a witness
ATTICISM witty remark; Attic salt
ATTICIZE to use Athenian idioms
ATTINGED touched lightly; affected
ATTIRING arraying; adorning; robing
ATTITUDE pose; posture; bearing
ATTORNED transferred homage
ATTORNEY lawyer; solicitor **Law**
ATTRITED worn away; abraded; erased
ATTRITUS a grade of coal **Min.**
ATTUNING harmonizing **Mus.**
AUBUSSON style of carpet
AUCUPATE to go bird-catching
AUDACITY boldness; effrontery; daring
AUDIENCE formal interview; listeners
AUDITING examining accounts
AUDITION a test of competency
AUDITIVE audible
AUDITORY an audience; auditorium
AUGURATE foretell by divination
AUGURIAL ominous
AUGURIES prognostications; portents
AUGURING presaging; prophesying
AUGUSTAN (Emperor Augustus)
AUGUSTLY majestically; imposingly
AULARIAN member of an Oxford Hall
AURELIAN (Emperor Aurelius)
AUREOLED in a halo **Eccl.**
AURICLED eared **B.**
AURICULA the primula **B.**
AURIFORM ear-shaped
AURILAVE an ear-washing instrument
AUROREAN rosy; dawning
AURULENT golden
AUSONIAN Italian
AUSTRIAN
AUTACOID a hormone; a chalone **Med.**
AUTARCHY autocracy; absolutism
AUTARKIC self-sufficient
AUTISTIC withdrawn **Psych.**
AUTOBAHN fast motorway
AUTOCADE motor cavalcade
AUTOCRAT absolute ruler **Eccl.**
AUTO-DA-FE Inquisitional judgment
AUTO-DYNE frequency stabilizer
AUTO-GAMY self-fertilization **B.**
AUTO-GENY spontaneous generation
AUTOGYRO a type of aircraft
AUTOLOGY the study of self
AUTOMATA automatons; robots
AUTOMATH a self-taught man
AUTONOMY self-government
AUTOPSIA autopsy; post-mortem **Med.**
AUTOPTIC seen with one's own eyes
AUTOSLED snow vehicle
AUTOTOMY amputation; cell division
AUTUMNAL peculiar to the autumn
AUTUNITE phosphate of uranium **Chem.**

AUXILIAR subsidiary; assisting
AVAILING profiting; sufficing; using
AVELLANE heraldic cross of filberts
AVENGING vindicating; retaliating
AVENTAIL visor; opening in a helmet
AVENTURE fatal accident **Law**
AVERAGED equated; proportional
AVERMENT affirmation
AVERNIAN Plutonic ; infernal
AVERRING declaring; alleging
AVERSANT heraldic reversal
AVERSELY unwillingly; reluctantly
AVERSION dislike; hatred; allergy
AVIARIST keeper of caged birds
AVIATING flying
AVIATION travel by air
AVIFAUNA local birds **Z.**
AVISEFUL wary; watchful; circumspect
AVOIDING eschewing; shunning
AVOIDISM trouble evasion
AVOUCHED guaranteed
AVOWABLE affirmable; declarable
AVOWABLY deposably; admittedly
AVOWANCE avowal; confession
AVOWEDLY openly; frankly
AVULSION forcible separation
AWAITING abiding; expecting
AWAKABLE not dead-asleep
AWAKENED spurred; stimulated
AWAKENER a rouser
AWANTING wanting; lacking; absent
AWARDING decreeing; bestowing
AWEARIED jaded; spent; worn
AWEATHER the weather-side **Naut.**
AXE-HELVE handle of an axe
AXE-STONE jade **Min.**
AXILLARY (armpit); branch angle **B.**
AXIOLOGY theory of value
AXLETREE spindle
AXOIDEAN axial
AYENBITE remorse
AZOTIZED nitrogenized

B

BABAKOTO a large lemur **Z.**
BABBLING prattling; gossiping
BABELDOM state of confusion
BABIRUSA pig-deer of Ceylon **Z.**
BABISHLY childishly
BABOODOM realm of red tape
BABOOISM plethora of verbiage
BABOUCHE oriental slipper
BABY-FACE term of endearment
BABY-FARM baby-boarding house
BABY-HOOD state of infancy
BACCARAT a card game
BACCHANT bacchanalian
BACILLAR like baccili **Med.**
BACILLUS rod-like organism **Med.**

BACHELOR a degree-man
BACK-BAND cart-saddle band
BACK-BITE to speak evil; asperse
BACK-BOND conditional deed **Law**
BACK-BONE reliability; spine **Med.**
BACK-CHAT impertinent rejoinder
BACK-DOOR clandestine; furtive
BACK-DROP drop scene
BACK-DUTY unpaid tax **Law**
BACK-FALL a wrestling throw
BACK-FIRE a blow back
BACK-FLAP folding shutter
BACK-HAND (writing); (stroke)
BACK-HEEL rugby football
BACKLASH gear wear
BACKMOST hindermost
BACK-RENT dues **Law**
BACK-ROOM behind the scenes
BACKSIDE posterior
BACKSPIN golf
BACK-STEP cycle mounting step
BACK-VELD back blocks (S. Africa)
BACKWARD hesitating; reluctant
BACKWASH backward current; wake
BACKWORM filanders; hawk-disease **Z.**
BACONIAN (Bacon); inductive
BACTERIA fungoid growths **Med.**
BACTRIAN two-humped camel **Z.**
BACULINE rod-like
BACULITE fossil cuttle-fish **Min.**
BADGERED pestered; worried
BADGERLY grey like a badger
BADIGEON sculptor's cement
BADINAGE persiflage; chaff
BAFFETAS Indian muslin
BAFFLING defeating; hoodwinking
BAGHEERA the black panther (India) **Z.**
BAGPIPER a piper **Mus.**
BAGUETTE round moulding (arch.)
BAILABLE able to be bailed **Law**
BAIL-BALL cricket ball bail high
BAIL-BOND security for appearance
BAIL-DOCK room at Old Bailey **Law**
BAILMENT delivery of goods in trust
BAILSMAN guarantor of bond **Law**
BAKELITE a plastic material
BAKEMEAT pastry; pies
BAKSHISH discount; commission; tip
BALANCED in equilibrium
BALANCER acrobat; tumbler
BALANITE fossil barnacle **Min.**
BALCONET miniature balcony
BALDCOOT baldicoot; coot; monk **Z.**
BALDHEAD no hair apparent
BALDNESS alopecia **Med.**
BALD-PATE species of wild duck **Z.**
BALDRICK shoulder belt
BALE-FIRE signal fire; funeral pyre
BALK-LINE baulk-line (billiards)
BALLADER ballad-monger

BALLADRY patriotic or epic verse
BALL-COCK stopcock in a cistern
BALLIAGE an export duty
BALLISTA ancient catapult
BALLONET small balloon; gas bag
BALLOTED drew lots for; voted
BALLROOM location for stately measures
BALLYHOO bunkum; false fame
BALLYRAG bullyrag; torment
BALMORAL bonnet; boot; petticoat
BALNEARY a bathroom
BALOTADE an equine feat
BALSAMIC soothing; demulcent
BALUSTER supporting column (arch.)
BANALITY triviality; triteness
BANDAGED surgically bound
BANDANNA Indian silk kerchief
BANDEAUX hair-bands or fillets
BANDELET bandlet (arch.)
BANDEROL bannerol; small banner
BANDFISH long lean fish   **Z.**
BANDITTI bandits; robbers; outlaws
BANDSMAN a player   **Mus.**
BANDSTER sheaf-binder
BANDYING tossing about
BANEWORT deadly nightshade   **B.**
BANGSTER braggart; victor
BANGTAIL square-cut tail
BANISHED expelled; outlawed
BANISTER baluster; stair railings
BANJOIST fretful player   **Mus.**
BANKABLE receivable at a bank
BANK-BILL note of exchange
BANK-BOOK pass-book
BANK-NOTE promissory note
BANK-RATE Bank of England rate
BANKRUPT insolvent; broke
BANKSMAN overseer at pit-mouth
BANLIEUE environs of a town (Fr.)
BANNERED beflagged
BANNERET knighthood
BANNEROL banderol; small banner
BANTERED railed; chaffed
BANTERER joker; jester
BANTLING young child; bratling
BANXRING insect-eating squirrel   **Z.**
BAPHOMET Templar's idol
BAPTIZED baptised; immersed   **Eccl.**
BARATHEA woven fabric
BARBACAN barbicon; outer defence
BARBARED shaved; shorn
BARBARIC foreign; savage; Hunnish
BARBATED bearded; awned   **B.**
BARBECUE out-door cookery
BARBERRY thorny shrub; berberry   **B.**
BARBETTE armoured defence
BARBICAN barbacan; gun-port
BARBITON antique form of lyre   **Mus.**
BARDLING bardlet; poetaster; rhymster
BAREBACK unsaddled

BAREBOAT chartering contract   **Law**
BAREBONE (Parliament); lean; thin
BAREFOOT bootless
BARESARK without shirt of mail
BARGEMAN barge owner; bargee
BARGHEST a dog-like goblin
BARILLET watch-spring case
BARITONE (between tenor and bass) **Mus.**
BARKMILL bark-crusher
BARNABAS cornflour   **B.**
BARNACLE a twitch; cirriped; goose **Z.**
BARN-DOOR a farm portal
BARNEKIN outermost castle ward
BARNYARD the rooster's realm
BAROLOGY the science of weight
BAROMETZ a fern   **B.**
BARONAGE cf. peerage
BARONESS wife or widow of baron
BARONIAL noble and spacious
BAROUCHE four-wheeled carriage
BAR-POSTS supports of field-gate
BARRACAN material of camel-hair
BARRACKS the soldier's home
BARRANCO barranca; deep gorge
BARRATOR encourager of litigation **Law**
BARRATRY traffic in church offices **Eccl.**
BARRENLY sterilely; unfruitfully
BARRULET horizontal heraldic bar
BAR-SHEAR bar-cutter   **Tool**
BARTERED exchanged commodities
BARTERER a dealer
BARTIZAN small overhanging turret
BASALTIC allied to basalt   **Min.**
BASANITE touchstone; flinty slate **Min.**
BASCINET helmet of XVth century
BASE-BALL national game (U.S.A.)
BASEBAND frequency modulation
                        Electron.
BASE-BORN of low parentage
BASE-BRED of low breeding
BASELESS lacking any foundation
BASE-LINE a surveyor's base   **Meas.**
BASEMENT floor below ground level
BASENESS vileness; meanness
BASE-VIOL bass-viol; violoncello **Mus.**
BASHLESS unashamed; undaunted
BASICITY ratio of acid to base   **Chem.**
BASIFIER an alkali   **Chem.**
BASILIAN monk of St. Basil   **Eccl.**
BASILICA church   **Eccl.**
BASILICA public hall (Roman)
BASILING grinding to an angle
BASILISK dragon; lizard; cannon   **Z.**
BASINFUL bowlful
BASKETED hampered
BASKETRY wickerwork
BASQUINE Basque outer petticoat
BASS-DRUM   **Mus.**
BASSETTE tenor or small bass viol
BASS-HORN deep-toned bassoon **Mus.**
BASSINET wickerwork perambulator

BASS-TUBA euphonium **Mus.**
BASS-VIOL base-viol; violoncello **Mus.**
BASSWOOD (N. Amer.) **B.**
BASTAARD Dutch half-breed (S. Afr.)
BASTARDY illegitimacy
BASTERNA mule-borne litter
BASTILLE old castle; state prison
BATAVIAN native of Batavia
BATELESS irrepressible
BATHABLE washable
BATHETIC anticlimatic; bombastic
BATHMISM inherent divergence
BATHORSE pack-horse **Z.**
BATH-RAIL side-grip
BATH-ROOM balneary
BATSWING flat gas flame
BATTELED (Oxford University)
BATTENED grew fat; secured
BATTERED pounded; shattered
BATTLING striving; warring
BATUCADA batuque; dance (Brazil) **Mus.**
BAUDEKIN silk brocade; canopy **Eccl.**
BAUDRONS Scottish name for the cat
BAULKING balking; checking
BAVARIAN
BAWDRICK baldrick; shoulder belt
BAYADERE Indian nautch girl
BAYARDLY blindly
BAYBERRY wax-myrtle **B.**
BDELLIUM aromatic gum-resin **B.**
BEACHING running ashore
BEACONED lit up
BEADLERY beadle's jurisdiction
BEAD-ROLL names for masses **Eccl.**
BEADSMAN almsman
BEAD-TREE the azedarac **B.**
BEAD-WORK ornamental work
BEAK-HEAD Romanesque ornament
BEAKIRON bickern; anvil point
BEAM-BIRD spotted flycatcher **Z.**
BEAMLESS emitting no rays
BEAM-TREE a hardwood tree **B.**
BEAN-KING king of the revels
BEARABLE tolerable; supportable
BEARABLY endurably; moderately
BEARBIND bearbine; bindweed **B.**
BEARDING meeting face to face
BEAR-HERD bear-keeper
BEARINGS
BEARLIKE rude and rough; ursine
BEAR'S-EAR primula auricula **B.**
BEARSKIN headdress of the guards
BEARWARD bear-leader; Arcturus
BEASTIES small animals **Z.**
BEASTISH brutal; animal
BEATIFIC ecstatic; rapturous
BEAT-NOTE (wireless)
BEAUFREY beam or joist
BEAUPERE father-in-law (Fr.)
BEAUTIES lovelies

BEAUTIFY adorn; array: garnish
BEAVERED covered with beaver fur
BEBEERIN quinine alkaloid **Med.**
BECALMED motionless; tranquillized
BECHAMEL savoury sauce
BECHANCE befall; accidentally
BECKONED nodded; called; invited
BECOMING befitting; graceful
BECURLED with ringlets
BEDABBLE dabble; sprinkle
BEDAGGLE drag through the mire
BEDARKEN obscure; eclipse
BEDASHED bespattered
BEDAUBED smeared; plastered
BED-CHAIR bed back-rest
BEDECKED robed; embellished
BEDEGUAR a rose scourge **B., Z.**
BEDESMAN see beadsman **Eccl.**
BEDEWEEN the birch tree **B.**
BEDEWING sprinkling
BED-GOING retiring
BEDIMMED blurred; tarnished; dulled
BED-LINEN sheets, etc.
BEDMAKER college servant
BEDPLATE foundation plate
BED-QUILT an overlay
BEDRENCH saturate; immerse; soak
BEDSTAFF cudgel; truncheon
BEDSTEAD a framework
BEDSTRAW a plant **B.**
BED-TABLE bead belt (Anagram)
BEDUCKED soused
BEDUSTED smothered with dust
BEDWARDS on the way to bed
BEE-BREAD pollen collected by bees **B.**
BEECH-OIL beech-nut oil
BEE-EATER a bird **Z.**
BEEFIEST heftiest; lustiest
BEEFWOOD an Australian wood **B.**
BEER-PUMP
BEERSHOP inn; alehouse; tavern
BEESWING dregs of port
BEETLING overhanging; projecting
BEET-RAVE beetroot **B.**
BEETROOT beetrave **B.**
BEFITTED suitable; becoming; worthy
BEFLOWER cover with flowers
BEFOGGED dimmed; confused
BEFOOLED deluded; hoaxed; gulled
BEFOULED polluted; begrimed
BEFRIEND favour; patronize; aid
BEFRINGE adorn with fringes
BEFURRED covered with fur
BEGETTER a sire
BEGGABLE borrowable
BEGGARED rendered penniless
BEGGARLY paltry; mean; abject
BEGINNER tyro; novice; neophyte
BEGIRDED belted
BEGIRDLE encompass; encircle

BEGOTTEN born; produced
BEGREASE lubricate
BEGRIMED soiled; grubby
BEGRUDGE envy
BEGUILED deluded; diverted
BEGUILER cheat; deceiver
BEHAVING comme il faut
BEHEADAL an execution
BEHEADED decapitated
BEHEMOTH Job's hippopotamus **Z.**
BEHOLDEN grateful; indebted
BEHOLDER observer; surveyor
BEHOVING being necessary
BEINNESS comfort; well-being
BEJESUIT initiate in Jesuitism **Eccl.**
BEKISSED smothered in kisses
BELABOUR to thrash; whack
BELACING adorning with lace
BELAMOUR a gallant; a fair lady
BELATING being late
BELAYING fastening **Naut.**
BELAUDED eulogized
BELCHING
BELFRIED having belfries
BELFRIES steeples; watch-towers **Eccl.**
BELIEVED credited; fancied
BELIEVER theist; devotee; pietist
BELITTLE disparage; deprecate
BELLBIND, BELL-BINE bindweed **B.**
BELL-BIRD New Zealand bird **Z.**
BELL-BUOY the sailor's warning **Naut.**
BELLCOTE small belfry
BELLOWED roared; bawled
BELL-PULL bell-rope
BELL-ROPE a ringer
BELL-TENT conical canvas tent
BELLWORT a campanula **B.**
BELLYFUL replete
BELLY-GOD greedy; epicure
BELLYING swelling; billowing
BELONGED owned by; pertained
BELOVING loving; fond; doting
BELZEBUB Beelzebub **Eccl.**
BEMASKED wearing a domino
BEMIRING soiling
BEMOANED bewailed; lamented
BEMUDDLE mess up
BEMUFFLE wrap up
BENCHING sitting on a bench
BENDABLE not rigid
BENEAPED aground at low tide **Naut.**
BENEDICK ⎫ newly married man;
BENEDICT ⎭ learned saint **Eccl.**
BENEFICE church living
BENIGNLY kindly; benevolently
BENITIER holy water vessel
BENJAMIN gum; overcoat
BENOTING noting fully
BENUMBED torpid
BENZOATE a salt **Chem.**

BEPEPPER shoot repeatedly
BEPESTER annoy persistently
BEPITIED commiserated
BEPLUMED with plumes
BEPOMMEL belabour
BEPOWDER pulverize
BEPRAISE laud
BEPUFFED flattered
BEQUEATH entrust
BERATING scolding
BERBERIN barberry extract **Chem.**
BERBERRY the barberry **B.**
BEREAVED bereft
BERGAMOT citron; perfume; pear **B.**
BERGMEHL crystalline earth **Min.**
BERGMOTE a miner's court
BERHYMED celebrated in verse
BERI-BERI a tropical disease **Med.**
BERNOUSE burnouse; Arab mantle
BERRYING producing berries
BERTHAGE dock fees
BERTHING docking **Naut.**
BESCRAWL scribble
BESCREAM yell the house down
BESCREEN shelter
BESEEMED befitted
BESEEMLY becoming; fit; suitable
BESETTER an assailant
BESHADOW overshadow
BESIDERY variety of pear **B.**
BESIEGED beleaguered; encircled
BESIEGER an investor
BESILVER electro-plate
BESLAVED enslaved
BESLAVER slobber
BESLIMED bemired
BESMIRCH besmutch; beslime
BESNOWED snowed up
BESOILED defiled
BESORTED suited; fitted
BESOTTED drunk; crapulous; inebriated
BESOUGHT entreated; implored
BESOULED endowed with a soul
BESPICED highly seasoned
BESPOKEN made to order
BESPREAD broadcast; disseminate
BESSEMER a steel process
BESTIARY book about beasts
BESTOWAL gift; grant; distribution
BESTOWED gave; presented; awarded
BESTOWER donor; feoffer
BESTREAK mark with streaks
BESTREWN scattered; dispersed
BESTRIDE astride
BESTRODE traversed; mounted
BETAKING removing to; applying to
BETA-RAYS radium-rays
BETATRON electron speeding machine
BETEARED tearful; bedimmed
BETEL-NUT areca nut palm **B.**

BETIDING happening; befalling
BETONGUE scold; rail; nag
BETOSSED thrown about
BETRAYAL breech of trust
BETRAYED ensnared; beguiled
BETRAYER seducer; a Judas; traitor
BETTERED ameliorated; improved
BETULINE birch camphor   **B.**
BEVELING rounded edge
BEVELLED basiled; on the slant
BEVERAGE drink; potion; potation
BEVILLED sloping lines (Her.)
BEWAILED lamented
BEWARING minding; avoiding
BEWIGGED with wig; scolded
BEWILDER perplex; confuse
BEWINTER to chill
BEWRAYED disclosed
BEWRAYER betrayer
BEZONIAN beggar; rascal
BHEESTIE Hindu water-carrier
BIANCONI Irish car
BIBATION tippling
BIBLICAL scriptured
BIBULOUS absorbing
BICAUDAL with two tails
BICKERED squabbled
BICOLOUR of two colours
BICONVEX lens   **Photo.**
BICRURAL two-legged
BICUSPID having two cusps   **B.**
BICYCLED cycled
BIDDABLE worthy of being bid
BIDENTAL with two teeth
BIENNIAL once in two years
BIER-BALK right of way for funerals
BIFACIAL doublefaced
BIFEROUS two crops each year   **B.**
BIFIDATE cleft in twain   **B.**
BIFORATE having two pores
BIGAMIST   **Law**
BIGAMOUS involving bigamy
BIGAROON white-heart cherry   **B.**
BIG-BONED bony; osseous
BIGGONET cap; deerstalker
BIGNONIA plant genus   **B.**
BIG-SWOLN ready to burst
BIJOUTRY bijouterie; trinkets
BIJUGATE twin   **B.**
BIJUGOUS paired
BIJWONER squatter (S. Africa)
BILANDER Dutch barge   **Naut.**
BILBERRY whortleberry   **B.**
BILEDUCT a canal   **Med.**
BILL-BOOK account book
BILLETED quartered
BILLETEE person billeted
BILLFISH lake fish (N. Amer.)   **Z.**
BILLHEAD letterhead, printing
BILLHOOK hedge cutting tool

BILLIARD (used for billiards)
BILLOWED surged; swelled
BILLY-BOY bluff-bowed ketch   **Naut.**
BILLY-CAN bush teapot
BILOBATE with two lobes
BIMANOUS two-headed
BIMARINE between two seas
BIMENSAL six times in one year
BIMESTER two-monthly
BINAURAL adapted for two ears
BINDWEED bearbine; convolvulus   **B.**
BINNACLE bittacle; compass box   **Naut.**
BINOMIAL consisting of two terms
BINOXIDE a peroxide   **Chem.**
BIOBLAST parturient protoplasm
BIOCYTIN vitamin in yeast
BIOGRAPH bioscope; zoetrope
BIOLYTIC destructive to life
BIOMETRY life mensuration
BIOPLASM protoplasm   **Z.**
BIOSCOPE early cinematograph
BIOSOPHY made of life
BIPAROUS twin-producing
BIPENNIS two-edged battle-axe
BIRAMOUS double-branched
BIRCHING corporal punishment
BIRD-BATH garden ornament
BIRD-BOLT blunt arrow
BIRD-CAGE London walk
BIRD-CALL bird whistle
BIRD-EYED quick-sighted; eagle-eyed
BIRD-LICE avian irritants   **Z.**
BIRDLIKE aviform
BIRD-LIME sticky stuff
BIRD-SEED not sown but cropped
BIRD'S-EYE seen from above; tobacco
BIRD-SONG
BIRRETUM judge's black cap   **Law**
BIRTHDAY an anniversary
BIRTHDOM privilege of birth
BISCAYAN Basque
BISCOTIN sweet biscuit
BISECTED halved; split in twain
BISECTOR an equal divisor
BISERIAL in two series
BISETOSE double-bristled   **B., Z.**
BISEXUAL   **B., Z.**
BISHOPED (horse coping)
BISTOURY surgical knife   **Med.**
BITING-IN (etching)
BITINGLY acidly; mordantly
BITMAKER lorimer; loriner
BITMOUTH bit of a bridle
BITNOBEN a bitumen salt   **Med.**
BITTACLE compass housing   **Naut.**
BITTERED soured
BITTERLY acrimoniously
BIVALENT diatomic valency   **Chem.**
BI-WEEKLY periodically
BIZCACHA chinchilla, rodent   **Z.**

BLABBING telling; tatling
BLACK-ART necromancy
BLACKCAP a warbler **Z.**
BLACK-FLY turnip-flea **Z.**
BLACK-GUM N. American tree **B.**
BLACKING a polish
BLACKISH somewhat dark
BLACKLEG strike-breaker
BLACK-NEB crow; crane, etc. **Z.**
BLACK-OUT airman's blindness
BLACKPOT coarse ceramic
BLACK-ROD Usher to House of Lords
BLACK-WAD ore of manganese **Min.**
BLADDERY vesicular **Med.**
BLAMABLE censurable
BLAMABLY reprehensibly
BLAMEFUL culpable
BLANCARD bleached woven cloth
BLANCHED deprived of colour
BLANCHER white-washer
BLANDEST smoothest; mildest
BLANDISH flatter; coax; cajole
BLANKEST most vacant
BLANKING frustrating
BLASTEMA an off-shoot **B.**
BLASTING detonating; cursing
BLAST-OFF launching of rocket
BLASTULAR embryonic cell **Biol.**
BLATANCY obtrusive vulgarity
BLAUWBOK antelope, (S. Africa) **Z.**
BLAZONED embellished
BLAZONER a broadcaster
BLAZONRY heraldic painting
BLEACHED blanched
BLEACHER colour extractor
BLEAKEST coldest; barest; chilliest
BLEAKISH cold and cheerless
BLEATING blethering
BLEEDING blood-letting
BLENCHED flinched; paled
BLENDING intermingling; harmonizing
BLENHEIM spaniel; apple; plane **Z., B.**
BLESSING divine favour; boon; gain
BLETTING decaying **Eccl.**
BLIGHTED mildewed
BLIGHTER pestilent fellow
BLIMBING a fruit **B.**
BLIMPERY blatant inefficiency
BLINDAGE camouflage
BLINDEST most ignorant and heedless
BLINDING hoodwinking
BLINDMAN G.P.O. official
BLINKARD a blinker or winker
BLINKERS eye-shades
BLINKING ignoring; winking; gleaming
BLISSFUL rapturous; ecstatic
BLISTERY vesicated
BLITHELY joyously
BLITHEST merriest
BLITZING bombing

BLIZZARD violent snowstorm
BLOATING smoking; inflating; swelling
BLOCKADE encirclement
BLOCKING obstructing; shaping
BLOCKISH like a blockhead
BLODWYTE fine for bloodshedding
BLONCKET gray
BLOOD-HOT 98.6 degrees, Fahr. **Med.**
BLOODIED stained with gore
BLOODILY sanguinely
BLOODING fox-hunting rite
BLOOD-RED a gory hue
BLOOD-TAX conscription
BLOOD-WON dearly bought
BLOOMERS garments; blunders
BLOOMERY forge for smelted iron
BLOOMING flourishing
BLOSSOMY full of blossom
BLOTCHED pimpled; maculose
BLOTTING obliterating
BLOW-BALL dandelion head **B.**
BLOW-HOLE a whale's nostril **Z.**
BLOW-MILK skim-milk
BLOW-PIPE a tube; blow-gun
BLUDGEON truncheon; heavy stick
BLUE-BACK the field-fare **Z.**
BLUE-BELL hare-bell **B.**
BLUE-BIRD American warbler **Z.**
BLUE-BOOK Parliamentary report
BLUECOAT Christ's Hospital schoolboy
BLUE-EYED
BLUE-FISH mackerel **Z.**
BLUE-FUNK alarm and despondency
BLUEGOWN King's bedesman
BLUENESS azureness
BLUENOSE a Nova Scotian
BLUE-PILL mercurial pill **Med.**
BLUE-POLL salmon type **Z.**
BLUE-WING a duck **Z.**
BLUFFEST most outspoken
BLUFFING acting deceptively
BLUISHLY rather blue
BLUNGING pudling clay
BLUNTING dulling; benumbing
BLUNTISH not sharp
BLURRING dimming; obscuring
BLURTING uttering hastily
BLUSHFUL modest
BLUSHING showing shame; flushing
BLUSTERY stormy
BOARDING embarking; lodging **Naut.**
BOARFISH red and silver fish **Z.**
BOASTFUL vaunting
BOASTING bragging; bucking; crowing
BOATABLE navigable
BOATBILL a heron **Z.**
BOAT-HOOK aduncous adjunct
BOAT-RACE aquatic contest
BOAT-ROPE a painter
BOBBINET netted lace

BOBOLINK the rice-bird   **Z.**
BOB-WHITE American partridge **Z.**
BOCK-BEER lager beer
BOCKELET a hawk   **Z.**
BOCKLAND freehold-land   **Law**
BODEMENT a presentiment
BODILESS incorporeal
BODLEIAN (Oxford Library)
BODY-LINE (bowling at cricket)
BOG-BERRY cranberry   **B.**
BOG-EARTH peat   **Min.**
BOGEYISM frightfulness
BOGEYMAN hobgoblin
BOGGLING wavering; havering
BOG-WHORT whortleberry   **B.**
BOHEMIAN unconventional
BOLD-FACE brazen
BOLDNESS courage; audacity
BOLIVIAN (Bolivia)
BOLL-WORM cotton-worm; weevil **Z.**
BOLOMETER head radiation meter
BOLT-BOAT cobble   **Naut.**
BOLT-HEAD a matrass
BOLT-HOLE escape hole
BOLT-ROPE rope round sail   **Naut.**
BOMB-FREE no raiders
BOMBIATE a bombic salt   **Chem.**
BONA-FIDE in good faith
BONDAGER helpful tenant
BOND-DEBT bond-held debt   **Law**
BOND-MAID slave
BONDSMAN surety; bondman   **Law**
BONE-ACHE a pain   **Med.**
BONE-CAVE (pre-historic bones)
BONE-DUST manure
BONE-IDLE inert
BONELACE bobbin-lace
BONELESS spineless
BONHOMIE geniality
BONIFACE an innkeeper
BONNETED (hat-smashing)
BONSPIEL curling match
BONTEBOK S. African antelope   **Z.**
BOOBY-HUT covered sleigh
BOOBYISH dullish
BOOBYISM stupidity
BOOHOOED lamented loudly
BOOKCASE shelved case
BOOK-CLUB literary association
BOOK-DEBT outstanding account
BOOKLAND bockland   **Law**
BOOKLESS unlearned
BOOK-MARK book-marker
BOOK-MATE schoolfellow
BOOK-NAME nonce name
BOOK-OATH Bible-oath
BOOK-POST a postal facility
BOOKSHOP voluminous emporium
BOOKWORM avid reader
BOOSTING advertising; pushing

BOOT HOOK helpful appliance
BOOTHOSE spats
BOOTIKIN leggings
BOOTJACK a boot remover
BOOTLACE a latchet
BOOTLAST last for boot-making
BOOTLESS unavailing
BOOTLICK a lickspittle
BOOT-TREE (for a shapely boot)
BORACHIO leather wine bag
BORACITE magnesium borate   **Chem.**
BORDEAUX claret
BORDERED edged
BORDERER border dweller
BORDLAND reserved domain land **Law**
BORD-LODE timber carrying
BORECOLE winter cabbage   **B.**
BOREWORM teredo   **Z.**
BORROWED assumed; hypothecated
BORROWER cadger
BORSTALL hill road
BOSTANGI Turkish seraglio guards
BOTANIST   **B.**
BOTANIZE
BOTCHERY patchwork
BOTCHING clumsy repair work
BOTHERED plagued
BOTRYOID like a bunch of grapes
BOTSWANA (Bechuanaland)
BOTTLING preserving
BOTTOMED fathomed
BOTTOMRY loan secured by ship
BOTULISM form of poisoning   **Med.**
BOUDERIE pouting; petulance
BOUFFANT puffed out
BOUGHTEN bought (archaic)
BOUILLON broth; soup
BOUNCING resilient
BOUNDARY limit; (cricket)
BOUNDING leaping; bordering
BOUNTREE see bourtree   **B.**
BOURGEON bud; sprout
BOURTREE the elder   **B.**
BOVIFORM ox-like
BOW-BRACE archer's string-guard
BOW-DRILL rotary drill
BOW-GRACE a fender   **Naut.**
BOWINGLY subserviently; courteously
BOW-PIECE bow-chaser, (gun)   **Naut.**
BOWSPRIT a spar   **Naut.**
BOX-DRAIN enclosed drain
BOX-ELDER ash-leaved maple   **B.**
BOX-LOBBY passage in theatre
BOX-PLEAT a double fold
BOX-THORN a shrub   **B.**
BOYISHLY puerilely
BOY'S-PLAY a prank; trifling
BRACCATE with feathered feet   **Z.**
BRACELET a handcuff; ornament
BRACHIAL belonging to the arm

BRACKISH somewhat salt	**BRETTICE** brattice; partition
BRACTEAL leaf formation **B.**	**BREVETCY** brevet rank
BRADBURY £1 note (obs.)	**BREVIARY** prayer-book, R.C. **Eccl.**
BRADSHAW railway guide	**BREVIATE** epitome; a brief **Law**
BRADYPOD a sloth **Z.**	**BREVIPED** short-legged **Z.**
BRAGGART boaster	**BREVIPEN** short-winged **Z.**
BRAGGING vaunting	**BREWSTER** brewer; maltster
BRAIDING plaiting; upbraiding	**BRIAREAN** many handed
BRAILING hauling in; trussing **Naut.**	**BRIBABLE** venal; corrupt
BRAIN-FAG nervous exhaustion	**BRICKBAT** half-a-brick
BRAINING dashing out the brains	**BRICKING** building; wrecking
BRAINISH brain-sick; furious	**BRICK-RED**
BRAINPAN part of the skull **Med.**	**BRICK-TEA** tea in blocks
BRAISING a form of cookery	**BRIDE-ALE** ale at a marriage
BRAKE-MAN a controller	**BRIDE-BED** marriage-bed
BRAKE-VAN the guard's domain	**BRIDGING** joining up
BRAMBLED overgrown	**BRIDLING** controlling; scorning; ruffling
BRANCARD horse-borne litter	**BRIEFING** giving final instructions
BRANCHED forked; ramified	**BRIEFMAN** brief compiler
BRANCHER young bird **Z.**	**BRIGADED** combined
BRANDIED laced with brandy	**BRIGHTEN** clarify
BRANDING stigmatizing; marking	**BRIGHTLY** brilliantly
BRANDISE a trivet	**BRIGUING** canvassing
BRANDISH flourish; wave; shake	**BRIMLESS** rimless
BRAND-NEW bran-new	**BRIMMING** full; verging
BRANGLED wrangled	**BRINDLED** streaky brown
BRANTAIL the redstart; a warbler **Z.**	**BRINEPAN**⎫ salt extraction
BRANT-FOX a kind of small fox **Z.**	**BRINEPIT** ⎭ by evaporation
BRASSAGE cost of mintage	**BRINGING** conveying; fetching
BRASSARD an armlet	**BRISANCE** shattering effect
BRASSART arm armour	**BRISKING** quickening
BRASS-HAT big-wig	**BRISKISH** rather spry
BRASSICA the cabbage genus **B.**	**BRISLING** small sardine or sprat **Z.**
BRASSOCK field mustard **B.**	**BRISTLED** ruffled
BRATLING small brat	**BRITTLED** (cooking venison)
BRATTICE brettice; partition	**BRITZSKA** Polish carriage
BRAUNITE manganese oxide **Chem.**	**BROACHED** pierced
BRAWLING wrangling	**BROACHER** first proposer
BRAZENED shameless	**BROAD-AXE** heavy axe **Tool**
BRAZENLY impudently; boldly	**BROADEST** vastest; amplest
BRAZENRY effrontery	**BROADISH** rather broad
BRAZILIN a red dye **B.**	**BROCADED** embroidered
BREACHED violated; tore open	**BROCATEL** coarse brocade
BREACHES gaps; violations	**BROCCOLI** cultivated cabbage **B.**
BREAD-NUT a fruit **B.**	**BROCHURE** pamphlet; leaflet
BREAKAGE rupture; fracture	**BRODEKIN** buskin; half-boot
BREAKING smashing; infringing	**BROIDERY** embroidery
BREAKMAN brake's-man	**BROILING** grilling
BREAKVOW a perjurer	**BROKENLY** disconnectedly
BREAMING cleaning ship's bottom	**BROKERLY** mean; low; servile
BREASTED confronted	**BROMELIA** the pineapple **B.**
BREATHED exhaled; respired	**BROMIDIC** dull; addict **Med.**
BREATHER a respite	**BROMIZED** **Chem.**
BREDSORE a whitlow **Med.**	**BRONCHIC** (windpipe)
BREECHED put into trousers	**BRONZIFY** make into bronze
BREECHES pantaloons	**BRONZITE** lustrous diallage **Min.**
BREEDING lineage; begetting	**BROODING** pondering; incubating
BRELOGUE watch-chain ornament	**BROOKING** bearing; enduring
BRENNAGE an ancient tribute	**BROOKLET** streamlet
BRETHREN brothers; kindred	**BROOMING** sweeping; breaming

BROUGHAM one-horsed carriage
BROWBEAT bully; overbear; haze
BROWLESS shameless
BROWNING a process; a rifle
BROWNISH somewhat sunburnt
BROWNIST congregationalist **Eccl.**
BROW-POST a main beam
BROWSICK dejected; melancholy
BROWSING pasturing
BRUISING contusing
BRUMAIRE November (Fr. Rev. Cal.)
BRUNETTE dark hair and eyes
BRUSHING sweeping; brisk
BRUSSELS (carpets); (sprouts)
BRUSTLED crackled; bullied
BRUTALLY ferociously; ruthlessly
BRYOLOGY study of mosses
BRYONINE extract of bryony **Chem.**
BUBBLING gurgling; cheating
BUCCANED (smoked meat)
BUCCINAL like a trumpet
BUCCINUM a whelk **Z.**
BUCKBEAN a water-plant **B.**
BUCKETED rode furiously
BUCKHORN buck's horn **Z.**
BUCK-JUMP quick plunging leap
BUCKLING curling; fastening
BUCKMAST beech-mast **B.**
BUCKSHEE gratuity; commission; free
BUCKSHOT large shot
BUCKSKIN soft yellow leather
BUCRANIA ornamental ox-skulls
BUDDHISM⎫ religion founded
BUDDHIST ⎭ by Sakyamuni **Eccl.**
BUDDLING ore washing
BUDGEREE good (Australian)
BUDGETED made provision
BUFFCOAT a soldier; a jacket
BUFFETED struck; clouted
BUFONITE toadstone **Min.**
BUHL-WORK inlaid tortoiseshell
BUILDING erecting; pile; structure
BULGARIC Bulgarian
BULKHEAD (ship construction)
BULKIEST largest; biggest
BULL-BEEF coarse-beef
BULL-CALF male calf **Z.**
BULLDOSE to haze; intimidate; coerce
BULLDOZE rase or level
BULLETIN official report
BULL-FROG North American frog **Z.**
BULLHEAD miller's thumb (fish) **Z.**
BULLIRAG to badger; ballyrag
BULLNOSE rounded edge **Arch.**
BULLRING Spanish arena
BULL'S-EYE glass window; sweet
BULLWEED knap-weed **B.**
BULLWORT bishop's-weed **B.**
BULLYING browbeating; threatening
BULLYISM hectoring; blustering

BULLYRAG abuse vehemently
BULRUSHY full of rushes **B.**
BUMMALOE Bombay duck (fish) **Z.**
BUMMAREE fish-factor; money-lender
BUMP-BALL cricket
BUNCHING clustering; grouping
BUNDLING faggoting
BUN-FIGHT tea party
BUNGALOW one-storied house
BUNGHOLE hole in a cask
BUNGLING awkward; clumsy
BUNGVENT spile-hole in bung
BUNKERED coaled; in difficulties
BUNODONT a dental malady **Med.**
BUNTLINE a sheet **Naut.**
BUOYANCY specific lightness
BURBERRY a water-proof
BURDENED laden; overloaded
BURGAMOT bergamot; citron **B.**
BURGANET⎫ Burgundian helmet;
BURGONET ⎭ helmet with visor
BURGLARY felony at night
BURGLING stealing; robbing
BURGRAVE German governor
BURGUNDY French wine
BURINIST engraver
BURLETTA burlesque; comic opera **Mus.**
BURNOOSE Arab cloak
BURNT-EAR corn-disease **B.**
BURROWED excavated; tunnelled
BURROWER a rabbit
BURR-PUMP large pump **Naut.**
BURSALIS a muscle **Med.**
BURSCHEN German students
BURSTING exploding; rending
BUSH-BABY night-ape (S. Africa) **Z.**
BUSH-BRED
BUSHBUCK antelope (S. Africa) **Z.**
BUSHELER a clothes-repairer (U.S.A.)
BUSH-ROPE a liana; a creeper **B.**
BUSH-VELD bush-country (S. Africa)
BUSINESS stage-craft; occupation
BUSKINED booted
BUSYBODY officious person
BUSYLESS being idle
BUSYNESS state of being busy
BUTCHERY slaughter; massacre
BUTCHING butchery (dialect)
BUTTERED missed
BUTTERIS farrier's knife **Tool**
BUTTONED fastened
BUTTRESS support; prop
BUTTRICE farrier's knife **Tool**
BUTYRATE salt of butyric acid **Chem.**
BUTYROUS buttery; oleaginous
BY-BIDDER auction-bid encourager
BYCOCKET peaked cap (XVth Cent.)
BY-CORNER odd corner
BY-DESIGN subsidiary purpose
BY-LANDER bilander; hoy **Naut.**

BY-MATTER something incidental
BY-MOTIVE unavowed motive
BY-PASSED avoided
BYRONISM (Lord Byron)
BY-SPEECH casual speech
BY-STREET side street
BY-STROKE sly stroke
BY-THE-BYE by the way

C

CABACHON jewel without facets
CABALISM occultism; mystic science
CABALIST an adept
CABALLED plotted; conspired
CABALLER schemer; intriguer
CABBAGED filched; purloined; stole
CABBLING smashing into small pieces
CABIN-BOY   **Naut.**
CABINING confining; cooping up
CABIRIAN fire-worshipper (Lemnos)
CABOBBED curried
CABOCHED⎱ heraldic head without
CABOSHED⎰ a neck
CABOODLE the whole lot
CABOTAGE coasting trade
CABRIOLE capriole; to leap; to caper
CAB-STAND a rank
CACHALOT⎱ the sperm whale   **Z.**
CACHOLOT⎰
CACHEMIC unhealthy   **Med.**
CACHEPOT ornamental flower-pot
CACHUCHA Spanish dance   **Mus.**
CACHUNDE aromatic medicine   **Med.**
CACKEREL a species of fish   **Z.**
CACKLING gossiping; chattering
CACODOXY erroneous opinion
CACOLOGY bad pronunciation
CADASTRE a survey of land
CADENCED modulated; rhythmical
CADILLAC a pear; motor car   **B.**
CADUCEUS Mercury's wand
CADUCITY frailty; transitoriness
CADUCOUS early falling (leaves)   **B.**
CAERLEON King Arthur's residence
CAESIOUS blue-grey
CAESURAL (metric pause)
CAFFEINE coffee alkaloid   **Chem.**
CAGELING a bird in a cage
CAILLACH an old woman (Gael.)
CAIMACAM Turkish governor
CAISSOON caisson; water-tight chest
CAJOLERY flattery; blandishment
CAJOLING wheedling; coaxing
CAKESHOP (confectionery)
CAKE-WALK a caper
CALABASH gourd   **B.**
CALADIUM plant genus   **B.**
CALAMARY cuttle-fish   **Z.**

CALAMBAC aloes-wood   **B.**
CALAMINE zinc ore   **Min.**
CALAMINT aromatic plant   **B.**
CALAMITE tremolite   **Min.**
CALAMITY disaster; affliction
CALANDER a lark   **Z.**
CALANDRA grain-weevil   **Z.**
CALANGAY white cockatoo   **Z.**
CALATHUS work-basket
CALCEATE shod; to shoe
CALCEDON opaline quartz   **Min.**
CALCINED reduced to quick-lime
CALC-SPAR calcite   **Min.**
CALC-TUFF a lime-stone   **Min.**
CALCULUS stone; (calculation)   **Med.**
CALENDAR almanac; register; list
CALENDER hot-rolling machine
CALFLESS spindle-shanked
CALF-LOVE an early attachment
CALF-SKIN
CALIBRED bored; gauged
CALIDITY warmth; fervency; ardency
CALIDUCT a heating pipe
CALIFATE rank of calif
CALIPASH green turtle fat
CALIPERS a measuring device   **Tool**
CALIPPIC (Metonic cycles)   **Meas.**
CALISAYA Peruvian bark   **B.**
CALIXTIN Hussite   **Eccl.**
CALL-BIRD a decoy   **Z.**
CALL-GIRL prostitute
CALLIOPE muse of epic poetry
CALL-LOAN cash on demand
CALL-NOTE bird-call
CALL-OVER a roll-call
CALMNESS placidity; tranquillity
CALORIST a heat theorist
CALOTYPE talbot-type (photo)
CALTROPS a plant   **B.**
CALVERED crimped; pickled
CALVILLE an apple   **B.**
CALYCINE cuplike   **B.**
CALYCOID like a calyx
CALYMENE trilobite genus   **Z.**
CALYPTRA a covering   **B.**
CAMASSIA kind of hyacinth   **B.**
CAMATINA acorns for tanning
CAMBERED slightly arched
CAMBRIAN Welsh
CAMELEER camel driver
CAMELEON chameleon   **Z.**
CAMELINE camlet; camel hair
CAMELISH obstinate
CAMELLIA an evergreen   **B.**
CAMERATE to build archshape
CAMISADE⎱ night attack with white
CAMISADO⎰ shirts over armour
CAMISOLE a straight-jacket
CAMISTER a clergyman   **Eccl**
CAMOMILE a bitter plant   **B**

CAMPAIGN open country; crusade
CAMP-FIRE
CAMPHENE camphine; camphor **Chem.**
CAMP-SHOT a pile revetment
CAM-SHAFT
CAMSTONE whitening for doorsteps
CAM-WHEEL an eccentric
CANADIAN Canuck
CANAIGRE Texan dock **B.**
CANALIZE make into a canal
CANARESE natives of Canara
CANASTER a kind of tobacco **B.**
CANCELLI bars of lattice-work **Eccl.**
CANCRINE crab-like **Z.**
CANCROID like cancer **Med.**
CANDIDLY frankly; sincerely; naively
CANDYING preserving in sugar
CANE-HOLE trench for sugar canes
CANE-MILL sugar crushing mill
CANEPHOR basket-bearing figure
CANICULA the dog-star; Sirius
CANISTER a tin; tea chest; case-shot
CANITIES whiteness of the hair **Med.**
CANKERED corroded; infected
CANNABIN cannabic extract **Chem.**
CANNABIS hemp; bhang **B.**
CANNELON mince-pie
CANNIBAL anthropophagite
CANNIKIN pannikin; a billy
CANNONED (billiards); collided
CANNULAR tubular
CANOEIST a paddler
CANON-BIT cannon-bit; (horse-bit)
CANONESS a beneficiary **Eccl.**
CANONIST ecclesiastical expert **Eccl.**
CANONIZE besaint **Eccl.**
CANON-LAW diocesan digest **Eccl.**
CANOODLE caress; fondle
CANOPIED with an awning
CANOROUS tuneful; musical; melodious
CANSTICK candlestick (Shak.)
CANTERED galloped easily
CANTHOOK lumberman's lever **Tool**
CANTICLE song or chant
CANTICUM a canticle **Eccl.**
CANTONAL referring to a district
CANTONED divided into cantons
CANTORIS of the precentor **Eccl.**
CANZONET air or song
CAPACITY volume; capability; faculty
CAPE-CART two-wheeled vehicle (S.A.)
CAPELINE bandage; lady's wrap **Med.**
CAPELLET enlarged hock
CAPERING frolicsome frisking
CAPER-TEA black tea **B.**
CAPIBARA ⎫ Brazilian rodent **Z.**
CAPYBARA ⎭ allied to the guinea-pig
CAPITANO a head-man
CAPITATE growing to a head **B.**
CAPNOMORE wood-tar extract **Chem.**

CAPONIER gallery in a fort
CAPONISE castrate; geld; emasculate
CAPOTING winning all tricks at piquet
CAP-PAPER wrapping or writing paper
CAPRIOLE sort of buck-jump
CAPRIPED goat-footed
CAPROATE a butric salt **Chem.**
CAPSICUM red pepper; chilli **B.**
CAPSTONE fossil sea-urchin **Min.**
CAPSULAR in capsule form
CAPTIOUS hyper-critical; censorious
CAPTURED caught; arrested
CAPUCCIO a hood or cowl
CAPUCHIN ⎱ monk; hooded cloak **Eccl.**
CAPUCINE ⎰ hooded monkey; pigeon **Z.**
CARABINE carbine; short rifle
CARACARA Brazilian carrion-hawk **Z.**
CARACOLE spiral staircase (arch.)
CARACOLE equestrian turn; shell **Z.**
CARACOLY alloy of gold and silver
CARAPACE tortoise shell, etc. **Z.**
CARAP-OIL crab-wood oil **B.**
CARBOLIC phenol **Chem.**
CARBONIC **Chem.**
CARBURET impregnate with carbon
CARCAJOU wolverine or glutton **Z.**
CARCANET collar of jewels
CARDAMOM aromatic spice **Med.**
CARD-CASE a receptacle
CARDIACE heart-shaped jewel
CARDIGAN woolly waistcoat
CARDINAL short cloak; principal **Eccl.**
CARDIOID heart-shaped curve
CARDITIS heartburn **Med.**
CAREENED laid on one side **Naut.**
CAREERED raced; rushed; dashed
CAREFREE joyous
CARELESS heedless; remiss; incautious
CARESSED fondled; embraced; petted
CAREWORN grief-stricken
CARGOOSE crested grebe **Z.**
CARIACOU Virginian deer **Z.**
CARIBBEE a Caribbean
CARICOUS like a fig **B.**
CARILLON a ring of bells
CARINATE keel-shaped
CARL-HEMP female hemp plant **B.**
CARNAGED slaughtered; butchered
CARNALLY sensuously
CARNAUBA Brazilian palm **B.**
CARNEOUS fleshy
CARNIFEX public executioner
CARNIVAL revelry; masquerade
CAROLINE (King Charles) **Coin**
CAROLLED warbled; sang **Mus.**
CAROTEEL East Indian weight **Meas.**
CAROTENE vitamin A
CAROUSAL a jollification; orgies
CAROUSED held carnival; feasted
CAROUSEL tournament; tourney

CAROUSER a noisy reveller		
CARPETED told off; rebuked		
CARRIAGE cab; burden; behaviour		
CARRIOLE open carriage; sledge		
CARRITCH catechism (Sc.)		
CARRYING transporting; conveying		
CART-LOAD a measure of capacity		
CARTOUCH cartouche; hieroglyph		
CARUCAGE tax on ploughs		
CARUCATE (plough-land)		
CARUNCEL fleshy excrescence	**Med.**	
CARYATIC (Caryatides)		
CARYATID a lady supporter (arch.)		
CARYOKAR butter-nut tree	**B.**	
CASCABEL swell on cannon's mouth		
CASCADED fell in torrents		
CASCALHO diamond-bearing earth		
CASEMATE armoured chamber		
CASEMENT hinged window		
CASE-SHOT short range ammunition		
CASE-WORM caddis-worm	**Z.**	
CASHMERE silky goat's hair		
CASKETED enshrined; coffined		
CASSETTE container		
CASS-WEED shepherd's purse	**B.**	
CASTANEA chestnut-tree	**B.**	
CASTANET a clapper	**Mus.**	
CASTAWAY wrecked; rejected		
CAST-IRON rigid; inflexible		
CASTLERY feudal castle control		
CASTLING (chess)		
CASTRATE geld; emasculate		
CASTRATO high voiced singer	**Mus.**	
CASUALLY accidentally; fortuitously		
CASUALTY killed or wounded		
CATACOMB cave sepulchre		
CATALYST⎱ (unchanged substance		
CATALYSE⎰ assisting chemical action)		
CATAPULT a pellet projector		
CATARACT waterfall; eye trouble	**Med.**	
CAT-BLOCK anchor-tackle	**Naut.**	
CATCH-ALL		
CATCHFLY certain plants	**B.**	
CATCHING infectious; charming		
CATEGORY order; class; division		
CATENARY like a chain		
CATERESS lady provider		
CATERING food and entertainment		
CATHEDRA bishop's throne	**Eccl.**	
CATHETUS perpendicular line		
CATHEXIS concentration of psychic energy		
CATHISMA part of the psalter		
CATHODAL (negative electrode)		
CATHOLIC universal; liberal; tolerant		
CATILINE daring conspirator		
CATODONT teeth on lower jaw only		
CATONIAN resembling Cato; severe		
CATOPSIS morbid keen-sightedness		
CAT'S-FOOT ground ivy	**B.**	
CAT'S-TAIL the reed mace	**B.**	

CAT-STICK tip-cat's stick		
CAUDATED having a tail; tailed		
CAUDICES stems of trees	**B.**	
CAUDICLE an orchid stalk	**B.**	
CAULDRON bowl-shaped boiler		
CAULICLE caudicle; small stalk	**B.**	
CAULKING filling in cracks	**Naut.**	
CAUSALLY resultantly; productively		
CAUSERIE gossip; small talk		
CAUSEUSE settee for two		
CAUSEWAY roadway over wet ground		
CAUTIOUS wary; discreet; watchful		
CAVALIER haughty; disdainful; beau		
CAVATINA short simple air	**Mus.**	
CAVATION excavation		
CAVEATED warned	**Law**	
CAVEATOR caveat lodger	**Law**	
CAVE-BEAR extinct animal	**Z.**	
CAVERNED hollowed out		
CAVESSON horse-breaking appliance		
CAVICORN hollow-horned	**Z.**	
CAVILLED objected; carped; criticized		
CAVILLER captious critic		
CAVORTED pranced		
CELERIAC turnip-rooted celery	**B.**	
CELERITY rapidity; swiftness; speed		
CELIBACY the unmarried state		
CELIBATE unwed		
CELLARER wine steward; Simon		
CELLARET small wine container		
CELLULAR honey-combed; alveolated		
CEMENTED glued; united; stuck		
CEMETERY burial ground; necropolis		
CENATION supping		
CENOBITE religious order	**Eccl.**	
CENOTAPH a monument; memorial		
CENOZIAC tertiary geological period		
CENSORED blue-pencilled		
CENSURED reprimanded; rebuked		
CENTAURY rose-pink flower	**B.**	
CENTERED centred; localized		
CENTIARE a square metre	**Meas.**	
CENTIBAR a meteor measurement	**Meas.**	
CENTOISM literary patchwork		
CENTOIST platitudinarian		
CENTRING (football); centering		
CENTROID centre of gravity		
CENTUPLE a hundredfold		
CEPHALGY head-ache	**Med.**	
CEPHALIC remedy for head-pains	**Med**	
CERAMICS pottery		
CERASINE plum gum	**B**	
CERASTES a horned snake	**Z**	
CERATITE species of ammonite	**Min**	
CERATODE horny structure		
CERATOID ceratose; horny		
CERBERUS hell's watch-dog	**Z**	
CEREALIA corn and grass	**B**	
CEREALIN a bran extract	**Chem**	
CEREBRAL brainy		

CEREBRIC cerebral	**Med.**
CEREBRIN something in the brain	
CEREBRUM part of the brain	**Med.**
CEREMENT shroud dipped in wax	
CEREMONY prescribed formality	
CERNUOUS drooping	**B.**
CERULEAN sky-blue	
CERULEIN olive-green	
CERUSITE white lead	**Min.**
CERVICAL relating to the neck	
CESAREAN (Julius Caesar)	**Med.**
CESSPOOL drainage pit; midden	
CETACEAN⎫ whale or dolphin;	**Z.**
CETOLOGY⎭ their natural history	**Z.**
CETRARIA lichen; Iceland moss	**B.**
CHACONNE slow dance and music	
CHADBAND a canting hypocrite	
CHAFEWAX sealing-wax officer	
CHAFFERY haggling; bargaining	
CHAFFING bantering; scoffing	
CHAFFRON horse armour	
CHAINING restraining; fettering	
CHAINLET small chain	
CHAIR-BED convertible contraption	
CHAIRING carrying in triumph	
CHAIRMAN president or carrier	
CHALDAIC Babylonian	
CHALDRON 25 cwt. of coal	**Meas.**
CHALICED cup-like	
CHALKING recording in chalk	
CHALKPIT a quarry	
CHAMBREL horse's hind leg joint	
CHAMFRON horse's head armour	
CHAMORRO native; language (Guam, Marianas)	
CHAMPING chewing; gnawing; biting	
CHAMPION defender; hero; victor	
CHANCERY court of justice	**Law**
CHANCING risking; happening	
CHANDLER candle-maker; dealer	
CHANFRIN fore-part of horse's head	
CHANGING altering; varying	
CHANTING intoning; reciting	
CHAPBOOK book hawked by chapmen	
CHAPELET stirrups and leathers	
CHAPELRY chapel district	**Eccl.**
CHAPERON an escort; a cap	
CHAPITER capital of a column	
CHAPLAIN a sky-pilot	**Eccl.**
CHAPLESS without a lower jaw	
CHAPPING cleaving	
CHAPTREL arch-supporting capital	
CHARCOAL charred wood	
CHARGING rushing; costing; enjoining	
CHARLIES night watchmen	
CHARLOCK wild mustard	**B.**
CHARMING fascinating; captivating	
CHARRING scorching; toasting	
CHARTING mapping; recording	
CHARTISM⎫ (universal suffrage;	
CHARTIST⎭ payment of M.P.s, etc.)	

CHASSEUR light-armed soldier	
CHASTELY virtuously; modestly	
CHASTISE flog; castigate; discipline	
CHASTITY sexual abstinence	
CHASUBLE vestment over alb	**Eccl.**
CHATELET small castle	
CHATTELS miscellaneous property	
CHATTING friendly converse	
CHATWOOD fuel; ducal mansion	
CHAUFFER portable furnace	
CHAUNTER chanter of bag-pipes	**Mus.**
CHAUSSES trunk-hose; leg-armour	
CHAY-ROOT Indian red dye	**B.**
CHEATERY fraud; deception	
CHEATING knavery; duping	
CHECHAKO tenderfoot (Alaska)	
CHECKERS a draughts game	
CHECKING reproving; impeding	
CHEEKING saucy behaviour	
CHEEPING piping; chirping	
CHEERFUL merry and bright	
CHEERILY joyfully; gaily; blithely	
CHEERING applause; comforting	
CHELIFER book-scorpion	**Z.**
CHELLEAN early Palaeolithic	
CHELONIA tortoises and turtles	**Z.**
CHEMICAL chymical	
CHEMURGY applied organic chemistry	
CHENILLE fluffy silk or cotton	
CHERUBIC angelic	
CHERUBIM a celestial spirit	
CHESHIRE cheese; (cat)	**Z.**
CHESIBLE see chasuble	**Eccl.**
CHESSMAN a piece	
CHESTING encasing; boxing	
CHESTNUT old joke; conker	**B.**
CHEVEREL⎫ kid-skin;	**Z.**
CHEVERIL⎭ flexible leather	
CHEVILLE bridge of a violin	**Mus.**
CHEVYING chasing; pursuing	
CHIASMUS inverse parallelism	
CHIASTIC crossed	
CHICANED cheated; tricked	
CHICANER a swindler; artful dodger	
CHICCORY chicory	**B.**
CHICKING sprouting	
CHICK-PEA small pea	**B.**
CHIEFAGE capitation; poll tax	
CHIEFRIE small feudal rent	**Law**
CHILD-BED lying in	
CHILDING bearing children	
CHILDISH puerile; infantile	
CHILDREN kids	
CHILIASM doctrine of millennium	
CHILIAST believer in that doctrine	
CHILLIER cooler; colder	
CHILLING discouraging; depressful	
CHILTERN (stewartship)	
CHIMAERA fabulous monster	**Z.**
CHIMERIC fanciful; delusive	

333

CHINAMAN Chinese	**CHUMMAGE** chamber-fellowship
CHINAMPA floating garden	**CHUMMERY** friendship; intimacy
CHIN-CHIN a toast	**CHUMMING** messing together
CHINKING jingling	**CHUMP-END** thick end
CHINOITE green mineral	**CHUPATTY** unleavened bread
CHINREST violin	**CHURINGA** Australian amulet
CHINSCAB a sheep-disease	**CHURLISH** surly and sullen
CHINSING caulking	**CHURNING** agitating; rotating; foaming
CHIPMUCK ⎱ the ground-squirrel	**CHYLIFIC** producing chyle **Med.**
CHIPMUNK ⎰ of North America **Z.**	**CHYMICAL** chemical
CHIPPING chaffing; chopping; fracturing	**CIBATION** feeding
CHIPSHOT golf	**CIBORIUM** eucharistic vessel **Eccl.**
CHIRAGRA gout in the hands **Med.**	**CICATRIX** a scar **Med.**
CHIRPING cheeping	**CICERONE** guide
CHIRRING cooing; curring; purring	**CICISBEI** sword-knots
CHIT-CHAT small talk	**CICISBEO** philanderer
CHIVALRY gallantry	**CICURATE** to tame
CHLOASMA a skin disease **Med.**	**CIDER-CUP** a beverage
CHLORATE **Chem.**	**CIDERIST** cider-maker
CHLORIDE **Chem.**	**CIDERKIN** inferior cider
CHLORINE a yellow gas **Chem.**	**CILIATED** with eye-lashes
CHLORITE olive-green mineral **Min.**	**CILIFORM** (fine filaments) **B.**
CHLOROID **Chem.**	**CIMBRIAN** a German tribe
CHLOROUS **Chem.**	**CIMOLITE** fuller's earth **Min.**
CHOANITE fossil sponge **Min.**	**CINCHONA** Peruvian bark **Med.**
CHOICELY discriminately; exquisitely	**CINCTURE** girdle; belt
CHOIR-BOY a sweet singer **Eccl.**	**CINDROUS** ashy
CHOIRING singing in unison	**CINEFILM**
CHOLERIC irascible; testy; petulant	**CINERAMA** wide screen film
CHOLIAMB iambic metre	**CINERARY** cindery
CHONDRAL cartilaginous **Med.**	**CINEREAL** like ashes
CHONDRIN gelatinous liquid **Med.**	**CINGULUM** band; zone; belt
CHOOSING selecting; picking	**CINNABAR** dragon's blood **Min.**
CHOP-CHOP hurry!	**CINNAMIC** cinnamon type **B.**
CHOPNESS kind of spade	**CINNAMON** a spicy bark **B.**
CHOPPING and changing; veering	**CIPHERED** written in code
CHOP-SUEY a succulent Chinese dish	**CIRCAEAN** infatuating (Circe)
CHORAGIC (musical production)	**CIRCINUS** the compasses (Astronomical)
CHORALLY (choir or chorus)	**CIRCLING** flying around
CHORDATA vertebrates, etc. **Z.**	**CIRCUITY** indirect approach
CHORDING stringing	**CIRCULAR** round; printed leaflet
CHOREGUS choragus **Mus.**	**CIRRHOSE** ⎱ terminating in a
CHORIAMB iambic metre	**CIRRHOUS** ⎰ tendril or curl **B**
CHORISIS separation **B.**	**CIRRIPED** a barnacle **Z**
CHORTLED chuckled loudly	**CISELEUR** engraver; chaser
CHORUSED concerted	**CISELURE** chased metal-work
CHOULTRY caravanserai; inn	**CISTELLA** capsular shield **B**
CHOUSING swindling	**CISTVAEN** stone tomb
CHOW-CHOW ginger chutney	**CITATION** mention in despatches
CHRISMAL (consecrated oil) **Eccl.**	**CITATORY** citing; summoning
CHRISTEN baptize **Eccl.**	**CITREOUS** citric; lemon flavoured
CHROMATE **Chem.**	**CITRININ** bacteriostat
CHROMITE **Chem.**	**CITY-BRED**
CHROMIUM a metallic element **Chem.**	**CIVET-CAT** pole-cat **Z.**
CHROMULE colouring matter **B.**	**CIVETING** scenting with civet
CHTHONIC subterranean	**CIVILIAN** doctor of civil law
CHUCKIES a game with pebbles	**CIVILIST** civil law expert
CHUCKING throwing; jerking; gripping	**CIVILITY** politeness; courtesy
CHUCKLED exulted	**CIVILIZE** reclaim from barbarism
CHUFFILY clownishly; churlishly	**CLACK-BOX** valve container

CLACKING clicking; jabbering
CLADDING **Arch.**
CLADONIA reindeer moss **B.**
CLAIMANT assertor of claims
CLAIMING demanding; arrogating
CLAMANCY urgency; exigency
CLAM-BAKE pic-nic food (U.S.A)
CLAMMING daubing; clogging
CLAMPING fastening; clumping
CLANGING resounding; clanking
CLANGOUR din; clamour
CLANGOUS resonant
CLANKING clanging; clashing
CLANNISH cliquish
CLANSHIP loyalty; sodality
CLANSMAN one of a clan
CLAP-DISH wooden platter
CLAPPING applauding; putting away
CLAP-SILL frame of lock-gates
CLAP-TRAP speciosity; theatrical
CLAQUEUR hired applauder
CLARENCE four-wheeled cab
CLARINET reed instrument **Mus.**
CLASHING colliding; jarring; differing
CLASPING fastening; grasping; hugging
CLASSIER superior; loftier; finer
CLASSIFY arrange; tabulate
CLASSING grading; grouping; ranging
CLASSMAN a graduate
CLASS-WAR engineered strife
CLAUDIAN (Roman Emperors)
CLAUSURE closure; stoppage
CLAVATED with knobs on
CLAVECIN harpsichord **Mus.**
CLAVIARY index of keys
CLAVICLE collar-bone **Med.**
CLAVIGER clubman; key-man
CLAWBACK a sycophant
CLAWLESS no claws
CLAWSICK foot-rot
CLAY-COLD lifeless
CLAY-MARL chalky clay **Min.**
CLAY-MILL clay mixing mill
CLAYMORE Scottish broad-sword
CLAYWEED colt's-foot **B.**
CLEANING washing; purifying; clearing
CLEANISH rather clean
CLEANSED purged; purified
CLEANSER a detergent; purifier
CLEARAGE removal
CLEAR-CUT sharply outlined
CLEAREST plainest; purest
CLEARING (banking; woodcutting)
CLEAVAGE fracture; fissure; separation
CLEAVERS goose-grass **B.**
CLEAVING splitting; riving
CLEAVING clinging; uniting; adhering
CLECKING a brood; a clutch **Z.**
CLEMATIS traveller's joy, etc. **B.**
CLEMENCY clemence; leniency; mercy

CLENCHED clinched; gripped
CLERICAL priestly
CLERKAGE clerical work
CLERKDOM babooism
CLERKERY accountancy
CLERKISH somewhat learned
CLEVEITE Norwegian pitchblende **Min.**
CLEVERER more astute; abler
CLEVERLY dexterously; adroitly
CLICKING progressing satisfactorily
CLIENTAL dependant
CLIENTED supplied with clients
CLIMATIC due to climate
CLIMBING scrambling; scaling
CLINCHED clenched; held fast
CLINCHER decisive reply
CLINGING embracing; tenacious
CLINICAL bedside **Med.**
CLINIQUE nursing-home **Med.**
CLINKANT glittering
CLINKING jingling
CLIPPERS cutting tools **Tool**
CLIPPING shearing; trimming
CLIQUISH clannish
CLIQUISM exclusiveness
CLITELLA bands of worms **Z.**
CLITHRAL completely roofed
CLOAKAGE disguise; pretext
CLOAK-BAG portmanteau
CLOAKING hiding; veiling; screening
CLOCKING checking in; timing
CLODDING clotting
CLODDISH boorish; rustic
CLODPATE dolt; blockhead
CLODPOOL dullard; clotpoll
CLOGGING coalescing; impeding
CLOISTER an ambulatory **Eccl.**
CLOSE-CUT close-bodied; cropped
CLOSETED secluded
CLOTHIER cloth merchant; tailor
CLOTHING garments; dress; draping
CLOTPOLL clodpate
CLOTTING coagulating; curdling
CLOUDAGE cloudiness
CLOUDERY cloudage
CLOUDILY mistily
CLOUDING obscuring; dimming
CLOUDLET a little cloud
CLOUTING patching; buffeting
CLOVERED in clover
CLOWNERY buffoonery; burlesque
CLOWNING playing the fool; jesting
CLOWNISH ungainly; rude; boorish
CLOYLESS insatiable
CLOYMENT a surfeit; a glut
CLOYSOME palling
CLUBBING combining; bludgeoning
CLUBBISH rustic; congenial
CLUBBISM the club system
CLUBBIST frequenter of clubs

CLUB-FIST large heavy fist	
CLUBFOOT taliped	**Med.**
CLUBHAUL tacking	**Naut.**
CLUB-LAND (Pall Mall, etc.)	
CLUB-MOSS lycopodium	**B.**
CLUB-ROOM a meeting room	
CLUB-ROOT a plant disease	**B.**
CLUB-RUSH bulrush	**B.**
CLUCKING hen-talk	
CLUELESS without a trace	
CLUMPING (bootmaking); bunching	
CLUMSIER more awkward	
CLUMSILY maladroitly	
CLUPEOID like a herring	**Z.**
CLUSTERY in clusters or bunches	**B.**
CLUTCHED caught; gripped; clasped	
CLYFAKER a pickpocket	
CLYPEATE like a shield; oscutate	
COACHBOX driver's seat	
COACH-DOG Dalmatian	**Z.**
COACHFUL full inside	
COACHING tutoring; driving; training	
COACHMAN a coachee	
COACTING alliance; working together	
COACTION compulsion; coercion	
COACTIVE working in unison	
COAGENCY joint action	
COAGULUM a blood clot	**Med.**
COALESCE mix; unite; amalgamate	
COALFISH black-backed cod	**Z.**
COAL-HOLE small coal-cellar	
COAL-MINE coal-pit	
COAL-SHIP a collier	**Naut.**
COALWORK a colliery	
COAMINGS raised work	**Naut.**
COARSELY crudely; churlishly	
COARSEST roughest; grossest	
COARSISH rather coarse	
CO-ASSUME agree	
COASTING (shipping, cycling)	**Naut.**
COAT-CARD court-card	
COAT-LINK two buttons and a link	
COBALTIC rather blue	
COBBLING shoe-repair	
COBCOALS cobbles	**Min.**
CO-BISHOP joint bishop	**Eccl.**
COBSTONE large rounded stone	**Min.**
COBWEBBY araneous	
COCCAGEE cider apple	**B.**
COCCIDIA parasites	**Med.**
COCCULUS narcotic plant	**B.**
COCHLEAN spiral	
COCHLEAR twisted; spiral	
COCKADED bearing a badge	
COCKATOO crested parrot	**Z.**
COCKAYNE cocaigne; land of plenty	
COCK-BILL (anchor-dropping)	**Naut.**
COCK-BOAT cog; small boat	**Naut.**
COCK-CROW dawn	
COCKERED pampered	

COCKEREL young cock	**Z.**
COCK-EYED asquint; crooked	**Med.**
COCKLING puckering; wrinkling	
COCKLOFT top loft	
COCK-SHOT cock-shy; random round	
COCKSHUT eventide; twilight	
COCKSPUR Virginian hawthorn	**B.**
COCKSURE absolutely certain	
COCKTAIL iced drink; beetle	**Z.**
COCOA-NUT cokernut	**B.**
COCTIBLE able to be cooked	
CODDLING pampering; indulging	
CODIFIED systematized	
CODIFIER a compiler; collator	
CO-EDITOR joint editor	
COENZYME	
COERCING compelling; curbing	
COERCION force; constraint	
COERCIVE repressive; compulsive	
COESTATE union of estates	
COEXPAND dilate simultaneously	
COEXTEND march together	
COFFERED in a box	
COFFERER a treasurer	
COFFINED enclosed	
COGENTLY forcibly; potently	
COGITATE ponder; meditate; ruminate	
COGNIZEE fine receiver	**Law**
COGNIZOR exacter of a fine	**Law**
COGNOMEN the surname	
COGNOSCE give judgment	**Law**
COGNOVIT acceptance of claim	**Law**
COGWHEEL spur-wheel	
COHERENT connected; consistent	
COHERING adhering; uniting	
COHESION congruity; adhesion	
COHESIVE sticky; gummy	
COHOBATE distill	**Chem.**
COIFFEUR hairdresser	
COIFFURE a headdress	
COIGNING extorting	
COINCIDE happen simultaneously	
CO-INHERE exist together	
COINLESS impecunious; broke	
COISTRIL a groom; see coystril	
COKERNUT coconut	**B.**
COLANDER perforated bowl	
COLATION filtration	
COLATURE straining	
COLDNESS frigidity	
COLD-TYPE printing	
COLE-RAPE the turnip	**B**
COLESEED cabbage seed	**B**
COLESLAW cabbage salad	
COLEWORT young cabbage	**B**
COLISEUM Roman ruin	
COLLAGEN gelatine	**Chem**
COLLAPSE breakdown; subside; faint	
COLLARED pressed; caught	
COLLARET small collar	

COLLATED collected; assembled
COLLATOR codifier; donor
COLLEGER Eton scholar
COLLETIC sticky; mucilaginous
COLLIDED crashed; encountered
COLLIERY coal-mine
COLLOGUE plot; confer
COLLOQUY dialogue; conversation
COLLUDED acted in collusion
COLLUDER conspirator; plotter
COLLYING fouling
COLONIAL colonist
COLONIST a settler in the colonies
COLONIZE establish a colony
COLOPHON publisher's tallymark
COLORATE coloured; dyed
COLORINE madder extract   **B.**
COLOSSAL gigantic; herculean; titanic
COLOSSUS Apollo's statue
COLOTOMY colon cutting   **Med.**
COLOURED specious; painted; tinged
COLSTAFF carrying pole
COLUMBIC containing niobium   **Min.**
COLUMNAR in columns
COLUMNED having pillars
COMATOSE lethargic; drowsy
COMATOUS sleepy; torpid
COMBINED united; coalesced
COMBINER a merger; blender
COMBLESS lacking comb or crest
COME-BACK repartee; return
COMEDIAN actor; player; performer
COMEDIST writer of comedy
COME-DOWN humiliation; snub
COMELILY attractively; gracefully
COMETARY planetarium; orrery
COMING-IN entrance; income
COMITIAL relating to assemblies
COMMANDO a fighting force
COMMATIC staccato; concise
COMMENCE initiate; begin; originate
COMMERCE barter; trade; traffic
COMMIXED blended; combined
COMMONED held in common
COMMONER an M.P.; not a nobleman
COMMONEY a playing-marble
COMMONLY usually; frequently
COMMONTY common land
COMMOVED agitated; disturbed
COMMUNAL public
COMMUNED held private converse
COMMUTED exchanged; altered
COMMUTER season ticket holder
COMPAGES a complex structure
COMPARED likened
COMPESCE to curb
COMPETED strove; emulated
COMPILED amassed; composed
COMPILER literary hack
COMPLAIN grumble; grouse; repine

COMPLECT embrace
COMPLETE ended; perfect; fulfil
COMPLICE an accomplice
COMPLIED met; yielded; fulfilled
COMPLIER an active agent
COMPLINE evening service, R.C.   **Eccl.**
COMPONED heraldic squares
COMPOSED calm; invented; produced
COMPOSER a creator; writer   **Mus.**
COMPOSTO compounded; medley **Mus.**
COMPOUND combine; agree; mingle
COMPRESS abridge; condense; bandage
COMPRINT pirate   **Law**
COMPRISE include; embrace; contain
COMPTOIR cash-desk
COMPUTED calculated; rated
COMPUTER actuary; reckoner
CONACRED sub-let
CONARIAL } relating to the
CONARIUM } pineal gland   **Med.**
CONATION volition
CONATIVE endeavouring
CONCAUSE secondary cause
CONCAVED hollowed
CONCEDED granted; allowed; yielded
CONCEDER a donor; relinquisher
CONCEIVE imagine; think; fancy; plan
CONCERTO full accompaniment   **Mus.**
CONCETTO a right merry conceit
CONCHITE fossil shell   **Min.**
CONCHOID shell-like curve
CONCLAVE synod; assembly; council
CONCLUDE close; terminate; infer
CONCOURS a gathering (Fr.)
CONCRETE not abstract; solid; cement
CONDENSE compress; solidify; shorten
CONDITED pickled; preserved
CONDOLED sympathized; commiserated
CONDONED pardoned; forgave
CONDUCED aided; led; promoted
CONFALON gonfalon; banneret
CONFERVA a seaweed   **B.**
CONFETTI scraps of paper
CONFETTI (substitute for rice)
CONFIDED entrusted; hoped; relied
CONFIDER teller of secrets
CONFINED limited; shut-up; restrained
CONFINER borderer; neighbour
CONFIXED fastened
CONFLATE collect; assemble
CONFLICT combat; clash; discord
CONFOUND amaze; mystify
CONFRERE colleague; companion
CONFRONT face; beard; oppose
CONFUSED in disarray; flurried
CONFUTED disproved; overcame
CONGENER an affinity
CONGIARY Roman gift of wine
CONGLOBE to ball; ensphere
CONGREET salute mutually

337

CONGRESS representative assembly
CONGREVE lucifer; rocket
CONICINE hemlock   **Med.**
CONICITY conicalness
CONIFORM conical
CONJOINT associated; connected
CONJUGAL matrimonial
CONJUNCT concurrent; united
CONJURED bound by oath
CONJURER } magician; juggler;
CONJUROR } wizard; marabout
CONJUSTO with gusto   **Mus.**
CONNIVED overlooked; permitted
CONNIVER confidence man; accessory
CONNOTED included; implied
CONOICAL almost conical
CONOIDIC conoidal
CONQUEST victory; subjugation
CONSERVE preserve; maintain
CONSIDER contemplate; regard; ponder
CONSOLED solaced; assuaged; cheered
CONSOLER a comforter; soother
CONSOMME clear soup
CONSPIRE plot; intrigue; machinate
CONSPUED defamed; execrated
CONSTANT unchangeable; perpetual
CONSTRUE translate; interpret
CONSULAR a service
CONSULTA council
CONSUMED dissipated; squandered
CONSUMER devourer; waster; eater
CONSUMPT quantity consumed
CONTANGO premium; discount
CONTEMPT disdain; scorn; derision
CONTENTS the inside
CONTERNO contour; outline (It.)
CONTINUE endure; extend; persist
CONTLINE intervening space
CONTOURA copying device
CONTRACT agreement; abridge
CONTRARY otherwise; opposite
CONTRAST difference; compare
CONTRATE opposed; mitred
CONTRITE penitent; repentant; humble
CONTRIVE bring about; scheme
CONTUSED bruised; crushed; knocked
CONUSANT knowing; cognizable
CONVENED called together; gathered
CONVENER summoner
CONVERGE approach; incline
CONVERSE talk; parley; reciprocal
CONVEXED vaulted
CONVEXLY in convex form
CONVEYED stolen; imparted
CONVEYER impostor; conveyancer
CONVEYOR transporter; carrier
CONVINCE persuade; satisfy; prove
CONVOKED convened; mustered
CONVOLVE roll together
CONVOYED escorted; guarded

CONVULSE writhe; agitate; perturb
CONY-SKIN rabbit-skin
CONY-WOOL rabbit's fur
COOEEING hailing in Australia
COOK-ROOM cook-house; caboose
COOK-SHOP eating-house
COOLNESS indifference; frigidity
COOPERED repaired; doctored
CO-OPTING electing
CO-OPTION adoption; election
COPATAIN high-crowned; pointed
COPEPODA water-boatmen   **Z.**
COPHOSIS deafness   **Med.**
COPHOUSE tool-house
COPOPSIA eye-strain   **Med.**
COPPERAS sulphate of iron   **Chem.**
COPPERED covered with copper
COPULATE united; couple
COPYBOOK exercise book; example
COPYHOLD not freehold   **Law**
COQUETRY flirtation; philandering
COQUETTE a flirt; a jilt
CORACITE uraninite   **Min.**
CORACOID like a crow's beak
CORANACH coronach; a dirge
CORDATED heart-shaped   **B.**
CORDINER cordwainer; shoemaker
CORDOVAN goat-skin leather
CORDUROY ribbed cloth
CORDWAIN Spanish leather
CORD-WOOD fire-wood
CO-REGENT joint ruler
CORK-SOLE inner shoe-sole
CORK-TREE quercus suber   **B.**
CORKWING a sea-fish   **Z**
CORKWOOD an American tree   **B.**
CORN-BALL pop-corn
CORN-BEEF corned beef
CORN-BIND convolvulus   **B.**
CORNCAKE Indian meal cake
CORNEOUS horny
CORNERED brought to bay; controlled
CORNETCY rank of a cornet
CORNFLAG gladiolus   **B.**
CORNICLE a little horn
CORNIFIC horn-producing
CORNLAND grain-land
CORNLOFT granary
CORN-MILL a grinder; quern
CORN-MINT calamint   **B.**
CORN-MOTH a pest   **Z**
CORN-PIPE straw-pipe
CORN-PONE bread (Indian corn)
CORN-RENT rent paid in corn
CORNUTED with horns
CORN-WAIN farm-cart
COROCORE Malay boat   **Nau**
COROLLET a floret   **B**
CORONACH coranach; a lament
CORONATE crowned

CORONIUM gaseous element **Chem.**
CORONOID coracoid
CORONULE downy tuft on seeds **B.**
CORPORAL bodily; material; an N.C.O.
CORPORAS fine linen **Eccl.**
CORRIDOR passage-way; gallery
CORRIVAL co-rival
CORRODED eaten away; rusted; eroded
CORSELET corslet; leather cuirass
CORSICAN (Napoleon)
CORTICAL external; made of bark **B.**
CORUNDUM emerald; ruby; sapphire
CORVETTE a warship **Naut.**
CORYBANT priest of Cybele
CORYMBUS top-knot
CORYPHEE ballet-dancer **Mus.**
CORYSTES masked crab **Z.**
COSECANT an inverse sine
COSENAGE⎫ cousinhood;
COSINAGE ⎭ a writ **Law**
COSHERED pampered; coddled
COSHERER (free board and lodgings)
COSINESS snugness
COSMETIC a beautifier
COSMICAL relating to the universe
COSSETED petted; fondled; caressed
COSTATED ribbed **B.**
COST-BOOK account book
COST-FREE free of charge
COSTLESS without price; free
COSTLIER more expensive; dearer
COSTMARY aromatic plant **B.**
COST-PLUS war contract price
COSTUMED garbed; dressed; robed
COSTUMER costumier; dressmaker
CO-SURETY joint security
COTELINE ribbed muslin
CO-TENANT joint tenant
COTHOUSE a cottar's house
COTILLON cotillion; round dance **Mus.**
COTQUEAN a womanly man
COTSWOLD sheep **Z.**
COTTABUS wine throwing contest
COTTAGED covered with cottages
COTTAGER small holder
COTTONED attracted to
COTYLOID cup-shaped
COUCHANT heraldic ease
COUCHING removing cataract **Med.**
COUGHING a raucous noise
COULISSE theatrical side-scene
COUMARIC from Tonka beans **B.**
COUMARIN a scent **B.**
COUNTESS wife of earl or count
COUNTING reckoning; enumerating
COUNT-OUT adjournment; boxing
COUPELET cabriolet
COUPLING linking; a link **[Mus.**
COURANTE French dance; a paper
COURANTO musical piece **Mus.**

COURSING racing; chasing; pursuing
COURT-DAY sessions-day **Law**
COURTESY polished manners
COURTIER courtesy personified
COURTING wooing; soliciting; inviting
COUSCOUS African food **B.**
COUSINLY friendly
COUSINRY kin; relations
COUTILLE material for corsets
COVENANT contract; bond; pact
COVENTRY ostracism
COVERAGE protection; insurance
COVER-ALL an overlay
COVERCLE a lid
COVERING protecting; including
COVERLET bed cover; counterpane
COVERLID coverlet
COVERTLY surreptitiously; insidiously
COVETING acquisitiveness
COVETOUS avaricious; rapacious
COVINOUS collusive; fraudulent
COWARDLY timidly; cravenly
COWBERRY whortleberry **B.**
COWERING crouching; cringing
COWGRASS meadow trefoil **B.**
COWHIDED whipped
COWHOUSE a byre
COW-LEECH cow doctor
CO-WORKER fellow toiler
COWPILOT West Indian fish **Z.**
COWPLANT plant, Ceylon **B.**
COW-THIEF a rustler
COW-WHEAT annual plant **B.**
COXALGIA hip disease **Med.**
COXINESS conceit; bumptiousness
COXSWAIN steersman; cox **Naut.**
COYSTREL⎫ coistral; a groom;
COYSTRIL ⎭ custrel; a knave
COZENAGE deception; deceit; fraud
COZENING cheating; swindling
CRABBING peevish criticism; grousing
CRABTREE crab-apple
CRABWOOD S. American tree **B.**
CRAB-YAWS foot disease **Med.**
CRACKING distilling; splitting
CRACK-JAW difficult to pronounce
CRACKLED crepitated
CRACKLIN china-ware
CRACKNEL a biscuit
CRACK-POT a maniac; crazy
CRACOWES pointed shoes
CRADLING timber framework
CRAFTIER slyer; more cunning
CRAFTILY shrewdly; pawkily
CRAGSMAN rock-climber
CRAMFULL no more room
CRAMMING stuffing; tutoring
CRAMOISY crimson; cremosin
CRAMPING restraining; impeding
CRAMPONS grappling-irons

CRANE-FLY daddy-longlegs   **Z.**
CRANKING winding; turning; twisting
CRANNIED full of chinks
CRANNIES nooks; fissures
CRASHING blundering; clashing
CRATCHES mangers; swollen pastern
CRAVENLY cowardly
CRAW-CRAW tropical skin disease **Med.**
CRAWFISH crayfish; langouste   **Z.**
CRAWLING on all fours; creeping
CRAYFISH crawfish   **Z.**
CRAYONED drawn on chalk
CRAZIEST maddest; most idiotic
CREAKING grating
CREAMERY milk-bar; dairy
CREAMING foaming; mantling
CREAM-NUT Brazil nut   **B.**
CREAM-POT cosmetic container
CREASING folding
CREASOTE creosote   **Chem.**
CREATINE kreatine; gristle   **Med.**
CREATING begetting; fashioning
CREATION the universe; cosmos
CREATIVE inventive; productive
CREATRIX a designing lady
CREATURE term of contempt
CREDENCE belief; credit; reliance **Eccl.**
CREDENDA articles of faith   **Eccl.**
CREDIBLE trustworthy; believable
CREDIBLY conceivably
CREDITED trusted; accepted
CREDITOR a lender; mortgagee
CREEPING crawling; cringing; stealing
CREMATED reduced to ashes
CREMATOR incinerator
CREMOSIN crimson; cramoisy
CRENATED notched
CRENELET small loophole
CRENELLE loophole
CREOLIAN Creole
CREOSOTE coal-tar derivative   **Chem.**
CREPANCE brushing (horse)
CREPITUS lung-rattle   **Med.**
CRESCENT Turkish emblem
CRESCIVE growing; increasing
CRESTING topping
CRETATED chalked
CRETONNE patterned cloth
CREUTZER Austrian copper coin **Coin**
CREVASSE fissure in glacier
CREVICED rent; cracked; flawed
CRIBBAGE card game
CRIBBING shift lining; copying
CRIBBLED sifted; riddled
CRIBRATE perforated
CRIBROSE full of holes
CRIB-WORK a form of structure
CRICETUS genus of rodents   **Z.**
CRICKETED played the game
CRICKETER a wielder of the willow

CRIMEFUL criminal; wicked; culpable
CRIMINAL felon; convict; illegal   **Law**
CRIMPAGE press-gang work
CRIMPING plaiting; crisping
CRIMPLED curled
CRINATED hairy
CRINGING fawning; crouching; servile
CRINKLED wrinkled; corrugated
CRIPPLED disabled; impaired; maimed
CRISPATE curly
CRISPING crimping; twisting; waving
CRISTATE crested; tufted
CRITERIA standards of judgment
CRITHMUM the samphire   **B.**
CRITICAL crucial; fault-finding
CRITIQUE literary notice
CROAKING woeful; calamitous
CROCEOUS yellow; like saffron
CROCKERY earthenware
CROCKING blackening with soot
CROCOITE chromate of lead   **Min.**
CROFTING farming
CROMLECH ancient stone circle
CROMORNA organ-stop   **Mus.**
CROODLED cowered
CROOKING bending; inflecting
CROONING moaning; lamenting
CROPPING harvesting; lopping; cutting
CROP-SICK sick of a surfeit
CROSS-BAR transverse bar
CROSSBIT cheated
CROSS-BOW a weapon
CROSS-BUN hot cross-bun
CROSS-CUT short cut
CROSSING a ford; traversing
CROSSLET small heraldic cross
CROSS-ROW the alphabet
CROSS-SEA choppy sea
CROSS-TIE railway sleeper
CROSSWAY by-way
CROTALUM castanet; small bell **Mus.**
CROTCHED forked   [**Mus.**
CROTCHET whimsey; fancy; conceit
CROTONIC (croton-oil)   **B.**
CROTTLES lichens used for dyeing **B.**
CROUCHED cringed; fawned; truckled
CROUPADE equestrian feat
CROUPIER a raker of shekels
CROUPOUS croupy   **Med.**
CROW-BILL forceps   **Med.**
CROWDING urging; pressing; swarming
CROWFOOT ranunculus   **B.**
CROWMILL crow-trap
CROWNING a coronation
CROWNING (mercy) completing
CROWNLET small crown
CROWN-SAW circular saw
CROW-SILK aquatic plant   **B.**
CRUCIATE cruciform
CRUCIBLE melting pot

CRUCIFER cross-bearer
CRUCIFIX religious emblem **Eccl.**
CRUELEST most ruthless; harshest
CRUISING voyaging; sailing
CRUMBING covering with crumbs
CRUMBLED disintegrated; crushed
CRUMENAL a purse
CRUMPLED ruffled; rumpled; wrinkled
CRUNCHED munched
CRUORINE haemoglobin **Med.**
CRUSADED
CRUSADER valiant enthusiast
CRUSHING subduing; overpowering
CRUSTILY morosely; sullenly
CRUTCHED on crutches
CRUTCHET the perch, fish **Z.**
CRUZEIRO (Brazil) **Coin**
CRY-BABY child; coward
CRYOLITE a transparent stone **Min.**
CUBATION ⎱ determination of
CUBATURE ⎰ cubic contents
CUBEBINE a carminative **Med.**
CUBIFORM cubical
CUBOIDAL cube-like
CUCHILLA uplands (S. Amer.)
CUCUMBER a creeping plant **B.**
CUCURBIT distilling vessel **Chem.**
CUDDLING fondling; petting; hugging
CUFFLINK
CUL-DE-SAC dead-end
CULINARY au cordon bleu
CULLYING imposing on
CULLYISM being a simpleton
CULPABLE censurable; blameworthy
CULPABLY guiltily; sinfully
CULTRATE knife-like
CULTURED intellectual; refined
CULVERIN a cannon
CUMBERED hampered; clogged
CUMBRIAN (Cumberland)
CUMBROUS unhandy; clumsy
CUMULATE amass; collect
CUMULOSE heaped
CUNABULA a cradle; incunabula
CUNABULA books prior to A.D. 1500
CUNARDER a Cunard ship
CUNEATED wedge-shaped; cuneiform
CUNIFORM Assyrian writing, etc.
CUPBOARD a repository
CUPIDITY covetousness; avarice; desire
CUPREOUS like copper
CURARINE curari extract **Chem.**
CURARISE to poison with curari
CURASSOW S. American turkey **Z.**
CURATIVE healing; restorative
CURATORY remedial; antidotal
CURBLESS without restraint
CURB-ROOF bent roof
CURCULIO corn-worm; weevil **Z.**
CURDLING congealing; thickening

CURLICUE a fantastic curl; pig's tail
CURLIWIG a curved piece
CURRENCY coin; flow; circulation
CURRICLE two-wheeled chaise
CURRYING (food; leather; horse)
CURSEDLY execrably
CURSITOR Chancery writ writer **Law**
CURSORES running birds **Z.**
CURTLEAX cutlass; curtal-ax
CURTNESS abruptness; terseness
CURTSIED made obeisance
CURVATED curved; bent
CURVITAL not straight
CUSPIDAL pointed
CUSPIDOR a spittoon
CUSTOMED wont; habituated
CUSTOMER purchaser; client; patron
CUT-AWAY a style of coat
CUTCHERY Indian court **Law**
CUT-GLASS
CUTHBERT Northumbrian apostle
CUTIKINS spats (Sc.) **[Eccl.**
CUT-PRICE cheap
CUTPURSE pickpocket
CUTWATER prow **Naut.**
CYANOGEN poisonous gas **Chem.**
CYANOSIS skin disease **Med.**
CYANOTIC (blue jaundice) **Med.**
CYCLAMEN primrose family **B.**
CYCLE-CAR a combination
CYCLICAL circular; epic
CYCLONIC like a hurricane
CYCLOPIC gigantic; monstrous
CYCLOSIS circulation; cell movement
CYLINDER solid roller
CYMATIUM cyme; a moulding (Arch.)
CYNANCHE quinsy **Med.**
CYNICISM misanthropy
CYNOSURE centre of attraction
CYRENAIC of Cyrene
CYRILLIC (Slavic alphabet)
CYSTICLE small cyst **Med.**
CYSTITIS inflammation **Med.**
CYTISINE laburnum alkaloid **Med.**
CYTOLOGY study of cells
CYOTOSINE nucleic base **Chem.**
CZECHISH Czech language

D

DABBLING meddling; trifling
DAB-CHICK also dob-chick **Z.**
DACRYOMA defective tear duct **Med.**
DACTYLAR (finger); (toe)
DACTYLIC (verse)
DADDLING tottering locomotion
DAEDELUS a maker of mazes
DAEMONIC diabolical; satanic

DAFFODIL Lent lily **B., Eccl.**	**DAUNTING** intimidating; dismaying
DAFTNESS lunacy; stupidity	**DAUPHINE** French princess
DAGGERED stabbed	**DAVY-LAMP** miner's lamp
DAGGLING trapesing	**DAWDLING** dallying; lagging; trifling
DAG-SWAIN coarse woollen fabric	**DAYBREAK** dawn; dawning; day-spring
DAHABIEH Nile boat **Naut.**	**DAY-DREAM** reverie; visionary scheme
DAINTILY delicately; elegantly	**DAYLIGHT** illumination
DAIQUIRI rum drink	**DAYSHIFT** working period (industrial)
DAIRYING farming	**DAY-SIGHT** night-blindness
DAIRYMAN dairy keeper; milkman	**DAY-TO-DAY** ephemeral
DALESMAN Lake district man	**DAY-WOMAN** daily woman
DALLYING trifling; delaying; fondling	**DAZZLING** bewildering; confusing
DALMAHOY bushy bob-wig	**DEAD-BEAT** exhausted; (clocks)
DALMATIC long white vestment **Eccl.**	**DEAD-BORN** still-born
DAMAGING injuring; impairing	**DEADENED** retarded; benumbed
DAMASKED variegated	**DEAD-FALL** animal trap
DAMASKIN Damascus sword	**DEAD-FIRE** death omen
DAMASSIN damask cloth	**DEAD-HEAD** (on the free list)
DAMBOARD draughtboard	**DEAD-HEAT** bracketed
DAME-WORT dame's violet **B.**	**DEADLIER** more malignant
DAMNABLE pernicious; execrable	**DEAD-LIFT** (no leverage or help)
DAMOCLES his sword was a hanger	**DEAD-LINE** a boundary; time-limit
DAMPENED moistened; discouraged	**DEAD-LOCK** no compromise; impasse
DAMPNESS humidity	**DEAD-LOSS** complete loss
DANCETTE Norman zig-zag moulding	**DEAD-MEAT** meat for market
DANDERED sauntered (Sc.)	**DEADNESS** inertness; inertia
DANDIEST neatest	**DEAD-PULL** dead-lift
DANDLING fondling; caressing	**DEAD-ROPE** fixed rope in dead-eye
DANDRUFF dandruff; scurf **Med.**	**DEAD-SHOT** unerring marksman
DANDYISE dress ostentatiously	**DEAD-WALL** windowless wall
DANDYISH foppish	**DEAD-WIND** calm
DANDYISM elegance in attire	**DEAD-WOOD** decayed or useless wood
DANE-GELD tribute paid to Danes	**DEAD-WORK** unprofitable work
DANELAGH Danish England (A.D. 878)	**DEAD-WORT** species of elder **B.**
DANE-WEED a plant **B.**	**DEAFENED** stunned
DANE-WORT dwarf elder **B.**	**DEAF-MUTE** deaf and dumb
DANGLING hanging by a thread	**DEAFNESS** hard of hearing **Med.**
DANSEUSE ballerina	**DEAL-FISH** a thin fish **Z.**
DANUBIAN (Danube)	**DEANSHIP** office of dean **Eccl.**
DAPEDIUS ganoid fish **Z**	**DEARNESS** costliness; tenderness
DAPPERLY variegated	**DEARNFUL** solitary; mournful
DAPPLING shading; spotting	**DEATH-BED** the passing place
DARING-DO derring-do	**DEATHFUL** fateful; moribund
DARINGLY intrepidly; bravely	**DE-BANNED** freed; de-restricted
DARKENED obscured; clouded	**DEBARKED** landed
DARKLING gloomy; sombre	**DEBARRED** excluded; prohibited
DARKNESS ignorance; blindness	**DEBASING** degrading; vitiating
DARK-ROOM a developing locality	**DEBATING** discussing; disputing
DARKSOME mysterious; dismal	**DEBILITY** functional weakness
DASTARDY cowardice; base timidity	**DEBITING** charging
DASYURES Australian marsupials **Z.**	**DEBONAIR** genial; cheerful; merry
DATELESS immemorial; timeless	**DEBOUCHE** an opening; a market
DATE-LINE where East meets West	**DEBOUTED** expelled; ejected
DATE-PALM Biblical palm **B., Eccl.**	**DEBTLESS** owing naught
DATE-PLUM persimmon **B.**	**DEBUNKED** shown up
DATE-TREE (many varieties) **B.**	**DEBUTANT** a starter
DATOLITE a silicate **Min.**	**DECADENT** degenerate
DATURINE thorn-apple alkaloid **Chem.**	**DECAGRAM** 10 grammes **Meas.**
DAUBSTER poor painter	**DECAMPED** sloped off; fled; bolted
DAUGHTER	**DECANTED** poured out

DECANTER glass wine bottle
DECAYING rotting; declining; ebbing
DECEASED dead; departed; defunct
DECEIVED beguiled; duped; gulled
DECEIVER impostor; trickster
DECEMBER 10th Roman month
DECEMFID ten-cleft **B.**
DECEMVIR Roman magistrate
DECENTLY comme il faut
DECERNED judged; decreed
DECIDING settling; resolving
DECIGRAM one-tenth of gramme **Meas.**
DECIMATE kill one in ten
DECIPHER decode
DECISION verdict; firmness
DECISIVE final; conclusive
DECISORY determining
DECK-GAME (bull-board, etc.)
DECK-HAND an A.B. **Naut.**
DECK-LOAD deck-cargo
DECLARED said; announced; averred
DECLINAL sloping downward
DECLINED pined; sank; shunned
DECLINER a refuser
DECLUTCH gear-changing (motoring)
DECOCTED cooked; digested
DECODING deciphering
DECOLOUR bleach
DECORATE deck; embellish; garnish
DECOROUS proper; befitting; seemly
DECOYING luring; enticing; inveigling
DECREASE minimize; reduce; curtail
DECREPIT broken down
DECRETAL a Papal decree **Eccl.**
DECRYING disparaging; vilifying
DECUPLED tenfold
DECURION controller of ten
DEDICANT dedicator
DEDICATE devote; consecrate; assign
DEDITION surrender
DEDUCING inferring; drawing; deriving
DEDUCTED subtracted; withdrawn
DEEDLESS inactive
DEED-POLL a legal instrument **Law**
DEEMSTER Manx judge **Law**
DEEP-DYED extreme; rascally
DEEPENED became more mysterious
DEEP-LAID cunning; intricate
DEEP-MOST uttermost
DEEPNESS profundity
DEEP-READ scholarly
DEERFOOT leathercraft **Tool**
DEER-HAIR heath club-rush **B.**
DEER-HERD a herd of deer
DEER-LICK salt lick
DEER-NECK scraggy
DEER-PARK paddock enclosure, zoo
DEERSKIN leather
DEFACING disfiguring; marring; spoiling
DEFAMING slandering; traducing

DEFEATED frustrated; overthrown
DEFECATE purify; purge
DEFENCED fortified; covered
DEFENDED warded off; shielded
DEFENDER protector; advocate
DEFERENT a conveyor; deferential
DEFERRED postponed; adjourned
DEFERRER a procrastinator
DEFIANCE a challenge; provocation
DEFILADE cf. enfilade
DEFILING polluting; corrupting
DEFINING explaining; specifying
DEFINITE precise; exact; certain
DEFLATED punctured
DEFLEXED bent
DEFLOWER sully; seduce; ravish
DEFLUENT flowing
DEFORCED resisted **Law**
DEFOREST clear of trees
DEFORMED disfigured; misshapen
DEFORMER destroyer of symmetry
DEFRAYAL payment
DEFRAYED met the cost; paid
DEFRAYER liquidator; settler
DEFTNESS adroitness; dexterity
DEGAUSSE neutralize magnetic mine
DEGRADED reduced in rank
DEGREASE remove the grease
DEHORNED dodded (cattle)
DEIFICAL making divine
DEIFYING idolizing; exalting
DEIGNING condescending; vouchsafing
DEISHEAL clockwise
DEJECTED downcast; chapfallen
DEJECTLY gloomily; dolefully
DEJEUNER breakfast; lunch **(Fr.)**
DELATING informing
DELATION informer's accusation
DELAYING retarding; hindering
DELECTUS classical anthology
DELEGACY representation
DELEGATE deputy; commissioner
DELETING obliterating; effacing
DELETION erasure; expunction
DELETIVE delible
DELETORY erasive; blotting
DELIBATE taste; sip
DELICACY consideration; tact; relish
DELICATE dainty; frail; slight
DELIRIUM mental aberration; mania
DELIVERY rescue; distribution
DELOUSED cleared of vermin
DELPHIAN oracular
DELPHINE (Dauphin); (dolphin) **Z.**
DELUBRUM shrine; sanctuary
DELUDING duping; gulling; misleading
DELUGING pouring; inundating
DELUSION fallacy; imposture
DELUSIVE deceptive; fallacious
DELUSORY illusory; deceitful

DEMAGOGY popular oration technique
DEMANDED queried; exacted; claimed
DEMARCHE ultimatum; counter-stroke
DEMEANED degraded; behaved
DEMENTED daft; crazy; deranged
DEMENTIA insanity; lunacy **Med.**
DEMERARA brown-sugar **B.**
DEMERSAL near sea bottom
DEMERSED sub-aqueous
DEMIBAIN small bath
DEMIJOHN bottle enclosed in wicker
DEMILUNE ravelin (fort.)
DEMISING bequeathing; devising
DEMISSLY humbly
DEMI-TINT a shade
DEMI-TONE a semitone
DEMITTED dismissed; resigned
DEMIURGE Plato's world-maker
DEMI-VOLT an equestrian trick
DEMI-WOLF progeny of dog and wolf **Z.**
DEMOBBED demobilized; discharged
DEMOCRAT upholder of democracy
DEMOLISH destroy; raze; dismantle
DEMOLOGY social statistics
DEMONESS a diabolical lady
DEMONIAC possessed; infernal
DEMONISM Satanic cult
DEMONIST devil worshipper
DEMONIZE turn into a devil
DEMONOMY dominion of devils
DEMPSTER see deemster
DEMURELY gravely; sedately; modestly
DEMURRED hesitated; wavered; paused
DEMURRER a plea; objector **Law**
DEMYSHIP an Oxford scholarship
DENARIUS English penny; d. **Coin**
DENATURE denaturalize
DENDRITE dendroit **Min.**
DENDROID tree-like
DENDROIT tree-like fossil **Min.**
DENEGATE deny; contradict; refute
DENEHOLE shaft cut in chalk
DENIABLE controvertible; refutable
DENOTATE denote; signify
DENOTING indicating; designating
DENOUNCE impeach; censure; threaten
DENTAGRA toothache **Med.**
DENTATED with teeth; notched
DENTICLE small projection
DENTIZED toothed
DENUDATE strip bare; divest
DENUDING strip teasing
DEPARTED left; gone away; withdrew
DEPARTER metal refiner
DEPENDED relief; trusted; hung
DEPICTED described; limned; portrayed
DEPICTOR painter; artist
DEPILATE remove hair
DEPLETED emptied; drained
DEPLORED lamented; bewailed; grieved

DEPLOYED extended; unfolded
DEPLUMED plucked
DEPONENT a witness **Law**
DEPONING testifying under oath **Law**
DEPORTED expelled; banished
DEPORTEE reported forcibly removed
DEPOSING ousting; removing
DEPRAVED corrupt; vicious; profligate
DEPRAVER vilifier; reprobate
DEPRIVED robbed; dispossessed
DEPRIVER a despoiler; brigand
DEPURATE cleanse; purify
DEPUTING authorizing; charging
DEPUTIZE delegate; act for another
DERAILED off the lines
DERAILER train-wrecker
DERANGED disordered; insane; mad
DERATING reducing liability
DERATION free from restriction
DERBY-DAY a Wednesday
DERBY-DOG also ran
DERBYITE volunteer of 1915
DERELICT abandoned; deserted; left
DERIDING mocking; lampooning
DERISION laughing stock; mockery
DERISIVE scoffing; ridiculous
DERISORY scornful; contemptuous
DERIVATE a derivative
DERIVING deducing; tracing; obtaining
DERMATIC relating to the skin **Med.**
DEROGATE disparage; detract
DESCRIBE portray; narrate; tell
DESCRIED observed; espied; discerned
DESERTED forlorn; left; abandoned
DESERTER quitter; renegade; turncoat
DESERVED justified; merited; earned
DESERVER meritorious person
DESIGNED projected; invented; drew
DESIGNER schemer; contriver
DESILVER extract silver from
DESIRING craving; wanting
DESIROUS covetous; eager; longing
DESISTED stopped; ceased; forbore
DESK-WORK clerical work
DESOLATE solitary; deserted
DESPATCH dispatch; hasten; kill
DESPISAL contempt; scorn
DESPISED disdained; ignored; scouted
DESPISER scorner; contemner
DESPITED vexed; offended; teased
DESPOTAT territory under despot
DESPOTIC tyrannical; arbitrary
DESTINED ordained; fated
DESTRIER second charger **Z**
DETACHED isolated; disengaged
DETAILED particularized; recounted
DETAILER enumerator; narrator
DETAINED delayed; restrained; held
DETAINER withholder of goods **La**
DETECTED found out; unmasked

DETECTOR detecter; discoverer
DETERGED cleansed; wiped
DETERRED prevented; hindered
DETESTED odious; abominated; loathed
DETESTER abhorrer
DETHRONE depose; discrown
DETONATE explode violently
DETONIZE fulminate
DETRITAL (detritus); residual
DETRITED worn down; eroded
DETRITUS disintegrated material
DETRUDED extruded; thrust
DETRUSOR a muscle **Med.**
DEUCE-ACE a throw at dice
DEUCEDLY confoundedly
DEVALUED depreciated
DEVELOPE evolve; unfold; amplify
DEVESTED divested; alienated
DEVIATED swerved; strayed; veered
DEVIATOR a wanderer
DEVILDOM kingdom of hell
DEVILESS demoness
DEVILISH fiendish; malignant; diabolic
DEVILISM devil worship
DEVILKIN imp
DEVILLED highly seasoned; curried
DEVILTRY devilry; devilship
DEVISING scheming; bequeathing
DEVOLUTE transfer; depute
DEVOLVED handed over
DEVONIAN geological formation **Min.**
DEVOTING dedicating; consecrating
DEVOTION zeal; piety; attachment
DEVOURED bolted; consumed; gobbled
DEVOURER absorber; destroyer
DEVOUTLY earnestly; piously; holily
DEWBERRY the bramble **B.**
DEWINESS precipitation
DEW-POINT a critical temperature
DEWSTONE a limestone **Min.**
DEXTRINE starch gum **Chem.**
DEXTRONE synthetic blood
DEXTROSE glucose sugar **Chem.**
DEXTROUS dexterous; skilful
DEZINKED freed from zinc
DIABASIC greenstone type **Min.**
DIABETES **Med.**
DIABETIC **Med.**
DIABLERY diableric; impishness
DIABOLIC satanic; demoniac; fiendish
DIACHYMA cellular tissue **B.**
DIACONAL (deacon) **Eccl.**
DIACTINE having two rays
DIADELPH twin **B.**
DIADEMED crowned
DIADEXIS disease mutation **Med.**
DIADOCHI ancient governors (Gk.)
DIAGLYTH an intaglio; carved gem
DIAGNOSE identify **Med.**
DIAGONAL cross-tie

DIAGRAPH drawing instrument
DIALLAGE rhetorical argument
DIALLING (telephoning)
DIALOGIC in dialogue form
DIALOGUE two talking
DIALYSIS debility **Chem., Med.**
DIALYTIC unbracing
DIALYZED } (analysis of soluble
DIALYZER } substances) **Chem.**
DIAMETER an exact bisector
DIANDRIA two-stemmed plants **B.**
DIANODAL traversing a node
DIANTHUS carnations, pinks, etc. **B.**
DIAPASON concord of sounds **Mus.**
DIAPENTE interval of a fifth **Mus.**
DIAPERED figured
DIAPHANE transparent woven silk
DIAPHONE electrical fog-signal
DIAPNOIC (perspiration) **Med.**
DIARIZED recorded in a diary
DIASPORA Jew dispersion
DIASPORE aluminium hydrate **Min.**
DIASTASE malt sugar
DIASTEMA space between teeth
DIASTOLE heart dilatation **Med.**
DIASTYLE spaced columns (arch.)
DIATOMIC (two atoms) **Chem.**
DIATONIC natural scale **Mus.**
DIATRIBE stream of invective; tirade
DIBBLING planting
DIBSTONE stone used in a game
DICE-COAL small coal **Min.**
DICENTRA bleeding-heart **B.**
DICE-PLAY dicing
DICHROIC double refraction
DICKERED bargained
DICLINIC crystalline shape
DICROTIC double pulsation **Med.**
DICTATED bid; prescribed; ordained
DICTATOR autocrat; despot; tyrant
DIDACTIC instructive; moral; directive
DIDACTYL having two toes **Z.**
DIDAPPER dabchick **Z.**
DIDDERED shivered
DIDDLING cheating; trifling; dawdling
DIDYMATE in pairs; twins **B., Z.**
DIDYMIUM a rare metal **Chem**
DIDYMOUS growing in pairs **B.**
DIEGESIS explanation; narrative
DIELYTRA the bleeding-heart **B.**
DIE-STOCK die-holder
DIETETIC (food regime)
DIFFERED disagreed; diverged; varied
DIFFRACT break; refract
DIFFUSED disseminated; spread
DIFFUSER a spray
DIGAMIST married twice
DIGESTED classified; codified; arranged
DIGESTER a stock-pot
DIGGABLE suitable for spade work

M

DIGGINGS (gold); lodgings
DIGITATE having five leaflets **B.**
DIGONOUS with two anglés **B.**
DIGYNIAN ⎱ flowers having
DIGYNOUS ⎰ cleft styles **B.**
DIHEDRAL angle between planes
DIHEDRON geometric figures
DIKAMALI medicinal gum **Med.**
DILATANT swelling; elastic
DILATING expanding; stretching
DILATION distention; amplification
DILATIVE expansive
DILATORY tardy; dallying; lagging
DILIGENT busy; industrious; assiduous
DILLY-BAG Australian rush-bag
DILUTING attenuating; weakening
DILUTION watering; reducing
DILUVIAL alluvial
DILUVIUM glacial or flood deposit
DIMERISM duplex arrangement
DIMEROUS in two parts
DIMETRIC tetragonal
DIMINISH cut; abate; lessen; curtail
DIMPLING smiling
DIMYARIA molluscs **Z.**
DINAMODE unit of work, metre-ton
DINARCHY dual control
DINER-OUT a table companion
DING-DONG hammer and tongs
DINGHIES small boats **Naut.**
DINGIEST dullest; dirtiest
DINORNIS moa-bird, N. Zealand **Z.**
DINOSAUR extinct lizard **Z.**
DIOCESAN a bishop **Eccl.**
DIOGENIC (Diogenes); cynical
DIOPSIDE augite **Min.**
DIOPTASE copper silicate **Min.**
DIOPTRIC (refraction of light)
DIORAMIC (peep-show)
DIORITIC (igneous rock, diorite) **Min.**
DIOSCURI Castor and Pollux
DIPCHICK dabchick **Z.**
DIPLEGIA paralysis **Med.**
DIPLEXER two-way transmitter
Electr.
DIPLOGEN deuterium; heavy hydrogen
DIPLOMAT ambassador; envoy
DIPLOPIA double vision **Med.**
DIPNOOUS having lungs and gills **Z.**
DIPROTON two-proton system
DIPSACUS the teasel **B.**
DIPSOSIS morbid thirst **Med.**
DIPTERAL with two wings **Z.**
DIPTERAN a fly **Z.**
DIPTEROS (double peristyle, arch.)
DIPTYCHA writing tablets
DIRECTED addressed; enjoined
DIRECTLY expressly; soon; forthwith
DIRECTOR manager; controller
DIRENESS horror; calamity
DIRIGENT directing

DIRTIEST filthiest; most sordid
DIRTYING fouling; soiling
DISABLED incapacitated; crippled
DISABUSE enlighten; undeceive
DISADORN deprive of ornament
DISAGREE differ; vary; deviate
DISALLOW reject; forbid; disclaim
DISANNEX disunite; disjoin
DISARMED subdued; stripped
DISARRAY disorder; undress
DISASTER calamity; catastrophe
DISBENCH unseat
DISBLOOM disbud
DISBOSOM reveal
DISBOWEL disembowel
DISBURSE expend; spend
DISCANDY melt; dissolve
DISCASED undressed
DISCHARM disenchant
DISCINCT ungirded
DISCIPLE learner; follower; pupil
DISCLAIM disown; reject; renounce
DISCLOSE reveal; tell; betray
DISCOUNT allowance; forestall; deduct
DISCOVER detect; espy; divulge
DISCRASE a silver salt **Chem.**
DISCREET circumspect; prudent
DISCRETE separate; distinct
DISCROWN depose; dethrone
DISCSEAL form of valve
DISEASED indisposed; unhealthy; sickly
DISEDGED blunted
DISEDIFY scandalize
DISENACT repeal; annul
DISENDOW deprive of endowments
DISENROL cashier
DISFLESH disembody
DISFROCK expel from clergy **Eccl.**
DISGAVEL a change in tenure **Law**
DISGORGE surrender; eject; vent
DISGRACE ignominy; dishonour
DISGRADE reduce in rank; disrate
DISGUISE conceal; mask; cloak
DISHABIT dislodge
DISHERIT disinherit
DISHEVEL disarray
DISHORSE unhorse
DISINTER exhume; unbury
DISINURE render unfamiliar
DISIPPUS an American butterfly **Z.**
DISJOINT dislocate
DISJUNCT discontinuous
DISLEAVE deprive of leaves
DISLIKED detested; hated; loathed
DISLIKEN made unlike
DISLODGE evict; eject; oust
DISLOYAL false; perfidious
DISMALLY drearily; dolefully
DISMAYED terror-struck; appalled
DISMOUNT alight; descend; unhorse

DISORBED thrown from its orbit
DISORDER confusion; turbulence
DISOWNED repudiated; denied
DISPATCH despatch; expedite; send
DISPATHY antipathy; allergy
DISPEACE unrest; unease
DISPENSE administer; dispence
DISPERSE scatter; diffuse; dispel
DISPIRIT discourage; dishearten
DISPLACE remove; discharge; oust
DISPLAIT untwist; unravel
DISPLANT uproot; eradicate
DISPLUME pluck
DISPONED disposed
DISPONEE⎱ (conveyance of property
DISPONER⎰ in legal form) **Law**
DISPONGE dispunge; expunge
DISPOPED deprived of popedom **Eccl.**
DISPOSAL right of bestowing
DISPOSED inclined; arranged; biassed
DISPOSER administrator
DISPREAD extend; expand
DISPRIZE undervalue; belittle
DISPROOF refutation; rebuttal
DISPROVE confute; refute
DISPUNGE disponge; expunge
DISPUTED contested; wrangled
DISPUTER arguer; debater
DISQUIET to vex; unease; anxiety
DISRATED reduced in rank; degraded
DISROBED divested; denuded
DISROBER raiment remover
DISSEIZE dispossess **Law**
DISSERVE to perform an ill turn
DISSEVER cut in two; rend
DISSIGHT an eyesore
DISSOLVE loosen; liquefy; end
DISSUADE deter; disincline
DISTALLY remote
DISTANCE interval; space; outstrip
DISTASTE aversion; antipathy
DISTHENE cyanite; kyanite **Min.**
DISTINCT definite; clear
DISTITLE deprive of right
DISTOMUM liver-fluke parasite **Z.**
DISTRACT divert; harass; bewilder
DISTRAIN seize for debt **Law**
DISTRAIT absent-minded
DISTREAM overflow
DISTRESS anguish; suffering; worry
DISTRICT territory; region; quarter
DISTRUST discredit; doubt; suspect
DISTUNED put out of tune
DISUNION breach of concord
DISUNITE separate; disrupt
DISUNITY isolation; dissension
DISUSAGE disuse; desuetude
DISUSING abandoning
DISVALUE underrate; disprize
DISYOKED untrammelled

DITCH-DOG dead dog **Z.**
DITCHING excavating; clearing
DITHECAL with two spore-cases **B.**
DITHEISM⎱ co-existence of a
DITHEIST⎰ good and an evil god
DITHERED shivered; hesitated
DITOKOUS having twins
DITTY-BAG sailor's kit-bag
DITTY-BOX sailor's treasure-box
DIURESIS, DIURETIC **Med.**
DIVAGATE digress; wander
DIVALENT bivalent **Chem.**
DIVE-BOMB aerial attack
DIVERGED deviated; digressed; veered
DIVERTED distracted; amused
DIVERTER an entertainer
DIVESTED stripped; deprived; bared
DIVIDEND interest; share; profit
DIVIDING cleaving; parting
DIVI-DIVI pods used in tanning **B.**
DIVIDUAL shared in common
DIVINELY heavenly; exquisitely
DIVINIFY treat as divine
DIVINITY Deity; theology **Eccl.**
DIVINIZE divinise; deify
DIVISION category; army unit
DIVISIVE dissentient; discordant
DIVORCED forced asunder
DIVORCEE person divorced
DIVORCER divorcing person
DIVULGED communicated; revealed
DIVULGER betrayer of secrets
DIZENING dressing gaudily
DIZZYING confusing
DOCETISM doctrine of a sect **Eccl.**
DOCETIST a 2nd-century heretic **Eccl.**
DOCHMIAC Greek metrical foot
DOCILITY pliancy; tameness
DOCIMACY metallurgy
DOCKIZED erected docks
DOCKYARD naval establishment **Naut.**
DOCTORAL (doctor)
DOCTORED treated; doped **Med.**
DOCTORLY scholarly
DOCTRINE dogma; creed; tenet
DOCUMENT writing; record; writ
DODDERED quaked; tottered
DODDERER senile senior
DODECANE paraffin **Chem.**
DODIPOLL dolt; numbskull
DODONIAN oracular
DOGBERRY ignorant parish official
DOG-BRIER dog-rose **B.**
DOG-CHEAP bargain price
DOG-EARED crinkled corner
DOGESHIP Venetian office
DOG-FACED unprepossessing
DOGGEDLY obstinately; stolidly
DOGGEREL bad verse
DOGGONED confounded

DOG-GRASS couch grass   **B.**
DOG-HOUSE kennel
DOG-LATIN barbarous Latin
DOG-LEECH a vet.
DOGMATIC dictatorial; arbitrary
DOG'S-BANE a poisonous plant   **B.**
DOG'S-BODY utility man
DOG-SLEEP cat-nap
DOG'S-MEAT offal
DOG'S-NOSE beer and gin
DOG-TIRED spent
DOG-TOOTH a Norman moulding
DOG-TRICK a currish wile
DOG-WATCH   **Naut.**
DOG-WEARY exhausted
DOG-WHEAT dog-grass   **B.**
DOG-WHELK   **Z.**
DOLDRUMS calm zone; depression ·
DOLERITE basalt   **Min.**
DOLESOME dismal; rueful
DOLICHOS hyacinth bean   **B.**
DO-LITTLE a lazy-bones
DOLLARED flush; wealthy
DOLLED-UP dressed showily
DOLLHOOD dollship
DOLLY-MOP handled mop
DOLLY-TUB washing tub
DOLOMITE magnesian limestone **Min.**
DOLOROSO pathetically   **Mus.**
DOLOROUS sorrowful; dolesome
DOMAINAL⎰ (landed estate)
DOMANIAL⎱ (scope)
DOMELIKE dome shaped
DOMESMAN judge; umpire
DOMESTIC household; maid
DOMICILE habitation; residence
DOMIFIED (horoscope)
DOMINANT prevailing; ruling
DOMINATE control; override
DOMINEER to hector; to sway
DOMINION sovereignty
DOMINIUM ownership
DOMINOES hooded capes; a game
DONATING giving; bestowing
DONATION presentation; offering; alms
DONATISM a Christian cult   **Eccl.**
DONATIVE gratuity; benefice; largesse
DONATORY recipient of land   **Law.**
DONNERED stunned (Sc.)
DOOLTREE duletree; the gallows
DOOM-PALM Egyptian palm   **B.**
DOOMSDAY domesday (Book)
DOOMSMAN domesman; judge
DOOR-BELL a ringer
DOOR-CASE door framework
DOOR-KNOB a handle
DOORLESS without portal
DOORNAIL considered as dead
DOOR-POST regarded as deaf
DOOR-SILL lower framework

DOOR-STEP slice of bread (slang)
DOOR-YARD an enclosure
DORICISM Doric in expression
DORMANCY abeyance; latency
DORMOUSE somnolent rodent   **Z.**
DORR-HAWK night-jar   **Z.**
DORSALLY backward
DOSOLOGY science of doses   **Med.**
DOTARDLY foolishly; senilely
DOTATION donation; dowry
DOTINGLY stupidly; fondly
DOTTEREL a plover   **Z.**
DOUANIER custom-house officer (Fr.)
DOUBLETS (dice)
DOUBLING folding; running
DOUBLOON Spanish guinea   **Coin**
DOUBLURE book-binding
DOUBTFUL uncertain; ambiguous
DOUBTING distrusting; querying
DOUBTIVE questionable; dubious
DOUCHING spraying
DOUGHBOY American soldier
DOUGHNUT a confection
DOUM-PALM doom-palm   **B.**
DOURNESS obstinacy; grimness
DOVECOTE pigeon house
DOVE-EYED meek-eyed
DOVELIKE gentle; innocent
DOVERING snoozing
DOVESHIP qualities of a dove
DOVETAIL a joint; synchronise
DOWDYISH rather slovenly
DOWDYISM shabbiness
DOWELLED pinned together
DOWEL-PIN a fastening
DOWERING endowing; bequeathing
DOWFNESS lethargy; dullness
DOWNBEAR depress
DOWNBORE discouraged
DOWNCAST dejected
DOWNCOME sudden fall
DOWNFALL debacle; ruin
DOWNHAUL a sheet   **Naut.**
DOWNHILL a declivity
DOWNLAND hilly pasture land
DOWN-LINE (railways)
DOWNPIPE rainwater runaway
DOWNPOUR continuous heavy rain
DOWNRUSH downward draught
DOWNTROD trampled; tyrannised
DOWNTOWN business centre
DOWNWARD descending
DOWNWEED cottonweed   **B.**
DOXOLOGY hymn of praise   **Eccl.**
DOZINESS drowsiness
DRABBETT⎰ twilled linen
DRABETTE⎱ used for smocks
DRABBISH slatternly; dowdy
DRABBLED fouled with mire
DRABBLER a sail extension   **Naut.**

DRACANTH gum; tragacanth; **B.**
DRACONIN dragon's blood
DRACONIC (Draco); severe
DRAFFISH dreggy; worthless
DRAFT-BAR swingle-tree
DRAFTING sketching; drawing
DRAG-BOLT draw-bar
DRAGGING tugging; tedious
DRAGGLED wet and dirty
DRAG-HOOK a connection
DRAG-HUNT foxing the hounds
DRAGOMAN guide; interpreter
DRAGONET small dragon; a fish **Z.**
DRAGONNE heraldic lion-dragon
DRAG-SHOE a brake
DRAGSMAN coach-driver
DRAILING trailing; draggling
DRAINAGE sewage system
DRAINING emptying; exhausting
DRAMATIC theatrical
DRAMBUIE whisky liqueur
DRAMMOCK drummock; skilly; gruel
DRAM-SHOP shebeen; illicit bar
DRAUGHTS a game
DRAUGHTY inconveniently airy
DRAWABLE representable
DRAWBACK detriment; defect
DRAWBOLT coupling pin
DRAWBORE carpentry
DRAWGATE sluice gate
DRAW-GEAR harness; railway coupling
DRAWLING droning
DRAW-LINK a couple
DRAW-WELL deep well
DREADFUL frightful; dire; horrific
DREADING fearing; awing
DREAMERY reverie
DREAMFUL fanciful; dreamy
DREAMILY vaguely
DREAMING imagining
DREARILY gloomily; dismally
DREDGING deepening; sprinkling
DREGGISH foul with lees
DRENCHED saturated; inundated
DRENCHER a soaker
DRESSING alignment; draping **Med.**
DRIBBLING inveigling
DRIBBLED slavered
DRIBBLER (footballer)
DRIBBLET a small drop
DRIFTAGE leeway **Naut.**
DRIFT-ICE
DRIFTING passively awaiting events
DRIFT-NET
DRIFT-WAY cattle-road; leeway
DRILL-BOW a boring device **Tool**
DRILL-BOX seed-box
DRILLING training; perforating
DRINKING inbibing; carousing
DRIP-FLAP part of balloon **Aeron.**

DRIPPING (fat); (tap)
DRIVABLE
DRIZZLED rained
DROGHING coastal trade, W. Indies
DROILING drudging; loitering
DROLLERY buffoonery; waggery
DROLLING jesting; clowning
DROLLISH fairly facetious
DROMICAL (race-course)
DRONE-FLY drone-bee **Z.**
DROOLING slavering; slobbering
DROOPING withering; languishing
DROP-GOAL four points
DROPKICK football
DROPPING flock of sheldrakes **Z.**
DROP-RIPE ready to fall
DROPSHOT tennis
DROPSIED **Med.**
DROPWISE in drops
DROPWORT meadow-sweet **B.**
DROTCHEL idle wench; slut
DROUGHTY thirsty; arid
DROWNING submerging; overwhelming
DROWSILY sleepily
DROWSING dozing
DRUBBING beating; mauling
DRUDGERY slavery; ignoble toil
DRUDGING moiling; plodding
DRUDGISM menial occupation
DRUGFAST drugproof; immune **Med.**
DRUGGING inducing stupor
DRUGGIST chemist; chymist
DRUIDESS
DRUIDISM Celtic cult
DRUMFIRE continuous fire
DRUMFISH North American fish **Z.**
DRUMHEAD (service; courtmartial)
DRUMMING vibrating
DRUNKARD toper; dipsomaniac
DRY-BIBLE cattle-disease **Z.**
DRY-CLEAN (without immersion)
DRY-GOODS drapery
DRY-PLATE photographic plate
DRY-POINT engraving needle
DRY-STEAM (no unevaporated water)
DRY-STONE (no mortar used)
DRY-STOVE hot-house
DUALIZED halved; split in twain
DUBITATE to doubt; to vacillate
DUCATOON scudo; silver coin **Coin.**
DUCHESSE a table-cover
DUCKBILL platypus **Z.**
DUCK-DIVE swimming-dive
DUCK-HAWK marsh-harrier **Z.**
DUCKLING young duck **Z.**
DUCK-MOLE duckbill **Z.**
DUCK'S-EGG a zero
DUCK-SHOT pellets for wild fowl
DUCK-WEED a water-weed **B.**
DUCTLESS endocrine gland **Med.**

DUELLING⎫ fighting in single combat
DUELLIST ⎭
DUELSOME prone to duelling
DUETTINO short duet   **Mus.**
DUETTIST a performer   **Mus.**
DUKELING a petty duke
DUKERIES ducal country seats
DUKESHIP ducal rank
DULCIMER stringed instrument   **Mus.**
DULCITOR saccharine
DULE-TREE dool-tree; the gallows
DULL-EYED lacking expression
DULL-HEAD a dolt
DULLNESS dulness; apathy
DUMB-BELL no ringing tone
DUMB-CAKE (baked on St. Mark's Eve)
DUMB-CANE (causing dumbness) **B.**
DUMBNESS muteness
DUMB-SHOW pantomime
DUMMERER bogus mute
DUMOSITY prickliness
DUMPLING pudding
DUNCEDOM the class of dunces
DUN-DIVER goosander   **Z.**
DUNGAREE Indian cloth; overalls
DUNG-FORK a gardening implement
DUNG-HILL cock's castle
DUNG-MERE⎫ manure pit
DUNG-YARD ⎭
DUODENAL ⎧ the first of the
DUODENUM ⎭ small intestines **Med.**
DUOLOGUE conversation
DURATION indefinite length of time
DUSKNESS twilight
DUST-BALL horse disease
DUST-CART rubbish conveyor
DUST-COAT light overcoat
DUST-HOLE ash-bin
DUTCHMAN Hollander
DUTIABLE subject to customs
DUTY-FREE not customary
DWARFING stunting; overshadowing
DWARFISH pygmy; undersized; tiny
DWELLING domicile; habitat
DWINDLED declined; shrank
DYE-HOUSE
DYE-STUFF dye material
DYEWORKS colouration factory
DYNAMICS masses in motion
DYNAMISM⎫ the theory of
DYNAMIST ⎭ immanent energy
DYNAMITE powerful explosive
DYNASTIC in succession
DYNATRON electrical oscillation
DYSCHROA skin-disease   **Med.**
DYSGENIC detrimental to the race
DYSLUITE manganese ore   **Min.**
DYSODILE lignite   **Min.**
DYSOPSIA dimness of sight **Med.**
DYSOREXY depraved appetite **Med.**

DYSPATHY antipathy
DYSPEPSY indigestion   **Med.**
DYSPHONY difficulty of speaking
DYSPNOEA difficult in breathing **Med.**
DYSTOMIC (imperfect fracture) **Min.**

E

EAGLE-OWL great horned owl   **Z.**
EAGLE-RAY devil-fish   **Z.**
EAR-BORED (for ear-rings)
EARPHONE a receiver
EAR-SHELL a sea-shell   **Z.**
EARTH-BAG sand bag
EARTH-FED earthly contented
EARTH-HOG aard-vark   **Z.**
EARTHING burrowing; burying
EARTH-NUT pig-nut; peanut **B.**
EARTH-PEA hog peanut   **B.**
EAR-TO-EAR a definite distance
EASELESS non-stop; uneasy
EASEMENT relief; privilege
EASINESS facility; comfort; quiet
EASTERLY oriental
EASTLAND the Orient
EASTMOST farthest east
EASTWARD toward the rising sun
EAU-DE-NIL dull green colour (Nile)
EAU-DE-VIE brandy; Akvavit
EBENEZER memorial stone; chapel
EBIONISE ⎫ (Jewish Christian sect
EBIONISM ⎬ that upheld
EBIONITE ⎭ the Mosaic laws) **Eccl.**
EBLANINE volatile crystal   **Chem.**
EBONIZED blackened
EBRIATED intoxicated
EBURNEAN⎫ like ivory
EBURNINE ⎭
ECAUDATE tailless; Manx   **Z.**
ECCLESIA an assembly; a church **Eccl.**
ECHINATE prickly; bristled
ECHINITE fossil sea-urchin **Min.**
ECHINOID like a sea-urchin **Z.**
ECHINOPS globe thistle, etc. **B.**
ECHIODON sand-eel type   **Z.**
ECHOLESS no repetition
ECLAMPSY epilepsy   **Med.**
ECLECTIC selected; picked
ECLIPSED obscured; disgraced
ECLIPTIC a great circle
ECLOGITE crystalline rock **Min.**
ECONOMIC frugal; thrifty; careful
ECOSTATE ribless   **B.**
ECPHASIS explicit declaration
ECRASEUR surgical instrument **Med.**
ECSTATIC rapturous; beatific
ECTODERM outer skin   **Med.**
ECTOZOAN an external parasite **Z.**
ECUMENIC universal; catholic; general
EDACIOUS greedy; voracious

EDDERING making up fences
EDDY-WIND back draught
EDENTATA } animal lacking
EDENTATE } front teeth **Z.**
EDGE-BONE aitch bone; rump bone
EDGELESS blunt
EDGE-RAIL an iron rail
EDGE-TOOL cutting tool **Tool**
EDGEWAYS } sideways
EDGEWISE }
EDGINESS angularity
EDIFYING enlightening; instructive
EDITRESS woman editor
EDUCABLE teachable
EDUCATED instructed; taught; literate
EDUCATOR tutor
EDUCIBLE deducible; extractible
EDUCTION extraction; deduction
EEL-GRASS grass-wrack **B.**
EEL-SPEAR fisherman's fork
EERINESS weirdness; creepiness
EFFACING expunging; deleting; erasing
EFFECTED accomplished; executed
EFFECTOR effecter; creator
EFFERENT conveying outward
EFFICACY production power
EFFIGIAL relating to images
EFFIGIES images; likenesses; guys
EFFLUENT a stream; outflow
EFFLUVIA noxious exhalations
EFFORCED ravished; compelled
EFFULGED shone; beamed
EFFUSING shedding; pouring
EFFUSION emanation
EFFUSIVE demonstrative
EFTSOONS soon after; again
EGESTING discharging
EGESTION excretion
EGG-APPLE brinjal; aubergine **B.**
EGG-DANCE ancient blindfold hop
EGG-GLASS sand-glass
EGG-PLANT brinjal; aubergine **B.**
EGG-SHELL thin porcelain; paint
EGG-SLICE fried egg conveyor
EGG-SPOON
EGG-TOOTH knob on chick's beak
EGG-WHISK wire brush
EGLATERE eglantine; sweetbriar **B.**
EGOISTIC self-assertive
EGOPHONY a pleurisy symptom **Med.**
EGOTIZED self-conceited
EGRESSED departed; left
EGYPTIAN a gipsy; a tiny peg (anag.)
EIGHTEEN 1½ dozen
EIGHTHLY an ordinal number
EJECTING rejecting; cashiering
EJECTION discharge; dismissal
EJECTIVE expulsive; emissive **[Chem.**
ELAIDATE } castor-oil derivative
ELAIODIC }

ELANCING darting; casting; launching
ELAPHINE like a stag **Z.**
ELAPSING slipping away
ELAPSION lapse; interval
ELATEDLY in high spirits
ELATERIN cucumber extract **Chem.**
ELBOWING jostling; nudging
ELDER-GUN pop-gun
ELDORADO land of fabulous wealth
ELDRITCH weird (Sc.)
ELECTING choosing; preferring
ELECTION freewill; choice; acceptance
ELECTIVE selective; preferential
ELECTRIC stimulating
ELECTRON (negative electricity)
ELECTRUM silver and gold alloy
ELEGANCE refinement; taste; grace
ELEGANCY beauty of propriety
ELEGANTE lady of fashion
ELEGIAST sorrowful bard
ELEGIZED lamented in verse
ELENCHIC elenctic; refutatory
ELENCHUS a sophism
ELEPHANT size of paper **Z.**
ELEUSINE tropical grass **B.**
ELEVATED high; exalted; dignified
ELEVATOR a lift; animator
ELEVENTH (hour)
ELF-ARROW flint arrow-head
ELF-CHILD a changeling
ELICITED deduced; extracted; evoked
ELIDABLE suppressible
ELIGIBLE fit; fully qualified
ELIGIBLY desirably; worthily
ELIMATED polished; smoothed
ELINGUID tongue-tied
ELLIPSIS gap; omission; hiatus
ELLIPTIC oval
ELOCULAR without partitions
ELOINING banishing
ELONGATE stretch; extend; lengthen
ELOQUENT fluent and impressive
ELSEWISE otherwise; differently
ELUDIBLE avoidable; escapable
ELVANITE crystalline rock **Min.**
ELVE-LOCK elf-lock
ELVISHLY mischievously; impishly
ELYDORIC oil and water-colour
ELYTRINE (beetle wing material) **Z.**
EMACIATE waste away; decline; pine
EMANATED derived from; originated
EMBALING bundling; packing
EMBALMED filled with sweet scent
EMBALMER preserver; mortician
EMBANKED mounded
EMBARKED ventured; undertook
EMBARRED encaged; shut in
EMBATTLE draw up for battle
EMBAYING enclosing in a bay
EMBEDDED firmly established

EMBEZZLE appropriate; peculate
EMBITTER exacerbate; exasperate
EMBLAZED displayed; bedecked
EMBLAZON blaze; adorn; embellish
EMBODIED incorporated; integrated
EMBODIER codifier; merger
EMBOGGED mired; bogged
EMBOGUED emptied; discharged; fell
EMBOLDEN encourage; reassure; impel
EMBOLISM intercalation
EMBOLITE a silver ore **Min.**
EMBORDER adorn with a border
EMBOSSED ornamented in relief
EMBOSSER a craftsman
EMBOTTLE to bottle
EMBOWING arching; vaulting
EMBRACED embodied; clasped; hugged
EMBRACER corrupter of a jury **Law**
EMBRAVED inspired (obs.)
EMBRONZE fashion in bronze
EMBRUTED brutalized
EMBRYOUS inaugural
EMBUSQUE shirker in a cushy job
EMBUSSED loaded on a bus
EMENDALS repair-work
EMENDATE to correct; to rectify
EMENDING amending; reforming
EMERGENT pressing; urgent
EMERGING issuing; arising
EMERITED put on retired list
EMERITUS retired with honour
EMERSION reappearance; emergence
EMETICAL ejective **Med.**
EMIGRANT distant home seeker
EMIGRATE migrate; remove
EMINENCE distinction; celebrity
EMINENCY a title
EMISSARV envoy; spy; agent
EMISSILE capable of being emitted
EMISSION discharge; ejection
EMISSIVE emanative; expulsive
EMISSORY a duct; channel **Med.**
EMITTING issuing; delivering
EMMANUEL Immanuel; Messiah **Eccl.**
EMMARBLE enmarble; petrify
EMMEWING confining; penning
EMPACKET to pack up
EMPALING transfixing
EMPARKED enclosed
EMPATRON patronise
EMPAWNED pledged
EMPEOPLE populate (obs.)
EMPERISH impair (obs.)
EMPHASIS stress; force; accent
EMPHATIC definite; positive; earnest
EMPIERCE pierce (obs.)
EMPLANED boarded an aeroplane
EMPLOYED at work; occupied
EMPLOYEE a wage earner; hand
EMPLOYER the boss

EMPLUMED plumed
EMPLUNGE plunge (obs.)
EMPOISON embitter; envenom
EMPORIUM large store; mart
EMPTYING exhausting; discharging
EMPTYSIS hæmorrhage **Med.**
EMPURPLE to dye
EMPUZZLE mystify; bewilder; nonplus
EMPYREAL ethereal aerial; sublime
EMPYREAN highest;heaven
EMULATED vied; strove; competed
EMULATOR rival; copyist
EMULGENT flowing; oozing
EMULSIFY liquate; blend
EMULSINE a fermented mixture
EMULSION milky liquid
EMULSIVE milk-like
ENABLING empowering; allowing
ENACTING decreeing; ordaining
ENACTIVE authoritative
ENACTURE purpose; action (Shak.)
ENALLAGE change of tense, etc.
ENALURON heraldic bordure
ENARCHED like a rainbow
ENASCENT being born
ENAUNTER lest by chance (obs.)
ENCAENIA festival; commemoration
ENCAGING confining; mewing
ENCAMPED pitched; settled
ENCARPUS festoon of fruit (Arch.)
ENCASHED realized; cashed
ENCASING boxing; packing
ENCAVING hiding in a cave
ENCEINTE pregnant
ENCHAFER warmed up (obs.)
ENCHARGE to trust
ENCHASED decorated
ENCHISEL to chisel
ENCHORIC demotic
ENCIRCLE encompass; hem; environ
ENCLISIS ⎱ (grammatical
ENCLITIC ⎰ accentuation)
ENCLOSED wrapped; enveloped
ENCLOSER incloser
ENCLOTHE to clothe
ENCOFFIN prepare for burial
ENCOLLAR encircle
ENCOLOUR tinge
ENCOLURE horse's mane
ENCOMIUM panegyric; eulogy
ENCORING calling for a repeat
ENCRADLE lay in a cradle
ENCRINAL ⎱ (fossilized sea-lilies) **Min.**
ENCRINIC ⎰
ENCROACH trench; intrude; infringe
ENCUMBER burden; clog; obstruct
ENCURLED interlaced
ENCYCLIC circular
ENCYSTED enclosed
ENCYSTIS a tumour **Med.**

ENDAMAGE cause loss; spoil	**ENLARGER** an amplifier
ENDANGER hazard; imperil; jeopardize	**ENLINKED** coupled; connected
ENDEARED beloved; made fond	**ENLISTED** enrolled; engaged
ENDEIXIS a symptom **Med.**	**ENLOCKED** enclosed; shut up
ENDEMIAL locally prevalent	**ENMARBLE** emmarble; harden
ENDENIZE naturalize	**ENMESHED** entrapped; caught
ENDERMIC (through the skin) **Med.**	**ENMOSSED** mossy
ENDOCARP inner coat of fruit **B.**	**ENMURING** immuring; imprisoning
ENDOCYST inner membrane **Z.**	**ENNEADIC** nine of
ENDODERM inner skin **Z.**	**ENNEAGON** nine-sided polygon
ENDOGAMY tribal intermarriage	**ENNEATIC** ninth
ENDORSED ratified; approved	**ENNOBLED** made illustrious
ENDORSEE the assignee	**ENORMITY** atrocity; depravity
ENDOSARC endoplasm **B.**	**ENORMOUS** vast; monstrous; gigantic
ENDOWING presenting; bequeathing	**ENOUNCED** proclaimed; enunciated
ENDRUDGE enslave	**ENPLANED** (cf. entrained)
ENDURING lasting; persisting	**ENQUIRED** inquired; investigated
ENERGICO with vitality **Mus.**	**ENQUIRER** a snooper; questioner
ENERGIZE animate; excite; force	**ENRAGING** maddening; exasperating
ENERVATE weaken; sap; relax	**ENRAVISH** enrapture; entrance
ENFACING (cf. endorsing)	**ENRICHED** endowed; adorned
ENFAMISH to famish	**ENRICHER** a fertilizer
ENFEEBLE debilitate; paralyse	**ENRIDGED** furrowed; corrugated
ENFETTER manacle; shackle	**ENRINGED** encircled
ENFILADE to rake	**ENROBING** dressing
ENFOLDED clasped; enclosed	**ENROLLED** registered; recorded
ENFORCED compelled; obliged	**ENROLLER** inscriber
ENFORCER active agent	**ENROOTED** firmly fixed; established
ENFOREST afforest	**ENSAMPLE** a pattern; a model
ENFORMED fashioned	**ENSCONCE** protect; hide; harbour
ENFRAMED	**ENSEALED** sealed up
ENGAGING winning; charming	**ENSEAMED** seamed
ENGENDER produce; beget	**ENSEARED** dried up
ENGILDED gilt	**ENSEMBLE** all together **Mus.**
ENGINEER scheme; a sapper	**ENSHIELD** guard; screen
ENGINERY implements of war	**ENSHRINE** treasure; cherish
ENGINING contriving; racking	**ENSHROUD** veil; mask; conceal
ENGIRDED encircled	**ENSIFORM** like a sword
ENGIRDLE encompass; encircle	**ENSIGNCY** rank of ensign
ENGLANTE heraldic acorns, etc.	**ENSIGNED** distinctively marked
ENGORGED glutted	**ENSILAGE** preservation of fodder
ENGOULED (heraldic absorption)	**ENSILING** storing in a pit
ENGRAVED scribed; chiselled; cut	**ENSLAVED** in bondage; enthralled
ENGRAVER carver; sculptor	**ENSLAVER** captor; subjugator
ENGROOVE cut a furrow	**ENSNARED** trapped; inveigled
ENGULFED devoured; overwhelmed	**ENSOULED** animated
ENHANCED heightened; raised	**ENSPHERE** englobe
ENHANCER augmenter	**ENSTYLED** by name of
ENHARDEN encourage; harden	**ENSURING** assuring; safe-guarding
ENHUNGER affamish	**ENSWATHE** bandage; wrap
ENHYDRIC containing moisture	**ENTACKLE** supply with gear
ENJAILED put in prison; jugged	**ENTAILED** settled on heirs
ENJOINED commanded; directed	**ENTAILER** a deviser
ENJOINER prohibiter	**ENTANGLE** mat; ravel; implicate
ENJOYING appreciating; delighting in	**ENTASTIC** spasmodic **Med.**
ENKERNEL put in a nutshell	**ENTELLUS** sacred monkey **Z.**
ENKINDLE rouse; inflame; ignite	**ENTENDER** treat kindly
ENLACING encircling; entwining	**ENTERING** penetrating; noting
ENLARDED basted	**ENTHRILL** to pierce (obs.)
ENLARGED dilated; expanded	**ENTHRONE** install; exalt; elevate

ENTHUSED became ardent
ENTICING alluring; coaxing
ENTIRELY fully; perfectly
ENTIRETY aggregate; completeness
ENTITLED styled; dubbed; empowered
ENTOILED snared; trapped
ENTOMBED buried; interred
ENTOMOID like an insect **Z.**
ENTOPTIC inner vision
ENTOZOIC ⎱ referring to **Z.**
ENTOZOON ⎰ internal parasites
ENTR'ACTE an interval **Mus.**
ENTRAILS internal parts; offal **Med.**
ENTRANCE entry; to ravish
ENTREATY urgent request; petition
ENTREMES entremets; snacks
ENTRENCH fortify; encroach
ENTREPAS an amble (Fr.)
ENTREPOT emporium; transit depot
ENTRESOL mezzanine story
ENTWINED woven; plaited; twisted
ENVAPOUR surround with vapour
ENVASSAL enslave; enthral
ENVEIGLE inveigle; lure; seduce
ENVELOPE a cover; surround
ENVIABLE most desirable
ENVIABLY covetously; grudgingly
ENVIRONS suburbs; vicinity
ENVISAGE to face; to consider
ENVOLUME include
ENZOOTIC (localized disease) **Z.**
EOLIENNE dress material; silk & wool
EOLIPILE experimental flask
EOLITHIC pre-palaeolithic
EPAGOGIC inductive
EPALPATE no feelers **Z.**
EPANODOS rhetorical recapitulation
EPENETIC laudatory
EPHEMERA may-flies, etc. **Z.**
EPHESIAN debauchee; (Ephesus)
EPIBLAST outer skin **Med.**
EPICALEX outer calyx **B.**
EPICERIE grocery; spices (Fr.)
EPICOLIC (abdomen over colon) **Med.**
EPICYCLE circulating circle
EPIDEMIC locally prevalent **Med.**
EPIDOTIC (vitreous ore) **Min.**
EPIGEOUS low growing **B.**
EPIGRAPH motto; inscription
EPILEPSY fits **Med.**
EPILOGIC concluding
EPILOGUE farewell speech
EPIMACUS heraldic griffin
EPIMERAL (segment above joint) **Z.**
EPINASTY curvature **B.**
EPIORNIS extinct bird (Madagascar) **Z.**
EPIPHANY January 6th. **Eccl.**
EPIPHORA streams of tears **Med.**
EPIPHYTE (mistletoe, orchids) **B.**
EPIPLOCE rhetorical climax

EPIPOLIC fluorescent
EPISCOPY superintendence; search **Eccl.**
EPISEMON city badge (Gk.)
EPISODAL digressive; accidental
EPISODIC incidental; subordinate
EPISPERM outer seed cover **B.**
EPISTLER letter-writer; scribe
EPISTYLE the architrave (arch.)
EPITASIS climax; culmination
EPITONIC overstrained
EPITRITE metrical foot
EPITROPE rhetorical concession
EPIZOOTY animal epidemic **Z.**
EPLICATE unplaited
EPONYMIC yclept
EPOPOEIA epic poetry
EPSOMITE Epsom salts **Min.**
EPULOTIC cicatrizing **Med.**
EQUALISE equalize; even
EQUALITY uniformity; sameness
EQUALLED rivalled
EQUATING balancing
EQUATION allowance for inaccuracy
EQUIFORM of equal shape; similar
EQUIPAGE outfit; effects; train
EQUIPPED accoutred; armed
EQUITANT riding astraddle
EQUIVOKE an equivocation
ERADIATE emit; sparkle
ERASABLE effaceable
ERASTIAN follower of Erastus
ERECTILE capable of elevation
ERECTING raising; building
ERECTION structure; edifice
ERECTIVE setting upright
EREMETIC secluded; solitary; hermetic
EREPTION snatching; wresting
ERETHISM acute irritation **Med.**
EREWHILE formerly
ERGOTINE ⎫ parasitical fungus
ERGOTISE ⎬ found in rye, etc, **B.**
ERGOTISM ⎭ of poisonous nature
ERIGERON flea-bane genus **B.**
ERMINOIS heraldic fur
EROTESIS rhetorical question
EROTETIC interrogatory
EROTICAL amatory; amorous
EROTICAL (Eros)
ERRANTLY like knights of old
ERRANTRY rambling; roving
ERRORIST fallacious fellow
ERUCTATE belch
ERUGATED wrinkled; corrugated
ERUMPENT breaking out **B**
ERUPTING casting out
ERUPTION outburst
ERUPTIVE explosive
ERYCINIA insect genus **Z**
ERYSIMUM hare's ear, etc. **B**
ERYTHEMA a skin disease **Med**

ESCALADE } attack by means of
ESCALADO } scaling ladders
ESCALLOP scallop; a bi-valve **Z.**
ESCAMBIO (transfer of bills, Sp.)
ESCAPADE prank; adventure; frolic
ESCAPADO desperado
ESCAPING evading; eluding
ESCAPISM } the quest of
ESCAPIST } a mental anodyne
ESCARPED steeply; sloped
ESCHALOT small onion **B.**
ESCHEWED shunned; avoided
ESCHEWER escapist
ESCORTED attended; conducted
ESCOTTED taxed; maintained
ESCOUADE a squad (Fr.)
ESCULENT edible
ESCURIAL Spanish royal palace
ESOTERIC secret; mysterious
ESPALIER trellised trees
ESPARCET sainfoin **B.**
ESPECIAL particular; special
ESPIBAWN ox-eye daisy **B.**
ESPIOTTE species of rye **B.**
ESPOUSAL betrothal
ESPOUSED married
ESPOUSER wooer
ESQUIRED escorted; protected
ESSAYING attempting; endeavouring
ESSAYISH experimental
ESSAYIST a scribe; writer
ESSAYKIN short essay
ESSENCED perfumed
ESSENISM Essene doctrine
ESSOINED excused for absence
ESSOINER attendance excuser **Law**
ESSONITE yellow garnet **Min.**
ESSORANT heraldic wings
ESTANCIA cattle ranch, S. America
ESTEEMED held in high regard
ESTEEMER valuer; admirer
ESTHETIO aesthetic; perceptive
ESTIMATE appraise; calculate
ESTIVAGE method of ship loading
ESTIVATE pass the summer
ESTONIAN (Baltic republic)
ESTOPPED impeded; barred **Law**
ESTOPPEL a plea **Law**
ESTOVERS timber supplies **Law**
ESTRANGE alienate; disaffect
ESTRAYED strayed
ESTRIDGE ostrich down **Z.**
ESURIENT greedy; hungry
ETA-PATCH balloon patch
ETCETERA etc; etc.
ETEOSTIC a chronogram
ETERNITY perpetuity
ETERNIZE eternise; immortalise
ETHEREAL airy; heavenly; celestial
ETHERENE etherine; a gas **Chem.**

ETHERISM effects of ether
ETHERIZE etherise; to gas **Med.**
ETHEROLE a light oil **Chem.**
ETHICIST moralist
ETHIOPIC Abyssinian; Ethiopian
ETHNARCH Greek governor
ETHNICAL racial; heathen; pagan
ETHOLOGY moral philosophy
ETHYLENE carburetted hydrogen **Chem.**
ETIOLATE to blanch
ETIOLOGY study of causes
ETRURIAN } native of Etruria
ETRUSCAN }
ETYPICAL exceptional; aberrant
EUCALYPT eucalyptus **B.**
EUCHARIS Amazon lilies, etc. **B.**
EUCTICAL supplicatory
EUGENICS eugenism
EUGENIST (race culture)
EUGUBINE (bronze tablets)
EULACHAN candle-fish oil
EULOGIST panegyrist
EULOGIUM laudatory speech; encomium
EULOGIZE extol; applaud; flatter
EUNICEAE a worm genus **Z.**
EUONYMIN } an extract from the
EUONYMUS } spindle tree **B.**
EUPATORY hemp agrimony **B.**
EUPATRID Athenian aristocrat
EUPEPSIA good digestion **Med.**
EUPEPTIC highly digestible
EUPHONIA smooth enunciation
EUPHONIC harmonious; felicitous
EUPHONON harmonium **Mus.**
EUPHORIA satisfaction of the artist
EUPHRASY the eye-bright plant **Med.**
EUPHUISM bombastic diction
EUPHUIST affected speaker; pedant
EUPHUIZE over-emphasize
EUPYRION a quick-match, etc.
EURASIAN European-Asiatic
EUROPEAN
EUROPIUM metallic element **Chem.**
EURYTHMY symmetry; regularity
EUSEBIAN (Eusebius) **Eccl.**
EUTECTIC easily melted
EUTHERIA genus of mammals **Z.**
EUTHROPY good digestion
EVACUANT purgative **Med.**
EVACUATE quit; abandon; forsake
EVADIBLE escapable; evasible
EVANESCE disappear; vanish
EVASIBLE avoidable; elusory
EVECTION convection
EVEN-DOWN downright
EVENFALL twilight
EVENNESS levelness; **regularity**
EVENSONG, a service **Eccl.**
EVENTFUL full of incident; stirring
EVENTIDE evenfall; evening

EVENTUAL last; ultimate; final
EVERMORE always; eternally
EVERSION turning inside out
EVERTING overturning; upsetting
EVERYDAY usual; common; routine
EVERYONE everybody
EVERYWAY in all ways
EVICTING expelling; ousting
EVICTION dispossession
EVIDENCE testimony; witness
EVILDOER malefactor; criminal
EVILNESS malignity; depravity
EVINCING demonstrating; exhibiting
EVINCIVE indicative
EVITABLE avoidable; escapable
EVOCATOR a summoner **Law**
EVOLATIC volatile
EVOLVENT involute
EVOLVING unfolding
EVULGATE publish; divulge
EVULSION extraction
EWIGKEIT eternity (Ger.)
EXACTING enforcing; critical; rigid
EXACTION extortion; tribute
EXALTING extolling; honouring
EXAMINED inquired; studied
EXAMINEE candidate
EXAMINER scrutinizer; inspector
EXAMPLAR model; exemplar; pattern
EXCAVATE delve; dig; scoop
EXCEEDED surpassed; capped; excelled
EXCEEDER outdoor; surpasser
EXCEPTED excluded; omitted
EXCEPTOR objector
EXCESSED exceeded
EXCESSES debaucheries
EXCERNED excreted; exuded
EXCHANGE barter; commute
EXCISING cutting out
EXCISION extirpation; amputation
EXCITANT a stimulant
EXCITING rousing; inciting; inflaming
EXCITIVE provocative
EXCLUDED banned; barred; vetoed
EXCURSED digressed; wandered
EXCURSUS supplemented treatise
EXCUSING remitting; condoning
EXCUSSED deciphered
EXECRATE curse; detest; abhor
EXECUTED beheaded; achieved
EXECUTER }
EXECUTOR } executioner; agent **Law**
EXEGESIS explanatory discourse
EXEGETIC elucidative
EXEMPLAR pattern; examplar; model
EXEMPTED excused; released
EXEQUIAL funereal
EXEQUIES burial rites
EXERCISE use; task; drill; exert
EXERGUAL date space on coin

EXERTING striving; wielding
EXERTION effort; strain; attempt
EXERTIVE labouring; toilsome
EXHALANT exhalent; evaporative
EXHALING breathing; emitting
EXHORTED encouraged; warned
EXHORTER incitor; adviser
EXHUMATE disinter; exhume
EXHUMING digging up
EXIGEANT exacting; importunate
EXIGENCY exigence; urgency
EXIGIBLE able to be levied
EXIGUITY scantiness; fineness
EXIGUOUS tiny; diminutive; minute
EXIMIOUS eminent; famous
EXINTINE floral membrane **B.**
EXISTENT extant; living
EXISTING being; continuing
EXITIOUS deadly; malignant; noxious
EX-LIBRIS (book-plate)
EXOPHAGY selective cannibalism
EXORABLE not relentless; lenient
EXORCISM } deliverance
EXORCIST } from evil spirits
EXORCIZE exorcise
EXORDIAL introductory
EXORDIUM the beginning; preamble
EXOSMOSE diffusion
EXOSTOME part of ovule **B.**
EXOTERIC openly professed; superficial
EXOTHERM heat liberator
EXPANDED stretched; dilated
EXPECTED awaited; forecast
EXPEDITE hasten; accelerate
EXPELLEE
EXPENDED consumed; dissipated
EXPERTLY dexterously; adroitly
EXPIABLE atonable
EXPIATED made reparation
EXPIATOR indemnifier
EXPIRANT a dying person
EX-PIRATE retired free-booter
EXPIRING at death's door
EXPLICIT clearly stated; categorical
EXPLODED burst; repudiated
EXPLODER a machine
EXPLORED scrutinized; plumbed
EXPLORER investigator
EXPONENT an executant
EXPORTED shipped; sent abroad
EXPORTER foreign trader
EXPOSING exhibiting; revealing
EXPOSURE disclosure; revelation
EXPUGNED overcome; conquered
EXPUNGED erased; deleted
EXSECTED cut off
EXSERTED projecting; protruding
EXTENDED stretched; protracted
EXTENDER dilator; expander
EXTENSOR a muscle **Med.**

EXTERIOR outer; outward
EXTERNAL outer; foreign; exotic
EXTERNAT day school
EXTOLLER eulogizer
EXTORTED wrested; extracted
EXTRADOS convex surface of vault
EXTRORSE turned outward
EXTRUDED expelled; ejected
EXULTANT triumphant; jubilant
EXULTING crowing; rejoicing
EXUVIATE moult; shed a skin
EYEGLASS monocle
EYEPIECE telescope lens
EYESALVE eyewash; ointment
EYESIGHT vision
EYESTONE optical adjunct **Med.**
EYETEETH
EYE-TO-EYE vis-a-vis; face to face
EYETOOTH a canine tooth
EYEWATER tear; lotion

F

FABLIAUX French metric poetry
FABULIST an Aesop
FABULIZE fabulise; romance
FABULOUS feigned; fictitious; unreal
FACE-ACHE neuralgia **Med.**
FACE-CARD court card
FACELESS lacking a physiognomy
FACE-PACK cosmetic
FACETIAE witticisms; pleasantries
FACETING cutting facets
FACIALLY superficially; externally
FACILITY dexterity; readiness; address
FACINGLY oppositely
FACTIOUS turbulent; riotous
FACTOTUM general agent
FACULOUS spotted
FADDLING trifling; playing
FADELESS imperishable; enduring
FADINGLY decreasingly; vapidly
FAE-BERRY fea-berry; gooseberry **B.**
FAGGOTED bundled
FAGOTING a kind of embroidery
FAILDYKE turf-wall (Sc.)
FAINEANT idler; do-nothing; sluggard
FAINTEST barely perceptible; dimmest
FAINTING swooning
FAINTISH giddy; languid
FAIR-COPY correct copy
FAIR-HAND freehand
FAIR-LEAD a rope-guide **Naut.**
FAIRNESS honest dealing; equity
FAIR-PLAY justice; impartiality
FAIRYDOM fairyland
FAIRYISM enchantment
FAITHFUL leal; loyal; steadfast
FAKEMENT makeshift; swindle
FAKIRISM mysticism; poverty

FALCATED like a sickle
FALCHION short curved sword
FALCONER a hawker
FALCONET small hawk; cannon **Z.**
FALCONRY hawking
FALDERAL meaningless refrain
FALDETTA hood and cape (Malta)
FALLABLE unstable; depreciable
FALLIBLE liable to error; deceptive
FALLIBLY erroneously
FALLOWED ploughed but not sown
FALL-TRAP a snare
FALSETTE⎫ shrill and unnatural
FALSETTO⎰ tone of voice **Mus.**
FALTERED wavered; hesitated
FAMELESS undistinguished
FAMILIAR unceremonious; intimate
FAMILIST (16th century sect) **Eccl.**
FAMISHED anhungered; starved
FAMOUSLY remarkably; eminently
FAMULIST magician's attendant
FAN-BLAST forced draught
FANCIFUL whimsical; capricious
FANCYING preferring; imagining **[Mus.**
FANDANGO Spanish national dance
FANFARON swaggering bully; braggart
FANGLESS toothless
FANLIGHT window over front-door
FANTASIA musical medley **Mus.**
FAN-WHEEL ventilating device
FARADAIC⎫ relating to a farad,
FARADISE⎬ the practical unit **Meas.**
FARADISM⎰ of electrical capacity
FARCICAL ludicrous; absurd; droll
FARCY-BUD (glanders)
FARDELED in bundles
FAREWELL adieu; good-bye; parting
FAR-FLUNG widely disseminated
FARINOSE mealy; floury
FARMABLE cultivatable
FARMYARD rooster's realm
FARRIERY veterinary work
FARROWED littered
FAR-SPENT well advanced
FARTHEST ultimate; yondmost
FARTHING four a penny **Coin**
FASCICLE a cluster **B.**
FASCISTI Italian fascists
FASCISTS opponents of socialism
FASHIOUS vexatious; provocative
FASTENED secured; bound; tied
FASTNESS a stronghold; security
FATALISM⎫ (belief in the inevitable)
FATALIST⎰
FATALITY a calamity; disaster
FATHERED adopted; begat; sired
FATHERLY paternal; benign
FATHOMED comprehended; plumbed
FATIGUED weary; jaded; tired
FATTENED overfed

FATTENER a fat producer
FATTRELS ends of ribbon (Sc.)
FAULTFUL defective
FAULTILY imperfectly
FAULTING accusing
FAUTEUIL arm-chair; stall
FAUVETTE garden warbler **Z.**
FAVONIAN (west wind)
FAVOURED encouraged; approved
FAVOURER patron; supporter
FAYALITE an iron ore **Min.**
FEABERRY faeberry; gooseberry **B.**
FEARLESS intrepid; undaunted; heroic
FEARSOME dread; awe inspiring
FEASIBLE workable; achievable
FEASIBLY practicably; possibly
FEAST-DAY a festival
FEASTFUL sumptuous; luxurious
FEASTING banqueting; carousing
FEAST-WON bribed by feasting
FEATEOUS dexterous; deft
FEATHERY with plumes
FEATNESS adroitness; neatness
FEATURED impersonated
FEBLESSE feebleness; irresoluteness
FEBRIFIC causing fever
FEBRUARY month of expiation
FECKLESS inefficient; spiritless
FECULENT muddy; turbid; fetid
FEDELINI macaroni
FEDERACY confederacy; alliance
FEDERARY a confederate
FEDERATE league together
FEEBLISH weakish
FEEDBACK electronics
FEED-HEAD cistern of a boiler
FEED-PIPE water-pipe
FEED-PUMP a force-pump
FEE-GRIEF a private grief
FEER-TYPE positive process **Photo.**
FEETLESS footless; apodal
FEIGNING counterfeiting; shamming
FEINTING pretending; misleading
FELDSPAR felspar **Min.**
FELICIDE cat-killing
FELICITY happiness; bliss; blessedness
FELINITY cattishness
FELLABLE capable of being felled
FELLAHIN Egyptian peasants
FELLINIC bilious **Med.**
FELLNESS ruthlessness; ferocity
FELLOWED matched
FELLOWLY companionable
FELLSIDE mountain side
FELO-DE-SE suicide **Law**
FELSITIC like porphyry **Min.**
FELSTONE (quartz and felspar) **Min.**
FELTERED matted together
FELTWORT the mullein **B.**
FEMALITY feminality

FEMERELL louvre or ventilator
FEMICIDE lady-killing
FEMININE female; effeminate; tender
FEMINISM (women's rights)
FEMINIST advocate of feminism
FEMINIZE to make effeminate
FENBERRY cranberry **B.**
FENCEFUL affording defence
FENCIBLE a home guard
FENESTER ⎫
FENESTRA ⎬ a window
FEN-GOOSE greylag goose **Z.**
FENUGREC sort of clover **B.**
FEOFFING granting a fief
FERACITY fecundity; fruitfulness
FERETORY shrine for relics **Eccl.**
FERINELY wildly; savagely
FERN-SEED sphores **B.**
FERNSHAW a thicket of ferns **B.**
FEROCITY cruelty; savagery
FERREOUS of iron
FERRETED unearthed
FERRETER investigator
FERRIAGE ferry charge
FERRITES ferro magnetic materials
(ceramics)
FERRITIN liver protein
FERRULED tipped
FERRYING transporting
FERRY-MAN Charon (river Styx)
FERULING caning
FERVENCY ardour; devotion; eagerness
FERVIDLY hotly; zealously; with heat
FESTALLY joyously; jovially; merrily
FESTERED rankled
FESTIVAL mirthful; an occasion
FETCHING attractive; bringing
FETERITA dwarf sorghum **B.**
FETISHES charms; talismans; amulets
FETTERED shackled; manacled
FETTLING conditioning
FEUDALLY
FEVERFEW a febrifuge **B.**
FEVERING agitating; heating
FEVERISH inconstant; sultry
FEVEROUS restless; excited
FEWTRILS trifles (dial.)
FIBROGEN protein
FIBRILLA a filament **B.**
FIBROSIS fibrous growth
FIBULATE ⎫
FIBULOUS ⎬ (leg bones) **Med.**
FIDDLING trifling; fidgeting **Mus.**
FIDELITY trust; staunchness
FIDGETED worried; fretted; chafed
FIDICULA small lute **Mus.**
FIDUCIAL confident; precise; exact
FIELD-BED camp-bed
FIELD-DAY tactical exercise
FIELD-GUN mobile gun

FIENDISH malicious; devilish	**FINNIKIN** crested pigeon	**Z.**
FIERCELY zealously; vehemently	**FINOCHIO** sweet fennel	**B.**
FIERCEST most ferocious	**FINSCALE** rudd, fish	**Z.**
FIERY-HOT blazing; impetuous	**FIN-WHALE** rorqual	**Z.**
FIERY-NEW brand-new	**FIREARMS** offensive weapons	
FIFE-RAIL belaying pin rack **Naut.**	**FIREBACK** ornamental plate	
FIFTIETH ordinal of fifty	**FIRE-BALL** incendiary weapon	
FIG-APPLE a coreless apple **B.**	**FIRE-BARS** furnace bars	
FIG-EATER garden warbler **Z.**	**FIRE-BOAT** fire-fighting steamboat	
FIGHTING contention; strife; faction	**FIRECLAY** used for fire-bricks **Min.**	
FIG-SHELL a univalve shell **Z.**	**FIRECOCK** hydrant connexion	
FIGULATE moulded	**FIREDAMP** explosive gas in mines	
FIGULINE potter's clay **Min.**	**FIRE-EYED** with fiery eyes	
FIGURANT male ballet dancer	**FIREFLAG** flash of lightning	
FIGURATE of determinate form	**FIRE-GIRL** (N.F.S.)	
FIGURIAL represented by a figure	**FIRE-HOOK** demolition hook	
FIGURINE small statuette (Fr.)	**FIRE-HOSE** portable piping	
FIGURING calculating; symbolizing	**FIRE-KILN** an oven	
FIGURIST one skilled in figures	**FIRELESS**	
FILAGREE filigree; metal lacework	**FIRELOCK** antique musket	
FILAMENT slender thread	**FIRE-PLUG** valve in a water-main	
FILATORY spinning machine	**FIRESHIP** incendiary ship **Naut.**	
FILATURE the reeling of silk	**FIRESIDE** the hearth	
FILCHING pilfering; purloining	**FIRE-STEP** firing step in trench	
FILE-FISH a sea-fish **Z.**	**FIRETAIL** the redstart **Z.**	
FILIALLY like a son or daughter	**FIRETRAP** (no means of escape)	
FILIATED adopted; amalgamated	**FIRE-WARD** fire-warden	
FILICORD fern-like plant **B.**	**FIRE-WEED** a plant **B.**	
FILIFORM thread-like	**FIRE-WOOD** chopped sticks	
FILIGREE filagree; metallic lacework	**FIRMLESS** wavering; unstable	
FILIOQUE (clause in Nicene creed) **Eccl.**	**FIRMNESS** solidity; resolution	
FILIPINO (Philippines)	**FIRST-AID**	
FILLETED strung together	**FIRST-DAY** Sunday	
FILLIBEG a kilt (Sc.)	**FISHABLE** capable of being fished	
FILLIPED flipped	**FISH-BALL** fish-cake	
FILMGOER a frequenter of cinemas	**FISHBEAM** beam of special form	
FILM-STAR	**FISH-CAKE** fish-ball	
FILOPINA ⎫	**FISH-COOP** box used for ice-fishing	
FILOPINO ⎭ philopina, a nut-game	**FISH-GLUE** an adhesive	
FILTERED percolated; strained	**FISH-HAWK** the osprey **Z.**	
FILTHIER grubbier	**FISH-HOOK** barbed hook	
FILTHILY dirtily	**FISH-MEAL** abstemious diet	
FILTRATE filtered solution	**FISH-POND**	
FINALISM conclusiveness	**FISH-ROOM** part of ship **Naut.**	
FINALIST in the last round	**FISH-SKIN**	
FINALITY kismet; eventuality	**FISH-TAIL** a gas jet; jewelry	
FINANCED capitalized	**FISH-WEIR** a fishgarth	
FINDABLE discoverable	**FISH-WIFE** fish vendor	
FINE-DRAW invisible mending	**FISSIPED** cloven hoof	
FINELESS endless; unlimited	**FISSURED** cleft; cracked	
FINENESS purity	**FISTIANA** boxing annals	
FINE-SPUN elaborated	**FISTINUT** pistachio nut **B.**	
FINESSED acted artfully	**FISTULAR** tubular	
FINESSER crafty person	**FITFULLY** spasmodically; inconstantly	
FINGERED handled	**FIVEFOLD** 500%	
FINGROMS woollen cloth	**FIVELEAF** cinquefoil	
FINISHED ended	**FIXATION** stability; firmness	
FINISHER final blow	**FIXATIVE** a stabilizer **Photo.**	
FINITELY within limits	**FIXATURE** hair cream	
FINITUDE limitation	**FIXIDITY** permanence; constancy	

FIZZLING sizzling
FLABBILY limply
FLAG-DAY
FLAGGING signalling; wilting
FLAGRANT notorious; glaring
FLAG-SHIP Naut.
FLAG-WORM green gentle Z.
FLAMBEAU a lighted torch
FLAMELET small flame
FLAMINGO Z.
FLAMMING deluding
FLAMMULE pictorial Japanese flame
FLANCHED heraldic term; flanged
FLANERIE lounging (Fr.)
FLANKING bordering; touching
FLAP-JACK a confection; a compact
FLAPPING flopping; waving; shaking
FLASHILY transiently; gaudily
FLASHING sparkling; gleaming
FLAT-BOAT a small craft Naut.
FLAT-FISH flounder, etc. Z.
FLAT-FOOT flattie; policeman (slang)
FLAT-HEAD a N. Amer. Indian
FLAT-IRON smoothing iron
FLATNESS monotony; depression
FLAT-RACE not a steeplechase
FLATTERY insincere compliment
FLATTEST dullest; lowest; very level
FLATTING a process
FLATTISH comparatively level
FLATWISE not edgewise
FLAT-WORM tape worm Z.
FLAUNTED vaunted; paraded
FLAUNTER ostentatious person
FLAUTIST flute-player Mus.
FLAWLESS perfect; without blemish
FLAX-COMB a heckle
FLAX-LILY New Zealand flax B.
FLAX-MILL a factory
FLAX-SEED linseed B.
FLAX-TAIL the reed-mace B.
FLAX-WEED B.
FLAX-WORT B.
FLEA-BANE B.
FLEA-BITE an inconvenient trifle
FLEAKING reed covering under thatch
FLEA-WORT a plantain B.
FLECKING dappling
FLECTION flexion; bending
FLEECING shearing; swindling
FLEERING mocking; taunting
FLEETEST fastest; swiftest
FLEETING transient; passing; brief
FLENCHED flensed
FLENSING a whaling operation
FLESH-FLY blow-fly; blue-bottle Z.
FLESHING tights; scraping leather
FLESHPOT stock-pot; luxury
FLETCHED feathered (arrows)
FLETCHER arrow maker

FLEXIBLE pliant; tractable; lissom
FLEXIBLY sinuously; not rigidly
FLEXUOSE } winding; wavering;
FLEXUOUS } curving; elastic
FLICHTER flutter; quiver (Sc.)
FLICKING flipping
FLIGHTED took wing
FLIMFLAM humbug; nonsense
FLIMSIES lingerie; carbon copies
FLIMSILY unsubstantially
FLINCHED winced; shrank back
FLINCHER shrinker; coward
FLINDERS fragments; flitters
FLINGING hurling; casting; pitching
FLINTIFY turn into flint
FLIPFLAP an entertaining device
FLIPFLOP noise of walking, electronics
FLIPPANT pert; saucy; glib
FLIPPING flicking
FLIRTING philandering; (fan)
FLIRTISH somewhat coquettish
FLITTERN a young oak (dial.)
FLITTERS flinders; fragments; glitter
FLITTING migrating; hastening
FLIXWEED a hedge plant B.
FLOATAGE } flotsam;
FLOATSAM } shipwrecked goods Law
FLOATING circulating; wafting
FLOCCOSE tufted
FLOCCULE small flock of wool
FLOCK-BED bed stuffed with flock
FLOCKING congregating; crowding
FLOGGING a chastisement
FLOODING inundating; swamping
FLOOD-LIT illuminated
FLOOKING cross vein or fissure
FLOORAGE floor space
FLOORING material for floors
FLOPPILY limply; flaccidly
FLOPPING breaking down
FLORALLY with flowers
FLORENCE wine; cloth Coin
FLORIAGE blossom
FLORICAN Indian bustard Z.
FLORIDLY ornately; exuberantly
FLOSCULE a floret; a bloom B.
FLOTILLA small fleet Naut.
FLOUNCED threw oneself about
FLOUNDER struggle; a fish Z.
FLOURING reducing to powder
FLOURISH (weapons); (trumpets) Mus.
FLOUTING mocking; jeering
FLOWERED blossomed
FLOWERET B.
FLUENTLY volubly; easily
FLUFFING muffing
FLUIDIFY fluidise
FLUIDITY fluidism; liquidity
FLUMMERY a drink; humbug
FLUORENE coal tar product Min.

FLUORIDE	**Min.**
FLUORINE a gas	**Chem.**
FLUORITE fluor-spar	**Min.**
FLUOROUS derived from fluor	
FLURRIED agitated; disconcerted	
FLUSHING blushing; colouring	
FLUSTERY confused; agitated	
FLUXIBLE fusible	
FLY-BLOWN	
FLY-MAKER (fishing)	
FLYPAPER a fly-trap	
FLY-SHEET handbill; broadside	
FLY-WATER an arsenical solution	
FLY-WHEEL a conserver of momentum	
FOAL-FOOT colt's foot	**B.**
FOAMLESS	
FOCALIZE focalise; converge	
FOCUSING (photography)	
FODDERER cattle-feeder	
FOG-BOUND	
FOGEYDOM senility	
FOGGIEST most obscure; murkiest	
FOG-SMOKE thick fog	
FOILABLE able to be frustrated	
FOILPLAY fencing	
FOILSMAN fencer	
FOLDEROL refrain of old song	
FOLDLESS uncreased	
FOLD-YARD cattle enclosure	
FOLIAGED leafy	
FOLIATED laminated	
FOLIOING paging	
FOLKLAND common land	**Law**
FOLK-LORE legendary traditions	
FOLKMOTE assembly of freemen	
FOLK-SONG	
FOLK-TALE	
FOLKWAYS group tradition	
FOLLICLE a pod	**B.**
FOLLOWED imitated; pursued	
FOLLOWER partisan; adherent; copier	
FOLLOW-ON cricket	
FOLLOW-UP second stage support	
FOMENTED excited; fanned	
FOMENTER agent provocateur	
FONDLING a beloved one	
FONDNESS affection; predilection	
FONTANEL a cavity	**Med.**
FONTANGE wire cap-frame	
FOOD-CARD a rational requirement	
FOODLESS lacking sustenance	
FOOLSCAP paper, 17 × 13½ inhces	
FOOL-TRAP snare for simpletons	
FOOTBALL	
FOOT-BATH	
FOOT-FALL footstep; tread	
FOOT-GEAR shoes and stockings	
FOOT-HALT a sheep disease	
FOOT-HILL an underfeature	
FOOTHOLD	

FOOT-IRON carriage step; fetter	
FOOTLESS	
FOOTLING trifling; trivial; trumpery	
FOOT-MARK foot-print	
FOOT-MUFF	
FOOT-NOTE an addendum	
FOOT-PACE slow rate of progression	
FOOT-PATH	
FOOT-POST pedestrian messenger	
FOOT-RACE	
FOOT-ROPE rope along a yard	**Naut.**
FOOT RULE a 12-inch measure	**Meas.**
FOOT-SLOG march; walk; tramp; hike	
FOOTSORE	
FOOTSTEP footfall	
FOOTWEAR foot-gear	
FOOTWORK movement (sport)	
FOOTWORN worn by many feet	
FOOZLING bungling	
FORAGING ravaging; searching	
FORAMINA openings; orifices	
FORAYING plundering; raiding	
FORBORNE refrained; spared	
FORGEDLY compulsorily; unnaturally	
FORCEFUL coercive	
FORCIBLE cogent	
FORCIBLY violently	
FORDABLE	
FORDOING ruining; exhausting	
FOREBEAR forbear; ancestor	
FOREBODE prognosticate; portended	
FORE-BODY forward part of ship	
FORECAST prediction; prognosis	
FOREDATE antedate	
FOREDECK in the bows	**Naut.**
FOREDONE overpowered	
FOREDOOM predestinate	
FOREDOOR front door	
FORE-EDGE front edge of book	
FOREFEEL sense in anticipation	
FOREFELT anticipated	
FOREFOOT foremost end of keel	**Naut.**
FOREGIFT lease premium	
FOREGOER vor-trekker	
FOREGONE already decided	
FOREHAND cf. backhand	
FOREHEAD brow; audacity; metope	
FORE-HOOK strengthening piece **Naut.**	
FOREKNEW foresaw	
FOREKNOW know already	
FORELAID previously arranged	
FORELAND headland; bluff; cape	
FORELEND lend in anticipation	
FORELENT previously loaned	
FORELOCK sometimes a quiff	
FOREMAST	**Naut.**
FOREMEAN intend	
FOREMOST in the van; leading	
FORENAME Christian name	
FORENOON from sunrise to noon	

FORENSAL ⎫ concerning law-court	**FORTUITY** luck; accident
FORENSIC ⎭ procedure	**FORTUNED** presaged
FOREPART the beginning	**FORWARDS** onward
FOREPEAK (in the bows) **Naut.**	**FORZANDO** emphatically **Mus.**
FOREPLAN to scheme	**FOSSDYKE** Roman canal, (Lincs.)
FORE-RANK front rank	**FOSSETTE** dimple
FORE-READ prognosticate	**FOSSORES** burrowers **Z.**
FORE-RENT rent due before reaping	**FOSTERED** brought up; cherished
FORESAID previously mentioned	**FOSTERER** a nurse
FORESAIL one of various sails **Naut.**	**FOSTRESS** foster-mother
FORESEEN expected; anticipated	**FOTHERED** stopped a leak **Naut.**
FORESEER prophet	**FOUGASSE** land-mine
FORESHIP fore-part of ship **Naut.**	**FOUL-FISH** fish when spawning **Z.**
FORESHOW rehearse; predict	**FOUL-HOOK** not hooked in gills
FORESIDE front side	**FOULNESS** dirt; grossness; scurrility
FORESTAL concerning forests	**FOUL-PLAY** unfair action
FORESTAY part of rigging **Naut.**	**FOUNDERY** foundry; (metal casting)
FORESTER (Ancient order of)	**FOUNDING** establishing; endowing
FORESTRY arboriculture	**FOUNTAIN** jet of water
FORETELL predict; augur	**FOUNTFUL** full of springs
FORETIME the past; days of yore	**FOURCHEE** cross (Heraldic)
FORETOLD presaged; warned	**FOURFOLD** quadruple
FOREWARD the van; the front	**FOURLING** one of a quadruplet
FOREWARN caution; admonish; advise	**FOURNEAU** explosion chamber (Fr.)
FOREWENT foregone; by-gone	**FOURSOME** (dance; game; golf)
FOREWIND favouring breeze	**FOURTEEN**
FOREWISH look forward to	**FOURTHLY**
FOREWORD preface; prologue	**FOX-BRUSH** a trophy of the chase
FOREYARD (yard on foremast) **Naut.**	**FOX-CHASE** hunting
FORFAIRN down and out (Sc.)	**FOX-EARTH** reynard's home
FORGEMAN coach-smith	**FOXGLOVE** digitalis **B.**
FORGIVEN condoned; absolved	**FOXGRAPE** variety of grape **B.**
FORGIVER pardoner; remitter	**FOXHOUND** **Z.**
FORGOING preceding	**FOXINESS** craftiness; slyness
FORKEDLY furcated	**FOX-SHARK** thresher shark **Z.**
FORKHEAD (knuckle-joint)	**FOX-SLEEP** pretended sleep
FORKLESS not branching	**FOZINESS** lack of spirit (Scot.)
FORKTAIL salmon; kite; crow **Z.**	**FRACTION** part; particle; fragment
FORMALIN an antiseptic **Chem.**	**FRACTURE** break; rift; fissure
FORMALLY precisely; ceremoniously	**FRAGARIA** the strawberry **B.**
FORMERLY ci-devant; whilom	**FRAGMENT** shard; scrap; remnant
FORMLESS shapeless; chaotic	**FRAGRANT** odoriferous; redolent
FORMULAE sets of symbols	**FRAILISH** somewhat weak; delicate
FORMULAR prescribed; formal	**FRAMABLE** can be framed
FORRADER further forward (slang)	**FRAME-SAW** Italian saw **Tool**
FORSAKEN left; abandoned; renounced	**FRANCATU** russetin apple **B.**
FORSLACK to relax (obs.)	**FRANK-FEE** tenure in fee-simple **Law**
FORSOOTH in truth; indeed	**FRANKING** remitting postage
FORSPEAK forbid; bewitch	**FRANKISH** (Frank)
FORSPEND exhaust; squander	**FRANKLIN** (Canterbury Tales)
FORSTALL forestall (obs.)	**FRANKLIN** old English freeholder
FORSWEAR deny upon oath: jaudre	**FRAPPING** binding; lashing **Naut.**
FORSWINK exhaust; wear out	**FRASLING** the perch **Z.**
FORSWONK over-laboured	**FRAUDFUL** dishonest; knavish
FORSWORE ⎫ pledged falsely;	**FRAULEIN** German spinster
FORSWORN ⎭ recanted	**FRAXININ** extract from ash bark **Chem.**
FORTHINK regret (obs.)	**FRAXINUS** ash-tree genus **B.**
FORTIETH	**FREAKFUL** ⎫ capricious; whimsical;
FORTRESS fortalice; citadel	**FREAKISH** ⎭ abnormal; erratic
FORTUIST believer in chance	**FRECKLED** maculate

FREEBORN not in vassalage
FREE-CITY
FREE-COST cost free
FREED-MAN emancipated slave
FREEHAND without instrumental aid
FREEHOLD held in fee-simple **Law**
FREE-LOVE promiscuity
FREENESS freedom; liberty
FREE-PORT (duties not levied)
FREE-REED vibrating reed **Mus.**
FREE-SHOT legendary hunter
FREE-SOIL (no slavery)
FREE-WILL voluntary; spontaneous
FREEZE-UP immobility; infrozen
FREEZING congealing; chilling
FREMITUS palpable vibration **Med.**
FRENETIC frenzied; distracted
FRENULUM a butterfly's bristle **Z.**
FRENZIED maddened; furious
FREQUENT oft repeated; recurrent
FRESCADE a cool walk
FRESCOED painted on plaster
FRESCOER a washy painter
FRESHISH almost fresh
FRESHMAN first year student
FRESH-NEW unpractised
FRETTING worrying; fuming; abrading
FRETWORK interlaced ornament
FREUDIAN psycho-analytic
FRIATION crumbling
FRIBBLED frivolled; tottered
FRIBBLER trifler
FRICTION attrition; abrasion
FRIENDED befriended; well-disposed
FRIENDLY kind; favourable; amicable
FRIESIAN Frisian; (Friesland)
FRIGHTED affrighted; dismayed
FRIGHTEN alarm; scare; intimidate
FRIGIDLY coldly; icily
FRILLING edging material
FRINGENT } encircling; bordering
FRINGING }
FRIPPERY fallals; old clothes
FRISETTE artificial curl
FRISKFUL lively; sportive
FRISKILY briskly; wantonly
FRISKING capering; skipping; romping
FRITTING (glass-making)
FRIZETTE see frisette
FRIZZLED curled; fried
FRIZZLER (hairdresser; cloth-worker)
FROCKING coarse jean
FROG-FISH angler-fish **Z.**
FROGGERY an abode of frogs
FROGLING small frog **Z.**
FROG-SPIT froth-fly **Z.**
FROMWARD away from
FRONDAGE leafage
FRONDENT } leafy
FRONDOSE, FRONDOUS } **B.**

FRONTAGE building line
FRONTATE widening like a leaf
FRONTIER boundary; border; march
FRONTING facing; opposing
FRONTLET fillet or browband
FRONTOON a pediment (arch.)
FROSTILY frigidly; icily; freezingly
FROSTING icing
FROTHERY mere froth; foam
FROTH-FLY numerous parasites **Z.**
FROTHILY verbosely
FROTHING bubbling
FROTTAGE coin-rubbing
FROU-FROU rustling like silk
FROUNCED plaited; frowned
FROWNING glowering; scowling
FRUCTIFY to make fruitful; teem
FRUCTOSE fruit sugar
FRUGALLY economically; thriftily
FRUITAGE crop; harvest; produce
FRUIT-BUD **B.**
FRUITERY fruit-loft
FRUIT-FLY a pest **Z.**
FRUITFUL productive; fecund; prolific
FRUITING bearing fruit
FRUITION fulfilment; realization
FRUITIVE enjoying; gratifying
FRUITLET a small fruit **B.**
FRUMENTY porridge of sorts
FRUMPING insulting; flouting
FRUMPISH old-fashioned; ill-natured
FRUSTULE shell of a diatom **B.**
FUDDLING getting drunk
FUELLING stoking
FUGACITY instability; uncertainty
FUGITIVE volatile; vagabond; refugee
FUGLEMAN exemplary soldier
FULCRATE with supports **B.**
FULGENCY effulgence; brilliance
FULGURAL (lightning); flashy
FULL-AGED of mature age
FULL-BACK (football)
FULL-BUTT head-on crash
FULL-EYED with prominent eyes
FULL-FACE cf. profile
FULLNESS fulness; repletion; profusion
FULL-STOP end of a period
FULL-TIME normal working hours
FULL-WAVE wireless rectifier
FULMINED fulminated; thundered
FULMINIC explosive; detonative
FUMAROLE volcanic smoke hole
FUMATORY fumigating chamber
FUMBLING clumsy; groping
FUMELESS smokeless
FUMEWORT the fumitory plant **B.**
FUMIGANT fume-producing
FUMIGATE disinfect
FUMITORY fumewort **B.**
FUMOSITY smokiness; flatulence

FUNCTION duty; power; office
FUNDABLE able to be financed
FUNDLESS broke
FUNEBRAL, FUNEREAL sombre; woeful
FUNERARY mournful; dismal
FUNGIBLE interchangeable
FUNK-HOLE coward's corner
FURBELOW puckered flounce
FURCATED forked; branching
FURCULAR fork-shaped
FURFUROL organic liquid **Chem.**
FURIBUND raging; furious; frenzied
FURLOUGH leave of absence
FURMENTY see frumenty
FURRIERY the fur trade
FURROWED corrugated; ploughed
FURTHEST most distant; remotest
FURUNCLE a boil **Med.**
FURY-LIKE furious; violent; frantic
FUSAROLE a classic moulding (arch.)
FUSELAGE body of aircraft
FUSEL-OIL malodorous spirit
FUSIFORM spindle-shaped
FUSILEER } armed with light
FUSILIER } flint-lock muskets
FUSTERIC a yellow dye **B.**
FUSTILUG fat unwieldy person
FUTILELY unavailingly; ineffectually
FUTILITY uselessness; vanity
FUTURELY in time to come
FUTURISE anticipate; antedate
FUTURISM art movement
FUTURIST (Biblical prophesies)
FUTURITY future time; the hereafter
FUZZ-BALL puff-ball fungus **B.**
FUZZLING confusing; intoxicating

G

GABARAGE packing cloth
GABBATHA Pilate's judgment seat
GABBLING chattering; jabbering
GABIONED with gabions
GABLE-END
GADABOUT roving busybody
GADHELIC Gaelic Celt language
GADLINGS steel spikes
GADZOOKS a mild expletive
GAGGLING noise of geese; cackling
GAG-TOOTH projecting tooth
GAIEMENT in lively style **Mus.**
GAIETIES vivacities; jollities
GAINABLE procurable; attainable
GAINLESS unprofitable; bootless
GAINSAID contradicted; denied
GAIR-FOWL gare-fowl; great auk **Z.**
GAITERED
GALACTIA excess of milk **Med.**
GALACTIC (the Milky Way)
GALACTIN sap of cow tree **B.**

GALALITH material made from milk
GALANGAL spicy tropical plant **B.**
GALATIAN inhabitant of Galatia
GALBANUM a gum **B.**
GALEATED floral helmet **B.**
GALENISM Dr. Galen's principles
GALENIST one of his followers
GALENITE sulphide of lead **Min.**
GALENOID (galenite)
GALERITE fossil sea-urchin **Min.**
GALILEAN (Galileo; Galilee)
GALL-DUCT **Med.**
GALLEASS } heavy type of
GALLIASS } galley **Naut.**
GALLIARD gay fellow; brisk; a dance
GALLICAN (Gaul or France)
GALLIPOT a glazed pot; artist's pot
GALLIVAT Malay pirate ship **Naut.**
GALLIZED (wine production)
GALLOPED rode at a gallop
GALLOPER mounted orderly; A.D.C.
GALLOWAY a hardy horse **Z.**
GALVANIC electric; (Galvani)
GAMBESON } doublet worn
GAMBISON } under armour
GAMBLING playing recklessly
GAMBOGIC (gamboge)
GAMBROON twilled linen cloth
GAMEBIRD
GAMECOCK fighting cock **Z.**
GAME-LAWS **Law**
GAMENESS courage; endurance
GAMESOME sportive; gay; playful
GAMESTER a gambler
GAMMARUS genus of crustaceans **Z.**
GAMMONED pickled; bamboozled
GAMMONER practical joker
GANCHING impaling
GANG-DAYS (Rogation week) **Eccl.**
GANGETIC (River Ganges)
GANGLAND criminal resort
GANGLIAC gangliaL; (ganglion)
GANGLING slender
GANGLION nerve centre **Med.**
GANGRENE mortification **Med.**
GANGSMAN foreman
GANGSTER desperado; ruffian
GANGWEEK (Rogation week) **Eccl.**
GANISTER sandstone; fire-brick **Min.**
GANNETRY haunt of solar geese **Z.**
GANYMEDE cupbearer to Zeus
GAOLBIRD an old lag
GAPINGLY widely open
GARBAGED eviscerated
GARBLING distorted; perverting
GARBOARD plank next to keel **Naut.**
GARCINIA plant genus; mangosteen **B**
GARDENED
GARDENER a cultivator
GARDENIA tropical shrub; flower **B.**

GARE-FOWL gair-fowl; great auk **Z.**
GARGANEY sea-duck **Z.**
GARGLING warbling
GARGOYLE grotesque gutter-spout
GARISHLY gaudily; showily; tawdrily
GARLICKY like garlic **B.**
GARNERED harvested; stored
GARRETED with watch-towers
GARRISON an armed force
GARROTTE strangle; throttle
GARRULUS crow genus; jay **Z.**
GARTERED
GASALIER⎫ hanging pendant
GASELIER⎭ for gas
GAS-GAUGE (for testing pressure)
GASIFIED
GASIFORM gaseous
GAS-LIGHT
GAS-METER (for measuring volume)
GAS-MOTOR a gas-engine
GASOGENE⎫
GAZOGENE⎭ aerating; apparatus
GASOLENE⎫ rectified petroleum;
GASOLINE⎭ petrol
GAS-STOVE cooking stove
GASTIGHT air-tight
GASTRAEA primordial organism **Z.**
GASTRULA embryonic cup **Z.**
GAS-WATER (coal-gas purification)
GAS-WORKS a source of illumination
GATE-BILL record of fines
GATE-FINE fine when gated
GATELESS without a gate
GATE-POST
GATE-VEIN portal vein **Med.**
GATHERED collected; acquired
GATHERER gleaner; collector
GAUDY-DAY festival
GAUDYING making merry
GAUNTLET iron glove
GAVELMAN tenant in gavelkind **Law**
GAVELOCK crowbar; javelin
GAWNTREE barrel stand; gantry
GAZETTED published; recorded
GAZOGENE a gasogene
GEAR-CASE
GELASTIC risible
GELATINE an animal jelly
GELATION solidification by cold
GELIDITY extreme cold
GEMATRIA a cabbalistic method
GEMINATE in pairs **B.**
GEMINIDS meteoric shower **Astron.**
GEMINOUS double
GEMMATED budded **B.**
GEMMEOUS gemlike
GEMSHORN an organ stop **Mus.**
GENDARME armed policeman (Fr.)
GENDERED begat; sired; bred
GENERALE general principle

GENERANT a cause of production
GENERATE originate; beget; produce
GENEROUS munificent; liberal
GENESIAC (Genesis)
GENETICS study of heredity
GENETRIX⎫ a mother,
GENITRIX⎭ female parent
GENEVESE Genevan
GENIALLY heartily; cordially; jovially
GENITIVE possessive case
GENITURE birth; procreation
GENOCIDE racial extermination
GENOVESE Genoese; (Genoa)
GENTILIC tribal; non-Jewish
GEODESIC⎫ relating to measurements
GEODETIC⎭ of the earth
GEOGNOST student of geognosy
GEOGNOSY petrography
GEOGONIC (formation of the earth)
GEOLATRY earth-worship
GEOMANCY a form of divination
GEOMETER a mathematician
GEOMETRY mensuration
GEONOMIC (physical laws)
GEOPHAGY earth-eating
GEOPONIC agricultural; husbandry
GEORDIES Tynesiders
GEORGIAN a period; caucasian
GEOSCOPY observational knowledge
GERANIUM **B.**
GERMANIC Teutonic
GERMCELL gamete
GERMINAL sprouting; French month
GEROCOMY regime for the aged **Med.**
GESTURAL gesticulating
GESTURED acted; posed; signalled
GHANAIAN native of Ghana
GHETTOES Jewish quarters
GHORKHAR Asiatic wild ass; onager
GHOULISH gruesome; fiendish
GIANTESS colossal lady
GIANTISM hugeness
GIANTIZE play the giant
GIBBERED spoke inarticulately
GIBINGLY scornfully; mockingly
GIB-STAFF water-gauge; pole
GIDDIEST most thoughtless
GIDDYING making dizzy
GIFTLING a small present
GIGANTIC enormous; elephantine
GIGGLING tittering; sniggering
GIG-LAMPS spectacles
GILLAROO species of trout **Z.**
GILLENIA rose genus **B.**
GILL-FLAP a membrane **Z.**
GILT-EDGE aureate
GILT-HEAD sea-bream **Z.**
GILT-TAIL species of worm **Z.**
GIMCRACK a gewgaw; jimcrack
GIMLETED holed; bored

GINGERLY cautiously; warily
GINGIVAL relating to the gums **Med.**
GIN-HORSE mill-horse **Z.**
GIN-HOUSE cotton factory
GIN-SLING a short drink
GIPSYDOM gipsy life
GIPSYISM cheating; flattery
GIRASOLE sun-flower **B.**
GIRDLING encompassing; surrounding
GIRLHOOD juvenile femininity
GIRONDIN moderate republican
GIRTHING saddling; girdling
GIRT-LINE rigging line **Naut.**
GIVEABLE bestowable; presentable
GIVE-AWAY unintended disclosure
GLABRATE ⎱ smooth; without
GLABROUS ⎰ hair or down **B.**
GLACIATE freeze; polish by ice
GLADDEST very cheerful; merriest
GLADDING rejoicing; delighting; elating
GLADIATE sword-shaped
GLADIOLE sword-lily **B.**
GLADIOLI plural of gladiolus **B.**
GLADNESS joy; joyfulness; cheer
GLAD-RAGS party frocks
GLADSOME pleasurable; pleasant
GLAIRING varnishing
GLAIROUS viscous
GLANCING glimpsing; ricocheting
GLANDAGE feeding on acorns
GLANDERS a horse disease **Med.**
GLANDULE small gland **Med.**
GLAREOUS glairous; viscous
GLASSEYE a horse disease
GLASSFUL a measure of content
GLASSILY in a vitreous manner
GLASSING glazing
GLASSITE one of a Scottish sect
GLASS-POT (used for melting glass)
GLAUCIUM the yellow poppy **B.**
GLAUCOMA an eye-disease **Med.**
GLAUCOUS a sea-green colour
GLEAMING resplendent; radiating
GLEANING harvesting; culling; picking
GLEDGING squinting
GLEESOME frolicsome; hilarious; lively
GLIADINE yellow extract **B.**
GLIBNESS gift of the gab
GLIDDERY slippery
GLIMPSED viewed hurriedly; glanced
GLINTING gleaming
GLISSADE a glide on a glacier
GLISSAUN the coal-fish **Z.**
GLOAMING dusk; twilight
GLOATING revelling; crowing; exulting
GLOBATED spherical
GLOBULAR spheric; round
GLOBULET round particle
GLOBULIN (a blood constituent) **Med.**
GLOOMILY despondently

GLOOMING obscuring; depressing
GLORIANA Queen Elizabeth
GLORIOLE a halo **Eccl.**
GLORIOSA a lily **B.**
GLORIOUS illustrious; noble; eminent
GLORYING exulting; boasting
GLORY-PEA an Australian pea **B.**
GLOSSARY explanatory vocabulary
GLOSSILY smoothly; sleekly
GLOSSINA the tsetse fly **Z.**
GLOSSING commenting; polishing
GLOWERED scowled; frowned
GLOW-LAMP incandescent lamp
GLOWWORM a beetle **Z.**
GLOXINIA flowering plant **B.**
GLUCINUM white metal; beryllium
GLUCOSID sugar compound **Chem.**
GLUE-LINE dielectric heating
GLUMMEST gloomiest; very morose
GLUMNESS sulkiness; depression
GLUMPISH sullen; splenetic; moody
GLUTAEUS posterior muscle **Med.**
GLUTTING sating; saturating; cloying
GLUTTONY voracity; greed
GLYCEROL glycerine **Chem.**
GLYCOGEN animal starch **Chem.**
GLYCONIC kind of verse
GLYPTICS gem engraving
GNARLING gnawing
GNARRING snarling; growling
GNASHING grinding the teeth
GNATHISM (jaw measurement)
GNATLING small gnat **Z.**
GNAT-WORM larva of gnat **Z.**
GNOMICAL ⎱ relating to the art of
GNOMONIC ⎰ dialling
GOA-CEDAR a cypress **B.**
GOAL-LINE back-line (football)
GOAL-POST football
GOATHERD goat-minder
GOATLING small goat **Z.**
GOAT-MOTH **Z.**
GOATSKIN
GOAT'S-RUE a plant **B.**
GOBBLING guzzling; turkey-noise
GODCHILD
GOD'S-ACRE a graveyard
GODSMITH idol maker
GOD-SPEED a benediction
GOETHIAN (Goethe, 1749-1832)
GOFFERED crimped
GO-GETTER pushing person
GOGGLING rolling the eyes
GOINGS-ON queer happenings
GOITERED ⎱ afflicted with the
GOITROUS ⎰ goitre **Med.**
GOLCONDA diamond mine, Hyderabad
GOLD-DUST a plant **B.**
GOLDENLY splendidly; aureately
GOLDFISH a carp **Z.**

GOLD-FOIL, GOLDLEAF thin gold	
GOLD-LACE	
GOLDLESS destitute of gold	
GOLD-LILY the yellow lily **B.**	
GOLD-MINE	
GOLD-RUSH prospectors' scramble	
GOLD-SIZE a varnish	
GOLD-WIRE	
GOLD-WORK	
GOLF-CLUB	
GOLGOTHA a charnel-house	
GOLLYWOG grotesque doll	
GOLOSHES overshoes	
GOMARIST opponent of Arminians	
GOMBROON Persian pottery	
GONALGIA pain in the knee **Med.**	
GONENESS that sinking feeling	
GONFALON a banner	
GONGYLUS (seaweed) **B.**	
GOOD-DOER benefactor; patron	
GOOD-FOLK the fairies	
GOOD-LACK expression of pity	
GOODLIER more excellent; fairer	
GOODNESS kindness; beneficence	
GOODWIFE a term of respect	
GOODWILL benevolence; an asset	
GOOGLIES deceptive spheres	
GOOSE-CAP a silly person	
GOOSE-EGG a zero; a duck **Z.**	
GORGEOUS splendid and showy	
GORGONIA corals **Z.**	
GOSSAMER filmy cobweb	
GOSSIPED chatted; tattled	
GOSSIPRY small talk; intimacy	
GOURMAND glutton; epicurean	
GOUTWEED goutwort **B.**	
GOVERNED controlled; ruled; swayed	
GOVERNOR regulator; guardian	
GOWNSMAN cf. townsman (university)	
GRABBING snatching; clutching	
GRACE-CUP loving cup	
GRACEFUL elegant and easy	
GRACIOSO Spanish clown **Mus.**	
GRACIOUS affable; polite; benign	
GRADATED graded; blended	
GRADATIM step by step	
GRADIENT slope; incline	
GRADUAND about to be a graduate	
GRADUATE pass; proportion; divide	
GRAECISM a Greek idiom	
GRAECIZE to turn into Greek	
GRAFFITI ancient wall scribblings	
GRAFFITO two colour plaster layers	
GRAFTING bribing; (gardening)	
GRAINAGE duties on grain	
GRAINING a process; a fish **Z.**	
GRAIN-TIN melted tin	
GRALLINE (wading birds) **Z.**	
GRALLOCK entrails of deer **Z.**	

GRAMARYE necromancy; magic	
GRANDDAD grandfather	
GRANDEST most magnificent; noblest	
GRANDEUR pomp; splendour; majesty	
GRANDSON son's son	
GRANITIC of granite **Min.**	
GRANTING conceding; conferring	
GRANULAR in grains	
GRAPHICS art of drawing	
GRAPHITE blacklead **Min.**	
GRAPHIUM a style (for writing)	
GRAPPLED seized; grasped; clutched	
GRASPING gripping; avaricious	
GRASSING turfing; laying low	
GRASS-OIL an essential oil **B.**	
GRATEFUL thankful; beholden	
GRATIOLA hedge hyssop **B.**	
GRATUITY tip; bonus; pourboire	
GRAVAMEN principal charge **Law**	
GRAVELLY full of gravel	
GRAY-EYED grey-eyed	
GRAYLING fresh-water fish **Z.**	
GRAZIOSO gracefully **Mus.**	
GREASILY unctuously	
GREASING lubricating; corrupting	
GREATEST largest; biggest; bulkiest	
GRECIZED Hellenized	
GREEDILY voraciously; eagerly	
GREENERY verdure; foliage	
GREEN-FLY a pest **Z.**	
GREENING hoaxing	
GREENISH somewhat green	
GREEN-TEA **B.**	
GREETING welcoming; weeping (Sc.)	
GREFFIER notary (Channel Isles) **Law**	
GREMLINS malignant aerial imps	
GREYCING greyhound racing	
GREYNESS grayness	
GRID-BIAS (wireless adjustment)	
GRIDELIN violet grey colour	
GRIDIRON a grill	
GRIEVOUS burdensome; heinous	
GRILLADE grilled meat (Fr.)	
GRILLAGE a cross-beam construction	
GRILLING broiling; interrogating	
GRIMACED smirked	
GRIMALDI an old clown	
GRIMMEST sternest; dourest	
GRIMNESS fierceness; dourness	
GRINDERY shoemakers' materials	
GRINDING pulverizing; crushing	
GRINNING	
GRIPEFUL distressing; colicky	
GRIPPING holding tight; clutching	
GRISELDA a very patient lady	
GRISEOUS grey; grizzled	
GRITTING grating; grinding; abrading	
GRIZZLED grey; grumbled	
GROANFUL mournful; lugubrious	
GROANING moaning; complaining	

GROGGERY a dram-shop
GROGGING (extracting spirit)
GROG-SHOP a pub
GROINING angular curves (arch.)
GROMWELL a plant **B.**
GROOMING making neat and tidy
GROOVING furrowing; scoring
GROSBEAK a finch **Z.**
GROSCHEN (Austrian) **Coin**
GROTTOES caves
GROUNDED on the ground
GROUNDER low ball at baseball
GROUPING arranging; disposing
GROUSING grumbling
GROUTING filling in with concrete
GROWABLE cultivatable
GROWLERY a private den
GROWLING grumbling; snarling
GRUBBIER dirtier
GRUBBING digging up
GRUBBLED groped
GRUDGING envying; coveting
GRUESOME horrible; grisly; grim
GRUMBLED complained; repined
GRUMBLER grouser
GRUMNESS surliness; dourness
GRUMPHIE a sow **Z.**
GRUNDSEL groundsel **B.**
GRYPOSIS ingrowing nails **Med.**
GRYSBOCK steinbok, (S. Africa) **Z.**
GUACHERO oil-bird, (S. Amer.) **Z.**
GUAIACOL an odorous liquid **Chem.**
GUAIACUM resinous lignum vitae **B.**
GUANCHOS natives of Canary Islands
GUARACHA a Cuban dance **Mus.**
GUARANTY basis of security
GUARDANT facing (Her.)
GUARDFUL wary; cautious
GUARDIAN warden; protector
GUARDING watching; defending
GUBBINGS wild Devonians
GUELPHIC a royal family
GUERILLA an irregular
GUERNSEY a garment; a cow **Z.**
GUESSING imagining
GUGGLING gurgling
GUICOWAR Galkwar
GUIDABLE steerable
GUIDANCE direction; government
GUILEFUL crafty; insiduous
GUILTILY criminally; culpably
GUIMAUVE marsh-mallow **B.**
GUJARATI language (Bombay)
GULF-WEED tropical sea-weed **B.**
GULLIBLE easily deceived
GULLIVER swift traveller
GULLYING making a channel
GULOSITY voracity
GUMPTION shrewd sense; nous
GUM-RESIN **B.**

GUN-LAYER
GUNMETAL alloy; copper and **tin**
GUN-REACH gunshot; range
GUNSMITH gun-maker
GUNSTICK ramrod
GUNSTOCK part of gun
GUNSTONE stone projectile
GURGLING purling; rippling
GURKHALI language Nepal
GUSTABLE tasty; savoury
GUTTATED sprinkled; bedewed
GUTTERED ran in drops
GUTTLING gorging; swallowing
GUTTURAL throaty
GUYANESE (Guyana, S. Amer.)
GUZZLING swilling; tippling; quaffing
GYMKHANA sports meeting
GYMNASIC gymnastic
GYMNICAL athletic
GYMNOTUS electric eel **Z.**
GYNANDER a plant **B.**
GYNARCHY female government
GYNECIUM women's quarters
GYNERIUM pampas grass **B.**
GYPSEOUS (gypsum) **Min.**
GYPSYISM gipsyism
GYRATING spinning; rotating; whirling
GYRATION rotation; revolution
GYRATORY circling; revolutionary
GIRODYNE speedy helicopter **Aeron.**
GYROIDAL spiral; winding
GYROPTER helicopter (aeroplane)
GYROSTAT gyroscope

H

HABENDUM descriptive clause **Law**
HABITANT inhabitant; native
HABITING dressing; arraying
HABITUAL customary; usual; wonted
HABITUDE customary manner
HACIENDA estate or ranch (S. Amer.)
HACKBOLT great shearwater gull **Z.**
HACKLING heckling; separating flax
HAEMATIC acting on the blood
HAEMATIN (haemoglobin) **Med.**
HAGBERRY bird-cherry **B.**
HAGGADAH⎫ Rabinical commentary
HAGGADIC⎭ on Old Testament **Eccl.**
HAGGLING chaffering; bargaining
HAGTAPER the mullein **B.**
HAILSHOT small shot
HAIRBELL a bluebell; campanula **B.**
HAIR-LACE hair ribbon
HAIRLESS bald
HAIRLINE a fine line
HAIR-SALT epsomite **Min.**
HAIRTAIL a tropical fish **Z.**
HAIRWORK work done with hair
HAIRWORM freshwater worm **Z.**

HALATION (photographic defect)
HALENESS robustness; health
HALF-BACK (football)
HALF-BOOT (half way to the knee)
HALF-BRED mongrel
HALF-COCK a safety position
HALF-DEAD almost dead
HALF-DECK half length deck **Naut.**
HALF-DONE incomplete; under-done
HALF-FACE the profile
HALF-INCH map scale
HALFLING a youth
HALF-MARK old coin, value 6/8 **Coin**
HALFMAST a sign of mourning
HALF-MILE athletics
HALF-MOON a semi-circle; demilune
HALF-NOTE a semitone
HALF-PAST, HALF-HOUR
HALF-PIKE short pike
HALF-SEAS half-way **Naut.**
HALF-SPAN lean-to **Arch.**
HALF-SUIT body armour
HALF-TIDE
HALF-TIME an interval
HALF-TINT intermediate tint
HALF-TONE a printing process
HALICORE dugong; sea-cow **Z.**
HALIOTIS mother-of-pearl shell **Z.**
HALL-DOOR front door
HALLIARD running rope **Naut.**
HALL-MARK a guarantee
HALLOOED shouted
HALLOWED reverenced; sanctified
HALTERED roped; tethered
HALTERES balancing wings **Z.**
HAMBLING mutilating the foot
HAMIFORM hook-shaped
HAMMERED (Stock Exchange)
HAMMERER hammer-man; smith
HAMPERED impeded; packed; clogged
HANDBALL an old pastime
HANDBELL **Mus.**
HANDBILL announcement; broadcast
HANDBOOK a manual
HANDCART
HANDCUFF manacle; fetter
HANDFAST hold; custody; betroth
HANDGEAR (manual control)
HANDGRIP, HANDHOLD climbing
HANDICAP penalty; allowance
HANDLESS awkward
HANDLINE line without a rod
HANDLING manipulation
HANDLIST convenient list
HANDLOOM
HAND-MADE
HANDMAID an Abigail
HANDMILL a quern
HANDPICK select carefully
HANDPOST finger-post; guide

HANDRAIL support
HAND-SALE handshake deal
HANDSOME generous; good-looking
HAND-WORK
HANDYMAN jack-of-all-trades
HANGABLE dependable; suspensible
HANGER-ON parasite; retainer
HANGNAIL agnail **Med.**
HANGNEST a bird **Z.**
HANG-OVER after-party reaction
HANKERED coveted; longed; yearned
HAPLODON mountain beaver **Z.**
HAPPENED chanced; occurred; befell
HAPPIEST
HAQUETON padded jacket
HARA-KIRI happy despatch (Jap.)
HARANGUE tirade; declaim
HARASSED wearied; persecuted
HARASSER a guerilla
HARDBAKE toffee almond cake
HARDBEAM horn beam **B.**
HARD-CASH ready money
HARD-CORE unwavering resistance
HARDENED inured; obdurate
HARDENER **Chem.**
HARD-FERN the northern fern **B.**
HARD-HACK steeple-bush **B.**
HARDIEST most robust; boldest
HARDNESS compactness; firmness
HARDSHIP injustice; tribulation
HARDTACK ship's biscuit **Naut.**
HARDWARE ironmongery
HARDWOOD close-grained timber **B.**
HAREBELL hairbell; campanula **B.**
HAREFOOT swift of foot
HAREPIPE a snare
HARE'S-EAR a yellow flower **B.**
HARI-KARI hara-kiri (Jap.)
HARLEIAN a literary society
HARLOTRY wantonness
HARMLESS innocuous; inoffensive
HARMONIC concordant; consonant
HARPINGS battens **Naut.**
HARROWED lacerated; tortured; torn
HARROWER sensationalist
HARRYING harassing; raiding; vexing
HARTWORT plant; seseli type **B.**
HASTATED spear-shaped **B.**
HASTENED expedited; urged
HASTENER urgent reminder
HASTINGS early peas **B.**
HATBRUSH
HATCHERY incubator
HATCHETY sharp featured
HATCHING plotting; shading; breeding
HATCHWAY deck opening **Naut.**
HATEABLE odious; detestable
HATSTAND
HATTERIA tuatara; lizard, (N.Z.) **Z.**
HAT-TRICK

369

HAUNCHED having haunches
HAUNTING frequenting; obsessing
HAURIANT (heraldic fish on end)
HAURLING dragging; trailing
HAUSFRAU housewife (Ger.)
HAVANNAH a cigar
HAVELOCK white cover for cap
HAVILDAR Warrant Officer (Ind.)
HAVOCKED devastated; wasted
HAWAIIAN (Hawai)
HAWFINCH grosbeak   **Z.**
HAWK-BELL small bell on hawk's foot
HAWK-EYED lynx-eyed
HAWK-MOTH genus of moth   **Z.**
HAWK-WEED   **B.**
HAWTHORN the may   **B.**
HAY-FEVER   **Med.**
HAY-FIELD
HAY-KNIFE stack-cutter
HAY-MAKER a swipe
HAY-STACK a hay-rick
HAZARDED imperilled; ventured
HAZARDER a gambler; speculator
HAZEL-HEN ruffled grouse   **Z.**
HAZEL-NUT filbert   **B.**
HAZINESS uncertainty; vagueness
HEADACHE occipital disorder   **Med.**
HEADACHY off colour
HEAD-BAND book top; fillet
HEAD-BOOM jib-boom   **Naut.**
HEADFAST mooring rope   **Naut.**
HEADGEAR head-dress
HEADIEST most exhilarating
HEADLAMP (motor-car)
HEADLAND cape; promontory; ness
HEADLESS decapitated
HEADLINE
HEADLONG precipitately; steep; hasty
HEAD-MAIN main water supply
HEAD-MARK outstanding feature
HEAD-MOLD skull; a moulding   **Med.**
HEADMOST most advanced
HEAD-NOTE introductory note
HEAD-PUMP sea-water pump   **Naut.**
HEAD-RACE lead to water-wheel
HEAD-RENT   **Law**
HEAD-REST a support
HEAD-RING Kaffir coiffure
HEADSHIP supreme authority
HEAD-TIRE head-dress
HEAD-WIND a contrary wind
HEAD-WORD title word
HEAD-WORK intellectual labour; sport
HEALABLE remediable; curable
HEARABLE audible
HEARTILY cordially; sincerely; warmly
HEARTLET small heart
HEART-ROT central decay   **B.**
HEATHERY heathy; heath-clad   **B.**
HEATH-HEN black grouse   **Z.**

HEATH-PEA   **B.**
HEAT-SPOT a freckle
HEAT-UNIT   **Meas.**
HEAT-WAVE calorific undulation
HEAVENLY celestial; seraphic
HEAVIEST most ponderous
HEBDOMAD a group of seven
HEBETANT making blunt; dulling
HEBETATE to dull; stupefy
HEBETUDE dulness; stupidity
HEBRAIST ⎤ concerned with
HEBRAISM ⎬ Hebrew customs
HEBRAIZE ⎦ and literature
HECATOMB sacrifice of 100
HECKLING hackling; combing
HECKYMAL blue tit   **Z.**
HECTORED boasted; swaggered
HECTORER brawler; bully; braggart
HECTORLY insolent; domineering
HEDGEHOG   **Z.**
HEDGEHOP a low flight
HEDGEPIG young hedgehog   **Z.**
HEDGEROW bushy boundary   **B.**
HEDONICS ⎤ doctrine that
HEDONISM ⎬ happiness is the
HEDONIST ⎦ highest good
HEEDLESS regardless; rash
HEELBALL black wax
HEFTIEST sturdiest; beefiest
HEGELIAN (process of the spirit)
HEGEMONY leadership
HEGUMENE prior   **Eccl.**
HEIGHTEN enhance
HEIRLESS no heir
HEIRLOOM   **Law**
HEIRSHIP inherent right
HELCOSIS ulceration   **Med.**
HELCOTIC ulcerous
HELIACAL (sun-light)
HELICOID spiral
HELIOSIS sunstroke   **Med**
HELIOZIA protozoa   **Z**
HELIPORT helicopter airfield   **Aeron.**
HELLBENT reckless
HELLBORN ⎤ of satanic origin
HELLBRED ⎦
HELLENIC Grecian
HELL-FIRE
HELL-GATE
HELL-KITE bird of ill omen   **Z**
HELLWARD devilish progress
HELMETED
HELMINTH a worm   **Z**
HELMLESS rudderless
HELMSMAN steersman
HELOTAGE ⎤ slavery; bondage;
HELOTISM ⎦ servitude; serfdom
HELPLESS impotent; weak; powerless
HELPMATE wife; partner
HELPMEET helpmate; helper

HELVETIA Switzerland		
HELVETIC Swiss		
HEMATINE haematin	**Med.**
HEMATITE haematite	**Min.**
HEMIGALE Malayan civet	**Z.**
HEMIOLIC 3 to 2 ratio	
HEMIONUS dziggetai	**Z.**
HEMIOPIA faulty vision	**Med.**
HEMIPODE sort of quail	**Z.**
HEMIPTER cicada or bug	**Z.**
HEMP-PALM	**B.**
HEMP-SEED gallow's bird (Shak.)	
HENCHMAN servant; page; varlet	
HENEQUEN, HENEQUIN sisal hemp	**B.**
HEN-HOUSE coop	
HEN-HUSSY a cotquean	
HEN-MOULD black spongy soil	
HEN-PARTY ladies' gossip group	
HEN-ROOST poultry park	
HEN-WOMAN hen-wife	
HEPATICA liver tonic	**Med.**
HEPATITE barium sulphate	**Min.**
HEPATIZE hepatise; livery-work	
HEPTAGON 7 sided figure	
HEPTARCH ruler of a heptarchy	
HERALDED proclaimed; blazoned	
HERALDIC | armorial bearings	
HERALDRY /	
HERBAGED grass covered	
HERBARIA hortus siccus	**B.**
HERBELET small herb	**B.**
HERBLESS lacking vegetation	
HERCULES labour member for Tiryns	
HERD-BOOK cattle stud-book	
HERDSMAN cow-puncher	
HEREAWAY hereabouts	
HEREDITY inherent propensity	
HEREINTO into this	
HERESIES schisms	
HEREUNTO unto this	
HEREUPON upon this; then	
HEREWITH	
HERISSON spiked obstruction	
HERITAGE patrimony; legacy	
HERMETIC air-tight; mystic; occult	
HERNIOID ruptured; hernial	**Med.**
HERNSHAW heronshaw; handsaw	**Z.**
HEROICAL intrepid; valiant; epic	
HEROICLY dauntlessly; daringly	
HEROIZED lionized; idealized	
HEROSHIP heroism	
HERPETIC shingly	**Med.**
HERTZIAN (low frequency waves)	
HERTZITE galena	**Min.**
HESITANT vacillating; doubtful	
HESITATE pause; waver; demur	
HESPERUS a wreck	
HEXAGRAM Solomon's seal	
HEXAPLAR sextuple	
HEY-GO-MAD joyous interjection	

HIAWATHA N. Amer. prophet-teacher	
HIBERNAL wintry	
HIBISCUS tropical mallow	**B.**
HICCATEE Cen. Amer. tortoise	**Z.**
HICCOUGH hiccup	
HICCUPED	
HICKWALL small woodpecker	**Z.**
HIDDENLY privily; furtively; covertly	
HIDE-ROPE a reim (S. Afr.)	
HIDROSIS sweat	**Med.**
HIELAMAN native shield (Aust.)	
HIERARCH chief priest	**Eccl.**
HIERATIC priestly	**Eccl.**
HIGGLING haggling; chaffering	
HIGH-BALL whisky and soda	
HIGHBORN of noble birth	
HIGHBRED not a hybrid	
HIGHBROW so called intellectual	
HIGH-HUNG elevated	
HIGH-JUMP athletics; dismissal	
HIGHLAND	
HIGH-LIFE	
HIGH-MASS special service	**Eccl.**
HIGHMOST topmost	
HIGHNESS a rank; altitude	
HIGHROAD thoroughfare	
HIGH-SPOT climax	
HIGH-TIDE	
HIGH-TIME almost overdue	
HIGTAPER the mullein	**B.**
HI-JACKED plundered a gang	
HI-JACKER super-pirate	
HILARITY gaiety; jollity; merriment	
HILL-FOLK hillmen; Covenanters	
HILL-FORT stronghold; fastness	
HILLOCKY hummocky	
HILLSIDE a declivity	
HINDERED delayed; thwarted; impeded	
HINDERER obstructionist; opposer	
HINDMOST last; posterior	
HINDUISM doctrine and rites	
HINGEING depending on	
HIP-JOINT	**Med.**
HIREABLE on hire	
HIRELESS wageless	
HIRELING mercenary	
HIRPLING running lamely	
HIRRIENT trilling sound	
HIRUDINE like a leech	
HISPANIC Spanish	
HISTIOID resembling tissue	**Med.**
HISTORIC authentic; genuine; famous	
HISTRION play-actor	
HITCHING fastening; attaching	
HITHERTO till now	
HIVELESS not a single skep	
HIVE-NEST multiple bird's nest	
HOACTZIN hoatzin; S. Amer. bird	**Z.**
HOARDING storing; treasuring; fence	
HOARSELY discordantly; raucously	

HOASTMAN member of a guild
HOBBLING walking lamely; limping
HOBBYISM cult of a favourite
HOBBYIST pursuit
HOCKCART (last harvest load)
HOCKHERB a mallow **B.**
HOCKLING mowing
HOCK-TIDE a festival
HOCUSSED drugged; doped
HOG-FRAME (ship-building) **Naut.**
HOGGEREL sheep of second year **Z.**
HOGMANAY Dec. 31st (Sc.)
HOG-REEVE medieval parish officer
HOG'S BEAN henbane **B.**
HOG-SCORE line on a curling rink
HOGSHEAD large cask
HOGSTEER wild boar **Z.**
HOISTING raising; lifting; elevating
HOISTWAY trap-door
HOLDBACK check; retainer
HOLDFAST catch; grip
HOLEWORT moschatel **B.**
HOLINESS sanctity; devoutness **Eccl.**
HOLLANDS geneva; schnapps
HOLLOAED shouted
HOLLOWED excavated; scooped
HOLLOWLY insincerely; vacantly
HOLYROOD holy cross **Eccl.**
HOLY-WEEK the week before Easter
HOLY-WRIT the Scriptures **Eccl.**
HOMAGING paying respects
HOME-BIRD stay-at-home
HOMEBORN native; domestic
HOMEBRED natural; unpolished
HOME-FARM
HOMEFELT inward; private
HOME-GOER
HOMELAND native land
HOMELESS on the streets
HOMELIKE not ornate
HOMELILY familiarly
HOME MADE
HOME-RULE autonomy
HOMESICK nostalgia
HOMESPUN
HOMEWARD return journey
HOMEWORK out of school task
HOMICIDE man-slaughter **Law**
HOMILIST sermonizer
HOMODONT teeth all alike **Z.**
HOMODYNE (wireless telephony)
HOMOGAMY hermaphrodite **B.**
HOMOGENY similarity of nature
HOMOLOGY affinity of structure
HOMONYMY (similar sounding words)
HOMOSOTE material for walls of huts
HOMOTYPE structural affinity
HOMOTYPY
HONDURAN (Honduras)
HONESTLY uprightly; sincerely

HONEY-BAG nectar sac of bee **Z.**
HONEY-BEE **Z.**
HONEYDEW tobacco; melon **B.**
HONEY-POT a grape (S. Afr.) **B.**
HONORARY gratuitous; unpaid
HONOURED respected; revered
HONOURER venerator
HOODWINK befool; cheat; delude
HOOFLESS
HOOFMARK imprint; slot
HOOK-WORM a parasite **Z.**
HOOLIGAN ruffian; rascal; bully
HOOP-IRON iron band
HOOT-TOOT toot-toot!
HOPELESS despairing; despondent
HOPINGLY thinking wishfully
HOPPLING hobbling
HORATIAN (Horace)
HORNBEAK garfish **Z.**
HORNBEAM a tree **B.**
HORNBILL picarian bird **Z.**
HORNFISH garfish **Z.**
HORNFOOT hoofed
HORNGATE gate of dreams
HORN-LEAD chloride of lead **Min.**
HORNLESS dodded
HORNPIPE air; dance **Mus.**
HORNWORT water-plant **B.**
HOROLOGY works on clocks
HORRIBLE revolting; fearful; dire
HORRIBLY hideously; appallingly
HORRIDLY foully; alarmingly
HORRIFIC terrific; awful; frightful
HORSE-BOX van
HORSE-BOY stable-boy
HORSE-CAR a carriage
HORSE-FLY **Z.**
HORSE-HOE a harrow
HORSEMAN rider; equestrian
HORSE-WAY road or track
HOSE-PIPE a duct
HOSE-REEL
HOSPITAL an almshouse
HOSPODOR Slav governor
HOSTELRY inn; tavern; local
HOT-BLAST pre-heated air
HOTCHPOT farrago; mixture; medley
HOTELIER hotel-keeper
HOTHOUSE
HOT-PLATE a heating appliance
HOT-PRESS a machine
HOT-SHORT brittle
HOTTONIA water-violet **B**
HOT-WATER trouble
HOUGHING ham stringing
HOUNDING pursuing; tracking; trailin
HOUR-HAND time indicator
HOUSE-BOY serving lad
HOUSE-DOG watch dog **Z**
HOUSE-FLY musca domestica **Z**

HOUSE-TAX a levy	**Law**	
HOVELLED meanly housed		
HOVELLER longshoreman		
HOVERING in suspense		
HOWITZER short cannon		
HUCKSTER an advertiser		
HUDDLING cowering in mass		
HUDIBRAS political satire by S. Butler		
HUGENESS bulk; immensity; vastness		
HUGUENOT French Protestant	**Eccl.**	
HUIA-BIRD New Zealand bird	**Z.**	
HUMANELY mercifully; benignly		
HUMANISM ⎫ pragmatism;		
HUMANIST ⎬ human interests,		
HUMANITY ⎭ grammar, rhetoric, etc.		
HUMANIZE enlighten; civilize		
HUMATION burial		
HUMBLENESS abasement		
HUMBLING abasing; shaming		
HUMEFIED moistened		
HUMIDIFY to dampen		
HUMIDITY moisture		
HUMILITY humbleness; meekness		
HUMMOCKY hillocky		
HUMORISM facetiousness; jocularity		
HUMORIST jester; merryman		
HUMOROUS witty; droll; comical		
HUMOURED indulged; pampered		
HUMPBACK a whale; road-bridge	**Z.**	
HUMPLESS no depression here		
HUMSTRUM humdrum; monotonous		
HUNG-BEEF dried beef		
HUNGERED famished; hankered		
HUNGRILY cravingly		
HUNKERED squatted		
HUNTRESS a Diana		
HUNTSMAN chasseur		
HURDLING (athletics)		
HURLBONE a horse bone	**Z.**	
HURLWIND whirlwind		
HURRYING urging; speeding		
HURTLESS uninjured; innoxious		
HURTLING whizzing		
HUSHED-UP undisclosed		
HUSH-HUSH very secret		
HUSH-MUSH high confidential		
HUSKIEST very hoarse		
HUSTINGS electioneering platform		
HUSTLING bustling; jostling; elbowing		
HUTCHING cooping		
HUZZAING shouting with joy		
HYACINTH a gem	**Min., B.**	
HYALITIS optic inflammation	**Med.**	
HYBODONT irregular teeth	**Med.**	
HYDATISM a watery sound	**Med.**	
HYDATOID aqueous		
HYDRATED combined with water		
HYDROFIN high speed motor boat		
HYDROGEL water soluble colloid		
	Chem.	
HYDROGEN gaseous element	**Chem.**	

HYDROMEL watered honey	
HYDROMYS water-rats, etc.	**Z.**
HYDROPIC thirsty	
HYDROPSY dropsy	**Med.**
HYDROSOL colloidal solution	
HYDROZOA jelly fish, etc.	**Z.**
HYDRURET hybrid	**Chem.**
HYGIENIC salubrious; healthy	
HYLICISM materialism	
HYLICIST a philosopher	
HYLOBATE a gibbon	**Z.**
HYLOZOIC materialistic	
HYMENEAL conjugal; matrimonial	
HYMENEAN nuptial; bridal	
HYMENIUM part of fungus	**B.**
HYMN-BOOK often A. & M.	**Eccl.**
HYOSCINE poisonous alkaloid	**Med.**
HYPALGIA insusceptibility	
HYPERION a Titan	
HYPHENED linked	
HYPHENIC jointed	
HYPNOSIS hypnotism	**Med.**
HYPNOTIC mesmeric	
HYPOBOLE form of argument	
HYPOCIST astringent medicine	**Med.**
HYPOGEAL underground	
HYPOGEAN subterranean	
HYPOGENE rock formation	**Min.**
HYPOGEUM foundation	
HYPOTHEC debt security	**Law**
HYPOZOAN ⎫ below the limit	
HYPOZOIC ⎭ of life (geol.)	
HYSTERIA nervous disorder	**Med.**
HYSTERIC hysterical	

I

IANTHINA purple sea-snails	**Z.**
IATRICAL medical	**Med.**
IBSENISM (Henrik Ibsen)	
ICE-BLINK a reflection; mirage	
ICE-BOUND	
ICE-BROOK frozen brook	
ICE-CREAM the content of a cornet	
ICE-FIELD ice-floe	
ICE-FLOAT ice-field	
ICE-HOUSE	
ICE-LEDGE	
ICE-PLANT	**B.**
ICE-SHEET glacial ice	
ICE-WATER	
ICE-YACHT	
ICHOROUS like ichor	**Med.**
ICHTHINE (fishes' eggs)	**Z.**
ICHTHYIC fishlike	
ICTERINE yellow	
IDEALISM transcendency	
IDEALIST visionary	
IDEALITY perfection	
IDEALIZE idealise	

IDEATING fancying
IDEATION conception
IDEATIVE imaginative
IDENTIFY recognize; integrate
IDENTITY individuality; sameness
IDEOGRAM ideograph
IDEOLOGY metaphysics
IDIOTISH doltish; fatuous; inane
IDIOTISM imbecility; inanity
IDIOTIZE ridicule; befool
IDLEHOOD idleness
IDLENESS dolce far niente
IDOCRASE silicate of lime **Min.**
IDOLATER a heretic
IDOLATRY image worship
IDOLIZED idolised
IDOLIZER a fan
IGNATIAN (St. Ignatius) **Eccl.**
IGNITING kindling; inflaming
IGNITION firing; lighting
IGNITRON mercury arc rectifier **Elect.**
IGNOMINY public disgrace; obloquy
IGNORANT uninstructed; unaware
IGNORING disregarding; overlooking
ILLAPSED glided
ILLATION inference
ILLATIVE deducive
ILL-BLOOD enmity; discord; rancour
ILL-FATED calamitous; unlucky
ILL-FAURD ill-favoured (Sc.)
ILLINIUM metallic element **Chem.**
ILLIQUID financial
ILL-TIMED ill-judged
ILL-TREAT maltreat
ILLUDING deceiving
ILLUMINE enlighten; irradiate
ILLUMING elucidating
ILL-USAGE harsh treatment
ILLUSION delusion; dream; fantasy
ILLUSIVE ⎫ deceptive; fugitive;
ILLUSORY ⎭ hallucinatory
ILLYRIAN a Jugoslav
ILMENITE titanate of iron **Min.**
IMAGINAL relating to an image **Z.**
IMAGINED fancied; thought
IMAGINER dreamer
IMBANDED banded together
IMBANKED embanked
IMBATHED immersed
IMBECILE idiot; moron; Bedlamite
IMBEDDED firmly fixed
IMBELLIC pacific
IMBIBING absorbing; swallowing
IMBITION dye transfer **Photo.**
IMBOWING arching
IMBRUING drenching
IMBRUTED degenerated
IMBUMENT deep tincture
IMBURSED supplied with cash
IMITABLE easy to forge

IMITANCY mimicry
IMITATED parodied; aped
IMITATOR copy-cat; impersonator
IMMANELY savagely; brutally
IMMANENT inherent; innate
IMMANITY cruelty; inhumanity
IMMANTLE to cloak
IMMANUEL Emmanuel
IMMASKED disguised
IMMATURE unripe; crude; untimely
IMMERGED ⎫ submerged; soused;
IMMERSED ⎭ plunged; inundated
IMMESHED entangled; ensnared
IMMINENT impending; perilous
IMMINGLE mix; blend; amalgamate
IMMITTED injected; introduced
IMMIXING mingling; combining
IMMOBILE still; motionless; static
IMMODEST bold; indelicate; coarse
IMMOLATE sacrifice; surrender
IMMORTAL imperishable; deathless
IMMUNITY privilege; freedom
IMMUNIZE immunise; exempt
IMPACTED collided; struck
IMPAIRED enfeebled; blemished
IMPAIRER saboteur; marrer
IMPALING transfixing
IMPALMED grasped; handled
IMPANATE to sandwich
IMPARITY inequality; disproportion
IMPARKED enclosed
IMPARLED conversed; discussed
IMPARTED communicated; divulged
IMPARTER bestower; donator
IMPASTED kneaded
IMPAWNED pledged; mortgaged
IMPEDING obstructing; thwarting
IMPELLED urged; induced; drove
IMPELLER instigator; inciter
IMPENDED threatened; hovered
IMPENNED enclosed; encompassed
IMPERIAL short beard; a goatee
IMPERIUM sovereignty
IMPETIGO an eruption **Med**
IMPIERCE bore; drill
IMPINGED touched upon; infringed
IMPISHLY mischievously; wantonly
IMPLATED sheathed
IMPLEACH interweave
IMPLEDGE pawn; hypothecate
IMPLICIT tacit; implied; inferred
IMPLORED entreated; craved
IMPLORER supplicant; petitioner
IMPLUMED plucked
IMPLUNGE immerse; dive
IMPLYING indicating; connoting
IMPOCKET filch; steal
IMPOISON envenom; infect
IMPOLICY inexpedience
IMPOLITE positively rude; insolent

IMPONENT a backer; imposer
IMPONING wagering; betting
IMPOROUS gas-tight; impermeable
IMPORTED conveyed; denoted
IMPORTER foreign dealer
IMPOSING impressive; stately
IMPOSTOR trickster; charlatan
IMPOTENT helpless; incapable
IMPRIMIS in the first place
IMPRISON incarcerate; immure
IMPROPER unseemly; indelicate
IMPROVED bettered; amended
IMPROVER developer; rectifier
IMPUDENT saucy; shameless
IMPUGNED gainsaid; contradicted
IMPUGNER attacker; assailant
IMPUNITY exemption; immunity
IMPURELY unchastely; licentiously
IMPURITY an adulterant
IMPURPLE empurple
IMPUTING charging; insinuating
INACTION inertia; sloth; indolence
INACTIVE idle; torpid; supine
INAQUATE turn into water
INARABLE unfit for tillage
INASMUCH because
INAURATE gild
INBONDED (brick-laying)
INCAGING confining; mewing
INCANTON merge into a canton
INCARNED incarnated
INCASING encasing; enclosing
INCASKED barrelled
INCAVATE hollow out
INCENSED inflamed; enraged (Her.)
INCENSOR incense burner
INCEPTOR beginner; inaugurator
INCHMEAL gradually
INCHOATE begun; immature; incipient
INCIDENT episode; event; casual
INCIRCLE encircle; encompass
INCISELY clear cut; acutely
INCISING scribing; engraving
INCISION cut; gash; slit
INCISIVE trenchant; sarcastic
INCISORY sharpness
INCISURE a cut; wound
INCITANT stimulant; provocative
INCITING goading; arousing; spurring
INCIVISM lack of communal spirit
INCLINED disposed; biassed; tilted
INCLINER sloping dial
INCLOSED enclosed; penned; enfolded
INCLOSER a fencer of common land
INCLUDED contained; embodied
INCOMING entrance; arrival
INCOMITY incivility; rudeness
INCORPSE incorporate (obs.)
INCREASE aggravate; augment
INCREATE create within

INCUBATE hatch
INCUBOUS (leaf formation)   **B.**
INCUMBER encumber; hinder
INCURRED contracted; ran into
INCURVED bent
INCUSING stamping
INCUSSED forged; struck
INDAGATE investigate
INDEBTED under obligation
INDECENT unbecoming; coarse
INDENTED notched; toothed
INDEVOTE disloyal; unloving
INDEVOUT irreverent; impious
INDEXING compiling an index
INDIAMAN trading ship   **Naut.**
INDICANT symptomatic
INDICATE show; suggest; denote
INDICTED impeached; charged
INDICTEE a defendant
INDICTER an accuser
INDIGENE a native; aboriginal
INDIGENT poor; needy; necessitous
INDIRECT devious; tortuous; oblique
INDITING dictating; writing; penning
INDOCILE intractible; stubborn
INDOLENT lazy; sluggish; inert
INDORSED sanctioned; ratified
INDORSEE endorsee
INDORSER ratifier; confirmer
INDRENCH soak; saturate; steep
INDUCING actuating; urging
INDUCTED invested; installed   **Eccl.**
INDUCTOR officiating minister
INDULGED gratified; humoured
INDULGER favourer
INDULINE a dye   **Chem.**
INDURATE harden; inure
INDUSIAL (caterpillar skins)   **Z.**
INDUSIUM skin or cover   **B.**
INDUSTRY trade; assiduity; diligence
INDUVIAE withered leaves   **B.**
INEDIBLE uneatable
INEDITED unpublished
INEQUITY injustice; unfairness
INERMOUS no prickles   **B.**
INERTION sluggishness; indolence
INEXPERT unskilled; unversed
INFAMING defaming; discrediting
INFAMISE } publicly brand
INFAMIZE } with infamy
INFAMOUS vile; notorious; heinous
INFANTLY childishly; infantile
INFANTRY foot-soldiers
INFECTED tainted; corrupted
INFECTER carrier of disease
INFECUND sterile; barren; unprolific
INFERIAE Roman sacrifices
INFERIOR poor; subordinate; mediocre
INFERNAL diabolical; fiendish; satanic
INFERRED deduced; argued; surmised

INFESTED overrun; thronged; beset
INFILTER permeate; seep
INFINITE boundless; unlimited
INFINITO perpetual   **Mus.**
INFINITY immensity
INFIRMLY irresolutely; feebly
INFLAMED exasperated; infuriated
INFLAMER agent provocateur
INFLATED distended; bloated; swollen
INFLATOR air-pump
INFLATUS inspiration
INFLEXED bent inwards
INFLOWED ran in
INFLUENT a tributary
INFOLDED embraced
INFORMAL unconventional; simple
INFORMED told; apprized; notified
INFORMER a sneak
INFRA-RED
INFRINGE violate; transgress
INFRUGAL prodigal; extravagant
INFUMATE to smoke
INFUSING inculcating; inspiring
INFUSION instillation; introduction
INFUSIVE penetrative
INFUSORY protozoic   **Z.**
INGENIUM bent of mind
INGROOVE engroove; furrow
INGROWTH
INGUINAL (groin)   **Med.**
INGULFED swallowed up
INHALANT } a vapourizer;   **Med.**
INHALENT } the vapour
INHALING breathing
INHERENT innate; congenital
INHERING sticking fast
INHERSED coffined
INHESION inherence
INHOOPED encaged; cooped
INHUMING burying; interring
INIMICAL allergic; hostile; contrary
INIQUITY vice; sinfulness; offence
INITIATE a novice; start; inaugurate
INJECTED forced in; introduced
INJECTOR kind of pump
INJURING damaging; maltreating
INKINESS
INKMAKER
INKSTAND ink-holder
INK-STONE sulphate of iron   **Min.**
INLACING enlacing
INLANDER not an islander
INLAWING clearing of attainder
INLAYING ornamenting
INLOCKED locked up
INNATELY instinctively; naturally
INNERVED invigorated
INNOCENT guileless; blameless; sinless
INNOVATE make changes; alter
INNUENDO an insinuation

INORNATE plain
INQUIRED asked; investigated
INQUIRER questioner; scrutineer
INRAILED enclosed   **[Naut.**
INRIGGED with rowlocks on gunwhale
INSANELY crazily; deliriously
INSANITY dementia; mania; lunacy
INSCIENT ignorant; illiterate; unread
INSCONCE ensconce; hide; lurk
INSCRIBE dedicate; engrave; imprint
INSCROLL write on a scroll
INSEAMED marked by a seam
INSECTED segmented
INSECURE uncertain; hazardous
INSERTED introduced; injected
INSETTED implanted
INSHADED tinted
INSHRINE enshrine; dedicate
INSIGNIA badges; emblems; tokens
INSISTED persisted; maintained; urge
INSITION ingraftment
INSNARED entangled; caught; ginned
INSNARER trapper
INSOLATE dry in the sun
INSOLENT contumacious; hubristic
INSOMNIA sleeplessness   **Med**
INSOMUCH so that
INSPHERE ensphere; englobe
INSPIRED inhaled; animated
INSPIRER spiritual leader
INSPIRIT enhearten; infuse
INSTABLE unstable; transient
INSTANCE specify; occurrence; incider
INSTANCY urgency; solicitation
INSTATED established
INSTINCT natural propensity
INSTREAM to flow
INSTRUCT edify; direct; enjoin; orde
INSTYLED entitled; named; yclept
INSUCKEN milling restriction   **La**
INSULATE isolate; enisle
INSULTED affronted; outraged
INSULTER taunter; abuser; offender
INSURANT policy holder
INSURING assuring; underwriting
INTAGLIO opposite to Cameo
INTARSIA pictorial inlay
INTEGRAL whole; entire; complete
INTENDED betrothed; meant; purpos
INTENDER contemplator
INTENTLY with fixed attention
INTERACT theatrical interval
INTER-COM inter-communication
INTEREST concern; attention; discou
INTERIOR inside; inward; inner
INTERLAY insert
INTERMIT suspend
INTERMIX blend; commingle
INTERNAL domestic; within; inside
INTERNED confined; imprisoned

INTERNEE arrested alien
INTERPOL international criminal police
INTERRED buried; inhumed; entombed
INTERREX a regent
INTERTIE connecting piece
INTERVAL gap; pause; interim
INTER-WAR during the war
INTEXINE pollen cover   **B.**
INTIMACY familiarity; friendship
INTIMATE near; close; declare
INTIMITY inwardness
INTONATE intone
INTONING chanting
INTRADOS lower surface of arch
INTRENCH encroach; infringe; trespass
INTREPID dauntless; doughty; daring
INTRIGUE cabal; interest; conspiracy
INTROMIT insert; admit
INTRORSE facing inwards
INTRUDED butted in; thrusted
INTRUDER trespasser; interloper
INTUBATE insert a tube
INUNDANT overflowing; overwhelming
INUNDATE flood; swamp; deluge
INURBANE rude; uncouth; discourteous
INURNING putting in an urn
INUSTION a branding
INVADING violating; raiding; entering
INVARIED set; constant; uniform
INVASION foray; attack; assault
INVASIVE aggressive
INVECKED ⎱ scalloped
INVECTED ⎰
INVECTED engrailed (Her.)
INVEIGLE entice; wheedle; decoy; lure
INVEILED veiled
INVENTED devised; created; fabricated
INVENTOR innovator; contriver
INVERTER electronics
INVESTED arrayed; indued; beset
INVESTOR buyer; purchaser
INVITING attractive; alluring
INVOCATE adjure; invoke; beseech
INVOICED billed
INVOKING conjuring; summoning
INVOLUTE spiral
INVOLVED complicated; complex
INWALLED enclosed
INWARDLY privily; secretly
INWORKED inset
IODIZING (iodine)   **Med.**
IODOFORM an antiseptic   **Med.**
IODYRITE iodide of silver   **Chem.**
IOLANTHE a fairy; an opera   **Mus.**
IONICIZE Grecianize
IONIZING electrolysing
IOTACISM excessive use of " I "
IREFULLY angrily, furiously
IRENICAL tranquil, pacific
IRENICON peace propaganda

IRIDITIS eye inflammation   **Med.**
IRISATED like a rainbow
IRISCOPE spectroscope
IRISHISM Celtic expression, humorous
IRISHMAN (Ireland)
IRONBARK eucalyptus   **B.**
IRONCLAD plated
IRON-CLAY yellow iron ore   **Min.**
IRONGREY a colour
IRONICAL satirical; sarcastic; derisive
IRON-SAND firework mixture   **Min.**
IRONSICK rusty and leaky
IRONSIDE a Cromwellian
IRONWARE ironmongery
IRONWOOD tough timber   **B.**
IRONWORK smithery
IRRIGATE supply with water; moisten
IRRISION derision; banter
IRRITANT annoying; exasperating
IRRITATE gall; nettle; provoke
IRRUPTED burst in; invaded; raided
ISABELLE yellowish grey
ISAGOGIC introductory
ISENGRIM a fabulous wolf   **Z.**
ISLAMISM Mohammedanism   **Eccl.**
ISLAMITE worshipper of Allah   **Eccl.**
ISLAMIZE proselytize   **Eccl.**
ISLANDED isolated
ISLANDER not an inlander
ISLESMAN (from the Hebrides)
ISOBARIC (equal barometric pressure)
ISOCHEIM line indicating equal winter
　temperatures
ISOCHORE gas pressure and temperature
ISOCRYME line indicating equal winter
　temperatures
ISODICON short anthem   **Eccl.**
ISODOMON ⎱ masonry composed of
ISODOMUM ⎰ uniform blocks
ISOGONAL equi-angular
ISOGONIC (equal magnetic angles)
ISOLATED solitary
ISOMERIC ⎱ different properties **Chem.**
ISONYMIC ⎰ of similar compounds
ISOPATHY homoeopathy   **Med.**
ISOPRENE synthetic rubber   **Chem.**
ISOSTACY a geological theory
ISOTHERE (equal summer heat)
ISOTHERM line of equal heat
ISOTONIC having equal tones
ISOTOPIC
ISSUABLE distributable
ISSUANCE delivery
ISTHMIAN Corinthian
ITALIOTE a Greek colonist in Italy
ITCH-MITE burrowing insect   **Z.**
ITERANCE repetition
ITERATED repeated; recapitulated
ITHURIEL cherub; guardian angel
IVORY-NUT a palm-nut   **B.**

N

J

JABBERED gabbled; chattered
JABBERER wind-bag
JACKAROO greenhorn squatter (Aust.)
JACKETED having a paper cover
JACKFISH pike **Z.**
JACK-FLAG **Naut.**
JACK-FOOL perfect fool
JACK-KNIFE diving; sport
JACKWOOD jaca-tree **B.**
JACKYARD a boom **Naut.**
JACOBEAN (James I)
JACOBITE partisan of James II
JACQUARD loom mechanism
JACULATE to throw; to dart
JAGGEDLY raggedly; unevenly
JAILBIRD old lag
JALOUSIE Venetian blind
JAMAICAN (Jamaica)
JAMBEAUS leggings
JAMBOREE rally; boisterous frolic
JAMPANEE chair carrier
JANGLING wrangling
JANUFORM double-faced
JAPANESE
JAPANNED varnished; enamelled
JAPANNER a shoeblack
JAPHETIC Armenian alphabet
JAPONICA Japanese quince **B.**
JARARAKA poisonous snake **Z.**
JASPONYX an onyx **Min.**
JAUNDICE to prejudice **Med.**
JAUNTIER more sprightly
JAUNTILY debonairly
JAUNTING an outing
JAVANESE an Indonesian
JAW-LEVER veterinary instrument
JAW-TOOTH a molar **Med.**
JEALOUSY green-eyed monster
JEANETTE coarse cloth
JEBUSITE a Canaanite
JEHOVIST Hebrew Theologian **Ecc.**
JELLYBAG a strainer
JENTLING Danube chub **Z.**
JEOPARDY danger; peril; hazard; risk
JEREMIAD lamentation
JEROBOAM super champagne bottle
JERQUING customs searching **Naut.**
JERRICAN 5 gallon petrol tin
JEST-BOOK collection of jokes
JESUITIC, JESUITRY craftiness, cunning
JET-BLACK deepest black
JET-CRAFT⎫
JET-PLANE⎭ jet propelled aircraft
JETTISON throw overboard **Naut.**
JETTYING projecting
JEWELLED set with gems
JEWELLER a craftsman with gems

JEWISHLY judaical
JEW'S-HARP **Mus.**
JICKAJOG a shake; a push
JIGGERED flabbergasted
JIGGLING wriggling; joggling
JIGMAKER a tool-maker
JINGLING tinkling; rhyming
JINGOISH super-patriotic
JINGOISM ultra-patriotism
JOBATION a tedious scolding
JOCKEYED jostled; outwitted; deluded
JOCOSELY facetiously; joyously
JOCOSITY sportiveness; fun
JOCUNDLY mirthfully; waggishly
JOGGLING shaking; jostling; elbowing
JOHANNES old Portugese gold **Coin**
JOHDPURS riding breeches
JOIN-HAND connected script
JOINTING (carpentry)
JOINT-OIL synovia **Med.**
JOINTURE a settlement **Law**
JOISTING fitting with laths
JOKINGLY in jest; hilariously
JOLLIEST very merry and bright
JOLT-HEAD dunderhead
JONATHON American John Bull
JONGLEUR wandering minstrel **Mus.**
JOSTLING pushing; hustling; crowding
JOUNCING shaking; jolting (slang)
JOUSTING a tourney
JOVIALLY festively; blithely
JOVIALTY merriment; conviviality
JOYFULLY rapturously; gladly
JOYOUSLY blissfully; happily
JOYSTICK aeroplane control lever
JUBILANT triumphant; exulting
JUBILATE celebrate; rejoice
JUDAICAL Jewish **[Eccl., Law.**
JUDAIZED conformed to Mosaic law
JUDAIZER opponent of St. Paul
JUDGMENT sentence; decree; award
JUDICIAL legal; legitimate; sagacious
JUGGLERY manual dexterity
JUGGLING conjuring; swindling
JUGO-SLAV Yugo-Slav
JULIENNE clear soup
JUMBLING confusing; mixing
JUMP-SEAT collapsible seat
JUNCTION union; coalition; coupling
JUNCTURE crisis; exigency; strait
JUNKETED feasted; caroused
JUNK-RING piston packing
JUNONIAN queenly
JURASSIC geological period
JURATORY comprising an oath
JURISTIC legal jurisdictive
JURYMAST temporary mast **Naut.**
JUSTLING jostling,; jolting
JUSTNESS equity; impartiality
JUVENILE young; puerile; adolescent

K

KAFFLEH Bedouin shawl
KAILWIFE cabbage-seller; a scold (Sc.)
KAILYARD kitchen-garden (Sc.)
KAKEMONO Japanese picture
KALAMDAN Persian writing case
KALAMKAR Indian printed cotton
KALENDAR calendar; almanac
KALERUNT cabbage stalk   **B.**
KALEVALA Finnish epic
KALEYARD kitchen-garden   **B.**
KALINITE alum   **Min.**
KALIYUGA Hindu mythological era
KALOLOGY science of beauty
KALOTYPE early photograph
KAMADEVA Indian Eros
KAMIKAZE suicide bomb; plane (Jap.)
KANARESE language (Mysore, India)
KANGAROO a marsupial   **Z.**
KANTIKOY religious dance **Eccl., Mus.**
KARELIAN (Finno-Russian)
KASHMIRI people and language (Kashmir)
KATAKANA Japanese script
KAURI-GUM a resin (Aust.)   **B.**
KAYMAKAM Turkish Governor
KECKLING binding rope   **Naut.**
KEDGEREE a breakfast-dish
KEEL-BOAT type of yacht   **Naut.**
KEEL-HAUL (punishment)   **Naut.**
KEENNESS acuity; astuteness
KEEPSAKE memento; relic
KENOTRON wireless valve
KERASINE, KERATOSE horn
KERCHIEF a head cover
KERN-BABY harvest image   **B.**
KERNELLY full of seeds   **B.**
KEROSENE paraffin   **Min.**
KEYBLOCK printing
KEYBOARD clavier   **Mus.**
KEY-BUGLE Kent bugle   **Mus.**
KEY-FRUIT ash, sycamore, etc.   **B.**
KEY-MONEY levy on a tenant
KEYPLATE keyhole escutcheon
KEYSTONE
KIBITZER critical observer (U.S.A.)
KICKABLE suitable for booting
KICKBACK return of stolen goods; wages
KICKSHAW a fallal
KID-GLOVE
KIEFEKIL meerschaum   **Min.**
KILL-CROP a changeling
KILLDEER American plover   **Z.**
KILLOGIE a kiln (Sc.)
KILL-TIME a pastime
KILN-HOLE mouth of kiln
KILODYNE 1,000 dynes   **Meas.**

KILOGRAM 1000 grammes   **Meas.**
KILOWATT 1000 watts   **Meas.**
KINDLESS unnatural; merciless
KINDLIER more forbearing
KINDLING animating; tinder
KINDNESS benevolence; generosity
KINEMICS gestural expression
KINESICS gestural body movements
KINETICS dynamics
KINGBIRD American fly-catcher   **Z.**
KING-CRAB tropical crab   **Z.**
KINGFISH the opah   **Z.**
KINGHOOD sovereignty
KINGLESS republican
KINGLIKE truly regal
KINGLING ruler of petty state
KINGPOST principal strut
KINGSHIP kingcraft
KINGWANA language
KINGWOOD ebony (S. Amer.)   **B.**
KINKAJOU racoon; honey-bear   **Z.**
KINSFOLK kindred; relations
KIPPERED cured
KIRIKANE gold foil application (Jap.)
KIRKYARD graveyard   **Eccl.**
KIROUMBO tropical bird   **Z.**
KISS-CURL a tempting lock
KISTVAEN stone sepulchre
KITEFOOT a tobacco plant   **B.**
KITTENED
KITTLISH ticklish
KLYSTRON electron converter
KNABBING gnawing
KNACKISH knavish
KNAPPING flint breaking
KNAPSACK haversack; ruksac
KNAPWEED batchelor's buttons   **B.**
KNEADING dough work
KNEE-DEEP ⎫
KNEE-HIGH ⎬ nearly thigh high
KNEEHOLM knee-holly   **B.**
KNEELING kotowing
KNEE-STOP organ lever   **Mus.**
KNELLING tolling
KNICKERS knickerbockers
KNIFE-BOY scullery lad
KNIGHTED now Sir ?
KNIGHTLY courtly
KNITTING uniting; interlacing
KNITWEAR reticulated fabric
KNOCKING rapping; hitting; motoring
KNOCK-OUT K.O.; dealer's auction
KNOLLING knelling
KNOTLESS free from ties
KNOTTIER more intricate
KNOTTING securing; entangling
KNOTWORK ornamental work
KNOUTING scourging
KNOWABLE ascertainable; scibile
KNOW-ALLS wiseacres

KNUCKLED yielded; jointed
KOFTGARI ⎫
KOFTWORK ⎭ inlaying steel with gold
KOHELETH Preacher (Solomon) **Eccl.**
KOHINOOR famous diamond **Min.**
KOHLRABI cole-turnip **B.**
KOLINSKY Siberian mink **Z.**
KOMITAJI Balkan guerilla band
KONISTRA orchestra of a Greek theatre
KOORBASH ⎫ whip made from
KOURBASH ⎭ rhino hide
KOTOWING making obeisance
KREASOTE creasote **Chem.**
KREUTZER small Austrian copper **Coin**
KUKUKUKU people (New Guinea)
KURVEYOR transport rider (S. Afr.)
KYANIZED cyanized **Chem.**
KYLOSSIS club-foot **Med.**

L

LABDANUM ladanum **Chem.**
LABELLED directed
LABELLUM lower petal **B.**
LABIALLY
LABIATED lipped
LABOURED strove
LABOURER a toiler
LABURNIC derived from laburnum
LABURNUM flowering tree **B.**
LACE-BARK bark of a tree **B.**
LACE-BOOT (no buttons)
LACE-LEAF aquatic plant **B.**
LACERATE tear
LACEWING an insect **Z.**
LACHESIS one of the Fates
LACK-A-DAY sorrowful exclamation
LACKEYED valeted
LACONISM brevity; pithiness
LACROSSE a Canadian game
LACRYMAL tearful
LACTEOUS milk-like
LACTIFIC milk producing
LACTUCIC (lettuce) **B.**
LACUNOSE pitted; furrowed
LADDERED (stockings)
LADLEFUL a measure
LADYBACK tandem cycle
LADYBIRD a helpful beetle **Z.**
LADY-FERN **B.**
LADY-HELP
LADYHOOD gentility
LADYLIKE well-bred; delicate
LADYLOVE a sweetheart
LADYSHIP a title
LAGTHING Norwegian upper house
LAICIZED opened to the laity
LAKE-LIKE merely ?
LAMANTIN the manatee **Z.**
LAMASERY Thibetan monastery **Eccl.**

LAMBDOID lamda-shaped (Gk.)
LAMBENCY play of light
LAMBLIKE gentle; meek
LAMBLING lambkin **Z.**
LAMBSKIN
LAME-DUCK a bankrupt
LAMELLAR of thin plates
LAMENESS halting; crippledness
LAMENTED deeply regretted
LAMENTER deplorer; bewailer
LAMINARY in thin plates
LAMINATE in layers
LAMPLESS
LAMP-POST
LANCEGAY a kind of spear
LANCELET primitive vertebrate **Z.**
LAND-CRAB **Z.**
LANDFALL landslip **Naut.**
LAND-FISH fish out of water
LAND-GIRL
LAND-HERD a herd of animals **Z.**
LANDLADY mine hostess
LANDLESS no holding
LANDLINE overhead cable
LANDLOCK protect from wind and sea
LANDLORD mine host
LANDMARK notable event
LANDMINE parachuted bomb
LANDNAMA Domesday Book (Ice.)
LANDRAIL corncrake **Z.**
LAND-ROLL clod-crusher
LAND-SHIP a tank
LANDSLIP landslide
LANDSMAN cf. seaman
LAND-TURN land-breeze
LANDWARD rural
LANDWEHR German militia
LAND-WIND off-shore wind
LANGRAGE grape shot
LANGSHAN black Chinese hen **Z.**
LANGSYNE time long past
LANGUAGE diction; vernacular
LANGUISH pine; droop; decline
LANIATED torn to pieces
LANKIEST leanest
LANKNESS length without breadth
LANNERET small falcon **Z.**
LANOLINE wool fat
LANTHORN hornsided lantern
LAP-BOARD board used by tailors
LAPELLED with lapels
LAPIDARY stone-cutter
LAPIDATE pelt with stones
LAPIDIFY turn into stone
LAPIDIST stone-worker
LAPILLUS fragment of lava **Min.**
LAP-JOINT an overlapping joint
LAPPETED with flaps
LAPSABLE terminal; transient
LAPSTONE (used by a shoemaker)

LARBOARD port   **Naut.**
LARCENER a thief; pilferer
LARDERER a store keeper
LARGESSE liberality; generosity
LARKSPUR a delphinium   **B.**
LARRIKIN Australian hooligan
LARVATED masked   **Z.**
LARYNGES larynxes; throats   **Med.**
LASER-RAY, L-GUN searing ray **Med.**
LASSLORN jilted
LASSOING
LATCH-KEY domestic open sesame
LATENESS tardiness
LATENTLY secretly; apparently not
LATERITE brick-clay   **Min.**
LATHERED soapy; larruped
LATHWORK lath and plaster
LATINISM Latin idiom
LATINIST Latin scholar
LATINITY purity of Latin style
LATINIZE latinise
LATITUDE width; scope; laxity
LATTERLY more recently; lately
LATTICED cross-barred
LAUDABLE praiseworthy; honourable
LAUDABLY commendably
LAUDANUM an opiate   **Med.**
LAUGHING riant
LAUGHTER convulsive merriment
LAUNCHED hurled; began; initiated
LAUREATE crowned with laurel
LAVA-LIKE
LAVATION washing; purification
LAVATORY a wash-house
LAVENDER greyish blue   **B.**
LAVEROCK skylark   **Z.**
LAVISHED spent; squandered
LAVISHLY prodigally; wastefully
LAWFULLY legally; justly; validly
LAWGIVER a legislator; a Solon   **Law.**
LAWMAKER an M.P.
LAWYERLY verbose
LAXATION relaxation; slackness
LAXATIVE opening mixture   **Med.**
LAY-ABOUT lazy; good for nothing
LAY-CLERK a responder   **Eccl.**
LAY-ELDER Presbyterian elder   **Eccl.**
LAYERING horticultural process
LAYSTALL byre
LAZARIST R.C. missionary   **Eccl.**
LAZARONE Neapolitan beggar
LAZINESS inertness; slackness
LAZULITE a blue stone   **Min.**
LEACHING making an alkali
LEAD-MILL lapidary's plate
LEADSMAN a lead-swinger   **Naut.**
LEAF-LARD leaf-fat lard
LEAFLESS destitute of leaves
LEAFSCAR a mark   **B.**
LEAGUING confederating; coalessing
LEANNESS thinness; gauntness

LEAPFROG a game
LEAP-YEAR a year of 366 days
LEARNING scholarship; erudition
LEASABLE able to be let
LEASHING binding; securing
LEATHERN made of leather
LEATHERY tough
LEAVENED modified; tempered
LEAVINGS residue; relics
LEBANESE a native of Lebanon
LECANORA lichen; manna   **B.**
LECITHIN egg tissue
LECTURED reprimanded; chided
LECTURER an expositor
LED-HORSE spare horse
LEE-BOARD anti-drift device   **Naut.**
LEECHING doctoring   **Med.**
LEEFANGE sheet guide   **Naut.**
LEE-SHORE windward shore   **Naut.**
LEFT-HAND sinister
LEFTWARD to the left
LEFT-WING (politics)
LEGACIES bequests; gifts
LEGALISE authorise; sanction
LEGALISM adherence to law   **Law**
LEGALIST stickler for law
LEGALITY lawfulness
LEGALIZE sanction; warrant
LEGATARY legatee   **Law**
LEGATINE relating to a legate
LEGATION an embassy
LEG-BREAK (cricket)
LEGERITY lightness
LEGUMINA pods   **B.**
LEGUMINE nitrogenous proteid   **B.**
LEMONADE a soft drink
LEMUROID, LEMURINE monkey-like
                                    Z.
LENDABLE loanable
LENGHTEN extend; elongate; protract
LENIENCE } mildness; clemency;
LENIENCY } mercifulness; forbearance
LENINISM, LENINIST follower of
   Lenin
LENITIVE mitigating; sedative
LENS-HOOD light-shield   **Photo.**
LENTANDO slowing up   **Mus.**
LENTICEL cell-formation   **B.**
LENT-LILY daffodil   **B.**
LEPEROUS leprous   **Med.**
LEPIDOID ganoid; scaly   **Z.**
LEPORINE like a hare   **Z.**
LESSENED diminished; decreased
LETHARGY dulness; apathy; oblivion
LETTERED learned; printed
LEUCITIC containing volcanic ore **Min.**
LEUCOSIS pallor; albinism   **Med.**
LEVANTED decamped; welshed
LEVANTER N. African wind
LEVELLED flattened; raged; demolished
381 LEVELLER ultra-republican, 1649

LEVERAGE mechanical advantage
LEVERING exerting pressure
LEVIABLE taxable; imposable
LEVIGATE to smooth; to polish
LEVIRATE Hebrew marriage custom
LEVITATE cause to float
LEVITIES frivolities; flippancies
LEVOLOSE fruit sugar
LEWDNESS licentiousness
LEWDSTER a profligate
LEWISITE poison gas **Chem.**
LIBATION a drink-offering
LIBATORY oblatory
LIBELLED slandered; defamed
LIBELLER lampooner; calumniator
LIBERATE set free; emancipate
LIBERIAN (Liberia)
LIBRATED balanced
LIBRETTO words of musical play
LICENSED authorized; allowed
LICENSEE holder of a license
LICENSER licence issuer
LICHENIC made from lichen **B.**
LICHENIN moss starch
LICHGATE lychgate
LICHWAKE likewake; death-watch
LICORICE liquorice **B.**
LIEGEMAN vassal; henchman
LIFEBELT
LIFEBOAT **Naut.**
LIFEBUOY **Naut.**
LIFEHOLD lease for life **Law**
LIFELESS dull; inanimate; extinct
LIFELIKE
LIFELINE vital cord
LIFELONG till death
LIFE-PEER (not hereditary)
LIFE-RAFT (for shipwreck) **Naut.**
LIFE-RATE (life insurance)
LIFE-RENT rent during lifetime **Law**
LIFE-SIZE full scale
LIFE-TIME an uncertain period
LIFE-WORK
LIFTABLE capable of elevation
LIGAMENT binder; tendon
LIGATING binding; bandaging **Med.**
LIGATION a fastening
LIGATURE bandage; band **Mus.**
LIGHTFUL cheery; happy; radiant
LIGHTING illuminating; kindling
LIGHTISH not heavy; fickle
LIGNEOUS wooden
LIGNITIC (lignite; brown coal) **Min.**
LIGULATE straplike **B.**
LIGURITE pea-green gem **Min.**
LIKEABLE pleasant enough
LIKENESS resemblance; similarity
LIKENING comparing
LIKEWAKE lichwake; death-watch
LIKEWISE also; moreover; besides

LILACINE extract of lilac **B.**
LILLIPUT land of the pygmies
LILY-IRON harpoon for swordfish
LILY-STAR feather-star **B.**
LIMACOID like a slug **Z.**
LIMATION filing; polishing
LIMATURE filings
LIMA-WOOD Peruvian red-wood **B.**
LIME-FREE clear of calcium
LIME-KILN a furnace
LIMERICK verse often perverse
LIME-SINK a depression
LIME-TREE linden tree **B.**
LIME-TWIG a snare
LIME-WASH whitewash
LIMEWORT lychnis viscaria **B.**
LIMITARY finite; bounded
LIMITING confining; restricting
LIMONITE haematite ore **Min.**
LINAMENT lint **Med.**
LINARITE a lead compound **Min.**
LINCHPIN keeps the wheel on
LINCTURE linctus; medicine **Med.**
LINEALLY in a direct line
LINEARLY directly
LINE-FISH fish taken on a line
LINESMAN referee's assistant
LING-BIRD meadow pipit **Z.**
LINGERED lagged; delayed; tarried
LINGERER dawdler; loiterer; dallier
LINGERIE undies
LINGUIST seldom tongue-tied ?
LINIMENT embrocation
LINNAEUS eminent botanist (1707-78)
LINOLEUM lino; floorcloth
LINOTYPE type-setting machine
LINSTOCK flame-holder
LIONIZED heroized
LIPAEMIA fatty blood **Med.**
LIPO-GRAM (letter omission)
LIPSTICK a cosmetic
LIQUABLE fusible; fluent
LIQUATED liquified
LIQUIDLY smoothly; fluidal
LIQUORED in drink; tipsy
LIRIPOOP hood; trick; nincompoop
LIROCONE floury; powdery
LISTENED hearkened; attended; heard
LISTENER eavesdropper
LISTEN-IN (B.B.C.)
LISTLESS languid; apathetic; torpid
LITERACY ability to read and write
LITERARY erudite; scholarly
LITERATE learned; studious
LITERATI men of letters
LITEROSE bookish
LITHARGE lead oxide **Min**
LITHERLY mischievous; lazy
LITIGANT engaged in a lawsuit **Law**
LITIGATE to go to law **Law**

LITTERED scattered; strewn; deranged	**LOGOTYPE** twin letters in printing
LITTLE-GO examination (Camb.)	**LOG-SLATE** recording slate **Naut.**
LITTORAL a coastal strip	**LOITERED** lingered; tarried
LITURATE blurred; spotted	**LOITERER** an idler; flaneur
LITURGIC ritualistic **Eccl.**	**LOKWEAVE** carpet-splice
LIVEABLE habitable; residential	**LOLLARDY** Lollard doctrine **Eccl.**
LIVE-AXLE driving axle	**LOLLIPOP** a sweet
LIVE-BAIT sometimes a worm	**LOLLOPED** lounged; lurched
LIVELILY vivaciously; briskly; alertly	**LOMONITE** a zeolite **Min.**
LIVELONG lasting; the orpine **B.**	**LONDONER**
LIVENING cheering up; animating	**LONENESS** seclusion; solitude
LIVE-RAIL rail carrying current	**LONESOME** solitary
LIVERIED in uniform	**LONGBOAT** **Naut.**
LIVERIES garbs; uniforms	**LONGERON** main spar of aeroplane
LIVERISH bilious; testy **Med.**	**LONGEVAL** long lived
LIVE-WELL kind of aquarium	**LONG-FIRM** swindling company
LIVE-WIRE human dynamo	**LONGHAND** handwriting
LIVIDITY discolouration	**LONG-LEGS** daddy long-legs **Z.**
LIVINGLY lively; energetically; agilely	**LONG-MOSS** tillandsia **B.**
LIXIVIAL residual **Chem.**	**LONG-SHIP** a galley **Naut.**
LIXIVIUM lye; residuum **Chem.**	**LONG-SLIP** (cricket)
LOAD-LINE Plimsoll's mark **Naut.**	**LONGSOME** tiresome; tedious; irksome
LOANABLE able to be lent	**LONG-SPUN** protracted; extended
LOAN-WORD borrowed word	**LONG-STOP** (cricket)
LOATHFUL abhorrent; detestable	**LONG-TAIL** not docked
LOATHING hating; antipathy	**LONG-TERM** far seeing
LOBBYING endeavouring to influence	**LONGWAYS** lengthways
LOBBYIST a journalist	**LONGWISE** in extenso
LOBLOLLY gruel; lout; attendant	**LONICERA** honey-suckle genus **B.**
LOCALISM provincialism	**LOOKER-ON** spectator; observer
LOCALITY situation; district; spot	**LOOM-GALE** gentle gale
LOCALIZE assign to a place	**LOOP-HOLE** an escape
LOCATING positioning; fixing	**LOOP-LINE** alternative route
LOCATION film rendez-vous	**LOOSE-BOX** a stall
LOCATIVE grammatical case	**LOOSENED** undone; relaxed; slackened
LOCKFAST firmly fastened	**LOOSENER** a laxative **Med.**
LOCK-GATE (on canal or river)	**LOP-EARED** with drooping ears
LOCKLESS without a lock	**LOP-SIDED** unbalanced; biased
LOCK-SILL threshold of a lock	**LORD-LIKE** haughty; imperious
LOCKSMAN a turnkey	**LORDLING** a would-be lord
LOCKSPIT digging mark	**LORDOSIS** spinal curvature **Med.**
LOCK-WEIR weir with lock	**LORD'S-DAY** Sunday
LOCO-FOCO lucifer; ultra-radical	**LORDSHIP** sway; dominion; control
LOCULATE ⎫ divided	**LORICATE** to incrust
LOCULOSE ⎬ internally	**LORIKEET** Australian parrot **Z.**
LOCULOUS ⎭ into cells **B.**	**LOSINGLY** wastefully
LOCUTION diction; phrase	**LOTHARIO** a libertine; a filly-buster
LOCUTORY place for conversation**Eccl.**	**LOUDNESS** uproar; clamour; resonance
LODESMAN pilot **Naut.**	**LOUNGING** reclining; lolling; idling
LODESTAR pole-star	**LOVEBIRD** a budgerigar **Z.**
LODGINGS digs; accommodation	**LOVECHILD**
LODGMENT occupation; golf	**LOVEKNOT** a tangle
LOG-BOARD rough log **Naut.**	**LOVELACE** a libertine
LOG-CABIN timber hut	**LOVELESS** passionless; frigid
LOG-CANOE dug-out **Naut.**	**LOVELIES** beauteous damsels
LOG-GLASS timing device **Naut.**	**LOVE-LIFE** romance
LOGICIAN one skilled in logic	**LOVELILY** delectably; enchantingly
LOGICIZE deduce from reasoning	**LOVELOCK** a manly curl
LOGISTIC logical	**LOVELORN** jilted
LOGOGRAM puzzle in verse	**LOVE-NEST** romantic abode

LOVESICK languishing
LOVESOME adorable
LOVESUIT courtship
LOVINGLY affectionately; fondly
LOWERING depressing; threatening
LOW-WATER at the ebb
LOYALIST patriot; faithful follower
LUBBERLY clumsily; maladroit
LUCIDITY clearness; luminosity
LUCKIEST most fortunate; happiest
LUCKLESS singularly unfortunate
LUCKY BAG ⎱ a bran pie
LUCKY DIP ⎰ with hidden gifts
LUCULENT translucent; lucid; clear
LUCULLUS an epicure
LUKEWARM tepid
LUMBERED rumbled along
LUMBERER woodman
LUMINANT shining; radiant
LUMINARY a heavenly body
LUMINATE illuminate; brighten
LUMINOUS phosphorescent; lucent
LUMPFISH a sea fish **Z.**
LUNARIAN a moon observer
LUNATION a lunar month
LUNCHEON midday repast
LUNCHING
LUNGEING fencing; horse training
LUNGFISH **Z.**
LUNGLESS
LUNGWORT a lichen **B.**
LUNIFORM moon-shaped
LUNULATE like a crescent
LUPERCAL Roman festival
LUPINITE a bitter extract **B.**
LURCHING stumbling; rolling; lurking
LUSCIOUS rich in flavour
LUSTIEST beefiest; heftiest
LUSTRATE purify
LUSTRING silk cloth
LUSTROUS shining; luminous
LUSTWORT the sun-dew **B.**
LUTANIST a lute player **Mus.**
LUTATION sealing
LUTECIUM a metallic element **Chem.**
LUTEOLIN yellow dye **B.**
LUTHERAN Protestant **Eccl.**
LUXATING displacing
LUXATION dislocation
LUXURIES unnecessary pleasures
LUXURIST an indulger
LYCHGATE lichgate **Eccl.**
LYCOPODE yellow powder **B.**
LYMPHOID (vaccine) **Med.**
LYNCHING mob law
LYNCH-LAW short shrift
LYNX-EYED keen of vision
LYRE-BIRD Australian bird **Z.**
LYRICISM lyric composition
LYTERIAN terminating a disease **Med.**

M

MACARIAN blessed
MACARISM a beatitude
MACARIZE to bless
MACARONI fop; food
MACAROON almond biscuit
MACASSAR hair oil
MACERATE harass; to steep; to rot
MACHINAL mechanical
MACHINED
MACHINER operative
MACKEREL scad; (sky) **Z.**
MACROPOD long-legged **Z.**
MACROPUS kangaroo genus **Z.**
MACULATE to spot; to stain
MADDENED infuriated; incensed
MADELINE French cake
MADHOUSE Bedlam; asylum
MADRIGAL pastoral ditty **Mus.**
MAECENAS rich art patron
MAENADIC bacchanalian
MAESTOSO majestically **Mus.**
MAFFLING a simpleton
MAGAZINE depot; store; periodical
MAGDALEN home for repentants
MAGICIAN wizard; marabout
MAGIRICS the culinary art
MAGISTER master; doctor
MAGNESIA a medicine **Med.**
MAGNETIC attractive; drawing
MAGNIFIC splendid; majestic
MAGNOLIA a flowering tree **B.**
MAGOT-PIE magpie **Z.**
MAHADENA Hindu god, Siva **Eccl.**
MAHARAJA Indian rajah
MAHOGANY tropical tree **B.**
MAIDENLY modest; demure; bashful
MAIDHOOD girlhood; virginity
MAIEUTIC delivering; evolving
MAILABLE postable
MAIL BOAT a packet **Naut.**
MAIL-CART
MAIL-CLAD armour-plated
MAIL-DRAG mail-coach
MAIN-BOOM **Naut.**
MAIN-DECK **Naut.**
MAINLAND
MAINMAST **Naut.**
MAINSAIL **Naut.**
MAINSTAY **Naut.**
MAINTAIN continue; assert; aver; hold
MAINYARD **Naut.**
MAJESTIC imperial; august; regal
MAJOLICA pottery (majorca)
MAJORATE rank of major
MAJORITY over 21
MAKEBATE quarrel-maker
MAKELESS matchless

MAKIMONO Jap picture
MALACOID soft-bodied
MALADIES disorders; ailments **Med.**
MALAGASH ⎱ relating to
MALAGASY ⎰ Madagascar
MALAMUTE Arctic sledge dog **Z.**
MALAPERT saucy; impertinent; flippant
MALAPROP misuser of words
MALARIAL (malaria) **Med.**
MAL-DE-MER sea-sickness **Med.**
MALE-FERN **B.**
MALEFICE evil deed; enchantment
MALETOLT ⎱ illegal exaction **Law**
MALETOTE ⎰
MALIGNED traduced; slandered
MALIGNER defamer; reviler; abuser
MALINGER feign illness
MALLEATE to hammer
MALLECHO villainy; mischief (Shak.)
MALMROCK sandstone **Min.**
MALODOUR a smell; stench
MALT-DUST malt grains
MALT-KILN
MALT-MILL
MALTREAT abuse; hurt; harm; injure
MALTSTER malt-maker
MALT-WORM a tippler; weevil **Z.**
MAMBRINO round steel hat
MAMELUKE Circassian cavalry-man
MAMMALIA suckers **Z.**
MAMMARED stammered
MAMMIFER a mammal **Z.**
MAMMILLA a nipple **Med.**
MAMMODIS Indian muslin
MANACLED shackled; fettered
MAN-CHILD a boy
MAN-EATER cannibal; tiger **Z.**
MAN-HATER allergic to man
MAN-HOURS labour measure
MAN-OF-WAR warship **Naut.**
MAN-POWER
MAN-SIZED adult dimensions
MAN-TO-MAN
MANAGING controlling; contriving
MANCIPLE a steward; purveyor
MANDAEAN Babylonian sect
MANDAMUS a writ **Law**
MANDARIN official; orange; language **B.**
MANDATOR commander; director
MANDELIC bitter almond extract **B.**
MANDIBLE a jaw **Z.**
MANDINGO tribe (South Sahara)
MANDIOCA cassava; manioc **B.**
MANDOLIN a guitar **Mus.**
MANDORLA oval panel
MANDRAKE white bryony **B.**
MANDRILL a baboon **Z.**
MANELESS without a mane
MANELIKE like a mane
MANEQUIN manikin; artist's model

MANFULLY boldly; courageously
MANGABEY Malagasy monkey **Z.**
MANGCORN mixed grain crop
MANGLING calendering; mutilating
MANGONEL a ballistic machine
MANGROVE a tree **B.**
MANIACAL raving; frenzied; lunatic
MANICATE hairy **B.**
MANICHEE a doctrinaire
MANICURE hand treatment
MANIFEST invoice of ship's cargo **Naut.**
MANIFEST evince; clear; obvious
MANIFOLD multiplied; numerous
MANNERLY of good address
MANNIKIN manikin; dwarf
MANORIAL referring to a manor
MANSUETE mild; gentle
MANTELET small cloak
MANTIGER (Her.)
MANTILLA lace veil (Sp.)
MANTISSA decimal part of logarithm
MANTLING blushing; flushing; suffusing
MANUALLY by hand
MANUCODE bird of paradise **Z.**
MANURING fertilizing
MANUTYPE hand-painted
MAORI-HEN the weka **Z.**
MARABOUT Indian stork **Z.**
MARABOUT Moslem priest or wizard
MARASMUS emaciation **Med.**
MARATHON long distance race
MARAUDED roved; plundered; pillaged
MARAUDER raider; bandit; outlaw
MARAVEDI small Spanish copper **Coin**
MARBLING form of decor
MARCANDO with precision **Mus.**
MARCHING bordering; foot slogging
MARGARIC pearly
MARGARIN ersatz butter
MARGARON a fatty substance
MARGINAL in the margin
MARGINED edged; bordered
MARGRAVE German Count
MARIGOLD **B.**
MARINADE pickled fish
MARINATE to preserve; to salt
MARITIME marine; naval; nautical
MARJORAM aromatic plant **B.**
MARKEDLY unmistakably; eminently
MARKETED sold; vended
MARKSMAN crack shot
MARLINED twined with twine **Naut.**
MARLITIC (clay) **Min.**
MARMOSET American monkey **Z.**
MAROCAIN dress fabric
MARONITE Jewish sect
MAROONED left on desert island
MAROONER
MAROQUIN morocco leather
MARQUESS a marquis

MARQUISE marchioness	
MARRIAGE wedlock; espousal	
MARRYING wedding; uniting	
MARSH-GAS methane	**Chem.**
MARSH-HEN moor-hen	**Z.**
MARSH-TIT blackheaded tom-tit	**Z.**
MARTAGON turk's cap lily	**B.**
MARTELLO circular tower	
MARTINET a disciplinarian	
MARTYRED victimized	
MARY-SOLE a flat-fish	**Z.**
MARYGOLD marigold	**B.**
MARZIPAN a sweetmeat	
MASCARON face on door-knocker	
MASORITE a theologist	
MASSACRE pogrom; carnage	
MASSAGED kneaded; rubbed	
MASS-BELL sacring-bell	**Eccl.**
MASS-BOOK R.C. missal	**Eccl.**
MASSETER a jaw muscle	**Med.**
MASSEUSE a manipulator	**Med.**
MASSICOT lead oxide	**Min.**
MASSORAH Hebrew tradition	
MASTERED conquered; overcame	
MASTERLY expertly; dexterously	
MASTHEAD	**Naut.**
MASTLESS	
MASTODON early mammoth	**Z.**
MASURIUM a metallic element	**Chem.**
MAT-GRASS	**B.**
MATADORE bull-fighter; domino game	
MATAMATA S. Amer. river tortoise	**Z.**
MATCHBOX chez Lucifer	
MATCHING equalling; suiting	
MATELOTE a sauce	
MATERIAL stuff; essential; relevant	
MATERIEL equipment	
MATERNAL motherly	
MATESHIP comradeship	
MATHESIS mathematics; learning	
MATHILDA a tank	
MATRONAL motherly; sedate	
MATRONLY elderly	
MATTERED signified; imported	
MATTRESS	
MATURANT a cataplasm	**Med.**
MATURATE to poultice	**Med.**
MATURELY deliberately; completely	
MATURING ripening; mellowing	
MATURITY readiness; fullness	
MAUNDRIL a pick-axe	**Tool**
MAVERICK unbranded animal	
MAXILLAR (jaw)	**Med.**
MAXIM-GUN	
MAXIMIST a dealer in old saws	
MAXIMIZE raise to maximum	
MAY-APPLE N. American fruit	**B.**
MAY-BLOBS marsh marigold	**B.**
MAY-BLOOM hawthorn	**B.**
MAY-QUEEN	

MAYORESS wife of mayor	
MAZARINE deep blue	
MAZDEISM Zoroastrianism	
MAZINESS perplexity; haziness	
MAZOLOGY a zoological science	**Z.**
MEAGRELY scantily; sparsely; meanly	
MEAL-POCK ⎫ beggar's meal-bag	
MEAL-POKE ⎭	
MEALTIME	
MEALWORM	**Z.**
MEAN-BORN of humble origin	
MEANNESS sordidness; paltriness	
MEANTIME meanwhile	
MEASURED meted; ascertained; steady	
MEASURER computor; gauger	
MEAT-BALL rissole	
MEAT-SAFE	
MECHANIC artisan	
MECONATE, MECONINE ⎫ **B.**	
MECONIUM poppy-juice; opium ⎭ **B.**	
MEDALIST a prize winner	
MEDALLIC relating to medals	
MEDDLING interfering; intruding	
MEDIATED intervened; reconciled	
MEDIATOR an intercessor; arbitrator	
MEDICATE to doctor; to dose	
MEDICEAN (Medici of Florence)	
MEDICINE the curative art	**Med.**
MEDIEVAL (Middle Ages)	
MEDIOCRE middling; ordinary	
MEDITATE ruminate; muse; intend	
MEDULLAR pithy	**B.**
MEDULLIN lilac cellulose	**B.**
MEEKENED became gentle	
MEEKNESS submissiveness; humility	
MEETNESS fitness; propriety	
MEGALITH stone monument	
MEGAPODE mound bird	**Z.**
MEGATRON light-house valve	
MEGAVOLT million volts	
MEGAWATT million watts	
MEIONITE a silicate	**Min.**
MELAMINE organic compound	**Chem.**
MELANISM black coloration	
MELANITE black garnet	**Min.**
MELANOUS dark-visaged	
MELANURE sea-bream	**Z.**
MELIBEAN alternately responsive	
MELINITE a high explosive	
MELLIFIC honeyed	
MELLOWED matured; ripened; enriched	
MELLOWLY sweetly; melodiously	
MELODEON harmonium	**Mus.**
MELODIST composer	
MELODIZE render harmonious	**Mus.**
MEMBERED having limbs	
MEMBRANE tissue	**B., Z.**
MEMORIAL relic; monument; memento	
MEMORIZE learn by heart	
MEMPHIAN, MEMPHITE (Memphis)	

MEMSAHIB white lady (India)		
MENACING threatening; intimidating		
MENDABLE repairable		
MENHADEN American herring	**Z.**	
MENILITE brown opal	**Min.**	
MENINGES brain tissues	**Med.**	
MENISCAL⎱ crescent shaped		
MENISCUS⎰ type of lens		
MENOLOGY Saint's calendar		
MENOPOME mud-devil	**Z.**	
MENSURAL measurable		
MENTALLY intellectually		
MEPHITIC noxious; pestilential		
MEPHITIS an exhalation; miasma		
MERCABLE saleable; vendible		
MERCHAND to traffic; to trade		
MERCHANT trader; dealer; monger		
MERCIFUL humane; clement; lenient		
MERCURIC mercurial; sprightly		
MERICARP seed carpel	**B.**	
MERIDIAN great circle; noon		
MERINGUE a sweet		
MERIONES Can. jumping mouse	**Z.**	
MERISTEM formative tissue		
MERITING deserving; earning		
MEROSOME a segment; a somite	**Z.**	
MERRIEST blythest; happiest		
MERRYMAN mountebank; jester		
MERYCISM rumination		
MESCALIN alkaloid 'truth drug'	**Med.**	
MESDAMES ladies		
MESHWORK net work; reticulation		
MESITITE a carbonate	**Min.**	
MESMEREE one mesmerized		
MESMERIC hypnotic		
MESOCARP central carpel	**B.**	
MESODERM inner skin	**Med.**	
MESOLITE needlestone	**Min.**	
MESOTRON electron-directing device		
MESOTYPE zeolitic mineral	**Min.**	
MESOZOIC Triassic period		
MESQUITE African thorn-bush	**B.**	
MESSIDOR June 19th–July 18th. (Fr.)		
MESSMATE table companion		
MESSROOM		
MESSUAGE premises and garden		
METACISM excess of 'M'		
METAIRIE (produce sharing) Fr.		
METALLED (roads); plated		
METALLIC lustrous		
METALMAN metal-worker		
METAPHOR allegory; image		
METATOME an architectural space		
METAYAGE see Metairie		
METAZOAN⎱ multicellular		
METAZOIC⎰ construction of an		
METAZOON⎰ animal	**Z.**	
METECORN a corn issue		
METEORIC transient; dazzling; flashing		
METERAGE measurement		

METEWAND⎱ yard-stick	**Meas.**	
METEYARD⎰		
METHANOL methyl alcohol	**Chem.**	
METHINKS I think		
METHODIC systematic; orderly		
METHYLIC (methyl)	**Chem.**	
METHYSIS drunkenness	**Med.**	
METONYMY a trope		
ME-TOOISM		
METOPISM (frontal suture)	**Med.**	
METOPRYL anaesthetic	**Chem.**	
METRICAL rhythmic		
MEZEREON aromatic shrub	**B.**	
MIASMATA nauseous exhalations		
MICROBIC microbial	**Z.**	
MICROZOA animalculae	**Z.**	
MIDDLING mediocre; medium; average		
MIDNIGHT 24.00 hours		
MIDSHIPS	**Naut.**	
MIDWIVES		
MIGHTFUL powerful; dynamic		
MIGHTILY vigorously; potently		
MIGRAINE the vapours	**Med.**	
MIGRATED left; moved		
MIGRATOR emigrant; nomad; rover		
MILANESE (Milan)		
MILDEWED mouldy; musty; rusty		
MILDNESS gentleness; blandness		
MILEPOST milestone		
MILESIAN early Irish race		
MILITANT eager to fight; warring		
MILITARY martial; soldierly; warlike		
MILITATE oppose; contend; fight		
MILK-MAID dairy-maid		
MILK-TREE the messaranduba	**B.**	
MILK-WALK (a district)		
MILK-WARM		
MILK-WEED the sow-thistle	**B.**	
MILK-WORT flowering plant	**B.**	
MILKY-WAY a galaxy		
MILL-HAND factory operative		
MILLEPED centipede	**Z.**	
MILLIARD a thousand millions		
MILLIARE thousandth of an are (Fr.)		
MILLIBAR unit of barometric pressure		
MILLINER bonnet-maker		
MILLIPED milleped	**Z.**	
MILLPOND mere quiescence ?		
MILLRACE actuating stream		
MILLTAIL water past mill-wheel		
MILLWORK mill machinery		
MILTONIC (Milton)		
MIMICKED aped; took off; imitated		
MIMICKER impersonator; mime		
MINATORY menacing; threatening		
MINCE-PIE		
MINDLESS stupid; heedless		
MINGLING mixing; blending		
MINIATED illuminated		
MINIFIED depreciated		

MINIMENT muniment (obs.)
MINIMIZE treat slightingly
MINISTER servant; pastor; succour
MINISTRY agency; cabinet
MINORITE Franciscan friar   **Eccl.**
MINORITY the smaller number
MINOTAUR half man, half bull
MINSTREL ballad-monger
MINTMARK identification mark
MINUTELY particularly; exactly
MINUTEST smallest; tiniest
MINUTIAE small details
MINUTING recording; noting
MIRE-CROW black-headed gull   **Z.**
MIRINESS muddiness; swampiness
MIRRORED reflected
MIRTHFUL festive; jocund; vivacious
MISAIMED ill-directed
MISAPPLY pervert; misuse; abuse
MISARRAY disarray; disorder
MISBEGOT shapeless (Shak.)
MISCARRY to fail; be abortive
MISCHIEF injury; harm; hurt; trouble
MISCHOSE made wrong choice
MISCIBLE mixable
MISCLAIM claim in error
MISCOUNT reckon wrongly
MISCREED false creed
MISCUING (billiards)
MISDATED
MISDEALT (cards)
MISDOING wronging; offending
MISDOUBT suspicion; irresolution
MISDRAWN badly drawn
MISDREAD regard with dread
MISENTER to enter wrongly
MISENTRY erroneous record
MISERERE 51st Psalm   **Eccl.**
MISFAITH distrust; perfidy
MISFEIGN to disguise
MISFIELD cricket
MISFIRED did not go off
MISGRAFF⎱ to graft amiss
MISGRAFT⎰
MISGUIDE lead astray
MISHEARD
MISHMASH medley
MISHNAIC (Jewish Oral Laws)   **Law.**
MISHNOTH Jewish Oral Laws   **Law.**
MISINFER deduce erroneously
MISJUDGE misconstrue; mistake
MISLABEL address incorrectly
MISLAYER untidy person
MISLETOE also mistletoe   **B.**
MISLIKED disapproved; disliked
MISMATCH out-class
MISNAMED wrong appellation
MISNOMER incorrect appellation
MISOGAMY hater of marriage
MISOGYNY hatred of women

MISPLACE displace; mislay
MISPLEAD
MISPOINT punctuate improperly
MISPRINT typographical error
MISPRISE to mistake
MISPRIZE slight; undervalue; belittle
MISQUOTE
MISRATED rated erroneously
MISRULED governed badly
MISSERVE serve unfaithfully
MISSHAPE to deform
MISSPEAK utter wrongly
MISSPELL
MISSPELT an error in orthography
MISSPEND squander; misuse
MISSPENT wasted; dissipated
MISSTATE state falsely
MISTAKEN in error; wrong; incorrect
MISTEACH teach wrongly
MISTHINK think ill of
MISTIMED chronologically erroneous
MISTITLE use wrong title
MISTRAIN to educate amiss
MISTRESS lady of the house
MISTRIAL (jury fail to agree)   **Law**
MISTRUST want of confidence
MISTRYST to deceive (Sc.)
MISTUNED discordant
MISTUTOR to instruct amiss
MISUSAGE abuse; perversion
MISUSING misapplying; profaning
MISVOUCH to bear false witness
MISWRITE write incorrectly
MISYOKED mismatched
MITCHELL hewn Purbeck stone
MITHRAIC (Mithras)
MITIGANT alleviating; lenitive
MITIGATE lessen; allay; assuage
MITTENED wearing mitts
MITTIMUS a writ   **Law**
MIZZLING clearing off; drizzling
MNEMONIC aiding the memory
MOBILITY changeability; fickleness
MOBILIZE gather resources
MOBOCRAT demagogue
MOCCASIN⎱ leather shoe;
MOCCASIN⎰ venomous snake   **Z.**
MOCKABLE ridiculous; derisive
MODALISM Sabellian doctrine
MODALIST theorist
MODALITY logical custom
MODELLED fashioned; designed
MODELLER copyist; plastic planner
MODERATE so-so; fair; pacify; mollify
MODERATO at moderate pace   **Mus.**
MODESTLY decently; unobtrusively
MODIFIED altered; varied; changed
MODIFIER moderator
MODIOLAR like a bushel measure
MODISHLY foppishly; fashionable

388

MODULATE regulate; harmonize
MOFUSSIL rural districts (Hind.)
MOHARRAM Mohammedan fast **Eccl.**
MOIDERED spent; toiled
MOISTFUL damp; humid
MOISTURE humidity
MOLASSES treacle
MOLE-CAST a molehill
MOLE-EYED having small eyes
MOLE-HILL miniature mountain
MOLE-SKIN strong cotton fustian
MOLECULE group of atoms **Chem.**
MOLESTED troubled; pestered
MOLESTER an annoyer; harasser
MOLINIST a Jesuit **Eccl.**
MOLLIENT assuaging; softening
MOLLUSCA invertebrates **Z.**
MOLYBDIC (molybdenum) **Chem.**
MOMENTLY every moment
MOMENTUM impetus; impulsive weight
MONACHAL monastic **Eccl.**
MONANDRY (one husband only)
MONARCHO fantastic person (Shak.)
MONARCHY a kingdom; an empire
MONASTIC a monk **Eccl.**
MONAZITE a phosphate **Min.**
MONDAINE woman of fashion
MONDAYNE mundane (obs.)
MONETARY relating to money
MONETIZE to coin bullion
MONEYBOX cash-box
MONGERED dealt in
MONGOOSE mungoose **Z.**
MONIMENT monument; image (Spens.)
MONISTIC single-minded
MONITION a summons **Law**
MONITIVE warning
MONITORY cautionary
MONITRIX woman instructor
MONKEYED played about with
MONKFISH angler-fish **Z.**
MONKHOOD monastic state **Eccl.**
MONK-SEAL **Z.**
MONNIKER sobriquet; nickname
MONOCARP an annual plant **B.**
MONOCLED wearing an eye-glass
MONOCRAT autocrat
MONODIST writer of dirges
MONOGAMY (one wife)
MONOGONY asexual reproduction
MONOGRAM interwoven initials
MONOGYNY (one wife)
MONOLITH stone monument
MONOLOGY soliloquizing
MONOLULU Epsom Downs tipster
MONOMARK identification mark
MONOMIAL expressed by one term
MONOPODE single-footed
MONOPOLY exclusive privilege
MONORAIL single rail system

MONOTINT picture in one colour
MONOTONE unvaried tone
MONOTONY dull uniformity; tedium
MONOTYPE printing machine
MONOXIDE **Chem.**
MONSIEUR a Frenchman
MONTANIC mountainous
MONTEITH punch-bowl; kerchief
MONTEURS artificial flower makers
MONTICLE hillock; molehill
MONUMENT a memorial; cenotaph
MOOCHING loitering
MOONBEAM a lunar ray
MOONCALF monster; dolt
MOON-EYED purblind
MOON-SAIL a small sail **Naut.**
MOON-TYPE embossed lettering
MOON-YEAR lunar year
MOONFACE a round face
MOONFISH **Z.**
MOONLESS
MOONLING simpleton
MOONSEED climbing plant **B.**
MOONSHEE Moslem linguist
MOONWORT a fern **B.**
MOORCOCK red grouse **Z.**
MOORFOWL moorcock **Z.**
MOORGAME grouse **Z.**
MOORHAWK marsh harrier **Z.**
MOORLAND moreland; peaty soil
MOORWHIN a genista **B.**
MOORWORT marsh andromeda **B.**
MOOT-CASE a moot-point
MOOT-HALL judgment hall
MOOT-HILL a rendez-vous
MOOTABLE debatable; doubtful
MOPE-EYED myopic; purblind
MOPISHLY gloomily; dejectedly
MOQUETTE a carpet (Fr.)
MORALIST virtuous man
MORALITY ethics; virtue
MORALIZE philosophize
MORATORY delaying
MORAVIAN (John Huss)
MORBIDLY unhealthily
MORBIFIC causing disease **Med.**
MORELAND moorland
MOREOVER besides; also; likewise
MORESQUE arabesque
MORIBUND dying
MORILLON grape; duck **B., Z.**
MORMYRUS Egyptian pike **Z.**
MOROCCAN (Morocco)
MOROLOGY foolish talk
MOROSELY sullenly; sourly
MOROXITE a phosphate **Min.**
MORPHEAN sleepy; dreamy
MORPHEUS god of sleep
MORPHINE morphia **Med**
MORTALLY fatally; deadly

MORTARED (gun-fire; brickwork)
MORTGAGE pledge   **Law**
MORTISED jointed
MORTLING morling; dead sheep   **Z.**
MORTMAIN inalienable property **Law**
MORTUARY charnel house; morgue
MOSLINGS curried leather
MOSQUITO a raider   **Z.**
MOSS-BACK a Rip van Winkle
MOSS-CLAD mossy
MOSS-PINK a phlox   **B.**
MOSS-ROSE   **B.**
MOSS-RUSH   **B.**
MOSSLAND peat-land
MOTHBALL naphthalene, anti-moth
MOTHERED adopted
MOTHERLY parental; tender
MOTILITY movement; mobility
MOTIONAL emotional
MOTIONED gestured; proposed
MOTIONER a mover
MOTIVATE actuate; impel; induce
MOTIVITY power of energizing
MOTOR-BUS
MOTOR-CAR
MOTORIAL motory; giving motion
MOTORING travelling by car
MOTORIST
MOTORISE equip with motors
MOTORMAN chauffeur
MOTORWAY fast main road
MOTTLING variegating
MOUCHING slouching; skulking
MOUFFLON wild sheep   **Z.**
MOULD-BOX box for casting
MOULDING shaping; fashioning
MOULINET drum of capstan
MOULTING shedding feathers
MOUNDING banking
MOUNTAIN a light wine
MOUNTANT photographic paste
MOUNTIES R. Can. Mounted Police
MOUNTING embellishment; ascending
MOURNFUL lugubrious; grievous
MOURNING lamenting; sorrow
MOUSE-EAR a herb   **B.**
MOUTHFUL
MOUTHING con molto espressione
MOVABLES personal belongings; chattels
MOVELESS fixed; stationary
MOVEMENT agitation; crusade
MOVINGLY affectingly; eloquently
MOWBURNT (hay)
MUCCHERO rose and violet infusion
MUCEDINE a fungus   **B.**
MUCHNESS almost abundance
MUCILAGE gum   **B.**
MUCIVORA insects   **Z.**
MUCK-HEAP midden

MUCK-HILL dung-hill
MUCK-RAKE
MUCK-WEED white goosefoot   **B.**
MUCK-WORM a miser; a grub   **Z.**
MUCKERED made a muck of
MUCOSITY mouldiness
MUCULENT slimy; viscous
MUD-VALVE sediment valve
MUDARINE an extract   **B.**
MUDDLING confusing; deranging
MUDDYING miring
MUDGUARD a screen
MUFFLING deadening; shrouding
MUG-HOUSE ale-house
MUHARRAM a Moslem month
MULBERRY a fruit-tree   **B.**
MULCHING fertilizing
MULCTING fining; amercing
MULE-DEER N. American deer   **Z.**
MULETEER mule-driver
MULEWORT a fern   **B.**
MULISHLY obstinately; stubbornly
MULTEITY multiplicity
MULTIFID many cleft
MULTIPED with many feet
MULTIPLE a factor; numerous
MULTIPLY increase; augment; spread
MUMBLING muttering
MUMMYING embalming
MUNCHING chewing; masticating
MUNERARY donative
MUNGOOSE mongoose   **Z.**
MUNIMENT title-deed; stronghold
MUNITION military stores; equipment
MURALLED painted on a wall
MURDERED assassinated; slain
MURDERER a Cain
MUREXIDE a crystal   **Min.**
MURIATED soaked in brine
MURIATIC hydrochloric   **Chem.**
MURICATE prickly; thorny; spiky
MURIFORM like a wall
MURKSOME darksome; obscure
MURMURED complained; repined
MURMURER grumbler; grouser
MURRHINE (fluor-spar)   **Min.**
MUSCADEL muscatel   **B.**
MUSCATEL grape; wine   **B.**
MUSCULAR brawny; sturdy; powerful
MUSELESS artless
MUSHROOM upstart; blewit   **B.**
MUSICALE private recital
MUSICIAN instrumentalist   **Mus.**
MUSINGLY in contemplative fashion
MUSK-BALL perfumed sachet
MUSK-CAVY a rodent   **Z.**
MUSK-DEER   **Z.**
MUSK-DUCK Muscovy duck   **Z.**
MUSK-PEAR   **B.**
MUSK-PLUM   **B.**

MUSK-ROSE **B.**
MUSK-WOOD **B.**
MUSKETRY rifle-shooting
MUSLINET coarse muslin
MUSQUASH musk-rat **Z.**
MUSQUITO mosquito **Z.**
MUSTACHE moustache
MUSTAIBA Brazilian hardwood **B.**
MUSTERED assembled; gathered
MUTACISM mytacism
MUTATION discontinuous variation
MUTCHKIN pint (Sc.) **Meas.**
MUTENESS dumbness
MUTILATE maim; dismember
MUTINEER insurgent
MUTINIED rebelled; revolted; struck
MUTINOUS seditious; unruly; turbulent
MUTTERED mumbled; whispered
MUTTERER grumbler; grouser
MUTUALLY reciprocally
MUZZLING restraining; silencing
MYCELIUM mushroom spawn **B.**
MYCETOMA a foot disease **Med.**
MYCODERM fungoid pellice **Med.**
MYCOLOGY study of fungi
MYELITIS spinal disease **Med.**
MYLODONT (extinct sloth) **Z.**
MYOBLAST muscle making cell
MYOGRAPH recording machine **Med.**
MYOMANCY divination by mice
MYONOSUS⎫ muscular disease **Med.**
MYOPATHY⎭ **[Med.**
MYOSITIC⎫ muscular inflammation
MYOSITIS⎭
MYOSOTIS the forget-me-not **B.**
MYRIAPOD centipede **Z.**
MYRIARCH a commander
MYRICINE (bee's wax)
MYRMIDON desperate ruffian
MYRRHINE (myrrh) **B.**
MYSTICAL enigmatical; occult
MYTACISM excess of 'm' in speaking
MYTHICAL legendary; fabulous
MYTILITE fossil mussel **Z.**
MYTILOID mussel-like
MYXOPODA protozoans **Z.**

N

NACREOUS pearly; iridescent
NAILFILE manicurist's implement
NAILWORT Whitlow grass **B.**
NAINSOOK jaconet muslin
NAISSANT issuing (heraldic)
NAMEABLE identifiable
NAMELESS obscure; inglorious
NAMESAKE having identical name
NAPIFORM turnip-shaped
NAPOLEON nap; 20 francs **Coin**
NAPOLITE volcanic substance **Min.**

NARCEINE opium extract **Med.**
NARCISSI flowers **B.**
NARCOSIS stupefaction; stupor **Med.**
NARCOTIC anodyne; sedative; opiate
NARGHILE hookah-pipe; hubble-bubble
NARICORN horny beak **Z.**
NARIFORM beak-like
NARRATED recited; related; recounted
NARRATOR story-teller; historian
NARROWED contracted; cramped
NARROWER closer; nearer
NARROWLY nearly; barely; scarcely
NASALITY nosiness
NASALIZE enunciate nasally
NASCENCY growth; production
NASICORN horn-beaked **Z.**
NASIFORM nose-shaped
NATANTES water-spiders **Z.**
NATANTLY buoyantly
NATATION swimming
NATATORY of aquatic habits
NATHLESS nevertheless
NATHMORE never more
NATIONAL public; general; racial
NATIVELY by birth; naturally
NATIVITY birth; a horoscope
NATTERED querulous; grumbled
NATTIEST neatest; smartest
NATURISM nature worship
NATURIST
NAUMACHY a sea-fight
NAUPLIUS a shell-fish **Z.**
NAUSCOPY ship-sighting
NAUSEANT disgusting; revolting
NAUSEATE to loathe; to sicken
NAUSEOUS offensive; repulsive **[Naut.**
NAUTICAL marine; maritime; naval
NAUTILUS cuttlefish; diving bell **Z.**
NAVALISM sea power **Naut.**
NAVARCHY admiralship **Naut.**
NAVICERT naval permit **Naut.**
NAVICULA incense-boat
NAVIFORM art; boat-like
NAVIGATE voyage; cruise; steer; pilot
NAVY-BLUE ultramarine **Naut.**
NAZARENE of Nazareth
NAZARITE⎫ a sect of early
NAZIRITE⎭ Christians **Eccl.**
NAZIFIED Satanized
NEALOGIC adolescent
NEARCTIC N. of N. America
NEARHAND nigh; nearly
NEARNESS propinquity; closeness
NEATHERD cow-herd
NEATNESS spick and span; dexterity
NEBULOSE⎫ nebular; cloudy; hazy;
NEBULOUS⎭ misty; obscure
NECKATEE kerchief
NECKBAND collar
NECKBEEF coarse flesh

NECKLACE rivière; dog-collar
NECKWEAR scarves; ties; collars
NECROPSY post-mortem
NECROSIS mortification **Med.**
NECROTIC moribund
NECTARED honeyed
NEED-FIRE fire by friction
NEEDLESS unnecessary; superfluous
NEEDLING embroidering; sewing
NEGATING denying; disclaiming
NEGATION denial; dementi
NEGATIVE right of veto
NEGLIGEE loose apparel
NEGRITOS pygmies (Malay)
NEGROISM peculiarity of negro speech
NEIGHING whinnying
NEMALINE fibrous
NEMALITE hydrate of magnesia **Min.**
NEMATOID like a thread
NEMERTEA worms **Z.**
NEMOROSE growing in groves
NEMOROUS woody
NENUPHAR water-lily **B.**
NEO-LATIN modern Latin
NEOCRACY rule by upstarts
NEOLOGIC (novel words)
NEOPHRON genus of vultures **Z.**
NEOPHYTE novice; tyro; proselyte
NEOPLASM new tissue
NEPALESE a native of Nepal
NEPENTHE drug causing oblivion **Med.**
NEPHRITE jade **Min.**
NEPHROID kidney-shaped
NEPOTISM favouritism
NEPOTIST partial dispenser of office
NERONIAN (Nero)
NERVE-WAR fearful agitation
NESCIENT ignorant; unlettered;
NESCIOUS unaware; agnostic
NESTLING young bird **Z.**
NETHINIM temple servants (Heb.)
NETTLING irritating; provoking
NEURALGY neuralgia **Med.**
NEURITIS nerve inflammation **Med.**
NEUROSAL neurotic; temperamental
NEUROSIS nervous disease **Med.**
NEUROTIC highly strung
NEWBLOWN just blossoming
NEW-COMER late arrival
NEW-MODEL (Parliamentary Army)
NEWS-HAWK a reporter
NEWS-REEL topical film
NEWS-ROOM reading room
NEXTNESS proximity; propinquity
NIBBLING
NIBELUNG mythical Norse King
NICENESS precision; discrimination
NICKELIC of nickel
NICKNACK a trifle; gewgaw
NICKNAME a monniker; sobriquet

NICOTINE tobacco juice **B**
NIDERING rascal; coward
NIDOROSE smelling of cookery
NIDOROUS smelling of cookery
NIDULANT nestling
NIDULATE nestling
NIELLURE metal-work
NIFFNAFF a trifle; nicknack
NIFLHEIM region of mist (Scand.)
NIGERIAN (Nigeria)
NIGGLING finicking; trifling
NIGHNESS nearness; proximity
NIGHT-CAP cap or drink; horsehood
NIGHT-DOG nocturnal venatic hound
NIGHT-FLY nocturnal moth **Z.**
NIGHT-HAG a witch
NIGHT-JAR night-churr; goat-sucker
NIGHT-MAN scavenger
NIGHT-OWL **Z.**
NIHILISM extreme scepticism
NIHILIST Russian revolutionary
NIHILITY nothingness
NINE-EYES lampreys **Z.**
NINEFOLD 9 times
NINEPINS skittles
NINETEEN
NINEVITE of Nineveh
NISBERRY naseberry; medlar **B.**
NITRATED (nitric acid) **Chem.**
NITROGEN an inert gas **Chem.**
NOACHIAN (Noah); archaic; bygone
NOBBLING doping; injuring; swindling
NOBILITY distinction; aristocracy
NOBLEMAN a peer
NOBLESSE the nobility
NOCENTLY guiltily; culpably
NOCTILIO bat-genus **Z.**
NOCTUARY night record
NOCTURNE night scene **Mus.**
NODECUSP a curve
NODIFORM knotted
NODOSITY an entanglement
NODULOSE knotty; nodulous
NOEMATIC intellectual;
NOETICAL mental; thoughtful
NOISETTE a rose; an entrée **B.**
NOMADISM gipsy life
NOMADIZE wander with flocks
NOMARCHY provincial rule
NOMINATE designate; name; appoint
NOMISTIC lawful
NOMOGENY life origin
NOMOLOGY pyschology
NON-CLAIM failure to claim **Law**
NON-CREEP smooth flow additive **Chem.**
NON-ELECT not of the elect
NON-JUROR (Jacobite clergy) **Eccl.**
NON-MORAL amoral
NON-PARTY independent
NON-RIGID

NON-TOXIC not poisonous   **Med.**
NON-UNION (trades union)
NONESUCH without parallel; paragon
NONSENSE balderdash; inanity; trash
NOONTIDE midday
NORMALCY regularity; standard
NORMALLY usually; ordinary
NORSEMAN Scandinavian
NORTHERN
NORTHING distance northward
NORTHMAN
NORWEYAN Norwegian
NOSE-DIVE a plunge
NOSE-LEAF a bat appendage   **Z.**
NOSE-RING
NOSEBAND part of bridle
NOSELESS
NOSOLOGY } classification   **Med.**
NOSONOMY } of diseases
NOTALGIA backache   **Med.**
NOTANDUM a memorandum
NOTARIAL clerical   **Law**
NOTATION system of figures
NOTCHING nicking; scoring
NOTEBOOK
NOTELESS insignificant; petty; trivial
NOTICING observing; remarking
NOTIFIED made known; apprised
NOTIONAL fanciful; imaginative
NOTORNIS coot, (extinct) N.Z.   **Z.**
NOTTURNO emotional piece   **Mus.**
NOTWHEAT unbearded wheat   **B.**
NOUMENAL not phenomenal
NOUMENON a definite conception
NOVATIAN puritanical sect   **Eccl.**
NOVATION debt transference   **Law**
NOVELIST romancer; innovator
NOVELIZE to spin yarns
NOVEMBER
NOVENARY nine collectively
NOVERCAL like a step-mother
NOVERINT a writ   **Law**
NOWADAYS in these days; at present
NUBECULA cloudiness   **Med.**
NUBILITY marriage
NUBILOSE }
NUBILOUS } cloudy; overcast
NUCAMENT a catkin   **B.**
NUCELLUS nucleus of ovule   **B.**
NUCIFORM nut-like
NUCLEATE having a nucleus
NUCLEOLE small nucleus
NUDATION stripping
NUDENESS bareness
NUDISTIC scantily attired
NUGATORY ineffectual; futile; bootless
NUISANCE pest; annoyance; bother
NUMBERED reckoned; computed
NUMBERER counter; numerator
NUMBNESS torpor; stupefaction

NUMERARY not supernumerary
NUMERATE to number; to tell
NUMEROUS many; manifold; frequent
NUMMULAR numismatic
NUMSKULL blockhead; dunce
NUNCHEON luncheon
NUNDINAL (market day)
NUPTIALS a marriage
NURIMONO lacquer-ware (Jap)
NURSLING an infant; child
NURTURED brought up; tended
NUT-BROWN
NUT-SCREW monkey wrench
NUTARIAN nut-eater
NUTATION nodding
NUTHATCH small bird   **Z.**
NUTHOUSE lunatic asylum
NUTMEGGY like a nutmeg
NUTRIENT nourishing; alimental
NUTSHELL   **B.**
NUZZLING nestling
NYMPHAEA water-lilies   **B.**
NYMPHEAN } maidenly;
NYMPHISH } like a nymph

O

OAK-APPLE   **B.**
OAK-PAPER a wall paper
OAT-GRASS   **B.**
OATHABLE capable of being sworn
OBDUCING enveloping; covering
OBDURACY stubbornness; callousness
OBDURATE harsh; hardened; inflexible
OBEDIENT dutiful; submissive
OBEISANT reverencing; respectful
OBELIZED marked as spurious, (†)
OBERHAUS upper house (Ger.)
OBITUARY list of the dead`
OBJECTED protested; interposed
OBJECTOR opposer; heckler
OBLATION an offering; libation
OBLATORY donative; sacrificial
OBLIGANT bound by contract   **Law**
OBLIGATE oblige; pledge; mortgage
OBLIGATO of special import   **Mus.**
OBLIGING gratifying; constraining
OBLIQUED slanted
OBLIVION forgetfulness; (nepenthe)
OBSCURED eclipsed; clouded; dimmed
OBSCURER a concealer; hider
OBSERVED saw; remarked; obeyed
OBSERVER spectator; commentator
OBSESSED besieged; beset; haunted
OBSIDIAN volcanic rock   **Min.**
OBSOLETE discarded; archaic; effete
OBSTACLE hindrance; barrier; check
OBSTRUCT block; clog; impede; choke
OBTAINED got; won; earned; acquired
OBTAINER procurer; achiever

OBTECTED covered; hidden
OBTEMPER to comply with (Sc.) **Law**
OBTESTED besought; protested
OBTRUDED interfered; ejected
OBTRUDER intrudor; gate-crasher
OBTUNDED blunted; deadened
OBTURATE to close up; seal; shut
OBTUSELY stolidly; stupidly
OBTUSION bluntness
OBVERTED faced; confronted
OBVIATED avoided; prevented
OBVOLUTE wavy; enfolded   **B.**
OCCAMISM ⎫
OCCAMIST ⎬ doctrine of Occam **Eccl.**
OCCASION create; event; incident
OCCIDENT the west
OCCLUDED absorbed; shut up
OCCLUSOR a shutter; a valve
OCCULTED concealed; eclipsed
OCCULTLY secretly; reconditely
OCCUPANT holder; tenant; resident
OCCUPIED engaged; employed
OCCUPIER inhabiter
OCCURRED chanced; happened; befell
OCEANIAN (Oceania)
OCELLARY ⎫
OCELLATE ⎬ with spots like eyes
OCHEROUS yellow
OCHIDORE shore-crab   **Z.**
OCHLESIS ⎫ illness due to
OCHLETIC ⎬ overcrowding   **Med.**
OCHREATE sheathing   **B.**
OCHREOUS yellowish
OCHROITE cerite   **Min.**
OCTAPODY verse of 8 feet
OCTARCHY government by 8
OCTONARY referring to 8
OCTOROON one-eighth negro blood
OCTUPLET (eight notes)   **Mus.**
OCULARLY visibly; demonstrably
ODIOUSLY hatefully; offensively
ODOGRAPH distance and course meter
ODOMETER mileage recorder
ODONTIST dentist   **Med.**
ODONTOID toothlike
OENANTHE water dropwort   **B.**
OENOLOGY study of wine
OERLIKON light A.A. gun
OESTROUS female reproductive cycle
OFF-BREAK (cricket)
OFF-PRINT a reprint
OFF-SHOOT branch
OFF-SHORE
OFF-STAGE off the record
OFF-WHITE pale cream
OFFENDED violated; affronted
OFFENDER transgressor; delinquent
OFFERING tendering; proposing
OFFICIAL functional; authorized
OFT-TIMES frequently repeatedly

OHMMETER (resistance)   **Meas.**
OIL-FIELD
OIL-FIRED boiler; furnace
OIL-GLAND   **Med.**
OIL-PAPER transparent paper
OIL-PRESS
OIL-SKINS weatherproof garments
OILCLOTH linoleum
OILINESS greasiness; lubricity
OILSTONE whetstone
OINTMENT an unguent   **Med.**
OLD-TIMER old-stager
OLD-WORLD antiquated
OLEANDER an evergreen   **B.**
OLEASTER wild olive   **B.**
OLEFIANT oil producing
OLEOBROM developing process **Photo.**
OLIBANUM frankincense   **B.**
OLIPHANT elephant (obs.)   **Z.**
OLIVE-OIL   **B.**
OLIVETAN a Benedictine   **Eccl.**
OLYMPIAD period of 4 years
OLYMPIAN godlike
OLYMPICS games
OMADHAUN madman (Ir.)
OMELETTE
OMISSION oversight; failure; disregard
OMISSIVE exclusive; neglectful
OMITTING missing; skipping; dropping
OMNIFORM of all shapes; protean
OMOHYOID (shoulder-blade)   **Med.**
OMOIDEUM pterygoid bone   **Med.**
OMOPLATE shoulder-blade   **Med.**
OMPHALIC (navel)   **Med.**
OMPHALOS boss on a shield; hub
ONCE-OVER comprehensive glance
ONCIDIUM orchid genus   **B.**
ONCOLOGY science of tumours **Med.**
ONCOMING approach; advance
ONCOTOMY cutting a tumour   **Med.**
ONE-HORSE poorly equipped
ONE-SIDED partial; biassed
ONE-TRACK single interest or file
ONISCOID like a woodlouse   **Z.**
ONLINESS loneliness
ONLOOKER spectator; observer
ONOFRITE a mercury salt   **Min.**
ONOMANCY divination
ONRUSHES onsets
ONTOGENY embryonic development
ONTOLOGY metaphysics
ONYMATIC generic   **Z.**
OOLOGIST collector of bird's eggs
OOSPHERE an egg   **Z.**
OPALESCE to be iridescent
OPALIZED make like an opal
OPEN-EYED watchful
OPEN-WELL   **Arch.**
OPEN-WORK
OPENCAST outcrop; surface coal **Min.**

OPENNESS frankness; sincerity
OPERA-HAT a gibus
OPERATED performed; worked **Med.**
OPERATIC
OPERATOR workman; artisan; hand
OPERETTA short opera **Mus.**
OPHIDIAN reptilian **Z.**
OPHIDION conger eel **Z.**
OPHIURAN star-fish **Z.**
OPIFICER artificer
OPINABLE conjecturable
OPIUM-DEN
OPOPONAX a perfume; a gum **B.**
OPPILATE block up; obstruct
OPPONENT foe; rival; antagonist
OPPOSING resisting; withstanding
OPPOSITE contrary; adverse; inimical
OPPUGNED contested; fought
OPPUGNER adversary; competitor
OPTATIVE optional; elective; voluntary
OPTICIAN spectacle-maker
OPTIMACY the nobility
OPTIMISM hopefulness
OPTIMIST a sanguine person
OPTIMIZE take a bright view
OPTIONAL left to choice; discretional
OPULENCE wealth; affluence; profusion
OPULENCY riches; possessions
OPUSCULE a small work
ORACULAR portentous; ominous
ORANGERY orange garden
ORANGISM (William of Orange)
ORANGITE thorium silicate **Min.**
ORATORIO sacred musical drama
ORATRESS a woman orator
ORCADIAN (Orkney Islands)
ORCHANET alkanet **B.**
ORCHESIS art of dancing
ORDAINED bid; decreed; enjoined
ORDAINER assignor; prescriber **Eccl.**
ORDERING disposing; directing
ORDINANT candidate for orders **Eccl.**
ORDINANT a prelate **Eccl.**
ORDINARY a dinner; usual; customary
ORDINATE methodical; orderly
ORDNANCE guns; cannon; artillery
ORGANDIE figured muslin
ORGANIFY add organic matter
ORGANISM living structure
ORGANIST a player **Mus.**
ORGANIZE frame; constitute; construct
ORICHALC imitation gold
ORIENTAL Eastern
ORIENTED
ORIGINAL primitive; primeval; novel
ORILLION a bastion
ORINASAL mouth and nose sound
ORNAMENT embellishment; decoration
ORNATELY elaborately; in florid style
ORNITHIC referring to birds **Z.**

ORPHANCY orphanhood
ORPHANED parentless
ORPIMENT arsenic sulphide **Chem.**
ORTHODOX true; conventional; correct
ORTHOEPY correct pronunciation
ORVIETAN an antidote **Med.**
ORYCTICS fossils **Min.**
OSCINIAN (singing birds) **Z.**
OSCITANT drowsy; yawning
OSCITATE to gape
OSCULANT kissing
OSCULATE to buss
OSETROVA sturgeon; caviar **Z.**
OSMAZOME meat extract
OSNABURG coarse linen
OSSIANIC (Ossian)
OSSIFIED turned into bone
OSTEOZOA the vertebrata **Med.**
OSTERICK bistort plant **B.**
OSTIOLAR cellular
OTOSCOPE ear examiner **Med.**
OUISTITI marmoset **Z.**
OUTBLUSH outflush
OUTBOARD
OUTBOUND outward bound
OUTBRAVE defy; dare; challenge
OUTBREAK fray; riot; broil; revolt
OUTBURST eruption; ebullition
OUTCLASS excel; outvie; surpass
OUTCROSS (cross-breeding)
OUTDARED defied; flouted
OUTDATED outmoded; old-fashioned
OUTDOING surpassing; outstripping
OUTDOORS not at home
OUTDWELL outstay
OUTFACED braved
OUTFIELD (cricket)
OUTFLANK overlap
OUTFLASH outshine
OUTFLING sharp retort
OUTFLOWN
OUTFLUSH sudden glow of heat
OUTFROWN
OUTGOING expenditure; outlay
OUTGROWN
OUTGUARD outpost
OUT-HEROD
OUTHOUSE shed; shack; shanty; barn
OUTLAWED beyond the pale
OUTLAWRY exile; banishment
OUTLEAPT jumped over
OUTLEARN excel in learning
OUTLINED delineated; sketched
OUTLIVED outlasted
OUTLYING far; remote; distant
OUTMARCH
OUTMODED out of fashion
OUTPACED
OUTPOINT win (sport)
OUTPOWER overpower; vanquish

OUTRAGED insulted; maltreated
OUTRANGE extend further
OUTRAZED exterminated
OUTREACH exceed; surpass
OUTREIGN
OUTRIDER mounted attendant
OUTRIGHT at once; utterly
OUTRIVAL excel; outvie; beat
OUTROPER kind of bailiff **Law**
OUTSCOLD upbraid excessively
OUTSCORN despise; disdain; contemn
OUTSHINE eclipse; overshadow
OUTSHONE outrivalled
OUTSIDER not a favourite
OUTSIGHT outlook
OUTSKIRT border
OUTSLEEP
OUTSLEPT
OUTSLIDE
OUTSMART diddle; outwit; overreach
OUTSPEAK speak boldly
OUTSPENT over tired
OUTSPOKE
OUTSPORT outdo in sport
OUTSTAND resist; withstand
OUTSTARE
OUTSTOOD withstood
OUTSTRIP outrun
OUTSWEAR
OUTSWELL overflow
OUT-TO-OUT overall measurement
OUTVALUE appraise too highly
OUTVENOM
OUTVOICE talk down
OUTVOTED
OUTVOTER
OUTWARDS externally
OUTWATCH
OUTWEARY bore stiff
OUTWEIGH ⎱ exceed in value;
OUTWORTH ⎰ offset; overbalance
OUTWOUND extricated
OUTWREST extort by violence
OVARIOUS consisting of eggs **Z.**
OVEN-BIRD a tree-creeper **Z.**
OVER-AGED time expired
OVERALLS garments
OVERARCH overhang
OVERAWED quelled; intimidated
OVERBEAR overwhelm; domineer
OVERBLOW cover with blossom
OVERBODY embody excessively
OVERBOIL
OVERBOLD impudent; presumptuous
OVERBOWL cricket
OVERBRIM overflow
OVERBROW project
OVERBULK loom large
OVERBURN burn with zeal
OVERBUSY officious

OVERCAME vanquished; subdued
OVERCAST lowering; cloudy
OVERCLOY to surfeit
OVERCOAT
OVERCOLD too cold
OVERCOME defeat
OVERCROW to insult; exult; brag
OVERDATE post-date
OVERDONE
OVERDOSE
OVERDRAW
OVERDREW
OVERFALL tidal effect
OVERFAST
OVERFEED glut; cloy; satiate
OVERFILL
OVERFISH
OVERFLOW overrun; inundate; swamp
OVERFOLD inverted strata
OVERFOND doting
OVERFULL too full
OVERGAZE look over
OVERGIVE give lavishly
OVERGROW
OVERHAIR long outside hair
OVERHAND overarm
OVERHANG jut; impend
OVERHAUL repair; overtake; examine
OVERHEAD aloft
OVERHEAR eavesdrop
OVERHEAT
OVERJUMP neglect; pass by
OVERKILL excess of casualties (nuclear war)
OVERKIND indulgent
OVERKING control lesser kings
OVERKNEE (above the knee)
OVERLADE overburdened
OVERLAID ⎱ smothered
OVERLAIN ⎰
OVERLAND cross-country
OVERLEAF on the next page
OVERLEAP
OVERLIVE survive
OVERLOAD encumber
OVERLOCK
OVERLONG too long
OVERLOOK to slight; connive; condone
OVERLORD feudal superior
OVERMOST highest; topmost
OVERMUCH in excess
OVERNAME nickname; recount
OVERNEAT finicky
OVERNICE fastidious
OVERPAID
OVERPART overtask
OVERPASS disregard
OVERPAST gone; spent
OVERPEER to look down on; overlook
OVERPLAY gambling
OVERPLUS remainder; surplus

OVERRAKE to sweep over like a wave	
OVERRATE esteem too highly	
OVERREAD peruse (Shak.)	
OVERRENT exact too high a rent	
OVERRIDE trample; quash; annul	
OVERRIPE passé; past the prime	
OVERRULE prevail; repudiate; rescind	
OVERSEAM a seam	
OVERSEAS abroad	
OVERSEEN observed; overlooked	
OVERSEER superintendent; foreman	
OVERSELL	
OVERSEWN	
OVERSHOE a galosh	
OVERSHOT	
OVERSIDE overboard	
OVERSIZE out-size	
OVERSKIP leap over; overtrip	
OVERSLIP pass without notice	
OVERSMAN overseer; umpire	
OVERSOLD	
OVERSOUL divine principle	
OVERSPIN cricket	
OVERSTAY outstay	
OVERSTEP exceed; transgress	
OVERSWAY overrule	
OVERTÁKE pass	
OVERTASK overtax; overtoil	
OVERTILE imbrex, building	
OVERTILT upset	
OVERTIME	
OVERTONE harmonic	**Mus.**
OVERTRIP to trip along	
OVERTURE offer; proposal; prelude	
OVERTURN upset; invert; perturb	
OVERVEIL to cover	
OVERVIEW an inspection	
OVERWASH glacial formation	
OVERWEAR outdoor clothing	
OVERWEEN to be conceited	
OVERWIND (springs)	
OVERWISE too clever	
OVERWORK overtask	
OVERWORN threadbare	
OVERYEAR last year's	
OVIPOSIT to lay eggs	
OWL-GLASS malicious character (Ger.)	
OWL-LIGHT dusk	
OX-PECKER African bird	**Z.**
OXIDABLE oxidisable	
OXIDATOR	**Chem.**
OXIDIZED combined with oxygen	
OXIDIZER	
OX-TONGUE a plant	**B.**
OXYGONAL having acute angles	
OXYMORON bitter-sweet	
OZOKERIT waxen material	
OZONIZED (ozone)	

P

PABULARY alimentary	
PABULOUS nourishing	
PACHYOTE thick-eared	
PACHYPOD thick-footed	
PACIFIED calmed; lulled; assuaged	
PACIFIER tranquillizer; conciliator	
PACIFISM appeasement	
PACIFIST peace-maker	
PACK-LOAD load for an animal	
PACK-MULE	**Z.**
PACKETED made into a parcel	
PAD-CLOTH numnah	
PADDLING	
PADELION lady's mantle	**B.**
PADISHAH Turkish title	
PADUASOY corded silk	
PAGANISH heathen	
PAGANISM idolatry	
PAGANIST paynim; infidel	
PAGANIZE	
PAGINATE to number the pages	
PAGODITE pagoda-stone	**Min.**
PAGURIAN (hermit-crabs)	**Z.**
PAINLESS pangless	
PAINTBOX box of colours	
PAINTING a picture; limning	
PAINTOUT test of pigment	
PAIR-WISE in pairs	
PAITRICK a partridge (Sc.)	**Z.**
PAKISTAN	
PALAMATE web-footed	**Z.**
PALATIAL royal; magnificent; stately	
PALATINE with royal privileges	
PALE-EYED	
PALE-FACE a white man	
PALEBUCK the oribi	**Z.**
PALENESS wanness	
PALESTRA wrestling school	
PALILOGY repetition	
PALINODE recantation	
PALISADE a fortification	
PALL-MALL ancient croquet	
PALLIATE extenuate; mitigate; gloss	
PALLIDLY palely; wanly	
PALM-WINE	
PALMETTE palm-leaf decor	
PALMETTO fan-palm; hat	**B.**
PALMIPED web-footed	**Z.**
PALMITIN natural oil fat	
PALPABLE preceptible; evidently	
PALPABLY obviously; tangibly	
PALPATED handled; felt	
PALPIFER lobe of maxilla	**Z.**
PALPLESS absence of palpi	**Z.**
PALSTAFF } Celtic stone axe	
PALSTAVE	
PALSYING paralyzing	
PALTERED shuffled; quibbled	

PALTERER dodger; prevaricator
PALTRILY equivocately
PALUDINE marshy
PALUDISM malaria **Med.**
PALUDOSE boggy
PAMPERED coddled; humoured
PAMPERER over-indulgent person
PAMPHLET a broadsheet; brochure
PANAGHIA bishop's pendant **Eccl.**
PANCAKED landed flat
PANCARTE royal charter
PANCHEON earthenware pan
PANCREAS sweetbread **Med.**
PANDANUS (screw-pines) **B.**
PANDEMIC epidemic
PANDERED procured; ministered
PANDOWDY apple-charlotte
PANEGYRYeulogy;encomium;adulation
PANEL-SAW a cutting tool **Tool**
PANELESS no glass
PANELLED (walls; a jury)
PANGOLIN scaly ant-eater **Z.**
PANICKED terrorized; affrighted
PANICLED in clusters **B.**
PANIONIC (Ionian people)
PANNIKEL brain-pan; skull
PANNIKIN small vessel
PANOPTIC all seeing
PANORAMA extensive view
PANOTYPE antique photograph
PANSOPHY all wisdom
PANTHEON complete mythology
PANURGIC skilled in all craft
PAPALISM popery **Eccl.**
PAPALIST an R.C. **Eccl.**
PAPALIZE proselytize **Eccl.**
PAPERBOY newsagents' delivery boy
PAPERING decorating
PAPILLAE nipples **Z.**
PAPILLAR warty
PAPISHER a papist **Eccl.**
PAPISTIC popish **Eccl.**
PAPULOSE pimply
PAPYRINE like paper
PARABEMA Byzantine sacristy **Eccl.**
PARABLED used a parable
PARABOLA a conic section
PARABOLE similitude
PARACHOR molecular volume
PARADIGM example; model
PARADING displaying; flaunting
PARADISE Heaven; Eden; Elysium
PARAFFIN an oil **Min.**
PARAFORM fumigant; formaldehyde
Chem.
PARAGOGE literal addition
PARAGRAM a pun
PARAKEET paroquet; small parrot **Z.**
PARAKITE tailless kite
PARALLAX alternation; displacement
PARALLEL side by side

PARALOGY false reasoning
PARALYZE benumb; deaden; unnerve
PARAMERE an antimere **Z.**
PARAMOUR a lover; mistress
PARANEMA paraphysis **B.**
PARANGON matchless jewel
PARANOEA⎫ chronic monomania;
PARANOIA ⎰ hallucination **Med.**
PARAPSIS (thorax) **Z.**
PARASANG about 4 miles (Pers.) **Meas.**
PARASEVE Jewish Saturday night **Eccl.**
PARASHOT an anti-parachutist
PARASITE a sycophant; toady **Z.**
PARAVAIL inferior; cf. paramount
PARAVANE mine remover **Naut.**
PARAXIAL near to axis **Photo.**
PARCENER co-heir **Law**
PARCHING scorching; drying
PARCLOSE screen **Eccl.**
PARDONED excused; absolved
PARDONER (papal indulgences) **Eccl.**
PARENTAL affectionate; fatherly
PARERGON subsidiary work
PARGETED daubed; painted
PARGETER plasterer
PARHELIA mock suns
PARIETAL partitional
PARISIAN (Paris)
PARISITE a marble **Min.**
PARLANCE mode of speech
PARLAYED conferred; discussed
PARMESAN a cheese
PARODIED took off; burlesqued
PARODIST caricaturist
PARONYME similar sounding word
PAROQUET small parrot; parakeet **Z.**
PAROUSIA second Advent **Eccl.**
PAROXYSM fit; convulsion **Med.**
PARROTER copyist
PARROTRY servile imitation
PARRYING warding; frustrating
PARSONIC like a parson
PART-SONG glee **Mus.**
PARTAKEN consumed
PARTAKER sharer; partner
PARTERRE (flower beds, etc.)
PARTHIAN (Parthia)
PARTIBLE divisible
PARTIBUS marginal note **Law**
PARTICLE an atom; scrap; fragment
PARTISAN votary; adherent; halberd
PARTNERS a framework **Naut**
PART-TIME
PARTYISM party loyalty
PASCUAGE grazing
PASCUOUS growing in pastures
PASHALIK pasha's jurisdiction
PASILALY universal speech
PASS-BOOK bank-book
PASSABLE tolerable

PASSABLY acceptably; currently
PASSER-BY non-stop pedestrian
PASSERES perching birds **Z.**
PASSLESS trackless
PASSOVER Jewish feast **Eccl.**
PASSPORT a permit
PASSWORD watchword; countersign
PASTICHE a medley
PASTILLE medicated lozenge **Med.**
PASTORAL rustic
PASTORLY pastorlike; priestly
PASTRIES confectionary
PASTURED grazed
PATAGIUM wing membrane **Z.**
PATCH-BOX
PATCHERY botchery
PATCHING repairing; cobbling
PATELLAR (knee-cap) **Med.**
PATENTED
PATENTEE ⎫ one to whom a patent
PATENTER ⎭ is granted
PATENTOR issuer of a patent
PATERERO pederero; ancient gun
PATERNAL fatherly; parental
PATHETIC sad; grievous; emotional
PATHLESS no beaten track
PATIENCE cards; an opera
PATONCEE heraldic cross
PATRONAL condescending
PATTENED wearing clogs
PATTERED (rain)
PATTERER cheap jack
PATTY-PAN baking dish
PATULOUS spreading
PAULDRON a shoulder plate
PAUNCHED obese
PAVEMENT footway; sidewalk
PAVILION large tent; canopy
PAVISADO galley defence
PAVONINE like a peacock
PAWNSHOP
PAYCLERK
PAYSHEET
PEACEFUL placid; serene; pacific
PEACHERY a hothouse
PEACHICK young peafowl **Z.**
PEACHING divulging; informing
PEAGREEN a colour
PEAK-LOAD maximum activity **El.**
PEARL-ASH potash **Min.**
PEARL-EYE cataract **Med.**
PEARLIES coster's buttons
PEARLING diving for pearls
PEARMAIN an apple **B.**
PEASECOD pea-pid **B.**
PEASTONE limestone **Min.**
PEAT-MOOR peat-bog
PEAT-MOSS sphagnum **B.**
PEAT-REEK peat smoke
PECCABLE weak; frail; erring

PECCANCY sinfulness; offence
PECTINAL like a comb
PECTORAL breast-plate
PECULATE embezzle; steal; purloin
PECULIAR odd; singular; unusual
PECULIUM prerogative; privilege
PEDAGOGY instruction
PEDALIAN referring to feet
PEDALIER pedal keyboard
PEDALITY foot measurement
PEDALLED worked by foot
PEDALLER cyclist
PEDANTIC finical; exact; precise
PEDANTRY priggishness; conceit
PEDDLERY hawking
PEDDLING retailing; trifling
PEDERERO paterero; swivel gun (Sp.)
PEDESTAL plinth; base
PEDIATRY childish diseases **Med.**
PEDICURE foot treatment **Med.**
PEDIGREE lineage; stock; genealogy
PEDIMENT portico decoration
PEDIPALP whip-scorpion **Z.**
PEDIREME a crustacean **Z.**
PEDUNCLE stalk **B.**
PEEP-HOLE a chink
PEEP-O'-DAY dawn
PEEP-SHOW galanty-show
PEERLESS unrivalled; matchless
PEESWEEP peewit **Z.**
PEETWEET spotted sandpiper **Z.**
PEGAMOID imitation leather
PEGASEAN (Pegasus)
PEIGNOIR loose wrapper
PEJORATE deteriorate
PEKINESE small pug-nosed dog **Z.**
PELAGIAN (deep sea)
PELARGIC stork-like
PELASGIC early Grecian
PELE-MELE in disorder
PELERINE a tippet or cape
PELL-MELL promiscuously; confusedly
PELLAGRA acute anaemia **Med.**
PELLICLE thin skin or crust
PELLUCID transparent; vitreous; clear
PELORISM abnormality **B.**
PELT-WOOL wool from a hide
PELTATED shield-shaped
PEMMICAN dried meat
PENALIZE handicap; punish
PENCHANT inclination; turn; bent
PENCRAFT penmanship
PENDENCE suspense
PENDENCY indecision
PENDULUM swinging weight
PENELOPE currasow-bird (S. Amer.) **Z.**
PENITENT contrite; repentant
PENKNIFE pocket-knife
PENNORTH a pennyworth
PENNY-DOG a kind of shark **Z.**

PENOLOGY prison management
PENSTOCK duct to waterwheel
PENT-ROOF single sloped roof
PENTACLE five-pointed star
PENTAFID cleft in five
PENTAGON five sided figure
PENTELIC (marble) **Min.**
PENUMBRA partial shadow
PENWIPER
PENWOMAN authoress
PEOPLING populating
PEPERINO granular tufa **Min.**
PEPPERED hit with shot
PEPTOGEN digestive principle
PEPTONIC digestive
PEPYSIAN (Samuel Pepys)
PERACUTE very sharp or violent
PERCEIVE apprehend; discern; descry
PERCHING roosting
PERCLOSE screen; railing (Her.)
PERDENDO dying away **Mus.**
PERDURED endured; lasted
PERFORCE of necessity; forcibly
PERFUMED scented; odoriferous
PERFUMER perfume seller
PERFUSED sprinkled; bedewed
PERIAGUA a canoe (Sp.)
PERIANTH floral envelope **B.**
PERICARP seed-vessel **B.**
PERICOPE scriptural passage **Eccl.**
PERIDERM outer bark **B.**
PERIGEAL ⎫ (when moon's orbit is
PERIGEAN ⎭ nearest to the earth)
PERIGONE perianth **B.**
PERILLED endangered; risked
PERILOUS hazardous; risky; parlous
PERIODIC at stated intervals
PERIOTIC around inner ear
PERIPETY climax; solution
PERIPLUS circumnavigation
PERISCII polar people
PERISHED decayed; died; expired
PERISSAD (odd atomic valency) **Chem.**
PERJURED perfidious; forsworn
PERJURER false witness
PERLITIC vitreous obsidian **Min.**
PERMEATE penetrate; percolate; seep
PERMUTED exchanged; transmuted
PERNANCY rent in kind **Law**
PERNETTI kiln support
PERONEAL (fibula) **Med.**
PERORATE declaim; harangue
PEROXIDE a bleacher **Chem.**
PERRUQUE peruke; a wig
PERSICOT peach cordial
PERSIMON date-plum **B.**
PERSONAL distinctive; individual
PERSPIRE sweat
PERSUADE induce; sway; entice
PERTNESS sauciness; flippancy

PERTUSED punched
PERUSING reading; scrutinizing
PERUVIAN (Peru)
PERUVINE Peruvian balsam **B.**
PERVADED permeated; diffused
PERVERSE stubborn; vexatious
PERVIOUS porous; permeable
PESTERED plagued; harassed; worried
PESTERER tormentor; teaser
PESTLING pounding; abrading
PETALINE (petal) **B.**
PETALISM banishment; ostracism
PETALITE silicate of alumina **Min.**
PETALOID petal-shaped **B.**
PETALOUS having petals **B.**
PETERING calling at cards
PETERMAN a fisherman
PETIOLAR having a leaf-stalk **B.**
PETITION supplication; ask; beseeching
PETITION (of Right)
PETITORY petitioning; craving
PETRIFIC turning to stone
PETRONEL horse pistol
PETTIFOG quibble over details
PETULANT irritable; querulous; testy
PETUNTSE China clay **Min.**
PETWORTH variety of marble **Min.**
PEWTERER worker in pewter
PHACITIS eye inflammation **Med.**
PHALANGE finger-bone **Med.**
PHANTASM spectre; chimera
PHANTASY airy speculation; fancy
PHARISEE formalist
PHARMACY drug-store
PHEASANT a game bird **Z.**
PHENGITE species of mica **Min.**
PHENOLIC plastic mould
PHIALLED bottled
PHILABEG ⎫ the kilt
PHILIBEG ⎭
PHILOMEL the nightingale **Z.**
PHOCENIC (dolphins) **Z.**
PHONATED gurgled
PHONE-BOX call-box
PHONETIC vocal
PHORMIUM New Zealand flax **B.**
PHOSGENE poisonous gas **Chem**
PHOSPHAM ammonia compound
PHOSPHOR morning star; Venus
PHOTOPSY an eye trouble **Med**
PHRASING expressing; describing;
PHRYGIAN a Montanist [uttering
PHTHISIS consumption **Med**
PHYLARCH Greek tribal leader
PHYLETIC tribal
PHYLLITE clay-slate **Min**
PHYLLIUM leaf insects **Z**
PHYLLODE a form of leaf
PHYLLODY ⎫ leaf-like structure **B**
PHYLLOID ⎭

PHYLLOME foliage	**B.**
PHYSALIA Portuguese man-of-war	
PHYSALIS Cape gooseberry	**B.**
PHYSETER sperm whale	**Z.**
PHYSICAL material; corporeal; tangible	
PHYSIQUE bodily structure	
PHYTOMER phyton; plant unit	**B.**
PHYTOSIS vegetable parasites	**B.**
PHYTOZOA sea-anemones, etc.	**Z.**
PIACULAR atrociously bad	
PIANETTE small piano	**Mus.**
PIASSABA⎱ Brazilian palm; fibre used	
PIASSAVA⎰ for ropes and brooms	**B.**
PIAZZIAN like a piazza	
PICARIAN (woodpeckers)	**Z.**
PICAROON pirate; rogue	
PICCADIL high collar	
PICIFORM woodpecker type	**Z.**
PICK-ME-UP a cordial	
PICKEREL pike; dunlin	**Z.**
PICKETED enclosed; guarded	
PICKLING preserving	
PICKLOCK skeleton key	
PICKWICK a club	
PICOTITE a spinel	**Min.**
PICROMEL bile extract	**Med.**
PICTURED described; represented	
PIECENER a piecer; joiner of threads	
PIECRUST tart pastry	
PIEDNESS spotted diversity	
PIERCING keen; shrill; acute	
PIERHEAD jetty	
PIERIDES the nine Muses	
PIFFLING trifling; peddling	
PIG-FACED	
PIGEONED fleeced; swindled	
PIGEONRY pigeon loft	
PIGOTITE aluminium compound	**Min.**
PIGSTIES pig-pens	
PIG'S-WASH swill	
PIKEHEAD head of a pike	
PILASTER square column (arch.)	
PILCHARD sea-fish	**Z.**
PILE-WORK foundation of piles	
PILE-WORM teredo; boring worm	**Z.**
PILE-WORN threadbare	
PILE-WORT celandine	**B.**
PILEATED capped	
PILFERED filched; peculated	
PILFERER purloiner; embezzler	
PILIFORM slender as a hair	
PILLAGED ransacked; looted	
PILLAGER plunderer; rifler; robber	
PILLARED columnar	
PILLCORN oats	**B.**
PILLOWED cushioned	
PILLWORT a plant	**B.**
PILOSELY hairily	
PILOSITY hairiness	
PILOTAGE pilot's fee	

PILOTING directing; guiding; steering	
PIMELITE aluminium silicate	**Min.**
PIN-WHEEL firework; (clockmaking)	
PINACOID crystalline structure	
PINAFORE an opera; long apron	
PINASTER the cluster-pine	**B.**
PINCE-NEZ eye-glasses	
PINCHERS pincers; pliers	
PINCHING nipping; being frugal	
PINDAREE Mogul freebooter	
PINDARIC in the style of Pindar	
PINE-CLAD crowned with pines	
PINE-CONE fir-cone	**B.**
PINE-WOOD deal	
PINE-WOOL fibrous substance	
PING-PONG table tennis	
PININGLY longingly; languishingly	
PINIONED bound; shackled	
PINK-EYED having small eyes	
PINK-ROOT a vermifuge	**B.**
PINKSTER Whitsuntide; a pink flower	
PINMAKER	**[Eccl.**
PINMONEY an allowance	
PINNACLE apex; acme; zenith; crown	
PINNATED feathered	
PINNIPED fin-footed; a seal	**Z.**
PINOLEUM wood and canvas sunblind	
PINPATCH periwinkle	**B.**
PINPOINT locate exactly	
PINTABLE bagatelle gambling	
PIPE-CASE	
PIPE-CLAY a kaolin-like clay	**Min.**
PIPE-FISH sea-horse type	**Z.**
PIPE-LINE oil or water pipes	
PIPE-RACK	
PIPE-ROLL Great Roll of Exchequer	
PIPE-TREE the lilac	**B.**
PIPE-WINE wine from the cask	
PIPE-WORK a pipe-vein of ore	**Min.**
PIPERINE extract of pepper	**B.**
PIPEWORT pepperwort	**B.**
PIQUANCY pungency; raciness	
PIRATING infringing a copyright	
PIRIFORM pearshaped	
PISCATOR Isaac Walton; fisherman	
PISCINAL (fishpond)	
PISIFORM fishlike	**Z.**
PISOLITE coarse oolite	**Min.**
PISTACIA the pistachio-tree	**B.**
PISTOLET small pistol	
PITCHING flinging; casting; lurching	
PIT-FRAME framework round mine	
PITHECUS an ape	**Z.**
PITHLESS lacking energy; sapless	
PITIABLE sad; rueful; woeful; sorry	
PITIABLY deplorably; movingly	
PITILESS merciless; ruthless	
PITTACAL a blue dye	
PITTANCE dole; small allowance	
PITUITAL (pituitary gland)	**Med.**

PITYROID branlike
PIVOT-GUN swivel-gun
PIVOT-MAN key-man
PIVOTING moving round; hingeing
PIXY-RING fairy-ring
PLACABLE relenting; forgiving
PLACATED pacified; appeased
PLACEMAN office-holder
PLACENTA the afterbirth
PLACIDLY serenely; tranquilly; calmly
PLAGIARY literary theft
PLAGUILY pestiferously
PLAGUING tormenting; pestering
PLAINANT plaintiff **Law**
PLAITING pleating; braiding
PLANCHED planked
PLANCHET disc; a blank
PLANETIC planetary; revolving
PLANGENT resounding; reverberating
PLANKING flooring; putting down
PLANKTON drifting organic life **Z.**
PLANLESS unsystematic; aimless
PLANNING scheming; plotting; devise
PLANTAIN banana; a weed **B.**
PLANTING inculcating; inserting
PLANTLET a small shrub **B.**
PLANTULE embryo of a plant **B.**
PLANULAR (embryo of hydrozoa) **Z.**
PLASHING dabbling; splashing
PLASTERY plasterwork **Arch.**
PLASTRON breastplate
PLAT-BAND a border
PLATEFUL
PLATFORM scheme of action
PLATINIC (platinum) **Chem.**
PLATINUM metallic element **Chem.**
PLATONIC philosophical
PLATTING plaiting; weaving
PLATYPUS duck-bill **Z.**
PLAUSIVE plausible
PLAY-DEBT gambling debt
PLAY-MARE hobby-horse
PLAYABLE dramatic
PLAYBILL programme
PLAYBOOK book of dramas
PLAYGOER stage fan
PLAYMATE sportive companion
PLAYSOME frolicsome; wanton
PLAYTIME recreation
PLEACHED interwoven; plaited; matted
PLEADING arguing; disputing
PLEASANT welcome; delectable
PLEASING grateful; charming
PLEASURE indulgence; gladness; joy
PLEATING folding
PLEBEIAN popular; vulgar; ignoble
PLECTRUM quill for lyre **Mus.**
PLEDGING plighting; pawning
PLEIADES group of 7 stars
PLENARTY (benefice) **Eccl.**

PLEONASM verbosity
PLEONAST a spouter; demagogue
PLETHORA superabundance; surfeit
PLEURISY lung inflammation **Med.**
PLIANTLY easily bent; flexibly
PLICATED folded; involved; intricate
PLIGHTED betrothed
PLIGHTER one who pledges
PLIMMING becoming plump
PLIOCENE a geological strata
PLODDING slow but sure
PLOPPING dropping into water
PLOTTING contriving; planning
PLOUGHED furrowed; failed
PLOUGHER a husbandman
PLUCKILY courageously; valorously
PLUCKING stripping; (examinations)
PLUG-UGLY street ruffian
PLUGGING stopping; insistent
PLUM-CAKE
PLUM-DUFF a pudding
PLUMB-BOB (test for uprightness)
PLUMBAGO graphite **Min.**
PLUMBAGO blue or violet flower **B.**
PLUMBEAN leaden; dull; heavy
PLUMBERY lead work
PLUMBING sounding
PLUMBISM lead poisoning **Med.**
PLUMELET downy feather **Z.**
PLUMIPED feathered feet **Z.**
PLUMMING sinking a shaft
PLUMPEST fattest
PLUMPING going all out
PLUNGEON a sea-bird **Z.**
PLUNGING immersing; ducking
PLURALLY more than once
PLUTARCH a lively 2nd-century writer
PLUTONIC infernal; dark; igneous
PLUVIOUS rainy; pluvial; humid
POACHING stabbing; trespassing
POCHETTE a wallet
POCKETED filched; pouched
POCKMARK a scar **Med.**
POCKWOOD a hard wood **B.**
PODAGRAL ⎫
PODAGRIC ⎬ gouty **Med.**
PODALGIA neuralgia in foot **Med.**
PODARGUS genus of nocturnal birds **Z.**
PODISMUS spasm of foot **Med.**
POEMATIC poetical; lyric; metrical
POETICAL imaginative; rhyming
POETIZED versified
POIGNANT acutely painful; caustic
POIGNARD small dagger
POINDING distraining **Law**
POINTING directing; aiming; indicating
POISONED corrupted; envenomed
POISONER
POLARITY united opposites
POLARIZE magnetize

POLE-JUMP
POLE-STAR Polaris; a lode-star
POLEMAST (without a topmast) **Naut.**
POLEMICS controversies
POLICIES lines of conduct; parks
POLICING maintaining order
POLISHED smooth; burnished
POLISHER
POLITELY courteously; urbanely
POLITICS art of government
POLL-BOOK register of voters
POLLICES thumbs or great toes **Med.**
POLLINAR covered with pollen **B.**
POLLIWOG, POLLYWOG tadpole **Z.**
POLLSTER opinion taker
POLLUTED profaned; corrupted
POLLUTER defiler
POLONIUM radio-active element
POLTROON coward; dastard; craven
POLYFOIL circular ornamentation
POLYGAMY plurality of wives
POLYGLOT in several languages
POLYGRAM many sided figure
POLYOPIA multiple vision **Med.**
POLYPARY hard covering of polyps
POLYPIDE compound polyzoan **Z.**
POLYPODE having many feet
POLYPODY a fern **B.**
POLYPOID } resembling polyps;
POLYPOUS } octopus type **Z.**
POLYPOSE multi-pose portrait **Photo.**
POLYTYPE cast of an engraving
POLYZOAN colony of polyzoa **Z.**
POLYZOIC zoolatrous; sporozoic **Z.**
POLYZOON barnacle type **Z.**
POMANDER perfumed ball
POMIFORM like an apple
POMOLOGY apple culture **B.**
POMPEIAN (Pompeii)
POND-LILY **B.**
POND-WEED **B.**
POND-WORT water-soldier plant **B.**
PONDERAL ascertained by weight
PONDERED meditated; thought
PONDERER cogitator; ruminator
PONTIFEX a Roman pontiff
PONTIFIC priestly; papal **Eccl.**
PONTINAL bridging
PONY-SKIN soft hide
PONY-TAIL girl's hairstyle
POOH-POOH sneer at; deride
POOL-ROOM billiard-room
POONSPAR an Indian tree **B.**
POOR-JOHN salted hake
POOR-LAWS **Law.**
POOR-RATE a tax
POORNESS poverty; indigency
POPE-JOAN a card game
POPELING a would-be pope **Eccl.**
POPE'S-EYE fatty gland **Z.**

POPESHIP popehood **Eccl.**
POPINJAY parrot; coxcomb; fop
POPISHLY in popish style **Eccl.**
POPLITIC (knee-joint or ham) **Med.**
POPPLING bubbling
POPULACE rabble; mob; masses
POPULATE propagate
POPULINE aspen bark extract **B.**
POPULOUS thronged; crowded; dense
PORIFERA the sponges
PORIFORM like a pore
PORISTIC porismatic; inferential
PORK-CHOP
PORKLING young pig **Z.**
POROSITY porousness
POROTYPE a reproduction
PORPHYRY igneous rock **Min.**
PORPOISE sea-hog **Z.**
PORRIDGE
PORTABLE easily carried
PORTERLY coarse; vulgar
PORTESSE a breviary **Eccl.**
PORTFIRE an igniter
PORTHOLE passage for steam
PORTIERE doorway curtain
PORTLAND (stone; cement) **Min.**
PORTLAST gunwale **Naut.**
PORTMOTE court held in port **Law**
PORTOISE gunwale **Naut.**
PORTRAIT likeness; representation
PORT-ROPE rope for porthole lid
PORTUARY portable breviary **Eccl.**
POSEIDON sea-god; Neptune
POSITRON sub-atomic particle
POSHTEEN sheepskin coat
POSINGLY so as to puzzle
POSITING postulating; affirming
POSITION spot; post; locality
POSITIVE actual; real; true
POSOLOGY science of quantity **Med.**
POSSIBLE feasible; likely
POSSIBLY practically
POST-BILL placard
POST-CARD
POST-DATE cf. antedate
POST-FACT a later occurrence
POST-FREE postage paid
POST-HORN **Mus.**
POSTICHE wig; false hair
POSTLUDE conclusion **Mus.**
POST-NATI born after a certain date
POST-NOTE promissory note
POST-OBIT payable after death
POST-PAID prepaid
POST-TIME hour of despatch
POST-TOWN
POSTABLE mailable
POSTICHE counterfeit; coil of false hair
POSTIQUE added ornament
POSTMARK date stamp

POSTPONE defer; adjourn; shelve
POSTURAL postulatory
POSTURED posed
POSTURER acrobat
POT-BELLY a paunch
POT-HOUSE drinking booth
POT-METAL lead and copper alloy
POT-PLANT (grown in a pot) **B.**
POT-ROAST braised meat
POT-STICK stirring stick
POT-STILL malt whiskey
POTATION drinking bout
POTATOES **B.**
POTATORY draughty
POTENTLY forcibly; powerfully
POTHERED bothered; harassed
POTSHARD⎫
POTSHARE⎬ broken piece of
POTSHERD⎭ earthenware
POTSTONE soapstone **Min.**
POTTERED dawdled
POTTERER desultory worker
POTTOROO rat kangaroo **Z.**
POTULENT rather tipsy
POUCHING pocketing
POUCHONG black tea **B.**
POULAINE long pointed shoe
POULTICE a cataplasm
POUNCING sudden onset
POUNDAGE discount; taxation
POUNDING bruising; braying
POWDERED sprinkled
POWERFUL potent; puissant
POWERGAS coal-gas
POW-WOWED conferred
PRACTICE performance; wont
PRACTICK skilful; deceitful
PRACTISE to perpetrate; pursue
PRACTIVE adept; dexterous
PRAECIPE writ or instruction **Law**
PRAEFECT magistrate **Law**
PRAISING lauding; exalting; eulogizing
PRANCING bounding; capering
PRANDIAL concerning dinner
PRANGING crashing; bombing **Aeron.**
PRANKING displaying; gambolling
PRANKISH freakish; impish
PRASITES type of wine
PRATIQUE clearance certificate **Naut.**
PRATTLED babbled; chattered
PRATTLER chatterbox
PRE-ELECT choose beforehand
PRE-ENTRY previous to joining
PRE-EXIST
PRE-STUDY con; cogitate; ponder
PREACHED proclaimed; exhorted
PREACHER pastor; divine; declarer
PREAMBLE an introduction; preface
PRECEDED anticipated; headed; led
PRECINCT a close; enclosure

PRECIOUS dear; prized; treasured
PRECLUDE shut out; obviate; debar
PRECURSE a prognostication
PREDABLE raptorial; predacious
PREDATED antedated
PREDELLA altar decoration; stool **Eccl.**
PREENING tidying up; cleaning
PREFACED introduced by
PREFACER preface writer
PREFINED limited beforehand
PREFIXED anticipated; put before
PREGNANT prolific; fertile; fraught
PREHNITE silicate of alumina **Min.**
PREJUDGE condemn unheard
PRELUDED prefaced; started
PRELUDER prelude player
PREMIANT incentive
PREMIATE to reward
PREMIERE first performance
PREMISED introduced
PREMISES a message **Law**
PREMOLAR bicuspid tooth **Med.**
PREMORSE ending abruptly
PRENASAL in front of your nose
PRENATAL before birth
PRENOMEN Christian name
PRENTICE apprentice
PREORDER arrange beforehand
PREPARED provided; planned; made
PREPARER arranger
PREPENSE premeditated
PRESAGED foreboded; foretold
PRESAGER seer; soothsayer
PRESBYTE a far-sighted person
PRESCIND cut off; distract
PRESENCE mien; demeanour; company
PRESERVE conserve; defend; keep
PRESIDED controlled; officiated
PRESS-BED collapsible bed
PRESS-BOX reporter's box
PRESSING urgent; importunate; vital
PRESSION compression
PRESSMAN journalist
PRESSURE straits; urgency; stress
PREST-MAN an enlisted man
PRESTIGE reputation; fame; renown
PRESUMED surmised; thought
PRESUMER conjecturer
PRETENCE cloak; mask; guise
PRETERIT the past tense
PRETRIAL
PRETTIFY beautify; adorn
PRETTILY neatly; daintily
PREVIOUS antecedent; prior; former
PREVISED foreseen
PRICKING inciting; spurring
PRICKLED spiky
PRIDEFUL haughty; scornful
PRIESTLY sacerdotal **Eccl.**
PRIGGERY petty theft; haggling

PRIGGING larceny; pinching
PRIGGISH conceited; prim; affected
PRIGGISM coxcombry; pedantry
PRIMATES monkeys; archbishops **Z.**
PRIMEVAL antediluvian; pristine
PRIMMING decking; pranking
PRIMNESS formality; demureness
PRIMROSE a badge **B.**
PRINCELY regal; stately; lavish
PRINCEPS the original
PRINCESS
PRINCOCK a prig; coxcomb
PRINKING strutting; pranking
PRINTING typography
PRIORATE office of prior **Eccl.**
PRIORESS lady prior **Eccl.**
PRIORITY precedence
PRISMOID prismatic
PRISONED incarcerated; gaoled
PRISONER captive
PRISTINE original; ancient
PRIZEMAN a winner
PROBABLE credible; likely
PROBABLY maybe; peradventure
PROBATOR examiner; approver
PROCEEDS results; produce
PROCHEIN next; nearest **Law**
PROCINCT complete preparation
PROCLAIM bruit; trumpet; blazon
PROCURED got; obtained; acquired
PROCURER a pandar
PRODDING goading
PRODIGAL wasteful; reckless; lavish
PRODITOR traitor
PRODROME preliminary treatise
PRODUCED created; caused; made
PRODUCER generator; manufacturer
PROEMIAL introductory
PROFANED violated; debased
PROFANER blasphemer; desecrater
PROFILED outlined
PROFITED benefited; gained
PROFITER profiteer
PROFOUND deep; abysmal; occult
PROGGING begging food
PROGRESS advancement; growth
PROHIBIT interdict; forbid; ban
PROLAPSE fall down
PROLIFIC productive; fertile; fecund
PROLIXLY at great length
PROLOGUE dramatic preface; proem
PROLONGE rope; rings and toggle
PROMISED guaranteed; engaged
PROMISEE assured person
PROMISER⎱ assuror; warranter;
PROMISOR⎰ pledger; stipulator
PROMOTED elevated; preferred
PROMOTEE advanced person
PROMOTER active agent
PROMPTED suggested

PROMPTER encourager; (theatre)
PROMPTLY readily; quickly
PROMULGE announce; publish
PRONATED bent
PRONATOR an arm muscle **Med.**
PRONG-HOE a gardening tool
PRO-NYMPH a stage of insect life **Z.**
PROOFING testing; making waterproof
PROPENSE inclined; disposed
PROPERLY correctly; formally; exactly
PROPERTY quality; wealth; chattels
PROPHECY forecast; divination
PROPHESY to prognosticate; foretell
PROPLASM mould; matrix
PROPOLIS beeswax
PROPOSAL suggestion; tender
PROPOSED intended; meant; planned
PROPOSER mover; instigator
PROPOUND advocate; enunciate
PROPPAGE support
PROPPING shoring up
PROPRIUM self-hood; egotism
PROPYLON temple gateway
PRORATED assessed
PROROGUE adjourn; defer; postpone
PROSAISM prose writing
PROSAIST prosy person
PROSEMAN writer of prose
PROSPECT aspect; outlook; survey
PROSTYLE pillared portico
PROTASIS maxim; prologue
PROTATIC introductory
PROTEASE protein enzyme **Chem.**
PROTEGEE a ward
PROTEIDS albuminoids
PROTELES the aard-wolf **Z.**
PROTENSE extension (obs.)
PROTISTA organisms **B., Z.**
PROTOCOL treaty; draft agreement
PROTOZOA early life forms **Z.**
PROTRACT draw out; prolong; delay
PROTRUDE bulge; jut; project
PROVABLE demonstrable
PROVABLY verifiably
PROVIANT provender
PROVIDED if; supplied; yielded
PROVIDER furnisher; caterer
PROVINCE department; tract
PROVINED (vine culture)
PROVISOR purveyor; treasurer
PROVOKED exasperated; stung; vexed
PROVOKER inciter; annoyer; offender
PROWLING roving for prey; slinking
PROXIMAL adjoining; adjacent
PRUDENCE discretion; judiciousness
PRUINOSE⎱ powdery; mealy
PRUINOUS⎰
PRUNELLA self-heal plant **B.**
PRUNELLO dried plum **B.**
PRURIENT uneasy with desire

PRUSSIAN
PRYINGLY inquisitively; curiously
PSALMIST inspired singer — **Eccl.**
PSALMODY psalms collectively — **Eccl.**
PSALTERY stringed instrument — **Mus.**
PSAMMITE sandstone — **Min.**
PSELLISM stammering — **Med.**
PSITTACI the parrot tribe — **Z.**
PSYCHICS mental phenomena
PSYCHISM spiritualism
PSYCHIST psychologist
PTEROMYS flying squirrel — **Z.**
PTEROPOD class of molluscs — **Z.**
PTERYLAE clump of feathers — **Z.**
PTILOSIS plumage — **Z.**
PTOMAINE organic poison — **Med.**
PTYALISM salivation — **Med.**
PUBCRAWL round of taverns
PUBLICAN collector of tribute
PUBLICLY open to all
PUCELAGE virginity
PUCKBALL puffball — **B.**
PUCKERED wrinkled; crinkled
PUDDLING (clay; iron)
PUDICITY modesty
PUFF-BALL lycoperdon — **B.**
PUFF-BIRD S. American bird — **Z.**
PUFF-PUFF onomatopoeic locomotive
PUG-FACED monkey-faced
PUGGAREE scarf round helmet
PUGILISM the noble art
PUGILIST a pug; a boxer
PUISSANT powerful; forcible
PULINGLY fretfully; whiningly
PULLBACK a restraint
PULLOVER jersey; sweater
PULMONIC consumptive — **Med.**
PULPITER preacher — **Eccl.**
PULSATOR vibrator
PULSIFIC throbbing
PULVINAR a cushion
PUMICATE polish; make smooth
PUMP-DALE water trough
PUMP-GEAR
PUMP-HEAD ⎱ frame covering top
PUMP-HOOD ⎰ of pump
PUMP-ROOM
PUMP-WELL
PUNCHEON steel tool; large cask
PUNCHING perforating; striking
PUNCTATE pointed
PUNCTUAL punctilious; timely
PUNCTURE a hole; perforate; prick
PUNGENCE acridness
PUNGENCY keeness; acuteness
PUNINESS feebleness; frailty
PUNISHED chastised; penalized
PUNISHER disciplinarian
PUNITIVE punishing; penal
PUNITORY corrective

PUNTILLA lace-work
PUNTSMAN
PUPARIAL, PUPI- ⎱ a chrysalis; — **Z.**
FORM, PUPARIUM ⎰ pupa
PUPATION incubation — **Z.**
PUPILAGE wardship; minority
PUPILARY in statu pupillari
PUPILATE having a central spot
PUPIPARA viviparous insects — **B.**
PUPPETRY puppet-show; finery
PUPPYISH conceited
PUPPYISM affectation
PURBLIND dim-sighted
PURCHASE buy; procure; leverage
PURENESS purity; chastity
PURFLING embroidering
PURIFIED ceremonially cleansed
PURIFIER a refiner
PURIFORM resembling pus — **Med.**
PURISTIC scrupulously stylish
PURPARTY share of an estate — **Law**
PURPLING dyeing with purple
PURPLISH somewhat purple
PURPOSED resolved; meant; intended
PURPURIC madder-purple
PURSEFUL enough to fill a purse
PURSE-NET purse with strings
PURSLANE salad herb
PURSUANT conformably
PURSUING prosecuting; chasing
PURULENT suppurating — **Med.**
PURVEYED procured; retailed
PURVEYOR caterer
PUSEYISM tractarianism — **Eccl.**
PUSEYITE high church doctrinaire **Eccl.**
PUSHBALL a great ball game
PUSHBIKE a cycle
PUSHCART barrow; handcart
PUSHOVER easy success
PUSHPULL amplifier — **Electr.**
PUSS-MOTH — **Z.**
PUSS-TAIL a bristle grass — **B.**
PUSSY-CAT willow-catkin — **B., Z.**
PUSTULAR pimpled — **Med.**
PUTATION computation; sum
PUTATIVE reputed; alleged
PUTCHOCK root used for incense — **B.**
PUTTYING fixing panes
PUZZLING bewildering; perplexing
PYRAMOID of pyramid form
PYRENOUS globular; nucleiform — **B.**
PYREXIAL feverish — **Med.**
PYRIDINE organic compound — **Chem.**
PYRIFORM pear-shaped
PYRITIZE turn into pyrites
PYRITOUS like pyrites — **Min.**
PYROGRAM mechanical firework
PYROLOGY blowpipe analysis
PYROSOMA luminous animalculae — **Z.**
PYROSTAT a thermostat

YROXENE augite   **Min.**
YROXYLE gun-cotton   **Chem.**
YRRHOUS reddish
YTHONIC oracular
YXIDIUM lidlike capsule   **B.**

Q

QUACKERY charlatanism; humbug
QUACKING boasting
QUACKISH somewhat bogus
QUACKISM medical pretence
QUACKLED almost choked
QUADRANS Roman farthing   **Coin**
QUADRANT quarter-circle
QUADRATE square; to agree
QUADRIGA four-horsed chariot
QUADROON (quarter negro blood)
QUADRUNE gritstone   **Min.**
QUAESTOR treasurer
QUAFFING swallowing; imbibing
QUAGMIRE a bog; swamp
QUAGMIRY yielding; boggy
QUAILING flinching; blenching
QUAINTER odder; stranger
QUAINTLY whimsically; fancifully
QUAKERLY soberly
QUALMISH squeamish; queasy
QUANDANG Australian peach   **B.**
QUANDARY dilemma; predicament
QUANTIFY determine quantity
QUANTITY measure; amount; bulk
QUARRIED hewn
QUARRIER quarryman
QUARRIES arrows; panes of glass
QUARTERN a gill; 4 lbs.   **Meas.**
QUARTERS living places
QUARTILE (a planet aspect)
QUARTINE a seed covering   **B.**
QUASHING annulling; crushing
QUASSINE extract of quassia;   **Med.**
QUASSITE a febrifuge
QUATERON a quadroon
QUATORZE a count in piquet
QUATRAIN four line stanza
QUAVERED quivered; shook; vibrated
QUAVERER a warbler
QUAY-WALL harbour-wall
QUEASILY squeamishly
QUEBRADA a ravine (Sp.)
QUEEN-BEE   **Z.**
QUEENDOM queenly state
QUEENING playing the queen
QUEENLET a petty queen
QUEEREST quaintest; oddest
QUEERING spoiling; disarranging
QUEERISH rather strange
QUELLERZ limonite   **Min.**
QUELLING crushing; subduing; curbing
QUENCHED extinguished

QUENCHER a long drink
QUENELLE forcemeat
QUERCITE acorn extract   **B.**
QUERLING twirling
QUERYING challenging; inquiring
QUESTFUL adventurous
QUESTING seeking; searching
QUESTION interrogation; catechize
QUESTMAN authorized inquirer
QUEUEING lining up
QUIBBLED evaded the question
QUIBBLER prevaricator
QUICKEST speediest; fastest
QUICKIES inferior short films
QUICKSET living plant   **B**
QUIDDANY a mess of quinces
QUIDDITY captious question; quibble
QUIDDLED wasted time; pottered
QUIDDLER a trifler
QUIDNUNC tatler; know-all
QUIESCED silenced; subsided
QUIETAGE tranquillity
QUIETEST calmest
QUIETISE pacify
QUIETISM placidness
QUIETIST a mystic
QUIETIVE sedative
QUIETUDE rest; repose
QUILLING crimping; goffering
QUILL-NIB
QUILTING quilted work
QUINABLE interval of a fifth   **Mus.**
QUINCUNX plantation of 5 trees
QUINTAIN balanced tilting beam
QUINTILE aspect of the planets
QUINTOLE five-stringed viol   **Mus.**
QUIPPING taunting; jesting
QUIPPISH sarcastic
QUIRINAL Italian Court
QUIRINUS deified Romulus
QUIRITES Roman citizens
QUIRKING twisting
QUIRKISH evasive
QUISLING traitor; betrayer
QUIT-RENT rent in lieu of service
QUITTING deserting; ratting
QUIXOTIC romantic and absurd
QUIXOTRY notions and actions
QUIZZERY ridicule
QUIZZIFY hoax; puzzle
QUIZZING bantering; chaffing
QUOTABLE citable
QUOTIENT how many times
QUOTIETY proportionate frequency

R

RABATINE turned-down collar
RABBETED grooved
RABBINIC Hebrew language, etc.

RABBITER rabbit catcher
RABBITRY enclosure for rabbits
RABELAIS indelicate satirist
RABIDITY raving madness; frenzy
RABIETIC maniacal; insane; demented
RACE-CARD record of runners
RACE-GOER watcher of winners
RACEMOSE⎫ in clusters   **B.**
RACEMOUS⎭
RACEMULE small bunch   **B.**
RACHILLA leaf-rib   **B.**
RACHITIC rickety   **Med.**
RACHITIS rickets   **Med.**
RACINESS piquancy
RACK-RAIL toothed rail
RACK-RENT exorbitant rent
RACK-TAIL part of clock
RACK-WORK rack and pinion
RACKETED frolicked; clamoured
RACKETER a noisy person
RACOVIAN Polish Socinian
RADARMAN Radar petty officer R.N.
RADIALLY like spokes of a wheel
RADIANCE effulgence; lustre
RADIANCY brilliancy; glitter; sheen
RADIATED shone; sparkled
RADIATOR heating apparatus
RADICANT taking root
RADICATE to plant; emplant
RADICOSE having a large root   **B.**
RADICULE a small root   **B.**
RADIOING transmitting by wireless
RADIOLUS part of a feather   **Z.**
RADULATE (rasping tongue)   **Z.**
RAFFLING
RAFT-DUCK black-headed duck   **Z.**
RAFT-PORT (timber loading)   **Naut.**
RAFT-ROPE
RAFTERED timbered
RAFTSMAN
RAG-PAPER
RAG-WHEEL polishing wheel
RAGABASH ragamuffin
RAGGEDLY in tatters
RAGINGLY furiously; rabidly
RAGNAROK twilight of the gods
RAGSTONE impure limestone   **Min.**
RAILHEAD a terminus
RAILLERY banter; chaff; ridicule
RAILROAD railway
RAINBAND band in solar spectrum
RAINBIRD Jamaican bird   **Z.**
RAINCOAT waterproof
RAINCROW   **Z.**
RAINDROP
RAINFALL shower
RAINLESS
RAINPOUR downpour
RAINTREE S. American tree   **B.**
RAINWASH alluvial deposit

RAISINEE a confection
RAKEHELL a rip; debauchée
RAKISHLY set at an angle
RAKSHASA Hindu ghoul
RALLYING reuniting; gathering
RAMAYANA Indian epic poem
RAMBLING roaming; wandering
RAMBOOZE a cordial
RAMBUTAN Malayan fruit tree   **B.**
RAMICORN horny sheath
RAMIFIED diverse
RAMIFORM like a branch
RAMPAGED romped; rioted; gambolled
RAMPANCY excessive prevalence
RAMPSMAN highwayman
RAMRODDY stiff
RAMSHORN an ammonite   **Min.**
RAMULOUS ramulose; branching
RANARIUM frog aquarium   **Z.**
RANCHERO cow-puncher
RANCHING cattle-raising
RANCHMAN stockbreeder
RANCIDLY fustily; mustily; sourly
RANDOMLY at a venture; fortuitously
RANGIFER a reindeer   **Z.**
RANIFORM froglike   **Z.**
RANKLING festering; smouldering
RANKNESS overgrowth; exuberance
RANSOMED redeemed; released
RANSOMER liberator; indemnifier
RAPACITY greed; avarice; voracity
RAPE-CAKE cattle fodder
RAPE-SEED (hence colza oil)
RAPHANIA ergotism; blight
RAPHANUS radish   **B.**
RAPHIDES crystals in plants
RAPIDITY celerity; despatch; speed
RAPPAREE Irish robber; bandit
RAPTORES birds of prey   **Z.**
RAPTURED ravished; ecstatic
RAREFIED tenuous
RARENESS infrequency; scarceness
RARERIPE early ripe; untimely
RASCALLY knavish; roguish; dishonest
RASHLING reckless fellow
RASHNESS foolhardiness; unwariness
RASORIAL scratching
RAT-GOOSE brent goose   **Z.**
RATAPLAN beat of drum
RATCHETY jerky
RATE-BOOK book of valuations
RATEABLE assessable
RATHRIPE early ripe
RATIFIED confirmed; endorsed
RATIFIER approver; authorizer
RATIONAL reasonable; judicious; sane
RATIONED on an allowance
RAT'S-BANE rat poison
RAT'S-TAIL tapering
RATSNAKE rat-killing snake   **Z.**

RATTINET a woollen stuff
RATTLING quick; lively; clattering
RAVAGING despoiling; plundering
RAVEHOOK ripping iron **Tool**
RAVELLED entangled; untwisted
RAVENING plundering; devouring
RAVENOUS starving; voracious
RAVINGLY with fury; frantically
RAVISHED enchanted; charmed
RAVISHER abductor
RAW-BONED
RAWLBOLT ⎫ nail or screw
RAWLPLUG ⎭ wall fixing system
REABSORB
REACCESS fresh approach
REACCUSE indict again
REACHING extending; attaining
REACTION counter-measure; recoil
REACTIVE power to react
READABLE interesting
READABLY legibly
READJUST reset
REAFFIRM state anew
REAGENCY reflex influence
REALIZED felt; understood
REALLEGE assert again
REALNESS actuality; verity; fact
REANOINT
REANSWER reply again
REAPPEAR
REARGUED
REAR-LINE behind the army
REAR-RANK
REARMING re-equipping
REARMOST last; ultimate
REARWARD rear-guard
REASCEND climb again
REASCENT a further climb
REASONED argued; disputed
REASONER debater
REASSERT re-affirm
REASSESS re-impose; revalue
REASSIGN
REASSURE
REATTACH refix
REATTAIN get again
REAVOWED
REBATING deducting from
REBELLED revolted; mutinied
REBELLER a rebel; insurgent
REBELLOW re-echo
REBITING re-engraving
REBITTEN
REBOILED
REBRACED restrengthened
REBUFFED repulsed; snubbed
REBUKING chiding; carpeting
REBURIED re-interred
REBUTTAL refutation; retort
REBUTTED confuted; refuted

REBUTTER a legal reply **Law**
RECALLED revoked; annulled; denied
RECANTED retracted; abjured
RECAPTOR one who retakes
RECEDING retreating; ebbing
RECEIVED got; allowed; welcomed
RECEIVER a recipient; receptionist **Law**
RECENTLY lately
RECESSED dimpled; secluded
RECESSES niches; vacations
RECESSUS a recess; a niche
RECHARGE attack anew; reload
RECISION cutting back; pruning
RECITING rehearsing; relating
RECKLESS heedless; rash; headstrong
RECKLING weakest in a litter **Z.**
RECKONED considered; judged
RECKONER calculator; computer
RECLINED leant; lay; reposed
RECLINER a reclining dial
RECLOSED shut again
RECLOTHE provide new garments
RECOALED refilled the bunkers
RECOILED retreated; reacted
RECOILER flincher
RECOINED minted afresh
RECOLLET Franciscan monk **Eccl.**
RECOLOUR repaint
RECOMMIT refer again; re-entrust
RECONVEY transfer back
RECORDED entered; minuted **Law**
RECORDER flageolet; judge **Mus.**
RECOUPED indemnified
RECOURSE reference; resort; refuge
RECOVERY convalescence; revival
RECREANT craven; apostate
RECREATE refresh; delight
RECTORAL rectorial **Eccl.**
RECUBANT recumbent
RECUMBED reclined; reposed
RECURRED remembered; repeated
RECURVED bent back
RECUSANT An Elizabethan R.C. **Eccl.**
RED-BELLY terrapin; char **Z.**
RED-CEDAR pencil-wood **B.**
RED-CHALK reddle **Min.**
RED-CORAL **Min.**
RED-CROSS humanitarian organization
RED-EARTH reddish loam **Min.**
RED-FACED florid; rubicund
RED-METAL a copper alloy
RED-SHIRT follower of Garibaldi
RED-SHORT brittle
RED-STAFF millstone trimmer
REDACTOR editor
REDARGUE to refute; disprove
REDDENDA rent clauses **Law**
REDDENDO (vassal's duties) **Law**
REDDENED blushed; flushed
REDEEMED ransomed; freed; retrieved

o

REDEEMER liberator; saviour
REDELESS unwise; ill-advised
REDEMAND request again
REDEMISE reconveyance **Law**
REDENTED indented
REDEPLOY movement of army; industrial
REDIGEST reduce to form again
REDIRECT re-address
REDITION return
REDIVIDE re-allot
REDNOSED
REDOLENT aromatic; fragrant
REDOUBLE a bridge call
REDRIVEN herded back again
REDSHANK red-leg sandpiper **Z.**
REDUBBER old clo' merchant
REDUCENT reducing
REDUCING curtailing; abating
REDUVIUS predacious bug **Z.**
RE-DYEING
RE-ECHOED reverberated; repeated
REED-BAND clarionets, etc. **Mus.**
REED-BIRD bobolink **Z.**
REED-MACE cat's tail **B.**
REED-PIPE an organ pipe **Mus.**
REED-STOP an organ stop **Mus.**
REED-WREN greater reedwarbler **Z.**
REEDLESS no rush
REEDLING bearded titmouse **Z.**
REEF-BAND strip of canvas **Naut.**
REEF-KNOT not a granny
REEF-LINE a rope **Naut.**
REEL-LINE fishing line
REEL-RALL topsy-turvy (Sc.)
REEL-SEAT reel housing on rod
REELABLE able to be wound
RE-EMBARK
RE-EMBODY
RE-EMERGE
RE-ENFORCE reinforce
RE-ENLIST
RE-EXPORT
REFASTEN
REFERRED attributed; assigned
REFERRER enquirer
REFIGURE present anew
REFILLED replenished
REFINERY
REFINING purifying
REFITTED re-equipped
REFLEXED curved back
REFLEXLY reactively
REFLOWED ebbed
REFLOWER bloom again
REFLUENT flowing back
REFOREST plan anew
REFORGED
REFORMED remodelled; restored
REFORMER innovator
REFRAMED

REFREEZE
REFRINGE infringe
REFUNDED reimbursed; repaid
REFUNDER
REFUSING declining; repudiating
REFUTING gainsaying; rebutting
REGAINED retrieved; recaptured
REGALIAN regal; sovereign
REGALING faring sumptuously
REGALISM sovereignty
REGALITY royalty
REGARDED noticed; heeded; gazed
REGARDER observer; watcher
REGATHER recollect
REGICIDE killer of a king
REGILDED
REGIMENT organize; a military unit
REGIONAL topographical
REGIONIC local
REGISTER record; chronicle; fit
REGISTRY labour agency
REGNANCY predominance; supremacy
REGORGED vomited
REGRATED freshened; scraped
REGRATER huckster; regrator
REGROUND (razors); resharpened
REGROWTH new growth
REGULATE adjust; control; arrange
REGULIZE refine chemically
REHANDLE
REHASHED furnished up
REHEARSE recapitulate
RE-HEATED réchauffé
REHOUSED given new homes
REIGNING prevailing; governing
RE-IGNITE rekindle
REIMBODY re-incorporate
REIMPORT bring back
REIMPOSE retax
REINCITE reanimate
REINDEER the caribou **Z.**
REINFECT
REINFORM renotify
REINFUND pour in again
REINFUSE reanimate
REIN-HOOK bearing-rein hook
REINLESS unchecked
REINSERT put in again
REINSMAN accomplished driver
REINSURE
REINVENT create anew
REINVEST
REINVITE ask again
REISSUED
REJECTED excluded; rebuffed
REJECTOR decliner; rejecter
REJOICED exulted; gloried; delighted
REJOICER reveller; merry-maker
REJOINED knit together; reunited
REJUDGED re-examined; reconsidered

REKINDLE arouse anew; relight
RELANDED
RELAPSED retrogressed
RELAPSER backslider
RELATING narrating; telling
RELATION connection; kinsman
RELATRIX female informant **Law**
RELAXANT a loosener
RELAXING slackening; unbending
RELAYING (carpets; wireless)
RELEASED emancipated; freed
RELEASEE discharged person
RELEASER releasor; liberator
RELEGATE consign; transfer
RELESSEE releasee
RELESSOR releaser **Law**
RELEVANT applicable; apt; pertinent
RELIABLE trustworthy; trusty; safe
RELIABLY dependably
RELIANCE confidence; trust
RELICTED left bare **Law**
RELIEVED palliated; soothed; eased
RELIEVER mitigator; assuager
RELIGION faith
RELISHED appreciated
RELISTEN
RELIVING
RELOADED
RELUCENT transparent; shining
RELUMINE rekindle
REMAINED left over; stopped
REMAKING rebuilding
REMANENT remaining
REMANNED provided with a new crew
REMARKED said; declared; mentioned
REMARKER commentator; observer
REMARQUE marginal etching
REMEDIAL curative; healing
REMEDIED repaired; rectified
REMEMBER recall; recollect
REMERCIE to thank (obs.)
REMIFORM oar-shaped
REMINDED brought to notice
REMINDER keepsake; souvenir
REMISING releasing **Law**
REMISSLY negligently; slackly
REMITTAL surrender; remittance
REMITTED relaxed; forgave
REMITTEE consignee
REMITTER pardoner; remittor
REMOBOTH Syrian society
REMODIFY remodel
REMOLADE salad dressing
REMOLTEN
REMOTELY faintly
REMOTION remoteness (obs.)
REMOVING dislodging; abstracting
REMURMUR complain again
RENAMING rechristening
RENDERED translated; gave

RENDERER supplier; assignor
RENDIBLE able to be torn
RENEGADE ⎤ quisling; apostate;
RENAGADO ⎬ runagate; traitor;
RENEGATE ⎦ recreant; rebel
RENEGING revoking at cards
RENEWING renovating; rejuvenating
RENIDIFY build a new nest
RENIFORM kidney-shaped
RENIGATE renegade
RENITENT allergic; resistant
RENOUNCE disclaim; forsake; abjure
RENOVATE renew; repair; refresh
RENOWNED famous; eminent
RENOWNER swaggerer; braggart
RENTABLE leasable
RENTERER invisible mender
RENT-FREE
RENT-ROLL
RENUMBER
RENVERSE inverted; reverse
REOBTAIN
REOCCUPY
REOPENED
REOPPOSE
REORDAIN
REORIENT arising again
REPACIFY
REPAIRED redressed; went
REPAIRER restorer
REPARTEE witty retort; riposte
REPASSED
REPASTED fed
REPAYING refunding
REPEALED rescinded; annulled
REPEALER abrogator; revoker
REPEATED iterated; echoed
REPEATER a watch
REPELLED repulsed; checked; rebuffed
REPELLER deterrer; rejecter
REPENTED truly contrite; rued
REPEOPLE
REPERTOR a finder
REPERUSE read again
REPETEND recurring decimal
REPINING fretting; murmuring
REPLACED reinstated; restored
REPLACER a substitute
REPLEDGE
REPLEVIN a legal action **Law**
REPLUNGE dive again
REPLYING answering
REPOLISH
REPONING replacing **Law**
REPORTED communicated; related
REPORTER announcer; journalist
REPOSING reclining; resting
REPOSURE repose; peace; tranquillity
REPOTTED (gardening)
REPOUSSE embossed

REPRIEVE respite; pardon; acquit
RE-PRIMER recapping machine
REPRISAL retaliation; revenge
REPROACH reprimand; upbraid
REPROVAL admonition; censure
REPROVED blamed; rebuked; chided
REPROVER reprehender
REPRUNED
REPTILIA snakes   **Z.**
REPUBLIC democratic state
REPUGNED resisted; opposed
REPUGNER a rebel
REPULPIT restore a preacher
REPULSED checked; refused; rebuffed
REPULSER repeller
REPURIFY
REPUTING esteeming
REQUIRED wanted; demanded; lacked
REQUIRER exactor; claimant
REQUITAL recompense; punishment
REQUITED reciprocated
REQUITER avenger
RE-RAILED
REREFIEF an under-fief (Sc.)   **Law.**
REREWARD rear-guard
REROOFED
RESAILED sailed again
RESALUTE
RE-SCORED rearranged   **Mus.**
RESCRIBE rewrite
RESCRIPT edict; decree
RESCUING extricating; liberating
RESEARCH scientific enquiry
RESEATED
RESEIZED } legal seizure of   **Law**
RESEIZER } disseized property
RESEMBLE liken; compare; collate
RESENTED strongly objected; resisted
RESENTER an injured party
RESERVED shy; distant; unsociable
RESERVER withholder
RESETTER receiver of stolen goods
RESETTLE
RESIANCE residence
RESIDENT political agent
RESIDUAL left over
RESIDUUM residue; surplus; excess
RESIGNED abdicated; relinquished
RESIGNEE
RESIGNER renouncer; quitter
RESILING recoiling
RESINATA } Grecian white wine
RESINATE } of resinous flavour
RESINIFY }
RESINISE } to make resinous
RESISTED withstood; repelled; opposed
RESISTER opposer
RESISTOR   **Electr.**
RESMOOTH
RESOLDER solder again

RESOLUTE steadfast; staunch
RESOLVED melted; determined
RESOLVER solver
RESONANT resounding; sonorous
RESONATE re-echo; vibrate
RESORBED absorbed
RESORCIN crystalline phenol   **Chem.**
RESORTED betook; repaired; flew
RESORTER frequenter
RESOURCE expedient; means; device
RESOWING
RESPECTS compliments
RESPERSE disperse; sprinkle
RESPIRED inhaled
RESPITED postponed; reprieved
RESPOKEN repeated
RESPONSE answer; reply; rejoinder
RESTATED reaffirmed
REST-CURE
RESTLESS agitated; turbulent; uneasy
RESTORED returned; renewed; cured
RESTORER reviver; healer
RESTRAIN check; curb; suppress
RESTRICT limit; confine; hamper
RESTRIKE
RESTRING tennis; violin
RESULTED caused; followed; ensued
RESUMING renewing; continuing
RESUMMON call again
RESUPINE lying on the back
RESURVEY review
RETAILED gossiped; peddled
RETAILER not a wholesale merchant
RETAILLE divided twice, (Her.)
RETAINED detained; kept; withheld
RETAINER henchman; lackey; servant
RETAKING recapturing
RETARDED slowed up; delayed
RETARDER hinderer; obstructionist
RETENTOR retaining muscle   **Med.**
RETEPORE a coral   **Z.**
RETICENT taciturn; reserved; quiet
RETICULE lady's workbag
RETIERCE heraldic arrangement
RETIFERA the true limpet   **Z.**
RETIFORM meshed; reticulated
RETINITE obsidian; amber   **Min.**
RETINOID resin-like
RETINULA pigmented cells   **Z.**
RETIRACY retirement
RETIRADE a retrenchment
RETIRING shy; unobtrusive; diffident
RETORTED rejoined; replied (Her.)
RETORTER responder
RETOSSED thrown back
RETRACED returned by same route
RETRAXIT loss of action   **Law**
RETRENCH curtail; economize
RETRIEVE recover; regain; rescue
RETROACT oppose

RETRORSE bent back
RETRUDED thrust back
RETRYING
RETUNDED blunted
RETURNED rendered; reverted
RETURNER remitter
REUNITED rejoined
REURGING
REUSSITE magnesium compound **Min.**
REVALUED re-assessed
REVAMPED repatched
REVANCHE revenge (Fr.)
REVEALED disclosed; published
REVEALER betrayer; divulger
REVEHENT taking away
REVEILLE trumpet-call; dawn
REVELLED wantoned; feasted
REVELLER carouser
REVENGED requited; repaid
REVENGER vindicator
REVEREND respectful epithet
REVERENT submissive; humble
REVERING venerating; honouring
REVERIST a dreamer
REVERSAL complete change
REVERSED subverted; overthrew
REVERSER mortgager of land **Law**
REVESTED reappointed
REVETTED faced with masonry
REVIEWAL a critique
REVIEWED revised; edited; surveyed
REVIEWER an inspector; critic
REVILING aspersing; maligning
REVISING checking; amending
REVISION re-examination
REVISORY correctional
REVIVIFY reanimate; revive
REVIVING renewing; rousing
REVOKING repealing; quashing
REVOLTED felt disgust
REVOLTED rebelled
REVOLTER guerilla; partisan
REVOLUTE rolled back
REVOLVED rotated; wheeled; circled
REVOLVER a firearm
REVULSOR h. & c. apparatus **Med.**
REWARDED decorated; requited
REWARDER guerdon giver
REWORDED redrafted
RHABDITE rod-like structure **Z.**
RHABDOID spindle-shaped body **Z.**
RHABDOME lense supporter **Med.**
RHAETIAN (Rhaetia)
RHAGADES fissures of the skin **Med.**
RHAGODIA grapelike genus **B.**
RHAPSODE rhapsodist
RHAPSODY rambling composition **Mus.**
RHEOCORD resistance wire
RHEOLOGY formation of matter **Phys.**
RHEOSTAT (variable resistance)

RHEOTOME a switch
RHETORIC florid oratory
RHINIDAE sharks **Z.**
RHINITIS nasal inflammation **Med.**
RHINODON immense shark **Z.**
RHIZANTH flowering root **B.**
RHIZOGEN parasite plant **B.**
RHIZOMYS genus of mole-rats **Z.**
RHIZOPOD locomotive protozoa **Z.**
RHODANIC roe-red colour **Chem.**
RHODEINA gold-fish **Z.**
RHODITES genus of gall-flies **Z.**
RHOEADIC (poppy extract) **Chem.**
RHOMBOID quadrilateral figure
RHONCHAL bronchial **Med.**
RHONCHUS a râle **Med.**
RHOPALIC a hexameter
RHUBARBY cathartic **Med.**
RHYOLITE a quartz **Min.**
RHYTHMIC harmonious; metric; lilting
RHYTHMUS rhythm; cadence; verse
RIB-GRASS ribwort **B.**
RIB-NOSED like a baboon
RIB-ROAST beat soundly
RIBALDRY⎫ irreverent jesting;
RIBAUDRY⎭ obscenity
RIBBONED striped; streaked
RICE-BIRD the bobolink **Z.**
RICE-DUST rice-meal
RICE-GLUE a cement
RICE-MEAL
RICE-MILK milk with rice
RICE-SOUP
RICH-LEFT richly endowed
RICHNESS wealth; opulence; affluence
RICINIAE mites; ticks, etc. **Z.**
RICINIUM Roman mantle
RICKETLY shaky; weak; tottering
RICK-RACK openwork edging
RICKSHAW Indian or Chinese vehicle
RICOCHET rebound
RICOLITE ornamental stone **Min.**
RIDDANCE deliverance; release
RIDDLING perforating; sieving
RIDEABLE broken in
RIDICULE deride; lampoon; mock
RIFENESS prevalence
RIFFRAFF sweepings; refuse; rabble
RIFLEMAN modern musketeer
RIFLE-PIT short trench
RIGADOON lively dance
RIGATION irrigation
RIGHTFUL genuine; true; lawful
RIGHTING doing justice; rectifying
RIGIDITY stiffness
RIGORISM austerity
RIGORIST a martinet
RIGOROUS inflexible; severe; harsh
RILL-MARK corrugation
RIMIFORM having a rim

RIMOSITY roughness		**ROCCELLA** dyers' lichen	**B.**
RIMULOSE fissured		**ROCK-ALUM** alum stone	**Min.**
RINABOUT vagrant (Sc.)		**ROCK-BIRD** a pigeon	**Z.**
RIND-CALL defect in timber		**ROCK-CAKE**	
RING-BARK make a circular cut		**ROCK-CIST** a plant	**B.**
RING-BILL ring-necked duck	**Z.**	**ROCK-COOK** rock-fish	**Z.**
RING-DIAL portable sundial		**ROCK-CORK** asbestos	**Min.**
RING-DOVE cushat; wood-pigeon	**Z.**	**ROCK-CRAB**	**Z.**
RING-GOAL a ball game		**ROCK-DOVE**	**Z.**
RING-LOCK a puzzle lock		**ROCK-FIRE** firework mixture	
RING-MAIL chain armour		**ROCK-FISH** wrasse, bass, etc.	**Z.**
RING-NECK ring-plover		**ROCK-GOAT** ibex	**Z.**
RING-ROAD by-pass		**ROCK-HAWK** merlin	**Z.**
RING-ROPE a cable rope	**Naut.**	**ROCK-HEAD** bed-rock	**Min.**
RING-SIDE close to the scene		**ROCK-HEWN**	
RING-TAIL hen-harrier	**Z.**	**ROCK-LARK**	**Z.**
RING-TIME time for marriage		**ROCK-LILY** (various types)	**B.**
RING-WALL ring fence		**ROCK-LING** cod; haddock	**Z.**
RINGWISE experienced (sport)		**ROCK-MOSS** lichen	**B.**
RING-WORK mail construction		**ROCK-ROSE**	**B.**
RING-WORM skin disease	**Med.**	**ROCK-RUBY** a garnet	**Min.**
RINGBOLT embedded ring		**ROCK-SALT** native salt	**Min.**
RINGBONE callus on pastern		**ROCK-SEAL** common seal	**Z.**
RINGLETY with ringlets		**ROCK-SOAP** a kind of bole	**Min.**
RIPARIAN riparial; riverbanks		**ROCK-WOOD** ligniform asbestos	**Min.**
RIPENESS maturity; mellowness		**ROCK-WORK** a rockery	
RIPPLING flax cleaning		**ROCK-WREN**	**Z.**
RIPTOWEL reaping gratuity		**ROCKAWAY** American carriage	
RISE-BUSH a faggot		**ROCKETED**	
RISE-WOOD hedge cuttings		**ROCKETER** a high flier	
RISKIEST most reckless		**ROCKETRY** science of rockets	
RISORIAL ludicrous		**ROCKLESS**	
RITUALLY ceremoniously		**RODENTIA** rats	**Z.**
RIVALISE compete		**RODOMONT** vain boaster; braggart	
RIVALITY equality in rank		**ROENTGEN** unit of radiation	**Meas.**
RIVALLED emulated; vied; matched		**ROE-STONE** oolite	**Min.**
RIVER-BED a channel		**ROGATION** litany; supplication	
RIVER-GOD tutelary deity		**ROGATORY** interrogatory	
RIVER-HOG the capybara	**Z.**	**ROISTING** blustering; bullying	
RIVER-MAN		**ROITELET** kinglet; gold-crest	**Z.**
RIVER-PIE water-ousel	**Z.**	**ROLLBACK** price legislation	
RIVERINE riparian		**ROLL-CALL** famous picture	
RIVETING clinching		**ROLY-POLY** Swiss roll	
RIVULOSE wavy; rivose		**ROMANCED** economized the truth	
RIXATION brawl; quarrel		**ROMANCER** tall tale teller	
RIZZERED salted and sun-dried		**ROMANESE** Wallachian language	
ROAD-BOOK guide-book		**ROMANIAN** (Romania)	
ROAD-POST signpost		**ROMANISH** Catholic	**Eccl.**
ROAD-WEED plantago	**B.**	**ROMANIST** R.C.	**Eccl.**
ROAD-WORK highway repairs		**ROMANIZE** Latinize; convert	**Eccl.**
ROADLESS		**ROMANSCH** Swiss dialect	
ROADSIDE footpath; wayside		**ROMANTIC** quixotic; fanciful	
ROADSMAN road reqairer		**ROME-SCOT** Peter's pence	**Eccl.**
ROADSTER coachdriver; cycle		**ROMEWARD** verging on Romanism	
ROAN-TREE rowan tree; mountain ash		**RONCADOR** Pacific fish	**Z.**
ROASTING parching; bantering		**RONDELET** form of poem	
ROBORANT a tonic	**Med.**	**RONDELLE** ladder rung	
ROBURITE an explosive		**ROOD-ARCH** (over rood-screen)	
ROBUSTLY lustily; stoutly; sturdily		**ROOD-BEAM** beam supporting rood	
ROCAILLE scroll ornament		**ROOD-LOFT** gallery over screen	

ROOD-TREE Holy-rood; the cross	**ROTIFORM** wheel-shaped
ROODEBOK bush-buck **Z.**	**ROTTENLY** putridly
ROOF-TREE a beam	**ROTTLERA** dye yielding plant **B.**
ROOFLESS	**ROTURIER** plebeian
ROOMSOME spacious	**ROUGHAGE** litter
ROOSTING perching; lodging	**ROUGH-DRY** not ironed
ROOT-BEER dandelion ale	**ROUGH-HEW**
ROOT-CROP (esculent roots)	**ROUGHING** (ice-nails)
ROOT-FAST firmly rooted	**ROUGHISH** rather boisterous
ROOT-FORM	**ROULEAUX** bundles of fascines
ROOT-HAIR delicate filament **B.**	**ROULETTE** a game of chance
ROOT-KNOT an abnormality **B.**	**ROUND-ALL** acrobatic feat
ROOT-LEAF **B.**	**ROUND-ARM** (bowling)
ROOTLESS	**ROUND-TOP** masthead platform **Naut.**
ROPE-PUMP (by an endless rope)	**ROUNDERS** a game
ROPE-RIPE fit to be hanged	**ROUNDING** encircling
ROPE-WALK shed for spinning ropes	**ROUNDISH** not quite spherical
ROPE-YARN manilla; hemp; sisal etc.	**ROUNDLET** a small circle
ROPINESS stringiness	**ROUT-CAKE** cake for parties
ROQUETED (croquet)	**ROUTEING** selecting a route
RORIDULA sundew plants **B.**	**ROVINGLY** wanderingly
RORULENT dewy	**ROWDY-DOW** hubbub; uproar
ROSARIAN a rose fancier	**ROWDYISH** riotous; noisy
ROSARIUM rose garden	**ROWDYISM** turbulence; brawling
ROSE-BUSH **B.**	**ROWELLED** spurred
ROSE-DROP rose-flavoured orange **B.**	**ROXBURGH** a book-binding
ROSE-GALL an excrescence	**ROYALISM**
ROSE-HUED rosy	**ROYALIST**
ROSE-KNOT a rosette	**ROYALIZE**
ROSE-PINK sentimental	**RUBBISHY** trashy
ROSE-RASH German measles **Med.**	**RUBECULA** robin redbreast **Z.**
ROSE-ROOT herbaceous plant **B.**	**RUBEDITY** ruddiness
ROSE-TREE a standard rose **B.**	**RUBELLAN** magnesia mica **Min.**
ROSE-WOOD Brazilian timber tree **B.**	**RUBEZAHL** mountain imp (Ger.)
ROSE-WORM a caterpillar **Z.**	**RUBIANIC** madder-coloured
ROSE-YARD rose garden	**RUBICUND** ruddy; florid
ROSELITE cobalt arseniate **Min.**	**RUBIDIUM** metallic element **Chem.**
ROSEMARY aromatic plant **B.**	**RUBIFORM** like a ruby
ROSETTED having a rosette	**RUBRICAL** marked in red
ROSINESS rubicundity	**RUBSTONE** whetstone
ROSINING impelling; hustling	**RUBY-TAIL** cuckoo-fly **Z.**
ROSIN-OIL a lubricant	**RUBY-WOOD** red sandalwood **B.**
ROSMARUS walruses, etc. **Z.**	**RUCERVUS** East Indian deer **Z.**
ROSOGLIO red wine of Malta	**RUCKLING** crumpling; creasing
ROSTRATE beaked	**RUCKSACK** knapsack
ROSTROID like a rostrum	**RUDDLING** marking with ochre
ROSULATE having rosetted leaves **B.**	**RUDENESS** unmannerliness
ROSY-DROP a grog blossom	**RUDENTED** ornamented
ROSY-WAVE a moth **Z.**	**RUDIMENT** first principle; embryo
ROT-GRASS butterwort **B.**	**RUEFULLY** sorrowfully; regretfully
ROT-STEEP cotton purification	**RUFFLING** disturbing; agitating
ROTALIAN ⎫ protozoan **Z.**	**RUFULOUS** somewhat rufous
ROTALINE ⎭	**RUGBEIAN** (Rugby)
ROTALITE fossil rotalian **Min.**	**RUGGEDLY** jaggedly; unevenly
ROTARIAN (Rotary Club)	**RUGOSELY** wrinkly
ROTATING spinning; turning	**RUGOSITY** roughness
ROTATION revolution; series	**RUGULOUS** creased; rumpled
ROTATIVE in succession	**RUINABLE**
ROTATORY circulatory	**RUINATED** demolished
ROTIFERA animalculae **Z.**	**RULE-CASE** a printing tray

RULE-WORK tabulation
RULINGLY dominantly
RUM-BARGE a warm drink
RUM-SHRUB an odd decoction
RUMANIAN (Romania)
RUMBLING
RUMINANT chewing the cud   **Z.**
RUMINATE meditate; muse; ponder
RUMMAGED ransacked; rifled
RUMMAGER searcher
RUMOROUS vaguely heard
RUMOURED bruited; reported
RUMOURER a gossip; tatler
RUMPLESS having no tail
RUMPLING puckering; rimpling
RUNABOUT flivver; vagabond
RUNAGATE renegade; vagabond
RUNMAKER cricket
RUNNER-UP second
RUNOLOGY rune-craft
RUNRIDGE open-field husbandry
RUN-ROUND railway shunting
RUPICOLA cocks of the rock   **Z.**
RURALISM country life
RURALIST country bumpkin
RURALITY ruralness
RURALIZE rusticate
RUSH-HOUR commuter-time
RUSH-LILY   **B.**
RUSH-LINE football
RUSH-TOAD the natterjack   **Z.**
RUSHLIKE reedy; weak
RUST-MITE gall-mite   **Z.**
RUSTICAL rustic; sylvan
RUSTLESS stainless
RUSTLING cattle lifting
RUTABAGA Swedish turnip   **B.**
RUTHLESS pitiless; barbarous
RUTILANT shining
RUTILATE emit rays of light
RYE-GRASS   **B.**
RYOT-WARI } system of land
RYOT-WARY } tenure of India

S

SABAEISM star worship
SABBATIA gentian   **B.**
SABBATIC restful
SABBATON armoured boot
SABELINE sable type or skin   **Z.**
SABLIERE sand-pit
SABOTAGE wanton destruction
SABOTEUR a wrecker
SABOTIER a wearer of wooden shoes
SABULOUS sandy; gritty
SACCATED pouched
SACCULAR baggy; saclike; vesiculate
SACCULUS a small sac or cyst   **Z.**
SACELLUM makeshift altar   **Eccl.**

SACKLESS quiet; simple (Sc.)
SACK-RACE
SACREDLY divinely; holily
SACRISTY the vestry   **Eccl.**
SADDENED mournful; downcast
SADDLERY horse furniture
SADDLING loading
SADDUCEE Jewish ritualist   **Eccl.**
SADFACED gloomy; depressed
SAFENESS security; trustiness
SAFFRONY saffron coloured
SAFRANIN saffron dye   **Chem.**
SAGACITY wisdom; shrewdness
SAGAMORE American Indian chief
SAGE-COCK American grouse   **Z.**
SAGE-ROSE an evergreen   **B.**
SAGENESS sapience; sagacity; wisdom
SAGENITE crystals of rutile   **Min.**
SAGINATE pamper; fatten
SAGITTAL like an arrow
SAGO-PALM   **B.**
SAGUINUS marmoset   **B.**
SAHIB-LOG Europeans
SAIBLING the char   **Z.**
SAIKLESS sackless
SAIL-BOAT   **Naut.**
SAIL-FISH basking shark   **Z.**
SAIL-HOOP mast-hoop   **Naut.**
SAIL-LOFT (where sails are made)
SAIL-PLAN   **Naut.**
SAIL-ROOM   **Naut.**
SAIL-YARD spar for sails   **Naut.**
SAILABLE navigable
SAILLESS
SAINFOIN a fodder-plant   **B.**
SAINTISH rather saintlike
SAINTISM sanctimoniousness
SALACITY lust
SALAD-OIL olive-oil
SALADING salad vegetables   **B.**
SALARIED receiving wages
SALE-ROOM auction room
SALE-WORK work carelessly done
SALEABLE marketable
SALEABLY vendibly
SALESMAN sometimes a drummer
SALICINE extract of willow bark
SALIENCE prominence
SALIFIED made into salt
SALINITY saltness
SALITRAL saltpetre mine
SALIVANT]
SALIVARY]
SALIVATE } referring to saliva   **Med.**
SALIVOUS]
SALLYING dashing out
SALMONET young salmon   **Z.**
SALOPIAN from Shropshire
SALPICON Spanish savoury dish
SALSILLA edible tuber   **B.**

SALT-BUSH Australian plant	**B.**
SALT-CAKE sulphate of soda	**Min.**
SALT-COTE salt-pit	
SALT-FOOT (below the salt)	
SALT-JUNK salted beef	
SALT-LICK animals' rendezvous	
SALT-MINE	
SALT-WELL salt spring	
SALT-WORK salt factory	
SALT-WORT (several species)	**B.**
SALTLESS insipid; tasteless	
SALTNESS salinity	
SALUTARY beneficial	
SALUTING greeting; hailing	
SALVABLE rescuable	
SALVAGED saved	
SALVINIA genus of ferns	**B.**
SAMARIUM spectroscopic metal	**Chem.**
SAMAROID (winged fruit)	
SAMAVEDA Veda with chants	**Eccl.**
SAMBUCUS honeysuckle type	**B.**
SAMENESS monotony; similarity	
SAMPHIRE a herb	**B.**
SAMPLARY an example (obs.)	
SAMPLING matching	
SANATION a cure	
SANATIVE healing	
SANATORY curative; remedial	
SANCTIFY make holy; hallow	**Eccl.**
SANCTION ratification; approve	
SANCTITY holiness; godliness	
SAND-BALL pumice soap	
SAND-BAND protecting band	
SAND-BANK a shoal	
SAND-BATH (used by chemists)	
SAND-BEAR Indian badger	**Z.**
SAND-BIRD sandpiper	**Z.**
SAND-COCK redshank	**Z.**
SAND-CRAB the lady-crab	**Z.**
SAND-DART a moth	**Z.**
SAND-DUNE a ridge of drifted sand	
SAND-FISH	**Z.**
SAND-FLAG a sandstone	**Min.**
SAND-FLEA chigoe or jigger	**Z.**
SAND-HEAT heat of sand-bath	**Chem.**
SAND-HILL	
SAND-IRON a niblick	
SAND-LARK a wading bird	**Z.**
SAND-MOLE S. African rodent	**Z.**
SAND-PEEP American stint	**Z.**
SAND-PUMP (rock drilling)	
SAND-REED a shore grass	**B.**
SAND-REEL a windlass	
SAND-ROLL a casting	
SAND-SHOT small shot	
SAND-STAR starfish	**Z.**
SAND-TRAP sand eliminator	
SAND-WASP the digger-wasp	**Z.**
SAND-WELD	
SAND-WORM lob-worm; lug-worm	**Z.**

SAND-WORT genus Arenia	**B.**
SANDARAC realgar; resin	**Min. B.**
SANDEVER } glass scum in state	
SANDIVER } of fusion	
SANDWICH to interpose; intrude	
SANENESS sanity; mental equilibrium	
SANGAREE W. Indian drink	
SANGLANT bleeding	
SANGLIER wild boar	**Z.**
SANGRAAL holy grail	**Eccl**
SANGRADO a blood-letter; a leech	**Med.**
SANGREAL sangraal	
SANGUIFY to make blood	
SANGUINE optimistic; hopeful	
SANIDINE a felspar	**Min.**
SANITARY hygienic; healthful	
SANSKRIT ancient Indian language	
SANTALIC (sandal-wood)	**B.**
SANTALIN red dye	
SANTALUM sandal-wood genus	**B.**
SANTONIN wormwood	**Chem.**
SAP-GREEN	
SAPIDITY tastiness	
SAPIENCE wisdom; sagacity; intellect	
SAPINDUS the soapberry	**B.**
SAPI-UTAN wild ox, (Celebes)	**Z.**
SAPONIFY convert into soap	
SAPONINE soapwort extract	
SAPOROUS tasty; piquant	
SAPPHIRE blue, green or red gem	**Min.**
SAPREMIA blood poisoning	**Med.**
SAPUCAIA Brazil nut-tree	**B.**
SARABAND Spanish dance	
SARATOGA American travelling trunk	
SARCELLE a teal	**Z.**
SARCENET sarsenet; woven silk	
SARCINIC fungoid	**B.**
SARCITIS eye inflammation	**Med.**
SARCOCOL gum Arabic	**B.**
SARCODIC protoplasmic	**Z.**
SARCOSIS a tumour	**Med.**
SARCOTIC generating flesh	**Med.**
SARDELLE herring-like fish	**Z.**
SARDONIC ironical; cynical	
SARDONYX variety of onyx	**Min.**
SARGASSO sea of seaweed	
SARPLIER packing cloth	
SARRASIN a portcullis	
SARRIZIN buckwheat	**B.**
SARSENET sarcenet; woven silk	
SASH-DOOR door having panes of glass	
SASSANID a Persian ruler	
SASSOLIN native boracic acid	**Min.**
SASSOROL rock-pigeon	**Z.**
SATANISM devil worship	
SATANITY devilry; diablery	
SATELESS insatiable	
SATHANAS Satan	
SATIABLE appeasable	
SATIATED glutted; gratified	

SATIRIST lampoonist; ironic writer
SATIRIZE ridicule
SATRAPAL province of a satrap
SATURANT saturating
SATURATE soak; drench
SATURDAY
SATURNIA a moth genus **Z.**
SATURNIC (lead poisoning)
SATYRIUM orchid genus **B.**
SAUCEBOX impudent fellow
SAUCEPAN
SAUCISSE powder bag for use in mines
SAURLESS savourless; tasteless (Sc.)
SAURODON fossil fish **Min.**
SAURURUS pepper plants **B.**
SAUTERNE white wine
SAUTOIRE heraldic ribbon
SAVAGELY barbarously; inhumanly
SAVAGERY ferocity; brutality
SAVAGING maltreating
SAVANNAH savanna; a treeless plain
SAVEABLE rescuable; salvable
SAVINGLY thriftily; frugally
SAVOURED tasted
SAVOURLY well seasoned
SAVOYARD Gilbert and Sullivan
SAW-FLIES boring insects **Z.**
SAW-FRAME blade holder **Tool**
SAW-GRASS a marsh grass **B.**
SAW-HORSE cradle for sawing logs
SAW-TABLE
SAW-WREST a saw-set
SAWBONES a surgeon **Med.**
SAXATILE rock-inhabiting
SAXICAVA mollusc genus **Z.**
SAXICOLA the stone-chats **Z.**
SAXONDOM Anglo-Saxon world
SAXONISM a Saxon idiom
SAXONIST Saxon scholar
SAXONIZE
SCABBARD sheath
SCABBLED rough hewn; scappled
SCABIOSA teasel plants **B.**
SCABIOUS scurfy; itchy **B.**
SCAB-MITE a parasite **Z.**
SCABROUS rough; rugged
SCAFFOLD temporary structure
SCALABLE climbable; measurable
SCALARIA ladder-shells **Z.**
SCALAWAG scallywag; scamp
SCALDING
SCALDINO Italian brazier
SCALENUM scalene triangle
SCALENUS a muscle **Med.**
SCALIOLA imitation marble
SCALLION shallot; leek **B.**
SCALPING
SCAMBLED mauled; mangled
SCAMBLER gate-crasher
SCAMMONY convolvulus **B.**

SCAMPING shirking; skimping
SCAMPISH knavish; rascally
SCANDENT climbing
SCANDIUM a metal **Chem.**
SCANNING scrutinizing; viewing
SCANSION rhythm
SCANTIES light attire
SCANTILY meagrely; sparingly
SCANTING stinting
SCANTLED in small pieces
SCANTLET a small pattern
SCAPANUS shrew-moles **Z.**
SCAPHISM a Persian torture
SCAPHITE fossil ammonite **Min.**
SCAPHIUM beetle genus **Z.**
SCAPHOID boat-shaped
SCAPPLED rough hewn; scabbled
SCAPULAR (shoulder-blade); scarf
SCARABEE scarab; beetle **Z.**
SCARCELY hardly; barely
SCARCITY dearth; rarity; lack
SCARE-BUG a bugbear
SCARFING uniting timber
SCARF-PIN
SCARIDAE parrot-fish **Z.**
SCARIOUS dry; scaly
SCARITID (carabid beetles) **Z.**
SCARLESS unwounded; scatheless
SCARN-BEE dung-beetle **Z.**
SCARPHED (a timber joint)
SCARRING wounding; injuring
SCATCHES stilts
SCATHING bitterly severe; caustic
SCATHOLD open pasture ground
SCATLAND peat and pasture land
SCATTERY dispersed
SCAVENGE to collect refuse
SCELERAT villain
SCELIDES the hind-legs **Z.**
SCENARIO plan of a play
SCENE-MAN scene shifter
SCENICAL scenic; dramatic
SCENT-BAG animal's pouch **Z.**
SCENT-BOX
SCENTFUL highly odoriferous
SCEPTRAL regal
SCEPTRED kingly
SCHEDULE catalogue; inventory; list
SCHELLUM rascal; rogue
SCHEMING planning; intriguing
SCHEMIST projector; astrologer
SCHEROMA dryness of the eye **Med.**
SCHIEDAM schnapps; gin
SCHILLER bronze lustre
SCHISTIC laminated; slaty **Min.**
SCHIZOID tendency to dementia **Psych.**
SCHLÄGER duelling sword (Ger.)
SCHMALTZ grease (Ger); sentimental
SCHMELZE enamel (Ger.)
SCHNAPPS akvavit; firewater

SCHOENUS a sedge genus   **B.**
SCHOLION⎫ marginal note
SCHOLIUM⎭ in old classics
SCHOOLED disciplined; trained
SCHOONER large drinking glass
SCHOONER covered wagon   **Naut.**
SCIATICA neuralgia   **Med.**
SCIENTER knowingly; deliberately
SCIENTLY fully aware
SCILICET to wit; namely
SCIMITAR curved sword
SCINCOID the skink   **Z.**
SCIOGRAM radio photograph
SCIOLISM superficiality
SCIOLIST a know-all
SCIOLOUS shallow; skin-deep
SCIOPTIC (camera obscura)
SCIRRHUS cancerous tumour   **Med.**
SCISSILE able to be cut
SCISSION division
SCISSORS acrobatic feat; forfex   **Tool**
SCISSURA fissure; cleft
SCISSURE rupture division
SCIURINE⎫ rodent mammals,   **Z.**
SCIUROID⎭ squirrels, etc.
SCLERITE hardened tissue   **Med.**
SCLEROID ossified
SCLEROMA sclerosis   **Med.**
SCLEROUS bony
SCOFFING deriding; taunting; jeering
SCOFF-LAW contemptuous to law
SCOLDING nagging; chiding; rating
SCOLEINA earth-worms, etc.   **Z.**
SCOLOPAX woodcock genus   **Z.**
SCOLYTUS destructive beetle   **Z.**
SCOMFISH to nauseate (Sc.)
SCOONING skimming
SCOOP-NET a hand-net
SCOOPING ladling
SCOOTING decamping
SCOPARIA sweet bromweed   **B.**
SCOPEFUL with wide prospect
SCOPIDAE African wading birds   **Z.**
SCOPIPED having brushy feet   **Z.**
SCORCHED parched; charred
SCORCHER road-hog
SCORDATO out of tune   **Mus.**
SCORIOUS ashy; clinkery
SCORNFUL mocking; insolent
SCORNING spurning; scouting
SCORPION native of Gibraltar   **Z.**
SCOT-FREE untaxed
SCOTCHED wounded; blocked
SCOTOPIC night vision
SCOTSMAN
SCOTTICE in Scottish manner
SCOTTIFY
SCOTTISH Scots
SCOURAGE refuse water
SCOURGED chastised

SCOURING scurrying; scrubbing
SCOUTHER to scorn (Sc.)
SCOUT-LAW Boy Scout Code
SCOUTING rejecting; scorning
SCOWLING glowering; frowning
SCOWTHER a brief shower (Sc.)
SCRABBLE scribble; scrawl
SCRAGGED strangled; throttled
SCRAGGLY rough-looking
SCRAMBLE hurry; strife; clamber
SCRAN-BAG   **Naut.**
SCRANNEL squeaking; slender; meagre
SCRAPING abrading; rasping
SCRAPPED discarded; fought
SCRAPPLE to grub about; scrabble
SCRATCHY ragged; sketchy
SCRATTLE to scuttle
SCRAWLED scribbled
SCRAWLER slovenly writer
SCREAMED yelled; cried; squalled
SCREAMER tropical bird   **Z.**
SCREECHY shrill and harsh
SCREENED veiled; hidden; sieved
SCREEVER begging-letter writer
SCREW-KEY a spanner   **Tool**
SCREW-POD screw-bean   **B.**
SCREWING exacting; twisting; racking
SCRIBBET painter's pencil
SCRIBBLE scrawl; write
SCRIBING recording
SCRIBISM Jewish literature
SCRIGGLE wriggle
SCRIMPED stinted
SCRIMPLY miserly
SCRIVANO Italian clerk
SCRODDLE to variegate
SCROFULA the king's evil   **Med.**
SCROGGIE full of brushwood
SCROLLED convoluted
SCROOPED grated; cracked
SCROUGED squeezed
SCROUGER a whopper
SCROUNGE win; acquire by stealth
SCRUB-OAK stunted oak   **B.**
SCRUBBED scoured
SCRUBBER charlady
SCRUPLED hesitated; wavered
SCRUPLER demurrer; doubter
SCRUTINY close inquiry; search
SCUDDICK scuttock; a trifle; a shilling
SCUDDING speeding
SCUFFLED tussled
SCUFFLER brawler
SCULLERY
SCULLING rowing
SCULLION dish-washer
SCULPSIT he engraved it
SCULPTOR
SCUMBLED painted over
SCURRIED scampered; hastened

SCURRIES pony races	**SEA-PERCH** bass	**Z.**
SCURRILE scurrilous	**SEA-PIECE** seascape	
SCURVILY basely; shabbily	**SEA-PLANE** hydroplane; floatplane	
SCUTCHED separated	**SEA-PLANT** a seaweed	**B.**
SCUTCHER hedger	**SEA-POWER** strategic	
SCUTELLA sea-urchin genus **Z.**	**SEA-PURSE** eggcase of skate	**Z.**
SCUTIFER shield-bearer	**SEA-QUAIL** the turnstone	**Z.**
SCUTIPED having scaly shanks **Z.**	**SEA-QUAKE** marine earthwake	
SCUTTLED ran; bolted; scampered	**SEA-RAVEN** cormorant	**Z.**
SCUTTLER ship-sinker	**SEA-REEVE** customs officer	
SCUTTOCK see scuddick	**SEA-ROBIN** gurnard fish	**Z.**
SCYTHIAN (Scythia)	**SEA-ROVER** pirate; pirate ship	**Naut.**
SCYTODES a genus of spiders **Z.**	**SEA-SHARK** man-eater shark	**Z.**
SEA-ACORN a barnacle **Z.**	**SEA-SHELL** marine shell	**Z.**
SEA-ADDER stickle-back **Z.**	**SEA-SHORE** the beach	
SEA-APRON a seaweed **B.**	**SEA-SHRUB** a sea-fan	**Z.**
SEA-ARROW flying squid **Z.**	**SEA-SNAIL** the periwinkle	**Z.**
SEA-BEACH sea-shore	**SEA-SNAKE** sea-serpent	**Z.**
SEA-BEAST a sea monster **Z.**	**SEA-SNIPE** sandpiper	**Z.**
SEA-BELLS bindweed **B.**	**SEA-SQUID** cuttle-fish	**Z.**
SEA-BOARD the coast	**SEA-STICK** herring cured at sea	
SEA-BORNE shipped	**SEA-SWINE** porpoise	**Z.**
SEA-BRANT brent goose **Z.**	**SEA-TENCH** black sea-bream	**Z.**
SEA-BREAM mackerel type **Z.**	**SEA-THONG** cord-like seaweed	**B.**
SEA-CHART	**SEA-TROUT**	**Z.**
SEA-COAST sea-shore	**SEA-WATER** brine	
SEA-CRAFT seamanship	**SEA-WOMAN** mermaid	
SEA-DAISY the lady's cushion **B.**	**SEA-WRACK** coarse seaweed	**Z.**
SEA-DEVIL ray; angel-fish **Z.**	**SEAFARER** voyager	
SEA-DRAKE sea-crow **Z.**	**SEAGOING** sea-worthy	
SEA-EAGLE the osprey **Z.**	**SEAL-PIPE** a dip pipe	
SEA-FIGHT marine engagement	**SEAL-RING** signet ring	
SEA-FRONT shore promenade	**SEAL-SKIN** pelt; fur	
SEA-FROTH foam	**SEAL-WORT** Solomon's seal	**B.**
SEA-GATES (tidal basin)	**SEAMANLY** seamanlike	
SEA-GAUGE ship's draught	**SEAMIEST** most sordid	
SEA-GOOSE a dolphin **Z.**	**SEAMLESS** in one piece	
SEA-GRAPE glasswort **B.**	**SEAM-RENT** a tear at the seam	
SEA-GRASS the thrift **B.**	**SEAMSTER** one who sews	
SEA-GREEN marine colour	**SEARCHED** quested; probed; sought	
SEA-GROVE under-water grove	**SEARCHER** inquirer; examiner	
SEA-HEATH **B.**	**SEARNESS** dryness; sereness	
SEA-HOLLY the eryngo **B.**	**SEARWOOD** dry wood	
SEA-HORSE the walrus **Z.**	**SEASCAPE** sea-piece	
SEA-HOUND dog-fish **Z.**	**SEASONAL**	
SEA-JELLY sea-blubber	**SEASONED** matured; inured	
SEA-LEECH an annelid **Z.**	**SEASONER** a relish	
SEA-LEMON a doridoid mullusc **Z.**	**SEAT-BACK** loose cover	
SEA-LEVEL mean tide level	**SEAT-LOCK** a catch	
SEA-LOACH a gadoid fish **Z.**	**SEAT-MILE** transport statistic	
SEA-LOUSE a parasite **Z.**	**SEAT-RAIL** a crosspiece	
SEA-LUNGS a comb-jelly **Z.**	**SEAT-WORM** pin-worm	**Z.**
SEA-MARGE sea-shore	**SEBESTAN** ⎱ a tree with	**B.**
SEA-MELON sea-cucumber **Z.**	**SEBESTEN** ⎰ plumlike fruit	
SEA-MOUSE the dunlin; a worm **Z.**	**SEBUNDEE** Indian militia-man	
SEA-NYMPH an Oceanid	**SECAMONE** shrubby climber	**B.**
SEA-ONION a squill **B.**	**SECATEUR** pruning shears	**Tool**
SEA-OTTER marine otter **Z.**	**SECEDING** withdrawing; retiring	
SEA-OXEYE sea-shore plant **B.**	**SECERNED** secreted	
SEA-PEACH sea-squirt **Z.**	**SECESHER** a secessionist	

SECLUDED aside; shut off
SECONDED aided; transferred
SECONDER supporter; abettor
SECONDLY
SECRETED cloaked; concealed
SECRETLY privily; covertly
SECTATOR an adherent
SECTORAL in a sector
SECUNDUM according to (Latin)
SECURELY fast; safely
SECURING acquiring; getting
SECURITE an explosive
SECURITY safety; surety; pledge
SEDATELY calmly; seriously; soberly
SEDATIVE tranquillizing; soothing **Med.**
SEDERUNT Court Session (Sc.) **Law**
SEDGE-HEN marsh-hen **Z.**
SEDILIUM chancel seat **Eccl.**
SEDIMENT lees; dregs; grounds
SEDITION treason; mutiny; rebellion
SEDUCING enticing; inveigling
SEDUCTOR tempter; corrupter
SEDULITY assiduity; diligence
SEDULOUS industrious; busy
SEED-BIRD water-wagtail **Z.**
SEED-CAKE
SEED-COAT husk **B.**
SEED-CORN **B.**
SEED-DOWN down on cotton, etc. **B.**
SEED-FISH spawn; roe **Z.**
SEED-FOWL grain-fed bird **Z.**
SEED-GALL
SEED-LEAF a cotyledon **B.**
SEED-LEAP seed-basket
SEED-LOBE seed-leaf **B.**
SEED-PLOT a hot-bed
SEED-TICK a parasite **Z.**
SEED-WOOL cotton-wool and seeds
SEEDLESS pipless
SEEDLING young plant **B.**
SEEDSMAN dealer; sower
SEEDTIME sowing season
SEEDY-TOE a horse disease
SEER-FISH seir-fish **Z.**
SEERSHIP (soothsaying)
SEESAWED oscillated
SEETHING boiling
SEGREANT rampant and salient (Her.)
SEIDLITZ mineral water **Min.**
SEIGNEUR lord of the manor
SEIGNIOR seigneur; feudal lord
SEIR-FISH seer-fish **Z.**
SEIZABLE apprehendable
SEIZLING the carp **Z.**
SEJUGOUS (six pairs of leaflets) **B.**
SELADANG Malayan tapir; bison **Z.**
SELAMLIK men's quarters (Turk)
SELECTED chosen; culled; preferred
SELECTOR picker
SELENATE a selenic salt **Chem.**

SELENIDE a compound **Chem.**
SELENITE gypsum **Min.**
SELENIUM a chemical element **Chem.**
SELF-BORN self-begotten
SELF-HEAL burnet saxifrage **B.**
SELF-HELP unaided effort
SELFHOOD conscious personality
SELFLESS unselfish
SELF-LIFE indulgence
SELF-LIKE twin
SELF-LOVE self-seeking
SELF-MADE
SELFNESS egotism
SELF-PITY
SELFSAME identical; equivalent
SELF-WILL obstinacy
SELF-WISE self-conceit
SELICTAR Turkish sword-bearer
SELLABLE saleable; marketable
SELVAGEE untwisted rope
SELVEDGE woven border
SEMANTIC significant; expressive
SEMBLANT resembling; like
SEMESTER period of six months
SEMI-ACID
SEMI-BULL a papal bull **Eccl.**
SEMI-COPE outer monastic garment
SEMI-DOME
SEMI-FLEX to half bend
SEMI-MUTE half deaf
SEMI-NUDE barely clothed
SEMI-OPAL **Min.**
SEMI-OPEN sport
SEMI-OVAL
SEMI-RING
SEMINARY academy; college; school
SEMINATE propagate; sow
SEMINOLE American Indian
SEMIOTIC sign language
SEMITAUR half-bull; half-man
SEMITISM Hebrew idiom
SEMITIST Hebrew scholar
SEMITONE musical interval **Mus.**
SEMOLINA⎱ granules of flour
SEMOLINO⎰ manna; grits
SEMPLICE simply **Mus.**
SEMPSTER seamstress
SEMUNCIA Roman coin **Coin**
SENARIUS verse of six feet
SEND-DOWN expel; rusticate
SENG-GUNG Java badger **Z.**
SENGREEN the houseleek **B.**
SENILITY dotage; old age
SENNIGHT a week
SENONIAN geological formation
SENORITA Spanish young lady
SENSEFUL judicious; rational
SENSIBLE intelligent; wise; discreet
SENSIBLY sagaciously; sanely
SENSIFIC exciting

SENSUISM sensuality
SENSUIST amorist; materialist
SENSUOUS aesthetic; voluptuous
SENTENCE doom; maxim; clause
SENTIENT perceptive
SENTINEL sentry; watchman; warder
SENTRIES watchers
SENTRY-GO sentry duty
SEPALINE (leaf of calyx) **B.**
SEPALODY ⎫ reversion of **B.**
SEPALOID ⎭ petals to sepals
SEPALOUS sepaline **B.**
SEPARATE sort; divorce; sever
SEPIACEA cuttlefish **Z.**
SEPIIDAE cephalopods **Z.**
SEPIMENT hedge; boundary
SEPTARIA turtle-stones **Min.**
SEPTATED divided into cells **B.**
SEPTETTE (seven performers) **Mus.**
SEPTFOIL the tormentil **B.**
SEPTICAL putrefying **Med.**
SEPTUARY group of seven
SEPTULUM small cell **B.**
SEPTUPLE sevenfold
SEQUENCE continuity; series
SERAFILE serrefile
SERAGLIO a harem
SERAPHIC angelic; sublime
SERAPHIM celestial being **Eccl.**
SERAPIAS genus of orchids **B.**
SERENADE ⎫ open air musical
SERENATA ⎭ composition **Mus.**
SERENELY tranquilly; calmly; placidly
SERENEST calmest; most tranquil
SERENISE glorify
SERENITY peacefulness; quiet
SERGEANT serjeant
SERGETTE thin serge
SERIALLY consecutively
SERIATIM in regular order
SERICATE silky; downy
SERICITE potash mica **Min.**
SERIFORM Chinese writing
SERINGHI Indian viol **Mus.**
SERJEANT sergeant
SERMONER preacher **Eccl.**
SERMONET short address
SERMONIC admonitive **Eccl.**
SEROSITY (exuding serum) **Med.**
SEROTINE species of bat **Z.**
SERPETTE pruning knife (Fr.) **Tool**
SERPLATH 80 stone (Sc.) **Meas.**
SERPOLET wild thyme **B.**
SERRANUS perch; bass **Z.**
SERRATED notched; like a saw
SERRATUS a thorax muscle **Z.**
SERRIPED with serrated feet **Z.**
SERVIENT subordinate; slavish; abject
SERVIOUS obsequious; sycophantic
SERVITOR waiter; henchman

SESAMOID (toe bones) **Med.**
SESTERCE Roman 2d. coin **Coin**
SESTETTE sextet **Mus.**
SESTOLET sextuplet **Mus.**
SET-ASIDE reserve(d)
SET-PIECE stage scene
SETIFORM bristly
SETTLING colonizing; deciding; fixing
SETULOSE prickly; spinate; spicate
SEVERELY rigorously; strictly
SEVERING disrupting; sundering
SEVERITY harshness; austerity
SEWELLEL mountain beaver **Z.**
SEWER-GAS
SEWERAGE drainage
SEXAGENE angle of 60 degrees
SEXANGLE a hexagon
SEXTETTE sextet **Mus.**
SEXTUPLE sixfold
SEXUALLY
SFORZATO emphatically **Mus.**
SHABBIER more ragged
SHABBILY despicably; meanly
SHABRACK saddle-cloth
SHACKING tramping; hibernating
SHACKLED fettered; manacled
SHAD-BIRD American snipe **Z.**
SHAD-BUSH the June-berry **B.**
SHAD-FROG jumping frog **Z.**
SHADDOCK grape fruit **B.**
SHADEFUL umbrageous
SHADIEST most obscure
SHADOWED followed; obscured
SHAFTING (machinery)
SHAGGING shredding
SHAGREEN shark's skin
SHAKE-OUT return to normal; econ-omics
SHALLOON woollen fabric
SHAMANIC magical
SHAMBLES slaughter-house; ruin
SHAMEFUL humiliating; heinous; base
SHAMMING feigning; counterfeiting
SHAMROCK Irish emblem **B.**
SHANGHAI kidnap
SHANKING mishitting at golf
SHANTIES sea songs; huts
SHANTUNG coarse silk
SHAPABLE fashionable
SHARP-CUT clearly defined
SHARPING tricking
SHARP-SET keen
SHATTERY brittle; rickety
SHAW-FOWL a wappenshaw fowl **Z.**
SHEADING district, Isle of Man
SHEALING shepherd's hut (Sc.)
SHEARHOG shorn sheep **Z.**
SHEARING clipping; shaving; fleecing
SHEARMAN cloth-cutter
SHEA-TREE butter tree **B.**
SHEATHED encased; sheeted

422

SHEAVING collecting; harvesting
SHEDDING discarding; diffusing
SHEELING shealing; shelter
SHEEP-DIP
SHEEP-PEN an enclosure
SHEEP-RUN tract of pasture
SHEEPDOG a chaperon   **Z.**
SHEEPFLY a parasite   **Z.**
SHEEPISH diffident; bashful
SHEER-LEG a spar
SHEERING moving aside
SHEETING cloth for sheets
SHEILING shealing; hut
SHEKINAH Divine Aura
SHELDUCK female sheldrake   **Z.**
SHELL-GUN a cannon
SHELL-ICE (no water below it)
SHELLING bombarding; husking
SHELTERY affording shelter
SHELVING sloping; shelves
SHEMITIC Semitic; (Shem)
SHEPHERD a swain
SHERATON furniture designer
SHIELDED sheltered; screened
SHIELDER protector
SHIELING Highland hut; sheiling
SHIFTILY deceitfully; evasively
SHIFTING moving; varying; changing
SHILLALY Irish blackthorn cudgel
SHILLING a bob   **Coin**
SHIMMING wedging
SHIN-BONE the tibia   **Med.**
SHINGLED bobbed
SHINGLES herpes   **Med.**
SHINNING climbing
SHIPLESS
SHIPLOAD a full cargo   **Naut.**
SHIPMATE
SHIPMENT embarkation
SHIPPING   **Naut.**
SHIP-TIRE head-dress
SHIP-WORM the teredo   **Z.**
SHIPYARD building yard   **Naut.**
SHIREMAN sheriff
SHIRKING evading; scamping
SHIRTING material for shirts
SHIVAREE mock serenade; charivari
SHIVERED shattered; quaked; trembled
SHOALING thronging
SHOCK-DOG a poodle   **Z.**
SHOCKING offensive; outrageous
SHOEBILL whale-headed heron   **Z.**
SHOEHORN
SHOELACE a latchet
SHOELESS
SHOGGING shaking; jogging
SHOGUNAL (Japanese C. in C.)
SHOOTING a game-preserve
SHOP-BELL
SHOPGIRL

SHOPLIFT pilfer; rob a store
SHOPPING
SHOPWORN faded
SHORLING newly shorn sheep   **Z.**
SHORTAGE deficiency; lack
SHORT-AND the ampersand; &
SHORT-CUT (tobacco); a quick way
SHORT-LEG (cricket)
SHORT-RIB a false rib   **Med.**
SHOT-BELT bandolier
SHOT-FREE Scot free; untaxed
SHOT-HOLE hole for explosives
SHOT-SILK iridescent silk
SHOTTING loading with shot
SHOULDER carry; hump; a prominence
SHOUTING cheering; crying; calling
SHOW-BILL a showcard
SHOW-CARD card of patterns
SHOW-CASE
SHOW-DOWN cards on the table
SHOW-ROOM
SHOW-YARD (horses and cattle)
SHOWERED bestowed liberally
SHRAPNEL a projectile
SHREDDED cut into strips
SHREWDLY sagaciously; astutely
SHREWISH vixenish
SHRIEKED yelled; squealed; cried
SHRIEKER screamer
SHRIEVAL (sheriff)
SHRILLED squeaked; piped
SHRIMPED
SHRIMPER boat or catcher
SHRINING enshrining
SHRINKER a contractor ?
SHRIVING absolving; pardoning
SHROUDED veiled; hidden; screened
SHROVING Shrove-tide festivity
SHRUGGED uplifted
SHUCKING husking; stripping
SHUFFLED (cards); evaded
SHUFFLER palterer; quibbler
SHUNNING avoiding; evading
SHUNPIKE a byroad
SHUNTING
SHUTDOWN closure
SHUTTING fastening; barring
SHWANPAN Chinese abacus
SIBERIAN
SIBERITE red tourmaline   **Min.**
SIBILANT hissing; buzzing
SIBILATE to hiss
SIBILOUS sibilant
SIBYLLIC oracular; prophetic
SICANIAN Sicilian
SICELIOT a Greek in Sicily
SICILIAN (Sicily)
SICK-CALL doctor's visit
SICK-FLAG quarantine-flag   **Naut.**
SICK-LIST register of patients

SICK-ROOM patients' room   **Med.**
SICKENED languished; ailed; wearied
SICKENER a cause of disgust
SICKLIED pallid; wan
SICKLILY languidly
SICKNESS malady; disease; illness
SICULIAN early Sicilian
SIDE-ACHE side stitch or pain
SIDE-ARMS sword or bayonet
SIDEBAND close frequencies   **Radio**
SIDE-BEAM (above crank-shaft)
SIDE-COMB ornamental comb
SIDE-DISH an entrée
SIDE-DRUM   **Mus.**
SIDE-LINE
SIDELING sideways; sloping
SIDE-LOCK a curl
SIDELONG obliquely
SIDE-NOTE marginal note
SIDEREAL astronomical; (stars)
SIDERITE ironstone   **Min.**
SIDE-SEAT
SIDE-SHOW
SIDE-SLIP a skid
SIDESMAN deputy churchwarden **Eccl.**
SIDE-STEP evade
SIDETONE telephony
SIDE-VIEW profile
SIDEWALK pavement
SIDEWAYS crabwise
SIDE-WIND undue influence
SIEGE-GUN heavy gun
SIFFLEUR whistler
SIFFLING whistling
SIGHTING spotting; aiming; viewing
SIGMATIC (sigma)
SIGNABLE
SIGNALLY eminently; notably
SIGNIEUR seignior; feudal lord
SIGNLESS making no sign
SIGN-POST
SILENCED stilled; hushed
SILENCER (cars, guns, etc.)
SILENTLY mutely; dumbly; taciturnly
SILICATE silicon compound   **Chem.**
SILICIFY make into silica
SILICITE labradorite   **Min.**
SILICIUM silicon   **Chem.**
SILICULA, SILICULE seed vessel **B.**
SILK-MILL
SILK-REEL
SILK-WORM   **Z.**
SILKENED made glossy
SILLABUB syllabub; a drink
SILLADAR Indian cavalryman
SILLY-HOW a caul
SILPHIUM rosin-weed   **B.**
SILURIAN rock formation   **Min.**
SILURIST a Silurian
SILVANUS a forest-god

SILVERLY like silver
SIMARUBA quassia; bitterwood **B.**
SIMILIZE compare; liken
SIMMERED boiled gently
SIMONIAC one guilty of simony **Eccl.**
SIMPERED smiled fatuously
SIMPERER smirker
SIMPLIFY make plain and easy
SIMPLING gathering herbs
SIMPLISM affected simplicity
SIMPLIST herbalist
SIMULANT like unto
SIMULATE pretend; imitate; sham
SIN-EATER (a Welsh custom)
SINAITIC (Mount Sinai)   **Eccl.**
SINAPISM mustard plaster   **Med.**
SINCIPUT the skull   **Med.**
SINECURE salary for no work
SINEWING strengthening
SINEWOUS strong; vigorous
SINFONIA a symphony   **Mus.**
SINFULLY unrighteously; naughtily
SING-SING a prison in U.S.A.
SING-SONG community singing
SINGABLE vocable
SINGEING scorching; searing
SINGLING selecting; picking
SINGULAR peculiar; unique; quaint
SINICISM a Chinese custom
SINISTER evil; unlucky; baneful
SINK-HOLE a vent
SINN-FEIN Irish home-ruler
SINOLOGY Chinese lore
SINOPHIL lover of China
SINUATED insinuated; wound
SINUSOID geometric curve
SIPHONAL ⎞ working on the
SIPHONIC ⎠ siphon principle
SIPHONED extracted to a lower level
SIPYLITE niobite of erbium **Chem.**
SIRENIZE entice; allure
SIRIASIS sunstroke   **Med.**
SIRVENTE troubadour's song
SISCOWET ⎞
SISKIWET ⎬ a variety of trout **Z.**
SISKOWET ⎠ from Lake Superior
SISTERLY affectionate; sororal
SISYPHUS stone-roller
SITOLOGY dietetics   **Med.**
SITUATED placed; located; sited
SITZ-BATH remedial bath
SIXPENCE a tanner   **Coin**
SIXPENNY worth sixpence
SIXTIETH
SIZEABLE of some bulk
SIZINESS adhesiveness
SIZZLING hissing; seething; frying
SKEAN-DHU Highland dirk
SKELETAL like a skeleton
SKELETON outline; nucleus; cadre

SKELLOCK squeal (Sc.)	**SLIDABLE** capable of sliding
SKETCHED drafted; depicted; drew	**SLIGHTED** insulted; peeved
SKETCHER delineator	**SLIGHTLY** slenderly; faintly; scantily
SKEWBACK an abutment	**SLIME-PIT** pit of viscous mire
SKEWBALD piebald	**SLIMMING** banting; reducing; dieting
SKEWERED impaled	**SLIMNESS** craftiness; artfulness
SKIAGRAM X-ray photograph **Med.**	**SLINGING** throwing; flinging; tossing
SKIDDING side-slipping	**SLINKING** skulking; lurking; sneaking
SKILLESS maladroit; artless	**SLIP-DOCK** slipway **Naut.**
SKILLING outhouse; bay of a barn	**SLIP-KNOT**
SKIM-MILK	**SLIPOVER** sleeveless sweater
SKIMMING scan superficially	**SLIP-RAIL** form of gate (Australian)
SKIMMITY a burlesque	**SLIP-ROAD** minor by-pass; siding
SKIMPING scamping; stinting	**SLIPPERY** evasive; shifty; elusive
SKIN-DEEP superficial	**SLIPPING** tripping; erring; sliding
SKINLESS	**SLIPSHOD** down at heel
SKINNING flaying	**SLIPSLOP** jejune; trash; slovenly
SKIN-WOOL wool from dead sheep	**SLITHERY** slimy; deceitful
SKIPETAR an Albanian	**SLITTING** splitting
SKIP-JACK upstart; click-beetle **Z.**	**SLIVERED** cut into strips
SKIPPING leaping; bounding; hopping	**SLOBBERY** moist
SKIRLING bagpipe music **Mus.**	**SLOGGING** smiting
SKIRMISH contest; brush; fray	**SLOP-BOWL** slop-basin
SKIRTING bordering	**SLOP-DASH** weak cold tea
SKITTISH mettlesome; fickle	**SLOP-PAIL** household bucket
SKITTLES ninepins	**SLOPPING** spilling
SKUA-GULL the great skua	**SLOPSHOP** (ready-made clothes) R.N.
SKULKING lurking; slinking	**SLOPWORK** slovenly work
SKULL-CAP the sinciput	**SLOTHFUL** idle; dronish; dilatory
SKUNKISH like a skunk **Z.**	**SLOTTERY** squalid; dirty
SKYLIGHT	**SLOTTING** grooving
SKY-PILOT aviator; padre **Eccl.**	**SLOUCHED** bent; depressed
SKYSCAPE	**SLOUGHED** cast off
SKY-SHADE lens; hood **Photo.**	**SLOVENLY** negligently; unkempt
SLABBING cutting into slabs	**SLOVENRY** slovenliness; disorder
SLABLINE a running rope **Naut.**	**SLOWBACK** lazy lubber
SLACKING relaxing; loosening	**SLOW-DOWN** ca' canny; reduce capacity
SLAISTER slovenly work (Sc.)	
SLAMMING banging	**SLOWNESS** tardiness; sluggishness
SLANGILY colloquially	**SLOW-WORM** limbless lizard **Z.**
SLANGING vituperating	**SLUBBING** twisting
SLANTING sloping; tilting; oblique	**SLUG-HORN** a trumpet **Mus.**
SLAP-BANG violently	**SLUGGARD** laggard; lounger; slacker
SLAP-DASH carelessly; rashly	**SLUGGING** slogging
SLAPJACK flapjack; pancake	**SLUGGISH** slothful; inert
SLAPPING large; strong; spanking	**SLUICING** flushing
SLASHING showy; severe; gashing	**SLUMBERY** somnolent; soporous
SLATE-AXE a seax **Tool**	**SLUMMING** visiting slums
SLATTERN slovenly person	**SLUMPING** falling heavily
SLAVERED dribbled	**SLURRIED** smeared
SLAVERER driveller; idiot	**SLURRING** disparaging
SLAVONIC (Czechs; Poles; etc.)	**SLUTTERY** dirt and disorder
SLEAVING separating	**SLUTTISH** slatternly
SLEDDING sled-transport	**SLY-BOOTS** a wag
SLEDGING sleighing	**SLY-GOOSE** the sheld-duck **Z.**
SLEEKING gliding; smoothing	**SMACKING** tasting of; slapping
SLEEPFUL somnolent	**SMALL-ALE** (no hops)
SLEEPILY drowsily	**SMALLAGE** wild celery **B.**
SLEEPING dormant; slumbering	**SMALLEST** minutest; tiniest
SLEETING rain, snow and hail	**SMALLISH** on the small side

SMALLPOX variola **Med.**

SMALTINE⎱ compound of cobalt **Min.**
SMALTITE⎰ and arsenic
SMARTING stinging; rankling
SMASH-HIT popular song; musical
SMASHING disrupting; shattering
SMEARING daubing; begriming
SMECTITE fuller's earth **Min.**
SMELLING redolent; scenting
SMELTERY foundry
SMELTING producing metal
SMIRCHED soiled; clouded
SMIRKING simpering
SMITCHEL a particle
SMITHERY a smiddy; a smithy
SMITHING iron-working
SMOCKING pleating
SMOKABLE fumable
SMOKE-BOX (steam locomotive)
SMOKE-DRY cure; bloat
SMOOTHED palliated; levelled
SMOOTHEN to allay; mollify
SMOOTHLY suavely; blandly
SMORBROD open sandwich (Scand.)
SMORZATO diminuendo **Mus.**
SMOTHERY stifling; stuffy
SMOULDER hangfire
SMOULDRY slow burning
SMUDGING blotting
SMUG-BOAT smuggling boat **Naut.**
SMUGGLED
SMUGGLER an owler
SMUGNESS self-satisfaction
SMUTBALL a fungus **B.**
SMUTCHED blackened with soot
SMYTERIE many small people (Sc.)
SNACK-BAR
SNAFFLED purloined; filched
SNAGBOAT (removing snags) **Naut.**
SNAGGING lopping trees
SNAILERY snail farm
SNAKE-EEL **Z.**
SNAP-VOTE sudden vote
SNAP-WEED balsams, etc. **B.**
SNAPPING biting; breaking; cracking
SNAPPISH short tempered
SNAPSHOT
SNARLING entangling
SNATCHED plucked; clutched; wrested
SNATCHER grasper; grabber
SNEAK-CUP insidious scoundrel
SNEAKING telling; secret; slinking
SNEERING taunting; jeering; mocking
SNEEZING snuff
SNICKING cutting; nicking
SNIFFING indicating incredulity
SNIGGLED snared
SNIPPETY fragmentary
SNIPPING shearing; clipping
SNIP-SNAP smart sharp dialogue
SNITCHER handcuff; informer

SNIVELLY whining
SNOBBERY tuft-hunting
SNOBBISH
SNOBBISM aping gentility
SNOBLING a little snob
SNOOPING furtive enquiry; prying
SNOOZING dozing; drowsing
SNORTING puffing
SNOWBALL guelder-rose **B.**
SNOWBIRD American finch **Z.**
SNOWBOOT
SNOWCAPT crowned with snow
SNOWCOLD cold as snow
SNOWDROP **B.**
SNOW-EYES snow goggles
SNOWFALL
SNOWLIKE
SNOWLINE line of perpetual snow
SNOWSHED railway protection
SNOWSHOE
SNOWSLIP avalanche
SNOWSUIT winter garments
SNUBBING checking a rope
SNUBBISH petulant
SNUB-NOSE
SNUFFBOX
SNUFFERS candle trimmers
SNUFFLED sniffed
SNUFFLER
SNUGGERY cosy quarters
SNUGGING lying close
SNUGGLED cuddled
SNUGNESS warmth and comfort
SO-CALLED
SOAPBALL
SOAPSUDS
SOAP-TEST (for hardness of water)
SOAP-TREE a Chilean tree **B.**
SOAPWORK soap factory
SOAPWORT a genus of plants **B.**
SOB-STORY false, pathetic tale
SOB-STUFF synthetic emotion
SOBERIZE to calm down
SOBRANJE Bulgarian; Sobranye
SOBRIETY dispassion; temperance
SOCIABLE companionable
SOCIABLY friendlily
SOCIALLY gregariously
SOCINIAN a polemic theologian
SOCKETED shanked
SOCMANRY feudal tenure **Law.**
SOCRATIC (Socrates)
SODA-LIME soda and quicklime
SODALITE a soda compound **Min.**
SODALITY comradeship; association
SODA-SALT **Chem.**
SODDENED saturated; drenched
SOFTENED mollified; melted; assuaged
SOFTENER mitigator; mollifier
SOFT-EYED compassionate

SOFTLING weakling	**SONG-BOOK**	**Mus.**
SOFTNESS tenderness	**SONGLESS**	**Mus.**
SOFT-SHOE light tap-dancing	**SONGSTER** vocalist	**Mus.**
SOFT-SOAP flattery	**SONORITY** resonance	**Mus.**
SOFT-WOOD sap-wood **B.**	**SONOROUS** melodious; audible	**Mus.**
SOILLESS untarnished	**SOOTHING** pleasing; calming; lulling	
SOIL-PIPE drain-pipe	**SOOTHSAY** foretell; augur; predict	
SOLACING consoling; comforting	**SOPHERIM** Hebrew scribes	
SOLANDER case for prints	**SOPITION** lethargy	
SOLANINE an alkaloid **B.**	**SOPOROUS** drowsy; somnolent	
SOLANOID potato-shaped **Med.**	**SORBONNE** University of Paris	
SOLARISM solar myths	**SORCERER** wizard; magician	
SOLARIST mythologist	**SORDIDLY** ignobly; basely; meanly	
SOLARIUM sun-dial; sun-parlour	**SOREDIUM** a brood-bud **B.**	
SOLARIZE injure by sun's rays	**SOREHEAD** disgruntled person	
SOLASTER star-fish **Z.**	**SORENESS** regret; rancour	
SOLATIUM compensation	**SORICINE** (shrew-mice) **Z.**	
SOLDANEL blue moonwort **B.**	**SORORISE** be a sister to	
SOLDERED cemented	**SORORITY** women's club (Amer. Univ.)	
SOLDERER a joiner of metals	**SORROWED** grieved; lamented; wept	
SOLDIERY the military	**SORROWER** mourner; repiner	
SOLECISM incongruity; impropriety	**SORTABLE** befitting; suitable	
SOLECIST ⎱ (breaches of manners	**SORTMENT** assortment; distribution	
SOLECIZE ⎰ or syntax)	**SOTADEAN** satirical and malicious	
SOLEMNLY gravely; formally; staidly	**SOTERIAL** about salvation	
SOLENESS singleness	**SOUCHONG** black China tea	
SOLENITE fossil razor-shell **Min.**	**SOUGHING** moaning; sighing	
SOLENOID copper coil	**SOUL-BELL** passing-bell **Eccl.**	
SOLFAISM ⎱ (singing by syllables) **Mus.**	**SOULLESS** dull; spiritless	
SOLFAIST ⎰	**SOUL-SCOT** ⎱ requiem fee **Eccl.**	
SOLIDIFY harden; congeal; petrify	**SOUL-SHOT** ⎰	
SOLIDISM ⎱ (medical theory of	**SOUL-SICK** morally diseased	
SOLIDIST ⎰ diseases) **Med.**	**SOUND-BOW** part of a bell	
SOLIDITY compactness	**SOUNDING** swinging the lead	
SOLITARY lonely; single; remote	**SOURDINE** a muffler; sordet **Mus.**	
SOLITUDE isolation; seclusion	**SOUR-DOCK** sorrel **B.**	
SOLLERET foot armour	**SOUR-EYED** morose	
SOLONIAN (Solon, a lawgiver) **Law.**	**SOURNESS** tartness; asperity	
SOLSTICE an ecliptic point	**SOUR-PUSS** a kill-joy	
SOLUTION release; elucidation	**SOUTHERN**	
SOLUTIVE loosening	**SOUTHING** towards the south	
SOLVABLE explainable; resolvable	**SOUVENIR** memento; relic; keepsake	
SOLVENCY all debts payable	**SOW-BREAD** a tuber **B.**	
SOMATISM a doctrine	**SOW-DRUNK** beastly drunk	
SOMATIST materialist	**SOZZLING** getting fuddled	
SOMATOME homologous segment	**SPACE-BAR** typewriter gadget	
SOMBRERO broad-brimmed hat (S. Amer.)	**SPACEMAN** astronaut	
SOMBROUS gloomy; sombre; doleful	**SPACIOUS** vast; roomy; ample; wide	
SOMEBODY	**SPADILLE** ⎱ ace of spades in	
SOMEDEAL in some degree	**SPADILIO** ⎰ ombre & quadrille	
SOMEGATE somewhere (Sc.)	**SPADROON** double-handed sword	
SOMERSET summersault	**SPAGIRIC** chemical	
SOMESUCH similar	**SPALLING** stonework fragmentation	
SOMETIME formerly; once	**SPALPEEN** scamp; rascal (Ir.)	
SOMEWHAT more or less	**SPANDREL** ⎱ triangular space	
SOMEWHEN some time or other	**SPANDRIL** ⎰ beside an arch	
SOMNIFIC inducing sleep; soporific	**SPANEMIA** anaemia **Med.**	
SON-IN-LAW	**SPANGLED** glittering	
SONATINA short sonata **Mus.**	**SPANGLER** sparkler	
SONG-BIRD **Z.** 427	**SPANIARD** an Iberian	

SPANKING dashing; slapping	
SPANLESS immeasurable	
SPAN-LONG nine inches	**Meas.**
SPANNING bridging; extending	
SPAN-ROOF roof with eaves	
SPAR-DECK the upper deck	**Naut.**
SPAR-HAWK sparrow-hawk	**Z.**
SPAR-HUNG (with fluor spar)	
SPARABLE shoe nail	
SPARERIB a piece of pork	
SPARGING sprinkling	
SPARKFUL lively; gay	
SPARKING playing the gallant	
SPARKISH well-dressed; airy	
SPARKLER a diamond	**Min.**
SPARKLET charge of gas	
SPARLING a smelt	**Z.**
SPARRING boxing	
SPARSELY thinly; meagrely	
SPARSILE scanty; infrequent	
SPATHOSE⎫ foliated or lamular	**B.**
SPATHOUS⎭	
SPATHURA humming-birds	**Z.**
SPAVINED (leg swelling)	
SPAWLING slobbering	
SPAWNING	
SPEAKING hailing; addressing	
SPEARING lancing	
SPEARMAN	
SPECIFIC distinctive; peculiar	
SPECIMEN sample; type; exemplar	
SPECIOUS plausible; ostensible	
SPECKING staining	
SPECKLED variegated	
SPECTANT expectant	
SPECTRAL ghostly; spooky	
SPECTRUM (colour bands)	
SPECULAR reflective	
SPECULUM a mirror	
SPEEDFUL speedy; hasty; impetuous	
SPEEDIER faster; quicker	
SPEEDILY with rapidity	
SPEEDWAY racing track	
SPEKBOOM S. African shrub	**B.**
SPELDING⎫ dried haddock; or fish	
SPELDRIN⎬ split and dried in	
SPELDRON⎭ the sun	
SPELLING charming	
SPEND-ALL spendthrift	
SPENDING exhausting; squandering	
SPERABLE hopeful	
SPERGULA spurry; sandweed	**B.**
SPERM-OIL	
SPHAGNUM bog-moss	**B.**
SPHECIUS digger-wasps	**Z.**
SPHENOID wedge-shaped	
SPHERICS spherical geometry	
SPHEROID almost a sphere	
SPHERULE small globe	
SPHRAGID ochreous clay	**Min.**

SPHYGMIC pulsative	**Med.**
SPICATUM herring-bone work	
SPICCATO clearly	**Mus.**
SPICE-BOX	
SPICEFUL aromatic	
SPICKNEL baldmoney plant	**B.**
SPICULAR spiky; pointed	
SPICULUM small spike	**B.**
SPIFFING delightful	
SPIGELIA worm-grass; pink-root	**B.**
SPIKELET	
SPILIKIN spillikin	
SPILLING upsetting; shedding	
SPILLWAY overflow	
SPILOTES a snake genus	**Z.**
SPINDLED tapering	
SPINIFEX porcupine grass	**Z.**
SPINITIS spinal fever	**Med.**
SPINNERY spinning mill	
SPINNING whirling; twirling	
SPINSTER	
SPINSTRY spinning industry	
SPIRACLE⎫ breathing-hole;	**Med.**
SPIRICLE⎭ pore	
SPIRALLY whorled	
SPIRIFER fossil brachiopod	**Min.**
SPIRITED sprightly; alert	
SPIRITUS aspiration; breathing	
SPIRTING spurting; sprinting	
SPIT-CURL soap-lock	
SPITEFUL vindictive; malicious	
SPITFIRE fighting aircraft; irascible	
SPITTING piercing	
SPITTOON a cuspidor	
SPLASHED spattered	
SPLASHER a mud-guard	
SPLATTER to splash	
SPLAYING sloping	
SPLEENED angered	
SPLENDID lustrous; refulgent	
SPLENIAL splint-like bone	**Med.**
SPLENIUS a neck muscle	**Med.**
SPLICING joining; binding	
SPLINTER fragment; cleave	
SPLITTER separator	
SPLOTCHY unevenly daubed	
SPLUTTER a bustle; a stir	
SPOFFISH fussy; officious	
SPOILFUL wasteful; rapacious	
SPOILING marring; vitiating	
SPOLIARY Roman mortuary	
SPOLIATE plunder; pillage	
SPONDIAC (spondee)	
SPONDIAS hog-plums, etc.	**B**
SPONDYLE a vertebra	**Med**
SPONGING cadging; sorning	
SPONSION sponsorship	
SPONTOON kind of halberd	
SPOOFING bluffing	
SPOOKISH ghostly	

SPOOLING winding on spools
SPOONFUL
SPOONILY amorously
SPOONING courting
SPORADIC scattered; irregular
SPOROSAC a gonophore **Z.**
SPORTFUL frolicsome; jocose
SPORTING generous
SPORTING romping; displaying
SPORTIVE wanton; hilarious
SPOT-BALL billiards
SPOTLESS pure; untainted
SPOTTING observing
SPOUTING orating; gushing
SPRACHLE ⎫ to clamber up
SPRACKLE ⎭ with difficulty
SPRAGGED scotched up
SPRAINED overstrained
SPRAINTS dung of an otter
SPRAWLED straggled; spread
SPRAWLER lounger
SPRAYING atomizing
SPREADER extender
SPRIGGED adorned with sprigs
SPRINGAL catapult; youth
SPRINGER arch support **Z.**
SPRINKLE bedew; perfuse
SPRINTED speeded; spurted
SPRINTER racer
SPROCKET a cog
SPRUCELY neatly; tidily
SPRUCIFY to smarten
SPRUCING refurbishing
SPRUNTED sprang; sprouted
SPUILZIE to spoil (Sc.)
SPUNYARN loosely twisted rope
SPUR-GALL wound with a spur
SPUR-GEAR gear wheels
SPURIOUS bastard; faked
SPURLESS without incentive
SPURLING the smelt **Z.**
SPURNING disdaining; scouting
SPURRIER spur-maker
SPURRING inciting
SPURTING gushing
SPURTLED showered
SPY-CRAFT secret service
SPY-GLASS a telescope
SPY-MONEY
SQUAB-PIE pigeon-pie
SQUABBED stuffed; crashed
SQUABBLE wrangle; brawl; printing
SQUADDED grouped
SQUADRON
SQUALLED yelled; cried
SQUALLER screamer; informer
SQUALOID like a shark **Z.**
SQUAMATA reptile genus **Z.**
SQUAMATE ⎫ covered with scales;
SQUAMOID ⎭ scaly

SQUAMOSE ⎫ squamous; **Z.**
SQUAMULA ⎬ a small scale **Z.**
SQUAMULE ⎭
SQUANDER dissipate; lavish; fritter
SQUARELY evenly; quadrilaterally
SQUARING adjusting; regulating
SQUARISH not quite square
SQUARSON squire-parson **Eccl.**
SQUASHED compressed; squeezed
SQUASHER suppresser
SQUATTED cowered; crouched; sat
SQUATTER settler without title
SQUATTLE to squat down (Sc.)
SQUAWKED squalled
SQUAWMAN (Indian wife)
SQUEAKED shrilled
SQUEAKER informer
SQUEALED squalled
SQUEEGEE rubber mop
SQUEEZED crushed; constricted
SQUEEZER playing card
SQUEGGER self-quenching circuit
SQUIBBED wrangled
SQUIGGLE squirm; wriggle
SQUILGEE squeegee
SQUINTED
SQUIREEN a petty squire
SQUIRELY gallantly
SQUIRING escorting
SQUIRMED wriggled
SQUIRREL **Z.**
SQUIRTED ejected; gushed
SQUIRTER a syringe
STABBING piercing; thrusting
STABLING accommodation for horses
STABLISH establish
STACCATO abruptly **Mus.**
STACKING piling
STADDLED supported
STAFFING providing personnel
STAG-EVIL horse disease
STAGGARD 4-year-old stag **Z.**
STAGGERS giddiness
STAGHORN large fern **B.**
STAGNANT motionless; inert
STAGNATE become dull
STAHLIAN ⎫ medical theory **Med.**
STAHLISM ⎭
STAINING sullying; discolouring
STAIR-ROD
STAIRWAY a staircase
STAKE-NET fishing net
STALKING approaching warily
STALLAGE stall rent
STALL-FED luxuriously nurtured
STALLING losing speed when flying
STALLION male horse **Z.**
STALLMAN stall-holder
STALWART resolute; sturdy; valiant
STAMENED having stamens

STAMINAL constitutional; vigorous
STAMPEDE panic; rush; flight
STAMPING pounding; impressing
STANCHED staunched; stopped
STANCHEL next (Sc.)
STANCHER a tourniquet
STANCHLY steadily; staunchly
STAND-OFF (Rugby football)
STAND-PAT decline to budge
STANDARD banner; colours; fruit tree
STANDING rank; duration; status
STANHOPE dog-cart
STANK-HEN moorhen   **Z.**
STANNARY tin mine
STANNATE a salt   **Chem.**
STANNINE a tin alloy
STANNOUS containing tin
STANZAIC (stanzas)
STAPELIA milkweed plants   **B.**
STAPHYLE the uvula   **Med.**
STAPLING sorting ; binding
STAR-DUST cosmic dust
STARE-CAT over-inquisitive neighbour
STAR-FISH an echinoderm   **Z.**
STAR-FORT angular redoubt
STAR-GAZE astronomise
STAR-LIKE stellate
STAR-NOSE N. American mole   **Z.**
STAR-REED Peruvian plant   **B.**
STARCHED formal; stiff
STARCHER stiffener
STARCHLY rigidly; punctiliously
STARLESS
STARLING ring of piles   **Z.**
STAROSTA Polish noble
STAROSTY life-estate
STARRING taking the lead
STARTFUL skittish; jumpy
STARTING inventing; evoking
STARTISH nervous; fearful; scared
STARTLED affrighted; dumbfounded
STARTLER a shock; a rouser
STAR-TURN revue or circus act
STARVING famished; hungry
STARWEED   **B.**
STARWORT aster genus   **B.**
STASIMON choral ode   **Eccl.**
STATABLE declarable; affirmable
STATEDLY regularly
STATICAL in equilibrium; restful
STATUARY sculpture
STATURED full grown
STAY-BOLT a holdfast
STAY-LACE corset cord
STAYSAIL   **Naut.**
STEADIED supported; upheld
STEADILY constantly; firmly
STEADING farm out-houses
STEALING filching; purloining
STEALTHY clandestine; furtive; sly

STEAM-GUN
STEAMING evaporating; reeking
STEAM-TUG   **Naut.**
STEANING well-shaft lining
STEARATE a fatty acid
STEARINE tallow; suet; etc.
STEATITE soapstone   **Min.**
STEATOMA wen or tumour   **Med.**
STEELING hardening; bracing; nerving
STEEL-PEN a nib
STEENING well-shaft lining
STEEPING soaking; macerating
STEEPLED
STEERAGE third class at sea   **Naut.**
STEERING directing; piloting; guiding
STEEVELY stiffly (Sc.)
STEEVING stowing
STEINBOK African antelope   **Z.**
STELLARY starry
STELLATE radiated
STELLION a lizard   **Z.**
STELLITE zeolitic mineral   **Min.**
STEM-HEAD top of stem
STEM-LEAF   **B.**
STEMLESS no stalk
STEMMING opposing; stopping
STENLOCH overgrown coalfish   **Z.**
STENOSED contracted
STENOSIS constriction
STEP-DAME step-mother
STEP-GIRL doorstep cleaner
STEPPING pacing; walking
STERLING genuine; pure; sound
STERNAGE steerage   **Naut.**
STERNITE part of an insect   **Z.**
STERNWAY backward movement
STIBBLER clerical locum tenens   **Eccl.**
STIBNITE antimony compound
STICCADO xylophone   **Mus.**
STICKING adhering; fixing; piercing
STICKJAW toffee
STICKLED interposed; obstructed
STICKLER purist over trifles
STIFF-BIT horse's bit
STIFFISH rather tight
STIFLING suffocating; muffling
STIGMATA sacred marks   **Eccl.**
STILBITE zeolitic mineral   **Min.**
STILETTO small dagger; high heel
STILLING calming; distilling; ceramics
STILLION stand for a cask
STIMULUS spur; incitement; goad
STING-RAY a fish   **Z.**
STINGILY parsimoniously; miserly
STINGING pricking; wounding
STINKARD teledu; badger   **Z.**
STINKPOT a grenade
STINTING limiting; pinching
STIPPLED dotted
STIPPLER engraver

STIPULAR | having pin-feathers;	**Z.**	
STIPULED / (leaf lobe)	**B.**	
STIRLESS quiescent; still; dull		
STIRRING rousing; exciting; lively		
STITCHED united; sewn		
STITCHEL a hairy wool		
STITCHER seamstress		
STOCCADE | a thrust in fencing		
STOCCADO /		
STOCKADE palisaded defence		
STOCKIER stouter built		
STOCKILY thickset		
STOCKING foot-wear; storing		
STOCKISH stupid; blockish		
STOCKIST a tradesman		
STOCKMAN herdsman		
STOCKPOT (gravy and soup)		
STOICISM imperturbation		
STOLIDLY impassively; obtusely		
STOLZITE lead tungstate	**Min.**	
STOMATIC mouth medicine	**Med.**	
STONE-BOW (for shooting stones)		
STONE-FLY a lure for trout	**Z.**	
STONE-OIL petroleum	**Min.**	
STONEPIT quarry		
STOOGERY clownish fraudulence		
STOOKING corn gathering		
STOOLING ramifying		
STOOMING fermenting		
STOOPING condescending; bending		
STOP-BATH developing accessory **Photo.**		
STOP-COCK regulating valve		
STOP-OVER intermediate landing		
STOPPAGE a deduction of pay		
STOPPING a filling; checking		
STOPPLED corked		
STORABLE reservable		
STORMILY angrily; tempestuously		
STORMING assaulting; ranting		
STORYING narrating		
STOVAINE an anaesthetic	**Med.**	
STOWAWAY	**Naut.**	
STOWDOWN arrange cargo		
STRADDLE bracket; striddle		
STRAGGLE stray; digress; wander		
STRAIGHT direct; honest; upright		
STRAINED stressed; exerted; taxed		
STRAINER a filter; percolator		
STRAITEN confine; perplex; constrict		
STRAITLY narrowly; closely		
STRAMASH a tumult (Sc.)		
STRAMMEL straw	**B.**	
STRANDED driven ashore; aground		
STRANGER odder; quainter; alien		
STRANGLE choke; suppress; smother		
STRAP-OIL a thrashing		
STRAPPED secured; stropped		
STRAPPER harness-maker		
STRATEGY military art		
STRATIFY laminate		

STRATULA thin rock layer		
STRAVAIG wander (Sc.)		
STRAW-HAT		
STRAYING roving; deviating; erring		
STREAKED variegated; striped		
STREAMED flowed; poured; gushed		
STREAMER a pennant		
STRELITZ Muscovite militia-man		
STRENGTH power; vigour; might		
STREPENT noisy; strident		
STREPERA crow-shrikes	**Z.**	
STREPHON love-sick swain		
STRESSED emphasized; accented		
STRETCHY elastic		
STREWING scattering; broadcasting		
STRIATED furrowed; streaked		
STRIATUM brain ganglion	**Med.**	
STRICKEN afflicted; smitten; struck		
STRICKLE a template		
STRICTLY exactly; literally; severely		
STRIDDEN strode		
STRIDDLE straddle; bracket		
STRIDENT harsh; grating; creaking		
STRIDING bestriding; stalking		
STRIGATE striped; variegated		
STRIGGED with fruit stalks removed		
STRIGINE owl-like	**Z.**	
STRIGOPS owl-parrots	**Z.**	
STRIGOSE | bristly; setous;	**B.**	
STRIGOUS / aciform; setiform		
STRIKING impressive; forcible		
STRINGED (rackets; billiards)	**Mus.**	
STRINGER horizontal tie rod		
STRINKLE sprinkle sparingly		
STRIPING making stripes		
STRIPPED deprived; naked; fleeced		
STRIPPER pillager; peeler; husker		
STROBILA tape-worm	**Z.**	
STROBILE hardened catkin	**B.**	
STROKING (rowing); caressing		
STROLLED sauntered; wandered		
STROLLER actor; vagrant		
STROMBUS wing-shells, etc.	**Z.**	
STRONGLY forcibly; mightily		
STRONTIA strontium oxide	**Chem.**	
STROPHIC choral		
STROPPED (razors)		
STRUCKEN struck		
STRUGGLE wrestle; strive; contend		
STRUMMED vamped	**Mus.**	
STRUMOUS scrofulous	**Med.**	
STRUMPET trollop; fly-by-night		
STRUTHIO ostrich genus	**Z.**	
STRUTTED braced		
STRUTTER proud walker		
STUB-IRON (used for gun-barrels)		
STUB-NAIL short thick nail		
STUBBING uprooting		
STUBBLED bristly		
STUBBORN refractory; wilful; perverse		

STUCCOED plastered	**SUBPOLAR** adjacent to polar sea
STUD-BOOK pedigree book	**SUBPRIOR** prior's deputy **Eccl.**
STUD-FARM (horse breeding)	**SUBRIGID** fairly stiff
STUDBOLT headless bolt	**SUBSERVE** help forward; promote
STUDDING putting in studs	**SUBSIDED** sank; abated; waned
STUDIOUS diligent; scholarly	**SUBSOLAR** under the sun
STUD-MARE breeding mare **Z.**	**SUBSONIC** slower than sound
STUDWORK form of brickwork	**SUBSTAGE** microscopic device
STUDYING conning; learning	**SUBSTYLE** line on sundial
STUFFING cramming; taxidermy	**SUBSUMED** logically included
STULTIFY befool; annul	**SUBTENSE** chord of an arc
STUMBLED tripped; lurched	**SUBTEPID** lukewarm
STUMBLER blunderer	**SUBTITLE** secondary title
STUMMING fermenting	**SUBTLETY** cunning; artfulness
STUMPING (cricket); nonplussing	**SUBTONIC** leading note of scale **Mus.**
STUNDISM⎫ (Russian dissenters)	**SUBTOPIA** suburban ideal
STUNDIST⎭	**SUBTRACT** withdraw; deduct; take
STUNNING dazing; marvellous	**SUBTRIBE** section of a tribe
STUNSAIL studding-sail **Naut.**	**SUBTRIST** somewhat sad
STUNTING dwarfing; performing	**SUBTUTOR** under-master
STUPEOUS with matted hair **Z., B.**	**SUBULATE** awl-shaped
STUPIDLY doltishly; senselessly	**SUBURBAN** subregional
STUPRATE to ravish	**SUBURBIA** the suburbs
STURDILY stoutly; stalwartly	**SUBVENED** relieved; subsidized
STURGEON caviare fish **Z.**	**SUBZONAL** below the belt
STURNOID (starlings) **Z.**	**SUCCINCT** concise; compact; terse
SUASIBLE persuasible	**SUCCINIC** derived from amber
SUBACRID pungent	**SUCCUBUS** night demon
SUBACUTE slightly blunt; dull	**SUCHLIKE** somewhat similar
SUB-AGENT an underling	**SUCHWISE** in like manner
SUBAHDAR Indian captain	**SUCKENER** a tenant (Sc.)
SUB-CLASS subdivision	**SUCKERED** with suckers removed
SUBDUING overpowering; mastering	**SUCKLING** unweaned child
SUBDUPLE ratio of one to two	**SUDAMINA** sweating fever **Med.**
SUB-EQUAL nearly equal	**SUDANESE** (Sudan)
SUBERATE⎫ compound derived	**SUDATION** perspiration
SUBERINE⎭ from cork	**SUDATORY** hot-house
SUBEROSE somewhat gnawed **B.**	**SUDDENLY** hastily; abruptly; quickly
SUBEROUS corky	**SUFFERED** underwent; allowed; bore
SUB-FLORA floral division **B.**	**SUFFERER** victim; martyr
SUB-GENUS subdivision	**SUFFICED** satisfied; was adequate
SUB-GIANT bright star **Astron.**	**SUFFIONI** volcanic fumes
SUB-GRADE	**SUFFIXED** added; subjoined; appended
SUB-GROUP	**SUFFLATE** inflate; blow up
SUB-HUMAN almost human	**SUFFRAGE** vote; prayers; intercession
SUBHYOID under the tongue **Med.**	**SUFFRAGO** hock joint **Med.**
SUB-IMAGO a state of change **Z.**	**SUFFUSED** permeated; overspread
SUBLATED taken away	**SUFISTIC** (Moslem pantheism) **Eccl.**
SUB-LEASE an underlet	**SUGARING** sweetening
SUBLIMED exalted	**SUICIDAL** self-destructive
SUBLUNAR under the moon	**SUITABLE** appropriate; convenient
SUBMERGE plunge; drown; flood	**SUITABLY** fittingly; aptly
SUBMERSE duck; douse; dive	**SUITCASE**
SUBNASAL under your nose	**SULCATED** grooved; furrowed
SUBNODAL below a node **B.**	**SULLENLY** morosely; gloomily
SUBORDER subdivision; sub-genus	**SULLYING** smirching
SUBORNED bribed; lead astray	**SULPHATE**⎫
SUBORNER perjurer; false witness	**SULPHIDE**⎬ sulphur compounds **Chem.**
SUBOVATE almost egg-shaped	**SULPHITE**⎭
SUBPOENA writ of attendance **Law**	**SULPHURY** containing sulphur

SULTANIC despotic
SULTANRY Sultan's dominion
SUMERIAN (Babylonian)
SUMMERED
SUMMONED bid; cited; arraigned
SUMMONER invoker; prosecutor
SUMPITAN Malay blow-pipe gun
SUN-BLIND window-shade
SUNBURNT tanned; bronzed
SUNBURST dazzling gleam
SUNCRACK a fissure
SUNDERED parted; severed; broken
SUNDRIED dehydrated
SUNDRIES miscellanea; odds and ends
SUNLIGHT illumination from Helios
SUNNITES orthodox Moslems   **Eccl.**
SUNPRINT photograph
SUNPROOF fadeless
SUNSHADE a parasol
SUNSHINE illumination
SUNSHINY sunny
SUNSTONE feldspar   **Min.**
SUPERADD increase the total
SUPERBLY magnificently; gorgeously
SUPERHET (wireless oscillations)
SUPERIOR head of a monastery   **Eccl.**
SUPERMAN an admirable Crichton
SUPERNAL celestial; heavenly
SUPERTAX a gross imposition
SUPINATE bring palm upward
SUPINELY inertly; languidly
SUPPLANT displace by intrigue
SUPPLIAL provision; provenance
SUPPLIED bestowed; furnished; gave
SUPPLIER contributor; provider
SUPPOSAL supposition; conjecture
SUPPOSED assumed; opined; imagined
SUPPOSER surmiser; thinker; fancier
SUPPRESS quell; check; smother
SURBASED (pedestal moulding)
SURCEASE cessation
SURCULUS a botanical sucker   **B.**
SURENESS certainty; infallibility
SURETIES sponsors
SURF-BIRD plover; sandpiper   **Z.**
SURF-BOAT   **Naut.**
SURF-DUCK the scoter   **Z.**
SURFACED smoothed
SURGICAL chirurgical   **Med.**
SURICATE the meercat   **Z.**
SURMISAL surmise; assumption
SURMISED took for granted
SURMISER conjecturer; supposer
SURMOUNT overcome; surpass; scale
SURMULOT brown rat   **Z.**
SURNAMED
SURPLICE linen vestment   **Eccl.**
SURPRISE shock; bewilder; astound
SURREBUT rebut a rebuttal   **Law**
SURRENAL above the kidneys   **Med.**

SURROUND eucircle; hem; beset; loop
SURSOLID fifth power (Math.)
SURVEYAL review; scrutiny; prospect
SURVEYED scrutinized; scanned
SURVEYOR inspector; land measurer
SURVIVAL an outliving; relic
SURVIVED outlasted; endured; outlive
SURVIVOR
SUSPENSE uncertainty; indecision
SUSPIRAL breathing-hole
SUSPIRED sighed
SUZERAIN paramount ruler
SWABBING mopping
SWADDLED swathed; wrapped
SWADDLER a Methodist   **Eccl.**
SWADESHI Indian boycott
SWAGGING sagging
SWAGSHOP where trash is sold
SWAINING lovemaking; courting
SWAINISH boorish; rustic
SWAMPING overwhelming; inundating
SWAMP-OAK a casuarina   **B.**
SWAMP-ORE bog-ore   **Min.**
SWAN-HERD tender of swans
SWAN-LIKE
SWAN-MARK identification mark
SWAN-NECK curved
SWANNERY (Abbotsbury)   **Z.**
SWAN-SHOT buck-shot
SWAN-SKIN soft flannel
SWAN-SONG last act or appearance
SWANKING bragging
SWAPPING bartering
SWARDING turfing
SWARMING thronging; crowding
SWARTISH tawny; swarthy
SWASHING splashing
SWASTIKA Nazi emblem; triskele
SWATHING wrapping; binding
SWATTING (killing flies)
SWEALING melting; singeing
SWEARING profaneness; avowing
SWEATILY laboriously
SWEATING toiling; extorting
SWEEPING comprehensive; extensive
SWEEP-NET
SWEET-BAY the true laurel   **B.**
SWEET-GUM a gum tree   **B.**
SWEETING sweet apple   **B.**
SWEETISH rather sweet
SWEET-OIL olive oil
SWEET-PEA   **B.**
SWEET-SOP an evergreen shrub   **B.**
SWELLDOM fashionable world
SWELLING bombastic; dilating
SWELLISH foppish
SWELL-MOB thieving gang
SWERVING deviating; diverging
SWIFTEST fastest; fleetest
SWIFTLET (bird's nest soup)   **Z.**

SWIGGING quaffing; drinking	
SWILLING rinsing; toping	
SWIMMING dizziness	
SWIMSUIT bathing costume	
SWINDLED defrauded; cheated	
SWINDLER sharper; trickster	
SWINE-OAT a coarse oat	**B.**
SWINE-POX	**Med.**
SWINE-STY a pig-sty	
SWINGING vibrating; dangling	
SWINGLED flailed	
SWINKING drudging; moiling; toiling	
SWIRLING twirling; gyrating; eddying	
SWISHING birching	
SWITCHED shunted; bypassed	
SWITCHEL treacle beer	
SWOONING a syncope	**Med.**
SWOOPING descending; rushing	
SWOPPING exchanging	
SWORD-ARM right arm	
SWORD-CUT a wound	
SWORD-LAW violence	
SWOTTING	
SYBARITE a voluptuary	
SYBOTISM pig culture	
SYCAMINE mulberry tree	**B.**
SYCAMORE species of maple	**B.**
SYCONIUM figlike fruit	**B.**
SYENITIC (syenite)	**Min.**
SYLLABIC in syllables	
SYLLABLE to utter	
SYLLABUB sillabub; a drink	
SYLLABUS an abstract; summary	
SYLPHISH SYLPHINE fairy like	
SYMBOLIC emblematic; representative	
SYMMETRY harmony; regularity	
SYMMORPH similar notion	
SYMPATHY fellow-feeling; affinity	
SYMPHONY unison of sound	**Mus.**
SYMPHYLA an insect genus	**Z.**
SYMPLOCE rhetorical repetition	
SYNACRAL (common vertex)	
SYNALGIA sympathetic pain	**Med.**
SYNANCIA fish genus	**Z.**
SYNARCHY joint rule	
SYNASTRY stellar coincidence	
SYNCLINE geological basin	
SYNCOPAL (alteration in	
SYNCOPIC rhythm)	**Mus.**
SYNDETIC linking together	
SYNDROME concurrence	
SYNECHIA an eye-disease	**Med.**
SYNEDRAL (angularity)	
SYNGRAPH signed deed	**Law**
SYNOCHAL feverish	**Med.**
SYNODIST (synod)	**Eccl.**
SYNOMOSY sworn brotherhood	
SYNONYME alternative word with	
SYNONOMY similar meaning	
SYNOPSIS abstract; short outline	

SYNOPTIC comprehensive	
SYNOVIAL (synovia)	**Med.**
SYNTAXIS syntax; grammar	
SYNTEXIS emaciation	**Med.**
SYNTONIC intense sharp	**Mus.**
SYNTONIN acid albumin	**Med.**
SYPHERED flush jointed	
SYRIARCH a chief priest	**Eccl.**
SYRIGMUS noises in the ear	**Med.**
SYSTASIS political union	
SYSTEMIC pertaining to the system	
	Med.
SYSTOLIC contractive	
SYZYGANT (quadratic function)	

T

TABARDER a herald	
TABASHIR mostly silica	**Min.**
TABBINET damask-like fabric	
TABBY-CAT a mouser	**Z.**
TABBYING watered fabric process	
TABITUDE emaciation; atrophy	**Med.**
TABLEAUX pictures (Fr.)	
TABLE-CUT flat-faced	
TABLEFUL	
TABLEMAT plate underlay	
TABOOING prohibiting; banning	
TABORINE tambourine	**Mus.**
TABORING drumming	**Mus.**
TABORITE extreme Hussite	**Eccl.**
TABOURET embroidery frame	
TABULATE enumerate; catalogue	
TAC-AU-TAC (fencing)	
TACAHOUT a leaf gall	**B.**
TACITURN mute; reticent; silent	
TACKLING harnessing; dealing with	
TACKSMAN tenant (Sc.)	
TACTICAL strategic	
TACTLESS insensitive; indiscreet	
TAENIOID ribbonlike	
TAFFRAIL tafereel; stern-rail	**Naut.**
TAGILITE copper phosphate	**Chem.**
TAIGLING entangling	
TAIL-BOOM an aeroplane spar	
TAILCOAT formal jacket	
TAILGATE trombone technique	**Mus.**
TAILINGS mining refuse	
TAILLESS Manx; without end	
TAILORED	
TAILRACE (mill stream)	
TAILROPE guide-rope	
TAINTING corrupting; sullying	
TAINTURE taint; stain; blot	
TAKE-OVER acquire control	
TAKER-OFF mimic; quantity surveyor	
TAKINGLY captivatingly; winningly	
TALAPOIN Buddhist monk	**Eccl.**
TALENTED accomplished; gifted	
TALESMAN a juror	

TALISMAN charm; amulet
TALKABLE conversable
TALK-DOWN landing technique **Aeron.**
TALLIAGE Crown tax;
TALLIATE imposition
TALLNESS height; loftiness
TALLOWED fattened
TALLOWER tallow-chandler
TALLYING recording; agreeing
TALLYMAN pedlar
TALMUDIC (the Talmud) **Eccl.**
TAMANDUA arboreal ant-eater **Z.**
TAMANOIR
TAMARACK American larch **B.**
TAMARIND tropical tree **B.**
TAMARISK evergreen shrub **B.**
TAMEABLE submissive; docile
TAMELESS intractable; wild
TAMENESS dullness; monotony
TAMPERED interfered; machinated
TAMPERER meddler; schemer; plotter
TAN-BALLS (refuse bark)
TAN-HOUSE tan-bark store
TAN-STOVE used for tan-bark
TANGENCY, TANGENCE a state of contact
TANGIBLE tactile; positive; corporeal
TANGIBLY palpably; obviously
TANGLING complicating; matting
TANISTRY Irish land tenure **Law.**
TANNABLE
TANNADAR Indian policeman
TANTALUM metallic element **Chem.**
TANTALUS spirit-stand
TANTICLE stickleback **Z.**
TANTRISM Indian doctrine
TANTRIST a devotee
TANZIMAT Turkish reform bill
TAPADERA leather stirrup guard
TAP-DANCE
TAPE-LINE tape measure
TAPERING slightly conical; pointed
TAPESTRY woven work
TAPEWORM a parasite **Z.**
TAPIROID like the tapirs **Z.**
TARA-FERN bracken (N.Z.) **B.**
TARBOOSH a fez
TARGETED armed with a buckler
TARGUMIC (Bible in Aramaic) **Eccl.**
TARIFFED dutiable; taxed
TARLATAN muslin; tarletan
TARPEIAN (Roman rock)
TARRAGON savoury herb **B.**
TARRYING awaiting; loitering; halting
TARSIPED kangaroo-footed **Z.**
TARSIPES small marsupial **Z.**
TARTARIC (Tartar)
TARTARIN potash **Chem.**
TARTARUM tartar compound
TARTARUS sunless abyss
TARTNESS sharpness; piquancy

TARTRATE a tartar salt **Chem.**
TARTUFFE a hypocrite
TAR-WATER an infusion **Med.**
TASKWORK piece-work
TASTABLE savoury; palatable
TASTE-BUD
TASTEFUL discriminative; elegant
TATTERED in rags; rent
TATTLERY idle gossip
TATTLING chatting; prattling
TATTOOER, TATTOOED skin artist
TAUNTING deriding; flouting; reviling
TAUROCOL bull's glue
TAUTENED tightened; stretched
TAUTNESS strain; tenseness
TAVERNER inn-keeper; Boniface
TAWDRILY gaudily; garishly; flashily
TAXATION imposition; levy; toll
TAXIARCH Greek commander
TAXIRANK cab queue
TAXODIUM swamp-cypress **B.**
TAXOLOGY,TAXONOMY classification
TAXPAYER
TEA-BOARD tea-tray
TEA-BREAK refreshment pause (industrial)
TEA-CADDY
TEA-CHEST
TEA-CLOTH
TEA-FIGHT a bun-worry
TEA-HOUSE
TEA-PARTY (Boston 1773)
TEA-PLANT **B.**
TEA-TABLE
TEA-SPOON
TEACHING instructing; enlightening
TEAMSTER waggoner; drayman
TEAMWISE harnessed together
TEAMWORK co-operation
TEARDROP a tear
TEAR-DUCT lachrymal duct **Med.**
TEARLESS unfeeling
TEATHING fertilizing
TECHNICS doctrine of arts
TECTARIA shell-fish **Z.**
TECTONIC constructive
TEEN-AGER youngster
TEETHING dentition
TEETOTAL dry; total abstinence
TEETOTUM small top
TEGUMENT,TEGMINAL the skin **Med.**
TELARIAN web-spinner **Z.**
TELECAST televised
TELEFILM television film
TELEGONY hereditary influence
TELEGRAM a wire
TELESTIC ending
TELETYPE teleprint (Telex)
TELEVIEW watch television programmes

TELLTALE sneak; revealer; indicator
TELLURAL earthy
TELLURIC (tellurium) **Chem.**
TELOOGOO Dravidian dialect
TELOTYPE printed telegram
TEMERITY rashness; audacity
TEMEROUS reckless; bold; foolhardy
TEMPERED toughened; moderated
TEMPLATE a pattern; a jig
TEMPORAL secular; transient
TEMPTING alluring; inveigling
TENACITY adhesiveness; cohesion
TENAILLE a rampart
TENANTED occupied; dwelt
TENANTRY the tenants
TENDANCE attendance; care; attention
TENDENCY bias; drift; inclination
TENDERED offered; estimated
TENDERLY leniently; gently; softly
TENEBRAE R.C. service **Eccl.**
TENEMENT a flat or house-block
TENONING mortising
TENON-SAW
TENORIST a tenor **Mus.**
TENOTOMY tendon-cutting **Med.**
TENSIBLE tensile; ductile
TENTACLE a feeler **Z.**
TENTERED stretched
TENTWORK embroidery
TENTWORT a fern **B.**
TEOCALLI Mexican temple
TEPEFIED warmed up
TEPHRITE andesite **Min.**
TEPIDITY lukewarmness
TERAPHIM Hebrew idols
TEREBENE (turpentine) **Chem.**
TEREDINE teredo, boring worm **Z.**
TERGETIC dorsal **Z.**
TERMATIC an artery **Med.**
TERMINAL binding screw
TERMINER a determination **Law**
TERMINUS the end of a line
TERMLESS boundless
TERRACED
TERRAPIN tortoise **Z.**
TERRAZO Venetian mosaic
TERRIBLE formidable; dire; gruesome
TERRIBLY frightfully; awfully
TERRIFIC horrific; dreadful
TERTIARY third in order
TERTIATE triplicate
TERYLENE artificial cloth
TERZETTO a trio **Mus.**
TESSELLA ⎫
TESSERAE ⎬ small tiles for paving
TESSERAL tesselated
TESSULAR like dice
TEST-CASE **Law**
TEST-TUBE glass tube **Chem.**
TESTABLE bequeathable; devisable

TESTACEA animals with shells **Z.**
TESTACEL a little shell **Z.**
TESTAMUR a certificate
TESTATOR will-maker; devisor **Law**
TETANIZE cause spasms **Med.**
TETANOID convulsive
TETCHILY peevishly; testily
TETHERED restricted; tied; fastened
TETRADIC fourfold **Chem.**
TETRAGON quadrangle
TETRAPLA Bible in four versions **Eccl.**
TETRAPOD four-footed
TETRARCH Roman governor
TEUTONIC Germanic
TEXT-BOOK a manual
TEXT-HAND large script
TEXTRINE (weaving); textile
TEXTUARY authoritative
TEXTUIST text reciter **Eccl.**
THALAMIA layers of cells **B.**
THALAMUS an inner room; brain **Med.**
THALLIUM metallic element **Chem.**
THANEDOM thane's jurisdiction
THANKFUL grateful; beholden
THANKING acknowledging gracefully
THATCHED covered with straw
THATCHER a craftsman
THEARCHY theocracy **Eccl.**
THEETSEE black varnish **B.**
THEIFORM like tea
THEMATIC dissertative
THEOCRAT divine ruler
THEODICY a philosophy
THEOGONY (genesis of the gods)
THEOLOGY divinity **Eccl.**
THEORIES speculations; hypothesis
THEORIST conjecturer
THEORIZE postulate
THEOSOPH inspired person
THEREFOR for that purpose
THEREOUT therefrom
THERIACA an opiate **Med.**
THERMITE incendiary mixture **Chem.**
THESPIAN barnstormer; trouper
THEURGIC magical
THEWLESS weak; frail; feeble
THICKEST densest; closest
THICKISH rather thick
THICKNEE the stone curlew **Z.**
THICKSET closely planted
THIEVERY larceny
THIEVING purloining; filching
THIEVISH sly; stealthy
THIGGING begging
THINGAMY thingumabob
THINKING ruminating; cogitating
THINNESS attenuation; emaciation
THINNEST lankiest; leanest
THINNING reducing; diminishing
THINNISH meagre; spare

THIRLAGE milling rights **Law**
THIRSTED craved; yearned; longed
THIRTEEN the baker's dozen
THISNESS individuality
THLIPSIS compression **Med.**
THOLE-PIN rowlock
THOMEANS Malabar Christians **Eccl.**
THORACIC (thorax) **Z.**
THORNBUT turbot **Z.**
THORNSET beset with thorns **B.**
THOROUGH complete; perfect
THOUSAND M; mille
THRALDOM slavery; bondage
THRANITE trireme rower
THRAPPLE windpipe; thropple **Z.**
THRASHED drubbed
THRASHER fox-shark; thrush **Z.**
THRAWART obstinate (Sc.)
THREADED strung
THREADEN made of thread
THREADER shuttle-worker
THREAPED contradicted (Sc.)
THREATEN menace; intimidate
THREE-PLY threefold; triple; treble
THRENODY, THRENODE sad song **Mus.**
THRESHED beat out grain; discussed
THRESHEL a flail
THRESHER mocking-bird **Z.**
THRESTLE three-legged stool
THRIDACE lettuce juice
THRILLED agitated; stirred; excited
THRILLER a gripping story; curdler
THRIVING flourishing; prospering
THROBBED pulsated; beat; palpitated
THROMBIN blood clotting enzyme **Med.**
THROMBUS blood-clot **Med.**
THRONGED crowded; flocked
THRONING enthroning
THROPPLE windpipe; thrapple **Z.**
THROSTLE missel thrush **Z.**
THROTTLE garrotte; strangle; stifle
THROWING casting; hurling; slinging
THROW-OUT rejected product
THRUMMED strummed
THRUMMER vamper **Mus.**
THRUSTED intruded; drove; pushed
THRUSTER reckless rider
THUDDING reverberating
THUGGERY ⎱ brutality; violence;
THUGGISM ⎰ criminal assault
THUMBING fingering
THUMB-NUT screwed by hand
THUMBPOT small flower pot
THUMPING enormous
THUNDERY gloomy; frowning
THURIBLE incense censer **Eccl.**
THURIFER incense bearer **Eccl.**
THURSDAY
THUSWISE like so
THWACKED thumped; belaboured

THWARTED frustrated; balked
THWARTER obstructionist
THYRSOID (Bacchus's ivied staff)
TIBIALIS tibial muscle **Med.**
TICK-BEAN horse bean **B.**
TICK-SEED coreopsis **B.**
TICK-SHOP (goods on credit)
TICK-TACK signalling system (racing)
TICK-TICK, TICK-TOCK watch or clock
TICKETED labelled
TICKLING titillation
TICKLISH critical; risky
TIDEGATE, TIDE-LOCK dock
TIDELESS
TIDEMARK H.W.M. or L.W.M.
TIDEMILL
TIDESMAN customs officer
TIDE-WAVE tidal wave
TIDINESS neatness; trimness
TIED-HOUSE accommodation dependent on job
TIGELLUM first bud on a stem **B.**
TIGELLUS an internode **B.**
TIGER-CAT margay; ocelot **Z.**
TIGERISH ferocious
TIGERISM voracity
TIGHT-WAD a miser
TILE-KILN tile factory
TILLABLE arable; cultivable
TILLERED produced offshoots
TILT-BOAT boat with roof **Naut.**
TILT-YARD tilting yard
TIMBERED wooded
TIME-BALL time signal
TIME-BILL time-table
TIME-BOMB
TIME-BOOK works record
TIME-CARD a register
TIME-FUSE time-fuze
TIMELESS untimely
TIME-WORK rate of pay
TIMEWORN decayed; weatherbeaten
TIMIDITY fearfulness; shyness
TIMONIST misanthrope
TIMONEER helmsman **Naut.**
TIMOROSO hesitatingly; timidly **Mus.**
TIMOROUS fearful; pusillanimous
TINCTURE tinge; solution **Med.**
TINE-TARE the vetch **B.**
TINEWALD, TYNEWALD Manx Parliament
TINGEING colouring
TINGLING thrilling
TINGLISH sensation
TINKERED botched
TINKERLY clumsily
TINKLING clinking
TINNITUS ringing in the ears **Med.**
TINPLATE
TINSELLY tawdry
TINSMITH tin worker
TINSTONE cassiterite **Min.**

TINSTUFF tin ore   **Min.**
TINTAMAR confused noise
TINTLESS colourless
TIPPLING toping; soaking steadily
TIPSTAFF court officer   **Law**
TIPULARY (crane-flies)   **Z.**
TIRELESS inexhaustible
TIRESOME tedious; fretful
TIRONIAN (Roman shorthand)
TIRRIVIE tantrum (Sc.)
TISSUING interweaving
TIT-TAT-TO a game; criss-cross
TITANESS a giantess
TITANIAN (titanium)   **Chem.**
TITANITE sphene   **Min.**
TITHABLE subject to tithes   **Eccl.**
TITHONIC actinic
TITIVATE tidy up
TITMOUSE a small bird   **Z.**
TITRATED saturated (solution)   **Med.**
TITTERED giggled
TITTEREL whimbrel; curlew   **Z.**
TITTERER sniggerer
TITTUPPY frisky; lively
TITUBANT stumbling
TITUBATE stagger
TITULARY nominal; titular
TIVERING marking sheep
TOAD-FISH the sapo   **Z.**
TOAD-FLAX snapdragon   **B.**
TOAD-PIPE a horsetail   **B.**
TOAD-SPIT cuckoo-spit
TOADYING fawning
TOADYISH sycophantic
TOADYISM obsequiousness
TOBOGGAN toboggin; taboggin
TOCOLOGY obstetrics   **Med.**
TODDLING strolling aimlessly
TOGETHER in unison
TOILETTE ceremonial wear
TOILLESS workless
TOILSOME arduous; laborious
TOILWORN fatigued; tired; weary
TOKOLOGY tocology   **Med.**
TOLBOOTH a toll-booth
TOLERANT forbearing; liberal
TOLERATE suffer; brook
TOLL-DISH (used in mills)   **Meas.**
TOLL-GATE
TOLLETAN of Toledo
TOLTECAN early Mexican
TOM-NODDY puffin; a dolt   **Z.**
TOMAHAWK war hatchet
TOMALLEY lobster-liver   **Z.**
TOMATOES love apples   **B.**
TOMBLESS no tomb
TOMENTUM a downy covering   **Med.**
TOMMY-BAR small lever
TOMMY-GUN a handy weapon
TOMMY-ROT balderdash; nonsense

TOMOGRAM X-Ray photograph   **Med.**
TOMORROW the following day
TOMUNDAR Baluchi chief
TONALITE igneous rock   **Min.**
TONALITY pitch   **Mus.**
TONEDEAF unmusical
TONELESS unmusical
TONGUING barking; licking
TONICITY healthiness   **Med.**
TONSILAR (tonsils)   **Med.**
TONSURED clerical; shaven   **Eccl.**
TOONWOOD Indian red wood   **B.**
TOOTHFUL a short drink
TOOTH-KEY forceps   **Med.**
TOOTLING playing the flute   **Mus.**
TOP-BOOTS
TOP-DRESS to manure
TOP-HEAVY tipsy; ill-proportioned
TOP-LEVEL, TOPNOTCH excellent
TOP-LOFTY bombastic
TOP-PROUD very proud
TOP-SHELL a mollusc   **Z.**
TOP-STONE a finial
TOPARCHY small state control
TOPAZINE (topaz)   **Min.**
TOPOLOGY an aid to memory
TOPONOMY⎫
TOPONYMY⎭ topical terminology
TOPPLING falling
TOR-OUZEL the ring-ousel   **Z.**
TORCHING night fishing
TORCULAR a tourniquet   **Med.**
TOREADOR bullfighter
TOREUTES artist in metal
TOREUTIC chased metal-work
TORMINAL colicky   **Med.**
TORNADIC (tornadoes); very stormy
TOROIDAL like an anchor-ring
TOROSITY muscularity
TORPIDLY apathetically; dully
TORQUATE collared
TORSHENT youngest child (U.S.A.)
TORTILLA maize cake; omelette (Sp.)
TORTIOUS injurious   **Law**
TORTOISE terrapin   **Z.**
TORTUOSE⎫ twisted; winding;
TORTUOUS⎭ wreathed; deceitful
TORTURED agonized; racked
TORTURER tormentor
TORULOID⎫
TORULOSE⎭ somewhat cylindrical
TOTALITY full amount; sum
TOTALIZE to add up
TOTEMISM symbolism
TOTITIVE (no common factor)
TOTTERED reeled; staggered
TOUCHILY peevishly; petulantly
TOUCHING concerning; pathetic
TOUCHPAN priming pan
TOUGHEST most stubborn

TOUGHISH stiffish; leathery
TOURELLE slender tower
TOURNURE turn; contour; curve
TOUSLING ruffling; rumpling
TOWARDLY toward; docile; tractile
TOWERING soaring; mounting
TOWN-HALL
TOWNLAND a township
TOWNLESS
TOWNSHIP a municipality
TOWNSMAN
TOWN-TALK local gossip
TOXAEMIA blood-poisoning **Med.**
TOXICANT poisonous
TOXICITY poisonousness
TOYISHLY playfully
TRACHEAL⎫ (windpipe) **Med.**
TRACHEAN⎭
TRACHOMA eye disease **Med.**
TRACHYTE volcanic rock **Min.**
TRACKAGE towing; traction
TRACKING spooring; trailing
TRACKMAN (railroad track)
TRACKWAY path or open road
TRACTATE a treatise; a tract
TRACTILE ductile; tractable
TRACTION attraction; towage; hauling
TRACTIVE pulling
TRACTORY tractive
TRACTRIX geometrical curve
TRADEFUL commercial
TRADITOR traitor; quisling; renegade
TRADUCED defamed; slandered
TRADUCER calumniator; libeller
TRAGICAL calamitous; disastrous
TRAGOPAN Chinese pheasant **Z.**
TRAILING hauling; dragging
TRAIL-NET a trawl
TRAINING drilling; schooling
TRAIN-OIL
TRAIPSED gadded about
TRAMPING trudging; hiking
TRAMPLED trod under foot
TRAMPLER
TRAMROAD tramway
TRANCING sleeping; dreaming
TRANGRAM a knick-knack
TRANQUIL placid; calm; serene
TRANSACT negotiate; conduct; enact
TRANSEPT cross-aisle **Eccl.**
TRANSFER make over; exchange
TRANSFIX penetrate; perforate; impale
TRANSHIP change conveyance
TRANSIRE customs pass
TRANSMEW transmute (obs.)
TRANSMIT despatch; forward; remit
TRANSUDE to sweat
TRAP-BALL an old game
TRAP-DOOR door in the floor
TRAP-FALL a trap

TRAP-TUFA⎫ rock of volcanic
TRAP-TUFF⎭ origin **Min.**
TRAPESED traipsed; tramped
TRAPEZIA trapeziums
TRAPPEAN (traprock) **Min.**
TRAPPING snaring
TRAPPIST Cistercian monk **Eccl.**
TRAPPOUS like traprock **Min.**
TRASHERY rubbish; balderdash
TRASHILY
TRASLING freshwater perch **Z.**
TRAVERSE thwart; obstruct
TRAVESTY a burlesque; parody
TRAWLING fishing
TRAY-TRIP a draughts game
TREACLED (moth catching)
TREADING trampling; pacing; stepping
TREADLED pedalled
TREADLER bicyclist
TREASURE preserve; hoard; garner
TREASURY a repository
TREATING entertaining; dealing
TREATISE written discourse; essay
TREBLING
TRECENTO 14th Century in Italian art
TREE-CALF leather binding
TREE-CRAB (lives on coco-nuts) **Z.**
TREE-DOVE Indian pigeon **Z.**
TREE-FERN tropical fern **B.**
TREE-FROG many species **Z.**
TREELESS
TREE-NAIL long wooden pin
TREKKING migrating
TREMANDO tremulously **Mus.**
TREMBLED quivered; shook; quaked
TREMBLER vibrator; oscillator
TREMLELA jelly-like fungi **B.**
TRENCHED encroached; furrowed
TRENCHER wooden platter
TRENDING inclining; tending
TREPHINE cutting tool **Med.**
TRESPASS sin; intrude; transgress
TRESSURE heraldic border
TREWSMAN (wearing trews)
TRIADIST composer of triads
TRIALISM (body, soul and spirit)
TRIALITY threeness
TRIANGLE flogging frame
TRIAPSAL having three apses
TRIARCHY rule of three
TRIARIAN of the third rank
TRIASSIC geological formation **Min.**
TRIAXIAL having three axes
TRIBASIC **Chem.**
TRIBELET a small tribe
TRIBONYX genus of water-hens **Z.**
TRIBRACH three short syllables
TRIBUNAL court of justice
TRIBUTED contributed
TRIBUTER piece-work miner

TRICHINA parasitic worm   **Med.**
TRICHITE hairlike fibre   **Min.**
TRICHODA hairy infusoria   **Z.**
TRICHOMA hair disease   **Med.**
TRICHOME hairy outgrowth   **B.**
TRICHORD three-stringed lyre   **Mus.**
TRICKERY chicanery; deception
TRICKILY artfully; cunningly
TRICKING duping; gulling
TRICKLED oozed; percolated
TRICKLET small rill
TRICKSEY wily; pretty
TRICOLOR flag of France
TRICTRAC variety of backgammon
TRICYCLE
TRIDACNA genus of molluscs   **Z.**
TRIFLING toying; trivial; paltry
TRIGGING stopping; skidding
TRIGLOID gurnard genus   **Z.**
TRIGLYPH Doric ornamentation
TRIGNESS trimness; neatness
TRIGONAL⎫ triangular
TRIGONIC⎭
TRIGONON a triangle
TRIGRAPH a triphthong
TRILEMMA (three alternatives)
TRILLING quavering; warbling   **Mus.**
TRILLION million³ (G.B.) million² (USA.)
TRILLIUM a lily genus   **B.**
TRILOBED trilobate   **B.**
TRIMETER (versification)
TRIMMING decorating; adjusting
TRIMNESS neatness; tidiness
TRIMURTI Hindu Trinity   **Eccl.**
TRINGINE⎫ genus of sandpipers   **Z.**
TRINGOID⎭
TRINODAL treble-jointed
TRIODION Greek prayer-book   **Eccl.**
TRIOLEIN fatty oil
TRIP-BOOK (fishing records)
TRIPEMAN tripeseller
TRIPHANE spodumene   **Min.**
TRIPLANE an aeroplane
TRIPLING trebling
TRIPLITE a phosphate   **Min.**
TRIPODAL tripedal; three-footed
TRIPPANT heraldic trotting
TRIPPING lapsing; dancing; felling
TRIP-SLIP tram ticket (U.S.A.)
TRIPTOTE having 3 cases only
TRIPTYCH painted screen   **Eccl.**
TRIP-WIRE obstacle; brake   **Naut.**
TRISEMIC iambic
TRISKELE swastika
TRISTFUL sorrowful; dejected; doleful
TRITICAL trite; common; hackneyed
TRITICUM wheat, etc.   **B.**
TRIUMVIR one of three (Rome)
TRIUNITY trinity
TRIVALVE with three valves

TROCHAIC (verse)
TROCHITE sea-urchin's joint   **Z.**
TROCHLEA a cartilage   **Med.**
TROCHOID cycloid
TROLLING singing; spinning
TROLLOPY slatternly
TROMBLON fire-arm support
TROMBONE   **Mus.**
TROOPIAL American starling   **Z.**
TROOPING collecting; parading
TROPHESY indigestion   **Med.**
TROPHIES emblems of victory
TROPICAL figurative; fervid
TROT-COSY head covering (Sc.)
TROTTING
TROTTOIR side-walk (Fr.)
TROUBLED incommoded; vexed
TROUBLER disturber; pest
TROUNCED thrashed; castigated
TROUPIAL American song-bird   **Z.**
TROUSERS trowsers
TROUTING fishing for trout
TROUTLET small trout   **Z.**
TROUVERE French lyric poets
TROWSERS trousers
TRUANTLY lazily; evasively
TRUCKAGE cost of conveyance
TRUCKING bartering; hawking
TRUCKLED cringed; yielded; stooped
TRUCKLER servile agent
TRUDGEON a swimming stroke
TRUDGING foot-slogging
TRUE-BLUE faithful partisan
TRUE-BORN⎫ not a mongrel
TRUE-BRED⎭
TRUE-LOVE sweetheart; a herb   **B.**
TRUENESS honesty; accuracy; veracity
TRUMPERY rubbish; trash; trifling
TRUMPING ruffing
TRUNCATE lopped
TRUNDLED rolled; bowled; revolved
TRUNKFUL
TRUNNION gun support
TRUSSING binding; fastening
TRUSTFUL confiding; trusty
TRUSTILY faithfully; staunchly
TRUSTING relying on; believing
TRY-HOUSE oil refinery
TRYPTONE pancreatic ferment   **Med.**
TRYSTING rendezvousing; meeting
TUB-WHEEL flat water-wheel
TUBE-FORM tubular
TUBERCLE tumour   **Med.**
TUBEROSE Mexican lily   **B.**
TUBEROUS knobbed
TUBE-WELL artesian well
TUBICOLE caddis-worm   **Z.**
TUBIFORM tubular
TUBIPORE a coral   **Z.**
TUBULATE formed of tubes

TUCKAHOE edible fungus **B.**
TUCKSHOP sweet-shop
TUCOTUCO small rodent **Z.**
TUG-OF-WAR
TUG-PLANE (gliders)
TUKUTUKU tucotuco; rodent (S.A.) **Z.**
TULA-WORK niello-work
TUMBLING falling; tripping
TUMEFIED swollen; distended
TUMIDITY bombast; pomposity
TUMOURED distended; enlarged
TUMP-LINE carrying strap
TUMULATE make a barrow
TUMULOSE tumulous; many mounds
TUN-BELLY pot-belly
TUNELESS unharmonious; unmusical
TUNGSTEN same as wolfram **Chem.**
TUNGSTIC (tungsten) **Chem.**
TUNICARY ascidian; sea-squirt **Z.**
TUNICATE coated; a mollusc **Z.**
TUNING-IN (wireless)
TUNISIAN (Tunis)
TURANIAN family of languages
TURBANED wearing a turban
TURBIDLY disorderly; opaquely
TURBINAL scroll-like bone **Med.**
TURBO-JET gas engine **Aeron.**
TURCOMAN ⎱ Turks of central Asia
TURKOMAN ⎰
TURF-CLAD grassy
TURF-MOSS boggy land
TURGIDLY pompously; grandiosely
TURLOUGH shallow pool (Ir.)
TURMERIC yellow dye **B.**
TURNAGRA thrush (N.Z.) **Z.**
TURNCOAT renegade
TURNCOCK water-man
TURNDOWN fold down; reject
TURNOVER a pasty
TURNPIKE toll-gate; a road
TURN-SICK giddy
TURN-SKIN a were-wolf
TURNSOLE sunflower **B.**
TURNSPIT kitchen-boy
TURRETED
TUSSOCKY tufty
TUTELAGE guardianship; charge; care
TUTELARY protective
TUTORAGE instruction
TUTORESS governess
TUTORIAL educational
TUTORING teaching
TUTORISM education; coaching
TWADDLED gabbled
TWADDLER tattler; chatter-box
TWANGING
TWANGLED twanged
TWATTLED prattled
TWATTLER a gossip
TWEAKING twisting

TWEEDLED fiddled
TWEELING twilling
TWEEZERS forceps **Tool**
TWIDDLED twisted
TWIDDLER thumb-twirler
TWIGGING understanding
TWILIGHT dusk
TWILLING weaving
TWIN-BORN contemporaneous
TWINGING twitching
TWINKLED sparkled
TWINKLER a star
TWINLING twin lamb **Z.**
TWIRLING revolving; whirling
TWISTING writhing; contorting
TWITCHED jerked; snatched
TWITCHER convulsive mover
TWITTING upbraiding; taunting
TWO-EDGED
TWO-FACED false; double-dealing
TWO-PENCE
TWOPENNY cheap; worthless
TWO-PIECE costume; suit
TYCHONIC astronomic; (Tycho Brahe)
TYMPANIC like a drum
TYMPANUM ear-drum **Med.**
TYNEWALD Manx Parliament
TYPE-CAST single-character actor
TYPE-HIGH standard height
TYPHLOPS earthworms, etc. **Z.**
TYPHONIC cyclonic
TYPIFIED exemplified; symbolized
TYPIFIER prototype
TYPOLITE fossil footstep **Min.**
TYPOLOGY symbolism
TYPORAMA fac-simile
TYROCINY pupilage
TYROLEAN, TYROLESE (Tyrol)
TYROLITE Tyrol sandstone **Min.**
TYRONISM apprenticeship
TYRRANIC despotic; autocratic
TYRTAEAN (warlike verse)
TZAREVNA ⎱ Empress of Russia;
TZARITSA ⎰ Tzarina

U

UBIQUITY omnipresence
UDOMETER rain gauge
UGLIFIED made hideous
UGLINESS repulsiveness; unsightliness
ULTERIOR remote; hidden; indirect
ULTIMATA plural of ultimatum
ULTIMATE furthest; final; eventual
ULTIMITY last consequence
ULTRAISM extreme views
ULTRAIST extremist
ULULATED howled; yowled; lamented
UMBELLAR form of inflorescence **B.**

UMBONATE having a boss
UMBRATIC shadowy; shady; obscure
UMBRELLA a gamp
UMBRETTE African heron **Z.**
UMBRIERE vizor of helmet
UMPIRAGE arbitration; adjudication
UMQUHILE formerly (Sc.)
UNABASED not degraded; unashamed
UNABATED undiminished; persistent
UNACHING free from pain
UNACTIVE inactive; inert; torpid
UNADMIRE view with tolerance
UNADORED unloved; unvenerated
UNAFRAID bold; valiant; undaunted
UNAIMING purposeless; random
UNALLIED alone; separate; isolated
UNAMAZED composed; unruffled
UNAMUSED not entertained; bored
UNANCHOR let loose
UNANELED unshriven; unanointed
UNARGUED not disputed
UNARTFUL simple; artless; naive
UNATONED not expiated
UNATTIRE disrobe; undress
UNAVOWED unconfessed; secret
UNAWARES suddenly; unexpectedly
UNBACKED unaided; unassisted
UNBAGGED trouserless; let loose
UNBANDED disbanded; disembodied
UNBANNED permitted; unrestricted
UNBARBED unshaven; pointless
UNBARKED stripped of bark
UNBARRED unfastened; opened
UNBATHED untubbed
UNBEATEN untrodden; undefeated
UNBEDDED uprooted
UNBEFOOL undeceive
UNBEHELD not visible
UNBELIEF incredulity; scepticism
UNBENIGN malignant; malevolent
UNBEREFT not bereaved; unspoiled
UNBESEEM to be unworthy
UNBIASED impartial; unprejudiced
UNBIDDEN spontaneous; unsolicited
UNBISHOP deprive of a bishopric **Eccl.**
UNBITTED unbridled; uncurbed **Naut.**
UNBLAMED uncensured; unrebuked
UNBLOODY not cruel
UNBODIED incorporeal
UNBODING not expecting; unforeseeing
UNBOILED raw
UNBOLTED unfastened; unbarred
UNBONNET remove the hat; uncap
UNBOOTED stripped of boots
UNBOUGHT not bribed; incorrupt
UNBOYISH sedate; unchildish
UNBRACED relaxed; unsupported
UNBREECH debag
UNBREWED pure; genuine
UNBRIBED not corrupt

UNBRIDLE free from restraint
UNBROKEN inviolate; continuous
UNBUCKLE unfasten; unclasp
UNBUDDED not yet in bud
UNBUNDLE unpack
UNBUOYED **Naut.**
UNBURDEN disclose; reveal
UNBURIED uninterred
UNBURNED uncharred
UNBURROW to ferret out
UNBUSIED idle; unemployed
UNBUTTON unfasten
UNCAGING releasing; liberating
UNCALLED not awakened
UNCANDID reserved; cautious
UNCAPPED unbonneted
UNCARTED unloaded
UNCASING disengaging; unpacking
UNCAUGHT still free
UNCAUSED no reason for
UNCHANCE misfortune
UNCHANCY uncanny; dangerous
UNCHARGE unload
UNCHASTE impure; lewd
UNCHEERY dull; gloomy
UNCHEWED not masticated
UNCHIDED unrebuked
UNCHURCH excommunicate **Eccl.**
UNCIATIM ounce by ounce
UNCIFORM hook-shaped
UNCINATA marine worms **Z.**
UNCINATE hooked
UNCLENCH ⎫
UNCLINCH ⎬ to open the hand
UNCLEWED unwound **Naut.**
UNCLOSED open; ajar
UNCLOTHE undress
UNCLOUDY clear
UNCLUTCH declutch
UNCOATED
UNCOCKED
UNCOIFED headdressless; unkempt
UNCOILED unwound
UNCOINED not minted
UNCOMBED unkempt
UNCOMELY lacking grace
UNCOMMON odd; rare; strange
UNCOOPED set free
UNCORDED unbound
UNCORKED
UNCOSTLY inexpensive
UNCOUPLE disconnect
UNCOWLED unveiled
UNCREATE kill
UNCTUOUS greasy; oily; fulsome
UNCULLED unpicked
UNCURBED licentious; loose; unbridled
UNCURLED straightened
UNCURSED not execrated
UNDAMPED free to vibrate

UNDASHED undaunted; undismayed
UNDAZZLE undaze
UNDECENT indecent (obs.)
UNDECKED not adorned   **Naut.**
UNDEEDED not noteworthy
UNDEFIED unchallenged
UNDEFINE make indefinite
UNDENTED
UNDERACT perform inadequately
UNDERAGE immature
UNDERAID help secretly
UNDERARM (bowling)
UNDERBID offer less
UNDERBUD
UNDERBUY cut the price
UNDERCUT the tenderloin
UNDERDID economized effort
UNDER-DOG
UNDERFED on short commons
UNDERLAP extend below
UNDERLAY foundation
UNDERLET sublet
UNDERLIE below the surface
UNDER-LIP
UNDERMAN (insufficient crew)   **Naut.**
UNDERPAY remunerate inadequately
UNDERPIN support
UNDERRAN
UNDERRUN
UNDERSAY minimize
UNDERSET a contrary current
UNDERSKY lower sky
UNDERTOW tidal current
UNDEVOUT irreligious; unholy
UNDIMMED untarnished
UNDINTED undented
UNDIPPED
UNDIVINE secular
UNDOCKED (tails)   **Naut.**
UNDOCTOR
UNDOUBLE unfold
UNDRAPED nude
UNDREAMT unimagined
UNDRIVEN not propelled
UNDROSSY free from impurity
UNDULANT wavy
UNDULATE vibrate
UNDULOUS undulating
UNEARNED
UNEASILY restlessly
UNEDIBLE inedible
UNELATED not puffed up
UNENDING everlasting; ceaseless
UNENVIED viewed with complacency
UNERRING certain; sure; exact
UNESPIED not observed
UNEVENLY ruggedly; unequally
UNEXEMPT liable
UNEXPERT unskilled
UNFABLED real; true

UNFADING everlasting; constant
UNFAIRLY dishonestly; falsely
UNFALLEN
UNFASTEN open; let loose
UNFAULTY free from blemish
UNFEARED not held in awe
UNFELLOW to dissociate
UNFENCED not enclosed; open
UNFETTER unchain; unshackle
UNFILIAL undutiful
UNFILLED empty
UNFILMED
UNFIXING detaching
UNFLATED deflated
UNFLAWED flawless; faultless
UNFLESHY skinny
UNFLOWER deflower
UNFLUENT tongue-tied
UNFOILED not baffled
UNFOLDED deployed; disclosed
UNFOOTED untrodden
UNFORCED easy; natural
UNFORGED
UNFORMAL informal; unconventional
UNFORMED shapeless
UNFOUGHT uncontested
UNFOULED clean; unsullied
UNFRAMED
UNFRIEND an enemy
UNFROZEN uncongealed
UNFRUGAL prodigal; lavish; wasteful
UNFUELED unfuelled
UNFUNDED floating
UNFURLED displayed
UNGAINLY uncouth; clumsy
UNGALLED unhurt
UNGEARED unharnessed
UNGENIAL uncongenial; cold
UNGENTLE rude; rough
UNGENTLY harshly; unkindly
UNGIFTED without talent
UNGILDED
UNGILLED (free fish from net)
UNGIRDED beltless; unenclosed
UNGIVING rigid
UNGLAZED paneless
UNGLOVED
UNGLUING ungumming
UNGOADED not harassed; unurged
UNGORGED not sated
UNGOTTEN not gained
UNGOWNED unrobed
UNGRACED awkward
UNGROUND not milled
UNGUICAL (snail, claw, hoof)
UNGUIDED unregulated
UNGUILTY innocent
UNGULATA hoofed mammals
UNGULATE having hoofs
UNGUMMED unstuck

UNHACKED not notched
UNHAIRED scalped
UNHALLOW profane
UNHANDED let go
UNHANGED not dependent
UNHARMED scatheless; immune
UNHASPED unlatched
UNHEADED beheaded
UNHEATED
UNHEDGED
UNHEEDED disregarded
UNHEIRED without an heir
UNHELMED rudderless
UNHELMET deprive of a helmet
UNHELPED unassisted
UNHEPPEN clumsy; maladroit
UNHEROIC timid; shrinking
UNHINGED unsettled
UNHIVING unhousing
UNHONEST dishonest (obs.)
UNHOODED
UNHOOKED unfastened
UNHOOPED
UNHORNED
UNHORSED
UNHOUSED dislodged
UNHUNTED
UNHUSKED
UNIAXIAL having a single axis
UNIBASAL   **Chem.**
UNICYCLE acrobat's cycle
UNIDEAED thoughtless
UNIFYING uniting; merging
UNILOBAR ⎫
UNILOBED ⎭ having one lobe   **B.**
UNIMBUED not saturated
UNINURED not hardened
UNINVITE cancel invitation
UNIONISM combination; alliance
UNIONIST confederate; conservative
UNIONITE lime silicate   **Min.**
UNIPOLAR
UNIQUELY peculiarly; exceptionally
UNIQUITY singularity
UNISONAL harmonious
UNITEDLY jointly; concertedly
UNITIZED treated as a unit
UNIVALVE a mollusc   **Z.**
UNIVERSE the world
UNIVOCAL unanimous
UNJOINED uncoupled
UNJOYFUL dull; mirthless; downcast
UNJOYOUS gloomy; melancholy; glum
UNJUDGED
UNJUSTLY prejudicially; unfairly
UNKENNED unknown
UNKENNEL release
UNKINDLY unfriendly; harshly
UNKINGED deposed
UNKINGLY

UNLACING unloosing
UNLADING unloading
UNLAPPED unwrapped
UNLARDED not intermixed
UNLASHED unfastened
UNLAVISH sparse; frugal
UNLAWFUL illegal; illicit
UNLAYING untwisting
UNLEARNT forgotten
UNLICKED ungainly; awkward
UNLIKELY improbable; risky
UNLIMBER get into action
UNLINEAL not in succession
UNLINING emptying
UNLINKED disconnected
UNLIVELY cheerless; listless
UNLOADED discharged
UNLOCKED open
UNLOOKED unheeded
UNLOOSED slackened
UNLOOSEN set free
UNLORDED not raised to peerage
UNLORDLY
UNLOVELY unpleasing; hideous
UNLOVING passionless
UNLUTING ungumming
UNMAIMED sound
UNMAKING destroying
UNMANNED disheartened
UNMANTLE unrobe
UNMAPPED uncharted
UNMARKED unobserved
UNMARRED unsullied
UNMARTYR debunk
UNMASKED exposed; unveiled
UNMEDDLE unmuddle
UNMEETLY improperly
UNMELTED undissolved
UNMILKED
UNMILLED unground
UNMINDED forgotten
UNMINGLE sort out
UNMISSED
UNMOANED not lamented
UNMOCKED
UNMODISH out of fashion
UNMOORED cast off
UN-MOSAIC contrary to Mosaic law
UNMOVING motionless; impassive
UNMUDDLE co-ordinate
UNMUFFLE (drums)
UNMUZZLE
UNNAPPED (smooth cloth)
UNNATIVE unnatural
UNNEEDED superfluous
UNNERVED frightened
UNNETTED
UNNIMBED without a nimbus
UNNOOKED guileless; straightforward
UNNOTIFY cancel

UNOPENED
UNPACKED
UNPACKER
UNPAINED
UNPAIRED
UNPANGED without remorse
UNPARTED
UNPATHED trackless
UNPAWNED not pledged
UNPEELED
UNPEGGED
UNPENNED released
UNPEOPLE depopulate
UNPICKED
UNPINION
UNPINKED not pierced
UNPINNED
UNPITIED
UNPLACED not in the first three
UNPLIANT stubborn; stiff; rigid
UNPLUMED plucked
UNPOETIC prosaic
UNPOISED out of balance
UNPOISON
UNPOLISH make rough
UNPOLITE unmannerly; impolite
UNPOLLED not voted
UNPOSTED
UNPRAISE crab; criticize
UNPRAYED
UNPREACH recant
UNPRETTY plain
UNPRICED priceless
UNPRIEST unfrock   Eccl.
UNPRINCE
UNPRISON release
UNPRIZED not valued
UNPROPER improper
UNPROVED untested
UNPRUNED
UNPUCKER uncrease
UNPURGED unpurified
UNRACKED unharassed
UNRAISED
UNRANGED in disorder
UNREALLY illusively
UNREAPED not harvested
UNREELED unwound
UNREINED unbridled
UNREPAID not requited
UNREPAIR in disrepair
UNRIDDLE solve; unravel; decipher
UNRIFLED not ransacked
UNRIGGED dismantled
UNRIPPED torn
UNROBING undressing
UNROLLED
UNROOFED
UNROOTED uprooted

UNROUTED
UNRUFFLE plume
UNRUINED
UNRUMPLE smooth
UNSADDLE
UNSAFELY perilously
UNSAFETY danger; hazard
UNSALTED fresh
UNSAPPED not undermined
UNSATING not filling
UNSAYING recanting
UNSCARED not alarmed; unruffled
UNSEALED
UNSEAMED ripped open
UNSEARED uncharred
UNSEASON mistime (obs.)
UNSEATED unhorsed
UNSECRET not trusty
UNSECURE insecure
UNSEEDED not sown
UNSEEING blind
UNSEEMLY unbecoming
UNSEIZED
UNSERVED
UNSETTLE unhinge; disturb
UNSEXUAL
UNSHADED
UNSHAKEN
UNSHAMED unabashed
UNSHAPEN formless
UNSHARED
UNSHAVED unbarbed
UNSHAVEN unshorn
UNSHELVE
UNSHROUD unveil
UNSHRUNK
UNSIFTED not examined
UNSINGED unseared
UNSLAKED unquenched
UNSLUICE open a sluice
UNSMOKED
UNSMOOTH rough
UNSOAPED unwashed
UNSOCIAL reserved
UNSOCKET dislocate
UNSOILED clean
UNSOLDER
UNSOLEMN
UNSOLVED enigmatic
UNSONCIE } unlucky (Sc.)
UNSONSIE }
UNSORTED mixed
UNSOUGHT
UNSOULED spiritless
UNSOURED
UNSPARED
UNSPEEDY deliberate
UNSPHERE
UNSPIKED
UNSPOILT

UNSPOKEN untold	**UNTWINED** untwisted
UNSPRUNG ready-set trap	**UNVAILED** untipped
UNSTABLE inconstant; irresolute	**UNVALUED** not prized
UNSTARCH	**UNVARIED** monotonous
UNSTATED not mentioned	**UNVASSAL** free; emancipate
UNSTAYED unrestrained	**UNVEILED** disclosed
UNSTEADY vacillating	**UNVEILER** revealer
UNSTITCH	**UNVENTED** unuttered
UNSTORED not warehoused	**UNVERSED** unskilled
UNSTRING	**UNVIRTUE** evil; sin; vice
UNSTRUCK not impressed	**UNVIZARD**
UNSTRUNG relaxed; loosed	**UNVOICED** not spoken; mute
UNSUCKED	**UNWAITED** unattended
UNSUITED unbecoming	**UNWALLED** not enclosed
UNSUNNED	**UNWARILY** rash; reckless
UNSURELY unsafely	**UNWARMED** unexcited
UNSWATHE unwrap	**UNWARNED** unadmonished
UNSWAYED unbiased	**UNWARPED** **Naut.**
UNTACKED disjoined	**UNWASHED**
UNTACKLE unhitch	**UNWASTED**
UNTALKED unspoken	**UNWEANED** unalienated
UNTANGLE unravel	**UNWEDDED** unwed
UNTANNED	**UNWEEDED**
UNTAPPED unbroached	**UNWIELDY** ponderous
UNTASKED	**UNWILFUL** docile; pliant
UNTASTED	**UNWILLED** involuntary
UNTAUGHT illiterate	**UNWINDED** not blown
UNTENANT evict	**UNWISDOM** folly; fatuity
UNTENDED neglected	**UNWISELY** irrationally
UNTENDER unsympathetic	**UNWONTED** unusual
UNTENTED uncared for (Sc.)	**UNWOODED**
UNTESTED unproved	**UNWORDED** silent
UNTETHER untie	**UNWORMED**
UNTHAWED	**UNWORTHY** undeserving
UNTHORNY	**UNYOKING**
UNTHREAD disentangle	**UPCAUGHT** caught up
UNTHRIFT a prodigal	**UPCOILED** coiled
UNTHRONE dethrone	**UPCOMING** impending; ascending
UNTHROWN	**UPCURLED**
UNTIDILY disorderly	**UPHEAVAL** earthquake
UNTILING unroofing	**UPHEAVED** lifted up; raised
UNTILLED fallow	**UPHOLDER** partisan
UNTIMELY premature	**UPLIFTED** exalted
UNTINGED uncoloured	**UPMAKING** filling pieces **Naut.**
UNTIRING unwearied	**UPPERCUT** boxing blow
UNTITHED **Eccl.**	**UPPER-TEN** the aristocracy
UNTITLED	**UP-PLOUGH** plough up
UNTOMBED disenterred	**UPRAISED** lifted
UNTONGUE to silence	**UPRIDGED** in ridges
UNTOWARD perverse; froward	**UPRISING** insurrection
UNTRACED untracked	**UPROOTED** eradicated
UNTRADED inexperienced	**UPROUSED** awoken
UNTRUCED without truce	**UPSNATCH** clutch
UNTRUISM a fallacy	**UPSTAIRS**
UNTRUSTY unfaithful	**UPSTAYED** upheld
UNTUCKED unfolded	**UPSTREAM**
UNTUFTED	**UPSTROKE**
UNTUNING disordering	**UPTHRUST** upheaval
UNTURFED stripped of turf	**UPTOSSED**
UNTURNED	**UPTURNED** inverted

UPWAFTED borne aloft
UPWARDLY upwards
URALITIC (uralite)   **Min.**
URBANISM town planning
URBANITY suaveness; courteousness
URBANIZE derusticate
URCEOLUS floral envelope   **B.**
URGENTLY momentously; pressingly
UROCHORD (sea-squirt)   **Z.**
UROCHROA humming-birds   **Z.**
UROCISSA Asiatic magpie   **Z.**
UROMERIC (tail-piece)   **Z.**
UROSTEGE a snake's scale   **Z.**
UROESTON a tail bone   **Z.**
UROSTYLE lengthy tail   **Z.**
URSIFORM like a bear   **Z.**
URSULINE a nun, (St. Ursula)   **Eccl.**
URTICATE to sting; cause a rash
USEFULLY advantageously
USHERDOM schoolmastery
USHERING heralding; introducing
USTILAGO genus of fungi   **B.**
USTULATE scorched
USUFRUCT temporary possession   **Law**
USURIOUS at high interest
USURPING arrogating; assuming
UTILIZED employed; used
UTOPIAST (Utopia)
UTRIFORM bottle-shaped
UTTEREST furthest; remotest
UTTERING disclosing; issuing
UXORIOUS wife-loving

V

VACATING quitting; annulling
VACATION intermission; recess; holiday
VACCINIA cow-pox   **Med.**
VAGABOND vagrant; nomad; wanderer
VAGARIES whims; caprices; crotchets
VAGINANT sheathing   **B.**
VAGINATE sheathed   **B.**
VAGRANCY nomadism; itinerance
VAINNESS vanity; conceit; inanity
VALANCED decorated; draped
VALENTIA woven material
VALERIAN all-heal, medicinal plant   **B.**
VALETING personal attendance
VALHALLA hall of heroes
VALIANCE bravery; intrepidity
VALIANCY courageousness; chivalry
VALIDATE confirm; legalize
VALIDITY soundness; justness
VALKYRIA the Valkyries
VALLANCY large wig
VALLATED cup-shaped; circumvallated
VALORIZE make a currency reform
VALOROUS intrepid; bold; heroic
VALUABLE precious; costly; expensive
VALUATOR appraiser; assessor

VALVELET small valve
VALVULAR containing valves
VAMBRACE arm-armour
VAMOOSED decamped; skedaddled
VAMPIRIC extortionate
VAMPLATE hand-guard of lance
VANADATE vanadium salt   **Chem**
VANADIUM metallic element   **Chem.**
VANDALIC Hunnish; barbarous; savage
VANDYKED indented; notched
VANGUARD forefront; front line
VANILLIC flavoured with vanilla
VANISHED disappeared; dissolved
VANISHER absconder
VANQUISH overpower; rout; subdue
VAPIDITY insipidity
VAPORIZE turn into gas
VAPOROSE unsubstantial; gaseous
VAPOROUS unreal; steamy
VAPOURED evaporated; peevish
VAPOURER boaster; vaunter; braggart
VAQUERIA cattle ranch
VARANOID lizardlike   **Z.**
VARGUENO writing table (Sp.)
VARIABLE mutable; fickle; mercurial
VARIABLY changeably; fitfully
VARIANCE discord; strife; dispute
VARIATED altered; variegated
VARICORN a horned beetle   **Z.**
VARICOSE ⎫ permanently dilated **Med.**
VARICOUS ⎭
VARIETAL mutative; subgeneric
VARIFORM protean; diverse
VARIOLAR pox-marked   **Med.**
VARIORUM commentated edition
VARLETRY the rabble; the crowd
VARTABED Armenian priest   **Eccl.**
VASALIUM vascular tissue   **Med.**
VASCULAR vessels, ducts, etc.   **Med.**
VASCULUM specimen-box   **B.**
VASELINE petroleum jelly   **Min.**
VASIFORM like a duct   **Med.**
VASSALED enslaved
VASSALRY bondage; feudal system
VASTNESS immensity; spaciousness
VATICIDE murder of a prophet
VAULTAGE arched work
VAULTING leaping; bounding
VAUNTERY boastfulness; arrogance
VAUNTFUL ostentatious; swaggering
VAUNTING bragging; crowing
VAUNTLAY (hound movement)
VAVASORY (land tenure)   **Law**
VAVASOUR feudal tenant
VEALSKIN a skin-disease   **Med.**
VEDANTIC (Hindu philosophy)   **Eccl.**
VEGETATE to sprout; (secluded life)
VEGETIVE a vegetable (Shak.)   **B.**
VEHEMENT impetuous; ardent
VEILLESS open to view; undisguised

VEINLESS lack of venation **B.**
VELARIUM awning; canopy
VELATION mystery; concealment
VELATURA picture glazing (It.)
VELLEITY volition; inclination
VELLOPED heraldic wattles
VELOCITY swiftness; rapidity; rate
VELOGRID a grid in a wireless valve
VELVERET ersatz velvet
VELVETED like velvet
VENALITY mercenariness; corruptness
VENATION bunting; pursuit of game
VENDETTA a blood feud; vengeance
VENDIBLE marketable; disposable
VENDIBLY saleably
VENEERED overlaid; disguised
VENENATE poisonous; poisoned; toxic
VENERATE esteem; respect; revere
VENETIAN (Venice)
VENGEFUL vindictive; retributive
VENIABLE pardonable
VENIALLY excusably; trivially
VENOMING poisoning
VENOMOUS venemous; poisonous
VENOSITY full-bloodedness
VENOUSLY veined
VENT-HOLE air-hole
VENT-PLUG barrel-peg
VENTURED hazarded; dared
VENTURER speculator; adventurer
VERACITY truth; truthfulness
VERANDAH covered balcony
VERATRIC hellebore extract **Chem.**
VERATRUM hellebore, etc. **B.**
VERBALLY orally; by word of mouth
VERBATIM word for word
VERBIAGE verbosity; prolixity
VERDANCY greenness
VERDERER forest-keeper
VERDITER green pigment
VERGENCY border; verge
VERGETTE heraldic pallet
VERIFIED confirmed; authenticated
VERIFIER corroborator
VERJUICE sour juice
VERMINLY verminously
VERMOUTH absinthe; wormwood
VERNICLE miraculous imprint
VERONESE (Verona)
VERONICA speedwell plants **B.**
VERRUGAS Peruvian skin disease **Med.**
VERSABLE reversible
VERSELET }
VERSICLE } brief ode
VERTEBRA segment of the spine **Med.**
VERTICAL upright; erect; perpendicular
VERTICES summits; apices; zeniths
VERTICIL a whorl **B.**
VESICANT blistering
VESICATE to blister

VESICULA a pustule **Med.**
VESPIARY wasp's nest
VESTIARY a wardrobe
VESTMENT garment; robe; dress **Eccl.**
VESTUARY vestiary
VESTURAL (robe; clothing)
VESTURER vestment keeper **Eccl.**
VESUVIAN fusee; fuzee
VEXATION affliction; torment; worry
VEXILLAR feathery **Z.**
VEXILLUM a banner; Roman standard
VEXINGLY provokingly; annoyingly
VIAMETER an odometer **Meas.**
VIATICUM Eucharist **Eccl.**
VIBRATED quivered; oscillated
VIBRATOR a trembler; buzzer
VIBRISSA whisker; bristle
VIBROGEN cellular tissue **B.**
VIBRONIC electronic vibrations
VIBURNUM guelder-rose **B.**
VICARAGE **Eccl.**
VICARIAL substituted
VICARIAN deputy
VICARIUS a vicar **Eccl.**
VICE-DEAN a canon **Eccl.**
VICE-KING regent; viceroy
VICENARY based on twenty
VICHYITE (Vichy)
VICINAGE } neighbourhood;
VICINITY } proximity
VICTORIA a vehicle
VICTRESS woman conqueror; victrix
VICTUALS provisions; sustenance
VIDENDUM thing to be seen
VIETMINH people of Vietnam
VIEWABLE able to be seen
VIEWLESS vistaless
VIEWSOME panoramic
VIGILANT circumspect; alert; wakeful
VIGNERON vine-grower (Fr.)
VIGNETTE character sketch
VIGOROSO forcibly **Mus.**
VIGOROUS lusty; powerful; virile
VILENESS baseness; depravity; vice
VILIFIED slandered; defamed; decried
VILIFIER traducer; maligner
VILIPEND disparage; calumniate
VILLADOM suburban villas
VILLAGER
VILLAINY depravity; fraud; rascality
VILLATIC (village)
VINCIBLE conquerable; surmountable
VINCULUM bond of union; link; chain
VINE-CLAD
VINE-GALL
VINE-GRUB a parasite **Z.**
VINE-LAND
VINEYARD grape plantation **B.**
VINOSITY wine flavour
VINTAGER grape gatherer

VINTNERY the wine trade
VINYLITE plastic glass
VIOLABLE transgressive
VIOLATOR ravisher; debaucher
VIOLENCE brute force
VIPERINE venomous　**Z.**
VIPERISH malignant
VIPEROUS treacherous
VIRGINAL early form of spinet　**Mus.**
VIRGINIA tobacco; creeper　**B.**
VIRIDIAN bluish-green colour
VIRIDITY verdure; greenness
VIRILITY manhood; energy; manliness
VIROLOGY virus diseases　**Med.**
VIRTUOSE expert in art
VIRTUOSO connoisseur; expert
VIRTUOUS upright; moral; chaste
VIRULENT bitter in enmity; toxic
VISCACHA pampas hare　**Z.**
VISCERAL abdominal　**Med.**
VISCOUNT a title
VISIGOTH Spanish Goth
VISIONAL illusory; chimerical
VISITANT guest; frequenter
VISITING inspecting; haunting; calling
VITALISM⎫ (hypothetical vital
VITALIST⎭　principle)
VITALITY vigour; life; energy
VITALIZE animate; quicken
VITELLIN a protein in egg
VITELLUS the yolk of an egg
VITIATED impaired; spoilt; debased
VITIATOR a pervert
VITICIDE a vine pest　**Z.**
VITREOUS glassy
VITULINE (veal)
VIVA-VOCE orally
VIVACITY sprightliness; liveliness
VIVARIUM small zoo　**Z.**
VIVIDITY vividness; clarity; lucidity
VIVIFIED quickened; enlivened
VIVISECT operate　**Med.**
VIXENISH quarrelsome; snappish
VIZERATE viziership
VOCALIST singer　**Mus.**
VOCALITY utterableness
VOCALIZE voice; articulate
VOCATION profession; calling; pursuit
VOCATIVE (invocation); a case
VOIDABLE able to be annulled
VOIDANCE evasion; annulment
VOIDNESS nullity; emptiness
VOIGTITE form of mica　**Min.**
VOLATILE lively; gay; capricious
VOLCANIC eruptive
VOLITANT able to fly
VOLITION freewill; choice; purpose
VOLITIVE wishful
VOLLEYED (tennis)
VOLPLANE glide

VOLSUNGS Norse legendary race
VOLTAISM galvanism
VOLTZITE zinc sulphide　**Min.**
VOLULITE petrified shell　**Min.**
VOLUMIST an author
VOLUTION convolution; spiral
VOLVULUS stoppage　**Med.**
VOMITING ejecting
VOMITION sickness　**Med.**
VOMITIVE vomitory
VOMITORY an emetic　**Med.**
VORACITY rapacity; greed
VORTEXES whirlpools; vortices
VORTICAL turning
VORTICES eddies; maelstroms
VOTARESS lady devotee
VOTARIST adherent; votary; zealot
VOTIVELY by way of vow
VOUCHING warranting; backing
VOUSSOIR arch stone
VOWELISM use of vowels
VOWELIST user of vowels
VOWELLED with vowels
VOYAGEUR Canadian boatman
VRAICING gathering seaweed (Ch. Is.)
VULCANIC volcanic
VULGARLY commonly; boorishly
VULSELLA forceps　**Med.**

W

WABBLING wobbling
WADDLING walking like a duck
WAESUCKS alas (Sc.)
WAFERING sealing
WAGE-FUND (a theory)
WAGE-WORK paid work
WAGELESS unpaid
WAGERING betting; laying; staking
WAGGLING swaying
WAGGONER wagoner
WAGGONET wagonette
WAGONAGE cost of transport
WAGONFUL
WAGONING carting
WAGON-LIT sleeping car (Fr.)
WAILMENT lamentation
WAINBOTE timber for carts
WAINROPE cart-rope
WAINSCOT panelling
WAIT-A-BIT (various shrubs)　**B.**
WAITRESS a nippy; maid
WAKENING rousing; stimulating
WAKERIFE wakeful (Sc.)
WALDHORN hunting horn (Ger.) **Mus.**
WALHALLA Valhalla
WALKABLE
WALK-MILL fulling mill
WALK-OVER easy victory

WALLAROO large Kangaroo		
WALL-EYED glaring; fierce		
WALL-GAME Eton football		
WALL-KNOT Turk's head	Naut.	
WALL-MOSS stonecrop	B.	
WALL-NEWT lizard; gecko	Z.	
WALL-TREE fruit tree	B.	
WALL-WORT dwarf-elder	B.	
WALLOPED thrashed		
WALLOPER a slogger		
WALLOWED floundered; weltered		
WALLOWER groveller		
WALLSEND house coal	Min.	
WALTZING dancing		
WAMBLING rumbling		
WANDERED strayed; roamed		
WANDERER rambler; nomad		
WANDEROO langur monkey	Z.	
WANGLING winning by craft		
WANTLESS fully satisfied; abundant		
WANTONED frolicked		
WANTONLY sportively; capriciously		
WAPPENED tearful		
WAPPERED blinked		
WARBLING quavering; trilling		
WAR-DANCE		
WARDCORN castle guard		
WARDENRY warden's district		
WARDMOTE court of inquiry		
WARDROBE		
WARD-ROOM mess-room	Naut.	
WARDSHIP guardianship		
WARE-ROOM show-room		
WARFARER combatant		
WAR-FIELD battle-field		
WAR-HORSE a charger	Z.	
WARINESS alertness; craftiness		
WARMNESS warmth; ardour		
WARPAINT		
WAR-PLANE fighting aircraft		
WAR-PLUME		
WARPROOF valorous		
WARRAGAL the dingo	Z.	
WARRANTY authority		
WARRENER warren keeper		
WARRISON healing (obs.)		
WARTLESS		
WARTWEED } spurge used for		
WARTWORT } curing warts	B.	
WAR-WEARY		
WAR-WHOOP a war-cry		
WASHABLE		
WASHAWAY a breach		
WASHBALL soap-ball		
WASHBOWL washbasin		
WASH-DIRT (mining)		
WASH-ROOM ablution room		
WASP-BITE wasp-sting		
WASTEFUL prodigal; improvident		
WATCHBOX sentry box		

WATCHDOG a guardian		Z.
WATCHFUL vigilant; alert; wary		
WATCHING wakefulness; vigil		
WATCH-KEY		
WATCHMAN a look-out; custodian		
WATERAGE transport dues		
WATER-BED waterproof bed	Med.	
WATERBUG various types		Z.
WATERCAN yellow waterlily		B.
WATER-DOG water spaniel		Z.
WATERFLY		Z.
WATER-FOX the carp		Z.
WATER-GAS illuminating gas		
WATER-GOD Neptune		
WATER-HEN moorhen		Z.
WATER-ICE a confection		
WATERING diluting; irrigating		
WATERISH insipid; moist; damp		
WATERLOG saturate		
WATERMAN ferryman; turncock		
WATER-POA species of grass		B.
WATERPOT watering can		
WATER-RAM hydraulic ram		
WATER-RAT water vole		Z.
WATER-RUG water spaniel		Z.
WATER-TAP		
WATERWAY a canal		
WATT-HOUR measure of work	Meas.	
WATTLING plaiting; hurdling		
WAVEBAND group of wave-lengths		
WAVEFORM characteristic of radio wave		
WAVELESS calm; undisturbed; serene		
WAVELIKE undulating; rippling		
WAVE-LINE stream-line		
WAVE-LOAF a wave-offering		
WAVERING tottering; vacillating		
WAVEROUS fluctuating; unsteady		
WAVE-TRAP		
WAVEWORN		
WAVINESS unsteadiness		
WAXCLOTH oil-cloth		
WAXLIGHT a taper		
WAX-PAPER stencil paper		
WAX-PLANT honeywort		B.
WAXWORKS an exhibition		
WAY-BOARD thin stratum	Min.	
WAYBREAD common plantain		B.
WAYFARER traveller; pedestrian		
WAYGOING departing		
WAYGOOSE a printer's festivity		
WAYLAYER intercepter; lurker		
WAYLEAVE right of way		
WAYMAKER a precursor		
WAY-SHAFT an engine shaft		
WAYTHORN buckthorn		B.
WAY-TRAIN slow train		
WAYWISER pedometer		
WEAKENED debilitated; enfeebled		
WEAKENER enervator		
WEAK-EYED		

WEAKLING delicate creature
WEAKNESS feebleness; frailty
WEANLING newly weaned
WEAPONED armed
WEARABLE fit to be worn
WEARIFUL wearisome; tedious
WEARYING tiring; fatiguing
WEED-HOOK garden tool
WEEDLESS
WEEVILED infested with weevils **Z.**
WEIGHAGE a toll
WEIGHING balancing; pondering
WEIGH-OUT (horse racing)
WEIGHTED
WEISSITE iolite **Min.**
WELCOMED greeted; hailed; saluted
WELCOMER polite host; receptionist
WELDABLE
WELD-IRON wrought iron
WELLADAY alas; alackaday
WELLAWAY welladay
WELL-BOAT fishing boat **Naut.**
WELL-BORN of noble birth
WELL-BRED of good stock
WELLCURB ring of masonry
WELLDECK open-deck **Naut.**
WELLDOER a benefactor
WELL-HEAD source of a spring
WELL-HOLE (flight of stairs)
WELL-KEPT carefully tended
WELL-KNIT compact; sturdy
WELLNIGH nearly; almost
WELL-READ learned; scholarly
WELL-SEEN experienced; skilful
WELL-TO-DO prosperous; affluent
WELLSIAN (H. G. Wells)
WELL-WORN threadbare; shabby
WELSHING absconding
WELSHMAN a man of Wales
WELTERED wallowed; floundered
WEREGILD compensation for homicide
WEREWOLF a changeling **Z.**
WESLEYAN (John Wesley) **Eccl.**
WESTERLY
WESTWARD
WET-NURSE
WHACKING astounding; a beating
WHALEMAN
WHALE-OIL
WHANGHEE bamboo cane **B.**
WHANGING whacking
WHARFAGE dock dues
WHARFING wharves
WHATEVER anything which
WHEATEAR fallowfinch **Z.**
WHEAT-EEL a wheat disease
WHEAT-FLY a pest **Z.**
WHEEDLED coaxed; cajoled; inveigled
WHEEDLER sycophant; fawner; toady
WHEELMAN cycling

WHEEL-ORE bournonite **Min.**
WHEEL-TAX carriage tax
WHEELAGE a toll
WHEELING cycling; turning; twirling
WHEELMAN cyclist
WHEEZILY asthmatically
WHEEZING breathing heavily
WHELMING overburdening; crushing
WHELPING littering
WHENEVER
WHEREOUT out of which
WHEREVER
WHETTING sharpening
WHEY-FACE pale face
WHIFFING puffing
WHIFFLER prevaricator
WHIGGERY ⎫
WHIGGISH ⎬ Liberalism
WHIGGISM ⎭
WHIM-WHAM a gadget
WHIMBREL wimbrel; curlew **Z,**
WHIMSIES notions; caprices; fancies
WHINCHAT singing bird **Z,**
WHINNIED neighed
WHINNOCK a milk-pail
WHINYARD sword; dirk
WHIPCORD string; material
WHIPHAND advantage over; control
WHIPLASH
WHIPPING lashing; castigating
WHIPSTER whippersnapper
WHIPTAIL slender tail
WHIRLBAT cestus
WHIRLING gyrating; rotating
WHIRRING spinning; twirling; turning
WHISKERS (Dundreary)
WHISKING brushing; seizing
WHISTLED piped **Mus.**
WHISTLER broken-winded horse **Z.**
WHITE-ANT a termite **Z.**
WHITE-ARM arme blanche
WHITE-BOY Irish white-shirt
WHITE-HOT
WHITE-LIE an evasion
WHITE-MAN a true and trusty man
WHITENED blanched
WHITENER bleacher
WHITEPOT a confection
WHITLING sea trout; bull trout **Z.**
WHITSOUR summer apple **B.**
WHITSTER a whitener
WHITTLED pared; cut; trimmed
WHITTRET the weasel **Z.**
WHIZZING
WHODUNIT a crime novel
WHOMEVER whomsoever
WHOOPING yelling; hooting
WHOPPING beating; colossal
WHURRING
WICKEDLY heinously; atrociously

WICKERED made of osiers		**WIRINESS** toughness	
WIDE-EYED		**WISEACRE** a simpleton	
WIDENESS breadth; width		**WISELING** wiseacre	
WIDENING extending; broadening		**WISERITE** manganese carbonate	**Min.**
WIDOWING bereaving		**WISHBONE** merrythought	
WIELDING brandishing; plying		**WISH-WASH** weak drink	
WIFEHOOD wivehood		**WISTARIA** a climbing plant	**B.**
WIFELESS unmarried		**WITCH-ELM**	**B.**
WIFELIKE wifely		**WITCHERY** fascination; sorcery	
WIG-BLOCK wigmaker's block		**WITCHING** enchanting; charming	
WIGGLING wriggling		**WITHDRAW** retire; recall; retract	
WIGMAKER		**WITHDREW** retreated; departed	
WILD-BOAR	**Z.**	**WITHERED** faded; shrunk; drooped	
WILD-BORN		**WITHE-ROD** American shrub	**B.**
WILD-DUCK	**Z.**	**WITHHELD** kept back; detained	
WILD-FIRE sheet lightning		**WITHHOLD** restrain; reserve	
WILD-FOWL	**Z.**	**WITHWIND** bindweed	**B.**
WILD-LAND uncultivated soil		**WITTOLLY** complacently	
WILD-WOOD forest		**WIVEHOOD** wifehood	
WILDERED bewildered (obs.)		**WIVELESS** wifeless	
WILDNESS savageness; recklessness		**WIZARDLY** magically	
WILFULLY obstinately; deliberately		**WIZARDRY** sorcery; necromancy	
WILINESS craftiness; artfulness		**WIZENING** withering	
WILLOWED full of willows	**B.**	**WOAD-MILL** dye extracting mill	
WILLYARD wilful; shy (Sc.)		**WOBEGONE** woebegone; calamitous	
WIMBLING boring		**WOEFULLY** sorrowfully; tragically	
WIMPLING rippling		**WOLF-FISH** catfish	**Z.**
WINCHMAN windlass operator		**WOLF-SKIN**	
WIND-BAND (wind instruments)	**Mus.**	**WOMANISH** effeminate	
WIND-PUMP		**WOMMERAH** stick for spear-throwing	
WIND-RODE riding at anchor	**Naut.**	**WONDERED** speculated; marvelled	
WIND-ROSE a diagram		**WONDERER** conjecturer; ponderer	
WIND-SEED	**B.**	**WONDROUS** marvellous; miraculous	
WINDBILL guarantee		**WONTLESS** unaccustomed; unused	
WINDERED fanned		**WOOD-ACID** acetic acid	**Chem.**
WINDFALL (fruit; legacy)	**B.**	**WOODBIND** } wild honeysuckle	**B.**
WIND-GALL puffy swelling		**WOODBINE**	
WINDLASS a winch; capstan	**Naut.**	**WOOD-BIRD**	**Z.**
WINDLESS calm; winded		**WOODCHAT** shrike; woodpecker	**Z.**
WINDMILL swimming stroke		**WOOD-COAL** charcoal; lignite	**Min.**
WINDOWED fenestrated		**WOODCOCK**	**Z.**
WINDPIPE the trachea	**Med.**	**WOOD-DOVE** stockdove	**Z.**
WINDSAIL ventilating funnel	**Naut.**	**WOOD-EVIL** cattle disease	
WINDWARD toward the wind		**WOOD-HOLE** woodstore	
WINE-CASK		**WOOD-IBIS** tantalus; stork	**Z.**
WINELESS		**WOOD-KERN** Irish outlaw	
WINESKIN		**WOODLAND** forest land	
WING-CASE horny cover	**Z.**	**WOODLARK**	**Z.**
WINGLESS apterous	**Z.**	**WOODLESS** treeless	
WING-SHOT flying shot		**WOOD-LICE** millepeds	**Z.**
WINNOWED sifted		**WOOD-LILY** lily of the valley	**B.**
WINNOWER chaff remover		**WOODLOCK** a stop	**Naut.**
WINTERED hibernated		**WOOD-MITE** a beetle	**Z.**
WINTERLY cheerless		**WOODMOTE** forest court	**Law**
WIREDRAW to make wire		**WOODNOTE** bird call	
WIRE-HEEL a foot disease		**WOOD-OPAL** silicified wood	**Min.**
WIRELESS		**WOOD-PULP** cellulose	
WIREROPE		**WOODROCK** asbestos	**Min.**
WIRE-WORM a centipede	**Z.**	**WOODROOF** } a plant	**B.**
WIRE-WOVE (glazed writing paper		**WOODRUFF**	

452

WOOD-SEAR	cuckoo-spit;	
WOOD-SEER	an insect;	**Z.**
WOOD-SERE	a season	

WOOD-SHED
WOODSKIN Guiana canoe
WOODSMAN a woodcutter
WOOD-SOOT charcoal soot
WOOD-TICK death-watch beetle **Z.**
WOOD-VINE clematis **B.**

WOODWALE	golden oriole;	**Z.**
WOODWALL	green woodpecker	**Z.**

WOODWARD forest keeper
WOODWORK carpentry
WOOD-WORM a grub **Z.**
WOOD-WREN willow-warbler **Z.**
WOOINGLY enticingly
WOOLBALL
WOOLDING binding **Naut.**
WOOL-DYED dyed in the wool
WOOLFELL skin with wool on it
WOOL-MILL cloth factory
WOOLPACK 240 lb. of wool
WOOLSACK Lord Chancellor's seat
WOOLWARD wearing wool
WOOLWORK
WORD-BOOK a vocabulary
WORDLESS silent; dumb; mute
WORD-PLAY punning; repartee
WORKABLE feasible
WORKADAY prosaic; ordinary
WORKFOLK toilers
WORKGIRL
WORKROOM
WORKSHOP
WORMCAST
WORMGEAR gear wheels, etc.
WORM-HOLE
WORMLIKE vermicular **Z.**
WORMSEED santonica **B.**
WORMWOOD absinthe; vermouth **B.**
WORRICOW hobgoblin
WORRYING harassing; fretting; chafing
WORSENED deteriorated
WORSTING besting; defeating
WORTHILY deservedly; meritoriously
WORTHITE silica compound **Min.**
WOUNDILY excessively
WOUNDING injuring
WRACKFUL ruinous; destructive
WRACKING gathering seaweed
WRANGLED brawled; bickered
WRANGLER disputant
WRANNOCK the wren **Z.**
WRAPPAGE a wrapper
WRAPPING inclosing; muffling
WRATHFUL irate; incensed; wroth
WRATHILY indignantly; furiously
WRAULING caterwauling
WREAKFUL revengeful; angry
WREAKING inflicting; punishing

WREATHED garlanded; festooned
WREATHEN entwined
WRECKAGE debris
WRECKFUL causing ruin
WRECKING sabotaging; destroying
WRENCHED twisted; strained; wrung
WRESTING extorting; forcing; usurped
WRESTLED strove; grappled
WRESTLER
WRETCHED miserable; paltry; sorry
WRICKING spraining; straining
WRIGGLED squirmed
WRIGGLER shuffler
WRIGHTIA tropical climber **B.**
WRINGING twisting; squeezing
WRINKLED furrowed; creased; rumpled
WRISTLET wrist-band
WRIST-PIN connecting pin
WRITE-OFF total loss
WRITHING wriggling; squirming
WRITHLED wrinkled
WRONGFUL injurious; unjust; unfair
WRONGING violating; maltreating
WRONGOUS illegal (Sc.)

X

XANTHATE a salt **Chem.**
XANTHEIN yellow colour
XANTHIAN from Xanthus
XANTHINE yellow dye
XANTHITE yellow idocrase **Min.**
XANTHIUM a plant **B.**
XANTHOMA skin disease **Med.**
XANTHOUS yellowish
XANTHURA American jay **Z.**
XANTIPPE termagant; wife of Socrates
XENOGAMY cross-fertilisation **B.**
XENOLITE aluminium silicate **Min.**
XENOTIME yttrium phosphate **Min.**
XENURINE armadillo-like **Z.**
XERANSIS dryness **Med.**
XERANTIC exsiccant **Med.**
XIPHIOID like a swordfish **Z.**
XYLOCARP hard woody fruit **B.**
XYLONITE form of celluloid

Y

YACHTING ice, ocean, or lake pastime
YAHOOING howling and yelping
YAMMERED lamented; whined
YANOLITE axinite **Min.**
YARDLAND usually 30 acres **Meas.**
YARDWAND yardstick **Meas.**
YARWHELP bar-tailed godwit **Z.**
YATAGHAN long Turkish dagger
YEANLING eanling; a lamb **Z.**

YEAR-BOOK voluminous annual
YEARLING one year old animal **Z.**
YEARLONG twelve months
YEARNFUL mournful; distressing
YEARNING longing; craving; desirous
YELDRING } yowley; yorling; **Z.**
YELDROCK } the yellow-bunting **Z.**
YELLOWED dyed yellow
YEOMANLY sturdily; staunchly
YEOMANRY volunteer cavalry
YESTREEN last evening (Sc.)
YIELDING bearing; affording
YODELLED sang falsetto
YOGEEISM abstract meditation
YOICKING shouting encouragingly
YOKELESS unrestrained
YOKEMATE an associate; a partner
YOKE-TOED pair-toed
YOKOHOMA a breed of fowls **Z.**
YONDMOST farthest; uttermost
YOUNGEST most youthful
YOUNGISH somewhat juvenile
YOURSELF
YOUTHFUL boyish; puerile; fresh
YTTERBIA oxide of ytterium **Chem.**
YTTERITE gadolinite **Min.**
YTTRIOUS containing yttrium **Chem.**
YUGO-SLAV Jugo-Slav
YULETIDE Christmas; Noel **Eccl.**

Z

ZALOPHUS seal genus **Z.**
ZAMBOMBA Spanish instrument **Mus.**
ZAMINDAR zemindar; tax-collector
ZAMPOGNO Italian bagpipe **Mus.**
ZANTIOTE native of Zante
ZARATITE nickel compound **Min.**
ZARZUELA Spanish operetta
ZEALLESS slack; apathetic
ZEALOTRY fanaticism; fervour; ardour
ZECCHINO sequin (Venice) **Coin**
ZELANIAN (New Zealand)
ZEMINDAR Indian tax collector

ZENITHAL culminating; crowning
ZEOLITIC (felspar) **Min.**
ZEPPELIN airship
ZERUMBET East Indian drug **B.**
ZETICULA a small room
ZIBELINE like a sable **Z.**
ZIGGURAT Sumerian temple
ZINCKIFY cover with zinc
ZINGIBER ginger, etc. **B.**
ZINNOBER vermilion pigment
ZIONWARD heavenward
ZIPHIOID like a swordfish **Z.**
ZIRCONIA zirconium oxide **Min.**
ZIZYPHUS jujube tree **B.**
ZOANTHUS sea-anemone **Z.**
ZODIACAL (zodiac)
ZOETROPE early form of cinema
ZOIATRIA veterinary surgery
ZOLOTNIK Russian weight **Meas.**
ZONELESS beltless
ZOOBLAST animal cell **Z.**
ZOOCHEMY animal chemistry **Chem.**
ZOOGENIC generative
ZOOGLOEA colony of bacteria **Med.**
ZOOGRAFT grafting tissue **Med.**
ZOOLATER animal worshipper
ZOOLATRY animal worship
ZOOLITIC (fossilized animals) **Min.**
ZOOMANCY divination
ZOOMETRY animal mensuration
ZOONITIC articulated **Z.**
ZOONOMIA animal physiology
ZOOPHAGA carnivorous animals **Z.**
ZOOPHILY love of animals
ZOOPHYTE plantlike animal **Z.**
ZOOSCOPY seeing snakes, etc. **Med.**
ZOOSPERM male seed-cell **Med.**
ZOOSPORE animated spore **B.**
ZOOTOMIC (vivisection) **Med.**
ZOOT-SUIT long coat and tight trousers
ZOPILOTE turkey-buzzard **Z.**
ZWEIBACK biscuit rusk
ZYGADITE aluminium compound **Min.**
ZYGODONT (molar teeth) **Med.**
ZYMOLOGY study of fermentation

GENERAL INFORMATION
WEIGHTS AND MEASURES.
With some approximate English equivalents.

TWO LETTERS

LI 2,115 feet	**China.**	
RI 2½ miles	**Japan.**	
TO 4 gallons		**Japan.**

THREE LETTERS

AAM 30-35 gallons	**E. Ind.**	**OKA** 3 lbs.		**Egypt.**
ARE 120 square yards	**France.**	**OKE** 2¾ lbs.		**Turkey.**
AUM 31 Imp. gallons	**S. Africa.**	**OZS** ounces		**Brit.**
CAB 3 pints	**Heb.**	**PIN** half a firkin		**Brit.**
CHO 5½ chains	**Japan.**	**RAI** ⅜ acre		**Siam.**
COR 8½ bushels	**Heb.**	**RIO** ounce		**Japan.**
CWT a hundredweight	**Brit.**	**ROD** 5½ yards		**Brit.**
DWT a pennyweight	**Brit.**	**SEN** 44 yards		**Siam.**
ELL (Eng.) 45 inches	**Brit.**	**SHO** ¼ peck		**Japan.**
ELL (Scot.) 37 inches	**Brit.**	**SUN** 1 inch	•	**Japan.**
FOU a bushel	**Scot.**	**TAN** 133 lbs.		**China.**
GUZ 33 inches	**E. Ind.**	**TOD** 2 stone		**Brit.**
HIN 6 quarts	**Heb.**	**TON** 20 cwt.		**Brit.**
KEN 2 yards	**Japan.**	**TUN** 252 gallons		**Brit.**
KIN 1½ lbs.	**Japan.**	**WAH** 80 inches		**Siam.**
LOG ¾ pint	**Heb.**	**WEY*** 13 stones		**Brit.**
NIU 1 inch	**Siam.**			

FOUR LETTERS

ACRE 4840 square yards	**Brit.**	**MILE** 2,240 yards	**Irish.**
BALE 10 reams	**Brit.**	**MOIO** 2¾ quarts	**Port.**
BATH 6 gallons	**Heb.**	**MUDD** 1 bushel	**Mor.**
BUTT 108 gallons	**Brit.**	**NAIL** 2¼ inches	**Brit.**
CH'IH 1 foot	**China.**	**NATR** 2 lbs.	**Abys.**
COSS about 1¾ miles	**India.**	**OKET** 1 oz. avoirdupois	**Abys.**
CRAN about 750 herrings	**Brit.**	**PAAL** 1½ metres	**Java.**
DRAH 22 inches	**Morocco.**	**PACK** 240 lbs.	**Brit.**
DRAM 1/16 oz.	**Brit.**	**PECK** 2 gallons	**Brit.**
EPHA a bushel	**Heb.**	**PINT** 4 gills	**Brit.**
FOOT 12 inches	**Brit.**	**PIPE** 126 gallons	**Brit.**
FUNT 1 lb.	**Russ.**	**POLE** 16½ feet	**Brit.**
GILL ¼ pint	**Brit.**	**POOD** 36 lbs.	**Russ.**
GRAM 15·4323 grains	**France**	**REAM** 20 quires	**Brit.**
HAND (horses) 4 inches	**Brit.**	**REED** 152 inches	**Heb.**
HIDE 120 acres	**Brit.**	**ROOD** ¼ acre	**Brit.**
INCH	**Brit.**	**ROTL** 1 lb.	**Egypt.**
KELA ½ bushel	**Egypt.**	**SACK** 2 weys	**Brit.**
KILO 2·205 lb.	**France**	**SAWK** 20 inches	**Siam.**
KNOT 6,080 feet	**Brit.**	**SEAH** 14 pints	**Heb.**
KOKU 5 bushels	**Japan.**	**SEAM** (glass) 24 stone	**Brit.**
KOSS 2,000 yards	**India.**	**SEER** 2 lbs.	**India.**
KWAN 8 lbs.	**Japan.**	**TAEL** 1 oz.	**China.**
LAKH 100,000 rupees	**India**	**TOLA** 180 grains	**India.**
LAST 12 sacks	**Brit.**	**TS'UN** 1 inch	**China.**
LINK 8 inches	**Brit.**	**VARA** 32 inches	**Honduras.**
MILE 1,760 yards	**Brit.**	**YARD** 3 feet	**Brit.**

FIVE LETTERS

ANKER 7½ gallons	**S. Africa.**	**CANNA** 2 yards	**Malta.**
ARDEB 5 bushels	**Egypt.**	**CARAT** 200 milligrams	**France.**
BAHAR 3½ cwt.	**E. Ind.**	**CATTY** 1 lb.	**China.**
CABLE 100 fathoms	**Brit.**	**CAWNY** 1 acre	**India.**
CANDY 500 lbs.	**India.**	**CHAIN** 22 yards	**Brit.**
CANEH 6 cubits	**Heb.**	**CHANG** 3 lbs.	**Siam.**

CHANG 12 feet	China.	**OKIEH** 1 oz.	Egypt.
CHEKI 509 lbs.	Turkey.	**OUNCE**	Brit.
CHIEN 1 lb.	China.	**PARAH** 15 gallons	India.
CLOVE 7 lb.	Brit.	**PECUL** 133 lbs.	China.
COOMB 4 bushels	Brit.	**PERCH** pole, 5½ yards	Brit.
CUBIT 18 inches	Brit.	**PICUL** 133 lbs.	China.
EPHAH a bushel	Heb.	**PIEDE** 11 inches	Malta.
GRAIN 1/24 pennyweight	Brit.	**POUND**	Brit.
GROSS 12 dozen	Brit.	**QIRAT** 209 square yards	Egypt.
HOMER 8 bushels	Heb.	**QUART**	Brit.
KANEH 6 cubits	Heb.	**QUIRE** 24 sheets	Brit.
KILEH 1 bushel	Turk.	**SAJEN** 7 feet	Russ.
LIANG an ounce	China.	**SHAKU** 12 inches	Japan.
LIBRA 1 lb	Malta & Brazil.	**STERE** cubic metre	France.
LIPPY half a gallon	Scot.	**STONE** 14 lbs.	Brit.
LITRE	Almost universal.	**TSUBO** 4 square yards	Japan.
LIVRE 1 lb.	Greece.	**UNGUL** 1 inch	India.
MAUND 82 lbs.	India.	**VEDRO** 3 gallons	Russ.
METRE	France.	**VERST** 1,166 yards	Russ.
OCQUE 3 lbs.	Greece.	**YOJAN** about 5 miles	E. Ind.

SIX LETTERS

ARROBA 32 lbs.	Brazil.	**FEDDAN** 1 acre	Egypt.
ARSHIN (cloth) 27 inches	Turk.	**FIRKIN** 9 gallons	Brit.
BANDLE 2 feet	Eire.	**GALLON** 4 quarts	Brit.
BARREL 36 gallon cask	Brit.	**GRAMME** a gram	France.
BATMAN 17 lbs.	Turk.	**KANTAR** 100 lbs.	Abys.
BUNDLE 2 reams	Brit.	**MICRON** millionth part of a metre	France.
BUSHEL 8 gallons	Brit.	**MUSCAL** 1½ drams	Turk.
CANDIE 500 lbs.	India.	**NOGGIN** small cup, ¼ pint	Brit.
CANTAR 124 lbs.	Turk.	**POTTLE** 4 pints	Brit.
CENTAL 100 lbs.	N. America.	**ROTOLO** 1¾ lbs.	Malta.
CHOPIN a quart	Scot.	**SCHENE** 7½ miles	Egypt.
DECARE 1,000 square metres	France.	**SHTOFF** 1 quart	Russ.
DJERIB 2½ acres	Turk.	**TIERCE** 42 gallons	Brit.
ENDAZE 25½ inches	Turk.	**VISHAM** 3 lbs.	India.
FANEGA 11 bushels	Costa Rica.	**YOJANA** about 5 miles	India.
FATHOM 6 feet	Brit.		

SEVEN LETTERS

BRACCIO a cubit	Italy.	**MEGA-ERG** a million ergs	Greece.
CALORIE unit of heat	France.	**MILLIER** 1000 kilos	France.
CENTNER 1 cwt.	Germany.	**POUNDAL** unit of force	Brit.
CHALDER 96 bushels	Brit.	**QUANTAR** 99 lbs.	Egypt.
DECIARE 1/10th are	France.	**QUARTER** 28 lbs.	Brit.
DECIBEL unit of noise	Brit.	**QUINTAL** 1 cwt.	France.
DIOPTER optical measure	Greece.	**ROTTOLO** a weight	Levant.
DRACHMA silver coin	Greece.	**SCRUPLE** 20 grains	Brit.
FURLONG 220 yards	Brit.	**VIRGATE** a quarter of a hide	Brit.
HECTARE 100 ares	France.		

EIGHT LETTERS

CENTIARE a square metre	France.	**MUTCHKIN** about a pint	Scot.
CENTIBAR meterological meas.	France.	**PARASANG** about 4 miles	Persia.
CHALDRON 25 cwt. of coal	France.	**PUNCHEON** a large cask	France.
DECAGRAM 10 grammes	France.	**QUADRANT** an arc of 90°	France.
DECIGRAM 1/10th gramme	France.	**QUARTERN** a gill; 4lbs.	Brit.
FOOT-RULE a 12 inch measure	Brit.	**SERPLATH** 80 stone	Scot.
HOGSHEAD a large cask	France.	**YARDLAND** usually 30 acres	Brit.
KILODYNE 1000 dynes	France.	**YARDWAND** yardstick	Brit.
KILOGRAM 1000 grammes	France.	**ZOLOTNIK** unit of weight	Russ.
KILOWATT 1000 watts	Univ.		

COINS AND MONIES
ANCIENT AND MODERN

TWO LETTERS
AS a bronze Roman coin

THREE LETTERS

BOB a shilling
COB Spanish
DAM Indian copper coin
ECU French five-franc piece
FEN Chinese
FIL Iraqui, Jordanian
KIP Laotian
LAT Latvian
LEU Romanian
LEV Bulgarian
MIL proposed coin, 1/1000

ORE Scandinavian
PIE Pakistani, Nepali
PYA Burmese
REE Portuguese money
REI of account
SEN Japanese, Indonesian
SOL old French halfpenny, Peruvian
SOU French five-centime piece
WON Korean
YEN Japanese

FOUR LETTERS

ANNA Pakistani
AURA Icelandic
BANI Romanian
BAHT Thai
BEKA ½ Shekel Hebrew
BUCK American dollar
CASH small Eastern coin
CENT (various countries)
CHIP a counter; a sovereign
DAWM dam; Indian copper coin
DIME American 10-cent piece
DOIT Dutch half-farthing
DONG N. Vietnamese
GELD ancient tribute
HWAN Korean
JOEY 4d. piece (Joseph Hume)
KRAN Persian
KYAT Burmese
LAKH 100,000 rupees

LIRA Italian, Turkish
LIRE plural of lira (Italian)
MARK German
MERK Scottish 13/4d.
MITE a very small coin
OBOL Charon's ferry fee, 1½d.
PARA Yugoslav, Turkish
PESO Filipino
PICE the fourth of an anna
PULS Afghani
QUID a sovereign
RAND S. African
REAL the fourth of a peseta
RIAL Iranian
RIEL Cambodian
RYAL gold coin; the rose noble
TAEL Chinese
YUAN Chinese

FIVE LETTERS

ANGEL old English gold coin
AUREI Roman gold coins
BELGA a Belgian coin
BETSO small Venetian coin
BRASS money colloquially
COLON Costa Rican
CROWN five-shilling piece
DARIC gold coin of Darius
DINAR Serbian, Iranian, Jordanian
DUCAT Italian, gold or silver
EAGLE 10-dollar gold coin
FRANC French
GROAT silver 4d. piece
KRONA Scandinavian
LEPTA Greek
LIARD old French farthing

LIBRA Peruvian
LITAS Lithuanian
LIVRE old French franc
LOCHO Venezuelan
LOUIS 20-franc piece
MEDIO Venezuelan
MOHUR 15-rupee gold coin
MONGO Mongolian
NOBLE old English coin, 6/8d.
PENCE plural of penny
PENNI Finnish
PENNY English copper coin
POUND twenty shillings
QURSH Arabian
RIYAL Sudanese
RUPEE Indian

SAUDI Arabian gold sovereign
SCUDI plural of scudo
SCUDO Italian
SEMIS half a Roman as
SOLDI plural of soldo
SOLDO Italian halfpenny (former)

STICA small Saxon coin
STYCA stica; Saxon coin
SUCRE Ecuadorean
TICAL Thai
TICCY S. African 3d. piece
ZLOTY Polish

SIX LETTERS

AMANIA Afghani
AUREUS Roman gold coin
BALBOA Panamanian
BAUBEE }Scottish halfpenny
BAWBEE
BEZANT Byzantine gold coin
BUKSHA Yemeni
CONDOR Chilean
COPANG Japanese gold coin
COPPER one penny
DECIME a tenth of a franc
DIRHAM Moroccan
DOBLON Chilean
DOLLAR (various countries)
ESCUDO Portuguese
FILLER Hungarian
FLORIN silver 2-shilling piece
FORINT Hungarian
GOURDE Haitian
GROSZY Polish
GUINEA 21 shillings (obs.)
GULDEN Dutch, Hungarian
HELLER Austrian
KOPECK Russian
KORUNA Czech

KURUSH Turkish
LEPTON Greek
MARKKA Finnish
NICKEL 5-cent piece, U.S.A.
OBOLUS obol; ancient Greek coin
PAGODA Indian gold coin
PESETA Spanish
PRUTAH Indonesian
RAPPEN Swiss
ROUBLE Russian
SATANG Thai
SEQUIN Venetian gold coin
SHEKEL Jewish half crown
SOMALO Somali
SOVRAN poetical sovereign
STATER Greek gold or silver coin
TALARI Abyssinian
TALENT Hebrew
TANNER sixpence
TESTER Henry VIII shilling
THALER German
TICKEY S. African 3d. piece
TOMAUN Persian gold coin
ZECHIN sequin; Venetian coin

SEVEN LETTERS

AFGHANI (100 puls) Afghani
ANGELOT a Louis XI gold coin
ANGOLAR Angolan escudo
BOLIVAR S. American
CAROLUS gold coin of Charles I
CENTAVO S. American
CENTIME one-hundreth of a franc
CORDOBA Nicaraguan
CRUSADO Portuguese
DENARII pence
DRACHMA Greek
GUARANI Paraguayan
GUILDER Dutch florin
JACOBUS gold coin of James I

LEMPIRA Brazilian
MANILLA W. African copper coin
MILREIS Brazilian
MOIDORE old Portuguese coin
PFENNIG German copper coin
PIASTRE Egyptian
PISTOLE old Spanish gold coin
QUARTER quarter of a dollar
QUETZAL Guatemalan
QUINTAR Albanian
SEXTANS ancient Roman bronze coin
TESTOON old Italian silver coin
TESTRIL tester; a sixpence
TUGHRIK Mongolian

EIGHT LETTERS

AMBROSIN Milanese coin
CRUZEIRO Brazilian
DENARIUS Roman silver coin
DOUBLOON 2 pistoles (Spanish)
DUCATOON Venetian silver coin
FARTHING a quarter of a penny (obs.)
FLORENCE Edward III gold florin
GROSCHEN Austrian
HALFMARK old English coin, 6/8d
JOHANNES old Portuguese coin

KREUTZER Austrian copper coin
LOUIS-D'OR 20-franc gold piece
MARAVEDI small Spanish copper coin
NAPOLEON French 20-franc gold coin
QUADRANS Roman copper coin
SESTERCE Roman silver coin
SHILLING English (12 pence)
SIXPENCE English silver coin
STOTINKA Bulgarian

DISTINCTIVE GROUP PHRASEOLOGY.

TERMS OF THE CHASE.

NYE of pheasants
RAG of colts
BEVY of roes or quails
CAST of hawks
CETE of badgers
DOWN of hares
DULE of turtles
FALL of woodcock
GANG of elks
HERD of cranes, curlew, deer
LEPE of leopards
NEST of rabbits
PACE of asses
PACK of hounds
ROUT of wolves
SORD of mallards
SUTE of mallards
STUD of mares
TEAM of oxen
WISP of snipe
BROOD of hens
CHARM of goldfinches
COVEY of partridges
DOYLT of tame swine
DROVE of kine
FLOCK of sheep
PLUMP of wild fowl
PRIDE of lions
SEDGE of herons
SHOAL of fish
SIEGE of herons
SKEIN of geese (flying)
SKULK of foxes
SLOTH of bears

SWARM of bees
TRIBE of goats
TROOP of monkeys
WATCH of nightingales
BARREN of mules
COLONY of gulls
COVERT of coots
DESERT of lapwings
GAGGLE of geese
HARRAS of horses
FLIGHT of doves
KENNEL of raches
KINDLE of kittens
LABOUR of moles
LITTER of whelps
MUSTER of peacocks
SCHOOL of porpoises
SPRING of teal
BADLING of ducks
CLOWDER of cats
COMPANY of widgeon
DOPPING of sheldrake
FESNYNG of ferrets
BUILDING of rooks
RICHESSE of martens
SOUNDER of swine
SINGULAR of boars
COWARDICE of curs
BADELYNGE of ducks
SHREWDNESS of apes
CHATTERING of choughs
MURMURATION of starlings
EXALTATION of larks
CONGREGATION of plovers

MISCELLANEOUS.

BLAST of hunters
BLUSH of boys
LYING of pardoners
SKULK of friars
STALK of foresters
STATE of princes
MELODY of harpers
RAYFUL of knaves
DRAUGHT of butlers
POVERTY of pipers
FIGHTING of beggars

MORBIDITY of majors
SAFEGUARD of porters
WANDERING of tinkers
DISGUISING of tailors
SIMPLICITY of subalterns
SUBTILNE of sergeants
OBSERVANCE of hermits
DRUNKENSHIP of cobblers
SUPERFLUITY of nuns
MALAPERTNESS of pedlars
INCREDIBILITY of cuckolds

MODERN.

BAND of musicians
NEST of machine guns
PARK of artillery
GANG of thieves
ROPE of pearls
TUFT of grass
CASTE of flower pots
CLUMP of trees

CROWD of people
FLEET of cars
HORDE of savages
POSSE of savages
SHEAF of corn
SKEIN of silk
STAND of arms
TRUSS of hay

BUDGET of papers
FLIGHT of aeroplanes
GALAXY of beauty
PUNNET of strawberries
TROUPE of actors

CLUSTER of stars
COMPANY of actors
SEQUENCE of cards
COMMUNITY of saints
GATHERING of the clans

THE CHEMICAL ELEMENTS.

Name	Symbol.	Name	Symbol.	Name	Symbol.
ALUMINIUM	Al.	HOLMIUM	Ho.	PRASEODYMIUM	Pr.
ANTIMONY	Sb.	HYDROGEN (gas)	H.	RADIUM	Ra.
ARGON (gas)	Ar.	ILLINIUM	Il.	RHENIUM	Rn.
ARSENIC	As.	INDIUM	In.	RHODIUM	Rh.
BARIUM	Ba.	IODINE	I.	RUBIDIUM	Rb.
BERYLLIUM	Be.	IRIDIUM	Ie.	RUTHENIUM	Ru.
BISMUTH	Bi.	IRON	Fe.	SAMARIUM	Sm.
BORON	B.	KRYPTON (gas)	Kr.	SCANDIUM	Sc.
BROMINE	Br.	LANTHANIUM	La.	SELENIUM	Se.
CADMIUM	Cd.	LEAD	Pb.	SILICON	Si.
CAESIUM	Cs.	LITHIUM	Li.	SILVER	Ag.
CALCIUM	Ca.	LUTECIUM	Lu.	SODIUM	Na.
CARBON	C.	MAGNESIUM	Mg.	STRONTIUM	Sr.
CERIUM	Ce.	MANGANESE	Mn.	SULPHUR	S.
CHLORINE (gas)	Cl.	MASURIUM	Ma.	TANTALUM	Ta.
CHROMIUM	Cr.	MERCURY	Hg.	TELLURIUM	Te.
COBALT	Co.	MOLYBDENUM	Mo.	TERBIUM	Tb.
COLUMBIUM	Cb.	NEODYMIUM	Nd.	THALLIUM	Tl.
COPPER	Cu.	NEON (gas)	Ne.	THORIUM	Th.
DYSPROSIUM	Dy.	NEOYTTERBIUM	Yb.	THULIUM	Tm.
ERBIUM	Er.	NEUTRON (gas)	Nu.	TIN	Sn.
EUROPIUM	Eu.	NICKEL	Ni.	TITANIUM	Ti.
FLUORINE (gas)	F.	NIOBIUM	Nb.	TUNGSTEN	W.
GADOLINIUM	Gd.	NITROGEN (gas)	N.	URANIUM	U.
GALLIUM	Ga.	OSMIUM	Os.	VANADIUM	V.
GERMANIUM	Ge.	OXYGEN (gas)	O.	WOLFRAM	W.
GLUCINUM	Gl.	PALLADIUM	Pd.	XENON (gas)	Xe.
GOLD	Au.	PHOSPHORUS	P.	YTTERBIUM	Yb
HAFNIUM	Hf.	PLATINUM	Pt.	YTTRIUM	Y
HELIUM (gas)	He.	POTASSIUM	K.	ZINC	Zn.
				ZIRCONIUM	Zr.

GASEOUS EMANATIONS.

ACTINIUM from Thorium
IONIUM from Uranium

NITON from Radium
POLONIUM from Radium

THE SEVEN SENSES.

SIGHT
HEARING
FEELING
TASTE

SMELL
UNDERSTANDING
SPEECH

THE SIGNS OF THE ZODIAC.

	Spring.			*Autumn.*	
ARIES Ram		(1)	LIBRA Balance		(7)
TAURUS Bull		(2)	SCORPIO Scorpion		(8)
GEMINI Twins		(3)	SAGITTARIUS Archer		(9)

	Summer.			*Winter.*	
CANCER Crab		(4)	CAPRICORNUS Goat		(10)
LEO Lion		(5)	AQUARIUS Water Carrier		(11)
VIRGO Virgin		(6)	PISCES Fishes		(12)

THE NINE MUSES.

CALLIOPE	Epic Song.	ERATO	Erotic Poetry.
CLIO	History.	TERPSICHORE	Dance.
EUTERPE	Lyric Poetry.	POLYHYMNIA	Hymns.
MELPOMENE	Tragedy.	URANIA	Astronomy.
THALIA	Comedy.		

THE GREEK FATES.

CLOTHO spins the thread of life	The Spinner.
LACHESIS controls its destiny	The Disposer of Lots.
ATROPOS cuts it off	The Inflexible One.

THE FURIES.

Avenging deities—Erinyes—sent from Tartarus to avenge wrong and punish crime.

ALECTO
MEGAERA
TISIPHONE

THE HARPIES.

(Malignant monsters with birds' wings and claws who snatched away the souls of the dead.)

AELLO
OCYPETE
CELAENO or PODARGE

THE PLANETS AND THEIR SATELLITES.

MARS	SATURN	URANUS
Deimos	Rhea	Ariel
Phobos	Dione	Titania
	Mimas	Oberon
	Titan	Umbriel
FLOTA	Phoebe	
	Tethys	JUPITER
EARTH	Themis ?	Io
Luna	Iapetus	Europa
	Hyperion	Callisto
	Enceladus	Ganymede
VENUS		MERCURY
		NEPTUNE
YGEIA		Triton

THE BOOKS OF THE APOCRYPHA.

ESDRAS
TOBIT
JUDITH
ESTHER
THE WISDOM OF SOLOMON
ECCLESIASTICUS
BARUCH
EPISTLE OF JEREMY
SONG OF THE THREE HOLY CHILDREN
HISTORY OF SUSANNA
BEL AND THE DRAGON
THE PRAYER OF MANASSES
MACCABEES

461

ALPHABETS

Greek

ALPHA	NU		
BETA	XI		
GAMMA	OMICRON		
DELTA	PI		
EPSILON	RHO		
ZETA	SIGMA		
ETA	TAU		
THETA	UPSILON		
IOTA	PHI		
KAPPA	CHI		
LAMBDA	PSI		
MU	OMEGA		

Hebrew

ALEPH	LAMED
BETH	MEM
GIMEL	NUN
DALETH	SAMECH or SAMEKH
HE	AIN or AYIN
VAU	PE
ZAIN or ZAYIN	TZADDI or ZADE
CHETH or HETH	KOPH
TETH	RESH
JOD or YOD	SCHIN or SHIN
CAPH or KAPH	TAU

THE SEVEN WONDERS OF THE WORLD.

1. The PYRAMIDS of Egypt.
2. The HANGING GARDENS of Babylon.
3. The TOMB of MAUSOLOS.
4. The TEMPLE of DIANA at Ephesus.
5. The COLOSSUS of Rhodes.
6. The STATUE of ZEUS by Phidias.
7. { The PHAROS of Egypt, or
     { The PALACE of CYRUS cemented with gold.

MONTHS OF THE JEWISH YEAR.

TISHRI	NISAN or ABIB
HESHVAN	IYAR
KISLEV	SIVAN
TEBET	TAMMUS
SHEBAT	AB
ADAR or VEADAR	ELUL

FRENCH REVOLUTIONARY CALENDAR.

FRENCH REPUBLIC 1794

VENDEMIAIRE	Vintage	Sept.	FLOREAL	Blossom	Apr.
BRUMAIRE	Fog	Oct.	PRAIRAL	Pasture	May.
FRIMAIRE	Sleet	Nov.	MESSIDOR	Harvest	June.
NIVOSE	Snow	Dec.	THERMIDOR }	Heat	July.
PLUVIOSE	Rain	Jan.	FERVIDOR }		
VENTOSE	Wind	Feb.	FRUCTIDOR	Fruit	Aug.
GERMINAL	Seed	Mar.			

THE STATES OF AMERICA.

ALABAMA	Ala.	FLORIDA	Fla.
ALASKA	Alas.	GEORGIA	Ga.
ARIZONA	Ariz.	HAWAII	No official abbreviation
ARKANSAS	Ark.	IDAHO	Id., Ida.
CALIFORNIA	Cal.	ILLINOIS	Ill.
COLORADO	Colo.	INDIANA	Ind.
COLUMBIA (District)	D.C.	IOWA	Ia.
CONNECTICUT	Conn.	KANSAS	Kan.
DELAWARE	Del.	KENTUCKY	Ky., Ken.

LOUISIANA	La.	OHIO	O.
MAINE	Me.	OKLAHOMA	Okla.
MARYLAND	Md.	OREGON	Ore., Oreg.
MASSACHUSETTS	Mass.	PENNSYLVANIA	Penn.
MICHIGAN	Mich.	RHODE ISLAND	R.I.
MINNESOTA	Minn.	SOUTH CAROLINA	S.C.
MISSISSIPPI	Miss.	SOUTH DAKOTA	S.Dak.
MISSOURI	Mo.	TENNESSEE	Tenn.
MONTANA	Mont.	TEXAS	Tex.
NEBRASKA	Neb.	UTAH	Ut.
NEVADA	Nev.	VERMONT	Vt.
NEW HAMPSHIRE	N.H.	VIRGINIA	Va.
NEW JERSEY	N.J.	WASHINGTON	Wash.
NEW MEXICO	N.M.	WEST VIRGINIA	W.Va.
NEW YORK	N.Y.	WISCONSIN	Wis.
NORTH CAROLINA	N.C.	WYOMING	Wyo.
NORTH DAKOTA	N.D.		

BRITISH PRIME MINISTERS.

From 1770

Lord NORTH	Lord John RUSSELL	A. J. BALFOUR
Lord ROCKINGHAM	Lord DERBY	Sir H. CAMPBELL-
Lord SHELBURNE	Lord ABERDEEN	BANNERMAN
Duke of PORTLAND	Lord PALMERSTON	H. H. ASQUITH **
William PITT	Lord DERBY	David LLOYD GEORGE
Henry ADDINGTON	Lord PALMERSTON	A. BONAR LAW
William PITT	Lord John RUSSELL	S. BALDWIN
Lord GRENVILLE	Lord DERBY	J. R. MACDONALD
Duke of PORTLAND	Benjamin DISRAELI	S. BALDWIN
Spencer PERCEVAL	W. E. GLADSTONE	J. R. MACDONALD **
Lord LIVERPOOL	Benjamin DISRAELI	S. BALDWIN **
George CANNING	Lord BEACONSFIELD	Neville CHAMBERLAIN**
Lord GODERICH	W. E. GLADSTONE	W. Spencer CHURCHILL**
Duke of WELLINGTON	Lord SALISBURY	Clement ATTLEE **
Lord GREY	W. E. GLADSTONE	Sir W. CHURCHILL
Lord MELBOURNE	Lord SALISBURY	Sir Anthony EDEN
Sir Robert PEEL	W. E. GLADSTONE	Harold MACMILLAN **
Lord MELBOURNE	Lord ROSEBERY	Sir Alec DOUGLAS-HOME
Sir Robert PEEL	Lord SALISBURY	Harold WILSON **

PRESIDENTS OF THE UNITED STATES.

George WASHINGTON	Millard FILLMORE	William McKINLEY
John ADAMS	Franklin PIERCE	Theodore ROOSEVELT
Thom. JEFFERSON **	James BUCHANAN	William TAFT
James MADISON	Abraham LINCOLN **	Woodrow WILSON
James MONROE	Andrew JOHNSON	Warren HARDING
John Quincy ADAMS	Ulysses GRANT	Calvin COOLIDGE
Andrew JACKSON	Rutherford HAYES	Herbert HOOVER
Martin van BUREN	James GARFIELD	F. D. ROOSEVELT ****
William HARRISON	Chester ARTHUR	Harry TRUMAN **
John TYLER	Grover CLEVELAND	Dwight D. EISENHOWER**
James Knox POLK	Benjamin HARRISON	John KENNEDY
Zachary TAYLOR	Grover CLEVELAND	Lyndon B. JOHNSON**

** Signifies the number of consecutive terms of office.

COUNTIES OF THE UNITED KINGDOM.

ENGLAND AND WALES		SCOTLAND	IRELAND
3	**7**	**3**	**4**
MON	BEDFORD	AYR	CORK
	DENBIGH		DOWN
4	LINCOLN	**4**	LEIX
	NORFOLK		MAYO
BEDS	RUTLAND	BUTE	
CAMS	SUFFOLK	FIFE	**5**
GLAM	WARWICK	ROSS	
GLOS			CAVAN
KENT	**8**	**5**	CLARE
OXON			KERRY
	ANGLESEY	ANGUS	LOUTH
5	CARDIGAN	BANFF	MEATH
	CHESHIRE	ELGIN	SLIGO
BERKS	CORNWALL	MORAY	
BUCKS	HEREFORD	NAIRN	**6**
CARDS	HERTFORD	PERTH	
CARMS	MONMOUTH		ANTRIM
DERBY	PEMBROKE	**6**	ARMAGH
DEVON	SOMERSET		CARLOW
ESSEX	STAFFORD	ARGYLL	DUBLIN
FLINT		FORFAR	GALWAY
HANTS		LANARK	OFFALY
HERTS		ORKNEY	TYRONE
HUNTS			ULSTER (P)
LANCS			
LEICS		**7**	**7**
LINGS			
NOTTS		BERWICK	DONEGAL
PEMBS		KINROSS	KILDARE
SALOP		PEEBLES	LEITRIM
WILTS		RENFREW	MUNSTER (P)
WORCS		SELKIRK	WEXFORD
YORKS		WIGTOWN	WICKLOW
6		**8**	**8**
BRECON			
DORSET		ABERDEEN	KILKENNY
LONDON		AYRSHIRE	LAOIGHIS
OXFORD		CROMARTY	LEINSTER (P)
RADNOR		DUMFRIES	LIMERICK
STAFFS		ROXBURGH	LONGFORD
SURREY		STIRLING	MONAGHAN
SUSSEX			

464

PREFIXES.

TWO LETTERS

AB	AM	CO	EC	EU	OB	RE
AC	AT	DE	EM	EX	OC	SE
AD	BE	DI	EN	IL	OF	TO
AG	BI	DO	EP	IM	ON	UN
AL	BY	DU	ES	IN	OP	UP

THREE LETTERS

ABS	BIO	DIA	FOR	MON	PAR	SUB
AMB	BIS	DIS	HOM	NEG	PER	SUR
ANA	CAT	DIF	MAL	NON	POR	SYN
ANT	COL	DYS	MEN	OFF	PRE	TOM
APH	CON	EPH	MET	OUT	PRO	TRA
APO	COR	EPI	MIS	PAN	RED	TRI

FOUR LETTERS

ALLO	BENE	ENDO	HOLO	META	PERI	SEMI
AMBI	BULL	FORE	HOME	METH	POLY	SINE
ANTE	CATA	GAIN	HOMO	MONO	POST	TELE
ANTI	CATH	HEMI	HYPH	MULT	POUR	VICE
ARCH	DEMI	HEPT	HYPO	OVER	PROS	WITH
AUTO	DINO	HEXA	MALE	PARA	PROT	

FIVE LETTERS

AFTER	ENTER	HORSE	INTRO	PENTA	QUASI	TETRA
AMPHI	EXTRA	HYPER	JUXTA	PROTO	RETRO	TRANS
ARCHE	FORTH	INTER	MULTI	QUADR	SUPER	ULTRA
ARCHI	HEPTA	INTRA	PANTO	QUART	SUPRA	UNDER

SIX LETTERS

CIRCUM	CONTRA	CONTRO	HETERO	PRETER
PSEUDO	SUBTER			

The PREFIXES and SUFFIXES may be found useful when coping with anagrams of lengthy words.

SUFFIXES.

TWO LETTERS

AC	CY	EN	EY	IE	ON	SY
AL	ED	ER	FY	LE	OR	TH
AN	EE	ES	IC	LY	RY	TY
AR	EL	ET	ID			

THREE LETTERS

ACY	ASM	ERY	ILE	ITE	OID	TER
ADE	ATE	ESE	INE	IVE	ORY	TOR
AGE	BLE	ESS	ING	IZE	OSE	TRE
AIN	CLE	EST	ION	KIN	OUR	ULE
ANE	DOM	FUL	ISE	LET	OUS	URE
ANT	EER	ICS	ISH	NCE	PLE	WAY
ARD	EHE	IDE	ISM	NCY	RED	YER
ARY	ERN	IER	IST	OCK	RIC	YSM

FOUR LETTERS

ABLE	EREL	HERD	LESS	MONY	TEEN	WARD
ANCE	ERLY	HOOD	LIKE	MOST	THER	WAYS
ANCY	ETTE	IBLE	LING	NESS	TION	WIFE
CULE	FAST	ICLE	LITE	SHIP	TORY	WISE
ENCE	FOLD	IQUE	LOGY	SION	TRIX	
ENCY	FULL	ITIS	LONG	SOME	TUDE	
EOUS	HEAD	LENT	MENT	STIR	UBLE	

FIVE LETTERS

ASTER	ATIVE	CRAFT	LENCE	OLOGY	RIGHT	SCOPY
ATION	ATORY	GRAPH	METER	PATHY	SCOPE	STEAD

SIX LETTERS

ACEOUS   ACIOUS   ANEOUS   ESCENT   FEROUS   GRAPHY
MONGER

PRONOUNS.

TWO LETTERS

HE	IT	ME	MY	US	WE	YE

THREE LETTERS

HER	HIS	ONE	SHE	THY	YOU	WHO
HIM	ITS	OUR				

FOUR LETTERS

HERS	NONE	OURS	THEE	THEY	THOU	WHOM
MINE	ONES	THAT	THEM	THIS	WHAT	YOUR

FIVE LETTERS

THEIR	THESE	THOSE	THINE	WHOSE	WHICH	YOURS

SIX LETTERS

ITSELF   MYSELF   THEIRS